Advances in Behavior Therapy, 1968

Contributors

BRUCE L. BAKER
ALLEN E. BERGIN
R. A. BRAGG
PETER BRY
BRADLEY BUCHER
ELAINE P. BURGESS
JOSEPH R. CAUTELA
PATRICIA LEE DARWIN
MARVIN DICHTER
LEONARD FEINGOLD
LUIS E. FERNANDEZ
CYRIL M. FRANKS
ROBERT FRIED
ZALMON H. GARFIELD
ALAN GOLDSTEIN
JOHN D. HENDERSON
RONALD A. KLEINKNECHT
FELICITAS KORT
JON E. KRAPFL
ARNOLD A. LAZARUS
PETER M. LEWINSOHN
ROBERT M. LIEBERT
IRWIN LUBLIN
JOHN F. McBREARTY
MICHAEL J. McMAINS
M. MIKE NAWAS
R. VANCE PEAVY
GERALD W. PIAGET
ERNEST G. POSER
STEWART PROCTOR
N. DICKON REPPUCCI
RICHARD D. RUBIN
LEONARD F. SALZMAN
HALMUTH H. SCHAEFER
ROBERT L. SCHWITZGEBEL
MICHAEL SERBER
DAVID A. SHAW
MICHAEL D. SPIEGLER
RICHARD B. STUART
DAVID C. TINLING
LEONARD P. ULLMANN
MERVYN K. WAGNER
ZEV W. WANDERER
MALCOLM S. WEINSTEIN
PATRICIA A. WISOCKI

Advances in Behavior Therapy, 1968

Association for the Advancement of Behavior Therapy
Symposium Held in San Francisco, August 1968

Program Chairman: Arnold A. Lazarus

President: Joseph Wolpe

Edited by

Richard D. Rubin

HELENE FULD HOSPITAL
TRENTON, NEW JERSEY

Cyril M. Franks

PSYCHOLOGY SERVICE AND RESEARCH CENTER
NEW JERSEY NEUROPSYCHIATRIC INSTITUTE
PRINCETON, NEW JERSEY

1969

ACADEMIC PRESS New York and London

ACADEMIC PRESS, INC.
111 Fifth Avenue, New York, New York 10003

United Kingdom Edition published by
ACADEMIC PRESS, INC. (LONDON) LTD.
Berkeley Square House, London WIX6BA

LIBRARY OF CONGRESS CATALOG CARD NUMBER: 79-84231

PRINTED IN THE UNITED STATES OF AMERICA

List of Contributors

Numbers in parentheses indicate the pages on which the authors' contributions begin.

BRUCE L. BAKER (151), Department of Social Relations, Harvard University, Cambridge, Massachusetts

ALLEN E. BERGIN (117), Teachers College, Columbia University, New York, New York

R. A. BRAGG (53), V. A. Hospital of Salisbury, Salisbury, North Carolina

PETER BRY (31), University of Missouri, Columbia, Missouri

BRADLEY BUCHER (59), University of California, Los Angeles, California

ELAINE P. BURGESS (193), Drake University, Des Moines, Iowa

JOSEPH R. CAUTELA (165), Boston College, Chestnut Hill, Massachusetts

PATRICIA LEE DARWIN (139), Temple University, Philadelphia, Pennsylvania

MARVIN DICHTER (97), Eagleville Hospital and Rehabilitation Center, Eagleville, Pennsylvania

LEONARD FEINGOLD (25), Haverford State Hospital, Haverford, Pennsylvania

LUIS E. FERNANDEZ (45), Vanderbilt University, Nashville, Tennessee

CYRIL M. FRANKS (37), Neuropsychiatric Institute, Princeton, New Jersey

ROBERT FRIED (37), Hunter College of the City University of New York, New York

ZALMON H. GARFIELD (97), Eagleville Hospital and Rehabilitation Center, Philadelphia, Pennsylvania

ALAN GOLDSTEIN (161), Temple University School of Medicine, and Eastern Pennsylvania Psychiatric Institute, Philadelphia, Pennsylvania

JOHN D. HENDERSON (201), Spruce House, Horizon House, Inc., Philadelphia, Pennsylvania

RONALD A. KLEINKNECHT* (211), Washington State University, Pullman, Washington

FELICITAS KORT (161), Temple University School of Medicine, and Eastern Pennsylvania Psychiatric Institute, Philadelphia, Pennsylvania

JON E. KRAPFL† (31), University of Missouri, Columbia, Missouri

ARNOLD A. LAZARUS (189), Temple University School of Medicine, and Eastern Pennsylvania Psychiatric Institute, Philadelphia, Pennsylvania

PETER M. LEWINSOHN (231), University of Oregon, Eugene, Oregon

ROBERT M. LIEBERT (45), Vanderbilt University, Nashville, Tennessee

IRWIN LUBLIN (73), California State College, Los Angeles, California

JOHN F. McBREARTY (97, 139), Temple University School of Medicine, and Eagleville Hospital and Rehabilitation Center, Philadelphia, Pennsylvania

MICHAEL J. McMAINS (45), Vanderbilt University, Nashville, Tennessee

M. MIKE NAWAS (31), University of Missouri, Columbia, Missouri

R. VANCE PEAVY (17), University of Victoria, Victoria, British Columbia, Canada

GERALD W. PIAGET (161), Temple University Medical School and Eastern Pennsylvania Psychiatric Institute, Philadelphia, Pennsylvania

ERNEST G. POSER (183), Douglas Hospital and McGill University, Montreal, Quebec, Canada

**Present address*: University of Oregon Medical School, Portland, Oregon.
†*Present address*: Drake University, Des Moines, Iowa.

STEWART PROCTOR* (105), Indiana University, Bloomington, Indiana

N. DICKON REPPUCCI† (151), Harvard University, Cambridge, Massachusetts

RICHARD D. RUBIN (37), Helene Fuld Hospital, Trenton, New Jersey

LEONARD F. SALZMAN (131), School of Medicine and Dentistry, University of Rochester, Rochester, New York

HALMUTH H. SCHAEFER (83), Patton State Hospital, Patton, California

ROBERT L. SCHWITZGEBEL (1), Claremont Graduate School, Claremont, California

MICHAEL SERBER (161), Temple University School of Medicine and Eastern Pennsylvania Psychiatric Institute, Philadelphia, Pennsylvania

DAVID A. SHAW (231), University of Oregon, Eugene, Oregon

MICHAEL D. SPIEGLER (45), Vanderbilt University, Nashville, Tennessee

RICHARD B. STUART (221), University of Michigan, Ann Arbor, Michigan

DAVID C. TINLING (11), University of Rochester, Rochester, New York

LEONARD P. ULLMANN (175), University of Illinois, Urbana, Illinois

MERVYN K. WAGNER (53), V. A. Hospital at Salisbury, Salisbury, North Carolina

ZEV W. WANDERER (93), The Center for Behavior Therapy, Beverly Hills, California

MALCOLM S. WEINSTEIN (231), University of Oregon, Eugene, Oregon

PATRICIA A. WISOCKI (165), Medfield State Hospital, Medfield, Massachusetts

**Present address*: University of Utah, Salt Lake City, Utah.

†*Present address*: Psychology Department, Yale University, New Haven, Connecticut.

Foreword

Behavior therapy is synonomous with *conditioning therapy.* The term *behavior therapy* was first put forward by Skinner & Lindsley (1953); and its general adoption was later vigorously propagated by Eysenck (1959, 1960, 1964). The term explicitly denotes the use of experimentally established principles of learning for the purpose of changing unadaptive behavior. Behavior therapy is thus, by definition, an applied science, similar to the other technologies constituting medical therapeutics.

It is natural for a person with a clear commitment to scientific method to accept the behavioristic approach to psychopathology, and to adopt the techniques of behavior therapy. People with other orientations – like the psychoanalyst, Burton Glick (1967) – may also rationally adopt those behavior therapy methods of whose efficacy they are persuaded, without necessarily becoming behaviorists. A question that has arisen is whether it is equally rational for a behavior therapist to use psychoanalytic or other nonbehavioristic techniques under any conditions. The answer is unequivocal. The behavior therapist will always do *what the evidence indicates.* Even though his preference is for methods whose action he can control because he knows the operative factors, he will in appropriate circumstances willingly employ other methods that have empirically been shown to be effective. Just as the physician of old used digitalis to alleviate heart disease before he knew how it worked because it was *demonstrably* effective, the present-day behavior therapist may use mixtures of carbon dioxide and oxygen to remove pervasive anxiety, or may try to overcome a phobia by "flooding" – without knowing the mechanisms upon which these measures depend. He is willing to do such things because in each instance there is compelling evidence of a relationship between the particular therapeutic intervention and specific clinical change. No technique can be claimed as empirically acceptable unless such evidence exists.

It follows that methods that are not empirically supported have no place in the armamentarium of a scientifically oriented therapist. It is on scientific grounds that the behavior therapist rejects the psychoanalysis treatment, because it has not been demonstrated to have empirical validity. And it is for exactly the same kind of reason that he eschews self-disclosure therapy, reality therapy, Gestalt therapy, and a host of other methods of diverse theoretical parentage with no visible empirical support that some individuals have interlarded with behavior therapy under such package titles as "technical eclecticism" and "broad spectrum behavior therapy."

Probably the most common reason for wanting to add other things to behavior therapy is the idea that it leaves out of account the cognitive side of patients' problems. Even if the allegation were true it would not justify the use of unvalidated methods. But it is not true. What the patient perceives is generally to the forefront of the behavior therapist's interest and effort. He bases his operations on the patient's reported experience. He corrects misconceptions that are the source of inappropriate reactions. Changing a verbal or imaginal habit of response involves the same learning function as changing an emotional habit. Behavior therapy is concerned with *all* kinds of unadaptive habits (Wolpe, 1958, 1969).

During the last three or four years, interest in behavior therapy has been rapidly increasing. Requests for treatment have multiplied; lectures and symposia have usually been filled to capacity; and there has been a growing demand for proper training.

It would have been pleasant to be able to report that the rising tide of professional interest in behavior therapy has been matched by the provision of abundant facilities for training. In fact, very little has developed. The acquisition of skills in behavior therapy still rests mainly on episodic measures like demonstrations and workshops; and many people still have to rely entirely on the printed word.

Only here and there are additions to these bare rations available. Training programs that incorporate behavior therapy to an important extent are available in the Department of Psychology at New York State University at Stony Brook, the University of Wisconsin, Stanford University, and the University of Illinois at Urbana. In the Department of Psychiatry at Temple University Medical Center, we have had several trainees on an apprenticeship basis for periods ranging from two to twelve months. Recently, we had a four-week full-time Institute of 28 members, about two-thirds of whom were clinical psychologists and most of the remainder psychiatrists. In addition to attendance at lectures, seminars, and demonstrations, the participants were able to treat patients under the supervision of experienced behavior therapists. We intend to make this kind of Institute an annual event—a necessity until proper training courses become generally available.

Research activity continues to expand. The number of papers in existing journals continues to grow. New journals dealing specifically with behavior therapy are about to appear. The articles contained in the present volume emphasize the inventiveness, enthusiasm, and vigor of those who are engaged in research in behavior therapy—the latest addition to the family of scientific disciplines in the area of therapeutics.

JOSEPH WOLPE
President

References

Eysenck, H. J., Learning theory and behavior therapy, *Journal of Mental Science,* 1959, **105**, 61-75.

Eysenck, H. J. (Ed.), *Behavior Therapy and the Neuroses.* Oxford; Pergamon Press, 1960.

Eysenck, H. J. (Ed.), *Experiments in Behavior Therapy.* Oxford; Pergamon Press, 1964.

Glick, B., Conditioning therapy by an analytic therapist, *Archives of General Psychiatry,* 1967, **17**, 577-583.

Skinner, B. F., & Lindsley, O. R., Studies in behavior therapy, *Status Report I.* Naval Research Contract N5, ori-7662, 1953.

Wolpe, J., *Psychotherapy by Reciprocal Inhibition.* Stanford, California; Stanford Univ. Press, 1958.

Wolpe, J., *Practice of Behavior Therapy.* Oxford; Pergamon Press, 1969.

Preface

Not uncommonly, nonbehavioral practicing psychologists and psychiatrists scoff at the notion that therapeutic techniques are of crucial importance. Many still adhere to the belief that the necessary and sufficient condition for constructive behavior change is a permissive, nonjudgmental, and empathic therapist-patient relationship. Experienced behavior therapists are aware of the fact that, while such a relationship in therapy may be useful, it is rarely sufficient.

Perhaps the most distinctive feature of behavior therapy is the readiness with which it can accommodate a wide range of specific techniques which can be applied in a deliberate and systematic manner. It was such thinking which motivated us to make "therapeutic technique innovations" the theme of the 1968 Annual Meeting of the AABT. The decision to publish the Proceedings of this meeting reflects the increasing demand for knowledge about behavior therapy.

Are any new techniques being developed? Are established methods being combined with one another and producing novel effects? Are any of these existing methods being altered so as to reach larger patient populations? Are refinements being put into effect to reduce the time and increase the efficiency of therapy? These and similar questions elicited some 80 manuscripts on novel and modified behavior therapy techniques. Preference was given to papers outlining straightforward technical procedures suitable for ready incorporation into everyday clinical practice. Some ingenious methods were rejected as being either too complex, costly, or time consuming for most practitioners. Others, although rapid and direct, required either the construction of elaborate apparatus or the use of very special facilities for their application.

The papers finally selected fall into four broad categories: 1. Those in which some type of readily available and relatively inexpensive apparatus was used in therapy. Here will be found novel applications for familiar electronic and other instruments as well as ways in which relatively new devices serve to overcome everyday problems. 2. A presentation of variations in desensitization procedures. As a technique, desensitization should be neither fixed nor rigid and here one will observe how diverse therapists have extended the range and overall impact of desensitization therapy. 3. A sampling of general technique innovations which may stimulate the clinician to reassess and broaden his own therapeutic base. 4. Papers devoted to the novel application to therapy of familiar reinforcement principles. In addition to the above, the papers comprising the symposia should prove thought-provoking.

We hope that the reader will be able to integrate this volume into his therapeutic repertoire and that this will prove a stimulus to his development as a behavior therapist.

August, 1969

ARNOLD A. LAZARUS
Program Chairman

RICHARD D. RUBIN
CYRIL M. FRANKS
Editors

Contents

Refinements and Extensions of Systematic Desensitization
(*Michael B. Conant,* Chairman)

General Technique Innovations
(*Gerald W. Piaget,* Chairman)

Models for the Teaching and Practice of Behavior Therapy
(*Michael Serber,* Chairman)

Novel Applications of Reinforcement Principles
(*Leonard Krasner*, Chairman)

A Remote Instrumentation System for Behavior Modification: Preliminary Report

Robert L. Schwitzgebel[1]
CLAREMONT GRADUATE SCHOOL

There is fairly wide agreement that unwanted behavior is often the result of disturbances or unfavorable conditions in the social environment. Yet techniques for obtaining valid information about such changes, and a patient's reaction to them, are markedly inadequate. Studies by Gray (1955) and by Cartwright (1962), for example, indicated substantial differences between self-reported and observed behavior. The general lack of accurate field data means that even in individual cases we may be forced to speculate on critical factors such as the actual reinforcement contingencies or important discriminative stimuli.

Furthermore, from both a theoretical and a practical standpoint, it may be impossible to create in the laboratory or clinic the frequency, duration, and complexity of particular conditions which may be of concern (cf. Barker, 1965). Almost all treatment procedures today rely on massive transfer of behavior from the clinic to the patient's usual environment (assuming the individual will come to the clinic in the first place). Recent advances in telemetry and electronic communication systems, however, may now make feasible the investigation of aspects of the therapeutic process which heretofore have been relatively inaccessible. New modes of intervention are also suggested.

[1]The author wishes to acknowledge the early contribution of his brother, Ralph Schwitzgebel, to the system design. The development reported herein was performed pursuant to a contract with the United States Department of Health, Education, and Welfare, Office of Education.

The potential value of remote instrumentation and data-recording systems in biomedical research and in medical practice has long been recognized. Among early reports are those of Einthoven (1906), who transmitted electrocardiac data over a telephone line a distance of approximately 1 mi, and of Winters (1921), who devised a radio telemetry system in order that similar data could be transmitted from a ship without a physician on board to a medical facility on shore. Efforts to introduce radio devices into psychotherapy and educational situations have been reported for at least a decade. Korner and Brown (1952) described a "mechanical third ear" to be used for supervising beginning therapists; Ward (1960) devised a similar system for the same purpose. More recently, Sanders (1966) reported an auditory prompting system. In this latter case, the therapist speaks into a microphone of an FM transmitter, and the output is fed into a wire loop encircling the perimeter of an adjoining therapy room. A person in the therapy room, wearing a wireless subminiature behind-the-ear-type receiver, is then able to hear the therapist. This system has been used to supervise trainees during interviewing and psychological testing. A more novel application was the use of the so-called Bug-in-the-Ear with parents while they were interacting with their children during play therapy (Welsh, 1966). Presumably, this prompting could facilitate generalization of certain parent-child interactions outside the clinic. Patterson, Jones, Whittier, and Wright (1965) have described an instrumental conditioning procedure with a hyperactive nine-year-old boy in a classroom in which the therapist sent messages to the child via a small radio headset. An earphone and miniature radio unit (held in place by suspenders) was given to the youngster, and he was instructed that a buzz over the earphone indicated that he had earned a piece of candy for sitting still.

The present paper reports the designing and field-testing of a prototype electronic communication system for use with adolescent delinquents in natural settings.

Rationale and System Description

Some previous work (R. L. Schwitzgebel & Kolb, 1964; R. L. Schwitzgebel, 1967) suggested that systematically arranged positive consequences for delinquents employed as experimental *S*s could alter the frequency of social behaviors. *S*s who had participated in 20 or 30 hours of experimental interviewing tended to emit verbal operants at a fairly high rate. For example, on days when there were no interviews, *S*s often called the *E* on the telephone. Conversations were usually lengthy (30 min or more) and had little informative content. This behavior is certainly not atypical of adolescents; but what is therapeutically interesting is the reinforcing potential of the behavior (cf. Premack, 1965).

In psychoanalytically-oriented treatment, patient-initiated contact may be interpreted as a "transference" phenomenon and deliberately extinguished. In typical school counseling programs, contact with the counselor is either behaviorally noncontingent (e.g., on a fixed interval schedule of once a week) or contingent upon misbehavior. The remote instrumentation system to be described here was an attempt to make a high-probability behavior and positive consequences contingent on prosocial behavior by *decreasing* the *duration* and *increasing* the *frequency* of *E–S* contact. This arrangement was believed to be particularly desirable when dealing with patients characterized by impulsivity (cf. Mischel, 1958).

A two-way vibra-tactile radio communication system was designed to meet the following functional specifications:

1. Direct communication is possible within a radius of 100 yards under adverse city conditions, including normal building attenuation of the signal. The system can function with either party in his normal location. The supplemental use of local repeater stations and rented telephone lines can link extended geographical distances.
2. The communication is nonverbal in order to assure privacy and to prevent third parties from being unknowingly recorded. Messages are sent by simple arbitrary code, based on the presence or absence of a vibra-tactile or light signal or both.
3. Either party may send, receive, and initiate communication.
4. Controls are simple to operate and do not interfere with normal activity.
5. Equipment is small, lightweight, and packaged in a manner to allow, and perhaps encourage, acceptance among potential users.

Probably the most distinctive physical feature of the system is a 6 × 3 × 2 in. transceiver unit housed in a belt which sends and receives messages via a ¾ in. tactile transducer (see Fig. 1). The belt also houses the antenna. By pressing a button, the sender activates a small coil on the receiver's unit which is felt as a "tap" in the abdominal region. Information is conveyed by the number and the timing of the signals—similar to standard audio-telegraphy systems. The development of this mode of communication was based primarily

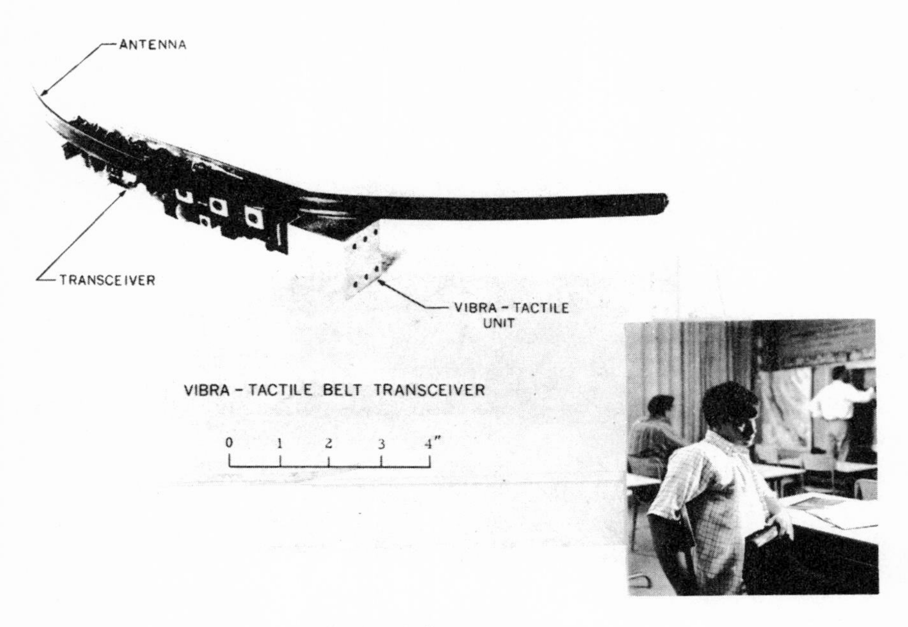

Fig. 1. Belt transceiver unit.

on the work of Geldard (1957, 1962) and his associates. A light and a barely audible tone accompanies the vibration. A multiple-frequency relay coil in the *E*'s belt allows him to communicate with four different *S*s without the *S*s themselves being able to communicate with each other.

The system is presently licensed by the FCC to operate two 12-W base stations at a frequency of 165.395 Mc/sec. and four 1-W belt units at 164.980 Mc/sec. One base station is located at the Fernald School (a nonresidential remedial school) on the North Campus of UCLA. This station transmits to, and receives messages from, the belt units worn by students in the school area. A similar base station serves the Psychology Department area in the South Campus. A rented commercial telephone line links the ¼ mile distance between the two stations.

Application

A small pilot study was conducted to estimate the feasibility of the system in terms of mechanical reliability and social acceptability.

Four male *S*s were selected from among volunteers on the basis of age (15-17 years), academic retardation, a history of antisocial aggressive behavior in the classroom, and reasonably high peer-group rating (or above-average physical size) in order to "protect" the equipment from students who might be jealous, curious, or hostile.

Because the system was designed to use code, the *S*s were given a series of five 1 hour practice sessions using telegraph practice-sets outside the classroom. Base-rate measures for classroom social and academic behaviors were obtained on a time-sampling basis from observers in an adjoining observation room and from self-reports of the *S*s. During certain hours, the *S*s were asked to report the frequency of four behaviors: 10 min or more of uninterrupted study, 10 min or more of idleness or socializing, hostile statements regarding academic work, and physical aggression toward other students. The validity of the self-reports was checked by concurrent independent observations of two lab assistants. The *E*'s signals to *S*s were limited to a query (e.g., "What are you doing now?"), acknowledgement of a communication, and notification of the *S* that he was eligible for some type of positive consequence (e.g., time out of the class visiting with the *E*). Various technical and procedural difficulties resulted in the consequences being given in what would have to be described as an unsystematic or haphazard manner.

Our work thus far has led us to several conclusions. These are undoubtedly biased by idiosyncratic factors in our particular project, but they may provide some tentative guide to therapists and researchers contemplating the use of remote instrumentation of this type.

1. Mechanical Reliability. In general, the basic design was found to be mechanically satisfactory, i.e., functional. However, a number of limitations should be noted. Attenuation of the signal by buildings was more severe than we had anticipated on the basis of published studies (e.g., Rice, 1965; Young, 1952). The belts did not withstand well the usual abuse given by active and curious adolescents. A very limited budget required that some military surplus components such as power transformers be installed in the base stations—resulting in a number of breakdowns and on one occasion a small fire. Fortunately most of the difficulties appear to be a matter of straightforward refinement of the components. The most serious design question involves the use of vibra-tactile signalization. The vibra-tactile transducer was often not powerful enough to produce a discrete signal through a layer of clothing; thus light and tone signals became important and necessary auxiliary information channels.

2. SOCIAL ACCEPTABILITY. The belts were generally well-received by members of the class. The novelty of the devices, an opportunity to spend some study periods outside the classroom, and attention from the *E*s probably accounted for much of the willingness of the *S*s to participate. *S*s tended to fantasize themselves as being "wire-up" in a manner similar to astronauts. Verbalizations about scientific research and about "trying something new" were encouraged by the *E*s; prosthetic or therapeutic connotations were purposefully avoided. Two of the *S*s asked to continue wearing the belts after the closing of the school year.

It should be noted that the belts were used only in the classroom of the clinic school where there is considerably more tolerance for experimentation than in typical public school classrooms. On the other hand, social deprivation in terms of positive adult attention is undoubtedly greater in the public school.

3. USE OF CODE. Our original plan to use Morse code was not found to be feasible due to the time and effort required to learn the code. The task appears to be roughly comparable to learning touch-typing and, of course, has less general practicality. A simple arbitrary code, conveying two or three bits of information, mutually decided upon by the *S*s and the *E* seemed to be adequate.

If verbal communication should be considered necessary, a small speaker (cordless hearing-aid style) could be added to the *S*'s unit, although the acceptance of this by adolescents is somewhat questionable. A "hearing aid"-microphone arrangement will not solve the problem, among delinquents at least, of a tendency to use socially unacceptable language. Furthermore, it may complicate, without any increased validity, eventual classification of the communications for research purposes (e.g., into digital code for computer analysis).

4. BEHAVIOR MODIFICATION. The results of the pilot study are inconclusive in terms of demonstrating replicable behavior change. All self-reported behaviors (i.e., time spent idle or working, hostile expressions regarding school work, and physical aggression toward other students) showed an apparent increase in frequency regardless of any attempted reinforcement or extinction via transceiver communication from the *E*. Direct counterconditioning or punishment was not used. Observer-subject reliability was high on three of the four dependent variables. By observers' standards, *S*s reported too infrequently the incidents of physical aggression. *S*s typically claimed that they were "just playing." Our impression is that the *S*s tried to report

accurately the behaviors of concern; they were also aware that observers might be present.

Simply requesting a *S* to report a specified behavior, which then became a condition for using the belt, seemingly prompted the behavior to a level consistently above the base rate (even for the too seldom reported physical aggression). Sensitization by frequent self-reporting and a desire to use the belt are factors associated with the use of the transceivers—beyond the usual application of contingent consequences—which might be effectively utilized to modify established response patterns. Generalization and extinction phenomena remain entirely unexplored.

Discussion

A judgment as to the usefulness of this type of instrumentation system obviously depends, in part, on the replicability of procedure and results. In order to increase the feasibility of other investigators developing remote communication devices similar to the units described here, the 165 Mc/sec range was selected because of the availability of nearby multiple-use citizen bands and relatively inexpensive equipment.[2] The eventual cost of materials in the individual belt units should be under $75.

Generally, studies employing telemetry must be viewed with considerable skepticism. Equipment and labor costs are still high because "off-the-shelf" components do not often meet all the requirements of novel application. Furthermore, there is an unfortunate tendency to assume that mechanization in itself produces "hard" and valid data. Remote systems are quite likely to have more "noise" in them than comparable laboratory arrangements. Like any innovation, remote instrumentation has its own costs and special limitations.

In order to provide a reasonably accurate and detailed report of the actual process of intervention, the system should be designed to automatically record all transceiver communications. This verification of procedure should prove to be one of the major advantages of using

[2] Investigators who contemplate using radio devices outside the frequency and power limitations of the citizen bands should be prepared for a minimum of 6 to 8 months processing time for licenses. Many frequencies are crowded or reserved for special purposes. One is also advised not to invest heavily in equipment prior to licensing as the final assignment is likely to vary to an unknown degree from the original request.

electromechanical interfaces in behavior therapy. Such recording will document, not necessarily eliminate, what may be seen later as the idiosyncratic (and perhaps valuable) "style" of the therapist.

Elsewhere (R. K. Schwitzgebel, Schwitzgebel, Pahnke, & Hurd, 1964) it has been suggested that remote instrumentation systems could have a fairly wide range of therapeutic application. Often before a serious crime is committed, for example, the potential offender will have strong ambivalent feelings. At times like these, it would require very little effort to signal for help. Presumably, the "cry for help" is also common prior to suicide attempts. This suggests that similar systems could be used with psychiatric patients in crisis situations, for alcoholics beginning treatment, or for hospitalized patients on their first few trips into town by themselves. Other potential applications would involve supportive or informational communications with retarded individuals or in geriatric cases.

It has been estimated that it will be possible within the next decade to manufacture all the circuits in a television set on a single slice of silicon at a cost of approximately 40 cents (Gifford, 1967). Whether or not this actually becomes possible, we can predict with some certainty that this type of technological advance will permit us, if we wish, to record and intervene in ongoing chains of behavior in more "natural" social situations. By and large our psychotherapeutic, educational, and correctional institutions have been slow to recognize the impact of this technosocial evolution. The boundaries of therapeutic or correctional systems no longer need be confined to the bricks and mortar of the pre-electronic age. "Therapeutic learning spaces" will be increasingly defined by the *possibility of communication* rather than by the designation of physical surfaces.

References

Barker, R. G. Explorations in ecological psychology. *American Psychologist*, 1965, **20**, 1-14.

Cartwright, A. Memory errors in a morbidity survey. *Milbank Memorial Fund Quarterly*, 1962, **16**, 5-24.

Einthoven, W. Le Telicardiogramme. *Archives of Internal Physiology*, 1906, **4**, 132.

Geldard, F. A. Adventures in tactile literacy. *American Psychologist*, 1957, **12**, 115-124.

Geldard, F. A. Virginia cutaneous project 1948-1962. Final report to the Office of Naval Research on Project NR-140-598, Psychology Laboratory, University of Virginia, 1962.

Gifford, J. The performance/ economics/ marketplace inter-relationships. *WESCON Technical Papers*, 1967, **2**, Part 2.

Gray, P. G. The memory factor in social surveys. *Journal of the American Statistical Association*, 1955, **50**, 344-352.

Korner, I. N., & Brown, W. H. The mechanical third ear. *Journal of Consulting Psychology*, 1952, **16**, 81-84.

Mischel, W. Delay of gratification, need for achievement, and acquiescence in another culture. *Journal of Abnormal and Social Psychology*, 1958, **57**, 13-16.

Patterson, G., Jones, R., Whittier, J., & Wright, M. A behavior modification technique for the hyperactive child. *Behaviour Research and Therapy*, 1965, **2**, 217-226.

Premack, D. Reinforcement theory. In D. Levine (Ed.), *Nebraska symposium on motivation*. Lincoln: University of Nebraska Press, 1965.

Rice, P. L. Transmission loss predictions for tropospheric communication circuits. *National Bureau of Standards (U.S.), Technical Note*, 1965, **1** & **2**, No. 101.

Sanders, R. A. The "Bug-in-the-ear": A device for training of clinical psychologists. Paper presented at the meeting of the Midwest Psychological Association, Chicago, May, 1966. (Mimeo., Northeast Nebraska Mental Health Clinic, Norfolk, Nebr.)

Schwitzgebel, R. K., Schwitzgebel, R. L., Pahnke, W., & Hurd, S. A program of research in behavioral electronics. *Behavioral Science*, 1964, **9**, 233-238.

Schwitzgebel, R. L. Short-term operant conditioning of adolescent offenders on socially relevant variables. *Journal of Abnormal Psychology*, 1967, **72**, 134-142.

Schwitzgebel, R. L., & Kolb, D. Inducing behavior change in adolescent delinquents. *Behaviour Research and Therapy*, 1964, **1**, 297-304.

Ward, C. H. An electronic aid for teaching interviewing techniques. *Archives of General Psychiatry*, 1960, **3**, 357-358.

Welsh, R. S. A highly efficient method of parental counseling: A mechanical third ear. Paper presented at the meeting of the Rocky Mountain Psychological Association, Denver, June, 1966.

Winters, S. R. Diagnosis by wireless. *Scientific American*, 1921, **124**, 465.

Young, W. R. Comparison of mobile radio transmission at 150, 450, 900, and 3700 Mc. *Bell System Technical Journal*, 1952, **31**, 1068-1085.

Auto-Desensitization to Phobic Fears with an Audiovisual Instructional Aid

David C. Tinling

UNIVERSITY OF ROCHESTER

Psychotherapy by reciprocal inhibition as described by Wolpe is an orderly and systematic process (Wolpe, 1958). Automated techniques might therefore be readily adapted to this therapy. Indeed, Migler and Wolpe have reported on automated self-desensitization (Migler & Wolpe, 1967). They designed a treatment for a man with a fear of public speaking; they used a specially modified tape recorder and a tape recording of the patient's own voice presenting relaxation instructions and instructions to visualize the hierarchy. The patient had control of the tape recorder so that he could press a pause switch to allow for good visualization or press a repeat button if he experienced any negative emotional responses to allow for a return to relaxation instructions and repeat stimulus presentation. The patient was able to take the equipment home and treat himself. Seven desensitization sessions were required to accomplish desensitization to all the scenes in the hierarchy. Follow-up indicated he was able to speak in public without anxiety or avoidance behavior. Migler and Wolpe cite another application in a personal communication from Lang, who apparently has used a rather elaborate apparatus with several tape recorders and electronic switching circuits to desensitize individuals with snake phobias. Apparently his results with automated treatment were slightly superior to standard practices. Recently Migler has reported on the use of an inexpensive tape recorder for automated self-desensitization (Migler, 1968). The advantages were that no modifications of the equipment were necessary and the machine was relatively inexpensive.

There are several reasons for exploring the development of techniques for automated self-desensitization: (*a*) The therapist has more time for other tasks, (*b*) treatment is less costly, (*c*) treatment can progress more rapidly, and (*d*) if he treats himself, the patient may develop a healthy sense of mastery which could generate new kinds of behavior in other areas of his life.

Method

An audio-visual instructional aid[1] was employed in the auto-desensitization of patients to phobic fears. It is a small, portable 12-lb unit which has been used mainly as an aid in teaching languages. The machine plays and records tape strips on cards. A student/instructor bar allows the operator to select the track on the tape that he desires to record on or listen to. The unit has a built-in microphone and speaker. Headphones may be used if desired. It is very simple to operate.

A group of prerecorded cards are available for language instruction. There are also blank cards available for instructor innovation. The cards come in four sizes, from 3 × 5 in. up to 8½ × 11 in. The cards are placed in a card slot and passed through a feed roller in order to record on or play the tape. The card velocity is 2¼ in. sec, so that on one large card a 5-sec stimulus can be presented. Two or more cards can be taped together to present a longer stimulus, although this has not been necessary.

Hierarchies were constructed in the standard way (Wolpe, 1958). The phobic stimulus was recorded by the author on the student track. Instructions to feel calm and relaxed were recorded on the instructor's track. One item of the hierarchy was recorded on each card. The cards were numbered in order from the lowest anxiety rating to the highest. All patients were trained in self-hypnosis and were able to induce comfortable states of relaxation. To guarantee relaxation some were given tapes with 10 min of hypnotic induction to play if this was needed at home. From time to time, this proved helpful.

The patient was given the machine to take home, a stack of stimulus cards, and a small record book which contained instructions for treatment as well as room to chart the progress of treatment.

In a treatment session, the patient began by inducing relaxation. When calm and comfortable, she began with the first card in her hierarchy. If the patient experienced any anxiety with the stimulus, she

[1]Bell & Howell Language Master.

was immediately to switch to the relaxation stimulus. She was to play that until she felt calm and relaxed and then return to the phobic stimulus. Once she could imagine the phobic stimulus three consecutive times without distress of any kind, she was to go on to the next card. She was to go at her own pace until she had completed the hierarchy.

Results

To date, five female patients have been treated in this fashion. All patients have found the machine easy to operate. They enjoy the convenience of being able to find their own space and time in which to perform the treatment.

Case 1. This 24-year-old woman came for treatment in December, 1966, after two years of intensive, analytically oriented therapy for multiple obsessions and phobias as well as a marked dependence on sedatives. She had been hospitalized four times and was considered to be a borderline schizophrenic. Thought-stopping techniques and escape-avoidance conditioning were used to treat her obsessions and her drug dependence. She was treated in the office with systematic desensitization for a fear of losing her teeth. Because she had so many fears, the Language Master was employed to help her use all the time available to her to diminish her phobic responses. She was given hierarchies for fears associated with dental care, being alone, sickness, school, being assertive, driving her car, and speaking in public. She worked at home for a few weeks with the Language Master until she could handle every stimulus card at least three times without anxiety. She felt there was a definite carry over into her real life. It is now eighteen months since her course of treatment. She takes no medicine, is an honor student in college, and has no phobic or obsessive symptoms.

Case 2. This 28-year-old, married, mother of two came for therapy in early 1967 because of many fears, depression, over-eating, over-drinking, obesity, frigidity, and marital discord. Many behavioral techniques were used in her case. Escape-avoidance conditioning was employed for her eating and drinking problem. Reciprocal inhibition was used for her frigidity. One fear which seemed very difficult for her was her fear of driving. She was a stranger to this city and felt particularly cut off by her inability to drive. At one time she had learned to drive an automatic shift in her home town and did this with some success. However, her husband owned a foreign car with a four-speed shift. This plus her unfamiliarity with the city led to a feeling of panic at even thinking about driving. She was given the audio-visual aid and 44 stimulus cards ranging from picturing the stationary car to driving at 65 mph in heavy thruway traffic. She was instructed to go slowly and practice with her husband in the car the scenes she had been able to experience without anxiety using the Language Master. For three months in the Autumn of 1967, she progressed to the point where she was comfortable driving at 45 mph in heavy traffic. When the winter snow came, she stopped driving and found by April, 1968, that she was once again afraid of driving. She had one office visit with a session of desensitization to driving. She was quickly able to resume her driving behavior and is currently driving alone around the city without anxiety. She has lost over 40 lb of weight, is sexually responsive, no longer drinks to excess, and currently exhibits no phobic behavior.

Case 3. This 29-year-old woman was referred for help in December, 1967, because of severe asthma, often precipitated by anxiety. It developed that she had many problems. She weighed 190 lb, felt she could not show herself in public, dreaded any sensations in her respiratory tree as a possible precipitant of an asthmatic attack, had severe premenstrual tension, and was locked in a very tense relationship with her chronically unhappy mother. Many techniques were employed in her care including a strong emphasis on assertive training, escape-avoidance conditioning for her obesity, and relaxation training for her problems with tension. The machine was employed to assist her in her concern about bodily sensations. She was given hierarchies for laughing, choking, nasal drip, tickle in the throat, wheezing, a catch in the throat, tightness in the throat, dryness in the throat, and a hurting sensation in the throat. In addition, she was given hierarchies for her fears of dogs, illnesses, and her mother's rejecting behavior. In the four months since she was treated for her fears, she has found that she no longer has an asthmatic attack when she has such sensations. The only thing now which will precipitate an attack is a rainy day. She now weighs 145 lb, continues to lose weight, demonstrates no phobic responses, and is seemingly much less troubled by her mother.

Case 4. She is a 34-year-old mother of two who presented with amphetamine and sedative dependence in December, 1967. She was treated for this with aversive conditioning in the hospital. Subsequently, she lost control of her eating behavior and gained 30 lb in a few weeks; she was readmitted to the hospital for a program of fasting. She has done well since discharge two months ago in spite of many family hardships. She is currently working at home on hierarchies relating to driving, flying, sickness, and aging. She is progressing well and notes a marked decrease in the amount of anxiety associated with these stimuli.

Case 5. A 33-year-old, married, mother of one came for help in the Fall of 1967 because of severe hypochondriasis and multiple phobic fears. She has done well with a combination of reciprocal inhibition and assertive training. She is currently working at home on a fear of pregnancy. Many of her hypochondriacal symptoms and phobic fears date from pregnancy experiences.

Discussion

Experience to date indicates that this equipment is well suited for automated desensitization. It readily allows for presentation of stimuli and control of the stimuli by the subject. One patient noticed that she had always been afraid of machines and felt this might have had something to do with her fear of driving. She now felt that machines could serve her interests and that she could control them. It may be that being able to handle the phobic stimulus in this real, concrete way, and manipulate it as well, generates other affects such as pride which would also inhibit anxiety. As Lazarus has noted, many different emotions can inhibit anxiety (Lazarus & Abramovitz, 1962).

None of the patients have had difficulty in operating the machine. It is important to remember that this machine was designed with children in mind and has been effectively used in schools with young children.

None of these patients was given visual stimuli, but the cards lend themselves to this. Pictures, photographs, or even cutting the card into various shapes could be employed as visual stimuli to match the auditory stimuli. One could vary the size, color, and content of the visual imagery to match the hierarchical position.

At this point more clinical experience is needed with more patients and with the added use of visual stimuli. It might be possible to develop a standard library of fear cards for the commonplace phobias. These could then be readily available to schools or clinics for use in auto-desensitization.

Summary

A simplified method of auto-desensitization to phobic fears using an audio-visual aid has been presented. Five patients have used this equipment without difficulty. The design of the machine lends itself to control of the stimulus presentation by the patient. Simultaneous presentation of visual and auditory stimuli is a potential advantage of this technique. The mastery of the phobic stimulus card may generate feelings which are important in inhibiting anxiety in addition to the relaxation employed. Further study seems warranted.

References

Lazarus, A. A., & Abramovitz, A. The use of "emotive imagery" in the treatment of children's phobias. *Journal of Mental Science,* 1962, **108**, 191-195.

Migler, B. A supplementary note on automated self-desensitization. *Behaviour Research and Therapy,* 1968, **6**, 243-244.

Migler, B., & Wolpe, J. Automated self-desensitization: A case report. *Behaviour Research and Therapy,* 1967, **5**, 133-135.

Wolpe, J. *Psychotherapy by reciprocal inhibition.* Stanford, Calif.: Stanford University Press, 1958.

Modification of Speech Patterns: An Example of a Cybernetic Training Design

R. Vance Peavy

UNIVERSITY OF VICTORIA

Recent advances in the design of electronic recording, transmission, and display instruments have provided the educator with powerful tools for redesigning human learning environments. This increased ability to extend (and simulate) the functions of the central nervous system and sensory systems through electronic instrumentation calls for a continuous re-examination of learning principles and of educational designs in which learning occurs.

Underlying many training and educational designs is the assumption that learning is primarily a process of learner response. This assumption focuses attention on teaching, on *re*active processes in the learner, and encourages the use of external guidance and motivational practices. Educational designs for the *re*acting learner stress reward, reinforcement, verbal persuasion, threat, and punishment.

Learning environments which are designed for the *ac*ting or *trans*-acting learner are less frequently encountered. Such designs encourage choice, problem solution, and relevancy. In general, they emphasize the self-regulating characteristics of a learner. Arguments in support of principles of learning and educational design which incorporate inherent motivational and energizing properties of the learner are emerging from perceptual and transactional psychology, from experimental studies of exploration and curiosity, and from communications and cybernetics theory.

Perceptual theorists (Combs, 1962; Rogers, 1951; F. Allport, 1955) give central importance to the self-governing characteristics of the individual. Gordon Allport (1961) terms mental set "the key to the edifice of psychology" and stresses the *ac*tive rather than *re*active nature of human behavior. Berne (1961) and Kilpatrick (1961) call attention to *trans*actional rather than reactive properties of an individual.

Representative studies of exploration (Nissen, 1930), manipulation (Harlow & McClearn, 1954) and activity (Brant & Kavanau, 1964) indicate intrinsic motivational properties of animals. In light of research into exploratory and curiosity behavior, White (1959) has formulated an innate "competency" motive. Life systems are conceptualized as inherently active, exploring, curious, and seeking mastery over their own behavior as well as over components of the environment.

Cybernetics yields further evidence for viewing the learner as self-regulating, (Smith & Smith, 1966). The term cybernetics is derived from the Greek word, *kybernetes*, meaning "steersman" or "governor." The formal analogy comparing self-regulating properties of living and nonliving systems was introduced by Wiener (1948). Cybernetics is defined as the science of control and communication in living and nonliving systems. Nonliving purposive systems are known as servomechanisms, (Rosenblueth, Wiener, & Bigelow, 1943). These devices, utilizing feedback control operations, function to regulate temperature, guide missiles and planes, control traffic flow, etc. The feedback control operations can generate movement toward a goal (motivation), detect errors in movement, and use the error for self-correction (learning). If the analogy of common properties between living and nonliving systems is accepted, then redefinition of the learner and learning environment using cybernetic principles is possible. The rest of this paper considers some of the principles involved in such a design and presents an example of a cybernetic educational design.

In behavioral cybernetic theory, it is assumed that the primary goal of the learner is to gain mastery over his own behavior as well as over elements of the environment. Energizing is intrinsic and the ability to detect differences (learn) is a functional characteristic of the living system. To be alive is to be motivated. The commonly held views that most learners "need motivating" or "lack incentive" are the result of incorrect conceptualizing about the nature of the learner and learning.

From the cybernetic view, the concept of motivation is not particularly helpful. The learner is seen as more interested in doing things in his own way (that is, as he can control them) than he is in gaining an extrinsic reward offered for some other response (Smith & Smith, 1966). A primary design goal is to establish an educational environment which will enable the learner to establish his own patterns of control over tasks, skills, and knowledge. Further, the cybernetic theorist is concerned with the *social utility* (relevance) of learning. If that which is being learned has no social utility to the learner, then he directs activities to other targets—asocial behavior, interpersonal conflict, discouragement, boredom, etc.

In summary, for the cybernetic theorist, the learner is self-initiating and is energized and directed at varying levels of organization by inherent feedback control systems. The educational design which implements cybernetic principles is one which (*a*) aims at increasing a learner's control over his own actions, (*b*) assigns high priority to intrinsic rather than extrinsic regulation factors, (*c*) gives attention to the degree of social utility accorded to the objects of learning by the learner, and (*d*) pays attention to overloading versus underloading (Senders, 1966). Cybernetic learning designs can be constructed for a wide variety of learning tasks such as speaking, teaching, interviewing, playing tennis, etc. Each individual design can incorporate selected cybernetic principles depending on the nature of the learning task, age of the learners, facilities available, and other conditions. In each instance, the design should provide a feedback control system which is intrinsic to the learner rather than including external guidance factors.

The design shown here (Fig. 1) is appropriate for modifying certain aspects of interview speech and includes corresponding design factors and principles.

Speech skills are learned; they are specific and can be analyzed into microscopic units. Pope and Siegman (1965) have shown that client speech output is dependent upon the specificity of interviewer questioning. Teaching open-ended questioning behavior to a naive interviewer should lead to greater client output—a condition which is generally held to be desirable in interviewing. The following example illustrates that speech pattern interactions between interviewer and interviewee can be effectively modified by a short, intensive training

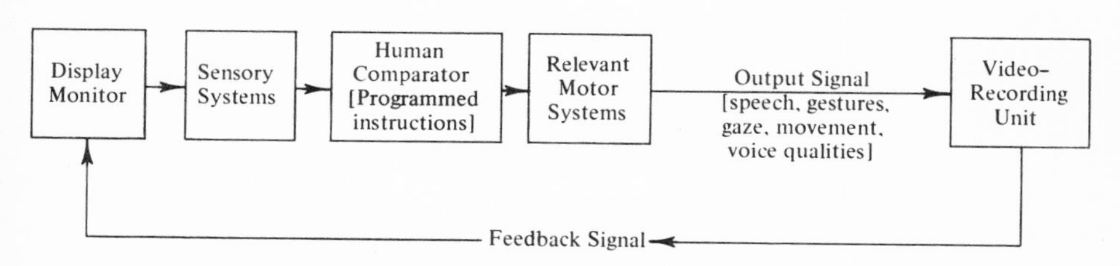

Fig. 1. Feedback control systems.

design which incorporates selected cybernetic learning principles outlined in Table 1.

Eighteen naive interviewers from an introductory class in counseling were randomly assigned to two groups (8 *E*s, 10 *C*s).

Hypothesis: Length of client speech utterance is increased as a result of increasing the open-endness of interviewer questions.

Procedure

All 18 subjects interviewed voluntary clients who were seeking assistance in obtaining summer employment. Following the initial interview, each of the 8 *E*s underwent three brief training cycles. Each interview was with a different client but the clients' request remained constant.

A *training cycle* consisted of five steps:

1. *E* read cues from specially prepared manual. The cues encouraged open-questioning.
2. *E* conducted a brief interview which was videotaped.
3. *E* read further cues from the manual which focused attention on questioning behavior.
4. *E* viewed his own videotape of the previous interview.
5. *E* rested briefly, talked with the instructor if he wished, and then repeated the cycle with a different client. Three such cycles were completed within 1½ hours.

Analysis

Twelve days after the completion of the training, all 18 subjects were taped while conducting posttraining interviews. The tapes were then analyzed for: (*a*) changes in average length of client speech utterance, (*b*) amount of interviewer talking time, (*c*) total number of interviewer utterances, and (*d*) number of questions asked by interviewers.

Table 2 shows changes in client speech for each of the first 4 min of the interview. As might be predicted, there was some gain in amount of client speech for both groups. The gain differences between *E*s and *C*s were found to be significant (01.,025.,025.,01.) by applying the Mann-Whitney U Test for each of the 4 min.

Table 1. Cybernetic Design Factors and Principles

Design factor	Principle
1. The trainee is given oral and written instructions about the specific skill to be learned. He is shown cues to watch for when viewing his own behavior on video-tape.	1. Built-in instructions are provided.
2. The trainee conducts a brief interview with focus on single skill. The interview is video-taped.	2. By analyzing interviewing into component parts, the level of complexity is held down to a level acceptable to a limited capacity system.
3. Immediately following the interview, the trainee is again given written cues to assist observation of his own behavior in the transactional situation (on video-tape).	3. Again, built-in instructions are used.
4. The trainee views video-tape without instructor's presence.	4. This illustrates the immediate feedback principle and blame-free atmosphere.
5. The trainee has a brief rest. He may ask for the instructor's comments but this is not compulsory.	5. Blame-free atmosphere, with rest allowing for integration.
6. Cycle 2, 3, 4, 5 is repeated but with different client.	6. All above principles operating plus practice under varied stress (different client).
7. Cycle 2, 3, 4, 5 repeated but with different client.	7. All of the above.

Table 2. CLIENT SPEECH OUTPUT DIFFERENCES

			Duration of interview (min.)			
			1	2	3	4
Average Duration of Speech Utterance (sec.)	*Es*	Pre-training	2.0	2.9	2.6	2.5
		Post-training	3.3	5.0	4.9	4.4
		Gain	1.3	2.1	2.3	1.9
	Cs	Pre-training	2.0	3.2	3.2	3.1
		Post-training	2.2	4.0	3.3	3.3
		Gain	0.2	0.8	0.1	0.2

Previous work by Matarazzo, Wiens, and Saslow (1965) has shown that increase in client output can be obtained by interrupting the client's speech. Analysis of the interruptions in this study revealed that, in the *E* group, the average number of questions declined, the total number of interviewer utterances decreased, and the average amount of interviewer talking time declined. In the *C* group, the number of questions increased, the number of utterances remained the same, and, like the *E* group, the average amount of talking time declined for interviewers. Thus, the increase in length of client utterance apparently did not result from being asked more questions, nor from being stimulated by a more talkative interviewer, but occurred as a result of the increased open-endness of questioning by the interviewer. This change in interviewer skill was accomplished in about 1½ hours of training time in a design which used maximum feedback, varied practice, and was essentially instructorless. The possibility of using a semiautomated training design such as this for the modification of a wide variety of communicative, social, and motor skills is worth considering.

References

Allport, F. *Theories of perception and the concept of structure.* New York: Wiley, 1955.

Allport, G. *Pattern and growth in personality.* New York: Holt, Rinehart & Winston, 1961.

Berne, E. *Transactional analysis in psychotherapy.* New York: Grove Press, 1961.

Brant, D., & Kavanau, J. "Unrewarded" exploration and learning of complex mazes by wild and domestic mice. *Nature*, 1964, **204**, 267–269.

Combs, A. (Ed.) *Perceiving, behaving, becoming: A new focus for education.* 1962 ASCD Yearbook. Washington, D.C.: Association for Supervision and Curriculum Development, 1962.

Harlow, H., & McClearn, G. Object manipulation learned by monkeys on the basis of manipulation motives. *Journal of Comparative and Physiological Psychology*, 1954, **47**, 73-76.

Kilpatrick, F. (Ed.) *Explorations in transactional psychology.* New York: New York University Press, 1961.

Matarazzo, J. D., Wiens, A. N., & Saslow, G. Studies in interview speech behavior. In L. Krasner & L. P. Ullman (Eds.), *Research in behavior modification: New developments and implications.* New York: Holt, Rinehart & Winston, 1965. Pp. 179-210.

Nissen, A study of exploratory behavior in the white rat by means of the obstruction method. *Journal of Genetic Psychology*, 1930, **37**, 361-376.

Pope, B., & Siegman, A. W. Interviewer specificity and topical focus in relation to interviewee productivity. *Journal of Verbal Learning and Verbal Behavior*, 1965, **4**, 188-192.

Rogers, C. *Client-centered therapy: Its current practice, implications, and theory.* Boston: Houghton Mifflin, 1951.

Rosenblueth, A., Wiener, N., & Bigelow, J. Behavior, purpose and teleology. *Philosophy of Science*, 1943, **10**, 18-24.

Senders, J. Human performance. *International Science and Technology*, 1966, July, 58-68.

Smith, K., & Smith, M. *Cybernetic principles of learning and educational design.* New York: Holt, Rinehart & Winston, 1966.

White, R. Motivation reconsidered: The concept of competence. *Psychological Review*, 1959, **66**, 297-333.

Wiener, N. *Cybernetics.* Cambridge, Mass.: M.I.T. Press, 1948.

An Automated Technique for Aversive Conditioning in Sexual Deviations

Leonard Feingold
HAVERFORD STATE HOSPITAL

The treatment of sexual deviations has been incorporating aversive conditioning procedures (Thorpe, Schmidt, Brown, & Castell, 1964; Feldman & MacCulloch, 1965; Bond & Evans, 1967). The techniques involve at least two elements and sometimes a third one.

1. Looking at or imagining the symbolic or real stimuli that are associated with the act. Touching the actual stimuli was used by Blakemore (Blakemore, Thorpe, Barker, Conway, & Lavin, 1963) in the case of transvestism.
2. The presentation of an aversive stimulus, usually electric shock, immediately following the looking at or imagining of the stimuli associated with the deviant act.
3. A third element that is more frequently included is differential conditioning (Solyom & Miller, 1965) in which a symbolic heterosexual stimulus is presented without shock or with the offset of shock. The purpose of this procedure is to condition approach behavior toward normal sexual behavior.

From a practicing therapist's point of reference, the aversive treatments are time-consuming and probably boring. Any movement toward automation of aversive techniques may lead to far greater applicability of these techniques. The technique developed here relies on the patient's imagination. The presentation of the stimuli for imagination and the aversive shock are all automatically programmed.

Apparatus and Procedure

The procedure for the automated treatment involves the patient imagining those situations associated with the deviant act as presented by a tape recorder and then receiving electric shocks to the leg. The shocks are programmed on the tape itself. In addition, the patient imagines heterosexual situations without electric shock.

Apparatus

The Uher Universal 5000 (about $300) lends itself to automation very easily. (A cheaper tape recorder—the Wollensak T-1600—can also be used.) The tape recorder was used in a fashion similar to the one in which Migler and Wolpe (1967) used it for automated self-desensitization. Two features to the recorder lend themselves to automated usage. It has a pause switch which makes it possible to stop the tape at any time. This pause switch is wired out to a remote control microswitch which the patient holds in his hand. The patient, by a simple depression of the microswitch, can easily stop the tape. The second feature allows for rewinding the tape to a preset place on the tape. This is necessary in order to repeat a scene. The recorder has two metal sensing guides on each side of the recording heads. When a metal foil on the tape makes contact with the sensing guides on the left, the tape recorder goes from playback to rewind. These two guides were bypassed by the tape and a push button was wired in parallel with the two guides, so that a momentary depression of the push button would rewind the tape. The second pair of sensing guides to the right of the recording heads functions to stop the rewinding and return to playback when the metal foil makes contact with the sensing guides. These guides were left alone.

On the tape each scene was preceded by a 1-in. metal foil. After each scene, the patient could either repeat the scene by pressing the rewind button or he could go on to the next scene by releasing the pause switch.

Shock is programed by putting a signal on tape with a Uher accessory called UHER DIA-PILOT. The tape bypasses the pick-up reel and goes around the heads of the DIA-PILOT. With this device, one can put an inaudible signal on the bottom one-quarter of the tape which, when played back through the device, triggers a built-in relay which is connected to the shock apparatus. Shock was delivered through an auto-transformer plugged into 120-V ac.

PROCEDURAL STEPS

1. The patient is asked to prepare a hierarchy of sexually deviant stimuli and rank the items from most stimulating to least stimulating.
2. The deviant scenes are put on tape in hierarchal order with the least exciting scene first and the most exciting scene last; 1-min relaxation instructions precede each scene in order to have the subject relaxed to enhance imagination. After every three or four deviant scenes, a heterosexual scene appears in which there are verbal descriptions of arousing heterosexual situations recorded by a seductive female voice. Each scene is preceded by 1-in. metal foil.
3. Shocks are programed on the tape following each deviant scene. The heterosexual scenes are not shocked and are only repeated once every three or four scenes.
4. The subject holds two remote control switches in his hand. The pause switch enables him to stop and start the recorder at any time. The rewind switch allows him to rewind the tape in order to repeat a scene if he feels any arousal on the scene.
5. The patient is instructed via the tape to imagine the deviant scene and stop the recorder until the scene is clear. He starts the recorder again as soon as he pictures the scene clearly and then automatically receives anywhere from one to three brief shocks. He is then asked if he felt any sexual arousal on the scene. If he felt any arousal, he is asked to press the rewind button which automatically rewinds the tape to the beginning of the scene, and the scene is repeated. He continues to repeat the scene until there is no arousal. If there is no arousal, he does not press the rewind button, and the tape proceeds to the next scene in the hierarchy. The patient goes as far as he can on the tape. The session runs anywhere from 45 min to 1½ hours. If he completes the tape in less than 45 min, he repeats the entire tape again.
6. The patients have usually been treated every day for the first week and then treatment has been thinned out. As a result of inquiries to the patient, new scenes may replace ones that no longer arouse him. Even though he may report no arousal, scenes are still repeated until arousal is not reported for more than five sessions.
7. There is no hard and fast rule for how long to treat a patient. It depends on his report of behavior outside the office. Generally, patients have been run 20 hours and booster treatments given after, if possible.

Results

Case 1. The first patient was a 17-year-old youth who was an in-patient in the hospital because of difficulties in adjusting at home and in school. He had been a promiscuous homosexual both before and during hospitalization, although this was not the reason for hospitalization. He reported impotence with girls, and at the time of the aversive conditioning, was seeing a girl at the hospital but was impotent. After three sessions on the tape, he reported a successful heterosexual experience with this girl, which she corroborated. After ten sessions with the tape, the patient stated that he did not want to give up his homosexuality but wanted to be bisexual. On a year followup, he reported bisexual activity.

Case 2. A 23-year-old exhibitionist was admitted to the hospital in lieu of going to jail. He had been arrested eleven times for exhibitionism and reported that he had been exhibiting two to three times a week for the last eight years. He received twenty treatments over four weeks while in the hospital, concurrently reporting a decrease in impulses. After leaving the hospital, he was seen weekly for ten weeks, biweekly for five weeks, and monthly for three months. He reported no acting-out for this period. Six months after the last treatment, he called up and reported an incident and asked for treatment. He was seen twice in a two-week period, receiving two treatments. On an eight-month follow-up, he reported no exhibitionism and increased adult heterosexual activity.

Case 3. A 17-year-old American youth came from West Germany for treatment. He had a history of homosexual activity from age 13 to 15 in various boarding schools. For the last two years there had been no acting-out, but he reported frequent and strong impulses to do so that were making him extremely anxious. He had little activity with females and in one case was impotent. He was seen for two months and received 25 treatments. He reported an immediate lessening of obsessive homosexual thoughts and later, during treatment, that female sexual stimuli were becoming arousing. One month after treatment, he reported a successful intercourse. One year after treatment, he reports that he still has homosexual thoughts which are considerably weaker and less frequent than previously. He continues to be aroused by females and has sexual contact with them.

Case 4. An 18-year-old youth was committed to the hospital because he had been caught in a pedophiliac incident with a 12-year-old boy. The patient reported that he had many pedophiliac impulses toward boys per day (10 to 12 per day). He had a diary which, from age 14, showed erotic interest in young boys. According to his diary he had 25 pedophiliac incidents in four years and no heterosexual ones. He received 23 treatments while in the hospital for ten weeks. He reported diminution of pedophiliac impulses to zero and no acting out. He was seen for six additional times during the next months, receiving a treatment each time. He reported that he had few deviant impulses and had begun dating girls. Contact was lost with this patient, preventing further follow-up.

Case 5. A 35-year-old married man came in for treatment of a pedophiliac problem with his six-year-old daughter. Two to three times a week he would fondle her and have an orgasm. Heterosexual contact with his wife was low in frequency and not rewarding. He reported pedophiliac tendencies toward little girls ever since he reached puberty. Previous to coming for treatment, he had seen a psychiatrist for five sessions with no diminution in the pedophiliac acts. He was extremely depressed and was having suicidal thoughts because he could not get over the problem. For the first three weeks, he received nine treatments. He reported no acts during this period and added that this was the longest interval in the last three years in which he did not have sexual contact with his daughter. After the third week, he had one pedophiliac incident. He felt extremely hopeless at this point. Because he lived a very long distance from the hospital, he was only able to come in once a week. The shock treatment was discontinued and we switched to covert sensitization for the next two sessions. On a year follow-up, he reports minimal pedophiliac impulses and no acts. When he does have the impulses, he uses covert sensitization. Heterosexual relations with his wife have considerably improved.

Case 6. A 35-year-old homosexual social worker came for private treatment. His sexual experience since puberty had been homosexual. At the time of treatment, he was seeing a girl and having successful intercourse with her. This was the first such experience in his life. He had not had homosexual experiences for the last year. However, he reported strong impulses in the homosexual direction and lack of satisfaction in the heterosexual relationship; the heterosexual aspect did not bring the same satisfaction as the homosexual one. He received 42 treatments over a three-month period. There was no change. He still reported strong homosexual impulses and lack of strong satisfaction in the heterosexual situation.

Discussion

The technique appears to be as successful as those reported in the literature. It has the advantage of minimal therapist time and long sessions to allow for overlearning. No special stimuli are needed. The only investment in time is the preparation of the tape and splicing in of the metal foils. Once the tapes have been spliced, they can easily be used with other patients by just erasing the old deviant scenes and putting new ones on. The author could never have given as many treatments as he did, and nor ones as long as he did, without this automated device. The machine makes it possible to have one patient running through the tape while another patient is being seen.

A word of caution is necessary in evaluating the technique. Other therapeutic maneuvers were going on more or less simultaneously with these patients in addition to the aversive conditioning. Such techniques as systematic desensitization, assertive training, and environmental manipulation were used with some of the above patients. Therefore, no claim is being put forward for the efficacy of aversive conditioning by itself. To the extent that the research literature indicates that aversive conditioning is of value, then the present technique may have value as an economical way of doing this conditioning.

References

Blakemore, C. B., Thorpe, J. G., Barker, J. C., Conway, C. G., & Lavin, N. I. The application of faradic aversion conditioning in a case of transvestism. *Behaviour Research and Therapy,* 1963, **1**, 29-34.

Bond, I. K., & Evans, D. R. Avoidance therapy: Its use in two cases of underwear fetishism. *Canadian Medical Association Journal,* 1967, **96**, 1160-1162.

Feldman, M. P., & MacCulloch, M. J. The application of anticipatory avoidance learning to the treatment of homosexuality. I. Theory, technique and preliminary results. *Behaviour Research and Therapy,* 1965, **2**, 165-183.

Migler, B., & Wolpe, J. Automated self-desensitization: A case report. *Behaviour Research and Therapy,* 1967, **5**, 133-135.

Solyom, L., & Miller, S. A differential conditioning procedure as the initial phase of the behaviour therapy of homosexuality. *Behaviour Research and Therapy,* 1965, **3**, 147-160.

Thorpe, J. G., Schmidt, E., Brown, P. T., & Castell, D. Aversion-relief therapy; a new method for general application. *Behaviour Research and Therapy,* 1964, **2**, 71-82.

Uses of the Bug-in-the-Ear in the Modification of Parents' Behavior

Jon E. Krapfl[1]
UNIVERSITY OF MISSOURI

Peter Bry
UNIVERSITY OF MISSOURI

M. Mike Nawas
UNIVERSITY OF MISSOURI

The Bug-in-the-Ear (BIE) is a small, battery-operated hearing-aid-like device. It is relatively inexpensive and has been used in a number of psychotherapy settings during the past few years. When using the BIE, in the manner to be discussed in this paper, the therapist observes through a one-way mirror as the parents and child interact in a playroom. The BIE, itself, has no wires and only the parent who places the device in his ear can hear the messages delivered through the therapist's microphone.

In the past, the BIE has proven to be of considerable value for therapy trainees because of its ability to provide feedback and to allow for the immediate reinforcement of appropriate responses and the correction of inappropriate ones. The fact that the BIE could provide immediate feedback and reinforcement led the authors to conclude that the device would be of value, not only in traditional settings, but also in the training of parents to manage their childrens' behavior, using the principles of operant conditioning.

[1]Now at Drake University.

Recently, it has been argued by some investigators that it may be more useful to attack behavioral problems in their natural environment. Consequently, there has been increased activity in the homes of disturbed children with the aim of training parents to deal appropriately with the aberrant behavior (Hawkins, Peterson, Schweid, & Bijou, 1966; Wahler, Winkel, Peterson, & Morrison, 1965).

While treatment in the home appears to offer many advantages over institutional behavior management, it carries with it a number of distinct disadvantages: the cost, the amount of professional time required, and the fact that the presence of the behavior modifier in the home may change the home environment and unduly influence the normal patterns of family interaction.

The BIE does not suffer from the disadvantages of treatment in the home setting and yet can often serve, first, to prepare the important figures in the patient's environment to maintain the patient's behavioral gains in the natural setting and, secondly, to obviate the necessity for institutionalization by providing important family figures with effective behavior control measures, thereby permitting treatment on an out-patient basis.

Often the failure to maintain gains of hospitalization has been attributed to parental "resistance" or inability to follow behavior modification training procedures outlined for parents upon their child's discharge. It may be that parents are often described as resisting when, in fact, they do not possess the appropriate child-controlling responses in their repertoire.

The use of the BIE provides an opportunity for the parent to demonstrate, and for the therapists to assess or to develop, the parents' ability to modify and control the child's behavior. Further, the use of this procedure requires only a short and fixed period of time. In addition, the appropriate controlling behaviors are made strikingly obvious to the parents through immediately consequated trials rather than through the use of instructions which may be misinterpreted or inappropriately applied. Thus the BIE provides a method for modifying the controlling behavior of parents who, in turn, are modifying their children's behavior. The procedure provides immediate feedback and the possibility for immediate correction of inappropriate behavior, thus insuring initial success with behavior modification techniques. It prevents misinterpretation or misunderstanding which may arise from reliance on verbal communication alone.

The following cases may serve to illustrate two different situations in which the use of the bug appeared particularly appropriate:

The first case illustrates the use of the bug in establishing a behavioral diagnosis, and in disrupting a firmly entrenched but maladaptive mother-son relationship and substituting instead more adaptive modes of relating.

Case 1. Paul is a nine-year-old boy who, at the beginning of treatment, had been living in the children's ward of our mental health center for about one year. Prior to his admission to the center, Paul had been living with his mother and brother (the father having abandoned the family several years earlier).

Before his admission to the center as an in-patient, Paul had been treated on an out-patient basis for approximately four years. He had never been able to attend public schools and his behavior was described as "quite autistic." Paul would typically spend his days playing by himself or wandering around the neighborhood, sometimes straying into homes uninvited. He was unable to relate in any way to other children his own age. Paul's psychiatric diagnosis was "schizophrenic reaction, childhood type."

Although the authors were involved in neither the planning nor the execution of Paul's treatment during his first eight months as an in-patient, they did have occasion to observe his behavior under many circumstances. The following behavioral problems were identified: making exploding noises, making machine gun noises, twirling around until quite dizzy, not concentrating for long periods while in the classroom or while involved in other activities, telling "tall tales," playing by himself even when with a group of other children, blowing on people, whining, screaming, compulsive construction of paper houses, and long and frequent conversations with himself and others about bridges, John F. Kennedy, and San Francisco.

A behavior modification program was devised which specifically concentrated on the correction of the identified inappropriate behaviors.

Rapid improvement in Paul's behavior patterns permitted his enrollment in the public school system for the first time. His teacher proved capable of handling the behavior modification program in the school setting and Paul's behavior improved with a rapidity which made it possible to extend his school attendance from the original one hour per day to full time attendance.

At this point, Paul's re-entry into the home setting was being considered. However, in spite of the fact that he continued to show improvement at the center and in school, it was noted that, following a visit to his home, he typically resorted to the previously mentioned forms of maladaptive behavior. The author's attention was, therefore, focused on the apparently problem-producing parent-child relationship.

To determine the factors in the relationship which were responsible for the behavioral deterioration, Paul and his mother were placed in an observation room, fitted with the BIE and a one-way mirror. Through observation it became apparent that the boy tyrannized his mother with the same type of "crazy" behaviors that he had used to gain his way in the ward. It also seemed clear that his mother inadvertently helped to maintain these behaviors by entering into long discussions with him about their appropriateness, rather than taking steps to extinguish or otherwise eliminate these behaviors. Clearly, the next step was to modify the mother's behavior so that she would no longer accelerate or maintain her son's inappropriate responses. To this end, the Bug-in-the-Ear device was employed.

In the first session, Paul's mother found it quite difficult to comply with the instructions of the therapist, particularly when they required change in long established behaviors, e.g., giving up a babyish nickname and substituting the name Paul.

She also found it difficult to give Paul direct instructions or to ignore his unrealistic demands. Toward the end of the first hour, the therapist instructed her to ask Paul to put away the toys with which he was playing. When she made the request, Paul asked, "Why should I?" Before the mother was given a chance to answer in her usual way and thus perpetuate her son's argumentative behavior, the therapist immediately and with firmness instructed her to tell him "because I said so." This appeared to have had a stunning effect on Paul for he was not used to this style of interaction. He complied without asking further questions. When the session was over his mother expressed surprise at her curt remark and Paul's equally surprising compliance. After that she appeared to place more faith in what the BIE and the simple, straightforward yet firm "yes" and "no" could do.

In the second session, Paul asked his mother for a new engine and more tracks to play with at the center. Mother began a long and involved explanation of reasons for considering the boy's request unreasonable. The therapist interrupted and instructed her to refuse his request with firmness and without apology. Paul responded: "If you don't buy another one I won't come home again." Mother seemed confused. The therapist instructed her to stand her ground. At this point Paul began blowing on his arm, screaming, and pounding the chair with his fists. The mother was instructed to inform him that he must stop immediately or she would leave. Much to her surprise, Paul accepted her statement without argument.

Sessions involving similar interactions were conducted on a weekly basis and served to modify the mother's behavior in such a manner that she no longer maintained Paul's bizarre responses. Considerable improvement was noted in Paul's behavior when returning from home visits. These visits were then made more frequent and of longer duration. Visits to the home by the therapist confirmed that the positive behaviors established in the center did, indeed, generalize to the home setting. Paul is presently living at home, spending weekdays at the center, and will resume public school classes this Fall.

It is noteworthy that throughout treatment the relationship between the therapist and Paul's mother was that of director to actress. The mother began to verbalize very genuine maternal feelings, even under the artificial circumstances. Paul also apparently found this structured mode of relationship more reinforcing. He began to greet his mother with a smile and sometimes even a hug. Although it is true that certain of Paul's behaviors have stagelike qualities, they are far more appropriate than his previous modes of relating.

The second case, to be presented now, has been followed for about one year.

Case 2. Henry, a five-year-old child, diagnosed as chronic brain syndrome with mental retardation, was admitted to the mental health center on an emergency basis because it had become impossible for his foster mother to control his behavior. Upon admission he was described as extremely hyperactive and physically abusive and threatening to younger children. His speech was almost completely unintelligible. His behavior was very disruptive: running, screaming, banging doors, urinating on the floors, throwing temper tantrums, interrupting group games, etc. The staff of the center felt that he should be kept there until an opening became available in one of the state schools for the retarded.

A program of behavior modification, focusing on the disruptive attention-seeking behaviors previously listed, was undertaken. The boy showed such progress that the staff decided that Henry's intellectual ability had been grossly underestimated and his foster mother decided that she wanted him back home.

In order to facilitate Henry's return to the home and the maintenance of the newly acquired adaptive behaviors, the therapist interviewed Henry's mother and gave her an orientation to the principles of behavior modification, illustrating his presentation by some of Henry's specific behaviors with which she was quite painfully familiar.

In order to insure a lasting effect for these instructions, Henry, his mother, and several siblings were placed in the playroom for three sessions with the BIE. An example of an early session follows. The mother was instructed to disregard Henry's inappropriate bids for attention from the beginning of the session. It was difficult for her to ignore him, especially as he began to whine, throw toys off the table, pull on her sleeves, and rub his head against her arm. She was given needed support by the therapist and urged to continue to disregard inappropriate bids for attention. Altogether, eleven separate bids for attention were made in a 15 min period. Then Henry gave up and stopped whining and disrupting the activities of his siblings. Instead he moved to the easel and began to draw. After a few minutes the foster mother was told to praise him verbally for his drawing but to do no more than that. Upon receiving the praise, Henry smiled and continued drawing for about 15 min—a rather unprecedented stretch of quiet and adaptive activity. The mother was asked to approach Henry, praise him again, and make complimentary comments about his drawing.

This episode and others like it appear to have had rather dramatic effects. In later sessions, the mother needed very little instruction from the therapist to ignore inappropriate attention-seeking behavior. From observations in these sessions and verbal reports of the mother in subsequent interviews, the gains made at the center were generally maintained at home and the mother was able to generalize her responses to the home in dealing with complex situations created by Henry or his siblings. The mother reported that Henry was able to develop constructive means for gaining attention, such as caring for the younger children and playing the role of mother's helper.

We do not claim that the BIE will prove useful in all situations involving parent-child interactions or even that the progress reported in these two cases could not have been attained without the use of this device. It is our feeling, however, that one session with the BIE might be worth many sessions of instruction. The BIE provides visual aid and on-the-spot corrections, feedback, and reinforcement of parents' behavior. It makes possible actual demonstrations which are carried out in an environment which approximates real life encounters. Finally, and perhaps most important, it utilizes the principles of operant conditioning to train parents rather than relying on more traditional instruction methods.

References

Hawkins, R., Peterson, R., Schweid, E. & Bijou, S. Behavior therapy in the home: Amelioration of problem parent-child relations with the parent in a therapeutic role. *Journal of Experimental Child Psychology*, 1966, 4, 99-107.

Wahler, R., Winkel, G., Peterson, R., & Morrison, C. Mothers as behavior therapists for their own children. *Behaviour Research and Therapy*, 1965 3, 113-134.

New Application of ECT

Richard D. Rubin

HELENE FULD HOSPITAL

Robert Fried

HUNTER COLLEGE

Cyril M. Franks

NEUROPSYCHIATRIC INSTITUTE

Prospectus

Although electroconvulsive shock (ECS) has been in use therapeutically for more than thirty years, studies establishing criteria for treatment and prediction of results in clinical practice are still lacking (Kalinowsky, 1966). However, parametric studies of the effects of ECS have been performed with animals, using the single ECS paradigm (Chevalier, 1965, Madsen & McGaugh, 1961). In these studies, the effects of ECS are attributed to retrograde amnesia (RA) produced by the disruptive effect of the ECS on memory trace consolidation (the structural encoding and consequent storage of memory). These studies demonstrate that RA gradually diminishes and finally disappears as the time between learning trial and ECS increases. For example, in the first of the systematic experimental studies of the effect of ECS on memory (Duncan, 1949), a conditioned avoidance response to an aversive stimulus was produced in animals, followed at different time intervals by ECS. If the avoidance responses were followed immediately (20 sec interval) by the ECS, the avoidance response was abolished. This indicated total RA. But, as the time interval between the avoidance response and the ECS was increased, the number of successful avoidance responses to the aversive stimulus increased until asymptote was reached at an interval of one hour between the avoidance response and ECS. At this point, there was no apparent memory loss for the avoidance response.

Indirectly, such studies lend support for the formulation of a testable hypothesis for the effective application of electroconvulsive therapy (ECT). Until now such a hypothesis has been lacking because ECT has proceeded largely on the basis of unrelated empirical findings, without a theoretical model of its effects to predict outcome in humans.

The proposed model and resulting hypothesis concern the effects of ECT on neurotic and psychotic symptoms and predict specific conditions under which treatment applications will be most effective in reducing overt symptom patterns and in maintaining a symptom-free state for considerable time periods.

Model

The model considers "attention" to be the effective "selector" of the *contents of consciousness,* i.e., the *memory event* (or memory trace) to be disrupted by ECS. Contents of consciousness have their neural correlates and essentially constitute the unique reaction of the subject to these neural events, e.g., . . . "An image of which I am not conscious now will appear in my imagination if appropriate stimuli activate some of my neurons ..." (Wolpe, 1958). Thus, suggesting imagery for a person's attention (providing *appropriate stimuli*) necessarily activates the neural correlates of that imagery. Suggesting the main psychopathological imagery for the attention of the patient necessarily activates ("selects") the neural correlates of *that* imagery. Giving ECT at that instant disrupts the neural correlates of the "selected" imagery and *pari passu,* ablates (by RA) the correlated psychopathological imagery and its conditional emotional response (CER). Thus, as stated in the hypothesis below, *contiguity* (the principle of conditioning) between memory event and ECS can be obtained and controlled. The model proposed is oversimplified, as most theoretical models are, but, ". . . Even a very oversimplified model may be quite useful in the early stages of a theoretical investigation . . ." (Rachevsky, 1966).

Ordinarily, routine ECT is given with the patient anesthetized, or, terrified, attending to what is going on in his immediate environment at the time of treatment. In either routine method, the psychopathology is not "uppermost in his mind"—"selected" as it were—when treatment is administered. The factor of contiguity between psychopathology and ECT consequently is not controlled.[1] Based on the preceding discussion, the following hypothesis is offered:

If the patient's attention is strongly directed, by hypnosis if necessary, to his most disturbing feelings and imagery (e.g. actively hallucinating, not just imagining he is hallucinating, carrying out a perverse activity, not just imagining doing so) and if he is instantly given ECT (awake), there should result a significantly greater amelioration and reduction of symptoms than that obtained when ECT is given in the usual way.

Patients whose psychopathology was refractory to all previous treatment would thus become "cured" by RA.

The purpose of the present study was to establish the validity of the above hypothesis which we describe as "aiming the treatment." To our knowledge, this is the first clinical study designed to apply the principles of conditioning to ECT.

Method

Fifteen patients hospitalized or with history of hospitalization because of mental illness voluntarily participated in this experiment. The ECS apparatus was a Medcraft, model B-24, set at 150 V; .6 sec. The procedure was as follows: Electrodes were attached as usual and a syringe containing 40 mg of Succinycholine was inserted in an antecubital vein. Then, patients with obsessions and compulsions were instructed to *act them out*. Those with hallucinations remained *ready* until hallucinations occurred. When symptoms were observable, the Succinylcholine was administered (to reduce fracture risk). At the *instant* fasciculation was observed (to prevent Succinylcholine from acting as an aversive stimulus), ECT was administered. Six cc of 2% solution of Pentothal was administered i.v. after the seizure while the patient was still comatose, to prevent the transient post-ictal confusion

[1]It is interesting to note, in support of this contention, that a review of the ECS literature (animal subjects) concluded that RA does not take place when the ECS is given under anesthesia (Lewis & Maher, 1965).

from acting as an aversive stimulus by keeping the patient asleep a few minutes, just as giving Pentothal in the routine way (before Succinylcholine) does. This method also served as control for any other effects of Pentothal, when comparing this method to routine treatment given with Pentothal, Succinylcholine, and ECT in that order.

Results

The fifteen patients thus treated included seven previously treated with routine ECT (with Pentothal anesthesia). These seven patients served as their own controls: In none of these patients had routine ECT been effective. Total number of previous routine treatments ranged from 5 to 28 (median = 10). All patients, following a single ECT given according to the above hypothesis, improved dramatically for periods of three months to three years to date. One relapsed after nine months but recovered after another treatment. The probability of the effectiveness of this treatment, resulting from chance factors only, is less than .1%. This estimate is based on the number of previous, ineffective, treatments (Fisher's exact probability test).

As an illustration, the first four consecutive patients treated in accordance with the hypothesis are herein presented.

Case 1. H.L., a 47-year-old woman, first became depressed about 20 years ago after her mother's death. While depressed, she ate canned peaches and became violently ill. From that day on, she blamed her depression on the peaches and spoke of little else. After about one month, she had several ECTs and recovered from all symptoms. Three months prior to her admission in June, 1965, her father-in-law died. She again became severely depressed and obsessed with the word "peaches." Prior to admission she had been unsuccessfully treated by the family doctor, who sent her to a psychiatrist who, after diagnosing involutional psychosis, administered eight ECTs with anesthesia, with no resulting improvement. He then referred her for admission to the hospital. On admission—and throughout hospitalization—she was obsessed with peaches. She would blush or cry if peaches were mentioned. Anything remotely resembling a peach (such as a door knob) frightened her. Staff concluded she had had insufficient ECT. After thirteen more ECTs with anesthesia, she improved as regards affect, but not as regards peaches, and she was discharged in August, 1965 as having received "maximum hospital benefit."

Though referred back to her psychiatrist, she failed to resume treatment. She was readmitted in October, 1965 after a suicide attempt. She said she could not get "peaches" out of her mind and lay on the floor weeping and mumbling "why did I ever eat one?" She was anorexic, insomniac, and inconsolable. Five more ECTs with anesthesia resulted in little improvement.

She was then treated, in accordance with the hypothesis, as follows: With electrodes attached to her temples, she was told vividly to imagine eating a peach. She began to cry. She was given Anectine, and in the 15 sec prior to its effect she was told she was to "eat the peach," that a bowl of peaches that she must eat was next to her, etc. At the instant fasciculation was observed, ECT was given. Later that day she was smiling and cheerful. She ate a peach that was offered to her. Elated, she called her husband and told him about it. A (psychoanalyst) colleague hypothesized that the Anectine had caused an aversive response to her "aversion to peaches," and that allowing respiratory distress to go on a few seconds (due to effect of Anectine) would enhance the "therapeutic effect" by increasing the "punishment." To test *his* hypothesis, she was given another treatment during which she was allowed to fasciculate for several seconds while she was told vividly to imagine eating a peach. Following that she continued to feel well, but she refused a third treatment because, she said, the last one frightened her. *She offered to eat a peach to prove she was well if we would not give her another treatment.* She was discharged, remaining well and working till June, 1966, when she saw a picture of a peach in a magazine. Her "obsession-depression syndrome" returned. She was then given one ECT with her hand in a bowl of canned peaches and a few drops of peach syrup on her tongue while the words "eat the peaches" were repeated. She recovered immediately from the syndrome and remained well until July, 1966 when she again saw a picture of a peach and burst into tears. The author was on vacation and she was treated by another psychiatrist who administered nine ECTs with anesthesia, with some improvement in affect, but none as regards peaches. She was discharged and referred back to the author. At this point she was well enough to participate in treatment by systematic desensitization to peaches and has been working (and eating peaches) since.

Case 2. I.C., a 30-year-old woman was obsessed for years with stabbing her mother and then herself. She had been in psychoanalysis previously, had received various medications, and had had sixteen ECTs elsewhere with evanescent improvement, but then slashed her wrist and was admitted in July, 1965. Six subsequent ECTs with anesthesia produced no noticeable improvement. She continued on medication and psychotherapy, and, being considered neither suicidal nor homicidal in the following weeks, was discharged. Despite continuing psychotherapy and dosages of as much as 75 mg of Tofranil q.i.d. along with 50 mg of Pertofane q.i.d. and 100 mg of Thorazine q.i.d., the "obsession-depression syndrome" got worse. She requested readmission in April, 1966. In accordance with the hypothesis, she was treated as follows: With electrodes in place, she was told to "act-out" her fantasy of stabbing her mother with a butcher knife. She raised her clenched fist with the imagined knife. She was told, "Kill her!" As she brought her fist down repeatedly she was given Anectine in the other arm and given ECT immediately on fasciculation. The next day, greatly improved, she went home and spoke kindly to her mother for the first time in years. She asked her mother, "Do you love me?" and then kissed her. When the author asked if she still felt like stabbing her mother, she laughed and said, "Oh, she doesn't deserve anything like that." The next day she was given a similar treatment in which she "acted-out" stabbing herself. The following day she was so greatly improved that she was discharged and went back to work. She remains free of the above symptoms as of October 25, 1968 and is currently being treated by systematic desensitization to various social situations.

Case 3. M.P., a 15-year-old boy, beat himself incessantly. On admission in March, 1966, he was covered with bruises. He said he "got a certain feeling inside" relieved only by beating himself. He admitted fantasizing killing his parents as he beat himself. Prior to admission, he had been treated unsuccessfully with psychotherapy and tranquilizers. In the first week in the hospital, while undergoing various examinations, he spent most of the leisure time available to him locked in his bathroom where he could be heard beating himself and cursing. He underwent a series of five ECTs with anesthesia, with no improvement. In accordance with the hypothesis, he was then treated while beating himself and shouting, "Kill!" After only one treatment, he had no desire to beat himself or kill his parents. He became sociable for the first time with other patients (even flirtatious with the student nurses). A week later while on a pass, his father said "Shhh" to him for interrupting. This resulted in his hitting himself once. He was given another treatment while beating himself and shouting "Kill!" while the author was saying in his ear "Shh-Shh-Shhh." Although his father subsequently has said "Shhh," M.P. has not beaten himself further and is now back in school, making a fairly good social adjustment (last seen on October 15, 1968).

Case 4. V.R., a 65-year-old male paretic (who had been treated for syphilitic meningio-encephalitis in a state hospital from 1941 to 1944) was admitted in March, 1966 with severe depression and the delusion "I am filling up with feces and when my head fills up I will die." He was given ten ECTs with anesthesia and became severely confused. When the confusion cleared, he eloped from the hospital "to get operated on to let the feces out." He was then treated, in accordance with the hypothesis, as follows: With electrodes in place, he was told he was gradually filling up with feces, that he was filling up to his throat, that feces was coming out of his mouth and ears. As he panicked, the ECT was given. After treatment, he felt perfectly well. He went around the hospital saying "It's a miracle—a miracle!" Ten days later, he confided that he was afraid he was getting "stopped-up" and was given an identical treatment, with an identical miraculous result. Three days later he ran into a nearby woods, explaining "God told me to come here to die." He willingly returned to the hospital and then, with electrodes in place, was asked if he heard God's voice. He did not. He was told to listen for it. After about 10 min he said, "I can hear Him now." When asked what God was saying, he replied, "My time has come." He was told to nod when he heard God again, and when he nodded a moment later, he was given the ECT instantly. Later in the day, he denied ever having heard God's voice. "You must have been mixed up with someone else." After two weeks of observation during which time he remained well, he was discharged to a boarding home where eventually he "got fresh" with a female resident. He was therefore asked to leave. He now resides in another institution pending placement in the community. As of October 22, 1968, he has none of the symptoms for which he had been treated, and no complaints of other psychiatric disturbance.

Discussion

Theoretically, reality and imagination differ: Neurones activated by one have connections not shared by the other. In psychosis, sharing increases: Hallucinations and delusions thus seem real, evoking a conditioned emotional response which can be ablated by RA produced by ECS. Generalizing from the model, symptoms treated by ECT can be divided into two broad categories: *Intermittent* states and *steady* states, and they can be discussed as corollaries to the hypothesis.

Corollary I (for intermittent states). Inappropriate cerebral neuronal assemblies (and their correlated psychopathology: hallucinations and delusions) may escape the effects of routine ECT since they are already inhibited by anesthesia or by the selector being linked to environmental and irrelevant stimuli. Since chronic schizophrenics are generally withdrawn, with a "poverty of associations," and may be selecting hallucinatory and delusional imagery only intermittently, it is to be expected that their improvement due to ECT may only follow an extremely long course of treatment, if at all. The model would explain and predict the results of a study in which one group of schizophrenics receiving 20 ECT treatments with thiopentathol anesthesia did not differ from the control patients receiving thiopentathol anesthesia without ECT (Miller, Clancy, & Cumming, 1953). Contradictory results (Brengelmann, 1959; Zamora & Kaebling, 1965) comparing relative memory loss with various modifications of techniques for routine ECT (unilateral, etc.) are regarded as factitious for therapeutic effect when viewed in the light cast by the proposed model: the most important factor, what the patient had "in mind" at the time of treatment, was *uniformly ignored.*

COROLLARY II (FOR STEADY STATES). Routine ECT is a tried and true remedy for depression because the symptoms of depression are primarily in a steady state: The neural correlates of affect involved are predominantly subcortical psychomotor centers which, since they are already conditioned to conscious content of everyday life, are comparatively unaffected by brief cortical anesthesia or wandering attention. Catatonia, which is also a steady state, may respond well to routine ECT for the same reasons: There is an RA effect on the neural correlates of that state. Acute schizophrenics are also in a steady state, virtually constantly selecting hallucinatory and delusional imagery. Predictably, they also respond well to routine ECT because, during the course of treatment, the pathological neural correlates are bound to be affected sooner or later.

Conclusions

The probability of successful treatment outcome can be increased by using the method described above and the following significant benefits may be obtained: (a) Increase in prediction of results of ECT, with consequent reduction of treatment failures. (b) Reduction in number of ECT given to each patient due to increased therapeutic effect of each treatment. (c) Decreased risk of bodily injury associated with decreased number of treatments. (d) Increased number of patients who can benefit from ECT. (e) Possible new applications of

ECT to parapsychiatric conditions, such as habitual criminality, drug addiction, etc. (f) Additionally, variations of the hypothesis presented could be used to study learning, recent and remote memory and recall, etc., in patients receiving ECT, in a manner parallel to the animal studies cited.

References

Brengelmann, J. C. *The effect of repeated electric shock on learning in depression.* Berlin: Springer, 1959.

Chevalier, J. A. Permanence of amnesia after a single post-trial electroconvulsive seizure. *Journal of Comparative and Physiological Psychology,* 1965, **59**, 125-127.

Duncan, C. P. The retroactive effect of electroshock on learning. *Journal of Comparative and Physiological Psychology,* 1949, **42**, 32-44.

Kalinowsky, L. B. Somatic treatments in psychiatry. *American Journal of Psychiatry,* 1966, **123**, 338-340.

Lewis, D. J., & Maher, B. A. Neural consolidation and electroconvulsive shock. *Psychological Review,* 1965, **72**, 225-239.

Madsen, M. C., & McGaugh, J. L. The effect of ECS on one-trial avoidance learning, *Journal of Comparative and Physiological Psychology,* 1961, **54**, 522-523.

Miller, D. H., Clancy, J., & Cumming, E. A comparison between unidirectional current non-convulsive electrical stimulation given with Reiter's Machine, standard a.c. ECS (Cerletti Method), and Pentothal in chronic schizophrenia. *American Journal of Psychiatry,* 1953, **109**, 617-620.

Rachevsky, N. A neurobiological model of schizophrenias and their possible treatment. *Bulletin of Mathematical Biophysics,* 1966, **26**, 167-185.

Wolpe, J. L. *Psychotherapy by reciprocal inhibition.* Stanford, Calif.: Stanford University Press, 1958.

Zamora, E. N., & Kaebling, R. Memory and electroconvulsive therapy. *American Journal of Psychiatry,* 1965, **122**, 546-554.

Experimental Development of a Modeling Treatment to Extinguish Persistent Avoidance Behavior[1]

Michael D. Spiegler, Robert M. Liebert, Michael J. McMains, Luis E. Fernandez

VANDERBILT UNIVERSITY

One of the fundamental problems recognized by clinicians of all theoretical persuasions is the development of short-term therapeutic techniques which can be economically administered. Furthermore, the depressing shortage of clinically trained workers in the face of the burgeoning number of persons who annually seek psychological assistance suggests that the development of treatment regimens which can be administered by nonprofessionals should be a central target for behavioral research.

However, the clinical implementation of new and purportedly economical therapeutic strategies has often antedated systematic laboratory research, resulting in the brief popularization of strategies and their subsequent devaluation as placebos rather than panaceas. Sensitive to this unfortunate historical trend, proponents of behaviorally oriented therapies have come to greatly value systematic accumulation of controlled laboratory evidence as a mandatory first step in the development of innovative techniques. Guided by this ethic, several recent experiments at our laboratory have been directed toward extinguishing persistent avoidance behavior through symbolic modeling procedures. The basic hypothesis that, under favorable circum-

[1]The authors wish to thank Mrs. John H. Dunlap and Betty Gay for serving as our models, and Jan Aitkenhead, Carol Ann Fernandez, Edith McFee, and Fran Owen for assisting in various stages of the research.

stances, behavior can be facilitated or inhibited through the mere observation of others has been amply documented (Flanders, 1968) and several pioneering demonstrations of its potential clinical application have been reported by Bandura and his colleagues (Bandura, 1968; Bandura, Grusec, & Menlove, 1967; Bandura & Menlove, 1968). Extensive review of these reports is beyond the scope of this paper which will be restricted to describing the systematic development of a modeling film to vicariously extinguish persistent avoidance of snakes.

An earlier study from our laboratory (Hill, Liebert, & Mott, 1968) demonstrated that nursery school boys' fear of dogs could be significantly reduced by a single presentation of an 11-min modeling film. This film differed from those used by Bandura and his associates in two significant respects. First, in our study two modeling *roles* were presented: an older boy who fearlessly interacted with the dog at the beginning of the film and a boy of nursery school age who gradually learned to emulate the former's approach behavior. Thus, not only did subjects observe the approach responses made by two models but, perhaps of even greater significance, they also observed the act of imitation itself. Second, whereas Bandura and his colleagues report that their model(s) appeared "fearless" throughout, the peer model in our movie initially appeared somewhat apprehensive. Studies of imitation have shown that under some circumstances increasing the similarity between the model and the observer may facilitate imitation. It therefore seemed plausible that a film in which the model initially exhibits a moderate degree of fear which he gradually overcomes will increase his perceived similarity to the observer and thus produce a situation which is maximally conducive to vicarious extinction.

In keeping with these considerations, a 14-min modeling film was produced to be used in reducing fear of nonpoisonous snakes in adults. The film first presents the meeting of an attractive female undergraduate (Model 1) and a noted female herpetologist (Model 2). In successive scenes, Model 1 gradually learns to approach and handle several snakes, following Model 2's demonstration of each behavior. While wearing gloves, Model 1 learns to stroke and pick up the smaller snake and then repeats this procedure with a larger snake. Next, Model 1 removes the gloves and repeats these successively more difficult tasks barehanded. Model 1 is then shown confidently holding the larger snake. Finally, Model 2 holds the snake close to her face in an affectionate gesture while it curls itself around her neck ("intimate interaction" scene). As the film progresses, Model 1 becomes noticeably more confident in handling the snakes and appears to be increasingly enjoying the procedure. A taped narrative, designed to be equally plausible with or without visual accompaniment, verbally describes what the film depicts and also includes information about snakes and their handling.

The first experiment employing these symbolic presentations was designed to provide an initial demonstration of the effectiveness of the sound film and to determine the relative contributions of the visual and narrative components of the treatment. A questionnaire dealing with feelings and attitudes toward nonpoisonous snakes was developed and administered to all female undergraduates in Vanderbilt University's introductory psychology classes. From this population 34 coeds who reported considerable fear of snakes were pretested twice by means of a graduated behavioral test. In turn, participants were asked to enter a room containing a caged 2-ft water snake, walk to the cage (a distance of about 15 ft), put on a pair of gloves, remove the lid of the cage and look in, reach into the cage and stroke the snake, pick up the snake, remove the gloves, stroke the snake, and finally hold the snake barehanded. Twenty of the women manifested avoidance behavior judged to be sufficiently stable and severe to warrant treatment. These subjects were assigned to one of four groups. One treatment consisted of a single viewing of the film with narrative, a second employed the film without the narrative, a third presented the narrative without the film, while members of a fourth group served as untreated controls.

Behavioral tests were conducted individually one week and one month after treatment by a female experimenter who was "blind" with respect to the treatment to which subjects had been exposed. As anticipated, greatest change was produced by the film with narration condition, the only group which significantly improved relative to the controls (Dunnett $t = 2.08$, $p < .05$). There was no significant effect for measures, revealing no change from one week to one month after treatment.

In a second experiment we re-examined the principal finding of our first study with another population. Ten undergraduate women from George Peabody College were selected in a manner analogous to the procedures described previously and were assigned to either the film with narrative or control treatment. Apart from deleting the "intimate interaction" scene,[2] the procedures were identical to those used previously. As in our earlier study, the treatment group showed signifi-

[2]Several subjects in the first experiment commented that they became distinctly disturbed during the "intimate interaction" scene, and, therefore, it was eliminated from the film for the second and third experiments.

cantly more approach behavior than the controls after treatment ($t = 2.56$, $p < .05$), but not before. Unfortunately, final examination schedules and subsequent vacations of our subjects precluded follow-up assessments.

The subjects used in the first two experiments were college students who, despite genuine fear and aversion toward snakes, could not properly be described as "phobic." It is doubtful that their avoidance behavior interfered seriously with any aspect of their daily lives. Further, these experiments were presented as an investigation of changes in attitude toward snakes over time. Thus, the participants were not highly motivated to modify their behavior and, moreover, were given no expectations about the effectiveness of the treatment. Both of these factors are typically salient features of clinical therapy of any orientation. It was therefore desirable to begin working with persons more troubled by their fear of snakes and to structure our treatment as therapeutic rather than merely experimental in nature. Thus, the participants in a recently completed third experiment, in which we collaborated with Martin Katahn and Charles Billings, were adults from the community-at-large (6 men and 15 women) who had responded to a newspaper advertisement asking for persons who were afraid of snakes and willing to participate in a study of new treatment methods. These subjects were selected by means of the assessment procedures used in the first two experiments and were also briefly interviewed and given comparable expectancies. They were then matched for level of avoidance behavior (as manifested on the behavioral test) and assigned to one of three treatment groups.

Several subjects in the first two experiments commented that although the film seemed to help in overcoming their fear, they became somewhat "anxious" while watching some of the scenes. We reasoned that if the participants were relaxed while viewing the film, its effectiveness would be enhanced. Thus, in the third experiment, subjects in the film with relaxation group ($n = 8$) were taught deep muscle relaxation by means of a 50-min prerecorded tape[3] and then shown the film. A second group was shown the film with narration ($n = 6$). Finally, in keeping with the strategy of examining the independent effectiveness of the logical components of the treatment, a third group ($n = 7$) was given only the relaxation training and, like the film with relaxation group, was instructed to practice relaxation and use it in future encounters with snakes.

[3]The tape was developed by Dr. Martin Katahn.

All participants were treated in groups and were seated in reclining lounge chairs during treatment. The treatments were administered in two sessions,[4] one week apart. During the second week, each group's treatment was repeated, with the exception that relaxation training was somewhat abbreviated.

Behavioral tests were individually administered after the first treatment session, before and after the second treatment, and one week after the second treatment with a new and substantially larger snake as a test for generalization. Mean raw scores (based on number of behavioral tests passed) at each assessment are presented in Fig. 1. As predicted, the addition of relaxation training to the modeling film substantially enhanced its effectiveness.

Subjects in the film with relaxation condition performed significantly better after the first treatment and on all subsequent tests than

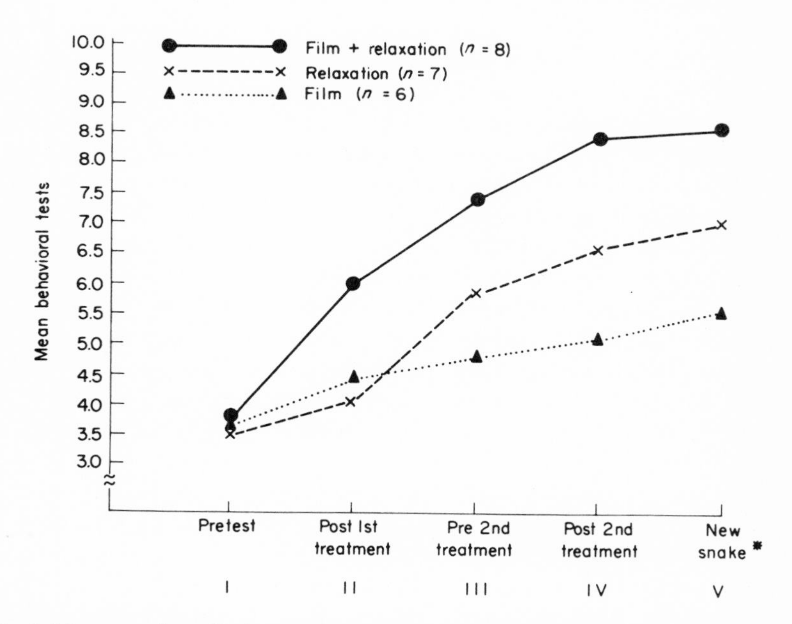

Fig. 1. Mean number of behavioral tests passed in the third experiment at each assessment as a function of treatment condition.

*Two subjects were unable to attend the final assessment (V), thereby reducing the number of subjects in the Film + Relaxation ($n = 7$) and Film ($n = 5$) conditions.

[4]Because relaxation training typically necessitates some practice (e.g., at home), it was decided to add an additional treatment session in the third experiment.

participants in either of the other two conditions. In the first posttreatment behavioral test, subjects in both the film only and film with relaxation conditions significantly increased their approach behavior relative to the pretest. The relaxation only group did not improve its performance from pretest to immediately after the first treatment, but thereafter showed significant improvement. As in the first two experiments, there was a significant decrease in avoidance behavior after only a single presentation of the modeling film. A second exposure to the film served to enhance its effectiveness. Additionally, it is apparent from Fig. 1 that no performance loss resulted from introducing the new and larger snake.

Most interesting is the fact that the relaxation only group showed greater improvement than the film only group, beginning with the third behavioral test, although never equaling the performance of participants given the film and relaxation treatment. Numerous previous experiments have shown that relaxation training alone (i.e., unassociated with anxiety provoking scenes) is ineffectual in reducing avoidance behavior (e.g., Davison, 1968; Rachman, 1965). However, a recent study by Zeisset (1968) found "relaxation-plus-application" to be an effective treatment which was not significantly different in its effects from standard desensitization procedures. Zeisset's relaxation procedures, like our own, emphasized that subjects should use the relaxation response in all situations in which feared objects or stressful situations were encountered. When relaxation training is presented in this way, it is plausible that the combination of self-induced relaxation and progressively more provoking encounters with real-life situations will produce *in vivo* desensitization. This hypothesis is indirectly supported by the finding that whereas the relaxation only group did not improve significantly immediately after its first treatment session, it did improve after having had an opportunity to use the relaxation in the first posttreatment behavioral test. However, the speculation that this process is operative must be substantiated by further experimentation.

The success of the film with relaxation group in the third experiment is not wholly revealed by citation of the several statistically reliable results which were obtained. It should be noted, for example, that participants in this group were, without exception, able to touch a large, unfamiliar snake with their bare hands after receiving only two treatments which required less than two hours of total time to administer. Moreover, the reports of these individuals uniformly suggested an alleviation of their previously long standing fear, and many reported an increased willingness to engage in gardening, camping, and other activities in which contact with snakes might reasonably occur.

Although the research reported in this paper cannot be considered more than a beginning in the development of film modeling therapy, the success which was realized in the foregoing experiments is impressive, especially in the light of the extremely economical means by which treatment was accomplished. Besides the brevity of treatment, in all three experiments the requisite materials consisted of an 8-mm film (which can now be easily reproduced for under $25), a movie projector, a reel of magnetic tape and tape recorder, and the availability of representative members of the class of feared objects. Extensive interaction with skilled therapists was entirely unnecessary, and the procedures were made even more economical by group administration.

References

Bandura, A. Modelling approaches to the modification of phobic disorders, *in* R. Porter (Ed.), *Ciba Foundation symposium: The role of learning in psychotherapy*. London: Churchill, 1968.

Bandura, A., Grusec, J. E., & Menlove, F. L. Vicarious extinction of avoidance behavior. *Journal of Personality and Social Psychology*, 1967, **5**, 16-23.

Bandura, A., & Menlove, F. L. Factors determining vicarious extinction of avoidance behavior through symbolic modeling. *Journal of Personality and Social Psychology*, 1968, **8**, 99-108.

Davison, G. C. Systematic desensitization as a counterconditioning process. *Journal of Abnormal Psychology*, 1968, **73**, 91-99.

Flanders, J. P. A review of research on imitative behavior. *Psychological Bulletin*, 1968, **69**, 316-337.

Hill, J. H., Liebert, R. M., & Mott, D. E. W. Vicarious extinction of avoidance behavior through films: An initial test. *Psychological Reports*, 1968, **22**, 192.

Rachman, S. Studies in desensitization—I: The separate effects of relaxation and desensitization. *Behaviour Research and Therapy*, 1965, **3**, 245-251.

Zeisset, R. M. Desensitization and relaxation in the modification of psychiatric patients' interview behavior. *Journal of Abnormal Psychology*, 1968, **73**, 18-24.

A Self-Administered Programmed Recording for Decreasing Cigarette Consumption[1]

Mervyn K. Wagner, R. A. Bragg

V. A. Hospital at Salisbury

The application of a specific combination of behavior modification methods to one experimental group in a recent study (Wagner & Bragg, 1968) suggested a procedure which might be effective in decreasing cigarette consumption. This particular approach appeared attractive because of its success, of course, but also because it could be programed and subsequently administered through the use of a recording.

The method hypothesizes that habituated responses such as smoking involve both positive and negative reinforcement. In other words, smoking is pleasurable while not smoking is painful, or at least uncomfortable. Experimental emphasis has been on the manipulation of the positive reinforcement aspects with the majority of studies involving some kind of punishment or aversive conditioning (Franks, Fried, & Ashem, 1966; Mullen, 1968; Powell & Azrin, 1968; Viernstein, 1968). Aversive procedures tend to be successful so long as the aversion is regularly applied; however, long-term effects are essentially poor. The aversive stimuli cause some changes in the positive reinforcement value of smoking in that it becomes less pleasurable, but the discomfort involved in going for increasing periods of time or being in particular situations without a cigarette is not relieved. Some

[1]Prepared within the framework of activities supported by the V. A. Psychiatric Program Evaluation Staff.

reference has been made to this aspect of the smoking habit in various studies, and informal but generally unsuccessful attempts have been made to control it. These informal attempts have amounted to some kind of substitution behavior such as chewing gum, eating candy, etc. The hypothesis upon which this particular selection of methods has been chosen is that modifying both aspects of the habit systematically will lead to a reduction of cigarette consumption. In other words, the attempt is to modify the pleasurable aspect of smoking (positive reinforcement) while at the same time effecting a change in one's ability to tolerate the discomfort experience (negative reinforcement) which follows going for long periods of time and being in particular situations without a cigarette.

Techniques

There are two separate aspects to the smoking recording—first, the techniques, and second, the programing of their use.

The first 16 min of the record give the *S*s accelerated relaxation training (Wolpe & Lazarus, 1966). This is the traditional procedure except that *S*s are told to practice without the record and that their goal for this practice should be learning to relax deeply and completely as quickly as possible.

The relaxation is then utilized during the systematic desensitization portion of the record which takes 17 min. Here again this procedure is essentially the same as that described by Wolpe, except for the fact that the hierarchy is on the record and thus the same for all *S*s rather than tailored specifically to the needs of the individual. These situations describe time without a cigarette and also predicted stressful situations such as, "Imagine yourself not having had a cigarette for a couple of hours; you are sitting there with someone, and he lights up a cigarette and offers you one." One definite difference between the procedure involved in the recording and the usual systematic desensitization is that rather than having *S* signal anxiety and then go back to the previous situation, he is instructed to move the arm of the record player forward when he can no longer remain relaxed and comfortable.

This third section, covert sensitization, is an aversion procedure described by Cautela (1967) in his treatment of alcoholics. The instructions for this procedure are to relax and then imagine going through the process of taking a cigarette out of the package, lighting up, etc. Concurrently, the record introduces systematically increased images of uncomfortable feelings, beginning with items such as, "The smoke is beginning to taste rather badly," continuing through, "You puke and vomit all over yourself," and ending with a combination of references to as many senses as possible.

At the point where the aversive condition is at its apex, instructions are given to crush out the cigarette, to break off the imagery, and to relax. The subsequent pairing of relaxation and not smoking constitutes the aversion relief principle described by Thorpe, Schmidt, Brown, and Castell (1964). The hypothesis is that the contiguity of smoking and aversive imagery will serve as a punishment situation for the smoking behavior while at the same time the aversion relief will serve as a positive reinforcement for the nonsmoking response.

Abbreviated Program[2]

INTRODUCTORY INSTRUCTIONS (On front of record cover)

This record can only help you quit smoking. Primarily it depends on your motivation. There are two aspects to the smoking habit—the first part is the pleasure it gives you and the second is the uncomfortable feeling that you get when you go without a cigarette for extended periods of time and in different situations. We will attempt to help you change both of these. Don't worry yet about trying to stop smoking.

(The *S*s are given ten postcards to return to the author with the number of cigarettes they smoke each day and the dates when they use the recording. For each card they return, they have $1.00 credit toward their $10.00 data-recording deposit. There is also a $5.00 breakage deposit.)

Results and Discussion

Too few *S*s have used the recording to be able to assess its effectiveness; however, the specific procedures duplicate one approach used (*in vivo*) in a study previous to derivation of the recording. Wagner and Bragg (1968) compared five different methods for modifying smoking behavior. The techniques used included systematic desensitization, covert sensitization, relaxation alone, counseling, and the treatment that combined systematic desensitization and covert sensitization. The focus for this study was not the termination of smoking *per se*, but

[2]Complete program may be obtained from the author. The record is also available at cost for research purposes only.

ABBREVIATED DAILY SCHEDULE (On back of record cover)

Day	No. of cigs.	No. times listened	Directions
1 2 7			Listen to Section 1 at least 3 times and practice twice daily during these first 7 days. When you can relax deeply and quickly, then go on.[a]
8			After completing Sections 2 and 3, then go on.
9 10 30[b]			Begin at Section 2. Stretch out the time between cigarettes. Relax instead of smoking. Don't carry cigarettes around. When you've gone as long as you can without a cigarette, then get one and imagine it as a "vomit cigarette." From now on, stop enjoying cigarettes. Relax when you don't smoke. Feel sick when you do. When you have reached these criteria, go on to the next section: (1) Completed Section 2 twice all the way through before having to go on to Section 3. (2) Have cut down substantially on your cigarette intake. (3) Have stretched out the time to at least 4 waking hours between cigarettes.
31 32 etc.			Now stop smoking. Relax instead. You are now a nonsmoker. Throw away all your cigarettes. Do whatever you have to, but don't smoke. About 4 times daily imagine smoking "vomit cigarettes." Continue listening to Side 2 every other day for 10 days, and then listen less frequently until you no longer feel the need to smoke. Do whatever you must to stop smoking at this time. If you have any problems, call.

[a] Each section of the schedule which is delineated by the horizontal lines is covered by a tear-strip which is removed after satisfying the requirements of that particular section.

[b] Of course the numbers would differ for different Ss, dependent upon their rate of progress through the program.

testing the effectiveness of the different methods for modifying a recalcitrant habit. Five of the nine Ss undergoing the systematic desensitization-covert sensitization treatment discontinued smoking after only five treatments. At a 90-day follow-up, only two of eight continued to abstain, even though the total group continued to smoke only 35% of their pre-experimental cigarette consumption.

Even though the success for this particular method cannot be reported at this time, there is increasing evidence in the literature that programed application of techniques adopted from learning theory models and experiments to behavior change are making rapid strides forward. For a change, the quest is not for principles that work but rather for the application of principles that do work.[3]

References

Cautela, J. R. Covert sensitization. *Psychological Reports*, 1967, **20**, 459-468.

Franks, C. M., Fried, R., & Ashem, B. An improved apparatus for the aversive conditioning of cigarette smokers. *Behaviour Research and Therapy*, 1966, **4**, 301-308.

Mullen, F. G., Jr. The effect of covert sensitization on smoking behavior. Unpublished manuscript, Queens College, Charlotte, N. C., 1968.

Powell, J. R., & Azrin, N. The effects of shock as a punisher for cigarette smoking. *Journal of Applied Behavior Analysis*, 1968, **1**, 63-71.

Thorpe, J. G., Schmidt, E., Brown, P. T., & Castell, D. Aversion-relief therapy: A new method for general application. *Behaviour Research and Therapy*, 1964, **2**, 71-82.

Viernstein, L. K. Evaluation of therapeutic techniques of covert sensitization of smoking behavior. Unpublished manuscript, Queens College, Charlotte, N. C., 1968.

Wagner, M. K., & Bragg, R. A. Comparing behavior modification methods for habit decrement—smoking. Unpublished manuscript, V. A. Hospital, Salisbury, N. C., 1968.

Wolpe, J., & Lazarus, A. A. *Behavior therapy techniques*. New York: Macmillan (Pergamon), 1966.

[3]Fourteen overweight Ss on a similar program which is tape recorded have lost a total of 122 lb, averaging .3 lb/day each for 30 treatment days; a record-keeping control group has lost .08 lb/day each for 56 days.

Some Ethical Issues in the Therapeutic Use of Punishment

Bradley Bucher
UNIVERSITY OF CALIFORNIA, LOS ANGELES

Traditionally psychotherapists have been highly critical of treatment methods that concentrate on direct changes in the patient's behavior or environment. The principal charge is that direct treatment neglects the more serious disturbances of which behavior is symptomatic and may result in deterioration of the patient's fragile psychic economy. However, this danger does not seem so serious to behavior therapists, whose models of behavior do not include many of the unobservable forces in dynamic theories, and who have not observed the predicted adverse effects in actual practice. However, traditional clinicians and behavior therapists not only use different models and techniques, they look at different behaviors. The data and methods of data analysis that are important to one system may seem irrelevant to the other. Thus, such problems as the relative depth of different therapies, the possible consequences of specific treatment methods, the manner of deciding how behavior and environmental events are related, etc., are not easily solvable to the satisfaction of both groups.

Ethical issues are not independent of this conceptual gap. For example, a behavior therapist may neglect to probe deeply into his patient's thoughts and subjective experiences, and thus become open to the charge of disregarding this important aspect of his patient's well-being. The behavior therapist may make a similar charge against the traditionalist, who sees so little merit in the reports of behavioral changes achieved through direct treatment methods. Both partisans see the patient as the loser. Unfortunately these differences in viewpoints do not permit mutually acceptable discussions of ethical questions. Therefore, the emphasis of this paper will be on ethical issues approached from the viewpoint of behavior modification, and problems arising from the criticisms of more traditional therapists will be ignored or presented in a translated form.

The use of aversive stimulation in behavior modification presents some special problems, in addition to those mentioned above. Many people object to use of such stimulation in principle, divorced from consequences. Objections on these grounds do not give much basis for discussion. Other critics point to the experimental evidence concerning the many side-effects of aversive stimulation. The recent review of punishment research, by Azrin and Holz (1966), gives many examples of effects that can occur under specific circumstances. The list includes the following: pain, emotional behavior, freezing, general disruption and breakdown of discriminations, flight, operant response suppression, physiological effects, acquisition of conditioned aversions, escape and avoidance behavior, operant aggression, masochism, ulcers, death, etc. Some of these reactions are temporary, others are more lasting. As extremes, pain is transitory; death is permanent. The character of some other possible side effects is less clear. For example, escape and avoidance behavior are very commonly observed in animal studies, where the training conditions make them possible. Such responses may be a result of transfer from previous learning in similar situations or they may be newly acquired or greatly strengthened during training. In the second case, they might later be observed in situations in which they would not previously have occurred, and so are more directly attributable to treatment.

The ethical issues raised by the possibilities of undesirable reactions can be included as part of more familiar research questions. What are the principal effects and effectiveness of specific treatment techniques, beyond the temporary discomfort they may entail? How may training be controlled so that the intended effects are achieved and undesirable reactions are minimized? Unfortunately, familiarity with the problems does not imply that ready answers are available. It does seem to be generally recognized that aversive techniques can produce quite powerful effects in animal research. However, results of use of such techniques with animals cannot be translated directly to humans with functional properties intact, so that much exploration needs to be done before treatment effects become predictable. In this paper some of the techniques that have received the most study in therapeutic use will be examined to see how far the problems outlined above have been answered from the data available.

There is one other aspect of treatment around which ethical issues collect; these are possibly even more serious than those described above. These arise from the practical problems of handling patients with whom it may seem desirable to use aversive stimulation in treatment; or in fact, with any patient who applies for therapy. In the preceding discussion, it was assumed that the therapist and client are in agreement about what treatment outcomes are desirable. In actual practice, this is often not the case. People with problems who come to therapists may be poorly "motivated," or in conflict about treatment, or not inclined to accept the therapist's view of things. To such patients, the therapist may feel some obligation to influence his client to accept treatment, or to continue it once it has begun. Particularly when an aversion technique is used, the therapist must be aware that the client may suffer pain and anxiety and may exhibit hostility and aggressiveness toward the therapist, or other reactions which may result in lack of cooperation, objections to the treatments, deterioration of the therapist-client relationship, termination of therapy, lawsuits, etc. Laboratory data is only indirectly relevant to understanding how the therapist may influence these behaviors, and hardly relevant at all to the ethical issues involved in the use of this influence. Animals are not paying volunteers, and the experimenter is not required to obtain their acquiescence for his treatment procedures; nor need he fear that treatment aversiveness will make them drop out of his experiment. Animals do not argue about their present behavior patterns or what the objectives of treatment should be. Of course, these behaviors do have some distant analogues in animal experimentation. They are subject to investigation, and they are certainly behaviors over which the therapist may want to obtain some control (Goldiamond & Dryad, 1968). But the use of this control involves serious ethical issues. As techniques for managing patients become highly developed, it will become more clear that the patient can be exposed to powerful coercion to accept treatment and treatment objectives that he might at first find objectionable or irrelevant. His freedom of choice, during therapy, may seem to him to be intact, while his decisions are manipulated by the therapist. This possibility bothers many traditional therapists about the practices of behavior modification techniques, since these therapists typically do not view their own therapy as subjecting patients to a high degree of external control. Certainly if the behavior modifier deliberately seeks such control, he must acknowledge his large measure of responsibility for the outcome, good or bad.

The ethical problems of patient management will become more clear as experience with the relevant techniques increases. It seems preferable to separate this issue from that of the effectiveness of treatment procedures, which will receive the main emphasis here.

The kinds of aversiveness that have been used vary greatly. At their most unpleasant, treatments have involved the use of drugs to induce nausea and emesis, at two-hour intervals, day and night, for a period of several days. At the other end of the continuum is such a treatment as brief time-out from some form of positive reinforcement. Some of the aspects of techniques that have been reported in the past few years, such as the continuous treatment procedure using drugs just mentioned, seem difficult to justify on grounds of learning research and appear to have been based partly on intuitions derived elsewhere (Bucher & Lovaas, 1968). Others have been the subject of thoughtful development using learning principles. The latter methods are easiest to evaluate, since the data given and the report of the method followed are generally more complete.

Electric shock has been used as an aversive stimulus for several behavior problems. Perhaps the most dramatic and revealing research comes from work with psychotic children. Several investigators have contributed to this development. The therapeutic aims have included suppression of self-injurious behavior and other high rate maladaptive acts such as self-stimulation, aggressiveness, and climbing. Other work has been aimed toward development of socially appropriate behavior and establishing actions of adults as cues and reinforcers, since appropriate behavior with adults is almost totally lacking in many of these children.

Suppression of self-injurious behavior has been reported in Tate and Baroff (1966), Wolf, Risley, and Mees (1964), Lovaas, Freitag, Gold, and Kassorla (1965a), and Bucher and Lovaas (1968). Results have been uniform. Self-injurious behavior, of a degree so extreme that caretakers in despair have kept the child in continuous restraints, can be eliminated very quickly, with a few applications of shock contingent on the behavior. Furthermore, there is no alternative therapy for the problem that has been shown to be comparable, either in speed or in the number of self-injurious behaviors that occur before suppression is complete.

Analysis of the variables that control this behavior has been equally valuable. Tate and Baroff observed self-injurious behavior of a child who accompanied two experimenters on a walk. The behavior was ignored for several days, then punished by withdrawal of attention and touch. Ignoring the child seemed to make little difference, but the mild punishment had a considerable effect, although the self-injurious behavior was not eliminated over 10 days, at which time it seemed to have reached a new steady rate of occurrence. The experimenters then resorted to a portable shock device. They remained sometimes with the boy in a treatment room, and sometimes watched over closed-circuit TV. When a self-injurious act occurred, they used the shock as quickly as they could reach the child. After almost complete initial suppression in the training room, self-injurious behaviors that occurred any other time during the day were also shocked. Tate and Baroff reported what appeared to be undesirable side effects of shock treatment. For several days, the boy appeared upset and sometimes refused food. Shock was then used to punish refusal to eat, drooling, and some self-stimulatory behavior, all of which were suppressed. Since these side-effects were not observed in the earlier sessions using withdrawal, they appear due to shock use rather than to suppression of the self-injurious behavior. The authors also observed desirable effects when self-injurious behaviors decreased. More appropriate behaviors took the place of the self-injurious acts, and the child began to interact with staff and with his environment in a more satisfactory manner. After six months, the boy appeared much happier and obviously lived a far more normal existence than before.

Lovaas *et al.* (1965a) investigated some factors maintaining self-injurious behavior in a detailed study of a single girl. They observed frequency of the behavior over a long series of sessions. In sessions when the experimenter remarked sympathetically, "I don't think you are bad" after a self-injurious act, the frequency rose sharply, and fell when this comment was withdrawn. That is, the behavior was reinforced by this contingent attention from adults. Withdrawal of reinforcement for other behavior also was found to result in increased rate of self-injurious responses.

When all adult attention for self-injury was withdrawn, frequency slowly decreased. Extinction by this technique was lengthy, when attempted with another child, as reported in Bucher and Lovaas (1968). However, contingent shocks from a portable shock device gave lasting suppression after only a few shocks over several sessions, although the suppressive effect was found to be virtually restricted to the experimenter and situation in which shock was delivered. The child quickly discriminated absence of shock in other settings, in which self-injurious acts continued or soon returned. Such discrimination was hardly to be anticipated in children who appear so indifferent to their environment. Risley (1968) found the same phenomenon. In all cases extension of shock use to a few new situations and persons gave more widely generalized suppression.

Also of interest are records taken of various other behaviors during sessions in which shock was used. In Bucher and Lovaas (1968), data is reported on the relation between frequency of self-injurious behavior, avoidance of adults, and crying. All three behaviors rose and fell together. Again, similar data appears in Risley (1968), for somewhat different behaviors.

Shock has also been used to build social behaviors in autistic children (Lovaas, Shaeffer, & Simmons, 1965b). Two children who had been quite unresponsive to adults were placed in a situation in which they could escape or avoid shock only by responding to adult requests to approach and show affection. This behavior was quickly established and persisted for many months. It was restored by a single noncontingent shock after it began to deteriorate. The apparent value of adults as secondary reinforcers was demonstrated by bar-press data. The child would press to see the experimenter's face after this training, although this stimulus did not reinforce the behavior before.

The findings outlined are of considerable significance for our understanding of human pathology or human behavior in general. Some allowance must certainly be made for the highly abnormal children studied here, but several impressive results are shown in carefully controlled experimentation that should aid in development and understanding of other behavior modification techniques. These findings include: (*a*) Positive relations appear to exist between quite different behaviors, in that changes in one may have extra benefits in increases or reductions of others. (*b*) Undesirable side-effects are absent or temporary in many situations, perhaps due to the availability of appropriate avoidance responses. (*c*) The suppression of high rate abnormal behavior permits development of more adaptive competing behaviors. (*d*) Affection and good intentions are inadequate for dealing with disturbed children, when these attitudes are not accompanied by knowledge of behavior principles. (*e*) Training using adults as stimuli for relief from anxiety or threat is valuable to establish adults as positively reinforcing stimuli. (*f*) Rapid discriminations can occur between different contingencies operating in different environmental circumstances, and these discriminations may be sharpened or decreased by use of different treatment variations.

Some of these findings are familiar in animal research, and some have been remarked on elsewhere as results of research or treatment with normal and disturbed children. All seem to be of immediate practical significance for work with behavior modification and deserve extensive investigation. They have already shown the value of use of aversion techniques in the situations described and point to powerful uses in others.

A second instructive use of aversion is in the use of adult attention withdrawal to reduce the rate of various behaviors in children. Many studies have appeared, most following a similar format, in which the experimenter or parent withholds attention for undesired behavior, while also reinforcing desired behavior with attention, approval, and perhaps more tangible rewards. Problems treated include crawling; hyperactivity; inappropriate interactions; emotional behaviors such as vomiting, crying, and tantrums; and others (Baer, 1968).

Most of the studies have intermixed attention withdrawal for undesired behavior with giving of attention for desirable behavior, where both consequences have been given or withdrawn together. Thus the positive and aversive qualities of the attention variable are not clearly separated.

Leitenberg (1965) discussed the question whether time-out or withdrawal of reinforcement should be considered aversive. He defined an event as aversive if behavior that prevents or terminates it is maintained above operant level. He concluded that, in general, time-out appeared to have aversive properties for a number of situations and a number of measures of aversiveness. In this interpretation of control by social reinforcement, certain behavior of the child is punished by time-out from reinforcement, so that these behaviors will be avoided; or, once begun, the aversiveness of the resulting time-out will be escaped by substitutions of socially reinforced behavior. The control that can be achieved through social reinforcing contingencies seems quite powerful, and the ease of application and pervasiveness of the reinforcers seems to make the techniques based on this research among the most widely useful that have yet been found in behavior modification, certainly for control of behavior in children.

The limitations of the techniques have not been exposed in research. Equally relevant in behavior modification is the development of techniques to make social reinforcement effective, by associating such stimuli with positive reinforcement or relief from aversive stimulation. The work with autistic children shows that abnormalities in responses to social reinforcement can be influenced by such controlled experiences. Etzel and Gewirtz (1967) found smiles and approving comments ineffective in the case of a six-week-old baby, not unexpectedly, but they became effective after shaping using more tangible reinforcers. It may be conjectured from other research in personality that attention and approval will be found not equally effective for all children or from all therapists. Such individual differences are of great interest to researchers in personality and in other schools of therapy.

The two preceding areas of research developed from single-subject studies. Generally this research does not include much investigation of the subjects treated, and the authors provide only brief comments on typical behavior patterns or other clinical descriptive information. However well controlled the specific manipulations used may be, it is quite possible that something unusual in the setting, or the patient, or some unnoticed variable in the manipulations used, or some combination of these, has been crucial for the outcome; so that attempts at replication of the reported manipulations will not be very successful. It might be thought that treatment of groups of subjects would reduce this problem, in that proportions of groups who responded successfully to treatment could be determined, but in fact this need not be so, as the following discussion of alcoholism will illustrate.

Treatment of alcoholism using conditioning techniques was one of the first, and largest applications of Pavlovian conditioning to therapy. The research done consists more in outlining the procedure followed and the results obtained, than in use of either control group or single-subject comparisons. An enormous number of alcoholics were treated by Voegtlin, Lemere, and associates, using a nausea-inducing drug, emetine, to condition aversion to alcohol. This research was begun in the 1930's, and the treatment of over 4000 cases was summarized in several papers, which can be traced from Lemere and Voegtlin (1950). Over 85% of cases treated were abstinent at least six months, according to follow-up findings on about 90% of the cases treated. Rates fell off slowly for longer follow-ups. The patients were treated in a short 5- to 10-day program, which included some unorganized group therapy, and sometimes social casework outside the hospital. In treatment, the patient was given an injection including emetine and was presented with a variety of alcoholic beverages, timed to precede onset of the waves of nausea induced by the drug. Thimann (1949) reported results for 245 patients given very similar treatment, supplemented by part-time hospitalization, psychotherapy, and social casework outside the hospital. Wallerstein (1957) treated 50 cases. Several other reports appeared on the use of emetine, apomorphine, shock, and other forms of aversive stimulation, in variations on the original procedure.

Franks (1960) reviewed a number of comments about these conditioning procedures that had appeared in various sources. Both Voegtlin's and Thimann's work have been severely criticized. Rejection of the technique appears to be the predominant reaction from those concerned with treatment of alcoholics, although the basis given for the rejection is frequently a distortion of the available data. Moore and Buchanan (1966) found that only 2% of 231 hospitals surveyed were using aversion therapy.

Assessment of the results of these studies is made difficult by absence of detailed observations that can be used for analysis of the factors operating in treatment. Even the fact that treatment results in establishment of a conditioned response to alcohol appears not to have been shown. Voegtlin reported casual observation of aversive reactions, and Wallerstein (1957) reported anecdotally that all of 50 patients treated became nauseous or vomited on seeing the conditioned stimulus after several days of conditioning; but these eyewitness reports are not supported by other data, nor are the conditions of observation specified.

A second important lack in these results is the absence of demonstration that aversion in the laboratory generalizes to different, and relevant, situations outside. Attempts to demonstrate generalization of responses classically conditioned in the laboratory show that subjects make quick discriminations between realistically threatening and nonthreatening situations, as recent reviews of Grings (1965) and Zeaman and Smith (1965) have noted, so that the absence of such discrimination in alcoholics would be of considerable interest. Even autistic children, normally so unresponsive to environmental events, have been found to discriminate quickly between situations in which punishment is or is not present, as was previously noted.

A third difficulty with the data on aversion conditioning of alcoholics is related to the large class of patients who appear relatively unresponsive to conditioning treatment. Voegtlin and Broz (1949) analyzed successes of their clients (over 3000 at the time) into various objective classifications, and found that indigents, separated but not divorced men, men with poor work histories, men not charged for treatment, and some other classes, showed relatively poor outcomes. The effects of this difference among patient types can perhaps be seen in the study of Wallerstein (1957). He treated 50 V.A. patients using the conditioning methods and obtained quite poor results: 25% were improved, and over 40% could not be followed up or did not report voluntarily for check-up or reconditioning. These patients fit the categories Voegtlin had found least suitable – indigents and men who did not pay for treatment. Also, they were not volunteers, in the sense that Voegtlin used the term, since they were assigned to the conditioning treatment by lot, after entering the hospital.

The comments above about generalization of the conditioned response indicate that aversion alone, especially in the attenuated form in which it may occur outside the hospital, may often be quite inadequate to mediate an avoidance or escape reaction to the numerous situations that may be associated with drinking. Some of these situations may be difficult to avoid and may contain many reinforcers for drinking other than the actual taste of alcohol. In the absence of a strong feeling of aversion, the sensation actually experienced may serve as a cue for alcohol avoidance behaviors, for which the reinforcement is not entirely escape or avoidance of aversive stimuli. That is, these cues may also serve to indicate the availability of positive reinforcement for carrying out a valued intention—continued sobriety. Whether or not the patient will use the cue will possibly depend on factors not highly related to the strength of the original conditioned response. The data at present show the importance of the patient class to which the patient belongs, and the environment to which the patient must return, but not the fine grain structure of the variables involved.

In spite of the large group of subjects reported on in the Voegtlin work, and other studies, it is not easy to make a general statement about the expectations for treatment at another clinic. The admissions policies for the Shadel sanitarium are unclear. Lemere and Voegtlin (1950) reported that 96 to 98% of admissions accepted aversion therapy. It seems impossible to judge how many alcoholics who inquired at the hospital actually went through the admissions procedure, or how many who would have inquired were put off by the reputation of the clinic for using unpleasant or unorthodox treatment. A. J. Carlson (1944) claimed that Voegtlin's success rate was common for well-motivated and highly selected patients, although he cited no data. Shadel (1944) attempted to clarify the nature of the admissions procedure. He stated that the reasons for rejecting potential applicants were chiefly lack of sincerity or physical incapacity. However, if lack of sincerity were very stringently interpreted, it might constitute the highly selective factor that Carlson assumed to be in operation. Although this seems unlikely, it does seem likely that the success rates to be expected for the classes of patients which Voegtlin and Broz analyzed would depend on such auxiliary factors as "motivation" to stop drinking, however this term might be interpreted.

Traditional research design would suggest use of groups of subjects assigned at random, and inclusion of "placebo" controls, as the preferred technique for investigation of these questions. The study of Wallerstein (1957), using four groups, gives an indication of how arduous this path would be. He treated four groups using four quite different therapies, among which only use of Antabuse seemed outstanding. The complexities of admissions selectivity, treatment related "motivational" conditions, etc., were no more than touched in this study, and of course variations in any of the four therapy methods might be suggested as more likely to have succeeded than those that were used. The careful study of individual subjects, to provide analytical information about the operation of specific treatment variables, seems potentially more fruitful.

Criticisms of the use of emetine or apomorphine have also been made on the grounds that the procedure fails to control certain variables that are known to be relevant in establishment of aversion reactions and in increasing their resistance to extinction. These include timing of the CS – US interval, use of partial reinforcement, and provision of a response to escape the CS and avoid the US. In some recent work, the earlier conditioning procedure has been modified in various ways. Sanderson, Campbell, and Laverty (1963) used the drug succinylcholine to induce a brief paralysis of respiration, as the unconditioned stimulus, in a one-trial conditioning study. Blake (1965) used shock as the US and added relaxation training and partial reinforcement. MacCulloch, Feldman, Orford, and MacCulloch (1966) used shock, partial reinforcement, and a response that permitted the subject to avoid shock on some trials. In none of these studies was a serious effort made to test if the subjects had actually acquired an aversion to alcohol; or if the aversion generalized to different situations; or if increased resistance to extinction from use of partial reinforcement or avoidance training would actually occur in situations that did not model closely the situations in which such resistance is customarily tested; or, in the MacCulloch *et al.* study, if the avoidance response that was learned in training would generalize to a different response that would avoid alcohol in some other situation. These approaches seem predicated on the assumption that failures in the earlier procedures, using drugs, were due to failure to establish a strong aversion to alcohol, or to use a training procedure that would result in a reaction resistant to repeated unreinforced elicitations under various conditions. It remains to be shown that these assumed defects are actually the most important ones or that these newer techniques have remedied them.

Enuresis is another problem to which much study has been given. The standard treatment is operationally a punishment procedure. A loud bell, buzzer, or shock apparatus is activated when a special pad is dampened by the child's release of urine during the night. Successful treatment is usually defined as 14 continuous dry nights. Retreatment of any relapsed cases has been common. Jones (1960) and Lovibond (1964) have reported on the many studies that have appeared. As with treatment of alcoholism, no single-subject studies have been done, perhaps because of the low rate of the behavior, and the uncertainty about the variables that control it. A few group comparison studies have appeared but until recently most reports have consisted of success rates for groups of subjects. They also include more or less adequate details of the procedure followed and a description of the class of patients treated. As was just seen in the review of alcoholism, this information is quite important in evaluating the reported rates of success.

To review these studies briefly, as reported in Lovibond, initial success rates have run from 30 to 100%. Relapses have run up to 45%, but the success rate of retreatment seems to be about as high as for original treatment. Relapses are variously defined, of course, so no lower limit can be given. One study surveyed buyers of a commercially available version of the device and found 50% reported cures among the approximately 50% of mail questionnaires returned. Side effects of treatment have been noted in many patients. These are principally reduction of tensions and conflict in the child and in the home. Reports of new undesirable behaviors are rare.

In a group comparison study done by Werry and Cohrssen (1965), the conditioning method was found superior to brief supportive and directive psychotherapy, and to a "no-treatment" condition, but the cure rate was only 30%. The improvement rate was 70%, however, compared to 35% for therapy, and 30% for the "no-treatment" condition. Werry and Cohrssen posited that their patients were hard core enuretics whose cases were more serious than those of the several studies reported earlier, although this is not clearly so. Another variable that might have entered was the closeness of supervision of the therapist over the parents who carried out the actual treatment. In this study, the therapist exercised no supervision after the initial instruction in the methods of operation. This was intended to reduce the effect of the therapist as a factor in treatment, but it clearly represents a less than optimal procedure, so that the results can hardly be used as an adequate measure of the value of the method. Of course the same comment of nonoptimality might be made for the psychotherapy used.

More adequate observation and control of treatment of individual subjects, with exploration of treatment variations within the conditioning technique, are needed. In the absence of such data, the rather disparate results of these conditioning studies may be due partly or largely to differences in the effectiveness of the variations in procedures followed, from study to study or case to case, and to as yet unspecified differences in the children treated.

In any case, treatment of enuresis using the conditioning device seems to have a record of demonstrated effectiveness beyond that of any competing psychological treatment. However, it will probably not be surprising to learn that Werry and Cohrssen report that psychotherapy is still considered the treatment of choice for this problem. The amount of investigation done with variations of the device also far exceeds research or data reported for other methods. Apparently the distrust of practitioners for direct treatment methods extends also to the data and research methods of their advocates. Unfortunately there is no currently viable alternative to collection of statistical evidence for treatment success and publication of carefully controlled research reports.

In conclusion, these four research applications demonstrate that uses of aversive stimulation in therapy have considerable merit. Some techniques in current use in therapy appear to have efficiency and effectiveness superior to the available competitors. Our knowledge about the potential of the techniques considered here is rudimentary, and many others are even less fully explored, but the promised gain seems sufficient to justify continuing investigation.

The undesirable side effects which have been so widely expected have not been observed in the work reported here, and current animal research gives support to the hope that such effects can be made inconsequential through use of appropriate controls. Present results do not justify ethical objections based on the belief that benefits from use of aversive stimulation will be outweighed by the negative consequences.

References

Azrin, N. H., & Holz, W. C. Punishment. In W. K. Honig (Ed.), *Operant Behavior*. New York: Appleton-Century-Crofts, 1966.

Baer, D. M. Some remedial uses of the reinforcement contingency. In J. M. Shlien (Ed.), *Research in psychotherapy*. Washington, D. C.: American Psychological Association, 1968.

Blake, B. G. The application of behaviour therapy to the treatment of alcoholism. *Behaviour Research and Therapy*, 1965, **3**, 75-85.

Bucher, B., & Lovaas, O. I. Use of aversive stimulation in behavior modification. In M. R. Jones (Ed.), *Miami symposium on the prediction of behavior: Aversive stimulation*. Coral Gables, Fla.: University of Miami Press, 1968.

Carlson, A. J. The conditioned reflex therapy of alcohol addiction. *Quarterly Journal of Studies on Alcohol*, 1944, **5**, 212-215.

Etzel, B. C., & Gewirtz, J. L. Experimental modification of caretaker-maintained high-rate operant crying in a six and twenty-week old infant (Infans tyrannotearus): Extinction of crying with reinforcement of eye contact and smiling. *Journal of Experimental Child Psychology*, 1967, **31**, 209-212.

Franks, C. M. Alcohol, alcoholism, and conditioning. In H. J. Eysenck (Ed.), *Behavior therapy and the neuroses*. New York: Macmillan, 1960.

Goldiamond, I., & Dryad, J. E. Some applications and implications of behavior analysis for psychotherapy. In J. M. Shlien (Ed.), *Research in psychotherapy.* Washington, D.C.: American Psychological Association, 1968.

Grings, W. W. Verbal-perceptual factors in the conditioning of autonomic responses. In W. F. Prokasy (Ed.), *Classical conditioning: A symposium.* New York: Appleton-Century-Crofts, 1965.

Jones, H. G. The behavioral treatment of enuresis nocturne. In H. J. Eysenck (Ed.), *Behaviour Therapy and the Neuroses.* New York: Macmillan, 1960.

Leitenberg, H. Is time-out from positive reinforcement an aversive event? A review of the experimental evidence. *Psychological Bulletin,* 1965, **64**, 428-441.

Lemere, F., & Voegtlin, W. L. An evaluation of the aversion treatment of alcoholism. *Quarterly Journal of Studies on Alcohol,* 1950, **11**, 199-204.

Lovaas, O. I., Freitag, G., Gold, V. J., & Kassorla, I. C. Experimental studies in childhood schizophrenia: Analysis of self-destructive behavior. *Journal of Experimental Child Psychology.* 1965, **2**, 67-84. (a)

Lovaas, O. I., Schaeffer, B., & Simmons, J. Q. Experimental studies in childhood schizophrenia: Building social behavior in autistic children by use of electric shock. *Journal of Experimental Research in Personality,* 1965 **1**, 99-109. (b)

Lovibond, S. H. *Conditioning and enuresis.* New York: Macmillan, 1964.

MacCulloch, M. J., Feldman, M. P., Orford, J. F., & MacCulloch, M. L. Anticipatory avoidance learning in the treatment of alcoholism: A record of therapeutic failure. *Behaviour Research and Therapy,* 1966, **4**, 187-196.

Moore, R. A., & Buchanan, T. K. State hospitals and alcoholism: A nationwide survey of treatment techniques and results. *Quarterly Journal of Studies on Alcohol,* 1966, **27**, 459-468.

Risley, T. R. The effects and side effects of punishing the autistic behaviors of a deviant child. *Journal of Applied Behavior Analysis,* 1968, **1**, 21-34.

Sanderson, R. E., Campbell, D., & Laverty, S. G. An investigation of a new aversive conditioning treatment for alcoholism. *Quarterly Journal of Studies on Alcohol,* 1963, **24**, 261-275.

Shadel, C. A. Aversion treatment of alcohol addiction. *Quarterly Journal of Studies on Alcohol,* 1944, **5**, 216-228.

Tate, B. G., & Baroff, G. S. Aversive conditioning of self-injurious behavior in a psychotic boy. *Behaviour Research and Therapy,* 1966, **4**, 281-287.

Thimann, J. Conditioned reflex treatment of alcoholism. II. The risks of its application, its indications, contraindications and psychotherapeutic aspects. *New England Journal of Medicine,* 1949, **241**, 406-410.

Voegtlin, W. L., & Broz, W. R. The conditioned reflex treatment of chronic alcoholism. X. Analysis of 3125 admissions. *Annals of Internal Medicine,* 1949, **30**, 580-597.

Wallerstein, R. S. *Hospital treatment of alcoholism.* New York: Basic Books, 1957.

Werry, J. S., & Cohrssen, J. Enuresis—an etiologic and therapeutic study. *Journal of Pediatrics,* 1965, **67**, 423-431.

Wolf, M., Risley, T., & Mees, H. Application of operant conditioning procedures to the behavior problems of an autistic child. *Behaviour Research and Therapy,* 1964, **1**, 305-312.

Zeaman, D., & Smith, R. W. Review of some recent findings in human cardiac conditioning. In W. F. Prokasy (Ed.), *Classical conditioning: A symposium.* New York: Appleton-Century-Crofts, 1965.

Principles Governing the Choice of Unconditioned Stimuli in Aversive Conditioning

Irwin Lublin

CALIFORNIA STATE COLLEGE, LOS ANGELES

Few psychologists would disagree with the following statement: If certain aversive conditioning techniques are more effective in eliminating given undesired behaviors than any other known method, and if whatever unpleasantness is associated with them can be adjudged slight in comparison with the undesirable effects on the subject's life and health of the continuation of the problem behaviors, then these aversive conditioning techniques should be used. In this manner, ethical questions can be answered in the light of empirical considerations. The important questions then become limited to decisions concerning what aversive stimulus to use, with what intensity, and how to manage the training procedure.

This paper will concern itself only with aversive conditioning of the classical, or autonomic, type—that is, where the focus is on altering the stimulus properties of an object formerly experienced as either neutral or attractive, until the same object is experienced as unpleasant or aversive. The change comes about through repeated pairing of the attractive object with a stimulus already known to be obnoxious or aversive to the subject. This paper will not discuss the use of aversive stimuli to suppress immediately preceding behavior, for which operation we use the term punishment, or the use of aversive stimuli to train escape and avoidance responses, in which case we are dealing with a standard operant paradigm.

In various behavior modification studies, such objects have been counterconditioned in the manner just described under the heading of classical aversive conditioning as alcoholic beverages, sexual fetish objects, persons of the same sex, transvestite costume, and so forth; however, the research which gave rise to these remarks dealt with cigarettes. This paper consists of some of the conclusions derived from 16 months of research with aversive conditioning of cigarette addicts (Lublin & Joslyn, 1968), as well as from a study of the aversive conditioning literature. The author hopes that these tentative conclusions may serve as contributions toward the founding of a science of aversive conditioning, a science which does not as yet exist, as Solomon (1964) and others have pointed out.

Proposed Principles in Aversive Conditioning of the Classical Type

1. The unconditioned aversive stimulus should only be electric shock when it is desired that *anxiety* responses be attached to formerly attractive stimuli.

Where conditioned anxiety is not desired, the use of pain and fear responses should be avoided. One reason for this recommendation becomes apparent when we consider what happens to subjects with whom the treatment fails. What we are implying here is that there is some ethical question about creating anxiety where there was none (or less), or so conditioning smokers, for example, that they are left not only with their undesired habit, but with enduring autonomic disturbance in conjunction with it. Even with subjects who succeed in stopping smoking, it remains a question whether strong shock conditioning has not raised their chronic anxiety levels. The irony here, of course, is that many heavy smokers are already using cigarettes to temporarily reduce chronically high tension levels. It follows that we may actually increase the strength or extent of the smoking habit by conditioning anxiety to cigarettes, not to mention the thought of cigarettes. Eysenck (1967), in a recent article, has noted that autonomic conditioning not only tends to resist extinction, but often shows intensification and generalization effects over time. This phenomenon has been referred to previously in the literature as the "incubation effect." Solomon has concluded from his research with dogs that conditioned anxiety under some circumstances may not be extinguishable at all (Solomon & Wynne, 1954). Pavlov and Liddell made similar observations many years ago. It should also be noted that strong learned anxiety responses which do effectively inhibit undesirable behavior may nevertheless give rise to psychosomatic disorder.

To clarify this principle, it will be helpful to give an example of a case where anxiety responses *may* be deemed preferable to approach or pleasure responses. Such an example is found in Feldman and MacCulloch's (1965) work with hardcore male homosexuals. After undergoing the carefully managed shock conditioning, the subjects became anxious in the presence of nude or "sexy" males. In other words, they achieved the learning accomplished much earlier by most heterosexual males in our culture. As a result, their lives changed markedly for the better, as judged by the subjects themselves.

It is important to add that sometimes anxiety responses may be deliberately trained because they are incompatible with previously troublesome responses. The obvious application to Feldman and MacCulloch's work is that when their homosexual subjects became anxious in the presence of nude males, they were unable to become sexually excited in their presence. It would not be stretching this experiment too far to say that the authors succeeded in training impotence where impotence was deemed appropriate. In a number of other studies, shock has been used effectively to cancel out sexual excitement, maladaptively occasioned and causing the subjects no little embarrassment and harassment. Thus success has been reported in counterconditioning fetish, exhibitionistic, and transvestite stimuli in this manner.

2. In the choice of unconditioned stimulus, most sensory modalities have been badly neglected, while others, especially electric shock, have been overemployed.

The overemployment of shock has probably carried over from animal studies, where the precise temporal and quantitative specification of the unconditioned stimulus has often been crucial to the theoretical parameters of the research. In behavior modification, which is clearly applied rather than basic science, we can be guided more by pragmatic considerations and less by strict precision of method.

The modalities of taste and olfaction have clearly been neglected. Yet in the writer's research, stale cigarette smoke, a US originally suggested by Wilde (1964), has appeared to be an excellent choice, partly for reasons yet to be elaborated (see Principle 6, below).

A single example will suffice to suggest the potential power of olfactory unconditioned stimuli (which on the appetitive end are already widely used by a variety of businesses and manufacturers).

Observation of animals, as well as young humans, seems to lead to the conclusion that the odor of feces is not innately obnoxious. And yet, in adult humans, this odor becomes strongly and almost universally aversive. The aversion seems to be the result of parental and other social conditioning, much of it connected with toilet training. This odor, and associated sensory elements, become so aversive that many neutral stimuli associated with it become, in turn, conditioned eliciters of disgust. The author has tried persuading friends that toilet paper is a satisfactory substitute for table napkins, but has only succeeded in diminishing their appetites. (Here we have a hint as to behavior therapy for overeating.)

It has recently come to the author's attention that Lazarus and Kort, at Temple, have found that smelling salts (presumably ammonia based) are a useful alternative to shock as a US in counterconditioning maladaptive sexual excitement. It is necessary to take a whiff of ammonia to appreciate that it provides a reliably aversive stimulus. No doubt the chemists are waiting even now with cabinets full of other stinks.

When one thinks of the extensive utilization of Wolpe's methods of systematic desensitization utilizing imaginative processes, it is really surprising that more has not been done with the negative possibilities of imagination, which should not be underrated. In systematic *sensitization,* the object which the person wishes to avoid is systematically paired with vividly imagined aversive imagery, involving any and all sensory modalities. The few studies already published by Anant (1967), Cautela (1967), and others, indicate that the technique has shown success with alcoholism, drug addiction, and other problems, and may have a great deal of unexploited potential. It is important to note that we are not dealing here with simple exhortation, or with scare verbalizations alone, but with the hierarchical and controlled pairing of vividly imagined conditioned stimuli and vividly imagined unconditioned stimuli, complete with varied sensory evocations and directly suggested aversive reactions.

It is worth adding briefly that, to the writer's knowledge, the tactile and temperature modalities have been totally neglected as a source of unconditioned stimuli.

All in all, it may be said that the possibilities for aversive stimulation have hardly been explored, but are only limited by the bounds of our fiendish imaginations. Electric shock, in retrospect, may turn out to have been a poor choice for many reasons.

3. Negative practice, or stimulus satiation, i.e., flooding the subject with the attractive stimulus itself, has likewise been neglected as a source of aversion. It is probably true that you *can* have too much of *any* good thing.

In this approach, we are reminded of the old homeopathic dictum that the cure resides within the "disease." Good examples are found in the work of Ayllon (1963) and Resnick (1968). Ayllon treated a psychotic towel hoarder by simply instructing the staff to bring towels endlessly to the patient's room instead of taking them away as they had been doing. As a result, the patient lost her interest in towels completely. Resnick treated heavy smokers by instructing them to *increase* their consumption to four packs a day. He reports that six of his eight subjects stopped smoking after the experimental period and maintained their abstinence for four months as of the date of this report.

Here we have the ingenious paradigm, discussed extensively by Hull (1943) and Dunlap (1930), where the conditioned stimulus becomes itself an aversive unconditioned stimulus by sheer repetition. Of course Hull and Dunlap had in mind primarily motor habits, where 'fatigue' and conditioned inhibition eventually overwhelmed the response potential. In the present context of autonomic conditioning, the emphasis is on changing the quality of the stimulus through quantitative overloading.

In this writer's research, the negative practice group was required to smoke rapidly to the beating of a metronome. First, they would puff every 3 sec, then, on the next trial, inhale every 6 sec, and so forth for as many trials as they could tolerate without becoming ill. Under these circumstances, on each trial, the subject's own cigarette became quite aversive after about 1 min.

4. Aversive stimulation (the unconditioned stimulus) should be optimal, rather than maximal.

A good example of a violation of this rule is found in the work of Sanderson, Campbell, and Laverty (1963) with chronic alcoholics. They employed succinylcholine chloride as an unconditioned stimulus and paired it with the ingestion of alcohol in a single trial. The subjects were not informed of the drug's effects, which include almost total temporary paralysis, including respiratory paralysis. The subjects thought they were dying.

Even if a single trial of this kind were impressively effective over the long run, which it was not (Madill, Campbell, Laverty, Sanderson, & Vanderwater, 1966), the saving in time would hardly justify the massive induction of fear. As a matter of fact, however, durable conditioning of the classical type is much more likely to be established by many repeated trials at a less than maximal level of the unconditioned stimulus.

It is also worth noting that higher than optimal levels of aversive stimulation may result in undesirable generalization of the conditioned response to a wide variety of unintended stimuli. It is not desirable that the former alcoholic become nauseated when in a room where liquor is consumed by others, for obvious reasons; and we do not wish our former smokers to have to give up their smoking friends along with their cigarettes. In a recent report by Farrar, Powell, and Martin (1968) testing the succinylcholine treatment of alcoholics, it was found that, of only two *S*s who succeeded in remaining abstinent for a year after the treatment, one avoided alcohol at some considerable cost. He became "extremely anxious" in the presence of anything containing alcohol, including mouthwash and hair spray, and even when attempting to take a tranquilizer that he had been taking when he had his succinylcholine session. According to the investigators, the patient himself feels that the cure is worse than the original condition.

Another point in this connection is that excessive aversiveness of a procedure will often result in escape from and avoidance of the learning situation, following the operant paradigm. Many physicians who have attempted to treat alcoholism by handing the patient a supply of Antabuse, which causes him to become acutely ill when he drinks, have reported that their patients simply stop taking the Antabuse. In a recent article, Powell and Azrin (1968) report that 17 of their 20 *S*s withdrew from an experiment in which they were severely shocked for smoking.

Many of the above remarks apply to marathon aversion sessions, a number of which have been reported in connection with the treatment of sexual fetishists. In a typical experiment of this kind, Cooper (1963) kept a female clothes fetishist awake day and night for a week while administering a nauseant drug every two hours and requiring the patient not only to carry out his fetishistic acts and remain in female clothing, but to re-enact in his mind every detail of his "disgusting perversion" while looking at himself in the mirror. For good measure, tape recordings were played for 20 min every two hours which stressed the "disgusting and unpleasant" nature of the patient's sexual deviation. Cooper's patient, as described by Feldman (1966), "finally broke down after seven days of this regime, having neither eaten nor slept for six days." Feldman remarks that this study and several very similar ones seem "marked by a rather moralistic overtone." It might be added that the methodology seems more characterized by punitiveness than by any requirement of learning theory.

5. Aversive qualities of the unconditioned stimulus depend strongly on individual thresholds, both sensory and evaluative.

Hence the "optimal" level of intensity of the aversive unconditioned stimulus, as referred to above, will actually vary from subject to subject. Ideally, the design should allow the *S* to control the input so as to produce enough, but not too much, aversiveness. In the writer's research, where *Ss* are asked to put out their cigarettes when they become "very unpleasant," a wide range of tolerance for the aversive stimulation has appeared. Some *Ss* become quite physically uncomfortable after a few seconds of either rapid puffing or exposure to the stale smoke. On the other hand, there are a few *Ss* who seem almost impervious to our supposedly aversive unconditioned stimulus. These have usually been very heavy smokers, in whom sensitivity to olfactory and chemical stimulation of the mucous membranes involved has presumably been grossly reduced.

A related problem that arises in this connection is that some *Ss* are very quick to pronounce the aversive stimulation as no longer bearable, while others force themselves to withstand the aversive stimulation to the point of becoming sick or even sustaining tissue damage. For this reason, and because of varying thresholds of aversion, it is desirable in work of this kind for trained experimenters to constantly monitor the situation and intervene where necessary, sometimes by chiding the *S* for being too self-indulgent, sometimes by reminding him that pain and suffering are not necessary. This requirement of sensitive monitoring means that well-trained therapists are needed for this work, and may prove a bar to automated aversive conditioning.

6. If the aversive unconditioned stimulus is so chosen as to be on a generalization gradient with the conditioned stimulus, i.e., perceptually similar to the attractive object, yet on the aversive end of the gradient, conditioning will be much more efficient and permanent.

Conditioning will be more efficient because many of the sensory cues will overlap and more permanent because stimulus discrimination between the laboratory and the life situation will be difficult for the subject to achieve. Ordinarily, the US should be presented in the same sensory modality as the CS, allowing primary stimulus generalization.

In many animal experiments over the years, from Pavlov to Wolpe, it has been reported that the subjects formed discriminations such that they only showed the conditioned response in the laboratory and failed to show it in other situations. Mowrer (1938) reported complete stimulus discrimination of a conditioned autonomic response, which did not occur when the electrodes were removed from the subject. This may be partly because the US in these experiments was almost always shock, having no 'natural' connection with the CS, and never encountered in the extra-laboratory environment.

A short while ago, pursuing my interest in aversive stimulation, I was a guest on the Joe Pyne TV show. Mr. Pyne asked this question: "If you wanted someone to hate tomatoes, I suppose you'd sock him in the face with a tomato a few times." My answer was, "No. That would be a good way to teach a person to hate me. If I wanted him to hate tomatoes, I'd feed him putrefied tomatoes every day for a week."

I think there is a good point here. Arbitrary unconditioned aversive stimuli have a way of backfiring: They not uncommonly produce anger directed at the trainer and rejection of the training procedure. On the other hand, children and others seem more inclined to react impunitively to 'natural' aversive stimuli, already associated with the conditioned stimuli. This is an additional reason, beyond efficiency and permanency of conditioning, to follow the proposed principle.

In accordance with the dictates of this principle, almost the entire impetus to the writer's smoking research came from Wilde's ingenious suggestion of stale cigarette smoke as an unconditioned stimulus for aversive conditioning of cigarette smokers.

References

Anant, S. S. Treatment of alcoholics and drug addicts by verbal aversion techniques. Paper presented at the meeting of the International Congress of Psychotherapy, Wiesbaden, August 1967.

Ayllon, T. Intensive treatment of psychotic behavior by stimulus satiation and food reinforcement. *Behaviour Research and Therapy*, 1963, **1**, 53-61.

Cautela, J. R. Covert sensitization. *Psychological Reports*, 1967, **20**, 459-468.

Cooper, A. J. A case of fetishism and impotence treated by behaviour therapy. *British Journal of Psychiatry*, 1963, **109**, 649-652.

Dunlap, K. Repetition in the breaking of habits. *Scientific Monthly*, 1930, **30**, 66-70.

Eysenck, H. J. Single-trial conditioning, neurosis, and the Napalkov phenomenon. *Behaviour Research and Therapy*, 1967, **5**, 63-65.

Farrar, C. H., Powell, B. J., & Martin, L. K. Punishment of alcohol consumption by apneic paralysis. *Behaviour Research and Therapy*, 1968, **6**, 13-16.

Feldman, M. P. Aversion therapy for sexual deviations: A critical review, *Psychological Bulletin*, 1966, **65**, 65-79.

Feldman, M. P., & MacCulloch, M. J. The application of anticipatory avoidance learning to the treatment of homosexuality. *Behaviour Research and Therapy*, 1965, **2**, 165-183.

Hull, C. L. *Principles of behavior*. New York: Appleton, 1943.

Lublin, I., & Joslyn, L. Aversive conditioning of cigarette addiction. Paper presented at the meeting of the American Psychological Association, San Francisco, September 1968.

Madill, M. F., Campbell, D., Laverty, S. G., Sanderson, K. E., & Vanderwater, S. L. Aversion treatment of alcoholics by succinylcholine-induced apneic paralysis, *Quarterly Journal of Studies on Alcohol*, 1966, **27**, 483-509.

Mowrer, O. H. Preparatory set (expectancy)—a determinant in motivation and learning. *Psychological Review*, 1938, **45**, 62-91.

Powell, J., & Azrin, N. The effects of shock as a punisher for cigarette smoking. *Journal of Applied Behavior Analysis*, 1968, **1**, 63-71.

Resnick, J. H. The control of smoking behavior by stimulus satiation. *Behaviour Research and Therapy*, 1968, **6**, 113-114.

Sanderson, R. E., Campbell, D., & Laverty, S. G. An investigation of a new aversive conditioning treatment for alcoholism. *Quarterly Journal of Studies on Alcohol*, 1963, **24**, 261-275.

Solomon, R. L. Punishment. *American Psychologist*, 1964, **19**, 239-253.

Solomon, R. L., & Wynne, L. C. Traumatic avoidance learning: The principles of anxiety conservation and partial irreversibility. *Psychological Review*, 1954, **61**, 353-385.

Wilde, G. J. S. Behaviour therapy for addicted cigarette smokers: A preliminary report. *Behaviour Research and Therapy*, 1964, **2**, 107-109.

The Ethics of Deprivation

Halmuth H. Schaefer

PATTON STATE HOSPITAL

Initially, it should be clear that there are two discrete meanings for the word *deprivation*: a popular one which denotes the taking or withholding—usually deliberately—of something from another to which he is used or otherwise entitled, and a technical one from the vocabulary of the behavioral scientist which refers to the absence of a variable from the environment of an organism. Popular convention regards deprivation most generally as negative, at worst not worthy of approval and at best a means of last resort. The technical use of the term is free of value judgments; it merely describes an existing condition which may or may not be desirable.

The technical convention of usage is much newer than the popular one. It is well established with behavioral scientists, but nonexistent for those outside the field. Much of the consternation which meets the behavioral scientist when he speaks to the public about deprivation comes from the mistaking by the public of the technical term for the popular one.

To enlarge upon the meaning of deprivation in common usage, it is enlightening and even grimly humorous to note some of the words which Roget's (1950) "Thesaurus of English Words and Phrases" places next to *deprivation*: *bereavement*, *divestment*, *disherison*, *distraint*, *distress*, *sequestration*, *confiscation*, *attachment*, *execution*, *eviction*, *rapacity*, *extortion*, *vampirism*, *predacity*, *blood-sucking*, *theft*, and others.

In all of these terms as well as in deprivation itself, there is contained the notion of a human or demonic planner whose goals are reprehensible. A fairly novel extension of deprivation which is free of this aspect of intentional planning is *cultural deprivation*, a concept traceable to behavioral science. But even here the culturally deprived, the victim as it were, is disadvantaged after deprivation and thus the negative flavor of deprivation is not diminished.

Another contributing factor to the general negative feeling about deprivation is the hypocrisy surrounding such deprivation as society does condone, especially in areas of sexual expression, free speech, and the rights of minority groups. Thus, mental patients committed by a court of law automatically lose over a dozen civil rights (more than twice those which a convicted felon loses), among them the right to hold public office, the right to engage in various businesses and professions, the right to vote, the right to obtain a marriage license or a driver's license, the right to convey property, and the right to procreate children. Yet, this is condoned publicly, and, indeed, recent efforts by lawmakers to remove these cruel deprivations met with considerable resistance by the very forces which would forbid behavioral therapy because it uses deprivation of various sorts during short, controlled periods for therapeutic purposes. Now, intuitively or consciously knowing that hypocrisy surrounds much deprivation that is actually practiced, causes the intellectual liberal especially to feel wary of deprivation of any kind.

The behavioral scientist also noted that deprivation is often an important immediate precedent to conditioning, although it is not, as some believe, the sole source of action nor is it possible to infer deprivation inescapably from a given mode of behavior. This latter point is of particular importance in that it demonstrates how deprivation is only one important factor in conditioning. Suppose, for example, that one were to observe in a laboratory a rat operating the lever in a box at a great rate for food reinforcement, while next to him another rat in an identical box operates the lever only occasionally. The absolute inference that one animal is hungry while the other is not, is not at all warranted without knowledge of the kinds of schedules of reinforcement to which these animals have been subjected. It may well be that one of them is on a schedule under which many responses (depressions of the lever) are required to obtain a morsel of food, while the other is on a schedule in which long periods of not responding are reinforced. In that situation, the deprivation for food of these two animals may be equal and yet result in entirely different patterns of behavior.

If the behavioral scientist expects to be successful in explaining his own work, and if he hopes that enlightened circles of society will avail themselves of the findings of his laboratory, he must face the fact that his technical understanding of deprivation does not readily remove the distaste, if not fear, with which mankind for millennia has regarded deprivation. The least he should do is to explain in detail, as I am trying to do here, what the technical meaning of deprivation is. But he should also come to grips with some of the problems which are caused when deprivation is used, especially in the kind of clinical setting to which conditioning in all its forms has recently been applied. And he should explain what the limits to the use of deprivation are to which he, as one professional, would and to which society in his opinion should, ascribe.

It is to the clinical aspects of deprivation to individuals that I wish to address myself specifically; this does not rule out the uses of deprivation in group settings, and I will be talking about those, although it cannot be stressed enough that even in wards for schizophrenics, behavioral treatment plans are tailored to the needs of individual patients.

Arguments against deprivation fall in two broad categories: those against deprivation of any kind, others against deprivation under most but not all conditions. All of the arguments touch peripherally on the issue of free will in the sense that they do not regard abstinence, i.e., the voluntary removal of a variable from an organism's own environment as a form of deprivation. In this, these arguments depart from the behaviorist view not only in relation to the free will issue, but also to the extent that the behavioral view of deprivation includes such involuntary deprivations as occur normally in life such as the night and day cycle, old age, and the like.

One absolute argument against deprivation holds that to deprive anybody of anything violates human rights and human dignity and is therefore reprehensible. Since any organization beyond the very limited social contact of single individuals requires, of course, the often unwilling abnegation of basic rights, this position leads to anarchism and the rejection of any and all authority. It is best expressed (Kropotkin & Smogorzewski, 1958) by a manifesto of the Anarchist International formulated in 1882 at a conference in Geneva: "Our ruler is our enemy. We anarchists, i.e., men without rulers, fight against all those who have usurped any power, or who wish to usurp it. Our enemy is the owner who keeps the land for himself...the manufacturer...the state...every thought of authority...."

Prince Peter Kropotkin, the most prominent theoretician of this movement, argues that man is essentially good and that only deprivation imposed by collective systems upon man causes him to commit evil acts. He also believes that horror of deprivation of any kind is quite alien to human nature, based on the observation that the very wording of anarchist thoughts remains essentially the same as, for example, one compares the fragmentary quotes of Zeno, the best exponent of anarchist thought in ancient Greece (ca. 300 B.C.) with the writings of Proudhon more than 2000 years later.

Most commonly, the counterargument to the anarchist position involves discussion of the basic nature of man. But a more practical counterargument is that in modern times the world is simply too small to allow the kind of individualism which an anarchist system would require. Every human being born today deprives, in however small a way, other human beings of living space and other freedoms. Furthermore, the humane benefits which state organizations can bring about by taxation are so substantial that only the gravest abuses of such exercise of deprivation lead even to questioning of this practice. In short, without abrogating the romantic charm of Kropotkin's philosophy, it seems enough to point to the utopian character of such thinking by reference to real and present conditions to refute this argument.

Still in the same category of general arguments against all form of deprivation falls one which holds that deprivation is to be condemned because of public policy. This argument can be based squarely on Hume's (1740, 1748) contributions to ethics. In his *Treatise of Human Nature*, Book iii (*Of Morals*), and in his later *Enquiry Concerning the Principles of Morals*, he holds on various grounds that "good" is anything approved by most men. Since presently most men would not approve the use of deprivation and even more men would probably disapprove of the use of deprivation as a therapeutic technique for the mentally ill or mentally retarded, it follows that deprivation cannot be considered to be "good" and consequently its use is unethical.

But Hume's reasoning is not satisfactory as a guide for judgment since any verdict to be valid must rest on the impossible polling of all men of all time. Historically, of course, it has been demonstrated sufficiently often to be acceptable that what the majority or even all men believed to be "good" at a given point in time appeared to be different in the light of subsequent knowledge. Less credibly, this argument could also be based on a professional's responsibility to the general public (Lucero, Vail, & Scherber, 1968; Lucero & Vail, 1968). This reasoning holds that the professional (especially in public employ), even though he may possess treatment techniques which in his own judgment and that of his peers are beneficial, must refrain from the use of such techniques if the public at that time regards them as bizarre and cruel until the public has become convinced that the techniques are indeed beneficial.

Since the argument, based in this way, would in effect have mob rule supersede considered professional judgment, it would not be worthy of an answer if it were not fairly common and if only recently it had not been used as a basis for public policy by representatives of a governmental body of this country.

Before countering this argument, it is well to point out that it is first of all vicious in that it would, if taken seriously, at once halt all progress. New techniques, no matter in what field, necessarily must seem bizarre and unusual to the general public. If not, they could not qualify as novel and revolutionary. Since they could, however, never be demonstrated as beneficial, they would forever seem strange to the general public and hence could never be tested. Ergo, all novel procedures would forever be banned.

Now, the argument itself contains an assumption which is neither in fact nor on philosophical grounds warranted: This assumption is that the professional, as a scientist, does not also have the duty to educate the general public to which, under this argument, he is responsible. But the scientist-professional, as his title doctor indicates, is also, if not primarily, a teacher and not, as it might seem, a giver of services which the public demands. Hence, the argument collapses because of faulty assumptions. Since the soundest form of teaching is practice, it must follow that novel techniques, such as the use of deprivation for therapeutic purposes, must be permitted in such teaching, and certainly cannot be precluded by this argument.

But the most tangible counterargument against the view that the public taste should dictate the conduct of treatment comes from the codes which professionals have formulated for their own guidance, such as the Oath of Hippocrates, the Declaration of Geneva, or the Declaration of Helsinki. In all of these, personal conscience is placed above all else, as for example in the wording of the Oath of Hippocrates: "I will follow that system of regimen which, according to *my ability and judgment, I* consider for the benefit of my patients, and abstain from whatever is deleterious and mischievous," or, in the Declaration of Geneva: "I will practice my profession *with conscience* and dignity; the health of my patient will be my first consideration." (Italics are mine.)

Of the arguments that would regard some though not all deprivation as unethical, the one which has the highest degree of apparent validity is that which holds that to deprive a sick or otherwise handicapped person of something to which in a civilized society he is normally entitled is wrong. This argument, in fact, forms the basis of many forms of procedures of dealing with juvenile delinquents and the mentally ill and the mentally retarded. Deprivation in the context of this argument is used in the vernacular, nontechnical sense. To avoid misunderstandings, two examples containing this argument may be useful. The case history of an emotionally disturbed 17-year-old girl shows that her family broke up when she was only three years old. Whatever love and affection the child may have experienced during the three years that father and mother were together must have been minimal, because the father was a drunkard and the mother was once haled into court for child beating. Subsequently the child was raised with relatives for a period of seven years, then spent time in various county and state institutions for difficult children. Her education was limited to the first four grades. She is now hospitalized for deviancy (lesbianism), suspected drug abuse (marijuana), and open hostility (assaulting a police officer). Circumstances of life have deprived her of most of what is considered a normal child's due: a mother's love, a father's guiding hand, the satisfaction of learning to succeed, the happiness of family and public holidays shared among friends, the security of a home, the foundation of a spiritual platform of any sort. To deprive such a creature of yet more, to deprive her of what is her due right now according to civil and moral law is not defensible, even though, of course, some things, such as free indulgence in sexual habits she has learned to enjoy is to be denied.

The mentally retarded who, because of his appearance and the demeanor which he cannot help, is denied love and affection by his very mother, is deprived of the joys of childhood, is deprived of pride in his abilities, his appearance; is it humane to subject him to a program of behavioral therapy which would deprive him of yet more, even though for a limited time?

The counterargument against deprivation in such instances must, of course, be based on the distinction between blind deprivation in the sense in which the public understands the concept, and purposeful therapeutic deprivation in the sense in which the behavioral scientist practices it. If deprivation brought about the damage that often it did, then it must be remembered that it was not deprivation per se, but the conditions under which it was used which brought about the deplorable result.

In other words, deprivation is a powerful behavioral tool, and like all tools it is neither good nor bad but can be used to either end. But even if the deprivation in part is inevitable (as for example with some aspects of mental retardation), adding more deprivation for therapeutic purposes is justifiable if by its use demonstrable benefits can be achieved by the deprived for himself. The demonstrable benefit here is most commonly the lessening of the wrongly assumed inevitable deprivation which results when the function of deprivation as a behavioral tool is not understood and when unwittingly so-called naturally occurring deprivation is unnecessarily tolerated.

Another argument with strong apparent validity is that there are some things so basic to a civilized society that no member of that society should ever be deprived of them. Among them is the regular availability of food, a place to sleep, and the protection of personal safety. In one form or another, these basic guarantees are expressed legally and it seems only just that such laws are enforced.

Since behavioral therapy is, however, in some instances based on the use of deprivation of food and other basic needs, it seems to infringe upon these laws. To avoid this, it should either proceed without the use of deprivation, or, if it cannot, not be practiced at all.

To counter this argument, it is only necessary to analyze the intent of laws that govern basic human rights to necessities. This can be done either by careful scrutiny of the wording of such laws or by common sense consideration of what is involved. The latter procedure brings to light the already evident, namely that such laws exist for the protection of individuals, but also invites the question, whether the absolute granting of basic necessities under all conditions actually benefits the individual. It clearly does not. The surgeon's knife should be permitted to penetrate a sick man's skin, even if under certain circumstances the patient cannot or will not give his consent. Similarly the diabetic must be deprived of certain foods if he is to be protected.

Now, most of the examples that can be marshalled fall in the medical domain, and society has learned to accept these as justifiable exceptions. In the course of time, the laws themselves have come to incorporate these exceptions, so that scrutiny of the law reveals that while it is criminal under most circumstances to stick knives into people, the surgeon in helping a patient is not only permitted but indeed required to do so.

The deprivation of food is entirely analogous. If it is done to starve people into submission, or if it is practiced with vengeance, or even without reason, then it is and should be a criminal act, totally devoid of any merit. But if it is practiced by a trained professional for the benefit, and let me add, for the clear and present benefit, of a patient, then it is not only permissible, but indeed obligatory, in lieu of other, less efficacious, techniques.

The basic rights to necessities, in other words, are not and cannot be absolute rights if the humane spirit in which these laws were drawn is to be preserved.

A last but no less compelling argument against the use of deprivation would allow under certain conditions the practice of deprivation by professionals in the behavioral and health sciences, but would insist that for the safeguard of the individual each case should be reviewed as to its merits prior to implementation of the regimen.

There could be no counterargument if it were not for the fact that sometimes delay in a decision to deprive can be detrimental to the patient. In that case, again, the intent of protection of the individual would, of course, be thwarted.

But there is also an attitude conveyed in this argument which must be highly objectionable to the serious professional. It says in effect that, even though he may have passed qualifying examinations by his peers and demonstrated his skill and knowledge in other ways, when he shows the very qualities for which his training has prepared him: resourcefulness, ingenuity, confidence in his ability, compassion to alleviate the suffering of a patient, he is then to be distrusted and to be prevented from acting on his conscience. I submit that only a country that has the lowest regard for her scientists can impose such a stipulation. Only a public that has been conditioned through a steady diet of Frankensteins and other mad movie scientists can seriously believe that such controls are necessary.

Quite true, there can be abuses of professional ethics and among the medical profession there were, during the last war, some almost unbelievable abuses which came to light at the Nuremberg trials. But the question is, whether these abuses could have been prevented by reviews of laymen or peers who are less informed than the applicant. Would not the semantic difficulties, which in the case of deprivation clearly play a role, require the professional to first educate the public and his peers before being able to present the very evidence that is to make such education convincing? No, the professional's conscience must be his own as well as the public's guide. At the same time, though, the professional should be prepared to defend his actions subsequently to his peers. If his judgment was correct it will be easy for him to do so. If it was faulty, he must bear the consequences.

It may well be that the philosophical theory of ethics has little to do with the everyday task of making moral decisions. It certainly is true that a history of ethics shows that man has made many attempts in many different directions to provide guidelines for the conduct of his affairs, but so far he has been unable to provide generally acceptable guidelines in the sense that scientific laws are universally acceptable.

But there is no reason for despair. Man has managed to conduct his affairs nevertheless. Ethics is the study of value concepts such as "good" and "evil." It is interesting to observe that whenever man felt most sure that he had found absolutes of "good" and "evil," that during such periods much suffering resulted. Such periods of certainty prevailed during and immediately following the major revolutions and religious revivals. It is as if man, during such periods, were so desperate in wanting to believe something, in wanting yardsticks by which to plan his action, that he closed his eyes to the imperfections of whatever beliefs he subscribed to.

In the absence of other evidence, a reasonable conclusion might be, and probably should be, that tolerance of many standards, as long as they are dictated by sincere dedication to a worthwhile cause and personal conscience, should be the keynote. Abuses are, of course, possible under such tolerance, but they also occur, and from what history tells us even more so, under conditions of most conservative intolerance. It seems to me to be easier to argue on the basis of tolerance, especially in view of the versatility and potential for growth of knowledge and experience which such argument entails. But that, of course, reflects my own prejudice and gets us into ethical arguments of a type which cannot be treated in this essay.

I believe that the climate of tolerance which must prevail has to be created by the scientist on the one hand, as he recognizes the problems which his novel ideas create and discusses them with his peers and the general public, and as he sets himself temporary limits which, hopefully, will be expanded as experience warrants, but more importantly, it must be created by the nonscientific public administrator, whose obligation ought not merely to be to give the public what it wants but also to make the public better informed. The administrator, as a hospital superintendent, a governor of a state, or a president of a country, ought not merely be responsive to public opinion, but also should help formulate it by taking the role of educator. He must not simply worry about being embarrassed by what the scientists under his administration do, but he must prepare the public to tolerate what these scientists may do. No doubt this makes his job more difficult, but also more responsible and, I believe, in the long run, more rewarding.

In an editorial in *Science*, Harris and Wolfle (1968) have pointed to the paradox which is of relevance here: "We view modern science as one of mankind's most remarkable intellectual attainments. We recognize its contributions to economic growth, national security, health and general well-being. At the same time we are bombarded with questions and statements such as: 'Is science misshaping our world?' 'There is danger in growing technology' . . ." There is no one but the public administrator who can deal with this paradox. He at once faces the scientist-professional and the public. He must bring about information exchange which is conducted not under hysteria, not in fear of either public opinion or scientific arrogance, but in a spirit of tolerance and with the aim of creating greater tolerance.

I believe that therapeutic deprivation is not only defensible but mandatory in programs of behavioral therapy. Others such as Ball (1968), Miron (1968), Cahoon (1968), and Bragg and Wagner (1968), to mention only those who have expressed themselves recently, agree with this view. The details and the persuasiveness of their writing are admirable and are an example of the educational role which the scientist must play. It is to be hoped that equally concerned—and parenthetically, equally well experienced and educated—administrators will do their share, so that standards acceptable to the conscience of the scientist as well as to the public's can be found. Once that is done, there will no longer be any need to discuss the ethics of deprivation as the repertoire of cultural habits will have been enlarged by one.

References

Ball, T. S. The re-establishment of social behavior. *Hospital and Community Psychiatry*, 1968, **19**, 230-232.

Bragg, R. A., & Wagner, M. K. Can deprivation be justified? *Hospital and Community Psychiatry*, 1968, **19**, 229-230.

Cahoon, D. D. Balancing procedures against outcomes. *Hospital and Community Psychiatry*, 1968, **19**, 228-229.

Harris, M., & Wolfle, D. The paradox of science in the universities. *Science*, 1968, **161**.

Hume, D. *Treatise of human nature.* Vol. III. 1740. (Reprinted: Everyman's Library, 1911.)

Hume, D. An enquiry concerning human understanding. 1748. In L. A. Selby-Bigge (Ed.), *David Hume*. 1896.

Kropotkin, P. A. & Smogorzewski, K. M. Anarchism. In *Encyclopaedia Britannica*. Chicago: Benton, 1958.

Lucero, R. J. & Vail, D. J. Public policy and public responsibility. *Hospital and Community Psychiatry*, 1968, **19**, 232-233.

Lucero, R. J., Vail, D. J. & Scherber, J. Regulating operant-conditioning programs. *Hospital and Community Psychiatry*, 1968, **19**, 53-54.

Miron, N. B. The primary ethical consideration. *Hospital and Community Psychiatry*, 1968, **19**, 226-228.

Roget, P. M. *Thesaurus of English words and phrases.* (Rev. & enlarged ed.) Philadelphia: McKay, 1950.

Orthodox Ethics and Unorthodox Techniques

Zev W. Wanderer

THE CENTER FOR BEHAVIOR THERAPY, BEVERLY HILLS

Ethical and legal problems arising out of the unusual techniques required by the behavior therapist in an outpatient community setting, and in private practice, may be summarized and discussed. Of major importance are the following legal and ethical restrictions that are currently in effect: (*a*) The therapist must conduct his practice in a professional setting. (*b*) Signed releases should be obtained before attempting experimental procedures (or before applying any technique which is not usual and customary for the location in which he practices). (*c*) The therapist has regard for the social and moral expectations of the community. (*d*) There is an unwritten stricture against physical contact with patients and collaterals.

A review of behavior-therapy techniques in technical manuals as well as in the periodical literature reveals that strict adherence to the above is inherently limiting.

Several behavior-therapy techniques which dramatically deviate from accepted community practice, but whose effectiveness has been demonstrated by published research, can be described. Illustrations include treating patients outside of the office, as with *in vivo* desensitizations of phobias in restaurants, cars, at airports, and even in washrooms.

Instrumentation, such as GSR (and even more elaborate polygraphic monitoring of psychophysiological responses to anxiety provoking stimuli), delayed audio feedback devices for stutterers, penile plethysmographic measurements, and behavior-shaping techniques for the treatment of sexual inadequacies in men are being used. The use of electric (nonconvulsive) shockers for aversive conditioning has a proper place in the practice of a behavior therapist.

The use of pornographic slides and films for the counterconditioning of homosexuality, pedophilia, and for sexual training, all of which have been reported as successful techniques in the literature, belong in the behavior therapist's office.

The strategic placement of students to act as behavioral analysts in classrooms, and in the home, is another appropriate innovation in the community practice of behavior therapy. The counterconditioning effects of carbon dioxide have been described and promulgated (Wolpe & Lazarus, 1967, pp. 121-124) and the use of this technique may be considered a proper part of the armamentarium of the behavior therapist, provided that carbon dioxide is not legally considered a medication. This last point needs to be further explored with legal experts in each state. Direct behavioral analyses by behavior therapists of social and sexual awkwardness and the provision of opportunities for correction of those problems by behavioral rehearsal and even by the encouragement of the use of professional women (Wolpe & Lazarus, 1967, p. 108) should, in the interest of answering the client's plea for help, be part of the proper function of the behavior therapist.

Recent work (Bandura, Grusec, & Menlove, 1967; Ritter, 1968) suggests that physical contact with phobic patients may accelerate the cure of specific phobias, under properly controlled conditions, so that certain phobias may be overcome in less than two hours.

A parallel to certain specialties within the medical profession may be drawn, wherein practices such as biopsy, gynecological and proctological examination, as well as obstetrics by male physicians, were not "accepted community practice" at one time, but by demonstrated augmentations in effectiveness a process of evolution took place within medicine. Similarly, behavior therapy and its unorthodox techniques can accelerate an evolution within psychology and psychiatry by continuing research and development to improve and demonstrate effectiveness, by efforts to encourage our colleagues to modify and update ethical and legal standards so that they can accommodate and take cognizance of behavior-therapy techniques, and, most important, by a program of public information so that community expectations of behavior therapy may be properly and accurately determined.

We propose that psychotherapists begin to take seriously the question of effectiveness of treatment in terms of preset objectives for the patient. Once a behavior therapist has undertaken treatment of a patient, it would appear that he should be ethically bound not to withhold from his patient the alternative options of techniques which have been demonstrated in the research literature to be effective, simply because they may deviate from accepted community practice. Provided that the therapist has a mature understanding with this patient and presents alternatives to the patient as options, and provided that the patient requests and authorizes a procedure which is unorthodox but which shows promise of accelerating a cure of the presenting problem, the therapist should feel free, if not obligated to commence with the unorthodox technique.

Professionals who wish to practice innovative therapeutic techniques have a responsibility to inform their colleagues as well as the public by giving precise descriptions of what they do together with some statement of probable effectiveness as demonstrated by published research reports.

We therefore propose that the Association for Advancement of Behavior Therapy explore the possibility of preparing a two-page public-information pamphlet, similar to those published by specialties within the American Medical Association, describing "How a Behavior Therapist Works."

A mutuality of responsibility exists between the therapeutic innovator and his more conventional colleagues. The therapeutic innovator has a responsibility to inform his colleagues of unconventional procedures that he proposes to use, and the rationale for their use—and, in return, he should be able to expect ethical, moral, and legal support from his colleagues in particular and from the profession in general.

If the above conditions are met, the individual patient, the helping professions, as well as society at large will benefit.

References

American Medical Association. *Medicolegal forms,* Chicago: AMA, 1961.

American Psychological Associations. *Casebook on ethical standards of psychologists,* Washington, D. C.: APA, 1967.

Bandura, A., Grusec, J. E., & Menlove, F. L. Vicarious extinction of avoidance behavior. *Journal of Personality and Social Psychology,* 1967, **5**, 16-23.

Ritter, B. The group desensitization of children's snake phobias using vicarious and contact desensitization procedures. *Behaviour Research and Therapy,* 1968, **6**, 1-6.

Wolpe, J., & Lazarus, A. F. *Behavior therapy techniques.* New York: Macmillan (Pergamon), 1967.

A Case of Impotence Successfully Treated with Desensitization Combined with *In Vivo* Operant Training and Thought Substitution

Zalmon H. Garfield

EAGLEVILLE HOSPITAL AND REHABILITATION CENTER

John F. McBrearty

TEMPLE UNIVERSITY
AND
EAGLEVILLE HOSPITAL AND REHABILITATION CENTER

Marvin Dichter

EAGLEVILLE HOSPITAL AND REHABILITATION CENTER

The case reported is one of impotence treated essentially with a broad spectrum approach. An aspect of the therapeutic program, previously unreported to the authors' knowledge, is the use of desensitization as a means of monitoring and controlling overly rapid and premature efforts to complete the sexual act. Control of this rapid series of behavioral components has been a repetitive problem in treating this particular behavioral deficit. The combination of thought stopping and thought substitution in the sexual situation represents another treatment innovation.

The subject was originally referred to the senior author because alternative efforts to assist with the problem were ineffective. The patient's impotence was so anxiety producing as to have substantially reduced his ability to benefit (or participate) from other therapy offered in the hospital for alcoholics where he was a resident.

Case History

Mr. C., a 45-year-old robust patient, suffered with total sexual impotence for a period of one year prior to seeking help. He described its gradual onset for a period of six months to a year prior to that time. This consisted of increasing inability to maintain an erection after it was achieved. The loss sometimes occurred after intromission. Occasionally no erection at all occurred. Finally he was unable to achieve an erection at any time.

Mr. C. was a rather handsome, gray haired man of slightly more than average height. He was trim and well built. In manner he was pleasant, soft spoken, and tended to be both passive and submissive. He agreed with the therapist, even when within ten minutes the therapist's statements were self-contradicting, and only rarely disagreed. When he did, however, he became doggedly, almost desperately stubborn in maintaining his position. He was overly respectful of authority.

Patient was a resident in a center for the treatment of alcoholism at the time the problem of his impotence was approached for the first time. There was no obvious connection between his impotence and his alcoholism in that he never attempted intercourse while drunk or drinking, nor had this ever been a pattern with him. He was sober for long periods (up to six months) between drinking binges. He had been sober for five months at the time treatment for impotence took place. The therapist who treated the impotence had nothing to do with the group therapy in which Mr. C. participated, nor with any other aspect of his therapy related to drinking or other maladaptive behaviors.

History

Patient was one of four children, all siblings being female and older. He described a somewhat seductive relationship with his mother as a boy ("she would lie down with me, sometimes cuddle me or play with my ear") and a fearful, submissive relationship with his father, whom he disliked because "he was mean to my mother." His father apparently returned his distaste and singled him out for frequent beatings with a frayed hose.

The parents' relationship to each other was described as tense and angry. The mother and children conspired to deceive the father to avoid his anger. Father was Catholic, mother Lutheran. The children pretended to go to the Catholic church at the father's insistence, but they avoided actually attending whenever possible, with approval from the mother.

The father was a powerful man, dark, stern, with virtually no interest outside the home other than his work as a plasterer. He was rigid and strict in all matters, especially sexual, refusing to allow any of the children, including Mr. C., to attend dances or have a friend of the opposite sex in the home at any time. The second sister was his father's favorite. He nicknamed her "Billy," and would tease the patient about his inadequacy compared to her. As a boy, Mr. C. heavily emphasized his participation in sports and he joined the paratroopers during World War II.

Patient's sexual history showed rather sparse activity and even more sparse information. He was seduced by a somewhat older neighborhood girl when he was in high school. This relationship continued on a furtive, occasional basis in her house for about a year. In his senior year in high school, he began to date his future wife. They had intercourse a few times, but with minimal response from her.

Mr. C.'s notion about orgasm in women ranged from an early concept that few women had orgasm and then rarely, to one in which he felt it was a man's duty to produce orgasm and that he failed as a man if it did not occur. The latter was his opinion when therapy began. His notions about sexual matters were consistently a product of impression rather than education; his sexual education in both home and school was negligible. He described his ideas in this area as largely acquired from peers, including an adolescent notion that masturbation and sexual intercourse were weakening.

Somewhere in his adolescence, or perhaps his early adult years, Mr. C. became emotionally attached to the Catholic church.

After separating from his wife, following 14 years of marriage, he took up a relationship with Miss M., a woman whom he had met earlier, and with whom he had had relations, but had left. Miss M. was the third and only other sexual partner of his lifetime and with her he achieved his first satisfactory sexual adjustment. They practiced contraception by coitus interruptus. He described condoms and diaphragms as "messy." (This conformed with an impression of overmeticulousness and overorderliness in his behavior, dress, and attitudes.)

Miss M. refused to marry him until he had been sober for a year. (He was drinking heavily by this time.) She was a registered nurse, supported her mother, maintained her own home, and, in general, according to Mr. C. was a "superior" person to him. She also was a woman who dominated her environment. Mr. C. said he always resented Miss M.'s condition for their marriage although he "understood" it. His religious scruples apparently added to this discomfort. She was, in person, short, round, good humored, and spoke with great assurance on all matters until confronted by a vigorous counterassertiveness. She appeared readily capable of asserting control over Mr. C.

Mr. C. reported that until his impotence became a problem, he was able to bring her to orgasm readily. He regarded this as a matter of great importance, it having never characterized his sexual relationship with his wife. This achievement became for him a "proof" of virility.

Miss M. persuaded Mr. C. to go to her church, a Protestant denomination. He felt guilty about going however because he felt his life made him unworthy of being in church.

Treatment

While history taking was being completed, relaxation instruction was begun. At the same time, Mr. C. was advised to engage in no sexual activity that had not been specifically approved in discussion with his therapist. He was told to think of himself and the therapist as an engineering or coaching team; no strategy was to be executed without full approval of the coaching team.

An analysis of Mr. C.'s behavior suggested that anxiety with reference to sexual behavior began with the most remote point in time and space at which he initiated approach behavior in the direction of Miss M. Just prior to experiencing his first signs of impotence, he reported a general feeling of unworthiness, including as a part of this his relationship with Miss M. He also reported having had achievement of orgasm by Miss M. on his mind at all times when they were engaged in intercourse. This was of primary importance. As anxiety about ability to perform increased, this factor became a major preoccupation and increased his anxiety.

It was determined that based on the behavioral analysis summarized above, treatment should include:

1. Desensitization to the temporal and spatial stimuli producing anxiety while approaching a time and place suitable for sexual relations to occur.
2. Thought stopping and thought substitution with reference to preoccupation with his partner's orgasm (Wolpe & Lazarus, 1966).

3. Practice in sexual assertiveness lagging a step or two behind desensitization and otherwise following the model described by Wolpe (1958).

In addition to the above, brief discussion took place with reference to Mr. C.'s worthiness as a human being and forgiveness as part of the Christian ethic. Mr. C. was encouraged to speak with a priest about his church association and negative feelings with reference to church attendance which appeared to be a response to his drinking behavior, as well as to the fact that he and Miss M. were not married. At the termination of the therapeutic relationship six weeks later, these discussions had had the initial effect of at least one church attendance and talk of visiting a priest.

Utilization of sexual assertiveness alone in an effort to attain the level of intercourse was attempted in this case independently by the patient early in the treatment program. It resulted in failure. It is, of course, unknown if it might have been successful if pursued more slowly in accordance with the Wolpe (1958) paradigm. It was felt at this stage, however, that the desensitization hierarchy would act as a supportive element in maintaining successful sexual approach behavior. It was also felt that it would act to inhibit responses which Mr. C.'s anxiety then would be likely to render unsuccessful. The procedure was successful in both respects.

The hierarchy constructed with Mr. C. was essentially one of temporal and spatial approach to the anxiety producing situation, sexual behavior. Fortunately for this purpose Mr. C.'s habits and behavior tended to be quite regular. Thus items in the hierarchy suggest the apparent remoteness of stimuli which can be anxiety producing. They involved such items as:

1. Closing the gas station where Mr. C. was working and delivering the cash to his employer's home.
2. Driving home and rounding the corner onto the street where he lived with Miss M.

On both these items, Mr. C. had initial anxiety reactions, but they occurred only one time. As he approached more closely the sexual situation anxiety became more acute. Such items as taking a bath before going to bed and kissing Miss M. good night required several repetitions, relaxation scenes, fractionation, etc.

As the hierarchy proceeded into sexual behavior and contacts (hugging, kissing, feeling, etc.), Mr. C. was strictly enjoined, under no circumstances, to proceed beyond the hierarchy level and advised to actually lag a step behind.

This injunction and advice relieved Mr. C.'s anxiety as to maintenance of an erection at crucial moments. The result of this was that very early in the sexual situation paralleling the hierarchy, Mr. C. developed and maintained an erection. By the time he arrived at stages just prior to intromission, he was sexually extremely excited and desirous to proceed to completion.

In fact, as stated above, one time quite early in the desensitization procedure paralleled by *in vivo* training, Mr. C. attempted to proceed at his own discretion to complete intercourse. He failed. This experience led to close adherence thereafter to procedures agreed upon with therapist.

The interaction of the relief of anxiety by reason of limitations placed on his actual behavior, plus relief generated by the desensitization procedure, led to steadily maintained relaxation in the situation as Mr. C. proceeded closer and closer to intercourse. His verbally expressed confidence in the therapy situation of his ability to carry the act to completion preceded by at least two weeks the actual accomplishment of the act.

It should perhaps be noted here that another method utilized by the therapist to relieve anxiety in the therapy situation as well as with reference to the sexual situation and discussion related to language. The therapist utilized common slang with reference to genitals and intercourse generally, picking up and continuing to use those expressions by Mr. C.

At the stage where Mr. C.'s confidence in ability to function sexually was quite high, such items were introduced into the hierarchy as:

1. "Miss M. plays with your prick for several minutes while you play with or suck her tits.
2. "You press against her pussy with your hard on.
3. "(Crucial item) You feel 'I could put it in if I wanted to.'
4. "You decide to put it in and do so for a very little while and take it out."

At the stage of item 3 above, the subject of Mr. C.'s preoccupation with Miss M.'s orgasm was reraised.

At this time, Mr. C. was instructed in thought stopping and thought substitution. He was told whenever during sex play he had any concern about his partner's orgasm he should instantly say to himself, "No, I will not think of that. I will think of enjoying myself." He was then instructed to think of the most pleasurably erotic situation he could while continuing sex play. Several such scenes were constructed involving situations particularly exciting to Mr. C. He was to continue these thoughts until the actual circumstances and activity became completely absorbing.

With this procedure and behavior added to his repertoire, the length of intromission was extended until it involved ejaculation. In these circumstances, as they recurred, Miss M. sometimes did not experience orgasm. The first experience of Mr. C. experiencing ejaculation took place a little more than four weeks after the first therapy session and three weeks after beginning desensitization procedures.

Mr. C. continued in therapy for several weeks beyond this point. Operant theory was utilized in designing behaviors to practice in developing further assertiveness in other areas with Miss M., her mother, in job situations, etc. These procedures were interrupted by Mr. C.'s departure from the hospital.

A footnote to this case is that Mr. C. returned to the hospital for a party. He reported at this time that he had experienced drinking "slips" sufficient to cause job loss, but that his sexual functioning had continued to remain intact up to that time.

Suggestive Conclusions

The case suggests once again the stability of responses developed by behavior-modification methods. The possible value is suggested of reinforcement and anxiety relief proceeding from feelings of strong potency in the sexual situation while being protected for a time from a test situation in a structured, authoritarian relationship. The combination of desensitization procedure with *in vivo* training appeared to accomplish this purpose, combining classical and operant conditioning methodology.

Finally the thought stopping followed by appropriate preplanned thought substitution appeared effective in this case in eliminating a sexually inhibiting stimulus from occurring.

References

Wolpe, J. *Psychotherapy by reciprocal inhibition.* Stanford, Calif.: Stanford University Press, 1958.

Wolpe, J., & Lazarus, A. A. *Behavior therapy techniques.* New York: Macmillan (Pergamon), 1966.

Duration of Exposure to Items and Pretreatment Training as Factors in Systematic Desensitization Therapy[1]

Stewart Proctor

INDIANA UNIVERSITY[2]

The most widely explored and employed of the behavior-therapy techniques at this time is certainly systematic desensitization, the development of which is largely credited to Joseph Wolpe. Simply stated, the theoretical explanation presented by Wolpe to account for the effects of this treatment is that anxiety (conceived of as a unified response) has, by some set of circumstances, come to be elicited by a specifiable object or situation (i.e., stimulus). Wolpe further proposes that a certain number of physiologically defined states—particularly, relaxation, assertion, and sexual arousal—are basically incompatible with anxiety: In his terms, they are reciprocally inhibiting responses. The fundamental process, Wolpe maintains, which accounts for successful systematic desensitization is the disappearance of the anxiety reaction through its progressive displacement by one of the incompatible responses he describes. Hence, if treatment continues nominally, the client proceeds through an imagined hierarchy (or hierarchies) of previously fear-arousing scenes and is eventually able to envision all the items without undue anxiety. Furthermore, he is

[1]This paper is based in part upon the author's dissertation which was submitted in partial fulfillment of the requirements for the degree Doctor of Philosophy, Indiana University, 1968.

[2]Now at the University of Utah.

also able to remain anxiety-free when actually in the previously fear-inducing circumstances, the result of a proposed generalization process from the imagined to the real stimuli. (A detailed account of both the treatment and theory can be found in Wolpe, 1958.)

Pretreatment Training and Systematic Desensitization

Wolpe's reciprocal inhibition paradigm presents numerous dimensions which lend themselves to systematic empirical investigation. Certainly, one critical consideration from both theoretical and empirical points of view is the idea that some response—most typically relaxation—must serve to displace the conditioned anxiety response. In point of fact, there has been reason to question the role of this variable for some time. For example, Rachman, (1965) wrote in a recent study:

> *In the normal therapeutic procedure, one does not present the next item on the hierarchy until the patient reports little or no disturbance from the item under consideration. For the purpose of this experiment, however, this precaution was disregarded. (p. 246).*

Hence, Rachman's subsequent conclusion that a state of relaxation is essential to effective desensitization is of dubious validity since no attempt was made to confirm, even subjectively, the supposed state. Cooke (1966) indirectly produced evidence that relaxation might not be crucial to systematic desensitization when he achieved equivalent success with two groups of subjects, one which was desensitized while reclining, the other while being presented live enactments of the hierarchy items while standing erect (and with no special training in selective relaxation). Finally, direct evidence that behavior modification can be attained using the systematic desensitization format but without muscle relaxation training, or even with subjects purposely tensing their muscles, was reported by Wolpin and Raines (1966). Speaking from a physiological standpoint, Davison (1966) has pointed out that muscle relaxation and anxiety may not be incompatible after all, and certainly the question of whether or not there exists a physiologically discernible "anxiety state" is far from settled (a negative argument is offered by Schachter, 1966).

To date, no studies have been published confirming directly any correlations between relaxation training and actual, physiologically defined relaxation attained, nor between physiologically defined relaxation and the degree of improvement in treatment. However, since we can say definitively whether or not a subject has been trained in deep muscle relaxation, it is suggested that pretreatment training be examined for the time being as a separate issue from the physiologically verified measures assumed to define relaxation itself. Chemically induced mild relaxation such as that described by Brady (1966) offers a potential means for systematically assessing the role of deep muscle relaxation independent of or combined with various types of pretreatment training. For the present, only variations in pretreatment training without physiological verification will be considered.

Timing Dimensions and Systematic Desensitization

Again from a theoretical as well as empirical point of view, the issue of timing in systematic desensitization and other behavior-therapy techniques warrants exploration. There are two basic time dimensions which suggest themselves in the systematic desensitization method: *intra-item duration* (duration of exposure), and *inter-item duration* (item spacing). Considered collectively, these two dimensions would be roughly equivalent to a third nonindependent dimension, *actual treatment duration* (apart from preparation for treatment). Curiously, none of these dimensions has been systematically studied. Paul (1969) has recently facilitated such research by exhaustively detailing the available information, and thus a review of the current data on timing in systematic desensitization will not be presented here. Suffice it to say, however, that, while most authors state the relevant durations employed in their research efforts, none to date has made an attempt at exploring the effects of varying duration factors in any systematic way.

It is apparent, then, that the relative functions in systematic desensitization of such potentially critical variables as duration of exposure to items and type of pretreatment training are as yet uncertain. Due to their obvious implications for both theoretical and applied considerations, they were selected from among the many which suggest themselves as topics of investigation for a research project.

The Use of Filmed Items in Systematic Desensitization

Before outlining the research conducted to investigate the above described variables and the implications of this research for practicing desensitization, an innovation in systematic desensitization research methodology will be presented. One of the inherent difficulties in using imagined scenes during systematic desensitization is that on-off times are not amenable to precise experimenter control. While Cooke's introduction of the use of real (as opposed to imagined) fear objects (1966) offers a variation, the method is beset with practical limitations which make it rather unwieldy in all but a small number of cases. Furthermore, experimental consistency across and within subjects cannot be insured.

In order to investigate more accurately the duration of exposure variable in the systematic desensitization paradigm, motion pictures were introduced as the medium for item presentation.[3] While films have been used successfully in other contexts (e.g., modeling behavior, stress response research), the technique has heretofore not been employed in systematic desensitization research despite numerous experimental advantages such as: (*a*) maximal experimental control of the content of item presentation; (*b*) maximal control of both inter- and intra-item durations; (*c*) the opportunity to systematically manipulate many variables such as the order of items, length of hierarchies, variations in accompanying sound tracks, etc. A more extensive exploration of this technique is described elsewhere (Proctor, 1968a).

Summary of Research

As a part of a large-scale study, duration of exposure to items and various types of pretreatment training in muscle tension states were employed as variables affecting a systematic desensitization analog treatment of phobic avoidance behavior. Two item exposure durations, 5 and 20 sec, were used in conjunction with three pretreatment training conditions: relaxation training, tension training, and a minimal neutral training. Training was conducted by prerecorded tapes in a single 20-min session prior to the initiation of four treatment sessions held twice weekly for two weeks. Assessments of treatment effects were made on three occasions: prior to treatment, immediately after treatment, and one month after treatment. Four measures were used in each assessment: (*a*) overt avoidance behavior as measured on a 13-point objective scale; (*b*) a subjective estimate of maximal fear level as measured on a 100-point scale; (*c*) the rate, in feet per second, with which the subject approached the fear-arousing object; and (*d*) a behavioral checklist consisting of items popularly assumed to imply anxiety. There were nine subjects in each of the six (2 × 3) treatment

[3]The research described was conducted in the spring of 1967.

groups as well as in a no-treatment control group the subjects of which were assessed at equivalent time intervals. The 63 subjects selected were those demonstrating the most avoidance behavior among some 150 who were tested after reporting strong fear of the phobic object (snakes).

Relaxation training followed the format established by Paul (1966a) and included an explanation of the principles of desensitization. Tension training, on the other hand, involved having the subjects progressively tense rather than relax each muscle group in a manner directly opposite to relaxation training. The rationale given to these subjects was that the treatment would enhance their tolerance for stress which was presently lower than it need be, thereby reducing their fear in the presence of the phobic object. Neutral pretreatment training consisted of a brief introduction to the fact that films of the phobic objects would be observed thus enabling subjects to make up a deficiency of nonstressful experience with the phobic objects, a deficiency which was suggested to be the basis of their fear. In the neutral pretreatment training no form of training in muscle tension states was given.

The two major variables and the three assessments produced a $2 \times 3 \times 3$ repeated measures design, and analyses of variance constituted the primary approach to data evaluation. Results were found to vary greatly according to the specific measures used in the analyses. In terms of the direct modification of overt avoidance behavior, duration of exposure to items proved to be a significant factor, longer exposures being associated with greater change. The duration of exposure effect is represented in Fig. 1, where pretreatment training conditions have been combined.

While duration of exposure to film-mediated items had a significant effect upon overt avoidance behavior, the rate with which subjects approached the previously fear-arousing object was significantly affected by the pretreatment training conditions in a rather curious way (neutrally-trained subjects manifesting the largest increase rate). The overall effect of pretreatment training (regardless of item exposure duration) is summarized in Fig. 2.

A third measure, subjective fear estimates on a 100-point scale, was influenced by a significant interaction between the two main variables, and a graphic presentation which summarizes this effect is given in Fig. 3. Results of the behavior checklist did not discriminate between any of the experimental conditions or between treated and untreated subjects.

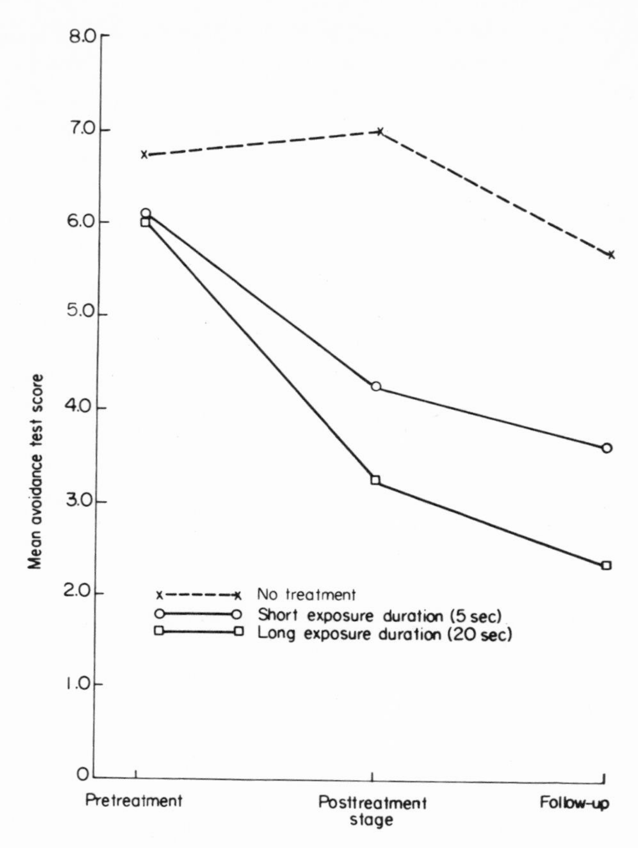

Fig. 1. Avoidance test results: differential effects of two item exposure durations (5 vs. 20 sec).

By way of both elaborating and summarizing these results, it can be stated that, on three of the four measures employed, treated subjects differed significantly from untreated subjects immediately after treatment. While these differences were selectively attenuated to some extent a month after treatment, the attenuation can be attributed partly to increased improvement by the untreated control subjects rather than to any remarkable decrement on the part of treated subjects. Furthermore, the distinction between treated and untreated subjects in terms of the "target" behavior—overt avoidance—did persist at a statistically significant level across time. The relative effectiveness of the systematic desensitization approach to behavior modification, even in this limited, short-term analog treatment, was again demonstrated. It was variation within the treated subjects that was attributable to the selective effects of duration of exposure to items and pretreatment training. By and large, treatment of any sort was still better than no treatment at all. Duration of exposure to items affected how *far* a subject would go toward handling a feared object, pretreatment training affected how *fast* he moved in this endeavor, and an interaction of the two affected how frightened the subject would say he was at the time.

Correlation analyses were conducted of both the extent to which the four measures used demonstrated some communality prior to experimental intervention (summarized in Table 1) and the extent to which they varied together following treatment (Table 2). It was found that

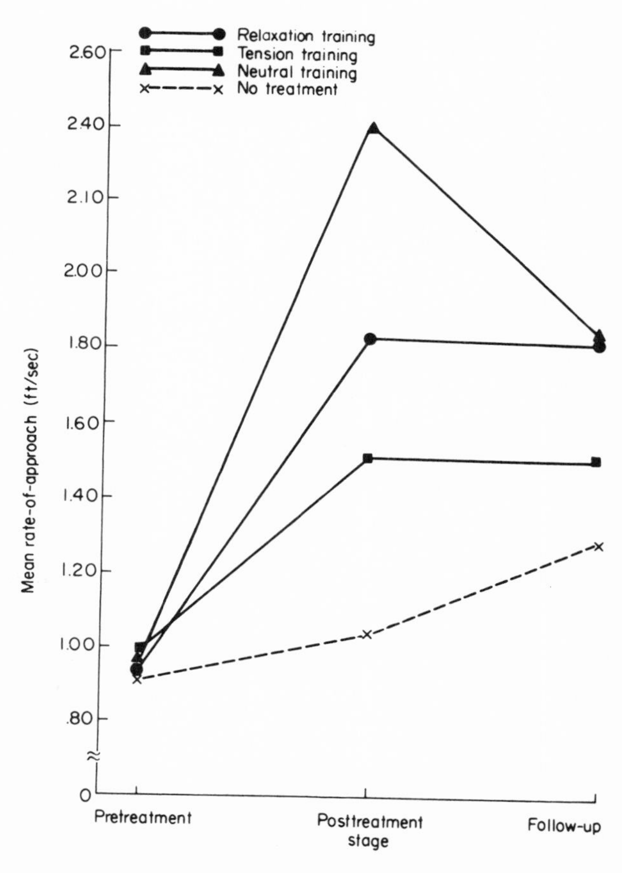

Fig. 2. Rate-of-approach results: pretreatment training effects.

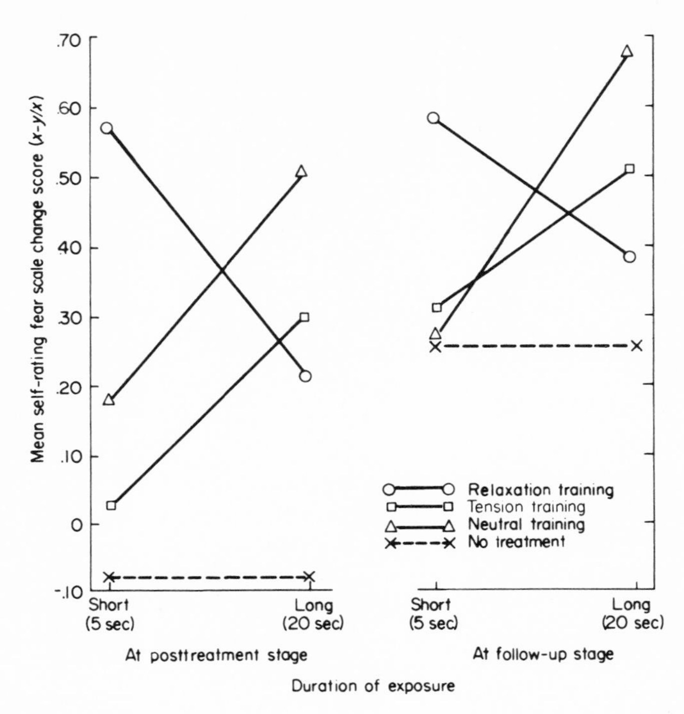

Fig. 3. Self-rating fear scale: mean percentage of change for all groups determined at posttreatment and follow-up stages.

the four measures manifested limited communality originally, but that (with the exception of the behavior checklist) they varied together to a considerable extent following treatment.

Implications for the Refinement of Systematic Desensitization

Many interesting theoretical implications emerge from the results described above. The measure-specific effects obtained, when combined with the correlational data and placed in the context of our accumulating knowledge in this area, suggest that it will be important in future work to determine more accurately not what theoretical process (e.g., extinction, reciprocal inhibition) accounts for treatment effects, but rather which process accounts for which changes (i.e., measures) under what conditions. The present data join others which cannot be reviewed here in implying that a single-process approach will be in-

TABLE 1
CORRELATION COEFFICIENT MATRIX FOR SCORES ON ALL MEASURES AT THE PRETREATMENT STAGE ($n = 63$)

Measure[a]	AT	SFS	RAP	BCL
AT	–	.27[c]	−.17	.37[b]
SFS		–	−.14	.11
RAP			–	−.01
BCL				–

[a]Key: AT = Avoidance Test, SFS = Self-Rating Fear Scale, RAP = Rate-of-Approach, and BCL = Behavior Checklist (items/sec).
[b]$p < .01$.
[c]$p < .05$.

adequate for explaining the variation both within and across response modalities following systematic desensitization psychotherapy. A more detailed exploration of the theoretical implications of these and other desensitization data is presented elsewhere (Proctor, 1968b).

The primary objective of this paper is not to discuss theoretical considerations, but rather to outline the implications of this research for the clinical use of systematic desensitization. Again, a number of points emerge. First, the filmed presentation of systematic desensiti-

TABLE 2
CORRELATION COEFFICIENT MATRIX OF THE INDICES OF CHANGE FOR EACH OF THE FOUR MEASURES ($n = 63$)

Measure[a]	AT	SFS	RAP	BCL
Post test				
AT	–	.55[b]	.56[b]	.03
SFS		–	.48[b]	.08
RAP			–	−.14
BCL				–
Follow up				
AT	–	.57[b]	.47[b]	.13
SFS		–	.44[b]	.16
RAP			–	−.21
BCL				–

[a]Key: AT = Avoidance Test, SFS = Self-Rating Fear Scale, RAP = Rate of Approach, and BCL = Behavior Checklist (items/sec).
[b]$p < .01$.

zation items has proved in this study to be an effective medium for enhancing stimulus control in addition to demonstrating its potential as a therapeutic tool. Bandura and Menlove (1968) have recently used a film medium in their "symbolic modeling" treatment method, and they cite research in progress (Bandura, Blanchard, & Ritter, 1968) which combines symbolic modeling with certain aspects of the systematic desensitization paradigm. Filmed item presentation is already being used in applied settings to a limited degree (Wanderer, 1968), and in view of these positive indications, it is suggested that the utility of filmed (or videotaped) item presentation be fully explored as both an experimental and a therapeutic instrument. A possible point of departure is the recent report of the successful automation of systematic desensitization through the use of electronically augmented audiotape recorders (Melamed & Lang, 1967). The same technical principles could be extended to the use of videotape recorders.

The aspect of this research, however, which bears the strongest implications for systematic desensitization practice is the measure-specific nature of the effects. Clinically, the practitioner is most commonly concerned with overt avoidance behavior modification in a gross sense. By this standard alone, the results of the present research imply that longer durations of exposure without aversive consequences have greater therapeutic value regardless of pretreatment training. Clearly, an extinction-like process is implied for this response mode.

According to the Wolpean formulation, the subjects given relaxation pretreatment training would be the only ones with whom a true reciprocal inhibition process could operate, since the relaxed state is required for the inhibition of the anxiety response. To demonstrate that an inhibition process may have been operating simultaneously, we must consider the effects obtained with a different measure, the self-rating fear scale. As can be seen in Fig. 3, the tension-trained and neutrally trained groups showed changes basically parallel to the results of the avoidance behavior mode (i.e., more change associated with longer exposure). The inverse, however, was true for the relaxation-trained groups. It is possible to speculate on the nature of this interaction. Paul (personal communication, 1968) has recently obtained data suggesting that the physiological correlates of anxiety take some number of seconds to mobilize completely following the onset of a fear-arousing event, thus confirming an hypothesis which he formulated earlier (Paul, 1966b). This finding has important implications for the managing of systematic desensitization treatment. It is conceivable that true reciprocal inhibition as a physiological process (and as defined by Wolpe) operates maximally for certain response modes when (*a*) initial exposures are limited in duration to levels which preclude the possibility of full anxiety arousal, and (*b*) relaxation training is employed. But it is equally conceivable that, simultaneously or alternatively, extinction-like processes occur, and that these processes may account for the modification of other response modes (revealed in different measures), or even in the same response modes under different circumstances.

Without further elaboration of the implications of these data for the practice of systematic desensitization, it is suggested that pursuing hypotheses suggested by an extinction model (e.g., longer exposure durations, repeated exposures) may be as important as pursuing hypotheses suggested by a reciprocal inhibition model (e.g., emphasis on not allowing the mobilization of anxiety during item presentation) or hypotheses suggested by any other model (e.g., social imitation). It behooves the practitioner to attend to all models and to the various measures of improvement with which he is concerned, for there is reason to believe that an interaction of models and response modes exists. Ford and Urban (1967) actually anticipated this situation when they wrote recently:

> *The most fruitful direction at this time would seem to be to try to apply the procedures related to specific learning situations, or to study the research on different response processes to isolate those learning conditions most effective with each kind. Different principles may govern the modification of different responses (p. 337).*

References

Bandura, A., Blanchard E. D., & Ritter, B. J. The relative efficacy of desensitization and modeling for inducing therapeutic behavioral, affective, and attitudinal changes. Unpublished manuscript, Stanford University, 1968.

Bandura, A., & Menlove, F. L. Factors determining vicarious extinction of avoidance behavior through symbolic modeling. *Journal of Personality and Social Psychology*, 1968, **8**, 99-108.

Brady, J. P. Brevital-relaxation treatment of frigidity. *Behaviour Research and Therapy*, 1966, **4**, 71-77.

Cooke, G. The efficacy of two desensitization procedures: An analogue study. *Behaviour Research and Therapy*, 1966, **4**, 17-24.

Davison, G. C. Anxiety under total curarization: Implications for the role of muscular relaxation in the desensitization of neurotic fears. *Journal of Nervous and Mental Diseases*, 1966, **143**, 443-448.

Ford, D. H., & Urban, H. B. Psychotherapy. *Annual Review of Psychology*, 1967, **18**, 333-372.

Melamed, B., & Lang, P. J. Study of the automated desensitization of fear. Paper presented at the meeting of the Midwestern Psychological Association, Chicago, May, 1967.

Paul, G. L. *Insight versus desensitization in psychotherapy.* Stanford, Calif.: Stanford University Press, 1966. (a)

Paul, G. L. The specific control of anxiety: "Hypnosis" and "conditioning." Paper presented at the meeting of the American Psychological Association, New York, Sept. 1966. (b)

Paul, G. L. Outcome of systematic desensitization. II: Controlled investigations of individual treatment, technique variations, and current status. In C. M. Franks (Ed.), *Behavior therapy: Appraisal of status.* New York: McGraw-Hill, 1969, in press.

Proctor, S. The role of innovation in behavior therapy research. Paper presented at the meeting of the California State Psychological Association, Santa Barbara. Jan. 1968. (a)

Proctor, S. The role of duration of exposure to items and pretreatment training in a systematic desensitization analog. Unpublished doctoral dissertation, Indiana University, 1968. (b)

Rachman, S. Studies in desensitization. I: The separate effects of relaxation and desensitization. *Behaviour Research and Therapy,* 1965, 3, 245-251.

Schachter, S. The interaction of cognitive and physiological determinants of emotional state. In C. D. Spielberger (Ed.), *Anxiety and behavior.* New York: Academic Press, 1966.

Wanderer, Z. Innovation in the private practice of behavior therapy. Paper presented at the meeting of the Western Psychological Association, San Diego, Mar. 1968.

Wolpe, J. *Psychotherapy by reciprocal inhibition.* Stanford, Calif.: Stanford University Press, 1958.

Wolpin, M., & Raines, J. Visual imagery, expected roles, and extinction as possible factors in reducing fear and avoidance behavior. *Behaviour Research and Therapy,* 1966, 4, 25-37.

A Technique for Improving Desensitization via Warmth, Empathy, and Emotional Reexperiencing of Hierarchy Events

Allen E. Bergin
COLUMBIA UNIVERSITY

As increasing numbers of psychotherapists have become convinced of the value of behavior-therapy techniques there has been a growing interest in developing ways of coordinating these approaches within a single repertoire of therapeutic methods. Weitzman (1967), working from a psychoanalytic point of view, has suggested specific modifications of both traditional techniques and of desensitization which require simultaneous application of procedures based upon both approaches. Truax and Carkhuff (1967), operating from a client-centered viewpoint, have suggested that many patients' poor social functioning is due to learning deficits that can be overcome by using warmth and empathy as reinforcers for human relating responses. Lazarus, as a behavior therapist, has proposed that his fellow mechanotropes give serious consideration to the value of empathy, interpretation, and other traditional procedures in their own work (1967).

The purpose of the following case experiment was to use some aspects of traditional procedures to deepen and accelerate the effects of desensitization. This procedure was a very significant part of the total therapy. The sessions in which it took place elicited the most profound reactions on the part of the patient, and her reports of greatest behavioral improvement followed a series of sessions where this type of desensitization was the focus.[1]

Diagnostic Evaluation

The client, a 24-year-old single female, presented her problems as being conflict over a recently developed homosexual relationship and an inability to relate effectively to men.

It soon became evident that her relationships with men had repeatedly proved traumatic and that this history created predispositions which made her vulnerable to the homosexual seduction which occurred after her arrival in a new place of employment. It was clear that her problems with men were primary, although it was the upset over having become involved in homosexual behavior that caused her to seek help.

The homosexual activity had occurred occasionally over a one-year period and intensified somewhat just prior to treatment. There were no previous episodes. She had dated men fairly often in the past and had become involved with a number to the extent of necking and petting, but had never experienced sexual relations or orgasm.

Her relationship with her father was a primary source of discomfort; the events involved in it seemed to permeate indiscriminately her thinking toward all males. Her father was a rigid, domineering person who expected success and perfection on a par with his own exacting behavior. His demands were exercised with unusual force upon the client and she grew up in total fear of his wrath.

In adulthood, her behavior with men was extremely guarded, and, as intimacy or intensity of the relationship developed, her fearful avoidance tendencies heightened proportionately. In addition, she sometimes felt intense anger toward specific men and toward men in general.

Her relationship with her mother had been positive and supportive although she saw her mother as weak and defenseless in relation to her father, thus making it difficult to identify fully with her mother's

[1]Additional procedures were utilized at different points during the therapy in order to move the client along on a broad front. Persuasion, instruction, and training in self-control were used to inhibit homosexual behavior, empathic relating was salient early in treatment to develop openness and willingness to relate to the therapist, interpretations were used to evoke restructuring of perceptions, and role-training in heterosexual behavior was used to promote learning of essential social skills. Nevertheless, the desensitization procedure was the special focus of the therapy and the primary changes were noted in association with it.

feminine role. Her affinity for her mother's support made it easy for her to respond to the entreaties of female friends, especially during periods of loneliness which were caused by removing herself from male companionship. The homosexual relationship that thus developed was chiefly a way of obtaining the warmth, intimacy, and support she had been lacking. This was hardly a satisfactory adjustment and she soon became depressed and anxious over feeling that she had slipped into an inadequate and unacceptable way of living. Indeed, this involvement had become moderately compulsive and she had all but lost her ability to withdraw from it.

Goals and Procedures of Treatment

The client was seen for a total of 41 sessions over an eight-month period and was then terminated by mutual agreement. The first 14 sessions were devoted to client self-exploration under conditions of therapist empathy, warmth, and questioning. This established a moderately trusting relationship and provided an in-depth evaluation of her pathology.

While this series of more traditional interviews aided understanding of the client's problems, it did not materially change them. It was concluded that her pathology was due in large part to maladaptive conditioned emotional responses to male figures. We therefore decided to treat the fears by means of desensitization. Several anxiety hierarchies were required in order to cover the domain of fears, which ranged from being criticized to being intimate.

Because of the unusual intensity of her fears, we decided to present the least disturbing hierarchy first and to then work toward the most disturbing theme. The initial set of items dealt with simple, positive interactions with men, such as the social and physical contacts of the first few dates. Five 50-min sessions were required to desensitize her to nine of the ten items involved. During that same time she began to report important changes in her feelings and behavior on dates. Dating was being encouraged as a way of building-up her heterosexual response repertoire and providing *in vivo* transfer of therapeutic learnings.

As treatment progressed, it was discovered that the client's anxiety was so intense in relation to the more disturbing themes that it was difficult to construct a hierarchy. We then decided to induce deep relaxation prior to discussing and constructing the hierarchy itself.

While deeply relaxed, the client was asked to name and describe a situation that would be least disturbing in a theme of being criticized by men. The relaxation apparently reduced her overall level of anxiety, since she was then able to describe experiences which had been hitherto only briefly mentioned because the topic was so upsetting.

Perhaps, because a number of prior self-exploration sessions had been held, it seemed desirable to have the client not only imagine but also actually explore her memories, thoughts, and feelings regarding the item being described. The process of hierarchy construction and the discussion of items under relaxation thus proceeded simultaneously and the client was regularly asked to report her anxiety level in "Subjective Units of Disturbance" (Wolpe & Lazarus, 1966).

Thus it became possible to stimulate discussion by means of empathic responses and questions and cause the client to gradually progress toward more anxiety provoking material. Whenever she became very upset (as subjectively reported or as observed by the therapist), discussion of that material was phased out, relaxation instructions were reintroduced, and the discussion returned to a less upsetting level.

This process is illustrated in the verbatim material below which is taken from the fourth session in which the procedure was used (the twenty-ninth session of the total series).

T: All right. Now I'd like you to search your own memory at this point, and for the moment let us not refer to your father. But in any other relationship with a man, try to imagine or think of a form of criticism or negative behavior on the part of the man.

P: "You don't know what you want. You think you want to be a career girl, but you need somebody to take care of you. But you're just" . . . Not exactly proposing, but trying to get some commitment.

T: Would this be a situation where you have shown some ambivalence toward a commitment?

P: Yes. It was true, and there was nothing I could do about it. I didn't admit it at the time.

T: How would you feel now if someone said that to you?

P: I'd probably be mad. I didn't have the implication that being a career girl was wrong. To him anything that went counter to motherhood was a sin....

T: All right.

P: He was very critical anyway.

T: Of you in particular or of things in general?

P: Well, he liked me and we were very good friends, and we both were cut off when he started criticizing me being a career girl. I backed away and sort of ruined everything.

T: All right. Where would you place that on the scale?

P: Oh, about 60. But it's more than anxiety. It's anger against the system.

T: Uh huh.

P: He was only expressing doctrine so to speak.

T: So, maybe it's really anger more than it is anxiety.

P: Except that he might be right about me.

T: So, maybe it's some of both. All right.

P: I feel like if he were really in touch it wouldn't bother him so much that I was a career girl.

T: So in a sense you feel critical of his naiveté or his rigidity.

P: Yea, except that I liked him very much and I thought maybe he was right. He's one of the few guys that I could really respect . . . And we sort of lost our friendship after that because he considered me kind of a sinner.

T: How did that make you feel, the idea that he thought of you as a sinner?

P: Not very good, it kind of ruined the relationship. We were never able to communicate again, and up until that time....

T: What had you told him that made him so concerned about you?

P: I don't remember. It wasn't any one thing, it was the impression.

T: All right. How do you feel right now?

P: About 10.

T: Now as you continue to relax can you bring forward another situation along this dimension?

P: Well, the person who was most critical of me was a doctor I used to go with. He was critical in kind of an insidious way because he kept wanting to psychoanalyze me and I'd never do it. He resented the fact that I wouldn't open up. He said that there was something too reserved about me, that I was afraid to.... I don't think he ever said it, but he implied that I should show him that I was a woman. And then when I did, he rejected me.

T: How did that happen?

P: Well, he just said that I showed myself to be very helpful and very warm. And, though I wouldn't give out any information, he could tell I was in love with him. And I had gone too far emotionally... and he didn't want to encourage me, that he was a very selfish person and that he would take all he could get, but that he was in love with someone else. And if I ever really wanted to get a man, I'd have to put out more effort to do it. In the physical things, that they really did matter, that I'd have to be more assertive sexually. He was always saying that I didn't push the sex bit, which I didn't. That I needed to work on my figure, that I needed to take better care of myself, that I needed to learn to become a real model type. That this was the only way I could compete for him.

T: How did you feel about all of those things?

P: I was furious. I said if a man really loves you, that sort of thing doesn't matter. He said, "You're just kidding yourself."

T: How do you feel about that now?

P: I'm still mad. He said every woman can do more than she does to make herself beautiful. And I agreed and I said I had done a lot, and he agreed that I had a lot more to do, that I couldn't be complacent about such a thing, especially when I had so many things going for me.

T: Where would you put that item in terms of subjective discomfort? Either fear, anger. I guess there's a lot of that here.

P: Oh, about 80 or 90.

T: What seemed to be so disturbing about that?

P: Well, it made me feel insecure and it reminded me of my father.

T: Do you feel like crying?

P: Yes....

T: I guess that whole situation then was...really fraught with meaning and implications plus pretty disturbing.

P: Yes....

T: If you really feel like crying, I think you shouldn't feel inhibited by me.... How do you feel right now on the scale?

P: Oh, about 30.

T: Not too bad?

P: No, I'm gaining control. I hate to cry.

T: That's sort of the way it seemed to me. Why do you hate to cry?

P: I hate to cry in front of anybody.

T: Yes, but you cry alone sometimes.

P: Yes.

T: You told me.... O.K., why don't you just relax for a moment. Forget about that item. . . Continuing to relax?

P: Yes....

T: All right. Now I'd like you to tell me a situation with your father.

P: I can remember several. Neither one seems to be any more important than the other. Should I just pick one?

T: Sure.

P: He and I got into a long argument, it ended up in an argument, about what men want in women, so to speak. He was criticizing the way I was going about things; that I shouldn't be too intellectual. And then he started on how I couldn't cook and how I couldn't sew and how I couldn't do any of the things a wife was supposed to be able to do.

T: Hmmm.

P: And that men want warmth and devotion and companionship. They don't want some intellectual that reads and...education is strictly an extra. That it's more important to...be sort of a slave to a man.

T: Hmmm.

P: And that I wasn't really worth (begins to cry)...

T: You weren't worth...?

P: (Sobs)

T: It's all right, go ahead. (Client appears to approach 100 on disturbance scale and to be having an *abreactive* experience.)

P: (Sobs profusely)...(After a period of crying and a long pause)

T: All right. (Pause) It's all right to continue crying, but I would like you to forget that situation for the moment. Sit back and relax and listen to the instructions to relax as deeply as you can. And while it's difficult, I'd like you to just gradually let that memory fade out now. You'll be able to remember it another time, but let's go gradually back to feeling relaxed and comfortable, as relaxed and comfortable as you can, concentrating again on the instructions of my voice and relaxing your hands and your arms and your body. I realize it's difficult to do that instantly, and I want you to feel as comfortable and as free as you can to phase out of that experience. But I also would like to know if there's anything you would like to say or discuss on that subject before you forget it and relax....

P: I never understood why my Mother didn't call him more sharply on it than she did. Because it seemed to me to be very obviously the wrong thing to say even if it were true.

T: Hmmm.

P: But perhaps my Mother felt I brought it on myself. I don't know.

T: Hmmm.

P: That I shouldn't have been arguing with him in the first place. He always said things in an argument so you couldn't ever win anyway. And no matter how badly I felt, I never cried. (Sobs)

T: Even then?

P: No.

T: So he really created terrific responses, but you wouldn't let him have the satisfaction of total victory.

P: No. I never gave him the satisfaction of having won. At least, emotionally, logically he sometimes would. Even if you proved him wrong logically, he countered or something. (Sobs)

T: How do you feel about crying here in my presence?

P: I don't like to.

T: It really doesn't bother me and I hope that you can feel increasingly comfortable. It's experiencing yourself here in my presence. And that's not a command. It's just a permission.

P: I feel like if a man can get you to cry, he feels like he can dominate you. That he's trying to reduce you to the lowest common denominator, forcing you into emotional submission. I don't think I feel that way about you, that you're deliberately trying to make me cry, but I feel that men would sometimes use it as an advantage. So, I would never want to be seen at that disadvantage.

T: Yes . . . All right. Are you feeling a little more relaxed?

P: Uh huh.

T: What would you say you feel?

P: Oh, about 40.

Several things seem evident from this material. Most obvious is the fact that under relaxation the client was much more capable than before of approaching the dreaded topics. Secondly, her reports of subjective disturbance peaked at the beginning of each item's discussion and then subsided significantly by the time that topic had been explored and a new one was about to be introduced. Third, there was evidence that anger was at times mixed with the fear response. It seems likely that such multiple affective responses occur in many cases and may simply decline in significance in correspondence with the changes in avoidance responses. Fourth, there was an intensification of the therapeutic process manifested by experiencing of strong feelings, recall of memories, and even abreaction as opposed to the typically more sedate quality of routine desensitization. Fifth, desensitization of feelings surrounding a given item or experience seemed to be greatly accelerated, as indicated by the sharp decline in reported disturbance level within a brief period.

It is worthy of note that the client reported more dramatic behavioral changes after these sessions than after more typical desensitization: she reported "I have experienced positive feelings for the first time in ages"; "I can more clearly see my father's role and how he's colored and blocked all my relationships with men." She also said she experienced a very real insight or strong feeling that she needed to differentiate reactions to her father from reactions to others and that, all things considered, a breakthrough had taken place.

Particularly interesting is her reference to the powerful influence of insight as a change-inducing process. Not only does insight appear to be produced by the desensitization process as Cautela argues (1965), but it also appears to strengthen specific changes that are occurring and to cause them to generalize more effectively to new situations. It is this factor of "transfer of training," of cementing change and generalizing it, that seems to occur as a function of symbolic, cognitive, and experiential mediating processes—it is exactly these factors that are made salient by the modified desensitization procedure described in this report.

Outcome of Treatment

The client terminated by mutual agreement after 41 sessions (eight months) of treatment. She had been able to sever her homosexual relationship and had been symptom free for six months in this regard. She had also moved significantly toward heterosexual adequacy and reported marked behavioral gains in her relationships with men. At follow-up one year later, she was happily married. A self-evaluation of change based on Knight's criteria as used by Wolpe was obtained at termination and is reproduced in Table 1. Pretherapy and follow-up MMPI and California Psychological Inventory (CPI) profiles were obtained and are reproduced in Figs. 1a and b and Fig. 2.

It is evident from the client's self-rating that she felt she had changed markedly and this is further confirmed by the therapist's independent ratings. Changes on the inventories are less dramatic but are observable.

Discussion

Obviously, this case study must be viewed as a demonstration of a technique rather than as a proof of its efficacy. It does, however, illustrate the potential of an approach which more frankly and openly utilizes experiential and relationship factors within a social learning framework. Many reports in the literature (e.g., Wolpe & Lazarus, 1966, p.28) indicate that such influences are present in all forms of behavior therapy but that they tend to be deemphasized. Because of

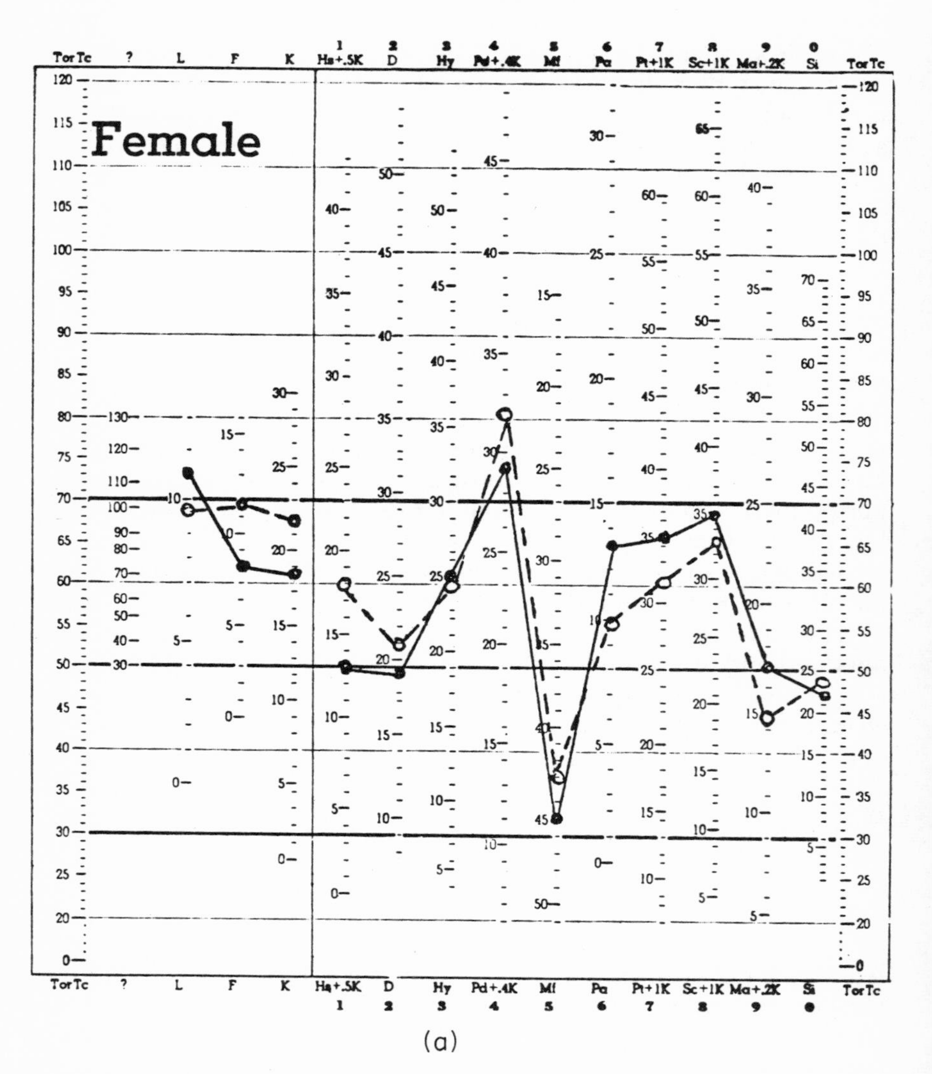

(a)

Fig. 1. (a) MMPI profile. (b) California psychological inventory profile. Solid lines, November, 1966; dashed lines August, 1967.

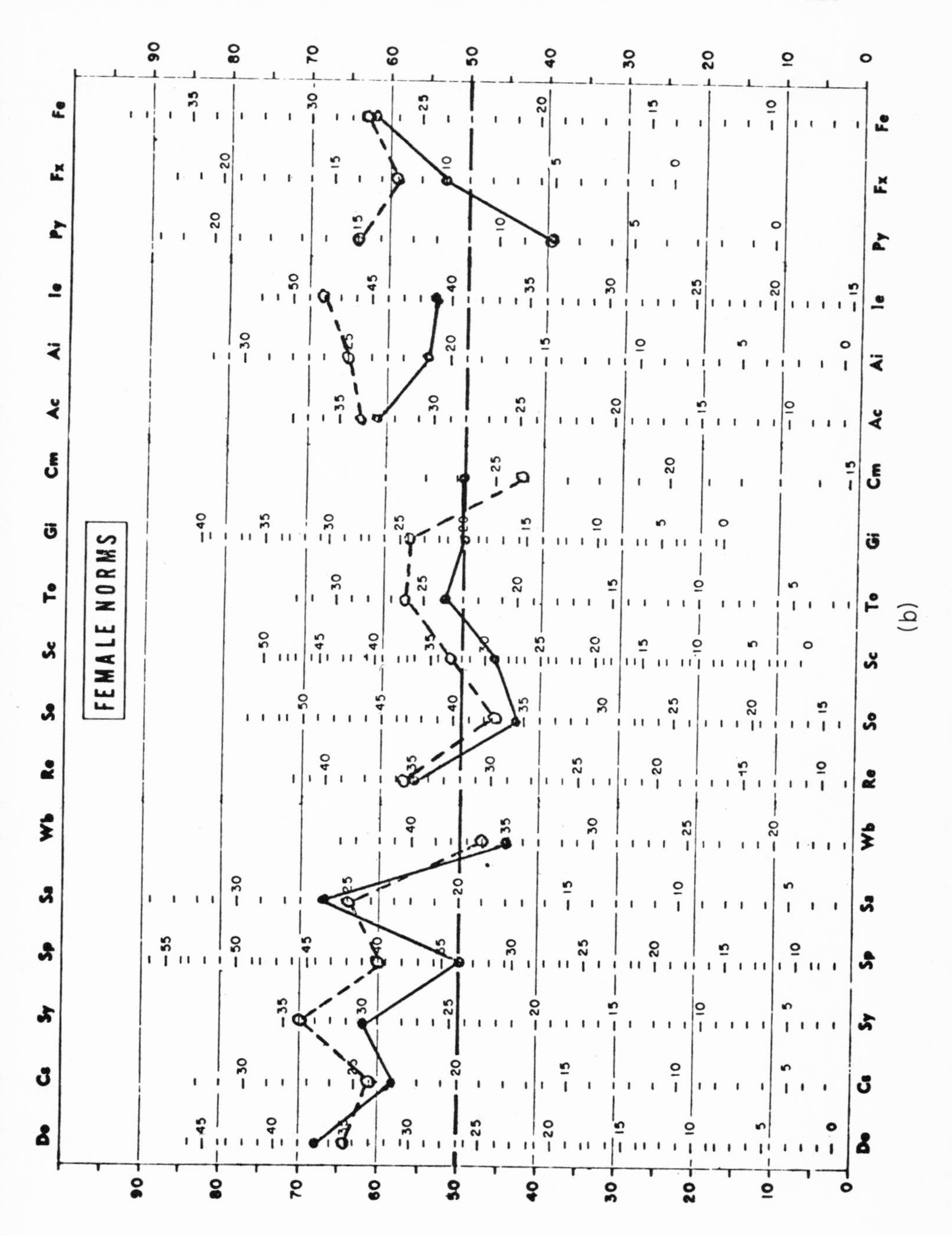

(b)

Table 1
CLIENT SELF-EVALUATION

Client self-evaluation			Evaluation by therapist
A. *Check the appropriate item regarding overall degree of change*			
1.	X	No more symptoms or feel only occasional transient symptoms when exposed to severe stresses	1. ___
2.	___	Marked improvement but symptoms still more than negligible	2. X
3.	___	Moderately improved but symptoms still quite significant	3. ___
4.	___	Slightly improved only	4. ___
5.	___	Unimproved. No change	5. ___
6.	___	Worse than before	6. ___
B. *Write the above number which best applies next to each of the following categories*			
a.	General productiveness in work, etc.	1	a. 1
b.	Adjustment and pleasure in sex	1	b. 2
c.	Interpersonal relationships	1	c. 2
d.	Ability to handle ordinary psychological conflicts and reality stresses	1-2	d. 2

this, their application and effects are unsystematic; and thus, behavior therapists may be guilty of unwittingly and unscientifically applying these influences, much as they accuse traditional therapists of unwittingly doing desensitization (Wolpe, 1958).

We are not appealing, by this argument, for a return to traditional techniques. We are only stating that elements of those techniques have therapeutic potency and that they should be systematically applied (Bergin, 1967). In the present case, the appropriate use of warmth and empathy proved these to be potent desensitizers of anxiety and reinforcers of prosocial responses, both behavioral and intrapsychic.

We may conclude that the range of events experienced during desensitization of a hierarchy item can be significantly broadened and intensified by virtue of these procedures because they, along with questioning and moderate interpretation, elicit a variety of cognitive and emotional responses which have been and are in the present consistently associated with the event structurally described by the item itself.

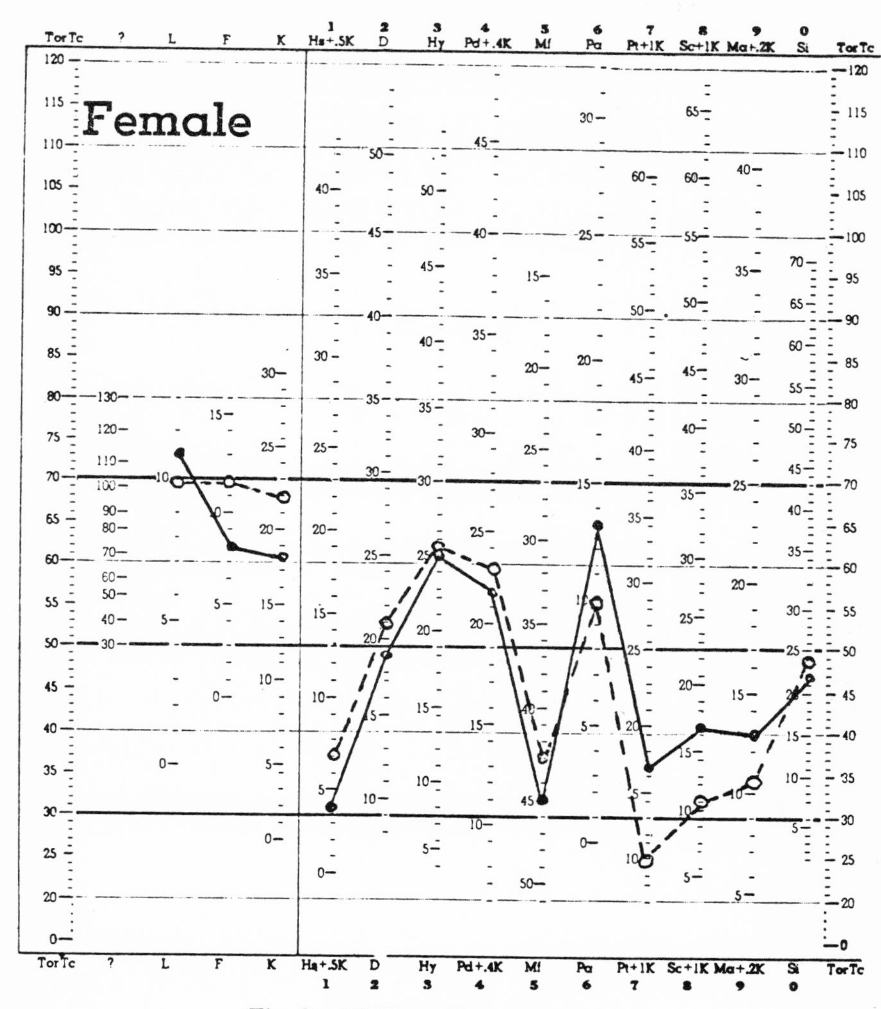

Fig. 2. MMPI profiles without "K."

We may argue that to embrace empathy as a technique and to become concerned with internal states is distinctly to leave the scientific substrate of our practice (Wolpe, 1968). This is unrealistic. We should be wedded more to empiricism than to behaviorism. They are not the same thing. Our scientific *style* or method is more important than any particular *content*, and we would argue that the phenomena we have dealt with in this case are subject to empiricism but that a portion of them do not fit adequately into a behavioral system. While neobehavioral theory may yet be stretched to embrace them systematically, we predict that such a modified conceptualization will no longer be recognizable as a behavioral theory. It will be something new, built upon the contributions of behavior research and theory, but distinctively different in its totality. Thus, the efficacious therapies of the future are unlikely to be behavioral therapies, but rather something built upon them and something far broader and more potent in relation to the full scope of human phenomena (Strupp and Bergin, 1969).

References

Bergin, A. E. Further comments on psychotherapy research and therapeutic practice. *International Journal of Psychiatry*, 1967, **3**, 317-323.

Cautela, J. Desensitization and insight. *Behaviour Research and Therapy*, 1965, **3**, 59-64.

Lazarus, A. A. In support of technical eclecticism. *Psychological Reports*, 1967, **21**, 415-416.

Strupp, H. H., & Bergin, A. E. Some empirical and conceptual bases for coordinated research in psychotherapy. *International Journal of Psychiatry*, 1969, **7**, 18-90.

Truax, C. B., & Carkhuff, R. R. *Toward effective counseling and psychotherapy*. Chicago: Aldine, 1967.

Weitzman, B. Behaviour therapy and psychotherapy. *Psychological Review*, 1967, **74**, 300-317.

Wolpe, J. *Psychotherapy by reciprocal inhibition*. Stanford, Calif.: Stanford University Press, 1958.

Wolpe, J. From the president. *Newsletter, Association for Advancement of the Behavioral Therapies*, 1968, **3**, 1-2.

Wolpe, J., & Lazarus, A. A. *Behaviour therapy techniques*. New York: Macmillan (Pergamon), 1966.

Systematic Desensitization of a Patient with Chronic Total Impotence

Leonard F. Salzman
UNIVERSITY OF ROCHESTER

This report is of interest because of the long-standing and absolute nature of the symptom, as well as the strong suggestion that the patient was, aside from his impotence, quite likely a latent or borderline schizophrenic. The successful use of hypnosis in such a patient and the need for revision of hierarchies as conditions changed are also noteworthy.

The patient was a 33-year-old man, married ten years, who had never had intercourse. Although earlier in his marriage he had on rare occasions been able to achieve partial and, at times, full erection in the company of his wife, he had never been able to sustain the erection for more than a few moments or to attempt intercourse. At the time I saw him, he was no longer experiencing any recognizable sexual impulse and would become acutely anxious at even the thought of a sexual relationship with his wife. He would experience acute anxiety at the prospect of seeing his wife undressed and reported rather bizarre and unusual feelings were he to attempt, or even imagine himself in, an intercourse position. When the prospect of sexual behavior would come to his attention, he would feel as if a glass wall existed between himself and the rest of the world. He would feel "disembodied" or "out of contact," feeling as if he would disappear or be engulfed by his wife's vagina, or that he was turning into a "werewolf," with feelings of change in his body image, and might commit horribly aggressive acts against her. The emergence of these thoughts and fantasies would result in near-panic states and there consequently was no longer any sort of sexual interest or attempt at physical contact with his wife.

The patient had discovered his impotence on his wedding night. He had never had any previous sexual experience, having come from a rigidly repressive family environment. Since his marriage he had undertaken intensive psychotherapy a number of times, accumulating a total of about six years of psychotherapeutic contacts with no result. He had, just prior to his being referred to me, been in psychoanalysis for six months, again with no sign of any change. It may also be of interest to note that some earlier attempts at treatment had employed hypnosis with the use of direct suggestion that he be capable of erection and intercourse, also with no success.

The patient had been given a full battery of psychological tests on two occasions, once in 1959 and again in 1966. On both examinations performed by different psychologists, the diagnostic impression was that of an incipient or latent schizophrenic reaction, primarily based on evidence of marked overinclusiveness of thought, a tendency to develop autistic perceptions, suggestions of poor reality testing, and especially on the second examination, the production of extremely primitive, morbid, and bizarre ideas with marked sexual preoccupation and poor affective control. He manifested a rigid, stereotyped, and perseverative quality to his thinking, the content of which was often suggestive of paranoid suspiciousness and sensitivity.

At the same time, however, the patient seemed capable of asserting some degree of control over these manifestations of underlying disorder, and detailed history taking revealed few, if any, indications of difficulty in his adaptation to his work or of difficulties in social and interpersonal relationships. It appears that his symptoms were largely restricted to the impotence, and its consequent interference with his relationship with his wife, who was by then considering divorce.

The method of using sexual responses (Wolpe & Lazarus, 1967) for overcoming the patient's anxiety and inhibition could not initially be of any great use since the patient was clearly experiencing a complete inhibition of sexual responsiveness. Nevertheless, the method was explained to the patient in anticipation that it would ultimately be a useful and important adjunct to the treatment. The major therapeutic effort, however, employed the method of systematic desensitization (Lazarus, 1963). Training was begun in relaxation and it was soon discovered that the patient would probably be an excellent hypnotic subject. In spite of some concern about the use of hypnosis here, it was decided to explore this by hypnotizing the patient and carefully observing the consequences. The patient was readily hypnotized and although some problems with this method did occur later on in the process of treatment, in the main it was a successful technique producing profound relaxation and calm.

The patient experienced acute distress even at the prospect of looking at a woman in a state of undress. The first hierarchy for desensitization concerned the dimension of observing a woman, at a distance, undressing. Initially it was necessary that the woman being observed have no relationship to the patient and the initial items in the hierarchy involved the patient imagining that he was observing a woman through a window in another apartment in the process of removing her clothing. Included later in the hierarchy, however, were items which involved the woman being aware that he was observing her. Further on in the hierarchy were items which involved increasing closeness, in spatial terms, to the woman who was undressing and finally, close-up observation of a woman's genitals with her awareness of his observation. This hierarchy led quite naturally into items which involved his wife as the object of observation and physical closeness, as well as being able to lie in bed next to his wife while looking at her scantily clad body.

Items in the first hierarchy involving the observation of a woman, other than his wife, removing her clothing were desensitized almost completely by the tenth session. (There were two half-hour sessions each week.) However, the last item on the hierarchy involving the direct observation of the genitals of a woman who was aware of his observation produced the first sign of acute disruption in the patient. In the tenth session, on being awakened from the hypnosis, after an unsuccessful attempt to desensitize this last item, the patient reported experiencing a number of "intruding images" of a bizarre nature which prevented him from visualizing clearly the item being presented, which made him acutely anxious, and which had, in fact, resulted in his near awakening from the hypnotic state. These primarily were of a woman completely disemboweled with her inner organs spilling out of a huge wound in her stomach. The first assumption was that too great a jump in the hierarchy had been attempted. However, further breakdown of hierarchy items still resulted in the intruding images. Further desensitizing of prior items also produced no diminution of the images. Next an effort was made to suppress the images by direct suggestion, but to no avail. My plan at this point was to see whether a hierarchy of those images could be constructed and then desensitized. The patient, however, reported that some diminution of the intensity of the intruding images had seemed to occur as he himself "lightened" the depth of the hypnosis as a consequence of his anxiety. He was then instructed, in the hypnotic state, to reach only a depth of hypnosis which produced profound calm and relaxation and to go no further. He was instructed that he should control the hypnotic state, lightening its depth, to the point where he could maintain a feeling of calm and relaxation without the intrusion of the images. This method was discovered to be extremely effective in preventing their appearance. The patient was then able to continue with the presentation of the hierarchy. The final item was then desensitized and the patient was able to contemplate observing a nude woman's genitals in detail with no discomfort.

The second hierarchy which was constructed was a rather long and detailed one which described the sequence of behaviors involved in initiating and carrying out sexual intercourse with his wife. The first item, for example, concerned the patient imagining himself lying beside his wife not touching but simply looking and experiencing affectionate feelings toward her. The items progressed through a detailed sequence descriptive of increasing physical contact, at first of a simply affectionate nature, but with increasing sexual implications, i.e., touching, stroking, and caressing his wife's body, and in addition, experiencing some reciprocal response on her part. By the fourteenth session we had been able to desensitize images of the patient touching, kissing, and caressing his wife. The patient reported experiencing his first erection in such a situation, which was sustained for 15 min while he petted his wife, although there was no genital contact between them. At this point the procedure and instructions for the direct use of sexual responses were repeated and reinforced. The patient was instructed to go no further than felt comfortable and pleasurable to him in the situation. The desensitization of images further in the hierarchy beyond simple affectionate and "petting" behavior was increasingly difficult, requiring many repetitions. It was, at times, necessary to break down an item in the hierarchy into four minor items in order to overcome the anxiety attached to the behavior at that point. For example, an item at the middle of the hierarchy which involved the patient moving into an intercourse position with his wife was so disruptive as to require the introduction of new items which simply involved minor degrees of change of his position and nonspecific physical movement before they could directly involve assuming the specific position in which the patient would lie between his wife's legs.

At approximately the nineteenth session, the patient again reported experiencing the earlier intruding "images" and others involving images of sexual contact with his mother. These were related to an item which involved imagining himself in a position astride his wife in which he was in close observation or contact with her genitals. The instructions for his controlling the hypnotic level were repeated and earlier items on the hierarchy were repeated with further desensitization.

In the twenty-first session, essentially at the same point in the hierarchy, the patient reported experiencing strong erections with much sexual drive. He reported having obtained and sustained an erection while in an intercourse position and reported "feeling alive down there." At this point, he attempted to go further, became anxious, and lost the erection. Again, he was cautioned not to attempt to go further than felt comfortable at the moment. The difficulty with intruding images disappeared and was never again observed subsequently.

In the twenty-fourth session, the patient reported achieving partial intromission, introducing the glans of his penis into his wife's vagina. This was accomplished after considerable effort on his part because of the physical resistance he encountered. The patient also reported that his wife had exclaimed in pain over this partial penetration, and further, that she no longer was exhibiting sexual excitement or lubrication of her vagina. As the patient evidenced a capacity for potency, problems of frigidity were becoming more apparent in his wife. The awareness of his wife's pain now became a major source of anxiety to the patient, and at this point, items dealing with his imagining some degree of discomfort on the part of his wife as he inserted his penis were introduced, and desensitization of these items was initiated. These items of images of the patient attempting strenuously to achieve intromission and producing more and more discomfort in his wife were quite difficult to desensitize and required six or seven sessions.

At this point, his wife's overt disinterest in the sexual act diminished considerably and changed to one of increased pressure that he continue the act where his own inclination was to stop. The patient then reported that he was now experiencing anxiety about the prospect of initiating sexual contact but failing to satisfy his wife. At this point, items descriptive of such thoughts were introduced into the hierarchy. It is noteworthy that when such a hierarchy was constructed, it had to begin at a point much earlier in the previously desensitized sexual hierarchy; for example, the first item in this subhierarchy involved the patient imagining that he might begin some sort of sexual play with his wife at the point that he was preparing for bed, brushing his teeth, etc. This subhierarchy continued with items which concerned his awareness of his wife's sexual excitement and her expectation of gratification. When items in this hierarchy were sufficiently desensitized, the patient again began reporting a capacity to experience an erection and to achieve partial intromission. He reported, in the forty-eighth session, increasing frequency of erections and partial intromission, which, however, was interrupted with the patient going on to manually induced orgasm.

In the forty-ninth session the patient reported having been able to carry out complete and satisfying intercourse for the first time in his life. In subsequent sessions he reported having intercourse every night, with no difficulty in sustaining an erection for a satisfactory length of time. In the fifty-second session the patient and his wife attempted intercourse in a different physical setting (not their bedroom) and the patient again had difficulty in sustaining an erection. A few such items concerned with initiating intercourse in different physical settings, such as the livingroom, etc., were introduced. These were easily desensitized; the patient resumed having intercourse at will and soon reported a suspicion that his wife was pregnant. The frequency of desensitization sessions was reduced after the patient reported a consistent frequency of highly pleasurable intercourse two to three times weekly. In addition, the patient reported many general changes in his feelings of well being, primarily in terms of feeling more adequate, feeling "more like a man," and considerable confidence about his ability to sustain sexual activity without any difficulty. He was encouraged to persist in the use of his own sexual responses for overcoming transient periods of anxiety. He reported that his sexual activity was now a completely spontaneous act with little or no rumination about his adequacy or about the question of whether or not he would be successful. Therapy was terminated at this point, but the patient was encouraged to return for consultation if he experienced any difficulty. Some months later he returned for a consultation at a point when his wife was in her seventh month of pregnancy, to report that she was experiencing considerable discomfort at intercourse, which was somewhat upsetting to him. It had also transpired that she was having a difficult pregnancy; there had been some vaginal bleeding and at times the continuation of her pregnancy was in doubt. The patient was instructed to abstain from intercourse until after his wife's delivery, but he was encouraged to continue indulging in any sort of sexual activity short of intercourse which was pleasurable both for himself and his wife.

In a follow-up session one year after his initial act of intercourse, the patient reported the birth of his child, the resumption of intercourse after the medically required period of abstention, and the initiation of contraceptive methods without any difficulty, with intercourse occurring approximately two to three times a week. He reported having experienced one or two episodes of difficulty in sustaining an erection but was aware that this had occurred at times when his motivation for intercourse was weak as a result of fatigue. He was not at all concerned about these episodes and felt quite gratified at the many positive changes which had taken place in his relationship with his wife.

Of interest here is the evidence that the treatment could progress successfully in spite of the fact that the patient's impotence and his complete inhibition of sexual responsiveness were to some extent a response to the threatened emergence of extremely bizarre and psychotic reactions in the sexual situation. For example, the experience of close psychological and physical contact with his wife produced acute feelings of being trapped in a catastrophic situation, feelings that he was giving up his "individuality" and that he would "disappear," but even more, there were reports of the feelings of "changing into an animal—a werewolf," in which the patient would actually experience the feeling of having his face change its shape, his features enlarge, etc. There were times when he would report the experience of having a thick growth of hair all over his body and of feeling that he looked detestable and ugly in a monstrous sort of way. There is no doubt in my mind that these responses were of a psychotic nature and it is instructive that the treatment could progress with the use of hypnosis, in spite of the emergence of bizarre thoughts. In this case, the successful approach was to give the patient an increased measure of control over the extent to which he was passive in the situation and of the depth of hypnosis which was reached. The suppression of these very primitive expressions of anxiety which led to major feelings of change in body image and self, permitted the desensitization of the stimuli which ordinarily evoked such bizarre responses. It is noteworthy that at the end of therapy the patient *could not even imagine* himself feeling in these ways that he had reported quite graphically only some three to four months earlier.

References

Lazarus, A. The treatment of chronic frigidity by systematic desensitization. *Journal of Nervous and Mental Diseases,* 1963, **136**, 272–278.

Wolpe, J., & Lazarus, A. *Behavior therapy techniques. A guide to the treatment of neuroses.* New York: Macmillan (Pergamon), 1967.

The Subject Speaks Up in Desensitization[1]

Patricia Lee Darwin, John F. McBrearty
TEMPLE UNIVERSITY

This research compared an experimental analogue of standard desensitization psychotherapy to a modification of desensitization. The target behavior selected for this purpose was speech anxiety.

Problem

It is recalled that, in the usual desensitization procedure (Wolpe, 1958), the therapist presents to the deeply relaxed subject imaginary scenes of graded anxiety levels arranged in a hierarchy, beginning with the least subjectively noxious and continuing until the most subjectively noxious scene has been presented. This research serves as a test of a promising modification suggested by Badri (1967) in which the *patient* rather than the therapist describes the visualized scenes.

Investigators have reported high claims (approximately 90%) of number of patients improved using the standard desensitization technique (Wolpe, 1958), including Paul's (1966) finding that 100% of speech-anxious subjects improved by desensitization for speech anxiety. Numerous variations of the usual desensitization procedure have been proposed which claim advantages (Brady, 1966; Davison, 1965; Friedman, 1966; Garfield, Darwin, Singer, & McBrearty, 1967; Kirch-

[1]This paper is based on the senior author's unpublished doctoral dissertation, Effect of greater subject activity and increased scene duration on rate of desensitization, Temple University, 1968.

ner & Hogan, 1966; etc.). However, few of the suggested variations have been compared by controlled experiments to standard desensitization as was done in this investigation.

Specifically, it was hypothesized that speech-anxious subjects who played a more active role in desensitization by *self*-description of scenes would desensitize more rapidly than speech-anxious subjects who played the traditional passive role by being exposed to therapist-description of scenes. It was further hypothesized that subjects exposed to an extended scene description would desensitize more rapidly than subjects exposed to the usual short scene description.

Thus, the independent variables were greater subject activity (i.e., self-description of scenes) and increased scene duration. The dependent variables were measures of basal skin conductance (BSC) and subjective report (subjective unit of disturbance, SUD, following Wolpe).

The scenes utilized in this study were from a speech-anxiety hierarchy (Paul, 1966) in which reading a book about giving speeches was low on the hierarchy, practicing giving a speech was about midway, and actually giving a speech was toward the top, with possible expansions in the hierarchy in terms of size and formality of audience.

Method

There were two phases to the procedures: a selection phase and an experimental phase. During the selection phase, 137 male 17- to 24-year-old college students in Introductory Psychology sections took a Speech Questionnaire comprised of the S-R Inventory of Anxiousness Speech Scale (Endler, 1962) and the Personal Report of Confidence as a Speaker (Paul's (1966) modification of Gilkenson's (1942) scale). Subjects were randomly drawn from the group of students scoring beyond a cut-off point. These subjects were contacted individually by phone and asked to come in for an appointment. Forty-six subjects went through the experimental treatment; six were dropped from the data analyses, leaving an *N* of 40, with 10 subjects to each of four treatment groups. These four groups were virtually indistinguishable on the basis of their Speech Questionnaire scores.

During the experimental phase, all subjects first received an identical explanation of the study and relaxation training, and were then required to give a short pretreatment speech test which was tape recorded. The content of the speech test was counterbalanced so that half of each treatment group first spoke about their "favorite leisure time hobby" and the other half first spoke about the "best weekend" they had had since they had been in college. Whichever topic was the content of the pretreatment speech test, the other topic became the content of the posttreatment speech test.

BSC measures and subjective reports were recorded before and after the relaxation training and before and after the pretreatment speech test. Up to this point, the procedures (explanation of study, relaxation training, and pretreatment speech test) had been administered in a double-blind fashion. Then, an envelope was opened containing information as to which of the four treatment groups the subject at hand had been assigned.

In Group 1, "passive-regular" subjects were exposed to hierarchy scenes described by the experimenter for about 10 sec (approximately the usual procedure, and thus serving as a control group); in Group 2, "passive-wide" subjects were exposed to speech hierarchy scenes described by the experimenter for 1½ min; in Group 3, "active-regular" subjects described scenes to the experimenter for 10 sec; and, in Group 4, "active-wide" subjects described scenes to the experimenter for 1½ min. During treatment, each subject was exposed to a neutral scene and the first five scenes from a speech-anxiety hierarchy.

Examples of the variation in style of treatment can be observed from the four modes of neutral scenes which follow. (The room is darkened, the subject is deeply relaxed, leaning back in a reclining chair and is told the following.)

GROUP 1, PASSIVE-REGULAR

"Now, I want you to visualize yourself lying in bed just before going to sleep. Look around you and see the familiar things in the room—the chair, the dresser, the mirror. See it vividly . . . make it very real . . . you are lying in bed just before drifting off to sleep."

GROUP 2, PASSIVE-WIDE

"Now, I want you to visualize yourself lying in bed just before going to sleep. See it vividly.

"It is nighttime and the room is dark except for a small light near your bed. You are dressed for sleep and stretched out full on the bed, with covers over you. Look around you and see the familiar things in the room—the chair, the dresser, the mirror, the lamp, the bed. See the shapes of things, see the colors. Picture everything very clearly.

"In the distance you can faintly hear soothing music . . . you feel drowsy and content.

"Feel things vividly, too: the fuzziness of the blanket under your fingers, the smooth, cool sheets and pillowcase, the comfort of the mattress, the warmth of the bed, the weight of the covers.

"Make it very real . . . you are lying in bed just before drifting off to sleep."

GROUP 3, ACTIVE-REGULAR

"Now, I want you to visualize yourself lying in bed just before going to sleep. See it vividly. Go ahead and describe it to me as you picture it."

GROUP 4, ACTIVE-WIDE

These subjects were told the same thing as the active-regular subjects, with the additional urging (if necessary): "Tell me *all* about it: what you see, what you hear, even what you smell or taste, what you feel . . . tell me more."

Subjects in all treatment groups were asked to hold the scene in their mind for 10 sec. The remainder of the time, aside from scene description and visualization, was spent in relaxing or revisualizing the neutral scene, so that regardless of treatment group, subjects were exposed to the same total experimental time of 50 min. The differences between treatments were whether the time was filled with active self-description or more passive listening to therapist description, and variations in the length of the description. BSC measures were recorded before and after each scene presentation.

Following one of the four modes of desensitization treatment, subjects were given a posttreatment speech test. BSC measures and subjective report were also taken before and after this second speech test. Finally, subjects were interviewed regarding subjective experiences, e.g., scene clarity, relaxation achieved, tension experiences, intrusive thoughts, shifts in scene, etc.

Results

Two analyses of variance were performed on the BSC measures: a four factor analysis of variance on obtained BSC measures (see Table 1) and a three factor analysis of variance on BSC difference scores (a measurement obtained by taking a difference between pre and post measurements at each of the two speech events, see Table 2). Similarly, two analyses of variance were performed on the SUD data: a three factor analysis of variance on SUD reports (see Table 3) and a three factor analysis of variance on SUD difference scores (Table 4).

Table 1
SUMMARY OF ANALYSIS OF VARIANCE FOR BSC SCORES

Source of variation	SS	df	MS	F
Between subjects				
A (passivity-activity)	266.84	1	266.84	.78
B (regular-wide)	66.43	1	66.43	.20
AB	4.67	1	4.67	.01
Subjects within groups (error)	12,267.20	36	340.75	
Within subjects				
C (nine events)	418.08	8	52.26	17.10[a]
AC	183.63	8	22.95	7.51[a]
BC	24.78	8	3.10	1.01
ABC	30.01	8	3.75	1.23
Cx subjects within groups (error)	880.26	288	3.06	
D (prepost)	95.21	1	95.21	22.97[a]
AD	14.20	1	14.20	3.43
BD	15.73	1	15.73	3.80
ABD	4.31	1	4.31	1.04
Dx subjects within groups (error)	149.19	36	4.14	
CD	463.03	8	57.88	32.62[a]
ACD	43.38	8	5.42	3.06[a]
BCD	6.06	8	.76	.43
ABCD	6.92	8	.87	.49
CDx subjects within groups (error)	511.02	288	1.77	
	15,450.95			

[a] $p < .01$.

In addition, *t* tests were performed where specific differences had been predicted. BSC measures and SUD reports were correlated. Several chi square tests were performed on peripheral information regarding various subjective experiences.

All subjects demonstrated (by both BSC and subjective report) the effectiveness of relaxation training. (This was in the face of considerable uneasiness—comments likening the reclining lounge chair to a dentist's chair and the GSR machine to getting a heart checkup.) All subjects also demonstrated (by BSC measures and subjective report) that the speech tests were anxiety arousing. (This was observable behaviorally as well, with much head-tossing, perspiring, and later such comments as, "What a horrible experience!".) Figure 1 gives an

Table 2
SUMMARY OF ANALYSIS OF VARIANCE ON BSC DIFFERENCE SCORES (DS)

Source of variation	SS	df	MS	F
Between subjects				
A (passivity-activity)	14.96	1	14.96	1.00
B (regular-wide)	4.04	1	4.04	.27
AB	20.34	1	20.34	1.36
Subjects within groups (error between)	537.24	36	14.92	
Within subjects				
C (speech 1 DS-speech 2 DS)	1.40	1	1.40	.69
AC	29.33	1	29.33	14.43[a]
BC	.59	1	.59	.29
ABC	.09	1	.09	.04
Cx subjects within groups (error within)	73.17	36	2.03	

[a] $p < .01$

Table 3
SUMMARY OF ANALYSIS OF VARIANCE FOR SUBJECTIVE UNITS OF DISTURBANCE DATA

Source of variation	SS	df	MS	F
Between subjects				
A (passivity-activity)	703.12	1	703.12	.53
B (regular-wide)	937.44	1	937.44	.71
AB	13.00	1	13.00	.01
Subjects within groups (error between)	47,826.22	36	1,328.51	
	49,479.78			
Within subjects				
C (five events)	21,224.52	4	5,306.13	31.43[a]
AC	688.90	4	172.22	1.02
BC	586.28	4	146.57	.87
ABC	129.42	4	32.36	.19
Cx subjects within groups (error within)	24,313.70	144	168.84	
	46,942.82			

[a] $p < .01$

Table 4
SUMMARY OF ANALYSIS OF VARIANCE
ON SUBJECTIVE UNIT OF DISTURBANCE DS

Source of variation	SS	df	MS	F
Between subjects				
A (passivity-activity)	.6	1	.6	.001
B (regular-wide)	678.6	1	678.6	1.54
AB	.6	1	.6	.001
Subjects within groups (error between)	16,608.7	36	461.4	
Within subjects				
C (speech 1 DS-speech 2 DS)	1,891.5	1	1,891.5	8.25[a]
AC	851.5	1	851.5	3.71
BC	165.3	1	165.3	.72
ABC	46.6	1	46.6	.20
Cx subjects within groups (error within)	8,269.6	36	229.7	

[a]$p < .01$

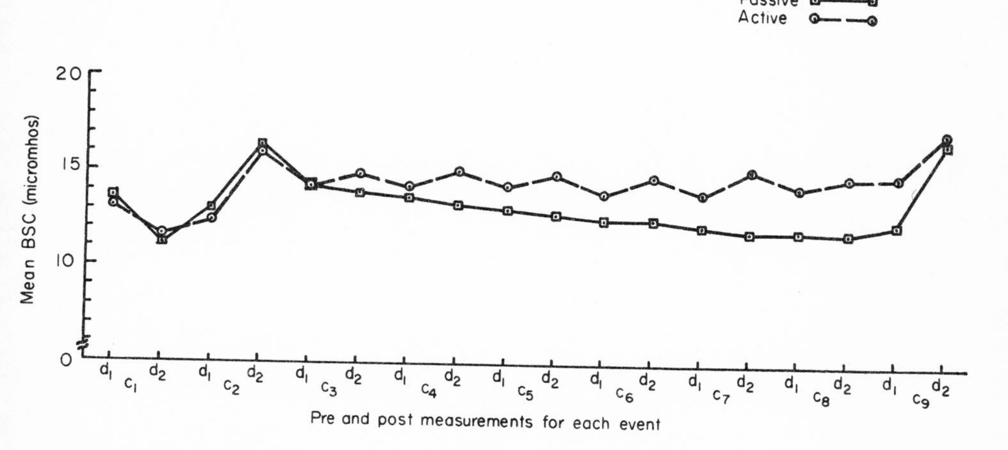

Fig. 1. Mean BSC response for activity (A) at pre-post measurements (D) for each event (C), ACD interaction. Relaxation training is represented by c_1, the first speech test by c_2, the scenes by c_3 to c_8, and the second speech test by c_9.

idea of the course of treatment in terms of BSC measures, while Fig. 2 depicts the course of treatment from a subjective point of view.

Substantial support was obtained for the major hypothesis that an active role facilitates desensitization. Active groups demonstrated (at a statistically significant level of at least .05): (*a*) less arousal (as measured by BSC difference scores) on speech 2 than passive groups (see Fig. 3). Some caution is necessary here, since one of the functions of the activity factor was to maintain the active groups at a higher level of arousal throughout treatment, while the passive groups became progressively more and more relaxed. This rendered passive and active groups at different levels of arousal prior to the posttreatment speech test. However, other evidence fortified the apparent superiority of active groups: (*b*) active groups exhibited less arousal (as measured by BSC) on speech 2 than their prior arousal on speech 1; (*c*) active groups also reported less subjectively experienced arousal on speech 2 than on speech 1 (see Fig. 4); while this difference was in the same decreasing direction for the passive groups, it was not statistically significant.

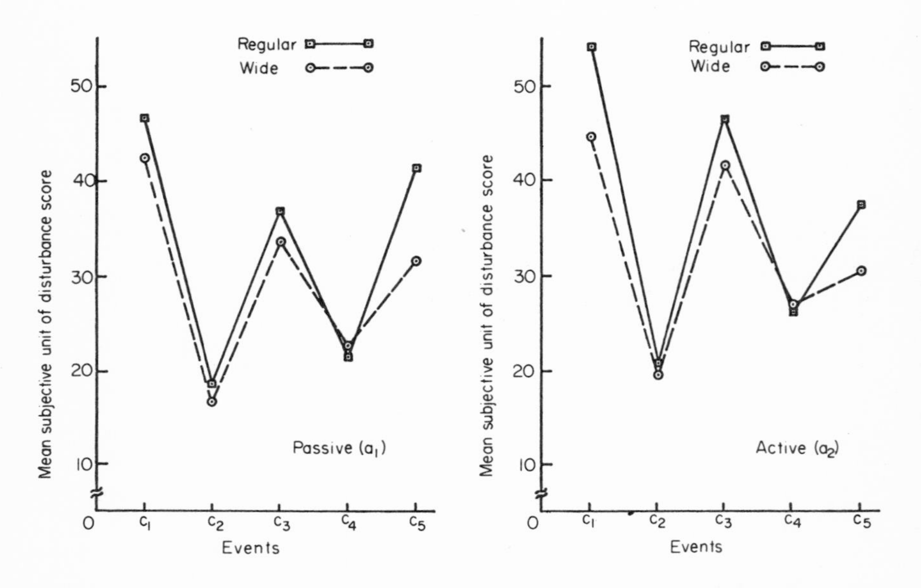

Fig. 2. Mean SUD response for regular and wide groups (B) at five events (C), in which c_1 was the subjective report given pre relaxation training, c_2 was given post relaxation training, c_3 was given after the first speech test, c_4 was given posttreatment, and c_5 after the second speech test.

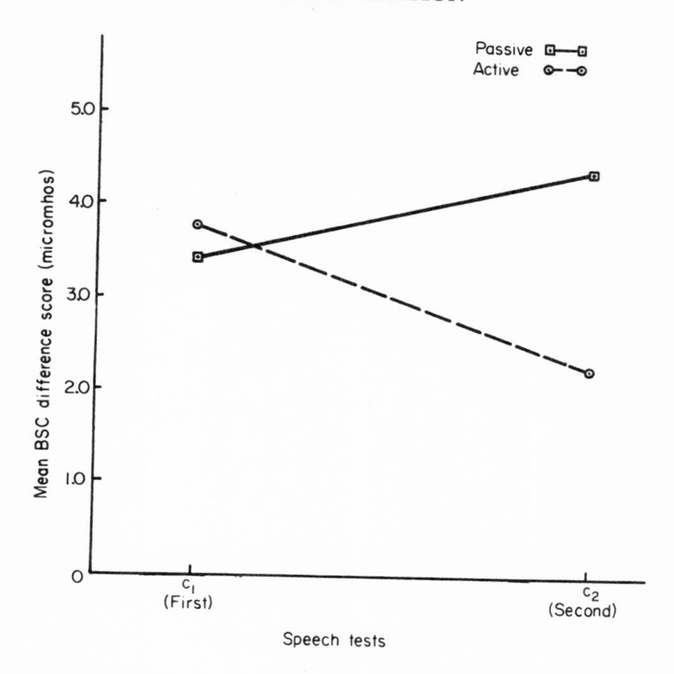

Fig. 3. Mean BSC difference score for active and passive groups (A) at speech tests (C), AC interaction.

Subjects reported on experiences of changes in the visualized content of scenes from the originally requested scene (e.g., frequently reported scene changes included shifts in physical location—from bed to living room, from classroom to movie theater; rejection of the scene—"Want to know what happened next? I got fed up and walked out of the room."; long stretches of road, view from a small plane; "Joe Pepitone hit a home run and the clapping stayed in my mind."). Many subjects reported these changes in scene, but (*d*) active groups reported significantly less scene changes. Active groups also reported less experiences of tension and they selected speech 1 as more difficult than speech 2 more often than passive groups, but these differences were not statistically significant. Nevertheless, in at least four comparisons, active groups exhibited superiority to passive groups. Correlations between subjective reports and BSC were negligible.

Wide groups were nonsignificantly different from regular groups on BSC measures, but they reported less subjectively experienced arousal on speech 2 than regular groups.

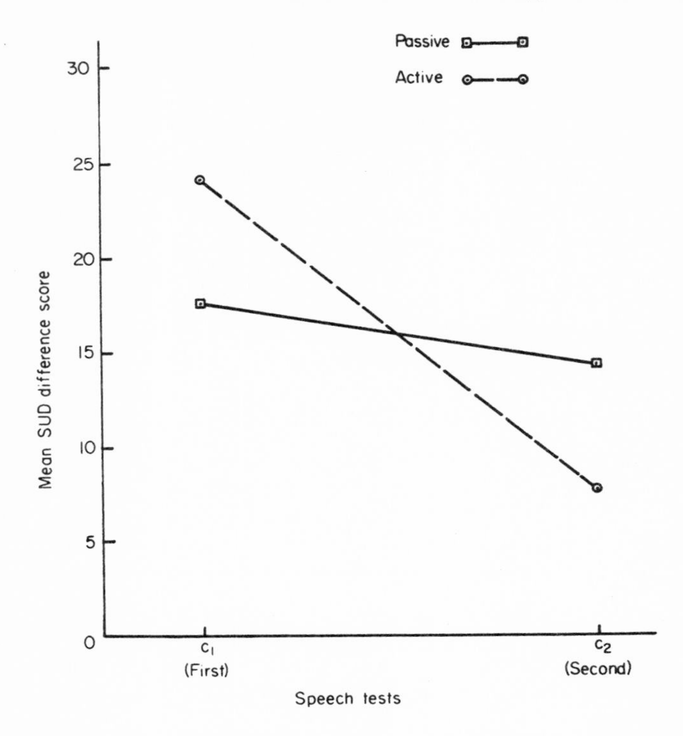

Fig. 4. Mean SUD difference score for active and passive groups (A) at speech tests (C), AC interaction.

Peripheral data regarding reported subjective experiences on various topics were also analyzed. Significantly more subjects from all the groups chose speech 1 as more difficult that speech 2. Subjects reported on the effect of the female experimenter (it seemed to have facilitated obtaining subjects). Most subjects reported there was no effect, they would have "responded about the same." Some found it favorable, mainly facilitating relaxation (e.g., "Your voice kind of sent me out . . ." or "It helped; a guy would say 'relax, or I'll smash you'."). Some found that it inhibited choice of words and content of speeches ("You don't tell females things like that" – regarding weedend activities – "I didn't want you to think terrible things about me."), while others found the effect mixed. No group differences were found. There is a possible limitation, however, in the sense that if active subjects who were speaking more frequently were more inhibited by the female experimenter, that inhibition could have depressed the extent of their superiority which could be even greater than was observed.

Approximately half of the subjects reporting on the following experiences stated that they had: difficulty getting or holding on to scenes, difficulty letting go of scenes, and experienced changes in the visualized content of scenes. A statistically significant majority of all subjects reported experiencing intrusive thoughts during scene visualization. The content of these changes and intrusive thoughts was intriguing, e.g., a recent nightmare about a friend who had been killed in Vietnam, how to perfect a golf swing, being affectionate with a girl, etc. Desensitization emerges as a more complex experience than its critics recognize and it appears that Weitzman's (1967) comment, in a review highly critical of behavior therapy, that desensitization has not been adequately characterized in the work of behavior therapists, has some validity. Whether or not these various subjective experiences effect the course of desensitization is not known, but their presence should be noted and described.

Summary

The major finding of this study is that self-description of scenes appears to accelerate the pace of desensitization for speech-anxious subjects. This finding suggests practical changes in the application of desensitization. The active role dimension should be explored for other target areas of desensitization.

References

Badri, M. B. A new technique for the systematic desensitization of pervasive anxiety and phobic reactions. *Journal of Psychology*, 1967, **65**, 201-208.

Brady, J. P. Brevital-relaxation treatment of frigidity. *Behaviour Research and Therapy*, 1966, **4**, 71-77.

Cooke, G. The efficacy of two desensitization procedures: An analogue study. *Behaviour Research and Therapy*, 1966, **4**, 17-24.

Davison, G. C. Relative contributions of differential relaxation and graded exposure to desensitization of a neurotic fear. *Proceedings of the 73rd Annual Convention of the American Psychological Association*, 1965, 209-210.

Endler, N. S., Hunt, J. Mc V., & Rosenstein, A. J. An S-R inventory of anxiousness. *Psychological Monographs*, 1962, **76**, Whole No. 536.

Friedman, D. A new technique for the systematic desensitization of phobic symptoms. *Behavior Research and Therapy*, 1966, **4**, 139-140.

Garfield, Z. H., Darwin, P. L., Singer, B. A., & McBrearty J. H. Effect of "in vivo" training on experimental desensitization of a phobia. *Psychological Reports*, 1967, **20**, 515-519.

Gilkenson, H. Social fears as reported by students in college speech classes. *Speech Monographs*, 1942, **9**, 141-160.

Kirchner, J. H., & Hogan, R. A. The therapist variable in the implosion of phobias. *Psychotherapy: Theory, Research and Practice*, 1966, **3**, 102-104.

Paul, G. L. *Insight versus desensitization in psychotherapy: An experiment in anxiety reduction*. Stanford, Calif.: Stanford University Press, 1966.

Weitzman, B. Behavior therapy and psychothery. *Psychological Review*, 1967, **74**, 300-317.

Wolpe, J. *Psychotherapy by reciprocal inhibition*. Stanford, Calif.: Stanford University Press, 1958.

Self-Desensitization: Implications for Treatment and Teaching[1]

N. Dickon Reppucci,[2] *Bruce L. Baker*
HARVARD UNIVERSITY

One question invariably raised in a discussion of behavior therapy regards its range of applicability. Typically the therapist is asked what types of *problems* he treats, and he responds by citing the wide range of disorders to which his colleagues have recently addressed themselves. But this question could be extended to ask: "What types of *people* respond best to these methods?" We have all heard the rejoinder that "the patients I see in practice are different" or "my patients wouldn't respond to such techniques." One focus of the present paper is this question of what personality dimensions relate to a successful outcome of behavior therapy.

A second focus of the paper concerns the potential educational uses of desensitization therapy. Recently Kahn and Baker (1968) reported a method for self-desensitization, reducing systematic desensitization to its simplest elements and thus providing a ready vehicle for teaching the approach. If personal involvement facilitates learning, as we believe it does, then the teaching of psychotherapy and psychopathology in the usual university curriculum suffers from being entirely too "academic." Yet it is difficult to give students a first-hand knowledge of specific therapies, especially from the patient's perspective. Self-desensitization, by its very simplicity, brevity, and automation,

[1]The authors are indebted to David Cohen, Lawrence Ephron, Paul Lehrer, John Muller, and Christine Reppucci for serving as judges. We also wish to thank Elizabeth Anderson and Susan Hole for their assistance. Research was supported by research grant G66-357 from the Foundations' Fund for Research in Psychiatry to Bruce L. Baker.

[2]Now at the Psychology Department, Yale University.

seemed to offer such a possibility; students could first program and then experience their own treatment. Hence, we are concerned herein with the usefulness of self-desensitization (*a*) to the educator, as a teaching device, and (*b*) to the therapist, as a treatment method.

A Teaching Method

The authors recently introduced a course, entitled Clinical Psychopathology, for advanced undergraduates at Harvard University. The main purpose of the course was to provide the students (24 boys and 15 girls) with an involving, first-hand experience of mental abnormality. The central focus was a superivised field placement for each student, in a community mental health center, a state school for the retarded, a state mental hospital, or a day care center for ex-mental patients. Reading assignments included case studies, first person accounts of pathological experience, and selected novels; assigned papers were addressed to aspects of the clinical experience. Class sessions included discussion of placement issues, lectures, films, therapy tapes, and several special ungraded exercises, which explored particular topics in depth. One of these was a self-desensitization exercise, in which the students were asked to desensitize themselves to one of their own "subclinical" phobias.

For our purpose, a phobia was defined as any situation which caused the student discomfort or anxiety which he wished to change. Each student was issued the do-it-yourself desensitization kit described by Kahn and Baker, consisting of a manual and a 12-in. long-playing phonograph record. The manual was designed to enable an intelligent and motivated individual to conduct the entire course of desensitization therapy with no therapist contact at all. It described the technique and then gave step-by-step instructions for building a hierarchy and proceeding with the desensitization. It also attempted to anticipate and deal with problems which might arise during the course of treatment. One side of the phonograph record was a 20-min course in relaxation training (adapted from Wolpe & Lazarus, 1966). The reverse side consisted of a 19-min recorded framework for a desensitization session. The actual hierarchy items did not appear on the record but were referred to as "the first item on your hierarchy," "the next item," etc. Thus, the record was standard for all subjects.

The presenting phobias included acrophobia, urinary stricture, test anxiety, fear of airplanes, blood, dogs, spiders, deep water, darkness, dentists, and many types of social anxieties, such as fear of public speaking, anxiety at social gatherings, and frigidity. After the students had practiced the relaxation exercises for three days and a sample hierarchy had been developed in the classroom, they constructed their own anxiety hierarchies. During the next two weeks, they were instructed to complete ten desensitization sessions. Students were issued a log book which had space for a daily account of progress, the anxiety hierarchy, and answers to questions concerning the nature and severity of the phobia. During the two months following treatment, each student tested the success of the treatment *in vivo* and submitted a report explaining exactly how he had tested the results and whether his phobia was changed in any way.

While completing the self-desensitization, the class was assigned Freud's case (1909) of a phobia in a five-year-old boy ("Little Hans") and selected chapters from *Psychopathology of Everyday Life* (1960). Following treatment, a classroom discussion was devoted to phobias. Similarities and differences between a learning theory and a psychoanalytic view of the cause and treatment of neurotic anxiety were explored. In addition, the experience with a subclinical phobia of one's own led into the question of what constitutes psychopathology. As a result of the exercise, many students developed an interest in behavior therapy, some asking for additional readings, others requesting guidance in applying behavior-therapy techniques in their field placements. At the conclusion of the course, an anonymous rating of the special assignments indicated that the students enjoyed this exercise and found it to be valuable. Thus, from a teaching point of view, self-desensitization was an extremely effective means of introducing behavior therapy and psychopathology to undergraduates.

Personality Dimensions Related to Outcome

Early in the course, as another special exercise, our students had completed a battery of psychological tests similar to those which a patient might receive upon admission to a mental hospital or clinic. The battery consisted of a shortened group Rorschach and TAT, the Incomplete Sentences Blank (Rotter & Rafferty, 1950), the Social Desirability Scale (Crowne & Marlowe, 1964), the Fear Survey Schedule (Wolpe & Lang, 1964), the Minnesota Multiphasic Personality Inventory, and the Interpersonal Adjective Check List (Leary, 1957). Personality measures from these instruments, with the exception of the Rorschach and TAT which are still being scored, were related to the degree of self-desensitization improvement.

On the basis of the students' report of their *in vivo* tests, four clinical psychologists independently rated degree of improvement on a five point scale (worse, no change, some improved, much improved, cured). Reliability coefficients between judges ranged from $r = .68$ to $r = .88$, with a mean of $r = .77$. As seen in Fig. 1, the average of the four judges' ratings classified 33 of the 39 subjects, or 85%, as showing some degree of improvement and over half as showing much improvement or cure. There were no sex differences.

The subjects were separated at the median total cure rating into a High Cure and a Low Cure group. One girl and three boys, who were on the median, were eliminated from the analysis, leaving a High Cure group of 17 subjects and a Low Cure group of 18 subjects. A comparison of these two groups on personality measures is shown in Table 1.

The High Cure subjects were significantly higher on the MMPI Mania (Ma) scale and lower on the Social Introversion (Si) scale than the Low Cure subjects. On the Leary IACL, the High Cure group was significantly higher on the managerial and autocratic dimensions and tended to be lower on dependency and masochism than the Low Cure group. On the social desirability scale, the High Cure subjects scored somewhat higher than the Low Cure subjects. A further analysis com-

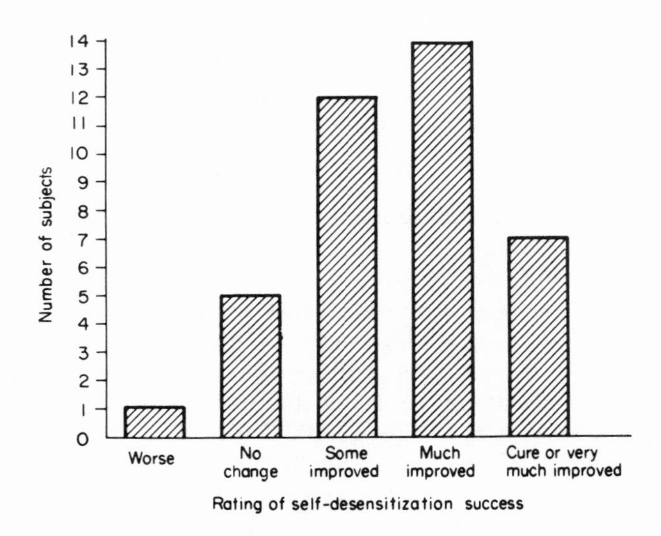

Fig. 1. Evaluation of self-desensitization success from students' reports: mean of four judges' ratings.

Table 1
MEAN SCORES ON PERSONALITY DIMENSIONS FOR HIGH CURE VERSUS LOW CURE SUBJECTS[a]

Variable Description	Low cure mean	High cure mean	d.f.	*t*-test	*p*
MMPI					
Lie(L)	45.3	44.8	33	.23	NS[b]
Nonconformity(F)	56.1	52.6	33	1.47	NS
Defensiveness(K)	54.3	57.4	33	1.31	NS
Hypochondriasis(Hs)	47.8	51.1	33	1.64	NS
Depression(D)	57.9	56.2	33	.60	NS
Hysteria(Hy)	57.9	60.6	33	1.13	NS
Psychopathic Deviance(Pd)	60.3	61.4	33	.32	NS
Paranoid(Pa)	59.2	58.7	33	.17	NS
Psychasthenia(Pt)	61.4	60.4	33	.31	NS
Schizophrenia(Sc)	60.4	63.2	33	.80	NS
Mania(Ma)	57.2	65.4	33	2.43	.02
Social Introversion(Si)	54.9	48.2	33	2.61	.01
Anxiety(A)	50.8	48.2	33	1.02	NS
Ego Strength(Es)	59.9	61.5	33	.66	NS
Rotter S.C.B. Maladjustment Scale	144.8	148.5	32	.69	NS
Marlowe-Crowne Social Desirability(SD)	9.8	12.2	33	1.74	.09
Fear Survey Schedule	140.3	136.4	33	.52	NS
Leary IACL					
Managerial	4.4	8.5	32	2.67	.01
Autocratic	8.8	11.1	32	1.70	.10
Competitive	6.6	7.9	30	1.09	NS
Narcissistic	4.8	5.2	31	.31	NS
Aggressive	7.1	9.0	31	1.35	NS
Sadistic	7.2	6.8	31	.36	NS
Rebellious	6.2	6.3	32	.10	NS
Distrustful	7.3	6.9	31	.37	NS
Self-Effacing	7.8	6.2	31	1.26	NS
Masochistic	6.5	4.1	32	1.77	.09
Docile	6.2	6.0	31	.17	NS
Dependent	10.7	7.9	31	1.91	.06
Cooperative	7.2	8.5	31	.86	NS
Over-Conventional	7.6	9.3	32	1.03	NS
Responsible	9.2	9.7	32	.30	NS
Hypernormal	5.2	7.8	32	1.54	NS

[a] High Cure indicates above the median total cure rating of the four judges ($N = 17$); Low Cure indicates below the median total cure rating of the four judges ($N = 18$).
[b] NS means $p > .10$; Two-tailed tests.

pared just those subjects in the top third versus those in the bottom third on cure rating. Although the differences between the Highest and Lowest Cure groups declined slightly on mania and social desirability, the differences on dependency and masochism were accentuated. In addition, the Highest Cure subjects were higher on the MMPI defensiveness (K) scale ($t = 1.78$; $p = .09$) and lower on the MMPI nonconformity (F) scale ($t = 2.20$; $p = .04$), than the Lowest Cure subjects. The Highest Cure group was the most deviant in comparison with normative data on these measures, being atypically high on hyperactivity (Ma) and managerial-autocratic traits and atypically low on masochism. The Lowest Cure group was atypically low on the need for social approval and somewhat prone to make themselves appear "sick" (F).

In addition to the personality variables *per se*, three other factors relating to treatment process were investigated: number of sessions, phobia seriousness, and phobia type.

NUMBER OF SESSIONS. The High Cure group completed the 10 treatment sessions as assigned while the Low Cure group completed only 8.6, or significantly fewer sessions ($t = 1.82$; $p = .08$). This difference may reflect a lower motivation for the self-desensitization assignment in Low Cure subjects, or simply a reaction to their lack of progress; in any case, their report of completing fewer sessions than assigned was consistent with their atypically low social desirability score.

SERIOUSNESS OF PHOBIA. It seemed possible that the seriousness of the student's phobia might be related to treatment success. Three advanced clinical psychology graduate students rated the degree of phobia seriousness, and a High Seriousness ($N = 20$) and a Low Seriousness ($N = 19$) group were formed by dividing the sum of these ratings at the median. A comparison of these groups on the outcome measure found no relation between phobia seriousness and treatment results ($t = .80$; $p = .43$).

The personality measures which differentiated the two groups were consistent with the seriousness dimension. Students with High Serious phobias scored higher on the Fear Survey Schedule ($t = 1.82$; $p = .08$), higher on the MMPI Anxiety scale ($t = 2.28$; $p = .03$), and lower on the MMPI Ego Strength scale ($t = 2.44$; $p = .02$) than those with Low Serious phobias. Also, the Low Serious group was much lower on the need for social approval ($t = 2.28$; $p = .03$) than the High Serious group.

TYPE OF PHOBIA. The phobias were categorized into two types: (*a*) those related to *noninterpersonal* fears such as airplanes, darkness, dogs, spiders, tests, and heights, and (*b*) those related to *interpersonal* anxieties, such as public speaking, social gatherings, frigidity, and making telephone calls. There were 20 noninterpersonal phobias and 19 interpersonal phobias. Phobia type was related to cure rating; individuals with noninterpersonal phobias were rated as more improved than those with interpersonal phobias ($t = 1.98$; $p = .06$), even though the two phobia groups completed the same number of desensitization sessions.

The two groups did not differ on the Fear Survey Schedule nor any of its 6 subscales, indicating that subjects generally had both types of phobias and their choice of a particular type to desensitize might have reflected more basic personality traits. In fact, Table 2 indicates that those subjects who chose noninterpersonal phobias tended to be autocratic and defensive, displaying repressive blandness (Hy) and some psychopathy (Pd). In comparison, subjects who chose interpersonal phobias tended to be socially introverted, reported few psychosomatic symptoms (Hs), and were somewhat uncooperative and very unconventional.

Table 2
MEAN SCORES ON PERSONALITY DIMENSIONS WHICH SIGNIFICANTLY[a] DIFFERENTIATE SUBJECTS WITH INTERPERSONAL PHOBIAS VERSUS SUBJECTS WITH NONINTERPERSONAL PHOBIAS

Variable	Interpersonal phobia mean	Noninterpersonal phobia mean	d.f.	*t*-test	*p*
MMPI:					
Defensiveness(K)	52.7	57.8	37	2.11	.04
Hypochondriasis(Hs)	46.6	51.4	37	2.50	.02
Hysteria(Hy)	55.8	61.8	37	2.90	.006
Psychopathic Deviance(Pd)	57.3	63.2	37	1.91	.06
Social Introversion(Si)	55.6	48.2	37	2.77	.009
Leary IACL:					
Autocratic	8.3	11.4	36	2.48	.02
Cooperative	6.1	9.0	35	1.99	.05
Hypernormal	4.7	8.0	36	2.25	.03

[a]Two-tailed tests. All other variables $p > .10$.

Discussion

The present findings suggest that self-desensitization is an exciting and valuable technique to introduce students to the study of psychopathology. The results also expand earlier findings, demonstrating that this method can be reasonably effective in the treatment of phobias, even though there is no therapist as such.

The first question which is inevitably raised when outcome measures are as subjective as ours is whether the results were greatly influenced by demand characteristics. This is especially relevant in the present study, since our patients were also our students and would have to be graded eventually. We did attempt to communicate that the self-desensitization treatment was ungraded and that in order to make it a profitable experience they should be as open and honest as possible. Yet we cannot be sure to what extent the reported success was no more than an apple on our desk. In defense of the results, however, we offer the following observations. Contrary to the assignment, a number of students did not report completing the full ten sessions, suggesting that there was not an overall tendency to comply with expectations. Also, our *in vivo* tests tended to be specific behavioral instances and progress was judged independently and with good reliability. Finally, our major findings were based on the relative position of subjects rather than the absolute amount of improvement, so that a slight overall bias would not alter the results.

Treatment effectiveness was related to both the nature of the phobia and some personality traits of the individual. Interpersonal phobias were less successfully treated than more situation specific ones. One explanation is that the more specific phobias were easier to conceptualize and arrange into hierarchies, providing fewer opportunities for the self-desensitization process to go astray. With an interpersonal phobia, the manual simply may not be detailed enough to put and keep the subject on the right track. However, the differential effectiveness might also have been related to the types of individuals who chose a complex interpersonal phobia to desensitize. As we have seen, these students tended to be generally more nonconforming and introverted. Since they reported as many fears on the Fear Survey Schedule as those choosing more specific phobias, it would be interesting to see if they could successfully desensitize one of their noninterpersonal problems; such an experiment might partial out whether our stumbling block was the type of person or the nature of his phobia.

Our outcome results begin to delineate two distinctly different personality types. Subjects who were High Cure resembled Leary's *Autocratic Personality*. Their MMPI profile peaked on mania. They were energetic, outgoing, and well-organized, viewing themselves as powerful, competent, and in charge. They tended to deny emotional feelings and picked a noninterpersonal phobia to treat. In comparison, subjects who were Low Cure tended to be masochistic and cynical, to avoid the conventional and the expected. Somewhat socially introverted and dependent, they were more thinkers than doers and conceived of themselves as complex and "sick" individuals; they picked interpersonal phobias to treat.[3]

A question which naturally arises is whether these types would predict success in regular desensitization therapy or only in self-desensitization. While the present data do not provide an answer, we would hypothesize that the presence of a therapist would tend to mitigate the outcome differences between the two types. Leary (1957) reported that the autocratic type is not well-motivated for conventional psychotherapy; 68% of these persons seen in a psychiatric clinic did not go into treatment. On the other hand, persons who are dependent, introverted, and unconventional tend to be well-motivated for psychotherapy. To the extent that the presence of a therapist in desensitization therapy would make it seem to the patient more like psychotherapy, our findings might even be reversed.

The present findings, then, suggest that it may be profitable to further consider the question of the range of applicability of behavior therapy techniques in an eventual effort to best suit the treatment to the person as well as to the problem.

References

Crowne, D. P., & Marlowe, D. *The approval motive.* New York: Wiley, 1964.

Freud, S. Analysis of a phobia in a five-year-old boy. 1909. *The collected papers.* Vol. III. (Translated by A. Strachey & J. Strachey) London: Hogarth Press, 1953. Pp. 149-295.

Freud, S. Psychopathology of everyday life. *The complete psychological works of Sigmund Freud.* Vol. VI. (Translated by J. Strachey) London: Hogarth Press, 1960.

Kahn, M., & Baker, B. L. Desensitization with minimal therapist contact. *Journal of Abnormal Psychology*, 1968, **73**, 198-200.

Leary, T. *Interpersonal diagnosis of personality.* New York: Ronald Press, 1957.

Rotter, J. B., & Rafferty, J. E. *Manual: The Rotter incomplete sentences blank.* New York: Psychological Corporation, 1950.

Wolpe, J., & Lang, P. J. A fear survey schedule for use in behavior therapy. *Behaviour Research and Therapy*, 1964, **2**, 27-30.

Wolpe, J., & Lazarus, A. A. *Behavior therapy techniques.* New York: Macmillan (Pergamon), 1966.

[3]An analysis of the data by sex found these types to emerge more distinctly in females though present in males.

The Use of Implosive-Expressive Therapy in Anxiety Reactions

Michael Serber, Alan Goldstein, Gerald W. Piaget, Felicitas Kort

TEMPLE UNIVERSITY

AND

EASTERN PENNSYLVANIA PSYCHIATRIC INSTITUTE

The anxiety reactions of numerous patients are not amenable to systematic desensitization. In certain instances the patient cannot be successfully desensitized because it may be impossible for him to reach the necessary degree of relaxation to countercondition the anxiety responses, or he may be unable to visualize the scenes presented to him with sufficient vividness.

Another problem in desensitizing some anxious patients is related to the spurious hierarchies which patients themselves present as the antecedents of their anxiety. At times it is impossible to find the pertinent antecedents of patients' anxiety reactions as they do not know exactly what makes them anxious and the material they present does not lead to clinically significant counterconditioning responses. In such cases, unadaptive anxiety may be evanescent, remission and exacerbation of symptoms not apparently being related to either the external or internal milieu.[1]

[1]This condition may be incorrectly attributed to so-called "symptom substitution," e.g., a young lady complained of feeling panicky in numerous situations to which she could not be desensitized with any degree of success. The sources of her discomfort kept changing and a clear description of the antecedents of her anxiety was never produced. If she were seen at infrequent intervals, it would appear that she suffered from different symptoms; her condition had been described as symptom substitution by several psychiatrists.

While it is important, of course, to get as complete a history as possible, the use of symbols (words) to describe autonomic states of discomfort often does not yield enough of the necessary information to desensitize some patients and another approach is needed. We employ in such cases a nonverbal approach.

Frequently recorded observations that the expression of emotion after an initial rise in intensity of feeling leads to a decline in the intensity of that feeling can be exemplified: Anger, when adequately expressed, permits the subject to feel less angry; examples in the sexual sphere of expression are part of our folklore and everyday experience; people expressing grief or fear subsequently feel less sad or anxious. In other words, the expressive component *per se* can alleviate or limit the extent of subjective discomfort felt by a patient.

Our nonverbal technique is used with those patients who, after a thorough history (and possibly trial desensitization), have made no statements about antecedents of anxiety that result in improvement. With the use of our technique, the patient need not verbalize what the feared feeling is, and valid therapeutic effects have been achieved with the patient not knowing specifically of what he was afraid.

As the title of our paper states, we use an implosive-expressive technique. A training period for the patient proceeds as follows for an average of two or three 45-min sessions.

The patient is first taught to sigh, modeling his sighs after the therapist's demonstration of what is expected, and is encouraged to express himself with his sighs. After a few minutes and some feelings of self-consciousness, the patient is generally able to sigh comfortably.

The patient is then taught to express anger. (Strangely enough, most of our patients learn to express anger much more easily than they can be taught to sigh). We teach vocalization of anger and appropriate facial expressions, and we encourage the hitting of a stuffed bolster with sound and energy. After being able to express anger with feeling, the patient is taught to express fright by opening his eyes and screaming; most importantly, he is encouraged to feel what he does. (Stanislowski frequently told his acting students, "Do what you do long enough, and you'll begin to feel it)." This is, of course, one of the premises of behaviorism. It is interesting to observe how many initially inhibited people get comfortable with nonverbal behavior after a short practice period.

At this point, after the patient is trained in basic emotive behavior (the period of training may vary from one to six sessions, not unlike the period of relaxation training in systematic desensitization), he is presented with a general scene that is beyond his present coping ability. He is again encouraged to express his anguish with appropriate vocalization and other motor behavior employing the entire body. The choice of expressive mode is his own. The patient is at all stages encouraged to feel what he is doing. The same scene is repeated on several occasions until the patient feels comfortable expressing himself in that particular imagined situation. When a patient begins on a specific scene, he is usually impressed with the gravity of the scene in his own life and the paucity of expression that accompanies it. Concurrent with practice of each scene, the discrepancy between affect and importance of the scene lessens considerably and the patient who feels capable of going on to the *in vivo* situation believes his affect for that particular scene to be qualitatively and quantitatively appropriate. This procedure is carried on for a number of troublesome scenes since we are most concerned with the affective component with which the patient is unable to cope. The patient is asked to implode himself simply by starting to think and to express what he feels. From three to ten sessions of implosive-expressive therapy is usually an adequate sample for the therapist to determine if any advantage from this approach is forthcoming.

As stated before, the patient, after becoming comfortable with the affective component, usually finds that as he is expressing a scene adequately his anxiety reaction subsides. The desirable end which we have frequently encountered is the ability to face the situation *in vivo* with markedly less or no anxiety. Generally the patient has no "insight" to explain the transformation of affective behavior.

The following cases are all varied in content and outcome and further illustrate the application of the technique:

Case I. A 41-year-old social worker with a long history of various phobias was treated by a succession of analytic and behavior therapists for several years. His symptoms and general apathy remained unchanged. Systematic desensitization appeared to work well for a limited period of time, but no lasting effects could be achieved. The patient was particularly anxious about being alone or doing anything without friends or family around him in case, as he put it, "something would happen to me."

The patient was taught basic emotive behavior and then imploded with various scenes which from his history were known to cause *in vivo* difficulties. After several sessions, the patient was able to cease calling the therapist because of acute anxiety attacks between therapeutic sessions. Also, he was able to take public transportation to work and to go to sports matches. His use of tranquilizers decreased markedly. The implosive-expressive therapy lasted ten sessions and a follow-up after a period of six months revealed no recurrence of acute symptoms. The patient felt that he had learned to face the situation internally without breaking down or becoming helpless.

Case II. A 40-year-old housewife was plagued with a number of hostile obsessions. She was afraid of going near any children because she might somehow hurt or kill them. Preparing meals also caused great anxiety because she was terrified at the prospect of accidently poisoning her family. Driving a car was equally forbidding because she could see herself running over children and animals.

Systematic desensitization proved of no value in her case because she could not imagine any anxiety provoking scene concomitant with relaxation. She was trained in emotive behavior and imploded over a period of five sessions. During the sessions she expressed much anger and fear but gradually became more comfortable with her feelings. Her family reported some improvement in her functioning and she reported that she felt appreciably more at ease when near children and when preparing food for the family. Her improvement did not deteriorate over a four-month follow-up.

Case III. A 45-year-old male was unable to drive his car farther than 5 mi from his home. He would, if trying to drive further, develop palpitations, dizziness, confusion, and the feeling he would somehow collapse. Systematic desensitization was employed for several sessions along several dimensions (time, distance, etc.) with no appreciable improvement in his mobility. He was taught expressive behavior and consequently imploded by having him imagine being lost on a desolate country road, out of gas and money. He first got furious, then cried, but got more comfortable with each successive presentation and expression of feeling. He volunteered the information that, in the midst of his crying and anger, he remembered his mother leaving him as a small child when he was sick. No interpretation was made and the emotive therapy went on for four sessions. Spontaneously, the patient began driving from Philadelphia to the shore (a distance of over 50 mi), going to New York, and, without difficulty, even flying to England for a vacation. Seven months later, the patient reported an increased freedom of movement and no recurrence of symptoms.

In summary, our experience indicates that the expression of emotion is of value in counterconditioning anxiety reactions by reciprocal inhibition. From observing our subjects, we conclude that their ability to express themselves adequately while imagining a tension or anxiety provoking scene prepares them to face the same provocative situation without anxiety and without having to "emote." As in successful systematic desensitization, when a patient has completed a hierarchy, it is usually unnecessary for him to imagine himself relaxed in the *in vivo* situation. We believe that emotive-expressive therapy both complements and extends the symptom relief offered to anxious patients, while broadening the range of patient problems accessible to direct therapeutic intervention.

The Use of Male and Female Therapists in the Treatment of Homosexual Behavior

Joseph R. Cautela
BOSTON COLLEGE

Patricia A. Wisocki
MEDFIELD STATE HOSPITAL

Behavior therapists have long contended that the behavior-therapy technique used for a maladaptive behavior problem is *the* primary agency of change in a therapeutic situation. This contention has been justified with the evidence of Lang, Lazovik, and Reynolds (1965) and Paul (1966), whose carefully controlled studies revealed the independent efficacy of the specific conditioning techniques used in the treatment of well-defined monophobic subjects. Other substantiating evidence for the effectiveness of the techniques exclusive of the therapist is available from the case reports of Wolpe (1962) and Lazarus, Davison, and Polefka (1965), in which therapists were interchanged without disrupting the successful desensitization of phobic subjects; from the use of a "Device for Automatic Desensitization" (DAD) developed by Melamed and Lang (1967) in which a programmed machine was about as effective as a human therapist in producing a reduction in fears; from a comparison study of tape recorded and live desensitization sessions by Krapfl and Nawas (1968) in which no differences were found between the desensitization groups, although both were significantly superior to the two control groups; and from the results of a study which compared the effectiveness of a conventional desensitization group with a "do-it-yourself" group which carried out the desensitization process at home and found that both groups were equally successful (Kahn & Baker, 1968).

As a result, behavior therapists have been criticized for failure to recognize the importance of the therapist in effecting behavioral change. Typical of the behavior therapist's stand on this point was Eysenck's (1960) statement (p. 19) that personal relations are not essential for cures of neurotic disorder, although "in certain cases . . . (they) may be required in order to provide a necessary step on the generalization gradient." The therapist's influence was not ruled out, only considered nonessential, except in "certain circumstances" which, unfortunately, were not specified.

Research findings by Rosenthal (1955), Noblin, Timmons, and Reynard (1963), and Truax (1966) have established the existence of behavior influence within the therapeutic relationship. Others (Lovaas, 1964; Staats, 1964; Krasner & Ullmann, 1965) have established that the therapist is a very powerful source of stimuli which act to manipulate a patient's behavior. In fact, two groups of investigators (Meyer & Gelder, 1963; Andrews, 1966), who reviewed the treatment of phobias, concluded that the therapist is *the* most important element for determining successful therapeutic outcome.

In a review article delineating specific critical variables involved in the therapist-patient relationship, Wilson, Hannon, and Evans (1968) cite evidence illustrating the importance in successful therapy of such variables as the success and prestige of the therapist, his attractiveness, his compatibility with the patient in socioeconomic status, sex, attitudes, and history of social reinforcement, his liking for the patient, and other factors which appear to significantly enhance the behavior modification process.

Psychoanalytic schools have also recognized the importance of the therapist in that he acts as a "transference figure" onto whom a patient can express his previously learned emotional responses. Ayllon and Michael (1959) and Bergin (1966) have even suggested that the therapist may produce *deleterious* effects on a patient's behavior.

From these two areas of research it seems clear that: (*a*) the technique of desensitization studied in these reports was the primary agent of change; (*b*) the therapist is an important source of behavioral change and can influence the outcome of therapy. Since both the technique and the therapist are viable factors and since the critical variables concerning the therapist have yet to be applied in a practical example of enhancing the therapeutic situation and thereby maximizing the effectiveness of the technique, we intend to present our program of treatment for homosexual clients in which the application of various behavior-therapy procedures is determined by a specific therapist variable.

Although we had been using covert sensitization (Cautela, 1966, 1967) exclusively, with great success in the elimination of the homosexual client's attraction to the same sex, many of these clients expressed feelings of despondency and loneliness because their entire social structure was disappearing and they were fearful of approaching females for various reasons. Also we noted that most of these clients experienced extreme anxiety in specific situations, such as being alone, rejected, etc.

From these observations, our treatment program was organized to include the following phases:

Phase I. Elimination of the patient's sexual attraction to the male by covert sensitization and thought stopping.
Phase II. Elimination of the patient's anxiety responses to females by relaxation, desensitization, instructions, and behavioral rehearsals.
Phase III. Elimination of anxiety responses to being alone, rejected, ignored, disapproved of, looking foolish, and other idiosyncratic fears by desensitization.
Phase IV. Training in assertive behavior.

Phases I and IV are assigned to the male therapist, Phase II to the female therapist, Phase III to either one, depending on how well the patient is progressing in the other sections. In cases where the homosexual client is female, the assignments are reversed, of course.

We believed this structure provided particularly well for discrimination learning—the client learns to associate the female therapist with anxiety-reduction while the male therapist is the recipient of any aggression resulting from the application of aversive conditioning. This idea is in accord with Gantt's work (1944) in which he found that the administration of aversion therapy sometimes produced conditioned responses to the immediate stimuli paired with the aversive stimulus (shock) and to other aspects of the environment, including the therapist.

During each therapy session, in response to any significant verbal statements by the client, each therapist is careful to provide reinforcement only in his own sphere—the female therapist remains noncommittal to statements about the client's attraction to males except to reinforce any negative statements he makes; the male therapist makes negative statements to positive remarks about the client's sexual attraction to males and gives positive verbal reinforcement to negative statements about it. Both therapists positively reinforce his descriptions of gains made with females and any positive verbal remarks about his own feelings of virility, normality, etc. That verbal conditioning is an effective means of producing changes in nonverbal behavior has been discussed by Krasner (1962, 1965) and demonstrated by Lovaas (1964).

There was another reason for alternating therapists in the treatment of homosexual clients—an incidental reason, but an important one. We were concerned with the possibility of stimulus generalization by the *therapist*. It is theoretically possible that the application of aversive conditioning to the sexual stimulus by the therapist might eventually affect him.

Outline of Procedure

Phase I

In the first session, clients are seen by the male therapist who explains the "division of labor" system and later introduces the female therapist. In the presence of the client, the male therapist explains to the female therapist the client's reason for seeking treatment and presents an outline of the behaviors to be treated. Usually at this point clients are somewhat nervous, but the female therapist listens dispassionately and often asks the client to elaborate on certain details dealing with his homosexual experiences. At the end of the session, the client makes an appointment to begin relaxation training with the female therapist. He also takes home with him six questionnaires to be completed by the following week—a Life History Questionnaire (Wolpe & Lazarus, 1966); a Fear Survey Schedule (Wolpe & Lang, 1964); a Reinforcement Survey Schedule (Cautela & Kastenbaum, 1967); a Reinforcement History Questionnaire (Cautela, 1968c); and two forms concerning specific information about his attraction to the same sex and reactions to the opposite sex (Cautela, 1968b).

We have found each of these questionnaires valuable in the overall treatment program. The Life History Questionnaire provides for a detailed account of the patient's pertinent history; the Reinforcement History Questionnaire provides an elaboration on methods used by parents to reward and punish; the Fear Survey Schedule gives us an idea of the number, type, and intensity of specific fearful items [some of these items (e.g., bats) are also used in conjunction with covert sensitization to make the stimulus more noxious]; the Reinforcement Survey Schedule supplies us with an idea of the reinforcers available to us for inclusion in anxiety-reduction scenes; the two description forms help to furnish a more comprehensive picture of the client's sexual history.

After this first interview, appointments are made on a biweekly basis—once a week with each therapist. Occasionally, owing to extreme anxiety in the presence of the female, the transfer to the female therapist must be made more gradually. In such cases both therapists will be present during each session (except while the client is taught relaxation techniques) until he feels comfortable enough to be alone with the female. At certain other times as well, during the course of treatment, both therapists are present during a session to present both viewpoints simultaneously to any problems the client may introduce.

When therapy has begun formally, a checklist (Wisocki & Cautela, 1968) is taken at the beginning of each session. It requires information concerning the number of times the client relaxed since the last session, practiced assigned scenes, masturbated—and with what stimulus (male or female), the number of urges he had toward males and females, the number of contacts he had with males and females, and the number of times he practiced thought stopping. In this way, we have an up-to-date tally of the client's sexual activities and progress.

The elimination of the client's sexual attraction to the same sex is brought about by the technique of covert sensitization (Cautela, 1966, 1967), applied exclusively by the male therapist. Covert sensitization is an aversive conditioning method in which the client, in imagination, pairs the pleasurable object (a sexually attractive male) within a noxious setting (e.g., a cesspool or dungeon) with the image of himself vomiting all over himself, the homosexual contact, and every aspect of the situation. The therapist builds a hierarchy of the desirable sexual objects and the contacts available to the client for sexual stimulation and then constructs extremely noxious scenes with this material. Covert sensitization is applied to all items in the hierarchy, with the most desirable sexual object usually treated first. Homework scenes are given to the client for practice outside the therapy session. The client is also told that whenever he sees someone to whom he is sexually attracted or whenever he begins to have a sexual fantasy about a male, he must immediately imagine that object covered with sores, scabs, and insects and imagine himself vomiting on it.

Covert sensitization seems to work very well in establishing an avoidance response to males. Some experimental evidence on its effectiveness in other sex-associated behaviors has been provided by Barlow, Leitenberg, and Agras (1968) and Davison (1968). It has also been applied successfully to such behavioral problems as alcoholism

(Anant, 1966, 1967; Ashem & Donner, 1968), smoking (Mullen, 1968; Viernstein, 1968), and overeating (Stuart, 1967).

In conjunction with covert sensitization, the male therapist also employs the method of thought stopping. The patient is instructed, after several practice sessions in the office, to shout "STOP" to himself whenever he feels he is beginning to get the urge to approach a male for sexual purposes, or even to think about a male in a sexual way. The use and effectiveness of this technique has been reported elsewhere (Cautela, 1968a).

PHASE II

The female therapist begins training the client in relaxation methods during the second therapy session. She teaches a version of Jacobsen's (1938) method of deep muscle relaxation. The client learns to relax sitting down, standing, and walking, in order to prepare him for any type of anxiety-provoking situation. We regard this period as the beginning of in vivo desensitization to the female therapist and to females in general, since the client is learning to relax in the presence of the female therapist.

After training the client in relaxation, the female therapist divides her session time between the following areas: (*a*) desensitization to various aspects of heterosexual situations and relationships, particularly ones in which he is expected to make some sort of sexual advance, such as making conversation, sitting on a couch, getting a drink for a girl, holding hands, kissing her good night, and later on, more intimate sexual behavior (each aspect requires a separate hierarchy in varying degrees of detail); (*b*) giving instructions in various dating procedures, such as methods of most comfortably kissing a girl in a car with bucket seats, places to go, what to wear, what is acceptable social conversation, etc.; and (*c*) answering questions about females, such as: Do girls enjoy sex; does lipstick come off in a kiss; what do girls "mean" when they invite a date into their houses. If the patient has reached the level where he is dating girls, some time is spent in discussing methods of obtaining more enjoyment from his dating experiences.

PHASE III

From the answers to the Fear Survey Schedule and in the course of applying the other treatment procedures, we usually find several specific areas of anxiety-provoking stimuli, such as being alone, rejected, ignored, criticized, being disapproved of, and looking foolish, common to these clients. When these areas are sex related, such as being rejected by a female, they are handled by the female therapist, either in separate hierarchies or as part of the related hierarchies with which she is working. Often, however, these areas are not sex related. For instance, homosexual clients usually have a fear of criticism by anyone, regardless of sex. When this is the case, separate hierarchies are constructed by either therapist, and desensitization is applied.

PHASE IV

We have found that homosexuals usually lack assertive behavior, both in heterosexual situations and normal social situations, such as in restaurants or movie theaters. Since it is especially necessary for males to be assertive, we thought it important to include this aspect in our treatment program.

Training in assertive behavior is under the control of the male therapist for the following reasons: (*a*) the association of assertiveness with a female might increase the client's anxiety toward females in general; and (*b*) the male therapist provides a model for imitation.

Assertive training consists of behavioral rehearsals, discussions, and desensitization when necessary.

Evaluation of the Program

This method of treatment for our homosexual clients has been in effect for less than a year and, therefore, we cannot yet properly gauge its value. We began with six homosexuals and gradually extended the program to include two other patients, nonhomosexual, but with anxiety reactions toward females in addition to other behavioral problems. Of the six homosexuals, two dropped out of therapy very early in treatment; a third has married after three months of intensive therapy and, as far as we know, is performing exclusively heterosexual behavior; a fourth had engaged in heavy petting and was engaged to be married, but was drafted into the army before treatment was terminated. The other two are still in therapy: One is dating females regularly and is looking for a girl he can marry; the other is beginning to date females more frequently.

Holding the number of sessions constant, however, we can say that the double-therapist approach has two added advantages over the previous program in which only the sexual attraction to the same sex was eliminated by covert sensitization. It seems to decrease resistance to therapy and facilitates approach behavior to females. The clients themselves have expressed a great deal of satisfaction with this arrangement.

An objection might be raised to this form of treatment on the grounds that the continuity of treatment is violated. We have found that frequent and thorough discussions of each case among the therapists overcome this problem. Both therapists are careful to relate as accurately as possible everything that occurred in each individual session. The checklist taken at the start of each session insures a measure of continuity as well, along with the other objective data from additional questionnaires. Furthermore, as mentioned previously, occasionally both therapists are present during the same therapy session.

The choice of the female therapist is also important for the success of the program. We expect clients to feel that a female who is young, attractive, active in dating, and at ease in the presence of males will be more up-to-date on dating practices than an older woman. Also, since our homosexual population is young (25-34 years of age), their target dating area is in a similar age range and it is, therefore, imperative that they feel comfortable with a young female.

With only these two cautionary measures raised (i.e., maintenance of continuity, and choice of the female therapist) and based on the success we have had to date, we feel this particular program can be successful in the treatment of homosexuals and can be a model for other behavior-therapy treatment programs designed to achieve a greater degree of total therapeutic efficacy.

References

Anant, S. S. The treatment of alcoholics by a verbal aversion technique: A case report. *Manas*, 1966, **13**, 78-86.

Anant, S. S. A note on the treatment of alcoholics by a verbal aversion technique. *Canadian Psychologist,* 1967, I, 19-22.

Andrews, J. D. Psychotherapy of phobias. *Psychological Bulletin*, 1966, **66**, 455-480.

Ashem, B., & Donner, L. Covert sensitization with alcoholics: A controlled replication. *Behaviour Research and Therapy*, 1968, **6**, 7-12.

Ayllon, T., & Michael, J. The psychiatric nurse as a behavioral engineer. *Journal of the Experimental Analysis of Behavior*, 1959, **2**, 323-334.

Barlow, D. H., Leitenberg, H., & Agras, W. S. Preliminary report on the experimental control of sexual deviation by manipulation of the US in covert sensitization. Paper presented at the meeting of the Eastern Psychological Association Convention, Washington, D.C., April 1968.

Bergin, A. E. Some implications of psychotherapy research for therapeutic practice. *Journal of Abnormal Psychology*, 1966, **71**, 235-246.

Cautela, J. R. Treatment of compulsive behavior by covert sensitization. *Psychological Record*, 1966, **16**, 33-41.

Cautela, J. R. Covert sensitization. *Psychological Reports*, 1967, **20**, 459-468.

Cautela, J. R. Behavior therapy and self-control: Techniques and implications. In C. M. Franks (Ed.), *Assessment and status of the behavior therapies and associated developments.* New York: McGraw-Hill, 1968. (a)

Cautela, J. R. Homosexual questionnaires. Questionnaire A—Attraction toward the same sex; Questionnaire B—Reactions toward the opposite sex. Unpublished manuscript, Boston College, Chestnut Hill, Massachusetts, 1968. (b)

Cautela, J. R. Reinforcement history questionnaire. Unpublished manuscript, Boston College, Chestnut Hill, Massachusetts 1968. (c)

Cautela, J. R., & Kastenbaum, R. A reinforcement survey schedule for use in therapy, training, and research. *Psychological Reports*, 1967, **20**, 115-130.

Davison, G. C. Elimination of a sadistic fantasy by a client-controlled counterconditioning technique: A case study. *Journal of Abnormal Psychology*, 1968, **73**, 84-89.

Eysenck, H. J. Learning theory and behavior therapy. In H. J. Eysenck (Ed.), *Behavior therapy and the neuroses.* New York: Macmillan (Pergamon), 1960. Pp. 4-21.

Gantt, W. H. *Experimental basis for neurotic behavior.* New York: Harper & Row (Hoeber), 1944.

Jacobsen, E. *Progressive relaxation.* Chicago: University of Chicago Press, 1938.

Kahn, M., & Baker, B. Desensitization with minimal therapist contact. *Journal of Abnormal Psychology*, 1968, **73**, 198-200.

Krapfl, J., & Nawas, M. The client-therapist relationship factor in systematic desensitization. Paper presented at the meeting of the Midwestern Psychological Association, Chicago, May, 1968.

Krasner, L. The therapist as a social reinforcement machine. In H. H. Strupp & L. Luborsky (Eds.), *Research in psychotherapy.* Vol. 2. Washington, D.C.: American Psychological Association, 1962. Pp. 61-94.

Krasner, L. Verbal conditioning and psychotherapy. In L. Krasner & L. P. Ullmann (Eds.), *Research in behavior modification.* New York: Holt, Rinehart & Winston, 1965.

Krasner, L., & Ullmann, L. *Research in behavior modification.* New York: Holt, Rinehart & Winston, 1965.

Lang, P. J., Lazovik, A. D., & Reynolds, D. J. Desensitization, suggestibility, and pseudotherapy. *Journal of Abnormal Psychology*, 1965, **70**, 395-402.

Lazarus, A. A., Davison, G. C., & Polofka, D. A. Classical and operant factors in the treatment of a school phobia. *Journal of Abnormal Psychology*, 1965, **70**, 225-229.

Lovaas, O. I. Interaction between verbal and non-verbal behavior. In H. J. Eysenck (Ed.), *Experiments in behavior therapy.* New York: Macmillan (Pergamon), 1964. Pp. 475-481.

Melamed, B., & Lang, P. J. Study of the automated desensitization of fear. Paper presented at the meeting of the Midwestern Psychological Association, Chicago, May, 1967.

Meyer, V., & Gelder, M. G. Behavior therapy and phobic disorders. *British Journal of Psychiatry*, 1963, **109**, 19-28.

Mullen, F. G., Jr. The effect of covert sensitization on smoking behavior. Unpublished manuscript, Queens College, Charlotteville, North Carolina, 1968.

Noblin, C. C., Timmons, E. O., & Reynard, M. C. Psychoanalytic interpretations as verbal reinforcers: Importance of interpretation content. *Journal of Clinical Psychology*, 1963, **19**, 479-481.

Paul, G. L. *Insight versus desensitization therapy.* Stanford, Calif.: Stanford University Press, 1966.

Rosenthal, D. Changes in some moral values following psychotherapy. *Journal of Consulting Psychology*, 1955, **19**, 431-436.

Staats, A. W. *Human learning*. New York: Holt, Rinehart & Winston, 1964.

Stuart, R. B. Behavioral control of overeating. *Behaviour Research and Therapy*, 1967, **5**, 357-365.

Truax, C. B. Reinforcement and nonreinforcement in Rogerian psychotherapy. *Journal of Abnormal Psychology*, 1966, **71**, 1-9.

Viernstein, L. Evaluation of therapeutic techniques of covert sensitization of smoking behavior. Unpublished manuscript, Queens College, Charlotteville, North Carolina, 1968.

Wilson, G. T., Hannon, A., & Evans, W. Behavior therapy and the therapist-patient relationship. *Journal of Consulting and Clinical Psychology*, 1968, **32**, 103-109.

Wisocki, P., & Cautela, J. Session checklist (homosexual clients). Unpublished manuscript, Boston College, Chestnut Hill, Massachusetts. 1968.

Wolpe, J. Isolation of a conditioning procedure as the crucial psychotherapeutic factor: A case study. *Journal of Nervous and Mental Diseases*, 1962, **134**, 316-329.

Wolpe, J., & Lang, P. A fear survey schedule for use in behavior therapy. *Behaviour Research and Therapy*, 1964, **2**, 27-30.

Wolpe, J., & Lazarus, A. *Behavior therapy techniques*. New York: Macmillan (Pergamon), 1966.

Making Use of Modeling in the Therapeutic Interview[1]

Leonard P. Ullmann

UNIVERSITY OF ILLINOIS

I am frequently asked, usually in an accusatory tone, "Why don't you behaviorists make use of work like Bandura's on modeling?" By "accusatory" I mean that many people act as if modeling is something antithetical to and outside of behavior modification. This is most certainly not the case and such a concept does not do justice to Bandura who is one of the prime authors in the field. One of the major concerns of this article is to counteract this notion and to have the opportunity for stating that Bandura's work on modeling is itself a model for behavior therapists. Here I shall indicate how behaviorists can and do use this corpus of data in clinical work with adult outpatients. A more general purpose of this paper, then, is to indicate how a behavioral technique may be systematically used within the structure of a seemingly traditional "talking" interaction.

Bandura (1965), Kanfer (1965), Berger (1962), and their co-workers developed in the first part of the 1960's a strong body of experimental evidence that information about how other people responded to situations altered the behavior of the recipients of that information. More recently Bandura (1968) and his colleagues (Bandura, Blanchard, & Ritter, 1968; Bandura, Grusec, & Menlove, 1967) have demonstrated the use of a modeling procedure in the amelioration of specific undesirable avoidance responses in both children and adults.

In modeling, the situation is one in which a person is provided with information about potential responses to a situation. While the current reaction against the portrayal of violence in mass media is welcome, it

[1]This work was supported in part by Public Health Service Grant MH 11938.

seems to me that the goal should not be a reduction of violence *per se*, but an increase in the portrayal (modeling) of nonviolent, prosocial, effective responses to situations to which the response of violence is now made. Too often, as in TV Westerns, it seems that violence is the only possible and proper response. What is needed are more instances of nonviolent responses to situations as proper behavior with favorable consequences.

At a later time, the person's behavior is more like that of the model than if he had not observed it. The effectiveness of modeling may be formulated in line with vicarious extinction, in the manner Bandura (1968) has admirably spelled out. I think that a difference between Bandura and myself is in the degree to which we follow a Pavlovian or Skinnerian model, although both of us make use of both models. It seems to me that Bandura's client is more passive and the focus is on his emotional responses; my view is one in which the client emits behavior that is reinforced. I think that this is in line with my view of modeling as prompting. A quotation from Bandura is presented to give the reader some more direct basis for comparison: "It has been shown in studies of vicarious emotional conditioning (Bandura & Rosenthal, 1966; Berger, 1962) that negative affective expressions by models can serve as powerful arousal cues for observers. One would expect modeled approach responses accompanied by positive affective expressions to engender less anxiety arousal and hence, faster extinction, than if the model manifested fearful reactions while performing the same behavior . . . Repeated modeling of approach responses decreases the arousal potential of aversive stimuli below the threshold for activating avoidance responses, thus enabling persons to engage, albeit somewhat anxiously, in approach behavior. The favorable outcomes resulting from direct contact with threatening events further extinguish any residual anxiety and avoidance tendencies . . . After approach behavior toward formerly avoided objects has been fully restored the resultant new experiences give rise to substantial reorganization of attitudes" (Bandura, 1968).

While agreeing that vicarious extinction is involved, I think that operant concepts of prompting and fading have a major role in the procedure. A crucial piece of work was accomplished by Baer and his colleagues (Baer, Peterson, & Sherman, 1967) who taught retardates how to imitate and who demonstrated how imitating may become a functional response class. That is, imitation may be developed by prompting the individual to do what the experimenter has done and fading the prompt until the person repeats without additional prompting what he has observed the teacher do. Reinforcement of imitative responses to some stimuli will maintain imitative responses to other stimuli even if these latter responses have not been reinforced. Metz (1965) and Lovaas, Berberich, Perloff, and Schaeffer (1966) have replicated the teaching of imitative responses with schizophrenic children and Risley and Wolf (1967) have applied prompting and fading techniques in a brilliant manner to echolalic speech. In summary, whether called modeling, imitation, vicarious reinforcement, or observational learning, there is a teachable skill that may be used to alter behavior and that has been shown to be effective in experiments conducted in the laboratory and clinic. The questions then become *what* behaviors should be modeled, i.e., selection of a behavior, and *how* modeling may be used, that is, guidelines for application.

The object of therapy is an increase of behavior that is variously called appropriate, normal, effective, or prosocial. When the behavior is in response to situations that the therapist can control or reconstruct in his office or institution, the procedures outlined by Bandura may be used with little modification. I am thinking here in particular of situations that are associated with unpleasant arousal and avoidance responses. In some situations, avoidance responses may be due to failure to acquire operant responses necessary for success in the situation. Here too, modeling, or prompting and fading, has been successfully used. While a behaviorist makes every effort to reduce his objectives to responses in limited, specific situations, there are occasions, especially with intelligent adult outpatients such as college students, when realistic or moral considerations make direct modeling within the therapy situation impossible. In many cases of this type, the person's own responses serve as stimuli for further responses. One of the major sources of stimuli in a person's environment is composed of his own behavior. The person may be said to observe his own behavior; he has information about that model (himself) and consequences to that model in prior similar situations; and finally he may be said to be influenced by what he has observed. If the consequences to the model, in this case himself, were favorable, it is likely that he will repeat what that model did. At this point the concept of modeling is so large as to subsume nearly all learning and hence becomes less useful. It seems, however, not logical to limit modeling stimuli to those external to the learning organism. I think this is an important aspect of behavior. It is one which Albert Ellis (1962) has dealt with more than any other psychotherapist. I also think it is one in which the modeling-during-interview approach has definite value.

In selecting a behavior to model, the therapist will do well to remember Hobart Mowrer's (1966, p. 451) penetrating comments on the subject. Mowrer points out "... a quite remarkable pedagogical paradox: the *therapist never does what he expects the patient to do!*"

Mowrer (1966) suggests the therapist exhibit to the patient a radical honesty and openness about his own life. In those cases where the therapist's evaluative procedures lead him to consider this a crucial behavior for the counselee, this procedure should be used. If what follows in this paper is correct, the therapist should go slowly in the intensity of the materials he reveals lest he move so rapidly the client cannot and does not follow the lead (prompt, model) provided him. Too rapid or unexpected deviation from the therapist pattern the client expects may upset him in the same way that the novelty of new approaches, including Mowrer's, tends to upset traditional therapists. Another reason for the suggestion of a progressive but conservative approach to openness is that the object is a set of behaviors that will serve the counselee in extratherapy situations. Just as the therapist must be careful not to move too fast, so the plan should be that the client emits behaviors that will be acceptable and hence increased and maintained. Too rapid a change to radical honesty in extratherapy situations may distress significant others. In this case, the modeling of the therapist may be as disturbing to other people as the novice in psychoanalytic therapy who interprets the acts of all his friends.

The object is to have the person make different and more effective responses to situations. The therapist may consider himself an expert in the control of behavior, but more accurately he is a person who teaches others what to do to control their own behavior. The task is to teach others to be their own therapists. This, by definition is a behavior a therapist can and does model.

This is what Goldiamond (1965) called self-control. The client is taught to make functional analyses of his own behavior, to control the stimuli in his own environment by altered behaviors. Another way of making this point is that if there is no difference between normal and abnormal behavior, the training of therapists follows the same principles as the training of patients (Ullmann, 1967b). Goldiamond (1965, p. 854) writes, "Initially *E* is the consultant, and eventually *S* becomes his own *E*." Having selected the goal, the next question is one of what things can be done to help the client attain this goal. What can be done to help the person become his own consultant?

The therapist will model the new behavior. An important point which can not be overemphasized is that a therapist does not start by exposing the final and perfect performance. Two important concepts are that he shapes toward the goal and that he fades his prompts. In his clinical work, Bandura has shown that the model gradually increases his proximity and degree of interaction with the previously difficult situation. If the model acts in a manner too far ahead of the subject's readiness, the situation is not unlike that of withholding reinforcement in a shaping procedure until the subject has made a major step forward. With nursery school children, if the model moves too quickly, the children may cry and look away. Second, if modeling is a form of prompting, then a crucial point is that over time, the prompt be faded so that the subject responds to the cues in the situation and the therapist changes his role to reinforcing or providing feedback for the acts emitted. The shift is demonstrated in work with mothers as therapists (Hawkins, Peterson, Schweid, & Bijou, 1966; Rickard & Mundy, 1965; Wahler, Winkel, Peterson, & Morrison, 1965).

A third point about technique is that what maintains the performance is the consequence of the behavior. The target situation is the world outside therapy; a new, more favorable reaction to the person's behavior should foster increased emission of the altered behavior. In the treatment situation, the therapist will seek information about favorable events as much as he will seek information about difficulties. He will respond with pleasure to reports of new behavior he considers appropriate and, a matter of equal importance which is frequently overlooked, he will focus the client's attention on what he did differently and what was different in the situation.

One of the major differences in practice between behavior therapists and evocative therapists is that the behavior therapist asks *what* rather than *why* questions. Having the client investigate situations for the stimuli that lead to disturbing responses is already a behavior different from making the disturbing responses to the situation. The therapist by asking *what* questions models a new response. He encourages the subject to ask himself these questions when in the actual situation.

Taking a hint from Kelly (1955), I ask students to make believe they are social anthropologists, or to use a loaded term, participant observers. As Franz Boaz or Margaret Mead among the Illini, they are asked to find out what people do in target situations, that is, what are the acts of normal models. As soon as possible, they are to write such material down. The new response is at minimum a focus on the actualities of the situation, rather than a focus on their presumed inadequacies or their unwanted physiological states. One may also view the imposition of the new, assigned task as a matter of increasing the length of the chain from previously disturbing stimulus to responses that are unprofitable and unwanted. Another aspect of this procedure returns to Hollingworth's (1930) concept of redintegration which may subsume respondent conditioning as the basis for avoidant or other maladaptive responses. In redintegration, the person responds to one aspect of a situation as if the total situation in which it had been embedded is present. The person has misidentified situations and investigation of the actual, current stimuli, especially in a matter-of fact manner, leads to emission of an alternative response on the one hand, and, on the other, to extinction (situation without visceral, unwanted response).

Having identified aspects of the situation, the therapist may question on possible alternative courses of action. This may be in terms of what responses the client has made, what responses he has seen others make, what responses he might consider making. The therapist may question to determine what conditions work against potential appropriate responses, or he may offer suggestions, first as to possible courses of action and then as to cues the person may provide himself in taking such actions. By such procedures, the therapist shows how a person can make a functional analysis of a situation. I think personal experiences of this sort should precede rather than follow more general academic training in the theory; however, it is a researchable question whether it is more effective for theory or personal experience to come first. Attention should be directed to what was effective and what can be done to repeat successes in the future and in increasingly different, broader situations.

If all goes well, fading enters. Questions asked by the therapist change from what was the situation to what did the person say to himself in the situation to what did he do in the situation.

In circumstances where the target behavior is the increase of an operant rather than reduction of an avoidance response and its correlated respondents, this procedure may be of particular value. To the extent that emission of an effective operant is one of the most important ways of reducing avoidance behavior in social situations, such prompting and fading, by questions and by other teaching procedures such as roleplaying, may be a useful adjunct to other techniques such as systematic desensitization.

In the teaching of relaxation, it may be very useful for the therapist to model each of the exercises: This lets the client know what will be asked of him and how to perform the act. The therapist may do well, especially where there are alternative possible exercises, to ask the subject to try the exercise and choose the one which gives him the greater feedback. On the one hand, this is a matter of selecting the most effective technique; on the other hand, the person is already engaging in the activity and thus is more likely to comply with suggestions later and obtain a deeper level of relaxation. That is, the procedure is a first step in the shaping of the relaxation response. Finally, some people, especially women, are reluctant to engage in behaviors such as nose-wrinkling. The therapist's having done so may indicate that such activity is not destructive of dignity.

This paper has brought together material from modeling, operant, respondent, and rational-emotive techniques. Shaping new responses by prompting and fading of prompts can be and is used widely in interview techniques. All the methods of teaching and social influence are potentially techniques of behavior therapy. The analysis of the techniques may also lead to a clarification of distinctions between evocative and behavioral therapies. At a more general level, teaching the person to be his own therapist and to control his own behavior is in keeping with the view that there is no distinction between normal and abnormal behavior (Ullmann, 1967a, 1969; Ullmann & Krasner, 1969). There is an increasing respect for the individual which is heightened rather than decreased by an increasing effectiveness of treatment.

References

Baer, D. M., Peterson, R. F., & Sherman, J. A. The development of imitation by reinforcing behavioral similarity to a model. *Journal of the Experimental Analysis of Behavior*, 1967, **10**, 405–416.

Bandura, A. Behavioral modification through modeling procedures. In L. Krasner & L. P. Ullmann (eds.), *Research in behavior modification.* New York: Holt, Rinehart & Winston, 1965.

Bandura, A. Modeling approaches to the modification of phobic disorders. In *Ciba Foundation symposium: The role of learning in psychotherapy.* London: Churchill, 1968.

Bandura, A., Blanchard, E. D., & Ritter, B. J. The relative efficacy of desensitization and modeling therapeutic approaches for inducing behavioral, affective and attitudinal changes. Unpublished manuscript, Stanford University, 1968.

Bandura, A., Grusec, J. E., & Menlove, F. L. Vicarious extinction of avoidance behavior. *Journal of Personality and Social Psychology*, 1967, **5**, 16–23.

Bandura, A., & Rosenthal, T. L. Vicarious classical conditioning as a function of arousal level. *Journal of Personality and Social Psychology*, 1966, **3**, 54–62.

Berger, S. M. Conditioning through vicarious instigation. *Psychological Review*, 1962, **69**, 450–466.

Ellis, A. *Reason and emotion in psychotherapy.* New York: Lyle Stuart, 1962.

Goldiamond, I. Self-control procedures in personal behavior problems. *Psychological Reports*, 1965, **17**, 851–868.

Hawkins, R. P., Peterson, R. F., Schweid, E., & Bijou, S. W. Behavior therapy in the home: Amelioration of problem parent-child relations with the parent in a therapeutic role. *Journal of Experimental Child Psychology*, 1966, **4**, 99–107.

Hollingworth, H. L., *Abnormal psychology,* New York: Ronald, 1930.

Kanfer, F. H. Vicarious human reinforcements: A glimpse into the black box. In L. Krasner & L. P. Ullmann (Eds.), *Research in behavior modification.* New York: Holt, Rinehart & Winston, 1965.

Kelly, G. A. *The psychology of personal constructs.* New York: Norton, 1955.

Lovaas, O. I., Berberich, J. P., Perloff, B. F., & Schaeffer, B. Acquisition of imitative speech by schizophrenic children. *Science,* 1966, **151**, 705-707.

Metz, J. R. Conditioning generalized imitation in autistic children. *Journal of Experimental Child Psychology,* 1965, **2**, 389-399.

Mowrer, O. H. The behavior therapies with special reference to modeling and imitation. *American Journal of Psychotherapy,* 1966, **20**, 439-461.

Rickard, H. C., & Mundy, M. B. Direct manipulation of stuttering behavior: An experimental-clinical approach. In L. P. Ullmann & L. Krasner (Eds.), *Case studies in behavior modification.* New York: Holt, Rinehart & Winston, 1965.

Risley, T., & Wolf, M. Establishing functional speech in echolalic children. *Behaviour Research and Therapy,* 1967, **5**, 73-88.

Ullmann, L. P. Abnormal psychology without anxiety. Paper presented at the meeting of the Western Psychological Association, San Francisco, Apr., 1967. (a)

Ullmann, L. P. The major concepts taught to behavior therapy trainees. Paper presented at the meeting of the American Psychological Association, Washington, D.C., Sept., 1967. (b)

Ullmann, L. P. Behavior therapy as social movement. In C. M. Franks (Ed.), *Assessment and status of the behavior therapies and associated developments.* New York: McGraw-Hill, 1969.

Ullmann, L. P., & Krasner, L. *A psychological approach to abnormal behavior.* Englewood Cliffs. N. J.: Prentice-Hall, 1969.

Wahler, R. G., Winkel, G. H., Peterson, R. F., & Morrison, D. C. Mothers as behavior therapists for their own children. *Behaviour Research and Therapy,* 1965, **3**, 113-124.

The Teaching of Behavior Modification in an Interdisciplinary Setting

Ernest G. Poser

DOUGLAS HOSPITAL
AND
MC GILL UNIVERSITY

Familiarity with techniques of behavior modification derived from learning principles is rapidly becoming *de rigueur* for clinical psychologists. This trend is now quite evident from the increasing space allotted to behavior therapy in clinical journals and the time devoted to that topic at conferences such as this. Also a recent survey of 74 Directors of Clinical Training and Chairmen of Psychology Departments revealed that 50% plan to increase course work or practicum training in behavior therapy and 90% expressed the opinion that well-trained behavior therapists will be able to find jobs.

On the other hand, the same survey showed that in most clinical training programs no more than one course or seminar is presently offered on the practice of clinical psychology from an experimental-behavioral-learning point of view, though 86% of the respondents felt that the growing popularity of that orientation was a desirable development for the field.

If these figures are representative, they suggest at least two conclusions. One, that there is a shortage of suitably qualified teaching staff for this area of specialization and two, that a lag exists between what clinical psychologists are being taught and what they are expected to do professionally.

Of these two problems, the second is by far the greater. It also has a long history as eminent psychotherapists like Carl Rogers and Albert

Ellis have been at pains to point out. Ever since World War II, little has been added to the traditional training program in clinical psychology to produce more competent psychotherapists. Hence it is not surprising that current emphasis on the use of nonprofessional psychotherapists is taken by some as an indictment of prevailing methods of professional training.

There are several reasons why the training of behavior therapists can and should avoid the pitfalls encountered by earlier schools of therapy. First, the theories and techniques germane to behavior therapy, based as they are on experimental studies of learning, are much more closely related to the mainstream of academic psychology than are those of dynamic psychotherapy. This important difference not only helps to integrate training in therapy with much subject matter already familiar to the student from his undergraduate course work, but also provides the budding clinician with a source of data unique to his discipline.

Secondly, attempts at behavior modification are typically preceded by an experimental analysis of the behavior to be modified which makes it easier to assess the outcome of treatment. This, and the fact that behavior therapy presents an open-ended system, both theoretically and methodologically, permit the activities of behavior therapists to be viewed in the context of research which is, after all, the focus of most doctoral training programs. It follows from this that behavior therapy is likely to narrow the gulf currently separating clinical and experimental psychology.

Lastly, behavior therapy, unlike traditional psychotherapy, is evolving techniques and instrumentation which can be applied by cotherapist technicians, parents, or even the patient himself. Not only does this greatly increase the scope of available treatment services but it also makes more urgent the establishment of training facilities for technicians who will work under the supervision of professionals. Hopefully, such a development would reverse the unfortunate present trend for professionals to become either researchers or practitioners. Instead we might expect to see a closer approximation to the scientist-professional type clinician envisaged ever since the Boulder conference. A dichotomy, based on the nature and intensity of training rather than on functional preferences of the graduate, would appear to be more economical and consistent with prevailing academic policy. There seems to be little justification for imposing the same kind and amount of training on candidates with very different professional aspirations.

The unifying effect behavior therapy is having at the intradisciplinary level has its counterpart at the interdisciplinary one. Perhaps for the first time in the history of the mental health professions, psychologists and psychiatrists have jointly elaborated treatment methods in which the experimental know-how of the behavioral scientist is combined with the clinical insights of the practitioner. From the start, this development was unlike that of psychoanalysis, client-centered therapy, or other theoretical contributions made by single individuals whose name typically became attached to the technique of therapy they developed.

Behavior therapy by contrast owes its substance, and indeed its name, to a number of innovators representing various disciplines from every corner of the globe.

The interdisciplinary heritage of the behavior therapies has already had a very salutary influence on the relationship between clinical psychologists and psychiatrists in many settings.

Douglas Hospital, a 1600-bed psychiatric institution affiliated with McGill University, is a case in point. A small behavior therapy unit was established there in 1966 for the primary purpose of providing an interdisciplinary setting in which all forms of behavior modification might be taught. The 13-bed unit is staffed by six nurses, four psychologists, a psychiatric resident, and a part-time social worker. Referrals are received from any service within the hospital or from other hospitals and agencies in the community. Limited out-patient services are also provided.

Admissions to and discharges or transfers from the unit are at the discretion of the psychologists in charge who also direct the treatment program for all patients. In administrative matters, such as staff appointments, budgetary appropriations, and space requirements, the director of the unit reports to the hospital's executive director or his deputy.

The psychiatric resident is in charge of the patient's physical welfare, medication, and any physical treatments that may be required. For this aspect of his work, he is responsible to the Regional Chief of Medical Services and through him to the Clinical Director of the Hospital. The resident, however, also receives training in behavior therapy and in this regard is supervised by one of the senior psychologists in the unit.

I have described the organizational hierarchy of this clinical teaching facility in some detail because it seems to me basic to the smooth operation of such an enterprise. The underlying principle is that authority is vested in whoever happens to have the most appropriate training and experience for the functions required. Thus the nurse is responsible for the day-to-day care of patients and the "housekeeping" of the ward, the physician looks after the patients' physical needs, while the overall direction of the behavioral treatment program is the psychologists' concern.

For many psychologists, this is a novel experience. Particularly those who came from traditional settings, where they were doing diagnostic appraisals or therapy without ever being placed in charge of patients, find the new approach challenging and at times a little disturbing.

It is plainly unsound to expect a professional person to accept even limited responsibility for a patient without also giving him authority to act on the outcome of his efforts, be they diagnostic or therapeutic. Yet this is precisely what has been and still is the case in many hospital psychology departments where psychologists, often highly trained, churn out test reports or do psychotherapy with patients over whose daily management and ultimate disposal they have no control whatever.

No one would deny that psychologists cannot take medical responsibility for patients. It should be equally evident that only trained behavior therapists should accept responsibility for the practice and teaching of that specialty. The time has come when members of allied professions, notably psychiatrists, seem ready to accept this principle as long as their domain, i.e., the assumption of medical responsibility for patients, is not violated. To guard this principle in the day-to-day operation of an interdisciplinary teaching unit is not without its difficulties. Yet, unless the general notion of division of labor and authority according to competence rather than tradition or status is more commonly recognized, it seems unlikely that the exciting prospects of this new approach to treatment will develop to their fullest potential. That is why every effort should be made to stress the interdisciplinary nature of this enterprise from the time a student first presents himself for training. It is not enough to pay lip service to the importance of interprofessional relations in our graduate schools without making sure that trainees experience the interdisciplinary learning situation in the course of their daily clinical activities.

For this reason, all personnel in our unit are involved in some phase of behavior therapy. Those with professional training and experience are expected to implement therapeutic strategies elaborated for each new patient at a weekly conference attended by all staff members. Less experienced personnel, nurses and trainees, are assigned to cases as cotherapists. They understudy the senior therapist and carry out certain procedures such as relaxation, desensitization, aversive conditioning, and operant schedules under supervision. We have found this system to provide gratifying results in terms of diversity and efficiency of training.

Formal teaching for nurses, psychiatric residents, postgraduate and postdoctoral students in clinical psychology is provided at three levels.

At the beginning of each academic year, a series of introductory lectures is given on the psychology of learning as it applies to the development of maladaptive behavior. Because the specialized vocabulary of experimental and clinical psychology often presents difficulty to students from other disciplines, they are advised to acquaint themselves with certain prerequisite reading prior to each lecture. Whenever possible, clinical case material is used to clarify the application of basic concepts such as reciprocal inhibition, counterconditioning, or reinforcement contingencies. We have also found it useful at this stage to show films and video tapes of earlier therapy sessions with patients still in the unit. In this way, trainees have an opportunity to judge for themselves the merits and limitations of various treatment procedures.

At the more advanced level, case study seminars are offered. These deal *in extenso* with the background, problem, treatment, and course of a particular patient still receiving treatment in the unit. Generally a trainee is asked to present the patient's history and to formulate the target problem at which treatment is to be aimed. At that point, each member of the seminar is invited to suggest an appropriate treatment strategy. Only then is the patient interviewed, mainly to give participants an opportunity to elicit whatever information they found lacking in the behavioral analysis of the problem as originally presented. Finally, the ongoing treatment program is described and discussed.

The third and perhaps most valuable training procedure takes the form of individual supervision while the trainee is in the process of doing therapy. Occasionally use is made of a one-way vision screen but more often the instructor is physically present in the treatment room.

Because the training situation is an interdisciplinary one, the informal learning experiences are particularly rewarding. This arises from the fact that a multidisciplinary setting also tends to be a multiorientational one. Most psychiatric residents have had considerable exposure to dynamic theory and analytically oriented practice. By contrast, the psychologist-trainees often come straight from the rigorous, well-controlled environment of the rat laboratory. Sharing an interest in the same patients provides an excellent opportunity for the clinicians to harness their speculations and for the erstwhile researchers to discover the degree to which their early therapeutic successes may be due to the "medical cellophane" conferred upon all who work in hospitals.[1]

No behavior-therapy teaching program would be complete without providing some research experience. In the Douglas Hospital Unit, facilities exist both for evaluational and psychophysiological studies relevant to behavior modification. All professional trainees participate in some project and here again collaboration between members of various disciplines has widened the scope of the research program. One study now in progress dealing with the role of state specific learning in the aversion treatment of alcoholics would have been quite impossible to do without the assistance of medically trained colleagues.

Throughout the six months training program with which we are currently experimenting, stress is laid upon the "unfinished" nature of the behavior therapies. In that sense we agree wholeheartedly with an observation recently made by an interdisciplinary team of authors, Drs. Hunt and Dyrad, when they say that, "despite the scientific coloring of its rhetoric, behavior therapy is still largely an art form." In their excellent commentary published in the Proceedings of the Third APA Conference on Research in Psychotherapy they describe, better than I could, the purpose of behavior therapy and its place in the contemporary scene. I should like to quote from their statement because it seems to me to express both the need and justification for keeping the behavior-therapy enterprise within the interdisciplinary arena. This is what they say: "Radical descriptive behaviorism then as compared with other views is not an attempt to contain man within its language nor to deny that other languages have validity, but is simply ordering the data of observation a different way to see if they can be made easier to manage."

Reference

Hunt, H. F. & Dyrad, J. E., Commentary: Perspectives in Behavior Therapy. *In* J. N. Shlier & H. F. Hunt (Eds.), *Research in Psychology*, Vol. III. Washington, D.C.: American Psychological Association, pp. 140–152.

[1]For this coinage I am indebted to Professor Sir Denis Hill of the Institute of Psychiatry, London, who used it to describe the anxiety reduction often experienced by psychiatric patients merely as a result of hospitalization.

The Content of Behavior-Therapy Training

Arnold A. Lazarus

TEMPLE UNIVERSITY
AND
EASTERN PENNSYLVANIA PSYCHIATRIC INSTITUTE

Is a behavior therapist best trained as a physician, a psychologist, a social worker, a minister of religion — all of these or none of these? Is it necessary for him to be well-versed in research methodology, learning theory, the history and philosophy of science, experimental psychology, and neurophysiology? Should he be familiar with traditional psychodynamic theory and practice? I have pondered over these questions ever since entering graduate school.

Five years ago, I concluded that it is not essential to have a thorough knowledge of the principles of learning in order to function as a competent behavior therapist. At that time, I was assigned the pleasant task of providing a year's intensive training for ten bright graduate students at Stanford University. Certainly, in that particular sample, therapeutic competence was unrelated to academic achievement. I came to see very clearly that intellectual and theoretical brilliance failed to prevent many individuals from committing serious clinical blunders. These impressions have subsequently been confirmed with different behavior-therapy trainees in several different settings.

Allied to the above is the question: At this stage of my career, what will make *me* a better behavior therapist? Should I take a course in cybernetics, or information processing models, or try to become really well-informed about the neurophysiology of learning? Would any of this knowledge assist me in helping the anxious, the depressed, or other tormented people who consult me? Or, as I believe, would my patients be better served if I took courses in drama and method acting to assist me with techniques like behavior rehearsal and assertive training?

I have had occasion to train a diverse range of professionals and nonprofessionals in behavior-therapy practices. They include newly qualified doctors, veteran physicians, experienced and inexperienced psychiatrists, psychologists, and social workers. I have trained nurses, teachers, graduate students, and ex-psychoanalysts. All this has led to the crystallization of certain impressions about whom to train, what to teach them, and how to go about it.

Postgraduates generally fare better than undergraduates, not because they acquire useful information during their courses or are necessarily brighter, but because they tend to have better reinforcement leverage in this status-conscious society. Furthermore, the holders of M.D.'s and Ph.D.'s usually have a fairly high level of endurance and a capacity to withstand monotony—two essential ingredients for any would-be fulltime behavior therapist! The best trainees, regardless of their backgrounds, were people who displayed kindness, tolerance, generosity, and compassion. Above all, those who were able to communicate a genuine desire to be of service were generally the most successful—as indicated by fewer patient drop-outs and more rapid therapeutic effect in areas which could be confirmed by outsiders. Regardless of intellectual abilities and technical skills, the worst trainees tended to be petty individuals, somewhat paranoid and self-opinionated, with a fondness for theories and a distaste for gaining proficiency at a wide range of specific techniques.

On the assumption that all trainees can read, the most efficient use of training time is to devote attention to those methods and procedures that cannot be acquired from books. It is useful for trainees to observe several behavior therapists in action and to participate as cotherapists in both individual and group sessions. But even after a year's intensive apprenticeship of this kind, the trainee can cover but a small fraction of the many possible clinical encounters and diverse maladaptive behaviors with which he is likely to be confronted. The use of *behavior rehearsal* as a training procedure is a most useful means of preparing the trainee to cope with an extremely wide range of likely and unlikely (but possible) therapeutic situations.

Typically, two or three trainees observe me playing the role of various kinds of patients with various kinds of problems while one of the trainees acts the part of the therapist. These sessions are tape recorded. I may act the part of an extremely compliant and acquiescent patient or respond in a belligerent and defensive fashion. I may come on as critical and condemnatory, or test my trainee's ability to handle vague, confused, and nonspecific complaints, or portray a phobic patient with an underlying psychosis. After some 10 to 15 min., the other trainees are invited to comment on the overall performance. The recording is then played back and the strengths and weaknesses of the trainee's responses are underscored. I might demonstrate what I regard as better ways of handling specific points of emphasis, with one of the trainees in the patient's role. In this manner, one can pitch many tricky clinical curves and thus reduce the probability that novice therapists will be caught unprepared to cope with difficult patients.

Careful reading combined with precise clinical demonstrations and a measure of practice enables most behavior-therapy trainees to become reasonably skilled at administering the various methods and techniques. It is much more difficult to teach people how to extract the crucial and relevant problem areas from the disjointed and somewhat nebulous material that many patients present, and thereafter to select the appropriate combination of techniques needed to quell the patient's discontent. The bulk of behavior-therapy training should therefore be focused on these two central aspects—problem identification and the selection of appropriate techniques. Above all, one has to acquire the ability to ferret out the primary areas and dimensions of patients' deviant behaviors. A claustrophobic patient may be suffering from no more than a fear of stuffy and constricted situations, in which case a course of desensitization may be the treatment of choice. But there is little point in desensitizing a claustrophobic patient to space constriction if his basic anxiety is a fear of death. There is still less point in desensitizing him if his claustrophobia is a product of his social ineptitude and personal timidity, resulting in avoidance behavior. Again, his claustrophobia might be one way of imposing limits on his spouse's range of movement as part of a dyadic marital impasse. Most behavior-therapy trainees have to be cautioned again and again not to take too many things at face value. In this connection, even the most experienced behavior therapists seem to require a refresher course from time to time.

Perhaps the best that can be said in favor of some varieties of academic training is that seemingly useless bits of information sometimes come in handy at the most unexpected times. Thus, my knowledge about an obscure African tribe, which I acquired during an undergraduate course in anthropology, was instrumental in facilitating rapport while treating a neurotic ethnologist.

Comprehensive sex education still remains sadly absent from most M.D. and Ph.D. training programs and yet is indispensible for anyone engaged in behavior-therapy practice. Trainees should be made familiar with the range of sexual deviates likely to end up in treatment as well as given a comprehensive knowledge of "normal" sex practices. It is necessary for a behavior therapist to acquire nonmoralistic insights into all matters pertaining to sex. Indeed, a nonpejorative outlook in general may be considered most essential.

Many trainees have found a personal course of behavior therapy extremely useful for many obvious reasons. I am becoming more inclined to the view that this feature is an important aspect of behavior-therapy training.

My presentation has dwelt on the training of efficient and effective behavior-therapy *practitioners*. Those who espouse the scientist-practitioner model will obviously call for somewhat different skills and points of emphasis. Similarly, the research-oriented (as distinct from service-oriented) behavior therapist will require much greater knowledge about scientific method, statistical procedures, and so forth. Broad spectrum behavior-therapy programs are urgently needed to disabuse those who have been misled into thinking that behavior-therapy skills can be culled from the writings of some individuals who, to paraphrase Perry London, believe that men leap from cliffs for the same reasons that animals salivate to bells. Hopefully, we will soon see the end of the do-it-yourself phase of behavior-therapy training and find more institutions eager to give behavior therapy a recognized place in their formal curriculum.

The Modification of Depressive Behaviors

Elaine P. Burgess

DRAKE UNIVERSITY

The treatment of depression with methods arising from the application of learning principles is remarkably absent from behavior-therapy literature. Ferster (1966) has described depression as a consequence of decreased reinforcement. Lazarus (1968) enumerated operational factors based on an S-R analysis which can account for depression, and more important, can designate implications for treatment. Basically, depression was viewed as the state of being in which a subject's response frequency or quality diminishes as a function of reduced reinforcement.

Lazarus suggested that reinforcing consequences maintain depressive behaviors; perhaps more attention should be paid to that aspect of depression. A broad class of active, task-oriented responses can be labeled a performing behavior class. Retarded motor-response rate, sad face and body appearances, and mournful verbalizations can be labeled a depressive behavior class. As the frequency of performing behaviors begins to diminish, the very absence of those behaviors becomes the occasion for reinforcement. Concurrent with the extinction of performing behaviors may be the conditioned acquisition of depressive behaviors. If this is the case, the client may not, in fact, be suffering from reinforcement deficiencies at the time he seeks treatment, for he obtains frequent reinforcements as a consequence to the emission of depressive behaviors. Individuals in the environment invite lengthy reiteration of his troubles, pay attention to his moods, attempt to "help" by performing tasks for him, and generally reorganize their behavior to accommodate his depressed state. Small wonder that the probability for response emission from a depressive behavior class exceeds that of a performing behavior class.

An analysis which assumes the progressive extinction of performing behaviors and acquisition of depressive behaviors must reverse contingencies for treatment. Reinforcement should be made contingent upon performing behaviors and extinction of depressive behaviors must be instituted. The general plan of treatment which I have been using to treat depression during the past year is based on that paradigm.

Six clients were treated in a traditional counseling setting; four were students between 19 and 22 years of age, one was a recent college graduate of 26, and one, at the Third Behavior Therapy Institute in Philadelphia in June, 1968, was a 40-year-old Ph.D. sociologist. All clients reported anxiety with respect to their inability to perform. Typical of depressed persons, the clients found the most simple tasks inordinately burdensome, had difficulty sleeping, noted a decrement in sexual response, failed to attend class or work, experienced diminished social activity and interactions, were given to long periods of morose ruminations concerned with their worthlessness, and had recently contemplated suicide.

General Treatment Plan

Initial Interviews

Only once, during the first interview, was the client allowed to verbalize his sad state of affairs. The history paid particular attention to the following areas: (*a*) enumeration of responses which were presently not being emitted, but which had formerly been in the client's repertoire, (*b*) assessment of the most potent client reinforcers and their current availability, (*c*) specification of the ways in which depressive behaviors were being maintained (reinforced), and (*d*) description of depression onset along with systematic investigation of any contiguous environmental changes.

Treatment Methods

If the history indicated the loss of a specific reinforcer which was available, or partially available, efforts to reinstate it were endeavored. If reinforcement losses were more generalized or nonspecific, the client was required from the first to emit a few performing behaviors which required minimal effort for successful completion.

Typically, depressed individuals undertake tasks which they fail to complete. The result is not only the loss of reinforcement for task completion, but also the occasion for anxiety arousal with respect to that failure. In addition, the interruption of a chain of responses is often reinforced by social attention. In order to achieve reinforcement for task completion it was important initially to select simple, easily executed performing behaviors for which the completion probability was high. The client's attention was drawn to the importance of successful completion, rather than to the nature or value of the task. Gradually task requirements were increased so that behaviors accelerated in frequency, duration, quality, and successively approximated former behaviors from the client's repertoire.

If available, a mate was taught to augment treatment by providing reinforcement specified according to prescribed contingencies. Clients were seen daily for the first week to maximize therapist reinforcing power, and with decreasing frequency as natural reinforcers began to be effective. Therapist attention and approval was used as a reinforcer during interviews which consisted of verbal or written reports concerned with activities or tasks endeavored and with planning the next behavior series. No time or attention was given to behaviors from a depressive class after the first interview. If possible, manipulations which decreased environmental reinforcement of depressive behaviors were instituted. It should be noted that techniques changed as a function of individual reinforcement histories, contingencies, and environmental components. The techniques described may not be important in their own right, or may not be applicable to other treatment situations, or both. The case reports which follow suggest, however, that methods based on the systematic implementation of an operant paradigm appear promising.

Reinforcement Reinstatement

Treatment began with an explanation of the client's depression in much the same fashion as has been presented above. Only one client, a bright, 19-year-old psychologist's son, took exception to this view of his dilemma on the philosophical ground that it was mechanistic. Owing to my own reluctance to insist on precise use of this new, experimental treatment method, I acquiesced and "went along" with his reinforcement contingency. Having been reared with interpretive material, he was able to supply "insights" which were as clever as those I could have provided. By careful manipulation of my reactions to his interpretations, it was possible to trick him into visiting the college and girl friend which he had abandoned at the time of depression onset. With the partial reinstatement of his valued acquaintances there and therapist reinforcement for current action-oriented behaviors combined with inattention to depressive behaviors, he began to evidence improvement. After three weeks, when he felt he was ready to discontinue treatment, the therapeutic plan and manipulations were revealed to him.

Therapy for two student cases was brief (four sessions) because reinstatement of past reinforcers was readily accomplished and the depressions disappeared. A bright, 21-year-old senior mathematics major sought treatment when he became concerned about persistent suicidal thoughts. Careful investigation of events surrounding the depression onset two months before led to the conclusion that he was without one of his prime reinforcers, self-satisfaction for academic pursuits. His history suggested consistent reinforcement during high school and college for sophisticated scientific endeavors. His recent marriage and the resulting shift of stimuli and reinforcers nearly masked the fact that for the first time he was unable to master theoretical concepts with facility. There was no one with whom he could discuss his difficulty due to the advanced and theoretical nature of the mathematics he was studying. Matters were further complicated because the professor had not tested or graded, which thus eliminated those standard reinforcers. The client was instructed to pick the brightest student in a class of 14 and to arrange to study and then socialize with him three nights a week. Two weeks later the client reported that: (*a*) It was a great relief to have someone with whom he could discuss mathematics, (*b*) the "brightest" student knew less than he about the material, and (*c*) he felt fine and was once more enthusiastic about the pursuit of a mathematics career.

The other client was an 18-year-old freshman who was attending college with financial assistance from Vocational Rehabilitation due to ulcerative colitis which he had suffered since age six. In addition to depression, he was aware of returning colitis symptoms. His history indicated a remarkable talent and motivation for money-making projects which he had undertaken since childhood. He not only took personal pride in his achievements but also valued the resulting financial gains. When he sought treatment he was not working, having been advised to use his time for study. Although he was not a bright fellow, his abilities exceeded his very poor scholastic performance. He was instructed to drop four of his sixteen hours and find part-time employment. Instructions were followed, except that he dropped only two hours. His scholastic performance improved measurably, but it was the excitement, challenge, and monetary rewards from a sales job which he reported with a glow of enthusiasm. The colitis symptoms disappeared along with the depression.

Contingency Management and Task Completion

The three remaining cases were not so quickly dealt with. A 26-year-old married Drake graduate described depression onset coincident with his first postgraduate employment, nine months prior to the initial interview. As a result of having overestimated his capabilities or having oversold himself to the firm, he needed considerable assistance in doing his work. He became increasingly less able to perform without help and tended to view this inability as his failure rather than as showing a need for structured training. Being an idealistic person, he found business practices at odds with his own ethics. At the time of the initial interview, he was acutely anxious with respect to his total failure to perform in any situation. Task planning began with easily accomplished behaviors such as making a telephone call, mowing the lawn, or drying dishes. These behaviors were praised by the therapist and became self-reinforcing when he felt satisfaction from having "done something." During interviews, he reported on the execution of tasks and planned successively more complicated activities such as job interviews, employment test taking, and vita writing. The client's wife was taught to reinforce completed performing behaviors with attention and praise, and to extinguish depressive behaviors by inattention. After two weeks the client reported that he felt "like a new man." His wife noted that he had initiated contact with friends and had written letters for the first time since their recent marriage. A crisis in her family caused the couple to move out of state before the behaviors were well established.

The sociologist who sought treatment at the Behavioral Science Department of the Eastern Pennsylvania Psychiatric Institute had undergone four and a half years of psychoanalysis. The presenting complaints were fears of student and family rejection, accompanied by pervasive anxiety. The client had recently lost his university position and was in the painful process of selling two properties preparatory to moving away. Assertive training was attempted but not pursued when the performance of those behaviors led to heightened anxiety. Task planning and reporting were then instituted for him while the co-therapist[1] instructed his wife with respect to the reinforcement and extinction of performing and depressive behaviors. Ultimately husband and wife were seen together once a week in an effort to effect, through practice, a modification of her habitually negative response style, and to alter the family's reinforcement of the client's depressive behaviors. Seen daily, the husband was required to perform increasing numbers of tasks beginning with receiving telephone calls, reading twenty textbook pages, and eating dinner with the family. Another required task was the keeping of a log which noted tasks performed, time spent, others' reactions, and anxiety level. (Anxiety level decreased following each task completion.)

A 22-year-old senior student reported that his general depressed state worsened when a girl in whom he was interested showed signs of involvement with another male. The young man was taught operant conditioning methods to assist him in strengthening the few remaining responses made toward him by the girl. When this proved ineffective, it was suggested that he date another girl. He was able to do so only because the intent was purported to provide the first girl with a modeling paradigm which might serve to change her view of the client. The maneuver was actually calculated to provide a reinforcer whose stimulus elements could approximate the first girl. No one was available from this student's surroundings to provide reinforcement for his performed behaviors. The reverse was the case; he received attention by reiterating troubles to his friends. It was necessary to require him to stay home and talk to no one unless he could assure the therapist that he engaged only in positive communications. These manipulations combined with graduated "car-fixing responses," which accomplished the eventual rehabilitation of his ailing sports car, resulted in the stable establishment of performing behaviors that proved resistant to the grim threat of impending draft following his graduation.

Particular care was taken to summarize the course of treatment for each patient; the purpose was to provide him with self-help, should he begin to feel depressed at some later time.

Follow-up indicated that the Drake graduate experienced a setback two months later. The sociologist was continuing with treatment a month later; reports stated that his performing behaviors had risen to an acceptable level and that desensitization of stimuli which evoked high anxiety had been added to the treatment program. Six to nine months after treatment the other four clients remained symptom free.

[1]Leonce Boudreau, Hospital St. Charles DeJoliette, Joliette, Quebec, Canada.

Conclusions

Contingency management, which promotes reinforcement for the completion of performing behaviors and extinction of depressive behaviors, seems to be effective for the treatment of depression when reinstatement of a reinforcer cannot be accomplished. All clients were able to perform in their life situation with at least passable facility within three weeks of treatment inauguration.

It will be noticed that no assertive training was employed. (This does *not* suggest that other methods should not be instituted in addition to contingency management and task completion, however.) The emergence of more assertive behaviors was noticed by the therapist as clients began to improve, in spite of the fact that no training had been endeavored. The lovelorn student came in one day waving his finger aggressively at the therapist, inquiring whether she was using additional techniques on him of which he was unaware. He then told of an incident in which he had behaved in an uncharacteristic and forceful fashion.

Another noteworthy aspect of treatment came to light when the therapist was forced to miss appointments due to an illness in her family. A colleague was quickly appraised of which behaviors to reinforce and which to extinguish; the transition from one therapist to another and back again was made with ease. A similar transition was equally effective for the sociologist when therapist transfer was necessary for his continued treatment. The "behavioral prescription" is easily written or communicated. Treatment success does not seem to depend upon the relationship between client and therapist.

Case reports, however, are not adequate to establish the efficacy of any treatment method. The need for controlled research is obvious.

References

Ferster, C. B. Animal behavior and mental illness. *Psychological Record*, 1966, **16**, 345-356.

Lazarus, A. A. Learning theory and the treatment of depression. *Behaviour Research and Therapy*, 1968, **6**, 83-89.

The Use of Dual Reinforcement in an Intensive Treatment System[1]

John D. Henderson

SPRUCE HOUSE, HORIZON HOUSE, INC.

The program described here is conducted within Spruce House, a community-based behavioral facility for emotionally disturbed men, operated under a token economy, which is described elsewhere (Henderson & Scoles, 1968; Scoles & Henderson, 1968; Henderson, 1968).

Because of its physical layout and small staff, the facility is particularly ill equipped to handle provocative, abusive, or bizarre patients. Acting-out behavior cannot be extinguished by ignoring it, since patients can enter unsupervised areas of the facility, break out, assault other patients, or damage the physical plant. Social reinforcement resulting from staff attention is inevitable when staff members must respond to hazardous behavior; such reinforcement usually results in an increase in the frequency and intensity of acting-out behavior.

Various special programs involving reinforcement of behaviors incompatible with acting-out, systems of fines for acting-out, and time-out programs have not been sufficiently speedy or powerful in dealing with provocative subjects.

In an attempt to modify the behavior of acting-out or unresponsive subjects, an intensive dual operant program was developed with the aim of enabling quick promotion of the subjects into the regular vocational programs of the facility. Dual reinforcement, attaching simulta-

[1]The program described in this paper is wholly supported by National Institutes of Mental Health Grant R11 NHO 2143, under a project entitled "Preventing Chronicity: a Study of Three Alternatives," Irvin D. Rutman, Project Director.

neously to the suppression of undesired behaviors and to the development of desired behaviors incompatible with the undesired ones, was employed because it was expected to be quickly effective.

Method

Subjects

The facility admits psychotic men, aged 18 to 55, excluding those who are known to be assaultive, suicidal, addicted to narcotics or alcohol, etc. Subjects who, after admission, are found to be acting-out or unresponsive to the regular programs of the facility are assigned to the Social Adjustment Laboratory. No more than three subjects are assigned to the laboratory at one time.

Apparatus

The Social Adjustment Laboratory (SAL) is a room measuring approximately 14 × 21 ft; three walls of the room are lined with work tables. Along the east wall are an entry door and an L-shaped counter which serves as a barrier between the staff member (called "SAL counselor") in charge and the subjects. Beyond the L-shaped counter is a second door which communicates with a tool room and office. There is a one-way mirror adjacent to the counter.

Midway along the east wall of the room is a panel of twelve electric clocks, three rows of four clocks each. Each row of clocks is identified by the name of the subject whose behavior is recorded by that row of clocks. From the subject's left to right his four clocks are labeled, "Bad Talk," "Good Talk," "Bad Action," "Good Work." Each "good" clock has a green background and a green indicator light; each "bad" clock has a red background and a red indicator light. An indicator is lighted when the corresponding clock is running.

A subject's four clocks are controlled by two single pole, triple throw switches; one switch for verbal behavior and the other for motor behavior. The switch positions are labeled V−, V+, and M−, M+, referring to undesired (negative) and desired (positive) verbal and motor behaviors. The six switches are mounted on a small box which can be held in the hand and is connected to the clock panel by a cord approximately 8 ft long which provides the SAL counselor with mobility both inside and outside of the laboratory. The clocks are rezeroed manually.

Work materials provided in the SAL include a printing press, materials and equipment for making signs, some woodworking equipment.

Work tasks include soap packaging, sign making, splicing of recording tape, construction of file boxes, pencil holders, toys, etc. When the laboratory has an assaultive subject assigned to it, only nonhazardous tools and materials are used.

On the south wall of the laboratory is a large chart upon which each person's earnings are portrayed once a day.

Procedures

Assignment to the Social Adjustment Laboratory is determined by the staff on the basis of problematic behavior or unresponsiveness to the regular vocational, instructional, social, and special programs conducted within the facility. Such assignments are ordinarily made during weekly staff meetings, but may be made as subjects' behavior requires.

For purposes of the SAL, symptom-defining behaviors such as abusive talk or action, provocative talk or action, bizarre (or delusional) talk or action are characterized as negative (−) and cumulatively recorded on a "bad" clock. Symptom-displacing or other desirable behaviors such as cooperative talk or action, work, etc. are characterized as positive (+) and cumulatively recorded on a "good" clock.

Performance is recorded as verbal (V) or motor (M) behavior. There are four behavior modes (dependent variables) which SAL procedures attempt to modify: V−, V+, M−, M+.

Three independent variables have been manipulated: (*a*) The limit of reinforced performance time within a SAL period, that is, accumulated minutes of performance after which no reinforcement is awarded. It is necessary to limit the amount of reinforcement awarded during a period so that it will not substantially exceed the amount available through the vocational program into which SAL subjects are to be promoted. (*b*) The performance interval between reinforcements upon which positive or negative reinforcement is contingent, that is, the number of minutes of performance required for a reinforcement to be awarded. (*c*) The rate of reinforcement, that is, the amount of positive or negative reinforcer awarded per unit time.

SAL programs are devised so as to quickly suppress negative verbal and motor behaviors, meanwhile enhancing positive verbal and motor behaviors. A second goal of the program is to lengthen the effective reinforcement interval so that subjects may be promoted into the first step of the regular vocational program of the facility where reinforcement is infrequent (maximum once per 120 min).

Subjects are assigned to the SAL from 8 A.M. until 3 P.M. Mondays through Fridays. Each day is divided into three 120 min periods, each period followed either by a coffee break or a meal. After 3 P.M., and on weekends, SAL subjects participate in ongoing social, instructional, and special programs, all of which involve the token economy.

The unit of secondary reinforcement is a token called a grickle (₲), which is employed in all other programs of the facility and is exchangeable for food extras, cigarettes, candy, passes, telephone calls, recreational activities, merchandise, etc. The token does not exist as such; token reinforcement is accomplished by a staff member recording the number of ₲ awarded on a "program card" carried by the subject. When a tangible token is necessary for immediate reinforcement, a ticket ("chit") worth 1 ₲ is employed. With some primitively organized patients, a combination of grickle (secondary) reinforcement and primary reinforcement such as candy or cigarettes is employed until the secondary reinforcing value of grickles is established. All token or primary reinforcements are accompanied by enthusiastic social reinforcement. The operation of the clocks and lights in response to the subjects' behavior also serves as a secondary or "feedback" reinforcement.

The initial schedules for subjects assigned to the laboratory are based upon the clinical judgment of the staff.

Grickles are deducted for specific *occurrences* of negative behavior when negative behavior is infrequent or results in accumulated clock time averaging less than 1 min per period. When negative behavior time exceeds 1 min per period, programs are devised providing for the deducting of grickles per minute or per minutes. Either of two methods of deducting is employed: (*a*) Grickles are deducted from an escrow allotment for occurrences or minutes of undesired behavior, any balance remaining at the end of the period being awarded as reinforcement for the suppression of the undesired behavior; (*b*) For each occurrence or time unit, grickles are subtracted from the subject's overall grickle balance; negative reinforcement thus effects not only the subject's SAL earnings, but his grickle balance from other program earnings as well.

When a subject's observed positive performances are at or near zero minutes per period, the program provides for grickle reinforcement per occurrence. When positive behavior averages 1 min or more per period, the program is rewritten so as to provide reinforcement for specified time intervals of positive behavior.

Upon entering the SAL, each subject is informed by the counselor of the reinforcement schedules which have been planned for him. He is told how many grickles will be deducted for each occurrence or each *n* minutes of V− behavior and whether the deduction will be taken from an allotment or from his balance. He is told how many grickles he will receive for *n* minutes of V+ behavior. He is similarly informed of the contingencies attaching to M− and M+ behaviors. V−, V+, M−, and M+ behavior complexes are defined for him; relevant examples from his own performance are provided.

The subject is given a work assignment. For the remainder of the period, the counselor operates the appropriate clock for the duration of any occurring V−, V+, M−, or M+ behavior. He occasionally attempts to elicit V+ behavior by addressing positive comments to each subject. When a subject attains his criterion on one of the dependent variables, he is immediately given enthusiastic social approval followed by a "chit" (ticket) for each grickle he has earned. When a primary reinforcer is additionally employed, it is awarded after the chit(s), in order to strengthen the secondary reinforcing value of grickles and of social approval. At the end of the 120 min period, the subject turns in his chits and has them recorded on his program card as grickles. This procedure permits token reinforcement immediately upon the attainment of a behavioral criterion, without permitting expenditure of the ₲ before the coffee break, meal, or store session which follows the SAL period.

Preliminary Results

Three independent variables have been manipulated in the SAL; learning theory suggests certain expectations for each:

1. Reinforcement limits (a ceiling on reinforced performance time per period) should have the effect of attenuating performance, their removal should enhance performance;
2. Brief intervals between reinforcements should facilitate performance, long intervals should tend to extinguish it;
3. High rates (grickles per unit time) of reinforcement should facilitate performance more than low rates do.

Suppression

The verbal performances of Duke, Art, and Pat are shown in Fig. 1. Duke was assigned to the SAL because of his threatening, abusive, and bizarre verbalizations, often accompanied by threatening gestures. Because of the high frequency of these behaviors, grickles were deducted from his overall balance. After five days in the SAL his V−

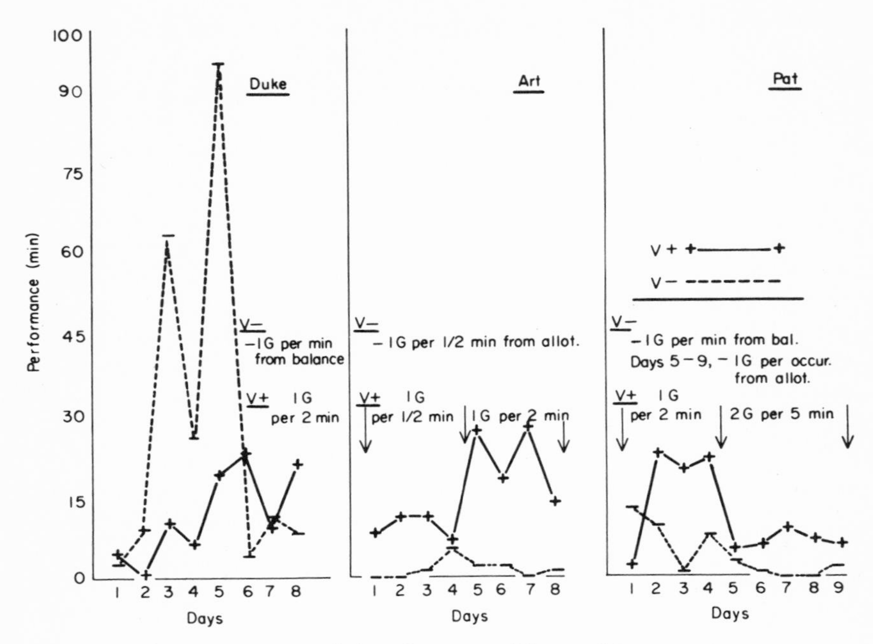

Fig. 1. Verbal performance of three subjects.

behavior was considerably reduced; Duke showed corresponding increases in his earnings in the evening social programs and his instructional program (conversation improvement practice).

Art was assigned to the SAL primarily because of his idiosyncratic, neologistic verbalizations. He was allotted 2₲/120 min period; 1 ₲ was deducted for each ½ min of bizarre or neologistic behavior. His V– behavior reached an acceptable level by the fifth day and was accompanied by corresponding increases in his earnings in the evening social programs and in his instructional program (conversation improvement practice and a programed interpersonal relations course).

Pat's V– behavior consisted mostly of hypochondriacal whining and complaining. One grickle was deducted from his overall grickle balance for each minute of such complaining. At the beginning of the fifth day, his program was changed to provide an allotted reinforcement of 4 ₲ per period for suppression of V– behavior; the reinforcement was reduced by 1 ₲ for each occurrence of V– behavior during the period. From the fifth through the ninth day, Pat's V– behavior was suppressed to an acceptable level with a corresponding increase in his performance in the evening social program. There was no increase in his instructional performance (a programed interpersonal relations course).

Motor performances of Duke, Art, and Pat are shown in Fig. 2. The M— behavior of Duke, Art, and Pat, though troublesome, accounted for relatively little SAL time. Duke produced about 5 min of M— behavior on the second and on the fourth day. Under a program which provided for the deduction of 1 ₲ from his overall grickle balance for each occurrence of M— behavior, Duke's M— behavior was suppressed to zero from the fifth through eighth days. Pat exhibited only one occurrence of M— behavior, on the third day. This was suppressed from the fourth through the ninth day under a program which provided for the deduction of 1 ₲ per occurrence from his overall grickle balance.

Reinforcement Limit

A reinforcement limit prevents the continued awarding of reinforcement as the SAL period progresses and thereby places a ceiling on the

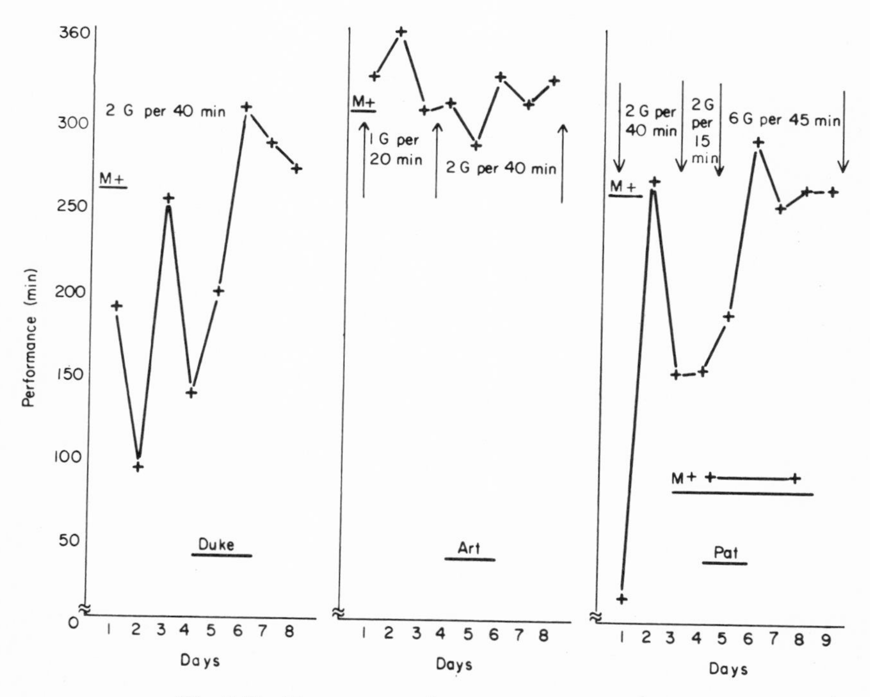

Fig. 2. Positive motor performance of three subjects.

number of minutes that can be reinforced. Performance would not be expected to substantially exceed the limit, since further performance would be unreinforced (extinguished). When Art (Fig. 1) was limited to one reinforced V+ minute per period (3 min/day) during the first through the fourth day, his V+ behavior did not exceed 11 min per day; when the limit was raised to permit ten reinforced minutes per period (30 min/day), his V+ performance rose to 27 min/day and remained above 14 min/day through the eighth day.

When Pat (Fig. 2) was limited to 60 reinforced M+ minutes per period (180 min/day), his M+ performance dropped. When the limit was raised with the beginning of the fifth day, M+ performance recovered; it remained above 190 min for the sixth through ninth day.

Interval and Rate

When Pat's V+ interval (Fig. 1) was lengthened and the rate of reinforcement decreased with the beginning of the fifth day, his V+ performance decreased from above 20 min/day to less than 9 min/day.

When Art's interval (Fig. 2) was lengthened at the beginning of the fourth day, his M+ performance showed an initial decrement, then recovery.

Hal's 30-day tenure in the SAL, shown in Fig. 3, permits examination of effects of varying interval and rate of reinforcement, with limit held constant, on M+ performance. Hal's initial program provided 2 ₵ for each 40 min of M+ behavior. This interval apparently provided insufficient frequency of reinforcement. During the fourth day, the program was changed to provide 2 ₵ for each 20 min of M+ behavior. The increases in frequency and rate of reinforcement seem to have produced a considerable performance increment from the seventh through eleventh days.

Beginning with the twelfth day, Hal's interval was lengthened but the rate of reinforcement was unchanged. Performance was attenuated from the twelfth through the seventeenth day. Beginning with the eighteenth day, the interval was shortened so that Hal could be given 1 ₵ for each 10 min of M+ behavior. Rate of reinforcement was unchanged. Performance tended to increase during the following several days.

Beginning with the twenty-third day there was a steady decline in performance, possibly due to "fatigue" factors. Both frequency and rate of reinforcement were increased in response to this decline; performance again climbed for three days but dropped on the thirtieth day to 150 min.

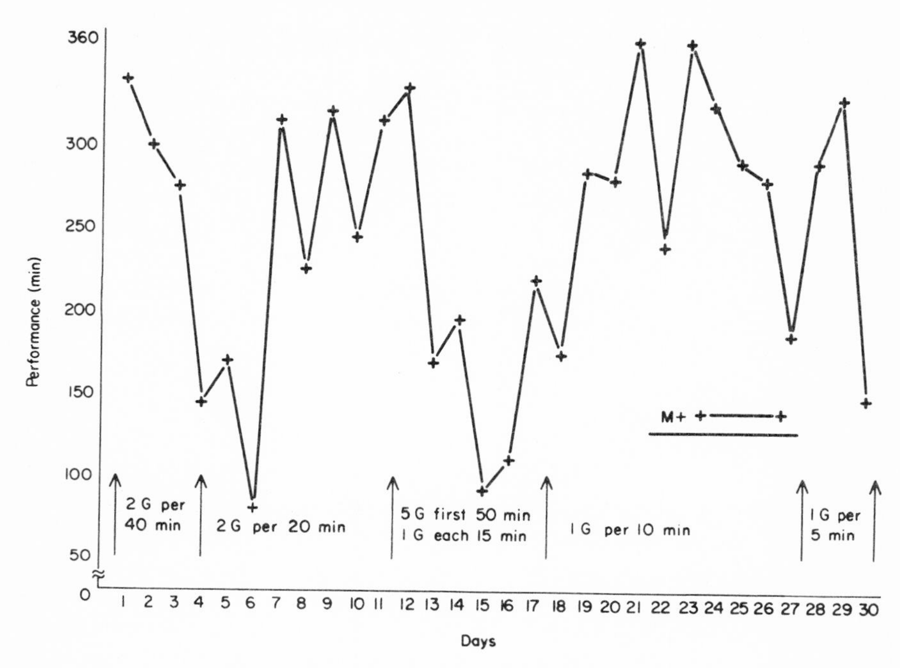

Fig. 3. Positive motor performance of Hal.

During these 30 days, Hal's performance in the evening social programs climbed steadily: He earned 1 ₲ the first week and 34 ₲ during the fifth week for social performance.

Discussion

The data presented above suggest that an intensive reinforcement system can be effective in reducing noxious behavior in a relatively short time. It is likely that this effect is augmented by the use of dual reinforcement. The program also appears to be of value in increasing desired verbal and motor behaviors such as friendly conversation and work. The variables examined are related to performance approximately as learning theory predicts: Positive performance increases with a shortened reinforcement interval or with an increased rate; performance decreases when the interval is lengthened or the rate is decreased; performance is not sustained appreciably beyond a limiting reinforcement. Finally, the behaviors developed in the intensive reinforcement situation do seem to generalize to related situations.

Since the work described here was exploratory, it has not dealt with several relevant issues. The relationships between reinforcement interval, magnitude, and frequency deserve systematic study in a setting such as the one described. Optimal shaping gradations for the prolongation of reinforcement interval must be discovered and sophisticated shaping techniques devised. The effects of social transactions among the subjects upon their performance should be studied, as should the mutual interactions between an intensive operant program and other concurrent programs (in the present case, social, instructional, and special programs). Study of these and other relevant variables might ultimately permit the prediction of an optimum program from other behavioral data.

Three alterations in the system described above are planned. Because of its confounding effect on other variables, the reinforcement limit will be discarded. The problem of promoting SAL subjects into the regular vocational program will probably be handled by increasing the ₵ reinforcement available in the regular vocational program. A procedure for gathering basal V−, V+, M−, and M+ data upon which to base reinforcement schedules is being instituted. Procedures are being sought for reducing or automating the observing, recording, and awarding of reinforcement so as to ease the burden on the counselor and increase the capacity of the SAL.

References

Henderson, J. D. Conditioning techniques in a community-based residential treatment facility for emotionally disturbed men. Unpublished manuscript, Spruce House, Horizon House, Philadelphia, 1968.

Henderson, J. D., & Scoles, P. E. A community-based behavioral milieu for psychotic men. Unpublished manuscript, Spruce House, Horizon House, Philadelphia, 1968.

Scoles, P. E., & Henderson, J. D. Effects of token reinforcement on the social performance of psychotic men. Unpublished manuscript, Spruce House, Horizon House, Philadelphia, 1968.

A Program of Behavior Modification for Problem Drivers[1]

Ronald A. Kleinknecht

WASHINGTON STATE UNIVERSITY[2]

Traffic violations and their frequent results—accidents, have become one of our society's gravest problems. The fact that more Americans have lost their lives on the highway than in all our wars speaks for the urgency of finding a solution to this increasingly serious problem. The majority of traffic violations, which are the best known predictors of accidents, are accounted for by a small minority of drivers. In the State of Washington in 1966, 3% of the 1.7 million drivers accounted for over one-half of the violations issued (O'Neall, 1967).

In light of this problem, there is a great need to change the behavior of this small but dangerous segment of the driving population. Psychologists, whose discipline has often been defined in terms of prediction and control of behavior, have largely ignored this most important class of human behavior—driving.

Current attempts to control driving behavior such as traffic court fines and forcing violators to observe gory, blood-stained movies of accidents are based largely on threat and punishment, both of which are generally inconsistently applied. Although punishment, under

[1]This research project was supported by the State of Washington Department of Motor Vehicles' Research Division. It was a preliminary report on a doctoral dissertation submitted to the Department of Psychology at Washington State University. The author wishes to thank his advisor, Warren K. Garlington, and committee members, Kenneth E. Lloyd and John D. Lillywhite, for their suggestions and guidance. Appreciation is expressed to Alfred Crancer, Chief Research Scientist, and Douglas Toms, Director of the Department of Motor Vehicles for their invaluable aid in making this project possible.

[2]Now at the University of Oregon Medical School, Portland, Oregon.

certain conditions, has been found to be effective in eliminating behavior, it is not generally considered by itself as the technique of choice for teaching new behavior owing to its emotional concomitants, social disruption, and operant and elicited aggression (Azrin & Holz, 1966). Another technique presently in vogue is nondirective group dynamics sessions aimed at changing the violator's attitude toward the traffic system, in hopes that this will effect a behavior change (Myrick, 1963). Few of these programs have been experimentally evaluated and fewer have produced statistically significant reductions in violation and accident frequency, while none, in the author's opinion, has shown a practically significant reduction.

Many diverse classes of operant behavior have been studied and brought under the experimental stimulus control. Another class of operant behavior in need of study is that of persistent traffic violating. The present study is an adaptation of the operant conditioning approach to a group of problem drivers in the state of Washington.

A Functional Analysis of Traffic Violations

A functional analysis of repeated traffic violating should help to clarify the behavior to be modified and present the rationale for the program to be described.

The first step in the analysis was to define the behavior of bad driving. Two indices of bad driving were used: (a) the receipt of traffic citations; and (b) the frequency of automobile accidents. The desired behavior is driving violation- and accident-free for a specified period of time.

A second step was identification of the reinforcing stimuli maintaining this high rate of traffic violating. On the surface it appears that all one would get from violations would be punishment in the form of fines and either the threat or occurrence of license suspension. However, the enduring effects of the punishment might be diminished since the aversive stimuli delivered by a traffic court is separated from the emitted behavior (violation) by delays as long as several months. Azrin (1956) has shown that immediacy of punishment is necessary for enduring response suppression. In addition, the punishing effects may be overshadowed by some immediate positive reinforcements. Azrin and Holz comment on this seemingly paradoxical situation: "If one fails to obtain a reduction of responses by an event that is known to be punishing, these results serve to indicate only that the variables maintaining the punished response are overriding the reductive effects of the punishment" (Azrin & Holz, 1966, p. 428).

Some consequences of traffic violating which might serve as reinforcers are peer approval and acceptance. These are known to be a powerful source of social control, especially characteristic of younger individuals (Sherif & Sherif, 1964; Garrison, 1965; Horracks, 1966). Here we note also that the age group with the highest rate of traffic violations and accidents is under 25 years of age, with a steadily decreasing rate beyond this age (Crancer, 1967). Possibly after this age, the peer influence loses its powerful reinforcing effects that earlier were able to override the reductive effects of punishment. At the same time, there appears to be a paucity of immediate positive reinforcement for safe driving in comparison to the reinforcement from one's peers for unsafe driving.

Another way of looking at this seemingly paradoxical behavior is in terms of the discriminative stimulus properties of punishment as shown by Holz and Azrin (1961). The fines, or other punishments imposed on the violator, may become associated with the reinforcement from one's peers and come to serve as discriminative stimuli for the presence of reinforcement. The punishment then acquires conditioned reinforcing properties.

Another reinforcing consequence of traffic violations such as speeding and running stop signs might simply be that by not stopping and speeding the driver reaches his destination sooner than if he had obeyed the traffic laws.

The final step in this analysis was to ascertain what environmental stimuli might be manipulated in order to alter the undesired behavior or instate a more adaptive or appropriate mode of behavior or both. In the case of the problem driver, there are several alternatives. First is removing the reinforcing stimuli such as peer approval and reaching one's destination sooner than if the traffic laws were obeyed. Removal of these stimuli should decrease the undesired behavior. A second alternative would be to positively reinforce a response which is incompatible with the undesired, maladaptive one. The first alternative of removing peer approval and faster arrival at one's destination would be an impossible task without complete environmental control. A more practical alternative would be to limit the driver's opportunity for positive reinforcement by restricting his opportunity to drive, constituting in effect, a period of time-out from reinforcement. Time-out periods have been shown to be aversive and to have response suppression properties similar to those of electric shock (Ferster, 1957).

Such a time-out for these drivers would probably be an aversive or punishing situation since it would also decrease the opportunity for other reinforcing activities such as social events, jobs, and freedom to come and go as one pleases. This driving restriction should serve to reduce the response rate of bad driving.

The second alternative presented was to reinforce some imcompatible, alternative behavior which is viewed as more adaptive. This would be to reinforce safe or violation- and accident-free driving. A logical reinforcer then would be the contingent withdrawal of the aversive driving restriction; the contingency being a specified period of violation- and accident-free driving.

A final consideration in the practical application of behavior modification techniques is the desirability of a transition from the artifically imposed or "arbitrary reinforcing stimuli" to a "natural reinforcement" which will maintain the behavior after the experimental intervention terminates. The imposition of an aversive driving restriction and its contingent withdrawal fits Ferster's definition of arbitrary reinforcement in that ". . . the outcome is reinforcing to the reinforcer over the long term and to the reinforcee over the short term" (Ferster, 1967, p. 341).

A natural reinforcer, one which meets the current repertoire of the reinforcee and occurs reliably in his milieu, will have to take over to maintain safe driving after the retraining period. The possibilities for such a natural reinforcer for safe driving are varied but might include lower insurance rates because of a better record, more ready cash since he no longer pays frequent fines to the traffic court, and hopefully, social reinforcement from parents, wives, and friends. These kinds of stimuli will have to begin functioning as reinforcers and maintain the desired behavior in order for the program to have long term effectiveness.

Following this analysis of behavior, a program was designed to modify the driving habits of a group of problem drivers.

Method

SUBJECTS

The subjects were 182 drivers from Seattle, Washington, who had received at least five traffic citations in the past two years, and had been interviewed by one of the Department of Motor Vehicles' Driver Improvement Analysts, placed on probation, and violated that probation. The mean age was 23.5 years, ranging from 18 to 36.

PROCEDURE

EXPERIMENTAL GROUP. The experimental group (*Ex*) was summoned to appear at one of the Driver Licensing facilities in Seattle. At this meeting they were shown a movie on safe driving habits, after which the restriction program was explained to them. Then they were issued a temporary driver license with the restricted driving times on it. Initially they were restricted to driving between 6 A.M. and 6 P.M. Monday through Friday only (no weekend or evening driving allowed). The restriction schedule is shown in Table 1. Two weeks later they returned to the licensing station where they were issued another license contingent upon driving violation- and accident-free for the preceding two weeks. The new license allowed them to drive an additional four hours each day. Every two weeks thereafter, over a three-month period, they returned for another license with more allotted driving time, until after six two-week steps they finally earned back their full driving privilege.

There was also a schedule of contingent punishing consequences for those who violated. Failure during the first month of the program resulted in a one month license suspension, after which they started the program over. If they violated during the second month they were not suspended, but had to start the restrictions over, and if the failure was in the final month, the penalty was reversion to step three, of the restriction schedule—driving from 6 A.M. to 12 P.M. Monday through Thursday, and 6 A.M. to 6 P.M. Friday.

CONTROL GROUP 1. Since most problem drivers tend to improve their driving records over time, with or without intervention, it was

Table 1
DRIVER RESTRICTION SCHEDULE

Step	Week	Restricted to	Penalty
1	1, 2	6AM-6PM, Mon-Fri	S1[a] and begin Step 1
2	3, 4	6AM-10PM, Mon-Thur; Fri-6PM	S1 and begin Step 1
3	5, 6	6AM-12PM, Mon-Thur; Fri 6AM-6PM	Return to Step 1
4	7, 8	Any time Mon-Thur; 6AM-6PM Fri, Sat, & Sun	Return to Step 1
5	9, 10	Anytime Sun-Thur; 6AM-6PM Fri & Sat	Return to Step 3
6	11, 12	Any time Sun-Fri; 6AM-6PM Sat	Return to Step 3
7	13	License returned	

[a] S1—suspension of all driving privileges for one month.

not practical to use the *Ex Ss* as their own controls and compare baseline frequencies with violation and accident frequencies after introducing the contingencies. For obvious reasons, a behavioral reversal was also an impractical technique for demonstrating stimulus control with problem drivers. To test the effects of the contingencies, a control group was subjected to the same initial treatment as *Ex* and were placed on the same driving restrictions. The difference between these two groups was that control group one (C1) received their new licenses and driving time automatically every two weeks whether they had violated or not. They were a noncontingent reinforcement control group, differing from *Ex* only in the absence of the no-violation contingency and no punishing consequences.

CONTROL GROUP 2. A second control group (C2) was summoned like the first two. They were shown the same movie about safe driving, told to behave themselves, and then released.

DEPENDENT VARIABLES. The dependent variables used to measure differences between the groups were number of citations and accidents per group, the number of subjects who failed in each group, and the mean time of failure of those who violated.

Results

The final data will be a six-month follow-up on the driving records beginning after the three-month retraining period. Data was not available for a six-month follow-up, but preliminary data for the three-month retraining period is presented in Table 2.

Statistically significant differences were found between the experimental group and the two control groups in the mean number of days before receiving a citation. For those who violated in *Ex*, an average of 37.1 days elapsed between initiation of the program and receipt of the citation. This figure is significantly longer than the 21.3 days for C1 ($P < .025$) and 23.6 days ($P < .05$) for C2.

Differences between the three groups in number of violations and accidents were in the expected direction but did not reach significance. The experimental group received 12 citations, C1 had 19, and C2 had 14.

Control Group 2 had the fewest accidents with two, while *Ex* had four and C1 had six. The data for some C2 *S*s, however, did not span the full three months. The experimental group had the longest mean time to accident involvement with 41.5 days, C1 was second with 29.0

Table 2
ACCIDENT AND VIOLATIONS DURING
THREE MONTHS OF RETRAINING

	Violations		Accidents	
Group	No.	Mean time to receipt of viol.[a]	Number	Mean time to Involvement
Experimental	12	37.1 days	4	41.5 days
Control 1[b]	19	21.3[d]	6	29.0
Control 2[c]	14	23.6[e]	2	16.5

[a] Based on first two months of the program since data were not available for some C2 *Ss*.
[b] Compared to *Ex*.
[c] Compared to *Ex*.
[d] $P < .025$.
[e] $P < .05$.

days, and C2 was last with 16.5 days. The number of accidents was too small for meaningful statistical comparisons.

Discussion

These preliminary data show that the contingent reinforcement group was significantly delayed in receiving citations during the retraining period. Although the number of citations received by the two control groups was not significantly different from *Ex*, the delay in violating indicates that during this period there was a significant degree of response reduction in the *Ex* group. The six month follow-up data now being collected will provide a more rigorous test of effectiveness of the contingencies imposed.[3]

The differences in time to violating might be explained by the fact that aversive control was the major treatment given the C1 group, which had the shortest mean time to violating. The C1 group was

[3] Although final data are not yet available at this time, the author has received some further data following the retraining period. These data suggest that although there was evidence of some behavior control during the retraining, this control did not carry over after the termination of the experiment intervention in that the groups did not differ significantly after three additional months.

In Ferster's terms (Ferster, 1967) there was some experimental control while the target behavior received arbitrary reinforcement, but upon its termination at the end of the retraining period, the desired behavior apparently was not reinforced and maintained by natural consequences from the driver's environment.

coerced to attend the program, had their licenses restricted, and got them back over time with no effort on their part. This treatment is solely an aversive situation with no real positive aspects. Several studies (Ulrich & Azrin, 1962; Azrin, 1964; Azrin, Hutchinson, & Hake, 1963; and others) have shown that elicited aggression frequently results from punishment. Driving behavior such as speeding, racing, failure to stop, etc., is a clear example of a potentially lethal form of aggression. The same might hold true for the C2 which also showed a significantly shorter mean time to violating than *Ex*. In contrast to the two control groups, *Ex* was presented with an aversive situation with even more punishing consequences, but it also had the additional variable of contingent reinforcement for safe driving, which served as a reinforcing stimulus. This latter positive stimulus may have kept the elicited aggression to a minimum in *Ex*, resulting in a longer time elapsed to failure.

If the hypothesis is correct that aggressive driving is elicited as a result of punishing consequences of traffic violations, then the traffic court system is actually serving to maintain the behavior that it is trying to eliminate. The fact that the majority of the traffic citations are issued to recidivists (O'Neall, 1967) indicates that the present system is, at best, minimally effective. This might be a function of either of the following factors: (*a*) aggression elicited from court fines, license suspension, jail sentences, coercion to observe accident victims in hospital emergency wards, or viewing movies of accidents; or (*b*) conditioned reinforcing properties of citations and fines as a function of the connection with peer approval and acceptance. Either or both of these consequences might be maintaining the high rate of traffic violating and accidents.

This data lend some support to the above hypothesis and indicates that the traditional traffic court system based largely on aversive control might be self-defeating and, therefore, in need of revision.

Other nonpunitive driver improvement programs such as defensive driving clinics and group therapy sessions designed to change driver attitudes have also been largely unsuccessful (Schuster, 1964; Scott, 1966). Schuster concludes: ". . . it appears that group psychotherapy for problem drivers, group driver improvement meetings and special training for adult drivers are not differentially effective in assisting the experimental group to improve. . ." (Schuster, 1964, p. 30).

In light of the problem presented by the chronic traffic violator and the ineffectiveness of the current corrective measures in changing driver behavior, a new experimentally sound technique for behavior change is needed. The present program of behavior modification is hopefully a step in that direction.

References

Azrin, N. H. Effects of two intermittent schedules of immediate and nonimmediate punishment. *Journal of Psychology*, 1956, **42**, 3-21.

Azrin, N. H. Aggressive responses of paired animals. Paper presented at symposium on medical aspect of stress. Walter Reed Institute of Research, Washington, D.C.: April 1964.

Azrin, N. H., & Holz, W. Punishment. In W. K. Honig (Ed.), *Operant behavior: Areas of research and application.* New York: Appleton-Century-Crofts, 1966. Pp. 380-447.

Azrin, N. H., Hutchinson, R. R., & Hake, D. F. Pain induced fighting in the squirrel monkey. *Journal of the Experimental Analysis of Behavior*, 1963, **6**, 141-148.

Crancer, A. Accident and violation rates for Washington drivers. Report 003, May 1967, Washington State Department of Motor Vehicles, Olympia, Washington.

Ferster, C. B. Withdrawal of reinforcement as punishment. *Science,* 1957, **126**, 509.

Ferster, C. B. Arbitrary and natural reinforcement. *Psychological Record,* 1967, **17**, 341-347.

Garrison, K. C. *Psychology of adolescence.* (6th ed.) Englewood Cliffs, N. J.: Prentice Hall, 1965.

Holz, W. C., & Azrin, N. H. Discriminative properties of punishment. *Journal of the Experimental Analysis of Behavior*, 1961, **4**, 225-232.

Horracks, J. E. The adolescent. In L. Carmichael (Ed.), *Manual of child psychology.* (2nd ed.) New York: Wiley, 1966. Pp. 697-734.

Myrick, R. Driver improvement clinic induces attitude change by group discussion. *Traffic Digest and Review*, 1963, **11**(5), 9-11.

O'Neall, P. A. Relation of accident involvement and number of citations. Report 006, November 1967, Washington State Department of Motor Vehicles, Olympia, Washington.

Scott, B. Effectiveness of group sessions in changing driver attitudes. Summary of proceedings: Research conference and workshop, American Association of Motor Vehicle Administrators, Sacramento, California, April 1966.

Schuster, D. H. Follow-up evaluation of the effectiveness of driver improvement classes for problem drivers. Proceedings of conference on safety in motoring, British Medical Association, Royal College of Surgeons and Society of Motor Manufactures and Traders, London, May 1964.

Sherif, M., & Sherif, C. *Reference groups.* New York: Harper & Row, 1964.

Ulrich, R. E., & Azrin, N. H. Reflexive fighting in response to aversive stimulation. *Journal of the Experimental Analysis of Behavior*, 1962, **5**, 511-520.

Token Reinforcement in Marital Treatment

Richard B. Stuart

UNIVERSITY OF MICHIGAN

Husbands and wives seeking treatment for marital discord typically complain of a lack of understanding and love shown by the other mate. If "understanding" is used to mean an emotion reflecting acceptance of and tolerance for the behavior of the spouse, the therapist is powerless to promote change. On the other hand, if "understanding" is used to mean an awareness of the events which stimulate and consequate the partner's behavior, the therapist can do much to aid in promoting changes. If "love" is viewed as a deeply personal emotional state with highly individual meaning, it must clearly be beyond the control of the therapist. On the other hand, if "loving" behavior is sought, such behavior can clearly be brought under therapist and spouse control in much the same manner as any other response can be controlled. Used in this sense, "loving" refers to " . . . an increased tendency to aid, favor, be with, and caress and a lowered tendency to injure in any way" [Skinner, 1953, p. 162]. The tasks of the marriage therapist are accordingly set as, first, to identify the desired ("loving") behaviors sought by each spouse from the other; second, to identify the contingencies which can be used to accelerate and maintain these behaviors; and third, to increase the probability that each of these behaviors will occur.

Communicational Problems in Disordered Marriages

Most parties to disordered marriages complain of an oppressive "lack of communication." At face value, this complaint would seem to have validity as recent research has shown that silence is far more prevalent in disordered as compared to "normal" families (Ferreira & Winter, 1968, p. 262). Closer analysis, however, would suggest that this complaint merely masks a persistent tendency to engage in negative communication. This analysis proceeds from the dictum of the interpersonal school which suggests that: "One cannot not communicate" (Watzlawick, 1964, p.2). In disordered marriages, the husband might ask his wife what is bothering her. She might respond with a grimace. Her grimace is not noncommunication; it says rather pointedly, first, that her husband should not ask for he alone is responsible for her distress and, second, that he is powerless to be of assistance to her. Therefore it would be more correct to say that while couples in marital conflict experience the same frequency of communications along the same range of communicational modes as their happier counterparts, their communication is more confined to a negative assortment of topics.

The emotional effect of this reliance upon negative or indirect communication is the feeling of despair expressed by so many prisoners of disturbed marriages. The functional effect is even more pernicious, however. When couples rely upon negative communication they express their wishes obliquely at best. To the extent that they fail to express their wishes directly, they reduce the probability that their wishes will be granted. For example, one recent study concluded that

> . . . the more family members explicitly tell each other about their likes and dislikes, the greater their likelihood of arriving at family decisions which better represent and fulfill the wishes of everyone concerned[Ferreira & Winter, 1968, pp. 260-261].

One major therapeutic goal must therefore stress the clear and unambiguous statement of the wishes and expectations of each partner.

Interactional Patterns in "Normal" and Disordered Marriages

Most persons entering marriage expect to enjoy reciprocal patterns of positive reinforcement. Reciprocity has the general sociological connotation that "each party has rights and duties" (Gouldner, 1960, p. 169) and the specific behavioral connotation that each party should dispense social reinforcement to the other at an equitable rate (Patterson & Reid, 1967, p. 1). When spouses elect to positively reward each other, this behavior can be understood to represent the best means available to each of maximizing individual rewards while maintaining minimal costs (Thibaut & Kelley, 1959, p. 12). When spouses elect to reduce the rate of positive reinforcement, this too can be understood in terms of the reward/cost balance. In such situations, each spouse has learned from past experience that his rewards dispensed to the other will not be reciprocated and each seeks to conserve his resources. Thus, whether or not one partner positively reinforces the other will be a function of his past experience with the other (Homans, 1961, pp. 53-59), while the presence of a reciprocal interaction suggests that: "Each individual has something to offer by way of reinforcing the other, and once established, the interaction sustains itself (Skinner, 1953, p. 310).

Normal marriages can be characterized by reliance upon reciprocal relationships. Each partner has learned that if he positively reinforces the other, he will be compensated in the same magnitude. In effect, each partner seeks to raise the rate at which he reinforces the other with the assurance that the rate at which he is reinforced will rise a like amount. In contrast, the partners in disordered marriages seek to minimize individual costs as they have little hope of receiving compensatory rewards. Two broad patterns are available. First, the partners may retreat entirely into patterns of withdrawal. Such patterns can be explained in functional terms as the failure of the social environment to maintain high rates of behavior. Second, the partners may rely heavily upon the use of negative reinforcement (the removal of an aversive event following the emission of a designated response). For example, while the wife in a successful marriage might tell her husband that she will put his favorite dessert on the table while he takes out the garbage, the wife in an unsuccessful marriage might nag him about having not taken out the garbage until he finally does so (if he does at all). He is unlikely to do so, however, as taking out the garbage would reinforce his wife's nagging at the same time that it would be yielding to her coercion.

Token Reinforcement in Marital Treatment

A token reinforcement system has proven useful in restoring functional communication and reciprocity in severely disordered marriages. In designing a token system, each partner is asked to specify exactly what responses he would like to see accelerated in the other. In specifying three such responses, each partner identifies the way in which he would like to be rewarded by the other. When a means is developed for the exchange of these responses, the partners can be assisted in recapturing reciprocity in their interaction. Token reinforcement can be used to "develop behaviors which lead to social reinforcement from others and to enhance the skills necessary for the individual to take a responsible social role . . . (Krasner, 1968, p. 2). Tokens have the following advantages: (*a*) They are tangible and unambiguously positive; (*b*) they permit the recipient to choose his reinforcement, thereby assuring the salience of the reinforcers which are proffered; (*c*) they are given immediately following a desired behavior; (*d*) they are typically given in association with some positive behavior; and (*e*) they may be retained and exchanged for actual reinforcement at a later time.

In establishing a token system with husbands and wives who are in conflict, it is typically necessary to overcome three myths. First, the myth that personality change must precede behavioral change must be overcome. This is done by indicating: (*a*) One knows "personality" through behavior; (*b*) it has been shown that changes may be brought about in behavior through rearrangement of the environment; and therefore, (*c*) "personality" can be changed through changing behavior through environmental control. Second, the myth that history is immutable must be overcome. Every event in every marriage, good or bad, has a history. While this history may contribute to an explanation of the conditions under which certain choices were made, the negative history does not preclude the possibility of positive choices in the present. Third, the myth that people in love "know without asking" the other's wishes must be refuted. This is a definitional matter and it is essential to designate effective participation in any relationship as both clearly stating one's wishes (stimulating the other to act) and rewarding his efforts (contingency management). Therefore, waiting for the other to anticipate one's wishes can be defined as low-level social behavior.

Procedure

The characteristics of the five couples who underwent behavior therapy for intense marital conflict are presented in Table 1. All couples sought treatment as a "last ditch" effort to work out solutions to marriage problems of long standing, and none of the couples indicated an expectation that treatment would succeed. In each instance, the wife complained that her husband neglected her conversational needs while the husband complained that his wife refused any and all sexual advances.

Following a discussion of the logic of the treatment and rejection of

Table 1
CHARACTERISTICS OF FIVE COUPLES WHO UNDERWENT OPERANT MARITAL THERAPY

	Couple	Age	Years married	No. Children	Years Education
1	Husband Wife	38 31	3	0	Ph.D. B.S.
2	Husband Wife	27 24	3	1	Ph.D. Ph.D.
3	Husband Wife	52 47	23	1	M.S. M.A.
4	Husband Wife	41 42	17	2	High School 2 Yrs. College
5	Husband Wife	36 35	11	2	M.S. M.S.

the interfering myths (where necessary), the wife was pressed for details about what "acceptable" conversation meant to her. Behavioral rehearsal during treatment sessions was often needed as a means of specifying the wife's expectations with precision. The wife was then instructed to purchase a kitchen timer which she could carry about the house. She was instructed to set the timer as soon as her husband entered and to give him one token when the bell sounded, if he met her conversational needs at her criterion level during that period. If he failed to behave at the criterion level by the end of the first 30 min, she was required to notify him of this and to offer constructive suggestions, cuing him as to how his performance could be improved upon. If she failed to do this, she was required to give her husband a token despite his failure to meet her conversational needs. At his request, at the half-hour cuing time, the timer could be reset so that he could earn a token within 60 min (rather than having to wait 90 min).

The criterion level for conversation was negotiable, with no husband being expected to engage in unending chatter with his wife. The criterion levels ranged from intense conversation to the wife's freedom to ask a casual question of her husband, with each couple employing a range of criteria as fit their changing situations.

The tokens were exchangeable by husbands for sexual favors from their wives. A different menu was constructed for each couple, taking into account their baseline level of sexual activity, the desired level of sexual activity, and the number of hours available for nonsexual (in this instance conversational) activity. Each of these couples had sex less than once per week (ranging from once in the year prior to treatment to once in the week prior to treatment), each desired sex an average of three times per week, and each had approximately five hours together on weeknights and 14 hours on weekends, making a total of approximately 52 to 54 hours per week. Accordingly, husbands were charged 3 tokens for kissing and "lightly petting" with their wives, 5 tokens for "heavy petting," and 15 tokens for intercourse.

With each of these couples, all therapeutic sessions were held jointly. Sessions were held during the first four, the sixth, eighth, and tenth weeks, for a total of seven sessions. When it is considered that these couples were each on the brink of filing for divorce, this could be considered relatively inexpensive treatment. Follow-up contacts were held by phone or by mail and all data, including that collected during sessions, were based upon self-report.

Results

The number of tokens earned and spent was recorded on a monitoring sheet on a daily basis. This sheet provided each spouse with visual feedback of his own performance. The data recorded for the five couples is presented in Table 2. It will be seen that each couple recorded a steady increase in the rate of conversational and sexual interaction.

Following the start of treatment with the third couple, the husband collected a fortune of 30 tokens. He then precipitated a major conflict with his wife and in the heat of battle threw 15 chips on the table and demanded intercourse. Following this, tokens were given a life of three days and became valueless unless spent within that time. In addition to reducing the likelihood of such abuses of the system, this modification increased the probability that husbands and wives would enjoy the maximum number of sexual encounters.

In addition to monitoring the rate of token and reinforcement exchange, each couple completed a brief attitude inventory adapted from the work of Farber (1957). The results of this inventory are presented in Table 3, which shows that husbands and wives both reported increased satisfaction in and commitment to their marriage following treatment.

Audio-tape recordings were made of all treatment sessions held with two couples (numbers 4 and 5). These tapes were analyzed to determine the number of clearly positive and clearly negative statements made by each partner about the other, whether directed to the therapist or to the spouse. The results of this analysis are presented in

Table 2
AVERAGE DAILY HOURS OF CONVERSATION AND WEEKLY RATE OF SEX OF FIVE COUPLES

Couple		Baseline	After ten weeks of treatment	At follow-up
1	Sex	0	2	3[a]
	Conversation	1	5	5.25[a]
2	Sex	.3	3	5[a]
	Conversation	1.25	4.75	4.50[a]
3	Sex	0	2	2[a]
	Conversation	.25	3	4[a]
4	Sex	.25	2	3[b]
	Conversation	1	5	6[b]
5	Sex	0	4	3[c]
	Conversation	.50	4.25	5[c]

[a] 52 weeks.
[b] 28 weeks.
[c] 24 weeks.

Table 4. (A full account of the procedure and findings for all couples will be published at a later date.) It will be seen that the verbal behavior of clients during interviews became markedly more positive over time, paralleling the reported increase in approach behaviors outside of treatment.

Discussion

Each spouse was directed to make specific modifications of his own behavior in an effort to modify the behavioral environment in which his partner's behavior occurred. The antecedents for changed behavior were probably twofold: Therapeutic recommendations exercised some S^D control as did the expectation of changes in the behavior of the spouse. The therapist suggested that each party engage in behavior which had doubtless been requested, cajoled, and demanded by the other party countless times before. As therapeutic directives, these new requests were differentiated from the old in four important respects. First, they were made more specific. Second, they were removed from the context of coercive demands in which granting the

Table 3
MARITAL SATISFACTION ASSESSMENT INVENTORY SCORES OF FIVE COUPLES

Source			Period		
Couple	Spouse	Rating self or spouse	Before	After	Follow-up
1	Husband	Self	5	14	14[a]
		Wife	2	8	12
	Wife	Husband	4	8	14
		Self	4	8	14
		Total	15	38	52
2	Husband	Self	3	15	15[a]
		Wife	2	5	13
	Wife	Husband	3	14	15
		Self	2	7	13
		Total	10	41	54
3	Husband	Self	4	8	10[a]
		Wife	0	7	10
	Wife	Husband	5	9	8
		Self	4	8	8
		Total	13	32	32
4	Husband	Self	5	10	10[b]
		Wife	2	4	10
	Wife	Husband	4	8	10
		Self	4	7	10
		Total	15	29	40
5	Husband	Self	2	10	12[c]
		Wife	4	10	12
	Wife	Husband	0	8	8
		Self	10	15	15
		Total	16	43	47

[a] 52 weeks.
[b] 28 weeks.
[c] 24 weeks.

request would have amounted to reinforcing unpleasant patterns of negative reinforcement. Third, it was possible to receive reciprocation immediately so that each partner had greater assurance that he would, in fact, receive his due. Finally, treatment was characterized as a "game" in which each partner could utilize strategies which would have greater payoff than he had experienced in the past.

Table 4
NUMBER OF POSITIVE AND NEGATIVE STATEMENTS MADE BY EACH SPOUSE ABOUT THE OTHER DURING OPERANT MARITAL TREATMENT

Couple		First week		Fourth week		Tenth week	
		Pos.	Neg.	Pos.	Neg.	Pos.	Neg.
4	Husband	8	11	14	2	14	3
	Wife	1	23	10	0	12	1
5	Husband	5	5	10	4	10	0
	Wife	0	3	3	0	8	0

It is difficult to assess the importance of any specific therapeutic technique. Every marriage therapist must be cognizant of the fact that his patients are torn between the actual distress of the present union and the imagined reward of future unions. When it is recognized that at best the subjects of one study treated "strangers more gently, and generally more nicely than they do their spouses" (Ryder, 1968, p. 237), one cannot overestimate the importance of increasing the rate and salience of positive reinforcements exchanged in a marriage. The use of token reinforcement is designed specifically to achieve this goal, and its effectiveness appears to have been indicated by changes in both the behavior (within and outside treatment) and attitude of patients who underwent this treatment.

The results of this study must, however, be qualified. The data concerning the rate of conversational and sexual behavior is the product of self-report. While it is impossible to assess the truth of such data, both partners concurred in the report. The data concerning attitude was taken from a crude attitude scale which may be more closely tied to hope than reality. Finally, the data concerning verbal behavior in the interview might have been influenced in important ways by differential responses of the therapist, despite the fact that care was taken to eliminate such influence.

References

Farber, B. An index of marital integration. *Sociometry*, 1957, **20**, 117-134.

Ferreira, A. J., & Winter, W. D. Information exchange and silence in normal and abnormal families. *Family Process*, 1968, **7**, 251-276.

Gouldner, A. W. The norm of reciprocity: A preliminary statement. *American Sociological Review*, 1960, **25**, 161-178.

Homans, G. *Social behavior: Its elementary forms.* New York: Harcourt, Brace & World, 1961.

Krasner, L. Assessment of token economy programs in psychiatric hospitals. Paper presented at Ciba Foundation symposium on Learning and Psychotherapy, London, January 1968.

Patterson, G. R., & Reid, J. Reciprocity and coercion: Two facets of social systems. Paper presented at the Ninth Annual Institute for Research in Clinical Psychology, sponsored by the University of Kansas, Department of Psychology, Lawrence, April 1967.

Ryder, R. G. Husband-wife dyads versus married strangers. *Family Process*, 1968, **7**, 233-238.

Skinner, B. F. *Science and human behavior.* New York: Free Press, 1953.

Thibaut, J. W., & Kelley, H. H. *The social psychology of groups.* New York: Wiley, 1959.

Watzlawick, P. *An anthology of human communication.* Palo Alto, Calif.: Science and Behavior Books, 1964.

Depression: A Clinical-Research Approach[1]

Peter M. Lewinsohn, Malcolm S. Weinstein, David A. Shaw

UNIVERSITY OF OREGON

As recently noted (Lazarus, 1968), the subject of depression[2] has been relatively neglected by behavior therapists. This is probably because a major symptom of depression refers to a subjective state, the term depression is elusive and ubiquitous, and the depressed patient is reluctant to verbalize his difficulties in behavioral or interpersonal terms.

This report constitutes an initial description of a program of clinical research on depression which has three major goals: (a) to test hypotheses about the socio-environmental reinforcement conditons associated with depression; (b) to develop systematic and replicable treatment strategies for depressed individuals; and (c) to design instruments with which to measure behavior change in depressed individuals. This presentation is concerned primarily with the description of a number of treatment methods which have been found to possess utility in the treatment of depressed individuals. Forthcoming reports will present the findings of several laboratory studies done as part of

[1]Portions of this paper were presented at the Joint Meeting of the Oregon and Washington State Psychological Associations, May 1968, and at the Conference on Behavioral Technology held at the University of Oregon, July 1968. This research has benefited greatly from many discussions with Dr. Gerald Patterson. The authors also are grateful to Dr. William Sheppard for his helpful suggestions in the writing of this paper.

[2]The term "depression" is used to refer to the syndrome of behaviors which has been identified in descriptive, factor-analytic studies of depressed patients (e.g., Grinker, Miller, Sabshin, Nunn, & Nunally, 1961) and which includes: (*a*) low rate of behavior, (*b*) verbal statements of dysphoria, self-depreciation, guilt, material burden, and fatigue; (*c*) somatic complaints such as sleeplessness, loss of appetite, headaches, etc.

the project (Lewinsohn & Flippo, 1969; Lewinsohn, Golding, Johansson, & Stewart, 1968b; Rosenberry, Weiss, & Lewinsohn, 1968).

The major assumptions underlying the approach to the depressed individual are:

1. A low rate of positive reinforcement acts as an eliciting stimulus for various respondents which in turn have operant consequences by setting the occasion for some depressive behaviors such as verbal statements of dysphoria, fatigue, and other somatic symptoms.

2. A low rate of positive reinforcement constitutes a sufficient explanation for other parts of the depressive syndrome such as the low rate of activity and verbal behavior. For the latter, the depressed person is considered to be on a prolonged extinction schedule.

3. The social environment provides reinforcements in the form of sympathy, interest, and concern which strengthen and maintain depressive behaviors. These reinforcements are typically provided by a small segment of the depressed person's social environment (e.g., his immediate family). However, since most people in the depressed person's environment (and eventually even his family) find these behaviors aversive, they will avoid him as much as possible, thus decreasing his rate of receiving positive reinforcement and further accentuating his depression.

4. A number of different environmental events (e.g., loss through death, separation, rejection, proverty, misfortune) and organismic states and traits (e.g., lack of social skill, ignorance) are presumed to be causally related to a state of low positive reinforcement. Social skill, defined as the emission of behaviors which are positively reinforced by others, is seen as an area of deficit especially important in the development of depressive behaviors.

Consistent with the above, the main goals of treatment are to restore an adequate schedule of positive reinforcement for the individual by training him to emit behaviors which are likely to be positively reinforced by others and to engage in activities which are intrinsically rewarding for him. A description of several treatment strategies found to be useful in accomplishing these goals follows.

Use of Home Observation as an Integral Part of the Treatment Process

The necessity of observing the depressed individual's interaction with his family in his own home as part of the diagnostic phase is stressed in the intake interview. The home visit typically becomes a focal point for discussion between therapist and client and requires the client to communicate and to plan with members of his family. The manner in which this is accomplished usually results in important diagnostic information. Home visits, lasting about an hour each, are scheduled around mealtime, when all members of the family are present. Observations are conducted during the beginning, middle, and ending phases of treatment. Interactions are coded in terms of the behaviors emitted by the client and the social consequences of his behavior. Other members of the family are also observed and their behavioral interactions are coded. Two or more observers are used and inter-observer agreement between trained raters has been found to be 90% or higher. The procedure is an adaptation of one developed by Patterson (1967). The methodology and the behavioral categories used in quantifying these observations are described elsewhere (Lewinsohn, 1968a).

The primary objective of the home observations is to obtain base level information with which to define treatment goals and to measure behavior change. On the basis of the home observations, the therapist identifies those interpersonal behavior patterns which he assumes to be causally related to the depression. These findings are presented to the client and his spouse in individual and joint interviews in close temporal proximity to the home visit. Behavioral terms, graphs, and other visual aids are used in order to present the "behavioral diagnosis" as clearly as possible. This sometimes requires several interviews during which the client is provided with information about his behavior and behavioral goals are identified and agreed upon. Interpersonal patterns which have emerged as critical have varied from case to case and have ranged from the complete absence of any interaction between client and spouse to very one-sided interactions, as well as to the observation that the client does not reinforce behavior which is directed toward him, that only a small proportion of the time is devoted to topics of interest to the client, or that his only "topic" is his depression. Detailed case descriptions illustrating the use of the home visit as part of treatment are available elsewhere (Lewinsohn & Atwood, 1968; Lewinsohn & Shaw, 1968; Martin, Weinstein, & Lewinsohn, 1968). In addition to the above, the home visits have also been found to have the following beneficial consequences: (*a*) They immediately focus the therapist-client interaction on behavioral and interpersonal problems. (*b*) They constitute an easy way of involving a significant part of the client's environment in the treatment process.

Daily Mood Ratings

Another strategy consists of having the patient rate his mood at the end of each day on one of the alternate forms of the Depressed Adjective Checklist (DACL) (Lubin, 1965). The objective is to sensitize the patient and the therapist to correlations of environmental changes and shifts in reinforcement contingencies with changes in the client's "depression." Figure 1 presents the DACL ratings of a patient described in a separate report (Lewinsohn & Atwood, 1968). In January, there was a drastic change in the direction of more depressed ratings which was discovered to be associated with a deterioration in her relationship with her husband. Similarly, the earlier change in the direction of less depressed ratings in December was associated with a shift in the direction of a more positive interaction with her husband. The mood ratings in this case not only helped to alert the therapist to a serious alteration in the clinical condition of the patient, but also were useful in demonstrating the importance to the client of modifying aspects of the relationship with her husband.

Three-Month Time Limit

A three-month time limit for treatment appears to facilitate behavior change. Originally instituted for practical reasons, it quickly became apparent that the inclusion of a time limit had a beneficial effect on the behavior of the client and the therapist. As the end of the three-month period approaches, both seem to increase their efforts. One might speculate that the provision of a definite period within which behavior change is to occur can serve as an SD to avoid the aversive consequences of terminating treatment without improvement.

Other Aids Found Useful

Other requirements used have included having the client keep a detailed record of his daily activities and the administration of vocational interest tests. The information provided by such records serves to focus the small amount of time the client spends on activities which he considers to be enjoyable. By means of such data, the therapist can pinpoint behavioral goals (e.g., spending more time outside the home, learning new skills, attending lectures, concerts, sports, etc.), as well as identify and reinforce desirable behavior change when it occurs.

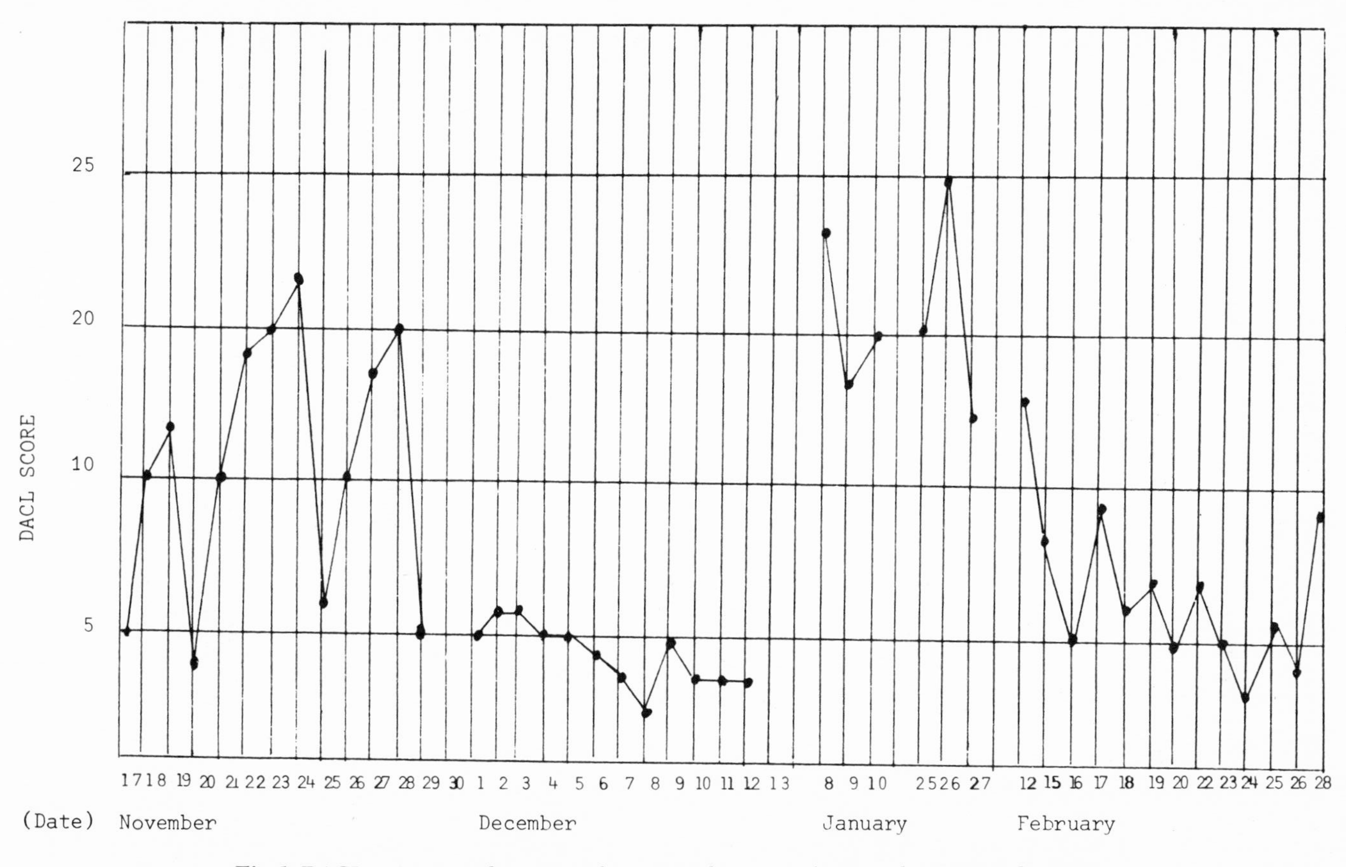

Fig. 1. DACL scores over the course of treatment for Mrs. G. (Lewinsohn & Atwood, 1968).

Application of the Premack Principle in the Treatment of the Depressed Individual

In many depressed clients, certain behaviors (e.g., verbal statements of dysphoria, guilt, self-depreciation, rejection, material burden) are emitted at a very high rate. Hence, according to Premack's principle (Premack, 1959), the occurrence of these high frequency behaviors should have reinforcing value for other, low-frequency behaviors. In other words, it should be possible to reinforce low frequency behaviors in the depressed individual (e.g., aggressive, self-assertive, realistic, and constructive behavior) by making high frequency (e.g., self-depreciatory statements) behaviors contingent upon them. Preliminary observation suggests that this is indeed the case. After initially deciding, with the client, on the low-frequency behaviors which should be increased in rate, the therapist can make the emission of the high frequency behaviors on the part of the client contingent upon his having emitted low frequency behaviors. An illustration of this is provided by the following case: A 22-year-old divorced male had spent several months roaming aimlessly around the country following the failure of his marriage. He appeared at the intake interview looking disheveled and unshaven, threatened suicide, and spent most of the hour in an animated account of the many details of his marital and other failures. In addition to being very critical of his past behavior, he reported serious financial and other material problems. It was clear from early discussions with him that many of his occupational goals (becoming a doctor, a journalist, or a biologist) were overly ambitious without drastic changes in his financial situation, status in school, etc. Working together, therapist and client decided upon a series of concrete steps which would enable the patient to come to some career decisions and to begin to work toward their realization. The behavioral steps involved such concrete actions as talking to his advisor, arranging for a loan, and inquiring into the availability of jobs of various kinds. Following this, the therapist would begin each interview by inquiring as to the amount of progress the patient had been making in regard to the positive steps agreed upon. If he had taken some definite action, the therapist would sit back and listen to the "depressive" kinds of things the client wished to talk about. On the other hand, if the patient had accomplished little since the last hour, the therapist would be polite but brief and end the hour within 10 or 15 min, suggesting that the client come back three or four days later. Within a few weeks, this client had made, and acted upon, many decisions such as finding a job, arranging for a loan, etc. He reported himself as feeling much better and as having gained many "insights" into himself.

A Behaviorally Oriented Approach to the Group Treatment of Depressed Persons

Since many depressed persons have very few friends, live by themselves, and emit very few interpersonal behaviors when they are with people, it seemed desirable to "create" an interpersonal situation which could provide the depressed person with information about his behavior and an opportunity to practice various social skills. A group consisting of nine depressed individuals was formed and met for 18 sessions over a three-month period with two therapists present. The main therapeutic strategy consisted of providing each client with information about his behavior in the group and its social consequences. On the basis of this information, we defined behavioral goals with him. Behavioral information was obtained by coding the ongoing interactions in the group, using a coding system similar to the one employed with the home observations. For each session, a complete record of who did what to whom and how often was available.

The group was structured as a "self-study" group where members would be able to learn about their own behavior and its consequences on others. They were given a talk emphasizing the behavioral aspects of depression, both in regard to its development and to its maintenance. Following this, the group members began to examine the aims and functions of the group, demanding to be given more structure by the therapist, talking about their respective problems, and in general behaving in ways commonly described for therapy groups in their early phases. However, instead of focusing primarily upon the attitudes, feelings, and content of the communications, the therapists focused on quantitative and qualitative aspects of the interactions between the members in the group setting. Each member of the group individually, as well as the group as a whole, was given information about his behavior at regular intervals. The data were individually plotted for each patient, with the aim of trying to focus his problems sharply for him. The interactional data permitted the quantitative identification of a number of different aspects of social skill.

THE RELATIONSHIP BETWEEN AMOUNT OF BEHAVIOR EMITTED BY THE INDIVIDUAL AND THE AMOUNT OF BEHAVIOR DIRECTED TOWARDS HIM. The interactional data included information about the number and kinds of behaviors emitted by the person, towards whom they were directed, and the number and kinds of behaviors directed towards him. Inspection of these data for each member of the group indicated that (*a*) there were large individual differences in the number of behaviors emitted per session and (*b*) for each individual, there was a very strong relationship between the number of behaviors emitted by him and the number of behaviors directed towards him. Spearman Rank-Difference Correlation Coefficients between the number of behaviors emitted by and directed towards each individual, over all sessions were in all instances found to be higher than .9. The concept of reciprocity (Patterson & Reid, 1967) was stressed with every client and especially with those for whom "passivity," i.e., a low rate of behavior, was a major problem. These individuals were strongly encouraged to emit more responses in the group, with the therapists and some members of the group reinforcing them whenever they took an active part. The largest self- and group-reported improvement was associated with those two members of the group who were initially quite passive and who progressively increased their rate of responding in the group.

INTERPERSONAL EFFICIENCY. Inspection of the reciprocity data for each person also revealed large differences between members in regard to their "interpersonal efficiency" (operationally defined as the ratio of the number of behaviors directed towards the individual divided by the number emitted by him). For some, the interpersonal efficiency ratio was close to 1 (i.e., almost as many behaviors were directed towards them personally as they were emitting), while for others it was much less than 1 (i.e., they were emitting many more behaviors than were being directed towards them personally). One member of the group was especially "inefficient." He was the most active member of the group but only a very small number of behaviors were directed towards him. When this was pointed out to him, he interpreted the behavior of the others as indicative of rejection of him, attributable to their narrow-mindedness. When this was brought up for discussion in the group, the group very forcefully confronted him with the observation, well documented, that whenever people directed behavior towards him, he provided them with aversive consequences in the form of hostility and criticism.

USE OF POSITIVE REACTION CATEGORIES. Analysis of their interactional data revealed that several individuals in the group emitted very few positive interpersonal reactions (e.g., verbal statements indicative of affection, approval, agreement, laughter, etc.). This was especially the case with one male member who was also very efficient, i.e., the others were attending to him. Inspection of his data revealed that he emitted many critical and challenging statements which resulted in defensive reactions on the part of the others (e.g., he informed another member of the group that her problem was trivial and easily soluble, whereupon she tried to convince him that this was not so). When presented with this information, the client expressed his concern over the fact that he had very few friends in spite of his concerted efforts. He was encouraged, whenever possible, to emit "positive" reactions and to cut down on the use of negative reactions.

The interactional and other data available for the group as a whole, such as the MMPI and interview ratings (Lewinsohn, Weinstein & Alper, 1968), indicate changes for most members of the group in the direction of increased social skill, along with changes in the direction of fewer depressive behaviors.

Summary

The treatment techniques described in this paper all follow from a behaviorally oriented conceptualization of the development and maintenance of depression. Most promising for future research appear to be the use of the home visit and the systematic use of the peer group, as agents of behavior change for depressed individuals. The strategies are all intended to restore an adequate schedule of positive reinforcement for the individual by training him to engage in more "constructive" behaviors (i.e., those which result in positive reinforcement from others and which maintain the behavior of others towards the individual). The techniques are based upon reinforcement principles even though, for the most part, the events in question are not under the direct control of the therapist. A quantitative method for coding interpersonal behavior is used to define behavioral goals and to measure behavior change. Major emphasis is placed upon providing the client with information about his own behavior and its consequences and upon reinforcing him for emitting "constructive" behaviors.

References

Grinker, R. R., Miller, I., Sabshin, M., Nunn, R. J., & Nunally, I. C. *The phenomena of depressions*. New York: Harper & Row, 1961.

Lazarus, A. A. Learning theory and the treatment of depression. *Behaviour Research and Therapy*, 1968, **6**, 83-89.

Lewinsohn, P. M., & Atwood, G. E. Depression: A clinical-research approach. *Psychotherapy: Theory, Research and Practice.* In Press.

Lewinsohn, P. M. Manual of instructions for the behavior ratings used for the observation of interpersonal behavior. Unpublished manuscript, University of Oregon, 1968. (a)

Lewinsohn, P. M., & Flippo, J. R. The differential effects of failure and success experiences on the self-evaluative ratings of depressed and non-depressed subjects. Unpublished manuscript, University of Oregon, 1969.

Lewinsohn, P. M., Golding, S. L., Johannson, S., & Stewart, R. Patterns of communication in depressed and non-depressed subjects. Unpublished manuscript, University of Oregon, 1968 (b)

Lewinsohn, P. M., & Shaw, D. A. Feedback about interpersonal behavior as an agent of behavior change: A case study in the treatment of depression. *Psychotherapy and Psychosomatics.* In Press.

Lewinsohn, P. M., Weinstein, M. S., & Alper, T. A behaviorally oriented approach to the group treatment of persons with depression. Unpublished manuscript, University of Oregon, 1968.

Lubin, B. Adjective check lists for the measurement of depression. *Archives of General Psychiatry,* 1965, **12**, 57-62.

Martin, M. L., Weinstein, M. S., & Lewinsohn, P. M. The use of home observations as an integral part of the treatment of depression: The case of Mrs. B. Unpublished manuscript, University of Oregon, 1968.

Patterson, G. R. Manual for the behavior check list. Unpublished manuscript, University of Oregon, July, 1967.

Patterson, G. R., & Reid, J. B. Reciprocity and coercion: Two facts of social systems. In M. J. Michaels & C. Neuringer (Eds.), *Behavior modification and clinical psychology.* New York: McGraw-Hill. In Press.

Premack, D. Toward empirical laws: I positive reinforcement. *Psychological Review,* 1959, **66**, 219-233.

Rosenberry, C. E., Weiss, R. L., & Lewinsohn, P. M. Frequency and skill of emitted social reinforcement in depressed and non-depressed subjects. Unpublished manuscript, University of Oregon, 1968.

Index

Ferster, C. B., 193, 213–214, 217

G

H

I

J

K

L

R

S

MIGRATIONS AND CULTURES

MIGRATIONS AND CULTURES

A WORLD VIEW

THOMAS SOWELL

BasicBooks
A Division of HarperCollins*Publishers*

Published by BasicBooks, A Division of HarperCollins Publishers, Inc.

Library of Congress Cataloging-in-Publication Data
Sowell, Thomas, 1930–
Migrations and cultures : a world view / Thomas Sowell.
p. cm.
Includes bibliographical references and index.
ISBN 0–465–04588–X
1. Emigration and immigration—Economic aspects. 2. Ethnic groups. 3. Ethnic relations. 4. Race. 5. Culture. I. Title.
JV6217.S69 1996
304.8'2—dc20
95–44316
CIP

96 97 98 99 ❖/HC 9 8 7 6 5 4 3 2 1

To the memory of Carter Goodrich, who made economic and social history come alive to a young graduate student.

CONTENTS

PREFACE

This book about the odysseys of peoples has had odysseys of its own. Evolving over a period of more than a dozen years, it has ended up being very different from what it was conceived to be at the outset in 1982 or what it was at various stages along the way. For example, what was conceived of as a single book has ended up as three (thus far). *Race and Culture,* published in 1994, was originally the last quarter of a huge manuscript of the same name, which included the histories now published here separately. Another spin-off was a study of affirmative action programs around the world entitled *Preferential Policies: An International Perspective,* published in 1991.

This has been an odyssey for the author as well—not only an odyssey of the mind but also a series of journeys that took me to 15 countries on four continents, some of these countries being visited two or three times over the years. Much of the data, literature, and expertise available in these countries was invaluable and virtually impossible to get while staying at home. Seeing the many peoples themselves, and their clearly very different ways and paces of working, often made their economic differences something that required no esoteric or sinister theories to explain.

History can be cruel to theories, as it has been cruel to peoples. Examples of both should be apparent in the chapters that follow. But history is what happened, not what we wish had happened, or what a theory says should have happened. History cannot be prettified in the interests of promoting "acceptance" or "mutual respect" among peoples and cultures. There is much in the history of every people that does not deserve respect. Whether with individuals or with groups, respect is something earned, not a door prize handed out to all. It cannot be prescribed by third parties, for what is to be respected depends on each individual's own values or the social values accepted by that individual—and "equal respect" is an internally contradictory evasion. If everything is respected equally, then the term respect has lost its meaning.

There is no way to begin honestly and know how the study of history will end, either as regards mutual respect among peoples or anything else. This book itself did not end up as planned, but turned instead into three very different books, each changing in content and conclusions with the passing years. Meanwhile, parts of the early manuscript dealing with multiethnic societies simply disappeared into oblivion, as I realized that a study of multiethnic societies was a much bigger project than originally envisaged, and therefore one appropriate to a much younger man.

The purpose of this book is, quite simply, that we should know what we are talking about when we talk about peoples and their cultures. That is a very large task in itself.

Thomas Sowell
The Hoover Institution

ACKNOWLEDGMENTS

Since this book was at the center of a study that produced two other books, I am indebted to many of the same people and institutions for all three. My greatest debt is to the Hoover Institution, which financed the worldwide travels, the voluminous literature of books, reports, and scholarly journals, and the years of work on my part and on the part of my research assistant, Na Liu, and my secretary during most of those years, Agnes Page. No separate accounting of the costs of this project was kept (perhaps fortunately), because it was not possible to separate out what part of three people's time went specifically to this work, as distinguished from other work that was going on during the same years. Nevertheless, the cost of the study that led to this book could not have been less than half a million dollars and might well have been twice that much. So my pride in what was accomplished must be tempered by a realization that very few other people have had an opportunity to do the same.

The nonfinancial contributions of others were also very large. The thousands of footnotes in this book suggest some of the sources of the information and insights that made my work possible, but there are many uncited works which made at least equal contributions by supplying not only information that corroborated the cited sources but, more importantly, provided the intellectual foundations in economics and other fields that helped to bring some order out of the chaos of otherwise overwhelming masses of information. In addition to this general intellectual indebtedness, there are many more direct obligations incurred for generous help given to me personally by a multitude of scholars, librarians, journalists, and officials, scattered literally around the world. Among them are, in alphabetical order, Dr. Bernard E. Anderson, Assistant Secretary of Labor at the U.S. Department of Labor, Professor Reginald Appleyard of the University of Western Australia (Perth), Dr. H. Avakian, Australian Institute of Multicultural Affairs (Melbourne), Dr. Alexandre Bennigsen of the École des Hautes Études en Sciences Sociales (Paris), Dr. André Béteille, University of Delhi, Professor Rondo Cameron of

Emory University, Dr. Suma Chitnis of the Tata Institute of Social Science (Bombay), Professor Gregory Clark of Stanford University, Professor Walker Connor, Trinity College (Connecticut), Professor John B. Cornell, University of Texas, Mr. Suman Dubey of *India Today* (New Delhi), Dr. Peter Duignan of the Hoover Institution (Stanford), Professor James Fawcett, Director of the East-West Center, University of Hawaii, Professor James R. Flynn of the University of Otago (New Zealand), Dr. Lewis Gann of the Hoover Institution (Stanford), Mr. Hu Gentles of the Private Sector Organisation of Jamaica, Mr. Petro Georgiou of the Australian Institute of Multicultural Affairs (Melbourne), Professor Margaret A. Gibson of California State University (Sacramento), Mr. Harvey Ginsberg of William Morrow Publishers, Professor Nathan Glazer of Harvard University, Professor Anthony G. Hopkins of Oxford University, Professor Donald L. Horowitz of Duke University, Professor James Jupp, Australian National University (Canberra), Professor Wolfgang Kasper of the Australian Defence Force Academy (Campbell), Professor Robert Klitgaard of the University of Natal (South Africa), Mr. Leslie Lenkowsky of the Hudson Institute, Mr. Greg Lindsay of the Centre for Independent Studies (Sydney), Professor Seymour Martin Lipset of Stanford University, Professor John McKay, Monash University (Australia), Dr. Ratna Murdia of the Tata Institute of Social Science (Bombay), Professor Charles A. Price of the Australian National University (Canberra), Dr. Alvin Rabushka of the Hoover Institution (Stanford), Mr. Sohindar S. Rana of the U.S. Information Service (New Delhi), Professor Peter I. Rose of Smith College (Massachusetts), Miss Claudia Rosett of the *Asian Wall Street Journal* (Hong Kong), Dr. Dominique Schnapper of the École des Hautes Études en Sciences Sociales (Paris), Dr. Sharon Siddique and Dr. Kernial Sandhu Singh of the Institute for Southeast Asian Studies (Singapore), Professor Sammy Smooha of the University of Haifa (Israel), Professor Leo Suryadinata of the National University of Singapore, Professor Malcolm Todd, University of Exeter (England), Mrs. Mary Lynn Tuck, American Historical Society of Germans from Russia (Nebraska), Professor Philip E. Vernon of the University of Calgary (Canada), Professor Myron Weiner and Mr. Steven Wilkinson of the Massachusetts Institute of Technology, and Dr. S. Enders Wimbush of Radio Free Europe (Munich).

CHAPTER 1

MIGRATION PATTERNS

In a world of 100 million immigrants—19 million of them refugees[1]—migration is a major social phenomenon, as it has been for thousands of years. While the drama of millions of human beings migrating across the oceans of the world has been limited to the past few centuries, when modern shipbuilding and seafaring methods have made this possible, migrations of individuals and relocations of whole peoples also took place on land, and across smaller bodies of water, for many centuries before that. Thus the English of today are not indigenous to England, nor the Malays to Malaysia, nor the Turks to Turkey. Migration and conquest put them where they are.

Conquest is only one of the ways in which peoples have migrated. Ahead of the conquerors, or sometimes in their wake, vast numbers of refugees may migrate to escape the carnage or the tyranny that has so often accompanied conquest. Others have migrated, not of their own volition, but in bondage. Whether on land or sea, they have been shipped like merchandise to wherever others wanted them to go—Slavs across Europe and Africans across the Atlantic, among many others. Free populations have also been involuntarily moved en masse, whether by expulsions, forcible resettlements such as the Ottoman Empire used to repopulate conquered areas with politically reliable people, or "ethnic cleansing," which acquired such grim connotations in the Balkans during the last decade of the twentieth century. Expulsions of Indians and Pakistanis from East Africa in the 1970s, and of fellow Africans from Nigeria in the 1980s, are part of a pattern also found in Central Europe: "Deportations and evacuations, exile and forcible repatriation, compulsory transfers and panic-stricken flight are an essential part of Central European history."[2] The peaceful and voluntary movements we think of as immigration are just one of the ways in which the populations of the world have been redistributed over the centuries.

Differences among peoples and among places lie at the heart of migrations. Moving has many and often heavy costs, including not simply the financial cost of transportation itself or even the additional expenses that go with searching for new work and new homes. Among the heaviest costs of all are the severing of personal ties in familiar surroundings to face new economic and social uncertainties in a strange land. Great dangers have often accompanied the voyage itself, whether the dangers from storms and rough seas that sank so many wooden ships in the Atlantic during the era of sails or the dangers that accompanied the mass exodus of the "boat people" from Southeast Asia in the late twentieth century, when both pirates and unseaworthy vessels cost the lives of many who set out in desperation and encountered tragedy on the high seas. Such risks are not run without major differences between where people are and where they are going.

The story of migration is not only about people who migrate but also about the lands to which they go and their impacts on those lands. To understand the impact of immigrants, it is first necessary to understand the cultures they take with them from their countries of origin. Sometimes it is highly specific skills which are salient, such as skills in clock-making among the Huguenots who migrated to Geneva in the sixteenth century and to London in the seventeenth, making both cities leading clock-making centers of the world for the first time.[3] Similarly, skills in optics, piano-building, and beer-brewing among Germans have led to German domination of one or more such industries in various countries around the world and to domination of all of them in the United States.

Sometimes it is not so much specific skills as a set of attitudes toward work and toward risk-taking, which may lead the immigrants to excel in some fields in which they had no experience before immigrating, as the Chinese and Japanese have done in many countries where they began as plantation laborers, moved on to become small businessmen, and—in later generations—rose to prominence in engineering, medicine, and other unrelated fields. Cultural transplants do not always involve a simple transfer of skills and achievements, and even less often a transfer of wealth. Nothing is more common than to have poverty-stricken immigrants become prosperous in a new country and to make that country more prosperous as well. The Chinese have done this throughout Southeast Asia, the Lebanese in West Africa, and numerous other groups in various other regions of the world.

Before turning to the histories of particular migrant groups in the chapters that follow, it will be helpful in putting their experiences in context to see some of the general patterns associated with migration and then to see how those patterns change over time. Such patterns include differences among the migrants themselves, in the circumstances from which they come, and in the changing settings in which their lives evolve.

DIFFERENCES AMONG MIGRANTS

Migrants differ not only in their respective points of origin and destination, and in the skills they bring, they differ also in their reasons for migrating and in such demographic characteristics as age distribution and sex ratios. Some groups acquire the culture of new lands rapidly, while others cling to their ancestral ways for generations or, in some cases, centuries. These differences are by no means always traceable to "national character," for the groups that differ are often much smaller than a nation-state, though occasionally larger. For example, different groups of people from different parts of India have by no means all had the same cultural patterns abroad, any more than they have had the same cultural patterns at home. Even in the much smaller area of the British Isles, Scottish and Welsh emigrants have not followed the same occupations or had the same general experiences overseas, any more than they have in Britain itself. On the other hand, some cultural patterns transcend national boundaries, as can be seen in the histories of Germanic peoples originating both inside and outside the boundaries of Germany. Not only was there much less illiteracy in nineteenth-century Germany than in contemporary Slavic nations, Germans living in the Russian Empire were more literate than the Slavs in that empire, and Germans in the Austrian Empire had an illiteracy rate of 6 percent in 1900, while Serbo-Croatians in the same empire at the same time had an illiteracy rate of 75 percent.[4] Conversely, Poles living in Prussia had higher illiteracy rates than the predominantly German population there.[5] Moreover, some cultural patterns are common not to a given race or nation, but to people from similar geographic settings, wherever those settings may be around the world.

Migrations of peoples have ranged from seasonal to permanent resettlement and from local to global. The seasonal migrations of shepherds and the perpetual movements of nomads long antedated the transoceanic migrations of the modern era. Migrants have varied not only in the duration of their stays, from sojourners to settlers, they have also differed in the roles they played in the societies to which they moved. Moreover, sojourners have differed among themselves in the economic roles they have played. Some have been agricultural laborers, harvesting the crops of other lands, some have been technicians and engineers who have created whole industries in other countries, and one of the most striking roles of sojourners has been that of middleman minorities in countries around the world. Among the differences to be explored here and in later chapters are differences in the origins and destinations of migrants, in the geographic settings from which they come and in which their respective cultures evolved, and the special roles played by some migrants who are sojourners or middleman minorities.

Origins and Destinations

Migrations tend to be selective, rather than random, in terms of skills and ambition, as well as in origins and destinations. The immigrant population from a given country living in another country is often highly atypical of the population in the country from which they came, in terms of their geographical and social origins. During the era of large-scale emigration from Sweden in the late nineteenth century, for example, few Swedes left their homeland from the favorably situated flatlands and forested regions of the country, while most left from regions lacking these advantages.[6] Similarly, migration from southern Italy began in remote mountain regions with the most backward agriculture.[7] Most of the Italian immigrants to Australia in the pre–World War II era came from areas which contained only 10 percent of the population of Italy.[8] In 1979, more than half of all the migrants to the countries of the Middle East from India came from a single state, Kerala[9]—a state containing less than 3 percent of India's population.[10]

Not only do immigrants often differ from the general populations of the respective countries from which they come, this selective migration is differently selective from one country to another. Thus late nineteenth-century immigrants to the United States from Greece and Spain were illiterate much less often than immigrants from Italy, even though illiteracy was more prevalent among the general populations of Greece and Spain than among the general population of Italy.[11] Destinations have likewise not been random. Rather, particular destination points have tended to be linked to particular points of origin.

Immigrants from particular towns in Lebanon often settled in clusters together in particular towns in Colombia.[12] Among Lebanese immigrants to the West African nations of Sierra Leone and the Ivory Coast, there was likewise a concentration of people from particular locations in Lebanon in particular parts of the new countries where they settled.[13] However, such patterns have not been peculiar to the Lebanese. Italian immigrants from Calabria settled in Calabrian farming communities in Australia.[14] Italian fishermen from North Messina and Molfetta provided most of the fishermen in the Australian port of Freemantle.[15] Italians from Stromboli created a predominantly Italian village in New Zealand.[16] Balkan immigrants from one region of southern Dalmatia settled together in one part of Santa Cruz, California.[17] Similar patterns of concentration have existed among Swedish immigrants to North Dakota, Macedonians settling in Toronto, and Japanese immigrants to the Philippines.[18] Often there have been occupational specializations accompanying regional concentrations of immigrants. For example, more than half the Greek immigrants from the Dodecanese island of Symi became fishermen in Australia, while those from Ithaca became caterers.[19] Similarly, in Indonesia in the late twentieth century, Hokkien Chinese were prominent in dealing in such products as rubber, coffee, pepper, and tobacco, while the Cantonese and Hakkas were more prominent in rice milling, lumber mills, machine shops, and soap factories.[20]

The linking of people from specific places of origin in one country to specific destinations in another has in some cases extended right down to the neighborhood level. Jewish immigrants from Poland settled in different streets on the lower east side of New York from the streets occupied by Jews from Russia, Hungary, or Romania, and German Jews lived in very different parts of the city from Eastern European Jews on the lower east side.[21] Italians from different regions of Italy have settled in different neighborhoods, whether in Buenos Aires, Toronto, New York, or other cities.[22] Recent Irish immigrants to Sydney, Australia, settled in different (and poorer) parts of the metropolitan area from those Irish immigrants who had arrived earlier.[23] In Bombay, particular streets are occupied by people who migrated there from particular regions or even particular villages in India.[24] Immigrants from Eastern and Southern Europe and their descendants remained geographically distributed in the United States in very different regional patterns from that of the American population as a whole, as late as 1980.[25] Asian Americans were likewise distributed among the regions of the country in their own distinctive patterns.[26]

Behind such migration patterns often lay particular beginnings of a new community in a new land when one pioneering individual, family, or group of families decided to try their luck overseas. Once established, immigrants from a particular village, city, or region became sources of *highly localized* information about the new country and, in the case of family members especially, often provided tangible help in moving and resettlement. Most of the Irish immigrants who left Ireland for the United States during the great famine of the 1840s had tickets for the voyage prepaid by family members already living in America.[27] Many Irish immigrants to Argentina also traveled on tickets prepaid either by earlier immigrants or by prospective employers.[28] It was once common for Lebanese businessmen in West Africa or Indian businessmen in East Africa to provide jobs for younger family members who later followed them to their new country of settlement, and Chinese businessmen have done the same in Southeast Asia.[29]

These linkages of successive waves of immigrants from particular families or communities have been called "chain migration." More than 90 percent of the immigrants to Australia, over a period of half a century, came via the chain migration process.[30] In Australia, as in the United States, letters sent back home were a major factor in others' decisions to follow in the footsteps of the early immigrants. Yet, while the majority of Southern Europeans settled in ethnic concentrations in Australia, most of these concentrations were not wholly unmixed communities representing people from only one town or village back home.[31] Similarly in late twentieth-century New York, a cluster of immigrants from India concentrated in a few buildings, though still interspersed among other groups in the neighborhood.[32] In these and other cases, it is not that a particular group could exclude immigrants from other countries or exclude citizens of the country in which they settled. Rather, they simply clustered together where they could. To one degree or another, however, immigrants have also tended to assimilate, first with compatriots from different parts of their country of origin, and later with members of the larger society around them in the country where they settled.

Sometimes the patterns have been more complicated. Polish and other Slavic immigrants from parts of Germany which had been taken from their ancestors by German conquerors often followed in the wake of German immigrants, with whose language and ways they were familiar. Thus American cities with large numbers of German immigrants—Milwaukee, Chicago, Cleveland, Detroit—later attracted large numbers of Polish immigrants from Prussia, who tended to settle in the German sections of town.[33] Similarly, Eastern European Jews often settled in the midst of, or adjacent to, Polish immigrants—Jews from Galicia near Poles from Galicia, Jews from Lublin near Poles from Lublin, and so forth for other regions.[34] This did not necessarily represent friendliness between Jews and Poles. On the contrary, Jews and Poles in Chicago were notoriously unfriendly toward one another but likewise found each other commercially indispensable as tradesmen and customers, respectively, who were used to one another's methods and languages.[35]

Sometimes the pattern is more complicated in another way. After members of a given immigrant family become established in a new land, they may send for relatives who are scattered at various locations. Thus a Greek family living in Sydney and Melbourne encouraged relatives living in Greece, Turkey, and Egypt to join them in Australia.[36] But although those who followed were not geographically concentrated, neither was the migration random in terms of the human connections involved.

Both the origins and the destinations of migrants have changed dramatically over time. Most Lebanese emigrants from the seventeenth century to the middle of the nineteenth century went either to Egypt or to European cities which had trade links to the Middle East, such as Livorno, Marseille, and Manchester. But, from the second half of the nineteenth century on into the early years of the twentieth century, Lebanese immigrants went to the Western Hemisphere, and after that they began to migrate to colonial West Africa.[37] Many factors were at work to produce these changes, but they did not produce randomness. Nor were the immigrants always culturally the same, even when they came from the same country. Emigrants from Syria-Lebanon to Egypt up through the middle of the nineteenth century tended to be either Christians or Jews from large cities such as Damascus and Beirut, while those who went to the Western Hemisphere in a later period tended to be Christians from mountain villages, and in a still later period those who immigrated to West Africa were predominantly Shiite Moslems from southern Lebanon.[38] The fact that others in their countries of destination might lump them all together as "Lebanese" or "Syrians"—or, in Argentina, "Turks," when the immigrants came as subjects of the Ottoman Empire—did not mean that these were the terms in which they thought of themselves or behaved toward one another. Often the hostilities which divided them in their country of origin continued to divide them after they settled overseas, whether in Sydney, Paris, London, New York, Dakar, or São Paulo.[39]

It is easy enough to understand how immigrants from an agricultural background in the cold lands of Scandinavia would settle in agricultural communities in the cold lands of Minnesota or Wisconsin, or how Chettyar money-lenders from India would become money-lenders in Burma or Malaya. What is more challenging is to understand how unskilled workers from southern China would become retailers throughout Southeast Asia and in the Caribbean and North America—

and how so many of their offspring would later become engineers, mathematicians, and physicians in these same countries.

Without assuming predestination, we may nevertheless find clues in the geographic settings in which their cultures evolved and in the historical influences which were also at work.

Geographical Settings

The geography of the Mediterranean world is quite different from the geography of Southeast Asia, not only in terms of such obvious things as soil and minerals, but also in terms of rivers, mountains, climates, disease environments, and other factors whose influences limit the possibilities of different peoples in different ways. The sense of a dependable abundance—"fish in the water, rice on the land," as a Thai saying has it[40]—could hardly have been common in the Mediterranean world, where the barren hills, scanty rainfall, and thin soils made survival a struggle and made the peoples of the region renowned for their frugality.[41] Moreover, geography cannot be thought of in two dimensions, as if we were looking down at a map or globe. While a whole region may be dominated by a particular culture, as the Middle East and North Africa have been by the Islamic culture, peoples living in mountainous parts of the same region—in Armenia or Abyssinia, for example—may preserve a very different religion and culture from that in the lower elevations.

Even when Islam became the religion of the Rif Mountains of Morocco, this happened centuries after Moroccans in the lowlands had become Moslems.[42] Similarly, the English language prevailed in the Scottish lowlands while Gaelic continued to survive in the highlands for generations, just as the Vlach language survived in the Pindus Mountains of Greece long after Greek prevailed in the lower elevations.[43] Mountains and uplands have in fact isolated peoples culturally and economically, from the Scottish highlands to the highlands of colonial Ceylon, which in both cases maintained their independence for many years after their respective lowlands were conquered and incorporated into another cultural universe. Even mountainous regions nominally under the control of a larger nation or empire have not always and in all places been effectively under such control—the mountains of Montenegro under the Ottoman Empire, the Rif Mountains under Moroccan sultans, and the uplands of India under the Moghal rulers, for example.[44] Isolation has been a key factor in both political autonomy and cultural separatism, as it has been in the enduring poverty of many mountain regions. In the Apennines Mountains of southern Italy, 91 out of 123 Lucanian villages had no roads whatsoever in 1860.[45] In parts of the Pindus Mountains of Greece, even in the twentieth century, there were places more accessible to mules and to people on foot than to wheeled vehicles, and one village acquired electricity as late as 1956.[46] In the Rif Mountains of Morocco, snow continued to cut off some communities completely in wintertime, even in the late twentieth century.[47]

The cultural isolation of mountainous communities has been partially relieved by the temporary migrations of its men to lower elevations in search of work, returning with at least a glimpse of another way of life, though the women who remained behind lacked even this.[48] Moreover, few people from other places have come to live in these mountain villages, to present a different viewpoint. Often the great majority of marriages have involved women and men not only from the same mountains but from the same village.[49] Finally, the poverty of many mountain peoples has often led them to utilize their children's labor from an early age, even at the expense of their education,[50] thereby cutting off yet another source of a broader exposure to the outside world.

Another pattern found among mountain people in various parts of the world, at least in recent centuries, has been the production of a wide variety of home-based arts and crafts during the long winter months when time is available. Swiss wood carvings, for example, have had their counterparts halfway around the world in Kashmir, as well as closer to home in Norway.[51] Numerous other products of home-based crafts, from weaving to metalwork, have issued from mountain communities and have been sold in the international markets as items of large value in a small physical size, able to bear the high transportation costs from mountain regions.

The toughness required to survive in many barren and backward mountain regions has produced renowned fighting men in many parts of the world, from the highland Scots[52] to the Gurkhas of India,[53] the Albanians,[54] the Moroccan Rifians,[55] the *Montagnards* of Vietnam,[56] and the

Swiss[57]—all formidable not only in their own homelands but also in the service of foreign countries. The elite Scottish highland regiments and Gurkha units of the British military forces had as counterparts the Albanians and Rifians who fought in the Ottoman armies, as well as the 50,000 to 60,000 Rifians who fought on the side of Franco during the Spanish civil war of the 1930s.[58] It has been estimated that somewhere in the vicinity of a million Swiss soldiers were killed in other people's wars between the fifteenth and the eighteenth centuries.[59]

The fighting qualities of mountain men have also taken the form of local brigandage and blood feuds in their homelands. Marauders from the highlands have preyed on more prosperous communities in the lowlands for centuries, whether Kurds raiding Armenian villages, Scottish highlanders raiding Scottish lowlanders, or similar activity in Italy, Spain, the Balkans, India, and Tibet.[60] Feuds have also been outlets for the fighting ability of mountain men. The celebrated "Hatfield and McCoy" feud of the American Appalachian region was not only an example of a custom that went back to the parts of Britain from which so many Southerners came,[61] it had its counterparts in similar tribal or clan feuds in the Rif Mountains of Morocco, in the Balkan mountains of Montenegro, in the mountains of the Caucasus, and in the mountains of Taiwan.[62]

The minerals found in some mountains present opportunities for mining and for the development of skills connected with mining. Thus the Germans in the Harz Mountains became renowned as miners, leading to a demand for Germans to work in the mines of other countries, whether in Bohemia, Norway, Spain, the Balkans, or Mexico.[63] However, the very fact that Germans were imported into all these countries suggests that geography presents opportunities which people are not predestined to grasp, for otherwise all the mountains and other sources of mineral deposits in all these other countries would have led to the development of indigenous miners, obviating the necessity to import Germans.

In geographical terms, mountains and highlands in general are important not only as obstacles in themselves, but also as features with both positive and negative effects on other parts of the environment. Rivers and streams flow more steadily because of the snows melting on the mountainsides, whereas their volume of water varies much more widely and more erratically where there are no mountain ranges, as in tropical Africa, where rainfall alone must sustain these waterways—or fail to sustain them. The Sierra Nevada in Spain and the Taurus Mountains in Turkey both supply the water that makes a flourishing irrigated agriculture possible on the plains below,[64] where rainfall alone would not be sufficient. In another sense, however, uplands have a negative effect on rivers, which must plunge more sharply downward, often with rapids and waterfalls, when the streams originate at higher elevations, whether on plateaus, mountains, or foothills. Rivers with steep gradients tend to be less navigable, or not navigable at all. Mountain ranges also drastically affect rainfall patterns. When moisture-laden air blows across a mountain range, it is not uncommon for the rainfall on the side where the moisture originates to be several times as great as in the "rain shadow" on the other side of the mountain, where the air goes after it has lost most of its moisture while rising over the crest. The net result is that people located on different sides of a range of mountains or foothills may have very different agricultural opportunities. On some western slopes of southern Italy's Apennines Mountains, for example, the annual rainfall reaches 2,000 millimeters, while parts of the eastern slopes get as little as 300–500 millimeters.[65] Similarly, in the American Pacific Northwest, precipitation on parts of the west side of the Cascade Mountains averages up to ten times as much as on parts of the Columbia Plateau to the east.[66]

Different sides of a mountain range often have not only different amounts of rainfall but also different slopes. This has had important military implications, where the people on one side have found it easier to climb the gentler slope and then descend upon the other side to invade their neighbors.[67] The locations and shapes of mountain passes have also had other military—and consequently cultural—impacts. The greater ease of Roman soldiers' entry through the mountain passes into Gaul, as compared to the more difficult mountain route into German regions, meant that Roman culture reached Gaul first and only later filtered secondhand into the lands inhabited by Germans.[68]

Coastal peoples have also tended to be culturally distinctive. In touch with more of the outside world, they have usually been more knowledgeable and more technologically and socially advanced than interior peoples.[69] As with other geographically related social patterns, these are not racial but locational. Sometimes the coastal peoples are racially or ethnically different—Germans being particularly represented on the coastal fringes of Russia at one time, for example[70]—but the differences between the interior and the coastal peoples remain, even when they are both of the same racial stock. Thus, in the Middle Ages, the largely Slavic population of the Adriatic port city of Dubrovnik was culturally far more advanced in literature, architecture, and painting, as well as in modern business methods, than the Slavs of the interior hinterlands.[71] In tropical Africa, likewise, the coastal peoples more in touch with outside influences were sufficiently more advanced technologically and organizationally to become enslavers of Africans farther inland.[72] One symptom of the importance of coastal areas as cultural crossroads is that many of the lingua francas of the world have originated in such settings, whether in the Levant, on the Swahili coast of Africa, or in the ports of China and Southeast Asia.[73]

Soil, of course, has profound effects on the kinds of agriculture that is possible—and therefore on the kinds of societies that are possible. A pattern of farms that are passed down through the same family for generations is possible in fertile regions, but not in places where the soil is exhausted in a few years and has to be abandoned and a new site found while the first land recovers its fertility. Whole societies may have to be mobile when the land in any given location cannot permanently sustain them. This means that there cannot be cities and all the cultural developments facilitated by cities. Mobile, slash-and-burn agriculture has been common in those parts of tropical Africa and Asia where great cities failed to develop and where the indigenous people long remained vulnerable to conquest or enslavement by peoples from more urbanized societies and larger nation-states elsewhere. In early medieval Europe as well, Slavs in East Central Europe practiced slash-and-burn agriculture, which necessitated very different forms of social organization from those which emerged after the use of the plow enabled them to create sedentary societies.[74] Moreover, just as the nature of agriculture has influenced where urban life is or is not feasible, so the economic and technological advances associated with cities influence agriculture. Thus, in the sixteenth century, the hinterlands of such flourishing cities as Venice, Milan, and Genoa saw great improvements in agricultural methods introduced.[75]

Deserts and steppes, such as those of North Africa, the Middle East, and Central Asia, have often produced societies on the move. These nomads have included some of the great conquerors of all time. Wave after wave of conquerors from Central Asia and the Caucasus have pushed other peoples before them into Eastern and Southern Europe over the centuries, creating a chain-reaction series of conquests in the Ukrainian, Polish, and Hungarian plains and in the Balkans, as those displaced moved on to displace others.[76] Less dramatic and less extreme have been the seasonal movements in places where sheep, goats, and other animals are herded in different places at different times of the year, rather than exhaust the vegetation in one place. Here there may be permanent dwellings where the women and children stay while the men migrate seasonally with their herds, as in the Balkans.

The significance of particular geographic features—mountains, rivers, climate, soil, etc.—is even greater when these features are viewed in combination. For example, the effect of rainfall on agriculture depends not only on how much rainfall there is but also on the ability of the soil to hold it. Thus a modest amount of rainfall may be sufficient for a flourishing agriculture on the absorbent loess soils of northern China, while rain falling on the limestone soils of the Balkans may disappear rapidly underground. Similarly, the economic value of navigable waterways depends on the lands adjacent to them. Navigable rivers which go through land without the resources for either industry or agriculture—the Amazon for example—are of little economic value,[77] even though navigable waterways in general have been crucial to the economic and cultural development of other regions more fully endowed with other resources. In Russia as well, waterways isolated from the major natural resources of the country, as well as from each other,[78] cannot match the economic role of rivers which flow into one another and into the sea after passing through agriculturally or industrially productive regions. Conversely, harbors that are not as deep, not as wide, nor as well-sheltered as other harbors may nevertheless become busy ports if they represent the only outlets for productive regions in the vicinity, as was the case of Genoa in northwestern Italy or Mombasa in East Africa.[79] Similarly, the port of Dubrovnik on the Dalmatian coast, strategically located for the international trade routes of the Middle Ages, flourished despite a harbor that was not particularly impressive in itself.[80]

Sometimes a variety of favorable geographical features exist in combination within a given region, as in northwestern Europe, and sometimes virtually all are lacking, as in parts of tropical Africa, while still other parts of the world have some of these favorable features but not others. The consequences include not only variations in economic well-being but, more fundamentally, variations in the skills and experience—the human capital—of the people themselves. Given the enormous range of combinations of geographical features, the peoples from different regions of the earth have had highly disparate opportunities to develop particular skills and work experience. International migrations then put these peoples with disparate skills, aptitudes, and outlooks in proximity to one another and in competition with one another in other lands, where they seldom have the same economic or social fate.

While geographical influences may distinguish one cultural universe from another, even another located nearby, the existence of similar geographical influences and similar social patterns in distant regions of the world—marauding and feuds among mountain men, for example—means that such patterns are not "national character" or "racial traits," but are international in scope and geographical in origin. Nor are these patterns necessarily racial characteristics even in the limited sense of characteristics differing from one race to another for non-genetic reasons. Particular cultural universes may be largely co-extensive with particular races—the Japanese culture for example—but this is not always or inherently so. In short, geographical influences cut across national borders and racial lines, producing similar effects in different countries and different effects in various regions of the same country or among culturally different members of the same race. This is not to say that there are no national cultural influences. Clearly there are. Language, religion, and political traditions are just some of the cultural values holding together nations composed of peoples subjected to disparate other influences. The point here is simply that a recognition of distinct cultural patterns, whether originating in geography, history, or otherwise, is not the same as a belief in "national character" or "racial traits." These things may overlap or even be congruent in some cases, but they may also be quite separate.

While continents or other regions of the world may not be geographically unique, nor homogeneous within themselves, nevertheless the ensemble of geographical influences operating in one region of the world has differed significantly from the geographical (and other) influences operating elsewhere. These differences are not confined to their original locations but are also imbedded in the cultures of peoples migrating from these different regions of the world.

One of the more geographically fortunate parts of the world, in terms of having the natural resources needed for the development of a modern industrial economy, has been Northern and Western Europe. Iron ore and coal deposits, the key ingredients of steel manufacturing and the heavy industry dependent on it, are concentrated in the Ruhr Valley, in Wales, in Sweden, and in the region so bitterly fought over by France and Germany, Alsace-Lorraine. The broad coastal plains of Northern Europe have also provided the peoples of that region with much prime agricultural land and with navigable rivers crisscrossing these lands, knitting large areas together economically and culturally. The fact that Europe has many peninsulas, islands, and numerous harbors gives the continent excellent access to the sea. The Gulf Stream warms Western Europe to give it milder winters than places at similar latitudes in the Western Hemisphere or in Asia. London, for example, is farther north than any place in the 48 contiguous United States, yet it has milder winters than New York City, much less cities in Minnesota or Wisconsin.

Eastern, Central, and Mediterranean Europe do not share all these advantages. The Gulf Stream's influence on the climate of European nations on the Atlantic becomes progressively less in the more distant central and eastern portions of the continent, where rivers are frozen for more days of the year and where winters are longer and more bitterly cold. The natural resources required for modern industry are also less abundant and in many places virtually non-existent in Central and Eastern Europe. The broad coastal plains of Northern Europe have no counterparts in the Balkans, where hills and mountains come down close to the sea and the coastal harbors often have no navigable rivers to link them to the hinterlands. Spain has likewise been lacking in navigable rivers[81] and Sicily lacking in both rivers and rainfall.[82]

These sharp differences in geographical advantages have been reflected not only in great disparities in wealth among the different regions of Europe, but also in similarly large differences in skills, industrial experience, and whole ways of life among the peoples of these regions. Thus, when the peoples of the Mediterranean migrated to the United States or to Australia, for example, they did not bring with them the industrial skills or the whole modern way of life found among German or English immigrants. What they did bring with them was a frugality born of centuries of struggle for survival in the less-productive lands and waters of the Mediterranean, and a power of endurance and persistence born of the same circumstances. The ability of the Italian immigrants to endure poor and cramped living conditions and to save out of very low wages, which caused comment among those around them, whether in other European countries or in the Western Hemisphere or Australia, had both geographical and historical roots. Similar characteristics have marked various other Mediterranean peoples, but the Italians are a particularly interesting group to study because they include not only the Mediterranean people of the south but also people from the industrial world of the Po River valley in the north, whose geographical, economic, and cultural characteristics are much more similar to those found among Northern and Western Europeans.

The enduring consequences of the different skills and experiences possessed by people from different parts of Europe can be seen in the fact that the average income of immigrants from Southern and Eastern Europe to the United States in the early twentieth century was equal to what was earned by the bottom 15 percent among immigrants from England, Scotland, Holland, or Norway.[83] Illiteracy was higher among immigrants from Southern and Eastern Europe.[84] In school, their children tended to lag behind the children of either native-born Americans or the children of immigrants from Northern and Western Europe,[85] and their I.Q. scores were often very similar to those of American blacks, and were sometimes lower.[86] Nor was all this peculiar to American society. In pre–World War II Australia, immigrants from southern Italy, Dalmatia, Macedonia, and the Greek countryside were typically illiterate and spoke primarily their local dialects rather than the official languages of their respective home countries.[87]

More than three quarters of these Southern European immigrants to Australia were from the rugged hills or mountains, the steep coastlines or islands of the region, rather than from the urban areas or plains.[88] Although these remote areas were eventually drawn into the modern world, the skills of their peoples continued to lag behind the skills of peoples in other parts of Europe that were more industrially advanced and this was reflected in their earnings in Australia, as in the United States. As late as the 1970s, the median earnings of immigrants to Australia from Greece, Italy, or Yugoslavia fell below the earnings of immigrants from West Germany or from English-speaking countries.[89] Southern Europeans in Australia remained under-represented in professional and technical occupations,[90] and from nearly half among the Italian immigrants to an absolute majority among the Greek and Yugoslavian immigrants were unskilled laborers.[91]

Asia has likewise had sharp cultural divisions, many growing out of its geography. The world's highest mountain range—the Himalayas—have separated Asia's two great ancient civilizations, those of China and India, which developed independently of one another to a greater extent than any of the civilizations of Europe or the Middle East. China, in particular, was a world of its own and clearly the most advanced nation on earth for many centuries. One sign of its preeminence was that Chinese goods were for long in great demand in Europe while Europe had nothing to offer in return except gold and silver. The compass was in use in China's maritime trade decades before it was introduced to Europeans by the Arabs, and books were printed in China centuries before the Gutenberg Bible was printed in Europe. Chinese silks and porcelain were in demand in Asia, Europe, and Africa.[92] While Chinese culture had a major impact on the cultures of Korea and Japan, and an influence felt as far away as Persia and Russia, there were few external cultural influences on China itself from the eighth through the thirteenth centuries.[93] Yet very little of China's culture was spread by migration—certainly nothing to compare with the later massive spread of European culture to the Western Hemisphere, not only by the movement of millions of Europeans but also by the Europeanization of both the indigenous populations of the Western Hemisphere and the millions of descendants of Africans brought to the New World.

The Japanese are a reminder that a meager natural resource base alone is not enough to prevent industrial development, though it may prevent such development from arising spontaneously from within the given society. Japan's industrialization was transplanted from Western Europe—notably England and Scotland—and from the United States, as a result of deliberate decisions made by the Japanese government amid a national fervor to catch up with the West. Why this happened in Japan, but not in India, Abyssinia, or the Balkans, is a profound question with few answers or even systematic explorations. Many centuries earlier, Japan was likewise very receptive to cultural and technological imports from China, which at that point represented the most advanced culture in the world. In short, geography is a major influence but not a predestination. Otherwise nations like Japan and Switzerland would be among the poorer nations of the world, instead of among the most prosperous.

Even after large numbers of Chinese, Japanese, and Indians migrated to other countries around the world, the cultures they took with them had little or no effect on others outside their own respective groups. To a greater or lesser extent, these migrants from Asia tended to assimilate at least the outward veneer of the Western societies in which they settled, though retaining their own work patterns and discipline which enabled them to rise to prosperity in these countries.

The southwestern part of Asia known as the Middle East has also sent abroad migrants whose cultural endowments reflect the geographical circumstances in which their societies evolved. Lacking both the spontaneous abundance of food found in parts of the tropics and the natural resources for modern industry found in Northern Europe, the peoples of the Middle East have historically had to struggle to make a living, whether in the nomadic pattern of the bedouins of the desert or in the irrigated farming of others, or—perhaps most striking of all—in the middleman traders who originated in this region and spread throughout the world. The economically strategic location of the Middle East, for centuries a crossroads of trade between Europe and Asia, fostered the development of many trading ports and many trading peoples,[94] of whom the Jews, the Armenians, and the Lebanese have been particularly prominent, not only in the Middle East itself but also in other countries on every inhabited continent. These kinds of immigrants—middleman minorities—from this part of the world have had patterns of skills and aptitudes strikingly similar to those of the overseas Chinese who originated in similarly demanding regions of southern China, where trade was part of their survival skills in a geographically unpromising region for industry, but which had trading ports.

Duration of Migrations

Migrations are not always permanent resettlements. Their duration may last from a few months to a few years to many generations. From ancient to modern times, shepherds have migrated with their flocks to summer grazing grounds and returned home for the harvest and to shelter in the winter. Agricultural laborers have likewise moved with the seasons, whether in their homelands, in neighboring countries, or from the Northern to the Southern Hemisphere, taking advantage of the reversal of the seasons to find work during two growing seasons in one year. Mountain men, whether in the French Alps and Central Massif or in the mountains of Switzerland or Austria, often left for the winter to work in the cities to supplement the meager incomes of their families. It was said of the high regions of the French province of Auvergne that "the subsistence of half the population is dependent on the seasonal migration of the other half."[95]

Similarly, migrants from northern Italy often left in the spring to work in other countries before returning home in the fall—the Lombards going to Switzerland, the Venetians to Austria, and the Piedmontese to France. Nor were these regional migrations within Europe incidental. More Italians migrated within Europe than migrated across the Atlantic to the United States, until late in the nineteenth century.[96] There were also long-established seasonal migration patterns in Central and Eastern Europe, with Polish women and children, for example, moving into the eastern region of Germany to work in the sugar beet fields there.[97] The topography and technological backwardness of the Balkans kept many of its poor from joining these international migrations until the latter part of the nineteenth century, when railroads finally reached into parts of this region, the first railroad reaching Serbia in 1878.[98] However, the seasonal migrations of Eastern and Central Europe long antedated the railroad, the plains of that region being accessible by wagon or even on foot,[99] unlike the rugged terrain of the Balkans.

Sojourners have not been limited to those who migrate for a season. Those working in commerce or industry usually have no reason to coordinate the length of their stay with the seasons and may remain abroad for whatever number of years is needed to accomplish their purposes.

Migrants who have been sojourners, rather than settlers, have included technicians, engineers, and businessmen who spread modern industrial knowledge and techniques from Britain to Japan in the nineteenth century, from Western Europe and the United States to Russia under both the czars and the Communists, and from Britain, France, and Germany to Argentina. Other sojourners have included the small retailers and other middleman minorities from China or Lebanon who long followed a pattern of spending their working years abroad and returning home in old age to retire—until their homelands became places to which fewer and fewer wished to return, whether because of oppression or violence.

However sharp the distinction between sojourners and settlers may be in principle, difficulties arise in applying that distinction in practice, when plans to sojourn or to settle change as a result of either external changes or changing dispositions on the part of the immigrants themselves. When Chinese and Lebanese sojourners found themselves stranded overseas after their respective homelands became places to which they no longer wished to return, they became settlers involuntarily, whether in the countries to which they had initially immigrated or in some other country to which they moved later. Maronite Christians among the Lebanese immigrants in Sierra Leone, for example, began to retire to Ireland in their older years, as a result of their contacts with Irish priests working as missionaries in Sierra Leone.[100] Conversely, immigrants who initially intended to settle may return to their homelands, or re-emigrate to another country, if disappointed in their hopes. Others, however, clearly intended from the outset to return, as shown by such things as men leaving their wives and children behind or by very high rates of saving while abroad, as among Sicilians, for example.[101]

Sojourners and returnees have often had major economic impacts on their countries of origin. Pakistan received 9 percent of its gross national product in 1981 from the remittances of its nationals working overseas and financed 86 percent of its trade deficit with those remittances. Altogether, Asian migrants working in the Middle East alone remitted more than $7 billion to their respective homelands in 1980.[102] Most of these were young males with wives and other dependents left at home[103]—obviously sojourners. In this case, the sojourners have also had a major impact in the countries to which they migrated, constituting 80 to 90 percent of the total labor force in Kuwait, Qatar, and the United Arab Emirates.[104] In other countries as well, remittances from abroad have been major items in their financial ledgers. As of 1979, remittances brought in 70 percent as much money as exports from Portugal, 80 percent as much as exports from Turkey, 93 percent as much as exports from Egypt, and 26 percent *more* than all exports from Jordan.[105] As one study of this phenomenon concludes: "It is hard to imagine a mechanism for the transfer of so much capital to so many (and often poor) countries and to the benefit of so many of their citizens."[106] Moreover, most of these remitters tended to be unskilled or semiskilled workers,[107] so that these benefits accrued to working-class families, rather than to elites, as foreign aid has so often tended to do. As of the late 1980s, remittances worldwide were greater than all the foreign aid dispensed by all the various governmental agencies around the world.[108]

Returnees not only bring back money but can also bring back new skills and changed attitudes. Stories of Italian immigrants returning home "arrayed like *signori*"[109] have been repeated among other immigrants in other countries, such as the Jains who returned to the state of Gujarat in India to live in a conspicuously prosperous lifestyle there, producing resentment among other Jains,[110] as Italian returnees were likewise resented in Italy.[111] Sometimes returnees have settled in enclaves with other returnees, whether in Italy or in India, perhaps a reflection of changed attitudes as much as a more prosperous lifestyle. For example, despite the low priority given to formal education in southern Italy, Italian emigrants returning home often showed much more interest in getting their children educated.[112] A study of Italian emigrants in the latter half of the twentieth century concluded:

> Today in southern Italy there is scarcely a village where a large percentage (often a majority) of the landowners are not returnees from the United States.
>
> Even more revealing is that one of the first acts of thousands upon thousands of Italian immigrants was to seek the best opportunities available by sending their children to institutions of higher education *in Italy*. My studies in southern Italian villages have shown that one

> of the most striking effects of emigration has been the creation of a vast army of teachers, lawyers, physicians, and other professionals who, their training paid for by the proceeds of their immigrant fathers' toil in America, have contributed a big share to the swelling middle class in Italian society.[113]

Such advancement was of course not true of all emigrants, Italian or otherwise. Some returned as failures and some returned to resume the life they had led before. Given the greater propensity of poorer and less-skilled people to migrate, whether as settlers or sojourners, it can hardly be surprising that many worked in lower-level occupations abroad and had no higher skills upon returning. Moreover, those intending from the outset to return home had little reason to acculturate to the society to which they went, even when they had the initiative and ambition to work very hard and save for the benefit of their families. The situation facing Greek emigrants who went to industrialized northwestern Europe may be indicative:

> The migrants were willing to take up any well paid job, irrespective of its prospects for promotion or for occupational training. Furthermore, the low level of schooling of most of the migrants did not allow them to avail themselves of the numerous educational and occupational training opportunities in the host country. Moreover, the migrants were willing to work long overtime hours and were left with little time and energy to improve themselves. Some skills acquired by migrants in highly specialized industrial processes are in low demand in Greece due to the relatively low level of technology prevailing. Many returnees do not like to work in the Greek manufacturing industry where wages are about one half of what they were earning abroad. . . . Returnees with skills often prefer self-employment anyway and do so in occupations and pursuits where their acquired skills have little usefulness. Also, it must be observed, that returnees tend to revert quickly to the somewhat relaxed approach to work characterizing the domestic labor force.[114]

These differing pictures of returnees need not contradict each other or even be indicative of differences between Italians and Greeks. Both patterns could undoubtedly be found in many countries—but seldom were returnees worse off than before they left. Those who returned with nothing more than their savings from abroad to resume the life they left were better off for being able to afford things they could not have afforded before, as well as for whatever insights they may have gleaned from their glimpses of another way of life. Among Greek sojourners, most came from an agricultural background in Greece but did not return to agriculture when they were repatriated. In addition to becoming more urbanized after living abroad, Greek returnees also tended to display changed attitudes toward family life, religion, and political issues.[115] Such modest improvements as better housing and a somewhat higher standard of living are not small things to people escaping from poverty. One study found that 22 percent of returning Pakistani migrants' savings went into the purchase or building of a house, while among returnees to Thailand 60 percent went for that purpose. Among returnees to Bangladesh, 6 percent of their savings went toward establishing a business, as did 23 percent of the savings of Sri Lankan returnees.[116]

Genuine returnees must be distinguished from immigrants who are only figuratively returning by going to a land whence their ancestors once emigrated. Millions of Germans who had settled in Eastern and Southeastern Europe over a period of centuries were expelled from these regions after World War II by nations reacting against the bitter experience of their wartime occupation by Nazi armies. Vast numbers of ethnic Germans thus "returned" to a country that they had never seen. The mass expulsions of Indians and Pakistanis from East Africa in the post-independence era were likewise represented politically as sending people "back" to their homelands, when in fact many had been born where they lived, never saw their ancestral homelands, and in many cases resettled in Britain, rather than on the Indian subcontinent. Early nineteenth-century American schemes to send slaves "back to Africa" were also attempts to "return" people to places they had never seen and which their parents and grandparents had never seen. While these back-to-Africa schemes were never carried out on the scale envisioned, some free blacks from the United States were in fact settled in Liberia, where their foreignness was painfully demonstrated by their lack of biological resistance to African diseases, which accordingly created a high death toll among them.

Migration is not always a once-and-for-all process, even for those who leave their homelands never to return. They may migrate from one foreign country to another before finally settling down. Most Polish immigrants to the United States, for example, lived outside of Poland before settling on American soil,[117] and many Southern Europeans lived outside their native lands before settling in Australia.[118] Some entrepreneurial refugees from Communist North Korea settled first in South Korea, then in Latin America, and finally in the United States.[119] The story of migration is often also a story of remigration. These repeated relocations also test the persistence of a group's culture in very different settings. The many large-scale relocations of Jews over many centuries, for example, has not destroyed either their cultural heritage or their cohesiveness, though both have been modified in the process.

The migrations of conquerors, refugees, slaves, and sojourners have been outstripped by the migrations of those going to settle permanently in a new land. However, even during the era of mass migrations across oceans during the past century and a half, vast numbers of people have continued to return home. It has been estimated that, between the mid-1830s and the late 1930s, approximately 30 million people left the Indian subcontinent and nearly 24 million returned[120]—even though these Indians were scattered across thousands of miles of ocean, from the South Pacific to the Caribbean to East Africa. At the other end of the spectrum, refugees seldom return, whether they have fled from famine (as among the Irish in the 1840s) or from persecution and mob violence (as among the Jews from Eastern Europe, beginning in the 1880s). Thus, during the early twentieth century, fewer than 10 percent of the Irish and Jewish immigrants to the United States returned, compared to about 60 percent of the southern Italian, Croatian, and Slovenian immigrants to the United States who returned home during the same era.[121] In the last decade of the twentieth century, the return flow of emigrants to Hong Kong was only 6 percent of those leaving—again, a refugee movement in anticipation of China's takeover of the colony in 1997.[122]

The widely varying reasons for migration have been reflected in very different patterns among the migrants. Refugees tend to be a relatively representative sample of the population from which they come, as far as age, sex, and other demographic characteristics are concerned, while sojourners are often predominantly male and predominantly young adults. During the era of mass emigration from China, Japan, and Italy, male emigrants outnumbered female emigrants several times over, whether their destinations were the United States, Latin America, Asia, or Australia.[123]

Where a migration begins to change in character from one of sojourning to one of permanent settlement, the sex ratio typically begins to shift—sometimes dramatically—toward one of male-female balance.[124] The earlier male predominance among the immigrant group may be followed by female majorities among later immigrants and, of course, sex-balanced offspring among descendants of the immigrants who are born in the new land. Sometimes the movement toward a balancing of the sexes is aided by a higher rate of return home among males still following the sojourning pattern, while females tend to stay. Often the females are the wives of those men who have decided to remain—whether or not that was their original intention—and who therefore send for their families to join them. Among groups where arranged marriages have been common, the women who migrate may be joining fiances whom they marry upon arrival. This was once common among Japanese immigrants to Canada and the United States, and was not unknown among Italian immigrants to Australia, especially for those men who could not afford a long trip back to Italy to find a bride.[125]

While refugees are, in principle, distinguishable from sojourners or other kinds of migrants, in practice this distinction has often been difficult to make. This has been especially so in the late twentieth century, when national and international policies designed to provide humane access to other countries for refugees have been taken advantage of by people declaring themselves to be refugees from persecution in order to circumvent immigration laws. Professional smugglers of illegal immigrants have included among their services briefing these immigrants on the fabrication of stories to tell, in order to gain asylum.[126] Moreover, even free-lance illegal immigrants often know that representing themselves as refugees increases their chances of being allowed to stay. The losers in this process include the legitimate immigrants and refugees who may find their access restricted as a result of the political backlash against other immigrants who abuse the trust and generosity of the receiving country.

Middleman Minorities

A special kind of migrant has been the middleman minority. These include retailers, ranging from pushcart peddlers to international merchants, and money-lenders, ranging from pawnbrokers and petty loan sharks to international financiers. Usually there are far fewer people at the higher levels of all these occupations than at the elementary levels requiring less money, experience, or sophistication. However, even modest prosperity among middleman minorities may be resented far more than real opulence among some other groups such as nobility or entertainers, and those relatively few members of middleman minorities who achieve genuine wealth tend to be regarded as representative rather than exceptional.

In one way or another, middlemen facilitate the movement of goods from the producer to the consumer, without necessarily physically producing anything themselves. Middleman *minorities* do this in communities where others are a majority of the population, whether in a particular ethnic enclave or in whole nations. For this to be a viable and lasting role, there must be some cultural difference between the middlemen and those they serve. Otherwise, each community or nation would supply its own middlemen. But, however large the role of racial and cultural differences in the histories of middleman minorities, this group of minorities does not represent a particular race or a particular culture.

Some are Africans, like the Ibos of Nigeria. Some are Middle Eastern, like the Lebanese and the Armenians, and some are Asians—though different races of Asians—like the overseas Chinese and the overseas Indians. The best known of the middleman minorities, the Jews, include both European and Middle Eastern peoples. Culturally, these various groups differ from one another in language, food, music, and social customs. Only when cultures are defined more narrowly in terms of work skills and work habits, as well as the fortitude needed to take on the demanding role of middleman minority, do these otherwise disparate groups show similarities. What they have in common is a particular kind of "human capital," as economists call the experience and knowledge used in economic activity.

Frictions that are all too familiar in intergroup relations tend to become extreme in the case of hostility toward middleman minorities. The word "pogrom" has often been used to characterize episodes of mob violence and atrocities that broke out against the Jews of Europe at various times in their history. However, the same kind of vindictive terror has been inflicted on other middleman minorities in countries around the world. The Ibos in Nigeria, Armenians in the Ottoman Empire, Tamils in Sri Lanka, and Chinese in Southeast Asia have likewise been on the receiving end of such inhuman treatment. In a horrifying contemporary example, a Tamil woman picked at random was dragged off a bus in Sri Lanka, doused with gasoline, and set ablaze by a Sinhalese mob in which people danced and clapped their hands while she died in agony.[127] During intergroup violence in Nigeria in 1966, tens of thousands of Ibos were slaughtered indiscriminately by mobs.[128] Back in 1895, Turkish mobs likewise massacred Armenians, including 3,000 men, women, and children who fled to a cathedral for refuge and were burned alive inside when the cathedral was set on fire with 30 cans of petroleum.[129]

What all these victims had in common was that they represented middleman minorities in these respective nations. Not all were personally engaged in middleman occupations, but members of the surrounding population were most likely to encounter people of their ethnic group in that role, even if a majority of the Tamils, Ibos, or Armenians worked less conspicuously in other occupations.

What is there about middleman minorities that provokes such venomous hostility? Other kinds of racial or ethnic minorities have also faced varying degrees of hostility, whether they were immigrants or descendants of slaves or of conquered indigenous people. Yet none of these other minorities has so often and on such a scale faced lethal mob violence. Tens of thousands of Ibos were slaughtered by their fellow Nigerians, the number of Armenians slaughtered in the Ottoman Empire was more than a million,[130] and Jews on many occasions over the centuries were slaughtered en masse by frenzied mobs in Europe, even before the government-controlled Nazi Holocaust claimed 6 million Jewish victims.[131] Moreover, middleman minorities have seldom been violent people themselves who might have initiated hostilities.

While hatred and even violence against various kinds of minorities have been all too widespread throughout history and in many regions of the world, this alone cannot explain the special kind or intensity of hatred and violence directed against middleman minorities. Perhaps what intensifies the feelings against them is that they perform economic functions which have been much misunderstood and condemned throughout history, regardless of who has performed these functions. Moreover, the social isolation of middleman minorities—"clannishness" is a phrase often used—makes it easy for others to imagine the worst about them and for skilled demagogues to play on that imagination to arouse the public to a frenzy of hatred against them.

While his economic functions define the middleman, the middleman *minority* usually exists where the local population does not provide its own middlemen, for one reason or another. It may be simply that such occupations do not attract many people from the local population. Often, however, local middlemen are simply not able to meet the competition from groups long experienced in such occupations. In Argentina, for example, native Argentine store owners found themselves losing business to Jewish immigrants charging lower prices and advancing credit to customers who before had to pay cash. Simply imitating the practices of the Jews was much easier said than done. To operate on a thinner profit margin required both finer calculation and a willingness to live on a lower economic level, at least until a large enough clientele could be attracted to offset the lower profit per item by a larger volume of business. Advancing credit also required a shrewd sense of when to lend, to whom, how much, and on what conditions. Here too, experience was indispensable—as well as a close knowledge of local individuals gained by observation and interaction. Groups with generations—or centuries—of experience as middleman minorities obviously have many advantages in this demanding field, where shrewd understanding, hard work, long hours, and inescapable risks are the norm and where bankruptcy is seldom far away for those who get careless.

While Jews are the most famous of the middleman minorities, so that others are analogized to them—the overseas Chinese as "the Jews of

Southeast Asia," the Lebanese as "the Jews of West Africa," Parsees as "the Jews of India," etc.—Jews are in fact not the most numerous of the world's middleman minorities nor are most Jews in such occupations in most countries today. Historically, however, Jews have been disproportionately concentrated in middleman occupations, going back at least as far as the times when Jewish peddlers followed in the wake of the Roman legions, selling to the peoples of the conquered lands. In more recent centuries and more open societies, Jews and other middleman minorities, after securing themselves financially through their earnings from business, have tended to educate their children for the professions. But, even before reaching that stage, middleman minorities have often also had skills in various kinds of production, such as shoemaking, textile and clothing manufacturing, gem cutting, or the work of gold- or silversmiths.

These occupations are not middleman functions, as such, though they are functions into which some middlemen have branched out—again, the Jews being the most notable example but by no means the only or most numerous examples. Middleman minorities such as the Parsees and Marwaris of India, for example, have likewise been prominent in the history of the textile industry in that country,[132] and the Lebanese have maintained an international network of textile dealers, centered in Manchester, England.[133] In eighteenth-century Russia, Armenians owned 209 of the 250 cloth factories in the province of Astrakhan.[134]

Very similar patterns can be found among the overseas Chinese concentrated in Malaysia, Indonesia, Thailand, and other countries of Southeast Asia, but following similar occupational patterns as far away as the Caribbean. They have not only been middlemen in such occupations as retailers and pawnbrokers, but have also branched out to become manufacturers of products ranging from clothing to computers. The overseas Chinese are the largest of the middleman minorities, consisting of about 36 million people scattered around the world, more than twice the entire Jewish population of the world. As will be seen in Chapter 5, the overseas Chinese have played a major role in the creation of businesses throughout Southeast Asia and elsewhere, and have played an even larger role in the economies of that region than the Jews have played in the economies of Europe or the Western Hemisphere.

It has not been uncommon at various periods of history for the Chinese minority in Southeast Asia—only about 10 percent of the population of that region—to own and operate a majority of the businesses in whole industries in Thailand, Malaysia, Vietnam, or Indonesia. Most of these enterprises have been of modest size and typically family-run operations, but the overseas Chinese dominance is felt as well in large corporations, where even international conglomerates are also often family-run.

Many other middleman minorities have dominated local commerce in particular regions of the world, such as the Indians and Pakistanis throughout East Africa, the Greeks and Armenians in the Ottoman Empire, Ibos in northern Nigeria, Koreans in black ghettos in the United States, and the Lebanese in numerous countries. Sometimes that dominance continues on into the present day, but in other cases these historical patterns have faded with time or the people themselves have been expelled en masse—a fate all too common in various countries of Europe, Asia, and Africa, for the hostility encountered by middleman minorities has been as striking and widespread as their success in rising from humble beginnings to at least modest prosperity and sometimes real riches for some in their ranks.

By the late twentieth century, when Thailand and Indonesia together had five billionaires, all five were overseas Chinese.[135] But seldom have middleman minorities begun their careers in a community or a country by bringing wealth with them. Almost invariably, they have *created* wealth, both for themselves and for the society around them, often creating not only particular businesses but in some cases whole industries and functions that did not exist before. Beginning often in poverty, middleman minorities have historically been hawkers and peddlers on a mass scale—for example, Jews in nineteenth-century America and Argentina and the Lebanese in South Australia, West Africa, and in many parts of the Western Hemisphere. It is from such humble beginnings that there ultimately emerged such businesses as Bloomingdale's, Haggar slacks, and Levis. Most peddlers, of course, never reached such economic heights, but many moved up to have their own stores and some eventually chains of stores.

Middleman minorities have typically been urban people, even in agricultural societies. Often an absolute majority of them living in a given country have concentrated in a single city. Thus studies during the 1980s showed that most of the Lebanese in France lived in Paris[136] and most of those in the Ivory Coast lived in Abidjan,[137] while three-quarters of the Lebanese in Australia lived in Sydney.[138] The great majority of the Parsees in India settled in Bombay.[139] Most of the nineteenth-century Jewish immigrants to the United States settled in New York City,[140] while in early nineteenth-century Australia more than two-thirds of the Jews in the colony of New South Wales lived in Sydney,[141] and in Argentina most lived in Buenos Aires.[142] Most of the Chinese living in Peru lived in Lima, while most of those in Argentina lived in Buenos Aires.[143]

The occupations of middleman minorities may explain their high degree of urbanization but their high levels of concentration in one or a few cities in each country suggests a social need for contact with compatriots, at least during the early generations of immigration. With the passage of time and the acculturation of later generations to the world of the host society, these concentrations tend to lessen, just as concentration in middleman occupations tends to decrease as later generations go into the professions.

In predominantly agricultural societies, middleman minorities have often financed the growing of peasants' crops, as the Chettyars from India once did in Burma and as the overseas Chinese did in Thailand and Malaysia. Indigenous farmers in East Africa—in what is now Kenya, Uganda, and Tanzania—were drawn into the world market by people from the Indian subcontinent who lent them money and purchased and marketed their crops. Modern transportation came to much of that region as a result of trucks owned and driven by Indians.

Despite these and other contributions of middleman minorities to the societies around them, they have often been seen as mere parasites who play no useful role in the economy. The uselessness of middlemen is a theme found among European colonial rulers in Asia and Africa, among the intellectuals and the ignorant, the religious and the secular. To make money from the mere transference of a physically unchanged product from the producer to the consumer "stinks of sorcery" to the economically uninitiated, according to F. A. Hayek,[144] and for a money-lender to demand more money back than he lent has been condemned by all three of the great religions that emerged from the Middle East—

Christianity, Judaism, and Islam. Even in the absence of racial or religious differences between middlemen and their customers, hostility to informal middleman activity arose in a World War II prisoner-of-war camp, much to the dismay of an economist among the prisoners.[145]

Clearly, the middleman could be easily circumvented if all that he did was to insert himself gratuitously between the producer and the ultimate consumer. Producers could simply open their own retail outlets or consumers could buy directly from the factory. Only where the costs and risks of these alternatives exceed what it would cost to use a middleman is the middleman able to sell and survive. The costs and risks are lower for the middleman simply because he is specialized and experienced in managing inventories, in dealing with customers, and in the other functions he performs. The middleman is also better able to advance credit to many low-income customers, simply because he knows them individually and at closer range than a distant manufacturing corporation or government bureau can. In short, the middleman lowers the costs of economic transactions for all concerned. Otherwise, either the customers or the manufacturers—or probably both—would take their business elsewhere.

The belief that middlemen are useless parasites has been tested empirically in different parts of the world and in various periods of history, when governments have expelled some middleman minority en masse. Only after prices and interest rates have risen in the wake of such actions, and in some cases the economy in general has collapsed, has it then become clear just what the middlemen contributed. However, even such painful lessons in economics have not always caused political re-evaluations, much less reversals of policy, though there have been instances where the expelled middleman minority has later been invited back. But the political embarrassment of such a reversal of policy has often served as a deterrent. Catherine the Great circumvented her own ban on Jews entering Russia by a secret communication to one of her officials in Riga saying that, in the interests of recruiting "some merchant people," passports could be issued without mentioning their nationality or religion. Lest he miss the hint, she added a postscript in German: "If you don't understand me, it will not be my fault." In the wake of this communication, Jews began to be recruited.[146]

Often middleman minorities are middlemen not only in a purely economic sense but also in social and political senses. Where a ruling class or race collects money from a large class of poorer people whom they do not wish to deal with directly, middleman minorities may take on the role of collecting rents or feudal dues for landlords, or taxes for government—all roles virtually guaranteeing unpopularity. Even in a modern capitalist economy, an imperial race may prefer having someone else deal directly with foreign peoples whose languages and customs they are unfamiliar with, or whom they may find distasteful, or who simply do not seem worth the trouble of investing time and energy in getting to understand. Thus the British East India Company dealt with the people of Bombay through Parsees as intermediaries in both tax collection and local marketing.[147] Large European commercial firms in West Africa often used Lebanese traders as intermediaries in dealing with the native peoples, just as they used Indian traders as intermediaries in East Africa.[148] On a more mundane level, middleman minorities have often been cultural intermediaries, facilitating economic transactions between individual members of other groups whose cultural differences made such transactions difficult to arrange. A nineteenth-century example from Eastern Europe may be illustrative. A Ruthenian man was asked what he would charge to shingle a roof but failed to respond:

> He was dismayed at the idea of undertaking such a contract, and refused to make any estimate. A Jew was then given the contract, and he came to the same man and offered him a fixed sum, which was accepted, for shingles and shingling, making of course his own profit on the business.[149]

Here the Jewish contractor played a role familiar to middleman minorities around the world, serving as a cultural intermediary to get things done which were mutually beneficial to parties who were prevented by cultural barriers from making the same transaction themselves. Often such middlemen are blamed for "exploitation" but the more fundamental problem is that the other transactors are in different cultural universes.

The story of middleman minorities is not just an economic story. It is a social and political story as well. The racial, religious, linguistic, and other differences among the middleman minorities of the world makes the prevalence of a general social and political pattern in their relations with those around them all the more striking. The special hatred directed at middleman minorities has chilling implications that reach well beyond racial and cultural issues. That people who have created much of the economic progress of a community or a society should be hated by those who have been the passive beneficiaries of that progress says something about the irrational side of human beings in general, and in particular their susceptibility to manipulation by skilled demagogues.

However vicious the attacks on middleman minorities, those attacks seldom arise spontaneously. Such groups often live at peace with the surrounding society for generations, or even centuries, until some special events or movements come along to make them targets. Very often the instigators of such disorders are business competitors, though sometimes they are simply political demagogues advancing their own careers, whether on the petty scale of "community leaders" who incite American blacks against Korean or Vietnamese store owners in ghetto neighborhoods or, at a national level, dictators like Idi Amin in Uganda or Hitler in Nazi Germany.

CHANGING PATTERNS

Whether migrations have taken place across land or water, there have been not only differences between countries of origin and countries of destination, there have also been differences among the various countries from which the immigrants originated. These latter differences have been reflected in different migration patterns. A very small percentage of the population of France migrated at all,[150] even during the era of massive worldwide migrations, while nearly two-fifths of all the people born in Ireland were living outside Ireland by 1891.[151] Differences among the migrants themselves have also been very large and very consequential.

Even when different immigrant groups arrived at their various destinations equally destitute in financial terms, they often arrived with very different mixtures of skills, work habits, and propensities to save, or to become alcoholic, violent, or criminal. Accordingly, immigrants from some nations have for centuries been more in demand than immigrants from other nations—and in some cases, more in demand than the native population of the countries to which they went.

In medieval Europe, for example, peasant farmers from the increasingly crowded lands of Western Europe were able to find more land, at lower prices, and with fewer feudal restrictions and obligations, in the eastern part of the continent or in Ireland[152] because these peasants were in demand by the lords of Eastern Europe, where Western European farmers were preferred to the indigenous farmers because they offered such things as skills in drainage among the Flemish and different plowing techniques among the Germans.[153] Landlords and rulers in Eastern Europe offered not only better economic terms for Western European peasants, but also greater personal freedom than that accorded to local peasants, and often the right to live under the laws they had been accustomed to in their lands of origin, rather than the unfamiliar laws of the new places of destination. Moreover, it was not only existing rulers who induced farmers to migrate. Potential conquerors likewise recruited supporters with promises of such benefits from military campaigns in Eastern Europe or in Ireland.[154]

International transfers of skills through migrations have been even more pronounced in urban communities. During the Middle Ages, most of the cities in Eastern Europe and the Balkans were populated primarily by foreigners with a variety of urban skills, rather than by the indigenous peoples who predominated in the countryside. Thus cities in Albania were often populated primarily by Greeks and cities in various parts of Eastern and Southeastern Europe by Germans.[155] In a later era, the same pattern would be found in colonial Malaya, where the Chinese outnumbered the Malays in Singapore, which subsequently became an independent city-state because its continued inclusion after independence would have threatened the national hegemony sought by ethnic Malays.

While some migrations have been from more advanced but more crowded countries, such as those of Western Europe, others have been from poorer countries to more prosperous countries. Even in the latter instances, however, seldom has it been the poorest of the poor who migrated, whether among the Irish,[156] the Italians,[157] or others. Those a notch or so higher on the economic scale could more readily gather together the passage money and might be a notch or so higher because they had more initiative or more skills or experience. The wealthy aristocracy seldom saw a need to suffer either the rigors of the voyage or the dislocations of resettlement. But how many of the poorer classes could seek a better life abroad depended critically on how much the voyage cost.

Late twentieth-century migrations to more developed countries have tended to be of people with more education, higher skills, and higher-level job experience than the general populations of the countries from which they emigrated—whether these countries have been in Europe, Asia, Africa, or Oceania. More than one-fifth the migrants from all four regions to the United States in fiscal year 1989 were in professional or technical occupations, with an additional 10 percent or more being in executive, administrative, and managerial positions. An absolute majority of those migrating from India to the United States were in these high-level occupations.[158] From the early 1970s through the mid-1980s, India sent more than 15,000 engineers and more than 15,000 physicians to the United States.[159] From Latin America, however, people of much lower skill levels have come to the United States.[160] These differences in skill levels among migrants from different parts of the world might be a function of the distance and expense required to reach North America from these regions. There have been large numbers of Asian lower-skilled emigrants but their destinations have tended to be quite different. Contract laborers from the Indian subcontinent, for example, went overwhelmingly to the Middle East.[161]

In gross terms, however, migration has continued to be from poorer countries to more prosperous countries. American engineers and physicians do not migrate in large numbers to India. Within the European nations, the same general pattern of migrants from poorer countries going to richer countries has likewise been the rule. In 1990, for example, there were nearly twice as many people born in Spain living in France as people born in France living in Spain. West Germany, the industrial giant of the continent, had the most migrants within its borders before reunification—more than 5 million people or more than one-third of all foreigners living in Europe. Conversely, the largest number of migrants in Europe came from poorer countries. More than a million were from Morocco, nearly a million and a half from Iran, more than a million and a half from Italy, and well over two million from Turkey. Like other migrants around the world, these did not settle randomly across the continent or evenly from one recipient nation to another. Italians were more than one-fourth of the foreigners living in Belgium and one-third of the foreigners living in Switzerland but they were only a tenth of the foreigners in West Germany, where Turks were nearly one-third of the foreign-born population. In the Netherlands, Italian immigrants were outnumbered nearly ten-to-one by Moroccans, even though there were more Italian immigrants than Moroccan immigrants in Europe as a whole.[162]

Migrants tend to differ not only from the general population of their respective countries of origin, they tend also to differ from the general population of the countries to which they are moving, as well as differing from migrants from other countries. The selective nature of many migrations is indicated by the fact that migrants often begin their life in a new land earning less than people of the same national, racial, or ethnic background who were born there—and yet, over a period of about 10 or 15 years, the migrants rise to higher income levels than their compatriots. Such patterns have been found among black, white, and Chinese immigrants to the United States and similar patterns have been found in Canada and Britain.[163]

Finally, the times themselves change, so that the conditions of migration, and consequently the sizes, origins, and destinations of migrations, also differ greatly. These differences in eras and peoples will be explored in turn. The purpose here will be not simply to assess the fates of the peoples who have migrated but also to assess what impact their migrations have had on the history of the world. For what migrations have meant has been not merely a relocation of bodies but, more fundamentally, a redistribution of skills, experience, and other "human capital" across the planet. It is this process of cultural change which has transformed nations and continents.

Changes in Transportation

Transoceanic travel has become so much taken for granted that it is easy to overlook how recently in human history it came into existence and how hazardous it remained long afterward. Intrepid explorers like Columbus, or like Cheng Ho in China more than half a century before him, traversed thousands of miles of open water, as did the Vikings who landed in Greenland under Leif Eriksson and others. But these were the feats of a few, not migrations of the many. Prior to Columbus, the great migrations were land migrations, often associated with conquest, or were migrations across the calm and enclosed waters of the Mediterranean or other bodies of water not comparable in size to the Atlantic or the Pacific. But, even after the development of the science of navigation and the technology of shipbuilding permitted large-scale movements of people across the oceans, these movements remained hazardous for centuries.

Accounts of the Atlantic crossing during the era of wind-driven ships depict the passengers packed into the ships' unhygienic holds as plagued with pox, blotches, and "devoured by lice." These immigrant holds were often a scene of fearful cries in the night or during storms at sea. Sometimes smallpox, yellow fever, typhus, or dysentery struck and spread through the crowded ship. In 1738, only two of fifteen ships arriving in Philadelphia disembarked most of their passengers in reasonable health. In 1749, an estimated two thousand German emigrants died at sea. On one ship in 1745 only fifty out of four hundred passengers arrived alive and in 1752 only nineteen out of two hundred. Between 1847 and 1851, forty British emigrant ships alone went down in the Atlantic, with a loss of more than a thousand lives. Moreover, even when ships arrived safely, many of those on board did not survive the rigors of the voyage. Seventeen percent of those on these crowded emigrant ships bound for America in the middle of the nineteenth century died either on the way or upon disembarking.[164] These were particularly disastrous episodes, however. Still, scattered data suggest perhaps a 4 to 6 percent average mortality rate en route during the eighteenth century, which then declined to less than one percent by the 1860s,[165] as the change from wind-driven ships to steamships drastically reduced deaths from both sinkings and disease.

Steamships had far-reaching effects because they not only made voyages faster and cheaper, they made the timing of these voyages far more exact. Before, when sailing ships depended on the wind, which was variable, their arrivals and departures could never be scheduled with any precision. Emigrants had to gather in port cities to await the unpredictable arrival of wind-driven ships, not only draining the emigrants' meager sums of money for food and lodgings while waiting, but also subjecting them to different disease environments, due to being in the midst of local strangers and other emigrants from other places, including other countries. The coming together of people from different disease environments, with different levels of resistance to one another's diseases, was likely to lead to more illnesses than normal, not only in port but also in the crowded and unsanitary conditions prevailing aboard ship during a long voyage when food and water supplies might run low and produce weakened resistance. A study of more than 2,800 eighteenth-century German emigrants with long waits in port before their voyage found mortality rates of 16 percent en route to America.[166]

The steamship changed all that. Where the time required to cross the Atlantic on a wind-driven ship ranged from one to three months, steam-driven ships crossed in a predictable ten days.[167] Now emigrants could arrive in port for scheduled departures, sparing themselves the costs of long stays in dockside lodgings and the hazards of health and crime that these stays often involved. The much shorter voyage in larger ships likewise reduced both the costs and the hazards at sea, including the dangers of declining resistance to diseases when food and water ran low and exhaustion from the voyage took its toll. After the changeover from sailing ships to steamships during the decade of the 1860s, immigration grew both larger in volume and more varied in the origins of the emigrants, now that an ocean crossing was more widely available in more regions of the world and at lower costs.

After the introduction of the steamship, the poorer peoples of Eastern and Southern Europe now began to predominate among those crossing the Atlantic and emigration across the Pacific also accelerated. Prior to the steamship, transoceanic emigration meant largely the emigration of Europeans—mostly Northern and Western Europeans—across the Atlantic, usually to the United States. If emigration across the Atlantic on ships with sails was an ordeal, emigration across the much larger Pacific on such ships was still more so. From China or Japan to Hawaii was farther than from London to New York, and to the mainland of North America was more than 2,000 miles farther than that. The advent of the steamship enabled more Chinese and Japanese emigrants to join the streams of emigrants heading for the Western Hemisphere. It also promoted large-scale migration from the Asian mainland to the South Pacific islands of Fiji and to the vast coast of East Africa, where people from the Indian subcontinent went as either sojourners or settlers. Although Fiji is 7,000 miles from India, people of Indian ancestry eventually became half the population of the country.

Steamships changed migration patterns in another way. In the era of ships with sail, poor emigrants were often carried on cargo ships, which had empty space heading west from Europe because the United States generally shipped bulky agricultural products to Europe in exchange for manufactured goods, which had much smaller bulk for a given value. Therefore the cost of carrying people westward in what would otherwise be empty space, or space that would have to be filled with ballast, was very low and the fares thus could be brought down to a level affordable to relatively poor people—provided that those poor people had access to ports which carried on trade with the United States. This meant that people in Northern and Western Europe, which had a large trade with the United States, were in a better position to find affordable means of crossing the Atlantic. Before the age of steam, destinations were constrained by the existing trade routes, since the migrants had to land wherever the cargoes landed. Steamships now made it economical to have ships designed and scheduled for passenger transport, making the Mediterranean as eligible as the Atlantic, and allowing the peoples of both regions to choose their own destinations in the New World of the Western Hemisphere.

In short, wholly new patterns of international migration were made possible by the steamship. While Northern and Western Europe supplied the great majority of immigrants to the United States during the first century of its history, the 1880s was the last decade for which that was true.[168] The rising proportions of immigrants from Southern and Eastern Europe became half of all immigrants to the United States in the 1890s and two-thirds during the first decade of the twentieth century.[169] Numbers also grew as origins changed in the wake of the steamship revolution. During the decade of the 1850s, 2.6 million immigrants arrived in the United States from around the world. By the 1880s, this had doubled to 5.2 million, and in the first decade of the twentieth century, immigration to the United States reached its peak of 8.8 million people.[170] The steamship also made seasonal migrations possible from Europe to the Western Hemisphere, leading to the phenomenon of Italian agricultural workers coming seasonally to Argentina and earning the nickname *golondrinas* (swallows).[171] In a later era, a revolution in air transportation would change international migration patterns yet again.

Even during the era of massive and growing transoceanic migrations, most European migration took place on land.[172] Some was rural-to-urban migration, or interregional migration within the same country, and some migrations were from one part of Europe to another. Like intercontinental movements of people, these migrations within Europe were not random. Typically, they were from the poorer to the more prosperous areas, whether these were cities, regions, or nations. Geographically disadvantaged areas—whether barren mountains, agricultural regions with poorer fertility, or technologically backward parts of the continent—tended especially to send their peoples out in search of a better life elsewhere. Thus there were outpourings of peoples from the mountains around Bohemia and from the Carpathians, the Pyrenees, France's Central Massif, and from the French Alps.[173]

Sometimes these were permanent relocations and sometimes they were seasonal migrations of men from mountain villages.[174] The less-developed eastern provinces of nineteenth-century Germany have been characterized as "the great reservoir of German labour" for the industrialized western regions of the country.[175] Not all these people were ethnically German, however, some being Poles originating in Prussia. An estimated quarter of a million Poles worked in the industrial Ruhr Valley of western Germany.[176] France was likewise a recipient of considerable immigration from other European countries. Thousands of foreigners, mostly Italians, worked in French coal mines, and altogether there were 400,000 foreign workers in the country as of 1900.[177]

In Europe during this era, as in the world at large during a later era, not all migrations were from poorer to richer countries, however. The more general pattern was from wherever the given people were less productive to wherever they were more productive. Therefore many people with higher skills migrated to where those skills were in shorter supply and would be more highly rewarded. The German and Flemish farmers who migrated into Eastern and Central Europe were by no means the only examples. Many of the towns in medieval Albania had an absolute majority of Greeks living in them, while the hinterlands were mostly Slavic.[178] Mining towns in many parts of Central, Eastern, and Southeastern Europe often had a population that was mostly German,[179] reflecting the more advanced skills of Germans in mining.

Railroads played a revolutionary role in land migrations comparable to that of the steamship at sea. Indeed, railroads played a major role in promoting transoceanic trade and transoceanic migration as well. Bulky agricultural products, for example, became easier and cheaper to transport to and from ports in various countries by rail, thus creating international markets which brought American grain to Europe, displacing European peasants—many of whom then went to America. The Argentine pampas likewise became a world supplier of wheat after rail lines connected its agricultural hinterlands to its own ports and thus to the port cities of the world. The coming of the railroad to Brazil likewise moved its huge coffee crops to its ports and from there to the ports of North America and Europe. More than that, however, rails moved landlocked peoples to the ports from which they could join the transoceanic migrations.

Land migrations have been of historic proportions and enduring significance in the Western Hemisphere as well. The mass movement of Americans from their original settlements on the eastern seaboard across the vast plains to the Pacific coast not only expanded a nation but also in the process transformed a people. The movement of blacks out of the South to the largely urban regions of the northeast and midwest in the twentieth century was comparable in magnitude to the mass migrations across the Atlantic from Ireland or Germany at their peaks in the previous century.[180] Even in the late twentieth century, the migrations of Americans from one region of the country to another was greater than the migrations of all peoples from all foreign countries to the United States.[181]

The era of relatively inexpensive air travel which began after World War II created new changes in international migration patterns. Caribbean migrants of modest means not only could reach the United States readily but could also choose their destinations within the United States—usually New York City and vicinity in the early postwar years—so as to skip over the South, which had racially discriminatory laws and practices that made it less attractive in the pre–civil rights era. Most of all, however, air travel brought the Western Hemisphere within reach of large numbers of emigrants from Asia. A negligible percentage of immigrants to the United States during most of its history, Asians became the largest single group of immigrants to the United States during the decade of the 1980s, when Vietnam and the Philippines together supplied more immigrants than all of Europe.[182] More than transportation alone was involved in this historic shift, however. Changing laws and policies also opened up the country more fully to migrants from non-European nations.

Migration Policies

Few countries have had consistent immigration policies over long periods of time. Japan, however, is one that has: It has consistently kept immigrants out throughout its history. With a population of 124 million people, Japan permitted 1.2 million aliens to be legally registered in 1991—less than one percent of its population.[183] Moreover, a significant fraction of these are people of Japanese ancestry from Brazil and other countries.[184] In addition, more than 100,000 illegal migrant workers were estimated to be living in Japan.[185] Few, if any, modern industrial nations have managed to remain as insulated from immigration as Japan and to retain as homogeneous a population. Even Australia, which once had a "white Australia" policy on immigration, let in nonwhite immigrants before and would later do so again, as well as letting in a variety of non-British Europeans all the while. By the late twentieth century, Australia was one of the few countries in the world with relatively open immigration policies. In proportion to its existing population, Australia accepted double or triple the proportions accepted in Europe.[186]

Most nations have had varying policies over time on whom they would admit as immigrants and some have had varying policies on whom they would allow to leave, and under what conditions. Both China and Japan prohibited all emigration, under pain of death, for centuries. The British attempted to prevent the emigration of British mechanics capable of carrying the techniques of its industrial revolution to other countries that might become rivals. In medieval Europe, serfs who left the land to which they were legally tied would be punished, sometimes with torture and mutilation.[187] Countries preparing for war have prohibited the emigration of young men of military service age. Most prohibitions, however, have been against migrants seeking to enter. Some of these prohibitions have been heartrending in their effects, when refugees fleeing deadly dangers have been turned away at the borders or at the dockside. Thus ships carrying Jewish refugees from Europe during the era of the Nazi persecutions were turned away from port after port[188] and, a generation later, "boat people" fleeing the Communist dictatorship in Vietnam and the killing fields of Kampuchea were turned away from Hong Kong, and interned upon landing in Malaysia.

The point here is not to evaluate migration policies politically or morally, but to see how they have changed historically—and what the causes and consequences of those changes have been. One of the major changes from the nineteenth to the twentieth centuries has been that nations which actively recruited immigrants and even subsidized their travel and resettlement in the nineteenth century began to restrict immigration—sometimes severely—in the twentieth. New countries of the Western Hemisphere, such as Canada, Argentina, and Brazil, helped subsidize the settlement of immigrants, in order to promote the economic development of their vast unoccupied lands and unused natural resources. The United States, as the world's leading recipient of immigrants, did not have to do that, but the American homesteading laws encouraged all who would settle on the land, whether immigrant or native.

Policies welcoming immigrants have not been confined to frontier societies, however. Medieval rulers in Eastern Europe often welcomed settlements of German farmers, from whose productivity the rulers would benefit, both directly in taxes and by having the Germans' more advanced agricultural practices spread to others in their domains.[189] Later, in the mid-eighteenth century, Catherine the Great brought German farmers into Russia for the same reasons. The Ottoman Empire offered refuge to the Jews expelled from Spain in 1492, not for humanitarian reasons, but because of an anticipation that Jews would benefit the empire both economically and by the information they would bring about military technology—an anticipation that proved to be correct on both counts.

Not all immigration policies have involved such rational calculations of national self-interest. Some policies have represented simply political expediency in giving in to the public passions of the moment. Many expulsions of productive groups—whether Jews in medieval Europe, Indian Chettyars in Burma, Moriscoes in Spain, or Indians and Pakistanis in Uganda—have represented these kinds of emotionally satisfying but economically self-damaging decisions.

The growing restrictions on immigration in Western Hemisphere nations in the twentieth century represented a variety of factors. As frontier conditions passed and the need to settle new regions subsided, the problems and potential dangers of continued unrestricted immigration prompted first the United States and Canada, and later countries in Latin America, to begin restricting either the numbers or the origins of immigrants, or both. The massive unemployment of the Great Depression of the 1930s made more potential job-seekers unwelcome.

Restrictions on the national or racial origins of immigrants fell into disrepute after World War II, which discredited the racist doctrines associated with Hitler and the Nazis. The "white Australia" policy and the stringent American restrictions on immigration from Asia both fell under criticism. Australia, aware that its small population made it vulnerable to invasion during the Second World War, began encouraging immigration from around the world in the postwar era, and subsidized many of the immigrants. In 1965, the United States produced a new immigration law, which no longer restricted immigration from Asia, so that Asians grew to become the most numerous of immigrants to the United States, with Latin Americans a close second. Together, Asia and Latin America supplied three-quarters of all immigrants to the United States during the decade of the 1980s.[190]

The Acculturation of Migrants

In addition to understanding the settings in which the various immigrants' cultures have evolved, it is necessary to understand the new countries in which these cultures are to function. The two things interact in various ways. The histories of particular racial and ethnic groups, and of particular nations and civilizations, can shed much light on the question as to what extent peoples carry enduring cultural patterns within themselves and the extent to which they are shaped, or their fates determined, by the actions of others in the society in which they currently find themselves. The implications of the answers to such questions are momentous, not only intellectually but also as a matter of immediate practical public policy in countries around the world. With statistical differences being so widely equated with moral inequities, empirical evidence on the persistence of cultural patterns within the same group from one country to another affects not only empirical questions but moral and political questions as well. When we study the history of Germans in Russia, in Paraguay, in Australia, and in other countries, do we find a set of occupational patterns, lifestyle patterns, and other patterns common to Germans in these very disparate societies? And do these patterns persist across the generations as they do across political borders? If so, how can such results be reconciled with the assumption that statistical disparities within a given nation demonstrate the effects of that society?

While we need not go to the extreme of attributing the fate of immigrants to the way they are treated by "society," neither can we ignore completely the fact that there is an interaction. Whether it is the internal cultural patterns of a group or the surrounding social and natural environment which predominates at a given time and place can only be determined by an examination of those times and places. Moreover, neither the culture of the immigrants nor the social or even natural environments around them remain fixed over time. Immigrants from different countries have tended to assimilate to the culture in their new societies to very different degrees, the German culture tending to be particularly tenacious, for example, while Scots have been readily absorbed into English-speaking cultures in the United States or Australia. However, even for a given immigrant group, how rapidly they acculturate has varied according to whether they perceive the surrounding culture as desirable or undesirable.

The Irish Catholic Church, for example, worked hard to assimilate Irish immigrants to American society in the nineteenth century, but worked equally hard to maintain a cultural separation of Irish immigrants from Argentine society at the same time.[191] The endurance of cultural patterns among emigrants varies both with the particular group and with the societies in which they settle. It has not been uncommon, for example, for the German language to remain the primary means of communication, including education, among German immigrants and their descendants a century after they immigrated to Russia, Argentina, or Australia. Yet Germans were more willing to assimilate in the United States than in other societies whose cultures they did not find as attractive. The overseas Chinese also acquired at least the outward veneer of American society more readily than they did the culture of colonial Malaya or post-colonial Malaysia. Immigrants from India and their descendants living in Fiji also made no effort to become like the Fijians, even when their local culture evolved away from that of India. Yet immigrants from India have blended into late-twentieth-century American society so well that they are little noticed as a separate group, even though they were, by 1980, more numerous than Koreans or Vietnamese living in the United States.[192]

Some of the most dramatic examples of cultural changes in a relatively short time have been among the immigrants to the United States from Eastern and Southern Europe and their descendants. Although notoriously uneducated and illiterate during the era of mass immigration—and indeed, often resistant to education for their children—Southern and Eastern Europeans eventually became, by 1980, as educated as other Americans and as well-represented in occupations requiring education, such as professional, technical, and managerial positions.[193] This entailed great differences between generations of these groups in education, occupations, and languages spoken.[194] The greater incidence of multiple ethnic ancestries reported by younger members of these groups suggests a growing amount of intermarriage,[195] one of the key indicators of acculturation. Not all statistics on intermarriage are necessarily evidence of either acculturation or assimilation, however. When Irish immigrants in postwar Australia married women who were Australian citizens, these statistical "intermarriages" were often marriages to Australian citizens of Irish ancestry.[196]

Not all cultural interaction resulting from migrations are one-way. Just as the larger society surrounding the immigrants may influence their culture, so can the immigrant culture affect the larger society. Thus the Spanish spoken in Argentina has acquired Italian words from the immigrants from Italy,[197] while such American cultural features as kindergarten, Christmas trees, and hamburgers derived from German immigrants. Migrating peoples can have a cultural impact on other peoples not only directly but indirectly. The mass migrations of Magyar invaders who settled the Hungarian plains during the Middle Ages split the vast areas of Eastern Europe where Slavic peoples lived. After the Slavs were thus separated from one another, their cultural developments diverged, as indicated by the separate Slavic languages that developed in different regions.[198]

The immigrant groups covered in the chapters that follow cannot of course represent all of the sweeping array of cultural patterns in the world. Nevertheless, they are sufficiently different from one another to provide some important insights into the role of culture in the economic and social fates of peoples, whether in their own countries or in a range of different countries to which they migrate. Because these groups have often settled in the same countries abroad, the very different patterns of their histories in these countries adds another dimension to the role of culture in history.

CHAPTER 2

GERMANS AROUND THE WORLD

Germans are an old people but Germany is a relatively new nation. The German language goes back more than a thousand years—longer than English, French, Spanish, or Italian[1]—and Germans were recognized as a distinct people in the days of the Roman Empire. Yet it was 1871 before the numerous, fragmented German states and principalities were united by Bismarck to form Germany as a state. But, centuries before that, large-scale emigration of Germans had begun, first to destinations within Europe and later across the Atlantic.

Even before they joined the great worldwide streams of emigration which followed the discovery of the Western Hemisphere, German peasants had settled in enclaves scattered through much of Eastern Europe during the Middle Ages. Authorities and rulers in these regions often encouraged these settlements by allowing these peasants to live under laws modeled after those of their homelands, rather than the laws and practices of Eastern Europe. Though called "German law," these laws applied to all who lived in certain settlements, including settlements whose populations were not predominantly German.[2] Many of these settlements absorbed into German culture some of the native inhabitants, with German land laws prevailing and creating more secure private property for peasants, with accompanying benefits of greater incentive-driven agricultural development more advanced than that generally prevailing in Eastern Europe. In short, Germans brought with them the cultural advantages of Western Europe into a generally more backward Eastern Europe. Polish, Czech, and Hungarian rulers welcomed German settlers into their lands for precisely this reason.[3]

Communities of German miners likewise spread down into the Balkans as mineral deposits were discovered in various parts of the region.[4] Major urban centers in medieval Eastern Europe were typically dominated by Germans, not only demographically but also culturally and economically, rather than by the indigenous peoples of the surrounding countryside.[5] Before the year 1312, the official municipal records of Cracow were kept in German. That year the change was made to Latin and it would be another century before a majority of the city's population was Polish.[6] German merchants spread through Eastern Europe and the Balkans,[7] with Nuremburgers, for example, taking over the metal trade of Bohemia.[8] Germans were also welcomed as formidable fighting men in the service of Eastern European rulers and German artillerymen served in the armies of the Ottoman Empire.[9] In addition, the Teutonic Order of Knights became a major military force in itself, conquering Prussia and engaging in warfare with Poland. Nor was German migration in Europe confined to Eastern Europe and the Balkans. German skilled craftsmen spread throughout Europe during the fifteenth, sixteenth, and seventeenth centuries.[10] In the fifteenth century many German craftsmen emigrated to Italy.[11] Clock-making was just one of the crafts in which Germans excelled. German clockmakers worked in Milan, Rome, and other Italian urban centers.[12] French royalty imported German craftsmen to make clocks for them.[13] As late as 1650, the French invited German clock-makers to Lyon,[14] which was already a leading clock-making center of Europe.

In short, Germans were a major part of the worldwide and centuries-old process of diffusion of skills from where they were abundant to where they were more scarce, whether those skills were agricultural, commercial, military, or the skills of many artisan occupations. This role preceded both the age of transoceanic migrations and the era of the industrial revolution, though both these epochs enhanced the world-wide role of Germans in spreading their skills to other countries and regions.

Emigration was not simply a search for an outlet for skills that were in more demand elsewhere. There were also reasons to seek to escape the German homelands. By the eighteenth century, several successive generations of Germans had experienced almost unremitting warfare on their territory. The southwestern regions, especially, were repeatedly devastated by armies of various nationalities—the crops destroyed or requisitioned, the people robbed, pillaged, and tortured, entire towns destroyed by blast and fire, and industries and agriculture paralyzed by fear and uncertainty. During the Thirty Years War, a single observer in the Palatinate counted twenty-three villages in flames in one day.[15] Altogether, the Palatinate lost four-fifths of its inhabitants during that war.[16] It is hardly surprising that emigration from the southwestern regions was particularly heavy in the eighteenth century.

Rulers of various southern German principalities issued edicts designed to impede or forbid emigration, but these had little effect. Indeed, emigration increased in size and in the diversity of destinations. In 1709, about 15,000 Germans went to Britain, of whom nearly 4,000 settled in Ireland. In addition, 3,000 crossed the Atlantic to New York, and other eighteenth-century German immigrants settled in North Carolina.[17] Pennsylvania became the principal American destination because of its religious toleration, which attracted especially various pacifist groups, such as the Mennonites, Amish, and Quakers. As early as 1745, there were an estimated 45,000 Germans living in Pennsylvania.[18] About 30,000 Germans settled in Russia in the mid-1760s[19] and nearly 20,000 Germans immigrated to Hungary in 1770 alone.[20]

Origins as well as destinations changed during the nineteenth century. As late as 1834, virtually all German emigrants were still from the southwestern region. But, a decade later, five-sixths of all German emigrants were from other regions. Half of the Germans who emigrated from 1816 to 1830 went to South America but, after 1830, about 90 percent went to the United States, on into the early twentieth century.[21]

As of the early nineteenth century, the German states and principalities were essentially an agrarian world where three-quarters of the population lived in villages and small towns. Such industry as textile manufacturing and the production of metal goods was carried on largely by artisans.[22] However more technologically and economically advanced the Germans were as compared to the peoples of Eastern Europe, compared to the peoples of Western Europe they were at that juncture followers rather than leaders in industry and, to some extent, in agriculture as well. More advanced and more scientific farming methods were imported from England,[23] though Germans also reorganized their own agriculture and introduced new crops.[24] In industry and transport, however, Germans were even more dependent on the technology already developed in England. Germany in the early nineteenth century had no modern steam-powered factories like those in England,[25] no railroads,[26] no sophisticated investment banking.[27]

Englishmen came over to Germany to install industrial equipment and teach German workers how to use it.[28] Englishmen built railroads in Germany and remained to run them, because Germans did not yet have the technical capability to do so.[29] Englishmen and English capital began the industrial manufacturing of wool in Germany and helped found the German steel industry. The Belgians and the French also provided some of the technological knowledge needed to get German industrialization going.[30] However, by the end of the century, Germany had surpassed them all as an industrial power. The number of steam engines in the country rose from 400 in 1834 to triple that number by 1850.[31] Coal production increased more than tenfold from 1815 to 1850.[32] By mid-century, Germany had nearly twice as many miles of railroad as France.[33] In the last decade of the nineteenth century, Germany overtook Great Britain in steel production.[34] By 1913, on the eve of the First World War, German steel output was double that of the British.[35]

As Germans emigrated to other countries in Europe, the Western Hemisphere, and Australia, many went as bearers of the most advanced science and technology. Others went with artisan skills that were in the process of being superseded by modern industry in Germany, but which still had a contribution to make in other lands that had not yet reached that stage of economic development. Some Germans also brought with them a tradition of military prowess and skill, going back at least as far as the Roman Empire, when German generals held supreme command of Roman legions.[36] Men of German ancestry were likewise to hold high command in the armies of czarist Russia,[37] in South America,[38] and in the United States from the Revolutionary War of 1776 to the two world wars of the twentieth century,[39] in both of which the U.S. Army was commanded by generals of German ancestry—Pershing and Eisenhower, respectively. Germany in general and Prussia in particular have long been famed for their military traditions and exploits. In both world wars, Germany inflicted far more casualties on opposing armies than the German army itself sustained.[40] In addition to a long list of famous military leaders over the centuries, Germany also produced the most famous theorist of the role of war, Karl von Clausewitz. Ironically, Germans around the world have also long been prominent among pacifist religious groups, as well as among military leaders.

A high value placed on education was another characteristic that German emigrants took with them to other parts of the world. As early as the seventeenth century, Germany was noted as a place where educators were respected more so than in other parts of Europe. In the nineteenth century Germany was one of the first European nations to have free and compulsory public education. Germany had more teachers per capita and a higher proportion of the national output was devoted to education than in many other European countries.[41] This high priority of education was more than a policy of a government, it was a cultural value of a people. Germans in the Austrian Empire had literacy rates many times higher than Serbo-Croatians in the same empire, just as Germans had several times higher rates of literacy than Russians in the Russian Empire and several times higher rates of literacy than Brazilians in Brazil.[42]

Kindergarten is a German word and a German institution which took root in other lands and, at the other end of the educational spectrum, the research-oriented German university likewise was imitated abroad, while great German intellectual and artistic figures such as Kant, Goethe, and Beethoven became part of the culture of Western civilization in general. Few German emigrants were at these Olympian levels, but their commitment to education and to the culture of their homeland found expression in the schoolhouses that sprang up wherever Germans settled, even in countries where the surrounding society had little or no interest in education and the bulk of the population was illiterate.

In addition to education and a desire for education, highly specific scientific and technological skills migrated with the Germans to their new lands of settlement. The first pianos in colonial America were built by Germans, and Germans likewise pioneered in building pianos in czarist Russia, Australia, France, and England.[43] A long German tradition of fine optical products, exemplified in such old optical firms as Zeiss, Schneider, and Voigtländer, lay behind the establishment of the leading optical firm in the United States, founded by two German emigrants named Bausch and Lomb. Germany's pre-eminence in the brewing of lager beer has been reflected in breweries established by German emigrants in other lands around the world. Germans were producing beer as far back as Roman times.[44] In 1991, Germany produced more than twice as much beer as Russia, despite having a much smaller population. In fact, Germany's output of beer was exceeded only by that of the United States,[45] where the leading breweries were founded by people of German ancestry.

In short, German emigrants did not simply leave Germany. They took part of Germany with them, preserving its culture not only for themselves but also making it part of the larger culture of the societies in which they settled.

RUSSIA

Germans became part of the population of czarist Russia in two very different ways: (1) as a result of Russian conquests of Baltic states which already had a substantial German population, and (2) through the immigration of Germans to Russia. As early as the sixteenth century, there was a colony of Germans living in Moscow. By the early eighteenth century, the Germans living in Moscow numbered 20,000 and another 50,000 lived in St. Petersburg.[46] But the first major immigration of Germans to Russia began later in the eighteenth century, during the reign of Catherine the Great—herself of German birth. By 1897, there were 1.8 million Germans living in the Russian Empire,[47] three-fourths of them in rural areas.[48] Though only 1 percent of the population of a vast empire, these Germans clustered in enclaves that remained German for generations, or even centuries.[49] Three of the main concentrations were in the Baltic, on the Black Sea, and along the Volga River.

Baltic Germans

Germans in the Baltic were a small proportion of all the Germans in Russia, and were less than one-tenth of the local population, even in the small Baltic states. There were about 100,000 Germans in the Baltic at the end of the eighteenth century and about 130,000 at the end of the nineteenth century—8 percent of the total population of the Baltic in the first period and 6 percent in the second.[50] However, the importance of the Baltic Germans to the local—and national—economies was out of all proportion to their numbers.

Germans in the Baltic were a dominant socioeconomic class rather than a disadvantaged minority.[51] In 1900, for example, Germans owned 60 percent of the arable land in Estonia. In 1908, German landowners held more land throughout the Baltic than the indigenous Baltic peasants and the Russian domain and church lands combined.[52] The Baltic port of Riga had one of the oldest entrepreneurial traditions in Russia. The fifth-largest city in the Russian Empire, Riga was founded by Germans during the Middle Ages and remained culturally a German city for centuries thereafter.[53] Its founding in 1201 A.D. was part of a long process of conquest of Latvia by German nobles,[54] and it became part of the Hanseatic League of German commercial cities.[55] Despite successive conquests by Poland, Sweden, and Russia over the centuries, Riga remained culturally German, though the city's population at the end of the nineteenth century was less than one-fourth German.[56] Most of Riga's technology and capital came from Germany, even after it was incorporated into the Russian Empire in 1721. Merchants, artisans, and industrialists in Riga were overwhelmingly German.[57] Riga German males had a 94 percent literacy rate as early as 1883—higher than that of Estonians, Latvians, Russians, or Jews in the same city,[58] and far higher than that in the Russian Empire as a whole.[59]

From the time of Peter the Great, Germans were a significant proportion of the Russian Empire's total professional manpower.[60] They filled many important scientific, scholarly, diplomatic, military and other high-level positions. In the 1880s, about 40 percent of the Russian army's high command was German, as were 57 percent of the Russian foreign ministry and 62 percent of those in the highest ranks of the Ministry of Posts and Commerce.[61] At one time, nearly all of the members of the St. Petersburg Academy of Sciences were German.[62] In short, Germans were over-represented in high-level positions, out of all proportion to their one percent of the total Russian Empire population. Moreover, these were mostly Baltic Germans. In the first half of the nineteenth century, Baltic Germans outnumbered all other Germans in Russia in high-level civil and military positions,[63] even though they were a minority within the German minority in the Russian Empire.

Germans in Russia were noted for traditional German orderliness, discipline, frugality, and calculation.[64] Germans in high government positions were noted for their efficiency and incorruptibility[65]—both characteristics in sharp contrast with Russian officials. Germans were also noted for their loyalty to Russia, even in the war against Germany in 1914.[66] During the Napoleonic wars, German generals were prominent in the leadership of the Russian army. It was one of these German generals (who was also partly Scottish) who devised the painful but ultimately successful strategy of a scorched-earth policy in retreat, which broke the back of Napoleon's invasion of Russia. He later led the triumphant procession of the Russian army into Paris and was made a field marshall and a prince by the czar. Most of these German generals in the Russian army were from the Baltic region.[67]

In the Baltic nations of Latvia and Estonia, the upper classes were German and the lower classes Latvian and Estonian. Most urban Latvians had to be able to speak German and those who rose up the economic scale became in the process Germanized in language and culture.[68] The two groups also intermarried, making for an indistinct ethnic boundary between them, despite German cultural and economic dominance. The 1881 census showed that more than 10 percent of those who spoke Latvian as their native language nevertheless spoke German as their customary language. Upwardly mobile Estonians and Jews likewise tended to become German-speaking.[69] Much of the educational activity of Riga was conducted in German, including education at Dorpat University, established by the czar in 1802.[70] During the early decades of its existence, Dorpat University drew nearly half of its faculty from Germany.[71]

For all their cultural and economic dominance, however, the Baltic Germans of the nineteenth century were not a conscious nationality group, much less an exclusive one. People who were ethnically Latvian were socially accepted as they became culturally German. Baltic Germans were, at this point,[72] cosmopolitan rather than nationalistic in outlook. But the rise of a newly emerging Latvian educated class, many educated at Dorpat University but refusing to become culturally German, signaled the beginning of nationality-group politics in the Baltic.[73] Germans in the Baltic long remained opposed to any arguments or policies based on race or nationality,[74] just as the Germans in Bohemia did in response to rising Czech nationalism there.[75] In both places, however, the indigenous nationalism not only grew but eventually provoked a German counter-nationalism. In Russia, however, the situation was complicated by the rise of Russian nationalism in the latter part of the nineteenth century, expressing itself in a drive for the imposition of Russian culture and language throughout the empire.

By the mid-1890s, every school in the Baltic—public or private—was forced to use Russian as the language of instruction. The police departments in the Baltic had to hire translators to translate their official reports from German into Russian—and this meant that German-staffed courts had to hire additional translators to translate the reports back from Russian to German, so that the judges could understand them.[76] As Russification proceeded, German schoolteachers, judges, university professors, and others began to lose their jobs, and many emigrated to Germany.[77] By the late 1890s, German nationalism was developing in the Baltic,[78] though historically Germans in the Baltic had never felt close to Germans in Germany.[79] Russian chauvinism had bred German counter-chauvinism.

The Baltic Germans no longer had the Russians to contend with after the Baltic states became independent as a result of World War I. However, World War II re-established Soviet—essentially Russian—control of the Baltic once more. But the Baltic Germans were at least spared the catastrophes which befell other Germans in Russia between the two world wars.

Volga Germans

One of the earliest large-scale migrations from Germany was to a region of Russia near the lower Volga River. This migration was largely concentrated in a very few years, from 1763 to 1766, under a special dispensation from Catherine the Great. Immigrants were recruited in the war-devastated southwestern portion of Germany and were conveyed en masse, with Russian government subsidies, via the Baltic Sea to St. Petersburg and then on a long journey down the Volga, settling eventually in a barren and desolate region near the frontier town of Saratov. The journey took many months on land and water, usually in crowded, uncomfortable quarters with poor food. What they found at the end of the journey was described by one of the early migrants as a "wilderness" where, as far as the eye could see, was "nothing but withered grass."[80]

By government design, the immigrants were settled as German enclaves, having both a separate legal status and a separate social existence from the Russian population in that part of the country. Catholics were also settled separately from Protestants. The purpose of the settlements was to provide more advanced demonstration models of efficient agriculture for the extremely backward Russian peasant masses.

Despite a substantial outlay of Russian government funds—more than 5 million rubles[81]—the early German colonists lived on the edge of desperation in the early years, and many perished. Corruption by Russian officials and civilians defrauded them of much of the money advanced by the government.[82] Contrary to official assurances, there was simply no shelter available when they arrived, nor even the kind of trees needed for building log cabins. These German immigrants spent their first harsh winter in Russia in holes that they dug out of the ground, in hillsides, and along river banks, covered with such miscellaneous material as they could salvage from their belongings or gather in the vicinity. Thus they faced the subzero temperatures, snowstorms, and blizzards of the long Russian winter. Food had to be bought locally at exorbitant prices from Russians who took advantage of their plight.[83] In the early years, the grain provided by the government for planting in the spring repeatedly arrived too late for effectively producing a crop.[84] Bandits and marauding remnants of the descendants of the once-great hordes of Genghis Khan robbed, terrorized, and devastated the region, even carrying off some of the Germans to be sold in the slave markets of Asia.[85]

Although the Volga German settlements had been promised local autonomy by Catherine the Great, Russian autocrats and bureaucrats constantly infringed and even openly violated these privileges. Village elders who complained about this policy were flogged. The fact that there were Baltic Germans among these government officials did not help, for Baltic Germans considered these south German peasants far beneath themselves.[86] A few settlers who attempted the desperate gamble of trying to find a way back to Germany from deep inside Russia were overtaken by Cossacks and forced to return to their villages. Some who paid a local guide to lead them out were murdered for their money on the way.[87]

These early hardships and tragedies took their toll on the population. Of about 30,000 immigrants recruited, about 27,000 reached the Volga settlements and a decade later there were about 23,000 alive in these settlements.[88] Over the first two years, the settlers built log cabins with logs floated down the Volga from northern Russia in warm weather. Altogether, there were more than 100 small colonies of German settlers. Here an eighteenth-century Rhineland style of life existed, largely unchanged, and with little contact with both Russian and German developments for more than a century. When some of these Volga Germans re-immigrated to America in the latter part of the nineteenth century, there were children among them who had never seen a Russian, and even many of the adults never spoke the Russian language and had never seen a train.[89] Intermarriage with the Russians was virtually out of the question, as was religious or other cultural assimilation. The Germans were sought by the Russian government and placed where they were precisely because they were more advanced than the ignorant Russian masses, and the Germans had no desire to retrogress to their level.

Nevertheless, some cultural borrowings took place in both directions. The Russian materials with which the initial colonists' homes were built led to dwellings with characteristically Eastern European features and heavy Russian clothing became necessary to cope with the harsh winters, while some Russian words became part of the local German dialects spoken by the various colonists. The wheat, barley, and oats planted by the Volga Germans were Russian varieties suited to the climate of the region. At the same time, Russian plows and wagons were improved upon by German adaptations and the Russian sickle was replaced by the German scythe and cradle.[90] Still, at the human level of day-to-day life, the German farmers lived in their own communities, apart from the Russian peasantry.[91]

Although only about half the settlers had been farmers in their homeland, virtually all had to become farmers on the Volga, in order to survive. Nevertheless, those who had artisan skills passed them along to sons during the long Russian winters indoors. Others passed along the rudiments of literacy. Artisan skills proved valuable in the self-contained little communities where the Volga Germans made their own shoes, bricks, and farm implements.[92]

Once normal living conditions were established among Germans in the Volga region—few actually lived within sight of the river which gave them their name—their population size was recovered and then expanded rapidly. The population rose from its low of 23,000 in 1775 and more than doubled, to 55,000, by 1811.[93] The Volga Germans had many children. Ten to twelve in a family was common. This represented a birth rate more than double that of families in their German homeland.[94] However, unwed motherhood remained rare throughout the history of these colonies.[95] By 1861, there were 200,000 Germans living in the Volga colonies and by the end of the nineteenth century 400,000.[96] Volga Germans constituted the largest group of Germans in Russia, even though there were other largely agricultural colonies of Germans in such regions as the Black Sea, Bessarabia, and Volhynia.[97]

German settlers introduced new crops—such as potatoes and sugar beets—in the lower Volga region,[98] developed improved strains of draft animals,[99] built the first public schools in that area, and introduced a variety of new tools and techniques. The crops already native to the region were also grown more efficiently by the Germans than by the Russians.[100] The Germans also built flour mills and manufactured cloth—both industries whose markets grew well beyond the narrow confines of the settler colonies to reach as far as St. Petersburg and even Finland.[101] In addition, the Germans developed sawmills, forges, and tanneries, and manufactured wagons, furniture, spinning wheels, and other wooden implements and conveniences for themselves and then for Russian customers.[102]

By the 1840s, the Germans were so prosperous that envy and hostility toward them was aroused among the neighboring Russians.[103] Yet with all these successes, the German farmers in Russia were not getting as high yields as contemporary German farmers in Germany,[104] where progress had continued. Nevertheless, the Germans in Russia—on the Black Sea as well as the Volga—were a major factor in Russia's becoming an important exporter of wheat in the early twentieth century.[105] One of the German farm settlements became a "show colony" of the entire Russian Empire, visited by dignitaries, writers, and educators.[106]

The economic development of the German colonies was achieved despite political mismanagement and large-scale fraud and corruption by the Russian officials in charge, who sought vainly to force them to grow mulberry trees for silkworms and silk production, and attempted to discourage the rise of industry in these farming communities. Changing policies, officials, and political institutions kept the German colonists disturbed and apprehensive for generations. For many, the final blow came when one of the basic privileges bestowed upon them by Catherine the Great was revoked by her successors—exemption from military service. Military service was enormously feared, not only by those German religious sects opposed to any form of participation in war, but even by others with no such philosophical objections. Russian soldiers were kept on active military duty for many years, treated brutally, and paid a pittance. Moreover, soldiers of German ancestry were treated even worse than others, and especially when they could not speak Russian—as most of the Volga Germans could not.

Military service requirements were also seen by the Germans as a major breach of faith by the czarist government and the harbinger of the destruction of whatever remaining guarantees they had. Moreover, a rising tide of Pan-Slavism and "Russification" policies threatened to destroy the whole way of life they had built up, with their own schools, churches, and other community institutions. In the early 1890s a major new migration began. By now practicing an agriculture adapted to the steppes of Russia, they sought out similar land in the great plains of the United States and western Canada, and in the Argentine pampas.[107] These three regions in the Western Hemisphere, like the Volga steppes, have been among the most productive grain-producing regions of the world.

Black Sea Germans

The German colonies in the region of the Black Sea were founded somewhat later in the eighteenth century than those on the Volga[108] and had a less hostile natural and political environment to contend with. Among the many separate colonies were those of the Mennonites, who were experienced farmers and prospered earlier than other Black Sea Germans, who had to adapt to agriculture. Observers noted the cleanliness and orderliness of the Mennonite villages. Their farming practices were so much more advanced than those of other farmers that the czarist government held them up as models and even forcibly imposed some of their farming methods on others.[109]

The rapidly growing population of Black Sea Germans reached about 150,000 by 1860. Despite dust storms, locusts, and other causes of recurring and devastating crop failures,[110] the Black Sea German colonies became more prosperous over the years. By building grain-storage facilities, the German colonies escaped the famines which sporadically afflicted others in Russia. From the decade of the 1830s onward, the Black Sea Germans began to sell commercially important amounts of grain.[111] Their prosperity was indicated by the expansion of their landholdings. Over a period of three decades, beginning in 1860, vast areas of land passed from the hands of the Russian nobility to the Black Sea German farmers, eventually totalling more than 11 million acres.[112] By 1912, an estimated 41 percent of the arable land in the Crimean peninsula was owned by Germans.[113] In four provinces of southern Russia, the land owned by the Germans in 1914 was more than six times what they had been allocated originally by the czars.[114]

For the Black Sea Germans, as for their compatriots on the Volga, the anti-German propaganda of Pan-Slav chauvinism, the Russification campaigns, and especially the imposition of military service were heavy blows that raised serious questions about their whole future in Russia. Moreover, despite the politicized resentment aroused against the Germans in Russia, other nations were anxious to have them. Brazil and Argentina sent agents to Russia to recruit them as immigrants, making promises and offering help in resettling. Canada and the United States, at about the same time, were making land available to immigrants in general.[115] About 18,000 Mennonites left Russia for the United States and Canada in the 1870s but the mass exodus of Germans in general from the Black Sea region took place later, after the assassination of Czar Alexander II in 1881 brought to power a new czar, far more hostile to foreigners in Russia. As the local autonomy of the German colonies was replaced by their direct rule by local Russian appointed officials, new harassments ensued. A massive emigration of Black Sea Germans began, to both North and South America. By the early twentieth century, the largest concentrations of Black Sea Germans in the Western Hemisphere were in the Dakotas. Most of the Germans who settled in western Canada during this era came from Russia, not Germany.[116]

Russian Policy

Like other prospering minorities in other countries, the Germans in Russia faced growing hostility. Envy was a major factor, not only as regards the Volga, Black Sea, and other German farm communities, but perhaps still more so for Baltic Germans, who had long been overrepresented at high levels in Moscow and St. Petersburg. Many Russians saw their careers blocked by the competition of the Germans. Pan-Slavism and intolerance of foreigners flourished in the Russian upper classes, who had the greatest stake in getting rid of competitors for lucrative and prestigious positions. Russian intellectuals were prominent in the anti-German campaigns.[117] Among the Russian masses, however, such idiomatic expressions as "as punctual as a German" or "as honest as a German"[118] suggest an appreciation of the qualities these people exhibited.

Germans and the Russians continued to live separate lives and intermarriage remained very rare. One index of their cultural differences was education. At the end of the nineteenth century, more than three-quarters of all Russians were still illiterate, while literacy was pervasive among the Germans, even the German farmers, who had set up their own schools in their own communities.[119] German newspapers and periodicals were a consequence and a reflection of this literacy.

The *Odessaer Zeitung* was just one of the newspapers which flourished among the Black Sea Germans, as the *Saratov Deutsche Zeitung* did among the Volga Germans, while the *St. Petersburger Zeitung* had been in existence since 1727.[120]

World War I—pitting Russia against Germany—and the staggering military losses suffered by the Russians raised anti-German feeling to new heights. Germans in Russia were accused of betraying the country to the kaiser, though no specific charge of treason was brought against any of the 2.4 million Germans in the country. About 200,000 Germans were forced to evacuate one of the Ukrainian provinces on short notice, and were shipped off to the Volga, Central Asia, and Siberia. Thousands perished in the packed, suffocating boxcars, where there was little food and no medical care. In 1915, Moscow mobs rampaged through a German suburb, destroying millions of rubles' worth of property, as well as injuring and killing innocent people. Hundreds of German businesses and homes were burned and looted.[121] In 1917 the czar issued an order banishing the Volga Germans, but the May revolution took place before this order could be carried out.

After the Kerensky government was replaced by the Communists in the fall of 1917, the Volga German Workers Commune was proclaimed, with its purpose being to "combat the big landowners and counter-revolutionaries in the German colonies." Though there were only 300 Communists among 400,000 Volga Germans, they were a "majority" in terms of brute force and political power. The material prosperity built up by generations of Volga Germans was depicted politically as their robbery of the have-nots, who were entitled to take it back.[122] By the standards of the Russian peasant, even the average German farmer was considered wealthy.[123] Marauding bands pillaged, tortured, raped, and devastated the Volga German community.[124] The number of cattle in those communities dropped from more than 700,000 to fewer than 300,000 in just one year.[125] Agricultural output in the region declined for several years.[126] The Volga Germans experienced their first great famine.[127] An estimated 166,000 people died of starvation in the Volga after their food and seed grains were repeatedly requisitioned and looted. Meanwhile, the Soviet government sold 282,000 metric tons of grain abroad to get foreign exchange.[128]

Like much of the Soviet Union, the Volga region recovered somewhat under Lenin's New Economic Policy in the early 1920s, which allowed some functioning of the marketplace and some private property. But the end of the New Economic Policy and the beginning of collectivized agriculture in 1927 marked the beginning of a new tragedy for the Volga Germans. Many of these German family farmers, even of very modest means, were considered "kulaks" or rich peasants—agricultural "capitalists" or "exploiters," in the political rhetoric of the day. Many were deported, directly "liquidated," or died of malnutrition, cold, abuse, or overwork in the slave labor camps. Disrupting the most productive segment of Soviet agriculture in turn had enormous impact on output, resulting in another famine. Again, the Soviet government made massive exports of grain while literally millions starved to death.[129]

Not all hostility to the Germans in Russia by the Communists was racial or ethnic. Much of it was ideological. Germans had a history of voting against Communists and Socialists, under both the czarist and Kerensky governments,[130] and in the civil war that followed the Bolshevik Revolution, Germans fought primarily on the side of the Whites against the Reds. Germans were also overwhelmingly a rural peasantry—a group which bore the brunt of Stalin's draconian collectivization policy in the 1930s. Urban Germans did not suffer nearly as much.[131] Throughout this era, as in centuries past, the Germans in Russia maintained their cultural traditions and their separate social cohesiveness. In the mid-1920s, 85 percent of German men in Russia married German women and 95 percent of all Germans in Russia spoke the German language. This reflected the continued rural, isolated existence of most Germans in the Soviet Union. Among Germans living in cities, intermarriage with Russian or Ukrainian women was not as rare as in the countryside.[132]

The end of the Volga Germans as a cohesive people in Russia came in 1941. After the Nazis invaded the U.S.S.R. in June of that year, Stalin ordered about 380,000 Volga Germans deported behind the Ural mountains.[133] Families were separated—the fathers and sons together and the others in separate trains. Once again, the cold, the packed conditions in the railroad cars, and the lack of food took their toll among the passengers. The corpses of those who died were strewn along the railroad tracks. Even those who survived the deportation and years in the forced labor camps were not allowed back after the war. Decades later, in the 1980s, the remnants of the Volga Germans in the Soviet Union were located principally in Central Asia, with many families not yet reunited, much less a cohesive community reconstituted. Some individuals even denied that they were Volga Germans, for fear of what might someday happen again.[134] By this time, identifiable Volga Germans existed mainly in the United States and Argentina. As late as 1975, about one-fifth the population of the Argentine province of Entre Ríos were Volga Germans.[135] Across the river from Entre Ríos—in Uruguay—there was another concentration of Germans from Russia.[136] As the Soviet Union became the Commonwealth of Independent States in the 1990s, the number of Volga Germans remaining in the territory of the former U.S.S.R. was approximately 2 million. They were now widely scattered, so assimilated that most no longer spoke German and many married outside the group. Heavy emigration to Germany also reduced their numbers.[137]

The experience of the Black Sea Germans in postrevolutionary Russia was very much the same as that of those hundreds of miles away on the Volga. After the Bolshevik Revolution in 1917, roving bands of Russian peasants seized food, clothing, horses, and cattle from the German communities—in the name of "sharing." The occupation of the Crimea by invading armies from Germany provided a brief respite in 1918, but the invaders' return to Germany after the end of World War I brought a return of Russian bands of robbers, who flourished in the anarchy of the civil war era. They spread a new reign of terror in the German communities. Houses were burned, people tortured, women raped, and men shot.[138] When the Red Army restored order, it was a very different order from what had existed before. Confiscations were now systematic rather than random. The dispossession of the most efficient farmers, politically branded as capitalists, despite the modest size of their farms, reduced agricultural output. Black Sea Germans now experienced their first famine, though famines were an old story to Russians.[139]

Another respite during Lenin's New Economic Policy allowed the Black Sea Germans to recover somewhat, but their unusual productivity, by Russian standards, only made them political targets again when Stalin's collectivization drive and liquidation of "kulaks" began.[140]

The invasion of the Soviet Union by Nazi armies in 1941 was followed by mass deportations of Black Sea Germans to the east by the Soviet government, even before the same fate befell the Volga Germans.[141] Those Black Sea Germans who were still in areas overrun by the Nazi invaders welcomed them as liberators, after the ordeals they had experienced under the Communists and, later, more than a quarter of a million Germans in Russia followed the retreating Nazi army back to Germany in 1943–44,[142] many dying along the way, in the brutal conditions of war and weather. After the war was over, tens of thousands were forcibly returned to Russia by the occupying Red Army, but tens of thousands of others hid under false identities. Some who were discovered committed suicide rather than go back.[143]

The wartime experiences of Germans throughout the Soviet Union had enduring consequences. The Autonomous German Republic of the Volga, established in 1922, was abolished in 1941 and never reconstituted during the era of the Soviet Union, nor the Germans deported to Central Asia and Siberia allowed to return to that region. When Germans as a group were more or less politically "rehabilitated" after Stalin's death and German-language newspapers were permitted once again, these papers carried special columns headed "Search for Missing Relatives." Many children had lost all contact with their parents during the wartime deportations, had no way of knowing whether they were dead or alive, and were themselves mistreated in orphanages or foster homes by Russians who regarded them as "little traitors."[144]

The neglect of this generation's education can be seen in later official Soviet data showing that 12 percent of Soviet Germans living in the Novosibirsk region of Siberia in 1967 had no education at all and another 25 percent only one to three years of schooling[145]—this among a people historically more educated than the Russians and with a record of strong interest in education in countries around the world. In the Central Asian republic of Kirgizia, where 70,000 or more Germans lived, there were fewer than 150 German students in institutions of higher education in academic year 1960–61, and from 1955 to 1966 none at all among scientific researchers with doctoral degrees. About half of all Germans in the Soviet Union now lived in Kazakhstan, and here too they remained statistically under-represented among students in higher education. With the post-Stalin relaxation of anti-German policies, however, the numbers of German students in Soviet institutions of higher education rose sharply. The number of German students in Kazakhstan more than tripled between 1960 and 1971; in Kirgizia they increased more than six-fold.[146]

Given their educational deficiencies and the fact that only about half of them were urbanized even in the 1980s,[147] the postwar Germans have tended to have lower incomes and occupations than other Soviet citizens.[148] The long years that many spent in forced labor camps under harsh conditions obviously did not benefit either their skills or their health.[149]

As of 1970, there were more than 1.8 million people of German ancestry in the Soviet Union, about two-thirds of whom spoke German as their mother tongue.[150] This was about the same as the number of Germans in the Russian Empire in 1897, and considerably less than the 2.4 million Germans in Russia in 1916.[151] This population decline in a predominantly rural population, historically noted for its high fertility, was one index of the devastations suffered by Germans in czarist Russia and in the Soviet Union. However, it may also reflect a reluctance of some people to identify themselves as German to the census-taker, or the census-takers' own bias toward having people identify themselves in assimilated terms, in keeping with official Soviet ideology.[152]

German culture was not completely obliterated in the Soviet Union, and in fact had a minor revival in the post-Stalin era. However, it had clearly declined from past generations. Even after the teaching of the German language in school was once more permitted in 1956 in Siberia and Kazakhstan, most Germans did not avail themselves of the opportunity in the years that followed, perhaps not wishing to call attention to themselves as German, after all that they had been through.[153] The German newspapers, which had disappeared completely during the war, were replaced in the post-Stalin era by a number of German-language papers set up by the Soviet government. The largest of these, *Neues Leben,* was first published in Moscow in 1957—and was still run by Russians in the 1980s.[154] The first German-language radio broadcasts of the postwar era also began in 1957, for a few hours daily on Radio Alma Ata, located in Kazakhstan. As of 1970, more than 90 percent of the Germans in the Soviet Union lived in Asia.

In the postwar era, Germans have been second only to Jews in the numbers emigrating from the Soviet Union. In both cases, such emigration was made possible only because of outside influences. In the case of the Germans, a desire to establish better relations with West Germany led the Soviet government to accede to requests from West German Chancellor Conrad Adenauer to permit some emigration. Likewise, after the collapse of the Soviet Union, Russian President Boris Yeltsin suggested, during an official visit to a united Germany, the revival of an autonomous Volga German republic.[155] An agreement between Russia and Germany in 1992 provided for the latter to invest in the Volga region, in order to create better conditions there to forestall a mass movement of people "returning" to a Germany they never knew, many of them no longer speaking German.[156] In peace as in war, Soviet Germans were pawns of forces beyond their control. Of the 2.8 million ethnic Germans who returned to Germany in the postwar world through 1992, just over half—1.5 million—came from the Eastern European countries of the former Soviet bloc after 1987.[157]

As an ironic footnote: Lenin's maternal grandmother was a Volga German.[158]

THE WESTERN HEMISPHERE

Germans came to the Western Hemisphere both as immigrants and as re-immigrants, the latter largely from czarist Russia and later the Soviet Union. There were also large numbers of people of German ancestry who came from Switzerland, Austria, and other parts of Europe where substantial numbers of Germans lived outside the Reich. A few also came from the German colonial empire in Africa. Nor were these Germans from outside Germany a minor part of the German immigration from Europe. Prior to World War I, only about 10 percent of the Germans who immigrated to Canada came from Germany.[159] While most German immigrants to the United States came from Germany, there were also by 1920 about 300,000 descendants of Germans from Russia living in the United States.[160] More than two-thirds were either Volga Germans or Black Sea Germans, about evenly divided.[161] As of 1928, there were also an estimated 100,000 Volga Germans living in Argentina.[162] Half a century later, there were still distinctive communities of Volga Germans in Argentina with their own *Asociación Argentina de los Alemanes del Volga*.[163] A visitor to a rural village in

Argentina in 1967 described this scene:

> I entered the church and heard something I did not remotely expect in this distant place—traditional German hymns of Holy Week, sung in typical Volga German style in which each voice remains distinct. I looked around; men, women and children were in their Sunday dress. Some of the women wore scarves. Beneath them were faces like those of the country people in Germany. In front of the nave the minister was preaching in common German to the parishioners.
>
> It was difficult to believe that I was in Latin America, that the ancestors of these people had left Germany for Russia 200 years ago.[164]

While this was an extreme example of the persistence of German culture, through centuries of living in very different surrounding societies, nevertheless it was indicative of a pattern that existed more widely in the Western Hemisphere and elsewhere. With Germans, as with other immigrants, the nature of the surrounding society affected the degree to which they wished to assimilate, though Germans were often especially slow to adopt the language or the outward cultural patterns of the countries in which they settled. Even after they did so, they still remained distinctive in the particular skills they brought and in their patterns of hard work, thrift, and law-abiding behavior.

Among the German immigrants to the Western Hemisphere were members of the Mennonite religious sect, whose immigrations and re-immigrations were part of a worldwide odyssey in search of security for their special way of life. Among the Mennonites who settled in Canada and the United States, some later immigrated again in groups to Mexico and then still later to Honduras.[165] Others re-immigrated to Paraguay. One of the descendants of the Germans in Paraguay became president of the country.[166] These moves by Mennonites were usually made in response to perceived threats to their way of life—notably government attempts to force their children to attend state schools, or to force their young men into the military, contrary to their religious tenets.

German immigrants to the Western Hemisphere, like German immigrants to other parts of the world, tended first to be family farmers and later to include more and more industrial workers and people from commerce, industry, science, and scholarship. Even in the earliest centuries of settlement in the Western Hemisphere, however, German technological know-how made its imprint. Germans were noted for their achievements in mining as early as the sixteenth century,[167] when Spain, Norway, and Mexico all imported Germans to build and operate silver mines, and England brought in Germans to open up copper mines.[168] Even earlier, Germans were noted as map makers, and it was a German map maker who gave the name "America" to the New World of the Western Hemisphere.[169] Germans also manufactured the first armor and swords in Mexico[170] and produced the first printing press in the Western Hemisphere,[171] as well as the first paper mill in North America.[172]

While the largest number of German immigrants went to the United States, some of their most dramatic impacts on the economic development of their new homelands were in South America. As of 1873, there were more than 40 German import-export businesses in Buenos Aires and a number of German breweries there drove English beer from the local market.[173] By the time of the First World War, German academics were dominant in Argentina's Institute of Physics, Astronomical Laboratory, Natural History Museum, National Bureau of Mines and Geology, and in its Institute of Military Geography.[174] In Brazil, the Germans' impact on the industrialization of the country was especially remarkable because the approximately 224,000 Germans who immigrated to Brazil between 1872 and 1972 were outnumbered by Japanese immigrants (248,000), by Spanish immigrants (716,000), by Italian immigrants (1.6 million), and by Portuguese immigrants (1.7 million).[175] Yet none of the others had the same impact on the development of Brazilian industry as the Germans did.

It was not in industry or commerce alone that the Germans transformed the lands to which they migrated. Whole virgin regions of Chile, Paraguay, Brazil, and Argentina were opened up to farming by Germans, often under arduous pioneering conditions.[176] German immigrants also made major contributions to the development of public education in Chile.[177] However, the earliest and largest migrations of Germans were to the United States, where more Germans immigrated in one year than the 224,000 who immigrated to Brazil in a century.[178] At one time, the United States was third in the world in the number of people who spoke German, exceeded in this respect only by Germany and Austria.[179]

The United States

The substantial number of German immigrants who settled in colonial America were but the beginning of a growing tide of immigration of Germans, not only from Germany itself but also from Austria, Switzerland, Russia, and elsewhere. After the emergence of the United States as an independent nation, Germans became the largest element in the massive immigrations of the nineteenth and early twentieth centuries. Between 1820 and 1970, approximately 7 million Germans immigrated to the United States, constituting 15 percent of all immigrants during that period. Between 1850 and 1900, Germans were never less than one-fourth of all immigrants to the U.S.[180]

During the colonial era, half or more of the German immigrants came as "redemptioners," people whose passage across the ocean was paid by others in exchange for a certain number of years of indentured labor thereafter.[181] While individual Germans settled in colonial America from the earliest days of the colonies, and scattered German settlements were attempted as well, the first permanent German settlement in the American colonies was Germantown, Pennsylvania, founded in 1683 near Philadelphia, which ultimately absorbed it in 1707.[182] Germantown was the first of many culturally German enclaves that would be established in the Western Hemisphere, as well as in Russia and Australia. After a poverty-stricken beginning, Germantown became an early focal point of German culture in America, distributing both German-language literature and new German immigrants to western Pennsylvania. The community became known for its hard-working people, its woven goods, the first paper mill in the colonies, its low crime rate, and the reluctance of its people to hold political office. It was here also that the first protest meeting against slavery in America was held in 1688.[183]

German farming communities in Pennsylvania became part of a whole string of German agricultural settlements scattered from upstate New York down through New Jersey, and from Pennsylvania southward, forming an almost unbroken chain of German-speaking communities, reaching down through the Cumberland Gap into the Shenandoah Valley, the Carolina Piedmont region, and on into Georgia.[184] Along these hundreds of miles, Germans tended to cluster together, though other elements, especially the Scotch-Irish, were also present in the region. This was frontier country at the time and Germans settled in these parts because land was cheap enough for them to afford it.

German pioneers cleared forests and built their own farmhouses, schoolhouses, and churches. They were widely known for their industriousness, thrift, neatness, punctuality, and reliability in meeting their financial obligations, as well as for retaining their own German language and customs. Their farms were more productive and their animals better cared for than those of most other groups. When they took over farms that others had worked, it was said that "they often grew rich on farms, on which their predecessors had nearly starved."[185] Early German pioneers often had contacts with the aboriginal American Indians, with whom they generally had better relations than did most other European settlers. This pattern of generally good relations between the Germans and the Indians[186] was to continue as the American frontier moved west,[187] though the Germans, like other settlers, were sometimes attacked by the natives and fought fiercely against them.[188]

Although German farmers established an enviable reputation, not all German immigrants were farmers. Urban Germans were often skilled artisans and craftsmen, who also soon became well known for the high quality of their work. Steuben glass, printing, iron works, the Conestoga wagon, and the Kentucky rifle (actually originating in Pennsylvania) were among their products. Beer was also brewed in many German settlements and German names such as Budweiser and Coors remained prominent among the leading American beer companies.

German military skills and traditions began playing a major role in American history with the war for independence. These military skills came not only from such German Americans as John Peter Mühlenberg, but also from a number of top military officers who arrived from Germany for the express purpose of helping to lead the American armies. Chief among these was General Friedrich Wilhelm von Steuben, who has been credited with turning the motley military forces of the American colonies into a real army.[189] German American military men of later times included those with Anglicized names such as General George Custer (Küster among his ancestors[190]), the Indian fighter, and General John J. Pershing (Pfoerschin[191]), commander of the American armies in World War I. German Americans in the military high command in World War II included General Dwight D. Eisenhower, who led the armies that invaded Normandy, Admiral Chester Nimitz, who commanded the Pacific Fleet, and General Carl Spaatz, whose bombers reduced much of Germany to rubble. General Norman Schwarzkopf, commander of the American and allied forces in the Persian Gulf War of 1991, represented yet another chapter in this long tradition.

After the American revolutionary war, German farmers continued to settle on or near the frontier, but that frontier was now much farther west—in Wisconsin, Missouri, and Texas, for example. Where eighteenth-century Germans had come from the southwestern part of Germany, nineteenth-century immigrants came from more diversified origins, and especially from the northwestern part of the country. Many German immigrants gained access to the upper midwest and the plains states overland from the east coast ports, but many others landed at New Orleans and came up the Mississippi River.[192] St. Louis, which was the terminus of steamboat lines from New Orleans, received such a concentration of Germans that, by 1845, the city had two German-language daily newspapers.[193] With the development of railroads and canals in the northern states, the immigrant traffic through the port of New Orleans tended to be limited to those headed for Texas[194] or remaining in New Orleans itself. By 1880, there were more than 17,000 Germans in Louisiana, nearly 14,000 of them living in New Orleans.[195] They were prominent in artisan crafts and became the sole producers of lager beer in that city.[196]

As early as 1850, the principal region in which German immigrants were concentrated was the upper midwest, especially Wisconsin, and this remained true as late as 1920. The next-largest concentration was in the middle Atlantic states, in which Germans had first settled in the eighteenth century. By 1960, the mid-Atlantic states were again the primary destinations of German immigrants.[197] These historic immigrant settlement patterns continued to be reflected in ethnic distribution patterns generations later. In the late twentieth century, people of

German ancestry constituted 56 percent of the population of Wisconsin and half or more of the population of four other midwestern and great plains states.[198]

During the era of mass immigration, people from particular small areas of Germany often settled together in very specific places in the United States. For example, immigrants from the county of Tecklenburg in the province of Westphalia settled in two adjoining counties in Missouri.[199] Villages "were practically transplanted from Germany to rural Missouri," according to one study.[200] Frankfort, Kentucky, was founded by Germans from Frankfurt, Germany, and Grand Island, Nebraska, by Schleswig-Holsteiners.[201] Lomira, Wisconsin, was settled almost exclusively by Prussians from Brandenburg, while the nearby towns of Hermann and Theresa were settled by Pomeranians.[202] Farther out on the northern plains, Germans re-immigrating from Russia also settled in clusters related to their places of origin.[203] Some of these communities were named for places in Russia (Odessa in North and South Dakota and in Washington state, and Moscow in both Dakotas) or were named for places in Germany (Leipzig, Berlin, and Strasburg, North Dakota, and Krupp, South Dakota[204]), not to mention Holstein and Kiel in Oklahoma.[205] In the nineteenth century there was already an American newspaper called the *Odessa Zeitung*.[206]

Germans from Russia long remained differentiated from other Americans, from Germans from Germany, and among themselves. For example, the Black Sea Germans led a separate existence in the United States, with social patterns quite distinctive from those of Volga Germans. At one time, 95 percent of the Black Sea Germans were wheat farmers,[207] while only about half the Volga Germans remained in agriculture[208] and these produced sugar beets. As late as the 1930s, it was estimated that more than half the sugar beet farms in Colorado, Nebraska, Montana, and Wyoming were in the hands of Volga Germans.[209] Germans from Russia were also differentiated by religion. It was estimated that more than four-fifths of all Catholic Black Sea Germans in the United States lived in either North or South Dakota.[210] Even when some of the later generations of Black Sea Germans and Volga Germans resettled in California, they settled separately—the former around Lodi and the latter around Fresno.[211]

Just as their forebears had had to adapt their crops to Russian conditions, so the Russian German immigrants had to adapt once more to American farming conditions and living conditions. The kinds of wheat, tobacco, and watermelons they had grown in Russia had to be replaced by American varieties. Moreover, American homestead laws promoted individual settlement, scattered among many other American and other immigrant farmers, rather than the re-creation of whole German colonies, as in Russia. However, where local conditions permitted, such colonies were re-created, as in Ellis County, Kansas, where large tracts of land were bought from the Kansas Pacific Railroad. Moreover, within these German colonies, there were Catholic villages and Protestant villages, with intermarriage between Catholics and Protestants remaining rare on into the 1920s.[212] Even in an urban setting, Volga German factory workers clustered together in Chicago as late as 1930.[213]

Germans immigrants' achievement as farmers in the United States remained outstanding in the nineteenth and twentieth centuries. In eastern Texas, German farmers were by 1880 producing a larger volume of output per farm—and on smaller farms—than other Texans.[214] In Nebraska, Colorado, Montana, and Wyoming, Germans who had re-immigrated from Russia established good reputations as farmers and had excellent credit ratings at banks.[215] Germans, both from Germany and from Russia, eventually achieved prosperity in Oklahoma, after harrowing years of pioneering in a virgin territory.[216]

The nineteenth century saw a general shift of the growing German population from the eastern seaboard states to the midwest particularly to the upper Mississippi and Ohio valleys. By the middle of the nineteenth century, this region contained more than half of all German-born people in the United States.[217] The midwest was not only the destination of nineteenth-century German immigrants but also a destination of east coast German Americans or their descendants. Not all these Germans were farmers, however. Cities such as Cincinnati, St. Louis, and above all Milwaukee, became centers of urban German populations in the nineteenth century. Only 5 percent of Cincinnati's population was German in 1830 but, by 1860, 30 percent of the city's inhabitants were German.[218] Milwaukee's Germans were 35 percent of the population.[219] A number of smaller communities were even more completely German, not only in population but in language as well. Hermann, Missouri, for example, had its street signs in German.[220] In rural areas, the concentration of German people and the dominance of the German language were even greater.[221]

Whether rural or urban, Germans in the nineteenth century tended to retain their culture, as their predecessors had done in earlier centuries. The German language could be heard spoken on the streets of Cincinnati or St. Louis[222] and German-language newspapers appeared daily in 15 American cities.[223] These daily newspapers ranged across the country, from *Die New Yorker Staats-Zeitung* to the *Cincinnati Volksblatt,* the *Chicago Abendpost,* the *Louisville Anzeiger,* and the *Deutsche Zeitung* in New Orleans.[224] Approximately four-fifths of the entire foreign-language press in the United States was German.[225] There were also innumerable German associations, whether gymnastic, musical, social, or literary. These existed not only in urban areas but even in such agricultural regions as the hill country of Texas.[226]

All in all, it was possible for many German Americans to live for generations in German enclaves, whether rural or urban, never having to venture into the English-speaking world for education, church, recreation, or marriage partners.[227] Not all did so, by any means, for American-born generations were attracted toward the cultural mainstream of the United States, even as the massive inflow of new German immigrants kept alive the culture of Germany. However, even the cultural mainstream of America began to take on features once peculiar to Germans. These included not only such old country traditions as lager beer, cole slaw, delicatessen, and the Christmas tree, but also such German improvisations on American soil as oatmeal and those "all-American" foods deriving their names from German cities, frankfurters and hamburgers.

Above all, perhaps, Germans profoundly influenced American recreational patterns. The innumerable innocent but secular and zestful recreations of the Germans—from songfests to bowling to parades, target shooting, and swimming—were at first viewed by other Americans with suspicion and reproach, especially when they took place on Sunday, in contravention of more Puritanical norms in the larger community. But, ultimately, such peaceful and enjoyable activities, often engaged in by family groups, began to become part of the American way of life. Germans played a major role in making music a part of

American life—not only by breaking down Puritanical prejudices against singing, but also by promoting all kinds of music, from folk music and marching bands to the great symphony orchestras. Many of the leading American classical music conductors of the nineteenth century were of German ancestry, as were the overwhelming majority of the members of the New York Philharmonic orchestra in the last half of the nineteenth century.[228]

Increasingly, as German immigration to the United States rose during the nineteenth century, the predominance of farmers among the immigrants declined. The rising urban component brought with them many artisan and industrial skills or entrepreneurial talents. Most Germans who worked in mid-nineteenth century New York, Boston, Detroit, St. Louis, or Milwaukee were either skilled manual workers or were in non-manual occupations, while the Irish, for example, were in mostly unskilled or semiskilled occupations in the same cities at the same time.[229] Similarly, in San Francisco in 1870, 38 percent of the Irish immigrants were unskilled, compared to only 7 percent of the Germans.[230] Germans also tended to be well-represented in business and the professions. In the middle of the nineteenth century, one-third of all the physicians in New York state were German.[231] In Milwaukee at about the same time, nearly half of all the shopkeepers were German.[232]

The success and prominence of Germans in agriculture, industry, commerce, and the professions was not repeated in politics, however. In the nineteenth century, as in the eighteenth century, Germans tended to be under-represented among those pursuing political careers and the German electorate tended to be apathetic as well. Moreover, those Americans of German ancestry who did achieve distinction in politics—notably the Mühlenbergs in the eighteenth century, Carl Schurz and John Peter Altgeld in the nineteenth, and Herbert Hoover and Dwight D. Eisenhower in the twentieth century—did so as spokesmen for the general population on broad national issues, not as ethnic representatives of German American community special interests.

The general political leanings of German Americans in the eighteenth and nineteenth centuries tended to be more liberal or progressive than those of their contemporaries. However, there was no monolithic German position on the issues of the day. Although Germans tended to be antislavery throughout the history of that institution,[233] there were many crosscurrents,[234] though no prominent German American leaders were pro-slavery.[235] Moreover, when a vote was taken in antebellum North Carolina to take away many legal rights of free Negroes, the German areas voted to let them keep those rights, while the state as a whole voted to abrogate their rights.[236] When the Civil War came, the large German population in Missouri was credited with keeping that state in the Union, despite many Confederate sympathizers.[237] On other issues of personal freedom, such as laws against drinking or laws restricting Sunday activities, the Germans voted for the freedom of the individual.[238] Within their own community enclaves, Germans welcomed German Jews as members of such organizations as the *Turnvereine*, singing groups, and other cultural organizations.[239]

German immigration to the United States peaked in the decade of the 1880s, when more than 1.4 million arrived on American shores. By the first decade of the twentieth century, however, German immigration had fallen to less than one-fourth of that.[240] The pioneering struggles of the eighteenth and nineteenth centuries gave way to very different kinds of adversity in the twentieth century. Economically, the rise of mass-production industry devalued and superseded many of the artisan skills among German workers, including many crafts associated with horse-and-buggy transportation, shoemaking, and furniture production. The rise of the meat-packing industry reduced the role of the German butcher shops, as the rise of mass marketing in general through department stores and supermarkets likewise eclipsed the German specialty shopkeepers.[241] The declining importance of family farms and the rise of mechanized, mass-production agriculture also could not help adversely affect the vast number of German family farmers scattered across many states.

International political developments likewise had their impact on German Americans. The outbreak of the First World War in Europe in 1914 brought much condemnation of Germany in the United States. German Americans were adversely affected, in part because of a generalized hostility to Germans and German culture, and perhaps more so because German American spokesmen tended to try to justify the actions of their ancestral homeland, which was waging a war of aggression in Europe. When the United States ultimately joined the war against Germany, feelings ran higher still among Americans in general, though German Americans loyally served in the U.S. military forces and America's leading fighter pilot was of German ancestry—Eddie Rickenbacker. Nevertheless, the German language was banished from many American high school curricula, as German music was banished from concert halls.[242] Some marriage ceremonies no longer used wedding marches by Mendelssohn or Wagner. German books were removed from library shelves and German American newspapers were boycotted by advertisers and readers. While this anti-German hysteria did not reach the levels it reached in some other countries, such as Russia, Brazil, or Australia, it was real enough and painful enough to German Americans. These attacks also hastened the demise of many German American associations.[243] Some of these organizations simply dropped any reference to Germany in their titles, as the Germania Life Insurance Company of New York changed its name to the Guardian Life Insurance Company,[244] for example.

While the anti-German hostility subsided quickly after the war, it nevertheless contributed to the already existing trend of declining cultural and social cohesion among Germans in the United States. In the early twentieth century, Germans in many parts of the United States still married mostly other Germans, even in an urban center like New York City, where 90 percent of the population was non-German. Intermarriage increased with the passing decades, however.[245] Other indices of assimilation included the decline of the large German-language press. German-language daily and weekly publications, numbering more than 700 in 1890, declined to barely 200 in 1920, and continued to decline to 81 in 1940 and to 33 by 1960.[246] German cultural organizations likewise declined sharply over the years, as German Americans became more assimilated and many disappeared into the larger society.

The rise of Hitler and the Nazis in Germany during the 1930s led to efforts to recruit German Americans to the cause, largely without success. A Nazi front organization, the German-American Bund, was established in 1936 with financial support from Germany, and made headlines with spectacular rallies and fiery rhetoric, but it made little headway with most German Americans. The organization disbanded when the United States entered the Second World War in 1941. In the larger society, there was no such hostility to German Americans during World War II as there had been in World War I, and few found it noteworthy, much less controversial, that the American army in Europe, the U.S. Pacific Fleet, and the American air force in Europe were all commanded by men of German ancestry.

Over the years, Germans have made major contributions to many aspects of American society. In addition to the contributions of broad masses of German people in agriculture and industry, and of German food, customs, and attitudes toward recreation, numerous individuals of German ancestry made historic contributions in various fields. Engineering history was made when John A. Roebling designed and built the Brooklyn Bridge, the first of many long-span suspension bridges which are now taken for granted, though the Brooklyn Bridge was a pioneering marvel in its day, made possible by the steel cables which Roebling also designed and produced. The genius of German-born engineer Charles Steinmetz provided the basis on which the General Electric Corporation was built.

Firms established by individuals of German ancestry have been among the leaders in many American industries, including optics (Bausch and Lomb), wood products (Weyerhauser), automobiles (Chrysler), pianos (Steinway, Schnabel), organs (Wurlitzer), candy (Hershey), prepared food (Heinz), language instruction (Berlitz), and innumerable beer companies, including Anheuser-Busch, Miller, Coors, Pabst, Schlitz, and Blatz. Germans are no longer a distinctive group in America because they have become so much a part of American society and that society has absorbed so many German cultural features, from kindergartens to Christmas trees to cole slaw. Yet it may be indicative of how long German cultural ties endured that the German language was spoken in childhood by such disparate twentieth-century American figures as famed writer H. L. Mencken, baseball stars Babe Ruth and Lou Gehrig, and by the Nobel Prize–winning economist George Stigler.

Brazil

Substantial German immigration to Brazil, as to South America in general, began early in the nineteenth century and included over the years not only immigrants from what is now Germany but also sizable numbers of Germans from Russia, Switzerland, and Austria.[247] Most settled in the southern part of Brazil, concentrated in the state of Rio Grande do Sul, where the first enduring German agricultural colony was established in 1824, though earlier unsuccessful attempts to establish German colonies in Brazil go back to the late eighteenth century. Settlements of Germans, in groups numbering in the hundreds or the thousands, continued to be made in the nineteenth century and well into the twentieth century.[248]

The initial German settlements were in an almost deserted region,[249] where the immigrants had to clear the forest before being able to farm. Until after the middle of the nineteenth century, the only immigrants to Rio Grande do Sul were Germans, and it was the last quarter of the century before the inflow of all other immigrants combined outnumbered the inflow of Germans.[250] For the period from 1844 to 1874, Germans constituted 87 percent of all immigrants to Rio Grande do Sul. Most of these immigrants were from western Germany.[251]

The German colonies remained culturally German for generations, and grew more by natural increase than by immigration.[252] The sexes were roughly balanced—a sign of permanent settlement—and German farm families tended to be large.[253] Self-contained German-speaking enclaves covered vast areas. Between 1824 and 1859, more than 20,000 Germans were brought to Brazil with Brazilian government aid in various forms.[254] The Germans not only lived separately from the Brazilians of Portuguese ancestry, but also in a very different way of life, which showed itself in the style of their better-constructed homes, the care of the land, and in the Germans' willingness to engage in hard manual labor disdained by the Portuguese.[255]

The two groups differed also in their attitudes toward education and cleanliness. In the German pioneering settlements, schools appeared in the first clearings in the woods,[256] while most native-born Brazilians remained illiterate on into the twentieth century.[257] Private German schools were not only more numerous than government schools but also of a higher quality. The Germans were also cleaner and healthier, better fed and better housed than the Portuguese.[258] Immigrants in general had higher standards of health and sanitation than the Brazilians, leading to a more rapid rate of immigrant population growth—the two groups having similar numbers of children per family, but with more of the immigrant children surviving to reach adulthood.[259] The Germans also had more skilled laborers, a fact resented by the unskilled and less-prosperous Brazilians.[260]

Even though Italian, Polish, and other immigrants began arriving in large numbers during the last quarter of the nineteenth century, the German enclaves remained largely isolated culturally.[261] As of 1882, the entire pioneering zone of southern Brazil was 71 percent German-speaking, 18 percent Italian-speaking, and only 10 percent Portuguese-speaking in a predominantly Portuguese-speaking country.[262] The Italians, and later the Poles, likewise tended to settle in their own colonies. The German colonies were noted as places where crime was virtually non-existent, where a woman could travel safely alone through the woods.[263]

In the late nineteenth century, Germans from Russia began to immigrate to Brazil in large numbers. Unlike the Germans from the Reich, who tended to settle in wooded areas like those in Germany, the Volga Germans tended to settle on grasslands like those in Russia. These latter areas proved to be very unproductive in Brazil, leading many Volga Germans to re-immigrate to neighboring Argentina, where they were more successful.[264] Indeed, Argentina's transformation from a wheat importer to one of the world's great wheat-exporting nations has been credited in part to the Volga Germans,[265] who introduced new agricultural practices and created new farm implements.[266]

Whether from Russia or from Germany, German farmers in Brazil tended to settle together, maintain their own language and customs, and resist both acculturation and assimilation into what they saw as an inferior culture.[267] There was little intermarriage in the areas of the German colonies, even well into the twentieth century,[268] though in cities and in rural areas with more diverse populations, acculturation and assimilation were more common.[269] But it was the German concentration, rather than the degree of urbanization, as such, that was crucial. Cultural assimilation was also slow. Even as late as the 1920s, 63 percent of the people in the town of Blumenau spoke German as their mother tongue, and throughout the region of German concentration in southern Brazil schools were conducted in the German language from the early nineteenth century until the Brazilian government put a stop to it in 1938.[270] As late as 1940, more than half the Germans in São Paulo, and nearly all in Rio Grande do Sul, spoke German in their homes.[271]

The economic rise of the German colonists in Brazil was from an initially primitive existence as pioneers. Indeed, in the early years they had to learn the crude agricultural techniques of the Portuguese Brazilians and the aborigines, in order to survive at a time when there was not sufficient capital to support more advanced methods.[272] There was a rapid growth of output in the German colonies around the middle of the nineteenth century. But exhaustion of the soil over the years brought declining yields in the older colonies[273] and in some places the poverty and isolation also took their cultural toll in a retrogression to a way of life reminiscent of the Brazilian rural poor.[274] However, newer colonies, established in the late nineteenth and early twentieth centuries, were more prosperous, not only because their soils were not exhausted, but also because their access to improved transportation made the marketing of their crops easier.[275]

By and large, the German farmers prospered, creating a rural middle class,[276] and introduced new crops such as tobacco, potatoes, rye, and wheat to Brazil.[277] As in Russia, their land expanded well beyond that originally allotted to them by the government. Despite the presence of huge landholdings by the Creole aristocracy of Brazil, Germans were able to buy up land, in small portions each, for their own use. Other European immigrant groups as well expanded beyond the land granted in their original colonies.[278] By the early twentieth century, there were few huge estates left in the areas of southern Brazil settled by European immigrants.[279] Even in the coffee-growing regions of the state of São Paulo, where the Brazilian elite owned virtually all the properties in 1905, by 1934 nearly half the coffee farms were owned by people of foreign birth.[280]

The persistence of huge landholdings and landless people in Latin America and elsewhere cannot be explained solely by the initial division of land, for small German farmers in czarist Russia bought out much of the landed aristocracy in the Crimea, just as their compatriots did in Brazil. It is the productivity of alternative landowners which is crucial in the long run, in determining whether or not they can bid land away from current owners. German farmers in Brazil, as elsewhere around the world, were noted for their productivity. They were brought to Brazil at the Brazilian government's initiative and with subsidies precisely because the government anticipated that they could achieve the arduous task of clearing virgin forests and making agriculture viable there. The Germans were noted as people who were not reluctant to engage in physical labor nor disdainful of it like many Portuguese Brazilians.[281] It was this pattern of hard work, not more advanced techniques of farming,[282] which accounted for the Germans' success in Brazil.

As elsewhere around the world, Germans in Brazil were "joiners." The first German club was established in Rio de Janeiro in 1830.[283] The *Germania* society was founded in Porto Alegre in 1855, followed over the years by mutual aid societies, athletic associations, photographer's clubs, singing groups, and many others.[284] Various sports were introduced to Brazil by Germans of an athletic bent. Soccer thus became the national sport of the country.[285] As a literate people in a largely illiterate society, the Germans produced their own newspapers and periodicals in urban centers. Publications with such names as the *Santa Cruz Anzeiger,* the *Deutsche Zeitung,* and the *Brasil Post* appeared in the nineteenth century and a flourishing German-language press continued publishing in Brazil well into the twentieth century.[286] These newspapers, like the people they served, tended to be nonpolitical. Government at all levels remained in the control of Brazilian landowners of Portuguese ancestry. Throughout the period up to World War I, most Germans in Brazil did not even bother to acquire Brazilian citizenship (which was easily obtainable), much less to vote.[287]

The passing years brought not only a growing prosperity to Rio Grande do Sul but also a larger and more varied immigration, as well as an in-migration of Brazilians of Portuguese ancestry. Declining German immigration into the state toward the end of the nineteenth century was surpassed several times over by that of Italian immigrants,[288] many of whom worked on the vast coffee plantations of the region, owned by Brazilians. Rio Grande do Sul continued to be one of the main recipients of immigrants to Brazil up until the beginning of World War I, these new immigrants now overshadowing the Germans numerically. In 1900, Germans were only 15 percent of the state's population, a proportion that remained relatively stable over the years, reaching 17 percent by the middle of the twentieth century.[289] In absolute numbers, however, the German population of Rio Grande do Sul rose from an estimated 60,000 in 1872 to 300,000 by 1917.[290]

Although the overwhelming majority of earlier German settlers were farmers, the passing generations saw the emergence of German artisans, merchants, and industrialists. The artisans were often taught trades that their fathers brought over from Germany, but which had not been practiced in Brazil because of the pressing need to develop the pioneering farms, in order to survive. These artisans initially divided their time between their respective trades and cultivation of the soil. Some, however, moved into villages or cities, opening their own one-man shops. They were well received in communities of Brazilian Portuguese ancestry. These artisans flourished in the late nineteenth century, but then declined with the rise of industry and the competition of Polish and especially Italian artisans.[291] Because Germans dominated the new industrial development, it is not clear how many German artisans failed and how many advanced into industry.

The first industrial firms in Rio Grande do Sul were founded by Germans in the mid-nineteenth century.[292] This state became the industrial heartland of Brazil, if not all of Latin America. By 1895 there were 30 corporations in Rio Grande do Sul, including 10 new industrial firms. Almost all were German. The largest employed more than 900 workers. By 1907 there were 212 industrial establishments and by 1908 over a hundred more than that. In many branches of industry, German names were the primary ones—and sometimes the only ones, as in the manufacture of metal furniture, trunks, stoves, paper, hats, neckties, leather, soap, glass, matches, beer, confections, and carriages, as well as in foundries and carpentry shops.[293] It was said that the German community at Novo Hamburgo passed, in a little over a century, from a green forest to electrometallurgy.[294]

The growing port city of Porto Alegre, long the major outlet for the shipment of agricultural products, became also a major center of industrial and commercial activity, including international shipments of commercial and industrial products. The majority of Porto Alegre's enterprises were German.[295] Small cigar factories were established in Porto Alegre as early as 1832,[296] processing tobacco grown in the German colonies.[297] Wood became one of the most important commodities in these colonies, as sawmills developed in the pioneering areas. Wood was one of the major exports of Porto Alegre, with two-thirds of it being shipped by German exporters at the end of the nineteenth century.[298]

Commercial activity increased in the older German colonies as agriculture declined over the years. The newer colonies, whose agriculture was more prosperous, were slower to develop commercial businessmen, but finally did so, and in growing numbers.[299] The German export business in Porto Alegre was initially tied very closely to the products of the German agricultural colonies in the area. Many of these export products remained predominantly in the hands of German exporters well into the twentieth century—leather, potatoes, and black beans, for example. Other products historically associated with the German colonies—sausage, ham, cheese, brandy—were increasingly exported by merchants of other ethnic groups, notably the Italians. In part this may represent a shift of production sites, more so than growing interethnic transactions. Woodwork, for example, was no longer centered in the German colonies.[300]

German importers began with strong links to the products of Germany, but they too became more diversified with the years, while rising to a dominant position among all exporters in Porto Alegre. As of 1858, less than one-fifth of that city's importers were German, but by 1890 more than half of the largest import houses were. By 1914, 96 out of 140 shipping firms in Porto Alegre were German.[301]

The movement of Germans out of their colonies, the growth of other colonies, and the general inflow of other immigrants and of Brazilians of Portuguese ancestry made some inroads into the cultural and social insularity of the Germans in Brazil. Still, as late as 1910, more than 70 percent of the marriages of persons of German ancestry were with others of the same ethnic background.[302] Nevertheless, this represented an increase of mixed marriages—an increase centered in the cities or in colonies near people of other ethnic backgrounds.[303] In the older German agricultural colony in São Leopoldo, in the center of a region still heavily populated by Germans, marriages remained almost 100 percent endogamous from the 1890s through the end of World War II.[304] However, in the urban areas of São Leopoldo, endogamous marriages fell sharply from 100 percent in 1878 to 59 percent by 1906.[305] In the city of Porto Alegre at about the same time, the rate of mixed marriages among the German Brazilians was almost identical.[306]

World War I proved to be a disaster for the Germans in Brazil, as in other countries. From the beginning, the sympathies of most Brazilians were with the Allies, that of the Germans with their homeland. About half of the Germans belonged to the Evangelical Church, which had institutional ties to the Prussian Church, from which they received most of their clergy and some of their money. The Evangelicals not only offered prayers for Germany's success in the war, but also raised money for the German Red Cross and bought German war bonds. This was not true of the German Catholics, nor was it true of those German Lutherans whose subsidies came from the Missouri Synod in the United States. Nevertheless, Germans as a whole were seen as pro-Germany in a country that was pro-Allies. Moreover, the Germans were a people whose prosperity and exclusivity were already resented. Finally, the Germans inadvertently hurt their own cause in 1916 by organizing a short-lived group called the *Germanische Bund für Süd Amerika,* a chauvinistic organization which provoked counter-chauvinism among other Brazilians.[307]

The spark which set off this explosive atmosphere came in April 1917, when a German submarine torpedoed and sank a Brazilian ship off the coast of France. Riots broke out in several Brazilian cities, with violence, arson, and looting aimed at German businesses and homes. Six months later, another Brazilian ship was torpedoed by a German submarine, setting off another series of riots in Rio de Janeiro and other Brazilian cities.[308] Brazil declared war on Germany, and while that had little practical meaning internationally—few Brazilians actually fought in Europe[309]—it had great impact on the Germans in Brazil. Under its special wartime powers, the Brazilian government imposed a military occupation in some German areas and closed down German-language newspapers and hundreds of German-language schools. Because of a lack of public schools in many areas where Germans were settled, this meant that thousands of children were simply deprived of education during the war. Many of these schools never reopened.[310] German business firms were blacklisted.[311] Many German organizations changed their names or dissolved.[312]

After the end of World War I, restrictions were lifted and life returned to normal, though there were lasting resentments among the

Germans in Brazil—resentments later exploited by Nazi agents in the 1930s. During the 1920s, when economic conditions were dire and chaotic in Germany, a huge new inflow of German immigration reached Brazil—nearly 76,000 German immigrants, by far the most in any decade of the country's history.[313] They joined a German community that was once again prosperous and was becoming more and more a part of Brazil's cultural and social life.

In 1920, more than half the leather products factories in the state of Rio Grande do Sul were owned by Germans or Brazilians of German ancestry.[314] Moreover, the top 15 German firms of that era produced twice as much leather as the top 14 firms owned by Brazilians of Portuguese ancestry. Firms owned by people of Italian, rather than Portuguese, ancestry provided the main competition to the Germans in many industrial areas. Sixty percent of the firms producing alcoholic beverages were German, with most of the remainder being Italian. About two-thirds of the tinware in the state was produced by 9 German firms. More than two-thirds of the nails, neckties, and dresses and all of the chocolate and products of glassworks came from German firms.[315] Yet Germans were a little more than one-fifth the population of the state.[316] All industrial machinery in Brazil was imported when the Germans built the first starch mill in Santa Catarina in the 1920s but, by the 1930s, a second starch mill was equipped with machines made in Brazil by German immigrant engineers.[317]

The postwar resurgence of the prestige of Germans was perhaps symbolized by the 1924 centenary celebration of the founding of the German colony and the government's expression of recognition of their contributions to Brazil.[318] There were also more tangible signs of how Germans had prospered in Brazil. When a country club was built in Porto Alegre in 1930, 40 percent of its members were of German ancestry.[319]

The rise of the Nazis to power in Germany in 1933 set in motion a chain of events which again compromised the position of Germans in Brazil. Nazis infiltrated most of the numerous German organizations in Brazil during the 1930s. The Nazi network was complete with its own secret police to take note of those opposed to Nazism, or even the hesitaters. Such people were subjected to boycotts and ostracism locally, and their relatives in Germany were subject to reprisals.[320] A few brave individuals and organizations in the German community publicly opposed the Nazis, but Germans as a group were perceived by other Brazilians as pro-Nazi. The Brazilian government took strong countermeasures in the late 1930s. The 1937 constitution forbad all political activity and in 1938 all private schools in the nation were nationalized. As of 1937 there were more than 2,000 private schools in the German colonies. Over a period of fifty years, the Brazilian government had built only 30 schools, but now they built more than 100 in five years, mostly in the German colonies. Still, these were small numbers by comparison with what had already existed there. These formerly private schools were now conducted in the Portuguese language and with a Brazilian orientation. These changes were decisive for the acculturation of a new generation of Germans in Brazil.[321]

World War II brought a new set of restrictions reminiscent of those in the previous war. German-language publications were prohibited, as was the speaking of German in public. German libraries were destroyed and German gun clubs disarmed. Some elements of the Brazilian police took advantage of the situation to commit violence and extortion. Once again the torpedoing of a Brazilian ship by a German submarine set off arson and looting against German businesses in Porto Alegre.[322]

During the war, young German men served in the Brazilian military, being exposed to the larger society and to regions of the country they might not have seen otherwise. The postwar world saw not merely a return to normalcy but further progress toward acculturation and integration into Brazilian society. Long apathetic about politics,[323] Germans began to elect more deputies than ever in the postwar elections.[324] While the rate of endogamous marriages remained high in most German agricultural settlements in the early postwar years—averaging 72 percent—in some towns and cities it dropped near or below 50 percent. In the city of Porto Alegre, endogamous marriages among Brazilians of German descent fell to 39 percent by 1949. At the other extreme, in the agricultural district of Teutonia, 100 percent of all marriages remained endogamous.[325]

The key role of the Germans in the industrial development of Brazil remained apparent in the postwar era. In the middle of the twentieth century, nearly half of the industrial enterprises in the southern Brazilian states were owned by people of German ancestry.[326] The German contribution is one reason why the southern Brazilian states became the industrial heartland of the country, as well as containing the most advanced agriculture. Indeed, São Paulo has been called "the industrial giant of Latin American."[327]

Paraguay

The landlocked nation of Paraguay, nestled between Argentina and Brazil, with Bolivia on its northern border, attracted relatively few immigrants—officially about 67,000 for the entire period from 1881 to 1958. Nearly one-fifth of these immigrants were German Mennonites;[328] but there were also other colonies of Germans who were not Mennonites.[329] German and other immigrant colonies began to be set up in the second half of the nineteenth century, as Paraguay sought to attract immigration, because of its small—and declining—population. There were fewer than a quarter of a million inhabitants of Paraguay in 1872—less than one-third as many people as in 1865.[330] A disastrous war had decimated its population. Foreigners were sought, not only for numbers, but also because of the skills and education desperately needed by the population of Paraguay, whose more cultured classes had long ago been suppressed or exiled under an anti-elitist dictatorship from 1814 to 1840.[331] The German colony established in 1881 was not the first foreign colony in Paraguay but it was the first to succeed and become an enduring settlement.[332]

Germans had been in Paraguay before these colonies were founded, but as individuals. There were Germans among the early Spanish explorers and conquerors. During a century and a half of Jesuit mission colonies in Paraguay, there were also Germans among the Jesuits, and these Germans often had skills and education lacking in their Spanish brethren, skills which improved the agriculture, health, and construction available to the native American Indians. One authority described the contributions of these German Jesuits as the "biggest cultural achievement of the Germans in South America during the seventeenth and eighteenth centuries."[333]

German colonies continued to be set up well into the twentieth century. Many of these Germans came not only from Germany but also from Russia, from German colonies in Africa, from Canada, and even from Samoa.[334] Among the contributions of Germans over the centuries were the introduction of the plow during the Jesuit colony era, participation in the creation of the first sugar manufacturing plant, cattle-breeding improvements, replanting of the Yerba trees in deforested areas, creation of a wine industry, and the development of a vast and barren region of western Paraguay called the *Chaco,* long thought to be impossible to farm.[335] The *Chaco* was quickly settled by a number of Mennonite villages in the late 1920s, despite many hardships and deaths.[336] Some Mennonites returned to Canada, some moved into the more developed eastern part of Paraguay, but others remained[337] and made this forbidding area more viable.[338] As in other areas of the Western Hemisphere, the German settlers in the *Chaco* tended to take a more conciliatory approach to the native American Indians in the area. Ironically, they thereby lost the respect of these Paraguayan Indians, who had been used to harsher treatment from whites.[339]

In Paraguay, as elsewhere around the world, German settlers established their own schools at their own expense. The first of these schools was built in 1889 and it was still in existence in the latter half of the twentieth century. There were eleven German schools in Paraguay by 1914, and on the eve of World War II there were 70 German schools, which provided a German education to an estimated 90 percent of the German children of school age.[340] However, the relatively small German population of Paraguay, living largely in scattered agricultural colonies, was unable to sustain its own newspapers until after the First World War. Before then, they obtained from Argentina the *Argentinisches Tageblatt* and other German papers. During the mid-1920s, however, the *Deutsche Zeitung für Paraguay* was published three times a week, and other German-language periodical literature developed.[341]

The largest minority in Paraguay, aside from the native American Indians, Germans maintained their cultural and social isolation in Paraguay on into the late 1930s. This isolation has been particularly characteristic of the large Mennonite element, which likewise isolated itself in Russia, Canada, Mexico, and elsewhere. Paraguay, with its once dire shortage of population, had agreed to granting the Mennonites the religious and educational autonomy they sought, together with exemption from military service. In addition, Paraguay had less stringent immigration requirements than some alternative destinations, such as Canada and Brazil.[342] The people and the country apparently met each other's needs.

New German colonies continued to be set up in Paraguay after World War II. Mennonite refugees from the Soviet Union fled first to Germany and then to Paraguay, when they feared being captured and sent back to the U.S.S.R.[343] Paraguay offered them the same religious freedom and guarantees for their own way of life which it had offered to others before them. The new Mennonite colonies encountered many of the same hardships as earlier ones, but now international humanitarian agencies and connections with Mennonites in Canada enabled some to leave—most for Canada, some for Brazil, and a few returning to Germany.

Paraguayans adopted some of the farming methods of the Mennonites and Paraguayan laborers often worked for them but they remained otherwise separate people.[344] Intermarriage has been quite rare.[345] In a world where few things have been so dangerous to ethnic minorities as high productivity, the appreciation of the Germans by Paraguay is a notable exception. Perhaps their isolation has reduced envy and minimized the opportunities for political claims of "exploitation" of others.

AUSTRALIA

There were some Germans among the earliest European settlers in Australia in the late eighteenth century. By the early nineteenth century, individual Germans were farmers, merchants, and vintners in Australia. In addition to establishing some of the earliest vineyards in the country, Germans also produced a light beer to replace British ale and stout. Many nineteenth century Germans settled in Australia, not as individuals but in groups. The first of these German settlements was made in 1838, marking also the first settlement of a large non-British group in the country.[346] Despite a voyage of three months or more to Australia, at a time when the United States could be reached in a matter of weeks, German immigration to Australia continued, though not on a scale comparable to that in the Western Hemisphere. However, as of 1861, Germans were the third-largest group in Australia, after people of British and Chinese ancestry, though in absolute numbers there were still only about 27,000 Germans. By 1891, however, the Germans had passed the Chinese and numbered 45,000 people, or just over half the total European-born immigrant population.[347]

Australia is a vast country—about the size of the continental United States—and the degree to which Germans formed separate communities in Australia varied considerably from region to region. This was in part related to the degree of urbanization and the ratio between the sexes among Germans in different areas. Over all, there was a surplus of males but it was not so extreme as to suggest a predominantly temporary or exploratory migration. As of 1861, there were more than twice as many male as female immigrants from Germany, but by 1881 there were less than twice as many. The sexes were closest to being balanced in the state of South Australia, where there were 82 female immigrants for every 100 male immigrants as early as 1861.[348] Here there were isolated German-speaking enclaves in which the food, customs, and even style of houses reproduced the life of Silesian peasant communities. However, in the gold fields in the state of Victoria, Germans were much more part of a general melting pot.[349]

In the 1840s and 1850s, several German villages were established in South Australia's Barossa valley, perhaps still the best-known German settlement area in Australia in the late twentieth century. The first settlements were crude, featuring thatched-roof cottages with dirt floors, arranged along a single road in a typical German manner. However, there were many people with such skills as carpentry, masonry, cabinetmaking, shoemaking, and tailoring, so these homes grew more comfortable as the villages thrived with the passing years. Still, the style of house, the furnishings and utensils, as well as the population of these farm communities remained entirely German. The tombstones from that era are inscribed entirely in German.[350] A visitor from Germany in 1851 declared: "The traveller would believe himself in some little village of the old country between the Rhine and the Oder."[351] The first German-language newspaper in Australia was published in the city of Adelaide in 1848[352] and continued to be published there in the late twentieth century.[353]

A very different picture was presented in the state of Victoria, where the lopsided sex ratio—nearly 4 times as many German men as German women in 1857[354]—militated against separate German enclaves. Given the very unbalanced sex ratio among Germans in Victoria, it is hardly surprising that they had a high rate of intermarriage. The fact that Germans were a very small fraction of the population throughout Victoria—perhaps 2 percent over all and only about 7 percent in the areas of their strongest concentration[355]—likewise tended to encourage both intermarriage and acculturation. The situation in the state of New South Wales was much like that in Victoria. Moreover, German immigrants to New South Wales increasingly settled in metropolitan and other urban areas, making those in the rural areas a minority as early as 1881.[356] These were not conditions that made for the preservation of a German culture. With the exception of rural groups, most of the 9,600 Germans in New South Wales in 1891 were soon absorbed into the general population.[357]

The state of Queensland, on the other hand, followed a pattern more like that of South Australia. There were more than two-thirds as many German female immigrants as German male immigrants in 1881. Most of these immigrants came in family groups, and the majority settled in rural areas. Queensland became a major area of German settlement. In 1891 almost one-third of all German immigrants to Australia settled in Queensland.[358] However, the Germans in Queensland were more diverse in their regional origins and dialects in Germany than were the Germans of South Australia.[359]

Most of the nineteenth-century immigration from Germany was from the Protestant eastern and central regions and largely ended in the 1880s. Although Germans in Australia were overwhelmingly Lutheran, they were split into two main Lutheran factions which differed culturally as well as theologically. The United Evangelical Lutheran Church maintained ties to Germany, from which many of its pastors came, speaking German and consciously maintaining the German language and culture in Australia. The other major faction, the Evangelical Lutheran Synod of Australia, developed ties to the Missouri Synod in the United States. By the 1890s, its many English-speaking pastors from the United States tended to make the latter group less resistant to cultural assimilation.[360]

On the whole, Germans in Australia were slow to take on the culture of the surrounding society. Although it was relatively easy to become naturalized in nineteenth-century Australia, most Germans did not become citizens.[361] They tended to maintain strong ties with each other, rather than with the surrounding society. In all the colonies, Germans were "joiners," forming associations or *Vereine.* As the *Deutsche Australische Post* said in 1893:

> Where there are two Germans they form a *Verein* but where there are four Germans they establish two *Vereine.*[362]

These clubs, associations, newspapers, and above all the Lutheran church, kept German culture alive for generations, for at least some of the Germans in Australia, though to highly varying degrees by region. While South Australian Germans remained thoroughly German for at least a century, Germans in Sydney were noted for becoming Anglicized. As early as 1893, a visitor from Germany claimed that his countrymen in Sydney believed only in God and the *Sydney Morning Herald.* Even where German clubs existed in Australia, they were by no means always restricted to Germans. Some of the German associations in Melbourne and Adelaide had substantial numbers of non-German members.[363]

As in Russia, the United States, and other parts of the world, the Germans in Australia were not very active politically. There were some German political figures in nineteenth-century Australia, but even in South Australia their numbers were very small and not in excess of the German proportion of the population. Some represented predominantly German constituencies but others represented constituencies in which their compatriots were a small minority.[364] By and large, Germans in Australia have historically been under-represented in politics.[365]

In Australia, as in other countries, Germans became known for hard work, thoroughness, honesty, thrift, sobriety, reliability, and respect for laws.[366] As in other countries, the rural German settlers were noted as successful farmers.[367] There were often pioneers on virgin land who had to create their own communities, schools, and cultural life in general, and maintain strong solidarity and cooperation.[368] Education was one of their commitments. As of the turn of the century, there were 46,000 Lutheran schools in South Australia alone.[369] The Lutheran church was the dominant religious and cultural influence, for few German Catholics immigrated to Australia.[370]

Approximately one-third of the German immigrants to Australia were farmers, slightly more were tradesmen, and only 12 percent were laborers. The wide range of skills among them enabled them to set up villages and even small towns as self-sufficient German enclaves.[371] The German language was retained in many communities until at least the beginning of the First World War.[372] Scattered evidence indicates that intermarriage was the exception rather than the rule in the nineteenth century but it became more common in the early decades of the twentieth century.[373] Similarly, although most Germans in the nineteenth century did not become Australian citizens, by 1921 a majority did.[374]

World War I dealt a blow to Germans in Australia, as elsewhere. About 4,000 of the 33,000 Germans in Australia at that time were interned,[375] some under brutal conditions.[376] German-language schools were closed.[377] The German-language press was also restricted in what it could report[378] and there was in general a reduced use of the German language, as well as a replacement by the Australian government of local German place names with names of English origin and of significance in British history.[379] Mueller Park in Western Australia became Kitchener Park, for example.[380] However, some of these names were later changed back.[381] Demagogic attacks on the entire German community were made by a number of politicians, some proposing to take away their basic rights.[382] In part, such reactions were the culmination of a growing unease over the years among the Australians, replacing their earlier acceptance and enthusiasm for the German immigrants. This prewar change in attitudes among Australians reflected changing attitudes among Germans in Australia, due to the rise of Pan-German doctrines. There were evidences of divided loyalty among Germans in Australia, especially after the unification of Germany in 1871 and its spectacular rise in economic achievement and military strength. A number of public embarrassments revealed the difficulty which many Germans in Australia had in reconciling their pride in their culture and fatherland with their role as citizens of another country.[383]

German-language newspapers made their appearance in Australia in the nineteenth century. The largest of these was the *Australische Zeitung*, published in Adelaide, near the center of the Australian German cultural stronghold. However, even this region was not impervious to the forces of cultural assimilation. When a new clubhouse was opened in 1913 in Tanunda, also in the German heartland of South

Australia, all the speeches for the occasion were in English.[384] The United Evangelical Lutheran-Protestant Church, the strongest bastion of German culture, began to offer services, confirmation, and Sunday-school instruction in English, though only gradually. It was 1930 before about half of the United Lutheran church services in Australia were given in English, and it was 8 years later before half of those in South Australia as a whole were in English. Most Sunday-school instruction and confirmations were in English earlier, perhaps reflecting the greater acculturation of the younger generation, though even here it was 1937 before half the South Australian United Evangelical Lutheran churches offered these services in English.[385]

The 1930s saw an infiltration of German organizations in Australia by Nazi agents, following a pattern found also in the United States, Brazil, Southwest Africa,[386] and elsewhere. Blackmail against people with relatives in Germany was part of the Nazi pattern, in Australia as elsewhere.[387] The Evangelical Lutheran Church rebuffed Nazi efforts and the United Evangelical Lutheran Church disavowed the Nazi ideology, but the latter's actions were more ambiguous and parts of the Nazi vision—including anti-Semitism—appeared in church publications. Nevertheless, when war came, it urged its members to fight for Australia and to cooperate with Australian authorities.[388] Once again, as in World War I, there were restrictions on what enemy aliens could do or where they could be. However, very few Australians of German ancestry were interned. Even in South Australia, there were only 27 Australians of German ancestry interned out of 30,000, though 88 German citizens were interned there and 350 German aliens nationally.[389]

In the postwar world, Germans continued to immigrate to Australia, and to prosper. From 1947 to 1969, 83,000 immigrants from Germany arrived in Australia. Most had their immigration subsidized by the Australian government.[390] These postwar German immigrants differed significantly from the immediate prewar German immigrants. Refugees from the Nazis, including a high proportion of professional people, predominated in the immediate prewar immigration from Germany, while the postwar immigrants were a broader cross-section of the German population. Relations between those who fled Nazi Germany and those who remained there until after the war were reportedly "politely reserved" in Australia.[391]

In addition to immigrants from Germany, the postwar German immigration has also included ethnic Germans from Hungary, Rumania, and Yugoslavia. Although resident outside Germany in some cases for centuries, these ethnic Germans—like those from Russia or in parts of Latin America—have often remained German in language and culture. Another component of the German population in Australia consisted of German nationals working for such multinational corporations as Volkswagen, Daimler-Benz, Bayer, and others.[392]

One area of Australia in which the postwar immigration has been studied in some detail is the Latrobe Valley of Victoria, a long-established dairying, and then mining and industrial, center. Germans were among a number of postwar immigrant groups settling there among a predominantly Australian-born population. For the valley as a whole, the immigration from Germany was 13 percent more male than female in 1954—and for Victoria as a whole, only 3 percent more male. Most of the Germans were Lutheran, had no kin in Australia, but immigrated with financial assistance from the Australian government.[393] After an average of 5 years' residence in Australia, less than one-fifth were unskilled laborers—next to the lowest proportion among all the immigrant groups. The lowest proportion was among immigrants from the Baltic, who may include, or even be predominantly, Baltic Germans.[394] The wages of immigrants from Germany in the Latrobe Valley were exceeded only by those of immigrants from Great Britain and the Baltic—the latter groups averaging several years' longer residence in Australia.[395] Just over half the German immigrants owned an automobile, putting them well ahead of most other immigrants in that regard.[396]

As for assimilation, about half the German immigrants in the Latrobe Valley spoke only German in their homes, more than a third spoke both German and English there, and less than one-sixth spoke mainly English at home. Most continued to read German-language publications, mainly from overseas, and 38 percent reported that friends who visited them were mainly German. While 40 percent reported that their visitors were both Australians and immigrants, only 11 percent reported that their visitors were mainly Australian. Nevertheless, there was little evidence that these postwar German immigrants intended to establish exclusive German enclaves in the manner of some earlier immigrants from Germany. Most of the postwar German immigrants in the Latrobe Valley did not teach German to their children.[397]

A similar pattern was found among German immigrants in the state of Western Australia. Here too, parents did not speak German exclusively at home, and the children in fact usually became proficient in English. Less than half the families stuck to German eating patterns and very few limited their social contacts to other Germans. Many of these postwar Germans came to Australia to sever their ties with a past that they wanted to forget, whether that past was World War II, Nazism, or Soviet occupation.[398] For the postwar German immigrants as a whole, more than 90 percent spoke English—including 42 percent who spoke only English.[399] These postwar German immigrants in Western Australia seemed to be on their way to a much speedier and more thorough assimilation than their nineteenth-century predecessors.

The number of Germans in Australia in the late twentieth century varies according to the definitions used—whether German nationals, German-born Australians, or Australians of full or partial German ancestry. By the most stringent definition, there were more than 110,000 persons in Australia who were born in Germany. By the most relaxed definition, there were estimated to be well over a million Australians with some degree of German ancestry.[400] By a more reasonable estimate of ethnic origin, there were approximately 581,000 Germans in Australia, and they were approximately 4 percent of the Australian population.[401] Official data, however, were available only for those born in Germany. By 1979, German-born males in Australia averaged 13 percent higher income than Australian males.[402] German immigrants achieved higher education more often than the Australian population as a whole[403] and were unemployed less often than the general population.[404]

IMPLICATIONS

A number of cultural characteristics have recurred or persisted for generations, or even centuries, among Germans—whether living in their homeland or in highly disparate societies around the world. The capacity of Germans for hard, thorough, unrelenting work has been noted in Germany itself, as well as in colonial America, czarist Russia, Honduras, Australia, Brazil, Ireland, Argentina, and Paraguay.[405] A counterpoint to this zeal for work has been an apathy about politics which has long been endemic in Germany itself and in the German states and principalities that preceded it,[406] as well as among German communities overseas. Along with this political apathy has gone a great deference to authorities, expressed in many ways, not only in Germany[407] but also in other lands where Germans have loyally served their adopted countries, even in wars against their ancestral homeland. Exceptions have occurred in countries which actively pursued anti-German policies internally, notably in such Eastern European nations as the Soviet Union and Czechoslovakia.

Both the strong German military tradition and antimilitary tradition have deep roots in Germany and have followed Germans around the world. The German respect for education is likewise a centuries-old phenomenon in Germany,[408] which pioneered in modern educational developments, from the kindergarten to the university. German emigrants have made education an important priority, even in countries where those around them have remained uneducated and unconcerned about education.

Loyalty to the German language and culture, while living in other countries, has seldom meant loyalty to the German government. However, both imperial Germany and the Third Reich attempted to manipulate Germans living in foreign countries, for national political advantage—and usually to the detriment of those German communities. Often the cultures to which Germans remained loyal were regional or local cultures, so that Palatine communities were re-created in upstate New York or Silesian villages in parts of Australia, or Volga or Black Sea communities when Germans from Russia resettled in the Western Hemisphere.

The local and regional nature of these cultures was exemplified in the local and regional dialects spoken by immigrants from different areas. The various regional dialects of German spoken in the many enclaves in the United States, for example, not only differed from one another but sometimes persisted after such dialects had begun to die out in Germany itself.[409] Moreover, German communities consisting of people who immigrated from countries outside the Reich tended to speak not only a particular dialect derived from their regional ancestral speech in Germany but also words and expressions from the Rumanian, Hungarian, Russian, or Ukrainian languages in the respective countries from which they immigrated to the United States, Canada, or elsewhere.[410] In short, German cultural persistence overseas was generally more a matter of clinging to the familiar, rather than political nationalism. Where German community solidarity did take a political form, such as support for Germany during the two world wars, the backlash which this provoked in the surrounding societies often ranged from social ostracism to economic blacklisting, repressive laws, internment, mob violence and—in Eastern Europe, after the Second World War, mass expulsions.

The dozen years of Germany's history dominated by the Nazis cast a long shadow over Germans, at home and abroad, for decades after the Hitler regime was buried in the dust and rubble at the end of World War II. While the Nazi movement exploited certain features of German culture, including obedience to authority and a romanticizing of power and violence,[411] in other ways the Nazis represented a sharp break with the more civilized aspects of German tradition. For example, the racial fanaticism of the Nazi era in Germany was in sharp contrast with the historic tolerant cosmopolitanism of Germans in the Baltic and Czechoslovakia, or the German antislavery position in Brazil and the United States,[412] their ability to get along with the indigenous American Indians in the Western Hemisphere,[413] their charitable efforts toward the aborigines in Australia,[414] and the widespread acceptance (including intermarriage) of Jews in pre-Hitler Germany.[415] Group prejudice and discrimination were by no means unknown among Germans, at home or abroad, but it tended to be less rather than more prevalent, as compared to other Europeans—or to Asians or Africans, for that matter.

The economic achievements of Germans were fundamental to the rise of Germany as a world power and to the agricultural and industrial progress of other nations with substantial contingents of German immigrants. The outstanding records of the Germans in family farming around the world in the eighteenth and nineteenth centuries was matched by their later achievements in science and technology. Even the particular industries in which they have historically been outstanding pioneers—brewing, optics, pianos, and industrial manufacturing, for example—have been reproduced among Germans in widely scattered countries.

While Germans abroad have been notable for their loyalty to the respective countries in which they settled, they have nevertheless suffered from Germany's actions in two world wars. The First World War led to the suppression of the German language and culture in the Western Hemisphere and Australia, while World War II brought the mass deportation of Germans from the European to the Asiatic regions of the U.S.S.R. The atrocities committed by the Nazis during their occupation of Eastern Europe and the Balkans came back to haunt the ethnic Germans of that region. Postwar realignments of borders were accompanied by expulsions of 15 million ethnic Germans, many of whom had family roots going back for centuries in Poland, Hungary, the Sudetenland of Czechoslovakia, and other parts of Eastern Europe, as well as in eastern regions of Germany which now became part of Poland as eastern portions of Poland became part of the Soviet Union. The embittered peoples of the region, who had suffered from the Nazi occupation, with which local ethnic Germans often collaborated, now took their revenge on Germans in general, with atrocities that contributed to the deaths of 2 million of these German expellees.[416] Winston Churchill, whose opposition to the Nazi regime began long before the war began, nevertheless spoke of "mass expulsions of millions of Germans on a scale grievous and undreamed-of" and said, "we must banish revenge against an entire race from our minds."[417]

The horrors of Hitler and the Nazis continued to be associated with Germany and with Germans, long after World War II, reducing the world influence of the economically vibrant West German nation,[418] even after the passing decades produced a German population largely born since the end of the Nazi era, including increasingly people whose *parents* had not yet been born at the time of Hitler. However, decades of peaceful coexistence and the development of democratic traditions in West Germany eventually allayed the fears of surrounding nations sufficiently to lead to widespread international acceptance of a reunited Germany in 1990. In the long view of history, few peoples have made such cultural and economic contributions to so many lands in so many parts of the planet as the Germans.

CHAPTER 3

JAPANESE AROUND THE WORLD

From 1638 to 1868, during the rule of the Tokugawa shoguns, emigration from Japan was forbidden, on pain of death. However, there was significant emigration both before and since. In 1606 there were 3,000 Japanese living in Manila alone and several times that number in the Philippines as a whole.[1] There was also Japanese emigration to Korea as early as the fifteenth century, and by the seventeenth century there were many Japanese communities in the countries of southeast Asia.[2]

The Meiji restoration's many changes included a resumption of emigration from Japan in the latter half of the nineteenth century. Despite its proximity to the Asian mainland, modern Japan's emigrants initially went primarily to the Western Hemisphere. As of 1900, more than half of all Japanese living abroad lived either on the mainland of the United States or in Hawaii—mostly the latter.[3] After the tightening of U.S. immigration restrictions in the early years of the twentieth century, the stream of Japanese emigrants shifted toward South America—notably Brazil and Peru. In short, before the creation of Japan's overseas empire, modern Japanese emigrants sought the higher-income,

European-offshoot nations of the Western Hemisphere. Even within its own Pacific region, more than three-quarters of the Japanese emigrants in that part of the world at the beginning of the twentieth century lived in another European-offshoot nation, Australia.[4]

Two things were to change this international distribution of Japanese emigrants, however: immigration restrictions by the recipient countries in the Western Hemisphere, Australia, and South Africa, and the development of an overseas Japanese empire in Asia. Early in the twentieth century, Canada, Australia, South Africa, and various countries in Central America and the Caribbean joined the United States in severely restricting immigration from Japan.[5] This shifted the stream of Japanese emigrants toward South America, where they were initially welcomed by countries with much undeveloped land and few people willing or able to develop it. However, by the mid to late 1930s, South American countries also began to restrict immigration from Japan.[6] Meanwhile Japan's conquest of such areas as Korea, Manchuria, and Formosa during the late nineteenth and early twentieth centuries provided new outlets for its emigrants. These conquests led to a great increase in the number of Japanese living overseas, as well as changing their global distribution. No longer were they concentrated in European-offshoot societies. As of 1935, there were more than a quarter of a million Japanese each in Manchuria and Formosa, and well over half a million in Korea, compared to about half a million in the entire Western Hemisphere and less than 200,000 in Southeast Asia, while Australia's "whites only" immigration policy (initiated in 1901) reduced the numbers of Japanese in that country to fewer than 2,000.[7]

The historic change in the overseas destinations of Japanese emigrants was dramatic. Whereas Manchuria received only 2 percent of Japanese emigrants between 1924 and 1934, it received 85 percent of all Japanese emigrants from 1935 to 1945.[8] By 1940, there were 1.7 million Japanese living abroad, of whom 1.2 million lived in Asia.[9] Those who lived in Japan's conquered territories were primarily government officials, industrial and transport workers, and businessmen—in short, representatives of the modern urban world. By contrast, those who settled in the Western Hemisphere were primarily agricultural laborers or farmers.[10] Moreover, the Japanese who emigrated at different periods represented also different stages in the evolution of modern Japan.

A modern Japanese scholar has said: "If you want to see Japan of the Taisho era (1912–1926) go to Brazil; if you want to see Japan of the Meiji era (1868–1912), go to America."[11] This difference was dramatically demonstrated during World War II, when Japanese Americans loyally supported the United States, despite receiving harsh treatment as enemy aliens, while the Japanese in Brazil (treated much better) remained so fanatically pro-Japan that many of them refused to believe that Japan had been defeated, even after its unconditional surrender in 1945. Thousands of Japanese in Brazil waited in port for the arrival of "victorious" Japanese military forces in the Western Hemisphere.[12] In both the United States and Brazil, the responses of the Japanese reflected the inner patterns of a people, rather than the effect of the surrounding society. Japan itself was quite different at the different times when they emigrated—very pro-Western in general and pro-American in particular during the earlier era and fanatically nationalist and racist during the later era.

In the wake of Japan's defeat in World War II, vast numbers of Japanese returned from Japan's overseas empire, now liberated by Allied troops. Nearly half a million returned from Formosa (Taiwan), more than half a million from South Korea, approximately 700,000 from Southeast Asia, a million from Manchuria, and 1.5 million from the conquered regions of China. This massive return of Japanese to their homeland took place over a period of about a decade following the end of the war, most arriving in a period of a year and a half following the end of the war. Altogether these returnees amounted to more than 6 million people.[13]

JAPAN

The history of Japan has been remarkable in a number of ways, and in some ways unique. Japan remained isolated from the rest of the world for two centuries, before American naval power forced the Japanese government to open up their ports to the outside world in 1854. Japan is also one of the few major nations of modern times to have a racially homogeneous population. Until 1945, the Japanese were also one of the few major nations or races never to have been conquered.

Japan is often thought of as a small country, but its area is larger than that of Great Britain, though smaller than that of California. Japan's vast economic output has tended to cause it to be compared to giant countries such as the United States and Russia—the only nations with a larger total output—and hence to be seen as little. But Japan is larger than a number of European nations, including Italy as well as the United Kingdom. In the past, Japan's successful wars against China (1895) and Russia (1905) likewise led to size comparisons with huge nations.

In terms of people, rather than land area, Japan has the seventh-largest population in the world, though less than half the population of the United States, and a small fraction of the population of China or India. Japan's gross national product is larger than that of all Latin America or the entire continent of Africa.[14] In another sense, however, Japan is smaller than it appears to be: Its hills and mountains leave relatively little land suitable for agriculture and it has little of the natural resources required by a modern industrial economy—iron ore, coal, petroleum, copper, lead, and zinc, all of which have to be imported.[15] Yet this meager natural resource base has to support the most densely populated major nation in the world.

Land suitable for farming has been not only scarce but scattered—in narrow river valleys or in mountain basins or along a coastal strip—so that Japan developed historically as a fragmented collection of settlements and domains. Even after a unified nation emerged, its prefect boundaries generally followed lines of natural geographic barriers that had historically divided the country.[16] Japan's rivers were usually navigable only for short distances, and so did not serve to knit the land together. The sea was Japan's great waterway, however, which meant that the coastal areas were in communication, even if the hinterlands were not. Still, no part of Japan is more than 70 miles from the sea,[17] though that distance was more formidable in the centuries before the modern transportation revolution.

Before the coming of Western science and technology, Japan was a poor country—and remained so for many years, even after its military power became impressive in the late nineteenth century. It has also been, historically, an isolated country. Just as Britain was once isolated by being off the mainland of Europe, Japan's historic development has taken place off the mainland of Asia—but several times farther off. Although Chinese cultural influences penetrated and transformed Japan more than a thousand years ago, Japan remained an isolated nation, developing, adapting, and modifying the Chinese cultural contributions in its own way. Until the development of ocean-going commerce in recent centuries, Japan had only the most intermittent contact even with Korea and China, much less with the world at large. There has been virtually no significant immigration into Japan, and the non-Japanese peoples in the country amount to less than 1 percent of its population.[18]

The forcible destruction of Japan's isolation by American naval vessels under Commodore Perry in 1854 was a turning point in Japanese history. It also demonstrated, with painful clarity, Japan's weakness and backwardness, compared to advanced Western industrial nations, and set the national agenda for Japanese development in the century that followed. Imitation of the West, admiration of the West, resentment of the West, and both national and racial ambivalence toward the West dominated Japanese thought and action in the generations that followed Perry's fateful opening of Japan to the outside world.

The United States, as the country powerful enough to break through Japan's historic isolation, was a special focus of Japanese attention. The American way of life was praised by Japanese leaders and intellectuals of the Meiji era, the United States was depicted as a benefactor to Japan by ending its isolation, and government-issued textbooks held up Abraham Lincoln and Benjamin Franklin as models to be imitated, even more so than Japanese heroes.[19] English was introduced into Japanese secondary schools in 1876, and there was even a suggestion that it be made the national language.[20] Euphoric descriptions of the United States as "an earthly paradise"[21] were part of a general depiction of Western peoples and nations as enviable, beautiful, and great.[22] Some enthusiasts not only adopted Western fashions, but even engaged in sweeping denigrations of all aspects of Japanese culture.[23]

Alongside such feelings, however, alternating with them and eventually overpowering them, was a growing Japanese desire to prove themselves, and to assert their own identity and mastery. By the early twentieth century, Japan had changed radically, to become an ultranationalistic country, shrill and belligerent toward other nations and fanatically devoted to their emperor. The Japanese themselves often saw these traits as defensive overcompensations for a sense of inferiority.[24] Those Japanese who immigrated to the United States earlier, during the Meiji era, were not brought up with such fanaticism, and Japanese American writings critical of emperor-worship or ultranationalism were often banned in Japan.[25] By the Taisho era (1912–1926), this nationalistic and racist arrogance and fanaticism were well underway in Japan. It was the immigrants of this era who settled in Brazil, carrying with them ideas that led to the tragi-comic denouement of their preparing to welcome "victorious" Japanese troops at the end of World War II, while Japan itself lay prostrate and hungry amid the rubble.

The consuming desire to "prove something" to themselves and to the world has been reflected in many aspects of modern Japanese history, especially the scope and nature of its wars and conquests. A Japanese editorial response to Japan's victory over China in 1895 saw it as demonstrating not only the military power of Japan as a nation, but also that the Japanese people "are not inferior to any race in the world," and declared: "We can hardly bear the happiness in our heart."[26] Victory over Russia in 1905—the first time a modern Asian nation had defeated a European nation—produced similar responses. Japan's conquests of the 1930s and early 1940s were marked by a special ruthlessness, murderous cruelty, and pointless humiliations of the conquered peoples—all characteristic of people trying to "prove something." The Japanese were noted for their wholesale rapes of the women in conquered countries,[27] their slapping the faces of men on the streets for no reason,[28] and for brutal tortures, mutilations, and executions of captured soldiers and civilians alike.[29] The infamous "Bataan death march," where several thousand captured American and Filipino soldiers were brutally—and often sadistically—killed, was part of this general pattern.

Postwar Japan has been one of the economic miracles of history, emerging not simply as an imitator of Western technology but as a pioneer in its development and application. The social and political miracle has been no less profound—an historically militaristic society becoming one of the most pacifist, and a nation of autocratic despotism becoming one of the leading democracies of the world. Much of this was the work of just one man—General Douglas MacArthur, who politically maneuvered his way to become the *de facto* ruler of postwar Japan and the shaper of its institutions, and even its psyche.

While MacArthur was implacable in his retribution against generals and top politicians responsible for Japan's war atrocities, he was equally rigid in his insistence that American troops repeat none of such behavior in their occupation of Japan.[30] For one of the few times in history, a conquering army was ordered to live only on its own rations, and neither to take nor buy food needed by the hungry conquered people.[31] MacArthur became a national hero to the Japanese for his shrewdly displayed kindness, generosity, and democratic actions.[32] A new pro-Americanism was rekindled in Japan, among a people whose wartime government had led them to expect a nightmare of horrors if Americans conquered their land.[33]

Some of the prominent and enduring traits of the Japanese people seem to reflect the peculiar circumstances of their environment and history. Their enormous capacity for sustained and meticulous work is readily understandable in a people whose food has had to be produced from relatively small amounts of not very fertile land, intensely cultivated and irrigated. The large irrigation systems on which their survival depended required much cooperation among people in a given area and subordination of individual interests and idiosyncracies to the common good. Their meager produce and thin margin of subsistence required an ability to live on little and put aside reserves for contingencies. The natural disasters to which Japan was particularly subject—earthquakes, typhoons, and volcanic eruptions—were reflected in a stoicism and tenacity that have marked the Japanese facing adversities of many kinds, from war to hostile peoples in other lands.

Japan's rise to become one of the leading industrial nations of the world by the second half of the twentieth century need not obscure the technological backwardness from which this rise began in the nineteenth century. Trains were unknown to the Japanese when Commodore Perry presented one as a present to an awe-struck group of Japanese dignitaries.[34] Yet, a century later, Japan's trains outstripped anything produced in the United States. Large, ocean-going ships had not been built in Japan during the long era when foreign travel was forbidden, and the first steel ship was built in Japan in the 1890s, with the quality of Japanese workmanship being inferior to that of European and

American producers,[35] but by 1960 Japan was the world's leading shipbuilder, and by 1969 it was producing half the world's tonnage.[36] A similarly dramatic rise of Japanese products took place in the automobile industry. Although the United States produced more than ten times the number of passenger cars produced in Japan as late as 1965, by 1983 Japanese production exceeded American production, and by 1990 Japan's output of passenger cars was more than 50 percent higher than that of the United States.[37] In photography, it was much the same story. As of 1990, the United States imported more than ten times as much photographic products from Japan as from any other country.[38] Yet the road to these pinnacles was far from smooth, and generations of painful efforts were behind these achievements.

Japan was a predominantly agricultural nation when it emerged from its isolation from the rest of the world in the mid-nineteenth century, and it remained so on into the twentieth century. As of 1881, raw silk and tea accounted for more than half the value of Japanese exports, but by 1910 manufactured goods accounted for more than two-thirds of Japan's exports.[39] Still, in terms of people, as late as 1920 more than half the working population of the country worked in agriculture.[40] The passing years, however, saw the transition of the Japanese economy into a more industrial one, first in light industry such as the production of textiles, bicycles, and other consumer goods, and later into such heavy industry as iron and steel, chemicals, and shipbuilding.[41] Moreover, increased industrial output was accompanied by improvements in the quality of Japanese work, which had been considered below the standards of established industrial nations.[42]

Although Japanese industry was largely devastated by American bombing during World War II, making agriculture again the mainstay of the economy during the period of postwar reconstruction, Japan soon resumed its role as an industrial nation and went on to become one of the leading industrial and technological powers of the world. By then, however, large-scale emigration from Japan had come to an end. Most of the emigrants who settled permanently around the world in countries outside the short-lived Japanese empire came from an agricultural Japan and carried with them predominantly agricultural skills. However, in addition to specific skills, they took with them the discipline and capacity for hard work which brought Japan itself to the economic forefront. Japan also had a long tradition of entrepreneurship, so that its historic industrial development was not a product of foreign entrepreneurs,[43] as in so many other countries. This economic initiative also became apparent in the histories of Japanese emigrants who settled overseas.

THE WESTERN HEMISPHERE

Although isolated instances of individual Japanese living in the Western Hemisphere are recorded as far back as the early seventeenth century,[44] substantial numbers of immigrants moved from Japan to the New World only in the late nineteenth century. Hawaii was the first recipient of substantial Japanese emigration, and for many decades remained one of their principal destinations. Japanese immigration to Hawaii began in 1868, before the government of Japan authorized emigration, and before Hawaii became an American territory. It was one of the few unauthorized, though well organized, emigrations from Japan. More than a hundred contract laborers for the Hawaiian plantations were shipped out of Yokohama without the permission of the newly installed Meiji government.

The arrangements proved unsatisfactory to everyone. The laborers, recruited in the city of Yokohama, were not familiar with farm work and turned out to be inadequate for their tasks on the plantations. At the same time, brutal plantation discipline provoked complaints to the Japanese government, which sent an investigator in 1869. As a result, more than *one-fourth* of the workers were released from their contracts and returned to Japan, at the expense of the Hawaiian government.[45] Perhaps as a result of this unhappy experience, the government of Japan took an active role in subsequent Japanese emigration—not merely regulating it, but also promoting and subsidizing it, as well as monitoring the progress of its nationals in other countries.

After World War II, nearly 6 million Japanese were sent back to Japan from lands in Asia which Japan had conquered,[46] leaving the Western Hemisphere once more as the home of most Japanese living outside their homeland. As of the middle of the twentieth century, more than 90 percent of all Japanese living in the Western Hemisphere were in just two countries—Brazil and the United States. Altogether, there were about three-quarters of a million Japanese in the Americas, of whom about 373,000 lived in Brazil and 326,000 in the United States.[47] These numbers have continued to grow, but the proportions have remained similar. By 1970, for example, there were nearly half a million Japanese in the United States and more than 650,000 in Brazil, followed by more than 50,000 in Peru and more than 30,000 in Canada. However, only ten Western Hemisphere nations had as many as a thousand Japanese.[48] The Japanese in Latin America generally have had incomes much higher than those of the general populace in the respective countries in which they lived.[49] So have the Japanese in the United States and Canada.[50] Many continued to send money to Japan long after they settled abroad—nearly half a million dollars a year from Brazil in 1967, upwards of three-quarters of a million dollars from Canada, and more than $25 million from the United States.[51]

The first major emigration from modern Japan began in 1885, when the Japanese government negotiated an agreement for agricultural laborers to go to Hawaii as contract workers, whose expenses were paid by their employers. The Japanese who went to the United States paid their own way. The other major destinations of Japanese emigrants in the nineteenth century were Canada, Australia, Mexico, and Peru, in order of the numbers admitted.[52] The Japanese government subsidized emigration to Latin America,[53] and even helped organize some emigrant colonies in Paraguay and Brazil.[54] But foreign governments later began introducing immigration restrictions against the Japanese—the United States, Mexico, Canada, and South Africa, in the early years of the twentieth century, followed in 1934 and 1936 by Brazil and Peru.[55]

The experiences of the Japanese in the various countries of the Western Hemisphere differed considerably, partly reflecting the terms and conditions under which they immigrated. The Japanese immigration to the Western Hemisphere was largely male, before the Japanese government gave direct financial subsidies, which enabled women to emigrate.[56] In Mexico and Bolivia, most Japanese men married local women,[57] but in Brazil, where there were almost as many Japanese women as men, intermarriage was virtually unheard of.[58] In Chile, most Japanese owned shops in the capital city, Santiago,[59] and in Peru most Japanese quickly became urbanized shopkeepers as well,[60] but in Brazil most Japanese have been agricultural workers and farmers.[61] Few Japanese have immigrated to the countries of northern South

America—Venezuela, Colombia, and Ecuador—and there were fewer than 2,000 Japanese in all of Central America, from which they were expelled during World War II and sent to the United States for internment.[62] Most of the Japanese in Bolivia did not come from Japan, but re-emigrated from Peru.[63]

Japanese colonies established in northeastern Argentina after World War II were among many foreign settlements there that pioneered in opening up that undeveloped region. The Japanese were among the most successful.[64] Similarly, in postwar Bolivia, unsuccessful attempts to develop a frontier area with native Bolivians led to the establishment of agricultural colonies of foreign settlers, including people from Japan. Here too, Japanese success was economically outstanding, whether in terms of output per acre or output per worker.[65]

From the beginning of major Japanese emigration in 1885 through 1963, nearly one-third of all Japanese emigrants in the world migrated either to the mainland of the United States or to Hawaii, another 22 percent to Brazil, 3 percent each to Canada and Peru, and 3 percent to all the rest of Latin America combined. Less than one-tenth went to Asia, except for Manchuria, which received one-fourth of all Japanese emigrants during this period,[66] all of whom were later forced to return to Japan after the Second World War. However, few Japanese who migrated to the Western Hemisphere returned to Japan, and in the postwar era, substantial immigration resumed to Brazil and the United States. The Japanese government again subsidized many emigrants—most of whom went to Brazil, while most of the self-financed emigrants went to the United States. As of 1968, half of all Japanese living outside Japan lived in Brazil.[67]

The United States

Hawaii was not only the first recipient of modern Japanese emigrants, but also resumed its role as one of the major destinations of emigrants from Japan some years after that initial ill-fated episode. A coincidence of economic conditions in Hawaii and Japan contributed to this result.

The Hawaiian sugar industry began booming in the 1870s and 1880s, at the same time when Japan's painful transition to a modern economy was producing large-scale unemployment, bankruptcies, and civil disorders. From 1885 to 1894, more than 28,000 Japanese migrated to Hawaii, the vast majority being single men. Unlike the first Japanese from Yokohama, these Japanese were farmers and farm laborers. They were sojourners rather than settlers. Initially, about three-quarters of them returned to Japan, though with the passing years this figure declined to only one-quarter.[68] Anticipating the application of American laws against contract labor to Hawaii in 1900, after the American takeover of the islands, Hawaiian plantation owners imported more than 26,000 contract laborers from Japan in 1899, in order to beat the ban—the largest number ever admitted in a single year. These contracts were then voided under American laws, however, leaving thousands of Japanese free to migrate to the U.S. mainland. But Hawaii remained the principal area of concentration for Japanese in the United States for many years. As late as 1910, there were about four times as many Japanese in Hawaii as on the mainland.[69] Among other factors, race relations were better in Hawaii.[70] The difference was sufficiently significant for the government of Japan to cease issuing passports for Japanese to go to the U.S. mainland, while continuing to authorize passports for Hawaii.[71] While ineffective as a means of controlling ultimate destinations, this policy at least demonstrated that differences in the treatment of Japanese had become known back in Japan.

A small but significant group of native-born people of Japanese ancestry arose in nineteenth-century Hawaii, at a time when such people were virtually non-existent on the mainland. By 1910, the native-born were about one-third as numerous as the foreign-born among the Japanese in Hawaii, while remaining less than 7 percent on the mainland. By 1930, native-born Japanese Americans exceeded those born in Japan by 80 percent in Hawaii, while on the mainland the number of native-born had not quite caught up to those born in Japan.[72] The regional distribution of Japanese also changed over the years, as their numbers grew. At the turn of the century, there were 85,000 Japanese in the United States, nearly two-thirds in Hawaii. By 1920, there were more than 220,000 Japanese, just over half living on the mainland.

Both on the mainland and in Hawaii, Japanese relations with the larger society were to some extent shaped by the fact that they followed in the wake of the Chinese. In both places, the Chinese had begun as unskilled laborers and many had worked their way up to become small businessmen—and were hated for their advancement and their competition. The Japanese were initially welcomed as substitutes for the Chinese as coolie labor, but then they too became increasingly resented, as they advanced to small farming and small business enterprise. Soon they were lumped together with the Chinese as "the yellow peril" threatening the living standards of American workers, businessmen, and American society in general. This reaction was more pronounced on the mainland than in Hawaii, but it was present in both places. Laws were passed in Hawaii to block the movement of the Japanese into skilled occupations,[73] and on the mainland to stop their purchase of land in California.[74]

Despite discriminatory laws and practices, the Japanese continued to advance economically. Among first-generation Japanese American family heads living on the mainland, a majority began either as farm laborers or as domestic servants, with less than 4 percent owning or managing farms, and less than 4 percent owning or managing businesses. But three-fifths of this generation of Japanese men eventually became owners or managers of either farms or businesses before World War II.[75] The largest number became farmers and more than two-thirds of these could speak only broken English or no English at all.[76] They also had to overcome the handicap of Alien Land Laws, which made it illegal for "aliens ineligible for citizenship" (Asians) to own land in California, where most mainland Japanese lived. Similar laws were passed in other states.[77] A variety of evasions developed, followed by a tightening of the legal loopholes, followed by more evasions.[78] However, time was on the side of the Japanese, as their American-born children were automatically citizens of the United States, to whom the land laws could not apply under the U.S. Constitution. In the decade of the 1930s, the land owned by Japanese Americans in California more than doubled.[79] A majority of employed Japanese males still worked in farming as late as 1940,[80] and they produced about one-third of the commercial truck farming crops sold in California.[81]

The Japanese gained their initial foothold in agriculture by working as agricultural laborers for lower wages than whites, and then acquired farms by paying more than whites for the land. Once established, they became formidable competitors. Where agricultural laborers were paid by piece-rate, as about half were, the Japanese earned substantially more than whites, through greater diligence and longer hours. As their reputation as hard workers spread, their hourly pay rose and eventually overtook that of whites.[82]

Japan's attack on Pearl Harbor on December 7, 1941, set the stage for a traumatic landmark in the history of Japanese Americans. In the shock and anger that followed this treacherous attack, which occurred in the midst of negotiations ostensibly aimed at peace, anti-Japanese feelings ran high, especially on the mainland. In Hawaii, where the attack occurred (killing many Japanese Americans, among others[83]), fewer than 1,500 Japanese Americans were taken into custody as enemy aliens, but on the mainland more than 100,000 were interned.[84] The economic impact was as devastating as the social trauma. Businesses built up over many years had to be liquidated in a matter of weeks, at ruinous losses. Nor could shattered careers be readily resumed after the war.

The wartime internment had lasting economic after-effects, reflected in occupational declines among Japanese Americans after the war. The proportion of first-generation Japanese Americans on the mainland who owned their own businesses or farms in the postwar years was only about half what it had been in the prewar years. The proportion of this generation who became house servants more than doubled the prewar level. Those who became farm laborers in the postwar years was more than triple the prewar percentage. The number who were professionals also declined.[85] But while these disastrous economic retrogressions struck the first-generation Japanese Americans (*Issei*), the second generation (*Nisei*) forged ahead at an accelerated rate. American citizens, American educated—with more years of schooling than whites—the *Nisei* sought lucrative professions. In colleges and universities, they seldom majored in liberal arts.[86] By 1959, Japanese Americans as a group had reached the family income of whites and by 1969 they exceeded the national average in family income by 32 percent. This trend has continued, with the 1990 census showing the median family income of Japanese Americans to be 45 percent higher than the median family income of native-born, non-Asian Americans.[87] Along with this economic progress came acculturation and social acceptance, including rising rates of intermarriage.[88] By 1980, three-quarters of all Japanese Americans spoke only English.[89]

Ironically, the Japanese on the mainland, who historically faced more discrimination, as well as wartime internment, achieved higher incomes and occupational levels than those in Hawaii.[90] The Japanese in Hawaii were also much more active politically, and by 1971 had a majority in the state legislature.[91] Yet these political advantages of the Japanese in Hawaii, together with the advantage of not having been subjected to the massive internments on the mainland, were still not enough to overcome other advantages of the Japanese on the mainland. Historically, the Japanese who immigrated to Hawaii came from poorer regions and poorer classes in Japan than did those who went to the U.S. mainland.[92] Apparently this social difference had enduring economic consequences, more so than differences in their treatment by the larger society, or differences in the political clout of Japanese Americans in Hawaii versus the mainland.

Canada

The first documented Japanese immigration to Canada occurred in 1877, but the numbers have never been large as a percentage of the total Canadian population. By 1979, there were nearly 50,000 Japanese in Canada, but they were less than one-half of one percent of the Canadian population. However, the Japanese immigrants were not evenly spread across Canada, but were initially concentrated in the western province of British Columbia. At the time of Pearl Harbor, more than three-quarters of all the Japanese in Canada lived within a 75-mile radius of the city of Vancouver.[93] As with other immigrant concentrations in various countries, this reflected ties with specific individuals, as well as a general desire to settle among compatriots. About half the prewar Japanese immigrants had relatives or friends in British Columbia.[94] Yet, even in prewar British Columbia, the Chinese and Japanese put together were still outnumbered more than ten to one by whites.[95]

Japanese immigration to Canada began very small but grew rapidly. As of 1896, there were fewer than a thousand Japanese in Canada, mostly fishermen on the Pacific coast of British Columbia, but increasing numbers came from Japan over the years to take jobs in such locally expanding Canadian industries as fishing, lumbering, mining, and railroad construction. By 1901, there were more than 4,700 Japanese in Canada—97 percent of them in British Columbia.[96] Perhaps as a result of Japan's mobilization for war with Russia, very few Japanese immigrants arrived in the first few years of the twentieth century. Canada received only about 2 percent of all emigrants from Japan during the entire 1885–1907 period, compared to nearly half who went either to the U.S. mainland or to such American possessions as Hawaii and the Philippines.[97] At the end of the Russo-Japanese War, Japanese immigration to Canada resumed—and on a larger scale. In less than three years, another 7,000 Japanese arrived in Canada. Partly this reflected the newly enacted American restrictions on Japanese settling on the U.S. mainland from Hawaii.[98]

The rapidly increasing numbers of the Japanese, and their geographic and occupational concentrations, caused them to be seen as a serious competitive threat, despite their relatively modest numbers on a national scale. Moreover, almost all of the Japanese immigrants were young single men, so that their proportion of the visible work force was much higher than their proportion in the general population, which of course included women and children. The Japanese also worked harder and for lower pay than whites, displacing them in many cases, and thereby becoming one of the most hated groups in the province.[99] As early as 1901, the Japanese constituted 22 percent of the work force in the seven largest mills in the Vancouver area.[100]

Canadian labor unions organized the first anti-Japanese rally in Canada, in August 1907. Weeks of anti-Japanese agitation in Vancouver culminated in a riot in which a mob of whites attacked the city's Chinese and Japanese neighborhoods. The mob rampaged through the Chinatown area but were turned back by the determined resistance of the Japanese.[101] This crisis led to an international "gentleman's agreement" between Canada and Japan, the net result of which was a restriction of Japanese immigration to Canada. Again, as in the American situation, the Japanese government's demonstrated strength during the war with Russia gave it the prestige and leverage to salvage some concessions for their people overseas.

Unlike the overwhelmingly male Chinese community in Canada, the Japanese young men were not left stranded without women when Asian immigration was curbed. As in the United States, wives could be brought from Japan to Canada, including the "picture brides" selected for them by their families overseas. After the so-called "gentleman's agreement," more females than males immigrated from Japan to Canada.[102] Over the years, the initially larger Chinese population of Canada declined, as the Chinese men died off or returned to China, without being replaced by children.[103] The Japanese community, however, continued to grow rapidly, composed as it was of young couples in the prime childbearing years. Their birthrate was more than double that of British Columbia as a whole.[104] However, this rapid increase moderated as the young Japanese population grew older.[105]

In the early years, the Japanese immigrants were concentrated in half a dozen laboring occupations, but by the 1930s they were represented in almost every occupation or sub-occupation listed by the Canadian census.[106] This occurred in the face of determined attempts by whites to prevent it. As early as 1902, a Royal Commission reported that the Japanese, living in shacks along the water, were able to undersell whites in boat-building. Employers, especially in the canneries, preferred the Japanese both as laborers and as fishermen, because of their skills and work habits. By 1921, the Japanese held more than 40 percent of the fishing licenses in the province—more than either whites or aboriginal Indians.[107] In the sawmills, Japanese workers competed so well by working for less that at least one mill refused to hire whites.[108] The Japanese even undercut the wages of Chinese workers, who had arrived earlier in Canada and had become established in this industry.[109]

The political counterattack against the Japanese began early in the fishing industry, where they were especially successful. In 1920, the Vancouver authorities began reducing the number of licenses issued to the Japanese. After several years of continuing reductions, the Japanese appealed to the courts and in 1928 the Canadian Supreme Court ruled that the government could not discriminate in this way. But the years that passed before this decision saw a decline in Japanese fisherman, and the *status quo ante* was not restored. In 1933, the Japanese held 28 percent fewer fishing licenses than in 1922, while whites and Indians each doubled their previous shares.[110]

In the lumbering industry, a different approach was used against the Japanese. Here the Japanese immigrants were typically very low-paid workers, so a minimum-wage law was used for the explicit purpose of pricing them out of jobs. This minimum-wage law was passed in British Columbia in 1925, when 45 percent of the lumbering workers were Orientals. A year later, more than a thousand white workers had been added and more than 400 Orientals eliminated. Like the displaced Japanese in the fishing industry, some of these workers returned to Japan.[111] In a number of occupations, government regulation, contracts, or franchises permitted local politicians to impose restrictions or prohibitions on the hiring of Japanese. Even where these efforts were subsequently overruled by higher national authorities, this took time and the Japanese were excluded until the legal processes ran their course.[112] Subcontractors for the provincial Department of Public Works, for example, were explicitly forbidden to hire Asians "directly or indirectly, upon, about or in connection with the works."[113]

Discrimination against the Japanese as employees led many into self-employment, notably in agriculture, but also in urban small businesses as well. Among berry growers in British Columbia, Asians held 29 percent of the acreage in 1920, rising to 45 percent by 1934. Because the Japanese cultivated much more intensively than the whites, their share of all the berries grown in the province was even larger than their share of the land, and reached an estimated 85 percent in 1934.[114] Urban Japanese likewise sought self-employment. As of 1931, 20 percent of the barbers' licenses granted in Vancouver went to the Japanese, as did nearly half the licenses for fish dealers and more than half the licenses as dressmakers.[115] By the mid-1930s, there were about 860 businesses run by the Japanese in Vancouver.[116] Just over half the Japanese working in that city remained laborers at this point, however.[117]

With the rise of the Japanese into the business class, the organized political opposition to them also rose from the working class to the businessmen. Whereas there was little anti-Japanese activity or feeling among white businessmen in British Columbia in 1913,[118] by 1919 the British Columbia Retail Merchants Association had organized a massive anti-Japanese letter-writing campaign, directed at elected officials.[119] They also tried to get stricter enforcement of retail store-closing laws, charging that the Japanese were gaining customers by staying open longer, or even by making sales on Sunday.[120] These efforts largely failed in the long run. From 1927 to 1937, the number of Japanese candy and fruit merchants in Vancouver increased from 58 to 80, and the number of grocers from 56 to 110.[121] By 1937, the Japanese held 20 percent of all grocers' licenses in Vancouver and 91 percent of all greengrocers' licenses.[122]

In the more strictly government-controlled occupations—civil service, logging on government land, or government-licensed professions, such as law, pharmacy, and dentistry—the Japanese were much more effectively kept out.[123] There were only 3 Japanese listed as working in public administration and defense (combined) in 1931.[124]

The first generation of Japanese immigrants in Canada spoke little English. As late as 1925, only about one-fourth of them declared that they could read and speak English.[125] The second generation—the *Nisei*—learned English in school and Japanese at home, but often did not learn either language well enough to be fluent and comfortable in it.[126] They were, however, noted for being well-behaved children in school[127] and their rate of juvenile delinquency was well below the national average.[128] The Japanese acculturated in superficial aspects, such as clothing and furnishings,[129] but retained their own sense of values and patterns of behavior. For example, they took care of their own needy, rather than leave them to public charity. Even during the Great Depression of the 1930s, only 4 percent of the Japanese in Canada received public relief, compared to 13 percent of the general population.[130]

World War II proved to be an even bigger disaster for the Japanese in Canada than in the United States. More than a thousand Japanese-owned fishing vessels were impounded. Japanese-language newspapers were closed. Then Japanese employees began to be fired, and political pressure groups in British Columbia began to demand that the Japanese be interned.[131] Neither the Canadian military authorities nor the Royal Canadian Mounted Police saw any danger from the Japanese in Canada,[132] and in fact none of them was ever convicted of any espionage or sabotage during the war.[133] Nevertheless, the political pressures from British Columbia caused the central government to give in to their demands.

Already regarded as security risks before Pearl Harbor, and registered and required to have papers on them at all times in Canada, the Japanese Canadians were now rounded up and interned. By this time,

60 percent of all Japanese in Canada were native born.[134] Three-quarters of those removed from the west coast of Canada were either Canadian-born citizens or naturalized citizens.[135] As in the United States, a sudden internment meant hasty sales of businesses and homes that represented a lifetime of work and savings. They typically sold for less than one-fourth their value.[136] Most of the Japanese-owned businesses were bought by members of other middleman minorities—Chinese, Greeks, and Jews.[137]

As in the United States, the Japanese were interned in remote places. Most spent the war in shacks hastily assembled in Canadian ghost towns, under the control of the Royal Canadian Mounted Police.[138] But the Japanese in Canada were interned earlier and kept interned longer than Japanese in the United States.[139] Moreover, when they were released, they were not allowed to return home like Japanese Americans. British Columbia did not want them back,[140] and they were not allowed to settle on the west coast until 1949.[141] The Canadian government presented them with the choice of relocating east of the Rocky Mountains or going to Japan. More than 40 percent of the Japanese said that they would rather go to war-devastated Japan than remain in Canada.[142] However, early reports from those who did in fact relocate to Japan depicted so many hardships there that many of those who had asked to go decided to relocate to eastern Canada instead.[143]

The postwar economic recovery of the Japanese in Canada has been at least as spectacular as that in the United States. The younger generation encountered less discrimination when scattered across parts of Canada with no history of organized anti-Japanese activity. While less than 1 percent of Japanese Canadians were in professional occupations in 1935, by 1971 more than one-third of the *Nisei* in Toronto were professionals. Japanese Canadians as a whole earned 16 percent higher income than the Canadian national average.[144] The average family income of the second-generation Japanese in Toronto was nearly twice the Canadian national average.[145] The Japanese were not only more dispersed nationally—with Toronto now superseding Vancouver as the main concentration—but were also so widely dispersed within the city that it was rare to find two Japanese living in the same block.[146] More than half the marriages of the third generation were intermarriages—compared to just 1 percent in 1941.[147] Yet the Japanese rose economically and were eventually accepted socially without ever having held a major elective office in Canada.[148] As in other countries and with other groups, political power has had little correlation with the economic success of Japanese in the Western Hemisphere.

Peru

In 1873, Peru became the first Latin American nation to establish diplomatic relations with Japan.[149] However, this grew out of isolated and bizarre international shipping incidents,[150] and led neither to important ties between the two countries nor to immigration. The first Japanese vessel did not call at a Peruvian port until 1883,[151] and the first significant numbers of Japanese immigrants did not arrive until fifteen years later.[152]

As in Canada and the United States, the Japanese arrived in Peru in the wake of the Chinese, and were often lumped together with them in popular perception, especially in the early years. Nearly 100,000 Chinese had immigrated to Peru between 1849 and 1874, and had aroused public animosity—expressed in riots and massacres—because of their economic competition as agricultural laborers and as small businessmen.[153] The Japanese who arrived in 1898 were overwhelmingly male and overwhelmingly agricultural laborers.[154] But, within a year of their arrival, most had moved to the cities.[155] This represented the first of many mutual disappointments between Japanese agricultural laborers and Peruvian landowners.

Around the turn of the century, Japanese workers were imported under indenture contracts which required them to work to pay off the cost of transporting them across the Pacific. Language and cultural differences, as well as unscrupulous employers and sometimes bungling emigration companies, led to many frictions and defections. The death rate among the young Japanese men was remarkably high. Among the first wave of 790 Japanese, there were 143 deaths the first year, from a variety of diseases.[156] Of the 984 Japanese who arrived in 1903 and 1904, nearly half died in the sugarcane fields.[157]

Japanese annual immigration to Peru went over one thousand for the first time in 1908, when it reached 2,442—a level never reached again in a single year. However, there were a number of years around World

War I when Japanese immigration exceeded one thousand annually, as it did again during the mid to late 1920s. After that, however, Japanese immigration to Peru was measured in the hundreds. Since 1950, immigration to Peru from Japan has been fewer than 100 annually, except for two years, and has been zero for three years.[158] Departures were also high, exceeding 1,000 in 1935. From the mid to late 1930s, the number of Japanese leaving Peru exceeded the number entering. Natural increase, however, led to a growing population of Japanese in the country. The number of Japanese living in Peru was more than 20,000 in 1930,[159] and this grew to more than 50,000 by 1970.[160]

Despite the relatively small size of the Japanese community in Peru, it had by 1930 become the most prominent foreign element,[161] in a country that received relatively little immigration. Their economic presence was especially notable as they moved from agricultural labor to urban occupations as artisans and small businessmen. Even as agricultural laborers, the Japanese were resented, for their work habits caused them to be sufficiently in demand to be paid more than Peruvian workers.[162]

Many of the Japanese moved from agricultural labor to jobs as urban domestic servants, a role which, among other things, aided their learning the Spanish language. Others became small shopkeepers, factory workers, or took miscellaneous other jobs that allowed them to move slowly but steadily up the economic ladder. Although most Japanese came to Peru as agricultural workers, most soon found their way to the capital city of Lima and its environs. As of 1909, there were 441 Japanese factory workers in the vicinity of Lima, along with 257 domestics and cooks, 35 carpenters, and 59 small merchants and peddlers.[163] The number of Japanese-owned barbershops in Lima rose from one in 1904 to 130 twenty years later—nearly three-quarters of all barbershops in the city in 1924.[164] A Japanese Chamber of Commerce was formed in Lima in 1915, with 27 members. Four years later, it had more than a hundred members. The number of Japanese grocery stores increased from 28 to about 200. Often the Japanese bought out Italian or Chinese shopkeepers.[165]

The Peruvian press attacked the growing range and competitive success of Japanese businesses. Attempts to promote boycotts of these businesses proved ineffective, however, for the Japanese typically charged lower prices.[166] Partly these reflected smaller profit margins and partly lower overhead costs, as the Japanese small businessman and/or his clerks often lived on the premises.[167] Unlike their Hispanic competitors, even prosperous Japanese businessmen seldom lived ostentatiously.[168] As in Canada, the Japanese reputation for fulfilling business obligations was high, leading to high credit ratings.[169] The Japanese also took more interest in educating their children than did other Peruvians,[170] building a foundation for their continued advancement.

In the city, as in the countryside, Japanese workers acquired a reputation for being more painstaking and conscientious than Peruvian workers. The Japanese thus became prominent among skilled workers and came to own nearly one-fourth of the mechanical and watch-repair shops in Lima.[171] They created the tire-repair trade in Peru, and dominated it for years.[172]

While economic boycotts against the Japanese did not prove to be viable, political action did. A law was passed requiring at least 80 percent of all employees to be Peruvians.[173] Immigration from Japan was severely restricted in the mid-1930s.[174] In May 1940, a Peruvian mob attack on the Japanese and their property in the cities of Lima and Callao also expressed the rising anti-Japanese feeling. The coming of World War II heightened anti-Japanese feelings and policies in Peru. More than 1,700 Japanese were identified as potentially dangerous enemy aliens, with the aid of the American F. B. I. and were shipped to the United States for wartime internment.

Peru was only one of a number of Latin American nations to ship parts of their own Japanese population to the United States. There was some thought that they might be exchanged for U.S. citizens held by Japan. But Peru participated in this operation with a vengeance, sending more than four-fifths of all the Japanese from Latin America who were interned in the U.S.A.[175] Hundreds were later shipped to Japan from the United States during the war on a neutral ship, and hundreds more were sent to Japan after the war.[176] Peru permitted only 79 to return.[177] However, 90 percent of the Japanese in Peru were not interned. They were simply subjected to many restrictions. Nor was there a mass exodus of Japanese after the war. As of 1970, Peru had a larger Japanese population than Canada, and was exceeded in this respect only by Brazil and the United States.[178]

The prosperity of the Japanese in postwar Peru was more striking than anywhere else in Latin America, except Brazil.[179] Historic popular resentment and political discrimination proved to be incapable of stopping their rise. Moreover, the history of Japanese economic success in Peru has also been a history of Japanese contributions to the Peruvian economy. These include contributions in agriculture, where the Japanese produced 25 percent of the cotton crop in the late 1930s, to the urban commercial sector, where they introduced modern merchandising methods, more ethical business practices, and greater cleanliness in food processing.[180] As in other countries, the Japanese in Peru acquired a reputation for hard work, reliability, and honesty.[181] While anti-Japanese snobbishness persisted on into the 1990s in some exclusive upper-class social clubs,[182] the general society increasingly accepted them. One sign of that greater social acceptance was that a little-known businessman of Japanese ancestry was elected president in 1990, defeating a world-famous Hispanic Peruvian writer. In 1995, he was re-elected in a landslide, defeating another famous Hispanic Peruvian who had been Secretary General of the United Nations. As in the United States, however, this political success followed economic success, and was neither a cause nor even a contributing factor.

Brazil

Significant emigration from Japan to Brazil began early in the twentieth century and was accelerated by the immigration restrictions of the United States, and by the curtailment of European immigration to Brazil, resulting from World War I. Fewer than a thousand Japanese arrived annually in Brazil as late as 1910, but in 1913 nearly 7,000 arrived.[183] By 1930, Japanese immigration to Brazil approached 14,000 annually, and there were more than 116,000 Japanese living in Brazil—78 percent of all Japanese in Latin America. The inflow from Japan around that time outnumbered the German and Italian inflows to Brazil, combined, and was second only to the Portuguese immigration.[184] Most Japanese settled in the state of São Paulo, in southern Brazil—223 out of 234 heads of families during the years 1908–1912 and 6,129 out of 6,518 family heads during the years 1933–1937, with comparably lopsided proportions in between.[185] Their origins were also not random. Prior to 1930, 60 percent of the immigrants from Japan came from just five of the country's 47 prefects, though greater diversity of origins appeared among later immigrants.[186] Their destinations, however, remained very similar throughout the prewar era. As late as 1940, 90 percent of the Japanese immigrants in Brazil still lived in the state of São Paulo. However, even in this state, the 200,000 to 250,000 Japanese were less than 3 percent of the population.[187] Return migration to Japan throughout the prewar era has been estimated at about 15,000 people.[188]

The peak of Japanese immigration to Brazil was reached in 1933, when more than 24,000 arrived—more than half of all immigrants to Brazil that year.[189] At that point, more than one-fifth of all Japanese living outside Japan lived in Brazil.[190] But after 1934, when immigration restrictions were applied, the decline of Japanese immigration to Brazil was sharp, in both absolute and relative terms. By 1941, there were only about 1,500 immigrants arriving from Japan, and they were less than 6 percent of all immigrants to Brazil at that time. After World War II, there was some resumption of Japanese immigration to Brazil, at somewhat more than the immediate prewar level, but not approaching the immigration in the peak years of the early 1930s. Most of the new postwar immigrants settled in the Amazon region of the northeast, rather than in the southern region where most Japanese were concentrated.[191] Altogether, about a quarter of a million Japanese immigrated to Brazil over the period from 1908 to 1975. After taking into account return migration and natural increase, there was a net Japanese population of three-quarters of a million living in Brazil at the latter date, 75 percent of whom lived in the state of São Paulo.[192]

The first Japanese immigrants to Brazil came as a group in 1908, as a result of a contract between the state of São Paulo and a private emigration corporation in Japan. As in Hawaii, this initial effort failed amid bitter recriminations, apparently due to lack of knowledge of local conditions, and the company went bankrupt.[193] But Japanese immigration continued, with sharp fluctuations but generally increasing from the hundreds initially entering annually to the thousands immigrating annually around World War I. As of 1918, the approximately 5,600 Japanese immigrants were more than one-fourth of all immigrants to Brazil.[194]

Japanese immigration to Brazil remained primarily an organized, corporate undertaking, rather than a matter of isolated immigrants crossing the Pacific. Japanese immigrants came in groups and lived together as groups in Brazil, in all-Japanese agricultural communities, sealed off from the rest of Brazilian society. This was the choice of the Japanese organizers rather than of the Brazilian authorities or populace. The purpose was to minimize frictions with the Brazilian population and forestall the kind of popular hostility that had led to the exclusion of the Japanese from other countries. Many immigrants who began as agricultural laborers in the Japanese colonies went on to become small, independent farmers, but still living within the Japanese enclaves.[195] More than 90 percent of the Japanese heads of families arriving in Brazil in the prewar era were farmers but more than three-quarters of them began working in Brazil as contract laborers in agriculture, though very few remained in that position very long. Nearly half left that status within two years and more than two-thirds within four years, with fewer than 1 percent remaining contract laborers permanently.[196]

Unlike other predominantly agricultural peoples in some other lands, the Japanese in Brazil were educated. During the entire period from the early twentieth century until 1941, Japanese immigrants to Brazil had higher literacy rates (74 percent) than those of Italian immigrants (60 percent), and much higher literacy rates than Portuguese (43 percent), Turkish (38 percent), or Spanish immigrants (28 percent). The Japanese literacy rate was exceeded only by that of Polish (77 percent) and German immigrants (87 percent) to Brazil.[197]

The Japanese colonies contained not only their own leaders, doctors, and social institutions, but also created their own rice mills, lumber mills, a sugar factory, and electric generating capacity. They also built roads, bridges, waterworks, and radio stations. The Japanese created the silk industry in Brazil, so that Brazil no longer imported silk. The Japanese, who were only 2 to 3 percent of the population of the state of São Paulo, and owned less than 2 percent of its land, nevertheless produced nearly 30 percent of its agricultural output in the early 1930s—including 46 percent of the cotton, 57 percent of the silk, and 75 percent of the tea. By 1943, the Japanese owned more than a million acres of land in São Paulo. A substantial proportion of the banana plantations and fishing were also in Japanese hands.[198]

These Japanese colonies were for years run by officials appointed in Tokyo. Moreover, banks in Japan opened offices in Brazil. This policy of establishing self-contained Japanese enclaves largely avoided obvious, direct economic competition between the Japanese and local workers, farmers, or businessmen—competition which had provoked great hostility elsewhere in the hemisphere, especially where the Japanese became a middleman minority, as in Peru. Moreover, the Japanese colonies were almost equally balanced between the sexes (60 percent male),[199] so that another source of interaction and competition with the local populace was avoided. More than 90 percent of all Japanese immigrants to Brazil from 1908 to 1941 came in family groups.[200]

The Japanese attempt in Brazil to avoid situations that caused trouble in other countries seemed at first to pay off well. The Japanese were so welcome in Brazil that even a local civil war blockade of the port of Santos in 1932 was lifted long enough to allow a ship full of Japanese immigrants to enter—the only ship allowed through the blockade during the whole period of military hostilities. A 1933 Brazilian study concluded that the Japanese settler was "of great efficiency, hard working, orderly, economical, obedient, and law abiding." Yet, even in Brazil, those few Japanese who became middlemen—storekeepers and petty traders—met resentment.[201] The fact that most Japanese in Brazil avoided such roles—and avoided open competition with Brazilians in general—undoubtedly had much to do with their acceptance. From a strictly economic viewpoint, the Japanese in their enclaves were as much in competition with other Brazilians as if they were living completely mingled with them, but *politically* the appearances were quite different, with many Brazilians paying little attention to the isolated Japanese, even though purchasing their output through the roundabout channels of commerce.

Although socially and culturally isolated, the Japanese in Brazil were not literally sealed off physically from all contact with others. In part of the agricultural Ribeira valley, located in the southern region of the state of São Paulo, the largely illiterate and barefoot day laborers known as *caboclos* outnumbered the Japanese by at least two to one in the early 1940s,[202] but they lived socially very distinct lives. In the

Ribeira valley town of Registro, 21 of the 25 stores were owned by Japanese and both the traders and the clerks were largely Japanese.[203] Under these circumstances, intermarriage between the Japanese and Brazilians was not only rare but was a sign of a loss of social status on the part of the Japanese involved.[204]

Despite the social cohesiveness and cultural persistence of the distinctive inner values of the Japanese, many outward cultural changes occurred in the very different geographic, climatic, and economic environment of Brazil. For example, while a peasant on horseback was a rare sight in Japan, this became a common sight among the Japanese farmers in the Ribeira valley, where distances were greater and the roads were of poorer quality.[205] The construction of houses was also adapted to local conditions and Western clothes became common. In a deliberate decision made by authorities in Japan, Japanese emigrants were instructed *not* to create Buddhist or Shinto institutions in Brazil, where in fact they became at least nominal Christians, though with some survivals of their ancestral religious practices continuing privately. The decision that these emigrants should wear Western clothing was also made by authorities in Japan.[206] The need to minimize frictions with the local Brazilians was clearly a high priority.

Japanese children born in Brazil learned the Portuguese language when they attended the public schools. In the school setting, the use of the Japanese language was an offense to be reported to the teacher. Accordingly, Japanese children in the Ribeira valley in the early 1940s spoke Portuguese without an accent, even though their parents generally spoke much poorer quality Portuguese. This mastery of the national language of Brazil not only represented an element of acculturation in itself but opened the door to further acculturation through reading Brazilian newspapers, books, and other publications, and facilitating business or social contacts with other Brazilians. At the same time, when Portuguese became the primary language of the younger generation, this made interactions with their own parents less easy. Often the parents spoke to their children in Japanese and the children replied in Portuguese.[207]

As farmers, the Japanese introduced new crops, new agricultural methods, scientific analysis of soils—and hard work. Their output per acre was more than 4 times that of other immigrant farmers in Brazil and more than 8 times that of Brazilian farmers.[208] For years the Japanese prospered in Brazil, while being largely ignored politically. But two developments eventually brought them unwelcome political attention: the rise of Japan as an imperialist power in the 1930s and the rise of nationalism in Brazil at the same time, which cast suspicion and resentment on separatist minorities, including Germans and Italians, as well as Japanese. In 1938, the Brazilian government began a conscious campaign of cultural Brazilianization requiring among other things that the Portuguese language be taught in all schools and shutting down private schools conducted in foreign languages, such as those which often supplemented public-school education among the Japanese in Brazil. With Japan being seen increasingly as a military menace and an economic rival, the presence of an enclave in Brazil controlled from Japan aroused serious concern. That concern was expressed first in restrictions on immigration from Japan in 1934 and then in increasing government supervision of the Japanese colonies, especially after Japan's entry into World War II. The Japanese, however, were not so much singled out as they were part of a general concern over unassimilated foreign enclaves in Brazil, particularly when the principal such enclaves were made up of nationals of the three countries of the Germany-Italy-Japan Axis powers, who were aggressive seeking new lands to conquer. In addition to banning foreign political activity in Brazil and passing laws making it easier to deport aliens, the Brazilian government also launched a campaign of "Brazilianisation" in the country's education system, requiring both public and private schools to teach the language of the country, Portuguese, as well as the history and geography of Brazil.[209]

A wartime government report on the Japanese colonies still praised their sanitary conditions, but now noted that all books and periodicals in the settlement were in the Japanese language and that textbooks in Japanese contained propaganda and military instructions.[210] This was in violation of the laws of the Brazilianization campaign but the Japanese continued to evade these laws by establishing clandestine schools using the Japanese language and promoting Japanese ideals.[211]

Although Brazil did not declare war on Japan until June 1945, when the war was almost over, the Japanese in Brazil were put under the same wartime restrictions imposed on Germans and Italians after

Brazil declared war on Germany and Italy in 1942. These included restrictions on travel, bans on possession of firearms or explosives, and a suspension of the constitutional rights of Germans, Italians, and Japanese in Brazil.[212] There was press hysteria and brief, apparently token, arrests of local Japanese leaders, along with confiscations of radios and firearms. About a thousand Japanese families were evacuated from the vicinity of the port of Santos.[213] But the measures taken fell far short of those against the Japanese in Peru, Canada, the United States, or Central America. Moreover, Brazil did not join other Latin American nations which shipped Japanese to the United States for wartime internment.[214] These national differences in wartime treatment of Japanese minorities reflected prewar political attitudes toward the Japanese in these countries, rather than differences in military vulnerability or even the loyalty of local Japanese. In Brazil, there was in fact far more pro-Japan sentiment and activity among the Japanese than in other Western Hemisphere nations where much harsher measures were taken.

In Brazil, more than 50,000 Japanese belonged to a pro-Japan organization whose activities included sabotage and terrorism against members of the Japanese community who were considered to be collaborators in the war effort against Japan. The utter isolation of some Japanese communities in Brazil made it possible for pro-Japan fanatics to maintain that Japan had won the war, even after its surrender in 1945. Sixteen Japanese Brazilian leaders who asserted that Japan had lost the war were assassinated,[215] the last being killed as late as 1947.[216] So convinced were many Japanese of Japan's victory that more than 2,000 of them journeyed to the port of Santos to meet a nonexistent Japanese naval force supposedly sent to take them back to their "victorious" homeland.[217] As with many movements, what began as an ideology ended as a racket, including the sale of land in the Japanese empire, and collections for arranging welcoming events for visiting Japanese officials celebrating their "victory" over the United States.[218] It was at this point that those Japanese Brazilians who proclaimed Japan's defeat were assassinated. They were now a threat to money, not simply to group morale.

Over the years, despite the success of Japanese agricultural colonies, there was a movement of people from the farms to the cities.

For example, during the period from 1945 to 1958, the number of Japanese families living in the city of São Paulo doubled and there was some regional dispersion of Japanese as well. By 1958, 45 percent of the Japanese in Brazil were urban. This was all the more remarkable because postwar Brazilian immigration policy favored agricultural immigration from Japan.[219] However, the movement to the cities was not by any means a completely new phenomenon. More than one-fourth of the original 781 Japanese immigrants to Brazil in 1908 moved on to the cities of Santos and São Paulo.[220] Only the continued inflow of Japanese immigrants to the agricultural colonies maintained the rural predominance among Japanese in Brazil. In the postwar era as well, most immigrants from Japan to Brazil went into agriculture, and were in fact recruited from the predominantly agricultural island of Kyushu.[221]

The changing rural-urban mix of the Japanese population in Brazil has been reflected in the share of Japanese farmers in the agricultural output of the state of São Paulo and of Brazil as a whole. From the mid-1930s to the mid-1950s, the growing role of the Japanese farmers was reflected in their rising proportions of the agricultural output of the state of São Paulo, where most of them lived. They produced 33 percent of the state's potatoes in the mid-1930s and 60 percent in the mid-1950s. They produced 75 percent of the tea in the earlier period and 100 percent in the later period. In the later period they also produced 90 percent of the state's eggs and peppermint, 99 percent of its tomatoes, and 100 percent of its peaches. However, the postwar urbanization of many second-generation Japanese in Brazil was reflected in declines in the Japanese share of various agricultural crops, though as late as 1978 they still produced 71 percent of the tomatoes in the state of São Paulo, 80 percent of the silkworms, 92 percent of the strawberries, and 94 percent of the tea.[222] At one time, more than half the tomatoes in the entire country were grown by the Japanese,[223] who were less than one percent of Brazil's population.[224]

Education has been an important part of the Japanese success story in Brazil. Even in São Paulo, where they have been concentrated, the Japanese were less than 3 percent of the population in the 1970s, but they were 10 percent of university enrollment.[225] In Brazil as a whole, the Japanese have had the highest proportion of college graduates of all the ethnic groups.[226] This was achieved despite the rural locations of most Japanese, which often necessitated sending their children away to boarding schools, even for high-school education.[227] As of 1988, 16 percent of the students at the University of São Paulo were Japanese—and were often resented by other students as "unfair competition" because they "work so hard." A physics professor at the university said: "In my classes, they are always the brilliant ones, the top 20 students."[228]

The economic success of the Japanese in Brazil has been particularly remarkable in view of their relatively recent arrival in the country, virtually all within the twentieth century. Moreover, their assimilation into Brazilian society has not been particularly rapid. During the entire period from 1908 to 1947, the intermarriage rate for Japanese females in Brazil never reached 1 percent and that of males reached only 4 percent.[229] As late as 1958, nearly two-thirds of all Japanese in Brazil spoke only the Japanese language, compared to 28 percent who spoke both Japanese and Portuguese, and only 8 percent who spoke Portuguese alone.[230] Their intermarriage rate was now 14 percent, and that represented a considerable rise over the years,[231] intermarriages being only 3 percent of all existing Japanese marriages.[232] Even their local origins in Japan still affected their marriage patterns in Brazil. In the extreme case, more than 90 percent of Okinawans who married in Brazil married other Okinawans.[233] Late marriages remained the rule among Japanese in Brazil, as in Japan.[234] In religion, there was some sign of assimilation, but 45 percent of the Japanese remained Buddhists, in an overwhelmingly Catholic country.[235] Some Westernized names, usually in combination with Japanese names, were given to the second generation—42 percent—but only 8 percent were given purely Westernized names and about half were given purely Japanese names.[236]

By the late twentieth century, there were estimated to be close to a million Japanese in Brazil,[237] and they owned almost three-fourths as much land in Brazil as there is in Japan.[238] They also prospered in Brazil's urban economy, where they owned banks and produced paper, plastics, fertilizer, and electronics. Japan's postwar re-entry into Brazil's economy, with investments exceeded only by those of the United States and West Germany, created further employment opportunities for Japanese Brazilians who worked by the hundreds for such firms as Sony, Mitsubishi, and Honda. Among the business advantages of the Japanese in Brazil was a reputation for honesty in a country noted for its corruption in both business and politics.[239]

Like other groups with a rapid economic rise and a slow assimilation rate, the Japanese in Brazil advanced to a large extent through self-employment. This was a long process, however. As of 1912, only 14 percent of the Japanese in Brazil were self-employed but, by 1958, 86 percent had achieved this status.[240] Most were farmers,[241] but among the Japanese in nonagricultural occupations, half were tradesmen. Less than 1 percent worked for the government.[242] It was the middle of the twentieth century before the first Japanese was elected as a representative in the state capital of São Paulo.[243] However, by 1988, two *Nisei* had served as cabinet members and three as members of Congress.[244] As elsewhere, their political success followed in the wake of economic success, rather than being a factor in producing that success.

IMPLICATIONS

The rise of the Japanese in country after country, from their initial role as low-paid, unskilled laborers to middle-class occupations in the second and later generations, has implications which reach well beyond the remarkable history of this remarkable group of emigrants. The methods and nature of their rise challenge widely held beliefs as to the historical causes or contemporary prospects for advancing poorer racial or ethnic minorities.

Neither political activities nor biological assimilation played significant roles in the rise of the Japanese, though both political success and substantial racial intermarriage occurred *after* their socioeconomic rise. Even the ability of Japanese emigrants to speak the European languages of the surrounding societies in the Western Hemisphere (and Australia) was very limited during the first generation, which led the Japanese to concentrate in occupations where there was little or no need to master languages radically different from their own. Working together as agricultural laborers, fishermen, or farmers, or performing routine tasks as domestic servants with minimal need for a vocabulary in the local language, the first generation of Japanese overseas—the *Issei*—began the long movement up the occupational ladder.

Second and later generations, at least partially familiar with the local language—and often no more than partially familiar with the Japanese language as well—not only rose further but often in entirely different occupations, such as the educated professions. It was not the specific skills brought from Japan which produced the greatest economic success for Japanese emigrants, but their more general "human capital" in work habits, perseverance, social cohesion, and law-abiding patterns of life. These found their outlets in whatever economic and social opportunities were available in the countries in which they settled.

Initially, the Japanese encountered not only nativist opposition but even increasing opposition, as their competition with the local populations pitted them first against other laborers and then against other farmers and businessmen, as they rose into these occupational strata. Eventually, however, over a period of generations, their success in the economy and their social patterns as a group with low incidences of crime, violence, and other social pathologies made them more acceptable, both in the economy and socially. The Japanese as a group acquired a reputation for honesty and reliability, whether in Brazil, the United States, or Peru.[245]

None of this happened quickly or easily, or without major setbacks, of which internment during World War II was the principal tragedy in both Western Hemisphere nations and Australia. The postwar experience of the Japanese has been radically different from their prewar experience, again both in the Western Hemisphere and in Australia. Once excluded under the "white Australia" policy, the Japanese were by the 1980s being encouraged to immigrate to Australia—though with little success.[246] The prosperity of postwar Japan meant that there was no longer such economic pressure as once existed for the island's people to seek a living in other countries. Regional and neighborhood concentrations of Japanese dissolved in the United States and in Canada, partly as a result of the wartime internment experience. In postwar Toronto, where many Japanese lived, it became rare to find two Japanese families living in the same block.[247]

The role of Japan as a military power spared Japanese abroad some of the worst oppression suffered by the Chinese emigrants who preceded them to the United States and Canada, where a predominantly male Chinese population was left stranded overseas without their wives and families, and without prospects of acquiring wives from their homelands. Japan also took a more direct interest in the colonies set up under its auspices in Brazil. However, it is by no means clear that Japan was, on net balance, a continuing beneficial influence on the lives of Japanese emigrants overseas.

The military aggressions of Japan in the 1930s and 1940s generated anti-Japanese sentiments in many countries, usually to the detriment of the Japanese living in those countries. The far greater acceptance of the Japanese overseas in the postwar era, after the fears and hostilities aroused by Japan's military threat had passed, suggests that hostility to the local Japanese was not purely racial or due simply to locally generated economic rivalry or social friction.

The response of the Japanese overseas to the hostile attitudes and government policies directed against them tended to be pragmatic rather than emotional. Reforming the racism of the surrounding society was not a major preoccupation, perhaps because the Japanese themselves have been highly ethnocentric, whether in Japan or overseas, and so could hardly have been surprised to discover similar feelings in others. Such minorities in Japan as the Koreans,[248] the Ainu,[249] or even the social pariah group of Burakamin among the Japanese themselves,[250] are severely excluded from social interaction with most Japanese, and even Japanese Americans who settle in Japan tend to find themselves not accepted as true Japanese.[251]

Whatever the historical origins of such attitudes among the Japanese, this meant that Japanese emigrants overseas seldom dissipated their energies in attempts to morally regenerate the majority population in the countries in which they settled, since universal acceptance was not part of their own outlook. The remarkable reversal of public attitudes toward the Japanese over the years—especially in Australia, Peru, and the United States—suggests that behavior and performance are more effective ways of changing other people's minds than moral crusades or emotional denunciations. The behavior and performance of Japanese emigrants have certainly produced remarkable economic advancement in the most varied countries on three continents.

CHAPTER 4

ITALIANS AROUND THE WORLD

Emigration from Italy belongs among the extraordinary movements of mankind. In its chief lineaments it has no like. Through the number of men it has involved and the courses it has pursued, through its long continuance on a grand scale and its rôle in other lands, it stands alone.

—Robert Foerster[1]

An estimated 26 million people emigrated from Italy in the century from 1876 to 1976.[2] Their primary destinations were Western Europe, North America, and South America, but significant numbers settled as far away as Australia. This was not a simple one-way migration. More than 8.5 million emigrants returned to Italy in just the period from 1905 to 1976.[3] Those who immigrated to other countries in Europe were the most likely to return—about 90 percent were returnees in the late nineteenth and early twentieth centuries[4]—but even those who crossed the Atlantic returned to Italy in surprisingly large numbers. Around the beginning of the twentieth century, approximately 40 percent of those who went to Brazil and to the United States returned, and even larger proportions returned from Argentina and Uruguay.[5]

Italy had a history of temporary migrations—first internal and then external—before the era of mass overseas migrations. Within Italy, men from one province often moved to another province in search of seasonal work as agricultural laborers, leaving their families behind, perhaps to farm their own small parcels of land. With the money earned while away, additional land could be bought or rented, until there was a large enough farm to support the family without continued migrations of the father. Behind such patterns was the basic economic insufficiency of their original locality and situation—often poverty-stricken, especially in southern Italy—combined with a local attachment too strong for permanent abandonment. Fishermen and others were also absent for long periods for similar reasons. Sometimes a sojourn of some years was necessary to earn the money to enable the family to survive, much less to improve their circumstance upon the return of fathers and older brothers who had been away working. In other cases—among stonemasons from the Piedmont region of northern Italy, for example—the seasonal migrations of males to other countries provided the main support of the community for centuries, while the women remained behind to do the farming.[6]

It was not wanderlust but grim poverty, and a tenacious determination to deal with it, that led many Italians to migrate—and to endure miserable living conditions and great personal deprivation in many lands while accumulating savings to send back home and take back home. As employment opportunities at close range dried up, or better opportunities opened up farther away, the migrations within Italy were increasingly overshadowed by longer-range migrations to Europe, to the Western Hemisphere, and eventually to Australia.

Northern Italians predominated among the late nineteenth-century emigration, and other European countries predominated among their destinations. Nearly two-thirds of the more than 5 million emigrants who left Italy in the last quarter of the nineteenth century were from the north, and two-thirds of the northerners emigrated to other countries in Europe, with the remaining third crossing the Atlantic. As emigration from Italy during the early twentieth century reached even more vast proportions, southern Italians came to predominate, and their primary destinations shifted from Europe to the Western Hemisphere. While northern Italian emigrants continued overwhelmingly to prefer Europe as a destination during the 1901–1913 period, 91 percent of the southern Italian emigrants crossed the Atlantic. Emigration from central Italy was relatively modest in both periods.[7]

During the height of the emigration from Italy in the twentieth century, northern and southern Italians were very similar in such demographic characteristics as age, marital status, and birthrate—and even in such general economic characteristics as proportions working in agriculture, industry, and commerce. But the per capita income in northern Italy was nearly 70 percent higher than in the south, and the illiteracy rate in the south was double that in the north.[8] These large economic and educational disparities reflected regional differences in history, culture, and geography so profound as to cause Italy to be called "a country in which two civilizations simultaneously exist in one national body."[9]

Northern Italy has long been the center of Italy's commerce and industry, home of the Renaissance, and the political spearhead of the forces that unified the long-fragmented regions of the Italian peninsula into one nation in 1861. By contrast, southern Italy has long been poorer, more agricultural, and a cultural backwater dominated by folk traditions. Lawlessness was more prevalent in such southern regions as Calabria and Sicily than in northern Italy.[10] Even geographically, the northern provinces have been more favored, benefitting agriculturally from more abundant rainfall and from the springtime water runoff from melting Alpine snows, while southern Italy's highlands have not been high enough to provide such snow or the spring runoff it produces, and much of its lower-lying area has been malarial.

While Italy has in recent centuries been one of the poorer countries of Europe, it was one of the richest, both economically and culturally, in the days of the Roman Empire and again in medieval times when it contained some of the most advanced regions of Europe. Before there was any such state as Italy, Venice was a major maritime republic, complete with its own powerful navy. Milan was a center for the production of armor. Italian merchants were to be found all over Europe. Banking was so highly developed in the region of Lombardy that its bankers spread to other countries, with Lombard Street in London's financial district being a result of their activities there in centuries past. The cultural and economic roles of Florence, Genoa, and other Italian cities were also historic. All of this, however, was in northern Italy.

Regional differences have been biological and social, as well as cultural. Northern Italians have tended to be slightly taller and with a higher proportion of people with lighter complexion, hair, and eyes. Socially, northern Italians have distanced themselves from southern Italians, both in Italy and overseas. It was northern Italians in the

United States who urged the American government to collect separate statistics for the two groups. American statistics also include as southern Italians people who are called central Italians in the statistics of Italy and other countries.[11] These finer regional, and even more local, breakdowns remained important in the history of Italians, both in Italy and overseas.

Among the nations of Europe, Italy had one of the highest rates of illiteracy—62 percent in 1871[12]—but the regional variations concealed by this national figure were both large and growing for decades. While illiteracy was 42 percent in the Piedmont and 85 percent in Sicily in 1871, this declined rapidly in the Piedmont to only 11 percent illiteracy by 1911, while the decline in Sicily was to just 58 percent, increasing the disparity between the two regions from two-to-one in the earlier period to more than five-to-one in the later period.[13] In parts of southern Italy, there was an active resistance to compulsory attendance laws, leading in some cases to riots in which schoolhouses were burned down.[14] This resistance was based partly on a need for children's work to help supplement meager family incomes and partly on a suspicion that schooling would produce few, if any, benefits for the lower classes in Italian society, while the orientation of the schools undermined family solidarity, which was crucial for survival.[15]

The different destinations of northern and southern Italian emigrants seem to reflect their economic and cultural differences. Northern Italians fit more readily into the cultural pattern of Western Europe or of Latin America, and could more readily afford the passage to their destinations of choice. Southern Italians sought destinations where there was a strong demand for unskilled labor and where they could afford the travel expense. The Western Hemisphere met the first requirement and the United States met both.[16] In the early twentieth century, the United States became the prime destination of emigrants from Italy, absorbing 41 percent of the total Italian emigration between 1906 and 1910, when emigration from the south surpassed that from the north of Italy.

Italian immigration to the United States was overwhelmingly from southern Italy and consisted overwhelmingly of unskilled workers.[17] The extreme case were the Sicilians, who were from an especially poor part of Italy, and whose destination was predominantly the United States as far back as 1886—and continued to be so for decades, with 95,000

Sicilian emigrants out of 109,000 going to the U.S. as late as 1920.[18] The relative proportions of northern and southern Italians among the total immigration from Italy over the years has been very different in Brazil and Argentina, for example, compared to the United States[19]—a fact reflected in the later history of Italians in these countries.

The temporary nature of much Italian emigration has been reflected in the relative proportions of men and women involved. One sign of temporary emigration or sojourning is an unbalanced sex ratio among the emigrants. In the early years of Italian emigration, nearly 90 percent of the emigrants were male. Many emigrated for the express purpose of returning with money to purchase land or a home in Italy.[20] Others emigrated with the plan of bringing their wives and families over to join them after establishing themselves in a foreign land. Some were simply exploring the possibilities. Neither those who planned to stay nor those who planned to return always carried out these plans.[21] Many repeatedly postponed their return and only later in life realized that they were going to remain permanently where they were. Others went back and forth across the ocean before making up their minds.[22] Even from distant Australia, 31 percent of the Italian men who arrived between 1922 and 1940 also departed permanently, while an additional 24 percent made trips back to Europe, though settled in Australia.[23] Finally, there were Italian seasonal migratory workers, whose migrations took them across the Atlantic, especially to South America, where seasons are the reverse of those in the Northern Hemisphere, permitting them to be harvest laborers in both places.

While it is impossible to know how many returnees to Italy were carrying out their original plans, how many were intentionally migratory workers, and how many were giving up hope of permanent settlement abroad, some general clues are provided by sex ratios and marital status. Three-fourths of the returnees from the United States in the early twentieth century were single and 90 percent were male, which suggests sojourning or exploratory emigration. But half the Italians returning from Brazil during the same time were women and three-quarters of all Italian returnees from Brazil were married,[24] suggesting disappointed hopes. The historical experiences of Italian immigrants in the two countries during that era add further support to these implications.

One effect of the massive Italian emigration, combined with large-scale return to Italy, was that considerable knowledge of foreign countries built up in Italy. But it was typically highly specific knowledge of particular places abroad, concentrated in particular places in Italy. One result was that rates of emigration varied enormously between very similar provinces and villages in Italy, even when they were located near each other,[25] for one community might have overseas contacts and the next community not.

Another result was a concentration of Italians from particular provinces, and even villages, in Italy living in particular cities or even neighborhoods in the lands to which they emigrated. For example, in the middle of the twentieth century, there were more than a thousand Italians from the small Sicilian town of Piggioreale living in Sydney, Australia—and virtually no one from the other Sicilian towns nearby.[26] Two towns in northern Italy, only four miles apart, sent the bulk of their respective emigrants to opposite sides of the Australian continent.[27] By 1939, there were more people from some Italian villages living in Australia than there were still remaining in Italy.[28] In the Western Hemisphere, there were similar patterns of regional, provincial, and village concentrations. In various American cities, Italians from specific towns and villages concentrated in particular neighborhoods or even streets.[29] The same was true in Buenos Aires and Toronto.[30]

Before considering the impact of Italian emigrants on other countries, it is worth noting their impact on Italy. In 1902, they sent back 9 million lira—more than 2 million American dollars at that time—and 7 million lira of this was from the United States. These remittances increased nearly ten-fold, to 84 million lira in 1914, 66 million of which came from the United States. By 1920, Italy was receiving 1 billion lira from abroad.[31] In addition, those who were repatriated brought back substantial savings with them. They also brought back new ideas—less deference to the local aristocracy, and more concern for educating their children, for example. Sometimes they had become so different from their neighbors that they tended to live apart, in enclaves of returnees.[32]

ITALY

In the absence of strong religious or political ties, among southern Italians especially, the family has long been the focus of intense loyalties in Italy. Although the family, and especially the family honor, has been a concept that extends far beyond the immediate nuclear family, southern Italy has not been an extended-family society. Intense loyalties within the nuclear family have eclipsed all other loyalties to the extent that even close relatives have counted for very little by comparison and have often been viewed suspiciously, competitively, or enviously.[33] Those outside the family counted for even less. Children seldom played with anyone except relatives,[34] and the concept of making friends outside the family was foreign to the culture.[35] The strength of these patterns varied not only by region but also by social class. Such patterns have been stronger in southern Italy than in the north, and strongest of all on the island of Sicily. By class, the traditional patterns were preserved most by the lower socioeconomic classes.[36]

The preservation of the family and the family honor, as conceived among the southern Italian masses, entailed the careful isolation of girls before marriage and of wives afterward. While working children have been more common in Italy than elsewhere in European civilization, working wives have been less common.[37] Both patterns have followed Italians around the world. Within Italy itself, as late as 1911, more than half of all children between the ages of ten and fifteen were gainfully employed.[38] Few southern Italian families of that era could afford to sacrifice their children's earnings for the sake of long years of schooling. Nor was formal education viewed as unambiguously beneficial, for it was often seen as a threat to traditional ways and to the solidarity of the family.[39] These attitudes too followed Italian emigrants around the world.

The emigrants who left Italy generally had very little in the way of financial assets and were in fact often destitute when they arrived at their various destinations. Their major assets consisted of cultural patterns developed in the hard struggle for existence, particularly in the south of Italy. They were willing to do hard, dirty, dangerous, and "menial" work, to work long hours without complaint, to remain sober and dependable—and to save. However, they brought no tradition of individual initiative as employees, being from a society where such initiative was considered offensive by employers and others above them on the social scale.[40] Moreover, southern Italian emigrants seldom had the technical or industrial skills that German emigrants had, and the agricultural techniques used in Italy were generally backward.[41]

Illiteracy was also relatively high among Italians,[42] again especially those from the south of Italy. But the Italian emigrants carried with them a pattern of extreme thrift and of family pooling of efforts and money—traits that proved useful in getting an economic foothold in foreign lands. Beyond the family, however, the southern Italians had relatively little tradition of organizing, whether for economic, political, cultural, or recreational purposes. This, too, was in sharp contrast with the German pattern.

While most Italians in the southern provinces worked on the land, they were usually *not* farmers living on farms or leading a rural life. Rather, they were generally village and town dwellers, who were either employed on the land by others or who were sharecroppers. Those who owned land often had tiny, scattered, uneconomic patches—a product of the division and redivision of farms with inheritance from generation to generation. In short, there was usually no rural way of life, nor even self-supporting family farms, but instead an insecure, poverty-stricken existence at the mercy of employers and landlords. It was a kind of life that they had no desire to re-create in other lands. Thus this agricultural people typically became an urban people abroad, and those who returned to Italy often did so after saving enough money to buy their own land in larger, self-sustaining sizes, with the prestige that being a genuine landowner brought in Italian society.[43] But southern Italian emigrants were seldom simply farmers in the old world who became farmers overseas, in the manner of many German or Scandinavian emigrants.

The proportions of agricultural and nonagricultural occupations among Italian emigrants varied over time, with shifts back and forth. Nonagricultural occupations predominated among the early emigrants, being overtaken by agricultural occupations for the first time in 1883, with the nonagricultural emigrants resuming predominance in the late 1890s and remaining predominant on into the twentieth century. The sex imbalance, however, tended to persist. Male emigrants from Italy outnumbered female emigrants several times over from 1876 until 1917, when female emigrants were briefly in the majority. After the First World War, male predominance resumed, though not on as extreme a scale as before.[44]

Italian emigration began a long decline in the early 1920s, when the United States and other Western Hemisphere nations imposed restrictive laws against further immigration. The Mussolini regime in Italy also restricted the outflow. The Great Depression of the 1930s reduced emigration still more drastically and the Second World War brought it to a complete halt.[45] When emigration resumed in the postwar era, most Italian emigrants went to Europe.[46]

The first postwar year, 1946, saw approximately 110,000 emigrants leave Italy—a number exceeded in every year thereafter until 1975. The peak of this postwar emigration was reached in 1961, when more than 387,000 people emigrated from Italy. However, even this peak was less than half of the Italian emigration of 1906.[47] Perhaps more important, Italy after 1975 became a net recipient of immigrants.[48]

EUROPE

People from the Italian peninsula spread across Europe long before modern Italy was formed in 1861—indeed, at least as far back as the Roman Empire. Modern Italian emigration has of course been a very different movement of people from that of the Roman conquerors. In most of twentieth-century Europe, Italians have come as seasonal or longer-term sojourners—seldom as permanent settlers—from a poorer country, seeking to earn more than they could in their homeland. Often they have taken the harder, dirtier, or more dangerous jobs disdained by the working populations of the host nation, or they have been willing to work for less, or for longer hours, or with more docility. This pattern was already well established before the First World War among Italian immigrants in France, Germany, Switzerland, and the Austro-Hungarian Empire.[49] However, there were also some highly skilled Italians, including architects who designed buildings and other structures in various countries around the world. The Kremlin was designed by Italian architects, as were many of the other onion-domed buildings in Russia.[50] Their numbers were of course much smaller than the numbers of unskilled laborers.

France was attracting large numbers of seasonal agricultural workers from Italy—men, women, and children—in the nineteenth century and there was an urban Italian colony in Marseilles as well. In 1851, there were more than 63,000 Italians in France and by 1911, more than 400,000—more than any other foreign group in France and more than one-fourth of all foreigners there.[51] The movement of Frenchmen from rural to urban life was offset by an importation of agricultural workers from other countries, principally from Italy.[52] Urban centers in France also attracted Italian immigrants. In 1911, there were nearly 34,000 in Paris and, at about the same time, at least 125,000 in Marseilles.[53] In Lyons, the glass industry—itself derived from Italy—employed at least 3,000 Italian boys, in work considered too exhausting for French boys.[54]

The sojourning Italians in France, as in much of the rest of Europe, the Western Hemisphere, and Australia, were noted for their extremely parsimonious manner of living, in order to save money to take back or send back to Italy.[55] Often this meant living not only in the most crowded quarters—several men per room was not uncommon—but also in the dirtiest, ill-ventilated places, with little sunlight and much exposure to disease. This pattern prevailed not only in France but also in Germany, Switzerland, and Britain.[56] Disliked by fellow workers for accepting low pay and hard work, Italians tended also to be socially disdained in general.[57] They seldom intermarried with the host population in France, Germany, or Switzerland.[58]

Among the Italians themselves, immigrants from northern Italy kept aloof from southern immigrants, and other regional, provincial, or local differences also fragmented Italian communities in other European countries,[59] as they were similarly fragmented in the Western Hemisphere and Australia. There was little attraction between Italians, as such. Unlike other immigrants to Switzerland, Italians did not concentrate in the regions populated by Swiss citizens of their own ancestry. Most Italian immigrants in Switzerland went to non-Italian regions of the country.[60]

Certain occupational patterns also recurred among Italian immigrants in Europe and elsewhere. Aside from the large contingent of unskilled laborers in industry and agriculture, Italians became notable as fishermen, from the Iberian peninsula to Greece and all around the Mediterranean to Turkey, Egypt, Tunisia, and Algiers, as well as further afield in the United States and Australia.[61] They became miners not only in France and Germany, as already noted, but also in Switzerland, Austria, Belgium, Luxemburg, Greece and Russia, as well as in such non-European nations of the Mediterranean region as Turkey, Egypt, and Tunisia.[62] Italians also became notable as street musicians from Britain to the Austro-Hungarian Empire to the Caucasus region of Russia.[63] Wine-making has been another characteristic Italian endeavor abroad as at home, in France, the Austro-Hungarian Empire, and Russia,[64] as well as in more remote parts of the world, such as Australia, Argentina, and the United States.

Construction work in general has attracted many Italians, all across Europe, as well as in other parts of the world. They helped build a railroad line to Sarajevo, as well as railroads in Switzerland, Greece, Rumania, Russia, and Turkey.[65] They helped build canals in Rumania, Greece, and Suez.[66] Among the skilled trades associated with construction, Italians have been prominent as masons. Switzerland had more than 5,500 Italian masons in 1909 and Italian masons were involved in the modernization of Sarajevo during the same era.[67]

The First World War brought emigration to an end and the domination of the Fascists in Italy from the early 1920s until the end of the Second World War also restricted emigration. For a brief period after World War II, Italy became a recipient of a massive return of Italians—more than half a million—from the Balkans and North Africa, as well as a recipient of refugees from Yugoslavia.[68] When large-scale emigration from Italy resumed after this long hiatus, Western Europe became the principal destination of Italian emigrants. Throughout the 1950s, Italy supplied more than half of all the immigrant labor in Europe.[69] France became one of the principal destinations of Italian emigrants, approximately 90,000 of them being employed there in 1957. They remained the principal group of foreign workers there until 1960, when they were still an absolute majority among immigrant workers in France.[70] However, during the 1960s, the flow of emigrants from Italy diverted to West Germany, as France drew more of its labor from Spain, Portugal, and Algeria.[71] By 1965, 32 percent of all Italian emigrants, worldwide, were in Germany, 37 percent in Switzerland, and only 7 percent in France. Just 18 percent went outside of Europe.[72] However, this did not mean that there were growing permanent settlements of Italians across Europe. Return migration from European countries was also heavy.[73]

Italians in Western Europe continued largely in their traditional role as sojourners, as contrasted with the permanent settling of Italians in the Western Hemisphere and Australia. By the early 1960s, return migration from Europe was more than four-fifths of direct migration, while outside Europe less than 10 percent of Italian emigrants returned. The net migration to European and non-European countries for the period from 1946 to 1965 was thus virtually the same, despite the much larger initial outflow to Europe.[74] Western Europe's importance to Italy has not been primarily as a settlement area but as a source of income. Emigrant remittances from Western Europe to Italy totalled $381 million in 1964—more than 3 times the emigrant remittances from North America, 15 times the emigrant remittances from South America, and nearly 21 times the emigrant remittances from Australia.[75] Italians in the other regions of the world were, by then, primarily permanent settlers overseas. Although Italy continued to be the largest European supplier of emigrants to the rest of the continent, by 1990 there were almost as many Iranian as Italian emigrants living in Europe and there were more Turks. While Italians living in Europe outside of Italy numbered more than 1.5 million people, there were nearly 1.5 million Iranians and 2.3 million Turks. Moreover, Italians were little more than 10 percent of all the foreigners living in Europe.[76]

THE WESTERN HEMISPHERE

Mass emigration from Italy to the Western Hemisphere in the last quarter of the nineteenth century coincided with a more general mass emigration of Europeans across the Atlantic. However, the destinations of the early Italian emigrants especially were not so concentrated on the United States as were the destinations of many other groups. Like the Spaniards, many Italians settled in South America. Argentina absorbed the largest number of Italian immigrants to the Western Hemisphere during the period from 1876 to 1890 and Brazil became the leading recipient nation for Italian emigrants in the first half of the 1890s. Then the United States took over the lead in the later 1890s, holding that lead on into the early decades of the twentieth century.[77] In 1920, on the eve of restrictive American immigration laws, more than half of all emigrants from Italy went to the United States.[78]

Argentina

Argentina was the prime destination of Italian emigrants in the early decades of mass emigration from Italy, and Italians long remained among the principal immigrants arriving in Argentina. As early as 1864, Italians were 40 percent of all immigrants in Argentina,[79] and they were nearly 40 percent of all foreigners in Argentina as late as 1914, still outnumbering the 35 percent of immigrants who came from Spain, the original colonizing country.[80] The large Italian population of Argentina grew by natural increase as well as by immigration. Italians had the highest birthrate of all the immigrants.[81]

More than 100,000 Italians arrived in Argentina during the 1860s—nearly ten times the immigration to the United States during the same decade. During the 1880s, Italian immigration to Argentina totalled nearly half a million (compared to 300,000 to the United States). In the first decade of the twentieth century, Italian immigration to Argentina peaked at nearly 800,000, though by then it was considerably surpassed by the 2 million Italian immigrants to the U.S.[82] Over the entire period from 1857 to 1950, more than 3.2 million Italians arrived in Argentina—and nearly 1.5 million departed.[83] Some were migratory agricultural workers, known locally as *golondrinas* (swallows), because they came and went with the seasons, taking advantage of Argentina's Southern Hemisphere opposite seasons from Italy's to work during the growing and harvesting seasons in both countries.[84]

The impact of the Italians on Argentine development was even greater than their numerical impact on the population. They brought a pattern of thrift, of hard work, and of entrepreneurship largely lacking in the existing Argentine population.

"*We don't know how to save,*" an Argentine writer of that era declared.[85] In Europe as well, the Argentine was known as "the spendthrift of the world."[86] No such characterization applied to the Italians in Argentina, who saved even out of low incomes. As early as 1860, nearly one-third of the depositors in the Banco de Buenos Aires were Italian.[87] By 1887, there were twice as many depositors of Italian citizenship as of Argentine citizenship.[88]

Italians likewise took on manual labor disdained by the Argentines. They became agricultural workers in huge numbers—more than half a million immigrant agricultural workers arrived between 1876 and 1897—virtually creating agriculture in Argentina, where the land under cultivation by 1895 was nearly nine times as large as it was less than a quarter of a century earlier.[89] Italian immigrants often began as peons, saved, and over the years rose to become sharecroppers and eventually landowners.[90] There were whole colonies which were predominantly Italian. For example, in 1905, more than 10,000 families in agricultural colonies in Cordoba were Italian—out of a total of 13,435 families in those colonies.[91] Here, by this time, four-fifths of the landowners were Italians, whether their land was owned free and clear or was mortgaged.[92] In Mendoza, at about the same time, Italians predominated in grape-growing and wine-making.[93]

In urban occupations as well, Italians were prominent among manual workers at various levels of skill. Among those Italians who immigrated to Argentina between 1876 and 1897, 94,000 were day laborers, 13,000 were masons, and another 33,000 were artisans and craftsmen of various sorts.[94] Most of the country's masons, seamen, tradespeople, architects, importers, engineers, restaurant and hotel owners were Italian.[95]

While Italians in Argentina worked in many of the same occupations as in Europe or the United States, they also reached many higher-level positions earlier in Argentina and became prominent, or even dominant, in some professions and as entrepreneurs. In addition to becoming prominent in law and medicine and as university professors, Italians long dominated as architects in Argentina. Many of the public buildings, churches, banks, and private homes were designed by Italian architects and built by Italian builders, employing Italian skilled labor. Much of modern Buenos Aires, including the water supply and sewage systems, was designed and built by Italians.[96] More than half the iron production of Argentina was attributed to Italians, as was the ownership of more than 600 flour mills. In Buenos Aires, they predominated in the production of alcoholic beverages—except beer, where the Germans were pre-eminent.[97]

The large, wealthy, landowning classes in Argentina were Spanish descendants of those who received huge grants of land from the government of Spain in colonial times. However, this wealthy Argentine aristocracy had little interest in commerce and industry. Over the years, as the economy became more industrialized and commercial, this was primarily the work of various immigrant groups, who became disproportionately the owners of the business enterprises of the country. By 1914, foreigners (who were about 30 percent of the Argentine population) owned 72 percent of the commercial firms in the country—82 percent in Buenos Aires.[98]

While native Argentines were a majority of all property owners, this reflected their continued dominance among rural landowners, but in Buenos Aires the foreign-born owned 60 percent of all the real estate.[99] The active economic role of foreigners during the immigrant era left enduring marks on the Argentinean social structure. As late as 1962, only about half the upper-class Argentines had Spanish surnames.[100] Italians were an important part of the foreign entrepreneurial class that emerged in the immigrant era, despite the initial poverty of Italian immigrants. By 1909, Italians in Buenos Aires owned more than twice as many food and drinking establishments as the native Argentines, more than three times as many shoe stores, and more than ten times as many barbershops.[101]

Although only 32 percent of the population of Buenos Aires in 1887, Italians owned 58 percent of the industrial establishments.[102] In Corrientes, Italian commercial houses were among the largest.[103] Italians were also more active in the Argentinean labor movement than were the Argentines.[104] Over the years, Italians came to be nationally the most numerous of the owners and workers in Argentina's industrial and commercial enterprises.[105] Even these sharp statistical differences between the Italians and the Argentines tended to understate the role of the Italians, for second-generation Italians were counted as Argentines.[106]

In agriculture, the Italians were noted for their "patience, energy, and frugality," as contrasted with the Argentine agricultural worker who was seen as "lazy, frivolous and totally lacking in ambition."[107] Much the same contrast was seen in the cities, where Italians were noted for having "the drive and ambition native *criollos* lacked." Unlike the Italian agriculturalists who were largely from northern Italy, the urban Italians were largely from southern Italy. Many of them became factory workers, artisans, mechanics, bricklayers, or tradesmen, and some became wealthy in the construction industry.[108]

Artistically and culturally, the Italians have had a major impact on Argentina at both elite and popular levels—in architecture, drama, sculpture, and painting,[109] on the one hand, and in cooking[110] on the other. The Argentinean version of the Spanish language has also acquired Italian words from this segment of the population.[111]

Prior to World War I, the overwhelming majority of Italians in Buenos Aires married other Italians, only a small percent acquired Argentine citizenship, and the language of the home (and of many workplaces) was Italian.[112] A variety of Italian-language newspapers appeared and disappeared, but the largest and longest-lasting of these achieved a circulation of 40,000 in 1904, making it the third-largest newspaper in Argentina at that time.[113] The Italian provincial, regional, and local-origin differences which fragmented Italian immigrant communities in other countries also appeared in Argentina. The many mutual aid societies set up by Italian immigrants reflected their exclusive admissions policies, which limited membership to those from particular parts of Italy.[114]

One of the areas of Argentine life in which the early generations of Italians played little role was government and politics.[115] Political appointees were almost invariably native Argentines,[116] though not because of any special skill they possessed, for these political appointees were in fact notoriously incompetent.[117] The exclusions of immigrants were only part of the story. The political apathy of Italians, observed in other countries, was also characteristic of Italian immigrants in Argentina.[118] Only in later generations did non-Hispanics in general, and Italians in particular, play an important role in Argentine politics. The most famous of all modern Argentine political leaders, Juan Perón, was half Italian.[119] He was, of course, *not* an ethnic Italian leader. Nor was an earlier Argentine president of Italian extraction in the nineteenth century, who paid little attention to the Italian community in Argentina.[120]

Argentina's Italians became, over the years, essentially Argentines, though Argentina itself changed culturally because of them and their forebears. Continuing immigration to Argentina from Italy had, by the early 1960s, dwindled to levels far below those of the immigrant era—and was more than counterbalanced by return migration.[121]

Brazil

There were few Italian immigrants in Brazil before the middle of the nineteenth century. One of these few, however, was a butcher-shop owner with a Brazilian wife. His name was Giuseppe Garibaldi,[122] later destined to return to his native land and to glory.

Massive European immigration into Brazil began in the last quarter of the nineteenth century. Italians were a major part of that immigration, as Brazil was a major recipient of Italian immigrants. During more than half a century of immigration, from 1884 to 1939, approximately one-third of all immigrants to Brazil were from Italy—more than from any other country, including Portugal, whose people dominated colonial Brazil.[123] Italian immigrants were especially prominent in the earlier part of this period. The one million Italians who immigrated to Brazil in the late nineteenth-century constituted almost half of all immigrants arriving there at that time.[124] These were predominantly northern Italians.[125] Later, by the early twentieth century, southern Italians predominated among the immigrants from Italy, but for the entire period 1876–1930, 57 percent of Italian immigration was from northern Italy and 43 percent was from the south.[126]

These changing immigration patterns reflected the recruiting patterns in Italy of the Brazilian coffee plantation owners and the availability of immigration subsidies by the Brazilian government. Recruiting officers for Brazilian planters operated only in the north of Italy, because northern Italians were preferred. At the height of Italian immigration to Brazil in the 1890s, 91 percent of the immigration to the state of São Paulo—where both coffee-growing and Italian immigration were centered—was subsidized. At the same time, immigration to the state of São Paulo was more than two-thirds of all immigration into Brazil. Because these government subsidies were designed to encourage whole families to settle, in order to minimize return migration, the Italian immigration to Brazil did not exhibit the drastic sex imbalance found in other countries. As the subsidizing of immigrants declined in the early twentieth century, however, the regional origins of Italian immigrants to Brazil began to reflect the general regional pattern of emigration from Italy at that time—which was more southern than northern.[127]

The coffee-growing regions of São Paulo, located north and west of the city of the same name, attracted immigrants from many countries. But, during the coffee boom of the late nineteenth century, nearly three-quarters of these immigrants were from Italy. Although substantial numbers of Japanese began arriving in the early twentieth century, joining large streams of immigrants from Germany, Spain, and Portugal, nevertheless Italians made up nearly half of all the immigrants to São Paulo during the period from 1887 to 1930, roughly from the end of slavery to the beginning of the Great Depression.[128] Because Italian immigrants were a substantial majority of the coffee plantation workers,[129] they contributed to the maintenance of Brazil's pre-eminence in the world market for coffee. More than half of the world's coffee came from Brazil, and 90 percent of Brazil's coffee was produced in the state of São Paulo,[130] which is roughly equal in size to Italy. The ownership of large coffee plantations remained primarily in the hands of the Brazilian elite,[131] though immigrants in general and Italians in particular later emerged as owners of more modest-sized farms producing coffee. That was, however, years after working under trying conditions as field hands.

Arriving in Brazil as the institution of slavery was being brought to an end there, many Italian indentured laborers on the coffee plantations found themselves being subjected to the abusive treatment that had been common under the slave regime. These practices included the flogging of male workers and sexual assaults on women and girls. Frauds and unhealthy living conditions added to their woes and many of these early Italian immigrants returned to Italy destitute.[132] Others stayed on, however, some saving enough to become landowners themselves.[133]

Given the availability of frontier land in the region, as well as other land not suitable for coffee-growing, there was a considerable turnover of coffee plantation workers, some of whom went on to become general farmers and some of whom became coffee growers themselves. Because coffee trees required a special combination of conditions, at no time was more than 15 percent of the land in the state of São Paulo producing coffee,[134] even during years when that state supplied half the coffee in the world.

A growing worldwide demand for coffee and the building of railroad lines in Brazil to facilitate movement of the crop to port for export led to an almost continuous expansion of the industry. Output doubled from the mid-1880s to the early 1890s and doubled again by the end of the nineteenth century.[135] This led to a growing demand for workers on the plantations, which was accentuated by a high rate of turnover among plantation workers,[136] many of whom used their savings to buy farms of their own. In order to maintain a labor supply and continue receiving immigrants from Italy, Brazilian coffee growers were forced to improve the conditions on their plantations. In the western plateau region of São Paulo, where coffee production flourished, by 1905 Italians owned about one-seventh of the rural properties, worth about one-tenth the value of such properties in the area.[137] By 1920, Italians owned nearly 16 percent of the land, now worth nearly 22 percent of the value.[138]

Coffee-growing was not the only rural occupation of Italian immigrants. Among the contributions of the Italians in Brazilian agriculture were the promotion of rice cultivation and the development of a wine industry.[139] While the Italian agricultural colonies in Rio Grande do Sul were not as wealthy as those of the Germans in the same region,[140] Italian artisans were able not only to compete with, but even to displace, the German artisans.[141] However, artisans in general were a declining group, smaller in number in 1950 than in 1890.[142]

In the early twentieth century, Italian firms arose to compete with German firms in metallurgy, and the principal oil refinery in Porto Alegre was Italian, again in competition principally with German firms.[143] Four-fifths of the butter production and almost nine-tenths of the wine production in the region were also in the hands of Italians.[144] Among the industries arising in the Italian sections of the state of São Paulo were rice mills, tanneries, paper mills, furniture factories, distilleries, and shoe factories.[145] Italians were prominent among the workers in this region, as well as among the owners. In 1911, the São Paulo textile industry employed approximately 10,000 workers, three-fifths of them Italian.[146] In Rio Grande do Sul and Santa Catarina, Italians owned 19 percent of all industrial enterprises, and in the metropolitan area of São Paulo, 48 percent. In both places, they and the Germans together owned over half the industrial enterprises, with the Portuguese and Brazilians of Portuguese ancestry owning less than one-fourth of such businesses.[147]

Neither the striking success of Italians in particular regions of the country or particular sectors of the economy, nor their general rise to respectable prosperity nationally, should create the impression that this great historical process was completed quickly, much less easily. An observer of the late nineteenth century arrivals of immigrants to Santa Catarina noted that, while German immigrants arrived with clothing, baggage, and work implements, the Italians came in rags. Among the early Italian immigrants to São Paulo, even modest savings could be accumulated only by painful sacrifices.

Most of the southern Italian immigrants were illiterate and many, if not most, of the northern Italian immigrants were as well. Schools in São Paulo in the immigrant era were declared to be "a horror and a shame"—both pedagogically and on sanitary grounds.[148] For many Italian immigrants, becoming a bootblack was the first step upward. Shining shoes in Rio de Janeiro, São Paulo, and Santos was almost exclusively an Italian occupation.[149]

Neither education nor special skills were keys to the progress of most Italians in Brazil but simply their willingness to work. They were preferred on the coffee plantations, for example, simply because they were regarded as more industrious than the local Brazilians.[150]

Social and cultural progress came no more easily than economic advancement. Child labor and lack of schooling long remained common. In the early years of the twentieth century, even reasonably prosperous Italians allowed their children to grow up without elementary education[151] and it was said that "every child past toddling earns more than its current cost."[152] Italians tended to cling to their own language and culture, especially in the agricultural regions, though this did not reflect any strong loyalty to Italy or any strong sense of being Italian. In Brazil as elsewhere, regional fragmentation was common among the Italians.[153] In the cities, Portuguese words began to find their way into the Italian language and Italian words into the Portuguese language,[154] but neither assimilation nor acculturation was rapid, either with the Portuguese majority or with other immigrant groups. Even in Santa Catarina, where there were more than 100,000 Germans and at least 30,000 Italians, there was seldom intermarriage between them.[155]

The Italian influence on Brazil reached well beyond their own enclaves. In addition to making possible Brazil's world pre-eminence in coffee production, and creating a considerable part of the industrial development of the country, Italians also made major contributions to architecture and to popular music in Brazil.[156] More broadly, they and other immigrants have transformed Brazil into a modern nation.

The United States

While the United States was the largest single recipient of Italian immigrants during the era of mass emigration, it was also receiving vast numbers of immigrants from other countries as well. This alone meant that the Italian impact on American society was not likely to be as dramatic as the impact of Italian immigrants in Argentina or Brazil. Moreover, the native-born American population was both larger and already relatively well endowed with the industrial and commercial skills and aptitudes that were so lacking in societies where Italian immigrants supplied these key elements of economic modernization. Finally, Italian immigrants to the United States came overwhelmingly from the more backward southern part of Italy. Despite all this, however, Italian immigrants played a significant role in American social history and included individuals who rose to national stature in a number of fields.

Italian immigrants were among the last and largest waves of immigrants from Europe. The mass exodus from famine-stricken Ireland to the United States in the middle of the nineteenth century exceeded 200,000 people in only one year (1851), while Italian immigration exceeded that total in eight different years during the first two decades of the twentieth century. Only the mass exodus of Jews from Eastern Europe to the United States during the same era was at all comparable in size.[157] Altogether, more than 5 million Italians immigrated to the United States between 1876 and 1930.[158] Of these, about 2 million returned to Italy.[159] Despite a preponderance of males over females among Italian immigrants, the still greater preponderance of males among those who returned to Italy led to a lessening imbalance between the sexes among those remaining in the United States. While there were well over three times as many males as females among Italian immigrants, the ratio was less than two to one among the resident Italian American population, as early as 1910.[160] With the passing years, especially after the virtual cutoff of immigration from Italy in the 1920s, the sexes became balanced.

In the era before mass emigration from Italy, those Italians who came to the United States were largely from the northern provinces. The total Italian population officially recorded in the United States in 1850 was less than 4,000 persons. By 1880 there were more than 44,000 and by 1900 there were 484,027. Between 1880 and 1900, southern Italians became predominant among the immigrants from Italy and remained so as the immigrant tide swelled in the twentieth century.[161]

A predominantly agricultural people in Italy, the immigrants became predominately urban in the United States, which no longer had the abundance of cheap land still found in Argentina or Brazil. In the cities, previous waves of immigrants had occupied other economic niches and neighborhoods, so that Italians became part of a more general pattern of ethnic succession in occupations, housing, schools, and even organized crime, which was dominated by Irish and Jewish gangsters before Italian gangsters began to take over during the 1920s. Because of the natural increase of other groups who had immigrated earlier, even the record-breaking immigration from Italy in the early twentieth century seldom made the Italians the largest foreign-origin group in American cities, with New York and New Orleans being notable exceptions. In no other major American city were Italians either the largest or the second-largest immigrant group.[162] Italian immigrants, at their peak, were just 1.5 percent of the U.S. population, compared to 3 percent of the total population of Brazil and 12.5 percent of the Argentine population.[163] In New York City, Italians were 7.4 percent of the population, compared to 20 percent in Buenos Aires and 35 percent in São Paulo.[164]

In one respect, however, Italian immigrants to the United States were very much like Italians who settled in South America. These immigrants typically began at the very bottom of the occupational ladder. Out of 474 foreign bootblacks in New York toward the end of the nineteenth century, 473 were Italians.[165] Italians were also prominent among ragpickers, sewer workers, and in whatever other hard, dirty, dangerous, or "menial" jobs others disdained. Italian children worked at an early age, as in Italy, even at the expense of their education.[166] But Italians seldom accepted charity or resorted to prostitution as some other immigrant groups, such as the Irish, did.[167] This, too, reflected patterns that went back to Italy.

Both in 1880 and in 1905, approximately three-fourths of the Italians working in New York City were blue-collar workers, with most of the remainder being peddlers, shopkeepers, and barbers. More than half the barbers in New York at that time were Italian. While the proportion of blue-collar workers was broadly similar to that in Buenos Aires, in the latter city significantly more of these were skilled workers. Moreover, the remainder in Buenos Aires included more owners of small industrial and commercial establishments, rather than peddlers and barbers. High white-collar occupations were rare for Italians in both cities, but higher (4 percent) in Buenos Aires than in New York (2 percent).[168]

In New York, as in Buenos Aires and other cities in other countries, Italians settled in clusters related to their places of origin in Italy. Not only did Neapolitans and Sicilians settle in different parts of New York; people from different parts of Sicily clustered on different streets.[169] The settling of Italians from particular towns in Italy on particular streets in American cities was also a pattern found in San Francisco, Chicago, New Haven, Cleveland, Buffalo, Kansas City, and Rochester, among other places.[170] What was seldom created in the United States, however, were all-Italian enclaves, rural or urban. Few Italians became rural in America and in the cities there were seldom any all-Italian neighborhoods. Rather, Italians typically lived interspersed among other immigrant groups, such as the Irish, the Jews, the Germans, and Poles,[171] even though the particular Italians interspersed in a given section might be predominantly from one province or village in Italy.

Initially, both in Chicago and in San Francisco, marriages among Italians were primarily between people whose families had originated in the same province or village in Italy.[172] Eventually, in the second generation and later, marriages began to occur among people from different geographical origins in Italy and also with non-Italians. Italians, however, were much slower than other groups to intermarry. In 1920, 97 percent of Italian men in the United States had Italian wives.[173] This was particularly true of southern Italians, especially those from smaller communities.[174] As late as 1950, more than three-quarters of Italian marriages were with other Italians.[175]

While immigrants from various parts of Italy might settle in the same American city, it was also true that different parts of the United States had different proportions of people from particular parts of Italy. Italians in New Orleans were mostly Sicilians,[176] for example, while Italians in San Francisco—and in California in general—were mostly from northern Italy.[177] Neapolitans and Calabrians became open-pit miners in Minnesota,[178] immigrants from Turin created an agricultural settlement in North Carolina,[179] and Piedmontese settled in the town of Genoa, Wisconsin.[180] More than half of all the Italians in the United States, however, were concentrated in the middle Atlantic states in 1910, New York state alone having more than 472,000 and Pennsylvania nearly 200,000. Four-fifths were urban.[181]

Wherever the early Italian immigrants lived, they tended to live in squalor. Overcrowded and filthy living quarters were common among them, whether in New York, Philadelphia, Boston, Milwaukee, Pittsburgh, St. Paul, or in agricultural laborers' camps or at temporary construction sites.[182] Italian laborers also tended to skimp on food—even as compared to other unskilled immigrant laborers—in a desperate effort to save money.[183] Frailty of physique among Italian immigrants was noted at the time, when they were considered less strong than Irish workmen, for example.[184] With the passage of time and the arising of new generations, however, this complaint disappeared. So too did the squalor of Italian homes. In later generations, Italian housewives took special pride in the cleanliness of their homes.[185]

The occupations of the Italians in the United States during the immigrant era of the late nineteenth and early twentieth centuries were much like those they held in other countries. At least half of all immigrant masons and barbers arriving in the United States were Italians.[186] Fishermen, shoemakers, waiters, and tradesmen were also common among Italian immigrants and the selling of fruits was a specialty in which Italians became prominent, both in New York and in New Orleans.[187] While not as well represented among skilled occupations in general as the Germans, Britons, or other Northern and Western European immigrants, Italians were better represented than the Croatians, Slovaks, Magyars, and other southern and Eastern European immigrants. Most Italian immigrants, however, were unskilled laborers.[188] As elsewhere, they often worked on construction projects, in mines, and on railroad-building projects. Often they succeeded other immigrant groups in these and other manual laboring occupations. Over the years, Italians replaced the Irish as unskilled laborers building railroads[189] and on the New York waterfront.[190] They also replaced the German and Irish workers in the petroleum industry of New Jersey;[191] the Irish, Germans, and Welsh in Pennsylvania's coal-mining region,[192] and Jewish workers in New York's clothing industry.[193] As early as 1890, 90 percent of the employees in New York's public works were Italian. Among 12,500 workers who built the Erie Canal, 10,500 were Italian. They were also predominant among the workers who built trolley lines in large eastern cities, and the subways of Boston and New York.[194]

Among the relatively few Italians to go into farming in the United States, most were from northern Italy.[195] Of these, the Italian (and Italian-Swiss) wine-makers of California became the best known. Italians also took over abandoned wastelands requiring great exertions to bring them under cultivation, and often became successful as truck farmers.[196] Occupations requiring education long remained rare among Italians in the United States—printers or newspaper reporters, for example,[197] as well as more exalted professions.

As workmen, Italians were noted for their diligence and sobriety—the latter often contrasted with the drinking of the Irish[198]—but also for a lack of initiative that required them to have considerable supervision. The pattern was similar to that noted in Europe during the same era, and was consonant with the docility expected of workers in Italy.[199] Child labor was another Italian pattern brought over from the homeland and it often interfered with, or even prevented, schooling.[200] Italian women worked more often in the United States than in Italy, though concern for preserving chastity and avoiding even the appearance of laxity in this regard affected what kind of work they did. Work performed in the home—so-called "sweatshop labor"—was acceptable and common, as it both preserved the reputation of the wife and facilitated work by the children.[201] Operating sewing machines with other women in a clothing factory was also common. However, Italian women tended to avoid working as domestic servants, which could be seen as potentially compromising, especially in an era of live-in maids.[202] Prostitution was virtually unknown among Italian American women.[203]

Like other workers entering a society with a different language and a very different culture, Italians often sought and performed work with a labor contractor of their own nationality and culture. The labor contractor or *padrone* was often from the same province or community in Italy as his workers. He understood both their culture and the business requirements of the American employer, and spoke both English and Italian. He was more than a middleman, however. The *padrone* often advanced money to the workmen, transported them to the job site, supervised them at work, took responsibility for their housing and for providing the kinds of food they were used to. These versatile entrepreneurs did not hesitate to protect their investment by maintaining a prison-like control over the workers to whom they had advanced money, including the use of armed guards.

Opportunities for defrauding or otherwise taking advantage of new people in a strange land were numerous, and the *padrone* system provided reformers and newspaper reporters with numerous scandals. However, the continuing use of *padroni* by the same workers, year after year, suggests that more than ignorance or gullibility was involved. Men with very limited options, and with serious economic exigencies, were able to find work all across the country, in places they had never seen, among people whose language and way of life they could not understand, and ended up with savings vital to themselves and their families. Repeated attempts by reformers to stamp out the *padrone* system failed, but it began to die out on its own after about 1920, as existing Italian immigrants grew more able to function independently in the United States and the second-generation Italian Americans had no need for *padrone* services.

Over the years, as Italians rose up the economic scale, they did so largely through acquiring job skills in blue-collar occupations, rather than by becoming educated and entering the professions. Acquiring knowledge of English and literacy enabled many to become low-level civil servants but few became doctors, lawyers, or intellectuals. Nor did politics attract many nor prove particularly rewarding for those it did attract. Irish politicians long continued to represent predominantly Italian districts. Even after experienced politicians arose within the Italian American communities, they could not count on the votes of their countrymen. There was no Pan-Italian solidarity in voting, any more than in the many other activities in which Italians remained regionally fragmented in the United States. The first major Italian American political figure was Fiorello H. LaGuardia (1882–1947), who became first a congressman and then the legendary mayor of New York for more than a decade, from 1934 to 1945. Yet even he failed to carry the Italian vote in his 1941 re-election campaign against an Irish opponent.[204]

Along with a general and gradual rise of Italians to higher occupational levels over the decades, there were particular instances of dramatic success. In California, and especially in its fertile Napa Valley, many highly successful wine-making businesses arose among Italians from northern Italy and from Switzerland.[205] Italians also excelled in the production of both fresh and canned fruit. By 1922, a California Italian, Giuseppe DiGiorgio, became the largest fruit-grower in the United States.[206] Another, in 1916, formed the company which produced Del Monte brand canned fruits and vegetables—the country's largest seller of canned produce.[207]

One of the most remarkable success stories in banking history was that of A. P. Giannini, also a California Italian. He founded the Bank of Italy, an American bank designed to attract Italian immigrants as depositors and borrowers. Being familiar with the culture and the parsimoniousness of his fellow Italians, Giannini was able to do a thriving business by serving a group largely overlooked by conventional American banks. By the middle of the 1920s, the Bank of Italy had branches in many of the urban centers of California. Ultimately renamed the Bank of America, it became the largest bank in the world.

Despite the prosperity achieved by Italian Americans in general and the spectacular success of a few, their role in American history has not matched their role in the development of Brazil and, especially, Argentina. As one indicator, Italians in the United States played nothing like the leadership role they played in both national labor organizations and national business organizations in Argentina. Italians in Argentina constituted 40 percent of the labor movement in its early formative years and provided key leaders, while in the United States Italians tended to lag behind other groups in unionization and still more so among the early union leaders. Similarly, Italians were prominent among employer organization leadership in Argentina in its formative years but were wholly unrepresented among the leadership of the National Association of Manufacturers in the United States during its first 20 years.[208]

Such differences partly reflected the fact that the United States was a far more developed country when the Italian immigrants arrived, that other immigrants preceded them and collectively outnumbered them greatly, while in both Argentina and Brazil the Italians were one of two groups that together constituted the bulk of the immigrant population. However, the complete dominance of northern Italians among the most outstanding Italian American entrepreneurs of the immigrant era—in the wine industry, canning, fresh fruits, and the Bank of America—suggests that the greater representation of northerners among the Italian immigrants in Argentina and Brazil may also be an important factor in the larger role played by immigrants from Italy in those two countries. Within the early labor movements in both these South American countries, for example, northern Italians tended to be leaders more so than southern Italians.[209] In the United States at about the same time, 40 percent of the northern Italians were unionized, compared to only 11 percent of the southern Italians.[210]

With both the business and labor history of Italians in the United States, Argentina, and Brazil reflecting regional differences in Italy, it is difficult to avoid the conclusion that this is yet another example of historic head starts that had enduring consequences.

AUSTRALIA

Although the land area of Australia is comparable in size to that of the continental United States, its population is smaller than that of California. Most Australians live on the coastal fringes of the island continent, leaving the geographically and climatically inhospitable interior largely uninhabited. In sparsely populated Australia, various ethnic groups became socially significant, even though their numbers would be small enough for them to pass virtually unnoticed in the United States. Italian immigration to Australia has never been on a scale comparable to the immigration from Italy to Western Europe or to North or South America. Yet Italians have been both a noticeable presence and a notable presence in Australia.

Most immigration from Italy to Australia has occurred since the early 1920s, when American immigration restrictions sent Italians in search of other destinations. Isolated individuals of Italian ancestry lived in Australia from the beginning of its history, having arrived there on the first ships of convicts transported from Britain, and on the first ships of free settlers as well.[211] Yet, as late as 1891, there were fewer than 4,000 Italian-born individuals in Australia[212] and they were outnumbered by Danes, Chinese, and German immigrants, and vastly outnumbered by British-born immigrants.[213] Most of these Italians were from the northern provinces of Italy and northerners maintained a slight majority among Italian immigrants in Australia as late as 1947.[214]

The early Italian immigrants had patterns characteristic of Italians in other countries. They were noted for their hard work, their "docility and temperance," and for saving steadily "by a simple and even primitive mode of life."[215] Some Australians said that the Italians could "live on the smell of an oil rag." For all these traits, they were preferred as workers by some employers—and were often disliked by Australian workers.[216] Many Italian immigrants were unskilled laborers, but those with occupational specialties were often miners, fishermen, fruit and vegetable vendors, and restaurant owners.[217] Children were sometimes used as street musicians,[218] as in other countries. In some places, Italian immigrants took over land considered unproductive by unsuccessful Australian farmers and made it successful by hard work.[219] Even in times of unemployment, Italians seldom accepted charity, public or private.[220]

As elsewhere, people from particular parts of Italy tended to settle together[221] and northern and southern Italians were antagonistic to one another. Social life tended to be limited to the family circle or to two or three families. There was little sense of an Italian community, as such, though Italians lived separately from Australians.[222] Neither religion nor education played a major role in their lives, and politics aroused little interest.[223] Italians established no schools or churches of their own and very few newspapers.[224]

Not only were most of the Italians who arrived in the last quarter of the nineteenth century from northern Italy, nearly half came from just one province in northern Italy, and there were highly localized origins within that province as well. Altogether, nearly 90 percent of the Italian immigrants to Australia during that era came from an area containing only 10 percent of Italy's population.[225] Yet immigration to Australia was often heavy from the isolated places where it originated. By 1939, there were more people from some Italian villages living in Australia than remained back in Italy.[226]

The first major increase of Italian immigration into Australia—called a "flood" by the standards of the times—began in the 1920s. More than 7,800 arrived in the peak year of 1927,[227] in a country with a total Italian immigrant population of only 4,500 as late as 1921.[228] Altogether, between 1921 and 1930, nearly 24,000 Italian immigrants entered Australia,[229] but subsequent immigration from Italy was sharply reduced by the Great Depression and then by World War II.

Although Italians in Australia showed little interest in politics, the politics of Italy—Mussolini's fascism—reached out to touch them, both directly and indirectly. The Italian government, through its representatives in Australia, promoted pro-Fascist organizations, which tapped an emotional attachment to Italy and Italian culture, even among immigrants not particularly susceptible to political ideology in general or to fascism in particular.[230] The Second World War also had its impact on Italians in Australia, where 3,650 were interned, out of a population of 70,000.[231] Moreover, those Italians remaining outside the internment camps still lived under various restrictions as "enemy aliens."[232]

The post–World War II era saw immigration from Italy to Australia resume and reach a scale never seen before. While fewer than a thousand Italians immigrated to Australia from 1945 to 1948, the number shot up to nearly 6,000 the following year and climbed to a peak of more than 30,000 per year in the middle of the 1950s, before beginning an uneven decline that continued until fewer than 10,000 per year were arriving in the early 1970s. Altogether, approximately 374,000 people immigrated from Italy to Australia from 1945 to 1972, making Italians by far the largest non-British ethnic group in the country,[233] and 4 percent of Australia's total population.[234] Even allowing for substantial return migration,[235] this large influx of immigrants significantly altered the composition of the Italian population in Australia.

By 1978 there were 595,000 people who were either first- or second-generation Italians living in the country.[236] Nearly half—approximately

286,000 people—had been born in Italy. The immigrant families may in fact have included a majority of all Italians in the country, for their children born on Australian soil were counted as part of the second generation, though still living in immigrant homes. Radically different age distributions between first-generation and second-generation Italians reinforce this inference. Two-thirds of the Italian-born population in Australia was between 25 and 54 years of age, while more than four-fifths of second-generation Italians were less than 20 years old.[237] Because of the relative recency of substantial Italian immigration, the adult second generation plus these immigrant families together constituted an estimated 90 percent of all Italians in Australia,[238] who in total would exceed 650,000 by this reckoning. However, counting all individuals with any trace of Italian ancestry, there might be close to a million Australians of Italian descent.[239]

Over the years, the Italian population in Australia has changed in many ways. Whereas the earlier Italian immigrants were predominantly rural, the postwar immigrants have been predominantly urban.[240] The regional origins of Italian immigrants have also changed over the years, from northern to southern Italy. From the late nineteenth century until early in World War II, most Italian immigrants to Australia came from northern Italy.[241] By 1976, however, the most common regional origins of Italian-born immigrants in Australia were southern, with Sicily and Calabria alone accounting for about one-third of the total immigration from Italy.[242] As elsewhere, there was little social mixing of northern and southern Italians in Australia,[243] though northern Italians manned a social welfare agency operating among southern Italians.[244] Marriage patterns have clearly shown the social separation. For the entire period from 1920 to 1954, the great majority of southern Italian males in Australia were married to southern Italian females, whether they were married in Italy or in Australia.[245]

Normal family life was easier to establish and maintain for the postwar immigrants from Italy to Australia than it was for their predecessors in an earlier era. A very unbalanced ratio between men and women immigrants, a very low rate of intermarriage with Australians, and the fact that many married men left their wives behind in Italy, all made it difficult for the early immigrants to establish families in Australia. In 1871, there were nearly 14 times as many males as females among the 860 Italians in Australia. As late as 1901, the ratio was more than six to one.[246] As of 1921, one-half of all Italian-born men in Australia were married but one-fourth of these married men had families in Italy.[247] Moreover, the preponderance of males continued for years. However, a greater tendency of males than of females to return to Italy[248] mitigated the sex imbalance, which fell to two to one by 1947.[249]

After the massive postwar immigration, the ratio of males to females among those born in Italy was only 1.2 to 1.[250] As with other groups and other countries, this sex-balanced immigration was a harbinger of permanent settlement. Rates of naturalization and of learning the English language were both much higher among the postwar Italian immigrants than among those of earlier times.

Along with more signs of assimilation, the new immigrants also showed some persistent Italian patterns common in other countries. For example, babies born out of wedlock remained very rare among Italians in Australia—one out of every 148 births to women born in Italy—in a community noted for an absence of sex education.[251] Italian schoolchildren have tended to have poor scholastic performances and to drop out of school earlier than Australian children in general[252]—a pattern long ago observed among Italian immigrants in other countries. Another pattern common to Italian immigrants was a below-average crime rate.[253] In religious practices as well, the pattern among Italian immigrants to Australia has been very similar to that observed in other countries: They have been overwhelmingly Catholic—and overwhelmingly nonparticipants in the church.[254]

Among the more recent Italian immigrants to Australia, as among the earlier, the desire to work and get ahead has been strong. They have preferred jobs that offered frequent opportunities for working overtime.[255] The desire for home ownership has been high among Italians in Australia, as in other countries. Home ownership has in fact been more common among Italians than among Australians in general.[256] More than four-fifths of Sicilian immigrants have become home owners,[257] though this often involved a real struggle to make the down payment.[258] Italians in Australia have been by no means an affluent group, however, though they have risen from their early poverty. As of 1933, the average Italian male in Australia earned 87 percent of what Australian males in general earned, and by 1976, 97 percent.[259] While this represented considerable progress for a group relatively recently immigrated, their income level could not explain the high home-ownership level of Italians in Australia.

As in other countries, Italian immigrants in Australia have had relatively low levels of education and have been statistically under-represented in professional and technical occupations.[260] Although there were more than twice as many Italian-born males as German-born males in Australia in the early 1980s, there were more than twice as many German-born males as Italian-born males in professional and technical occupations.[261] Nevertheless, Italians have apparently been considered desirable workers in the occupations in which they worked, for even in a period of sharp unemployment in the economy as a whole in 1972, their unemployment rates were not substantially different from those of native-born Australians.[262] Moreover, Italians were self-employed as tradesmen to a greater extent than the Australian population as a whole.[263]

Along with these signs of persistent Italian patterns have been signs of assimilation to a new society, at least in such outward forms as language, citizenship, and occupational mobility. More than 90 percent of the Italians under the age of 15 were born in Australia.[264] But, even among the Italian-born population, by 1976 four-fifths spoke English, even if not exclusively,[265] and a majority were citizens of Australia.[266] Italians from northern Italy more readily adopted some Australian child-rearing practices,[267] but many Sicilians adjusted in various ways as well.[268] Education became increasingly valued by Italians in Australia, but the prerequisites for it may not have been fully understood, or not yet present.[269] Occupationally, there were significant changes over the years as well, with Italians no longer being over-represented among fishermen in Australia, for example.[270] Whereas the early Italian immigrants were primarily laborers, by 1947 more were employers or self-employed than were employees.[271] By the late 1970s, less than one-sixth were unskilled laborers.[272] Italians did not simply melt into the general population, however. There were still distinctively Italian neighborhoods,[273] though many Italians lived outside such neighborhoods.[274] Perhaps most significant, intermarriage remained the exception rather than the rule among men and women born in Italy.[275]

IMPLICATIONS

Emigration from Italy—perhaps the largest emigration from any country anywhere in history—illustrates many facets of the process of human migration. The enormous importance of specific and reliable knowledge about destinations has been reflected in the linkage between highly specific places of origin in Italy and highly specific destinations in other countries—including places 10,000 miles away in Australia. The human linkages behind these geographical facts suggest something of the psychic costs of loneliness in a strange land, as well as the actuarial risks associated with settling abroad. More than 90 percent of Italian immigrants to Australia, for example, came via these human linkages rather than as isolated individuals seeking a new life at random among the Australian population.[276]

Italian emigration also illustrates the different roles that the emigration process can play in the lives of individuals and families. Sojourners and remittances from sojourners have played a key role in the survival of desperately poor families in Italy. Men living in crowded and squalid conditions abroad, skimping on their personal expenses even to the detriment of their health, were often objects of pity or contempt, when in fact they were heroic in their quiet tenacity and self-sacrifice for their loved ones back home. Too proud to take charity, they were not too proud to wear rags and to do the hardest and dirtiest work spurned by others—all the while sending money home from foreign countries to fulfill their family responsibilities. Their reliability in fulfilling their financial obligations was not lost on Australian lending institutions, which readily lent them money to buy land,[277] or on the California institution first known as the Bank of Italy and later as the Bank of America.

The time that Italian-born men were away from their wives and children ranged from several months for migratory workers to several years for those who slowly accumulated the money required to bring their families to join them in a foreign land. That such human dramas were re-enacted literally millions of times in the far reaches of the globe is not only a tribute to the Italians but also an inspiration as showing what the human spirit is capable of—and perhaps also a rebuke to those who whine over much less formidable problems.

Those Italians blessed with skills tended to take those skills where they were most scarce and thus likely to be more rewarded. Thus the greatest entrepreneurial success of the Italian emigrants came in underdeveloped countries of the immigrant era, like Argentina and Brazil—and in California, when it was an underdeveloped part of the United States. In each of these places, it was principally northern Italians who reached the economic peaks, but those northern Italians with entrepreneurial skills and capital had the option of settling in more developed regions or nations, and chose instead the route that led to such striking success.

Whether high or low in the outside world's economic or social ranking, Italian returnees were impressive to their compatriots when they came back home "arrayed like *signori*,"[278] buying land or otherwise raising their families' economic and social positions. Poverty-stricken though much of Italy has been, it has sent forth millions of people with the inner strength and inner values to prosper in more promising lands abroad—sometimes to prosper beyond the natives of those lands. Most of these Italian emigrants took with them no skills, as these are conventionally defined in occupational terms.

Among those who did have special callings, however, these were often the same in the many countries to which they went as fishermen, wine-makers, masons, musicians, architects, fruit and vegetable growers and sellers, or restaurant and hotel owners. However, Italians abroad did not merely transfer skills from Italy and they certainly did not transfer much capital. They accumulated both skills and capital in their new settings. But while they absorbed, at varying rates and to varying degrees, the cultures of new lands, they also brought to those lands some of the cultural treasures of Italy, whether in music, art, or architecture, or at the more mundane level of cooking, masonry, and a certain flair seen in Italian writers or entertainers. In these and other ways, the influence of the Italian culture extended farther than it did in the days of the Roman Empire.

CHAPTER 5

THE OVERSEAS CHINESE

The "overseas Chinese" are the largest of the world's middleman minorities. At the beginning of the twentieth century, there were an estimated 7 million Chinese living outside of China. By mid-century this had doubled to 14 million[1] and by 1993 there were an estimated 36 million overseas Chinese.[2] While Chinese communities arose in such far-flung locations as Britain, Peru, New Zealand, and the Caribbean,[3] the chief concentrations of the overseas Chinese have been in the nations of Southeast Asia. The worldwide distribution of the overseas Chinese in 1993 was as follows:[4]

AFRICA	108,000
EUROPE	757,000
WESTERN HEMISPHERE	3,802,000
OCEANIA	407,000
ASIA	31,054,000
TOTAL	36,128,000

The overseas Chinese have often been called "the Jews of Asia," but perhaps the Jews might be called the Chinese of the West. The overseas Chinese are not only far more numerous than the Jews, but have also played a far larger economic role in the countries of Southeast Asia than even the considerable economic role of the Jews in Europe and America. The largest conglomerate in Indonesia is controlled by an overseas Chinese businessman, one of a number of ethnically Chinese billionaires in Southeast Asia. Though less than 5 percent of the Indonesian population, the overseas Chinese have controlled an estimated 70 percent of the country's private domestic capital and run three-quarters of its 200 largest businesses. In Thailand, ethnic Chinese, about 10 percent of the population, have controlled all four of the largest private banks. Altogether, ethnic Chinese living outside of China produced as much wealth as China itself in the early 1990s.[5] Of the five billionaires in Indonesia and Thailand in the late twentieth century, all were ethnically Chinese.[6] Although this level of prosperity did not occur overnight, there has long been a pattern throughout Southeast Asia of most of the firms, and most of the investment in whole industries, being in the hands of the Chinese minority, which has been less than 10 percent of the population of that region.[7] Typically, their enterprises have been family-controlled and family-run, even when they have been giant multinational corporations.

The Chinese have also been a numerically small but economically significant factor in a number of Western Hemisphere nations. In the Jamaican capital of Kingston, the Chinese at one time owned most of the grocery stores.[8] They also owned most of the grocery stores in Peru's capital city, Lima—as well as most of the shoe stores, department stores, and hotels in that city.[9] They have had similar success in retail trade in Panama, where most of the towns have had Chinese grocery stores, restaurants, and dry goods stores.[10]

Like most middleman minorities, the overseas Chinese have been a predominantly urban people, concentrated especially in the principal metropolises of the nations in which they have settled. In various times and countries, more than half the Chinese population has been concentrated in one city—Bangkok in Thailand, Manila in the Philippines, Lima in Peru, Buenos Aires in Argentina, Saigon in South Vietnam, Vientienne in Laos, and Phnom Penh in Cambodia. Most of the

Chinese in Brazil lived either in São Paulo or in Rio de Janeiro.[11]

Like other minorities, Chinese may "all look alike" to outsiders, but their internal differences are sharp and enduring, both in China and overseas. Chinese from different parts of China not only speak in ways that are mutually unintelligible, but also operate overseas in different social networks that are often mutually exclusive in both personal and business matters.[12]

But, while these networks typically do not include all the Chinese in a given country, they link similar groups of Chinese internationally. Regional networks link the Hokkiens or Yunnanese of Indonesia or Singapore with people of similar ancestral origins in south China who live on the other side of the Pacific.[13]

The regional mixture of the overseas Chinese does not match the regional mixture of people in China, nor is this mixture the same in all overseas countries. The primary source of the overseas Chinese emigration were the two southern provinces of Fukien and Kwangtung, which in the nineteenth century contained only about 10 to 15 percent of the population of China.[14] Even within these two southern provinces, the origins of people immigrating to particular places has varied considerably. The Cantonese have historically constituted the bulk of Chinese immigrants to the United States, Canada, and Latin America, but in Southeast Asian countries the Cantonese have been a minority within the Chinese minority.[15] More broadly, the Chinese of Thailand, the Indochina region, and the United States originated mostly in China's Kwangtung (now Guangdong) province, which contains the city of Canton (now Guangzhou), while the Chinese in the Philippines, Malaysia, and Singapore originated mostly in the province of Fukien.[16]

The localization of origins and destinations has sometimes been even more specific. Of all the Chinese who immigrated to the United States before World War I, a majority came from Toishan, just one of 98 districts in Kwangtung province.[17] Moreover, the occupations of the overseas Chinese have historically been highly correlated with their respective places of origin in China—and have remained so, decades or even generations later.[18] The strong regional ties of the overseas Chinese are also reflected in more than a thousand regional organizations to which they belong. Overseas Chinese have long been known as "joiners" and have more than 8,000 organizations altogether.[19] Almost all overseas Chinese belong to some Chinese organization.[20]

Enormous diversity may be concealed in a common label: To speak of China during the Ming dynasty is to refer to an area ten times the size of France and an era longer than the entire history of the United States. To speak of the Chinese "language" and its "dialects," as if we were speaking of English as spoken by the Scots and the Irish, is to ignore profound linguistic differences which made Chinese "dialects" mutually unintelligible as spoken words, though people educated in written *non-phonetic* Chinese characters could communicate on paper in that medium, much as Spaniards and Russians can understand the same written Arabic numerals, while pronouncing them in entirely different ways.

Although Chinese traders, immigrants, or sojourners have been found in various parts of Southeast Asia for many centuries, large-scale emigration from China is much more recent in history. There were only an estimated 100,000 Chinese living in the region prior to the mass immigration of Chinese laborers in the nineteenth century.[21] This emigration coincided with turbulent times in China, including famines and wars. The consolidation of European imperialism in Southeast Asia provided security, order, and economic opportunities sorely lacking in the declining Manchu dynasty. One measure of China's travails was an absolute decline in population—from approximately 391 million in 1842 to 307 million by 1885.[22] This was not due to emigration alone, by any means. All 7 million Chinese overseas at the turn of the century would account for only a small fraction of the population decline. What was happening in China was the disintegration of a nation that had a history and a culture that went back thousands of years—and which had once been the leading nation in the world in technology, scholarship, commerce, and organization.[23]

China was a nation centuries before Christ. Confucius was born nearly a century before Socrates. Cast iron was produced in China a thousand years before it was produced in Europe[24] and the tonnage of cast iron produced in China in 1078 greatly exceeded that produced in England seven centuries later.[25] Printing existed in China centuries before its first appearance in Europe.[26] Gunpowder likewise originated in China. Chinese metropolises of more than 2 million people each existed at a time when the largest city in Europe contained no more than 54,000 residents.[27] Commerce, though officially deplored in Confucian philosophy, flourished in China.[28] Economic development in China in the eleventh century was at a level reached by no European nation until the eighteenth century.[29] In the fourteenth century, China had the most advanced agriculture in the world,[30] and as late as the sixteenth century, China had the world's highest standard of living.[31] Yet China was not simply overtaken by the later progress of European nations. Internal decline and disintegration appeared in many forms, including technological stagnation under stifling government economic controls,[32] neglect of military defenses,[33] widespread corruption,[34] and eventually a fragmenting of the country as local warlords gained control of particular regions and foreigners—both Japanese and Europeans—began to prey on a weakened China.[35] It was from this China that massive emigration began in the nineteenth century.

Although the overseas Chinese have become widely known as a middleman minority, Chinese immigrants seldom began overseas as businessmen. In the era of mass Chinese immigration, most of these immigrants began overseas as coolie laborers—destitute, illiterate, unskilled workers, often in debt for their passage and indentured to whoever paid for it. Early Chinese immigrants almost always began in the lowliest unskilled tasks—often jobs considered too dirty, difficult, dangerous, or "menial" for the local peoples to accept. The different rates at which individual Chinese rose from such occupations contributed to the economic diversity of the overseas Chinese communities. As with the Jews, the more successful Chinese provided the stereotypes which the larger society associated with the group as a whole, even when Chinese peddlers and small shopkeepers outnumbered commercial giants and Chinese laborers outnumbered them all.[36] Overall, however, the overseas Chinese as a group have usually averaged considerably higher incomes than the surrounding populations of the countries in which they lived. As of 1969, for example, Chinese American families earned 12 percent higher incomes than the average American family, and in less-developed countries the differences have usually been far greater. In Malaysia, the Chinese have usually averaged about double the income of the Malays, and in Jamaica more than double the income of the average Jamaican.[37] This did not mean that the overseas Chinese were rich, especially not in Third World countries, where general economic levels have been low.

It was once a common practice for those who succeeded overseas to return to China to spend their old age. However, post–World War II political developments, and especially the takeover of China itself by the Communists, sharply reduced the repatriation of overseas Chinese to the homeland and made them more of a permanent part of the societies in which they lived. Because Chinese immigrations to many nations began as virtually all-male immigrations, many have throughout history married with local women, producing mixed offspring who have become culturally Chinese in some places and times, and culturally assimilated into the larger society in other places and times. Some Chinese families have remained culturally Chinese for generations, whether or not they remained biologically pure Chinese. Sometimes the same individual would present himself as a member of the indigenous culture and society when dealing with indigenous customers and as Chinese when dealing with other Chinese businessmen.[38] Many Chinese never became citizens of the countries in which they lived, though their families remained there for generations. Others did become citizens, especially after World War II, and particularly after the Communist victory in China made their return highly unlikely. In recent years, the very phrase "overseas Chinese" has been challenged as obsolete, insofar as it connotes people temporarily absent from China.

Such wide diversities in social reality have been reflected in huge disparities in statistics on the number of Chinese in various countries. A 1936 census in Indochina, for example, listed 326,000 Chinese but an independent scholar put the figure at more than 1 million.[39] Much depends on whether one counts as Chinese only Chinese nationals or includes people of Chinese ancestry who hold citizenship in the local country, or whose citizenship is in doubt, or whether one counts as Chinese only those who consider themselves Chinese, omitting others of the same racial mixture who consider themselves Thais, Burmese, or Filipino, for example. Australian census statistics on the Chinese, for example, refer to persons born in China, even though these are (1) a minority of the ethnically Chinese in Australia, and (2) include many White Russians who were born in China.[40] Our definition of the overseas Chinese will be based on those who are ethnically Chinese, regardless of citizenship or nativity. Racial mixtures also complicate the count of Chinese. In some cases, the part-Chinese may be not only estranged from the Chinese community but even hostile to it. In some countries of Southeast Asia, part-Chinese politicians have spearheaded anti-Chinese movements.[41] This parallels the situation among Spanish Jews whose fifteenth-century expulsion from Spain was partly the work of Jewish converts to Christianity.[42]

Although it may seem paradoxical that the Chinese generally prosper in other countries, where they have historically been subjected to both sweeping discrimination and sporadic mob violence, but remain very poor in China, that is nevertheless the case. Per capita income in China in the late twentieth century was less than half that of Taiwan, and less than one-seventh that of Singapore, to compare it only with other Chinese states in the area.[43] On the world scene, China remained one of the poorest nations—after having once been the richest.

SOUTHEAST ASIA

China, its people, and its culture have spread into Southeast Asia for many centuries. However, most Chinese in Southeast Asia in the twentieth century are not descendants of those Chinese who moved into this region in the early centuries of the Christian era or during the Sung, Yuan, or early Ming dynasties.[44] Large-scale emigration from China into Southeast Asia began only after European colonial powers—Portuguese, Spanish, Dutch, and British—consolidated their control in the region in the sixteenth and early seventeenth centuries, and created stable conditions in which Chinese immigrants could feel secure. Before then, the Chinese were neither a large nor a predominant element among the foreigners in the region, who included Arabs, Persians, and people from India.[45] The high tide of Chinese immigration into Southeast Asia—the late nineteenth and early twentieth centuries—coincided with the high tide of European imperialism in the region.

The initial wave of Chinese immigrants to Southeast Asia usually brought with them no special skills other than a capacity for long and hard work, and a tenacity in seeking to advance themselves through painful thrift and the risks of setting up their own tiny businesses with their savings. In the process, the overseas Chinese have brought retail stores and eventually other elements of a modern commercial and industrial world into traditional, rural peasant societies in Southeast Asia. With the passing generations and increasing prosperity, the overseas Chinese have branched out into a variety of economic ventures, and have established their own schools in which their children could be educated. Among the factors in their entrepreneurial success has been their ability to conduct business among themselves and with others on the strength of verbal agreements. This gave them an advantage over local businessmen who lacked the same credibility—even with local clienteles and creditors.[46]

The ties of the overseas Chinese to their homeland have historically been reflected in their remittances to families in China, as well as in repatriation in old age or after achieving prosperity. These remittances to China, and returns to China with the savings of many years, have been a source of bitter political accusations that the overseas Chinese were draining away the wealth of the countries in which they lived and worked. These political charges proceeded on the implicit assumption that there is either a fixed or a preordained level of wealth in the host country, from which the Chinese subtract the sums that they send or take back to China. From an economic standpoint, such charges collapse when the sums sent or taken by the overseas Chinese are seen as (1) a fraction of the wealth they have created and added to the host country's economy, and (2) representing what the Chinese would have spent on themselves and their families, wherever they were located, leaving the rest of the population no better or worse off because of the remittances or residential choices of the Chinese. But, however economically questionable, these charges have been politically effective.

The rise of the Communist government on the mainland of China has led to a sharp decline in both repatriation and remittances from overseas —the latter due to confiscatory practices of the Communists.[47] Taiwan, however, continued to receive large sums from the overseas Chinese, who invested more than $147 million there in 1979.[48] Moreover, hostility and discrimination toward the Chinese by no means declined with the decline in remittances and repatriation to China. On the contrary, escalating discrimination in Indonesia and Malaysia, for example, led to outflows of Chinese capital to Singapore, Hong Kong, and elsewhere.[49]

Thailand

For several centuries the Chinese have been part of the history of Thailand or Siam, as it was known for a large part of its history. During much of that time, the Chinese were well received by the Thais[50] and there was considerable intermarriage, extending all the way to the royal family.[51] There was a Chinese high official in the Thai government as early as the fifteenth century, the first of many Chinese to hold high office and receive official honors.[52] Moreover, the prestige of Chinese civilization was high in Thailand.[53] But, despite this historical background, severe interethnic tensions and discrimination developed in twentieth-century Thailand, in the wake of major social, and especially political, changes.

While Chinese immigration to Thailand goes back for centuries, neither data nor reliable estimates were available until the late nineteenth century, when from 13,000 to 34,000 Chinese per year were entering the country. Altogether, nearly a million and a half Chinese immigrants entered Thailand from 1882 to 1917—a huge number for a small country to absorb—but about two-thirds of these immigrants returned to China,[54] a pattern common among the overseas Chinese of that era. Nevertheless, those who remained and propagated created a growing Chinese population estimated at 100,000 in 1825, increasing to 349,000 by 1917—rising from about 5 percent of the total population of Thailand in 1825 to about 10 percent in 1917.[55] The Chinese were concentrated disproportionately in and around Bangkok, where they constituted about half of the local population by the mid-nineteenth century.[56] But, even in areas where the Chinese were more thinly spread, their economic impact was out of all proportion to their numbers.

Most of the Chinese who immigrated to Thailand were themselves poor and came from poor southern coastal provinces of China, areas subject to flood and drought, with attendant widespread hunger. Thailand, by contrast, has historically been a country of abundant fertile land. Against this background, it is not surprising that contrasting attitudes and behavior patterns have long been observed between the Chinese and the Thais. Extreme thrift has been one of the striking characteristics of the Chinese, in Thailand as elsewhere. Even the Chinese common laborer in nineteenth-century Bangkok could save more than half his earnings.[57] No such frugality was necessary for the Thais, whose adage "rice on the lands, fish in the waters," expressed the ready availability of subsistence.[58] Thais who worked on construction of the first railroad in Thailand in the late nineteenth century were noted for leaving after a few days to go spend their earnings in the nearest town. Most of the work had to be done by Chinese immigrants.[59]

Thais tended to remain peasants in traditional agriculture, while the Chinese predominated in occupations requiring arduous labor, skills, or entrepreneurship. Chinese workers were noted as the first people to get up in the morning in Bangkok,[60] where large numbers of Chinese blacksmiths were found forging iron before daybreak by a British visitor in 1833.[61] Canals and railroads were built with Chinese labor.[62] The Chinese also pulled rickshaws—a job spurned by the Thais.[63] An ethnic division of labor emerged, in which the growing Thai population was absorbed producing rice, while the Chinese dominated virtually all other labor, business, and industrial activity, except for fields where other foreigners made major contributions. Even in agriculture, it was the Chinese who introduced new crops and new methods,[64] supplied most of the labor on rubber plantations,[65] as well as financing the Thai peasant, purchasing his rice production, owning the rice mills, and managing the distribution of rice, both domestically and internationally.[66]

The Chinese immigrants of the pre–World War I era were at least 90 percent male, and among the few females a significant proportion went into brothels.[67] About half the Chinese males who remained in Thailand for five years or more married Thai women. Their offspring could choose whether to be regarded as Thai or Chinese, for both social and legal purposes—but a choice was necessary.[68]

The Chinese were by no means a homogeneous group within themselves. The various dialect groups were not only socially separate—each had its own separate cemetery in Bangkok[69]—but in some cases had a history of mutual hostility in China. During the 1860s, fights between the Hakkas and the Cantonese in China's Kwantung province cost an estimated 100,000 lives.[70] In Thailand as well, their feuds sometimes led to armed battles between the *tongs* or secret societies that flourished among the Chinese in countries around the world.[71]

For all the wide range of occupations engaged in and even dominated by the Chinese, they seldom pursued political careers or engaged in organized and sustained political activity for ethnic interests in Thailand. Even those Chinese who achieved important government positions typically did so as individuals, rather than as spokesmen for an organized Chinese political constituency, and their elevation to office often removed them further from the Chinese community and its special interests.[72] The politics that mattered to the Chinese in Thailand were the politics of China. Within Thailand they were submissive to the Thai royalty and aristocracy,[73] and on the few occasions when they were not, their uprisings were quickly and bloodily crushed.[74]

Those Chinese who elected to become naturalized Thais were subject to all the duties that fell to the Thai masses under an autocratic government. Those who chose to remain Chinese citizens had to pay a special tax. A nineteenth-century observer noted that "there is nothing that the Siamese policeman so much enjoys as leading some unfortunate Chinaman to pay the tax." The whole set of procedures surrounding this tax demeaned the Chinese.[75] This and a variety of other taxes on things largely confined to the Chinese, such as opium and gambling, led to the Thai government's receiving nearly half its total revenue from the Chinese minority.[76]

By and large, the Chinese and the Thais coexisted with relatively little friction,[77] on into the early twentieth century. Events in China, however, promoted a growing sense of nationalism among the overseas Chinese, including those in Thailand. Japan's successful war against China in 1895 was the first of a series of events promoting a sense of national consciousness among Chinese notorious for their regional or local perspectives. The Chinese revolution of 1911, and the long struggle of Sun Yat-sen to unify the country, all captured the imagination of the overseas Chinese, who contributed financially to his efforts. A second round of Japanese aggression against China, beginning in the 1930s, aroused still more Chinese nationalism overseas.

Coinciding with these political trends was a social trend that reinforced separation of the Chinese from the Thais: an increase in the number of Chinese women immigrating into the country. As of 1910, a Chinese woman was a rare sight in Bangkok, but by 1930 they were a substantial social phenomenon[78]—and growing. From about 15 percent of all Chinese immigrants in the early 1920s, women became 27 percent from the decade beginning in 1932, and 32 percent of the immigrants settling permanently. One consequence of this was a sharp decline in the rate of intermarriage between Chinese men and Thai women.[79] The preference of Chinese men for Chinese women was shown in the higher bride prices these women commanded, as compared to the bride price for Thai or mixed Thai-Chinese women.[80]

Along with a drop in biological assimilation went a decline in cultural assimilation, as Chinese immigration hit record levels between the end of World War I and the beginning of the Great Depression of the 1930s. An annual immigration of 68,000 rose to a peak of 155,000 in the 1927–28 official year. For the entire period 1918–1931, more than 1.3 million Chinese immigrants entered Thailand and, while most continued to depart as well, there was a net addition of about half a million to the Chinese population of the country.[81] Along with the more or less automatic reinforcement of the Chinese culture implied by growing immigration and declining intermarriage, there were conscious efforts to perpetuate a separate ethnic identity among the Chinese in Thailand through the creation, beginning around 1911, of Chinese schools emphasizing the Chinese language and culture—and Chinese politics.[82] The first decade of the twentieth century also saw the first community-wide Chinese organizations in Thailand, cutting across dialect lines—yet another sign of growing Chinese nationalism.

At about the same time, a new European-educated Thai elite was developing Thai nationalism, and with it a growing suspicion, resentment, and hostility toward the Chinese. A Chinese protest boycott against tax law changes in 1910 shut down the city of Bangkok, engendering enormous and lasting resentment among the Thais—without having any effect on the tax laws.[83] Chinese separatism, Chinese domination of the economy in general and their role as money-lenders to Thai peasants in particular, all came in for critical re-examination. An era of Thai-Chinese antagonism was beginning, with political power firmly in the hands of the Thais.

In the economy, the Chinese were as dominant as ever in the years between the two world wars. The four major exports of Thailand—rice, timber, tin, and rubber—were all largely in Chinese hands, with competition coming primarily from foreigners—Europeans, Australians, and Americans—and with the Thais virtually spectators at the economic development of their country. Westerners tended to compete best with the Chinese in industries requiring very large capital investments, such as dredge mining, forestry, and steam-powered rice mills. Europeans remained dominant in forestry, though the Chinese owned three of the nine modern sawmills in Bangkok in 1924, and the labor in all nine sawmills was predominantly Chinese. In mining, the Chinese lacked the capital for dredging equipment, but most of the miners were Chinese. In rubber, the Chinese dominated at every level, from the plantation workers to the owners and rubber merchants. Market-gardening, sugar production, and fish exporting were among the other industries where the Chinese remained supreme.[84]

While Westerners could command more vast capital resources than the Chinese, the advantage of the Chinese was in a far more intimate knowledge of the country, its people, and customs. In credit operations, such as those involving the Thai peasant, this meant knowing each farmer so well as to be able to gauge repayment prospects that varied greatly from individual to individual, according to a host of attitudinal as well as objective conditions. The boundary between Chinese and Western predominance in sectors of the Thai economy tended to run along lines reflecting the relative importance of huge capital investments versus knowledge of the local scene. Industries which simply extracted raw material for shipment overseas required less local knowledge and more vast capital, so it is hardly surprising to find Western firms predominating in tin-mining or forestry. But local retailing was overwhelmingly Chinese in Thailand, as throughout Southeast Asia. Large Western-owned commercial establishments usually lacked the knowledge of the local languages, customs, or conditions necessary to deal directly with Thai customers or with Chinese retailers, and so employed Chinese agents to act as intermediaries. Theoretically, they could have hired Thai intermediaries but they found the Chinese more industrious and knowledgeable and the Thais too easygoing for their business purposes.[85]

The evolution of the rice-milling industry in Thailand illustrates the changing relations of Western and Chinese advantages. Initially, when rice was milled by hand, the rice exported from Thailand came almost entirely from Chinese mills. But Western mechanized and steam-powered rice mills, built in the 1850s and 1860s, began to make inroads—until the Chinese ordered similar equipment from England in the 1870s. By 1879, the Chinese owned as many steam-powered rice mills as the Westerners, and by 1919 all Western-owned rice mills had either closed down or had been sold to the Chinese.[86]

Conversely, where very large capital investments held decisive advantages, Westerners tended to prevail. In the import-export trade, for example, the Chinese in Thailand were dominant for centuries,[87] but huge Western square-rigged sailing ships began displacing the smaller, more shallow-draft Chinese junks in the nineteenth century, and the appearance of steam-powered ships added to the Western advantage. By 1890, the British alone carried two-thirds of the foreign trade, with other Western ships carrying more than one-third, and only 2 percent of the tonnage being carried in junks.[88] Nevertheless, this drastic reduction in Chinese shipping, where capital was decisive, did not similarly reduce the Chinese role in the trading end of the import-export business, where knowledge was decisive. In 1890, despite British dominance in shipping to Bangkok, the Chinese still conducted 62 percent of the import-export business, operating as agents for Western shippers as well as on their own.[89]

Although many leading businessmen in Thailand were Chinese, this did not mean that most Chinese in Thailand were prosperous. Numerous Chinese lived in huts with the earth for a floor in the countryside, or lived in the back of the shop in town, often without electricity or toilet facilities.[90] Nor were all Chinese businessmen. In the nonagricultural sector of the Thai economy, approximately 70 percent of the workers were Chinese.[91] A nineteenth-century observer described Chinese vegetable gardeners in Bangkok as living "in small dirty huts within their premises, guarded by a multitude of dogs, and a horrible stench of pigsties."[92] Still, what struck many Thais was the prominence of the Chinese among the affluent members of the society. The historic role of the Chinese in the economic development of Thailand was often forgotten and their prosperity was attributed to some undefined "exploitation." Chinese money-lenders were often blamed for the poverty of the Thai peasant. In reality, money-lending was a highly competitive business, and Thai lenders offered no better terms than the Chinese.[93]

Sometimes resentments have been based on charges of sharp business practices by the Chinese. Such charges are difficult to assess in a country where buyer and seller alike engaged in widespread petty cheating that was mutually expected and—within limits—accepted.[94] Were the Chinese to engage in more cheating than local businessmen, or otherwise charge higher prices or offer inferior merchandise, local competition could undercut them and replace them. Yet, throughout Southeast Asia, Chinese businessmen were seldom matched by locals for price, credit terms, or conditions of sale. It was the Chinese who undercut—a fact lamented by those who also complained (inconsistently) of Chinese "exploitation" of the consumer.[95] Their low profit margins have made them formidable competitors for Europeans and Southeast Asians alike.[96]

During the Great Depression of the 1930s, the Thai government began a nationalistic policy designed to secure employment to Thai nationals. Since the overwhelming majority of foreigners in Thailand were Chinese, this was in effect a blow to them, though many Chinese were also Thai citizens. Taxi-driving was restricted to Thai nationals. Remittances to China were restricted.[97] Chinese schools were restricted in their curriculum, Chinese nationalistic propaganda banned, and some schools were closed for violations or evasions.[98] More anti-Chinese laws and edicts followed during World War II, especially after the Japanese took control of Thailand.

Despite decades of laws and policies designed to move Thais out of traditional agriculture and into the modern economy, and especially into commerce and industry, the Thais took relatively little advantage of the opportunities. A law in the mid-1930s required rice mills to employ at least 50 percent Thai workers but proved impossible to carry out, due to a lack of such labor.[99] In 1939, a new law authorized the government to require up to 75 percent Thai employees in both public and private enterprises, but a lack of qualified Thais prevented the government from implementing it, for fear of damage to the economy.[100] During World War II, a forced evacuation of Chinese from various parts of Thailand caused many Chinese businessmen to sell their businesses to Thais at a fraction of their value,[101] but this did not lead to a large Thai business class. Most of the better economic opportunities created by wartime restrictions on the Chinese were seized by Japanese businessmen, not Thais.[102] Even in postwar Thailand, Thai neighborhoods still had Chinese shops.[103]

The very attempts at preventing the development of Chinese separatism had the effect of fostering a heightened sense of ethnic identity in the beleaguered group,[104] and the economic advantages of the Chinese persisted as well. They continued to own from 80 to 90 percent of the rice mills—the largest enterprises in the country. Moreover, the Chinese dominated every phase of rice production except the actual farming. Chinese bought the rice, transported it, milled it, and did three-quarters of the exporting of rice from Thailand.[105] Even some of the government-owned enterprises, set up to reduce the role of the Chinese in the economy, ended up hiring Chinese managers.[106]

What the growing restrictions on the Chinese, and the growing preferences for Thais, accomplished was to make it necessary for the Chinese to bribe Thai officials, both directly and indirectly, to allow them to perform economic functions that only they could perform. High officials of the Thai government became directors and "partners" of Chinese businesses, lending their political influence to get the Chinese businesses through the growing maze of government regulations and preferential policies[107] ostensibly for the benefit of the Thai masses.

One of the ironies of the overseas Chinese is that this historically accomplished capitalist group has also become prominent on the political left, including the Communist movement. The Chinese greatly outnumbered the Thais in the Communist movement in Thailand.[108] The overseas Chinese also constituted a majority of the Communist movements in Malaysia.[109] A similar pattern of over-representation on the political left has also been observed among another historically capitalistic middleman minority, the Jews. This does not mean that most overseas Chinese (or Jews) have been Communist, or even part of the political left. It does mean that, among those on the political left in those countries, this consummately capitalist group has supplied more than its share.

Malaysia

While Thailand has the largest number of overseas Chinese of any nation in Southeast Asia—an estimated 6 million people—Malaysia has the highest *proportion* of overseas Chinese in its population, 29 percent.[110] Socially, the Chinese have been more clearly separated from the majority population in Malaysia than in Thailand, for the great majority of Malays are Moslems, for whom intermarriage with non-Moslems is out of the question, and such features of the Chinese culture as fondness for pork and gambling tend to limit social interactions in general. There have been few interracial neighborhoods in Malaysia, as well as little intermarriage,[111] even when there was a substantial surplus of males in both the Chinese and Indian minorities.[112]

The British colony of Malaya received its independence in 1957 as the Federation of Malaya. With the addition of Singapore and parts of the island of Borneo in 1963, it became Malaysia. Two years later, Singapore became a separate and independent city-state.

Like the Thais, the Malays were not a people ground into poverty by lack of land or resources. On the contrary, abundant land and ample rainfall made it possible for the Malay peasant to live all year on one crop, produced in a few months, even though the land was quite capable of producing two crops a year, if necessary. This left leisure for the development of a relaxed life-style, as seen by some, or laziness as seen by others.[113] Malaya was also richly endowed with some of the most extensive deposits of tin ore in the world, as well as rich petroleum deposits and other minerals. The climate and soil were also suitable for growing rubber trees, eventually making Malaya the world's leading producer of rubber. But the development of all these resources was largely the work of foreigners, not Malays. Those Malays with wealth usually did not choose to invest it in such enterprises and, among less affluent Malays, relatively few were willing to work on rubber plantations or in tin mines, when they had the option of a less arduous life on their own land.[114]

Capital for the development of Malaya's resources was largely supplied by Western nations, while the labor needed came largely from China, India, and Ceylon. These workers were typically illiterate and very poor people, from nations where making a living was much harder than for the Malays, and where the dangers of hunger and starvation had created habits of thrift, as well as hard work. Where some Malays did work alongside the Chinese on rubber plantations, both performing identical unskilled labor, the output per worker was more than twice as high among the Chinese as among the Malays.[115] Unlike the Chinese and the Indians, Malays were also notorious for free spending and for going into debt for the sake of social celebrations.[116]

The numbers of Chinese in the region that was eventually consolidated into Malaysia were quite small before the era of European colonialism. However, as early as 1794, a British report on the Penang settlement described the Chinese as "the most valuable part of our inhabitants," possessing a variety of artisan skills, as well as being shopkeepers, planters, and boatmen. The Chinese were also described as "indefatigable" in the pursuit of money.[117]

Under British rule, there was substantial Chinese immigration, into the whole region, many fleeing a breakdown of law and order in China during and after the Taiping Rebellion in the middle of the nineteenth century.[118] In the Malay states (not counting Singapore, Penang or Malacca), the Chinese population rose from an estimated 100,000 in 1881 to more than a million just 50 years later.[119] By 1941, the Chinese actually outnumbered the Malays in British Malaya.[120]

These Chinese played a major role in the economic development of the country. At the turn of the century, Malaya produced one-half the tin in the world[121] and Chinese miners helped develop this industry.[122] By 1931, there were nearly 79,000 Chinese miners and more than 160,000 Chinese growing rubber.[123] Over the years, they spread out into other occupations. Beginning at the very bottom, in occupations rejected by most Malays, the Chinese rose economically, many using their savings to open tiny businesses, some of which grew into more substantial enterprises. Whereas more than half of all Chinese in Malaya in 1911 were either agricultural laborers or mining laborers, just twenty years later only 11 percent of the Chinese were in these two occupations.[124] The Chinese came ultimately to own 85 percent of all retail outlets in the country.[125]

Although a vital part of the economy and a substantial portion of the population—about one-third by 1931[126]—the Chinese remained in separate enclaves, speaking their own languages, establishing their own community institutions, and having little interest in Malay culture or social life, which they looked down upon.[127] Their social, cultural, and political orientations were all toward China. But along with these sojourning Chinese, looking to return to China after achieving some financial success in Malaya, there also developed a native-born community of Chinese with local roots, the so-called "Straits Chinese."[128]

As in Thailand, much of the commercial and industrial competition faced by the Chinese in Malaya came from foreigners, rather than from the indigenous population. Indian laborers came to predominate on the rubber plantations and Indian businessmen were significant in the Malay economy.[129] European capital and technology competed with the Chinese in tin-mining, and eventually became predominant. As of 1920, the Chinese-owned mines produced nearly two-thirds of the tin in Malaya, but by 1938 the European mines produced two-thirds.[130] The Malays themselves played a negligible role as investors, owners, or managers. As of 1931, non-Malays owned 99 percent of the rubber holdings in Malaya—the Europeans and Americans owning 84 percent, the Chinese 13 percent, and the Indians 2 percent.[131] Even as workers, the Malays were seldom involved in this major industry of the Malayan economy.[132]

The British colonial government gave various legal preferences to the Malays, such as providing free schooling to Malay children but not Chinese children[133] and preferentially hiring Malays for the civil service.[134] But the initially illiterate Chinese began to establish private schools for their children to be educated.[135] Moreover, the Malays, even at the university level, tended to be educated in subjects that prepared them only to be clerks, while the Chinese university students specialized in medicine, science, and technical fields.[136] Nevertheless, in education as in the economy, the relative success of the Chinese should not obscure the reality that many Chinese were far less fortunate than those whose striking success generated envy and resentment among the Malays. As late as 1950, less than half the Chinese children of school age received even primary schooling, and less than one-third the total Chinese population of the country was literate.[137]

World War II and its aftermath tended to alienate Malays and Chinese from one another. Ten days after Japan bombed Pearl Harbor, crippling the American Pacific Fleet and gaining naval superiority throughout the Far East—Japanese troops invaded Penang. Two months later Singapore surrendered and the long nightmare of Japanese occupation began for the Chinese in Malaya. Chinese who had contributed money or other support to China in its resistance to the Japanese invaders, or to the defense of Malaya, were cited by informers and executed by the Japanese. So were many other categories of Chinese considered potentially bothersome by the occupation authorities. The massacres lasted for days. Altogether, about 5,000 Chinese were killed.[138] Meanwhile, many Malays collaborated with the Japanese during the war, creating a bitterness between Chinese and Malays that lasted into the postwar era.

Although the British had long before established political machinery for moving Malaya toward independence, the divisiveness in postwar Malaya made this more difficult. Economic differences compounded political differences, and the demographic makeup of the population further complicated matters. The average Chinese male earned more than double the income of the average Malay male.[139] In Malaya as it was constituted in 1948, the population was divided—truly divided—into 45 percent Chinese, 43 percent Malay, and 10 percent Indian.[140] Moreover, the anti-Japanese guerrilla movement from World War II—virtually all Chinese—turned into a Communist-led guerrilla movement, trying to take over the country.

In hopes of reconciling the three major ethnic groups enough to permit a viable nation after independence, the principal political parties representing each group formed a coalition called the Alliance Party. In this alliance, the Malayan Chinese Association and the Malayan Indian Congress were subordinated to the Malays' political representative, the United Malays National Organization. The compromise by which they hoped to avert intergroup strife and carnage after independence involved political priority for the Malays as an offset to the economic predominance of the Chinese. Rural and urban votes were weighted in such a way as to guarantee Malay predominance, since the Chinese were largely urban and the Malays largely rural. Moreover, the constitution provided that the head of state had to be a Malay, that the state religion was Islam, and that Malay was the national language. In the social and economic sphere, the constitution established preferential treatment of the Malays in government employment, university scholarships, and in the issuance of business permits and licenses. In exchange, non-Malays received somewhat more liberalized citizenship qualifications and—crucial to the Chinese and the Indians—freedom to continue engaging in business, with relatively little government interference.[141]

This compromise was by no means universally accepted. It was in fact attacked politically by both Chinese and Malay parties outside the Alliance. Some dissident Chinese criticized the plan for giving too much to the Malays, while dissident Malays demanded still more. Singapore's People's Action Party demanded a Malaysia without any ethnic privileges or restrictions, where all Malaysians would be equal under the law. This principle was seen by the ruling Alliance Party as a threat to the basic compromise on which hopes of a peaceful transition to independence were based. Moreover, the People's Action Party's wily leader, Lee Kwan Yew, was seen as a potential mobilizer of the Chinese throughout the country, who outnumbered the Malays with Singapore (his political base) included in Malaysia. In 1965, Singapore was separated from Malaysia to forestall this. It was one of the rare—if not unique—examples of a nation voluntarily divesting itself of territory and people—in this case, the largest port in Asia. The removal of predominantly Chinese Singapore now made the Malays a numerical as well as political majority in Malaysia.

Economically, however, the Chinese remained dominant, but against a background of growing demands that more be done for the Malays. The Chinese were often seen as not merely more fortunate but as "exploiting" the Malay peasantry. Despite attempts to depict the Malay peasant as virtually in bondage to the Chinese middleman or moneylender, only about half the farmers in Malaysia in the 1950s and 1960s were in debt, and most debts were repaid within the year. A similar pattern has been found in Thailand and Laos.[142] But political rhetoric overwhelmed facts.

Although the Alliance Party was re-elected in 1969, it lost both Malay and Chinese voters to more militant parties from each community. More important, massive race riots broke out in the capital city, Kuala Lumpur. Hundreds of Chinese were killed, amid widespread burning and looting of Chinese businesses. These riots marked a watershed in Malaysia's political history.

The original political compromise was readjusted to give wider and more sweeping preferences to Malays, now extending into the private sector and including new government credit sources designed to end the presumed dependence of the Malay peasant on the Chinese middleman. More fundamentally, the government committed itself to a long-range effort to "eliminate the identification of race with economic function"[143]—that is, to produce statistical parity of representation of Malays throughout the economy. The Malay *bumiputras* or "sons of the soil" were to have an institutionalized "special position" in the Malaysian economy and society.

The actual consequences of these policies have been considerably less dramatic than the political rhetoric. Overall, Chinese income remained approximately double that of the Malays, with minor variations from survey to survey, as in the past.[144] However, for particular sectors and classes, there were striking changes, though not usually to the benefit of the Malay masses, in whose names the preferential policies existed. The proportion of all the poor households in peninsula Malaysia that were Malay households actually increased slightly.[145] At the other end of the economic scale, however, the more fortunate Malays advanced still further. Government-run enterprises provided managerial positions for members of the Malay elite, including royalty.[146] Malays with political connections served on boards of directors of large corporations, though still outnumbered by Chinese directors, who usually came from a business background. Both were still outnumbered by foreign directors.[147]

There has been a growing Malay share in the stock of businesses in Malaysia, but these shares have usually been held by the government in the name of the Malay people, rather than by individual Malay stockholders.[148] These industries have usually been unprofitable in direct proportion to the percentage of government ownership.[149] Malay private businesses likewise made little headway in competition with the Chinese, for even Malay customers often preferred doing business with non-Malay firms.[150] Chinese businesses seeking to circumvent government restrictions have operated behind Malay "front" men so widely as to give rise to the popular expression "Ali-Baba" enterprises, where Ali is a Malay and Baba is Chinese. In one study of a local Malaysian trucking industry, 102 out of the 105 people owning and managing trucking firms were Chinese, and so were most of their employees, even though trucking was one of the licensed businesses in which Malays received preferential privileges.[151]

The most successful displacement of the Chinese was in areas totally controlled by government, notably government employment and university admissions. More than 90 percent of all new government jobs created in 1979–80 went to Malays. Whereas Malays were only 40 percent of the university students in the country in 1970, after a decade of stronger preferences they were 67 percent. The number of Chinese students in the country's universities declined absolutely during the decade of the 1970s, even though total university enrollment more than doubled. One consequence was that nearly 30,000 Malaysian students went abroad to study—three-quarters of them non-Malays.[152] Chinese capital also began to flow out of Malaysia, along with Chinese professionals.[153]

Even in the late twentieth century, there were many Chinese families among the urban poor of Malaysia, including many squatters in the capital city of Kuala Lumpur. There was also a rising rate of unemployment among young urban Chinese who entered a job market that legally discriminated against them in the land of their birth. But what was politically salient was that the Chinese remained disproportionately represented among the economic leaders of the country, and that the Malays saw this as a "problem" to be "solved."

Singapore

In less than two centuries, Singapore has gone from an almost uninhabited tropical island on the tip of the Malay peninsula to the fourth-largest port in the world. It is also the anomaly of a city-state created in the twentieth century, a status it has maintained since its separation from Malaysia in 1965. Aside from its harbor, Singapore has virtually no natural resources and has even had to import water, piped in from Malaysia. Yet it achieved an average income approximately double that of Malaysia and one of the highest standards of living in Asia.

Sir Thomas Stamford Raffles founded the British colony of Singapore in 1819. At that time the only inhabitants were 120 Malays and 30 Chinese. Under British rule the population grew rapidly, approaching 5,000 by 1821 and surpassing 10,000 just two years later. As elsewhere, the colonial authorities considered the Chinese as the most valuable part of the local population "beyond doubt," even though people from different provinces of China had to be kept separated from one another in the interest of tranquility.[154] Over the years, the Chinese population of Singapore rose both absolutely and relative to the total population. From a minority in the 1820s, the Chinese rose to become about half of the population of Singapore by 1840, three-fifths by 1881, and three-quarters by 1931.[155]

The Chinese immigration to Singapore showed the familiar pattern of young men from southern China coming as sojourners in hopes of returning home with money for a better life. Between the sex imbalance and tropical diseases, there was no natural increase of the resident Chinese population until the 1920s. By then, there were enough women and permanently settled men to create a Singapore-born population of Chinese, in addition to the immigrant population. By 1931 there were half as many Chinese women as men in Singapore and by 1947 just over half the population was native-born.[156]

Located centrally with respect to the other great ports of Asia, Singapore became a leading entrepôt port and a strategic link in British military power during the heyday of the empire. The fall of Singapore to the Japanese during World War II was a blow to British power throughout the region and ultimately to European colonialism in general. The Japanese occupation was also a bitter experience for the people of Singapore. Thousands were rounded up as suspected supporters of China in its war with Japan, and some were shot.[157]

In the postwar world, as independence approached for Singapore and Malaya, Western-educated Lee Kwan Yew and his People's Action Party attempted to promote the idea of "equal citizenship rights for peoples of all races" in newly formed Malaysia. Although this idea was rejected in Malaysia, Singapore's separation presented an opportunity for this approach to be tried in that independent and multiracial city-state.

The population of Singapore, when it began as an independent state in 1963, was 1.8 million people, including a Chinese majority (1.4 million) and sizable minorities of Malays (257,000), Indians (132,000), and others (36,500).[158] Intergroup frictions and animosities existed in Singapore as in Malaysia, and violence was by no means absent from Singapore's history. The various Chinese groups in the city had many bloody battles among themselves in the nineteenth century, with hundreds left dead,[159] and Moslem riots against Europeans erupted as recently as 1950. Politically inspired riots also rocked Singapore in

1955, requiring more than 10,000 soldiers and policemen to restore order.[160] Against this background, the challenge was to create a viable society out of these disparate and volatile elements, living in the shadow of a much larger Malaysia, equally volatile and with conflicting racial policies—a Malaysia whose ability to cut off the water supply alone meant that policies and events in Singapore could not be allowed to provoke the Malay government.

De-emphasis of race and ethnicity, promotion of Singaporean patriotism, equality before the law, and acceptance of cultural differences became the cornerstones of Singapore's efforts at nation-building. Four different languages were officially recognized, to accommodate the disparate groups. Among the Chinese, public policy promoted the speaking of Mandarin—a foreign language to the various southern Chinese groups, but a way of eroding the dialect-group separatism which has historically plagued the Chinese in countries around the world. Urban redevelopment and public housing policies tended to break up some ethnic enclaves and, together with racially integrated military and police forces, eroded some of the group insularity that existed. While the government did not impose a single language in the school system, and in fact required bilingualism, over the years an increasing proportion of students chose English as their second language. By 1975, nearly 70 percent of Singapore students were studying English, providing a *lingua franca* across ethnic lines, though each group spoke its own language at home.[161] At the same time, among the adults, one-fourth of the population had no schooling at all, 43 percent had completed only six grades, and only one percent had college degrees.[162] These data were a reminder of the grim past from which the prosperous and educated Singapore of recent years has arisen.

By 1983, English was overwhelmingly the language of instruction in the public schools, from primary grades through junior college. More than 400,000 students were being taught in English, compared to fewer than 40,000 in Chinese, fewer than 500 in Malay, and fewer than 50 in Tamil.[163] In short, most members of all three major ethnic groups were being educated in English.

Despite legal equality and official de-emphasis of racial and ethnic differences, the various groups in Singapore remained largely separate socially and different economically. Less than 5 percent of the non-

Moslem marriages in Singapore were intermarriages. Among these rare intermarriages, the most common was between Chinese and Europeans, with the wife being Chinese in nearly nine-tenths of these marriages. Moslem marriages were fewer but more diverse. Almost four-fifths of all Moslem marriages in Singapore were between the Malays, another 5 percent between the Indians, and 16 percent were intermarriages—usually between Malays and Indians. Less than 3 percent of all Moslem marriages were between Chinese and Malays, and less than 1 percent of all non-Moslem marriages were between Chinese and Malays.[164] Thus members of the two largest groups in Singapore were the least likely to marry each other.

Economic differences among the three ethnic groups also remain substantial. As of 1980, the Chinese earned 43 percent higher incomes than Malays. However, this was less of a differential than in Malaysia. Indians in Singapore earned incomes substantially the same as the Chinese, whereas they earned much less in Malaysia. However, Singapore Indians have historically been educated professional people to a much greater extent than the Indians in Malaysia, where about half still worked as plantation laborers. That the Malays should be doing better, relative to the Chinese, in Singapore than in their own country is especially striking in view of the sweeping preferential treatment of *bumiputras* in Malaysia.

Indonesia

The mass immigration of Chinese to what is now Indonesia began when it was a string of islands called the Dutch East Indies. These islands, including Java and Sumatra, separate the Pacific Ocean from the Indian Ocean at the Equator. Chinese traders visited Java at least as far back as the ninth century,[165] but large-scale immigration began only after the Dutch took over in the seventeenth century. Although there were fewer than five hundred Chinese in the city of Batavia in 1619, while the Dutch were consolidating their rule, by 1733 there were 80,000 Chinese in the same city.[166] As early as the mid-seventeenth century, the Chinese predominated among the artisans there. They also established the first sugar cane industry in Java, where the natives had used more primitive means of producing sugar. Under the Chinese, sugar production rose to many times its previous level and prices fell.[167] As money-lenders, the Chinese undercut their Japanese competitors by charging lower interest with less security. All in all, the Chinese were businessmen in both petty and large-scale enterprises, and many prospered visibly—to the visible resentment of both the Dutch and the indigenous people of the islands.

The Dutch authorities' attempts to control the movements and activities of the Chinese population, which included an important criminal element, led to many arbitrary edicts, harassment, and extortion. This led, in 1740, to a revolt among the Chinese—and to their slaughter by the thousands.[168] Nevertheless, despite many vicissitudes, the Chinese gained control of most domestic and foreign commerce in Java by the beginning of the nineteenth century.[169] However, this total dominance of the private economy was not destined to last. After about 1870 an inflow of European capital established large agricultural and industrial enterprises that eclipsed the smaller, family-run businesses of the Chinese. These large-scale undertakings, whether plantation agriculture, wholesaling, banking, or industrial enterprises, tended to be in the hands of the Europeans or of a new group, the Japanese. By 1921, the Dutch held 73 percent of all investments in plantations, wholesale trade, transport, and banking, while the Chinese held only 11 percent.[170] The Chinese continued prominent in small business, where most continued to work,[171] and they continued to be more prosperous than the Indonesians, though not nearly as prosperous as the Europeans.[172]

By 1930, there were more than a million Chinese in the Dutch East Indies, more than two-thirds of whom had been born there. Half a million Chinese had fathers who were also native-born, so the Chinese population had local roots, even though it was socially distinct. The Chinese were also internally differentiated, with groups whose origins were in different parts of China being concentrated in different parts of the Dutch East Indies, working in different occupations, and varying in their respective proportions of native-born and foreign-born, as well as in male-female ratios.[173]

Earlier immigrants, predominantly male, married local women and tended to assimilate culturally, speaking the local vernacular rather than Chinese, eating local foods, wearing local clothing, and observing local customs. These immigrants and their descendants became known as *peranakans* ("mixed bloods") but the connotations extended beyond the biological to a whole way of life and set of values. When substantial numbers of Chinese women began arriving in the islands in the 1920s, a new kind of Chinese community came into being—the *totoks* ("pure bloods"), who lived in a Chinese world, linguistically and culturally, and separate from the social worlds of either the Indonesians or the *peranakans.*[174]

The split between the *peranakans* and the *totoks* has been an enduring one, but the passing years have changed the relative proportions of the two groups. As of 1920, 70 percent of the Chinese population were *peranakans,* but by 1950, this had dropped to approximately 60 percent.[175] Although these two groups were initially defined in terms of racially mixed versus racially unmixed ancestry, over the years the terms have come to be used in social and cultural senses, rather than in strictly racial, citizenship, or generational senses. During the interwar period, a leading Chinese newspaper in the East Indies was published in the Malay language for the *peranakans* and in Chinese for the *totoks*—and with differing proportions of news items relating to the Indies and to China.[176] *Peranakans* and *totoks* also had different political organizations with conflicting goals.[177]

To the indigenous Indonesians, however, both were Chinese and neither were welcome as full-fledged members of the Indonesian nationalist movement trying to secure independence from Dutch rule.[178] Indonesian nationalists tended to be defined in racial terms. Moreover, many Chinese were well aware of the envy and hostility of the Indonesians, and some Chinese openly preferred the continuance of Dutch rule, though others were sympathetic to Indonesian nationalism, while still others saw no reason to take sides and many dangers in doing so.

Economic differences between the Chinese and the Indonesians were very large. In 1939, there were more Chinese than Indonesians in the top income bracket in absolute numbers, even though the Chinese were a small minority in the population. Most Chinese were in the middle income bracket, while more than four-fifths of the Europeans were in the top bracket. But with more than two-thirds of the Indonesians in the bottom bracket, the Chinese looked rich.[179] Moreover, they were a safer target to attack, both politically and in terms of violence.[180] As elsewhere in Southeast Asia, the presence of the colonial power protected the Chinese to some extent, but the early World War II victories of the Japanese jeopardized them. When it became clear, after the Japanese invasion, that there was no longer anyone to protect the Chinese, first criminals and then the general population in Java began to rob, murder, and rape in the Chinese community.[181] As in Thailand and Malaysia, the Chinese were generally pro-Western during the war, while the native peoples were generally pro-Japanese,[182] though there were also some Chinese collaborators and some Indonesians who did not collaborate.[183]

Neither the Japanese during the war nor the Indonesians after the war paid much attention to the distinction between *totok* and *peranakan* Chinese.[184] In the confusion following the surrender of Japan, when Indonesian nationalists proclaimed independence while the Dutch returned to re-establish colonial rule, the Chinese attempted to be neutral but were in various places assaulted by Indonesians. In 1946, some of the most assimilated Chinese, who had lived peacefully with the Indonesians for years, were slaughtered by the hundreds in the suburbs of Tangerang. More massacres followed in other places. Altogether an estimated 1,000 Chinese were killed and 100,000 made homeless.[185] More died in the military conflicts between Indonesian and Dutch military forces, particularly at the hands of Indonesian guerrillas.[186] Nor were the Chinese population's troubles over when peace returned as an independent Indonesia was declared in 1949.

There were more than 2 million Chinese in newly independent Indonesia, nearly three-quarters of whom were born there.[187] Yet that did not automatically make them citizens. As late as the mid-1960s, less than half the Chinese in Indonesia were citizens.[188] Partly this reflected the complexities of international relations involving Communist China, the Chinese Nationalist government on Taiwan, and Indonesia, for China had long claimed overseas Chinese as its own citizens and new treaties were required to remove ambiguities on this point. More fundamentally, however, the problem was a reluctance of Indonesians to grant automatic citizenship to the Chinese born on their soil—and the reluctance of some Chinese to seek a citizenship which would not mean equal treatment in Indonesia, but only a cutting off of ties with China. Informed estimates of the Chinese who rejected

Indonesian citizenship ranged from 10 percent in Semarang to 25 percent in Jakarta.[189]

The fears of the Chinese that they would receive only second-class citizenship were amply confirmed by a series of laws distinguishing "indigenous" Indonesians from citizens of "foreign" ancestry or citizens with dual citizenship. For example, import licenses, government credit, and other privileges were reserved for "national" importers—in practice, indigenous Indonesians, as distinguished from citizens of nonindigenous origin, such as the Chinese.[190] "Alien" Chinese, who included people born in Indonesia but not Indonesian citizens, were even more discriminated against. They were banned from operating retail businesses in small towns or villages, or owning rice mills.[191] People with both Indonesian citizenship and other citizenship were banned from another range of economic activities—a blow at those Chinese whose status remained unclear as China and Indonesia negotiated a citizenship treaty. Accompanying these and many other economic constraints on the Chinese were numerous restrictions on the publication of Chinese-language newspapers and magazines, or the operation of private Chinese schools.[192]

Reactions among the Chinese were varied. More than 100,000 simply left Indonesia in 1960 and much Chinese-owned capital also flowed out of the country.[193] Others operated businesses behind Indonesian "front" men who officially held the required licenses. This became such a widespread and widely known phenomenon that such businesses were known (as in Malaysia) as "Ali-Baba" enterprises—Ali being the Indonesian "front" and Baba the Chinese actually owning and operating the business. Yet another strategy was for Chinese businessmen to contribute to influential or powerful government officials, to get the rules bent, suspended, or ignored, or even to receive government contracts and favors.[194] In a variety of ways, the Chinese accommodated themselves to what Indonesian President Sukarno called The New Order and Sukarno in turn began to moderate the anti-Chinese policies in Indonesia, while seeking closer international ties with China. The government was also aware that the full implementation of its proclaimed intention to "indigenize" business ownership would damage an economy already suffering from many problems. However, the failure to do so, and the continuing prosperity of many

Chinese, created public discontent, often manipulated by enemies of the regime, leading increasingly in 1963 to outbreaks of anti-Chinese violence in various parts of the country.

Most politically active Chinese came eventually to support Sukarno's left-wing, pro-China government—and suffered greatly in the violent backlash in 1965 that brought to power a conservative military government headed by General Suharto. Anti-Chinese violence erupted sporadically and demands for stronger anti-Chinese policies were almost constant, during the first two years after the military accession to power. However, by the end of 1967, both the political and the violent phases of anti-Chinese activity were in retreat. While making token concessions to the more extreme anti-Chinese elements, notably Moslem business rivals and Indonesian university students, the Suharto government held fast against demands that would have crippled the economy by forcing Chinese businessmen to abandon economic activities for which there were not enough indigenous substitutes.[195]

Some previously nationalized Chinese enterprises were returned to their owners after 1967.[196] As elsewhere in Southeast Asia, Chinese businessmen in Indonesia attempted to buy security by various forms of payoffs to Indonesian officials, ranging from common soldiers to the highest levels of government. This was a continuation of a long-standing pattern, antedating the Suharto government.[197] The price of peace for the Chinese went beyond money. They had to accept the government's banning of most of their cultural, social, and political organizations,[198] as part of a general policy of pressure toward assimilation—one of the remarkable features of which was the mass changing of Chinese names to Indonesian names individually and "voluntarily," but under pressure.[199] Despite such attempts at accommodation, riots against the Chinese continued to break out sporadically during the 1970s and 1980s.[200] The Chinese in Indonesia have long been considered the most assimilated Chinese community in Southeast Asia[201] but this has not prevented them from being also the most repeatedly and violently attacked. A large community in absolute numbers—4 million people in the late twentieth century—the Chinese in Indonesia were less than 3 percent of the country's population, while the 4.3 million Chinese in neighboring Malaysia constituted 29 percent of that country's total population.[202] Neither assimilation nor inconspicuous size has spared the Chinese the dire consequences of envy, resentment, and the politicization of race.

The Philippines

The Chinese population of the Philippines has historically been one of the smallest in any Southeast Asian nation, both absolutely and relative to the general population. In the middle of the twentieth century, the Chinese population of the Philippines was estimated at less than a quarter of a million people—about one-twelfth that of the Chinese population in Thailand, and only 1 percent of the total Philippine population.[203] By the late twentieth century, there were an estimated 700,000 Chinese in the Philippines, not quite one and a half percent of the total population.[204] The extreme smallness of the Chinese minority in the Philippines makes their historic role in the development of the Philippine economy all the more remarkable.

European colonialism and large-scale immigration of Chinese both came to the Philippines somewhat earlier than in some other parts of the Far East. There were Chinese already living in the Philippines before the arrival of the Spaniards in the sixteenth century and there were many more when Spanish rule came to an end four centuries later. However, there were highly variable estimates of how many Chinese lived in the Philippines at many points in between.[205] There were enough, however, for several thousand Chinese to be killed by the Spaniards on each of three occasions when revolts were drowned in blood during the seventeenth century.[206] In addition to the resident Chinese, there were traders from China who came and went, supplying a variety of commodities. The Chinese were also the principal laborers and artisans in the country, and built many churches, forts, and convents that remained standing as late as the Second World War.[207] The Chinese were also bakers, porters, tailors, shoemakers, locksmiths, weavers, and worked in other trades. Moreover, they produced goods at low prices.[208] The economic success of the Chinese aroused not only the usual envy and resentment but also, in this age of mercantilism, fears that gold was being drained away to China.[209]

In the Philippines, as elsewhere in Southeast Asia during the colonial era, the Chinese were often sojourners rather than settlers. They came to earn money with which to return to China—whether or not they actually achieved their goals, and regardless of whether the goal itself changed over the years. Many left families behind, to whom they returned, but some brought their families over to join them in the Philippines. During the late nineteenth century, from 10,000 to 12,000 Chinese arrived in Manila annually, and 7,000 to 8,000 departed for China. The resident Chinese population in the Philippines grew to about 40,000 by the end of the Spanish colonial period, just over half concentrated in Manila. Most of the Chinese of this era were uneducated males, but the Chinese dominated both wholesale and retail trade.[210] Chinese domination of skilled occupations lasted for centuries. Even as late as the early twentieth century, American businessmen in the Philippines were pressing for allowing immigration from China, because of insufficient skilled labor among the Filipinos.[211]

Because the Chinese were prominent in skilled and entrepreneurial roles did not mean that most Chinese worked in such occupations. Many were coolies doing simple arduous labor. However, the change to American rule in the Philippines after the Spanish-American War meant that American restrictions on Chinese coolie immigration now applied. Thereafter, the Chinese who came to the Philippines tended to be tradesmen. Here, as elsewhere in the world, the Chinese shopkeeper became known for his hard work, long hours, and frugality. The Chinese community—or rather communities, split along lines deriving from their places of origin in China—was also noted for supplying credit and other aid to newcomers from the homeland.[212]

During the period of American colonial rule in the Philippines, Chinese investments grew to become second only to U.S. investments. The Chinese also conducted about three-quarters of all retail trade and owned about three-quarters of all the rice mills in the Philippines.[213] However, this did not mean that affluence was common among the Chinese in the Philippines. The average Chinese shop was described as a "miserable" little shack, smelly, and containing a small inventory.[214] Nevertheless, it was enough to inspire envy among Filipinos who had less, and who were often in debt to the Chinese storekeeper or other middleman. After the Philippines became an autonomous commonwealth in 1935, it began to pass discriminatory legislation restricting the economic activities of the Chinese and creating government-subsidized Filipino competition.[215] By 1939, according to Philippine President Manuel Quezon, the Filipino share of retail trade had risen from its previous 15–20 percent to 37 percent. Quezon tried to moderate anti-Chinese feeling in the Philippines by pointing out that the Chinese "have helped in the development of our country when our own people were not engaging in business enterprises."[216]

There were fewer barriers to intermarriage between the Filipinos and Chinese, under the Catholic religion and Spanish rule, than to intermarriage in Moslem Malaysia, for example. Moreover, these Chinese-Filipino *mestizos* were more readily merged with the general Filipino population than were the mixed populations of Malaysia or Indonesia.[217] The *mestizos* of the Philippines have been characterized as "one of the most capable, prosperous and powerful elements of the Filipino people." Even after a massive increase of immigration from China under American colonial rule, the *mestizos* still greatly outnumbered the ethnically Chinese. By the 1940s there were about three-quarters of a million *mestizos*. Some of those who entered politics were among the most strongly anti-Chinese elements in the Philippines.[218]

The Chinese community in the Philippines evolved socially as well as economically. With the passing years, more and more Chinese women immigrated into the Philippines, reducing the vast sex imbalance, and creating a purely Chinese generation of substantial size for the first time. While there were still five Chinese men for every Chinese woman in the Philippines as late as 1933, this was less than half the ratio just 15 years earlier, and the ratio continued declining over the years. The second-generation Chinese were raised in a Chinese culture. By 1935 there were 58 Chinese schools in the Philippines, enrolling more than 7,000 students. Nevertheless, this second generation also acquired Filipino culture and, unlike their parents, had never seen China and were unlikely to be able to visit it as war raged there for more than a decade.[219] Moreover, after the Philippines gained complete independence in 1946, a renewed series of laws discriminating against aliens prompted many second-generation Chinese to seek Filipino citizenship, despite the costs and difficulties of doing so.[220]

There were many influences tending to bring Filipinos and Chinese closer together, as well as other influences tending to pull them apart.

The fact that so many of the Chinese in the countryside lived surrounded by Filipinos meant that they—and especially their children—tended to acquire local languages, customs, and attitudes. The experiences of the two groups during World War II also tended to bring them closer together. Unlike the situation in other Southeast Asian nations, both the Filipinos and the Chinese opposed the Japanese invaders of the Philippines, both remained loyal to the Allied cause, and Filipinos often helped the Chinese hide out from the Japanese occupation authorities.[221] In the postwar era, the civil war in China prompted the Philippine government to suspend immigration from that country, to avoid being swamped by refugees. This had the side effect of making the Chinese population of the Philippines one that was increasingly Philippine-born and bred, without an influx of new Chinese to replace the older generation of China-born people as they died out. Moreover, intermarriage between Chinese and Filipinos continued. In the middle of the twentieth century, nearly one-fourth of all marriages of Chinese males were with Filipino women. In addition, common-law relationships were widespread, especially among lower-level merchants, many of whom operated behind the facade of the woman's Philippine citizenship (and ostensible ownership) to evade anti-alien laws and restrictions aimed at the Chinese. Marriages between Filipino males and Chinese females remained extremely rare, however.[222]

Social interactions in general between Chinese and Filipinos tended to be greater in the provinces, where the Chinese have been more thinly spread among the indigenous population, while in Manila the large Chinese community has been more self-sufficient in its social and cultural life. As of 1958, for example, there were 36 Chinese schools in and around Manila, with approximately 23,000 students.[223]

Through all the changes in the country, the Chinese remained a middleman minority. By the late twentieth century, more than four-fifths of all adult Chinese males in the Philippines owned and operated some kind of business. These were by no means all large or even prosperous businesses, and failure rates were high.[224] Nevertheless, the Chinese community was essentially a business community. With the severe restrictions imposed on immigration after World War II, and with the virtual severance of ties with China by the Philippine Chinese after the Communists took power in 1949, the Chinese community in the Philippines now had its roots locally, though its culture, and especially its economic patterns, remained distinctively Chinese. The more successful found it expedient to establish relationships with Filipinos in high places, for political protection from discriminatory laws and policies.[225]

Indochina

Chinese influence in the Indochina region goes back to the ancient Han dynasty, which was contemporaneous with the Roman Empire. The relationships of China with this region were military, economic, and cultural. The Han dynasty established a military garrison in Hanoi, for example, and cultural artifacts from ancient China have been found not only in Indochina but also as far away as Borneo, Java, and Sumatra.[226] It was 939 A.D. before Vietnam freed itself from China and it remained independent, except for the epoch of Mongol rule, until it was again briefly part of the Chinese empire during the early Ming dynasty.[227] All in all, Vietnam was under Chinese rule for more than a thousand years.[228] Cambodia recognized Chinese suzerainty, in the T'ang dynasty of the seventh century.[229] China also traded extensively with the Indochina region, as it did with other parts of Asia and with Europe and the Western Hemisphere. At this juncture, China was an exporter of finished products and an importer of raw material.[230] New strains of rice imported from Vietnam during the Sung dynasty greatly improved rice production in China.[231] In later centuries, the Indochina region also became a refuge for the defeated Chinese supporters of fallen dynasties.[232]

Indochina derived its name from its geographical location between the great civilizations of India and of China, and its history has reflected the cultural influence of both. Chinese culture remained particularly influential, even after Chinese rule was thrown off or tribute paid to China discontinued. Chinese populations in the Indochina region long antedated French colonial rule. The indigenous peoples of Indochina were far from being homogeneous or harmonious among themselves, and their reactions to the Chinese also varied greatly. Hostility between the Cambodia's Khmer people and the Vietnamese, for example, goes back for centuries and has historically been greater than that between the Khmer and the Chinese.[233] While the Vietnamese massacred more than 10,000 Chinese in a community near Saigon in the eighteenth century,[234] Cambodia had no such history of anti-Chinese hostility as that in Vietnam, and in fact relations between the Khmer and the Chinese were generally amicable, with significant intermarriage.[235]

French colonial rule in Indochina began in the mid-nineteenth century and lasted until just after the middle of the twentieth century. Under the French, the Chinese population of the region grew rapidly, despite various efforts of the French authorities to restrict their immigration. By 1931, there were approximately 418,000 Chinese in Indochina.[236] Around the middle of the century, there were nearly this many Chinese in the Saigon-Cholon area alone,[237] more than 800,000 in South Vietnam altogether, as well as an estimated 50,000 to 60,000 in North Vietnam, 40,000 in Laos, and 218,000 in Cambodia.[238] These are all estimates and, in the absence of official census data, different estimates have varied considerably.[239] What has been consistent among the estimates is that (1) South Vietnam contained the largest concentration of Chinese, with Cambodia next, and (2) the Chinese in all these countries were less than 10 percent of the population.

This small Chinese minority played a disproportionately large role in the economies of Indochina. They owned approximately 70 percent of small-scale industry in Laos and conducted more than 70 percent of the retail trade in Vietnam and Cambodia.[240] In South Vietnam in 1974, the Chinese owned 60 percent of all capital invested in paper manufacturing and in fisheries, and 80 percent of all capital invested in the manufacturing of textiles, iron and steel, and chemical and allied products.[241] This reflected a long history of Chinese businessmen in Indochina being too much competition for both the indigenous businessmen and for the French.

The Annamites and Cambodians, for example, lacked the frugality and perseverance of the Chinese in business, and Annamite fishermen were neither as efficient nor as venturesome as Chinese fishermen, who fished on the open seas while the Annamites fished only the coastal waters. The French were unable or unwilling to live as cheaply as the Chinese, to accept as low a rate of profit, or to learn the local languages and cultures as a way of facilitating business transactions. Therefore the Chinese acted as middlemen, not only in the sense of being intermediaries in the economic chain of transactions, but also in the sense of being intermediaries between the French and indigenous races.[242] The Chinese also undersold the French businessmen selling to the French government during the colonial era.[243]

The effectiveness of the Chinese in extending credit to each other and to the local population depended upon extensive, firsthand knowledge of the individual recipients, rather than simply on such "objective" data as financial assets.[244] This meant, among other things, that the Chinese could generally lend to each other at lower rates of interest than to Vietnamese businessmen, and in turn the Chinese could sell with smaller profit margins and more liberal credit terms to customers than the Vietnamese businessmen could.[245] In Cambodia the Chinese dominated commercial gardening and truck farming around the country's urban centers, and dominated the cultivation of pepper from before the French came until the guerilla warfare of the postwar era made it too hazardous.[246] On the eve of World War II, the Chinese owned and operated 23 out of 27 large, mechanized rice-processing mills in the main coastal port cities, as well as being prominent in a wide range of commercial and industrial enterprises, ranging from distilleries to shipbuilding.[247]

Indochina escaped direct Japanese occupation during most of World War II because it was run by the Vichy regime in France, which was collaborating with Japan's ally, Nazi Germany. In the last year of the war and for decades into the postwar era, Indochina became a battleground where, at various times and places, troops of the Communist-led insurgents, the Chinese Nationalists (Kuomintang), the British, the French, and eventually the Americans, fought over the destiny of this strategically located country.[248] As French Indochina disappeared, Vietnam, Cambodia, and Laos went their separate ways as independent states. All discriminated against the Chinese with laws forbidding them to engage in many occupations.[249] When the Communists established control in these states during the 1970s, the Chinese were doubly hated as "capitalists" and doubly targeted for oppression. Of the one million refugees who fled Vietnam between 1975 and 1979, an estimated 70 percent were Chinese.[250] Many were "boat people" who often put themselves and their families on flimsy and leaking river craft and took the desperate gamble of setting sail on the high seas, where hundreds of thousands drowned. Many "boat people" were also victimized on the high seas by crews of other vessels who boarded their defenseless boats to rob, rape, and murder the hated Chinese.

After 1979, the exodus declined but did not stop. With the Communist takeover of Cambodia, renamed Kampuchea, a new wave of mass barbarities fostered a new wave of refugees, sometimes called "land people," who tried to escape across the land to Thailand. Many were killed on the way. Those who remained were caught in the greatest mass murders of the postwar era by Communist leader Pol Pot's Khmer Rouge troops. Half of Kampuchea's Chinese population of 400,000 were killed during the 1975–79 period.[251] They were only part of the millions slaughtered in the infamous "killing fields" of Kampuchea. China, which protested vehemently about Indonesia's mistreatment of its Chinese minority, made no such protests over what was happening in Kampuchea. Pol Pot was an ally.

THE WESTERN HEMISPHERE

The immigration of Chinese to the Western Hemisphere does not go back as many centuries as their immigration to Southeast Asia, nor has it involved as large numbers. Yet some aspects of the economic and social patterns of the overseas Chinese have reappeared, adapted to local circumstances. Significant Chinese immigration to the Western Hemisphere dates generally from the middle of the nineteenth century, though about two hundred were brought to Trinidad experimentally in 1806 by the British.[252]

That most Chinese immigrants to Southeast Asia should have come from China's southern provinces seems explainable by geographical proximity, but that the same should be true of Chinese immigrants to the Caribbean and the United States suggests that geography was hardly the only factor. Virtually all the Chinese immigrants to Cuba came from southern China, with 41 percent coming from the Toishan district alone,[253] which also supplied a majority of the Chinese immigrants to the United States prior to World War I.[254]

Internal distinctions among the Chinese have persisted in the Western Hemisphere, as in Southeast Asia. The Cantonese and the Hakkas, for example, have remained residentially and socially separate throughout the Caribbean region, despite the small size of the Chinese communities there. Moreover, their usual destinations have differed as well. The former have tended to re-emigrate from British Guiana to Suriname, the latter to Trinidad.[255] In the United States, the postwar "Hong Kong Chinese" immigrants remained socially and economically quite distinct from the Chinese whose forebears immigrated largely before World War I.[256]

Chinese communities of various sizes have been scattered throughout the Western Hemisphere, from Canada to Argentina. Chinese laborers helped build the Panama Canal and many remained to engage in retail trade, setting up grocery stores and dry goods stores, as well as restaurants and coffee shops. By the middle of the twentieth century, there were more than 5,000 Chinese in Brazil, including some who operated factories and engaged in the import and export trade. In Ecuador, the Chinese owned the largest rice mill in the country.[257] The Chinese in Canada have had a history very much like that of the Chinese in the United States, including both their oppressions and exclusions, on the one hand, and their eventual emergence as a prosperous and respected community on the other. One sign of changed times was a 1957 upset victory in a Canadian Parliamentary election by a Chinese candidate who defeated an incumbent minister.[258] In much of the Western Hemisphere, however, the Chinese went through many vicissitudes before achieving such general acceptance.

The Caribbean and South America

Perhaps the most tragic of all immigrations from China have been those of the "coolie trade" from the Portuguese-held port of Macao to the Western Hemisphere in the nineteenth century. These Chinese coolies, or immigrant laborers, have been described as "more slaves than immigrants,"[259] for many of these nominally free immigrants were in fact prisoners from the time that they were locked into holding compounds in Macao until they completed years of contract labor under brutal conditions in Cuba, Peru, or other destinations in Latin America. While some of these poor and often illiterate Chinese came voluntarily, others were gotten into the compounds by trickery, drugs, or force. Once inside, they had little chance of escape, though many were judged physically unfit and let go. But those retained for Macao's coolie trade faced years without freedom, during which they were subject to flogging and other punishments. Inside the Macao compounds, Chinese men could be seen "dripping with blood, the result of chastisements."[260] Legal formalities of contract were observed, but under conditions that made a mockery of the process.[261] Fortunately, not all Chinese immigrants to the Western Hemisphere embarked from Macao, nor were they all in the semi-slave condition of those who did.

Although the term "coolie" was applied to immigrant Chinese laborers in general,[262] not all came as indentured workers. Most Chinese who immigrated to the United States, for example, did not.[263] Moreover, as the horrors of the semi-slave trade became known in China and the West, various nations began to forbid their ships to engage in it. The British closed the port of Hong Kong to this trade, as China closed its ports and made the recruiters or kidnappers subject to beheading, while some were lynched by angry Chinese mobs.[264]

By 1859, only the Portuguese port of Macao on the south China coast continued to carry on this kind of coolie trade.[265] But through Macao hundreds of thousands of Chinese were shipped to the Western Hemisphere. In the quarter of a century beginning in 1849, approximately 90,000 Chinese were shipped from Macao to Peru,[266] and for the period 1847–1874 an estimated 125,000 were shipped to Cuba.[267] Most never saw China again,[268] and many did not live to complete their terms of indenture, though they were sent as young men in their prime. A majority of those sent to Cuba died before completing the eight years of their labor contracts.[269]

The high death rates were due to unhealthy living conditions, brutal working conditions, and suicides. The suicides began in the holding compounds in Macao, continued during the long voyage to the Americas, and after the Chinese were placed on plantations as laborers. In nineteenth-century Cuba, there were years when more than a hundred Chinese committed suicide.[270] In Peru, guards were posted to prevent suicide among the Chinese performing the grueling task of shovelling bird manure into sacks for export as fertilizer, under stifling heat and stench.[271]

The ships that carried the Chinese coolies from Macao to the Caribbean and South America were set up as floating prisons, with barred doors and cannon pointed at those doors. Packed in like sardines in filthy conditions, for a voyage that took four months to Peru, many Chinese died en route. For the period 1860–1870, more than 4,600 died out of a total of 43,000 shipped to the Peruvian port of Callao.[272] Earlier death rates were higher.[273] Among Cuban-bound vessels that landed in Havana from 1847 to 1859, there were more than 7,700 deaths among 50,000 coolies who embarked from China.[274] These mortality figures from the ports of arrival do not include deaths on ships that never reached their destinations, whether because of natural or man-made disasters. There were also many mutinies among the Chinese, and those that succeeded forced the ships to turn back to China, so the mortality figures do not include those who died in the bloody battles for control of those ships. The mortality rates to Cuba and Peru were not due merely to the general conditions of voyages at that time, for British ships carrying Chinese laborers from Canton and Hong Kong to British Guiana during the same era averaged far lower mortality rates.[275]

In Peru, more than 90 percent of the men worked on the huge plantations run by wealthy Peruvian landowners, some of whom would buy an entire shipload of coolies at a time. Here too, they were locked up and subjected to flogging, among other punishments. Their contracts gave them three days off *per year*—for Chinese New Year celebrations.[276] There were from time to time escapes and riots by the Chinese and, in 1870, a major uprising of more than a thousand coolies who went on a rampage, spreading beyond the plantations into nearby communities, committing rape and murder. In the end, the uprising was suppressed, with 150 deaths among the Chinese and 16 among the whites.[277] The whole system of importation of indentured coolies from Macao was ended in 1874. The life of the Chinese in Cuba was not very different, and the end of the coolie trade from Macao came the same year. The Cubans also flogged the Chinese, with this refinement:

> A current practice was that of obliging the victim to count the lashes himself. If in his agony he lost count, the result could be to his disadvantage.[278]

A contemporary Cuban journalist who observed the plantation

declared: "There is no pretense on the part of any one to regard them in any other light than as slaves."[279]

While Chinese in the Western Hemisphere in general were not treated in such a horrifying way as in Cuba and Peru, their lives were at best arduous throughout the Americas. Yet, by the end of the nineteenth century, the Chinese were starting their economic rise, from very lowly beginnings. As of 1899, there were more than 8,000 Chinese day laborers in Cuba and more than 2,700 servants, but also nearly 2,000 merchants. Many of these were itinerant peddlers or proprietors of small eating places. The Chinese had become predominant in the growing and selling of vegetables in Cuba, and owned many grocery stores.[280] In Peru, the descendants of the coolies came eventually to own more than half the grocery stores in the capital city of Lima.[281] Because there were no Chinese women sent to Peru, the men married Peruvian women when they could, producing offspring with a combination of Chinese, American Indian, and Caucasian ancestry.[282]

Although most immigrant groups tend to increase in population size over the generations, the Chinese population in the Western Hemisphere declined substantially in various countries. During the nineteenth century, 125,000 Chinese went to Cuba as contract laborers in one generation, but there were only 14,000 Chinese living there in the middle of the twentieth century.[283] In British Guiana, nearly 16,000 Chinese arrived over a period of 60 years but fewer than 3,000 remained as of 1911.[284] In the United States, the Chinese population exceeded 100,000 in 1890 but was down to about 60,000 by 1920.[285] Among the causes for the decline of the Chinese population, a massive sex imbalance was clearly of major importance, but was not necessarily decisive, for there was also a large sex imbalance among the Chinese population in Jamaica, which nevertheless grew more or less steadily over the years.[286] But a large sex imbalance in countries where marriage with the women of other races was rare had very different consequences than in Jamaica, where Chinese intermarriage was widespread. Decimation by death in the prime of life was another factor, especially in countries like Cuba or Peru, where brutal working and living conditions took a toll. Little of the declining Chinese population can be attributed to people returning to China, because this seldom happened,[287] largely due to the utter inability of most coolies to save enough money to finance a voyage back across the Pacific. For better or worse, the fate of the Chinese immigrants to the Western Hemisphere now lay in the Western Hemisphere.

While Cuba and Peru stand out for the special criminality and brutality with which they brought masses of Chinese to the Western Hemisphere, the principal occupation of the Chinese upon arrival was very much the same—agricultural laborers—whether in Cuba and Peru or in Jamaica, Trinidad, Suriname, British Guiana, or other countries in the Caribbean and South America. Yet, in later years, the Chinese have emerged as shopkeepers throughout the region.

So dominant did the Chinese become as retailers that grocery stores in the area were called generically "China Shops."[288] They also became prominent in other kinds of retailing. In Peru, Chinese merchants were noted for selling at cheaper prices.[289] In Chile, by 1914 there were 456 businesses owned by a Chinese population of only a few thousand people.[290] By 1943, nearly two-thirds of the Chinese working in British Guiana were in retailing.[291] The Chinese also became dominant in the retail trade in Jamaica, where they were less than one percent of the population.[292] The competition faced by the Chinese in retailing in the West Indies came principally from such other international middleman minorities as the East Indians, the Jews, and the Portuguese, rather than from West Indian Creoles. Even the elite among the Creole Jamaicans and Trinidadians tended to shun entrepreneurial activity in favor of the professions and politics.[293] As in other parts of the world, the Chinese tended to ignore local politics in the West Indies.[294]

By 1943, there were more than 12,000 Chinese in Jamaica, nearly half of whom were "colored" Chinese of mixed ancestry. By 1960 this had grown to nearly 22,000 Chinese, again nearly half being "colored" Chinese. With the passing years, the proportion of the Jamaica Chinese born in China declined from more than one-fifth in 1943 to less than one-tenth by 1960. The sex ratio had become virtually even by 1960, as compared to a five-to-one male predominance in 1911. As a proportion of the total population of Jamaica, the Chinese were just over 1 percent.[295] In Guyana, the Chinese are just under 1 percent.[296] There were about 3,000 Chinese in Suriname.[297] In Trinidad, the Chinese were also less than 1 percent of the population and numbered about 8,000.[298] Yet they have historically played a major role in the development of the distribution of goods at the retail level throughout the West Indies.[299]

As elsewhere, the Chinese in the Caribbean were highly urbanized. More than one-third of the Chinese in Trinidad lived in the capital city and principal seaport, Port-of-Spain.[300] Precisely because they were so small a portion of the population and politically uninvolved, the Chinese have been entrusted with mediating roles in Trinidad and Guyana,[301] where hostility between blacks and East Indians caused each group to distrust the other. The first president of Guyana was Chinese, as was the first governor-general of Trinidad.[302]

The same characteristics associated with the Chinese elsewhere were widely noted of them in the Caribbean—the central role of the family, frugality, social separateness (even when culturally assimilated), and a willingness to sacrifice the present for the future. Although the Chinese in the West Indies became largely Creoles in terms of external culture, their values and prosperity were distinctive. Not only were the Chinese more entrepreneurial; they were also better educated. In Jamaica and Trinidad, a higher proportion of the Chinese than of any of the other ethnic groups attended secondary school. Chinese were therefore over-represented in the professions and civil service, as well as in business. In mid-twentieth-century Jamaica, the average income of the Chinese was three times that of "colored" Jamaicans and five times that of black Jamaicans.[303]

Residentially, the Chinese in the West Indies tended to be widely scattered, partly because their retail stores served many areas. The more prosperous later generations often lived in white upper-class neighborhoods in and around the respective capital cities of Trinidad, Jamaica, Guyana, and Suriname.

In the earlier years, intermarriage between Chinese men and "colored" women was commonplace around the Caribbean when the largely male Chinese first arrived, so that racially mixed Chinese were almost as numerous as pure Chinese in the Caribbean—and as socially accepted in the Chinese community.[304] Nevertheless, the Chinese remained outside the value system of West Indian society—unaffected by its Creole patterns of conspicuous consumption, distribution of largesse, forgiveness of debts, and other traits that operate against business success.[305] The social sanctions of Creole society were ineffective against the Chinese, who—in a fundamental value sense—lived outside that society, even when located in it, exhibiting its outward manifestations in language, food, and clothing, or even a degree of biological amalgamation.

The great prominence of the Chinese in retailing provoked the same social hostility and political antagonism in the Caribbean as in Southeast Asia. There were sporadic outbreaks of destruction of Chinese shops by mobs and arson at various times in the history of Jamaica,[306] including a 1965 riot in which Chinese shops were looted and burned after an accusation that a black employee had been mistreated by a Chinese employer. Decisions by Chinese West Indian umpires in international cricket matches have also set off riots in Trinidad, Guyana, and Jamaica.[307] These were simply sparks that ignited combustible emotions. However, the anti-Chinese hostility of the Caribbean has apparently been far less than in Southeast Asia. This may be due to the generally more relaxed racial feelings in the region or to the existence of other middleman minorities there who are more numerous (the East Indians) or more prominent (the Jews), and who serve as alternative targets of local envy and resentment.

The United States

The first documented record of a Chinese person in the United States goes back to the eighteenth century, and there have been claims of Chinese being in the area that is now the United States even earlier.[308] However, large-scale immigration of Chinese began around the middle of the nineteenth century, in response to the discovery of gold in California. Between 1850 and 1882, when American legislation abruptly cut off immigration from China, more than 322,000 Chinese entered the United States. However, the resident Chinese population remained far below that number in the nineteenth century, as many immigrants returned to China. As of 1880, there were approximately 105,000 Chinese in the United States and 107,000 in 1890, before a long decline in the Chinese population to 62,000 in 1920.[309]

Partly these numbers reflected the continuing return of immigrants to China while replacements were forbidden to enter the United States. Partly too, it reflected a lopsided imbalance between males and females among the Chinese immigrants—a ratio of about 19 to 1 in 1860, rising to a peak of nearly 27 to 1 by 1890.[310] Few Chinese men remained in the United States long enough, or prospered well enough, to bring over their wives from China before the Chinese Exclusion Act went into effect in 1882, though more than one-fourth of them had wives.[311] Indeed, many Chinese men did not prosper well enough to be able to return to China, and were permanently cut off from wives and children on the other side of the Pacific Ocean. This was a particularly bitter blow to a people so family-centered as the Chinese. Many lived out their lives as lonely and destitute men in a country where there was little hope of intermarriage. With very few Chinese marriages and very few Chinese children being born to replace the older generation as they died off, the Chinese population of the United States continued to decline for decades.

There was little to indicate that this tragic fate was in store when the first Chinese immigrants landed in the mid-nineteenth century and were largely welcomed by Americans. However, these first few Chinese were predominantly prosperous merchants, along with skilled artisans, fishermen, and hotel and restaurant owners. Race alone was not enough to bar them from participation in municipal festivities and ceremonies in San Francisco.[312] It was when a much larger mass of coolie laborers arrived from China that American attitudes became negative and hostile. However, this change did not happen all at once. During the first few years, the Chinese workers were welcomed by the public, by government officials, and especially by employers, for the Chinese were noted for their hard work and dependability.[313] The concentration of this coolie immigration in time and space added to its shock. By 1851, there were 25,000 Chinese working in California.[314] They were concentrated in and around San Francisco and out in the "gold rush" region about a hundred miles to the east. Several thousand Chinese clustered together here and there in the gold rush country in 1852, working hard and living frugally—both patterns being in sharp contrast with the patterns among the rowdy masses of American gold-seekers around them. Many of these Americans were Southern whites, who constituted about one-third of the vast numbers of men attracted by California gold. The virulent racial attitudes they brought with them from the antebellum South were felt in both laws and attitudes in California in the years that followed. Blacks as well as Chinese suffered from adverse changes in the racial atmosphere in mid-century California.[315]

The Chinese not only mined gold, both for themselves and as employees of mining companies, but also worked as cooks, peddlers, and storekeepers in the mother lode country. Discriminatory laws and practices, the latter often backed by violence that was endemic in gold rush communities, forced many Chinese out of direct competition with white miners. However, the Chinese were allowed into some areas abandoned by white miners as unprofitable. Here the remarkable patience of the Chinese often paid off, as they carefully panned the streams and painstakingly picked through the dust to find bits of gold overlooked by the disappointed white miners.[316] Tremendous amounts of gold came out of California, and later Nevada, in the gold rush years. The large element of luck made these years of fabulous wealth and dire poverty among gold miners—the latter predominating. How the Chinese in particular fared economically is not known directly. However, as a group, in 1876 alone they sent an estimated $11 million back to Kwangtung province, where nearly all the Chinese in the United States originated, making it one of the most prosperous and modernized provinces in China.[317] A high personal price was paid by the Chinese immigrants, however. Many failed in the search for gold or ended up in poverty and many were killed in the violent frontier area. Eighty-eight were reported as murdered in 1862 alone. Even those who employed Chinese workers were sometimes targets of violence.[318]

The gold rush changed San Francisco from a little town with about a thousand people (including troops stationed there) to a city to rival those of the east coast in population and wealth. It too was a violent place, both in terms of murders and vigilante retribution. This was the home of more than half the Chinese in the United States in the 1850s.[319] The Chinese in nineteenth-century San Francisco engaged in a wide range of occupations. In 1850, when there were only about 700 Chinese in the city, they owned restaurants, laundries, and shops. An area known as "little Canton" had 33 retail stores, 15 pharmacies, and 5 restaurants, serving both Chinese and non-Chinese customers. By 1870, there were about two thousand Chinese laundries dominating this trade in San Francisco.[320] The Chinese were also the main providers of firewood and supplied fruit, vegetables, and flowers. They were also in great demand as domestic servants and were widely used in construction work, ranging from landfill operations and street grading, which created many parts of San Francisco as it is today, to stone masonry and other artisan work that erected the first stone building in the city—with stone imported from China.[321]

With the passing years, the Chinese spread out somewhat geographically and diversified occupationally during the nineteenth century. The building of the transcontinental railroad alone ultimately employed more than one-fourth of all the Chinese in the country. In the course of this backbreaking and dangerous work of building a railroad across rugged mountains, more than a thousand Chinese ended up with their bones being shipped back to China to be buried.[322] However, when the president of the Central Pacific Railroad, Leland Stanford, was photographed in 1869 driving the historic golden spike, connecting the eastern and western United States by rail, none of those in the famous picture taken at Promontory Point was Chinese—even though nine-tenths of the 14,000 railroad workers on the Central Pacific side were Chinese. However, their contribution was publicly acknowledged that day and later.[323]

As in other countries around the world, the Chinese in the United States encountered growing resentment from those unable to compete with them. This began as early as the beginning of the 1850s among white laborers.[324] Miners in the gold rush region took the law into their own hands early on, driving the Chinese out of various mining areas with violence.[325] For decades violent attacks continued sporadically, usually by white workers, urban and agricultural.[326] As the California gold rush tapered off, many Chinese sought work in new occupations and communities, and their success quickly provoked backlashes from white workers and then, as the Chinese went into business for themselves, from white businessmen and small farmers. Large landowners who hired many Chinese coolies lined up politically against a growing list of anti-Chinese legislation, as did the railroads and other large white-owned businesses with many Chinese workers.[327] Politically, however, the anti-Chinese forces prevailed, as laws excluded or harassed the Chinese from industry after industry. Mob violence against the Chinese, or against those hiring Chinese, exploded in communities across the state.[328] The physical violence was successful in forcing employers to stop hiring Chinese. Organized labor unions were especially prominent in anti-Chinese agitation and politically. Numerous anti-Chinese laws in California were capped by a federal law cutting off further immigration from China.

Before being forced out, the Chinese had been a majority of the work force in some industries and localities. At one time, they were more than four-fifths of all agricultural workers in California, including vineyard workers.[329] They were half the work force in the California shrimp-fishing industry[330] and received five-sixths of the payroll of the Columbia River canneries in Oregon in 1872. As late as 1888, they were 86 percent of the cannery workers in California.[331] In San Francisco cigar factories in 1877, the Chinese were 5,500 workers out of a total work force of 6,500 and half the cigar factories were Chinese owned.[332] In 1873, half the shoes and boots manufactured in San Francisco were made by Chinese workers and many of the factories were also Chinese owned.[333] However, the Chinese were not found in large, unionized industries.[334] The American Federation of Labor would not admit them as members and AFL President Samuel Gompers was an active supporter of anti-Chinese legislation.[335]

The Chinese were forced into economic retreat along a broad front. Eventually they were backed into two principal occupations—workers in laundries and restaurants. Together, these two occupations accounted for more than half of all Chinese employed in 1920.[336] The small Chinese hand laundry, usually operated by one man,[337] became an American institution across the country. So too was the Chinese restaurant, often operated in a Chinatown section of town. What these occupations had in common was that they were not in direct competition with whites. Similarly, the Chinese set up many small retail stores in rural black communities across the South, operating again without being in direct competition with whites.[338]

As in other parts of the world, the Chinese in the United States responded to repressive laws with a variety of schemes to circumvent them. In one decade, more than 7,000 Chinese were smuggled into the United States, at a conservative estimate.[339] These included women who had chosen, or been tricked or forced into, prostitution.[340] White prostitutes also operated in Chinatowns. Drugs and gambling were other common features of Chinatowns, along with violent clashes among various tongs who controlled vice. The Chinatowns of this era had a wholly unsavory reputation in the surrounding society.

Because the Chinese were excluded by federal law from becoming naturalized citizens of the United States, California and other states were able to circumvent the Fourteenth Amendment's barriers against racial discrimination by passing laws against all persons "ineligible for citizenship" instead of against the Chinese as such.[341] These laws worked for many years, depriving the Chinese of many opportunities and basic rights—but they could not work indefinitely. Chinese children born in the United States, unlike those born in Southeast Asia, automatically became citizens and these anti-Chinese laws did not apply to them. These American-born Chinese were a small group, but a growing one. Most Chinese females in the United States were American-born at least as early as 1910 but it was 1940 before this would be true of the Chinese population as a whole.[342] The geographical dispersion of the Chinese population over the years also made them less noticeable.

The development of family life was decisive for the future of Chinatowns and of the Chinese American population. The physically and socially sordid Chinatowns of the era of lonely men were no longer acceptable to Chinese families and to leaders of the Chinese community. Tongs went into legitimate businesses as Chinatown residents began cooperating with police to stamp out crime and violence, and Chinese businessmen began refusing to continue to pay extortion. Community organizations behind these actions also began to upgrade the physical appearance of Chinatowns, making them more attractive to visitors from the surrounding society. Chinatowns now began to become known as places with far lower crime rates than American cities as a whole.[343]

Other factors also worked to improve the situation of Chinese Americans. Their withdrawal from direct competition with whites made it impossible for the anti-Chinese animosity of earlier years to be maintained at the same emotional pitch. Moreover, as Chinatowns changed from being crime-ridden, drug-ridden places, and became quiet and colorful tourist attractions, the image as well as the incomes of the Chinese benefitted. Finally, the well-behaved and academically conscientious Chinese children were welcomed by public school teachers. Americans in general also became more sympathetic to China after Japan invaded it in the 1930s, and especially after the United States and China became allies during the Second World War.

All this set the stage for repeal of the Chinese Exclusion Act of 1882 in 1943. When immigration from China resumed, most of the new immigrants were female, including thousands of wives of Chinese men in the United States. Many couples were reunited after decades apart.[344] Meanwhile, housing barriers and other barriers were coming down. By the middle of the twentieth century, most Chinese Americans no longer lived in Chinatowns but were moving out into white, middle-class neighborhoods. A new generation of American-born Chinese began to go to college and enter professions. Their higher education tended to focus on fields that led to well-paying jobs in the sciences, accounting, or engineering. By 1959, the family income of the Chinese was virtually the same as the U.S. national average and, a decade later, exceeded it.[345] By 1990, the median family income of native-born Chinese Americans was 60 percent higher than the median family income of native-born, non-Asian Americans.[346]

Along with a general prosperity, Chinese Americans had some outstanding achievements. In 1957, two Chinese Americans won Nobel Prizes in physics, as did another in 1976.[347] I. M. Pei became an internationally renowned architect. While most Chinese-owned businesses remained modest in size, there was a Chinese-owned chain of stores in California as early as 1939 and in the postwar era a Chinese-owned Wall Street firm, one of the world's largest individual shipowners, and a multinational computer company, owned by Chinese American An Wang.

The postwar era also brought a new wave of immigrants and refugees from China, often through Hong Kong, to the United States. Many of them began at the bottom, in low-wage jobs in Chinatown restaurants and garment factories, working long hours to eke out a living and repay debts incurred in getting to the United States. Their lack of knowledge of English or of American society tied them to Chinatowns and limited their economic options. Crime rates again soared in Chinatowns, as the offspring of these postwar immigrants grew up, often unsupervised by parents working long hours at low pay. Some postwar Chinese youth gangs organized criminal activities with branches in several cities.

The postwar influx of Chinese immigrants has been large enough to swamp the American-born Chinese population. By the late twentieth century, just over half the Chinese in Los Angeles and San Francisco were foreign-born, as well as two-thirds of those in New York.[348] Moreover, the new immigrants did not have the same regional and cultural origins as the existing Chinese American community, and so could not socially integrate readily with them. The 1990 median family income of Chinese immigrants who had arrived during the previous decade was below that of non-Asian Americans and only about half the median family income of native-born Chinese Americans.[349] However, the new immigrants also included some well-educated, prosperous, and sometimes wealthy individuals. Even those in the lower economic levels seemed unlikely to remain there indefinitely, if the history of the overseas Chinese is any guide. Even in the poverty-stricken Chinatown on New York's lower east side, Chinese banks had the longest hours of any banks in the city.[350]

IMPLICATIONS

The highly disparate societies in which the overseas Chinese have risen from poverty to prosperity make it difficult to attribute their success to peculiarities of particular places and times.[351] The almost universal hostility and resentment they have encountered around the world make it insupportable to claim that Eurocentric stereotypes about "the yellow peril" are at the heart of this phenomenon, when Asians have reacted in very similar ways—and often more violently.

Many of the charges made against the overseas Chinese likewise show little correlation with the actual patterns of hostility. For example, the claim was often made that remittances back to China were draining the wealth of the host country, and that the Chinese were only sojourners who did not put down local roots. Over the years, however, both the remittances and repatriation of the overseas Chinese declined and then fell drastically, following the Communist revolution in China—but hostility to the overseas Chinese was not reduced. Similarly, despite bitter complaints that the Chinese do not assimilate, hostility toward them has been no less in Indonesia where they are perhaps most assimilated—and most subjected to mob violence during the postwar era.

Resentments against the overseas Chinese have been quite real, however little relationship these resentments have had with the reasons given for it. Nor is simple envy a sufficient explanation. Other groups, both domestic and foreign, have often been much more prosperous than the Chinese, without arousing nearly as much hostility. What distinguished the Chinese were (1) the low economic level at which they began their careers overseas and (2) the path they took upward. Not only did the overseas Chinese usually begin destitute in a foreign country at a given historical period; new destitute Chinese continued arriving over the years, even after the original immigrants and their descendants had achieved prosperity. Thus the indigenous populations had continuously before their eyes the spectacle of foreigners arriving poorer than they were and yet rising to surpass them. Inspirational as such stories may be to some, they have proved galling to many others in countries around the world—whether these rises from poverty to affluence were achieved by Ibos in Nigeria, Indians in Fiji, Lebanese in West Africa, Jews in Eastern Europe, or Chinese in Southeast Asia. The prosperity of people born prosperous may evoke envy but they are no such blow to the ego as the achievements of upstarts.

The paths taken by the Chinese during their economic rise compounded the resentments. The activities of middleman minorities, whether a racially distinct group or not, have long been condemned as "exploitative" by people who do not understand economics—which include many otherwise educated people. Selling the physically identical product to the consumers at a higher price than that paid to the manufacturer or supplier has long been regarded as cheating in some way, even when what has added value to the product has not been a physical change in itself but a change in its location and availability, which may entail not only transportation costs and inventory risks but also enormously long hours of work in a store to accommodate customers' convenience. Similarly misunderstood has been another middleman function, the extension of credit, whether through money-lending or by making sales on the installment plan. Being forced to pay back more than was lent has long been condemned by many as "usury," often forbidden by law, especially in past centuries. Just as in the retailing of products, the crucial fallacy is the assumption that the same thing is being given two different values. The very fact that people voluntarily borrow means that money now and money later are not the same thing—otherwise they could wait and accumulate the money that they use for repayments, saving themselves the interest.

Some critics of middlemen have conceded that they in fact perform an economic function of value to others (otherwise they would have no customers) but claim that they charge "too much" for this function. This same nebulous charge could of course be made against anyone in any walk of life, from taxi drivers to schoolteachers to people who sell newspapers. In the case of the overseas Chinese, they often achieved their prominence in particular industries by charging lower prices than their competitors and became prominent as creditors by charging lower interest rates or requiring less collateral.[352] Accusations of engaging in "ruinous" or "cutthroat" competition have been made against Chinese middlemen as often as they have been accused of charging excessive prices—and sometimes both accusations have been made by the same individual,[353] though these accusations contradict each other.

None of this means that the overseas Chinese have always been blameless or exemplary. In societies where haggling and sharp practices have been the norm, with buyers and sellers both seeking to outdo each other, the Chinese have played such games skillfully. However, their faithful fulfillment of contracts and even verbal agreements among themselves have been crucial to maintaining their own access to credit, without which most small businesses could not survive. Indeed, access to more credit on better terms has been one of the keys to the ability of the overseas Chinese to undersell their competition.[354] That is often called an "advantage" but the word loses its essential meaning if it confounds a differential benefit among identical performers and an earned recognition of different performance.

Banks have tended to extend more credit to Chinese businessmen because they proved to be better credit risks. The ability of the Chinese themselves to extend credit to others on better terms than their competitors has often been due to a greater investment of time in getting to know individuals, so as to be able to assess their repayment prospects in societies where neither formal records nor legal collection processes can be relied upon.[355]

The personal behavior of the overseas Chinese has often been objected to on many grounds. Easygoing and polite people like the Malays tend to regard the Chinese as brusque or even rude. In many countries, especially in past eras, complaints have been made that the Chinese lived in unhygienic or unesthetic conditions and had disgusting personal habits. Such charges cannot be dismissed arbitrarily as prejudice, especially in light of the fact that early Chinese immigrants were illiterate and destitute people, preoccupied with a struggle for survival and desperate to save money to get ahead. The Chinese in the Philippines are an illustration:

> In the past, Chinese store owners and their Chinese shop helpers both young and old worked sixteen to eighteen hours daily including Sundays. During the lulls, these tired men, especially the old ones, dozed off to relieve their fatigue. As they slept, their mouths would open, letting the saliva out. . . . To many Filipinos *intsik beho* [old pig] was an accurate description of the Chinese. The stereotype *intsik baboy* meaning Chinaman pig referred to the early Chinese lack of attention to personal cleanliness and environmental hygiene. The poor Chinese coolie or peddler in his ambition to save a few more centaros lived an austere, spartan, unpretentious life. His indifference to a healthy sanitary environment was not helped by his habit of spitting anywhere after clearing his throat.[356]

Again, however, history showed no correlation between the complaints and the level of hostility. It was precisely in the post–World War II era, after growing proportions of overseas Chinese had become educated, professional, and had higher behavioral standards, that discrimination and mob violence against them became more pronounced.

Throughout the history of the Chinese in Southeast Asia, the criminal activities and violence of the secret societies or tongs and the corruption of public officials by the Chinese have complicated their lives and those of the societies around them. The history of the secret societies went back many centuries and, during the period of Manchu rule, tongs enjoyed wide popular support as resistance movements against foreign overlords.[357] Like the Sicilian Mafia, however, the secret societies evolved from this role into the role of extortionists and specialists in other criminal activities and violence. Their influence seems to have been greater in the earlier years of Chinese mass immigration. Bribery and corruption, however, seem to have varied with the severity of government regulation in general and racially discriminatory policies in particular. Thus, corruption of public officials by the Chinese was greater during Spanish rule in the Philippines than under the more laissez-faire rule of the Americans.[358] In other countries as well, corruption of officials varied with the economic or other powers wielded by those officials. As the newly independent nations of Southeast Asia generally increased the role of government in their economies, and escalated their anti-Chinese policies in particular, the Chinese responded with both ad hoc bribery and more enduring economic connections with government officials.

Aside from such pragmatic relationships with officials, the overseas Chinese have usually had little or no interest in political activity in the various countries in which they settled. Preoccupied with economic achievement rather than politics, the Chinese began in the twentieth century to take an interest in the politics of China. The idealistic nationalism of Sun Yat-sen struck a responsive chord among overseas Chinese and the 1911 revolution that ended Manchu and dynastic rule in China aroused patriotic feelings among Chinese abroad as well as at home. These feelings took the very tangible form of substantial financial contributions to Sun Yat-sen's Nationalist movement and then to the new Republic of China. This new government's currency was in fact printed by overseas Chinese in San Francisco.[359] The Japanese invasion of China in the 1930s heightened the patriotic feelings of the overseas Chinese, who organized anti-Japanese boycotts, in addition to raising money to help China defend itself. These activities brought brutal retaliation later, when Japan invaded and occupied many parts of Southeast Asia.

China has usually been able to do very little to help the overseas Chinese, and in some ways its influence has been negative in its effects on them. China's announcement, early in the twentieth century, that it considered the overseas Chinese to be citizens of China created political backlashes and legal complications that lasted for decades in Southeast Asia. A surge of Chinese nationalism among the overseas Chinese at about the same time added to the perception that they were aliens and provoked counter-nationalism in the majority populations of Southeast Asian nations. Both the Kuomintang government and later the Communist government of China were active politically and culturally in overseas Chinese communities, promoting political loyalty to China among people who were citizens of another country and infiltrating Chinese schools and other cultural organizations to propagandize and manipulate.[360] Such activities achieved little beyond a heightened hostility to the overseas Chinese among the indigenous populations around them.

For much of its modern history during the era of mass emigration, China was too weak to offer much protection to the overseas Chinese. The Americans' abrupt cutoff of Chinese immigration in 1882 was much more complete and unilateral than the "gentlemen's agreement" with Japan that later curtailed Japanese immigration. As a stronger nation, Japan was able to get an important concession for Japanese men living in the United States—that their wives be allowed to join them and that fiancees from Japan be allowed to enter the U.S. to marry them. Moreover, the bilateral nature of the agreement meant that Japan was not openly insulted, as China was, by a unilateral policy change toward its nationals. With the unification of China under the Communists in 1949 and the subsequent growth of its military power, the effect on Southeast Asian nations was often to make them see China as a threat and their own Chinese populations as potential fifth columnists. China's power was not great enough to prevent mistreatment of the overseas Chinese but only great enough to provoke such mistreatment.

Like some other nations, China used its overseas compatriots politically as pawns in its own maneuvers for national advantage—turning a blind eye to their sufferings in countries with which China had good relations, such as Kampuchea, and ostentatiously coming to their rescue in countries with which China was already at odds, such as Indonesia. All in all, the overseas Chinese have contributed more to China than vice versa, especially during the era that saw creation of the Republic of China by Sun Yat-sen and China's long resistance to Japanese invasions that began in the 1930s. Some observers have lamented the political noninvolvement of the overseas Chinese in the countries in which they settled. However, the rise of the Chinese from poverty to prosperity in many countries around the world has generally been more dramatic than that of groups such as the Irish, who were heavily involved in politics and quite successful at it. Moreover, where the Chinese were more politically active, as in Indonesia, there is little evidence that they did better than in countries where they stayed away from politics. Indeed, an argument could be made that they were treated worse in Indonesia than in most other Southeast Asian nations. Chinese political activity in Malaysia, and especially their public gloating at the results of the 1969 election, set off the race riots which led to the "new economic policy" of widespread official discrimination against the Chinese in education, government, and the economy. However plausible the view that more political activity would have helped the overseas Chinese, the historical record suggests the opposite.

As it is, the achievements of the overseas Chinese have been as remarkable as the hostility of others who benefitted from Chinese economic endeavors that advanced many nations. Such patterns of response may be a grim reflection on human nature, especially as similar patterns are found in the history of other middleman minorities, whether in Asia, Europe, Africa, or the Western Hemisphere.

CHAPTER 6

JEWS OF THE DIASPORA

When in 1882 an Odessa cantor chanted "all the nations reside on their land, but Israel wanders the earth like a shadow finding no rest, receiving no brotherly welcome," his congregants audibly sobbed.

—Eugene F. Sofer[1]

The tragic history of the Jews as a people wandering the world through centuries of persecution has been equally remarkable for their achievements, perhaps unique for any population of similar size. Even after the modern state of Israel was created in the middle of the twentieth century, most of the Jews in the world were still the Jews of the Diaspora.

As of 1990, there were approximately 13 million Jews in the world, of whom 90 percent lived in just 5 countries, with nearly three-quarters living either in the United States or in Israel. There were nearly 9 million Jews of the Diaspora and almost 4 million Jews living in their historic homeland of Israel, which contained 31 percent of all the Jews in the world.[2] Unlike any other people, the Jews of the world are today a smaller population than they were more than half a century ago, before the Holocaust.[3]

The Jews of the Diaspora have been very thinly spread among the populations of the countries in which they live. Even in the United States, with the largest Jewish population in the world, Jews were only about 2 percent of the population.[4] Yet the only country with a higher percentage was Israel. The world Jewish population in 1990 was distributed as followed:[5]

UNITED STATES	5,535,000
ISRAEL	3,946,700
SOVIET UNION	1,150,000
FRANCE	530,000
BRITAIN	315,000
ALL OTHERS	1,329,700
TOTAL	12,806,400

The Diaspora of the Jews has been more than simply a worldwide dispersion. Many peoples have been widely dispersed throughout the world, but the bulk of those peoples have usually remained in their respective homelands. What has been historically unique about the Jewish Diaspora has been a combination of features, including (1) the vast majority of a whole people living outside their historic homeland, (2) the loss of that homeland, both demographically and politically, to other peoples, and (3) an ever-changing pattern of dispersion, with the largest concentration of Jews in the world being at one time in Eastern Europe, at another time in the Islamic countries, and today in the United States.

If the overseas Chinese are numerically the largest of the world's middleman minorities, Jews are the best known in that role—the classic image of the middleman. The Chinese have been called "the Jews of Southeast Asia" and the Lebanese "the Jews of West Africa." Shakespeare's merchant of Venice was Jewish. Jewish peddlers, shopkeepers, pawnbrokers, merchants, and bankers have historically created an image that still survives, even in countries where contemporary Jews are more likely to be doctors, lawyers, or intellectuals. Their history has been profoundly affected by the fact that so many Jews were middlemen, whatever they may be today.

ANCIENT TIMES

In ancient times, Jews were neither a race of middlemen[6] nor a people without a country. However, there were Jewish communities far from Israel, centuries before Christ. The conquest of Israel by the Assyrians in the eighth century B.C. led to the removal of more than 27,000 Jews—the "lost tribes," who disappeared without a trace in the lands of the conquerors. Successive conquerors dispersed more and more Jews over the centuries, whether as prisoners, refugees, or migrants, but these Jews retained their identity and loyalty, exemplified in the phrase, "If I forget thee, O Jerusalem. . . ." There were not only mass exoduses of Jews but also mass returns. In the sixth century B.C., the Persian conquerors of Babylon permitted its Jewish population to return to their homeland and rebuild the temple at Jerusalem. Although 50,000 returned, many others remained abroad.[7] But these Jews of the Diaspora continued to make financial contributions, as well as pilgrimages, to the temple in Jerusalem.[8]

In the first century B.C., the Romans captured Jerusalem. They ruled for the next several centuries, despite two massive revolts in the first and second centuries A.D., which led only to the destruction of the temple, the obliteration of Israel as a political entity, and the dispersal of the great majority of the Jewish people. The Jews became, and remained for almost two thousand years, a people without a country. They were a minority everywhere, including the area once known as Israel but now renamed by the Romans *Syria Palaestina.*

Even before the obliteration of ancient Israel as a political entity, Jews were widely scattered throughout the Roman Empire. Out of an estimated 8 million Jews in the world at that time, only about 2.5 million lived in Palestine. Approximately 4 million lived in the rest of the Roman Empire and another million in Babylonia. Jews were about 10 percent of the total population of the Roman Empire[9] and they tended to concentrate in urban areas. There were about 50,000 Jews living in Rome itself and Jews constituted about 40 percent of the population of Alexandria, where they were prominent in the grain-export trade, both as shipowners and as sailors.

The range of occupations open to Jews at this period was greater than in later, medieval times. In addition to being merchants trading domestically and internationally, Jews were also artisans, farmers, and mercenary soldiers. While wealthy Jews attracted attention, most Jews were in fact poor. Most earned their livings from manual labor and some were beggars on the streets, in both Rome and Alexandria. Nevertheless, the success of Jewish businessmen, though it advanced the economies in which they settled, provoked envy and hostility among non-Jewish businessmen—mostly pagans rather than Christians in the early era of the Diaspora.[10]

The vicissitudes of the Jews under the Roman Empire—or in the contemporary Persian empire—were very different from their troubles in medieval and modern times. Both empires were multiethnic and multireligious. Tolerance was a necessity for the survival of the realm. Each of the numerous groups in the Roman Empire was expected to respect the rights of others, the gods of others, and to pay homage both to the political rulers and to the gods of Rome. Otherwise, they were free to pursue their own religion and their own way of life.

Jews had a special difficulty in fitting into this Roman scheme. While other peoples had their own gods for themselves, the God of the Jews was conceived as the one God of all mankind and of the universe. While this might, in one sense, suggest the brotherhood of man, in another sense it led to the conclusion that all other religions were false, that it was a sacrilege to accept them in any way, much less pay even formal homage to them. It was this feature of Judaism—and later, Christianity—that provoked special *political* problems for the Jews (and later, the Christians) in the Roman Empire. This view was also characteristic of the third great religion of the Middle East, Islam, which emerged in a still later era. Pagans were not intolerant of other religions.[11] It was the Judeo-Christian tradition that introduced religious intolerance into the Roman Empire and, through it, into Western civilization. Over the ensuing centuries, no one suffered more as a result than the Jews.

Not all anti-Jewish hostiliy was religiously based, even when it invoked religious feelings. The prime modern examples were the Nazis, who were by no means religious. Hostility among peoples, as such, goes far back into human history. Hostility between Greeks and Jews, for example, led to violence in many cities during Roman times,[12] despite strong measures taken by the Romans to suppress such outbreaks, which were seen as a threat to public order and, ultimately, to the stability of the empire.

By and large, the Romans attempted to accommodate the special religious views of the Jews, though particular Roman rulers offended their religion in various ways. Nevertheless, Roman rule was found burdensome in other respects, including taxation, and the Romans could be implacable in vengeance against Jews, as against other peoples. After the second revolt in Jerusalem, vast numbers of Jews were either slaughtered or sold into slavery. But the singling out of Jews for special oppression and violence, just for being Jews, was something that still lay centuries into the future.

THE MIDDLE AGES

When the last Roman emperor was overthrown in 476 A.D., marking the end of the ancient world and the beginning of the Middle Ages, Jews were widely scattered around the Mediterranean and could be found farther north in Europe, as well as farther south in the Arabian peninsula. Much of this region was destined to be conquered in later centuries by adherents of the new and crusading religion of Islam. During the Middle Ages, most Jews lived in the Islamic world.[13] That world extended from Spain across North Africa and the Middle East into Central Asia. Moreover, it was an expanding world that would eventually conquer the Balkans in Europe, establish the Mogul Empire in India, and reach Southeast Asia via Arab traders to make Islam the religion of regions that later became Malaysia and Indonesia.

Like Christians and other non-Moslems, Jews in the Islamic lands were legally placed on an inferior plane but, in practice, they were treated far better in much of the Moslem world at that time than in the contemporary Christian world.[14] However, the treatment of Jews varied among Islamic countries, as among Christian countries, and in both their treatment changed over time as well. Throughout the Islamic world, a non-Moslem dared not strike a Moslem, even in self-defense, and merely verbal retaliation was dangerous. Small children threw rocks at Christians or Jews with impunity[15]—a fate not uncommon for Jews in parts of contemporary Christendom.[16] Self-protection being forbidden and fatally dangerous, the protection of non-Moslem minorities in Islamic countries depended crucially on the practices of the authorities and the attitudes of the populace. Religious differences provided the basis for hostility to Jews in both the Christian world and the Islamic world, but the wide variations in the actual treatment of Jews within each world did not correspond with religious variations. Certainly the historic reversal of the positions of the two civilizations, over a period of centuries, in their respective treatment of Jews cannot readily be attributed to religion. Indeed, slaughters of Jews occurred in North Africa and the Middle East before the rise of either Christianity or Islam.

Among the factors influencing the better treatment of Jews in Moslem lands during the early Middle Ages was that Jews were less conspicuous, as only one of a number of non-Moslem minorities in the Islamic world, while they stood out sharply as the only non-Christian people in Christian Europe[17]—at a time when religion was an enormous influence. Moreover, the early Islamic world was a confident, dynamic world—a world expanding for a thousand years, winning repeated military victories over European powers, singly or in combination. The Ottoman Empire became the most powerful military force on earth. Nor were all its achievements on the battlefield. The culture of the Islamic world was in many respects more advanced and more sophisticated than that of contemporary Europe,[18] especially in mathematics and philosophy, for example.[19] In later centuries, when the great tides of history turned in favor of Europe, it was the Ottoman Empire and the Islamic world in general that suffered innumerable crushing defeats, saw their conquered territories in Europe lost, and saw Moslems across North Africa and the Middle East become subjugated by Europeans. In this later era of defeat and dangers, the confident cosmopolitanism of the early Ottoman Empire gave way to more bitter reactions to non-Moslems, of whom Jews were the most vulnerable.

The history of Jews in medieval Europe took a very different course from the history of Jews in Islamic lands. In the fragmented Europe left after the fall of the Roman Empire, barbarian invaders took over many areas where Jews had lived since ancient times. Like other pagans, these barbarian conquerors were tolerant of religious differences and Jews were able to survive, and in some places thrive, among them. With the passing centuries, however, the barbarians became Christianized and that entailed affiliation with an international church dedicated to stamping out deviations from Christian orthodoxy. Even after the pagans became Christianized, there remained a social toleration and mutual interaction for centuries more, giving little foreshadowing of the persecutions of Jews that would become widespread in Europe during the later Middle Ages. As a literate people during the widespread ignorance of a dark age, Jews enjoyed a certain prestige among their Christian neighbors. Even Jewish peddlers brought products and ideas from a wider world to the provincial communities of early medieval Europe. Centuries of religious preaching against Jews were required to turn them into pariahs in the popular mind.[20]

Jews as artisans, peddlers, and merchants played a role in the revival of European urban communities after the collapse of the Roman Empire.[21] Jews lived in many European cities, including Rome, Frankfurt, and Lyons. Their urban occupations included goldsmiths and physicians, and their rural occupations owners of farms and vineyards. Jews were in the entourages of aristocrats, and supplied them with exotic luxuries from the East. Christians during this era socialized with Jews and dined in their homes—and many converted to Judaism, though few Jews converted to Christianity.[22] Recognizing the dangers to Christianity, and to itself as an institution in such situations, the Catholic Church counterattacked in various ways, intellectual and political. The net result was a growth of policies, laws, and practices which kept Christians and Jews apart, forbad proselytizing by Jews, and restricted or harassed them in the practice of their own religion. Ironically, these policies worked so effectively that eventually popular anti-Jewish hostility reached levels that caused a succession of popes to issue edicts against anti-Jewish violence and libels—the most infamous libel being that Jews killed Christian babies and drank their blood. In an earlier era, the same accusation had been made by pagans against the Christians.[23]

Despite growing restrictions and persecutions, many Jews continued to prosper. Indeed, Jews became pre-eminent in international trade between Christian Europe and the Moslem lands,[24] partly because both saw them as neutrals in the great Christian-Moslem struggles of that era, allowing them to function economically in both worlds, where Christians restricted Moslems and Moslems restricted Christians.[25]

These functions as both economic and cultural intermediaries could be carried out because the Jews of Europe had contacts with fellow Jews in North Africa and the Middle East, many of the latter also being merchants.

Part of the exports from Europe to the Islamic world during this era—and for centuries to come—were European slaves. In an era when large landownership in Europe often meant holding serfs and slaves, Jewish landowners were no exception. Moreover, in their role as international traders in various merchandise, the Jews—like the Arabs in Africa—included slaves among that merchandise. As the Germanic peoples of Western Europe invaded the Slavic lands to the east, they often sold members of the conquered population as slaves to Jews, who then resold them elsewhere in the Christian or Islamic world. Jews became major dealers in the European slave trade, as in other trade.[26] The growing spread of Christianity in Europe and its influence on secular law increasingly made it illegal for Jews to own Christian slaves and also increasingly difficult for them to own land.[27] Christians, Jews, and Moslems all banned the holding of their own people as slaves, but all three held other peoples as slaves. In the Ottoman Empire, Jews continued to function as slave traders for centuries, selling European Christians to Moslems. With castration being forbidden to Moslems, Jews were the principal suppliers of white eunuchs to the Ottoman Empire in the fifteenth century, the supply coming largely from the Caucasus region.[28]

In Europe, along with a growing antagonism toward the Jews by Christian religious authorities and those influenced by them, there was a more pragmatic and more ambivalent response to the Jews by rulers of nations. The skills and entrepreneurship of the Jews were important economic contributions to national development, as well as providing contributions more directly to the rulers in loans and taxes. Therefore rulers often protected Jews from the violence of mobs. At other times, however, rulers found it expedient to use Jews as scapegoats for popular discontents. One symptom of this ambivalence among rulers was that Jews were sometimes expelled and later invited back into the same realm.

Despite the use of religious intolerance to stir public feeling against the Jews, various attacks, expulsions, and confiscations had pragmatic goals—including being rid of creditors and the debts owed to them. When King Philip of France expelled the Jews in 1306, the reason given was that they charged excessively high interest rates. However, he did not cancel the debts owed to Jews, but instead set about collecting them for his own treasury. To his disappointment, the king discovered that the money collected in this way was less than the taxes that Jews had been paying. Moreover, when Christian money-lenders replaced Jews, complaints arose that Christians charged higher interest rates than the Jews had. The net result was that the Jews were invited back.[29] The same cycle of expulsion followed by an invitation to return appeared in several medieval German cities.[30] There was a more lasting expulsion of Jews from England in 1290 and from France in 1394. Various cities and regions also expelled Jews—Cologne in 1424, Augsburg in 1439, and Moravia in 1454, for example.[31]

The series of Crusades of Christian Europe against the Moslems in Palestine produced major tragedies for Jews in Europe. As bands of Crusaders marched across the continent, unruly elements among them paused to attack Jews. The slaughters of 1096 took 10,000 Jewish lives in Central Europe.[32] Violent attacks on Jews likewise marked later Crusades. Popular hostility to Jews again vented itself in the wake of the Black Death or bubonic plague of the fourteenth century, which killed between a fourth and a half of the entire population of Europe. Rumors spread that the Jews had somehow caused the plague and this set off murderous violence against Jewish inhabitants in hundreds of European cities.[33]

While the ignorance of the masses in Europe during this era was no doubt a factor in such attacks on Jews, it was often the educated clergy who were leaders in whipping up anti-Jewish feeling, in the interests of solidifying Christian hegemony, and often it was years before the anti-Judaism of the educated took root in the masses.[34] This pattern was to be repeated in later eras of secular intellectuals, who also required long years of determined effort to inculcate anti-Jewish hostility into the masses.[35]

With the passing centuries and growing intolerance, the occupations open to Jews began to narrow, as did their choice of residence, or even the clothing they were permitted to wear. Landownership, military careers, and many occupations represented by the emerging guilds were closed to Jews in many parts of medieval Europe. In many countries, they were left with occupations peripheral to feudal society—peddlers, artisans, or money-lenders on a small or large scale, for example. In some places, Jews also became rent collectors for noble landlords or tax collectors for governments—roles which added to their unpopularity. Rulers began to require Jews to wear clothes or insignia that distinguished them from Christians. Similar requirements to wear special clothing were imposed on Jews in some Islamic lands, to distinguish them from Moslems. Jews in much of Europe were also required to live in separate communities from Christians. Sometimes these were walled communities which Jews were forbidden to leave at night—the ghettoes, which later in history became a generic term for residential enclaves of other groups around the world.

As the Jews settled for centuries in lands with different races, religions, languages, and cultures, the evolution of Jewish culture reflected these differences in the respective cultures around them, as well as reflecting the opportunities and rights those cultures permitted or denied to Jews. Language was the most obvious example. Jews of the Byzantine Empire typically spoke Greek,[36] while those in Arab lands spoke Arabic, and those in various parts of Europe spoke either the regionally dominant language or a Jewish dialect derived from it, such as Yiddish derived from German or Ladino from Spanish.[37]

Within their own enclaves, Jews typically maintained autonomous institutions, both secular and religious, and were collectively responsible through their leaders to the ruling powers for order and for taxes. The world of the ghettoes was in many countries and for many centuries a narrow world, largely insulated from the cultural developments of Christian Europe and preoccupied with Jewish traditions and contemporary Jewish problems. Education remained more common among the Jews than among many of the Christian communities around them, but for most it was an education as circumscribed as the lives they led. Contacts were maintained, at least intermittently, by the more educated classes with other Jewish communities in other lands, though the language barriers that increasingly separated world Jewry were formidable to those who were not multilingual. Commerce likewise connected the Jews in different lands, as the Jews themselves connected in trade countries that were hostile to one another, especially those of Christian Europe and the Islamic world.

One of the major divisions within world Jewry developed between the *Ashkenazic* Jews of Germany and the *Sephardic* Jews of Spain—each named for the Hebrew word for their respective countries of residence, though the names stuck long after later migrations took them far from these countries. The late fifteenth century, for example, saw two mass migrations of historic consequence—Ashkenazic Jews migrating from German lands into Poland and Sephardic Jews migrating from Spain to the Mediterranean Islamic countries. Throughout the centuries of the Diaspora, whether the circumstances of the Jews in particular lands were good or bad, these circumstances were subject to sudden and drastic change. Centuries of persecution in the Byzantine Empire, for example, were followed by an era of renewed toleration and economic advancement, leading to a prosperous Jewish community in Constantinople.[38] Elsewhere the sequence was the reverse, from toleration and prosperity to intolerance and spoliation. Spain went through the latter cycle, on a large scale, more than once.

Spain

A large and prosperous Jewish population lived in Spain for centuries before the Visigoths established a kingdom there in the fifth century A.D. In the early Middle Ages in Spain, as in other parts of Europe, Jews were not as limited in their occupations as they became in a later era. In addition to being merchants in both domestic and international trade, Jews also held civil and military offices in the Visigothic government, and were large landowners and slave-holders.[39] After the Visigoths began to abandon paganism for Christianity, beginning with the Visigothic King Reccared in 589, a new era began. Reccared himself did not begin persecuting Jews, nor did his immediate successors, but his religious conversion and that of his kingdom provided a religious basis for severe seventh-century restrictions on Jews by later kings, typically for political reasons or economic gain.[40] Religion was an enabling rather than an impelling force. Most of the Catholic Visigothic kings did not adopt anti-Jewish policies and, even in the late seventh century, some Catholic clergy themselves continued the illegal practice of selling Christian slaves to Jews.[41]

Whatever the reasons behind growing restrictions on Jews in Spain, these restrictions became widespread and severe. The death penalty was decreed for Jews who proselytized Christians, and Jews were ordered expelled from government posts where they exercised power over Christians. When Jews were forbidden to hold Christian slaves, this was an economic blow both to slave-owners and to landowners, especially since Jewish landowners were also forbidden from hiring Christian employees. After these and other anti-Jewish policies decreed by King Sisebut were applied unevenly across the country against various resistance, neglect, and evasion by local civil and church authorities, he eventually simply ordered that Jews either convert to Christianity or leave the country. However, Sisebut died in 621 A.D. before this draconian policy could be fully carried out, and his successor reversed Sisebut's anti-Jewish policies in general. But a decade later, these anti-Jewish policies resumed under a new regime. However, their implementation continued to be problematical, as both civil and religious authorities often found it expedient to use the talents of Jews, who sometimes even administered ecclesiastical estates of Catholic clergy.[42] In short, the actual implementation of policy toward the Jews reflected the conflict between the economic usefulness of Jews and their political, social, and religious unpopularity.

Although many Jews remained in Spain and some continued to engage in lucrative but forbidden economic activities at the end of the seventh century,[43] they nevertheless welcomed the Moors who invaded Spain in the early eighth century. The conquering Moors brought to the Jews more than a respite from persecution. The vast Islamic domains, of which Spain now became part, offered many opportunities for trade, not only within itself but also between itself and Christian Europe. The Jews, widely scattered in both civilizations, and yet in contact with fellow Jews living in both Christian and Islamic countries, were in an ideal position to conduct that trade. They became a conduit, not only for trade but also for intellectual and cultural interchanges between the two hostile blocs of nations.[44]

The seven centuries of Moorish rule in Spain included three centuries (900–1200 A.D.) which have often been called the "golden age" of Jews, not only for their economic achievements but also for their intellectual and cultural development. The Islamic world of this era was itself a source of new ideas in science, poetry, and philosophy.[45] A rich Moorish architectural tradition left its monuments across Spain. Many cultural treasures came in the Arabic language, including classics not only from the Middle East and North Africa, but also classics of Greek civilization and even from as far away as India—all written in Arabic or translated into Arabic. In this way, a whole new system of numbers, originating in India, reached Europe and replaced the cumbersome system of Roman numerals. Because these numbers came to Europe by way of the Arabs, they were mistakenly called Arabic numerals. Chess likewise originated in India and reached Europe via the Arab conquerors. Much of the literature that entered Spain in Arabic was retranslated into European languages and became part of the cultural heritage of European civilization. Jews were an important part of this translation process.[46]

Standing at the crossroads of two great civilizations, the Jews were peculiarly well situated to deal in the ideas and cultures of both the Islamic and the Christian worlds, as well as in their material goods—and to advance themselves culturally and materially as well. It was not simply that they received knowledge from different directions but that these cultural crosscurrents also stimulated their own thinking and the development of their own Jewish culture. For example, the Islamic world's concern for the purity of the Arabic language stimulated Jews to re-examine Hebrew grammar and style.[47] After many centuries in which Jewish intellectual efforts, as embodied in their writings, concentrated on specifically Jewish matters and virtually ignored science, now in the wake of Arab science Jews began to produce numerous scientific works during the centuries of Islamic rule in Spain.[48] The most famous Jewish philosopher of the Middle Ages, Maimonides, was a product of such cultural crosscurrents, being familiar with both Greek and Arab philosophers, as well as with his own Judaic traditions. At less-exalted levels of the Jewish community as well, both Islamic and Christian cultural features influenced the Jewish culture.[49]

Despite the duration and achievements of Islamic rule in Spain and Portugal, the Moors never fully occupied the Iberian peninsula. A band of Christian-ruled regions across the northern edge of the country held out and eventually became bases for a long process of Christian reconquest that lasted for centuries. Portugal became independent in the twelfth century and the Christian kingdoms of Spain won major victories in the early thirteenth century that gave them control of most of their country's territory, but the Moors still retained the kingdom of Granada in the south. The military struggle in Spain continued on through most of the fifteenth century. But, as early as the thirteenth century, Christian-ruled Spain encompassed a majority of Sephardic Jews.[50]

Most of these Jews were in such occupations as craftsmen, shopkeepers, or money-lenders, but some reached higher levels as owners of large textile factories in Seville, Córdoba, and Toledo, or as government financial administrators and tax collectors. The Jews excelled in those mundane skills neglected by Castilian society and this complementarily benefitted both economically. However, the prosperity and influence of the Jews were increasingly resented by the Spanish populace, who were held in check only by a strong central government, well aware of the benefit it derived from the work of Jews. When the bubonic plague or Black Death that swept across Europe struck Spain, it contributed to a social disruption that undermined the power of the Spanish monarchy. A civil war within Christian Spain from 1369 to 1371 likewise weakened the government's control. During this disruption of order, a wave of anti-Jewish violence swept across the country, culminating in the forced conversion of tens of thousands of Jews in 1391. Neither church nor state was successful in their attempts to control these mob outbreaks or the forced conversions. Many other Jews, not directly coerced, chose on their own to become Christians as it became increasingly dangerous to be a Jew.[51]

These events had lasting effects on the history of the Jews and on the history of Spain. The ethnically Jewish population was now split religiously three ways: (1) those converted Jews who adhered to the Christian religion and who were called *conversos;* (2) those converts who secretly maintained Jewish religious observances and whom the Spaniards bitterly called *marranos* or swine; and (3) those Jews who remained open adherents of Judaism. The interactions among these three groups were to have fateful consequences.

The *conversos,* now freed of the discriminatory laws that applied to Jews, became even more prosperous and influential, reaching high positions in church and state alike, and even marrying into the Christian aristocracy. *Conversos* became especially influential in municipal governments. But, however much their legal, economic, and social status may have changed, the *conversos* still aroused the envy and hostility of the populace, just as they had when they were Jews. Bloody outbreaks against *conversos* erupted in Toledo in 1448, in Sepúlveda in 1468, in Córdoba in 1473, and in Segovia and Jaén in 1474. There was also a widespread questioning of the large role of *conversos* in Spanish life, and charges that many *conversos* were actually *marranos,* secretly practicing Judaism. The charge of religious apostasy from Christianity brought in the Spanish Inquisition. Though the Inquisition's powers were sweeping and its methods ruthless, still the *conversos'* power and influence enabled many to escape with their lives and much of their property.[52]

Attempts to curb the prosperity and influence of the *conversos* centered on making a legal distinction between them and people born into the Christian community, the so-called Old Christians. In self-defense, the *conversos* insisted on the unity of all Christians, whether by birth or conversion—as against the Jews. Both the logic of the argument and the social exigencies of the times led the *conversos* into promoting anti-Jewish beliefs and policies,[53] in a country already seething with hostility to Jews. Although the royal government still needed the skills, talents, and wealth of the Jews while engaged in a military struggle against the Moors, once Granada fell in 1492, ending Moorish rule in Spain, the Jews became expendable. A royal decree issued that same year expelled all religious Jews from the country. Unlike the expulsions of relatively small populations of Jews from England and France in previous centuries, the number of Jews suddenly forced out of Spain on short notice reached the hundreds of thousands.[54] Wealth that the Jews were forced to leave behind helped finance the other great historic event of that year—the voyage of Columbus that led to discovery of the Western Hemisphere.[55]

Most of the Sephardic Jews went to the Islamic lands of North Africa and the Middle East and, in particular, to the Ottoman Empire. Not all Sephardic Jews settled in the Ottoman Empire, however. Many settled in those European countries noted for their tolerance toward Jews, such as Italy, England, and Holland.[56] The Spanish Jews who settled in Holland helped to make Amsterdam one of the world's great commercial ports,[57] and came ultimately to own one-fourth of the shares in the Dutch East India Company.[58]

Existing Jewish communities scattered across the vast Ottoman Empire were not only swamped demographically by the huge influx of Jews from Spain, as well as from other parts of Europe, but were also revitalized by these new people, who were more advanced in both knowledge and wealth.[59] Sephardic exiles rapidly rose to commercial prominence in the Balkans.[60] The cosmopolitan Sephardim who settled in southern France as *marranos* were both more prosperous and more accepted culturally than the poor, alien, and openly Jewish Ashkenazim who settled in eastern France, which became strongly anti-Jewish.[61] The Sephardic Jews who settled in Algeria became the acknowledged leaders of the Jewish community there, and leaders also of the commercial activities of the nation.[62] Although the Spanish government had confiscated the wealth of the Sephardic Jews, they could not confiscate the skills and traits that created that wealth in the first place—and would create it again in many other nations, as far away as the Caribbean.

The Ottoman Empire

As of the late fifteenth century, the Ottoman Empire offered far greater tolerance and far more opportunities than the Jews were likely to find in most other places, Christian or Islamic. At that juncture, the Ottoman Empire was the most powerful military force in an expanding Islamic world—and more powerful than any European nation or empire. The Ottoman Turks climaxed their rise from a nomadic people to a world power by their invasion of the Byzantine Empire and capture of its capital, Constantinople, in 1453. Renamed Istanbul, this city now became the capital of the Ottoman Empire. As conquerors of a large, racially and religiously diverse region, the Ottoman Turks ruled with tolerance and shrewdness. The welcome they offered to Jews exiled from Spain reflected that shrewdness.

Among the skills that the Sephardim brought to the Ottoman Empire was a knowledge of the military technology of the West[63] and a knowledge of Western languages and Western politics. All this was valuable to the Ottoman rulers in their centuries-long hostilities against Christian Europe. The Ottoman Empire much preferred Jews to Christians in sensitive positions.[64] For example, Jews were sometimes sent abroad as interpreters for Ottoman envoys[65] and even as unofficial emissaries themselves.[66] Moreover, unlike the larger Christian minority within the Ottoman Empire, the Jews were under no cloud of suspicion of being sympathetic to the Christian nations, after the persecutions they had suffered there. Indeed, the Ottoman rulers followed a policy of moving Jews into recently conquered Christian cities, whether because these cities were depopulated or as a counterweight to potentially disloyal Christian inhabitants. Jews in the Ottoman Empire were encouraged—or even ordered—to move into Istanbul,[67] where they were 11 percent of the city's population by 1477. After the later arrival of Spanish and Italian exiles, the Jewish population of Istanbul grew to be several times as large by 1535,[68] though the migration of many other groups to Istanbul[69] make it uncertain how much the relative proportions may have changed. The same policy was later applied to the strategic port of Salonika, which had a negligible Jewish population in 1519 but became more than two-thirds Jewish in less than a century.[70]

Jews in the Ottoman Empire were allowed to engage in a much wider range of economic activities than in much of contemporary Europe. Indeed, their particular skills were more widely needed.[71] Jewish peddlers were common in towns like Gallipoli and Salonika, and in the villages in their vicinity. Often these peddlers dealt in barter.[72] At the other end of the economic scale, Jews were also prominent in international trade, particularly with countries where other Jews engaged in international trade. Thus Jews played an important role in the Ottoman trade with Italy but not in its trade with the Persian Gulf region or with India.[73] The principal commodities traded by Ottoman Jews, both domestically and internationally, were textiles, clothing, threads, and leathers.[74] Having been active in the textile industry of Spain,[75] Jews were among the pioneers of the textile industry in the Ottoman Empire and supplied a large proportion of the uniforms worn by the military corps of the Janissaries.[76] Jews were so common in the customs service that many of the Ottoman customs receipts of that era were written in Hebrew.[77]

In the medical profession, in this earlier and more tolerant era, Jews in the Islamic world worked as colleagues of Moslem or Christian physicians.[78] The Moslem world, once in advance of Europe in science and medicine, had fallen behind by the time the Jewish refugees from Spain, Italy, and other parts of Europe began arriving in large numbers during the fifteenth century. As bearers of medical skills now more advanced than those of the Islamic world, Jews became prominent as physicians,[79] including some who became physicians to sultans of the Ottoman Empire. By the early sixteenth century, the palace medical staff consisted of 41 Jews and 21 Moslems.[80] With the passage of time, however, the source of the Jews' superiority—their knowledge of Western medicine—declined as they lost touch with ongoing medical developments in the West. As second- and third-generation Sephardic Jews fell behind in medicine, they were replaced by Western-educated Greeks.[81]

In general, Christian minorities in the Ottoman Empire, such as Greeks and Armenians, kept in touch with Christian Europe, often sending their children there to be educated. Ottoman Christians were therefore more abreast of Western progress and retained their facility with Western languages and their contacts in Western countries. As the Western knowledge and connections of the Ottoman Jews became obsolete over time, they began to be displaced by Christians in field after field. Not only were Jewish doctors replaced by better qualified Greeks; Jewish merchants likewise saw their share of the empire's international trade dwindle to the vanishing point in competition with Christians.[82] Armenian merchants, shipowners, entrepreneurs, and bankers played an increasing role in the Ottoman Empire—at the expense of Jews—from the late eighteenth century.[83] Even in the theater, an early Jewish predominance eventually gave way to Armenian predominance.[84] In addition to ousting Jews from various commercial and professional positions through the competition of superior skills, Christian minorities also actively promoted hostility to the Jews in Christian Europe and in the Islamic world, bringing to the latter the old claim that Jews killed children and drank their blood.[85] As the Jews of the Ottoman Empire declined both economically and demographically, their growing poverty was reflected in very low levels of education, and growing persecutions added to their demoralization.[86] The new intellectual currents of European civilization in the era of the French Revolution made no such impact among Ottoman Jews as among Greeks and Armenians. Jews in the Ottoman Empire remained isolated even from contemporary intellectual currents among the Jews of Europe.[87]

As the position of the Jews was declining within the Ottoman Empire, so the empire itself was declining relative to its chief rival, Christian Europe. This represented a drastic reversal of international power, and its domestic repercussions had grim implications for non-Moslem minorities. After centuries of territorial expansion, the Ottoman Turks began to experience setbacks and then defeats. In its era of ascendancy, the Ottoman Empire repeatedly inflicted crushing military defeats on the Europeans, conquered Greece and the Balkans, and by 1529 were besieging Vienna. Only with the help of other European powers, who feared that the Turks would overrun the continent, was the fall of Vienna averted—and only barely averted at that. Centuries of expansion of the Islamic world in all directions gave the Ottoman Turks not only confidence in themselves and in their mission, but also contempt for the "infidels" of Europe, whom they so long surpassed in science and medicine as well as on the battlefield, and whom they continually enslaved in great numbers. For centuries, Ottoman rulers and even Ottoman scholars had no interest in European culture, and often lacked very basic knowledge of the continent and its inhabitants, beyond those with whom they had common frontiers. In short, Europe was regarded as beneath their notice, even though Ottoman scholars produced serious studies of India, China, and other foreign countries.[88]

With this attitude of utter disdain toward Europe, it was a special shock for the Ottoman Empire to begin to encounter a series of major military defeats from European powers using more advanced weapons and techniques of war. The year 1571 saw the loss of Ottoman control of the Mediterranean in a decisive naval battle against a combined Papal, Spanish, and Venetian fleet. On land, it was 1664 when the Habsburg Empire inflicted the first major defeat suffered by the Ottoman Empire in a pitched battle. In 1683, when the Ottomans returned to besiege Vienna, they were not only resisted but routed, despite having numerical superiority. It marked an historic turning point in the relationship between the two empires and, more broadly, between Christian Europe and the Islamic world.[89]

The degree of tolerance toward non-Moslem minorities within the

Ottoman Empire during its long era of ascendancy was no longer maintained as the Ottomans began to experience the shocks of military defeat and of uprisings among European subject peoples, together with European subjugation of Moslems in North Africa and the Middle East, threatening the very survival of the empire. In this beleaguered and embittered atmosphere, non-Moslems in general were viewed less charitably and more suspiciously, as weak links or potential traitors. Legal restrictions against the activities of non-Moslems that had been only loosely or intermittently applied during the more cosmopolitan era of Ottoman expansion now began to be applied more rigorously.[90] While Christians were more suspect than Jews, it was the Jews who were more vulnerable, both because they were less numerous and because they had no foreign homeland whose influence could be used in their behalf.[91] In addition to official discrimination, Jews, like other non-Moslems, were subject to being harassed with impunity by Moslems, including children who could throw rocks at them, spit on them, or hit them, secure in the knowledge that no retaliation was possible, under pain of death.[92] These developments were not peculiar to the Ottoman Empire, but were widespread throughout the Islamic world—and were worse in many other parts of that world.

In parts of Morocco, Jews were required to go barefoot when they ventured outside their own enclave, and an eighteenth-century Jewish visitor to Morocco described his co-religionists there as "oppressed, miserable creatures, having neither the mouth to answer an Arab or the cheek to raise their head." Jews were even pulled out of their synagogues on their Sabbath to do forced labor. As late as the nineteenth century, in Cairo, even the lowliest Arab did not hesitate to beat a Jew for such trivial things as daring to pass a Moslem on the right.[93] In Yemen, Jews were required to clean the public latrines and Jewish orphans were taken away to be raised as Moslems.[94]

Ironically, Jews living in parts of North Africa and the Middle East after European imperial powers conquered these areas now found themselves better off than under their former Moslem rulers, even though many of their ancestors had fled European persecution to find more security in the Islamic lands. Over the centuries Europe had changed, as the Islamic world had changed. Under pressure from European powers, the Ottoman Empire began to reform and modernize, ultimately granting equal citizenship to all in 1869, regardless of religion.[95] But by then, the Jews of the Ottoman Empire had fallen far behind the Jews in other parts of the world.

MODERN EUROPE

The modern era that began for the world when the two hemispheres learned of each other's existence and began to interact was, for the Jews of Europe, an era when both progress and tragedy reached unprecedented dimensions. At the dawning of the early modern era, most of the Jews of the world were still living in the Islamic countries. However, with the passing centuries, the Jews' deteriorating position in a declining empire led many to immigrate to Europe, where the worst persecutions of the Middle Ages now seemed to be over and where, in any event, economies were advancing and political systems were relatively stable.

Law and order were especially important to Jews, who were a small, vulnerable, and conspicuous minority in country after country. By and large, Jews supported the emerging and growing nation-states of Europe, which had the power to protect them, even when those states did not provide equal rights. Secessionist nationalities seeking "self-determination" seldom had Jewish support—a fact bitterly remembered and revenged when these nationalistic movements eventually succeeded in establishing independent nations, as during the disintegration of the Habsburg and Ottoman empires after the First World War.[96]

In early modern Europe, the Jews lived separate lives, symbolized by the ghettoes that existed in various forms across the continent. The separation was more than physical, however. Christians and Jews lived in separate worlds of the mind and spirit. They followed different traditions, not only in religion—immensely important as that was to both in that era—but also in customs, dress, language, food, education, and demeanor.[97] The separation of Christian and Jew, initiated by a militant Catholic Church during the era of the Crusades, was virtually complete in much of early modern Europe. Yet the Jews, whose occupations from peddlers to international financiers kept them in contact and continual interaction with Christians, could not remain wholly unaffected by dramatic changes in the European world around them, which was moving to the forefront in science, philosophy, technology, and economic achievement. Those Jews who were urban, educated, and working in professions that brought them into more contact with the higher levels of European culture were of course more cognizant of these changes and their implications than were the masses of Jewish peddlers or artisans scattered through the agricultural hinterlands or gathered in small villages where life seemed to go on as always since time immemorial.

All regions of Europe did not advance equally. Throughout most of the modern era, the spearhead of the progress of European civilization was in Western Europe—England, France, the Netherlands, and the Germanic lands, stretching from the North Sea through what is today Austria. Jews were forced out of much of this region during the late Middle Ages, so that the population center and cultural center of European Jewry had shifted from Western Europe to Eastern Europe by the early modern era.[98] Most Ashkenazic Jews no longer lived in the Germanic lands from which their name derived, but in largely Slavic regions to the east. More important, Jews began the modern era living in the more backward lands of Europe, and those Jews remaining in the more advanced parts of Europe were largely insulated from the intellectual and cultural sources of that advance. Even within the Poland-Lithuania region, where most European Jews were now concentrated, the more advanced western and northern regions were served by a German middle class, while in the more backward eastern region Jews dominated trade.[99]

Modernizing tendencies of various sorts slowly but inexorably began eroding the barriers between Christians and Jews in Europe—and eventually eroded also much of the traditional meaning of Christianity and Judaism. Intellectually, one of the by-products of the Renaissance of the late medieval and early modern period was a renewed interest in scholarly research on the ancient world, which included the Old Testament that Christians and Jews shared as a sacred text. Associated with this was an interest in the Hebrew language and in Judaic writings. A linguistic and philosophic basis was thus created for discourse among Christian and Jewish scholars, though that discourse began haltingly, sporadically, and amid warnings against it by co-religionists on both sides. Politically and economically, the rising nation-states and empires in Europe found the skills, entrepreneurship, and capital of the Jews very useful in strengthening their respective countries' military forces. During the Thirty Years' War (1618–1648), many discriminatory restrictions against Jews were removed as the contending European countries sought the aid of Jewish financiers to carry on their expensive struggles against one another.[100]

The erosion of restrictions against Jews within Christian Europe was accompanied by an erosion of control over individual Jews by autonomous Jewish community authorities who were progressively undermined as the rising secular nation-states strengthened their direct rule of subjects or citizens, at the expense of intermediary institutions such as the nobility or religious bodies. To varying degrees, individual Jews were attracted away from Jewish traditions—not necessarily so much as to convert to Christianity, though that happened in some cases—but one could remain a Jew and yet adopt some ideas or practices of the surrounding Christian world. In places and times where the Gentiles' hostility abated—amid the *philo*-Semitism in vogue in some high places in the second half of the seventeenth century in Europe,[101] for example—there need be no sense of betrayal of one's people in reaching out to a wider intellectual or social world. Nevertheless, the process was not painless, as different segments of the Jewish community differed greatly, and sometimes vehemently, as to how far to go.

Some men would shave their beards and discard traditional Jewish dress in order to move more easily among Gentiles in their business or profession. Some rabbis would countenance Jews going to the theaters or opera houses of the Gentiles.[102] Some venturesome Jewish congregations would introduce choirs, stained-glass windows, or other external features borrowed from Christian churches into their own houses of worship. Yet, few went so far as Spinoza, who denied the divine origin of Judaism and was expelled from the Sephardic community of Amsterdam.

The loosening of traditional religious ties and discipline among Christians facilitated a reaching out of those on the fringes of both communities toward each other. The Catholic-Protestant split of the sixteenth century and the bitter, devastating, and ultimately futile wars that grew out of their struggle for supremacy made religious tolerance seem more attractive and, for some, made religion itself seem less attractive. Movements to grant civil rights to Jews spread across Europe, beginning in the early eighteenth century in France, though it would be generations later before civil equality before the law was achieved, at varying dates, in different parts of the continent.[103] The historically decisive event was the granting of civil equality to all French citizens in 1791, in the wake of the French Revolution—making this the first time in Europe that Jews were recognized as equal before the law. This civic equality then spread across the continent in the wake of Napoleon's conquering armies, and though the reconstitution of the old regimes after Waterloo marked a setback for civil equality for Jews, the *status quo ante* was not wholly restored everywhere and by the mid-nineteenth century civil equality for Jews was becoming more widely accepted.[104]

Along with this movement for civic equality of individuals, there developed an appreciation of Jewish traditions. Both tendencies originated within the educated elite of Christian Europe and the resistance they encountered among both the elite and the masses was formidable. Nevertheless, the groping toward mutual understanding between Christians and Jews was historic in itself and in its longer-run consequences. When eminent individuals of the non-Jewish world, such as Milton and Rembrandt, showed respect for and interest in Jewish tradition—Rembrandt actually lived in the Jewish quarter of Amsterdam[105]—it was perhaps inevitable that such eminent Jewish individuals as Moses Mendelssohn should reach out toward the ideas and philosophy of the wider European world.

Unlike Spinoza, Mendelssohn remained a Jew and a defender of Judaism, but set it in the broader context of the eighteenth-century Enlightenment and of Western philosophy in general. He was an historic bridge between the Jewish and Christian worlds, not only by what he said and did, but also by the respect and admiration he evoked from the Christian world, including the praises of Immanuel Kant.[106] Gentiles as well as Jews mourned his death and other Jews followed in his footsteps to participate more fully in European culture and contribute to its advancement. Among Christians, Mendelssohn's call for religious toleration and separation of church and state continued to be echoed after he was gone.[107] His son became a leading banker in Berlin and his grandson one of the great composers of classical music.

With the passing generations and centuries, Jews increasingly produced historic figures, not simply within the Jewish tradition, but in Western civilization and of world stature. The great classical economist David Ricardo was descended from Sephardic Jews in Holland, though he himself no longer followed Judaism and lived in England. Many of the intellectual giants of the nineteenth and twentieth centuries were likewise of Jewish descent—Marx, Freud, and Einstein being perhaps the best known. Although no Jew was awarded a Nobel Prize until 1905, 16 percent of all Nobel Prizes over the next 70 years went to Jews, who were never as much as 1 percent of the world's population.[108] At more mundane levels as well, Jews became not only a part of Western civilization but also a major influence in its development. The nature and strength of that influence varied greatly from country to country, and especially as between Eastern Europe and Western Europe. At the level of the masses, as well as the elite, the Jews of these two regions of Europe grew more dissimilar over time—the Western European Jews becoming more assimilated and part of the larger society around them, while Eastern European Jews remained more isolated in their own traditions and their own social world.

The modern era also saw a subtle but fateful change in the character of anti-Jewish hostility. In medieval Europe, as in the Islamic lands, religion was the central pivot of anti-Jewish animosities, even if the impelling force was envy or resentment of their success. However, Jews who converted to Christianity, or to Islam in the Moslem world, were relieved of the disabilities which applied to those who continued to adhere to the Judaic faith. In some particulars, both social and legal, converts might encounter some barriers or limitations but even these tended to erode away with the passing generations, both in Christian and Moslem lands.[109] *Conversos* in medieval Spain were not the only offspring of Jewish ancestors to rise to prominence or power after religious conversion. This happened in Moslem countries as well and, in nineteenth-century England, Disraeli became prime minister at a time when no practicing Jew was permitted to sit in Parliament. By contrast, later anti-Semitism focused on *ancestry,* on descent from the "race" of Semites. This racial and pseudo-scientific anti-Semitism emerged in the late nineteenth century and was the kind of anti-Jewish animosity that later actuated Hitler and the Nazis, to whom an individual's religious or non-religious views meant nothing during the Holocaust. This hostility to Jews as a people, quite aside from religious differences, was articulated at least as far back as Voltaire in the eighteenth century.[110]

Eastern Europe

The widely shifting national boundaries of Eastern Europe over the centuries, including the appearance and disappearance of whole nations such as Poland, makes the separate national histories of the Jews in this region not only more difficult to follow but also less meaningful. Jews in a given location might belong to several different countries in a span of a few generations. In addition, Jewish settlements expanded territorially with the expansion of the Polish Empire in the sixteenth and seventeenth centuries, and many Jews were later incorporated into Russia as the czars took over formerly Polish territories. Similarly, some Ottoman Jews became Eastern European Jews without moving, as the boundaries of the Ottoman Empire were pushed back toward Turkey. Despite many local variations, the history of Eastern European Jews can therefore be considered as a regional history, rather than national histories.

Substantial numbers of Jews lived in Eastern Europe since medieval times, at least. Many fled there as a refuge from the lethal mass violence that struck them when the Crusaders passed through Western Europe. In addition, Polish ruler Boleslav specifically invited Jews to settle in his domains in the thirteenth century, providing for their protection as well as their separation from Christians. Eastern Europe, then as later, lagged behind Western Europe in economic development, education, urbanization, skills, and the general cultural development of its masses, however much its elite might produce geniuses of world stature like Tolstoy or Dostoyevsky. Jews were sought as a source of Western European skills much lacking in Poland. In other parts of Eastern Europe, though without such formal recognition of their role, Jews likewise provided much-needed artisan skills and provided a largely backward peasant society with such complementary occupations as peddlers, merchants, money-lenders, and manufacturers. As a literate people in the predominantly illiterate world of Eastern Europe,

Jews were also useful to the landowning nobility as rent collectors and to the government as tax collectors—both roles tending to provoke hostility from the general populace.

The Christian religion and the Catholic Church as an institution were both relatively recent features of Polish life when the Ashkenazic Jews began arriving there in medieval times, so religiously based hostility toward Jews was far less prevalent then than in later centuries, when the Christian clergy eventually succeeded in turning Poland into one of the most anti-Jewish countries in Europe. Christian merchants, artisans, and others who competed in the same occupations as Jews were also contributors to Polish anti-Jewish hostility. The offsetting liberalizing influences of the Renaissance and of early modern thought were slow to reach Eastern Europe, historically a region on the fringes of European culture, as exemplified by the relatively late arrival of Christianity in Poland in the tenth century. The two great regions of Europe had in fact differed since ancient times, when the Roman Empire extended over Western Europe and became an enduring cultural influence there. The Slavic lands of the east remained beyond the borders of the empire, and for many centuries thereafter looked to the West for new technology and new ideas. Jews were only one of the conduits of Western European culture to Eastern Europe.

As the modern age dawned, an enormous transfer of Europe's Jewish population was already underway. Waves of persecutions, expulsions, and mob violence in various parts of Western Europe, from the mid-fifteenth to the late sixteenth century, led to an exodus of Jews to the east—to Eastern Europe as well as to the Ottoman territories in the Balkans and the Middle East.[111] Whatever the variety of immediate causes of these anti-Jewish outbreaks, the larger pattern of expulsion of Jews from the West and their acceptance in the East reflected the widely differing need for their skills and talents in the two regions.

Western Europe was well supplied with Christian artisans, merchants, literate professionals, money-lenders, and other occupations in which Jews specialized. Indeed, it was often these Christian competitors who whipped up popular hostility and promoted official discrimination against Jews. This common pattern existed even in Spain, where many of the Christian competitors had themselves been Jews before the mass forced conversions of the fourteenth and fifteenth centuries. In those regions where the particular skills and talents of the Jews were in especially great demand—Eastern Europe and the Balkans, for example—rulers found it worthwhile to encourage Jewish settlement and to protect them from popular hostility.

In the year 1500, there were an estimated 30,000 Jews in Poland, but by 1575 there were an estimated 100,000 to 150,000 there.[112] This rapid growth of the Jewish population continued, as most German Jews migrated into Poland.[113] The Jewish population was not evenly spread across Poland but became concentrated in the less-developed eastern regions of the country, while German artisans and merchants remained dominant in the western and northern Baltic regions of Poland.[114] For the Jews, Poland was not simply a country with less persecution than they had known in Western Europe. It was a place where a far wider range of occupations was open to them. Jews were tanners, soap-makers, glaziers, fur-processors, distillers, and clothiers, as well as middlemen marketing agricultural produce and managers of the estates of noblemen.[115] The jewelry business in Poland was almost entirely in Jewish hands.[116]

Culturally, Poland became the new capital of world Jewry. Talmudic academies, which had once flourished in Germany, now became prominent in Poland as the Ashkenazim settled there. Literacy became widespread among Polish Jews, as even the children of poor Jews were enabled to attend school with subsidies from the Jewish community at large. With the spread of printing, costly handwritten manuscripts were replaced by much less expensive books, thereby spreading Jewish writings even to families scattered in isolated villages in the rural countryside in Poland or the Ukraine. Behind these economic and institutional facts was a strong tradition of respect for learning and intellectual endeavor, which made many individuals and communities sacrifice to achieve education.[117] Literacy and an emphasis on intellect added to the other sharp differences between the Jews and the largely illiterate Polish peasant masses by whom they were surrounded. They literally spoke different languages. The Ashkenazic Jews of Poland continued to speak Yiddish—a dialect of German, as it existed before the exodus from Germany, together with an admixture of Hebrew, Slavic, and other words, varying in proportions from place to place.[118]

Polish military expansion to the east in the seventeenth century brought Jews into the Ukraine, where thousands worked as peddlers, small tradesmen, or craftsmen,[119] and some as managers of Polish noblemen's estates in the newly conquered lands. Eventually, the oppressions suffered by the Ukrainians led to an armed revolt in 1648, led by Cossacks with the help of Tatars from the Crimea. The brutal and indiscriminate massacres of the vengeful Cossacks, especially, took thousands of lives of Polish noblemen, Catholic clergy, and Jews. Being more numerous than the other targeted groups, Jews bore the brunt of the losses. For the Jews, it was a loss of life not to be exceeded until the Nazi Holocaust nearly three centuries later.[120] Nevertheless, the Jewish population recovered demographically and economically within a generation.[121]

By the end of the seventeenth century, the combined kingdoms of Poland and Lithuania contained an estimated 350,000 Jews. Among other Eastern European countries, Bohemia-Moravia's Jewish population was approximately 50,000 and that of Hungary 10,000.[122] As of 1700, Prague alone had 11,000 Jewish residents, making it the largest Ashkenazic community in Europe.[123] As elsewhere, most of the Bohemian Jews were poor peddlers and traders.[124] In general, Eastern European Jews tended to live in self-governing communities, autonomous in their internal affairs and watchful over their members lest they provoke the surrounding society by ostentatious dress, rowdy behavior, or ill-advised words.[125] Such self-governing Jewish communities were not unique to Eastern Europe—they occurred elsewhere across the continent and in Islamic countries—but Eastern European self-restriction was tighter. Among other things, this meant that Eastern European Jews were more sealed off in their own world from the intellectual currents of modern Europe.[126]

Within their world, the Jews developed their own trends and fashions but these had little or no connection with the outside world of Christian Europe. Among the Messianic Jewish movements originating in Eastern Europe was Hasidism, which emphasized spiritual, more so than intellectual, devotion to Judaism.[127] But, as regards the outside world, neither the eighteenth-century Enlightenment nor nineteenth-century attempts at assimilation or accommodation to the outward practices of the larger society had nearly the influence among Eastern European Jews as among Jews in the West. This meant that Eastern

European Jews remained not only alienated from Christians but also, to an increasing extent, from their changing co-religionists in Western Europe as well. This alienation among Jews was felt on both sides. By the mid-nineteenth century, followers of Eastern Europe's own Jewish modernizing "enlightenment" or *Haskalah* movement were referred to sarcastically by their more traditional compatriots as "Berlinchiks"—imitators of German Jews.[128]

Poland, the heartland of Eastern European Jewry, disappeared from the map in the late eighteenth century, as Russia, Prussia, and Austria divided its territory among themselves. Along with the territory of Poland, Russia acquired large numbers of Jews. In 1795 there were approximately 800,000 Jews in Russia,[129] a country with a centuries-old tradition of anti-Jewish policies, including a 1727 decree by Catherine I banning them from the country. The czarist regime did not want its newly acquired Jewish population spreading throughout the country, so the government confined them to regions including some—but not all—of what had been Poland and some less-developed regions in the southern part of the Russian Empire. This was called the Pale of Settlement and Jews were forbidden to live "beyond the Pale." Moscow and St. Petersburg, for example, were beyond the Pale, as were Warsaw and Kiev, at least for a time. Thus the Jews, though highly urbanized elsewhere, had less than 20 percent of their population living in cities of 10,000 people or more in czarist Russia.

The Russian government also began a decades-long campaign to "Russify" the Jews through such heavy-handed methods as conscripting their young men for more than 30 years of military service (other conscripts served 25 years), during which they were forced to eat pork, make the sign of the cross, and otherwise violate Jewish tradition and be pressured to become Christian in religion and Russian in culture. The long beards and long coats traditional among Jewish men were also forbidden and policemen carried scissors with which they were authorized to trim the beards of any Jews they encountered on the streets who were caught violating this law.[130]

One of the underdeveloped regions of the Russian Empire in which Jews were permitted to live was the area around the Black Sea—land recently conquered by Russia from the Ottoman Empire. Here there developed the port of Odessa, where Jews were one among a number of non-Russian minorities who settled and contributed to the economic growth of the area. Agricultural colonists in this region produced nearly one-fourth of Russia's grain exports. Odessa's businessmen were noted for their indefatigable pursuit of money, its workers were paid far more than similar work brought elsewhere, and Odessa became the primary port of entry for goods from Asia on their way to markets throughout Europe.[131] Like other nationalities, the Jews specialized in particular sectors—as bankers, agents, brokers, and traders in tobacco and Oriental goods.[132] By 1842, Jews owned 228 businesses in Odessa and constituted just over half the people engaged in trade in the city.[133] In this developing frontier region, Jews were free of many of the restrictions which applied elsewhere as to where they could live or the occupations they could follow. Their success, however, came back to haunt them. In 1871, there was an outbreak of mob violence against the Jews of Odessa, instigated by their business competitors.[134]

Anti-Semitic policies in Russia were at their peak during the reign of Czar Nicholas I (1825–1855). His son, Alexander II, began a process of reducing or repealing some anti-Jewish policies but, despite hopes raised earlier in his reign, his policies stopped far short of the "emancipation" or civic equality found in other European states.[135] When Alexander II was assassinated in 1881 by a member of a group in which Jews and other minorities were prominent, anti-Semitic riots broke out in Russia and the new czar, Alexander III, began a new wave of anti-Semitic policies. Sporadic outbursts of anti-Jewish mob violence, often unchecked by police or even with the active participation of policemen and soldiers, became recurrent events in the Russian Empire—on through the decades leading up to the First World War.[136]

The shock of these first *pogroms* of the 1880s set off one of the great mass exoduses in history. Between 1881 and 1914, more than a million and a half Jews immigrated from Russia to the United States alone. From all of Eastern Europe, more than 2 million Jews immigrated to the United States during this period.[137] Many other Jews fled to other European countries, or to North Africa or the Middle East, but at least three-quarters went to the United States, just as three-quarters of the Jewish emigrants of this era originated in Russia.

During the period between the two World Wars, and especially during the 1930s, the political, social, and economic position of Jews in

Eastern and Central Europe deteriorated drastically. Many of the newly independent nations of this region were carved out of the old Austro-Hungarian Empire, after its defeat in World War I. Poland reappeared as a nation after more than a century, and Czechoslovakia, Yugoslavia, and Latvia were created as sovereign states by the victors at the conference table. As in the case of newly emerging nations in Asia and Africa after World War II, the small, largely peasant, Eastern European nations turned their newly won power against their own domestic minorities, of whom the Jews were the prime targets.

Although the Jews of this region were by no means all prosperous, and many were in fact very poor, a disproportionate amount of the commerce of the area was conducted by Jews, who were also prominent in the professions and the press. As of 1921, more than three-fifths of all the commerce in Poland was conducted by Jews, who were only 11 percent of the population.[138] In 1931, just over half the private physicians in Poland were Jewish.[139] The Jewish working class consisted largely of craftsmen—shoemakers, bakers, tailors—rather than workers in large factories or mines, who tended to be Polish. Of the Polish Jews in commerce, nearly four-fifths were in one-man operations—small shopkeepers rather than owners of businesses large enough to have employees.[140] Few Jews were hired by the Polish government, however. Out of nearly 29,000 railroad employees, for example, fewer than 50 were Jews. Less than 3 percent of schoolteachers hired by the government were Jews, and Jewish professors were virtually unheard of in Polish universities. Nor were Jewish doctors hired in state hospitals or Jewish lawyers retained by state institutions.[141]

Much the same situation existed in Hungary. On the eve of World War I, 60 percent of all merchants in Hungary were Jews. In the capital city of Budapest, Jews were 42 percent of the journalists, 45 percent of the lawyers, and 49 percent of the doctors. Many also held important government posts and hundreds held titles of nobility.[142] By 1920, half of all lawyers and three-fifths of all doctors were Jewish—in a country where Jews were only 6 percent of the population. While there were many poor Jews in Hungary, Jews were also prominent among the more prosperous classes. Nearly half of all industrial enterprises in Hungary were owned by Jews, as were more than three-fifths of all large commercial firms. Most Hungarian Christians were in agriculture—a sector in which only 4 percent of the Jews worked.[143] In short, there were two entirely different occupational patterns as between the Jews and the Gentiles in Hungary. The same was true in Rumania, where nearly three-quarters of the non-Jewish population worked in agriculture, while four-fifths of the Jews were in commerce or industry.[144]

The over-representation of Jews in commerce, industry, and the professions was usually an indication of the backwardness of the particular region. In the more backward eastern areas of Poland, 88 percent of all commerce was conducted by Jews, while in the more advanced western areas, formerly part of Germany, just under 8 percent of the commerce was conducted by Jews.[145] In Lithuania, a much poorer country than Poland, Jews conducted more than three-quarters of all commerce.[146] In Rumania, as in Poland, the more backward areas were where Jewish predominance in commerce was greatest.[147] The relatively small numbers of truly wealthy Jews were more likely to be found in the great commercial and industrial centers, where they were seldom a majority, while the masses of Jewish peddlers, small shopkeepers, and others at this much lower economic level were often virtually the only nonagricultural people in many backward peasant communities. Here this latter kind of Jewish economic "dominance" was particularly likely to excite envy and anti-Semitism among the ignorant population and provide a statistical basis for political demagoguery.

As in so many other backward countries with more advanced minorities, the newly rising indigenous middle classes of Eastern Europe spearheaded the attack on those whose competition threatened their career aspirations. Universities in Eastern Europe became centers of anti-Semitism and fascism in the interwar period.[148] In some Polish universities during the 1930s, Jewish students were forced to sit in segregated areas of classrooms and were subjected to violence, including several murders.[149] In 1934, Nazi propaganda minister Josef Goebbels gave a lecture at the University of Warsaw, attended by leading Polish officials. Among the subjects covered were the Nazi views on the Jews.[150] Throughout Eastern Europe, by one means or another, the proportion of Jews among university students generally declined.[151]

Responding to widespread convictions that the emerging Polish middle class could advance only by displacing Jews, the Polish government established control over those industries in which Jews predominated, such as tobacco, liquor, salt, and matches.[152] Boycotts of Jewish businesses in Poland during the 1930s—sometimes supplemented with violence against their owners or customers—led to a decline in Jewish-owned stores, both absolutely and relative to the total numbers of stores. Occupational licensing laws and the rules of medical and journalistic professional associations also excluded Jews from many occupations.[153] In Hungary, similar restrictions were imposed during the 1930s, though less effectively administered. One ironic casualty of this anti-Jewish atmosphere was the anti-Semitic prime minister, Béla Imrédy, who was forced to resign when his political enemies revealed that he had a Jewish great-grandfather.[154]

The crucial role of rising indigenous middle-class aspirants as the political base for obsessive anti-Semitism is indicated by lower levels of anti-Semitism in places and times where such classes had not yet emerged—for example, in late nineteenth-century Hungary or in Lithuania as late as the immediate post–World War I years[155]—or in places where a long-established, non-Jewish middle class was well able to hold their own in competition, as in the Bohemian province of Czechoslovakia or in Latvia. Among these latter middle classes, however, were members of the German minority who, during the 1930s, came more and more under the influence of Nazi Germany,[156] adding to the problems of the Jews. The assimilation of many Eastern European Jews to the German language and culture—in parts of Czechoslovakia, Rumania, and Latvia,[157] for example—did not help. Nor did the high degree of assimilation of Hungarian Jews.[158] More generally, the degree of Jewish acculturation or assimilation to the society around them had little or no effect on their ultimate fate.

During World War II, approximately 2.7 million Polish Jews were murdered by the Nazis and another 350,000 escaped into the Soviet Union. By 1945, only 85,000 remained alive in Poland, and another 230,000 in the U.S.S.R. Some of the survivors were killed in anti-Semitic outbreaks of violence by the Poles. Initially, many Jews returning from the Soviet Union after World War II benefitted from the establishment of a Communist satellite government in Poland. Although the prewar Communist Party in Poland had only 5,000 Jewish members out of a total Jewish population of more than 3 million, nevertheless Jews were 26 percent of the Communist membership. They received many important posts in the government and economy of early postwar Poland.

While this brought Jews some immediate material benefits, it also made them the focus of much Polish hatred of a dictatorial regime imposed by their historic enemies, the Russians. When anti-government agitation and riots erupted in the 1950s and 1960s, Jews were special targets—and were especially treated as expendable by the Communist authorities. Many were purged. More than half the Jews in Poland emigrated to Israel between 1950 and 1958, and another 17,000 left between 1969 and 1970. By the late twentieth century, there were only about 10,000 Jews (including offspring of mixed marriages) in Poland[159]—this in a country which had more than 3 million Jews before the war.

The tragedy of the Jews in Poland was repeated, with local variations, in other parts of Eastern Europe and the Balkans. In Hungary, Rumania, and Czechoslovakia, for example, Jews were historically over-represented in the leadership of the Communist Party, as they were in Poland. When a Communist dictatorship was briefly imposed in Hungary after the First World War, its leadership was overwhelmingly Jewish—and the political retaliation after its overthrow was, as in Germany, anti-Semitic. In Hungary, the reaction included the murder of 1,800 Jews in 1920 and a heightened and lasting anti-Semitism throughout the society.[160] In the Nazi Holocaust a generation later, half or more of the total Jewish population of Hungary perished, despite resistance by the Hungarian government and the heroic efforts of Sweden's Raoul Wallenberg to aid their escape. The postwar imposition of a Communist government on Hungary again brought many Jews to prominence—and they were, as in Poland, later sacrificed in purges to appease both Stalin and domestic anti-Semites. By the late twentieth century, there were an estimated 75,000 Jews in Hungary—less than 10 percent of the prewar Jewish population.[161]

Postwar Czechoslovakia, Rumania, and other Eastern bloc countries also went through periods of the waxing and waning of Jewish fortunes, associated with (1) the early installation of Communist satellite governments, (2) Stalin's anti-Semitic purge policies in the late 1940s and early 1950s, and (3) the changing foreign policies of the Communist bloc toward Israel and the Islamic nations of the Middle East. Native anti-Semitism also played a role, and this varied from country to country and by region within countries. Backward Slovakia was a particularly anti-Semitic region of Czechoslovakia, for example,[162] while Bulgaria was historically much less anti-Semitic and had the highest rate of survival of Jews during World War II of any Axis nation. Throughout Eastern Europe and the Balkans, the postwar Jewish population was a tiny fraction of its prewar size, with aging and intermarriage producing further declines.

The key nation in Eastern Europe was of course the Soviet Union. The Bolshevik Revolution of 1917 which created the U.S.S.R. had a disproportionate number of Jews among its leaders—Leon Trotsky being the most prominent—and raised hopes among other Jews of an end to the savage anti-Semitism that had marked so much of Russian history. Many of the Jews among the Communist leadership had long since ceased to think of themselves as Jews, even in a social or cultural sense, much less a religious sense. Yet many of them later learned to their shock and disillusionment that others—including their comrades—still thought of them that way and singled them out for hostile treatment.

Like other ethnic groups in the U.S.S.R., the Jews were initially allowed a certain cultural autonomy in the 1920s. But the reaction set in during the 1930s, when Stalin's purges struck. Thousands of Jews were among the intellectuals purged.[163] Jews aroused a special suspicion as a highly visible group with international kinship and cultural ties, in a totalitarian state attempting to seal its population off from outside "corrupting" influences, such as Trotskyism, democracy, or knowledge of the higher standards of living in other countries. Jews were even more of a political problem during the period of Stalin's collaboration with Hitler, beginning with the Nazi-Soviet pact of August 1939, which paved the way for World War II. The Soviet Union's Jewish foreign minister, Maxim Litvinov, was replaced by V. M. Molotov prior to the accord with Nazi Germany.[164]

In the nearly two years that elapsed between the Nazi-Soviet pact and the Nazi invasion of the U.S.S.R., the Soviet Union annexed vast areas of Eastern Europe containing approximately 2 million Jews, among the other peoples of that region. Located in the area of bitterest fighting during the Nazi-Soviet war—and of Nazi extermination campaigns in occupied territories—Jewish casualty rates were proportionately several times those of the Soviet population as a whole.[165] Nevertheless, Jews remained under suspicion as the only Soviet people with strong kinship ties to Western nations and the democratic tradition. The emergence of the modern state of Israel made the loyalty of Soviet Jews still more suspect.

Communist press campaigns against "homeless cosmopolitans" stopped short of explicit anti-Semitism, but government policy did not. Jewish cultural organizations were shut down. Purged individuals were often referred to by their Jewish names even when they had long been known by Russified names. Executions on bizarre charges eliminated virtually the entire cultural leadership of Soviet Jewry. Jews were barred from the Soviet foreign service, where they had once been prominent. Many Jewish students and professors were purged from institutions of higher learning. In the last days of Stalin, a "plot" by Jewish doctors was fabricated and publicized—the fabrication later being admitted by the Soviet government itself after Stalin's death.[166]

The entire period of World War II and the postwar era were times of greatly heightened *Russian* nationalism, with attendant subordination of the role of minority cultural identities. Jews suffered from this general pattern, as well as from being singled out as special targets. The focus of the Soviet attack was primarily Jewish identity rather than Jewish ancestry. Soviet Jews without ties to the Jewish people and willing to be hostile to Israel, for example, could and did survive and thrive. One of the leading Soviet intellectuals of this era was Ilya Ehrenburg, who was of Jewish ancestry, but who declared "there is no such entity as the Jewish people."[167]

People of Jewish ancestry thus continued to be over-represented among the educated classes, among Communist Party members, among doctors and lawyers, and in the Soviet Academy of Sciences, even though restricted *de facto* from the foreign ministry and the top levels of the armed forces. Nevertheless, the emergence of newly educated classes among some Soviet nationalities, such as Central Asians, led to notions of "ethnic balance" in organizations open to such people—and "ethnic balance" meant career obstacles to Jews, an overachieving group without the political clout to protect themselves like the Slavs.[168]

Despite official attempts to undermine Jewish identity, the effect of Israel on Soviet Jews was electrifying. The first appearance of Golda Meir at a Moscow synagogue in 1948 caused the usual High Holy Days attendance of 2,000 to rise suddenly to nearly 50,000 demonstrative people.[169] The longer-run effect was even more dramatic. Between January 1968 and June 1973, more than 62,000 Soviet Jews immigrated to Israel, despite enormous obstacles put in their way. This was more than all the other Soviet peoples to emigrate in half a century of Communist rule.[170]

The reaction of the Soviet government took many forms. They tightened emigration restrictions, drastically reducing the outflow, creating an entire class of rejected emigration applicants known as "refuseniks"—people not allowed to leave and also subjected to discrimination and harassment for having applied. The most famous of these was Anatoly Scharansky, later known as Natan Scharansky, once he was free to take the Jewish name his mother preferred, but which she had dared not give him in the U.S.S.R. The Soviet government also sharply restricted the opportunities of Jews in general. Between 1970 and 1977, the number of Jews admitted to Soviet universities dropped by 40 percent, from approximately 112,000 to just 67,000. Almost none were admitted to Moscow State University. Jews were especially excluded from the sciences. In the mathematics department at Moscow State University, Jews were once 30 percent of all students in the late 1940s but by the early 1970s were only 1 percent.[171]

These repressive measures in turn brought into play the special access of Soviet Jews to the West, and especially the Western media. An estimated one-third to one-half of the leadership of the Soviet dissident movement was Jewish.[172] This was an especially ironic role, in view of earlier Jewish prominence among those in the forefront of the drive to create communism in Russia and the Western world.

Western Europe

Although Jews were expelled from many parts of Western Europe during the late Middle Ages, many returned during the early modern era. By 1582 a general synod of German Jewry was convened, for now there were Jewish communities in various German towns and cities. At around the same time, Jews settled in other places from which they had once been expelled in France, the Netherlands, and in Tuscany, for example. In Venice, the number of Jews in the ghetto rose from 900 in 1552 to about 1,700 by 1586. While the Jews of Western Europe were growing in numbers, they were also subjected to fewer restrictions.[173] The trends were not all in one direction everywhere, however. Spain did not relent in its intolerance and, as late as 1670–71, Jews were expelled from Vienna and lower Austria.[174] There were also expulsions from parts of Italy in the mid-sixteenth century, even as other Italian regions welcomed those expelled.[175] Nevertheless, the broad pattern over the ensuing centuries was a growing Jewish presence in Western Europe, not only demographically but also economically and intellectually.

The Germanic lands—including Austria as well as the German states and principalities—became the central focus of Western European Jewry. It was here that the Jews became most acculturated and most prosperous, and it was to Germanic Europe that the Jews of the Slavic lands fled for refuge from successive waves of persecution. By the time of the First World War, there were approximately 617,000 Jews in Germany and 2.2 million in Austria—far more than the 100,000 in France or the 250,000 in Britain, and exceeded in Europe only by the 6 million Jews in the Russian Empire.[176] German Jewry was at the same time the leaders of European Jewry and intensely patriotic, often calling themselves "Germans of the Mosaic faith."

Even within the ethnically and culturally diverse Habsburg Empire, most Jews spoke German, not only in Austria but also in regions where they lived among populations that were predominantly Czech or Rumanian.[177] Substantial numbers, especially among the educated, also spoke German in predominantly Polish Galicia or in the Hungarian portion of the Austro-Hungarian Empire,[178] as the Habsburg realm became known. What was involved was not simply a language preference but a conscious choice or commitment to become part of the cultural advance of Western European society as a whole, to escape from the narrower traditions of Orthodox Jewry and to reject the cultures of Eastern European Gentiles in favor of the more advanced German culture. Language was more than symbolic, however. The language chosen determined the whole philosophic, scientific, and other literature to which one had access. The choice was fundamentally cultural—to cast one's lot with Western European civilization—and that underlying choice often involved the German language because so many Western European Jews lived in Germanic lands. Those who lived in England made the same choice in the form of speaking the English language and adopting an English way of life.

France has not had a particularly large Jewish population but it has played a significant role—both positive and negative—in Jewish history. The first granting of civil equality to Jews, in many parts of Europe, occurred in the wake of the Napoleonic conquests, which spread the egalitarian principles of the French Revolution. Even after the defeat of Napoleon at Waterloo in 1815 and the subsequent restoration of old monarchies and their old policies, the concept of civil equality for Jews would not go away, and in fact triumphed over much of Europe during the next two generations. However, France also exemplified the strong undercurrent of anti-Semitism, even in Western European nations that have not had the history of pogroms found in Eastern Europe. The Dreyfus case, involving the false conviction and imprisonment of a Jewish captain in the French army, became a major scandal when it was exposed. More important, the anti-Semitism aroused by the initial conviction and the exultation in Dreyfus' disgrace revealed an ugly undercurrent of French society. Still more grim in its consequences was the turning over of French Jews to the Nazis by the collaborationist Vichy government during World War II. The zeal with which the French ferreted out Jews for the Nazi concentration camps was a painful contrast to efforts to aid or conceal Jews in other Western European countries such as Holland, Denmark, Norway, and even Hitler's wartime ally, Italy.

England, with a larger Jewish population than France, played a less dramatic role in the history of world Jewry—at least until World War I. Many Jews prospered in England and some rose to great prominence—not only converts like Ricardo in economics and Disraeli as a novelist and later a political leader, but also Baron Lionel Nathan de Rothschild, international financier and the first practicing Jew to sit in Parliament in 1858. But Britain's historic contribution to world Jewry came in 1915, when their conquest of Palestine during military operations against the Ottoman Empire was followed by the Balfour Declaration, declaring the right of Jews to settle in Palestine. The influx of Jewish settlers changed the region, "made the desert bloom" in Churchill's words,[179] and set the stage for the eventual re-creation of the state of Israel.

As the modernizing trends of Western Europe opened up new opportunities for Jews, those who wished to remain within the older Jewish tradition, culturally as well as religiously—to dress and talk and behave in the old way—struggled for control of Jewish communities with the modernizers, with varying degrees of success, from Holland to the Habsburg Empire, and this cultural battle continued across the oceans, in the United States and Australia. However, this cultural struggle was far less urgent in countries where it was not also a political struggle for control of autonomous Jewish communities. As the medieval political and legal institutions of separate Jewish communities dissolved over time with the emergence of modern states, cultural differences among Jews could be resolved by differing individual and social choices, rather than by a struggle for political supremacy and imposed conformity.

Depoliticization of internal Jewish cultural differences permitted separate Jewish communities to develop, socially as well as religiously—these communities being identified in many countries, including the United States, as German Jews versus Eastern European Jews. But, in broader historical terms, these differences represented in part earlier community and individual choices, as well as accidents of geography, history, and biological descent. In Australia, the acculturated, Westernized Jews were both English and German, and they stood in contrast to the Eastern European Jews who formed communities in the older tradition. The former tended to settle in Sydney, the latter in Melbourne.[180] In New York, the distinction was between the more acculturated "uptown Jews" (initially German) and the "downtown Jews" who retained the old ways from Eastern Europe. Similar neighborhood divisions existed in Chicago.[181]

The Habsburg Empire extended into both Eastern and Western Europe, not only geographically but culturally as well—and so did the Habsburg Jews. Vienna's wealthy Jews with titles of nobility—Baron Salmon de Rothschild being the most prominent example—epitomized the thoroughly Westernized ideal, while the despair of ever finding a real home in Europe was symbolized by the doctrine of Zionism, formulated in late nineteenth-century Vienna by Hungarian-born Theodor Herzl. Zionism was widely rejected by the leaders of Western European Jewry, but it struck a responsive chord in Eastern European Jews, who became its principal supporters. Yet, in Vienna itself, the very word Zionism could not be mentioned in the Jewish-owned newspaper for which Herzl wrote.[182]

Vienna had a unique history in which Jews in general long remained banned from the city, while specified individual exceptions—"tolerated" Jews—lived there and became prominent in the national economy and influential with government. Some were ennobled by the emperor. These wealthy and socially prominent Jews were thoroughly Westernized, with a Germanic culture, a cosmopolitan outlook, and were devoted to the Emperor Franz Joseph and the house of Habsburg, from whom their privileges and protection flowed. The smallness of this particular group of Jews long resident in Vienna is indicated by the fact that the total Jewish population of the city was less than 2,000 people, as late as 1847. But even after large numbers of Jews entered Vienna, legally or illegally, with the passing decades, these special families of historically "tolerated" Jews remained special. Their whole way of life was far removed from that of the masses of Habsburg Jews, their religion tended to be a modernized Reform Judaism and a few converted to Christianity. Yet this relatively small wealthy class of Viennese Jews continued over the years to attract disproportionate attention—and resentment—from other Austrians, including an impoverished and embittered young man named Adolf Hitler.

In between the enormously wealthy Jews of Vienna, with titles of nobility, and the destitute Jews of the eastern hinterlands were many Jews working in middle-class occupations, in a proportion much greater than their proportion of the population. Jews were approximately one percent of the population of Vienna in 1857, 6 percent in 1869, and 12 percent within the original boundaries of the city in 1890. Yet Jews were more than one-fifth of all law students and more than one-third of all medical students in Vienna in 1880, as well as approximately one-third of all university students there in 1890. They also owned most of the leading newspapers in Vienna and, for a generation before World War I, dominated Viennese cultural life with prominent figures who included Gustav Mahler and Sigmund Freud. Much the same story could be told of other Habsburg cities such as Prague or regions such as Bukowina.

Similarly, elsewhere in Germanic Europe, Jews were statistically much over-represented in the Berlin schools and in the Prussian universities. They dominated journalism in Berlin, where they were less than 6 percent of the population in 1895.[183] However, Jews moving into the mainstream of German life found their acceptance varying in an uneven pattern from place to place, from time to time, from class to class, and from activity to activity. As early as 1790, Jews were admitted to German universities on an equal footing with other students.[184] But there were still difficulties for Jews seeking faculty appointments a hundred years later.[185] However, for the period 1870–1933, Jews (by ancestry or religion) were over-represented among both students and professors at German universities.[186]

In the early nineteenth century, Germany was an agrarian nation, less developed economically than some other nations of Western Europe. German Jews were correspondingly less economically advanced than the Sephardic Jews in Holland, for example.[187] But the sharp economic rise of Germany in the nineteenth century was also a rise of German Jewry, who shared the pride of other Germans in their country's emergence as a leading nation in Europe and the world. The political unification of Germany in 1871 was a milestone in this progress. German Jews were noted for their patriotism and their pride in German achievements and culture, both in Germany and abroad.

In the early nineteenth century, as German Jews sought to regain the civil equality they had enjoyed under French occupation during the Napoleonic wars, their foreignness in dress, customs, and outlook were among the barriers to their social acceptance and legal equality. Some of the wealthier and more acculturated Jews simply converted to Christianity and left their former Jewish life behind them (Karl Marx's father was one of these). Others promoted deliberate efforts to reduce jarring external differences between Jews and Gentiles, while retaining the essentials of Judaism and a Jewish community. Reform Judaism grew out of these efforts. Synagogue services began to be conducted in the German language and included mixed choirs, organ music, and other characteristics of Christian churches. For many, the word "temple" replaced "synagogue" and traditional restrictions on food and individual conduct were relaxed.

Such changes were anathema to Orthodox Jews and made little headway in Eastern Europe, but Reform Judaism quickly spread as far as the United States in the early nineteenth century, varying in its degree of deviation from Orthodox Judaism from country to country.[188] The relative proportions of the two branches of Judaism—and of Conservative Judaism which developed somewhere between them—also varied from country to country. Reform Judaism symbolized a wider assimilationist tendency among German Jews, just as German Jews epitomized assimilationism among European Jewry as a whole. While many Vienna Jews were also thoroughly acculturated, that was not true of the much larger number of Eastern European Jews in the Habsburg Empire.

By the end of the nineteenth century, there were nearly 600,000 Jews in Germany, generally prosperous, German-speaking, with more than half of them in commerce, one-fifth in industry and trade, and about 6 percent in the professions and government.[189] Even the most religiously orthodox Jews considered themselves thoroughly German.[190] This remained true even after immigration to other countries: Nineteenth-century German Jewish immigrants in the United States, Chile, and Czechoslovakia often took part in the general cultural life of the German enclaves in these countries,[191] while retaining their own religious institutions. In calling themselves "Germans of the Mosaic faith," German Jews used a terminology which had relevance to their social reality, but no such corresponding term took hold among Eastern European Jews, in circumstances where to be a Jew was to be wholly outside the social world of the Gentiles.

In the first decade of the twentieth century, one-fourth of all law students and medical students in Germany were Jews, though Jews were only 1 percent of the population. One-third of the graduate students in philosophy were also Jews. In some German cities, Jews were a majority of all doctors. Jews were only 5 percent of the Berlin population in 1905, but they paid 31 percent of all income tax collected in that city, averaging more than twice the income tax per person of either Protestants or Catholics. In various other cities, Jews paid from three times to nine times the taxes of other citizens.[192] For Germany as a whole, Jewish income was more than three times the national average.[193] The integration of the Jews into German life was social as well as economic. Nearly half of all Jews who married in Germany during the 1920s married Gentiles. Thousands converted to Christianity or simply abandoned Judaism or drifted away from the Jewish community.[194] The tragic irony was that German Jews were among the most assimilated and accepted Jews in the world in the decade before the Nazis came to power.

Despite the extremely small and declining Jewish population of Germany, Jews were highly visible—and vulnerable to resentment—for a number of reasons. They were concentrated in urban areas and in a relatively few occupations, which they often dominated. By the early 1930s, just before Hitler came to power, one-half of all the theater directors in Germany were Jews and three-quarters of all the plays produced were written by Jews.[195] Jews owned 4,000 wholesale textile businesses—40 percent of all such businesses in Germany—as well as 60 percent of all wholesale and retail clothing businesses.[196] Jewish politicians were long prominent on the political left—usually much further left than the Jewish voters—and Jews predominated in a short-lived Communist government established in Germany after the country's defeat in World War I. The unpopularity of that regime gave a boost to anti-Semitism in Germany and was used for years afterwards in anti-Semitic propaganda by the Nazis and others.[197]

Other historical developments added to the unpopularity of Jews. Jews prominent on the political left were highly critical of Germany's participation in World War I, and some in the Reichstag voted against military appropriations. This too left bitter memories among other Germans, especially after the catastrophic defeat, international humiliation, and dire economic distress suffered by Germany in the wake of the war. It was politically easy to depict the Jews as unpatriotic, subversive elements who had stabbed Germany in the back and tried to impose Communism. No one made these arguments more vehemently than the Nazis. Events in Eastern Europe added to the problems of Jews in Germany. Jewish refugees from the east—with far less education, money, or assimilation than German Jews—flooded into Germany after World War I. By 1933, one-fifth of all Jews in Germany were foreign. Many were an embarrassment to the German Jews, some of whom advocated immigration restriction.[198] Eastern European Jews were referred to generically as "Polacks," by Jews and non-Jews alike.[199]

Anti-Semitic appeals had long been a feature of German political life, but the parties that relied primarily on anti-Semitism tended to do poorly at the polls. The Nazis did not rely solely—or even primarily—on anti-Semitism, and in fact tried to be all things to all people. Before coming to power they even had a Jewish following.[200] Moreover, the Nazi Party was never a serious political contender during the decade of the 1920s, however much sensation they created with their rabble-rousing and violence. Most Germans during that period regarded them as a joke.[201] In the election of 1928, the Nazis polled less than a million votes, out of 31 million votes cast.[202]

The desperate years of the Great Depression, under an ineffective German government headed by the now-senile military hero Paul von Hindenburg, gave Hitler his chance. From less than 3 percent of the vote in 1928, the Nazis shot up to 18 percent in 1930 and to 37 percent in 1932—the highest level of support they ever achieved in a free election.[203] It was also the largest support of any of the numerous German political parties. In January 1933, Hitler became Chancellor of Germany and 15 months later was voted dictatorial powers.

Anti-Semitic policies began immediately and increased at a measured pace. Laws barred Jews from many professions and made their lives miserable with innumerable legal restrictions, supplemented by ad hoc harassment and violence by Nazi thugs. But Hitler shrewdly avoided outpacing what German public opinion would support. When a boycott of Jewish businesses in 1933 failed to get the expected support, the Nazis called it off after four days.[204] But by 1935, after much anti-Semitic propaganda, Hitler instituted the Nuremburg Laws, which stripped Jews of the rights of German citizens and initiated new prohibitions and restrictions. His first serious miscalculation came when he launched the notorious *Kristallnacht*—the night of broken glass—in November 1938, in response to an assassination of a German official by a Jewish youth. Publicly billed as a "spontaneous" outburst of rage by the German people against the Jews, it was a night of violence and vandalism against Jewish homes and property, orchestrated and carried out by the Nazis.

A preliminary report listed more than a hundred homes set on fire, more than a hundred synagogues burned, hundreds of shops destroyed, and dozens of murders of Jews. Later estimates were much larger—the shops looted ran into the thousands rather than the hundreds—and the full extent of the disaster may never be known.[205] But, as the Nazi leaders themselves quickly discovered, they had miscalculated German public reaction—which was a revulsion, even among many Nazi Party members. Thereafter, the remainder of the Nazi actions against the Jews were taken with extraordinary secrecy and in calculated stages. Jews themselves did not realize the full extent of what was happening until it was too late. Germans heard only rumors, amid the numerous rumors that circulate during wartime. Concentration camps had existed for years in Nazi Germany, and contained both Jews and non-Jews. But when many of these became mass extermination camps during World War II, those who knew firsthand about the mass murders were under threat of death if they told anyone.[206]

While Nazi propaganda depicted anti-Semitic outbursts as the righteous wrath of the whole German people against the Jews, internal Nazi documents throughout the Hitler era complained bitterly of inadequate public support and cooperation with anti-Jewish policies,[207] despite years of brainwashing. A few brave souls even actively opposed or sabotaged these policies, though that risked brutal punishment for both the individual and his family.[208] Against this grim background, it is all the more remarkable that some Jews were hidden by other Germans. Estimates for Berlin alone run into the thousands.[209] Most Germans, like most other people, were not heroes. But the difference in attitudes between the German populace and the Nazi government was indicated by the fact that Jews, lacking legal protection in Nazi Germany even before the war, suffered no such pogroms as they suffered from the general populations of Eastern Europe, or parts of the Islamic world, under such circumstances.

The official persecutions that preceded the Holocaust were enough to drive most Jews from Germany. Between 1933 and 1938, approximately 150,000 of the half-million Jews in Germany emigrated. An equal number fled in the year before World War II began in 1939. This mass exodus saved a majority of the German Jews from the fate that overtook other Jews in the conquered lands of Europe.[210] Of the millions of Jews killed by the Nazis, less than 200,000 were German.[211]

Nevertheless, the slaughter of those who remained represented the destruction of one-third the German Jews of the pre-Nazi period, just as the Holocaust represented the killing of one-third of all the Jews in the world. As if such staggering massacres of defenseless men, women, and children were not enough, the Nazis imposed a pervasive dehumanization that sadistically scarred the souls before the mass murders and the burning of bodies. If one historical episode can be singled out as the nadir of human civilization—indeed, as a bitter mockery of that term—it must surely be the Holocaust.

Postwar Germany had fewer than 25,000 Jews remaining—less than 5 percent of the German Jewish population just a decade earlier. Moreover, many Jews around the world were bitterly opposed to any Jews at all remaining in Germany after the Holocaust. While several thousand emigrated from Germany, to either Israel or the United States, most stayed.[212] Communist East Germany ("The Democratic Republic of Germany") was at first a country where individual Jews rose to prominence after the war, but Stalin's anti-Semitic policies in the early 1950s were echoed in so-called "anti-Zionist" purges in East Germany.[213] From 1952 to 1961, approximately 5,000 East German Jews fled to West Germany as part of a general influx of 20,000 Jews to the Federal Republic of Germany.

The state of Israel made claims for reparations against both German governments, on behalf of victims of Nazism—many of whom were settled in Israel at great expense to the Israeli government. East Germany rejected these claims but West Germany paid more than $10 billion directly to individuals over a period of two decades. In addition, vast amounts of equipment and supplies were given as reparations to the new nation of Israel, which desperately needed them.[214] Some individuals among the postwar German youth came to work in Israel as a symbolic gesture. Perhaps what it symbolized went beyond Germans and Jews—the flickering light of common humanity persisting against the dark background of enormous evils.

The Holocaust's lasting impact can be seen in many ways, including demographically. On the eve of the Second World War, the Jewish population of the world was nearly 17 million people. But, by the end of the war, this population was reduced to 11 million—and, half a century later, it still had not recovered its prewar level but was less than 13 million. Moreover, the primacy of European Jewry was gone. In 1939, more than half the Jews of the world lived in Europe, but by 1991 Europe contained less than a sixth of world's Jewish population.[215] Most now lived in the Western Hemisphere.

THE WESTERN HEMISPHERE

By the twentieth century, Jews in the Western Hemisphere meant primarily Jews in the United States. However, the first Jewish settlements in the New World were in Latin America. The earliest community of Jews in the thirteen North American colonies came from Brazil in 1654. Jewish communities in Latin America are very old, even if not very large. Moreover, Jews have contributed disproportionately to the commercial and industrial development of a number of Latin American nations.

Persecutions in fifteenth- and sixteenth-century Spain and Portugal sent many Jews fleeing, not only to countries with greater tolerance but also to Western Hemisphere colonies, where intolerance would be harder to enforce, including Spanish and Portuguese colonies. Jews also settled in Dutch colonies, which exhibited the religious tolerance characteristic of Holland. In mid-seventeenth-century Dutch Brazil, an estimated one-half of the small white population were Jews.[216] In Curaçao, another Dutch colony, Jews constituted an estimated 36 percent of the whole population.[217] As in Holland itself, these were Sephardic Jews.

In addition to those who were openly and explicitly Jewish in a religious sense, many descendants of Jews forcibly converted to Christianity in Spain and Portugal in previous centuries also settled in Latin America, some resuming the Jewish faith overtly or covertly, and others remaining Catholic, with some of these latter intermarrying with the Spanish and Portuguese. These converted Jews, however, exhibited much the same economic patterns as their kinsmen who followed the traditional faith. They also fell under various political bans against Jews occupying high positions,[218] or even settling in some colonies. Some were pursued by the Inquisition on charges of having secretly remained Jews after their conversions to Christianity, and at least one was burned at the stake as a result of such charges.[219]

The skills possessed by the Jews and converted Jews were often in short supply in the Latin American colonies. The two largest occupational categories of converted Jews called before the Inquisition in Peru were merchants and "commercial travelers."[220] Nearly one-third of the Portuguese *conversos* investigated by the Inquisition in Bahia province in Brazil worked in the professions, including lawyers and judges.[221] Only about 12 percent of the converted Jews in Bahia were working class, and these included shoemakers, musicians, and other skilled people. More than a third were either stationary or itinerant merchants.[222] As early as the seventeenth century, Jews owned dozens of sugar mills on Brazil's northern coast, perhaps half of all the sugar mills there.[223]

Despite a bitter early history of persecution by the Inquisition in the colonial era, Jews later found both religious tolerance and economic opportunities in many of the nations of Latin America, some of which were actively seeking to attract immigrants from Europe, in the wake of achieving independence. In the nineteenth century, Jewish immigrants to Latin America brought industrial, scientific, and entrepreneurial skills, all in short supply in the recipient nations.[224] Retailing was a major occupation of Jews economically active in Argentina,[225] Brazil,[226] Chile,[227] Mexico,[228] Peru,[229] and Curaçao.[230] Jews were also prominent in industrial enterprises in Argentina,[231] Mexico,[232] Peru,[233] and Guatemala.[234] In Rio de Janeiro, Jews were the dominant element in the gem trade,[235] an occupation they also followed in Peru.[236] Altogether, there were only a few thousand Jews in all of Latin America as late as 1889,[237] despite their prominence in particular industries and high-level occupations. However, even these few Jews were not a socially cohesive group, but were fragmented along lines of national origin and according to their respective degrees of assimilation into the various cultures of the region.

The French Jews of Brazil and Mexico assimilated almost completely,[238] as did the Sephardic Jews of Santo Domingo and Colombia,[239] but the Sephardics of Curaçao remained a separate enclave from the time of their arrival in the mid-seventeenth century, marrying among themselves so much that some families were linked to each other several times over.[240] This pattern persisted in Curaçao until the generation born in the early decades of the twentieth century reached marriageable age in the 1930s and 1940s.[241] Among eighteenth- and nineteenth-century Sephardim in Brazil, marrying one's cousins was as common as it was in New York.[242] Over the centuries, however, so many Jews in Latin America had disappeared by biological absorption into the larger society that many Hispanics in the late twentieth century claimed Jewish ancestry, partly because of the prestige of the early Jews but also because it marked them as Caucasian in societies where admixtures of Indians and Africans were common.[243]

Even among Jews who remained Jews, the social separation of Sephardim and Ashkenazim was carried over from Europe. The Sephardim of Curaçao remained aloof from the later-arriving Ashkenazim, who ultimately grew to be a larger community.[244] Even after intermarriage became common among these Sephardim during World War II, the Sephardic women of Curaçao usually married Dutch men and the Sephardic men usually married Latin women.[245] Moreover, Arabic-speaking Sephardim—so-called "Oriental Jews"—were another separate community in Latin America.

However much the larger societies might lump them all together as Jews, the various internal divisions were sufficiently important to the Jews themselves for them to maintain separate existences, separate synagogues, and separate burial grounds—a pattern still continued in late twentieth-century Latin America.[246] Jews from the Middle East and North Africa enjoyed none of the prestige of Sephardim in Holland, for example, and sometimes compromised the prestige of the Sephardic community as a whole in Argentina,[247] though Argentine Sephardim tended on average to be quite comparable to Argentine Ashkenazim in economic level.[248] Moreover, even within the Sephardic community of Buenos Aires, Jews from Morocco tended to concentrate in different neighborhoods from Jews from Turkey or Syria, and all tended to maintain separate organizations.[249]

Both in Latin America and in the United States, those Jews who established themselves in colonial times or who immigrated prior to the 1880s were very different from, and were subsequently overwhelmed numerically by, Jewish immigrants from the era of the massive exodus from Eastern Europe that began in the last two decades of the nineteenth century. Both in the United States and in Latin America, many of these Jewish immigrants brought with them from Eastern Europe the skills of the garment industry, whose expansion after their arrival changed the clothing patterns of the poor and the working classes in both regions of the hemisphere. Mass-produced, ready-made clothes were the exception rather than the rule prior to the expansion of the garment industry in the late nineteenth century. Two key ingredients were the perfection of the sewing machine and the arrival of large numbers of Jewish immigrants.

The well-to-do were able to buy clothes made to order by tailors or seamstresses, but the poor and the working classes generally relied on either homemade clothes or secondhand clothes cast off by the more affluent classes. Both in Europe and in the Western Hemisphere, the buying, renovating, and selling of secondhand clothing was a major economic activity in the nineteenth century. As later as 1880, less than half the men's clothing in the United States was purchased ready to wear.[250] It was much the same story in Latin America. Sewing machines and fabric-cutting machines provided the technological basis for the change to mass-produced clothing, but the massive influx of Jewish immigrants from Eastern Europe provided much of the labor, skills, and entrepreneurship. In both regions of the hemisphere, piecework at meager wages for the workers and uncertain profits by the "sweatshop" operator were the basis of clothing priced low enough to be affordable by the masses. By the time of the First World War, even in Latin America, the ready-made suit had replaced secondhand, homemade, or tailor-made clothing for most people.[251]

Throughout Latin America, the Jews' work habits—their willingness to work relentlessly for long hours at almost any job—contrasted sharply with the more relaxed life-style of the surrounding population. Many of the Jews who arrived in the Latin American republics around the beginning of the twentieth century began their careers in the New World as peddlers.[252] Much retailing was the work of peddlers carrying their wares on their backs, sometimes for lack of ordinary employment, and in some times and places such peddling was not clearly distinct from begging.[253]

Despite such tenuous beginnings, the contributions of Jews to the economic development of the Western Hemisphere remained impressive in the twentieth century, as in earlier times. They created much of the clothing and textile industry of the United States, Chile, Brazil, and

Argentina,[254] founded Avianca airlines in Colombia,[255] produced some of Mexico's most prominent engineers and doctors,[256] and established hundreds of factories in Venezuela.[257] While Jewish community organizations have flourished in Latin America as social organizations, the specifically religious aspect of these organizations has tended to be less than crucial.[258] Estimates of Jewish intermarriages in Brazil range from 25 to 30 percent.[259]

Although there have been sporadic outbursts of anti-Semitism here and there in parts of Latin America, the independent nations of the region have by no means maintained the traditions of persecution from the days of the Spanish Inquisition. Jews have not only flourished economically, but have also become socially acceptable enough to reach such prominent positions as vice president of Panama, commander of Chile's air force, and generals in the Brazilian army.[260] Nevertheless, when shiploads of Jewish refugees from Nazi persecution in Europe tried to escape to the Western Hemisphere on the eve of World War II, many were turned away. The most famous of these ships carrying Jewish refugees was the liner *St. Louis* which, in 1939, was turned away from Cuba and the United States and was forced to return to Europe, where Holland, England, and France accepted portions of the refugees. However, other ships carrying Jewish refugees were turned away from Uruguay and Paraguay, and those briefly landed at Costa Rica were subsequently expelled.[261] Partly this reflected a reluctance of some countries to accept more immigrants in general, but various Latin American countries accepted other immigrants and refugees, while turning away Jews.[262]

Argentina

Colonial Argentina in the sixteenth and seventeenth centuries was subject to the Spanish Inquisition, which claimed the lives of many Jews and converted Jews. Throughout the colonial era, Jews lived under a precarious tolerance. Even after Argentine independence, it was 1860 before the first Jewish wedding was performed in Buenos Aires, after much legal and political maneuvering.[263] But in the late nineteenth century, Argentina began to encourage immigration from Europe, including the immigration of Jews, and that meant allowing greater religious toleration.[264] By this time, however, the few Jews from the colonial era had long since been absorbed into the general population. As of 1888, the Jewish population of the entire country was estimated as only 1,500 people.[265] A year later, a ship docked in the port of Buenos Aires carrying more than 800 Jews, the beginning of the modern era of Jewish immigration to Argentina.[266]

Today's Jewish communities in Argentina date from the mass immigration era, the quarter of a century between 1889 and World War I. Although there were fewer than 2,000 Jews in the country when this era began, there were an estimated 10,000 by 1895, then 100,000 by World War I, and more than 200,000 by the end of the decade of the 1920s.[267] Unlike the earlier settlements of Sephardim, these later communities were of Ashkenazic Jews, primarily from Eastern Europe.[268] Just one decade after the first Russian immigrants arrived, more than 90 percent of all Jews in Argentina were from Eastern Europe.[269] As late as 1936, half the Jewish population of Buenos Aires was born in Eastern Europe, and they constituted more than four-fifths of the foreign-born Jewish population, which still outnumbered the native-born Jews by more than two to one.[270]

At first, during the early years of immigration, many immigrants settled in the numerous agricultural colonies established for Jews in the Western Hemisphere by Baron Maurice de Hirsch, a very wealthy Bavarian Jew who saw an agricultural life as the solution of the Jews' ages-old problems in the cities. Baron de Hirsch donated $40 million[271] so that each Jewish family could begin life in these agricultural colonies with a house, fenced land of from 185 to 370 acres, credit for the first year's expenses, seed, farm implements, draft animals, and livestock. The farms were subsequently sold to them in installments over the years at below market value.[272] As of 1909, more than 19,000 Jews lived in these agricultural colonies in Argentina, compared to fewer than 17,000 Jews in Buenos Aires, and 13,000 in the rest of the country.[273]

Baron de Hirsch's agricultural colonies were scattered across Argentina and also (to a lesser extent) in Brazil, the United States, and Canada.[274] Neither the baron nor the Jews who settled in these colonies knew much about agriculture. He often bought the wrong kind of land,[275] and the early settlers made very elementary mistakes in farming,[276] an occupation most of them had never known before. Primitive Argentine farmers in the vicinity often had to teach the first Jewish settlers how to farm.[277] Over the early decades, into the 1920s, the population of the agricultural colonies grew, but this numerical growth concealed a large turnover, as many left for city life that was more familiar and were replaced by a growing number of new Jewish immigrants to Argentina.

In one sense these colonies succeeded, and in another they failed. Eventually, the settlers became better farmers and in fact introduced new crops and new techniques, leading to greater prosperity for themselves and new food for Argentine domestic consumption and export.[278] But in terms of their original purpose—an agricultural way of life for Jews—they failed. Settlers sold their land, often at a profit during the wheat boom around World War I, and moved into the cities, many carrying bitter memories of clashes with the heavy-handed administrators in charge of these colonies.

By the late twentieth century, the colonies were in disrepair and less than a thousand Jewish families remained there.[279] Other Jewish agricultural colonies failed throughout the Western Hemisphere[280]—monuments to the difficulty of deliberately changing a people from above. The Jews who left the colonies—essentially the young—entered professions in which Jews had been prominent for centuries. Some of the Argentine Jewish families spoke of "sowing wheat and reaping doctors."[281]

Some farmers sold out and used the money to open businesses in Buenos Aires.[282] By the mid-1930s, only 11 percent of the Jewish people of Argentina still remained in the agricultural colonies, though a new influx of refugees from Nazi Germany temporarily repopulated these colonies over the next few years.[283] Large changes in population size over the generations marked the rise and fall of the agricultural colonies. There were fewer than 7,000 people in these colonies in 1896, but their population grew to a peak of more than 20,000 in 1925, and then declined to about 6,000 in 1961[284]—a decline that has continued, as Argentine Jews became an increasingly urban people.[285] As early as World War I, more than half of the Jews in Argentina—65,000 out of 110,000—were living in Buenos Aires.[286]

During the era of mass immigration, most Jewish immigrants to Latin America arrived in the lowest class accommodations on the ships that brought them,[287] and many of them began life in Argentina destitute.[288] Among those who settled in urban areas, principally Buenos Aires, peddling was the first occupation of many, if not most—as it was among Jews throughout Latin America.[289] In Argentina, their willingness to sell on credit to the local people without collateral gave them an advantage over Argentine retailers, who insisted on cash and a large profit margin.[290]

During these economically precarious times, some Jewish women were drawn into prostitution rings, often by the deception and trickery of Jewish pimps, who operated as far away as Eastern Europe, from which they recruited girls to work in Buenos Aires, then one of the world centers of prostitution.[291] As of 1909, approximately half the brothels in Buenos Aires were run by Jews and nearly half of the more than 500 registered prostitutes in the city were Jewish.[292] Although these pimps and prostitutes usually encountered little trouble from public officials, who were often paid off, they were targets of vigilante raids by other Jews who were outraged at what was going on and apprehensive as to how this would affect the Argentines' attitudes toward the Jewish community as a whole.[293]

Although the early Jewish immigrants began at the bottom of the economy and society, like many other immigrants, they brought with them skills—some obsolescent artisan skills, but still skills of value in the Argentine economy of that era—and experience in retail commerce, even if at the lowly level of the peddler in many cases. In this they were unlike many Italian or Spanish immigrants, for example,[294] and unlike the native Argentines. For the period from 1895 to 1930, the largest category of workers among the Jews were skilled workers, who were an absolute majority of all Jewish workers throughout that period.[295] After many vicissitudes, these skills paid off as Jews became prominent in the garment industry.[296] They also became shoemakers, jewelers, bakers, watchmakers, and furniture makers. In addition, Jews eventually became prominent in heavy industry—machinery, chemicals, automobiles, electrical equipment—in Argentina, unlike their experience in the United States, where Jews played little role in such sectors of the economy.[297]

The prosperity achieved by Jews, though usually modest, was

resented by many and this resentment was exploited by demagogues. As early as 1910, Argentine mobs raged through the Jewish quarter of Buenos Aires, beating and raping.[298] Even worse outbreaks occurred in 1919, including pillage and the murder of hundreds, as police stood passively by.[299]

More genteel Argentines attacked the Jews verbally, in the press, in novels, and in drama.[300] Among other things, it was said that "the great stores" of the Argentines were often empty while the shops of the Jews were "constantly crowded with customers."[301] This was part of a more general Argentine reaction against economically rising immigrants, and particularly those who were small businessmen, such as Jews and Levantines, who were said to fill no real need but were simply "driving many already established shopkeepers to poverty."[302] How they could do this without giving the Argentine customer a better deal was not explained. Some of the strongest criticisms were directed against the Jewish agricultural colonies, which neither competed with Argentines nor had enough contact even to be accused of "exploitation." The criticism here was precisely that they kept to themselves and did not assimilate.[303]

The economic rise of Jews in Argentina was by no means smooth, however, nor always permanent. The records of a Jewish community organization in Buenos Aires revealed that most of its members who rose from the working class in early twentieth-century Argentina to become businessmen were workers again by 1945.[304] Nevertheless, over the generations, Argentine Jews generally rose.[305] The once-ubiquitous Jewish peddler—the two terms being virtually interchangeable to many Argentines—gradually faded away as Jews found other occupations and created businesses in a variety of industries.[306] In 1909, for example, the first Jewish-owned sawmill was opened, and by 1940 approximately one-third of all the sawmills in Buenos Aires were owned by Jews.[307] As in the United States, Jewish immigrants in Argentina put to use the garment and textile industry skills they brought with them from Eastern Europe, beginning with small "sweatshop" operations and eventually expanding into larger enterprises and into retail shops offering cloth, fur, and leather goods.[308] As of 1960, nearly half of all Argentine Jews who worked in manufacturing worked in the manufacture of clothing and textiles.[309] At the same time, nearly one-fourth of all Jewish men were proprietors of stores, and more than a third were in commerce of some sort, and another 10 percent were executives. About 20 percent were factory workers, but even these were often in skilled jobs as tailors, furriers, shoemakers, electricians, and makers of precision instruments. About 8 percent were in the professions—doctors being the most numerous, followed by architects and engineers. There were more than ten times more Jewish artists and writers than there were Jewish cooks and domestic servants.[310] The Jewish proletariat virtually disappeared in Argentina.[311]

When compared to the Argentine population as a whole, the economic position of the Jews is particularly striking. While 45 percent of Jews in manufacturing were in clothing and textiles, only 13 percent of all Argentines in manufacturing worked in these fields.[312] German Jewish refugees of the 1930s were by the 1950s operating some of the nation's largest clothing factories and Jews of various national backgrounds were prominent in a variety of other industries.[313] While from 41 to 60 percent of Argentines were classified as lower class in 1961, fewer than 4 percent of Jews were in that category.[314]

Although the Jewish population in general achieved socioeconomic levels far higher than those of the Argentine population as a whole, to some extent this reflects the fact that the Jewish males in Argentina have a higher average age (42) than that of the country as a whole (36).[315] Still, that can hardly explain all of most of the distinctive achievements of Jews—distinctive as to the economic sectors in which they achieved success, as well as the level of success achieved.

Jewish participation in industry, commerce, the professions, and technology has helped make Argentina the most modern, industrialized, and highest income nation in Latin America.[316] But in Argentina, as elsewhere, Jews have tended to avoid politics, and especially ethnic community politics. They have even publicly deplored political appeals to the Jewish community by others. What Jewish political activity there has been in Argentina has tended to be universalistic and of the political left, whether moderate or radical. This too has been a common pattern among Jews, from the United States to South Africa. Political power was virtually out of the question for Jews in Argentina, where they were just 2 percent of the population nationally and only 5 percent even in Buenos Aires, where they were concentrated.[317] The total Jewish population of Argentina in the late twentieth century was estimated as perhaps half a million people, though there was considerable uncertainty and controversy about this, with other estimates being lower than a quarter of a million.[318]

Anti-Semitism has waxed and waned in Argentina. Ironically, President Juan Perón, pro-Fascist and a protector of Nazi war criminals, was less anti-Semitic than the government that preceded him or perhaps governments that succeeded him. His protectionist policies benefitted Jewish manufacturers.[319] A Jewish finance minister under the Perón regime was widely credited with stabilizing the Argentine economy and currency, despite Perón's idiosyncratic administration.[320] His exile after a new junta seized control was followed by runaway inflation.

In 1980, more than a thousand Jews were known to be arrested and detained in Argentina,[321] Jacobo Timerman being the best known. How much of this represented anti-Semitism is hard to know, in a country where such repression has extended well beyond Jews. The return of democracy—and of Timerman—to Argentina represented a hopeful sign. Still, as the head of B'nai B'rith in Buenos Aires said, democracy "very rapidly becomes anarchy in this country." He added: "That's our danger."[322]

No one had more stake in stability and order in Argentina than its Jewish population. Their prosperity and prominence in intellectual and business pursuits made them obvious targets for demagogues, mobs, or anyone looking for a scapegoat. While Jews were only about 1 percent of the Argentine population, they were 20 percent of the university student body.[323]

The United States

The first Jews to reach colonial America were a small group of Sephardim among the passengers who arrived aboard the *Santa Catarina* in 1654—from Brazil. After Dutch rule in Brazil was replaced by Portuguese rule, the religious tolerance characteristic of Holland was replaced by the persecutions characteristic of Portugal, causing Jews to flee to many destinations, including the colonies in North America.[324] Two years after the *Santa Catarina* put the first Sephardim ashore, the first Jewish congregation was established in the Dutch colony of New Amsterdam, later to become New York. Twenty-one years later, another congregation was established at Newport, Rhode Island, and, before the middle of the eighteenth century, there were also Sephardic congregations in Savannah, Philadelphia, and Charleston.[325]

The first Ashkenazic Jews from Germanic Europe arrived in 1702 but it was decades later before the first Ashkenazic synagogues were established.[326] In the meantime, the small numbers of Ashkenazim joined the larger Sephardic congregations and adjusted to Sephardic rituals. At first the Sephardim looked down upon their German co-religionists, some Sephardic families even disinheriting children who married Ashkenazim,[327] but eventually the German Jews began to establish themselves, some becoming elected leaders in the congregations, and their "intermarriages" with Sephardim became more frequent.[328] The numbers of both groups remained relatively small. At the time of the American Revolution, the total Jewish population of the American colonies was only about 2,000.[329]

In no part of colonial America did Jews enjoy equal legal rights with the Christian population.[330] The first Sephardim to land at New Amsterdam encountered resistance to their settling there by the governor of the colonies, Peter Stuyvesant. However, the colony was controlled by the Dutch West India Company in Holland, which had Sephardim on its board of directors, and Stuyvesant was overruled. In general, however, anti-Jewish hostility in the colonies was never on a scale approaching that of Europe. Jews in America were simply one of a number of immigrant groups, while in Europe they were for centuries the single conspicuous minority. Thinly spread among the general population and acculturated in dress and manner, Jews were accepted members, and sometimes officials, in colonial organizations, public and private.[331]

In 1774, the first Jew was elected to public office in America, serving in the Provincial Congress as a representative from South Carolina. He may also have been the first Jew elected to any public office anywhere in the modern world.[332] The few remaining political restrictions on Jews began to break down in the wake of the American Revolution and the universalistic ideals it promoted. Before the middle of the nineteenth century, the first Jew was elected to the United States Senate, from Florida.[333]

With the passing years and continuing immigration, German Jews gradually came to predominate among American Jewry, not only numerically but also by achievement. They often began as peddlers in both settled and frontier areas of America, spread thinly among the general population but playing an important role in retail distribution. The more successful moved up from their backpack or pushcart to a horse and wagon, or to a store, and a very few ultimately established major department stores with such well-known names as Macy, Gimbel, Abraham & Strauss, Bloomingdale, Altman, and Saks in New York, Bamberger in New Jersey, Filene in Boston, and Hecht in Washington, D.C.[334] Perhaps the most dramatic rise was that of a pushcart peddler named Levi Strauss in California's gold rush days. The tough trousers he produced for miners eventually made him a millionaire and made Levi's a world famous trade name. Another German Jew, Julius Rosenwald, was instrumental in turning Sears into a leading retail chain.

Family networks were one source of the success of the early Jews through which a poor peddler in the hinterlands could receive goods on credit from established relatives in the big city who might not trust a stranger.[335] Peddling was a major economic function in colonial America and in the early era of the United States, when stores were scarce outside of large cities and travelling back and forth to town from scattered farm communities was difficult, time-consuming, and sometimes dangerous. The peddler who brought goods to the door was welcome as a source of products and of news from the outside world. His religion was seldom a matter of concern.[336] German Jews tended to become more popular than the Yankee peddlers they replaced.[337]

The great mass of the German Jewish immigrants of the nineteenth century had at least some elementary education before they reached the United States. Like German Jews elsewhere during this period, they were proud of and loyal to the German culture, and were often welcomed into the institutional and cultural life of other Germans in America.[338] Within the Jewish community itself, sermons were usually delivered in German, Jews spoke among themselves in German, and established German-language newspapers.[339] With the passing generations, however, the German Jews became as Americanized as they had once been Germanized. The 1860s and 1870s were years of struggle between the German and English languages within the Jewish community, to some extent between generations, and thus a struggle that necessarily ended with the victory of the later generations.[340]

The era of German predominance among American Jewry lasted until the 1880s, when the massive immigration of Jews from Eastern Europe swamped the existing Jewish community in the United States. However, German Jews continued to leave their mark on many aspects of American life, in such well-known companies as Hart, Schaeffner & Marx, Bache and Co., Florsheim, Kuhn, Loeb & Co., Goldman Sachs, Simon & Schuster, and many others. In music, Jerome Kern and Oscar Hammerstein, in publishing, Joseph Pulitzer and Adolph Ochs (*N.Y. Times*), in science, A. A. Michelson and Albert Einstein, were just some of the German Jews who made enduring contributions to American life.

Beginning in the early 1880s and continuing on a mass scale until the beginning of the First World War in 1914, more than 2 million Eastern European Jews immigrated to the United States. More than four-fifths came from czarist Russia, and so included Polish and Lithuanian Jews, as well as Jews who had lived in Russia before its absorption of Poland and Lithuania.[341] Altogether, more than one-third of all the Jews in Eastern Europe emigrated and more than 90 percent of them came to the United States, most settling in New York City.[342] The lower east side of Manhattan became the principal home of the Eastern European Jews and the most densely populated section of the city.[343] It long remained common for people in this neighborhood to sleep three or more to a room.[344]

In many respects, the lower east side was a classic slum, with overcrowded and deteriorating buildings, seldom repaired, and with shared toilets—two to a floor in many tenements and outdoor backyard toilets in others. The sewage in backyard toilets either collected there until the sanitation department periodically carted it away or else ran off in open channels, creating foul stenches either way. Very similar conditions existed in Chicago.[345]

The people who lived in Manhattan's lower east side slums were generally not used to city life, having come from the villages and towns of agricultural Eastern Europe. They were Yiddish-speaking Jews from a separate, poor, and narrow world, wholly unlike the educated, prosperous, and cosmopolitan German Jews who lived farther uptown. The conspicuously foreign demeanor, dress, and attitudes of the "downtown" Jews were a painful embarrassment to the "uptown" Jews, who sought to get them to speak English, practice cleanliness, and avoid loud and demonstrative behavior. Much the same relationship existed in Chicago between the German Jews and the Eastern European Jews there.

In both cities, the German Jews provided charity and did volunteer work among their Eastern European brethren but maintained a social distance and often betrayed their distaste. When Eastern European Jews moved into the Halsted Street section of Chicago, the German Jews moved out.[346] Usually, however, both in New York and Chicago the Eastern European Jews were in no financial condition to live in the middle-class neighborhoods inhabited by German Jews. Some flavor of the lives of the early immigrants was captured by the famous bandleader Benny Goodman, reminiscing about his childhood in an Eastern European Jewish neighborhood in Chicago:

> I can remember a time when we lived in a basement without heat during the winter, and a couple of times when there wasn't anything to eat. I don't mean *much* to eat. I mean *anything*. That isn't an experience you forget in a hurry. I haven't ever forgotten it.[347]

While the German Jews and the Eastern European Jews were united by religion, in another sense they were divided by religion. The Orthodox Judaism of Eastern Europe was a more strict doctrine, used a more traditional service, and was a more central part of life than the much-transformed Reform Judaism common among German Jews, who were accused by the Orthodox of "aping the Christians" by having church-like temples rather than synagogues, and observing the Sabbath on Sunday rather than Saturday. Eastern European Jews were by no means all very religious. Many worked on Saturdays or did not adhere strictly to the dietary laws. But the Judaism which played either a larger or smaller role in their life was Orthodox Judaism. Intermarriage with Gentiles was much rarer among Eastern European Jews. Indeed marriage between Eastern European Jews and German Jews was not common.

Neither the economic level nor the occupational skills of the Jewish immigrants who arrived in the United States during the mass immigration era were the same as those of the existing American Jewish population. However, the newcomers had more skills than many other immigrant groups of the time. Rarely were these professional skills but seldom were the Eastern European Jews unskilled laborers. They had a variety of artisan skills, many associated with clothing and related fields such as shoemaking. Nearly two-thirds of the Jewish immigrants to the United States from 1899 to 1914 were skilled workers and just over half these skills were in the clothing industry.[348] This was not counting leather goods or animal products, though significant numbers of Jews had skills associated with the production and sale of shoes and furs. Indeed, three-quarters of all furriers among the immigrants of this era were Jews.[349]

Overall, the skill mix among Eastern European Jews meshed with the industrial concentrations of German Jews. As of 1880, when most American Jews were still of German extraction, half of all Jewish firms were in clothing and allied fields. Moreover, Jewish firms dominated these fields. By the end of the nineteenth century, German Jews owned 80 percent of all retail clothing stores in New York City and 90 percent of the wholesale clothing trade.[350] Decades earlier, Jews already owned the largest wholesale shoe company in the country.[351] The match of Eastern European Jews' skills and the industries dominated by German Jews often made for an economically symbiotic relationship between the two groups. In the clothing industry, centered in New York, it became a common pattern for Eastern European Jews to work as employees of German Jews. Moreover, the vast influx of immigrants contributed to a rapid expansion of the whole industry. The number of men's clothing factories in New York more than doubled during the decade of the 1880s.[352] In addition, much clothing production was contracted out to be performed at home, in the lower east side tenements—the "sweatshops."

The much-criticized "sweatshops," with their low piece rates necessitating long hours of work, often by whole families, served a crucial function for the Jewish immigrants. It was work immediately available when they arrived, usually destitute, in the United States. Because the work was done in the home and home was in a Yiddish-speaking neighborhood, there was no need to know English, American customs, or even how to get to work. Parents did not have to leave their children unattended to go to work, and while the children themselves were often used in the work, they were not roaming the streets at random, getting into trouble. Moreover, not all the long hours of work and overcrowded living in poor surroundings were due solely to poverty. Even the well-known journalist-reformer Jacob Riis acknowledged that much of the money earned by Jews in the lower east side tenements was saved. Many were saving to bring over their family members still left in Europe.[353] Two-thirds of all Eastern European Jewish immigrants arriving during this era had their passage to America paid by family members.[354] Some sweatshop workers were saving to start their own businesses someday or to give their children a better chance in life in America than they themselves had ever had in Europe.

These aspirations were often fulfilled. The rise of the lower east side Jews, and of their counterparts in Chicago and elsewhere, became one of the American sagas of success. After years of travail, with much suffering and even tragedies along the way, the Eastern European Jews began to rise occupationally—first in business, then professionally, and in a wide range of fields. The role of pushcart peddler, with which so many began as new immigrants, declined rapidly as they made their way into more promising occupations. Jewish children, though initially struggling with their schoolwork, like other children with a foreign language and culture, eventually became over-represented among those who graduated from high school and went on to college. The free municipal colleges of New York were a special boon to a group like the Jews, with a long tradition of reverence for education, who had long lacked the means or the opportunity to pursue it to higher levels in Eastern Europe.

In the most prestigious of these institutions, the College of the City of New York (known as "the poor man's Harvard"), eventually nearly three-quarters of the students were Jews.[355] By the late 1930s, more than half the physicians in New York were Jewish, as were nearly two-thirds of the dentists and lawyers.[356] The distinction between German Jews and Eastern European Jews is not made in these data. However, the fact that the latter predominate numerically among American Jewry assures that such results would be virtually impossible unless they had achieved prosperity. In retrospect, it may seem easy to ridicule the fears of the German American Jews that the mass immigration of Eastern European Jews would be a calamity for American Jewry as a whole. However, anti-Semitism did in fact escalate as masses of visibly foreign Jews made a negative impression on the surrounding society, as they did in other countries. With the passing generations, as they ceased to be foreign, the fact that they were Jews proved to be insufficient to sustain the same level of anti-Semitism.

By 1969, Jews averaged 80 percent higher family income than other Americans.[357] Heads of Jewish families were also older, averaging 50 years of age, as compared to 44 years of age for Chinese Americans and 36 years of age for Puerto Ricans.[358] Not only greater age—which encompasses more job experience—but also education has contributed to the prosperity of American Jews, most of whom are no longer middlemen. As of 1990, most Jews over the age of 25 had at least completed college, with about half of these having gone on to graduate study. By contrast, only 12 percent of the corresponding age bracket in the general white population of the United States had completed college.[359] Not surprisingly, nearly 40 percent of all employed Jews were working in the professions and another 17 percent in managerial occupations.[360]

AUSTRALIA

Jews came to Australia among the first settlers in 1788, arriving as most people arrived in that era—as convicts from Britain.[361] As late as 1841, convicts and ex-convicts constituted just over half of the total population of New South Wales.[362] Most Jews of that period were likewise convicts or ex-convicts.[363] Altogether, there were only about a thousand Jews in Australia in 1841 and not quite two thousand in 1851.[364] However, Jewish immigration increased sharply during the mid-century gold rush. Unlike others who crowded into the gold fields, however, the Jews came not primarily as prospectors or miners, but more often to sell provisions and merchandise to those who were seeking gold.[365] The Jewish population in Australia grew to well over 5,000 in 1861 and to nearly 14,000 thousand by 1891.[366] Many of the early Jewish settlers during the colonial era were retailers, ranging from peddlers working in the bush country to urban shopkeepers and an occasional wealthy merchant. As in the United States, some began as peddlers and went on to own their own stores or even chains of stores. Jews often became liquor dealers and tavern keepers as well, their own low rates of alcoholism giving them a competitive advantage over others who might succumb to their own wares.[367] As of 1828, more than a third of Australian Jews were merchants and only one-fifth were laborers. By 1845 there were 25 clothing stores in Melbourne owned by Jews—compared to 21 owned by all others.[368]

As in many frontier societies, men outnumbered women among the Jews in colonial Australia. The sex imbalance and the wide dispersal of Jewish men among Gentiles led to some intermarriage and abandonment of Judaism, though not by most Jews. While it was hazardous for women to migrate alone to Australia, without someone to protect them from unwanted male attentions during the voyage, increasing migrations of free families (as distinguished from convicts) to Australia brought the Jewish population closer to a male-female balance.[369] By 1861, there were nearly two-thirds as many Jewish women as men in Australia, though ratios varied considerably from region to region, being nearly equal in South Australia and nearly a two-to-one male predominance in Victoria. With the passing decades, the imbalance became much less pronounced.[370] The perpetuation of Jewish communities was thus made possible demographically, while their cultural and religious survival was made possible by the fact that even small and isolated groups of Jews attempted to keep their traditions and communities alive.[371] As early as 1817, for example, there was a Jewish cemetery in Australia.[372] The maintenance of Jewish communities was facilitated by the fact that in Australia, as in other countries, Jews were concentrated in urban centers. As early as 1833, more than two-thirds of the Jews in the colony of New South Wales lived in Sydney.[373]

Both the nature of Australian society and of the early Jews themselves facilitated their social acceptance, legal freedom, and economic opportunities. A frontier society with many ex-convicts, Australia was not a place of rigid social status, nor one that inquired too closely into people's backgrounds. As an offshoot of Britain, it inherited the legal traditions of a free society and tended to liberalize them even further so that Jews, for example, could be members of the colonial parliament before they could legally enter the Parliament in London.[374] Most of the early Jewish immigrants to Australia were from Britain,[375] and were culturally Anglicized, so that they readily fit in with the rest of the population. Thus began a pattern of Jewish cultural assimilation, religious distinctiveness, and widespread participation in Australian public life.

There were many indicators of the integration of Jews into Australian society. For example, Jews often became members of Masonic lodges, achieved high offices in these lodges, and some set up Masonic lodges themselves.[376] High intermarriage rates were a further indication of social acceptance.[377] So was an even rarer phenomenon among Jews around the world—an over-representation in nineteenth-century Australian political and public life. A Jew was appointed as one of the commissioners when the new colony of South Australia was founded in 1836.[378] Over the years, seven Jews became lord mayors of Melbourne and there were also Jewish mayors of Adelaide, Warwick, and other communities. There were more than a dozen Jewish members of the Victoria State Parliament between 1860 and 1901. In New South Wales, Jews at various times held such state offices as Speaker of the House and chief justice. At a national level, the first Australian-born governor general was a Jew.[379] This political success was seldom, if ever, a result of Jewish voting power, since Jews were never as much as 1 percent of the Australian population.[380]

While many Australian Jews in public life were also active in their religious congregations and in the Jewish community in general, the Jewish community itself tended to keep a low profile, to blend in culturally and socially. Nor was this all a matter of caution toward the outer world. The assimilation was often inward as well. Like the Jews of Western Europe, Australian Jews conceived of themselves as Englishmen of the Mosaic faith[381]—a religious "denomination" but not a "nationality" in the sense of a separate cultural-political entity. Moreover, Judaism itself tended to be less a fervent conviction than a social focus. Violations of the dietary laws were widespread, as was the practice of keeping Jewish-owned businesses open on the Sabbath. Those who attended synagogues were often inattentive or even talking and visiting during the services. Most Jewish children in nineteenth-century Australia were educated in non-Jewish schools.[382]

With the passing decades of the nineteenth century, the internal composition of Australian Jewry began to change—and with it their religious and cultural patterns began to change as well. As late as the middle of the nineteenth century, British Jews constituted 90 percent of the Jewish population in Australia. However, the gold rush brought in so many Jews from continental Europe that Anglo-Jews were only half the Jewish population of the country by 1861—and a declining proportion thereafter.[383] German and Austrian Jews were especially prominent in the new waves of Jewish immigrants but Eastern European, Palestinian, and other Jews also settled in Australia.[384] While German and Austrian Jews shared the "modern" or acculturated social patterns of the Anglo-Jews, the more traditional Jews from Eastern Europe did not blend in nearly as well, either with Australian society in general or with the existing Jewish community.

Eastern European Jews, who began arriving in substantial numbers in the 1890s, during the era of pogroms in Europe, were not simply a religious "denomination." They lived an entirely Jewish way of life, spoke Yiddish, wore beards, dressed in the clothes long common in Eastern Europe, and were used to very traditional religious services—not such things as English-language liturgy, mixed choirs, or clean-shaven rabbis dressed like English parsons.[385] Australian Judaism was predominantly Orthodox rather than Reform, but its innovations have caused it to be analogized to Conservative Judaism in the United States, rather than to American Orthodox Judaism.[386] Eastern European Jews began to establish their own separate congregations as early as 1878 in Sydney, where their synagogue featured a more traditional and more emotional service.[387]

As in other parts of the world, the arrival of Eastern European Jews—unmistakably foreigners—was followed by an increase of anti-Semitism, from which all Jews suffered. One symptom of the internal differences—and frictions—among the increasingly diverse Jewish population of Australia was that Zionism was almost totally rejected by the leadership of the Anglo-Jews, while it was embraced by those from Eastern Europe.[388] As in other countries, complaints against the newcomers from Eastern Europe included charges that they were too loud, conspicuous, and did not use enough soap and water.[389] As in other countries, attempts by Westernized Australian Jews to get them to change were resented by the immigrants from Eastern Europe.[390] These were not problems of immigrants as such but specifically of Eastern European (usually Polish) Jews. German and Austrian Jews tended to assimilate more readily, not only into the Australian Jewish community, where they established some Reform synagogues, but also into the wider Australian society, where they or their children sometimes converted to Christianity.[391]

The various national groups of Jews differed occupationally, as well as socially and religiously. Polish Jews tended to concentrate in and around Melbourne, while Perth was the most common destination of Palestinian Jews and Sydney that of Austrian Jews.[392] This pattern of people from particular places abroad settling in particular localities in Australia included not only Jews from specific provinces or cities abroad grouping in specific cities in Australia,[393] but even clustering sometimes in particular neighborhoods.[394] Yet Jews in Australia did not transplant ghettoes, either on a national-origin basis or as Jews in general. Greeks and Italians lived intermixed among Jews from various nations. Jews in Australia were apparently not as concentrated as in some American Jewish ghettoes—though even in the latter, they were sometimes outnumbered by non-Jews.[395] Few Jews from any part of the world worked in agriculture or as unskilled laborers in Australia, but their occupational distributions varied considerably by country of origin. For the period from 1881 to 1920, 30 percent of Russian Jews worked in textiles, compared to only 6 percent among German Jews, and much less among the non-Jewish Australians.[396]

As the twentieth century dawned, there were more than 15,000 Jews in Australia and this total rose to more than 20,000 by 1921.[397] Although the national origins of Jewish immigrants to Australia were more diverse than in the early colonial period, fewer than half of the 6,000 Jewish immigrants to Australia between 1881 and the onset of the First World War in 1914 were from Eastern Europe. As in the period from 1830 to 1880, most who were not from Britain were from Germanic Europe[398]—Germany or Austria, the latter narrowly defined to exclude Eastern European regions of the Habsburg Empire.[399] However, when Jewish immigration resumed after World War I, most of the more than 1,000 immigrants who came to Australia during the 1920s came from Eastern Europe and well over half of them settled in Melbourne.[400] The religiously more strictly Orthodox and culturally more traditional Jews who settled in Melbourne long continued to be contrasted with the more cosmopolitan and reserved Jews of Sydney. It was said that Sydney was a warm city with cold Jews, while Melbourne was a cold city with warm Jews.[401]

Despite a growing diversity within Australian Jewry, their most prominent leaders long continued to come from the so-called Anglo-Jews, whose culture by this time was distinctly Australian, rather than English.[402] From this group came the best-known Australian Jew and the country's most famous military leader, Sir John Monash. Educated in the public schools, like so many nineteenth-century Jews, Monash went on to become an engineer and a military officer. As General Monash, he was commander in chief of Australia's troops in Europe during the First World War. An Australian national hero, he was knighted and given numerous decorations. When he died in 1931, a quarter of a million people attended his funeral—clearly a national tribute, for this was several times the total Jewish population in Australia. Monash University, near Melbourne, is named for him.

The national origins of Jewish immigrants to Australia changed again in the decade of the 1930s. After the rise of the Nazis in Germany and Austria during that decade, most Jews came from these two countries. When immigration resumed after World War II, national origins shifted again. Eastern European Jews were once more a majority among Jewish immigrants to Australia.[403] Numbers were growing while these changes were taking place. The Jewish population in Australia rose to more than 30,000 by 1947[404]—a doubling of its size since the beginning of the century. It nearly doubled again by 1981.[405] This huge population growth was due to immigration rather than natural increase. Jewish families in Australia have historically had fewer children than the national average.[406] As early as 1948, most of the Jews living in Australia had been born outside Australia,[407] and, as late as 1984, two-thirds of all adult Jews in Australia had once lived in Nazi-occupied Europe.[408] In short, the postwar Jewish population of Australia was radically different in composition from what it had been a century earlier—or even a half-century earlier.

The postwar generation was a different Jewry in a different Australia. The European immigrants—predominantly Eastern European—

had wrested control of Jewish life from the older, Anglo-Jewish assimilationist elite.[409] Moreover, the Holocaust and the founding of Israel brought all Jews together and heightened a sense of identity and purpose. The large, postwar immigration of other groups to Australia meant that Jews were no longer in danger of being a lone conspicuous minority, but were now part of a larger ethnic mosaic in a society where multiculturalism was promoted. The postwar generation established many synagogues and Jewish schools. By the mid-1980s, three out of five Jewish children in Australia were receiving Jewish day-school education. In Melbourne, it was four out of five.[410] One day school with 2,500 students may have been the largest Jewish school in the Diaspora.[411]

The resurgence of Jewish identity in Australia, the growing size of the Jewish population, and its concentration in a few urban centers have all contributed toward lower rates of intermarriage. As of 1971, the overwhelming majority of Jews in Australia were married to other Jews—much more so than 50 years earlier.[412] This seemed to reflect choice rather than rejection by the larger society. Most Jews surveyed claimed to have experienced no anti-Semitism in Australia.[413] Jewish social welfare agencies continued a long tradition of taking care of their own needy in Australia, as they did around the world. In addition, Jews have long been prominent contributors to charities serving Australian society as a whole.[414] Almost the entire Jewish community in Australia contributed money to Jewish causes.[415]

By and large, the Jewish community in Australia was prosperous and educated. Among young people between the ages of 16 and 22, nearly three-quarters of the Jews were full-time students, compared to about 20 percent of their contemporaries in the general population.[416] While only one-half of one percent of the Australian population in general worked in law or medicine, 15 percent of the Jewish population of British or Australian origin worked in these professions. More than two-thirds of all Australian Jews were either employers or self-employed, compared to 10 percent of the general population.[417] Alcoholism, delinquency, and crime were virtually unknown among the Jewish population in Australia.[418]

There have been many evidences of Jewish acceptance in Australia. While postwar Jews were not as over-represented among prominent public figures in Australia as in the earlier years of Anglo-Jewish predominance, an estimated 10 percent of all barristers in Sydney and Melbourne were Jewish, at least one or two Jews have usually been in the cabinet, and from 1977 to 1982 the governor general of Australia was a Jew.[419] On lists of the 200 richest people in Australia during the 1980s, about one-fourth were Jewish.[420] One of the few sources of criticism of Australian Jews has been its own well-educated younger generation, which has sometimes seen its elders as having "a crudeness and coarseness" and a "nouveau riche pattern."[421] Whatever the merits or demerits of such charges, the freedom to utter them publicly is another indication of the sense of security of Jews in Australia.

IMPLICATIONS

A number of social, economic, and cultural patterns have been characteristic of Jews in many very different societies, widely scattered around the world. The Jews of the Diaspora have been identified for centuries as people of commerce—whether at the level of the lowly peddler or in the rarefied atmosphere of the international banker. Like other middleman minorities, Jews have, over time, often converted business success into higher education and professional training for their offspring. An ancient religious tradition of reverence for learning has in many countries been translated into secular intellectualism. Over a period of seventy-five years, Jews have won 16 percent of all Nobel Prizes awarded in the entire world, including more than one-third of those awarded in economics,[422] though they are much less than 1 percent of the world's population, and no more than 3 percent of the population of any country except Israel. There are fewer Jews in the world than there are Kazakhs or Sri Lankans.

Similarly disproportionate "over-representation" of Jewish achievements in universities, commerce, industry, and the professions has marked their history in societies as different as medieval Spain, the Soviet Union, Australia, Argentina, Poland, the United States, and many others. Such achievements have been only part of a larger social pattern found repeatedly among Jews around the world. For example, unusually low rates of alcoholism have been found in studies of Jews in Poland, Canada, Prussia, Australia, and the United

States.[423] Widespread philanthropy has likewise been characteristic of Jews from Europe to South Africa and from the Western Hemisphere to Australia.[424]

Although Jewish incomes have almost invariably been above the national average of the countries in which they lived, Jewish politics have consistently been of the political left, whether moderate or radical. They have opposed apartheid in South Africa, Franco in Spain, and have advocated the welfare state in France, Germany, the United States, Australia, and Israel. The creation of the Soviet Union and of Eastern bloc Communist nations owed much to Jews, though these governments later became antagonistic to the Jews of Israel abroad and to Jews in their own countries. Only belatedly and on a much smaller scale have Jews become prominent among opponents of the political left—Raymond Aron in France and Milton Friedman and the leaders of the neoconservative movement in the United States being notable examples.

Within the working class, as well as among businessmen, intellectuals, and political figures, Jews have long had a distinctive pattern. Their artisan and technical skills have ranged widely, from shoemaking to diamond-cutting, tailoring, and many other garment-trade skills. Even where Jewish immigrants have arrived in many countries destitute, ill-educated, and lacking a knowledge of the national language, they have nevertheless brought with them the ingredients of future success, for their children if not for themselves.

The history of Jews has not of course been merely a history of achievements but also of suffering and catastrophe. The achievements and the anguish have not been unrelated. Like many other groups with strikingly higher achievements than those around them, Jews have been resented, hated, and made the targets of politicians and of mobs. Where the skills of the Jews have been especially rare in the surrounding population—in Eastern Europe or the Arab countries, for example—Jews have been especially hated. The nations most noted for tolerance of Jews—Britain, Scandinavia, Holland, the United States, and Australia, for example—have usually had no lack of skills and talents in their general populations. In short, it has often been precisely in those societies most desperately in need of the special skills of Jews that anti-Jewish hostility has flourished most.

Anti-Semitism in Nazi Germany represented a very different phenomenon—the power of modern mass communications propaganda, in a totalitarian state, to produce fanatics who were neither representative of the history of the country nor able to sustain their influence after competing views were free to be heard. What made the Holocaust unique were the technical and organizational resources available to the Nazis, which made mass-production methods applicable to the slaughter of human beings by a small fraction of the German population. Other historic mass murders were accomplished one by one, by members of the general population, whether against the Jews in medieval Europe, the Chinese in Southeast Asia, the Ibos in Nigeria, or the Armenians in the Ottoman Empire.

The internal patterns of Jews have also varied greatly from place to place and from time to time. Where anti-Semitism was strongest and most implacable—Eastern Europe being again a prime example—Jews tended to be least assimilated in language or culture. Where acceptance was greater—in Western Europe and their offshoot societies in North America or Australia—Jews tended much more to become culturally assimilated, citizens, and patriots.

Nothing has so heightened or re-awakened a sense of Jewish identity around the world as the Holocaust. For generations prior to World War II, culturally assimilated Jews in many countries drifted away from the Jewish religion, culture, and community, some intermarrying, and their offspring often losing all sense of connection with the Jewish people. Among Marxists, there was a conscious rejection of such tribal links, in favor of ideological ties with comrades in the political struggle. But the Nazi horror suddenly made all sorts of social, national, political, and other differences among Jews irrelevant. Centuries of internal differences between Sephardim and Ashkenazim, or between the secular and the religious, rich and poor, etc., did not vanish around the world, but were reduced to a smaller scale against the historic background of Auschwitz or Buchenwald. One of the fruits of this heightened cohesion among Jews of the world was the state of Israel.

CHAPTER 7

THE OVERSEAS INDIANS

The overseas Indians are no longer Indians of India.
—Hugh Tinker[1]

"Indian" may well be the group designation with the most varied and disparate meanings. Its most straightforward meaning is the people of India. But, in the Western Hemisphere, the term more often refers to the aboriginal population, mistakenly called "Indians" by Columbus. Some definitions encompass also the peoples of those Pacific islands once called the East Indies. By extension, the peoples of the various Atlantic islands called the West Indies are called "West Indians," though they have no connection with any of the other "Indians" of the world. Moreover, all inhabitants of the Indian subcontinent were once referred to as Indians, while post-independence citizens of India, Pakistan, and Bangladesh have subsequently been given separate designations. To add to the confusion, people from India are called "East Indians" in the Western Hemisphere and are often called "Asians" in Africa—a term more likely to conjure up an image of Chinese or Japanese in the United States. Here, the term "overseas Indians" will refer to people from India as the country was defined as of the time of emigration, which is to say, the whole subcontinent in colonial times and the independent nation of India thereafter.

The diverse peoples of India have sharp differences in race, language, culture, and religion. India's population of 844 million is about one-sixth of the human race.[2] As of 1981, the number of people born in India and living outside of India was estimated at more than 13 million—more than 400,000 in the United States, 440,000 in Trinidad, 500,000 in Britain, 800,000 in South Africa, more than a million each in Burma and Malaysia, and more than 3 million in Nepal.[3]

The size, composition, and destinations of overseas Indians have changed drastically over the years. For the period prior to 1920, Trinidad and Guyana received more than 100,000 Indian immigrants each, while the United States and various Middle East countries such as Saudi Arabia or the United Arab Emirates received either no immigrants at all from India or negligible numbers. Yet, by the 1970s immigration from India to Trinidad and Guyana had ceased, while the United States and some Middle East nations received in a decade numbers of immigrants from India comparable to what Trinidad and Guyana had received throughout their entire histories. The once massive immigration of Indians into East Africa during the colonial era ended in the 1960s and turned into a net outflow of Indians after Kenya, Uganda, and Tanzania became independent[4]—and discriminatory against Indians.

The composition of the flow of emigrants from India has varied as much as their numbers and destinations. Much of the nineteenth-century migration of Indians was a mass movement of indentured laborers to the plantations of colonial Ceylon, Malaya, Fiji, Trinidad, British Guiana, and Mauritius. At least four-fifths of all sugar plantation workers in Fiji, British Guiana, Mauritius, and Trinidad were from India.[5] Indian workers also predominated on the tea plantations of Ceylon and on the rubber plantations of Malaya. However, joining these low-caste laborers during the nineteenth century, and becoming an ever more prominent part of the migration stream from India in the twentieth century, were people from other castes and other regions of the country who worked in such middleman occupations as street vendors, small shopkeepers, and the like.[6]

By the late twentieth century, Indian businessmen had risen to worldwide prominence in the diamond trade, being second only to the

Jews in that field. One Indian sect—the Jains—were operating in such diamond centers as New York, Tel Aviv, and Antwerp, and accounted for about one-third of all purchases of rough diamonds.[7] Overseas Indians as a whole have prospered in many of the same industries and occupations in which Jews have prospered, such as apparel, real estate, trading, finance, entertainment, and diamonds.[8] In addition, overseas Indians have become prominent in technical fields such as computers. Altogether, more than half of all the graduates from the Indian Institutes of Technology went overseas to work, with more than 20,000 engineers from India working in the United States alone.[9] In Hong Kong, Indians owned the Star Ferry line,[10] whose ferries connected the two main areas—Hong Kong Island and Kowloon peninsula. In Britain, there were more than 300 Indian multimillionaires.[11] Worldwide, overseas Indians owned an estimated $100 billion in real estate.[12]

Not only have Indians moved into higher occupational levels over time, the relative proportions of laborers and middlemen among the emigrants from India were often very different from their relative proportions among the Indian population living overseas. During the era of mass emigration from India, vast numbers of laborers returned home, often with passage prepaid under the terms of their original indenture agreements. Thus, despite the tens of thousands of laborers brought into East Africa to build a railroad from the coast to Lake Victoria, most of the population remaining after this project was completed were the entrepreneurial Gujaratis from western India. In some other countries, however, both the original emigrants and the later overseas Indian populations were agricultural workers, whether working for others or themselves. Fiji and Guyana exhibit this pattern.

The enormous diversity of the peoples of India is reflected in their emigrant population. Different groups tend to predominate among the Indian populations of different nations. The Gujaratis have been the dominant element among the Indians scattered across the vast regions of Africa bordering the Indian Ocean, from Kenya to South Africa. Tamils from southern India have historically been the overwhelming majority of the huge migrations of unskilled laborers who worked on the plantations of colonial Malaya and Ceylon. But the plantation workers brought from India to the Western Hemisphere, to British colonies in Trinidad and Guiana, originated in the northeastern part of the country, in the Ganges River basin. The economic fate of these Indians overseas has largely reflected their origins in India. The same has been true of smaller groups from India. The money-lending Chettyars, for example, have also been money-lenders in other countries, notably Burma, Ceylon, and Malaya,[13] as the Jains have been prominent in the diamond trade overseas, often having the diamonds cut back in India.[14]

The internal composition of overseas Indian populations has varied in much more complex ways as well. Their occupational distribution has varied enormously, according to the kind of country to which they emigrated. Among the nearly three-quarters of a million overseas Indians who have settled permanently in modern industrial nations during the late twentieth century—44 percent of them in Britain—highly skilled professionals constituted nearly half the total, while such high-level personnel have been only about 10 percent of the Indians who migrated to poorer or "underdeveloped" countries.[15] In the United States, immigrants from India have worked in professional and technical occupations to a greater extent than the American population as a whole.[16] But most overseas Indians—about four-fifths—worked in less-developed countries and have had an entirely different mix of skills and occupations. In Malaysia, for example, fewer than 10 percent of the immigrants from India are in either professional, technical, managerial, or administrative occupations, put together. In the Middle East, where nearly a million Indians lived in 1981, just 10 percent of those in the labor force worked in these kinds of occupations.[17]

Emigration from India has been vast in absolute terms, modest in proportion to the huge population of the country, and quite modest in terms of the proportion of Indians who remained abroad permanently. One "extremely rough" estimate of the total number of people who left India during the period between the mid-1830s and the late 1930s was that 30 million left and nearly 24 million returned.[18] As of 1971, Indians living abroad amounted to only about 1 percent of the population of India itself, while people of European ancestry living outside Europe amounted to 40 percent of the total population of Europe, and the number of people of British ancestry living outside Britain was 67 percent *more* than the total population of the United Kingdom.[19] Whether the overseas Indians are defined as people born in India and living elsewhere (about 5 million people as of 1981) or people of Indian ancestry living abroad (more than 13 million), they were still a negligible percentage of the vast population of India.[20] The mere *increment* to India's population has for several decades been many times as large as the total emigration from the country.[21]

However modest the overseas Indian population may be when compared to the population of India, in many of the small countries in which Indians have settled around the world, overseas Indians have become a substantial part of the local population. As of about 1960, Indians were more than one-third of the population of Trinidad and of Suriname, nearly half the population of Guyana and Fiji, and two-thirds of the population of Mauritius.[22] Their economic roles in these countries have often been even larger than their proportions of the population would indicate.

Like the overseas Chinese, the Indians come from a country of ancient glory and modern poverty, but they often prosper among poor indigenous peoples in many countries around the world. Virtually no wealthy people emigrated from India to Africa,[23] for example, even though there have been Indians who acquired great wealth in various African countries. Many—in some countries, most—of those who came from India did so as indentured laborers. Almost invariably, they began poor and often also illiterate and unskilled. The story of the overseas Indians is in many countries the story of how they rose to prosperity, sometimes affluence, and occasionally considerable wealth. It is also the story of how they transformed the countries in which this happened.

AFRICA

Indians have traded with Africa for many centuries. There are passing references to Indian traders in Africa as early as the second century A.D., but this did not imply any immigration or permanent settlements.[24] However, Indian trading communities have existed in Africa for hundreds of years, even if the people in these communities were sojourners whose families remained in India.[25] By the nineteenth century, the island of Zanzibar, off the east coast of Africa, was regarded as an outpost of India.[26] In 1860, an official report stated: "All the shopkeepers and artisans at Zanzibar are natives of India." There were about 5,000 "British Indian subjects" on the island and nearly all foreign trade was conducted by them.[27] There were even some very large Indian financial institutions in Zanzibar. As of 1872, an American trader on the island owed Indian financiers about $2 million, and a single French commercial house owed them at least $4 million.[28] Rupees became the principal currency in much of East Africa.[29] All of this, however, predated the mass movement of Indians to the mainland or to the interior of Africa.

Indian traders established outposts in various East African mainland ports in the nineteenth century. Indian merchants were noted for their "industriousness, frugality, and perseverance,"[30] for their "punctuality of payment and probity,"[31] for their "commercial integrity," and for the fact that they "work all day, rarely enjoying the siesta."[32] Indian merchants outfitted David Livingstone's famous expeditions and also sold supplies to Henry Stanley, who later searched for him.[33] A British nobleman who toured various East African ports reported only a handful of exceptions to the rule that "every shopkeeper was an Indian."[34] While this was the situation in those areas traditionally thought of as East Africa—Uganda, Kenya, Tanganyika—things were somewhat different further south, in Zambia, Malawi, and Rhodesia. Here the Europeans dominated trade initially, though Indians began to supplant them until restrictive legislation kept the Indians in check.[35] Further south, Indians were brought into the South African province of Natal, primarily as indentured sugar plantation laborers, although even here many subsequently became small businessmen, notably in truck farming.[36]

Still, the Indian presence in Africa was largely confined to some coastal areas of East Africa and the offshore island of Zanzibar, until the British opened up the interior of the continent with the great railroad line that reached from the Kenyan port of Mombasa all the way to Lake Victoria in Uganda. The East Africa Railway began to be constructed late in the nineteenth century. Of the approximately 16,000 laborers at work on its construction at one time or other, 15,000 thousand were Indians,[37] mostly indentured "coolies." They were expensive laborers, however. Not only were they paid more than they earned in India,[38] their passage was also paid both ways across the Indian Ocean, and in addition their rations and medical expenses were provided by the British. That such expenses were incurred is one measure of how much more valuable they were considered to be than African workers available locally. Africans, who owned their own land, from which they gained their chief subsistence, would work for brief and intermittent periods—quitting whenever they felt the need or desire to do so to return home.[39]

The building of the East Africa Railway marked the beginning of large-scale Indian immigration to Africa. Not only were great numbers of Indians employed in its construction—most of whom returned to India—but the auxiliary services associated with that effort, the manning of the railroad after it was built, and the opportunities for much wider trade which it presented, all attracted substantial immigration from India as well. While the building of the railroad was characterized as "the driving of a wedge of India two miles broad across East Africa,"[40] the poor and illiterate coolies who performed this task were only the vanguard of a larger and quite different Indian population movement into East Africa. For generations to come, a sharp distinction would be made within the Indian community in Africa between the descendants of the "indentured" Indians brought over by the British and the "passenger" Indians who paid their own way.[41]

Work on the East Africa Railway had many perils and handicaps. More than half the Indian workers—and all the European staff—were sick at one time or other, and the railway work force was said to resemble "a gigantic hospital on the move."[42] More than two thousand Indians died and more than six thousand were sent home incapacitated by disease.[43] Less than one-sixth signed up for another tour after their indenture contracts expired.[44] Altogether, counting replacements, about 32,000 Indians were imported to build the railroad, of whom fewer than 7,000 remained to settle in Africa.[45]

Railroad workers were not the only Indians brought into Africa at this time. Even the building of the railroad entailed the use of Indian troops to put down African raids and rebellions. Moreover, after the completion of the railroad, most of the skilled jobs in running it went to Indians,[46] and Indians—chiefly from Goa—were used throughout East Africa as subordinate administrative employees in the British imperial apparatus.[47] Plantation owners in central Africa also imported Indian indentured servants, as in South Africa. In the German colonies (in what is now largely Tanzania) Indians were also encouraged to immigrate.[48] All these efforts to import Indians across more than 2,000 miles of ocean again suggest important work differences between Indians and Africans, who were right at hand.

Many Africans refused to work on the East Africa Railway[49]—an understandable decision, given that more than one-fourth of the preselected, healthy young men brought over from India returned either dead or disabled. This unwillingness of Africans to undertake many tasks performed by the Indians was not confined to East Africa. The Zulus of South Africa were considered to be "well-qualified both by intelligence and strength,"[50] but would not remain continuously at work, nor give notice when they decided to go back to their tribal villages, nor indicate when they might return to work.[51]

The Indians of Africa are not a single people but are internally segmented by language, religion, and caste, or the remnants of caste. Most of the Indians in East Africa originated in the state of Gujarat and spoke Gujarati. They were mostly Hindus, separated by caste differences that did not survive the voyage or transplanting to Africa entirely intact, but which nevertheless remained strong enough to make marriage across caste lines rare even in the late twentieth century, after many Indians had begun to deny that caste still existed.[52] In India itself, Gujaratis were—and are—notable as businessmen.[53] About 70 percent of the Indians in East Africa were Gujaratis.[54] However, those Indians who came to dominate the colonial civil service were from the Portuguese colony of Goa,[55] were Catholics, thoroughly Westernized, and in the early years referred to themselves as Portuguese rather than as Indians.[56] There were also many Indians from the Punjab region and smaller scatterings from elsewhere in India, Ceylon, and what is now Pakistan.

The proportions of people from various parts of India varied considerably, even in a given country. In South Africa, where Indians were concentrated primarily in Natal province, 80 percent of the Indian population in that province in 1936 were Hindus, while just over half those in the Transvaal were Moslems, and those in the Cape Province were divided among the Hindu (29 percent), Moslem (44 percent), and Christian (19 percent) religions, with more than a thousand Buddhists as well. Linguistic differences were equally striking among the Indians of South Africa. Nearly half the Hindus in Natal spoke Tamil, but more than a third spoke Hindi, and sizeable numbers spoke Telugu. Among the Moslems in Natal, Urdu and Gujarati were the two main languages in all three provinces, the former primarily in Natal and the Cape, but the latter overwhelmingly in the Transvaal.[57] Caste differences, superimposed on these religious and linguistic differences, caused parents to choose spouses for their children from members of the same caste and religion back in India, rather than from members of a different caste or religion living in South Africa.[58] The various cultural groups tended to live in separate residential clusters within the Indian community.[59]

Uganda

The Indian workers who built the first railroad to Uganda attracted Indian shopkeepers who sold to them. These Indian shopkeepers remained after the railroad was completed, selling not only to their countrymen but also to the British and—primarily—to the much larger indigenous African population. In many cases, these Indian shops were the first permanent commercial retail establishments the African villagers had ever encountered.[60] The Asians in East Africa were also the first to import and sell cereal.[61] They served as middlemen who bought the African farmers' produce for cash on the spot[62] and assumed responsibility for its marketing. While there were some European wholesalers, Indians conducted the bulk of the retail trade with African natives.[63] They transformed East Africa from a largely subsistence and barter economy into a money economy. Taxes were paid in kind in Uganda until the turn of the century, but were paid thereafter in money—rupees.

A young Winston Churchill, after touring Africa, wrote of the Indian trader in Africa who was "penetrating and maintaining himself in all sorts of places to which no white man would go."[64] A 1905 report in Kenya declared that "fully 80 percent of the present capital and business energy of the country is Indian."[65] A 1919 report in Kenya declared that the Indians were "firmly established" in all the leading towns and districts."[66] Indians collected and purchased virtually all the cotton crop in Uganda[67] and by 1919 had built 17 cotton gins there.[68] They also built flour mills in Kenya,[69] and one Indian trader alone exported 20 tons of Kenyan maize.[70] As late as 1948, Indians owned about 90 percent of all cotton gins in Uganda.[71]

Numerous contemporary observers commented that Europeans simply could not compete with the small Indian trader,[72] either in the city or in the bush. Throughout East Africa, the Indian operated on a very small profit margin, lived extremely cheaply, took the risks of selling on credit, and worked long hours in remote places under what would be impossible conditions for Europeans.[73] He was, in short, performing an economic function which no one else was available to perform—a point also noted by various contemporary observers.[74] A British observer in the 1920s commented on the Indians driving their trucks, often "without lights, without brakes, apparently without tyres, and with an engine which looks like conking out at any moment, pushing trade through the most inaccessible places."[75]

Most Indians in Uganda were and remained small retailers, petty money-lenders, and the like, but Indians were also disproportionately represented among the few large-scale entrepreneurs of the country. Two large Indian conglomerates, Madhvani and Company and Mehta Sons, were based on sugar production but the former also spread out to encompass cornmeal, soap, margarine, beer, glass, and other products, while the latter included tea, iron, engineering products, and electrical equipment among their products.[76] Both firms began in Uganda cotton production and spread across international boundaries as well as across industrial fields.[77] There were no African entrepreneurs of comparable scope or magnitude.

While Indian business and financial relations with Africa go back for centuries, and many Indian businessmen in Africa have had family, trading, and banking relations with India, the wealthy Indian businessmen of Africa were not simply people who transferred their wealth from India. Virtually all the wealthy Indian businessmen in Africa made their fortunes in Africa,[78] usually from humble beginnings, sometimes as indentured laborers.

One of the earliest business magnates on the African mainland was Allidina Visram, who rose from a small caravan trader to develop a business empire with more than 30 branches in East Africa, stretching from Dar es Salaam in Tanganyika to the Kenyan port of Mombasa, and across hundreds of miles to Uganda's port of Entebbe on Lake Victoria.

He also had land investments in almost every town developing in early Kenya and Uganda, a fleet of sailing vessels on Lake Victoria, and he pioneered in cart transport services on land as well.[79] That this was not merely "self-perpetuating wealth" was underscored by the future of this financial empire after his death. Two generations later, the firm was bankrupt, with his family appealing to the government for financial aid.[80]

Most Indians in Uganda were nowhere near the economic levels of the Madhvanis or the Mehtas, though they were somewhat more prosperous than the indigenous Africans. Still, about half the Indians in Uganda owned their own businesses.[81]

The enormous economic role of Indians in transforming the economies of East Africa is all the more remarkable because of their relatively small number in proportion to the total populations of those countries. At the peak of their population size in Uganda in the late 1960s, Indians, Pakistanis, and Goans together added up to fewer than 100,000 people, in a nation of more than 8 million.[82] They were just over one percent of the population. The Asian population was of course much smaller in the earlier years, though rapidly growing, both through natural increase and by immigration—much of it by the successive bringing over of family members by those already settled in Africa. As of the early 1920s, there were between 5,000 and 6,000 Asians in Uganda. This more than doubled in a decade, and after World War II there were 35,000 in 1948, growing to about 63,000 by 1956.[83]

As with the Chinese, the Jews, and other middleman minorities around the world, the economic contributions and success of the Indians in Africa have been in sharp contrast with the social and political opposition they have encountered. European settlers—who generally arrived in Uganda after the Indians—were their earliest and most vocal critics. During World War I, Europeans were able to get government controls and restrictions on the cotton industry introduced, with the net effect of benefitting Europeans who were having difficulties competing with the Indians.[84] However, anti-Asian feeling has generally been less in Uganda than in Kenya.[85] Nevertheless, such antagonism grew, as the passing years saw the emergence of small native African businessmen and some educated Africans in Uganda, both of whom aspired to positions in the economy and in the civil service already held by Indians.

These African groups tended to be anti-Indian in outlook[86]—and to try to turn other Africans against the Indians.

As of 1952, there were more than twice as many African traders as Indian traders in Uganda, but non-African traders (mostly Indians) did an estimated three times as much business as the Africans. This was despite governmental regulations which hampered non-Africans from setting up shops in some locations. At the same time, Indians owned approximately 90 percent of the cotton gins in Uganda, many purchased from Europeans in financial trouble between the two World Wars. Most of the cotton produced in Uganda was sent to Bombay. All 34 cottonseed-oil mills in Uganda were also owned by Indians. More than three-quarters of all factories in Uganda were likewise owned by Indians.[87] In government employment, however, Indians were very much a minority. Europeans dominated the senior civil service and Africans dominated the junior civil service, with Indians being less than one-fifth of the latter.[88]

The numerical predominance of African traders may have had little economic significance, but it provided political force to anti-Indian feelings. High rates of business failures among the African traders fed their resentment of the Indians, whose own high failure rates in the past were seldom remembered.[89] After the mid-1950s, open hostility to Indian traders spread among Africans, sometimes expressed in destruction and looting.[90] The first major anti-Indian trade boycott in East Africa took place in Uganda in 1959, lasting seven months, and involved race riots and the burning down of the farms of those African peasants who did not adhere to the boycott of the Indians.[91] It was a foretaste of what was to come in the next decade.

These and other anti-Asian outbursts[92] in the years preceding Uganda's independence in 1962 left the Indian population ambiguous as to their future in general and their immediate citizenship decisions in particular. They could apply for Ugandan citizenship or seek various forms of British protection, or remain stateless. About 30,000 Asians applied for Ugandan citizenship under the 1962 constitution but, years later, more than half their applications were still pending.[93] Uganda's 1967 constitution included a "grandfather clause" under which even native-born people could become citizens only if one of their parents or grandparents had been citizens[94]—clearly an obstacle created to block Indians from achieving citizenship. At the same time, restrictions on non-citizens in government employment and in the private economy were used to "Africanize" Uganda in accordance with prevailing post-independence ideology.

The number of Asians in Uganda's civil service declined from about 2,000 in 1961 to about 1,300 by 1968—even though the bureaucracy itself was growing rapidly.[95] Restrictions were also placed on how much money emigrants could take out of the country with them.

Government jobs were particularly prized. They paid substantially more than the average wage in private industry. In both sectors, however, Asians earned several times the income of Africans, even after Ugandan independence, though much less than Europeans earned.[96] Still, there were far more Asians than Europeans, so that more job opportunities for Africans were to be had by displacing Asians. Many of the Asians also had no place to go and no government to protect them, so that they were an easier target. In the days when India was a colony of Great Britain, the British colonial government in India did not hesitate to intervene on behalf of Indians in Africa.[97] But, after India's independence, its government's international role as a leader in Third World politics made India unwilling to offend African or other Third World governments by championing the rights of Indians in these countries.[98] Indians in Uganda became pawns in political games, domestic and international.

The final tragedy for Indians in Uganda came with the rise to power of Idi Amin. His grossness and butchery were imposed on Ugandans by force, but much of the rest of the world, and especially African leaders, shared a certain complicity for their good-natured tolerance of Amin as an anti-colonialist who could twist the nose of whites. As one journalist wrote: "The world chuckled, Africans applauded, and Ugandans died, often at the rate of 100 to 150 a day."[99]

Amin directed a special venom toward the Asians. He accused them, among other things, of both "overpricing" and "undercutting,"[100] and warned of dire consequences if they did not collectively mend their ways. In August 1972, he ordered 50,000 Asians expelled, citizens and non-citizens alike[101]—and severely limited how much money (£55) they could take with them.[102] The Asian population of Uganda, which had been 96,000 in 1968,[103] was estimated at only 1,000 at the end of

1972.[104] Many landed, destitute, in England or in whatever other countries would take them.

The economic role of the Indians in Uganda can perhaps best be appreciated by considering what happened after they left. The economy collapsed.[105] The Asian shops were often simply turned over to Amin's favorites, who sold everything and then closed them down.[106] The confiscated wealth was not simply redistributed; the total wealth of the country was diminished. In agriculture, the Asians' coffee and tea plantations, which required constant care, were neglected after their departure and became breeding grounds for deadly tsetse flies. Ugandan soldiers who smuggled the coffee across Uganda and into Kenya helped spread sleeping sickness and make it a major health hazard in the region again.[107]

As of 1972, at least 35 percent of Uganda's national output was produced by Asians, with some estimates ranging to more than half. Twenty years after the expulsions of the Asians from Uganda, the economy still had not recovered from the havoc created by those expulsions. According to the head of Uganda's own chamber of commerce, most of the Africans who took over the running of former Asian businesses were "untrained" and became "business failures." With cracked and crumbling streets in the capital city of Kampala, and with half-completed construction sites still untouched since 1972, economic desperation and pressure from the World Bank and other Western aid donors led the Ugandan government to seek the return of Asian businessman. Efforts to attract these exiled businessmen have centered on the restoration of the thousands of confiscated properties belonging to them. Yet relatively few of the Indians and Pakistanis returned from abroad to reclaim their businesses.[108]

The hostile environment of Uganda made returning there an unattractive option. Despite the economic losses suffered by Ugandans as a result of the expulsions of the Asians, resentments against Indians and Pakistanis remained high. In addition to this more or less spontaneous animosity, there was organized opposition to the return of the Asians by those Africans who had taken over their businesses. The Uganda African Trade Movement issued a public statement plainly stating that its members "intend to wage an atrocious war everywhere in Uganda on any Asian returnee." Lest there be any doubt, the statement continued:

> We intend to harm, maim, cause them a lot of suffering, even killing them in the most despicable way ever . . . if they don't leave our land and country immediately.[109]

As in so many other settings, economic productivity has provoked political antagonism, especially in the case of middleman minorities.

Kenya

Kenya has historically had far more Indians than Uganda or any of the other countries of East Africa or Central Africa.[110] Yet, even in Kenya, Asians were only 2 percent of the population at their peak in 1962.[111] There were approximately 177,000 in Kenya at that time, most born in the country, out of a total population of more than 8 million people. Even this relatively small number of Indians in Kenya represented a substantial increase from about 44,000 in 1931, when only about half were born in the colony.[112] But these modest numbers of Indians were no measure of their contemporary or historic importance. Their large role in the modern urban economy was indicated by the fact that they were one-third of the population in the city of Nairobi,[113] where their businesses dominated the main street.[114] Nor was Nairobi unique in its Indian influence. The whole coastal fringe of East African ports was long known for being more representative of the culture of India than of the culture of the interior of their respective African countries.[115]

The East Africa Railway that brought the first large-scale migrations of Indians to the African mainland began at the Kenyan port of Mombasa toward the end of the nineteenth century. At a time when most Africans were unwilling to be wage workers for more than the one or two months needed to raise money to pay their taxes,[116] and showed little interest in selling their crops in the market,[117] the Indians established a reputation for their relentless work and economic competitiveness. Indians were not only the vast majority of those building the railroad across Kenya to Uganda, they also became almost all the stationmasters after it was built, as well as filling most of the subordinate posts in the colonial bureaucracy.[118] Throughout the British East African territories of Kenya, Uganda, and Zanzibar, Indians filled the government's middle-level jobs as clerks, cashiers, typists, mechanics, carpenters, policemen, and many other subordinate but important positions.[119]

In the private sector as well, Indians became the bulk of the skilled and unskilled labor force in Kenya, holding such jobs as masons, blacksmiths, tailors, building contractors, and shoemakers.[120] But, more than anything else, the Indians became tradesmen[121]—mostly small retailers in the cities, towns, and even remote interior African villages. In many cases they provided "the first slender means of communication"[122] with African settlements deep in the bush. One ingredient in the Indian retailer's success was that he was "willing to buy and sell in very small lots such as no European would care to deal in," as a report noted in the 1920s.[123]

Because the highland region of western Kenya had a temperate climate especially attractive to Europeans, it was reserved for whites only and quickly attracted a large influx of European settlers. With them came a growing hostility to the Indians. The Europeans could not compete with the Indians, either in the private or the public sector. Indians in both places simply produced more at lower cost. European cotton ginners could not pay African cotton growers as much as the Indians offered.[124] As a contemporary report stated: "The European cannot afford to trade on the small scale and with the small margins on which the Indians subsist and the African generally is not yet sufficiently advanced to do so."[125] The complete dominance of the Indians in small retailing may be indicated by the fact that it was 1966 before the first African-owned shop was opened on Kenyatta Street in Nairobi.[126] Their narrow profit margin and extreme thriftiness have remained the hallmark of Indian traders.[127]

Europeans objected to the Indians in their own self-interest and in the ostensible interest of the Africans. Indians were decried as "unfair competition" and it was claimed that "the Asiatic takes away all his earnings to his native country."[128] How he could do that and yet have growing business interests in Africa was not explained. European settlers launched increasingly vocal campaigns to keep the Indians out of the Kenyan highlands, out of certain residential areas of the cities, and, if possible, out of Kenya itself altogether. Indians were denounced as mere "hucksters and usurers," and white missionaries spoke of the "ill effect" of the Indians' dealings with Africans.[129] However, Winston

Churchill during a visit to Kenya in the early twentieth century said:

> It was by Indian labour that the one vital railway on which everything else depends was constructed. It is the Indian banker who supplies perhaps the larger part of the capital yet available for business and enterprise, and to whom the white settlers have not hesitated to recur for financial aid. The Indian was here long before the first British Official. He may point to as many generations of useful industry on the coast and inland as the white settlers—especially the most recently arrived contingents from South Africa (the loudest against him of all)—can count years of residence. Is it possible for any Government, with a scrap of respect for honest dealing between man and man, to embark on a policy of deliberately squeezing out the native of India from regions in which he has established himself under every security of public faith.[130]

Nevertheless, by and large, European settlers in Kenya succeeded in getting discriminatory laws and policies instituted against the Asians. The Kenyan highlands were reserved for whites, some sections of some towns were indirectly made purchasable only by Europeans, and there were differences in trial procedures between Europeans and Asians, as well as a banning of Asians from holding certain offices.[131] In the early twentieth century, an outbreak of cholera that struck Nairobi led to the burning down of an Indian bazaar there with "extremely unhygienic conditions."[132] A variety of observers, including Indians, reported "sharp practices" by Indian traders,[133] especially in the early years of dealing with less-sophisticated Africans in remote villages. Moreover, most Indians were still poor by European standards and their jerry-built, unaesthetic, and unsanitary urban settlements were an eyesore to the whites. However, these factors had all been present during the earlier years, when Indian immigration was welcomed. What was different now was that the Indians had advanced to the point of being rivals to the Europeans.

Indians, in their early years, were politically apathetic,[134] like most middleman minorities. However, the success of political organization among European settlers in getting the British colonial authorities to grant whites discriminatory privileges in Kenya encouraged the Indians to organize themselves politically as well, to press for equal rights. But these Indian organizations remained largely ineffective until after World War I, by which time increasingly discriminatory policies had aroused more Indians to greater concern and efforts. Indians at this point began also to help the nascent African protest movement in East Africa, providing such organizations as the Young Kikuyu Association with office space, newspaper space in Indian publications, and the use of Indian printing facilities.[135] Half a century later, there would be great Indian resentment at how these African political movements turned against them after achieving national independence.[136]

Despite the growing political setbacks suffered by Indians in Kenya, they continued to advance economically. Increasing numbers began to graduate from the ranks of petty traders to become more substantial businessmen engaging in sawmilling, building, and manufacturing. Others followed a pattern common among middleman minorities by using their business-based prosperity to educate the next generation in the professions.[137]

As in Uganda, the government intervened increasingly in the Kenyan economy under various rationales of fairness or preventing "reckless competition,"[138] but with the net effect of undermining the positions Indians had achieved in the competition of the marketplace. Business licensing and government marketing facilities were used to reduce the role of Indian middlemen during the 1930s. Transport-licensing legislation protected the existing railroad from the growing competition of trucks, in which Indians had long had important interests.[139] The taxation of income was also instituted—again, an apparently racially neutral measure, but one which hit Indians harder because they received less government expenditure per capita on many public services, including education.[140] As late as the 1950s, the colonial administration spent $180 a year for the education of each European child, compared to only $65 for each Asian child (and $5 for each African child).[141]

With the passing years, the power of the Europeans and the European colonial government was increasingly challenged by rising African nationalism—much of it seconded by Asians, politically, intellectually, and financially.[142] An Indian attorney participated in the legal defense of Jomo Kenyatta, and an Indian businessman supported Kenyatta's daughter while he was in prison.[143] Yet Asians and Africans remained separate, distant, suspicious, and resentful of each other. The economic and social gap between them has always been vast, and with the coming of independence, what the Indians had achieved economically became a prize to be sought politically by Africans. Moreover, both were well aware of this. As in Uganda, the average Asian in Kenya earned several times the income of the average African, though less than half the income of Europeans in Kenya.[144] Nevertheless, Asians were more numerous than Europeans[145] and their jobs and businesses more within striking distance of educated and vocal Africans.

Large Indian donations to African political causes were discounted by Africans as bribes with an eye to the future.[146] Indian-African relations were historically formal rather than personal—a customer-seller relationship or an African servant for an Asian employer. The only intimate contact was between Asian men and African concubines, but not the reverse, and intermarriage was virtually out of the question.[147] There were no more than 5,000 people of mixed Asian and African ancestry in all the countries of East Africa put together, even though early generations of Indians were nearly all male, and it is from these times that most Afro-Asians derive.[148]

Asians have not been admirers of African culture, African habits, or African appearance.[149] This was not peculiar to Kenya or even to East Africa. Despite the pious public "unity" of Third World politics, a delegate from India at the famous Bandung conference of Third World nations summed up the relations between Asians and Africans to an Indian writer by confiding: "We and the Africans couldn't care less for each other."[150]

As independence for Kenya approached, Asians began transferring their capital out of the country, and continued to do so.[151] Their lack of faith in their future in Kenya was also apparent in their reluctance to acquire Kenyan citizenship.[152] Kenya became independent in 1962 under a constitution—shaped in London—that assured equal rights without distinction of race.[153] Nevertheless, the political pressures for "Africanization" proved irresistible. While explicit racism was not proclaimed, a crucial distinction between "citizen" and "non-citizen" was made in a constitutional amendment added after independence. Only "citizens" have equal rights—and being born in the country did not make an individual a citizen.[154] As elsewhere in Africa, many Indians were hesitant to acquire local citizenship immediately after independence, when their future was uncertain. Later, the restrictions on naturalization made citizenship more difficult to obtain—and left many Asians vulnerable to political trends.

The Kenyan government confiscated thousands of shops owned by "non-citizen" Asians, forbad their commercial activities in rural areas, and a government official announced: "The Asians should go home."[155] However, few Asians were citizens of either India or Pakistan.[156] Kenya was the only home they had known. But they had no one to protect their interests. Such foreign pressures as were exerted in their behalf came from Britain, not India—and the British were anxious to avoid being deluged with more Asian refugees. The British government negotiated with Kenya to restrain itself from forcing out too many Asians, and with India to accept 15,000 of the refugees provisionally. More than 90 percent of these "provisional" refugees remained in India, however. The example of Uganda's mass expulsions of Indians in 1972 created political pressures in neighboring Kenya to do likewise. Although Kenya did not follow suit, it did pressure more and more Asians to leave.

The Asian population of more than 176,000 in Kenya in 1962 was by 1975 reduced to about 25,000.[157] Those remaining were almost all either professionals or skilled workers. The Indian businessman who had played a large role in building the economy of Kenya was now driven from it.

South Africa

Indians were brought to southern Africa as indentured laborers, beginning in 1860, and their numbers grew rapidly. By 1875 there were 10,000 Indians in the colony of Natal, and by the turn of the century there were 100,000.[158] Indians in South Africa have tended to remain concentrated in Natal province, with some also living in the Transvaal.[159] In the middle of the twentieth century, about 40 percent of all Indians in South Africa were living in the city of Durban, and 80 percent in the province of Natal, of which it is part.[160]

The growth of a resident Indian population in South Africa was never intended by the white officials there, was opposed by official policy, but was effectively stopped only in the Orange Free State, which brought in no indentured laborers. In Natal, the indentured laborers often remained after their contracts had expired, even though they were entitled to a free return trip to India. Indian labor was wanted in South Africa, but not an Indian community. At first, Indians were indentured for five years, required to remain for an additional five years (thus supplying the local labor market), and at the end of that time could choose either free passage to India or a grant of land in South Africa. After many Indians chose the land, that option was removed.[161] Indians who remained in South Africa after their indentures expired were required to purchase a pass from the government, at a price which was expected to be prohibitive in relation to their income. Moreover, the law made no provision for an Indian to become a naturalized citizen of South Africa.[162] Only the need to placate the British colonial government of India prevented the law from being harsher and prescribing criminal penalties for failure to return home.

While many Indians did return to India, many others did not. The latter either made the financial sacrifices necessary to purchase the pass or else simply evaded the law. While the Transvaal did not import indentured laborers from India, many of those from Natal moved into the Transvaal after their contracts expired, often as small traders. Their relative prosperity led others in India to sail directly to the Transvaal. As a resident Indian population grew, whites in the Transvaal created political pressure for restrictions on the Indians. The Orange Free State simply barred Indians entirely, and only a negligible number settled there in violation of the law. The Cape colony had no restrictions on Asian immigration during the nineteenth century, but few came there, and those who did were often from Natal or the Transvaal,[163] rather than from India.

The geographic and social origins of the Indians changed as the successive waves of indentured laborers were succeeded by waves of "passenger" Indians paying their own way. Untouchables from Madras and Calcutta were prominent in the early indentured migration, but the later waves that came as commercial traders were more likely to come from western India, with Gujaratis being prominent among them. Even these "passenger" Indians, however, were poor by Western standards, and their commercial activity often began as marginal peddlers selling fruits and vegetables door-to-door at cheap prices. Indians in South

Africa also went into a variety of other occupations. Those who spoke English could work as cooks, waiters, junior clerks, or drivers, while others went into construction, painting, fishing, and other trades and occupations. In heavy manual labor, they could not compete with the bigger and stronger Africans.[164]

In agriculture, Indians in Natal often converted wasteland, unused by either Europeans or Africans, into gardens from which they supplied fruits and vegetables in the local markets. As early as 1886, an official report said:

> Before there was a free Indian population, the towns of Pietermaritzburg and Durban had no supply of fruit, vegetables and fish; at present all these things are fully supplied. We have never had any immigrants from Europe who have shown any inclination to become market-gardeners and fishermen.[165]

The early Indian market-gardeners were largely illiterate people, living in shanty housing, and carrying baskets of produce door-to-door, to eke out a living.[166] They were noted for their long hours of work, through the day and into the night. Some were seen weeding their gardens by moonlight.[167] Only slowly, over the years, did they rise to a modest level of living, in some cases eventually buying a truck to deliver their produce, or moving from a shanty into a tiny house.

While agriculture was a natural progression for former plantation laborers, Gujaratis often began in commerce upon their arrival from India, setting up small businesses in competition with whites in Natal, the Transvaal, and the Orange Free State.[168] As elsewhere, the Indian retailer was willing to adjust his transactions to the special needs of his clientele, often poor Africans. Indian stores tended to be open long hours,[169] to charge lower prices than the Europeans charged, and to extend credit.[170] Many Indians learned an African language and employed African assistants.[171] They were hated by the Europeans as "unfair" competition and denounced by the Africans as "exploiters."

The reactions of the whites began to make themselves felt politically in policies designed to hamstring Indian economic activities and personal life with special restrictions and taxes. Discrimination against Indians as employees was strongest in the government itself, where the principle that no European could be subordinate to a non-European restricted the Indians to the lowest jobs. The government's issuance of licenses to engage in various trades likewise discriminated against the Indians, though it did not wholly exclude them. The government also restricted Indians' right to purchase land.[172] The same discriminatory approach was manifested in the provision of government services, notably education.[173] Indian resistance to discriminatory policies was organized by a young attorney from India named Mohandas K. Gandhi. His political career and nonviolent resistance techniques began in South Africa before they were applied in India.[174] By and large, however, the repression of the Indians, among others, remained an enduring feature of South African life, especially after *apartheid.*

Relations between Indians and black Africans were also often marked by antagonism. In Durban in 1949, a fight between a black youth and an Indian shopkeeper escalated into a mass riot, in which 142 people were killed.[175] Despite the opposition of both blacks and Indians to apartheid, it was difficult for them to make common cause politically, though some cooperation slowly emerged.[176] Still, ironically, black and Indian opposition to apartheid was itself largely separate racially. Another African-Indian riot erupted in Durban in 1985, with African mobs looting Indian stores and destroying Indian homes.

Asians—almost all Indians—have historically been from 2 to 3 percent of the population of South Africa,[177] and have been about as urbanized as the whites.[178] Asians' average family income has historically been more than double that of black Africans in South Africa, but less than a third that of whites.[179] Asians have worked in commerce and industry to about the same extent as the whites and much more so than blacks.[180] As in other countries, intergroup income comparisons that ignore regional and rural-urban differences can be misleading, as are differences which ignore family size. As of 1951, the per capita income of Indians in Durban was slightly lower than that of Africans in Durban, significantly less than that of "Coloureds" in Durban, and only one-seventh that of whites in Durban.[181] As of 1982, the average monthly earnings of Asians in South Africa (almost all Indians) was still just over half that of whites and was just over one-third more than that of blacks.[182]

As elsewhere, the caste system has not survived completely intact among the overseas Indians in South Africa, but neither has it vanished entirely or lost all significance.[183] It remains strongest among Hindu Gujaratis.[184] Gujaratis also have by far the highest average income among the various Indian groups in South Africa—more than 60 percent higher than among Indians who speak English in the home, and more than double the incomes of Indians who speak Urdu, Hindi, Tamil, or Telugu.[185]

Most Indians in South Africa speak English as one of their languages, for English serves as a *lingua franca* within a polyglot community. A growing minority of Indians also speak English at home, especially among the younger generation.[186] As in other groups and other societies, the Indian culture is most self-consciously promoted by Indian intellectuals, who are themselves thoroughly Westernized.[187]

Internal differences among Indians have been sharp in South Africa, as in India itself and in other countries around the world. Intermarriage is rare among the various language groups of Indians in South Africa, much less between Hindus and Moslems.[188] Internally fragmented and facing antagonism from blacks and whites alike, Indians have been very vulnerable in South Africa, both during the era of white minority rule and in the subsequent era of black rule.

THE WESTERN HEMISPHERE

Indians who immigrated to the Western Hemisphere went largely to the lands in and around the Caribbean. This immigration occurred mainly from just before the middle of the nineteenth century through World War I. During that period, more than 20,000 Indians went to Jamaica, between 30,000 and 40,000 each went to Suriname and Guadaloupe, more than 100,000 to Trinidad, and more than 200,000 to what was then called British Guiana.[189] As a proportion of the total local population, Indians have been from 2 to 4 percent of the people of Jamaica, Martinique, and Guadaloupe, and have ranged from one-third to one-half the population of Trinidad, Guyana, and Suriname.[190] Since the 1960s, a significant number of emigrants from India have also gone to the United States[191]—but this was still far less than 1 percent of the American population. About 40,000 Indians from the Caribbean re-emigrated to Canada, where they lived a social life largely apart from Indians from India.[192]

As in Africa, the caste system of India declined in importance in the Western Hemisphere, where the conditions for its full maintenance did not exist. The crowded ocean voyage and crowded barracks for indentured servants in the early years of emigration from India began the process of breaking down caste distinctions. Moreover, Indians were assigned tasks on Western Hemisphere plantations without regard to their caste origins in India. In addition, the "passenger" Indians, who were less subject to these conditions and who retained more of their caste traditions in Africa, seem to have been a much smaller proportion of the Indian population in the Western Hemisphere. Still, caste did not disappear entirely as a social consideration.[193] However, marriage across caste lines became the rule rather than the exception among Indians in Guyana and Trinidad.[194]

The history of people from India living in the Western Hemisphere has been in some ways similar to their history in Africa, but in other ways quite different. Their immigration to the Western Hemisphere was initially in very similar roles as manual laborers, often indentured servants. Here, as in Africa, they were imported *en masse* from a great distance, in preference to employing the local black population. In colonial Guiana and Trinidad, the "East Indians" (as they were called to distinguish them from aboriginal "Indians") largely replaced blacks on plantations after the era of slavery ended. "East Indians" were generally regarded as harder working and less troublesome.

The differences from the situation in Africa have also been quite striking. Indians in the Western Hemisphere have tended to remain rural agricultural workers, in contrast to the great urbanization of Indians in Africa. Moreover, the black population averages higher incomes than the Indians in Trinidad.[195] Part of the explanation lies in the different origins of the emigrants from India to different parts of the world. While most of those who went to Africa from India were Gujaratis from western India, those who went to the Western Hemisphere were predominantly from the Ganges River basin in the eastern end of the subcontinent. There are vast differences among the various peoples of India within the country itself, where the Gujaratis are disproportionately represented in commerce and the educated professions. As with other nationalities, these internal differences persisted for generations in other countries where they settled.

Guyana

During the colonial era, British Guiana was the only British colony on the South American mainland. Indentured emigration from British India to British Guiana began in 1838, shortly after the abolition of slavery. Indians were one of a number of foreign workers (including Portuguese and Chinese) imported to do work formerly performed on the sugar plantations by Afro-American slaves. The former slaves worked irregularly after emancipation—often only as many days as required to meet their subsistence needs in a tropical country where food was readily obtainable from nature,[196] and where clothing and housing requirements were modest. Many worked their own plots of land, even when employed on plantations.[197]

Between 1838 and 1917, approximately 239,000 laborers arrived from India.[198] Indians were harder and steadier workers, in part because the strict terms of their five-year indenture contracts left them little choice. They inherited not only the work but also the harsh treatment of the era of slavery. Flogging was common in the early years. An official report in the nineteenth century noted that Indians were flogged until they bled.[199] Between ill-treatment and exposure to new diseases, the Indians of Guyana had a death rate that went as high as 12 percent a year in 1839[200]—among people imported in the youthful prime of life.[201]

However, the harsh regime under which indentured servants lived could not alone explain the productivity of the Indians. The Portuguese and West Indians imported for similar work proved to be unsatisfactory, as did Indians from Madras.[202] Nor were the advantages of those Indians who remained the mainstay of the plantation labor force due either to skill or strength. Blacks were prominent among the more skilled workers on the plantations,[203] and were regarded as stronger and better workers—when they chose to work.[204]

The evidence suggests that Indians simply represented the best option available for the plantation owners in British Guiana—and that British Guiana represented the best option available to people from the Ganges River basin in India. Not only did the inflow continue for decades, despite the difficult conditions of indentureship; British Guiana by the 1880s and 1890s became the principal foreign destination of emigrants from India.[205]

In the early years, mistreatment of Indian indentured laborers in Guiana was so notorious that the British colonial government in India refused to allow any more to be shipped there. But with various assurances and reforms—variously enforced—the indenture traffic resumed in 1844.[206] For a few years in the 1850s, a British official responsible for the well-being of Indian indentured laborers performed his job so conscientiously that plantation owners used their political influence to get his work hamstrung and his authority reduced to impotence.[207] Though the office was ultimately restored to independence and authority, the episode showed the political muscle of the plantation owners—and the corresponding vulnerability of the Indians.

That political muscle was also demonstrated by harsh vagrancy laws, and by ordinances raising the price of government-owned land, which was sold only in large parcels—all designed to reduce the options of Negro and Indian workers, thereby pressuring them to work on the white-owned plantations.[208]

By 1890, at least 70,000 of the 100,000 Indians in British Guiana lived on sugar plantations and only 5 percent in the cities. At about the same time, only 10 percent of their children attended even elementary school. The first compulsory attendance laws in the colony exempted the Indians, who did not want their children proselytized in schools run by Christian missionaries.[209] There were no secular schools.[210]

With the passage of time and the expiration of indenture contracts, more and more former indentured laborers from India settled in British Guiana as independent peasants. Only about one-third returned to India.[211] As elsewhere around the world, Indians in British Guiana were noted for their thriftiness, saving out of wages disdained as too low by Afro-Americans there. But while the Indians had the advantage in saving, black Guianans had the advantage in education. Afro-Americans were the main beneficiaries of compulsory education, and soon filled the teaching profession, civil service, and skilled trades in the colony.[212]

As of 1925, when the Indians outnumbered the Afro-Americans slightly (42 percent of the population versus 39 percent), 85 percent of the employees in the colonial bureaucracy were Negroes.[213] As of 1931, Indians still constituted just 7 percent of the teachers and 8 percent of the civil servants.[214] Their lack of education was an enduring handicap. As late as 1946, just one-half of the Indians were literate in English,[215] which was the only language that most of them knew.

While Indians in British Guiana remained concentrated in agriculture, they were important factors in that field. Their arrival in the nineteenth century revived the collapsing sugar industry in British Guiana, which suffered from the massive withdrawals of blacks from the plantations after emancipation. Indians also played a major role, as independent farmers, in developing the rice production of the country. By the latter part of the twentieth century, 42 percent of the total exports of the independent nation of Guyana consisted of these two crops.[216]

Although the last indenture contract did not run out until 1920, most Indians advanced beyond the status of indentured laborer years before that. By 1911, about half of all Indians in British Guiana lived away from the sugar estates.[217] Nor were all those on the estates indentured. Even after the end of indentureship, Indians continued to live on the sugar estates in large numbers, constituting about four-fifths of all persons on such estates in 1931, when they were still almost equally divided between this and all other places of residence.[218] Many lived in villages in the vicinity of the plantations.[219]

The total Indian population of British Guiana grew from less than 8,000 in the middle of the nineteenth century to over 100,000 in 1886, to about 180,000 by 1948. The Indian proportion of the total population rose from about 6 percent in 1851 to about 40 percent by 1893.[220] The Indian population overtook the Afro-American population by 1917, and by 1964 the Indians constituted just a shade over half of the total population of the country, which also included 6 percent who are either Europeans, Chinese, or the aboriginal "Amerindians."[221] Historically, the birthrate among Indians has been the highest for any group except (in some years) the aborigines, who had a far higher death rate.[222] In short, the Indians were not only more numerous than their chief rivals, the blacks, but were also the fastest-growing portion of the entire population. This was all the more remarkable, in view of the historically unbalanced sex ratio among Indians. There were fewer than 50 women per 100 men among the Indians in 1880, and only 70 women per 100 men as late as 1917.[223]

While Indians in British Guiana have historically been more represented in commercial occupations than in government employment,[224] they were never as prominent as traders or retailers as the Indians in Africa. The Portuguese and Chinese dominated commercial trading in British Guiana,[225] where there were few Gujaratis among the Indians to contest their predominance. Indians continued to predominate in agriculture, however. As of 1968, they were 70 percent of the independent farmers, and of those working on the sugar estates. Moreover, even within agriculture, the Africans and Indians functioned very differently. Indians were dominant in commercial farming, especially in producing the two main cash crops, sugar and rice. Afro-American farmers tended to be subsistence farmers.[226] Partly this reflected the great saving propensities of the Indians, which enabled them to buy the larger amounts of land required for commercial farming.

Relations between peoples of African and of Indian ancestry have been strained and often hostile, as in Africa and in the Caribbean islands. The two groups have been separated residentially, occupationally, socially, and politically. Even in the last half of the twentieth century, nearly half of all Guianans of African ancestry lived in urban areas, while nearly nine-tenths of all Guianans of Indian ancestry lived in rural areas.[227]

The differing urban-rural distributions of the two groups were only one factor in their separate existences, however. The relatively few Indians who lived among Afro-Americans, and vice versa, encountered frictions. As a result of race riots in the 1960s, villages became less mixed than before. Similar residential separation between the two groups was common in the French Antilles, Suriname, and Trinidad. Even in Jamaica, where Indians were too small a group to form separate residential communities, or to resist outward cultural assimilation, hostility between them and Afro-American Jamaicans was reported by both sides.[228]

However widespread the frictions and conflicts between peoples of African and Indian ancestries, their cultural and other differences did not create constant or fixed levels of contention.

The era of their more extreme separation, both residentially and occupationally, during colonial times was an era when they were not as polarized—and indeed, when they formed a multiracial movement seeking independence. This movement split apart only as independence was at hand and the political struggle for the spoils of power began.[229]

Colonial British Guiana had an economic and social pattern similar in many ways to that in other British colonies in the Caribbean, Africa, or Asia. A small white colonial aristocracy controlled both the government and the commercial economy, and made its culture the standard to which the subject peoples aspired.[230] Meanwhile, a small middle class began to emerge among the colonial subjects, those educated or semi-educated in English taking jobs in the colonial government, and gradually acquiring civil and political rights over the years—eventually leading to demands for independence. In the case of British Guiana, these colonial subjects were not primarily the indigenous American Indians but people whose ancestors came to the colony from Africa or India. By 1940, those of African ancestry were 15 percent of the top civil servants and, while no Indians had yet reached that level, 10 percent of the pensionable staff was Indian, compared to 67 percent Afro-American. The colonial peoples were rising and the end of white minority rule was a clear prospect.

Both the Indian and African populations were united in support of independence. The two leaders of the independence movement were Dr. Cheddi Jagan, an Indian Marxist who founded the movement, and Forbes Burnham, an Afro-American who later joined. Both men were educated abroad, Jagan in the United States and Burnham in England. This biracial leadership led to an overwhelming victory of the People's Progressive Party in the election of 1950, held as part of a phased movement toward self-government, as the colony of British Guiana evolved toward becoming the independent nation of Guyana. The period 1950–1953 has been called "the Golden Age of racial harmony in Guyana." It was destined to last less than five years. As in other countries, racial harmony was turned into racial polarization by politics.

The racial "imbalance" in the government jobs became a major point of contention, as in other Third World countries emerging into independence. As late as 1957 the Indians, who were half of the population, still had only about a third of the government jobs—and were especially under-represented in the police and other security forces, where they had only one-fifth of the jobs.[231]

The radical proposals of Cheddi Jagan's government, including the nationalization of foreign companies, caused the British to suspend Guyana's constitution and remove his party from office. This crisis, after less than six months in power, split the People's Progressive Party into two wings—the radical wing still led by Cheddi Jagan and a more moderate wing led by Forbes Burnham. The ideological split, however, quickly became a racial split, with the Indians largely supporting Jagan and the blacks largely supporting Burnham. As the election of 1957 approached, racial appeals were widely used at the grass roots levels.[232] This resort to racial appeals was far more fateful for the future of Guyana than the outcome of the election itself.

Cheddi Jagan won—but he found himself the leader of a government whose black bureaucracy was against him, and whose black-dominated security forces were of doubtful reliability to him. Strikes, demonstrations, and disruptions plagued the Jagan government. Racial outbreaks required British troops to maintain order. When Burnham won the 1964 elections, Jagan's forces retaliated with similar strikes and boycotts by his Indian supporters.[233] But, with the Burnham government commanding black security forces, these strikes were more readily dealt with.

The Burnham government instituted authoritarian controls, including long detentions without trial. This polarization of the races jeopardized Guyana's emergence into independence, as intergroup violence unsettled the country in the early 1960s and the political parties representing the opposing races became deadlocked over a constitution proposed for the new nation. The British resolved the outstanding constitutional issues in a way that undermined Cheddi Jagan's party, whose representation in Parliament exceeded its share of the popular vote.

The first election under proportional representation in 1964 saw a sharp reduction in Jagan's parliamentary support, to a level closely corresponding to his party's share of the vote (46 percent). While this still left him with the largest single party support, a coalition led by Burnham's Afro-American-based party and buttressed by support from those opposed to Jagan's radicalism put the opposition in power. Each of the two major rival parties treated the 1964 elections as decisive for the future, hence their deadlock on a constitution. Each regarded the holding of power at the time of independence—1966—as determining the whole future course of political power, which neither party would be willing to relinquish. So it turned out to be.[234]

Despite disastrous economic policies which, among other things, led to rice production's falling to half its previous level,[235] the ruling Afro-Americans consolidated their position with ever-growing majorities in the elections of 1968, 1973, and 1980, even though blacks were still a minority of the country's population—only 30 percent in 1980, compared to the Indians' 51 percent. The honesty of those elections has been widely questioned. In addition, some Indians, either opposed to Jagan or opportunistically aware of the unlikelihood of the ruling party's losing power, switched their support. Nevertheless, despite some token concessions to Indians, the ruling party leadership remained overwhelmingly Afro-American in a country where Indians were the largest ethnic group in the population.[236] One symptom of the kind of government that ruled Guyana was that the police and auxiliary armed forces, which numbered fewer than 4,000 in 1964, rose to more than 21,000 thousand by 1977.[237]

External pressures and the death of Prime Minister Forbes Burnham in 1985 led to major political and economic changes in Guyana. The deterioration of the economy, with such side-effects as a rising infant mortality rate, and the inability of Guyana to pay its external debts brought growing pressure on Burnham's successor, Desmond Hoyte, to restructure the economy and hold genuine elections. Needing international financial assistance, the government acceded to these requests, beginning a program of privatization of government-owned enterprises and arranging to hold elections that would have international credibility. When these elections were held in 1992, a coalition headed by the People's Progressive Party won, bringing Cheddi Jagan to power once again. However, during the intervening decades since he was last in power, Jagan's People's Progressive Party had pulled back from its Marxist ideology and its pro-Soviet stances, which became obsolete with the collapse of the Soviet Union. Ironically, the socialist policies instituted by the once-moderate PNC were now dismantled by the once-Marxist PPP. From an ethnic perspective, the 48 percent of the Guyanan population of East Indian ancestry was no long disfranchised, nor power monopolized by leaders of the 32 percent of the population of African ancestry.[238]

Trinidad

In Trinidad, as in Guyana, Indians tended to be rural and the blacks urban.[239] In both places, this was a legacy from the era of indentured Indian plantation labor. Work in the sugarcane fields long remained an occupation dominated by Indians.[240] Approximately 143,000 indentured workers were brought from India to Trinidad between 1845 and 1917, when indentureship was abolished.[241] The resident Indian population in 1921 was about 122,000, of whom just 37,000 had been born in India. The total population of Trinidad was about 366,000.[242] The Indians in Trinidad have long been cut off from the source of their culture, so that they gradually absorbed much of the outward culture of the Caribbean, while retaining such inner values as thrift and strictness concerning sex. Moreover, much of what they retained as traditions from India had in fact changed in India itself.[243] The caste system did not survive completely intact in Trinidad, but neither did it disappear as a social factor among Indians living there.[244] Yet, however much Indians in Trinidad came to differ from the people of India, they remained apart from other Trinidadians as well. Indians in Trinidad maintained a pattern of residential and social separateness common to them in the Caribbean. As of 1950, there were fifty separate Indian schools in Trinidad.[245]

From the earliest times, the Indians established a remarkable reputation for thrift. Their remittances to India between 1890 and 1912 totalled more than £65,000. In a period of one decade in the early twentieth century, the Indians also purchased a total of more than £72,837 worth of land and saved each year from about £60,000 to £80,000—all this on wages of 25 cents a day.[246]

The Indians were not only a large but growing proportion of the population. By 1946, the Indians numbered about 200,000—35 percent of Trinidad's population[247]—and by 1962 they were 40 percent of the population.[248] The political influence of Indians, however, was far less than their share of the population might suggest. Like Indians in other countries, they tended to be politically apathetic, divided internally, and without strong leadership. One consequence was that they received relatively little of the spoils of politics. Indians in Trinidad were only 11 percent of the civil service and less than 3 percent of the police force.[249] They did much better in the private sector, where they constituted 34 percent of the doctors and 42 percent of the lawyers.[250] In the twenty years following the end of World War II, the number of Indian doctors increased more than fivefold.[251] However, the fact that the Indians largely remained a rural people in Trinidad has meant generally lower educational levels and lower money incomes—in 1960, 25 percent below the incomes of blacks and only about one-sixth the income of whites.[252]

Relations between Trinidadian blacks and Indians have generally been antagonistic, especially after the rise of "black power" ideology in the 1960s. At first, during the 1950s when Trinidad was approaching independence, the leading political figure in Trinidad—black intellectual Eric Williams—spoke for a political agenda addressed to "have-nots" in general, not to particular racial or ethnic groups. However, after Trinidad achieved independence in 1962, Williams' party became essentially the party of blacks, and their chief opposition was essentially a party of Indians.[253]

The internationally renowned Indian writer V. S. Naipul has written that his native Trinidad "teeters on the brink of a racial war." Naipul said of the Trinidadian Negro that "his values are the values of white imperialism at its most bigoted" and that the Indian "despises the Negro for not being an Indian."[254] However it might be phrased, the antagonism between these two races in Trinidad repeated an antagonism between them found in other countries, often thousands of miles apart.

The United States

Substantial migration from the Indian subcontinent to the United States is a relatively recent phenomenon. For the entire period from 1946 to 1964, fewer than 7,000 people migrated from India to the United States[255] and, as late as 1970–71, there were only an estimated 32,000 Indians, Pakistanis, and Bangladeshis living in the country.[256] Later, nearly 32,000 would arrive in just one year (1977).[257]

Although very small numbers of immigrants from India to the United States can be traced back into the nineteenth century, and nearly five thousand arrived during the first decade of the twentieth century, the highly restrictive American immigration laws and policies that began in the 1920s reduced the numbers below 500 for the entire decade of the 1930s.[258] Significant increases in immigration from India began after new American immigration laws and policies went into effect in the late 1960s, and the numbers grew progressively in the decades that followed.

The first of this new wave of people from India were Sikhs and Punjabis,[259] many of whom went into farming. As the population of South Asians in the United States grew, however, both their geographical and social origins changed as well. The 1980 American census showed more than 387,000 people born in India or of Indian ancestry.[260] The sexes were balanced, suggesting a permanent settlement, and nearly half of their occupations were professional, technical, and the like.[261] As a whole, Indian males living in the United States averaged 10 percent higher incomes than white American males.[262] This was all the more remarkable because three-quarters of the Indian immigrants had arrived in the United States only within the previous decade.[263]

A decade later, the 1990 census showed that the Asian Indian population of the United States had grown to more than 786,000 people. The great majority had been born outside the United States and most of these had entered the country only during the past decade. Only a little more than one-fourth of all Asian Indians in the United States were naturalized American citizens.[264] Despite their relatively recent arrival in the United States, Indians still had higher family incomes than native-born Americans. Whereas the median family income for native-born Americans was about $35,000 in 1990, the median family income of Indians who arrived between 1980 and 1990 was more than $40,000 and of those who arrived before 1980 was more than $60,000.[265] The prosperity of Indians in the United States was clearly related to their high levels of education and occupations. As of 1980, nearly two-thirds of all employed Indians were college graduates. Employed Indians as a group averaged 4 years more education than employed white Americans as a group. But, for any given level of education and for most occupations, whites received higher incomes than

Indians.[266] It was just that Indians' educational qualifications were so much better that they received higher incomes overall. They have made very little mark in politics—though the first Indian was elected to the Congress of the United States in 1956[267]—nor have they been particularly vocal or even noticeable as a social group, despite being a larger group than either Koreans or Vietnamese.[268]

Among the occupations in which Indians have been concentrated have been engineering and medicine. Between the early 1970s and the mid-1980s, more than 15,000 engineers and more than 15,000 physicians migrated from India to the United States.[269] This is in addition to the students from India who were trained in these professions in the United States. They tended to specialize in electronic engineering. By the late 1980s, California's Silicon Valley alone had 5,000 Indian engineers and nationally there were more than 20,000.[270] Indian engineers played prominent roles in founding computer companies such as Sun Microsystems, some becoming millionaires in the process.[271] There were also 28,000 physicians from India working in the United States, including 10 percent of all anesthesiologists in the country.[272] People from India were well represented in business as well, owning nearly 40 percent of all small motels in the United States, including about one-fourth of the franchises in the Days Inn chain. Most of these Indian motel owners have been Gujaratis.[273]

ASIA

Both the peoples and the cultures of India have spread across Southeast Asia for many centuries. While Indians and Indian culture have a long history in the nations of Southeast Asia, massive immigration from the subcontinent to these other nations occurred only after the establishment of European colonial governments and the development of ports, industry, and commercial agriculture in this region. But, once begun, the immigration of Indians to other parts of Asia reached impressive proportions. In the decade of the 1880s, for example, about 140,000 Indians immigrated to Malaya, about 165,000 to Burma, and nearly half a million to Ceylon.[274] By the late twentieth century, the two largest concentrations of Indians abroad were in Asia—in Sri Lanka and Malaysia. Indians have also been an important minority in Burma, and a small but significant middleman minority in Thailand, Indochina, and Indonesia.

Most of the Indians in Thailand and Indonesia have historically been merchants.[275] Some in Burma, Malaysia, and Indochina have been notable as money-lenders.[276] Both occupations have made Indians conspicuous—and often bitterly resented—in the region. Nevertheless, the numerical bulk of the Indian population in some of these countries consisted of laborers, as in Burma,[277] Malaysia,[278] or Sumatra,[279] for example. Yet the *image* of the Indian projected politically was that of the monied elite, "the Chettyar with the bloated abdomen," as Burmese Prime Minister U Nu put it.[280] The geographical concentration of Indians, who were more than half the total population of Rangoon in 1931,[281] contributed to the distorted perception of them.

As in India itself, those who shared the broad label "Indian" have been highly diverse, and these diversities have followed them in other countries. The Chettyars from southern India have been prominent as money-lenders in Burma, Malaya, and Indochina. Sikhs from northern India have also been prominent as money-lenders in Malaya where, in the middle of the twentieth century, approximately 10,000 of them engaged in this occupation in the Malay Federation alone.[282] But five-sixths of all Indians in prewar Malaya were Tamils from southern India,[283] as were the bulk of the Indians in Ceylon, now Sri Lanka. As of 1980, four-fifths of all the Indians in Malaysia were Tamils.[284] In prewar Malaya, these southern Indians were usually laborers on rubber plantations, while northern Indians were in business and the professions.[285] Tamils in Malaya remained largely uneducated as late as the middle of the twentieth century.[286] At the same time, the Indian children of Singapore were in school to a greater degree than the Chinese or Malay children—the adult Indians of Singapore being mainly businessmen and professionals.[287]

Indians in Thailand have tended to be sojourners rather than settlers,[288] while in Malaya and Indonesia, half the Indian population was born locally,[289] as was more than half of the million Indians living in prewar Burma.[290] Although Indians were only about 8 percent of the work force in Burma during the 1930s,[291] they nevertheless played an important role in the Burmese economy. As of 1931, approximately half the income-tax payers in Burma were Indians.[292] A decade later, Indians were more than half of all the physicians, businessmen, and bankers in the country and more than two-thirds of all the port workers and railway personnel.[293] As with other groups in similar circumstances, the Indians were targets of hostility in Burma. Violence took more than 200 lives in 1938 and Indians were expelled from the country *en masse*. Despite the usual charges that foreign money-lenders were impoverishing the native people, interest rates charged by the Burmese money-lenders who replaced the Chettyars were usually higher.[294]

Malaysia

Indians were in Malaya many centuries before the Europeans. So were many aspects of Indian culture, adopted by the ruling Malay elite.[295] However, the twentieth-century Indian population in Malaysia did not derive from the Indians who came in those ancient times. An estimated 95 percent of all Indians who have immigrated to Malaya and Malaysia in the past two millennia have done so since the late eighteenth century.[296] The British founding of the port of Penang in 1786, and later Singapore in 1819, were crucial for the immigration of Indians and Chinese, and for the transformation of Malaya from a land of forests and swamps into a developed economy—a transformation in which the indigenous Malays played virtually no role.[297]

Even unskilled labor had to be imported, for the Malays possessed land or engaged in fishing, and seldom had need or inclination to become wage laborers for others on unfamiliar and demanding tasks.[298] Indians played an important role in the development of the Malay economy, largely as unskilled labor. The Tamil Indians in Malaya—later Malaysia—never became as predominant in the economy in general, or in commerce in particular, as the Gujaratis did in Africa or the Chettyars in Burma. The vast majority of the Indians in Malaya came as laborers, and many remained laborers and returned to India in the same occupation.[299] The importance of regional and social origins in India was underscored by the historic concentration of Bengalis, Sikhs, Chettyars, and Tamils in different occupations in Malaysia.[300] But the preponderant majority were Tamils.[301]

Many of the Indians who entered Malaya in the nineteenth century came as indentured laborers or under some other variety of labor contract or verbal agreement with a recruiting agent for the plantations in Malaya. Few migrated on their own and then looked for work. The so-called "assisted" immigrants consistently outnumbered those who came as independent individuals paying their own passage.[302] The early immigration was nearly all male. As late as 1901, there were only 171 Indian women for every 1,000 Indian men in Malaya.[303] The work of a nineteenth-century Indian laborer lasted about nine to ten hours per day, six days a week, and discipline was enforced by flogging. In addition, an Indian worker might often be trapped by debt for years,[304] unable to return home until long after his initial indenture period.

Despite the harsh conditions and the fraud often connected with debts to plantation owners or to labor contractors, Indians continued to pour into Malaya, overwhelmingly from among the untouchables of the poverty-stricken Tamil regions of southern India. Altogether, more than 2,700,000 people immigrated into Malaya from India between 1844 and 1941.[305] Wages in Malaya were considerably higher than those in southern India—perhaps as much as double—for work that was not as arduous. Hours were shortened and working conditions improved in the early twentieth century, so that plantation work in Malaya compared favorably with similar work in other countries of the region.[306] Even after the Great Depression of the 1930s produced mass unemployment and very low wages in Malaya, a revival of the rubber plantations caused a massive inflow of Indians. Nor were these Indians unaware of economic conditions in Malaya. Though illiterate, they remained well informed about conditions in Malaya, even while living in the districts of southern India from which they were recruited.[307]

Over the period from the founding of Penang in 1786 to Malayan independence in 1957, more than 4.2 million Indians arrived in the country.[308] However, the resident Indian population of Malaya did not grow correspondingly, for there was a huge return migration to India as the plantation workers completed their contracts. More than 3 million of the 4.2 million who arrived between 1786 and 1957 returned to India.[309] The total Indian population resident in Malaya was less than a million—about 820,000—in 1957.[310] Return migration was not, however, the only reason for this large disparity between the size of the immigration from India and the size of the Indian population in Malaya at a given time. The mortality rate on the plantations was very high.

On some plantations, half the workers died within a year of their arrival. Overwork, malnutrition, malaria, snakes, and wild animals all contributed to these deaths. So did the Indian laborer's own lack of hygiene and his tendency to skimp on food, in order to enjoy alcohol or tobacco. Moreover, the brutal conditions imposed by the Japanese conquerors during World War II also led to the deaths of an estimated 50,000 Indian laborers.[311] After the war was over, there were fewer Indians in Malaya in 1947 than there had been in 1931.[312]

Over the years, the Indians of Malaya gradually ceased being sojourners and became a native-born group. As late as 1921, only 12 percent of the Indians in Malaya had been born there, but by 1947 the proportion had risen to about half, and by 1967 to an estimated 70 percent.[313] Indians also became a more urbanized group, rising from 24 percent urban in 1911 to 47 percent urban by 1957.[314] However, agriculture has remained the largest single employer of Indians in Malaya, though declining from about 61 percent in 1931 to 45 percent by 1965.[315] Indians played an historic role as workers on the rubber plantation that made Malaya the world's leading producer of rubber. As of 1937, the rubber industry employed 300,000 Indians and 200,000 Chinese, compared to only 30,000 Malays.[316] Indians remained more than half of all rubber plantation workers as late as 1957 and 41 percent as late as 1970.[317]

In the twentieth century, Indians have been a growing number, but a declining proportion, of the population of the Malay Peninsula. The Indian population (including Pakistanis and Ceylonese) of the Malay Peninsula numbered 439,000 in 1921 and this nearly doubled to 933,000 by 1970, but the proportion of Indians in the population declined from 15 percent to 11 percent.[318]

Economically, the Indians of Malaysia, until the late twentieth century, earned incomes in between those of the Malays and the Chinese. In 1957–58, Indian households earned 70 percent more than Malay households and 21 percent less than Chinese households. In 1970, the Indians earned 75 percent more than the Malays and 22 percent less than the Chinese.[319] While Malay households outnumbered Indian households by five to one in 1970, there were more Indian than Malay households in the top income bracket, in absolute numbers.[320] The relative economic positions of the three groups long remained in the same order, with percentages fluctuating somewhat by year and by type of survey. Educationally, the rank order was also similar in scientific and technical fields—the Chinese students at the University of Malaya in 1962–63 vastly outnumbering the Malays in engineering, and even the Indians—numerically the smallest of the three groups—outnumbering the Malays 41 to 16 in science and 24 to 5 in engineering, while the Malays outnumbered the Indians 247 to 90 in liberal arts.[321] All of this was despite preferential admissions and preferential scholarships for Malay students.

Intermarriage has remained rare among these three groups, despite the fact that Indian males outnumbered Indian females in the early years—two to one as late as 1932.[322] Urban Tamil Moslems have, however, intermarried somewhat with urban Malays,[323] who are overwhelmingly Moslem. Most of the Indians in Malaysia are Hindus, however.[324] But, within the Indian community, caste distinctions have not been as restrictive as in India.[325]

While the nativistic riots of May 1969 were directed primarily at the Chinese, Indians remained behind locked doors, and some Indians were attacked and killed by Malay rioters, weeks later.[326] In the political aftermath of those riots, Malays were given still more privileges vis-à-vis both Indians and Chinese. In the nation's universities, for example, Indians declined from 7 percent of those enrolled in degree courses to 6 percent between 1970 and 1980. Still, this was not as drastic a cutback as the Chinese suffered—from 49 percent to 26 percent.[327] In income, however, Indians fell behind the Malays by 1976, after more than a decade of increased Malay preferences in the economy.[328]

Sri Lanka

The largest number of overseas Indians in any nation have been the more than two and a half Indians in the island nation of Sri Lanka—formerly Ceylon—off the southeast coast of India. While Sri Lanka is a Third World country, its 15 million people have been materially better off than the peoples of India. Life expectancy in Sri Lanka exceeded that in India by 17 years, and its infant mortality rate was only about one-third that in India, while its adult literacy rate was more than twice as high as India's.[329]

The island of Ceylon was populated by people from India many centuries ago—but by different people from different parts of India. The Sinhalese, who form approximately three-quarters of the population, originated in northern India, centuries before Christ. The Tamils, a darker group constituting nearly one-fifth of the population, originated in southeastern India, in the state of Tamil Nadu, about 20 miles across the water from the island of Ceylon. There have long been two distinct groups of Tamils in Sri Lanka, even aside from caste and class differences. The so-called "Ceylon Tamils" or "Sri Lanka Tamils" have been on the island for many centuries—perhaps as long as, or longer than, the Sinhalese—and are citizens of Sri Lanka. But approximately one-third of the Tamils in the country have been so-called "Indian Tamils," largely descendants of immigrants who arrived from India between the 1830s and the 1930s. There are also several smaller minorities.

To a considerable extent, these three major groups in Sri Lanka have been separated geographically. The Ceylon Tamils—approximately 1.9 million people in 1981[330]—have been concentrated on the northern tip of the island, nearest the Indian state of Tamil Nadu, and along a contiguous strip going down the east coast of Sri Lanka. In some of these areas, the Ceylon Tamils vastly outnumber the Sinhalese, the national majority.[331] The Indian Tamils—about 1.2 million people—have historically been concentrated in the south-central region, where they have worked primarily as agricultural laborers on plantations producing coffee, tea, and rubber. The Sinhalese majority—more than 9 million people—have been numerically dominant everywhere else, as well as politically dominant in the nation as a whole.

The three groups have had very different histories and cultures. Most Sinhalese are Buddhist, most Tamils Hindu. Sinhala is the language of the Sinhalese and the Tamil language is spoken by both Ceylon and Indian Tamils. Even before the British took control of Ceylon at the end of the eighteenth and the beginning of the nineteenth centuries (succeeding Portuguese and Dutch colonial rule), missionaries began establishing schools, first in the north, where the Ceylon Tamils were concentrated.[332] This gave the Ceylon Tamils an historic educational advantage. Like other historic advantages in other countries, this proved to have enduring consequences over the generations. Schools in

Sinhalese areas came later,[333] and the education of the Indian Tamils on the plantations tended to be neglected most and longest.[334] It was 1929 before even half the Tamil children on the estates were attending school and 1950 before 60 percent were.[335]

The growth of an immigrant Tamil community in colonial Ceylon was closely linked to the development of British-owned plantations in the south-central region. By 1837, there were 5,000 acres under cultivation growing coffee, employing 10,000 immigrants from India—predominantly Tamils.[336] However, these Tamil immigrants were a very separate community from the Ceylon Tamils. Many centuries of separation of Ceylon Tamils from India meant that there were cultural differences between Tamils from the two countries, their differences and separateness being reinforced by their geographic separation in Ceylon.[337] The British imported Tamils, rather than other Indian groups, for plantation work not only because the Tamil regions of India were nearby, but also because the Tamil untouchables were preferred for such work. The same was true in more distant Malaya, where untouchables were especially preferred for the highly regimented work on plantations, since they were used to doing as they were told.[338] Ceylon Tamils were used for higher positions in Malaya.[339]

Because of the short voyage from India to Ceylon, the caste system survived intact more so among Indians in Ceylon than among Indians in more distant lands, where the voyage itself compromised caste separation and eating arrangements.[340] Moreover, the wide range of occupations on large plantations permitted various castes to work in their traditional occupational specialties.[341] Virtually all castes, except Brahmins, migrated to Ceylon in substantial numbers, but the early migration was as much as one-half untouchables. As late as 1930, untouchables were still 38 percent of all Indian immigrants on the Ceylon plantations.[342] The persistence of Indian caste traditions complicated the administration of British plantations in Ceylon[343] and continued to complicate the performance of even simple tasks, long after independence.[344] Nevertheless, the degree and extent to which caste behavior was practiced in Ceylon was not the same as in India.[345]

The first substantial migrations of Indians to Ceylon in the eighteenth century led to rapid growth of the migration stream in the nineteenth century. Fewer than 3,000 Tamil laborers immigrated in 1839, but by 1843 more than 36,000 immigrated, and in 1865 nearly 90,000 Tamils immigrated to Ceylon.[346] The early immigration was overwhelmingly male. It was 1847 before the number of female immigrants passed one thousand per year. From 1839 to 1859, more than 900,000 Tamils immigrated to Ceylon, but only 7 percent were women and 2 percent were children.[347] The percentage of women and children rose in succeeding years, but was still only 19 percent for the years 1860 to 1870.[348]

Working conditions on the plantations were harsh. Corporal punishment and fines deducted from meager wages were among the penalties inflicted on those who failed to produce as much as expected.[349] Cheating by labor contractors and plantation managements also occurred.[350] Yet the poverty of India was sufficient to keep the stream of immigrants coming—and growing. More than 100,000 Indians immigrated to Ceylon in 1910 and more than 200,000 in 1925 and 1930.[351] Although elements of fraud were present in both the recruiting and the payment of Indian plantation workers, the Indians' continued and growing migration to Ceylon cannot be accounted for by ignorance on their part because, by 1923, half of all Indian recruits to the plantations in Ceylon had been there before.[352] Since then, a majority of the Indian immigrants continued to be returnees rather than first-time migrants.[353]

Most of the early immigrants in the nineteenth century were contract laborers who were free to return to India after their contracts expired. Nearly half a million Tamils returned home during the period from 1839 to 1859—almost half of those who arrived in Ceylon during that period. More than half a million also departed during the years from 1860 to 1870, or more than two-thirds as many as arrived. Nevertheless, a resident Indian Tamil population began to develop in Ceylon. It grew not only by the excess of arrivals over departures, but also by natural increase. The departure rate for women was much lower than for men.[354] As with so many other migrations, the migration of women marked a more permanent settlement. However, even the Ceylon-born descendants of these Indian Tamils continued to be called Indian Tamils and to remain a separate community from Ceylon Tamils, as well as from the general society. By 1911, the growing Indian Tamil population slightly outnumbered the Ceylon Tamils, and continued to do so as late as 1953, though by 1971 the Ceylon Tamils had once more become the largest component of the Tamil population of Sri Lanka.[355]

The historic role of Indian Tamils as plantation laborers in south-central Ceylon persisted over the generations. As late as 1971, more than four-fifths of the more than 1 million persons working on plantations in Sri Lanka were Indian Tamils. Conversely, about four-fifths of all Indian Tamils in Sri Lanka worked on plantations. Nevertheless, there also were more than 240,000 Indian Tamils in Sri Lanka who were not plantation workers.[356] Some were laborers, servants, rickshaw-pullers, and performed similar unskilled work.[357] Some Indians, however, were traders, businessmen, and money-lenders.[358] These entrepreneurial groups followed historically in the wake of the Indian laborers, much as in East Africa, the Caribbean, and Fiji. In Ceylon, as in other countries, these Indian businessmen were from castes and ethnic groups noted for their entrepreneurship in India itself, but they by no means confined their clientele to Indians.

Gujaratis were merchants of various sorts and sizes, and Chettyars were money-lenders. At one time, 40 percent of all the credit extended by pawnbrokers in Ceylon was extended by Chettyars. Nearly 90 percent of the rice imports of Ceylon were handled by Indians (and the rest by Europeans). As of 1945, there were an estimated 750 Chettyar firms in Ceylon, with an aggregate capital of £7.5 million.[359] The textile trade was also largely in the hands of Indians, as was retailing, wholesaling, and importing.[360] Thus, despite the humble position of most Indian Tamils, the Sinhalese saw major parts of the economy in Indian hands—and resented it.

The Ceylon Tamils also outperformed the Sinhalese economically, but in a different way. Concentrated in the agriculturally unpromising north—an area with few natural resources[361]—the Ceylon Tamils were especially attracted to education, leading to careers in the colonial government. The top echelons of the colonial civil service were dominated by Englishmen, and the Sinhalese were a majority of the native-Ceylonese civil servants, but the Ceylon Tamils were nevertheless much over-represented relative to their percentage of the Ceylonese population.[362] Even after the establishment of schools for the Sinhalese, the Ceylon Tamils—11 percent of the population—were more than 30 percent of all the students in Ceylon University College as late as 1942.[363] Ceylon Tamils also occupied 30 percent of the posts in the

Ceylon civil service and 40 percent of the judicial posts, as late as 1946, two years before independence.[364] In the universities, Tamils were particularly successful in the scientific and technical fields, in which the Ceylon Tamils had exceptional educational preparation.[365] As of 1948, 40 percent of the engineers in the government's irrigation department were Tamils.[366]

In short, the success of Tamils in both business and the professions provided reasons for the Sinhalese to be envious and resentful. Sinhalese politicians were not slow to mobilize these feelings. Even during the British colonial era, laws were passed in 1938 restricting the activities of Indian businessmen and establishing quotas for Ceylon employees. In the years that followed, new restrictions and discriminations against Indian businessmen emerged.[367] Nevertheless, in 1955 a Sinhalese politician could still complain that "in the towns and villages, in business houses and in boutiques most of the work is in the hands of the Tamil-speaking people."[368]

Despite these cultural differences and economic disparities, the Sinhalese and the Tamils coexisted peacefully and even amicably during much of the colonial era in Ceylon. The rising Westernized middle class of both groups shared a similar cosmopolitan outlook, spoke English, manned the colonial civil service, and worked side-by-side in British businesses. Educated together in English-language schools, the Westernized Sinhalese and Westernized Tamils lived apart from their respective ethnic communities, both locationally and otherwise. Moreover, each considered it a badge of modernity to disdain ethnic chauvinism. In the cities, the Westernized Sinhalese and Westernized Tamils lived intermingled residentially, but their good relations with each other did not extend to such intimacies as intermarriage. Against this background, there was much optimism that, when Ceylon achieved independence, it would not degenerate into intergroup strife.[369] The initial internal dissensions after independence were not between Sinhalese and Tamils, but polarization quickly led in that direction.

As in many Third World countries, the central intergroup battle was over white-collar government jobs, which not only paid far more than the indigenous people could earn in the marketplace, but also carried the status of nonmanual labor and the prestige of government established in colonial times. There were vast intergroup differences in representation and access to such jobs. Nor were these simply Sinhalese-Tamil differences.

Historically, the part-European Ceylonese group known as "Burghers" (many being part Dutch) were the first in time and predominance in the colonial civil service. As of 1870, the vast majority of Ceylonese doctors and surgeons employed by the colonial government were these Eurasian Burghers, who were less than one percent of the Ceylon population.[370] This reflected in part the fact that the majority of Burghers spoke English, a key prerequisite for employment by the British colonial government. As of 1911, more than three-quarters of all Eurasians spoke English, compared to less than 1 percent of the Sinhalese from the Kandyan highlands, 4 percent of the lowland Sinhalese, and 6 percent of the Ceylon Tamils. The Kandyan Sinhalese in the highlands had held out longest against British colonial conquest (until 1815), and were consequently exposed to British culture for a shorter time—a fact that continued to be reflected in their under-representation in higher education and higher-level occupations more than a century later, in an independent Sri Lanka.

With the passing years, the very tiny minority of Burghers was overtaken in government employment by larger groups, but among these larger groups the rank order of their acculturation (and especially their English-language ability) in colonial times continued to dominate their educational and employment patterns for generations. As of 1921, the percentage of Ceylonese lawyers who were Kandyan Sinhalese was only 4 percent, compared to 46 percent who were lowland Sinhalese, even though the highlanders were about half as numerous as the lowlanders in the population. Ceylon Tamils, who were only about half as numerous as the Kandyans, nevertheless constituted 28 percent of all Ceylonese lawyers. But there were no Indian Tamil lawyers, even though Indian Tamils at that point slightly outnumbered Ceylon Tamils in the population. In the medical profession, Ceylon Tamils actually led with 44 percent of all the positions, compared to 34 percent held by all Sinhalese (only a tenth of whom were Kandyan physicians or medical practitioners), 12 percent Burghers, 1 percent Ceylon Moors—and no Indian Tamils.[371]

In the marketplace, however, where European acculturation in general and the English language in particular were not so crucial, the representation of groups tended to be quite different. For example, among drapers and cloth dealers in Ceylon in 1921, 44 percent were Ceylon Moors, followed by lowland Sinhalese (15 percent), Ceylon Tamils (9 percent), Kandyan Sinhalese (half of one percent)—and no Indian Tamils. Among plantation owners and supervisors, 89 percent were lowland Sinhalese, 4 percent Kandyan Sinhalese, 4 percent Ceylon Moors, 3 percent Ceylon Tamils—and again, no Indian Tamils.[372] In short, each ethnic group had its own distinctive pattern of occupational concentration, whether self-employed or employed by others, and Indian Tamils were the most concentrated in plantation labor, which required neither English, skills, nor capital. Indian Tamils lived in a separate world and took no active part in the economic and political struggles around them.

Independence found a small, highly Westernized, English-speaking, educated, often Christian elite in positions of power, wealth, and prestige, in a nation whose majority was Buddhist and Sinhala-speaking, while its principal minority was Hindu and spoke Tamil. Militant nationalism rebelled against this condition, demanding new leaders and a new emphasis on the indigenous culture, religion, and languages. Rising numbers of educated but non-English-speaking Sinhalese spearheaded this reaction against Western culture, language, and religion.[373] Buddhist extremists resented the large role of Christian missionary schools in the education of Ceylonese and the large government grants which such schools received. There was also a demand that the affairs of the Ceylonese government no longer be conducted in English but in the Ceylonese people's "own language"—which would make a profound difference in access to coveted government careers.

Seizing the leadership of this upsurge of nationalistic and religious militancy was S. W. R. D. Bandaranaike—an Oxford-educated, Christian, Sinhalese aristocrat (his godfather was the British colonial governor) who grew up unable to speak Sinhala. By this time, however, he had followed a pattern among some other Sinhalese politicians by becoming Buddhist, Sinhala-speaking, and an extremist on language, religion, and Sinhalese culture.[374] His election to the prime ministership in 1956 marked the turning point toward religious and language extremism and ethnic polarization. Despite political slogans about wanting their "own language" instead of English, there was no "own language" of the Ceylonese people. There were two main languages representing the two major population groups. From the "own language" slogan there was a swift transition to a "Sinhala only" slogan, accompanied by attempts to redress ethnic imbalances inherited from the colonial era, by giving preferential treatment to the Sinhalese majority. What began as nationalism had become ethnic polarization. It was now a question of the Sinhalese versus the Tamils.

Among the first victims of the polarization that began with independence in 1948 were the Indian Tamils, one of the poorest segments of the population, whose only benefit from colonialism was the opportunity to become plantation laborers in Ceylon. With the independence of Ceylon in 1948 came the task of defining citizenship and allocating the political power once held by the British colonial government. Indian Tamils were excluded from citizenship and deprived of the right to vote, which immediately removed eight Tamil members from Parliament. After negotiations with India, more than half a million Indian Tamils were repatriated over the years.[375] Only in the wake of these repatriations did the Ceylon Tamils again become a majority of the resident Tamil population.

Discrimination was not limited to the political rights of Indian Tamils. After the government nationalized the port facilities of Colombo, large numbers of Indian Tamil dockworkers were replaced by Sinhalese. The number of schools available for the education of the children of Indian Tamils on the plantations declined under the independent government of Sri Lanka from what it had been under the British colonial regime.[376]

Tamil demonstrations against the new language policy in 1958 were met by Sinhalese reactions that escalated into widespread—and lethal—violence. Cars and trains were stopped by Sinhalese mobs and their Tamil occupants killed. Houses were burned down with people inside them. Before the army could restore order, hundreds of people were killed in these inter-ethnic clashes—mostly Tamils.[377] As in other countries and times, chauvinism bred counter-chauvinism. The moderate Ceylon Tamil political party lost virtually all support to more militant political leaders who demanded autonomy in Ceylon Tamil areas and, finally, a separate state.[378]

Nevertheless, preferential treatment for the Sinhalese majority was pushed further. Universities became a political battleground, with university admissions policy being taken out of academic hands and being determined politically at the cabinet level.[379] As of 1969—before the politicization of admissions policy—Tamils constituted 15 percent of all university admissions but 40 percent of all admissions in the sciences, including 48 percent in engineering and 49 percent in medicine.[380] In 1972, a new system of grading entrance examinations was introduced, giving different weights according to ethnicity and region. Two years later, quotas were added.[381] The proportion of Tamil students declined sharply. By 1975, Tamils gained only 14 percent of the engineering admissions.[382] Similar trends emerged in government employment. Tamils declined from 40 percent of the clerical service in 1949 to 5 percent in 1978–81.[383] Only 6 percent of new teachers and less than 5 percent of police recruits hired were Tamils.[384] In the armed forces, between 1956 and 1970, Tamils declined from 40 percent to one percent.[385] In the more scientific and technical occupations, however, the Tamils held their own.[386]

Growing Sinhalese-Tamil polarization developed around these policies. In the 1977 elections, Tamils gave more than two-thirds of their votes to a party pledged to a separate state. Riots between the two groups also erupted in 1977, leaving an official death toll of 97 Tamils and 24 Sinhalese, along with more than 14,000 people turned into refugees.[387] In 1978, young Tamils formed a militant group called the Liberation Tigers, which claimed credit for 11 killings. Stringent curtailment of civil liberties failed to stop the violence.

The 1977 elections in Sri Lanka were the first in which Sinhalese-Tamil issues were not paramount. Sri Lanka's free-spending welfare state, with government ownership extended to more than 90 percent of all businesses, had produced runaway inflation, 24 percent unemployment, and the migration of local talent to other countries. The rejection of these policies by the voters brought to power a government which not only restored a greater freedom of private economic activity—reducing inflation and unemployment, and greatly increasing the per capita growth in real income[388]—but also a party with a history of somewhat less militant Sinhalese chauvinism, and with some significant Tamil voter support. In 1978, this government attempted to ameliorate the language issue by voting the Tamil language some official recognition and making some administrative gestures toward local autonomy.

Together with the lack of unanimity among the Tamils on the secession issue, these policies seemed to promise a de-escalation of ethnic polarization. However, the returning prosperity of Indian businessmen under free-market conditions, the resentments of their Sinhalese business competitors, and suspicions that this government was not as zealous as previous governments in preserving Sinhalese privileges, created a political backlash. Moreover, Tamil extremists saw the need to disrupt efforts at mutual accommodation by terrorist violence, certain to increase polarization.[389]

In June and July of 1983, both Sinhalese and Tamils initiated local violence—the Sinhalese against Tamil businesses (in methodically organized looting and arson, rather than spontaneous rioting) and Tamils in ambushes of Sinhalese soldiers, provoking new rounds of Sinhalese violence, both by the military and by civilians.

These new outbursts of violence between the Sinhalese and the Tamils took hundreds of lives in 1983 and left tens of thousands homeless. The overwhelming majority of the victims were Tamils and many of the killings were done in gruesome and sadistic fashion, leaving burned and mutilated corpses.[390] However, some Sinhalese individuals have hidden Tamils from mobs, at risk to their own lives.[391] But such individual acts of honor and courage showed little sign of prevailing over politicized polarization.

Riots, assassinations, and other acts of violence became no longer sporadic but self-sustaining, as revenge and counter-revenge acquired a continuing momentum of their own. As the national army—overwhelmingly Sinhalese—was sent into the Tamil areas of the north to restore order, in practice it spread the disorder, engaging in indiscriminate killings of Tamil civilians in retaliation for Tamil guerilla ambushes or fatal land-mine explosions. When guerrillas killed 13 soldiers in a 1983 ambush, for example, Sinhalese troops retaliated by pulling 20 Tamils off a bus and killing them.[392] When Sinhalese troops suffered large casualties from land-mine explosions, they sometimes massacred whole Tamil settlements, or at least all the young males.[393] Meanwhile, various Tamil guerilla groups fought among themselves for political supremacy in the north, while a Sinhalese extremist organization took shape in the south and conducted its own terrorism there.

In addition to these military and paramilitary clashes, mob violence continued to erupt against the Tamils living in the predominantly Sinhalese south, reaching a climax in the massive riots in the summer of 1983. After Tamil guerrillas bombed an army patrol and then shot the survivors in the northern city of Jaffna, Sinhalese mobs in the capital city of Colombo in the south rioted against the Tamils living there. Deaths ran into the thousands and a majority of the Tamil population of the city became refugees. The violence then spread out beyond the city along the coast and up into the highlands.[394] These riots have been considered the "point of no return" in the escalation of sporadic violence into outright civil war.[395]

Thousands of Tamils fled to refugee centers in the south, others fled north to the Tamil areas, and still others fled to India, especially to the Tamil regions of southeastern India. This massive influx of refugees into India, with their stories of widespread atrocities, and with more than 50 million sympathetic fellow Tamils being citizens of India, put pressure on the Indian government to "do something." It attempted both to mediate among the factions in Sri Lanka and—in a barely clandestine way—to arm and train Tamil guerrillas on Indian soil. As the Sri Lankan army besieged the city of Jaffna in 1987, Indian planes dropped food and supplies to the Tamils who were holding out. Finally, about 50,000 Indian troops landed in the Tamil regions of Sri Lanka, after an "accord" forced upon the Sri Lankan government, providing for the Indian troops to substitute for the Sri Lankan troops in maintaining order in the northern Tamil regions and to disarm the guerrillas operating there. Greater autonomy was also promised the Tamils, but well short of independence.

This accord was bitterly resented by Sinhalese in general and by Buddhist extremists in particular, leading to new outbreaks of terrorism and assassinations in the south. Within one year of the agreement, Sinhalese extremists killed over 200 of those who supported it, and narrowly missed an assassination attempt on the president himself.[396] Meanwhile, Tamil extremists in the north were also opposed to the accord, which stopped short of their demand for independence and hampered their own drive for political hegemony within the Tamil areas by trying to disarm them. Eventually, renewed guerilla warfare broke out, this time against the occupying army from India. Again the fighting was ugly and vicious, with thousands of civilians being killed, some while being used as human shields by the guerrillas or as targets of indiscriminate shooting, bombing, and shelling by the Indian army.

All these complex and tragic events unfolded from a relatively simple cause—group polarization, promoted in justification of preferential policies designed to get one man elected prime minister of Sri Lanka in 1956. That man, S. W. R. D. Bandaranaike, was neither a racial nor a religious fanatic. He simply seized upon the mood of the moment as a way to get elected prime minister, after which he was prepared to negotiate a more reasonable set of policies with the Tamils. But having unleashed fanaticism, he was unable to contain it, and his subsequent attempts at conciliation with the Tamils brought on his own assassination by a Buddhist extremist. There is also reason to believe that the assassination of Indian Prime Minister Rajiv Gandhi in 1991 grew out of India's intervention in Sri Lanka and the bitter disappointments of Sri Lanka's Tamils at the atrocities committed against them by the Indian army, which had initially been welcomed as their saviors.[397]

The political attempt to reverse the greater economic successes of the Tamils in Sri Lanka led to a seemingly irreversible escalation of polarization and hostility, in which every segment of the population eventually lost. While the earliest and more severe losses were inflicted upon the Tamils, everyone suffered from the destruction of the country's economy by both war and the loss of tourist revenues due to the war, and by the loss of political freedom as the national emergency was used to justify dictatorial rule that left the same corrupt party in power for more than a decade without an election. Economically, the losses from the conflict—over a six-year period—have been estimated as equal to two-thirds of the annual output of the country.[398] The supreme irony is that all this happened in a country once justly held up as a model of harmonious intergroup relations.

Moderate Tamil leaders receptive to the government's efforts at compromise and rapprochement have been assassinated by Tamil separatists. There were now those on both sides with a vested interest in conflict as such, for a return to peace and harmony would mean a diminution of their own significance and power.

Fiji

The South Pacific tropical islands of Fiji were annexed by Great Britain in 1874. After attempts of British sugar, cotton, and coffee plantation owners to use Fijian and Polynesian workers failed, indentured labor from India was used—more than 7,000 in the first decade and growing numbers thereafter. Between 1900 and 1911, nearly 3,000 Indians arrived annually in Fiji, less than 10 percent at their own expense and the rest as indentured laborers. Fewer than 500 annually returned to India.[399] Altogether, between 1878 and 1916, when indentures were abolished, more than 60,000 Indians were brought to Fiji, about three-quarters of whom originated in northeastern India (in what are now the states of Uttar Pradesh and Bihar) and the rest from southern India.[400]

In theory, each worker had the terms and conditions of his contract explained to him in India, and a local magistrate was needed to certify this, to make the contract legal. In practice, however, such a requirement was not easily fulfilled in a largely illiterate population, with magistrates of varying interest in their well-being. The labor recruiters, who were paid a commission for each indentured laborer they delivered, were even less concerned about informed consent. Some even told the illiterate that Fiji was near Calcutta,[401] when in fact it is 7,000 miles southeast of Calcutta—farther than the distance from New York to Moscow or Jerusalem, for example.

As with other long-distance transportation of indentured labor, the voyage itself—with its crowded conditions of living and eating—wreaked havoc with the caste distinctions with which people left India. They were also treated largely as an undifferentiated mass by the companies that employed them in Fiji, where families or groups of individuals lived in partitioned cubicles in huge, barracks-like structures.

The work on the plantations was long and arduous under a tropical sun, with discipline enforced by corporal punishment, and with a failure to produce the assigned output being punishable by loss of pay or even legal prosecution. Conditions tended to be worse on smaller plantations, surviving on a narrower margin of profit.

Although there was a government requirement that each shipload of people brought from India be at least 40 percent female, this requirement was not always met. As late as 1912, only 30 percent of the Indians in Fiji were female. During the era of indentured labor, from 1879 to 1916, prostitution was rampant on the plantations, as was violence—both among workers living in overcrowded barracks and in acts of revenge by workers against overseers. Perhaps the most telling evidence of how bad conditions were was the suicide rate among Indians in Fiji, which was more than twice as high as in other contemporary societies with indentured Indian labor, such as British Guiana, Trinidad, and Jamaica. The suicide rate was also 15 times as high as in those parts of India from which the indentured laborers came.[402]

At the end of their indenture contracts, the workers were free to return to India, at their own expense. At the end of a second indenture, they could return to India with their passage paid, but more long years of work under harsh conditions were not always appealing, even though many were able to save significant sums of money as indentured laborers. Altogether, about 25,000 returned to India, out of more than 60,000 who left during the era of the indenture system. Most of those who remained became tenant farmers, leasing land from the native Fijians, who by law could not sell it.

The first home built by an Indian who leased land after completing his indenture was usually either a Fijian-style hut or a crude shack of some sort, made from packing cases, kerosene cans, and old corrugated iron, all on a wooden frame. These dwellings were often inferior in construction, sanitation, and water supply to the plantation barracks they had left, but they were private and they were homes.[403] Living conditions improved over the years, as the free Indians gradually established themselves economically. Most of their leased acreage was planted in sugar, as on the plantations, but the Indians also grew rice, which they sold to the plantations as food for laborers. By 1911, the Indians on Fiji also owned more than 10,000 head of cattle,[404] nearly one-third of all cattle in Fiji.[405] An Indian society emerged in Fiji that was neither a replica of the societies from which its members came in India, nor an undifferentiated mass—but certainly a society very different from that of the indigenous Fijians, with whom they very seldom intermarried. Initially, plantation laborers who completed their indentures leased whatever available land they could as they became free, and so settled in a more or less random pattern, in terms of their backgrounds in

India. Only with the passage of years and a turnover of leaseholds did they begin to cluster with kin, with co-religionists, or with others who spoke the same language.

Still, the full range of the intricate social patterns of India was not re-created. Caste distinctions eroded after the crowded living conditions of the voyage and the plantations, Indian widows could remarry in Fiji, and Hindus and Moslems drew closer after shared sufferings. When the first mosque was built in Fiji, most of the money was donated by Hindus.[406] However, caste intermarriage was still resisted, though relations between different castes were not as rigid as in India.[407] While India-based social distinctions eroded somewhat, some Fiji-based distinctions also emerged and became important parts of the local social pattern. Indentured Indians were not accepted as being on the same plane as free Indians, especially after some free Indian farmers began using indentured laborers in the early twentieth century. In addition, larger and smaller tenant farmers were differentiated, and those few able to own some of the small amount of land legally available for outright purchase were in a still more fortunate class.[408]

Among the indentured Indians, conditions improved somewhat over the years, partly as a result of pressures on the plantation owners from the colonial governments in Fiji and India, and pressures from the colonial officials in London. The growing profitability of sugar helped finance these improvements. One index of the improvement was a declining mortality rate among indentured laborers, from 53 per thousand in 1895 to 38 per thousand in 1910 and 22 per thousand in 1912. However, the death rate among Indians in Fiji who were not indentured laborers was only 9 per 1,000 in 1912.[409]

Over the years, the Indian community in Fiji grew considerably and changed in its internal composition. Indentured laborers were just over half of the nearly 8,000 Indians in Fiji in 1891. But, by 1901, the free Indians were in the majority, and by 1911 they were two-thirds of the more than 44,000 Indians in the islands. Increasing numbers and proportions of the Indians in Fiji were born there—27 percent in 1911 and 44 percent by 1921.[410] In addition to the indentured laborers, former indentured laborers, and their descendants, the Indian community also included small but growing numbers of "free immigrants"—people who paid their own way to Fiji. These people usually did not become plantation laborers but instead tended to work in towns, often as peddlers or storekeepers, or they leased land in the country. These free immigrants included Sikhs and Gujaratis, the latter becoming the main traders in Fiji.[411] The Gujaratis were known for being thrifty and hardworking, with a strong sense of loyalty to one another.[412] In one sense, the Gujaratis and their success imparted pride to the other Indians and provided leadership. Socially, however, the Gujaratis kept to themselves.[413]

The sex imbalance was slow to correct itself. Despite the growth of a sex-balanced, Fiji-born Indian generation, the immigrants from India continued to be predominantly male. As late as 1921, females were still only 39 percent of the Indian population in Fiji. Much violence, including murder, grew out of sexual infidelity or the exploitations of suitors.[414] However, with the passing years, the sex imbalance was concentrated among the older Indians, while the marriage-age Indian population was more evenly balanced between men and women, leading to a growing population of locally born children.[415]

The Indian population of Fiji increased both absolutely and as a percentage of the total population. As of 1881, Indians were only about 1 percent of the Fijian population and the native Fijians 90 percent. By 1901 the Indians were 14 percent, and just a decade later this had more than doubled to 29 percent. By 1946, the Indian population overtook the indigenous Fijian population, 46 percent to 45 percent, with Europeans, Chinese, and others accounting for the remainder. The Indian population of Fiji remained slightly larger than that of the Fijians for decades,[416] until the Fijians regained the edge in the late 1980s.[417]

In the commercial economy of the islands—rural and urban—the Indians surpassed the Fijians decisively. As early as 1936, an estimated 90 percent of all sugarcane grown in Fiji was grown by Indians[418]—and sugar was the colony's major industry, as it remained after independence. Indians likewise predominated in retailing, transport, and other small businesses in Fiji, while Europeans and Chinese predominated in the larger enterprises. As of the mid-1960s, Indians averaged significantly higher cash income than the Fijians, but when cash and in-kind subsistence were averaged together, there was very little difference.[419] Fijians in traditional villages lived comfortably on two or three days' work per week, and the Fijian community's ownership of the bulk of the land ensured large rental receipts from Indian tenant farmers. Since taxes were based on cash income, however, Fijians paid only 5 percent of the country's personal taxes, compared to 40 percent paid by Indians, and 49 percent by Europeans.[420]

As in many other Third World countries, intergroup disparities in education and government employment sparked racial polarization in Fiji. The British colonial government took little interest in the education of either Fijians or Indians until 1916. In view of their vulnerability as tenants on Fijian land, the Indians were especially eager to take advantage of educational opportunities and the employment opportunities in government to which these could lead. Indians spent heavily on improving standards in their schools and Indian students outperformed Fijians in school, in the university, and in civil service examinations. These differences were enduring.

After World War II, Indians even began displacing Europeans in higher-level occupations. Meanwhile, Fijian students tended to suffer more attrition as they moved through the educational system. As late as 1968, among 643 recipients of university degrees, 464 were Indians and only 77 were Fijians, the latter having barely more than the 63 degrees received by members of the tiny Chinese minority in Fiji. The educational advantages of the Indians at first translated into a large representation of Indians in the civil service. However, after independence, the Fijian government instituted policies of racial "balance" in employment, leading to a Fijian majority among its employees, despite the fact that Indians did better on both entrance examinations and on internal examinations within the civil service.[421] In the university as well, Fijian students were admitted with lower qualifications than Indian students were required to have.[422]

Politically, the Fijian system of voting has, since colonial times, made the Fijians the political majority, despite the larger numbers of Indians in the population for many years. Not surprisingly, this led to indigenous Fijian dominance in the government, both civilian and military. This pattern lasted from independence in 1970 until April 1987, when an Indian-dominated government took power. Within a month, however, the Fijian-dominated military staged a *coup d'etat,* reclaiming political supremacy at gunpoint. Civilian violence against Indians by

Fijians also erupted. In the wake of these unsettling developments, tourism declined sharply, reducing revenues to the economy and to the government alike. Fiji's real per capita income fell and its government's deficit rose. Educated and skilled people began leaving the country—mostly Indians but also some Fijians and expatriates.[423]

All this was an especially ironic tragedy in a country which many long saw as a place of harmony, and which Pope John Paul II had called "a symbol of hope for the world."[424]

IMPLICATIONS

The history of Indians in various countries around the world has by no means been uniform. In some countries, Indians have enjoyed an income or occupational level above that of the majority population. This has been true not only in such African nations as Kenya, Uganda, and Tanzania, but also in such disparate societies as Malaysia, Fiji, and the United States. This has not been the case, however, in Guyana, where the local African-American population has historically been economically somewhat ahead of the Indians, though that was changing by 1967.[425] While the Indians of South Africa have been economically ahead of the black majority there, they have been well behind the long-dominant white minority. Partly these different fates of Indians in different countries reflect conditions and policies in the countries themselves—quite clearly in South Africa, for example—or in the degree of urbanization of the Indians, as in Guyana, where rural concentration has obvious negative implications for money income and urban occupational status.

By and large, however, the economic positions of Indians abroad reflected the economic positions of the numerous divisions of the Indian people in India itself. The striking business success of the Gujaratis has been apparent in Bombay or in East Africa, and Gujaratis have outpaced other Indians economically as businessmen in Guyana, Fiji, and South Africa.[426] Chettyars have likewise extended their prominent role as bankers, money-lenders, and traders from southern India and Ceylon to Burma, Malaysia, Thailand, Indonesia, and Mauritius.[427] The Tamils who have dominated Indian migration to the plantations of Sri Lanka and Malaysia have no such record of entrepreneurial success in those countries, but neither do they match the Gujaratis or the Chettyars in this respect in India itself. The economically superior position of the Indians in Singapore, as compared to Indians on the Malay Peninsula, goes back to colonial times and likewise reflects differences that have long existed between the same groups in India. Indians in Guyana are products of a poverty-stricken region of northeast India and have no such pattern of striking economic success abroad as the commercial Gujaratis or the money-lending Chettyars.

In short, Indians in some countries have been middleman minorities, and in others not. Where they have been businessmen, their commercial success has to varying degrees tended to be reflected in rising levels of education over time and in a movement into the professions, much in the pattern of the overseas Chinese and the Jews. Also like these other middleman minorities, Indians in these roles have tended to keep a low political profile. Few have pursued political careers overseas, and politics has had little or nothing to do with their rise to affluence in foreign lands. Often politics has been an obstacle to that rise and, especially in post-colonial times in Africa and Asia, politics has been a threat to positions already achieved in the economy. Idi Amin's brutal expulsions of 50,000 Indians and Pakistanis from Uganda was the worst and most dramatic example of hostile political processes at work, more subtly and insidiously, in much of post-colonial Africa, in Burma, and to a lesser extent, in Malaysia and Fiji. The vicissitudes of the overseas Indians also follow a pattern of long standing in the history of the overseas Chinese, the Jews, the Armenians, the Ibos of Nigeria, the Lebanese in West Africa, and other middleman minorities.

Despite many tragedies and injustices, overseas Indians seem to have suffered less severely than other leading middleman minorities, whether due to historical happenstances or to differences in the behavior of the Indians themselves. However, like the overseas Chinese and the Jews, overseas Indians have generally held themselves separate and aloof from the surrounding populations. Indians have in fact tended to be much more resistant to intermarriage with the surrounding population than the overseas Chinese. The oft-repeated claim that hostility to Jews, Chinese, or other middleman minorities is due to their clannishness is belied by the fact that even greater clannishness among the overseas Indians seems not to have provoked as much hostility as the Jews, Chinese, and others have faced. Moreover, the deliberate decision of the Aga Khan to have his Ismaili followers in Africa adopt the language and culture of the surrounding society, and to seek local citizenship, did not spare the Ismailis the same fate as other overseas Indians in Africa.[428]

Even among those overseas Indians who were not middleman minorities, a certain tenacity, persistence, and frugality have been observed,[429] as among other peoples from lands where survival has historically been difficult (the Scots or the Japanese, for example). Transplanted to countries where subsistence is more easily obtained, such as Fiji or Malaysia, these Indians have eventually surpassed those indigenous to the country and whose way of life evolved under its more favorable conditions.

That Indians have prospered in other countries around the world, while India itself has been poverty-stricken, remains a paradox, even after allowance for the fact that many of these prosperous Indian groups are also prosperous at home. In colonial East Africa, for example, Indians did not simply transfer their wealth to those countries but usually began at quite modest and even precarious economic levels, from which they rose to affluence and sometimes riches. The more modest economic achievements of Indians in Guyana nevertheless represent a substantial rise from their original status as plantation laborers treated little better than slaves.

Whether the pattern of prosperity abroad and poverty at home reflects simply selective migration, or reflects as well barriers to economic development within Indian society, is a question of more than theoretical interest—and in fact a question of momentous practical implications. What is known is that the overseas Indians working in professional, technical, managerial, and administrative occupations around the world in 1981 added up to more than a quarter of a million people.[430] Because of high levels of unemployment among people in such occupations in India,[431] it is not clear that their skills and talents would have been put to use had they remained at home. Both India's doctors and engineers seek employment overseas in substantial numbers.[432]

Official efforts to get Indians to return from overseas to help develop their homeland have had meager results,[433] despite preferential treatment of their investments, relative to the treatment of investment by other non-citizens or by citizens living in India.[434] However, remittances from overseas Indians—more than $5 billion in 1981—amounted to more than all the foreign aid used by India that year. The overseas Indians have thus made a significant contribution to their country of origin, even without being there personally. In many cases, they have made even more of a contribution to the development of the countries to which they migrated.

CHAPTER 8

HISTORY AND CULTURES

The study of history is a powerful antidote to contemporary arrogance. It is humbling to discover how many of our glib assumptions, which seem to us novel and plausible, have been tested before, not once but many times and in innumerable guises; and discovered to be, at great human cost, wholly false.

—Paul Johnson[1]

History cannot provide direct answers to the quandaries of the present because there are too many variables that change between one era and another. But if history cannot provide answers, it can at least help in defining questions, and in some cases it can utterly destroy theories which might otherwise seem plausible within the narrow confines of a particular time and place. History is an anchor in reality against the rhetorical winds of the *zeitgeist*. For example, one of the clearest facts to emerge from these worldwide histories of various racial and ethnic groups is that gross statistical disparities in the "representation" of groups in different occupations, industries, income levels, and educational institutions have been the rule—not the exception—all across the planet. Moreover, many of these disparities have persisted for generations or even centuries.

The histories presented here are not the only ones illustrating the pervasiveness of distinctive cultural patterns and economic achievements. As the French historian Fernand Braudel put it, in his *A History of Civilizations:* "In no society have all regions and all parts of the population developed equally."[2] In the Austrian Empire, for example, rates of illiteracy in 1900 varied from 3 percent in Bohemia to 73 percent in Dalmatia[3] and per capita income in the former was nearly three times what it was in the latter during the same era.[4] In Nigeria in 1926, only 10 percent of the children attending secondary school were from the northern part of the country, where a majority of the population lived.[5] An international study of military and police forces later in the twentieth century could find no multiethnic society in which either organization was ethnically representative of the general population.[6] Another worldwide study of multiethnic societies found "few, if any" which even approximated proportional representation of the different ethnic groups in different levels or sectors of the economy.[7]

The racial, ethnic, or national minorities who have owned or directed more than half of particular industries in particular nations have included not only the six groups considered here but also the Lebanese in West Africa,[8] Greeks in the Ottoman Empire,[9] Britons in Argentina,[10] Belgians in Russia,[11] and Spaniards in Chile.[12] In the words of Braudel, it was immigrants who "created modern Brazil, modern Argentina, modern Chile."[13] Minority predominance in particular industries and occupations has been common at local levels as well. In the early nineteenth century, over half the newspapers in Alexandria were owned by Syrians.[14] In the Russian Empire in the eighteenth century, Armenians owned 209 of the 250 cotton cloth factories in the province of Astrakhan.[15] Beginning in the 1960s, most of the installers of underground cable in Sydney, Australia, were Irish.[16] In the 1990s, more than four-fifths of all the doughnut shops in California were owned by people of Cambodian ancestry.[17]

Sometimes it is not one specific racial, ethnic, or national group which dominates an industry or an occupation but foreigners in general, leaving the majority population of a country a minority, or even non-existent, in whole segments of its own economy. At one period of history or another, this has been true of the majority populations of Peru,[18] Malaya,[19] Argentina,[20] Switzerland,[21] Russia,[22] and much of the Balkans,[23] the Middle East,[24] and Southeast Asia.[25] Indeed, it has been a worldwide phenomenon, found even in some economically advanced countries, as well as being common in less advanced countries.

Nothing has been more common than for cities to be dominated by one ethnic group—either demographically or economically, or both—while the population of the surrounding countryside has been predominantly of a different ethnic group. Examples include the long history of German dominance in Prague, Cracow, and Riga, for example, in centuries past, while the surrounding population was Czech, Polish, and Latvian, respectively. On the other side of the world, there was Chinese domination of Phnom Penh, Saigon, and Singapore, while the surrounding populations in the countryside were Cambodian, Vietnamese, and Malay. Similar patterns could be found at one time with Indians in the Kenyan capital of Nairobi or the Burmese capital of Rangoon.

In military matters as well, foreigners have been disproportionately represented at all levels in many countries. From the fifteenth through the seventeenth centuries, most of the gunners aboard Portuguese warships were either Flemish or German.[26] In the twentieth century, an estimated 50 percent of the pilots in the Malaysian air force were Chinese.[27] In the Ottoman Empire, Italians, Greeks, and Catalans manned the fleet, while Germans manned the artillery, and the elite infantry corps of the Janissaries consisted also of non-Turks in a Turkish empire.[28] In producing military technology, foreigners brought the technology of cannons to China, Spain, and Russia, among others, and foreigners made the United States the first nuclear power.[29]

Behind such striking patterns around the world and down through history is the simple fact that skills have never been evenly or randomly distributed, whether between ethnic groups, nations, regions, or civilizations. The high level of modern optical skills developed among Germans, for example, has been apparent not only in such old German optical firms as Zeiss, Schneider, and Voigtländer, but also in the role of German immigrants and their descendants in the American optical industry. The first cameras produced by the leading American photographic company, Eastman Kodak, used lenses manufactured by the leading American optical firm, Bausch & Lomb, founded by German immigrants. A number of Kodak's top-quality and highest-priced cameras, notably the Retina line, were manufactured in Germany during the pre–World War II era and in the immediate postwar period.[30] Kodak's top-quality rollfilm camera of the midcentury decades, the Medalist, was first manufactured during World War II when, of course, Kodak had no access to the German optical industry. However, the lens on the Medalist was a variation of a lens design created earlier in Germany.[31] A number of American press cameras and reflex cameras in the midcentury decades used American-made Wollensak lenses, named for a German immigrant who established the company producing these lenses and other photographic equipment.[32] The leading Swedish camera of the late twentieth century, the Hasselblad, has used lenses manufactured in Germany by Zeiss.

While the virtual monopoly of Germans in top-quality lenses was broken by the emergence of the Japanese as leading photographic lens manufacturers in the middle of the twentieth century, nevertheless there were few other rivals to the lens makers in these two countries. During the earlier decades, when Americans designed and produced some of the top-quality lenses, these were disproprotionately Americans of German ancestry or American lenses that were variations of German lenses.[33] During earlier centuries, the lead in optical skills was in other countries—in northern Italy during the Renaissance, for example.[34] The point here is not that one particular country or race has had permanent possession of the leading optical skills. The point is that these skills have never been randomly or evenly distributed, but have been highly concentrated, though concentrated in different places in different centuries. Nor are optical skills peculiar in this respect. They illustrate a pattern common in many other fields.

Physical settings have been no more even or random than the peoples who evolved in these settings. There are 76 mountain peaks in Asia higher than 20,000 feet and none in Africa.[35] More than one-third of the total land area of Europe consists of islands and peninsulas, compared to only one percent of the land area of South America.[36] As a noted geographer has said:

> Nothing in the physical or human spheres is evenly distributed. No spatula has spread human and environmental elements evenly over the face of the earth. If human and environmental elements, whether population, resources, or environmental conditions such as climate were uniformly distributed, then all areas and peoples of the world would have exactly the same potential. Absence of differences would eliminate trade and the necessity for exchange of goods and ideas.[37]

The geographical differences in the settings in which peoples and cultures have evolved are just one of the factors making such uniformity unlikely or impossible. Nothing has been even or random in the histories of migrating groups. Neither their geographic origins or destinations have been random, nor have the skills and aptitudes they brought with them, which have often been as specific as the points from which they originated and the points to which they moved. If there is one pattern that emerges from all these histories it is that each group has its own cultural pattern—and that these patterns do not disappear upon crossing a border or an ocean. Nor are these patterns always coextensive with national or racial groups. Among migrants from India, for example, Tamils have not had the same experience, either at home or abroad, as Gujaratis. Southern Italians have differed from northern Italians, whether in Argentina, Australia, the United States, or in Italy itself. Jews from Poland have had very different economic histories from the ethnic Poles, whether in Poland or overseas—and different histories from those of Jews from Germany or Britain.

Both hereditary and environmental explanations of group differences encounter serious problems in the light of history. Middleman minorities such as the overseas Chinese, the Jews of the Diaspora, and the overseas Indians show some striking similarities in their experiences in a variety of nations, and yet they are racially quite distinct from one another. Other middleman minorities, such as the Koreans in the United States, the Ibos in Nigeria, or the Lebanese around the world, exhibit similar middleman characteristics, while being racially distinct from each other and from the three middleman minorities studied here.

Over long spans of history, the radical reshuffling of the relative technological rankings of different races and nations makes it hard to conclude that such standings are genetically determined. Not only was China as far in advance of Europe a thousand years ago as the reverse has been true for the past few centuries, Southeastern Europe was likewise as far in advance of northwestern Europe two thousand years ago as the reverse has been true in the modern industrial era. Moreover, twentieth-century Chinese have prospered all around the world—except in China. The productivity of people of the same race has been so radically different that Chinese living outside of China were in 1994 estimated to have produced as much wealth as the entire population of China,[38] which was of course dozens of times larger.

Many environmental explanations of socioeconomic differences—that groups are what they are and have the economic fates that they do because of "society"—arbitrarily limit the environment to the surrounding world in which they are currently living, when the environments in which their cultures have evolved may be thousands of miles away from the society in which they now live. How much effect the existing society has is an empirical question, not a foregone conclusion. In extreme cases—slavery or genocide, for example—the prior culture of the group has had very little effect on their fate. But, fortunately, such extremes are rare. Even in less extreme circumstances, such as the systematic biases against the admissions of Tamils to universities in Sri Lanka or Chinese to universities in Malaysia, the consequences have been both apparent and significant, just as similar campaigns of exclusions against Germans in Russia under Stalin, or against Jews in interwar Poland, took their toll. General historical patterns are suggestive, not all-determining.

The dogma that the immediate environment or the history of the surrounding society is virtually all that matters need not be replaced by a dogma that only internal cultural patterns matter. But the balance between them cannot be struck by any *a priori* formula. That is why history has to be studied and not constructed from theories. Unique events, specific leaders, passions of the moment, and accidental confluences of circumstances all make history more than a simple pattern predetermined by social, geographic, or other forces. Nevertheless, the skills, habits, and values which constitute the cultural endowment of a people usually play a powerful role in shaping the kinds of outcomes experienced by that people. The fashionable but false dichotomy between "blaming the victim" and blaming "society" ignores factors for which no blame is in order. Clearly, no one can be blamed for cultural developments which took place before he was born, or for the geographical settings in which those cultural developments took place.

With most of the cities of the world being located on navigable waterways, it has been virtually inevitable that Africa would be the least urbanized continent, given its dearth of navigable rivers or natural harbors. Contrast that with the great cities of the world located at or near the terminus of great rivers emptying into the open seas (New York, London, Rotterdam, Buenos Aires, Shanghai), cities beside huge lakes or inland seas (Geneva, Chicago, Detroit, Odessa), or cities on great harbors emptying into the open seas (Sydney, Singapore, Hong Kong, San Francisco, Tokyo, Rio de Janeiro). The geographical prerequisites for such cities simply have not existed over most of the African continent, and such sites have been especially scarce south of the Sahara. It is not a matter of blame, for either Africans or for the urban societies in which their descendants have found themselves in the Western Hemisphere, that the kinds of urban and industrial skills which many others brought with them to the New World had not developed in most of Africa. Had Africans migrated voluntarily to the Western Hemisphere, there would still be no reason to expect the black population of the hemisphere to have the same economic history as the white population—especially since different segments of the white population have differed so sharply from one another, in part reflecting the geographical advantages and disadvantages of the particular regions of Europe from which they came.

Expectations of similarity are inconsistent with the fact that differences lie at the heart of migrations. There would be no point in crossing an ocean if things were the same on both sides. There would usually be no point in incurring the high costs and high risks of migrations if everyone were equally productive where they were and where they were going. Even refugees flee because of differences in safety at different locations. When people come from different worlds, it can hardly be surprising that they differ in their new worlds. Nor can all these differences be reduced to things for which the new society can be blamed or for which policy-makers can offer solutions. The past, like geography, lies beyond the reach of policy-makers, though various policies may moderate or exacerbate the consequences of such factors. While societal guilt may often be as irrelevant as individual blame, many who reject the genetic inheritance of intelligence nevertheless promote the collective inheritance of guilt.

A given culture is of course not stamped on a given people for all time, but neither does it evaporate in a few years or even in a given lifetime. Moreover, a culture is not a symbolic pattern, preserved like a butterfly in amber. Its place is not in a museum but in the practical activities of daily life, where it evolves under the stress of competing goals and other competing cultures. Cultures do not exist as simply static "differences" to be celebrated but compete with one another as better and worse ways of getting things done—better and worse, not from the standpoint of some observer, but from the standpoint of the peoples themselves,[39] as they cope and aspire amid the gritty realities of life. To say that books have almost invariably displaced scrolls and guns have almost invariably displaced bows and arrows, whenever a given people has had the choice, is not to say that some observer pronounces a moral benediction on either.[40] Weapons may of course inflict harm—that is what makes them weapons—and so may some books, Hitler's *Mein Kampf* being a prime example. The point is very different—namely, that cultural relativism has neither explanatory power nor historical relevance to the way that the many and disparate peoples of the world have actually behaved. Its role is, at best, that of a polite evasion of otherwise embarrassing differences in performance and, at worst, a distraction from the task of acquiring the requisite human capital behind other people's good fortune, instead of resenting that good fortune and attributing it to "exploitation" of those who have had precious little to exploit.

The importance of politics, and especially of protest politics, in advancing groups economically receives little or no support from the histories we have surveyed. Some of the most strikingly successful groups, such as the Germans and the Chinese, have been noted for their political apathy in countries around the world. So have Italians. Immigrants from India have been virtually invisible in American political life, even as their numbers and their prosperity have grown remarkably in the late twentieth century. In a few countries, such as Australia in the nineteenth century and the United States in the twentieth century, Jews have been prominent as elected officials. But, even in these particular places and times, Jewish officials have usually been representatives of broader political constituencies rather than ethnic leaders. The Japanese overseas have been politically prominent only in Hawaii—but Japanese Americans have been even more successful economically on the mainland of the United States, where their political strength has been negligible. The election and re-election of a man of Japanese ancestry to be president of Peru in the 1990s was another case of a political leader arising as a representative of a broad constituency, *not* as an ethnic leader.

CULTURAL CAPITAL

While our survey of half a dozen groups in two dozen countries represents only a modest sample of the vast numbers of groups who have migrated across the planet over the centuries, the cultural histories sketched here provide revealing glimpses of the enormous role of cultural heritages and their far-reaching implications. Cultures cover a broad spectrum of human concerns, from things as superficial as modes of dress to things as deeply felt as what one is prepared to die for. What some people think of as culture, or as "high culture"—art, music, literature—is only a small part of the vast spectrum of skills, values, traditions, and unarticulated habits of thought and action encompassed by a given culture.

Cultures are not merely customs to which people have a sentimental attachment, or badges of "identity" which permit them to engage in breast-beating. Cultures are particular ways of accomplishing the things that make life possible—the perpetuation of the species, the transmission of knowledge, and the absorption of the shocks of change and death, among other things. Cultures differ in the relative significance they attach to time, noise, safety, cleanliness, violence, thrift, intellect, sex, and art. These differences in turn imply differences in social choices, economic efficiency, and political stability. Though cultures transcend race, particular cultures are obviously often associated with particular racial and ethnic groups. Australians are Europeans, regardless of what geography may say. Not only their language and physical appearance, but also their fertility patterns, technology, philosophy, social customs, and institutions of government make them part of a culture that exists 10,000 miles away, and foreign to the culture of their neighbors in Papua New Guinea or Indonesia.

When cultures are seen as more than group differentiations, their role as vast accumulations of human capital can be better appreciated. To realize how Western Europe retrogressed after the collapse of the Roman Empire, and how many centuries it took to recover the economic level, the physical infrastructure, and the social and political cohesion achieved in Roman times, is to see the role of a generation or a whole race reduced to humbling perspective. After the fall of Rome, the races of Western Europe were the same as they had been before, but the dissolution of their cultural institutions left them far below the material and intellectual levels achieved by their ancestors. Cities and towns shriveled and some disappeared, industries vanished, law and order broke down, and in some places illiteracy became the norm, even among the aristocracy. Medieval Europe presented a grim picture:

> A thousand years ago, most of Western Europe was covered by great forests swarming with wild animals and, according to the imagination of the people of the time, with fairies, dwarfs, and evil spirits. Marshes too were numerous and widespread and in the south the malarial mosquito created around them a depressing atmosphere of misery and death. The few towns, located within the geographical limits of the old Roman Empire, looked more like villages than towns proper and elsewhere there were no towns at all but only a handful of small and dirty villages.[41]

Those regions of Europe which had never been part of the Roman Empire in the first place were even less advanced. Towns were even more rare in medieval Eastern Europe than in Western Europe.[42] The Slavs who poured into East Central Europe and the Balkans during the Middle Ages were not only illiterate but had no written language in which they could even conceivably have been literate.

The recovery of Europe from the collapse of the Roman Empire took centuries as regards some cultural aspects, but for others it took more than a thousand years. As late as the nineteenth century, there was said to be no city in Europe whose water supply was as dependable as it had been in Roman times.[43] This massive and tragic retrogression is a sobering reminder of the enormous importance of a civilization's cultural capital, as compared to the isolated "ability" of individuals or even the efforts and talents of a whole generation. There is no reason to doubt that individual mental capacity was as great as ever, or that as many potential geniuses were born during the darkest of the Dark Ages in Europe as during its eras of the most shining achievements. What was lacking was an ability to "avail themselves of the great bank and capital of nations and of ages,"[44] as Burke phrased it in a different context. The institutions of such cultural transmission were simply gone with the collapse of Roman society.

Conversely, a rapid accumulation of cultural capital—usually possible only by borrowing from the cultures of others, at least initially—has also produced dramatic economic and social changes. In modern times, the sudden bursting of the Scots upon the world scene as leading figures in a variety of fields of endeavor in the eighteenth century,[45] after having been on the backward fringes of European civilization for many centuries,[46] illustrates the power of cultural development. The similarly meteoric rise of Japan to the economic and technological forefront in just one century likewise shows the power of the acquisition of a new cultural capital, even in a country lacking most of the natural resources required for the spontaneous internal generation of modern industry. Whatever heartening implications such historic developments may have for the hidden potential of peoples, the implication must also be faced that that potential can remain hidden for a very long time, with very serious consequences.

It may sound noble to say that cultures are merely different, not better or worse in any way, and that it is all a matter of perceptions and preferences. But this argument contradicts itself by saying that one way of looking at cultural differences is *better*—the way of cultural relativism preferred by a fringe of contemporary intellectuals, rather than the way preferred by the vast majority of other human beings around the world and down through the centuries.

These cultural differences do not matter only if cause and effect do not matter. But those who wish to be spared the devastations of diseases which have plagued the human race from time immemorial must either have the cultural capital of modern medical science themselves or have access to others who do. Smallpox, for example, continued to ravage the peoples of Eastern Europe and the Balkans, long after vaccination had brought it under control elsewhere in Europe,[47] because this was one of the many forms of cultural capital that came belatedly to these regions. Even after modern medicine became accessible to the poorer peoples of Europe, the same diseases continued to ravage poorer peoples more remote from the centers of Western medical advancement. It was not just a matter of perceptions and preferences.

Widely varying amounts and kinds of cultural capital make economic and social disparities among groups and nations virtually inevitable. Yet the political temptation is to overlook the causal influences of differences in cultural capital which often go far back into history and, instead, to attribute these disparities to current failures of society. For example, the head of the leading black civil rights organization in the United States declared in 1994:

> Almost half of all African-American children live in poverty. Black unemployment is twice that of whites. The infant mortality rate in many black communities is equal to that of many third world nations. The statistics for housing, crime and education deliver a tragic statement of despair and inequality. Yet, in polls, more than 60 percent of whites say blacks now have equal opportunity.[48]

The very possibility that these disparities might be due to cultural differences affecting behavior and attitudes, or to differences in the human capital brought into the workplace, rather than to the behavior of the larger society, received no attention whatever, either in this statement or in much of the media or the academic world. Yet, when all this was being said, black American married couples with college degrees were at the same income level as white American married couples with college degrees.[49] Even a quarter of a century earlier, black males raised in homes with books and library cards were at the same income level as white males raised in homes with similar advantages and similar education.[50] While infant mortality rates were higher among blacks in general than among whites in general, infant mortality rates among black intact families were lower than among white female-headed families, even when those white females had more education than black females living with their husbands.[51] In short, life-style differences have had major impacts on social misfortunes—though only minor impact on much thinking about those misfortunes. The issues reach beyond questions of blaming a group or assigning guilt to society. Future improvements depend upon how much of present efforts go into developing the internal resources of a group and how much into seeking political changes in the surrounding society.

The implications of cultural development, as well as cultural differentiation, affect not only such issues as intergroup differences in economic progress, but also race and racism as factors in such progress. Each will be explored separately.

INTERGROUP DIFFERENCES

Dramatic rises from poverty to prosperity, whether among nations or among various immigrant groups in countries around the world, undermine the notion of "haves" and "have-nots" as enduring categories of people frozen into their respective positions by social and economic forces. Indeed, the histories reviewed in the preceding chapters suggest that a more fruitful dichotomy might be between the *doers* and the *do-nots.* Since many peoples and nations have played both roles at different times in their histories, questions arise as to how and why wealth is created abundantly under some conditions and not under others. But to put that question on the agenda would be to abandon much of the intellectual and political agenda of those who focus on the distribution of wealth, as if its creation could be taken for granted, as something that happens *somehow*—and as if its uneven distribution, either within a given country or between nations, could only be explained by malign forces or sinister machinations. Moreover, once inherent prerequisites for producing wealth are recognized, such unevenness is neither surprising nor inherently suspect, since there is no *a priori* reason to expect those prerequisites to be evenly distributed. Therefore academic standards, employment standards, and other criteria can no longer be dismissed as arbitrary impositions of barriers with "disparate impact" by race, class, gender, or other social groupings.

While cultures compete, and while this competition results in winners and losers among the products of different cultures, this does not mean that the flesh-and-blood human beings whose cultural artifacts no longer remain functional are necessarily losers in the process. On the contrary, in many cases, they gain a higher standard of living and a wider cultural exposure which they themselves come to value and embrace. Again, this represents not simply the values of an observer but the preferences revealed by the behavior of the people concerned, as they abandon their own traditional ways of doing particular things in favor of ways they have discovered in the cultures of others. Nor is this a particularly modern development. The earliest known civilizations borrowed extensively from one another. Thousands of years before Christ, metallurgical techniques from the Middle East diffused into the steppes of Central Asia.[52] Horseback-riding techniques and musical instruments developed in Central Asia spread to China[53] and a great variety of products and processes flowed from China to the West over the centuries—gunpowder, paper, printing, porcelain, silk, canal locks, wheelbarrows, rudders for boats and ships, and playing cards, for example.[54] In the other direction, art styles from ancient Greece and Rome made their way along the Silk Road to China.[55] The culture of ancient Korea was almost all of Chinese origin.[56]

Happy endings are of course not guaranteed in all cultural encounters. Some groups have been oppressed in many ways for many generations, or even centuries, because they would not give up their cultures. This was the fate of the Jews in Europe and Central Asians under both the czars and the Communists. The point here is not to assess whether most cultural competition ends happily or unhappily, but rather to indicate that the competition of cultures takes place both within societies and between societies.

Cultures compete at many levels. They compete most obviously in warfare, for the outcomes of wars of conquest can determine what language the descendants of the combatants will speak for centuries to come, what concepts will organize their thoughts, and what values will shape their moral universe. The Western Hemisphere is an outpost of European civilization because Europeans won the wars of conquest in this part of the world. Today, even those in the Western Hemisphere who hate European civilization express that hatred in a European language and denounce it as immoral by European standards of morality. The alternatives they propose likewise tend to follow European concepts. Pan-Africanism, for example, is not an African concept but a European concept applied to Africa, paralleling such notions as Pan-Slavism and Pan-Germanism, but having little in common with the strong local and tribal loyalties of Africa. A whole generation of post-independence African leaders, educated in Europe and the United States, has proclaimed the ideology of Pan-Africanism, while having their hands full trying to hold together countries torn apart by internal tribal rivalries.

Wars are only one of the ways in which cultures compete. More continuously and more pervasively, they compete in the many practical ways that cultures serve human purposes, from the growing of food to trying to understand the motions of the stars. Agricultural methods and astronomy are just two of many features taken over by one culture from another and spread around the world. Yet, even when one culture supersedes another, seldom is it more satisfactory in every way, so that laments for the lost virtues of abandoned cultures have been both common and understandable. But there is no need for nostalgia to corrupt history or for rejected cultural artifacts to be resurrected at public expense, much less imposed on others for obligatory admiration. Above all, there is no need to encourage those who have progressed by cultural borrowings to retrogress by painting themselves into their own cultural corner and taking upon themselves the arduous burden of advancing solely by what their own subgroup can accomplish in isolation from the wider world which has long been the cultural resource of peoples, nations, and whole civilizations.

Migrations have long been part of the process of cultural diffusion. However, intergroup differences present not only an opportunity for cultural interchanges and economic advancement, but also for negative consequences, ranging from social frictions to the spread of disease to the disintegration of whole societies. Even immigrant groups contributing greatly to the economic development of the countries to which they go may also harbor criminal elements in their midst whose depredations and corruption of law enforcement agencies affect the larger surrounding society. The tongs among the overseas Chinese and the Mafia among Italian immigrants have been obvious examples. International terrorists hiding among Moslem immigrant populations in Europe and the United States are more recent examples.

Diseases have long been spread by migrations. Nineteenth-century emigrants from Russia, for example, often departed on transatlantic voyages from the German port of Bremen—and in 1892 they brought a devastating cholera epidemic with them to Bremen, killing nearly ten thousand people.[57] Earlier in the century, caravans from Central Asia brought cholera into Europe, where the population had less resistance than in parts of Asia where the disease was endemic.[58] In East Africa as well, movements of people—in this case, slaves—often spread both cholera and smallpox along their routes as they were forcibly marched from where they were captured to where they would be sold, through areas inhabited by various other peoples.[59] Perhaps the most disastrous of all disease-spreading migrations was that of Europeans to the Western Hemisphere, annihilating by disease the majority of the indigenous population—and, in some places such as the Caribbean, virtually all of the indigenous population. Nor has the modern era been immune to the biological consequences of the movements of people from different disease environments. The United States in the late twentieth century found various diseases which had become virtually extinct in the American population suddenly resurgent as they were re-introduced by immigrants from countries where such diseases were still prevalent—tuberculosis, leprosy, measles, cholera, and malaria, for example.[60] Internal migrations have also spread diseases, at various times and places throughout history, especially when refugees fleeing epidemics have spread the epidemic to others.

Animals, as well as human beings, are struck by diseases transmitted through migration. One diseased ewe brought into Northumberland from Spain in the thirteenth century has been blamed for a spread of murrain in Britain that lasted more than a quarter of a century.[61] Rinderpest, which struck Western Europe in the eighteenth century, killing vast numbers of cattle, later spread into parts of Africa, with similarly devastating results for both wild and domesticated animals there. From another perspective, however, the transportation of animals to environments where their usual predators are lacking, and the usual animal diseases less prevalent, has often led to higher-than-usual survival rates. More favorable conditions in new lands have also had similarly beneficial effects on the health and survival of plants and human beings. Wheat in the Delaware Valley, sheep in New Zealand, and Britons in Massachusetts, Australia, and New Zealand all thrived better than in their native lands.[62]

Among the many crosscurrents of positive and negative consequences of migrations are frictions among peoples with different cultural backgrounds, priorities, taboos, and imperatives. From differences in the way that people look at each other to differences in the way they respond to noise or dispose of their garbage, immigrants may differ from the peoples of their host countries. A sufficiently cohesive group of foreigners may even pose a threat to the territorial integrity of the nation in which they settle. Americans who settled in parts of Mexico in the early nineteenth century agreed to accept the laws, language, religion, and citizenship of that country, but in fact later revolted, seceded, and eventually joined that part of Mexican territory to the United States. In ancient times, the peaceful settlement of barbarians in parts of the Roman Empire was a prelude to their later attacks on the empire that brought it down in ruins. The entire modern state of Israel was created as a result of demands and insurrections by a population that had largely immigrated to that part of the Middle East within the previous century. The question here is not whether these particular events were good or bad developments. The point is that immigration can profoundly affect the fabric of a society and even dissolve the ties that hold a nation together.

The demands of immigrants need not be territorial to be divisive or disruptive. Indeed, it need not even be the immigrants themselves who make demands. In Britain and British offshoot nations such as the United States, Canada, and Australia, ideological proponents of "multiculturalism" among the native populations have promoted sweeping ranges of programs aimed at preserving foreign cultures and languages, often with more than a hint of hostility to the institutions and traditions of the host country. In the United States, many immigrants are legally entitled to preferential treatment under "affirmative action" programs set up ostensibly to remedy historic wrongs that occurred before contemporary immigrants arrived. Both multiculturalism and affirmative action programs thus add to the cost of absorbing immigrants, not least by increasing the resentment of them by the native population.

Government-provided benefits in general have made immigrants more costly to absorb, quite aside from the question whether they cause more immigrants to come, or reduce the selectivity of the immigrant population by including many without the initiative or ambition of those who immigrated when there was little or no help available from government. Anti-immigrant feelings and movements have grown in the welfare states of Western Europe and the United States. Unfortunately, among ideological zealots who have promoted immigrants as a symbolic cause, this resentment by the masses may only confirm their own sense of moral superiority, rather than serving as a warning that the combination of lax immigration laws, welfare state benefits, and schemes to keep foreigners foreign are leading to potentially explosive conflicts.

These social conflicts may be especially tragic in an era when persecutions and armed conflicts around the world are producing vast numbers of refugees seeking asylum but discovering that such asylum is increasingly difficult to find. The human tragedies caused by turning away desperate people from borders are made doubly tragic when much of the opposition comes not simply from objections to the immigrants themselves but also from objections to the social and political agendas being promoted by ideologues who use the immigrants as part of their general opposition to the values and traditions of their own society.

Just as there are both positive and negative consequences of immigration, the immigrants themselves differ greatly. Fewer than 5 percent of the immigrants from Britain or Germany went on welfare after arriving in late twentieth-century America, but more than one-fourth of the immigrants from Vietnam and nearly half of those from Cambodia did.[63] Again, domestic ideological agendas may make it impossible to be selective in admitting immigrants from different nations, leaving as alternatives only loss of control of the borders or restrictive policies toward immigrants in general.

THE PAST AND THE FUTURE

The historic role of migrations in spreading skills, technology, and manpower from where they are abundant to where they are more scarce has been monumental in its consequences. However, such achievements have not come merely from the movement of bodies. It has been the movement of knowledge, of skills, and of technology that has been crucial. What the passage of time and the development of modern industry and instant electronic communications has done has been to make the transmission of knowledge, skills, and technology less and less dependent on the transportation of bodies—all the while making such transportation so inexpensive as to permit larger migrations, over greater distances, of immigrants who may be less and less selective.

Whether they are in fact less selective may be difficult to determine, especially when the crucial selectivity in terms of ambition and perseverance are unquantifiable and selectivity in terms of education is ambiguous in some cases—immigrants to the United States during the 1980s, for example, having rising numbers of years of schooling but falling further behind the years of schooling of Americans, which was rising faster.[64] Moreover, it would be a great mistake to equate formal schooling with human capital. Many of the immigrants who helped bring whole nations into the modern commercial world—the Lebanese in West Africa and the Chinese in Southeast Asia, for example—arrived with little or no formal education. Conversely, much schooling produces no skills, however much it may expand expectations, contributing to political instability in some Third World countries especially. Whatever the empirical facts about the quality of immigrants may be in particular countries in particular years, the transportation of bodies and the dissemination of human capital have become increasingly separable operations, so that the historic role of immigration in advancing nations need not apply to its future role. Those countries with the most human capital to contribute to the rest of the world have tended to send fewer and fewer emigrants abroad, so that nothing resembling the massive migrations from Japan and Germany in earlier generations existed by the late twentieth century. Refugees with valuable human capital, such as the Jews or the Huguenots in the past, have migrated simply to escape persecution, thereby benefitting the recipient countries, whether the Ottoman Empire, Switzerland, England, or the United States. But many refugees have no such human capital and refugees to the United States in the late twentieth century tended to stay on welfare longer than either American citizens or other kinds of immigrants.[65]

In short, international migrations have tended to become a less and less effective way of transferring human capital, at least as compared to alternatives that have emerged or grown in importance. One alternative way of sharing the human capital of the world has been international trade and the setting up of businesses in each other's countries. Japan, for example, has permitted virtually no immigration but has become one of the leading international trading nations of the world and has also set up Japanese businesses, turning out Japanese products, produced by Japanese methods, in countries around the world. As of 1992, for example, Toyota produced more than 345,000 cars in the United States and Honda more than 450,000. Meanwhile, only about half of General Motors' worldwide passenger car output was being produced in the United States.[66] Neither technological nor managerial human capital requires mass immigration for its diffusion.

Even in centuries past, sojourners have played crucial roles in the economic development of nations without remaining to become permanent residents. When Britain was the leading industrial nation of the world, its technicians and engineers took its technology to Germany and the United States in the early nineteenth century and to Japan later in that century, providing the foundation for the later rise of each of these nations to major positions as industrial powers that later eclipsed Britain itself. In many other countries as well, British railroads and British textile machinery became standard from India to Africa to South America. Sojourners from various nations have also gone to Britain—and, in a later era, to the United States, Germany, and other industrial nations—to acquire the human capital needed to advance their own countries economically. This human capital has been not only in the form of technological knowledge but has also included knowledge of the science behind the technology and the organizational skills needed to turn technology into products and produce these products in economically viable enterprises. Moreover, once a sufficient human capital has been transferred to another nation in this way, its own people can train others at home, while staying abreast of international developments.

One of the historically important ways of transferring human capital by immigration has been by the return of sojourners bearing knowledge, skills, and attitudes acquired during their stays in more advanced societies. This, however, makes a stronger case for the sending countries to permit emigrants to leave freely than for recipient countries to allow immigrants to enter freely. This method of transferring human capital has, if anything, become more important over time. During the late twentieth century, the proportion of Ph.D.s awarded to foreigners by universities in the United States increased in a variety of fields, but particularly in mathematics and engineering.[67] As of 1993, American citizens received only 39 percent of the doctorates in engineering awarded in the United States.[68] In addition to transfers of technology by education, specialized books and journals, multinational corporations, international computer networks, consulting firms, and government agencies all facilitate the international transfer of human capital, without the need for permanent resettlement.

The history of immigration in all its various forms is an important part of the history of the advancement of the human race. The causes and consequences of immigration remain relevant for the present and future, even where mass immigration itself is no longer an urgent priority for the recipient countries, now that less costly and less socially disruptive ways of transferring human capital have become more feasible. The history of immigrants who began in poverty and achieved prosperity, while at the same time advancing the economic level of the society around them, brings into sharper focus the importance of *creating* wealth, especially important when so many are preoccupied with its distribution. Such immigrants have left a legacy not only of economic examples but also of human inspiration.

NOTES

CHAPTER 1: MIGRATION PATTERNS

1. Myron Weiner, *The Global Migration Crisis: Challenge to States and to Human Rights* (New York: HarperCollins, 1995), p. 2.
2. Dariusz Stola, "Forced Migrations in Central European History," *International Migration Review,* Vol. XXVI, No. 2 (Summer 1992), p. 324.
3. Carlo M. Cipolla, *Clocks and Culture: 1300–1700* (New York: Norton, 1978), pp. 64–69.
4. See Carlo M. Cipolla, *Literacy and Development in the West* (New York: Penguin, 1969), pp. 17, 51, 115; Robert J. Kaiser, *The Geography of Nationalism in Russia and the USSR* (Princeton, N.J.: Princeton University Press, 1994), p. 70; Piotr S. Wandycz, *The Lands of Partitioned Poland, 1795–1918* (Seattle: University of Washington Press, 1974), p. 185.
5. Carlo M. Cipolla, *Literacy and Development in the West,* pp. 84–85.
6. Walter Nugent, *Crossings: The Great Transatlantic Migrations, 1870–1914* (Bloomington: Indiana University Press, 1992), p. 62.
7. Ibid., p. 99.
8. Helen Ware, *A Profile of the Italian Community in Australia* (Melbourne:

Australian Institute of Multicultural Affairs and Co.As.It. Italian Assistance Association, 1981), p. 12.

9. Leela Gulati, "The Impact on the Family of Male Migration to the Middle East," *Asian Labor Migration: Pipeline to the Middle East,* edited by Fred Arnold and Nasra M. Shah (Boulder, Colo.: Westview Press, 1986), p. 196.
10. Myron Weiner, *The Global Migration Crisis,* p. 37; *The World Almanac and Book of Facts: 1995* (Mahwah, N.J.: Funk and Wagnalls, 1994), p. 775.
11. Carlo M. Cipolla, *Literacy and Development in the West,* pp. 95–96.
12. Louise L'Estrange Fawcett, "Lebanese, Palestinians and Syrians in Colombia," *The Lebanese in the World: A Century of Emigration,* edited by Albert Hourani and Nadim Shehadi (London: I. B. Tauris & Co., Ltd., 1992), p. 368.
13. Ibid., p. 513; H. L. van der Laan, *The Lebanese Traders in Sierra Leone* (The Hague: Mouton, 1975), pp. 236–237, 239.
14. Charles A. Price, *Southern Europeans in Australia* (Melbourne: Australian National University, 1979), p. 282.
15. Ibid., pp. 31–32.
16. Ibid., p. 110.
17. Ibid., p. 132.
18. Robert C. Ostergren, "Prairie Bound: Migration Patterns to a Swedish Settlement on the Dakota Frontier," *Ethnicity on the Great Plains,* edited by Frederick C. Luebke (Lincoln: University of Nebraska Press, 1980), pp. 84–88; Charles A. Price, *Southern Europeans in Australia,* p. 114; Yasuo Wakatsuki, "Japanese Emigration to the United States, 1866–1924: A Monograph," *Perspectives in American History,* Vol. XII (1979), p. 428.
19. Charles A. Price, *Southern Europeans in Australia,* p. 161.
20. Yuan-li Wu and Chun-hsi Wu, *Economic Development in Southeast Asia: The Chinese Dimension* (Stanford, Calif.: Hoover Institution Press, 1980), pp. 60–61.
21. Moses Rischin, *The Promised City: New York's Jews, 1870–1914* (Cambridge, Mass.: Harvard University Press, 1962), pp. 76, 78.
22. Samuel L. Bailey, "The Adjustment of Italian Immigrants in Buenos Aires and New York," *American Historical Review,* April 1983, p. 291; Robert F. Foerster, *The Italian Emigration of Our Times* (New York: Arno Press, 1969), p. 393; Dino Cinel, *From Italy to San Francisco: The Immigrant Experience* (Stanford, Calif.: Stanford University Press, 1982), p. 28; John E. Zucchi, *Italians in Toronto: Development of a National Identity, 1875–1935* (Kingston, Ontario: McGill-Queen's University Press, 1988), pp. 41, 53–55, 58.

23. Seamus Grimes, "Friendship Patterns and Social Networks Among Post-War Irish Migrants in Sydney," *The Irish World Wide,* Volume 1: *Patterns of Migration,* edited by Patrick O'Sullivan, pp. 169–171.
24. Mary Fainsod Katzenstein, *Ethnicity and Equality: The Shiv Sena Party and Preferential Policies in Bombay* (Ithaca, N.Y.: Cornell University Press, 1979), pp. 31–32.
25. U.S. Commission on Civil Rights, *The Economic Status of Americans of Southern and Eastern European Ancestry* (Washington, D.C.: U.S. Commission on Civil Rights, 1986), p. 25.
26. Peter Xenos, Herbert Barringer, and Michael J. Levin, *Asian Indians in the United States: A 1980 Census Profile* (Honolulu: East-West Population Institute, 1989), p. 22.
27. Oliver MacDonagh, "The Irish Famine Emigration to the United States," *Perspectives in American History,* Vol. X (1976), pp. 394–395.
28. Patrick McKenna, "Irish Immigration to Argentina," *The Irish World Wide,* Volume I: *Patterns of Migration,* edited by Patrick O'Sullivan, p. 71.
29. See, for example, H. L. van der Laan, *The Lebanese Traders in Sierra Leone* (The Hague: Mouton, 1975), pp. 242–243; Floyd Dotson and Lillian O. Dotson, *The Indian Minority of Zambia, Rhodesia, and Malawi* (New Haven, Conn.: Yale University Press, 1968), pp. 73–75; Robert G. Gregory, *South Asians in East Africa: An Economic and Social History* (Boulder, Colo.: Westview Press, 1993), p. 300; Edgar Wickberg, *The Chinese in Philippine Life: 1850–1898* (New Haven, Conn.: Yale University Press, 1965), p. 172; Ng Bickleen Fong, *The Chinese in New Zealand: A Study in Assimilation* (Hong Hong: Hong Kong University Press, 1959), pp. 15, 172.
30. Charles A. Price, *Southern Europeans in Australia,* p. 109.
31. See ibid., pp. 248, 251.
32. Madhullike S. Khandelwal, "Indian Immigrants in Queens, New York City: Patterns of Spatial Concentration and Distribution, 1965–1990," *Nation and Migration: The Politics of Space in the South Asian Diaspora,* edited by Peter van der Veer (Philadelphia: University of Pennsylvania Press, 1995), p. 184.
33. Caroline Golab, *Immigrant Destinations* (Philadelphia: Temple University Press, 1977), pp. 24–25.
34. Ibid., p. 132.
35. Louis Wirth, *The Ghetto* (Chicago: University of Chicago Press, 1958), p. 229.
36. Charles A. Price, *Southern Europeans in Australia,* p. 111.
37. Albert Hourani, "Introduction," *The Lebanese in the World,* p. 5.

38. Ibid., p. 6.
39. Ibid., p. 8. See also Trevor Batrowney, "The Lebanese in Australia, 1880–1989," ibid., pp. 432, 434–435; Michael Humphrey, "Sectarianism and the Politics of Identity: The Lebanese in Sydney," ibid., pp. 444, 449; H. L. van der Laan, *The Lebanese Traders in Sierra Leone*, p. 245.
40. James A. Haetner, "Market Gardening in Thailand: The Origins of an Ethnic Chinese Monopoly," *The Chinese in Southeast Asia*, edited by Linda Y. C. Lim and L. A. Peter Gosling (Singapore: Maruzen Asia, 1983), Volume I: *Ethnicity and Economic Activity*, p. 40.
41. Fernand Braudel, *The Mediterranean and the Mediterranean World in the Age of Philip II*, translated by Sian Reynolds, Volume I (New York: Harper & Row, 1972), pp. 238, 241–243. See also John R. Lampe, "Imperial Borderlands or Capitalist Periphery? Redefining Balkan Backwardness, 1520–1914," *The Origins of Backwardness in Eastern Europe: Economics and Politics from the Middle Ages until the Early Twentieth Century*, edited by Daniel Chirot (Berkeley: University of California Press, 1989), p. 180.
42. J. R. McNeill, *The Mountains of the Mediterranean World: An Environmental History* (Cambridge: Cambridge University Press, 1992), p. 47.
43. Ibid., p. 29.
44. Ibid., p. 206; William H. McNeill, *The Age of Gunpowder Empires: 1450–1800* (Washington, D.C.: American Historical Association, 1989), p. 38.
45. J. R. McNeill, *The Mountains of the Mediterranean*, p. 143.
46. Ibid., pp. 27, 54.
47. Ibid., p. 46.
48. See, for example, ibid., p. 110.
49. Ibid., pp. 142–143.
50. Ibid., pp. 116–117, 139.
51. Ellen Churchill Semple, *Influences of Geographic Environment* (New York: Holt, 1911), pp. 578–579.
52. William S. Brockington, "Scottish Military Emigrants in the Early Modern Era," *Proceedings of the South Carolina Historical Association* (1991), pp. 95–101.
53. Byron Farwell, *The Gurkhas* (New York: Norton, 1984).
54. Fernand Braudel, *The Mediterranean and the Mediterranean World in the Age of Philip II*, Volume I, pp. 48–49.
55. J. R. McNeill, *The Mountains of the Mediterranean*, pp. 205–206.
56. Gary Snyder, "Beyond Cathay: The Hill Tribes of China," *Mountain Peo-*

ple, edited by Michael Tobias (Norman: University of Oklahoma Press, 1986), pp. 150–151.

57. N. J. G. Pounds, *An Historical Geography of Europe: 1500–1840* (Cambridge: Cambridge University Press, 1988), p. 102.
58. J. R. McNeill, *The Mountains of the Mediterranean,* pp. 119, 213.
59. N. J. G. Pounds, *An Historical Geography of Europe: 1500–1840,* p. 102.
60. Ellen Churchill Semple, *Influences of Geographic Environment,* pp. 586–588.
61. David Hackett Fischer, *Albion's Seed: Four British Folkways in America* (New York: Oxford University Press, 1989), p. 767.
62. J. R. McNeill, *The Mountains of the Mediterranean,* pp. 48, 205, 206; Ellen Churchill Semple, *Influences of Geographical Environment,* pp. 592, 599.
63. See, for example, William H. McNeill, *The Age of Gunpowder Empires: 1450–1800* (Washington, D.C.: American Historical Association, 1989), p. 4; Jean W. Sedlar, *East Central Europe in the Middle Ages, 1000–1500* (Seattle: University of Washington Press, 1994), pp. 115, 126, 131; Wolfgang von Hagen, *The German People in America,* pp. 75–76.
64. J. R. McNeill, *The Mountains of the Mediterranean,* pp. 20, 35, 41.
65. Ibid., p. 31.
66. H. J. de Blij and Peter O. Mueller, *Physical Geography of the Global Environment* (New York: Wiley, 1993), pp. 132–133.
67. Ellen Churchill Semple, *Influences of Geographical Environment,* pp. 542–543.
68. Ibid., pp. 532–533.
69. Ibid., Chapter VIII.
70. Ibid., p. 272.
71. Peter F. Sugar, *Southeastern Europe under Ottoman Rule, 1354–1804* (Seattle: University of Washington Press, 1993), pp. 178–183; Jean W. Sedlar, *East Central Europe in the Middle Ages, 1000–1500,* pp. 454–457.
72. Francois Renault, "The Structures of the Slave Trade in Central Africa in the 19th Century," *The Economics of the Indian Ocean Slave Trade in the Nineteenth Century,* edited by William Gervase Clarence-Smith (London: Frank Cass & Co., Ltd., 1989), pp. 148–149; James S. Coleman, *Nigeria: Background to Nationalism* (Berkeley: University of California Press, 1971), p. 65.
73. Ellen Churchill Semple, *Influences of Geographic Environment,* p. 276.
74. Jean W. Sedlar, *East Central Europe in the Middle Ages, 1000–1500*, p. 84.

75. Fernand Braudel, *The Mediterranean and the Mediterranean World in the Age of Philip II,* Volume I, p. 84.
76. Jean W. Sedlar, *East Central Europe in the Middle Ages, 1000–1500,* pp. 3–13.
77. The Amazon, for example, is by far the world's greatest river but the soils in its region have been characterized as "startlingly poor" and it has led to no great cities being established along its banks. See Jonathan B. Tourtellot, "The Amazon: Sailing a Jungle Sea," *Great Rivers of the World,* edited by Margaret Sedeen (Washington, D.C.: National Geographic Society, 1984), p. 302.
78. William L. Blackwell, *The Industrialization of Russia: A Historical Perspective,* third edition (Arlington Heights, Ill.: Harland Davidson, 1994), p. 2.
79. Ellen Churchill Semple, *Influences of Geographic Environment,* pp. 263, 283.
80. Josip Roglic, "The Geographical Setting of Medieval Dubrovnik," *Geographical Essays on Eastern Europe,* edited by Norman J. G. Pounds (Bloomington: Indiana University Press, 1961), p. 147.
81. James Vicens Vives, *An Economic History of Spain* (Princeton, N.J.: Princeton University Press, 1969), p. 365.
82. Constance Cronin, *The Sting of Change: Sicilians in Sicily and Australia* (Chicago: University of Chicago Press, 1970), p. 35.
83. U.S. Commission on Civil Rights, *The Economic Status of Americans of Southern and Eastern European Ancestry* (Washington, D.C.: U.S. Commission on Civil Rights, 1986), p. 15. It also took the immigrants from southern and eastern Europe, and from Ireland and the French-speaking regions of Canada, more years to reach the average income of native-born Americans. Barry R. Chiswick, "The Economic Progress of Immigrants: Some Apparently Universal Patterns," *The Gateway: U.S. Immigration Issues and Policies* (Washington, D.C.: The American Enterprise Institute, 1982), p. 147.
84. Stanley Lieberson, *Ethnic Patterns in American Cities* (New York: Free Press of Glencoe, 1963), p. 72.
85. See, for example, Peter Fox, *The Poles in America* (New York: Arno Press, 1970), p. 96; Leonard P. Ayres, *Laggards in Our Schools: A Study of Retardation and Elimination in City School Systems* (New York: Russell Sage Foundation, 1909), pp. 107–108; *Reports of the Immigration Commission,* 61st Congress, 3rd Session, Volume I: *The Children of Immigrants in Schools* (Washington, D.C.: U.S. Government Printing Office, 1911), pp. 48–49, 89, 90.
86. Thomas Sowell, "Race and I.Q. Reconsidered," *Essays and Data on*

American Ethnic Groups, edited by Thomas Sowell (Washington, D.C.: The Urban Institute, 1978), p. 207.

87. Charles A. Price, *Southern Europeans in Australia,* p. 58.
88. Ibid., p. 24. See also pp. 16, 17n.
89. Helen Ware, *A Profile of the Italian Community in Australia* (Melbourne: Australian Institute of Multicultural Affairs, 1981), p. 68.
90. Ibid., p. 47.
91. Ibid., p. 63.
92. John K. Fairbank, Edwin O. Reischauer, and Albert M. Craig, *East Asia: Tradition and Transformation* (Boston: Houghton-Mifflin, 1989), pp. 133, 135.
93. John K. Fairbank et al., *East Asia,* pp. 143, 174.
94. Ellen Churchill Semple, *Influences of Geographic Environment,* pp. 266–271.
95. N. J. G. Pounds, *An Historical Geography of Europe: 1500–1840,* p. 86.
96. Walter Nugent, *Crossings,* p. 35.
97. Ibid., pp. 35–36, 84.
98. Ibid., p. 84.
99. Ibid., p. 84.
100. H. L. van der Laan, *The Lebanese Traders in Sierra Leone,* p. 241.
101. Emilio Reyneri and Clara Mughini, "Return Migration and Sending Areas: From the Myth of Development to the Reality of Stagnation," *The Politics of Return: International Return Migration in Europe* (New York: Center for Migration Studies, 1984), p. 34.
102. Fred Arnold and Nasra M. Shah, "Asia's Labor Pipeline: An Overview," *Asian Labor Migration: Pipeline to the Middle East* (Boulder, Colo.: Westview Press, 1986), p. 7.
103. Ibid., p. 6.
104. Ibid., p. 4.
105. Charles B. Keely and Bao Nga Tran, "Remittances from Labor Migration: Evaluations, Performance and Implications," *International Migration Review,* Vol. 23, No. 87 (Fall 1989), p. 519.
106. Ibid., p. 514.
107. Reginald T. Appleyard, "Migration and Development: Myth and Reality," *International Migration Review,* Vol. 23, No. 87 (Fall 1989), pp. 493–494.
108. Myron Weiner, *The Global Migration Crisis: Challenge to States and to Human Rights* (New York: HarperCollins, 1995), p. 68.
109. Robert F. Foerster, *The Italian Emigration of Our Times,* p. 417.
110. Judith M. Brown and Rosemary Foot, "Introduction: Migration—the

Asian Experience," *Migration: The Asian Experience* (London: St. Martin's, 1994), p. 6.

111. Dino Cinel, *From Italy to San Francisco,* pp. 95, 278 (n. 152).
112. Ibid., pp. 86–88; Joseph Lopreato, *Italian Americans* (New York: Random House, 1970), pp. 158–159; Humbert S. Nelli, *The Italians in Chicago, 1880–1930: A Study in Ethnic Mobility* (New York: Oxford University Press, 1970), p. 72.
113. Joseph Lopreato, *Italian Americans*, pp. 158–159.
114. Ross Fakiolas, "Return Migration to Greece and Its Structural and Socio-Political Effects," *The Politics of Return,* edited by Daniel Kubat, p. 40.
115. Ibid., pp. 41–43.
116. Reginald T. Appleyard, "Migration and Development: Myth and Reality," *International Migration Review,* Vol. 23, No. 87 (Fall 1989), p. 493.
117. Walter Nugent, *Crossings,* p. 175.
118. Charles A. Price, *Southern Europeans in Australia,* pp. 105–107.
119. Ilsoo Kim, *New Urban Immigrants: The Korean Community in New York* (Princeton, N.J.: Princeton University Press, 1981), p. 113.
120. Kingsley Davis, *The Population of India and Pakistan* (Princeton, N.J.: Princeton University Press, 1951), p. 99.
121. Walter Nugent, *Crossings,* p. 160.
122. Ai Leng Choo, "When Many Are Fleeing Hong Kong, Others Find It's Profitable to Go Back," *Wall Street Journal,* January 24, 1992, p. A10.
123. See, for example, Anna Maria Martellone, "Italian Mass Emigration to the United States, 1876–1930: A Historical Survey," *Perspectives in American History,* New Series, Vol. 1 (1984), pp. 406–407; W. D. Borrie, *Italians and Germans in Australia: A Study of Assimilation* (Melbourne: Australian National University, 1954), pp. 36, 51; Herbert S. Klein, "The Integration of Italian Immigrants into the United States and Argentina," *American Historical Review,* Vol. 88, No. 2 (April 1983), p. 316; Robert F. Foerster, *The Italian Emigration of Our Times* (New York: Arno Press, 1969), p. 242; Victor Purcell, *The Overseas Chinese in Southeast Asia,* second edition (Kuala Lumpur: Oxford University Press, 1980), pp. 41, 85, 179, 223, 387, 499; Yasuo Wakatsuki, "Japanese Emigration to the United States, 1866–1924: A Monograph," *Perspectives in American History,* Vol. XII (1979), p. 514; C. Harvey Gardiner, *The Japanese and Peru, 1873–1973* (Albuquerque: University of New Mexico Press, 1975), p. 34.
124. See, for example, Moses Rischin, *The Promised City,* pp. 80–81; Betty Lee Sung, *The Story of the Chinese in America* (New York: Collier Books,

1967), pp. 85, 87; Ira de A. Reid, *The Negro Immigrant: His Background, Characteristics and Social Adjustment, 1899–1937* (New York: AMS Press, 1970), p. 236; W. D. Borrie, *Italians and Germans in Australia: A Study of Assimilation* (Melbourne: F. W. Cheshire, 1954), p. 132; Charles H. Young and Helen R. Y. Reid, *The Japanese Canadians* (Toronto: University of Toronto Press, 1938), pp. 16–17.

125. Yugi Ichioka, *The Issei: The World of the First Generation Japanese Immigrants, 1885–1924* (New York: The Free Press, 1988), pp. 164–165; Ken Adachi, *The Enemy That Never Was: A History of the Japanese Canadians* (Toronto: McClelland and Stewart, 1976), Chapter 4; Ellie Vasta, "Cultural and Social Change: Italian-Australian Women and the Second Generation," *The Columbua People: Perspectives in Italian Immigration to the Americas and Australia* (New York: Center for Migration Studies, 1994), p. 407.
126. Myron Weiner, *The Global Migration Crisis,* p. 10.
127. William McGowan, *And Only Man Is Vile: The Tragedy of Sri Lanka* (New York: Farrar, Straus & Giroux, 1992), p. 98.
128. David Lamb, *The Africans* (New York: Random House, 1982), p. 308.
129. Lord Kinross, *The Ottoman Centuries: The Rise and Fall of the Turkish Empire* (New York: Morrow, 1977), p. 560.
130. David Marshall Lang, *The Armenians: A People in Exile* (London: George Allen & Unwin, 1982), p. 125.
131. See, for example, Solomon Grayzel, *A History of the Jews* (New York: Mentor Book, 1968), pp. 306, 440–442, 547–548; Paul Johnson, *A History of the Jews* (New York: Harper & Row, 1987), pp. 216–217; Stephen H. Haliczer, "The Castilian Urban Patriciate and the Jewish Expulsions of 1480–92," *American Historical Review,* February 1973, pp. 41–42; Benjamin Pinkus, *The Jews of the Soviet Union,* pp. 27–30.
132. Ashok V. Desai, "The Origins of Parsi Enterprise," *Indian Economic and Social History Review,* June 1968, pp. 307, 312; Christine Dobbin, "From Middleman Minorities to Industrial Entrepreneurs: The Chinese in Java and the Parsis in Western India, 1619–1939," *Itinerario,* Vol. XIII, No. 1 (1989), p. 122.
133. Albert Hourani, "Introduction," *The Lebanese in the World,* edited by Albert Hourani and Nadim Shehadi, p. 8.
134. Roger P. Bartlett, *Human Capital: The Settlement of Foreigners in Russia, 1762–1804* (Cambridge: Cambridge University Press, 1979), p. 151.
135. Joel Kotkin, *Tribes: How Race, Religion and Identity Determine Success in the New Global Economy* (New York: Random House, 1993), p. 180.
136. Amir Abdul-Kaim, "Lebanese Business in France," *The Lebanese in the*

World, edited by Albert Hourani and Nadim Shehadi, p. 697.

137. Didier Bigo, "The Lebanese Community in the Ivory Coast: A Non-native Network at the Heart of Power?" ibid., p. 514.
138. I. H. Burnley, "Lebanese Migration and Settlement in Sydney, Australia," *International Migration Review*, Vol. XVI, No. 1 (Spring 1982), p. 102.
139. John J. Ray, "The Traits of Immigrants: A Case Study of the Sydney Parsees," *Journal of Comparative Family Studies*, Vol. XVII, No. 1 (Spring 1986), p. 127.
140. Moses Rischin, *The Promised City*, p. 33.
141. Hilary Rubinstein, *Chosen: The Jews in Australia* (Sydney: Allen & Unwin, 1987), p. 9.
142. Judith Laikin Elkin, *Jews of the Latin American Republics* (Chapel Hill: University of North Carolina Press, 1980), p. 59.
143. S. W. Kung, *Chinese in American Life: Some Aspects of Their History, Status, Problems, and Contributions* (Seattle: University of Washington Press, 1962), pp. 22–23.
144. F. A. Hayek, *The Collected Works of F. A. Hayek*, Volume I: *The Fatal Conceit: The Errors of Socialism*, edited by W. W. Bartley III (Chicago: University of Chicago Press, 1988), p. 91.
145. R. A. Radford, "The Economic Organisation of a P.O.W. Camp," *Economica*, November 1945, pp. 189–201.
146. Roger P. Bartlett, *Human Capital*, pp. 86–87.
147. Ashok V. Desai, "The Origins of Parsi Enterprise," *Indian Economic and Social History Review*, June 1968, pp. 310, 311.
148. See, for example, Didier Bigo, "The Lebanese Community in the Ivory Coast: A Non-native Network at the Heart of Power?" *The Lebanese in the World*, edited by Albert Hourani and Nadim Shehadi, pp. 511–512; H. L. van der Laan, *The Lebanese Traders in Sierra Leone* (The Hague: Mouton, 1975), pp. 27–28; J. S. Mangat, *A History of the Asians in East Africa*, pp. 8–9.
149. Emily Green Balch, *Our Slavic Fellow Citizens* (New York: Arno Press, 1969), p. 61.
150. Walter Nugent, *Crossings*, pp. 12, 41, 43.
151. Robert E. Kennedy, Jr., *The Irish: Emigration, Marriage and Fertility* (Berkeley: University of California Press, 1973), p. 27.
152. Robert Bartlett, *The Making of Europe: Conquest, Colonization and Cultural Change, 950–1350* (Princeton, N.J.: Princeton University Press, 1993), pp. 126–132; Jean W. Sedlar, *East Central Europe in the Middle Ages, 1000–1500*, pp. 98–99.

153. Robert Bartlett, *The Making of Europe,* pp. 114–115, 149; Jean W. Sedlar, *East Central Europe in the Middle Ages, 1000–1500,* p. 86.
154. Robert Bartlett, *The Making of Europe,* pp. 90–92.
155. Jean W. Sedlar, *East Central Europe in the Middle Ages, 1000–1500,* pp. 115, 136, 411.
156. Oliver MacDonagh, "The Irish Famine Emigration to the United States," *Perspectives in American History,* Vol. X (1976), pp. 423, 425.
157. Walter Nugent, *Crossings,* p. 99.
158. Robert W. Gardner, "Asian Immigration: The View from the United States," *Asian and Pacific Migration Journal,* Vol. 1, No. 1 (1992), pp. 78–79.
159. Paul M. Ong, Lucie Cheng, and Leslie Evans, "Migration of Highly Educated Asians and Global Dynamics," *Asian and Pacific Migration Journal,* Vol. 1, Nos. 3–4 (1992), p. 545.
160. George J. Borgas and Richard B. Freeman, "Introduction and Summary," *Immigration and the Work Force,* edited by George J. Borgas and Richard B. Freeman, p. 7.
161. Charles W. Stahl, Reginald T. Appleyard, and Toshikazu Nagayama, "Introduction," *Asian and Pacific Migration Journal,* Vol. 1, Nos. 3–4 (1992), p. 409.
162. D. A. Coleman, "International Migration: Demographic and Socioeconomic Consequences in the United Kingdom and Europe," *International Migration Review,* Vol. XXIX, No. 1 (Spring 1995), p. 163.
163. Barry R. Chiswick, "The Economic Progress of Immigrants: Some Apparently Universal Patterns," *The Gateway,* pp. 119–158.
164. Walter Nugent, *Crossings,* p. 31.
165. Henry A. Gemery, "European Emigration to North America, 1720–1800: Numbers and Quasi-Numbers," *Perspectives in American History,* Vol. I (1984), pp. 300–301.
166. Ibid., p. 299.
167. Maldwyn Allen Jones, *American Immigration,* pp. 184–185.
168. Alice Kessler-Harris and Virginia Yans-McLaughlin, "European Immigrant Groups," *Essays and Data on American Ethnic Groups,* edited by Thomas Sowell (Washington, D.C.: The Urban Institute, 1978), p. 108; U.S. Commission on Civil Rights, *The Economic Status of Americans of Southern and Eastern European Ancestry,* pp. 11–13.
169. U.S. Commission on Civil Rights, *The Economic Status of Americans of Southern and Eastern European Ancestry,* p. 11.
170. Ibid.
171. Samuel L. Baily, "The Adjustment of Italian Immigrants in Buenos Aires

and New York," *American Historical Review,* April 1983, p. 303.

172. N. J. G. Pounds, *An Historical Geography of Europe: 1800–1914* (Cambridge: Cambridge University Press, 1985), p. 79.
173. Ibid., pp. 79, 84.
174. N. J. G. Pounds, *An Historical Geography of Europe: 1500–1840,* pp. 86–87.
175. N. J. G. Pounds, *An Historical Geography of Europe: 1800–1914,* pp. 81–82.
176. Ibid., p. 84.
177. Ibid., p. 81.
178. Jean W. Sedlar, *East Central Europe in the Middle Ages, 1000–1500,* p. 136.
179. Ibid., p. 115.
180. Compare Daniel M. Johnson and Rex R. Campbell, *Black Migration in America: A Social Demographic History* (Durham, N.C.: Duke University Press, 1981), pp. 74–75, 95, 127, 156–157, 170; U.S. Bureau of the Census, *Historical Statistics of the United States: Colonial Times to 1970* (Washington, D.C.: U.S. Government Printing Office, 1975), pp. 105–106.
181. U.S. Bureau of the Census, *Geographical Mobility: March 1990 to March 1991,* Series P-20, No. 463 (Washington, D.C.: U.S. Government Printing Office, 1992), p. xiii.
182. Robert W. Gardner, "Asian Immigration: The View from the United States," *Asian and Pacific Migration Journal,* Vol. 1, No. 1 (1992), pp. 68–69.
183. Susumu Watanabe, "The Lewisian Turning Point and International Migration: The Case of Japan," *Asian and Pacific Migration Journal,* Vol. 3, No. 1 (1994), p. 136.
184. Ibid., p. 135.
185. Toshikazu Nagayama, "Clandestine Migrant Workers in Japan," *Asian and Pacific Migration Journal,* Vol. 1, Nos. 3–4 (1992), p. 629.
186. D. A. Coleman, "International Migration: Demographic and Socioeconomic Consequences in the United Kingdom and Europe," *International Migration Review,* Vol. 29, No. 109 (Spring 1995), p. 157.
187. Ibid., p. 95.
188. Leonardo Senkman, "Argentina's Immigration Policy during the Holocaust (1938–1945)," *Yad Vashem Studies,* Vol. 21 (1991), pp. 165–169 (published in Israel).
189. Peter Gunst, "Agrarian Systems of Central and Eastern Europe," *The Origins of Backwardness in Eastern Europe,* edited by Daniel Chirot, p. 63.

190. See U.S. Immigration and Naturalization Service, *Statistical Yearbook of the Immigration and Naturalization Service, 1991* (Washington, D.C.: U.S. Government Printing Office, 1992), p. 30.
191. Patrick McKenna, "Irish Immigration to Argentina," *Patterns of Migration,* pp. 77–80.
192. Peter Xenos, Herbert Barringer, Michael Levin, *Asian Indians in the United States: A 1980 Census Profile* (Honolulu: East-West Population Institute, 1989), pp. 2–3, 17.
193. U.S. Commission on Civil Rights, *The Economic Status of Americans of Southern and Eastern European Ancestry,* pp. 29, 35.
194. Ibid., pp. 28–29, 33, 46.
195. Ibid., p. 44.
196. Seamus Grimes, "Friendship Patterns and Social Networks among Post-War Irish Migrants in Sydney," *Patterns of Migration,* edited by Patrick O'Sullivan, p. 178.
197. Thomas E. Weil et al., *Area Handbook for Argentina* (Washington, D.C.: U.S. Government Printing Office, 1975), p. 8.
198. Jean W. Sedlar, *East Central Europe in the Middle Ages, 1000–1500,* pp. 12–13.

CHAPTER 2: GERMANS AROUND THE WORLD

1. Roy E. Mellor and E. Alistair Smith, *Europe: A Geographical Survey of the Continent* (New York: Columbia University Press, 1979), p. 24.
2. Jean W. Sedlar, *East Central Europe in the Middle Ages, 1000–1500* (Seattle: University of Washington Press, 1994), pp. 100–101.
3. Peter Gunst, "Agrarian Systems of Central and Eastern Europe," *The Origins of Backwardness in Eastern Europe: Economics and Politics from the Middle Ages until the Early Twentieth Century,* edited by Daniel Chirot (Berkeley: University of California Press, 1989), pp. 63–66. See also Jean W. Sedlar, *East Central Europe in the Middle Ages, 1000–1500,* pp. 17, 326, 417.
4. Jean W. Sedlar, *East Central Europe in the Middle Ages, 1000–1500,* pp. 115, 126, 131.
5. Ibid., pp. 288, 402, 410–411.
6. Robert Bartlett, *The Making of Europe: Conquest, Colonization and Cultural Change, 950–1350* (Princeton, N.J.: Princeton University Press, 1993), p. 235.
7. Ibid., p. 124.

8. Ibid., p. 349.
9. Ibid., pp. 229–230, 266, 267.
10. Carlo M. Cipolla, *Clocks and Culture: 1300–1700* (New York: Norton, 1978), p. 31.
11. Ibid., p. 117.
12. Ibid., p. 52.
13. Ibid.
14. Ibid., p. 117.
15. Victor Wolfgang von Hagen, *The Germanic People in America* (Norman: Oklahoma University Press, 1976), p. 83. See also Albert Bernhardt Faust, *The German Element in the United States,* Volume I (New York: Arno Press, 1969), pp. 54–58.
16. Gordon Craig, *The Germans* (New York: G. P. Putnam and Sons, 1982), p. 20.
17. Hattie Plum Williams, *The Czar's Germans: With Particular Reference to the Volga Germans* (Lincoln, Neb.: American Historical Society of Germans from Russia, 1975), pp. 10, 12.
18. Virginia Brainard Kunz, *The Germans in America* (Minneapolis: Lerner Publications Company, 1966), p. 9.
19. Fred C. Koch, *The Volga Germans: In Russia and the Americas, from 1763 to the Present* (University Park: Pennsylvania State University Press, 1978), p. 8.
20. Ibid., p. 26.
21. Wolfgang Köllman and Peter Marschalck, "German Emigration to the United States," translated by Thomas C. Childers, *Perspectives in American History,* Vol. VII (1973), p. 518.
22. W. O. Henderson, *The Rise of German Industrial Power: 1834–1914* (Berkeley: University of California Press, 1975), p. 23.
23. Ibid., pp. 24, 29.
24. Ibid., p. 24.
25. Ibid., pp. 25, 27.
26. Ibid., p. 44.
27. Ibid., p. 26.
28. Ibid., p. 25.
29. Ibid., p. 44.
30. Ibid., pp. 53, 57.
31. Ibid., p. 53.
32. Ibid., p. 55.
33. Ibid., p. 49.
34. B. R. Mitchell, *European Historical Statistics, 1750–1970,* abridged edi-

tion (New York: Columbia University Press, 1975), p. 223.

35. Ibid., pp. 224, 225.
36. William Chase Greene, *The Achievement of Rome: A Chapter in Civilization* (New York: Cooper Square Publishers, Inc., 1973), p. 85.
37. Adam Giesinger, *From Catherine to Khrushchev: The Story of Russia's Germans* (Lincoln, Neb.: American Historical Society of Germans from Russia, 1974), pp. 143–144.
38. Larry V. Thompson, book review, *Journal of Latin American Studies,* May 1976, p. 159. See also Victor Wolfgang von Hagen, *The Germanic People in America,* pp. 242–243, 270; Ronald C. Newton, *German Buenos Aires, 1900–1933: Social Change and Cultural Crisis* (Austin: University of Texas Press, 1977), pp. 7–8, 22.
39. Albert Bernhardt Faust, *The German Element in the United States,* Volume I, pp. 320–327; Virginia Brainard Kunz, *The Germans in America,* pp. 48–51, 55, 60–61.
40. T. N. Dupuy, *A Genius for War: The German Army and General Staff, 1807–1945* (Englewood Cliffs, N.J.: Prentice-Hall, 1977), p. 4.
41. Carlo M. Cipolla, *Literacy and Development in the West* (New York: Penguin, 1969), pp. 24, 28, 30–31, 70.
42. Carlo M. Cipolla, *Literacy and Development in the West,* p. 17; Richard Sallet, *Russian-German Settlements in the United States,* p. 14; Frederick C. Luebke, *Germans in Brazil: A Comparative History of Cultural Conflict during World War I* (Baton Rouge: Louisiana State University Press, 1987), p. 50.
43. Victor Wolfgang von Hagen, *The Germanic People in America,* p. 326; Alfred Dolge, *Pianos and Their Makers* (Covina, Calif.: Covina Publishing Company, 1911), pp. 172, 264; Edwin M. Good, *Giraffes, Black Dragons, and Other Pianos: A Technological History from Cristofori to the Modern Concert Grand* (Stanford, Calif.: Stanford University Press, 1982), p. 137n; W. D. Borrie, "Australia," *The Positive Contribution by Immigrants,* edited by Oscar Handlin (Paris: United Nations Educational, Scientific, and Cultural Organization, 1955), p. 94.
44. Fernand Braudel, *The Mediterranean and the Mediterranean World in the Age of Philip II,* translated by Sian Reynolds, Volume I (New York: Harper & Row, 1972), p. 189.
45. Beer Institute, *Brewer's Almanac: 1992* (Washington, D.C.: Beer Institute, 1992), p. 1.
46. La Vern J. Rippley, "Germans from Russia," *Harvard Encyclopedia of American Ethnic Groups,* edited by Stephan Thernstrom et al. (Cambridge, Mass.: Harvard University Press, 1981), p. 426.

47. Richard Sallet, *Russian-German Settlements in the United States,* translated by La Vern J. Rippley and Armand Bauer (Fargo: North Dakota Institute for Regional Studies, 1974), p. 13.
48. Ingeborg Fleischhauer, "The Germans' Role in Tsarist Russia: A Reappraisal," *The Soviet Germans: Past and Present,* edited by Edith Rogovin Frankel (New York: St. Martin's, 1986), p. 13.
49. See, for example, Richard Sallet, *Russian-German Settlements in the United States,* translated by LaVern J. Rippley and Armand Bauer, p. 3.
50. John A. Armstrong, "Mobilized Diaspora in Tsarist Russia: The Case of the Baltic Germans," *Soviet Nationality Policies and Practices,* edited by Jeremy R. Azrael (New York: Praeger Publishers, 1978), pp. 63–64.
51. Adam Giesinger, *From Catherine to Khrushchev,* p. 139. See also Robert P. Bartlett, *Human Capital: The Settlement of Foreigners in Russia 1762–1804* (Cambridge: Cambridge University Press, 1979), p. 89.
52. Ingeborg Fleischhauer, "The Germans' Role in Tsarist Russia: A Reappraisal," *The Soviet Germans,* edited by Edith Rogovin Frankel, p. 16.
53. See Robert Bartlett, *The Making of Europe,* p. 194; Anders Henriksson, *The Tsar's Loyal Germans* (New York: Columbia University Press, 1983), pp. x, 1.
54. Frederic T. Harned, "Latvia and the Latvians," *Handbook of Major Soviet Nationalities,* edited by Zev Katz et al. (New York: The Free Press, 1975), p. 94.
55. N. J. G. Pounds, *An Historical Geography of Europe* (Cambridge: Cambridge University Press, 1990), p. 205.
56. Ingeborg Fleischhauer, "The Germans' Role in Tsarist Russia: A Reappraisal," *The Soviet Germans,* edited by Edith Rogovin Frankel, p. 16.
57. Anders Henriksson, *The Tsar's Loyal Germans,* pp. 1, 4.
58. John A. Armstrong, "Mobilized Diaspora in Tsarist Russia," *Soviet Nationality Policies and Practices,* edited by Jeremy R. Azrael, p. 68; Richard Sallet, *Russian-German Settlements in the United States,* translated by La Vern J. Rippley and Armand Bauer, p. 14.
59. Richard Sallet, *Russian-German Settlements in the United States,* translated by La Vern J. Rippley and Armand Bauer, p. 14.
60. John A. Armstrong, "Socializing for Modernization in a Multiethnic Elite," *Entrepreneurship in Imperial Russia and the Soviet Union,* edited by Gregory Guroff and Fred V. Carstensen (Princeton, N.J.: Princeton University Press, 1983), p. 99.
61. Ingeborg Fleischhauer, "The Germans' Role in Tsarist Russia: A Reappraisal," *The Soviet Germans,* edited by Edith Rogovin Frankel, pp. 17–18.

62. Fred C. Koch, *The Volga Germans,* p. 195.
63. John A. Armstrong, "Mobilized Diaspora in Tsarist Russia," *Soviet Nationality Policies and Practices,* edited by Jeremy R. Azrael, p. 68.
64. John A. Armstrong, "Socializing for Modernization in a Multiethnic Elite," *Entrepreneurship in Imperial Russia and the Soviet Union,* edited by Gregory Guroff and Fred V. Carstensen, p. 100.
65. Adam Giesinger, *From Catherine to Khrushchev,* p. 153.
66. John A. Armstrong, "Mobilized Diaspora in Tsarist Russia," *Soviet Nationality Policies and Practices,* edited by Jeremy R. Azrael, pp. 95–96.
67. Adam Giesinger, *From Catherine to Khrushchev,* p. 143.
68. Anders Henriksson, *The Tsar's Loyal Germans,* p. 2.
69. Ibid., p. 37.
70. Ibid., p. 2.
71. John A. Armstrong, "Mobilized Diaspora in Tsarist Russia," *Soviet Nationality Policies and Practices,* edited by Jeremy R. Azrael, p. 69.
72. Earlier, there was anti-Latvian discrimination. Roger P. Bartlett, *Human Capital,* p. 89.
73. Anders Henriksson, *The Tsar's Loyal Germans,* pp. 15, 35, 54.
74. Ibid., p. 35.
75. Gary B. Cohen, *The Politics of Ethnic Survival: Germans in Prague, 1861–1914* (Princeton, N.J.: Princeton University Press, 1981), pp. 24–26.
76. Anders Henriksson, *The Tsar's Loyal Germans,* p. 50.
77. Ibid., pp. 55–56.
78. Ibid., p. 59.
79. Ibid., pp. 61–62.
80. Timothy J. Kloberdanz, "Plainsmen of Three Continents: Volga German Adaptation to Steppe, Prairie, and Pampa," *Ethnicity on the Great Plains,* edited by Frederick C. Luebke (Lincoln: University of Nebraska Press, 1980), p. 55.
81. Fred C. Koch, *The Volga Germans,* p. 19.
82. Hattie Plum Williams, *The Czar's Germans,* pp. 120–122.
83. Fred C. Koch, *The Volga Germans,* p. 25.
84. Adam Giesinger, *From Catherine to Khrushchev,* p. 16.
85. Hattie Plum Williams, *The Czar's Germans,* p. 117.
86. Fred C. Koch, *The Volga Germans,* pp. 40–42.
87. Ibid., p. 47.
88. Ibid., pp. 35–36.
89. Hattie Plum Williams, *The Czar's Germans,* pp. xi–xii; Fred C. Koch,

The Volga Germans, p. 212. As late as 1900, virtually all the Russian-born individuals in North Dakota were German-speaking. Frederick C. Luebke, "Introduction," *Ethnicity on the Great Plains,* edited by Frederick C. Luebke, p. xviii.

90. Timothy J. Kloberdanz, "Plainsmen of Three Continents," ibid., pp. 56–57.
91. Timothy J. Kloberdanz, "Plainsmen of Three Continents," ibid., pp. 58–59.
92. Fred C. Koch, *The Volga Germans,* pp. 64–65.
93. Ibid., p. 69.
94. Ibid., p. 83.
95. Ibid., p. 176.
96. Ingeborg Fleischhauer, "The Germans' Role in Tsarist Russia: A Reappraisal," *The Soviet Germans,* edited by Edith Rogovin Frankel, p. 20.
97. Timothy J. Kloberdanz, "Plainsmen of Three Continents," *Ethnicity on the Great Plains,* edited by Frederick C. Luebke, p. 55.
98. Hattie Plum Williams, *The Czar's Germans,* p. 141.
99. Fred C. Koch, *The Volga Germans,* p. 98.
100. Hattie Plum Williams, *The Czar's Germans,* p. 141.
101. Ibid., p. 146; Fred C. Koch, *The Volga Germans,* p. 62.
102. Fred C. Koch, *The Volga Germans,* pp. 64–65.
103. Hattie Plum Williams, *The Czar's Germans,* p. 159.
104. Fred C. Koch, *The Volga Germans,* p. 54.
105. Ibid., p. 55.
106. Ibid., p. 33.
107. Timothy J. Kloberdanz, "Plainsmen of Three Continents," *Ethnicity on the Great Plains,* edited by Frederick C. Luebke, pp. 60–61.
108. Adam Giesinger, *From Catherine to Khrushchev,* pp. 94–95.
109. Ibid., pp. 63–65.
110. Ibid., p. 62.
111. Ibid., pp. 62–63.
112. Richard Sallet, *Russian-German Settlements in the United States,* translated by La Vern J. Rippley and Armand Bauer, p. 4. See also Adam Giesinger, *From Catherine to Khrushchev,* pp. 71–72.
113. Adam Giesinger, *From Catherine to Khrushchev,* p. 72.
114. Ingeborg Fleischhauer, "The Germans' Role in Tsarist Russia: A Reappraisal," *The Soviet Germans,* edited by Edith Rogovin Frankel, p. 21.
115. Adam Giesinger, *From Catherine to Khrushchev,* p. 229.
116. Ibid., pp. 230–234.

117. Ibid., p. 223.
118. Karl Stumpp, *The German-Russians: Two Centuries of Pioneering* (Bonn: Edition Atlantic-Forum, 1966), pp. 140–141.
119. Ibid., p. 28.
120. Ibid., pp. 8–9.
121. Adam Giesinger, *From Catherine to Khrushchev,* p. 249.
122. Fred C. Koch, *The Volga Germans,* p. 257.
123. Adam Giesinger, *From Catherine to Khrushchev,* p. 261.
124. Fred C. Koch, *The Volga Germans,* pp. 258–259.
125. Ibid., p. 263.
126. Adam Giesinger, *From Catherine to Khrushchev,* p. 259.
127. Ibid., p. 260.
128. Fred C. Koch, *The Volga Germans,* pp. 266–267.
129. Ibid., pp. 281–282.
130. Ingeborg Fleischhauer, "The Germans' Role in Tsarist Russia: A Reappraisal," *The Soviet Germans,* edited by Edith Rogovin Frankel, p. 29; Benjamin Pinkus, "From the October Revolution to the Second World War," ibid., p. 32.
131. Benjamin Pinkus, "From the October Revolution to the Second World War," ibid., pp. 44, 46–47.
132. Ibid., p. 61.
133. Ibid., p. 88.
134. Fred C. Koch, *The Volga Germans,* p. 294.
135. Ibid., p. 298.
136. Ibid., p. 226.
137. Anthony Hyman, "Refugees and Citizens: The Case of the Volga Germans," *The World Today,* Vol. 48 (March 1992), pp. 41–43.
138. Adam Giesinger, *From Catherine to Khrushchev,* pp. 262–263.
139. Ibid., p. 267.
140. Ibid., pp. 287–288.
141. Ibid., p. 307.
142. Ibid., p. 311.
143. Ibid., pp. 313–314.
144. Benjamin Pinkus, "The Germans in the Soviet Union since 1945," *The Soviet Germans,* edited by Edith Rogovin Frankel, pp. 106, 106n.
145. Ibid., pp. 119–120.
146. Ibid., pp. 121–122.
147. Ibid., p. 122.
148. Ibid., pp. 122–125.

149. Ibid., p. 118.
150. Adam Giesinger, *From Catherine to Khrushchev,* p. 335.
151. Karl Stumpp, *The German-Russians,* p. 144.
152. Benjamin Pinkus, "The Germans in the Soviet Union since 1945," *The Soviet Germans,* edited by Edith Rogovin Frankel, p. 138.
153. Ibid., pp. 125–127.
154. Ibid., p. 132.
155. Anthony Hyman, "Refugees and Citizens: The Case of the Volga Germans," *The World Today,* Vol. 48 (March 1992), p. 41.
156. Myron Weiner, *The Global Migration Crisis: Challenge to States and to Human Rights* (New York: HarperCollins, 1995), p. 58.
157. Hans Jürgen, "Ethnic Germans (*Aussiedler*) from Eastern Europe and the Former Soviet Union in Germany," *Migration World Magazine,* Vol. 22, No. 1, p. 12.
158. Roger P. Bartlett, *Human Capital,* p. xiv.
159. George K. Weissenborn, "Three Hundred Years of German Presence in Canada," *Language and Society,* Spring 1983, p. 16.
160. Richard Sallet, *Russian-German Settlements in the United States,* translated by La Vern J. Rippley and Armand Bauer, p. 17.
161. Fred C. Koch, *The Volga Germans,* p. 3.
162. Ibid., p. 226.
163. Iris Barbara Graefe, "Cultural Changes among Germans from Russia in Argentina, 1967–1977," *Germans from Russia in Colorado,* edited by Sidney Heitman (Fort Collins, Colo.: The Western Social Science Association, 1978), p. 64.
164. Ibid., p. 58.
165. Harry Leonard Sawatzky, *They Sought a Country: Mennonite Colonization in Mexico* (Berkeley: University of California Press, 1971), passim.
166. Victor Wolfgang von Hagen, *The Germanic People in America,* p. 270.
167. Ibid., p. 75.
168. Christopher Hibbert, *The English: A Social History, 1066–1954* (New York: Norton, 1987), p. 175.
169. Victor Wolfgang von Hagen, *The Germanic People in America,* pp. 13, 14, 17.
170. Ibid., p. 77.
171. Ibid., p. 72.
172. Ibid., p. 105.
173. Ronald C. Newton, *German Buenos Aires, 1900–1933,* p. 9.
174. Ibid., p. 21.

175. Thomas W. Merrick and Douglas H. Graham, *Population and Economic Development in Brazil: 1800 to the Present* (Baltimore: Johns Hopkins University Press, 1979), p. 91.
176. See, for example, George F. W. Young, *Germans in Chile: Immigration and Colonization, 1849–1914* (Staten Island, N.Y.: The Center for Migration Studies, 1974), Chapters II, III, IV, V.
177. Markos J. Mamalakis, *The Growth and Structure of the Chilean Economy: From Independence to Allende* (New Haven, Conn.: Yale University Press, 1976), pp. 76–77. See also William Walter Sywak, "Values in Nineteenth-Century Chilean Education: The Germanic Reform of Chilean Public Education," Ph.D. dissertation, University of California at Los Angeles, 1977.
178. A quarter of a million immigrants came from Germany to the United States in 1882. U.S. Bureau of the Census, *Historical Statistics of the United States: Colonial Times to 1970* (Washington, D.C.: U.S. Government Printing Office, 1975), p. 106.
179. Glenn G. Gilbert, *The German Language in America: A Symposium* (Austin: University of Texas Press, 1971), pp. viii–ix.
180. Kathleen Neils Conzen, "Germans," *Harvard Encyclopedia of American Ethnic Groups,* edited by Stephan Thernstrom et al., p. 406.
181. Ibid., p. 407.
182. Albert Bernhardt Faust, *The German Element in the United States,* Volume I, pp. 36, 43.
183. Ibid., pp. 36, 37, 38, 39, 40–41, 45–46.
184. Frederick Merk, *History of the Westward Movement* (New York: Knopf, 1978), p. 49.
185. Albert Bernhardt Faust, *The German Element in the United States,* Volume I, pp. 131–139, 147–148, passim.
186. Ibid., pp. 98–99, 103, 112, 232, 240, 278, 392, 396, 463; Joseph Wandel, *The German Dimension of American History* (Chicago: Nelson-Hall Inc., 1979), pp. 15, 16, 20, 27, 51, 65.
187. R. L. Biesle, "The Relations between the German Settlers and the Indians in Texas, 1844–1860," *Southwestern Historical Quarterly,* July 1927, pp. 116–129.
188. Albert Bernhardt Faust, *The German Element in the United States,* Volume I, pp. 199, 213–214, 268–269, 270–271, 280, 305, 309, 310, 316–319, 371, 376, 393, 394, 402–403, 415, 484, 489, 491.
189. Ibid., pp. 320–328.
190. Ibid., p. 517.
191. Joseph Wandel, *The German Dimension of American History,* p. 187.

192. Thomas Sowell, *Ethnic America: A History* (New York: Basic Books, 1981), p. 57.
193. Albert Bernhardt Faust, *The German Element in the United States,* Volume I, pp. 447–448.
194. John Fredrick Nau, *The German People of New Orleans, 1850–1900* (Leiden: E. J. Brill, 1958), p. 9.
195. Ibid., p. 12.
196. Ibid., pp. 59, 68.
197. Kathleen Neils Conzen, "Germans," *Harvard Encyclopedia of American Ethnic Groups,* edited by Stephan Thernstrom et al., p. 412.
198. "The Great Melting Pot," *U.S. News and World Report,* July 7, 1986, p. 30.
199. Walter Kamphoefner, "Transplanted Westfalians: Persistence and Transformation of Socioeconomic and Cultural Patterns in the Northwest German Migration to Missouri," unpublished Ph.D. dissertation, University of Missouri (Columbia), 1978, especially Chapter 6.
200. Walter D. Kamphoefner, "The German Agricultural Frontier: Crucible or Cocoon," *Ethnic Forum,* Spring 1984, p. 25.
201. Theodore Huebener, *The Germans in America* (Philadelphia: Chilton Company, 1962), p. 84; Hildegard Binder Johnson, "The Location of German Immigrants in the Middle West," *Annals of the Association of American Geographers,* March 1951, pp. 24–25.
202. Joseph Wandel, *The German Dimension of American History,* p. 56.
203. Richard Sallet, *Russian-German Settlements in the United States,* translated by La Vern J. Rippley and Armand Bauer, pp. 21–32, 35–53.
204. Ibid., pp. 28, 31, 37, 74.
205. Ibid., p. 77; Douglas Hale, *The Germans from Russia in Oklahoma* (Norman: University of Oklahoma Press, 1980), p. 15. Kiel's name was changed to Loyal during the anti-German hysteria of World War I. Richard C. Rohrs, *The Germans in Oklahoma* (Norman: University of Oklahoma Press, 1980), p. 47.
206. Richard Sallet, *Russian-German Settlements in the United States,* p. 30.
207. La Vern J. Rippley, "Germans from Russia," *Harvard Encyclopedia of American Ethnic Groups,* edited by Stephan Thernstrom et al., p. 427.
208. Timothy J. Kloberdanz, "Plainsmen of Three Continents," *Ethnicity on the Great Plains,* edited by Frederick C. Luebke, p. 63.
209. Richard Sallet, *Russian-German Settlements in the United States,* p. 49.
210. Ibid., p. 40.
211. LaVern J. Rippley, "Germans from Russia," *Harvard Encyclopedia of American Ethnic Groups,* edited by Stephan Thernstrom et al., p. 427.

212. Timothy J. Kloberdanz, "Plainsmen of Three Continents," *Ethnicity on the Great Plains,* edited by Frederick C. Luebke, pp. 62–63.
213. Ibid., pp. 63–64.
214. Terry G. Jordan, *German Seed in Texas Soil* (Austin: University of Texas Press, 1982), p. 108.
215. Fred C. Koch, *The Volga Germans,* pp. 214–215; Richard Sallet, *Russian-German Settlements in the United States,* pp. 42–62.
216. Richard C. Rohrs, *The Germans in Oklahoma,* passim; Douglas Hale, *The Germans from Russia in Oklahoma,* passim.
217. Maldwyn Allen Jones, *American Immigration* (Chicago: University of Chicago Press, 1970), p. 118; Hildegard Binder Johnson, "The Location of German Immigrants in the Middle West," *Annals of the Association of American Geographers,* March 1951, p. 4.
218. Albert Bernhardt Faust, *The German Element in the United States,* Volume I, p. 426.
219. Kathleen Neils Conzen, *Immigrant Milwaukee, 1836–1860: Accommodation and Community in a Frontier City* (Cambridge, Mass.: Harvard University Press, 1976), p. 14.
220. Carl Wittke, *The Germans in America* (New York: Columbia University Teachers College Press, 1967), p. 9.
221. Walter Kamphoefner, "The German Agricultural Frontier: Crucible or Cocoon," *Ethnic Forum,* Spring 1984, pp. 21–35.
222. Carl Wittke, *We Who Built America: The Saga of the Immigrant* (Cleveland: The Press of Case Western Reserve University, 1967), pp. 207–208.
223. J. C. Furnas, *The Americans: A Social History of the United States 1587–1914* (New York: G. P. Putnam and Sons, 1969), p. 390.
224. Carl Wittke, *We Who Built America,* pp. 225–226.
225. Kathleen Neils Conzen, "Germans," *Harvard Encyclopedia of American Ethnic Groups,* edited by Stephan Thernstrom et al., p. 420.
226. Terry G. Jordan, "A Religious Geography of the Hill Country Germans of Texas," *Ethnicity on the Great Plains,* edited by Frederick C. Luebke, pp. 114, 116.
227. Ibid., p. 416; Carl Wittke, *We Who Built America,* p. 207.
228. Albert Bernhardt Faust, *The German Element in the United States* (New York: Arno Press, 1969), Volume II, pp. 250–293.
229. Kathleen Neils Conzen, *Immigrant Milwaukee,* p. 73.
230. R. A. Burchell, *The San Francisco Irish, 1848–1880* (Berkeley: University of California Press, 1980), p. 60.
231. Victor Wolfgang von Hagen, *The Germanic People in America,* p. 322.
232. Kathleen Neils Conzen, *Immigrant Milwaukee,* p. 69.

233. Albert Bernhardt Faust, *The German Element in the United States,* Volume I, pp. 45–46, 182, 242; Carl Wittke, *The German Language Press in America* (New York: Haskell House Publishers Ltd., 1973), pp. 51–52, 79, 82, 85, 100–101, 110–111, 115, 121, 122, 124, 135–137, 149, 152–153, 154, 180; Carl Wittke, *We Who Built America,* p. 233.
234. James M. Berquist, "The Mid-Nineteenth Century Slavery Crisis and German Americans," *States of Progress,* edited by Randall M. Miller (Philadelphia: The German Society of Philadelphia, 1989), pp. 55–71.
235. Ibid., p. 57.
236. Thomas Sowell, *Ethnic America,* pp. 191–192. See also John Hope Franklin, *The Free Negro in North Carolina, 1790–1860* (New York: Norton, 1971), pp. 8, 114–115.
237. Virginia Brainard Kunz, *The Germans in America,* p. 50.
238. Albert Bernhardt Faust, *The German Element in the United States,* Volume II, pp. 146, 148.
239. Carl Wittke, *We Who Built America,* p. 329.
240. Kathleen Neils Conzen, "Germans," *Harvard Encyclopedia of American Ethnic Groups,* edited by Stephan Thernstrom et al., p. 410.
241. Hartmut Keil, "Chicago's German Working Class in 1900," *German Workers in Industrial Chicago, 1850–1910: A Comparative Perspective,* edited by Hartmut Keil and John B. Jentz (DeKalb: Northern Illinois University Press, 1983), pp. 24–29; Nora Faires, "Occupational Patterns of German-Americans in Nineteenth-Century Cities," ibid., pp. 37–51.
242. Carl Wittke, *We Who Built America,* p. 247.
243. Kathleen Neils Conzen, "Germans," *Harvard Encyclopedia of American Ethnic Groups,* edited by Stephan Thernstrom et al., p. 423.
244. Virginia Brainard Kunz, *The Germans in America,* p. 54.
245. Charles H. Anderson, *White Protestant Americans* (Englewood Cliffs, N.J.: Prentice-Hall, 1970) p. 85; U.S. Bureau of Census, *Current Population Reports,* series P-20, no. 221 (Washington, D.C.: U.S. Government Printing Office, 1971), p. 7.
246. Albert Bernhardt Faust, *The German Element in the United States,* Volume II, p. 371; Kathleen Neils Conzen, "Germans," *Harvard Encyclopedia of American Ethnic Groups,* edited by Stephan Thernstrom et al., p. 423.
247. Fred C. Koch, *The Volga Germans,* pp. 222–226; E. Bradford Burns, *A History of Brazil* (New York: Columbia University Press, 1970), p. 186; Jean Roche, *La Colonisation Allemande et le Rio Grande do Sul* (Paris: Institute des Hautes Études de L'Amérique Latine, 1959), p. 115.

248. Hans Juergen Hoyer, "Germans in Paraguay, 1881–1945: A Study of Cultural and Social Isolation," unpublished Ph.D. dissertation, American University, 1973, pp. 4–11.
249. Jean Roche, *La Colonisation Allemande et le Rio Grande do Sul,* p. 123.
250. Ibid., p. 78.
251. Ibid., p. 125.
252. T. Lynn Smith, *Brazil: People and Institutions* (Baton Rouge: Louisiana State University Press, 1972), pp. 134–135. See also Preston E. James, "The Expanding Settlements of Southern Brazil," *Geographical Review,* October 1940, p. 609; Jean Roche, *La Colonisation Allemande et le Rio Grande do Sul,* p. 134.
253. Jean Roche, *La Colonisation Allemande et le Rio Grande do Sul,* pp. 125, 128–131.
254. Preston E. James, "The Expanding Settlements of Southern Brazil," *Geographical Review,* October 1940, p. 608. See also Terry G. Jordan, "Aspects of German Colonization in Southern Brazil," *Southwestern Social Science Quarterly,* March 1962, p. 348.
255. Preston E. James, "The Expanding Settlements of Southern Brazil," *Geographical Review,* October 1940, pp. 613, 616; Charles Wagley, *An Introduction to Brazil* (New York: Columbia University Press, 1971), p. 79.
256. T. Lynn Smith, *Brazil,* p. 134.
257. Thomas W. Merrick and Douglas H. Graham, *Population and Economic Development in Brazil: 1800 to the Present,* p. 111.
258. Terry G. Jordan, "Aspects of German Colonization in Southern Brazil," *Southwestern Social Science Quarterly,* March 1962, p. 350.
259. Rollie E. Poppino, *Brazil: The Land and the People* (New York: Oxford University Press, 1973), pp. 186–187.
260. Terry G. Jordan, "Aspects of German Colonization in Southern Brazil," *Southwestern Social Science Quarterly,* March 1962, p. 350.
261. T. Lynn Smith, *Brazil,* pp. 134–135.
262. Preston E. James, "The Expanding Settlements of Southern Brazil," *Geographical Review,* October 1940, p. 617.
263. T. Lynn Smith, *Brazil,* p. 134.
264. Terry G. Jordan, "Aspects of German Colonization in Southern Brazil," *Southwestern Social Science Quarterly,* March 1962, pp. 349–350; Fred C. Koch, *The Volga Germans,* pp. 225–226; Timothy J. Kloberdanz, "Plainsmen of Three Continents," *Ethnicity on the Great Plains,* edited by Frederick C. Luebke, pp. 65–66.
265. Fred C. Koch, *The Volga Germans,* p. 227.
266. Timothy J. Kloberdanz, "Plainsmen on Three Continents," *Ethnicity on*

the Great Plains, edited by Frederick C. Luebke, p. 66.

267. Charles Wagley, *An Introduction to Brazil,* p. 78; Preston E. James, "The Expanding Settlements in Southern Brazil," *Geographical Review,* October 1940, pp. 619–620; Fred C. Koch, *The Volga Germans,* p. 226.
268. Preston E. James, "The Expanding Settlements of Southern Brazil," *Geographical Review,* October 1940, p. 620.
269. Hans Juergen Hoyer, "Germans in Paraguay, 1881–1945," pp. 5, 6, 9.
270. Preston E. James, "The Expanding Settlements of Southern Brazil," *Geographical Review,* October 1940, pp. 618–619.
271. Frederick C. Luebke, *Germans in Brazil: A Comparative History of Cultural Conflict during World War I* (Baton Rouge: Louisiana State University Press, 1987), p. 57.
272. Jean Roche, *La Colonisation Allemande et le Rio Grande do Sul,* p. 585. See also Leo Waibel, "European Colonization in Southern Brazil," *Geographical Review,* October 1959, pp. 532–536.
273. Jean Roche, *La Colonisation Allemande et le Rio Grande do Sul,* pp. 215–219.
274. Leo Waibel, "European Colonization in Southern Brazil," *Geographical Review,* October 1950, p. 532.
275. Jean Roche, *La Colonisation Allemande et le Rio Grande do Sul,* pp. 225–226.
276. Eric N. Baklanoff, "External Factors in the Economic Development of Brazil's Heartland: The Center-South, 1850–1930," *The Shaping of Modern Brazil,* edited by Eric N. Baklanoff (Baton Rouge: Louisiana State University Press, 1969), p. 30; Frederick C. Luebke, "A Prelude to Conflict: The German Ethnic Group in Brazilian Society, 1890–1917," *Ethnic and Racial Studies,* January 1983, p. 3.
277. Emilio Willems, "Brazil," *The Positive Contribution by Immigrants,* edited by Oscar Handlin et al., p. 124.
278. Rollie E. Poppino, *Brazil,* pp. 186–187.
279. Preston E. James, "The Expanding Settlements of Southern Brazil," *Geographical Review,* October 1940, p. 612.
280. Thomas H. Holloway, *Immigrants on the Land: Coffee and Society in São Paulo, 1886–1934* (Chapel Hill: University of North Carolina Press, 1980), pp. 150–161.
281. Preston E. James, "The Expanding Settlements of Southern Brazil," *Geographical Review,* October 1940, pp. 613–614, 625; Charles Wagley, *An Introduction to Brazil,* p. 79; Reinhard Maack, "The Germans of South Brazil: A German View," *Quarterly Journal of Inter-American Relations,* July 1939, p. 11. See also Terry G. Jordan, "Aspects of German Colo-

nization in Southern Brazil," *Southwestern Social Science Quarterly*, March 1962, pp. 346, 348.

282. Jean Roche, *La Colonisation Allemande et le Rio Grande do Sul*, p. 585.
283. Hans Juergen Hoyer, "Germans in Paraguay, 1881–1945," p. 10.
284. Jean Roche, *La Colonisation Allemande et le Rio Grande do Sul*, pp. 483–484, 487.
285. Ibid., pp. 449, 488.
286. Ibid., pp. 499–500.
287. Frederick C. Luebke, *Germans in Brazil*, pp. 64, 66.
288. Jean Roche, *La Colonisation Allemande et le Rio Grande do Sul*, p. 126.
289. Ibid., p. 127.
290. Ibid., pp. 133, 134.
291. Ibid., pp. 362–384.
292. Ibid., pp. 385–386.
293. Ibid., pp. 388–389.
294. Ibid., p. 147.
295. Ibid.
296. Ibid., p. 197.
297. Ibid., p. 338.
298. Ibid., p. 335.
299. Ibid., pp. 322–323.
300. Ibid., pp. 335–339.
301. Ibid., pp. 339–340.
302. Ibid., p. 445.
303. Ibid., p. 460.
304. Ibid., p. 457.
305. Ibid., pp. 457, 459.
306. Ibid., p. 66.
307. Frederick C. Luebke, "The German Ethnic Group in Brazil: The Ordeal of World War II," paper presented to the 1982 Annual Meeting of the American Historical Association, pp. 7–9; Frederick C. Luebke, *Germans in Brazil*, pp. 106–111.
308. Frederick C. Luebke, "The German Ethnic Group in Brazil," pp. 9–10; Frederick C. Luebke, *Germans in Brazil*, Chapters 5, 7.
309. Frederick C. Luebke, *Germans in Brazil*, p. 199.
310. Frederick C. Luebke, "The German Ethnic Group in Brazil," p. 12.
311. Jean Roche, *La Colonisation Allemande et le Rio Grande do Sul*, p. 539.
312. Frederick C. Luebke, "The German Ethnic Group in Brazil," p. 14. See also Jean Roche, *La Colonisation Allemande et le Rio Grande do Sul*, p. 539.

313. Thomas W. Merrick and Douglas H. Graham, *Population and Economic Development in Brazil: 1800 to the Present,* p. 91.
314. Emilio Willems, "Brazil," *The Positive Contribution by Immigrants,* edited by Oscar Handlin et al., p. 127.
315. Jean Roche, *La Colonisation Allemande et le Rio Grande do Sul,* pp. 391–392.
316. Ibid., p. 407.
317. Emilio Willems, "Brazil," *The Positive Contribution by Immigrants,* edited by Oscar Handlin et al., p. 129.
318. Jean Roche, *La Colonisation Allemande et le Rio Grande do Sul,* p. 540.
319. Ibid., p. 449.
320. Ibid., pp. 541–542; Richard F. Behrendt, "Germans in Latin America," *Inter-American Monthly,* April 1943, p. 23.
321. Jean Roche, *La Colonisation Allemande et le Rio Grande do Sul,* pp. 545–546.
322. Ibid., pp. 547–548.
323. Ibid., pp. 551, 557, 587.
324. Ibid., pp. 551–575.
325. Ibid., pp. 456–468.
326. Emilio Willems, "Brazil," *The Positive Contribution by Immigrants,* edited by Oscar Handlin et al., p. 133.
327. Rollie E. Poppino, *Brazil,* pp. 31–35.
328. Hans Juergen Hoyer, "Germans in Paraguay, 1881–1945," p. iii.
329. Philip Raine, *Paraguay* (New Brunswick, N.J.: Scarecrow Press, 1956), pp. 298–299, 302.
330. Ibid., p. 295.
331. Ibid., pp. 91, 99, 103, 111.
332. Ibid., pp. 297–305; Hans Juergen Hoyer, "Germans in Paraguay, 1881–1945," pp. 43, 50.
333. Hans Juergen Hoyer, "Germans in Paraguay, 1881–1945," pp. 44–47.
334. Philip Raine, *Paraguay,* p. 301; Fred C. Koch, *The Volga Germans,* pp. 231–232.
335. Hans Juergen Hoyer, "Germans in Paraguay, 1881–1945," pp. 46, 49, 51–56.
336. Ibid., pp. 54–55.
337. Fred C. Koch, *The Volga Germans,* p. 232.
338. Philip Raine, *Paraguay,* pp. 302–305.
339. Ibid., p. 304.
340. Hans Juergen Hoyer, "Germans in Paraguay, 1881–1945," pp. 76–78.
341. Ibid., pp. 102–103.

342. Ibid., pp. 145–150.
343. Joseph Winfield Fretz, *Immigrant Group Settlements in Paraguay* (North Newton, Kan.: Bethel College, 1962), pp. 62, 95.
344. Ibid., pp. 131–135.
345. Ibid., pp. 115, 134.
346. Ian Harmstorf and Michael Cigler, *The Germans in Australia* (Melbourne: Australasian Educa. Press Pty. Ltd., 1985), pp. 4–5. See also Captain Hahn of the Zebra, *Emigrants to Hahndorf: A Remarkable Voyage* (Adelaide: Lutheran Publishing House, 1988).
347. W. D. Borrie, *Italians and Germans in Australia* (Melbourne: Australian National University, 1954), p. 157.
348. Ibid., p. 158.
349. Charles A. Price, *German Settlers in South Australia* (Melbourne: Melbourne University Press, 1945), pp. 13–15.
350. Author's observations in 1989.
351. Ian Harmstorf and Michael Cigler, *The Germans in Australia,* pp. 18, 20–21, 64–70.
352. Ibid., p. 99.
353. The author bought a copy in December 1989.
354. W. D. Borrie, *Italians and Germans in Australia,* p. 158.
355. Ibid., pp. 164, 165.
356. Ibid., p. 167.
357. Ian Harmstorf and Michael Cigler, *The Germans in Australia,* p. 56.
358. W. D. Borrie, *Italians and Germans in Australia,* pp. 167–170.
359. Ian Harmstorf and Michael Cigler, *The Germans in Australia,* pp. 158–159.
360. Charles A. Price, *German Settlers in South Australia,* pp. 10, 63–64.
361. W. D. Borrie, *Italians and Germans in Australia,* pp. 185–189; R. B. Walker, "Some Social and Political Aspects of German Settlement in Australia to 1914," *Journal of the Royal Australian Historical Society,* March 1975, p. 26.
362. R. B. Walker, "Some Social and Political Aspects of German Settlement in Australia to 1914," *Journal of the Royal Australian Historical Society,* March 1975, p. 28.
363. Ibid., pp. 28–29. See also Ian Harmstorf and Michael Cigler, *The Germans in Australia,* pp. 39–40, 120.
364. R. B. Walker, "Some Social and Political Aspects of German Settlement in Australia to 1914," *Journal of the Royal Australian Historical Society,* March 1975, pp. 36–37.
365. "Germans," *The Australian People: An Encyclopedia of the Nation, Its*

People and Their Origins, edited by James Jupp (North Ryde, Australia: Angus and Robertson Publishers, 1988), p. 485.

366. Ibid., pp. 478, 487; W. D. Borrie, *Italians and Germans in Australia,* pp. 193, 210; Charles A. Price, *German Settlers in South Australia,* pp. 23, 24.
367. W. D. Borrie, *Italians and Germans in Australia,* p. 211.
368. Ibid., p. 192.
369. Ibid., p. 196.
370. Ian Harmstorf and Michael Cigler, *The Germans in Australia,* pp. 75–76.
371. "Germans," *The Australian People,* edited by James Jupp, p. 479.
372. Ibid., p. 486.
373. W. D. Borrie, *Italians and Germans in Australia,* pp. 182, 184.
374. Ibid., p. 188.
375. Ibid., p. 208. See also Ian Harmstorf and Michael Cigler, *The Germans in Australia,* pp. 172–173.
376. Ian Harmstorf and Michael Cigler, *The Germans in Australia,* pp. 129–133.
377. Charles A. Price, *German Settlers in South Australia,* p. 68.
378. W. D. Borrie, *Italians and Germans in Australia,* p. 208.
379. Ibid., p. 153; Charles A. Price, *German Settlers in South Australia,* p. 57.
380. Ian Harmstorf and Michael Cigler, *The Germans in Australia,* p. 63.
381. G. Kinne, "Nazi Stratagems and Their Effects on Germans in Australia up to 1945," *Journal of the Royal Australian Historical Society,* June 1980, p. 8.
382. Ian Harmstorf and Michael Cigler, *The Germans in Australia,* pp. 125–126, 128.
383. R. B. Walker, "Some Social and Political Aspects of German Settlement in Australia to 1914," *Journal of the Royal Australian Historical Society,* March 1975, pp. 32–33, 35.
384. Ibid., p. 27.
385. Ibid., p. 76.
386. Ibid., pp. 77–78.
387. G. Kinne, "Nazi Stratagems and Their Effects on Germans in Australia up to 1945," *Journal of the Royal Australian Historical Society,* June 1980, p. 16.
388. Charles A. Price, *German Settlers in South Australia,* Chapter VI; G. Kinne, "Nazi Stratagems and Their Effects on Germans in Australia up to 1945," *Journal of the Royal Australian Historical Society,* June 1980, pp. 1–19.
389. G. Kinne, "Nazi Stratagems and Their Effects on Germans in Australia

up to 1945," *Journal of the Royal Australian Historical Society,* June 1980, p. 16.

390. Geoffrey Sherington, *Australia's Immigrants* (Sydney: George Allen & Unwin, 1980), pp. 144, 147.
391. Ian Harmstorf and Michael Cigler, *The Germans in Australia,* p. 150.
392. Ibid., pp. 148, 155.
393. Jerzy Zubrzycki, *Settlers of the Latrobe Valley: A Sociological Study of Immigrants in the Brown Coal Industry in Australia* (Canberra: The Australian National University, 1964), pp. 14, 27, 53, 59.
394. See ibid., pp. 74–75.
395. Ibid., pp. 68, 92.
396. Ibid., p. 105.
397. Ibid., pp. 131, 139, 143.
398. Ruth Johnston, "British, German and Polish Immigrants," *Immigrants in Western Australia,* edited by Ruth Johnston (Nedlands, Australia: University of Western Australia Press, 1979), pp. 38, 39, 41, 44.
399. G. T. Kaplan, "Post-war German Immigration," *The Australian People,* edited by James Jupp, p. 498.
400. Ian Harmstorf and Michael Cigler, *The Germans in Australia,* pp. 164, 174.
401. Charles A. Price, "The Ethnic Composition of the Australian Population," *Immigration and Ethnicity in the 1980s,* edited by I. H. Burnley, S. Encel, and Grant McCall (Melbourne: Longman-Cheshire Pty. Ltd., 1985), pp. 48, 51.
402. Helen Ware, *A Profile of the Italian Community in Australia* (Hawthorn, Australia: Citadel Press, 1981), p. 68.
403. Jerzy Zubrzycki, "Cultural Pluralism and Discrimination in Australia: With Special Reference to White Minority Groups," *Case Studies on Human Rights and Fundamental Freedoms: A World Survey,* Volume III, edited by Willem A. Veenhoven and Winifred Crum Ewing (The Hague: Martinus Nijhoff, 1976), p. 407.
404. G. T. Kaplan, "Post-war German Immigration," *The Australian People,* edited by James Jupp, p. 500.
405. See, for example, Gordon Craig, *The Germans,* p. 11; Luigi Barzini, *The Europeans* (New York: Simon & Schuster, 1983), p. 81; Albert Bernhardt Faust, *The German Element in the United States,* Volume I, pp. 130–134; Harry Leonard Sawatsky, *They Sought a Country: Mennonite Colonization in Mexico* (Berkeley: University of California Press, 1970), pp. 344, 356, 365; Roger P. Bartlett, *Human Capital,* p. 214; Charles Wagley, *An*

Introduction to Brazil, p. 79; Arthur Young, *A Tour of Ireland* (Shannon, Ireland: Irish University Press, 1970), Volume I, p. 378.

406. Gordon Craig, *The Germans,* pp. 9–10, 31, 32, 67, 174.
407. Ibid., pp. 9–10, 22, 23, 32, 63, 84–85.
408. Ibid., pp. 170–172.
409. Glenn G. Gilbert, *The German Language in America,* p. xi. Moreover, even after later generations of people in these enclaves began to speak English, their English also often contained archaic words and expressions once peculiar to the local region of the United States where they first learned English. Carroll E. Reed, "The Dialectology of American Colonial German," ibid., pp. 7–8.
410. Carroll E. Reed, "The Dialectology of American Colonial German," ibid., p. 8.
411. Ibid., pp. 22, 32, 84–85, 190–203.
412. Frederick C. Luebke, *Germans in Brazil,* p. 81. There has been a challenge to the idea that Germans in the United States had amicable relations with blacks, or were abolitionist in their view of slavery. See, for example, the papers in *States of Progress,* edited by Randall M. Miller. However, the issue is not whether the Germans met some absolute standard in either their relations with blacks or in their views of slavery. The point is that their record compares favorably with that of other contemporary whites. Even the volume devoted to reassessing the history of Germans' relations with blacks in the United States, and their attitudes toward slavery, does not claim that the Germans were more racist than other whites, and some of the historical facts cited in that volume include the admission of some blacks as members of German churches in colonial Pennsylvania and the Moravians' missionary work among slaves (p. 6), the inclusion of blacks in a predominantly German union in Chicago at the beginning of the twentieth century (pp. 17–18), and the fact that it would be difficult "to find any significant German leaders who were advocates of slavery" during the antebellum era (p. 57).
413. Albert Bernhardt Faust, *The German Element in the United States,* Volume I, pp. 98–99, 103, 104, 112, 213; Volume II, p. 423.
414. Ian Harmstorf and Michael Cigler, *The Germans in Australia,* pp. 49, 80–81.
415. Raphael Patai, *The Vanished Worlds of Jewry* (New York: Macmillan, 1980), p. 57; Daniel L. Niewyk, *The Jews in Weimar Germany* (Baton Rouge: Louisiana State University Press, 1980), p. 98. See also Gary B. Cohen, *The Politics of Ethnic Survival,* pp. 76, 82, 96.

416. Alfred-Maurice de Zayas, *A Terrible Revenge: The Ethnic Cleansing of the East European Germans, 1944–1950* (New York: St. Martin's, 1994).
417. Winston S. Churchill, *Churchill Speaks: Winston S. Churchill in Peace and War, Collected Speeches, 1897–1963,* edited by Robert Rhodes James (New York: Chelsea House, 1980), pp. 882, 890.
418. Roger Thurow, "Bonn's Policy Makers Are Still Handicapped by the Nazis' Misdeeds," *Wall Street Journal,* February 19, 1985, pp. 1ff. See also Henrik Bering Jensen, "Struggling Against the Bonds of History," *Insight,* March 20, 1989, pp. 8–9; idem, "A Nation Haunted Still," ibid., pp. 13–17.

CHAPTER 3: JAPANESE AROUND THE WORLD

1. James L. Tigner, "Japanese Immigration into Latin America: A Survey," *Journal of Interamerican Studies and World Affairs,* Vol. 26, No. 4 (November 1981) p. 457.
2. Yukio Fujii and T. Lynn Smith, *The Acculturation of the Japanese Immigrants in Brazil* (Gainesville: University of Florida Press, 1959), p. 2.
3. Kazuichiro Ono, "The Problem of Japanese Emigration," *Kyoto University Economic Review,* April 1958, pp. 48–49.
4. Ibid., p. 49.
5. James L. Tigner, "Japanese Immigration into Latin America," *Journal of Interamerican Studies and World Affairs,* Vol. 26, No. 4 (November 1981), pp. 459, 463–464.
6. Ibid., pp. 459, 463–464, 468.
7. Ibid., pp. 48–49.
8. Teiiti Suzuki, *The Japanese Immigrant in Brazil* (Tokyo: University of Tokyo Press, 1969), p. 14.
9. James L. Tigner, "Japanese Immigration into Latin America," *Journal of Interamerican Studies and World Affairs,* November 1981, p. 459.
10. Kazuichiro Ono, "The Problem of Japanese Emigration," *Kyoto University Economic Review,* April 1958, p. 49.
11. Yasuo Wakatsuki, "Japanese Emigration to the United States, 1866–1924: A Monograph," *Perspectives in American History,* Vol. XII (1979), p. 465.
12. See, for example, William Petersen, *Japanese Americans: Oppression and Success* (New York: Random House, 1971), pp. 82–87; James Lawrence Tigner, "Shindo Remmei: Japanese Nationalism in Brazil," *Hispanic American Historical Review,* November 1961, pp. 515–532; Yukio Fujii and T. Lynn Smith, *The Acculturation of the Japanese Immigrants in Brazil,* p. 50.

13. Anthony T. Bouscaren, *International Migrations since 1945* (New York: Frederick A. Praeger, 1963), p. 122.
14. Edwin O. Reischauer, *The Japanese* (Cambridge, Mass.: Harvard University Press, 1981), pp. 6, 7.
15. Ibid., pp. 24–25. See also Ellen Churchill Semple, *Influences of Geographic Environment* (New York: Holt, 1947), p. 457.
16. Edwin O. Reischauer, *The Japanese,* p. 8.
17. Ibid., p. 9.
18. Ibid., p. 35.
19. Yasuo Wakatsuki, "Japanese Emigration to the United States, 1866–1924," *Perspectives in American History,* Vol. XII (1979), p. 440.
20. Ibid., pp. 430, 438.
21. Ibid., p. 431. See also p. 434.
22. Ibid., pp. 430–434.
23. Neil Pedlar, *The Imported Pioneers: Westerners Who Helped Build Modern Japan* (New York: St. Martin's, 1990), pp. 22–23; Yasuo Wakatsuki, "Japanese Emigration to the United States, 1866–1924," *Perspectives in American History,* Vol. XII (1979), pp. 430, 440–442; Robert A. Wilson and Bill Hosokawa, *East to America: A History of Japanese in the United States* (New York: Morrow, 1980), p. 41.
24. Yasuo Wakatsuki, "Japanese Emigration to the United States, 1866–1924," *Perspectives in American History,* Vol. XII (1979), p. 443.
25. Ibid., pp. 419–420.
26. Ibid., p. 443.
27. Victor Purcell, *The Chinese in Southeast Asia* (Kuala Lumpur: Oxford University Press, 1980), p. 305; William Manchester, *American Caesar: Douglas MacArthur, 1880–1964* (Boston: Little, Brown, 1978), p. 227; "Sorry," *The Economist,* August 17, 1991, p. 30; Yuri Kageyama, "Japanese Tells of 'Sex Slaves' in Second War," *San Francisco Chronicle,* June 3, 1992, p. A10.
28. Victor Purcell, *The Chinese in Southeast Asia,* p. 307.
29. Haruko Taya Cook and Theodore Cook, *Japan at War: An Oral History* (New York: The New Press, 1992), pp. 25, 41–42, 74, 110–111, 146–151, 154–156, 161–166; William Manchester, *American Caeser,* pp. 227–228, 296, 413–414.
30. Ibid., pp. 473–474.
31. Ibid., p. 448.
32. Ibid., pp. 447, 452, 454, 465–477, 509–510.
33. Ibid., pp. 439–440.
34. Irokawa Daikichi, *The Culture of the Meiji Period,* translation edited by

Marius B. Jansen (Princeton, N.J.: Princeton University Press, 1985), p. 7.

35. G. C. Allen, *A Short Economic History of Modern Japan: 1867–1937*, revised edition (London: George Allen & Unwin, Ltd., 1972), p. 82.
36. Ibid., p. 179.
37. *World Motor Vehicle Data: 1992 Edition* (Detroit: Motor Vehicle Manufacturers Association of America, Inc., 1992), p. 14.
38. *1990–1991 Wolfman Report on the Photographic Imaging Industry in the United States* (New York: Hachette Magazines, 1991), p. 95.
39. Allen C. Kelley and Jeffrey G. Williamson, *Lessons from Japanese Development: An Analytical Economic History* (Chicago: University of Chicago Press, 1974), p. 198.
40. G. C. Allen, *A Short Economic History of Modern Japan*, p. 210.
41. Ibid., Chapters VII, IX.
42. Ibid., p. 150.
43. Ibid., p. 95.
44. Robert A. Wilson and Bill Hosokawa, *East to America*, pp. 18–19.
45. Ibid., p. 27. See also William Petersen, *Japanese Americans*, pp. 9–10.
46. Chitoshi Yanaga, *Japan since Perry* (Hamden, Conn.: Archon Books, 1966), p. 626.
47. Yukio Fujii and T. Lynn Smith, *The Acculturation of the Japanese Immigrants in Brazil*, p. 3.
48. C. Harvey Gardiner, *The Japanese and Peru, 1873–1973* (Albuquerque: University of New Mexico Press, 1975), p. 133.
49. James L. Tigner, "Japanese Immigration into Latin America," *Journal of Interamerican Studies and World Affairs*, November 1981, p. 476.
50. Peter S. Li, "Income Achievement and Adaptive Capacity: An Empirical Comparison of Chinese and Japanese in Canada," *Visible Minorities and Multiculturalism in Canada*, edited by K. Victor Ujimoto and Gordon Hirabayash (Toronto: Buttersworth, 1980), p. 365; Thomas Sowell, *Ethnic America: A History* (New York: Basic Books, 1981), p. 5.
51. C. Harvey Gardiner, *The Japanese and Peru, 1873–1973*, p. 132.
52. James L. Tigner, "Japanese Immigration into Latin America," *Journal of Interamerican Studies and World Affairs*, November 1981, p. 458.
53. Ibid., pp. 460–461.
54. Ibid., pp. 468–469.
55. Ibid., p. 459.
56. Ibid., p. 461.
57. Ibid., pp. 463, 466.
58. Ibid., p. 472.

59. Ibid., p. 467.
60. Ibid., p. 465.
61. Teiiti Suzuki, *The Japanese Immigrant in Brazil,* p. 221.
62. James L. Tigner, "Japanese Immigration into Latin America," *Journal of Interamerican Studies and World Affairs,* November 1981, p. 464.
63. Ibid., p. 466.
64. Robert C. Eidt, *Pioneer Settlement in Northeast Argentina* (Madison: University of Wisconsin Press, 1971), pp. 175–176, 213.
65. Stephen Ide Thompson, "San Juan Yapacani: A Japanese Pioneer Colony in Eastern Bolivia," Ph.D. dissertation in anthropology, University of Illinois at Champaign-Urbana, 1970, pp. 18–19, 182.
66. Teiiti Suzuki, *The Japanese Immigrant in Brazil,* p. 14.
67. Harold D. Sims, "Japanese Postwar Migration to Brazil: An Analysis of Data Presently Available," *International Migration Review,* Fall 1972, p. 247.
68. Robert A. Wilson and Bill Hosokawa, *East to America,* pp. 141–142.
69. Ibid., p. 152.
70. Ibid., p. 153.
71. Ibid., p. 146.
72. William Petersen, *Japanese Americans,* p. 20.
73. Ibid., pp. 23–24.
74. Robert Higgs, "Landless by Law: Japanese Immigrants in California Agriculture to 1941," *Journal of Economic History,* March 1978, pp. 215–223.
75. Eric Woodrum, Colbert Rhodes, and Joe R. Feagin, "Japanese American Economic Behavior: Its Types, Determinants, and Consequences," *Social Forces,* June 1980, p. 1238.
76. Ibid., p. 1247.
77. William Petersen, *Japanese Americans,* p. 52.
78. Robert Higgs, "Landless by Law: Japanese Immigrants in California Agriculture to 1941," *Journal of Economic History,* March 1978, pp. 215–223.
79. Ibid., p. 222.
80. Ibid., p. 221.
81. Robert Higgs, "Landless by Law: Japanese Immigrants in California Agriculture to 1941," *Journal of Economic History,* March 1978, p. 207.
82. Ibid., p. 209.
83. Robert A. Wilson and Bill Hosokawa, *East to America,* p. 154.
84. Ibid., pp. 156, 210.
85. Eric Woodrum, Colbert Rhodes, and Joe R. Feagin, "Japanese American

Economic Behavior: Its Types, Determinants, and Consequences," *Social Forces,* June 1980, p. 1238.

86. William Petersen, *Japanese Americans,* pp. 114, 116.
87. See U.S. Bureau of the Census, *1990 Census of Population: Asian and Pacific Islanders in the United States* (Washington, D.C.: U.S. Government Printing Office, 1993), pp. 142, 151.
88. See, for example, U.S. Bureau of the Census, *1970 Census of Population, Subject Report PC(2)-1G,* p. 17; Akemi Kihumura and Harry H. L. Kitano, "Interracial Marriage: A Picture of the Japanese Americans," *Journal of Social Issues,* Vol. 29, No. 2 (1973), pp. 69, 73.
89. Peter Xenos, Herbert Barringer, and Michael J. Levin, *Asian Indians in the United States: A 1980 Census Profile* (Honolulu: East-West Population Institute, 1989), p. 29.
90. Ibid., pp. 124–125.
91. Robert A. Wilson and Bill Hosokawa, *East to America,* pp. 156–159.
92. William Petersen, *Japanese Americans,* p. 13.
93. Tomoko Makabe, "The Theory of the Split Labor Market: A Comparison of the Japanese Experiment in Brazil and Canada," *Social Forces,* March 1981, pp. 788–789.
94. Charles H. Young and Helen R. Y. Reid, *The Japanese Canadians* (Toronto: University of Toronto Press, 1938), p. 22.
95. Ibid., p. xxi.
96. Ibid., p. 6.
97. Ibid., p. 39.
98. Ibid., pp. 8–9.
99. Ibid., p. 172.
100. Tomoko Makabe, "The Theory of the Split Labor Market: A Comparison of the Japanese Experiment in Brazil and Canada," *Social Forces,* March 1981, p. 795.
101. Charles H. Young and Helen R. Y. Reid, *The Japanese Canadians,* pp. 9–10.
102. Ibid., p. 17.
103. Ibid., p. 204.
104. Ibid., p. 26.
105. Ibid., p. 30.
106. Ibid., pp. 34–35.
107. Tomoko Makabe, "The Theory of the Split Labor Market: A Comparison of the Japanese Experiment in Brazil and Canada," *Social Forces,* March 1981, p. 794. See also Charles H. Young and Helen R. Y. Reid, *The Japanese Canadians,* p. 42.

108. Tomoko Makabe, "The Theory of the Split Labor Market: A Comparison of the Japanese Experiment in Brazil and Canada," *Social Forces*, March 1981, p. 796.
109. Charles H. Young and Helen R. Y. Reid, *The Japanese Canadians*, p. 47.
110. Ibid., pp. 43–45.
111. Ibid., p. 50.
112. Ellen Bar, "Issei, Nisei, and Sansei," *Modernization and the Canadian State*, edited by Daniel Glenday, Hurbert Guindon, and Allan Turowetz (Toronto: Macmillan of Canada, 1978), p. 341.
113. Ken Adachi, *The Enemy That Never Was* (Toronto: McClelland and Stewart, Ltd., 1976), p. 52.
114. Charles H. Young and Helen R. Y. Reid, *The Japanese Canadians*, pp. 56, 269.
115. Ibid., p. 74.
116. Tomoko Makabe, "The Theory of the Split Labor Market: A Comparison of the Japanese Experiment in Brazil and Canada," *Social Forces*, March 1981, p. 797.
117. Charles H. Young and Helen R. Y. Reid, *The Japanese Canadians*, pp. 72–73.
118. Patricia E. Roy, "Protecting Their Pocket Books and Preserving Their Race: White Merchants and Oriental Competition," *Cities in the West: Papers of the Western Canadian Urban History Conference—University of Winnipeg, October 1974*, edited by A. R. McCormack and Ian MacPherson (Ottawa: National Museums of Canada, 1975), p. 116.
119. Ibid., p. 119.
120. Ibid., pp. 120–126.
121. Ibid., p. 125.
122. Ibid., pp. 127–128.
123. Tomoko Makabe, "The Theory of the Split Labor Market: A Comparison of the Japanese Experiment in Brazil and Canada," *Social Forces*, March 1981, p. 804.
124. Charles H. Young and Helen R. Y. Reid, *The Japanese Canadians*, p. 243.
125. Ken Adachi, *The Enemy That Never Was*, p. 111.
126. Ibid., pp. 129, 130.
127. Ibid., p. 167.
128. Ibid., p. 121.
129. Ibid., p. 131.
130. Ibid., p. 121.
131. Ibid., pp. 200, 202.

132. Ibid., p. 203.
133. Ibid., pp. 205, 276.
134. Ellen Bar, "Issei, Nisei, and Sansei," *Modernization and the Canadian State,* edited by Daniel Glenday, Hurbert Guindon, and Allan Turowetz, pp. 343–344.
135. Ken Adachi, *The Enemy That Never Was,* p. 210.
136. Ellen Bar, "Issei, Nisei, and Sansei," *Modernization and the Canadian State,* edited by Daniel Glenday, Hurbert Guindon, and Allan Turowetz, p. 346.
137. Patricia E. Roy, "Protecting Their Pocket Books and Preserving Their Race: White Merchants and Oriental Competition," *Cities in the West,* p. 132.
138. Ellen Bar, "Issei, Nisei, and Sansei," *Modernization and the Canadian State,* edited by Daniel Glenday, Hurbert Guindon, and Allan Turowetz, p. 347.
139. Tomoko Makabe, "The Theory of the Split Labor Market: A Comparison of the Japanese Experiment in Brazil and Canada," *Social Forces,* March 1981, p. 807.
140. Ellen Bar, "Issei, Nisei, and Sansei," *Modernization and the Canadian State,* edited by Daniel Glenday, Hurbert Guindon, and Allan Turowetz, p. 347.
141. Tomoko Makabe, "The Theory of the Split Labor Market: A Comparison of the Japanese Experiment in Brazil and Canada," *Social Forces,* March 1981, p. 807.
142. Ellen Bar, "Issei, Nisei, and Sansei," *Modernization and the Canadian State,* edited by Daniel Glenday, Hurbert Guindon, and Allan Turowetz, p. 348.
143. Ibid., pp. 348–349.
144. K. Victor Ujimoto and Gordon Hirabayashi, *Visible Minorities and Multiculturalism,* p. 365.
145. Ellen Bar, "Issei, Nisei, and Sansei," *Modernization and the Canadian State,* edited by Daniel Glenday, Hurbert Guindon, and Allan Turowetz, pp. 349–350.
146. Ken Adachi, *The Enemy That Never Was,* p. 356.
147. Ibid., pp. 362–363.
148. Ibid., p. 359.
149. J. F. Normano and Antonello Gerbi, *The Japanese in South America* (New York: Institute of Pacific Relations, 1943), p. 66.
150. C. Harvey Gardiner, *The Japanese and Peru, 1873–1973,* pp. 1–21.
151. Ibid., p. 18.

152. J. F. Normano and Antonello Gerbi, *The Japanese in South America,* p. 70.
153. Ibid., p. 68.
154. Ibid., p. 69.
155. James L. Tigner, "Japanese Immigration into Latin America," *Journal of Interamerican Studies and World Affairs,* November 1981, p. 465.
156. C. Harvey Gardiner, *The Japanese and Peru, 1873–1973,* p. 25.
157. J. F. Normano and Antonello Gerbi, *The Japanese in South America,* p. 70.
158. C. Harvey Gardiner, *The Japanese and Peru, 1873–1973,* pp. 30, 34, 36, 38, 100.
159. J. F. Normano and Antonello Gerbi, *The Japanese in South America,* pp. 74–75.
160. C. Harvey Gardiner, *The Japanese and Peru, 1873–1973,* p. 133.
161. J. F. Normano and Antonello Gerbi, *The Japanese in South America,* p. 75.
162. C. Harvey Gardiner, *The Japanese and Peru, 1873–1973,* pp. 61–62.
163. Ibid., p. 62.
164. Ibid., p. 64.
165. Toraji Irie, "History of Japanese Immigration to Peru, Part II," translated by William Himel, *Hispanic American Historical Review,* November 1951, p. 662.
166. C. Harvey Gardiner, *The Japanese and Peru, 1873–1973,* p. 68; J. F. Normano and Antonello Gerbi, *The Japanese in South America,* p. 109.
167. J. F. Normano and Antonello Gerbi, *The Japanese in South America,* p. 96.
168. Ibid., p. 97.
169. Ibid., p. 98.
170. C. Harvey Gardiner, *The Japanese and Peru, 1873–1973,* p. 75.
171. J. F. Normano and Antonello Gerbi, *The Japanese in South America,* p. 100.
172. Ibid., p. 92.
173. C. Harvey Gardiner, *The Japanese and Peru, 1873–1973,* p. 68.
174. J. F. Normano and Antonello Gerbi, *The Japanese in South America,* pp. 77, 113–114.
175. C. Harvey Gardiner, *The Japanese and Peru, 1873–1973,* pp. 85–87.
176. Ibid., pp. 88, 91.
177. Ibid., p. 92.
178. Ibid., p. 133.
179. James L. Tigner, "Japanese Immigration into Latin America," *Journal of Interamerican Studies and World Affairs,* November 1981, p. 476.
180. Ibid., p. 476.
181. William R. Long, "New Pride for *Nikkei* in Peru," *Los Angeles Times,* April 28, 1995, p. A1.

182. Ibid., p. A14.
183. J. F. Normano, "Japanese Emigration to Brazil," *Pacific Affairs,* March 1934, p. 44.
184. Ibid., p. 45.
185. Patrick Makoto Fukunaga, "The Brazilian Experience: The Japanese Immigrants during the Period of the Vargas Regime and the Immediate Aftermath, 1930–1946," unpublished doctoral dissertation in history, University of California at Santa Barbara, 1983, p. 44.
186. Ibid., p. 36.
187. Ibid., pp. 62–63.
188. Ibid., pp. 71–72.
189. Yukio Fujii and T. Lynn Smith, *The Acculturation of the Japanese Immigrants in Brazil,* p. 7.
190. J. F. Normano and Antonello Gerbi, *The Japanese in South America,* p. 12.
191. Yukio Fujii and T. Lynn Smith, *The Acculturation of the Japanese Immigrants in Brazil,* pp. 7–8.
192. James L. Tigner, "Japanese Immigration into Latin America," *Journal of Interamerican Studies and World Affairs,* November 1981, p. 471.
193. Yukio Fujii and T. Lynn Smith, *The Acculturation of the Japanese Immigrants in Brazil,* p. 3; J. F. Normano and Antonello Gerbi, *The Japanese in South America,* p. 25.
194. Yukio Fujii and T. Lynn Smith, *The Acculturation of the Japanese Immigrants in Brazil,* p. 5.
195. J. F. Normano and Antonello Gerbi, *The Japanese in South America,* pp. 31–33.
196. Patrick Makoto Fukunaga, "The Brazilian Experience," pp. 53–54.
197. Ibid., p. 39.
198. Ibid., pp. 36–42.
199. Ibid., p. 49.
200. Yukio Fujii and T. Lynn Smith, *The Acculturation of the Japanese Immigrants in Brazil,* p. 10.
201. J. F. Normano and Antonello Gerbi, *The Japanese in South America,* pp. 49–51.
202. Emilio Willems and Herbert Baldus, "Cultural Change among Japanese Immigrants in Brazil," *Sociology and Social Research,* Vol. 26, No. 6 (July–August 1942), p. 532.
203. Ibid., pp. 531, 533.
204. Ibid., p. 533.
205. Ibid., p. 531.
206. Ibid., pp. 526, 528–529.

207. Emilio Willems and Herbert Baldus, "Cultural Change among Japanese Immigrants in Brazil," *Sociology and Social Research,* Vol. 26, No. 6 (July–August 1942), p. 534.
208. James L. Tigner, "Japanese Settlement in Eastern Bolivia and Brazil," *Journal of Interamerican Studies and World Affairs,* Vol. 24, No. 4 (November 1982), p. 511.
209. Patrick Makoto Fukunaga, "The Brazilian Experience," pp. 97–99.
210. J. F. Normano and Antonello Gerbi, *The Japanese in South America,* pp. 52–53.
211. Patrick Makoto Fukunaga, "The Brazilian Experience," p. 117.
212. Ibid., p. 120.
213. James Lawrence Tigner, "Shindo Remmei: Japanese Nationalism in Brazil," *Hispanic American Historical Review,* November 1961, p. 516.
214. C. Harvey Gardiner, *The Japanese and Peru, 1873–1973,* p. 87.
215. James Lawrence Tigner, "Shindo Remmei: Japanese Nationalism in Brazil," *Hispanic American Historical Review,* November 1961, pp. 515–532.
216. James L. Tigner, *The Okinawans in Latin America* (Washington, D.C.: Pacific Science Board, 1954), p. 45.
217. Yukio Fujii and T. Lynn Smith, *The Acculturation of the Japanese Immigrants in Brazil,* p. 50.
218. James Lawrence Tigner, "Shindo Remmei: Japanese Nationalism in Brazil," *Hispanic American Historical Review,* November 1961, p. 520.
219. Harold D. Sims, "Japanese Postwar Migration to Brazil: An Analysis of Data Presently Available," *International Migration Review,* Fall 1972, pp. 248, 257.
220. Robert J. Smith, "Assimilation and Acculturation of Urban Japanese in South Brazil," *VIIIth Congress of Anthropological and Ethnological Sciences* (Moscow: Navka, 1964), p. 212.
221. Harold D. Sims, "Japanese Postwar Migration to Brazil: An Analysis of Data Presently Available," *International Migration Review,* Fall 1972, pp. 247, 248.
222. James L. Tigner, "Japanese Settlement in Eastern Bolivia and Brazil," *Journal of Interamerican Studies and World Affairs,* Vol. 24, No. 4 (November 1982), p. 512.
223. Harold D. Sims, "Japanese Postwar Migration to Brazil: An Analysis of Data Presently Available," *International Migration Review,* Fall 1972, p. 251.
224. Teiiti Suzuki, *The Japanese Immigrant in Brazil,* p. 33.

225. Thomas E. Weil et al., *Area Handbook for Brazil* (Washington, D.C.: U.S. Government Printing Office, 1975), p. 84.
226. Preston E. James, *Latin America,* fourth edition (Indianapolis: Odyssey Press, 1942), p. 792.
227. Fr. John T. Sasaki, "Japanese Immigrant Farmers in Brazil," *Migration News,* January/February 1972, p. 5.
228. Marlise Simons, "Japanese Gone Brazilian: Unhurried Workaholics," *New York Times,* International Section, May 8, 1988, p. 4.
229. Patrick Makoto Fukunaga, "The Brazilian Experience," p. 42.
230. Teiiti Suzuki, *The Japanese Immigrant in Brazil,* p. 131.
231. Ibid., p. 159.
232. Ibid., p. 116.
233. Ibid., p. 109.
234. Harold D. Sims, "Japanese Postwar Migration to Brazil: An Analysis of Data Presently Available," *International Migration Review,* Fall 1972, pp. 261–262.
235. Teiiti Suzuki, *The Japanese Immigrant in Brazil,* p. 121.
236. Ibid., p. 144.
237. Marlise Simons, "Japanese Gone Brazilian: Unhurried Workaholics," *New York Times,* International Section, May 8, 1988, p. 4.
238. Teiiti Suzuki, *The Japanese Immigrant in Brazil,* p. 91.
239. Marlise Simons, "Japanese Gone Brazilian: Unhurried Workaholics," *New York Times,* International Section, May 8, 1988, p. 4.
240. Teiiti Suzuki, *The Japanese Immigrant in Brazil,* p. 240.
241. Ibid., p. 219.
242. Ibid., p. 234.
243. Emilio Willems, "Immigrants and Their Assimilation in Brazil," *Brazil: Portrait of Half a Continent,* edited by T. Lynn Smith and Alexander Marchant (New York: The Dryden Press, 1951), p. 224.
244. Marlise Simons, "Japanese Gone Brazilian: Unhurried Workaholics," *New York Times,* International Section, May 8, 1988, p. 4.
245. James L. Tigner, *The Okinawans in Latin America,* p. 246; Marlise Simons, "Japanese Gone Brazilian: Unhurried Workaholics," *New York Times,* International Section, May 8, 1988, p. 4; William R. Long, "New Pride for *Nikkei* in Peru," *Los Angeles Times,* April 28, 1995, p. A1.
246. D. C. S. Sissons, "Japanese," *The Australian People: An Encyclopedia of the Nation, Its People and Their Origins,* edited by James Jupp (North Ryde, Australia: Angus & Robertson Publishers, 1988), p. 637.
247. Ken Adachi, *The Enemy That Never Was,* p. 356.

248. Stewart S. Lee, "The Korean Minority in Postwar Japan," *Muhlenberg Essays: In Honor of the College Centennial*, edited by Katherine S. Van Eerde and Nelvin L. Vos (Allentown, Pa.: Muhlenberg College, 1968), pp. 418–435.
249. William Wetherall and George Devos, "Ethnic Minorities in Japan," *Case Studies in Human Rights*, edited by Willem A. Veenhoven et al. (The Hague: Martinus Nijhoff, 1975), pp. 344–346.
250. Ibid., pp. 340–344; I. Roger Yoshina, "The Buraku Minority of Japan," *Patterns of Prejudice*, January 1983, pp. 39–47.
251. Urban C. Lehrer, "Japanese-Americans Viewed as Oddity in Land of Ancestors, but Number Grows," *Wall Street Journal*, December 8, 1983, p. 34.

CHAPTER 4: ITALIANS AROUND THE WORLD

1. Robert F. Foerster, *The Italian Emigration of Our Times* (New York: Arno Press, 1969), p. 3.
2. Anna Maria Martellone, "Italian Mass Emigration to the United States, 1876–1930: A Historical Survey," *Perspectives in American History*, New Series, Vol. I (1984), p. 380.
3. Ibid., p. 399.
4. Robert F. Foerster, *The Italian Emigration of Our Times*, p. 28.
5. Ibid., p. 32.
6. Patrizia Audencio, "The Path of the Trade: Italian Stonemasons in the United States," *International Migration Review*, Vol. XX, No. 4 (Winter 1986), p. 779.
7. Computed from Anna Maria Martellone, "Italian Mass Emigration to the United States," *Perspectives in American History*, New Series, Vol. I (1984), p. 389.
8. Herbert S. Klein, "The Integration of Italian Immigrants into the United States and Argentina: A Comparative Analysis," *American Historical Review*, April 1983, p. 312.
9. Leonard Covello, *The Social Background of the Italo-American School Child: A Study of the Southern Italian Family Mores and Their Effect on the School Situation in Italy and America* (Totowa, N.J.: Rowman and Littlefield, 1972), p. 25.
10. Charles A. Price, *Southern Europeans in Australia* (Melbourne: Australian National University, 1979), p. 80.
11. Charles A. Price, *The Methods and Statistics of "Southern Europeans in*

Australia" (Canberra: Research School of Social Sciences, Australian National University, 1963), p. 6.

12. Carlo M. Cipolla, *Literacy and Development in the West* (New York: Penguin, 1969), p. 14.
13. Ibid., p. 19.
14. Richard Gambino, *Blood of My Blood: The Dilemma of the Italian-Americans* (Garden City, N.Y.: Anchor Books, 1974), p. 247. See also Leonard Covello, *The Social Background of the Italo-American School Child,* Chapter 8.
15. Leonard Covello, *The Social Background of the Italo-American School Child,* pp. 251–254; Richard Gambino, *Blood of My Blood,* pp. 247–248.
16. Anna Maria Martellone, "Italian Mass Emigration to the United States," *Perspectives in American History,* New Series, Vol. I (1984), p. 409.
17. Thomas W. Merrick and Douglas H. Graham, *Population and Economic Development in Brazil: 1800 to the Present* (Baltimore: Johns Hopkins University Press, 1979), p. 95; Anna Maria Martellone, "Italian Mass Emigration to the United States," *Perspectives in American History,* New Series, Vol. I (1984), p. 405.
18. Anna Maria Martellone, "Italian Mass Emigration to the United States," *Perspectives in American History,* New Series, Vol. I (1984), p. 413.
19. Thomas W. Merrick and Douglas H. Graham, *Population and Economic Development in Brazil,* p. 95.
20. Dino Cinel, *From Italy to San Francisco: The Immigrant Experience* (Stanford, Calif.: Stanford University Press, 1982), pp. 59–65.
21. Ibid., pp. 46–48.
22. Robert F. Foerster, *The Italian Emigration of Our Times,* pp. 426–430. See also Leonard Covello, *The Social Background of the Italo-American School Child,* pp. 297–298.
23. Charles A. Price, *The Methods and Statistics of "Southern Europeans in Australia,"* p. 11.
24. Dino Cinel, *From Italy to San Francisco,* p. 49.
25. Ibid., p. 45.
26. Constance Cronin, *The Sting of Change: Sicilians in Sicily and Australia* (Chicago: University of Chicago Press, 1970), p. 186.
27. Charles A. Price, *Southern Europeans in Australia,* pp. 163–164.
28. G. Cresciani, "Italian Immigrants, 1920–1945," *The Australian People: An Encyclopedia of the Nation, Its People and Their Origins,* edited by James Jupp (North Ryde, Australia: Angus and Robertson Publishers, 1988), p. 609.

29. Dino Cinel, *From Italy to San Francisco,* p. 28.
30. Samuel L. Baily, "The Adjustment of Italian Immigrants in Buenos Aires and New York, 1870–1914," *American Historical Review,* April 1983, p. 291; John E. Zucchi, *Italians in Toronto: Development of a National Identity, 1875–1935* (Kingston, Ontario: McGill-Queen's University Press, 1988), pp. 53–59.
31. Dino Cinel, *From Italy to San Francisco,* p. 75.
32. Ibid., pp. 74–75.
33. Constance Cronin, *The Sting of Change,* Chapter 4; Edward C. Banfield, *The Moral Basis of a Backward Society* (New York: The Free Press, 1958), pp. 110–111; Leonard Covello, *The Social Background of the Italo-American School Child,* pp. 169–170.
34. Leonard Covello, *The Social Background of the Italo-American School Child,* p. 161.
35. Ibid., pp. 186, 188, 190.
36. Luigi Barzini, *The Italians: A Full-length Portrait Featuring Their Manners and Morals* (New York: Atheneum, 1981), p. 206.
37. See, for example, Leonard Covello, *The Social Background of the Italo-American School Child,* p. 230; Constance Sorrentino, "International Comparisons of Labor Force Participation, 1960–81," *Monthly Labor Review,* February 1983, pp. 24, 25.
38. Leonard Covello, *The Social Background of the Italo-American School Child,* p. 230.
39. Ibid., pp. 251, 254–274, 287–288, 292, 295–296; Richard Gambino, *Blood of My Blood,* pp. 247–248.
40. See, for example, Leonard Covello, *The Social Background of the Italo-American School Child,* p. 191; Edward C. Banfield, *The Moral Basis of a Backward Society,* pp. 18–19, 20–21; Robert F. Foerster, *The Italian Emigration of Our Times,* pp. 120, 132, 142; Rudolf Glanz, *Jew and Italian: Historic Group Relations and the New Immigration* (New York: Shulsinger Brothers, 1970), p. 29.
41. Dino Cinel, *From Italy to San Francisco,* p. 24.
42. Ibid., p. 23.
43. Ibid., pp. 59–65.
44. Anna Maria Martellone, "Italian Mass Emigration to the United States," *Perspectives in American History,* New Series, Vol. I (1984), pp. 406–407.
45. Ibid., pp. 391–393.
46. Ibid., p. 382; Francesco Cerase, "Italy," *The Politics of Migration Policies: The First World in the 1970s,* edited by Daniel Kubat (New York: Center for Migration Studies, 1979), p. 235.

47. Anna Maria Martellone, "Italian Mass Emigration to the United States," *Perspectives in American History,* New Series, Vol. I (1984), pp. 391–393.
48. Myron Weiner, *The Global Migration Crisis: Challenge to States and to Human Rights* (New York: HarperCollins, 1995), p. 59.
49. Robert F. Foerster, *The Italian Emigration of Our Times,* pp. 129–202.
50. Luigi Barzini, *The Italians* (New York: Atheneum, 1981), p. x; Fernand Braudel, *The Mediterranean and the Mediterranean World in the Age of Philip II,* translated by Sian Reynolds, Volume I (New York: Harper & Row, 1972), p. 192.
51. Robert F. Foerster, *The Italian Emigration of Our Times,* p. 129.
52. Ibid., p. 131.
53. Ibid., pp. 134, 136.
54. Ibid., pp. 137, 145–146.
55. Ibid., pp. 144, 185–186, 199; Thomas Kessner, *The Golden Door: Italian and Jewish Immigrant Mobility in New York City, 1880–1915* (New York: Oxford University Press, 1977), p. 27; W. D. Borrie, *Italians and Germans in Australia: A Study in Assimilation* (Melbourne: Australian National University, 1954), p. 147.
56. Robert F. Foerster, *The Italian Emigration of Our Times,* pp. 145, 147, 166, 167–168, 185, 186; Lucio Sponza, *Halian Immigrants in Nineteenth Century Britain: Realities and Images* (Leicester: Leicester University Press, 1988), pp. 195–216.
57. See, for example, Robert F. Foerster, *The Italian Emigration of Our Times,* pp. 140–145, 181–182.
58. Ibid., pp. 143, 161, 181.
59. Ibid., pp. 139, 146, 161, 170, 187.
60. Ibid., p. 171.
61. Ibid., pp. 195, 206, 207, 211, 213, 214, 215, 220, 222, 325, 419.
62. Ibid., pp. 138, 153, 156, 172, 192, 205, 206, 211, 213.
63. Ibid., pp. 195, 203, 210.
64. Ibid., pp. 132, 189, 210.
65. Ibid., pp. 171, 176, 196, 207, 209, 210, 211.
66. Ibid., pp. 207, 209, 212.
67. Ibid., pp. 177, 196, 212.
68. Anthony T. Bouscaren, *International Migrations since 1945* (New York: Frederick A. Praeger, 1963), p. 73.
69. John Salt, "International Labor Migration in Western Europe: A Geographical Review," *Global Trends in Migration: Theory and Research on International Population Movements,* edited by Mary M. Kritz, Charles

B. Keely, and Silvano M. Tomasi (New York: Center for Migration Studies, 1981), p. 137.

70. Yann Moulier and Georges Tapinos, "France," *The Politics of Migration Policies,* edited by Daniel Kubat, p. 131.
71. John Salt, "International Labor Migration in Western Europe: A Geographical Review" *Global Trends in Migration,* edited by Mary M. Kritz et al., pp. 138, 139; Yann Moulier and Georges Tapinos, "France," *The Politics of Migration Policies,* p. 131.
72. Francesco Cerase, "Italy," *The Politics of Migration Policies,* edited by Daniel Kubat, p. 235.
73. Ibid., p. 240.
74. Giuseppe Lecrezio Monticelli, "Italian Emigration: Basic Characteristics and Trends with Special Reference to the Last Twenty Years," *International Migration Review,* Summer 1967, p. 13.
75. "Italian Emigration: Some Aspects of Migration in 1964 International Agreements Emigrant Remittances," *International Migration Review,* Vol. 4, No. 2 (1966), p. 125.
76. D. A. Coleman, "International Migration: Demographic and Socioeconomic Consequences in the United Kingdom and Europe," *International Migration Review,* Vol. XXIX, No. 1 (Spring 1995), p. 163.
77. Herbert S. Klein, "The Integration of Italian Immigrants into the United States and Argentina," *American Historical Review,* April 1983, p. 308; Anna Maria Martellone, "Italian Mass Emigration to the United States," *Perspectives in American History,* New Series, Vol. I (1984), p. 389.
78. Anna Maria Martellone, "Italian Mass Emigration to the United States," *Perspectives in American History,* New Series, Vol. I (1984), p. 392.
79. Robert F. Foerster, *The Italian Emigration of Our Times,* pp. 228–229.
80. Ibid., p. 236.
81. Carl Solberg, *Immigration and Nationalism: Argentina and Chile, 1890–1914* (Austin: Institute of Latin American Studies, University of Texas, 1970), p. 38.
82. Jorge Hechen, "The Argentine Republic," *The Positive Contribution by Immigrants,* edited by Oscar Handlin et al. (Paris: United Nations Educational, Scientific, and Cultural Organization, 1960), p. 151.
83. Robert F. Foerster, *The Italian Emigration of Our Times,* p. 227.
84. Samuel L. Baily, "The Adjustment of Italian Immigrants in Buenos Aires and New York," *American Historical Review,* April 1983, p. 303.
85. Jorge Hechen, "The Argentine Republic," *The Positive Contribution by Immigrants,* edited by Oscar Handlin et al., p. 150.

86. Mark Jefferson, *Peopling the Argentine Pampa* (New York: Kennikat Press, 1971), p. 1.
87. Robert F. Foerster, *The Italian Emigration of Our Times,* p. 227.
88. Carl Solberg, *Immigration and Nationalism,* p. 50.
89. Robert F. Foerster, *The Italian Emigration of Our Times,* p. 230.
90. Ibid., p. 243.
91. Ibid., p. 235.
92. Ibid., pp. 242–243.
93. Ibid., p. 240.
94. Ibid., p. 255.
95. Ibid., p. 256.
96. Ibid., pp. 257–259.
97. Ibid., pp. 260–261.
98. Carl Solberg, *Immigration and Nationalism,* p. 51.
99. Ibid., p. 57.
100. Ibid., p. 62.
101. Robert F. Foerster, *The Italian Emigration of Our Times,* p. 262.
102. Samuel L. Baily, "The Adjustment of Italian Immigrants in Buenos Aires and New York," *American Historical Review,* April 1983, p. 284.
103. Robert F. Foerster, *The Italian Emigration of Our Times,* p. 256.
104. Samuel L. Baily, "The Italians and the Development of Organized Labor in Argentina, Brazil and the United States," *Journal of Social History,* Winter 1969–70, pp. 124–125.
105. Samuel L. Baily, "The Role of Two Newspapers in the Assimilation of Italians in Buenos Aires and São Paulo, 1893–1913," *International Migration Review,* Fall 1978, p. 324.
106. Samuel L. Baily, "The Adjustment of Italian Immigrants in Buenos Aires and New York," *American Historical Review,* April 1983, p. 284.
107. Carl Solberg, *Immigration and Nationalism,* p. 13.
108. James Bruce, *Those Perplexing Argentines* (New York: Longmans, Green and Co., 1953), pp. 101, 102.
109. Robert F. Foerster, *The Italian Emigration of Our Times,* p. 270.
110. Carl Solberg, *Immigration and Nationalism,* p. 37.
111. Thomas E. Weil, et. al., *Area Handbook for Argentina* (Washington, D.C.: U.S. Government Printing Office, 1975), p. 8.
112. Samuel L. Baily, "The Role of Two Newspapers in the Assimilation of Italians in Buenos Aires and São Paulo, 1893–1913," *International Migration Review,* Fall 1978, p. 339.
113. Ibid., p. 327.
114. Robert F. Foerster, *The Italian Emigration of Our Times,* p. 272.

115. Ibid., p. 273.
116. Mark Jefferson, *Peopling the Argentine Pampa,* p. 120.
117. Ibid.
118. Robert F. Foerster, *The Italian Emigration of Our Times,* p. 273.
119. Thomas E. Weil, *Area Handbook for Argentina,* p. 22.
120. Robert F. Foerster, *The Italian Emigration of Our Times,* p. 274.
121. "Italian Emigration," *International Migration,* Vol. 4, No. 2 (1966), p. 122.
122. Robert F. Foerster, *The Italian Emigration of Our Times,* p. 279.
123. Emilio Willems, "Brazil," *The Positive Contribution by Immigrants,* edited by Oscar Handlin et al., p. 121.
124. Robert F. Foerster, *The Italian Emigration of Our Times,* p. 287.
125. Ibid., p. 289.
126. Thomas W. Merrick and Douglas H. Graham, *Population and Economic Development in Brazil,* p. 95.
127. Ibid., pp. 92–95, 103.
128. Thomas H. Holloway, *Immigrants on the Land: Coffee and Society in São Paulo, 1886–1934* (Chapel Hill: University of North Carolina Press, 1980), p. 42.
129. Robert F. Foerster, *The Italian Emigration of Our Times,* p. 290.
130. Thomas W. Merrick and Douglas H. Graham, *Population and Economic Development in Brazil,* p. 96.
131. Thomas H. Holloway, *Immigrants on the Land,* pp. 155–157.
132. Robert F. Foerster, *The Italian Emigration of Our Times,* pp. 295, 296, 297.
133. Ibid., p. 297.
134. Thomas H. Holloway, *Immigrants on the Land,* p. 28.
135. Ibid., p. 26.
136. Ibid., p. 60.
137. Ibid., pp. 149, 151.
138. Ibid., p. 152.
139. Emilio Willems, "Brazil," *The Positive Contribution by Immigrants,* edited by Oscar Handlin et al., p. 124.
140. Jean Roche, *La Colonisation Allemande et le Rio Grande do Sul* (Paris: Institute des Hautes Études de L'Amérique Latine, 1959), p. 163.
141. Ibid., p. 374.
142. Ibid., p. 377.
143. Ibid., p. 391.
144. Ibid., p. 392.

145. Emilio Willems, "Brazil," *The Positive Contribution by Immigrants,* edited by Oscar Handlin et al., p. 128.
146. Samuel L. Baily, "The Italians and the Development of Organized Labor in Argentina, Brazil and the United States," *Journal of Social History,* Winter 1969–70, p. 131.
147. Emilio Willems, "Brazil," *The Positive Contribution by Immigrants,* edited by Oscar Handlin et al., p. 133.
148. Robert F. Foerster, *The Italian Emigration of Our Times,* pp. 316–317.
149. Ibid., p. 314.
150. Thomas H. Holloway, *Immigrants on the Land,* p. 172.
151. Robert F. Foerster, *The Italian Emigration of Our Times,* p. 298.
152. Ibid., p. 319.
153. Ibid., pp. 317–318.
154. Ibid., p. 319.
155. Ibid., pp. 303, 305.
156. Emilio Willems, "Brazil," *The Positive Contribution by Immigrants,* edited by Oscar Handlin et al., pp. 131, 132.
157. U.S. Bureau of the Census, *Historical Statistics of the United States: Colonial Times to 1970* (Washington, D.C.: U.S. Government Printing Office, 1975), p. 105.
158. Anna Marie Martellone, "Italian Mass Emigration to the United States," *Perspectives in American History,* New Series, Vol. I (1984), p. 389.
159. Ibid., p. 399.
160. Herbert S. Klein, "The Integration of Italian Immigrants into the United States and Argentina," *American Historical Review,* April 1983, p. 316.
161. Robert F. Foerster, *The Italian Emigration of Our Times,* pp. 323, 327.
162. Ibid., p. 329.
163. Samuel L. Baily, "The Italians and the Development of Organized Labor in Argentina, Brazil and the United States," *Journal of Social History,* Winter 1969–70, p. 129.
164. Ibid., pp. 129–130.
165. Robert F. Foerster, *The Italian Emigration of Our Times,* p. 335.
166. Leonard Covello, *The Social Background of the Italo-American School Child,* pp. 257–258; Thomas Kessner, *The Golden Door,* pp. 84, 96.
167. Thomas Sowell, *Ethnic America: A History* (New York: Basic Books, 1981), p. 280.
168. Herbert S. Klein, "The Integration of Italian Immigrants into the United States and Argentina," *American Historical Review,* April 1983, p. 285.

169. Ibid., p. 291; Robert F. Foerster, *The Italian Emigration of Our Times,* p. 393; Dino Cinel, *From Italy to San Francisco,* p. 28.
170. Dino Cinel, *From Italy to San Francisco,* pp. 28, 117–118; Virginia Yans-McLaughlin, *Family and Community, Italian Immigrants in Buffalo, 1880–1930* (Ithaca, N.Y.: Cornell University Press, 1977), p. 130; Joseph Lopreato, *Italian Americans,* pp. 41–42.
171. Joseph Lopreato, *Italian Americans,* p. 42; Humbert S. Nelli, "Italians," *Harvard Encyclopedia of American Ethnic Groups,* edited by Stephan Thernstrom et al. (Cambridge, Mass.: Harvard University Press, 1981), p. 548.
172. Dino Cinel, *From Italy to San Francisco,* p. 178; Humbert S. Nelli, *Italians in Chicago, 1880–1930,* p. 195.
173. Dino Cinel, *From Italy to San Francisco,* p. 177.
174. Ibid., p. 178.
175. Joseph Lopreato, *Italian Americans,* p. 135.
176. Anna Maria Martellone, "Italian Mass Emigration to the United States," *Perspectives in American History,* New Series, Vol. I (1984), p. 416.
177. Dino Cinel, *From Italy to San Francisco,* p. 21.
178. Robert F. Foerster, *The Italian Emigration of Our Times,* p. 351.
179. Ibid., p. 367.
180. Andrew F. Rolle, *The Immigrant Upraised: Italian Adventurers and Colonists in an Expanding America* (Norman: University of Oklahoma Press, 1970), p. 68.
181. Robert F. Foerster, *The Italian Emigration of Our Times,* pp. 328n, 329.
182. Ibid., pp. 324, 384–385.
183. Ibid., p. 386.
184. Ibid., pp. 356, 386.
185. See, for example, Herbert J. Gans, *The Urban Villagers: Group and Class in the Life of Italian-Americans* (New York: The Free Press, 1962), p. 20; Virginia Yans-McLaughlin, *Family and Community,* pp. 223–224.
186. Robert F. Foerster, *The Italian Emigration of Our Times,* p. 333.
187. Ibid., pp. 333–338, passim.
188. Ibid., p. 347.
189. Ibid., p. 358.
190. Ibid., p. 356.
191. Ibid., p. 345.
192. Ibid., p. 350.
193. Ibid., p. 347.
194. Ibid., pp. 353–355.
195. Humbert S. Nelli, "Italians," *Harvard Encyclopedia of American Ethnic*

Groups, edited by Stephan Thernstrom et al., p. 549.

196. Robert F. Foerster, *The Italian Emigration of Our Times,* p. 371.
197. Ibid., pp. 329–330, 343.
198. Nathan Glazer and Daniel Patrick Moynihan, *Beyond the Melting Pot: The Negroes, Puerto Ricans, Jews, Italians, and Irish of New York City* (Cambridge, Mass.: MIT Press, 1963), pp. 257–258.
199. See, for example, Robert F. Foerster, *The Italian Emigration of Our Times,* pp. 99, 120, 132.
200. Leonard Covello, *The Social Background of the Italo-American School Child,* pp. 289–310.
201. Humbert S. Nelli, "Italians," *Harvard Encyclopedia of American Ethnic Groups,* edited by Stephan Thernstrom et al., p. 551.
202. Thomas Sowell, *Ethnic America,* pp. 112–113.
203. Rudolf Glanz, *Jew and Italian,* p. 61.
204. Nathan Glazer and Daniel Patrick Moynihan, *Beyond the Melting Pot,* p. 213.
205. Robert F. Foerster, *The Italian Emigration of Our Times,* p. 369.
206. Dino Cinel, *From Italy to San Francisco,* p. 233.
207. Ibid., p. 231.
208. Samuel L. Baily, "The Adjustment of Italian Immigrants in Buenos Aires and New York," *American Historical Review,* April 1983, p. 287.
209. Samuel L. Baily, "The Italians and the Development of Organized Labor in Argentina, Brazil and the United States," *Journal of Social History,* Winter 1969–70, pp. 125, 126.
210. Ibid., p. 124.
211. R. Pascoe, "Italian Settlement until 1914," *The Australian People,* edited by James Jupp, p. 596.
212. Charles A. Price, *Southern Europeans in Australia,* p. 11.
213. W. D. Borrie, "Australia," *The Positive Contribution by Immigrants,* edited by Oscar Handlin et al., p. 88.
214. Charles A. Price, *Southern Europeans in Australia,* p. 11.
215. N. O. P. Pyke, "An Outline of Italian Immigration into Australia," *The Australian Quarterly,* September 1948, p. 103.
216. W. D. Borrie, *Italians and Germans in Australia* (Melbourne: Australian National University, 1934), p. 147; N. O. P. Pyke, "An Outline of Italian Immigration into Australia," *The Australian Quarterly,* September 1948, p. 102.
217. W. D. Borrie, *Italians and Germans in Australia,* pp. 128, 129.
218. R. Pascoe, "Italian Settlement until 1914," *The Australian People,* edited by James Jupp, p. 597.

219. G. Cresciani, "Italian Immigrants 1920–1945," ibid., p. 610.
220. W. D. Borrie, *Italians and Germans in Australia,* p. 146.
221. D. Menghetti, "Italians in North Queensland," *The Australian People,* edited by James Jupp, pp. 600–601.
222. W. D. Borrie, *Italians and Germans in Australia,* pp. 144–145.
223. Ibid., p. 145; R. Pascoe, "Italian Settlement until 1914," *The Australian People,* edited by James Jupp, p. 596.
224. R. Pascoe, "Italian Settlement until 1914," *The Australian People,* edited by James Jupp, p. 596.
225. Helen Ware, *A Profile of the Italian Community in Australia* (Melbourne: Australian Institute of Multicultural Affairs and Co.As.It. Italian Assistance Association, 1981), p. 12.
226. G. Cresciani, "Italian Immigrants 1920–1945," *The Australian People,* edited by James Jupp, p. 609.
227. N. O. P. Pyke, "An Outline of Italian Immigration into Australia," *The Australian Quarterly,* September 1948, p. 105.
228. Charles A. Price, *Southern Europeans in Australia,* p. 11.
229. N. O. P. Pyke, "An Outline of Italian Immigration into Australia," *The Australian Quarterly,* September 1948, p. 105.
230. D. Menghetti, "Italians in North Queensland," *The Australian People,* edited by James Jupp, p. 601; G. Cresciani, "Italian Immigrants 1920–1945," ibid., pp. 610, 611, 612.
231. Helen Ware, *A Profile of the Italian Community in Australia,* p. 15.
232. D. Menghetti, "Italians in North Queensland," *The Australian People,* edited by James Jupp, p. 602.
233. Australian Government Commission of Inquiry into Poverty, *Welfare of Migrants* (Canberra: Australian Government Publishing Service, 1975), pp. 37–38.
234. Helen Ware, *A Profile of the Italian Community in Australia,* p. 24.
235. Ibid., p. 18.
236. Charles A. Price, "The Ethnic Composition of the Australian Population," *Immigration and Ethnicity in the 1980s,* edited by Ian Burnley, Sol Encel, and Grant McCall (Melbourne: Longman Cheshire, 1985), p. 47.
237. Helen Ware, *A Profile of the Italian Community in Australia,* pp. 22–23.
238. Ibid., pp. 11, 21.
239. Ibid., p. 26.
240. Australian Government Commission of Inquiry into Poverty, *Welfare of Migrants,* p. 39.
241. Ibid., p. 38.
242. Helen Ware, *A Profile of the Italian Community in Australia,* p. 7.

243. Ibid., p. 28.
244. Australian Government Commission of Inquiry into Poverty, *Welfare of Migrants,* p. 51.
245. Charles A. Price, *The Methods and Statistics of "Southern Europeans in Australia,"* p. 40. The terms used in the table cited are defined on pp. 38–39 and are more fully explained in Charles A. Price and J. Zubrycki, "The Use of Intermarriage Statistics as an Index of Assimilation," *Population Studies,* Vol. 16, No. 1 (1968), pp. 58–69.
246. Helen Ware, *A Profile of the Italian Community in Australia,* p. 13.
247. W. D. Borrie, *Italians and Germans in Australia,* p. 132.
248. Charles A. Price, *Southern Europeans in Australia,* pp. 93, 94.
249. W. D. Borrie, *Italians and Germans in Australia,* p. 131.
250. Helen Ware, *A Profile of the Italian Community in Australia,* p. 22.
251. Ibid., p. 91.
252. Des Storer, "Italians in Australia: A Social Overview," *Mosaics or Melting Pot: Cultural Evolution in Australia,* edited by Philip R. de Lacey and Millicent E. Poole (Sydney: Harcourt Brace Jovanovich Group, 1979), pp. 294–295; Helen Ware, *A Profile of the Italian Community in Australia,* p. 36.
253. Helen Ware, *A Profile of the Italian Community in Australia,* p. 43; Thomas Sowell, *Ethnic America,* pp. 118, 125.
254. Helen Ware, *A Profile of the Italian Community in Australia,* pp. 33–34; Thomas Sowell, *Ethnic America,* pp. 115–116.
255. Constance Cronin, *The Sting of Change,* p. 163.
256. Helen Ware, *A Profile of the Italian Community in Australia,* pp. 34, 35.
257. Constance Cronin, *The Sting of Change,* p. 162.
258. Ibid., p. 163.
259. Peter R. Shergold, "Discrimination against Australian Immigrants: An Historical Methodology," *Immigration and Ethnicity in the 1980s,* edited by Ian Burnley, Sol Encel, and Grant McCall, p. 72.
260. Australian Government Commission of Inquiry into Poverty, *Welfare of Migrants,* p. 39.
261. Australian Bureau of Statistics, *Census of Population and Housing, 30 June 1981: Cross-Classified Characteristics of Persons and Dwellings, Australia,* Catalogue No. 2452.0, October 1983, pp. 11, 12.
262. Australian Government Commission of Inquiry into Poverty, *Welfare of Migrants,* p. 43.
263. Helen Ware, *A Profile of the Italian Community in Australia,* p. 47. See also W. D. Borrie, *Italians and Germans in Australia,* p. 142.
264. Helen Ware, *A Profile of the Italian Community in Australia,* p. 26.

265. Ibid., pp. 30–31.
266. Ibid., pp. 32, 33.
267. Constance Cronin, *The Sting of Change,* pp. 231–232.
268. Ibid., Chapters 10, 11.
269. Ibid., pp. 239–240.
270. Helen Ware, *A Profile of the Italian Community in Australia,* p. 48.
271. Ibid., p. 62.
272. Ibid., p. 63.
273. Constance Cronin, *The Sting of Change,* p. 161.
274. Australian Government Commission of Inquiry into Poverty, *Welfare of Migrants,* p. 39.
275. Lado Ruzicka, "Premarital Pregnancies in Australia," *Journal of Marriage and the Family,* May 1977, pp. 109, 392.
276. Charles A. Price, *Southern Europeans in Australia,* p. 109.
277. W. D. Borrie, "Australia," *The Positive Contribution by Immigrants,* edited by Oscar Handlin et al., p. 101.
278. Robert F. Foerster, *The Italian Emigration of Our Times,* p. 417.

CHAPTER 5: THE OVERSEAS CHINESE

1. S. W. Kung, *Chinese in American Life: Some Aspects of Their History, Status, Problems, and Contributions* (Seattle: University of Washington Press, 1962), pp. 9, 11.
2. 中華 民國 僑務 統計／僑務 委員會 編. --〔臺北〕：該會 [The Republic of China, *Overseas Chinese Affairs Statistics*] (Taipei, Taiwan: Overseas Chinese Affairs Commission, 1994), p. 8. See also "The Chinese Abroad—Rich, Not Red," *The Economist,* April 28, 1984, p. 80.
3. 中華 民國 僑務 統計／僑務 委員會 編. --〔臺北〕：該會 [The Republic of China, *Overseas Chinese Affairs Statistics*], p. 6; Ng Kwee Choo, *The Chinese in London* (London: Oxford University Press, 1968); Watt Stewart, *Chinese Bondage in Peru: A History of Chinese Coolie in Peru, 1849–1874* (Durham, N.C.: Duke University Press, 1951); Ng Bickleen Fong, *The Chinese in New Zealand: A Study in Assimilation* (Hong Kong: Hong Kong University Press, 1959); David Lowenthal, *West Indian Societies* (New York: Oxford University Press, 1972), pp. 202–208; Duvon Clough Corbitt, *A Study of the Chinese in Cuba: 1847–1947* (Wilmore, Ky.: Asbury College Press, 1971); Cecil Clementi, *The Chinese in British Guiana* (Georgetown, British Guiana: "The Argosy" Company, Ltd., 1915).

4. 中華 民國 僑務 統計／僑務 委員會 編. --〔臺北〕：該會 [The Republic of China, *Overseas Chinese Affairs Statistics*], p. 8.
5. Andrew Tanzer, "The Bamboo Network," *Forbes*, July 18, 1994, pp. 138–145.
6. Joel Kotkin, *Tribes: How Race, Religion, and Identity Determine Success in the New Global Economy* (New York: Random House, 1993), p. 180.
7. See, for example, Lea E. Williams, *The Future of the Overseas Chinese in Southeast Asia* (New York: McGraw-Hill, 1966), p. 11; Victor Purcell, *The Chinese in Southeast Asia*, second edition (Kuala Lumpur: Oxford University Press, 1980), pp. 3, 7, 83, 128, 195, 540; Yuan-li Wu and Chun-hsi Wu, *Economic Development in Southeast Asia: The Chinese Dimension* (Stanford, Calif.: Hoover Institution Press, 1980), pp. 30, 51, 71, 85.
8. S. W. Kung, *Chinese in American Life*, p. 22.
9. Ibid., p. 23.
10. Ibid., p. 22.
11. Ibid., pp. 21, 22, 23.
12. Lea E. Williams, *The Future of the Overseas Chinese in Southeast Asia*, pp. 17–18; David Lowenthal, *West Indian Societies*, p. 203; "Chinese Abroad—Rich, Not Red," *The Economist*, April 28, 1984, p. 81; G. William Skinner, *Chinese Society in Thailand: An Analytical History* (Ithaca, N.Y.: Cornell University Press, 1957), pp. 134–143; Jack Chen, *The Chinese of America* (San Francisco: Harper & Row, 1980), p. 19; Naosaku Uchida, *The Overseas Chinese: A Bibliographical Essay Based on the Resources of the Hoover Institution* (Stanford, Calif.: Hoover Institution Press, 1960), pp. 21–46, 52.
13. Joel Kotkin, *Tribes*, p. 188.
14. Victor Simpao Limlingan, *Overseas Chinese in ASEAN: Business Strategies and Management Practices* (Manila: Vita Development Corporation, 1986), p. 35.
15. S. W. Kung, *Chinese in American Life*, p. 24.
16. *China Yearbook, 1980* (Taipei, Taiwan: China Publishing Company, 1980), p. 364.
17. Jack Chen, *The Chinese of America*, p. 18.
18. Yuan-li Wu and Chun-hsi Wu, *Economic Development in Southeast Asia*, pp. 84, 134–136; Victor Purcell, *The Chinese in Southeast Asia*, p. 176.
19. The Republic of China, *Overseas Chinese Affairs Statistics*, pp. 7, 72; *China Yearbook, 1980*, pp. 364–365.
20. Naosaku Uchida, *The Overseas Chinese*, p. 43. See also L. A. Peter Gosling, "Chinese Crop Dealers in Malaysia and Thailand: The Myth of

the Merciless Monopsonistic Middleman," *The Chinese in Southeast Asia,* edited by Linda Y. C. Lim & L. A. Peter Gosling (Singapore: Maruzen Asia, 1983), Volume I: *Ethnicity and Economic Activity,* p. 152; Jack Chen, *The Chinese of America,* p. 27.

21. Victor Simpao Limlingan, *Overseas Chinese in ASEAN,* p. 28.
22. Ibid., p. 35.
23. Charles O. Hucker, *China's Imperial Past: An Introduction to Chinese History and Culture* (Stanford, Calif.: University Press, 1975), pp. 324, 336, 349, 351, 352; Jacques Gernet, *A History of Chinese Civilization* (Cambridge: Cambridge University Press, 1983), p. 347.
24. Charles O. Hucker, *China's Imperial Past,* p. 65; Jacques Gernet, *A History of Chinese Civilization,* pp. 69, 138, 140.
25. Jacques Gernet, *A History of Chinese Civilization,* p. 320.
26. Charles O. Hucker, *China's Imperial Past,* p. 336; Jacques Gernet, *A History of Chinese Civilization,* pp. 332–337; *The Concise Columbia Encyclopedia,* edited by Judith S. Levey and Agnes Greenhall (New York: Columbia University Press, 1983), p. 2812.
27. Charles O. Hucker, *China's Imperial Past,* pp. 331, 333.
28. Frederic Wakeman, Jr., *The Fall of Imperial China* (New York: The Free Press, 1975), p. 39.
29. Charles O. Hucker, *China's Imperial Past,* p. 342.
30. Frederic Wakeman, Jr., *The Fall of Imperial China,* p. 12.
31. Charles O. Hucker, *China's Imperial Past,* p. 356.
32. Ibid., p. 356.
33. Ibid., pp. 323–328; Frederic Wakeman, Jr., *The Fall of Imperial China,* p. 66.
34. Frederic Wakeman, Jr., *The Fall of Imperial China,* p. 32; Jacques Gernet, *A History of Chinese Civilization,* pp. 491–492.
35. Jacques Gernet, *A History of Chinese Civilization,* pp. 579–580; Charles O. Hucker, *China's Imperial Past,* p. 356.
36. Lea E. Williams, *The Future of the Overseas Chinese in Southeast Asia,* p. 20.
37. Yuan-li Wu and Chun-hsi Wu, *Economic Development in Southeast Asia,* p. 57; Irving Kaplan et al., *Area Handbook for Jamaica* (Washington, D.C.: U.S. Government Printing Office, 1976), p. 102.
38. Clifton A. Barton, "Trust and Credit: Some Observations Regarding Business Strategies of Overseas Chinese Traders in South Vietnam," *The Chinese in Southeast Asia,* edited by Linda Y. C. Lim and L. A. Peter Gosling, Volume I: *Ethnicity and Economic Activity,* p. 62; L. A. Peter Gosling, "Changing Chinese Identities in Southeast Asia: An Introduc-

tory Review," ibid., Volume II: *Identity, Culture, and Politics,* pp. 4–5; Victor Purcell, *The Chinese in Southeast Asia,* second edition, p. 32.

39. S. W. Kung, *Chinese in American Life,* p. 9.
40. Australian Government Commission of Inquiry into Poverty, *Welfare of Migrants* (Canberra: Australian Government Publishing Service, 1975), pp. 116–118.
41. Victor Purcell, *The Chinese in Southeast Asia,* second edition, pp. 116–117, 538–539, 546.
42. Stephen H. Haliczer, "The Castilian Urban Patriciate and the Jewish Expulsions of 1480–92," *American Historical Review,* February 1973, pp. 47–49.
43. *The World Almanac and Book of Facts, 1983* (New York: Newspaper Enterprise Association, 1983), pp. 510, 511, 560.
44. Jacques Gernet, *A History of Chinese Civilization,* pp. 126–127, 398–399.
45. Victor Simpao Limlingan, *Overseas Chinese in ASEAN,* pp. 23–25.
46. Yuan-li Wu, "Chinese Entrepreneurs in Southeast Asia," *American Economic Review,* May 1983, pp. 113–114.
47. Chun-hsi Wu, *Dollars, Dependents and Dogma: Overseas Chinese Remittances to Communist China* (Stanford, Calif.: The Hoover Institution Press, 1967), pp. 41–42.
48. *China Yearbook, 1980,* p. 367.
49. Yuan-li Wu, "Chinese Entrepreneurs in Southeast Asia," *American Economic Review,* May 1983, p. 116.
50. Victor Purcell, *The Chinese in Southeast Asia,* second edition, p. 90.
51. G. William Skinner, *Chinese Society in Thailand,* pp. 20–21, 26–27, 45.
52. Ibid., pp. 4, 10, 15, 19, 148, 149–154.
53. Victor Purcell, *The Chinese in Southeast Asia,* second edition, p. 91.
54. G. William Skinner, *Chinese Society in Thailand,* p. 61.
55. Ibid., pp. 79, 183.
56. Ibid., pp. 81–82.
57. Ibid., p. 116.
58. James A. Haetner, "Market Gardening in Thailand: The Origins of an Ethnic Chinese Monopoly," *The Chinese in Southeast Asia,* edited by Linda Y. C. Lim & L. A. Peter Gosling, Volume I: *Ethnicity and Economic Activity,* p. 40; see also G. William Skinner, *Chinese Society in Thailand,* p. 98.
59. G. William Skinner, *Chinese Society in Thailand,* p. 114.
60. Victor Purcell, *The Chinese in Southeast Asia,* second edition, p. 107.
61. Ibid., p. 97.

62. G. William Skinner, *Chinese Society in Thailand,* pp. 64, 114.
63. Victor Purcell, *The Chinese in Southeast Asia,* second edition, p. 107.
64. Yuan-li Wu and Chun-hsi Wu, *Economic Development in Southeast Asia: The Chinese Dimension,* p. 70.
65. G. William Skinner, *Chinese Society in Thailand,* p. 216.
66. Victor Purcell, *The Chinese in Southeast Asia,* second edition, p. 128.
67. G. William Skinner, *Chinese Society in Thailand,* pp. 126, 190.
68. Ibid., pp. 127–128.
69. Ibid., p. 139.
70. Ibid., p. 31.
71. Victor Purcell, *The Chinese in Southeast Asia,* second edition, p. 261. See also G. William Skinner, *Chinese Society in Thailand,* p. 141.
72. G. William Skinner, *Chinese Society in Thailand,* p. 154.
73. Victor Purcell, *The Chinese in Southeast Asia,* second edition, pp. 100, 104.
74. Ibid., p. 101.
75. G. William Skinner, *Chinese Society in Thailand,* pp. 147–148.
76. Ibid., p. 125.
77. Victor Purcell, *The Chinese in Southeast Asia,* second edition, p. 119.
78. Ibid., p. 85.
79. G. William Skinner, *Chinese Society in Thailand,* pp. 190–191.
80. Ibid., p. 196.
81. Ibid., p. 173.
82. Ibid., p. 158.
83. Ibid., pp. 159–164.
84. Ibid., pp. 216–218.
85. Ibid., pp. 102–103.
86. Ibid., pp. 103–104, 213.
87. Ibid., pp. 10, 99.
88. Ibid., pp. 101–102.
89. Ibid., pp. 101–102.
90. Victor Purcell, *The Chinese in Southeast Asia,* second edition, p. 131.
91. Ibid., p. 129.
92. G. William Skinner, *Chinese Society in Thailand,* p. 113.
93. Ibid., pp. 221–222.
94. L. A. Peter Gosling, "Chinese Crop Dealers in Malaysia and Thailand: The Myth of the Merciless Monopsonistic Middleman," *The Chinese in Southeast Asia,* edited by Linda Y. C. Lim & L. A. Peter Gosling, Volume I: *Ethnicity and Economic Activity,* pp. 138–141, 156.
95. Victor Purcell, *The Chinese in Southeast Asia,* second edition, pp. 469n,

546. See also A. L. Peter Gosling, "Chinese Crop Dealers in Malaysia and Thailand: The Myth of the Merciless Monopsonistic Middleman," *The Chinese in Southeast Asia,* edited by Linda Y. C. Lim and L. A. Peter Gosling, Volume I: *Ethnicity and Economic Activity,* pp. 131–170.

96. See, for example, L. A. Peter Gosling, "Chinese Crop Dealers in Malaysia and Thailand: The Myth of the Merciless Monopsonistic Middleman," *The Chinese in Southeast Asia,* edited by Linda Y. C. Lim and L. A. Peter Gosling, Volume I: *Ethnicity and Economic Activity,* pp. 139, 153.
97. G. William Skinner, *Chinese Society in Thailand,* p. 225.
98. Ibid., pp. 228–229.
99. Victor Purcell, *The Chinese in Southeast Asia,* second edition, p. 139n.
100. G. William Skinner, *Chinese Society in Thailand,* p. 264.
101. Ibid., p. 271.
102. Ibid., p. 275.
103. Ibid., p. 311.
104. Victor Purcell, *The Chinese in Southeast Asia,* second edition, p. 127.
105. Ibid., p. 128.
106. Lennox A. Mills, *Southeast Asia: Illusion and Reality in Politics and Economics,* (Minneapolis: University of Minnesota Press, 1964), p. 130.
107. G. William Skinner, *Chinese Society in Thailand,* pp. 359–360.
108. Ibid., p. 336.
109. Karl von Vorys, *Democracy without Consensus: Communalism and Political Stability in Malaysia* (Kuala Lumpur: Oxford University Press, 1976), p. 88n.
110. "The Chinese Abroad—Rich Not Red," *The Economist,* April 28, 1984, pp. 80, 81.
111. Nena Vreeland et al., *Area Handbook for Malaysia* (Washington, D.C.: U.S. Government Printing Office, 1977), p. 89.
112. Ibid., p. 88.
113. See, for example, Mahathir bin Mohamad, *The Malay Dilemma* (Kuala Lumpur: Federal Publications, 1982), p. 21; Nena Vreeland et al., *Area Handbook for Malaysia,* p. 89.
114. Nena Vreeland et al., *Area Handbook for Malaysia,* p. 82.
115. P. T. Bauer, *Reality and Rhetoric: Studies in the Economics of Development* (Cambridge, Mass.: Harvard University Press, 1984), p. 7.
116. D. G. E. Hall, *A History of South-East Asia,* (London: Macmillan and Company, Ltd., 1981), p. 835.
117. Victor Purcell, *The Chinese in Southeast Asia,* second edition, p. 244.
118. Alvin Rabushka, *Race and Politics in Urban Malays,* second edition

(Stanford, Calif.: Hoover Institution Press, 1973), p. 17; Lennox A. Mills, *Southeast Asia*, p. 41.

119. Victor Simpao Limlingan, *Overseas Chinese in ASEAN*, p. 29.
120. Ibid., p. 30.
121. D. G. E. Hall, *A History of South-East Asia*, p. 606.
122. Donald R. Snodgrass, *Inequality and Economic Development in Malaysia* (Kuala Lumpur: Oxford University Press, 1980), pp. 16–17.
123. D. G. E. Hall, *A History of South-East Asia*, p. 83; Victor Purcell, *The Chinese in Southeast Asia*, second edition, p. 284.
124. Donald R. Snodgrass, *Inequality and Economic Development in Malaysia*, p. 38.
125. Yuan-li Wu and Chun-hsi Wu, *Economic Development in Southeast Asia*, p. 51.
126. Nena Vreeland et al., *Area Handbook for Malaysia*, p. 83.
127. Ibid., pp. 87–88.
128. D. G. E. Hall, *A History of South-East Asia*, p. 836.
129. See, for example, Usha Mahajani, *The Role of Indian Minorities in Burma and Malaysia* (Westport, Conn.: Greenwood Press, 1973), Chapter IV.
130. Victor Purcell, *The Chinese in Southeast Asia*, second edition, p. 283n.
131. Ibid., p. 284.
132. P. T. Bauer, *The Rubber Industry: A Study in Competition and Monopoly* (Cambridge, Mass.: Harvard University Press, 1948), pp. 217–218.
133. Victor Purcell, *The Chinese in Southeast Asia*, second edition, p. 277.
134. Ibid., p. 277; Nena Vreeland et al., *Area Handbook for Malaysia*, p. 96.
135. Victor Purcell, *The Chinese in Southeast Asia*, second edition, pp. 277–279.
136. Yuan-li Wu and Chun-hsi Wu, *Economic Development in Southeast Asia*, p. 57.
137. Virginia Thompson and Richard Adloff, *Minority Problems in Southeast Asia* (New York: Russell and Russell, 1970), p. 41.
138. Victor Purcell, *The Chinese in Southeast Asia*, second edition, pp. 305–306.
139. T. H. Silcock, "Approximate Racial Division of National Income," *The Political Economy of Independent Malaya: A Case Study in Development*, edited by T. H. Silcock and E. K. Fisk (Berkeley: University of California Press, 1963), p. 279.
140. Lennox A. Mills, *Southeast Asia*, p. 42.
141. Nena Vreeland et al., *Area Handbook for Malaysia*, pp. 231–232.
142. L. A. Peter Gosling, "Chinese Crop Dealers in Malaysia and Thailand:

The Myth of the Merciless Monopsonistic Middleman," *The Chinese in Southeast Asia,* edited by Linda Y. C. Lim & L. A. Peter Gosling, Volume I: *Ethnicity and Economic Activity,* p. 142.

143. Donald R. Snodgrass, *Inequality and Economic Development in Malaysia,* p. 78.
144. Ibid., p. 82; Robert Klitgaard and Ruth Katz, "Overcoming Ethnic Inequalities: Lessons for Malaysia," *Journal of Policy Analysis and Management,* Vol. II, no. 3 (1983), pp. 335, 343; Pang Eng Fong, "Race, Income Distribution, and Development in Malaysia and Singapore," *The Chinese in Southeast Asia,* edited by Linda Y. C. Lim and L. A. Peter Gosling, Volume I: *Ethnicity and Economic Activity,* p. 321.
145. Mavis Puthucheary, "Public Policies Relating to Business and Land and Their Impact on Ethnic Relations in Peninsular Malaysia," *From Independence to Statehood: Managing Ethnic Conflict in Five African and Asian States,* edited by Robert B. Goldmann and A. Jeyaratnam Wilson (London: France Pinter, 1984), p. 158.
146. Donald R. Snodgrass, *Inequality and Economic Development in Malaysia,* p. 221.
147. Lim Mah Hui, "The Ownership and Control of Large Corporations in Malaysia: The Role of Chinese Businessmen," *The Chinese in Southeast Asia,* edited by Linda Y. C. Lim and L. A. Peter Gosling, Volume I: *Ethnicity and Economic Activity*, p. 278.
148. Tai Yoke Lin, "Ethnic Restructuring in Malaysia 1979–1980: The Employment Perspective," *From Independence to Statehood,* edited by Robert B. Goldmann and A. Jeyaratnam Wilson, p. 52; Donald R. Snodgrass, *Inequality and Economic Development in Malaysia,* p. 221.
149. Tai Yoke Lin, "Ethnic Restructuring in Malaysia 1979–1980: The Employment Perspective," *From Independence to Statehood,* edited by Robert B. Goldmann and A. Jeyaratnam Wilson, p. 53.
150. Donald R. Snodgrass, *Inequality and Economic Development in Malaysia,* pp. 223–224.
151. Donald M. Nonini, "The Chinese Truck Transport 'Industry' of a Peninsular Malaysia Market Town," *The Chinese in Southeast Asia,* edited by Linda Y. C. Lim and L. A. Peter Gosling, Volume I: *Ethnicity and Economic Activity,* pp. 180, 195–196.
152. Tai Yoke Lin, "Ethnic Restructuring in Malaysia 1979–1980: The Employment Perspective," *From Independence to Statehood,* edited by Robert B. Goldmann and A. Jeyaratnam Wilson, pp. 48–50.
153. Ibid., p. 57.
154. Victor Purcell, *The Chinese in Southeast Asia,* second edition, p. 249.

155. Ibid., p. 234.
156. Nena Vreeland et al., *Area Handbook for Singapore* (Washington, D.C.: U.S. Government Printing Office, 1977), p. 18.
157. Ibid., p. 47.
158. *Economic and Social Statistics: Singapore 1960–1982* (Singapore: Department of Statistics, 1983), p. 7.
159. Victor Purcell, *The Chinese in Southeast Asia,* second edition, pp. 251–252.
160. Nena Vreeland et al., *Area Handbook for Singapore,* pp. 48–50.
161. Ibid., p. 69.
162. Ibid., p. 76.
163. *Key Education Statistics, 1983* (Singapore: Ministry of Education, 1983), p. 9.
164. *Statistics of Marriage, 1983* (Singapore: Department of Statistics, 1984), pp. 7–8, 12–13.
165. Victor Purcell, *The Chinese in Southeast Asia,* second edition, p. 389.
166. Ibid., pp. 397, 404.
167. Ibid., p. 396.
168. Ibid., p. 404.
169. Ibid., p. 410.
170. Ibid., pp. 461–462; J. A. C. Mackie and Charles A. Coppel, "A Preliminary Survey," *The Chinese in Indonesia,* edited by J. A. C. Mackie (Melbourne: The Australian Institute of International Affairs, 1976), pp. 4–5.
171. Virginia Thompson and Richard Adloff, *Minority Problems in Southeast Asia,* p. 49; J. A. C. Mackie and Charles A. Coppel, "A Preliminary Survey," *The Chinese in Indonesia,* edited by J. A. C. Mackie, p. 7.
172. J. A. C. Mackie and Charles A. Coppel, "A Preliminary Survey," *The Chinese in Indonesia,* edited by J. A. C. Mackie, p. 7.
173. Victor Purcell, *The Chinese in Southeast Asia,* second edition, pp. 385–388; Wilfred T. Neill, *Twentieth-Century Indonesia* (New York: Columbia University Press, 1973), p. 347. See also Charles A. Coppel, *Indonesian Chinese in Crisis* (Kuala Lumpur: Oxford University Press, 1983), p. 2.
174. J. A. C. Mackie and Charles A. Coppel, "A Preliminary Survey," *The Chinese in Indonesia,* edited by J. A. C. Mackie, p. 5; Leo Suryadinata, *Peranakan Chinese Politics in Java: 1917–1942,* revised edition (Singapore: Singapore University Press, 1981), pp. xiv, 7.
175. Leo Suryadinata, *Peranakan Chinese Politics in Java,* p. xiv.
176. Ibid., pp. 100–101.
177. Ibid., passim.

178. Ibid., pp. 124–130. See also Charles A. Coppel, *Indonesia Chinese in Crisis,* pp. 2–3.
179. Charles A. Coppel, *Indonesian Chinese in Crisis,* p. 20.
180. Leo Suryadinata, *Peranakan Chinese Politics in Java,* pp. 152–153.
181. Victor Purcell, *The Chinese in Southeast Asia,* second edition, p. 472.
182. Ibid., p. 473.
183. Leo Suryadinata, *Pribumi Indonesians, the Chinese Minority and China: A Study of Perceptions and Policies* (Singapore: Heinemann Asia, 1986), pp. 58–59.
184. Ibid., pp. 128, 147.
185. Victor Purcell, *The Chinese in Southeast Asia,* second edition, pp. 473–478.
186. Mary F. Somers-Heidhues, "Citizenship and Identity: Ethnic Chinese and the Indonesian Revolution," *Changing Identities of the Southeast Asian Chinese since World War II,* edited by Jennifer Cushman and Wang Gungwu (Hong Kong: Hong Kong University Press, 1988), pp. 121–122.
187. Victor Purcell, *The Chinese in Southeast Asia,* second edition, p. 383.
188. Mary F. Somers-Heidhues, "Citizenship and Identity," *Changing Identities of the Southeast Asian Chinese since World War II,* edited by Jennifer Cushman and Wang Gungwu, p. 115.
189. Victor Purcell, *The Chinese in Southeast Asia,* second edition, p. 486.
190. Leo Suryadinata, *Pribumi Indonesians, the Chinese Minority and China,* p. 130; Victor Purcell, *The Chinese in Southeast Asia,* second edition, pp. 487–488.
191. Leo Suryadinata, *Pribumi Indonesians, the Chinese Minority and China,* p. 132; Victor Purcell, *The Chinese in Southeast Asia,* second edition, pp. 488, 489.
192. Victor Purcell, *The Chinese in Southeast Asia,* second edition, pp. 487, 488.
193. J. A. C. Mackie, "Anti-Chinese Outbreaks in Indonesia, 1959–68," *The Chinese in Indonesia,* edited by J. A. C. Mackie, pp. 83, 92.
194. Leo Suryadinata, *Pribumi Indonesians, the Chinese Minority and China,* pp. 141–142; Richard Robison, *Indonesia: The Rise of Capital* (North Sydney: Allen & Unwin, 1987), pp. 271–328.
195. Charles A. Coppel, *Indonesian Chinese in Crisis,* Chapter 7.
196. Yuan-li Wu and Chun-hsi Wu, *Economic Development in Southeast Asia,* p. 63.
197. Charles A. Coppel, *Indonesian Chinese in Crisis,* pp. 40, 152, 153, 159, 173.
198. Ibid., pp. 160–166, 167.

199. Ibid., pp. 82–85, 110–111, 144.
200. Joseph P. Manguno, "Suharto Angling for Political Dividends in Expansionary Budget for New Year," *The Asian Wall Street Journal Weekly,* January 12, 1981, p. 12; "Now a Spate of Bombings," *Asiaweek,* October 19, 1984, pp. 8–9; Susumu Awanohara, "Bombs in Chinatown," *Far Eastern Economic Review,* October 18, 1984, p. 18.
201. Virginia Thompson and Richard Adloff, *Minority Problems in Southeast Asia,* p. 48.
202. See "The Chinese Abroad—Rich Not Red," *The Economist,* April 28, 1984, pp. 80, 81.
203. Jacques Amyot, *The Manila Chinese, Familism in the Philippine Environment* (Quezon City: Institute of Philippine Culture, 1973), p. 2.
204. "The Chinese Abroad—Rich Not Red," *The Economist,* April 28, 1984, pp. 80, 81.
205. Victor Purcell, *The Chinese in Southeast Asia,* second edition, pp. 500–504.
206. Ibid., pp. 514, 519, 527.
207. Ibid., p. 508.
208. Ibid., p. 512.
209. Ibid., pp. 511, 524.
210. Jacques Amyot, *The Manila Chinese, Familism in the Philippine Environment,* pp. 11, 42.
211. Victor Purcell, *The Chinese in Southeast Asia,* second edition, pp. 536–537.
212. Jacques Amyot, *The Manila Chinese, Familism in the Philippine Environment,* pp. 63–66.
213. Victor Purcell, *The Chinese in Southeast Asia,* second edition, p. 540.
214. Ibid., p. 548.
215. Ibid., pp. 544, 546; Antonio S. Tan, "The Changing Identity of the Philippine Chinese, 1946–1984," *Changing Identities of the Southeast Asian Chinese since World War II,* edited by Jennifer Cushman and Wang Gungwu, pp. 183–184.
216. Victor Purcell, *The Chinese in Southeast Asia,* second edition, pp. 545–546.
217. Charles A. Coppel, *The Chinese in Indonesia, the Philippines and Malaysia* (London: Minority Rights Group, 1982), p. 18.
218. Victor Purcell, *The Chinese in Southeast Asia,* second edition, pp. 538–539.
219. Antonio S. Tan, "The Changing Identity of the Philippine Chinese,

1946–1984," *Changing Identities of the Southeast Asian Chinese since World War II*, edited by Jennifer Cushman and Wang Gungwu, pp. 182–183.

220. Ibid., pp. 184–185.
221. Ibid., pp. 186–187.
222. Jacques Amyot, *The Manila Chinese, Familism in the Philippine Environment*, pp. 128, 131, 132.
223. Ibid., pp. 76–78.
224. John T. Omohundro, "Social Networks and Business Success for the Philippine Chinese," *The Chinese in Southeast Asia*, edited by Linda Y. C. Lim & L. A. Peter Gosling, Volume I: *Ethnicity and Economic Activity*, pp. 66–67.
225. Ibid., p. 78.
226. Jacques Gernet, *A History of Chinese Civilization*, pp. 126–127; Victor Purcell, *The Chinese in Southeast Asia*, second edition, p. 11.
227. Jacques Gernet, *A History of Chinese Civilization*, p. 262.
228. Ibid., pp. 301–302.
229. Ibid., p. 238.
230. Ibid., p. 485.
231. Charles O. Hucker, *China's Imperial Past: An Introduction to Chinese History and Culture*, p. 343.
232. Victor Purcell, *The Chinese in Southeast Asia*, second edition, p. 181; William E. Willmott, *The Chinese in Cambodia* (Vancouver: University of British Columbia, 1967), p. 6.
233. William E. Willmott, *The Chinese in Cambodia*, pp. 33–36.
234. Victor Purcell, *The Chinese in Southeast Asia*, second edition, p. 184.
235. William E. Willmott, *The Chinese in Cambodia*, pp. 40–42.
236. Victor Purcell, *The Chinese in Southeast Asia*, second edition, pp. 177–178.
237. Virginia Thompson and Richard Adloff, *Minority Problems in Southeast Asia*, p. 56.
238. Victor Purcell, *The Chinese in Southeast Asia*, second edition, pp. 168, 170, 171.
239. Cf. ibid., pp. 168–171; William E. Willmott, *The Chinese in Cambodia*, p. 15; Lea E. Williams, *The Future of the Overseas Chinese in Southeast Asia*, p. 11. More estimates are compared in Yuan-li Wu and Chun-hsi Wu, *Economic Development in Southeast Asia*, p. 84.
240. Yuan-li Wu and Chun-hsi Wu, *Economic Development in Southeast Asia*, pp. 51, 88.

241. Ibid., p. 85.
242. Victor Purcell, *The Chinese in Southeast Asia,* second edition, pp. 193, 195, 204.
243. William E. Willmott, *The Chinese in Cambodia,* p. 47.
244. Clifton A. Barton, "Trust and Credit: Some Observations Regarding Business Strategies of Overseas Chinese Traders in South Vietnam," *The Chinese in Southeast Asia,* edited by Linda Y. C. Lim and L. A. Peter Gosling, Volume I: *Ethnicity and Economic Activity,* pp. 46–63.
245. Ibid., pp. 61–62.
246. William E. Willmott, *The Chinese in Cambodia,* pp. 49–51.
247. Martin J. Murray, *The Development of Capitalism in Colonial Indo-China, 1870–1940* (Berkeley: University of California Press, 1980), p. 221.
248. Victor Purcell, *The Chinese in Southeast Asia,* second edition, pp. 210–211.
249. Ibid., pp. 215–221.
250. "Emergency," *The New Republic,* June 30, 1979, p. 6.
251. Ben Kiernan, "Kampuchea's Ethnic Chinese under Pol Pot: A Case of Systematic Social Discrimination," *Changing Identities of the Southeast Asian Chinese since World War II,* edited by Jennifer Cushman and Wang Gungwu, p. 211.
252. B. W. Higman, "The Chinese in Trinidad, 1806–1838," *Caribbean Studies,* October 1972, pp. 21–44.
253. Duvon Clough Corbitt, *A Study of the Chinese in Cuba,* p. 115.
254. Jack Chen, *The Chinese of America,* p. 18.
255. David Lowenthal, *West Indian Societies,* p. 203.
256. Thomas Sowell, *Ethnic America,* pp. 149–152.
257. S. W. Kung, *Chinese in American Life,* pp. 22–23.
258. Ibid., p. 21.
259. Watt Stewart, *Chinese Bondage in Peru,* p. 119.
260. Ibid., p. 46.
261. Ibid., Chapter II; Duvon Clough Corbitt, *A Study of the Chinese in Cuba,* pp. 18–19, 27–29.
262. Watt Stewart, *Chinese Bondage in Peru,* p. 16n.
263. Jack Chen, *The Chinese of America,* p. 25.
264. Duvon Clough Corbitt, *A Study of the Chinese in Cuba,* pp. 18–19, 21, 42, 46; Watt Stewart, *Chinese Bondage in Peru,* pp. 19, 30–33.
265. Duvon Clough Corbitt, *A Study of the Chinese in Cuba,* p. 19.
266. Watt Stewart, *Chinese Bondage in Peru,* p. 74.
267. Duvon Clough Corbitt, *A Study of the Chinese in Cuba,* p. 117.
268. Ibid., p. 80; Watt Stewart, *Chinese Bondage in Peru,* pp. 124, 228.

269. Duvon Clough Corbitt, *A Study of the Chinese in Cuba,* p. 80.
270. Ibid., p. 80.
271. Watt Stewart, *Chinese Bondage in Peru,* p. 98.
272. Ibid., p. 75.
273. Ibid., p. 62.
274. Duvon Clough Corbitt, *A Study of the Chinese in Cuba,* p. 52.
275. Cecil Clementi, *The Chinese in British Guiana,* pp. 103–104, 111, 126, 128, 129, 133, 184, 185, 191, 277.
276. Watt Stewart, *Chinese Bondage in Peru,* p. 116.
277. Ibid., pp. 120–123.
278. Duvon Clough Corbitt, *A Study of the Chinese in Cuba,* p. 70.
279. Ibid., p. 83.
280. Ibid., Chapter VII.
281. S. W. Kung, *Chinese in American Life,* p. 23.
282. Watt Stewart, *Chinese Bondage in Peru,* p. 129.
283. Duvon Clough Corbitt, *A Study of the Chinese in Cuba,* p. 117.
284. Cecil Clementi, *The Chinese in British Guiana,* p. 318.
285. Stanford M. Lyman, *The Asian in the West* (Reno: University of Nevada System, 1970), p. 79.
286. Orlando Patterson, "Context and Choice in Ethnic Allegiance: A Theoretical Framework and Caribbean Case Study," *Ethnicity: Theory and Experience,* edited by Nathan Glazer and Daniel P. Moynihan (Cambridge, Mass.: Harvard University Press, 1981), p. 324.
287. Watt Stewart, *Chinese Bondage in Peru,* p. 228; Cecil Clementi, *The Chinese in British Guiana,* pp. 195–196.
288. David Lowenthal, *West Indian Societies,* p. 203; Jan Knippers Black et al., *Area Handbook for Trinidad and Tobago* (Washington, D.C.: U.S. Government Printing Office, 1976), p. 88.
289. Watt Stewart, *Chinese Bondage in Peru,* p. 228.
290. Carl Solberg, *Immigration and Nationalism: Argentina and Chile, 1890–1914* (Austin: University of Texas Press, 1970), p. 70.
291. Orlando Patterson, "Context and Choice in Ethnic Allegiance," *Ethnicity,* edited by Nathan Glazer and Daniel P. Moynihan, p. 341.
292. Ibid., p. 327.
293. Jan Knippers Black et al., *Area Handbook for Trinidad and Tobago,* p. 3; Irving Kaplan et al., *Area Handbook for Jamaica* (Washington, D.C.: U.S. Government Printing Office, 1976), p. 100; David Lowenthal, *West Indian Societies,* p. 194.
294. Jan Knippers Black et al., *Area Handbook for Trinidad and Tobago,* p. 53; S. W. Kung, *Chinese in American Life,* p. 23.

295. Orlando Patterson, "Context and Choice in Ethnic Allegiance," *Ethnicity,* edited by Nathan Glazer and Daniel P. Moynihan, pp. 324, 325.
296. David Lowenthal, *West Indian Societies,* pp. 203–204.
297. Ibid., p. 207.
298. Jan Knippers Black et al., *Area Handbook for Trinidad and Tobago,* pp. 82, 87; Orlando Patterson, "Context and Choice in Ethnic Allegiance," *Ethnicity,* edited by Nathan Glazer and Daniel Moynihan, pp. 326–327.
299. Jan Knippers Black et al., *Area Handbook for Trinidad and Tobago,* p. 88; David Lowenthal, *West Indian Societies,* p. 203.
300. Jan Knippers Black et al., *Area Handbook for Trinidad and Tobago,* p. 88.
301. Ibid., p. 90; David Lowenthal, *West Indian Societies,* p. 207. See also Orlando Patterson, "Context and Choice in Ethnic Allegiance," *Ethnicity,* edited by Nathan Glazer and Daniel P. Moynihan, p. 324.
302. David Lowenthal, *West Indian Societies,* pp. 207–208.
303. Ibid., pp. 203–204.
304. Ibid., p. 204.
305. Ibid., p. 193.
306. Ibid., pp. 145, 207.
307. Ibid., p. 207.
308. H. M. Lai, "Chinese," *Harvard Encyclopedia of American Ethnic Groups,* edited by Stephan Thernstrom et al. (Cambridge, Mass.: Harvard University Press, 1981), pp. 217–218; Jack Chen, *The Chinese of America,* pp. 5–6.
309. H. M. Lai, "Chinese," *Harvard Encyclopedia of American Ethnic Groups,* edited by Stephan Thernstrom et al., p. 223.
310. Ibid.
311. S. W. Kung, *Chinese in American Life,* p. 35.
312. Jack Chen, *The Chinese of America,* p. 35.
313. S. W. Kung, *Chinese in American Life,* p. 67.
314. Jack Chen, *The Chinese of America,* p. 47.
315. Ibid., pp. 44–45.
316. Betty Lee Sung, *The Story of the Chinese in America* (New York: Collier Books, 1967), p. 26. See also Jack Chen, *The Chinese of America,* pp. 48–49.
317. Jack Chen, *The Chinese of America,* p. 53; S. W. Kung, *Chinese in American Life,* p. 66.
318. S. W. Kung, *Chinese in American Life,* p. 67.
319. Jack Chen, *The Chinese of America,* pp. 55–56.
320. Ibid., pp. 57, 58.
321. Ibid., pp. 59, 60.

322. Ibid., pp. 70, 72.
323. Ibid., pp. 72, 73.
324. S. W. Kung, *Chinese in American Life,* p. 67.
325. Stanford M. Lyman, *Chinese Americans* (New York: Random House, 1974), pp. 59–60.
326. Jack Chen, *The Chinese of America,* pp. 89, 90.
327. H. M. Lai, "Chinese," *Harvard Encyclopedia of American Ethnic Groups,* edited by Stephan Thernstrom et al., p. 220.
328. S. W. Kung, *Chinese in American Life,* p. 87; Jack Chen, *The Chinese of America,* pp. 89–91, 99, 109.
329. Jack Chen, *The Chinese of America,* pp. 83, 93.
330. Ibid., p. 99.
331. Ibid., pp. 105, 106.
332. Ibid., p. 109.
333. Ibid., p. 113.
334. Ibid., p. 115.
335. Stanford M. Lyman, *Chinese Americans,* p. 76; Jack Chen, *The Chinese of America,* pp. 108–109, 144–145.
336. S. W. Kung, *Chinese in American Life,* p. 57.
337. Ibid., p. 183.
338. H. M. Lai, "Chinese," *Harvard Encyclopedia of American Ethnic Groups,* edited by Stephan Thernstrom et al., p. 224.
339. Stanford M. Lyman, *Chinese Americans,* p. 106.
340. Ibid., pp. 94–95.
341. Ibid., pp. 115, 126.
342. S. W. Kung, *Chinese in American Life,* p. 40.
343. Betty Lee Sung, *The Story of the Chinese in America,* p. 132.
344. Thomas Sowell, *Ethnic America,* p. 143.
345. Betty Lee Sung, *The Story of the Chinese in America,* p. 322; Thomas Sowell, *Ethnic America,* p. 5.
346. See U.S. Bureau of the Census, *1990 Census of Population: Asians and Pacific Islanders in the United States* (Washington, D.C.: U.S. Government Printing Office, 1993), pp. 142, 146, 147.
347. H. M. Lai, "Chinese," *Harvard Encyclopedia of American Ethnic Groups,* edited by Stephan Thernstrom et al., p. 227.
348. Jack Chen, *The Chinese of America,* p. 239.
349. U.S. Bureau of the Census, *1990 Census of Population: Asians and Pacific Islanders in the United States,* pp. 142, 146, 147.
350. Gwen Kinkead, "Chinatown-1," *The New Yorker,* June 10, 1991, p. 63.
351. Cf. Orlando Patterson, "Context and Choice in Ethnic Allegiance," *Eth-*

nicity, edited by Nathan Glazer and Daniel P. Moynihan, pp. 326–327.

352. Linda Y. C. Lim, "Chinese Economic Activity in Southeast Asia: An Introductory Review," *The Chinese in Southeast Asia,,* edited by Linda Y. C. Lim & L. A. Peter Gosling, Volume I: *Ethnicity and Economic Activity,* pp. 4, 8; Victor Purcell, *The Chinese in Southeast Asia,* second edition, pp. 199, 546, 547.
353. Victor Purcell, *The Chinese in Southeast Asia,* second edition, p. 546.
354. Janet T. Landa, "The Political Economy of the Ethnically Homogeneous Chinese Middleman Group in Southeast Asia: Ethnicity and Entrepreneurship in a Plural Society," *The Chinese in Southeast Asia,* edited by Linda Y. C. Lim and L. A. Peter Gosling, Volume I: *Ethnicity and Economic Activity,* pp. 90–93.
355. L. A. Peter Gosling, "Chinese Crop Dealers in Malaysia and Thailand: The Myth of the Merciless Monopsonistic Middleman," ibid., pp. 134–135; Clifton A. Barton, "Trust and Credit: Some Observations Regarding Business Strategies of Overseas Chinese Traders in South Vietnam," ibid., pp. 49–50, 52.
356. Antonio S. Tan, "The Changing Identity of the Philippine Chinese, 1946–1984," *Changing Identities of the Southeast Asian Chinese since World War II,* edited by Jennifer Cushman and Wang Gungwu, p. 192.
357. Victor Purcell, *The Chinese in Southeast Asia,* second edition, p. 272; Charles O. Hucker, *China's Imperial Past,* pp. 337–338. See also Jacques Gernet, *A History of Chinese Civilization,* pp. 315, 372–373, 491, 531, 545, 555, 586, 604.
358. Victor Purcell, *The Chinese in Southeast Asia,* second edition, p. 539.
359. Stanford M. Lyman, *Chinese Americans,* pp. 38–39.
360. Ibid., p. 159; G. William Skinner, *Chinese Society in Thailand,* pp. 213, 324–325; Leo Suryadinata, *Pribumi Indonesians, the Chinese Minority and China,* pp. 149–150.

CHAPTER 6: JEWS OF THE DIASPORA

1. Eugene F. Sofer, *From Pale to Pampa: A Social History of the Jews of Buenos Aires* (New York: Holmes & Meier, 1982), p. 15.
2. U. O. Schmelz and Sergio DellaPergola, "World Jewish Population, 1990," *American Jewish Yearbook: 1992,* edited by David Singer and Ruth R. Seldin (New York: American Jewish Committee, 1992), pp. 493, 511.
3. See Sergio DellaPergola, "Jews in the European Community: Sociodemographic Trends and Challenges," *American Jewish Yearbook: 1993,*

edited by David Singer and Ruth R. Seldin (New York: American Jewish Committee, 1993), p. 66.

4. Ibid., p. 495.
5. Ibid., pp. 493, 511.
6. Michael Grant, *The Jews in the Roman World* (New York: Dorset Press, 1984), pp. 34, 62.
7. Ibid., pp. 16–19.
8. Ibid., p. 48.
9. Jane S. Gerber, *The Jews of Spain: A History of the Sephardic Experience* (New York: The Free Press, 1992), p. 3.
10. Solomon Grayzel, *A History of the Jews* (New York: Mentor Books, 1968), pp. 138–140.
11. Michael Grant, *The Jews in the Roman World,* p. 60.
12. Ibid., pp. 60, 123, 124, 183, 192, 242; Nicholas de Lange, *Atlas of the Jewish World* (New York: Facts on File Publications, 1984), p. 28.
13. Bernard Lewis, *The Jews of Islam* (Princeton, N.J.: Princeton University Press, 1984), p. 67.
14. Ibid., Chapter I.
15. Ibid., p. 36.
16. See, for example, Louis Wirth, *The Ghetto* (Chicago: University of Chicago Press, 1958), pp. 43, 44.
17. In Moslem countries such as Morocco and Yemen, where Jews were the only non-Moslem minority, their treatment was particularly bad, suggesting that it was their uniqueness, rather than Islam or Christianity as such, which was a key factor in the hostility they faced. This conclusion is further reinforced by the history of Jews in colonial North America, where sharp religious differences among Christians—Protestants versus Catholics, Anglicans versus Quakers, Shakers, and others—made the Jews seem like just another religious minority. See Jane S. Gerber, *The Jews of Spain,* pp. 207, 224.
18. Solomon Grayzel, *A History of the Jews,* pp. 291, 303; Bernard Lewis, *The Jews of Islam,* p. 67.
19. W. Montgomery Watt, *The Influence of Islam on Medieval Europe* (Edinburgh: Edinburgh University Press, 1972), pp. 33–39.
20. Solomon Grayzel, *A History of the Jews,* pp. 271–273, 275.
21. Ibid., pp. 281–282.
22. Pierre Riché, *Daily Life in the World of Charlemagne,* translated by Jo Ann McNamara (Philadelphia: University of Pennsylvania Press, 1978), pp. 126–128.
23. Solomon Grayzel, *A History of the Jews,* p. 314.

24. Ibid., pp. 278, 280.
25. Jane S. Gerber, *The Jews of Spain,* p. 34.
26. Solomon Grayzel, *A History of the Jews,* pp. 280–281.
27. Ibid., pp. 276–278.
28. Lord Kinross, *The Ottoman Centuries: The Rise and Fall of the Turkish Empire* (New York: Morrow, 1977), p. 146.
29. Solomon Grayzel, *A History of the Jews,* p. 342.
30. Ibid., pp. 345–347.
31. Jonathan I. Israel, *European Jewry in the Age of Mercantilism: 1550–1750* (Oxford: Oxford University Press, 1985), pp. 5, 6.
32. Solomon Grayzel, *A History of the Jews,* p. 306.
33. Paul Johnson, *A History of the Jews* (New York: Harper & Row, 1987), pp. 216–217.
34. Solomon Grayzel, *A History of the Jews,* pp. 271–272, 391.
35. Nathaniel Katzburg, *Hungary and the Jews: Policy and Legislation, 1920–1943* (Jerusalem: Bar-Ilan University Press, 1981), p. 20. See also Peter Pulzer, *The Rise of Political Anti-Semitism in Germany and Austria* (Cambridge, Mass.: Harvard University Press, 1988), pp. 69, 273, 275; Richard S. Levy, *The Downfall of the Anti-Semitic Political Parties in Imperial Germany* (New Haven, Conn.: Yale University Press, 1975), passim.
36. Steven B. Bowman, *The Jews of Byzantium, 1204–1453* (Tuscaloosa: University of Alabama Press, 1985), pp. 164–168.
37. Solomon Grayzel, *A History of the Jews,* pp. 251, 299, 397–398; Raphael Patai, *The Jewish Mind* (New York: Charles Scribner's Sons, 1977), p. 100; Paul Johnson, *A History of the Jews,* p. 230.
38. Steven B. Bowman, *The Jews of Byzantium, 1204–1453,* pp. 4, 39–40, 50, 52.
39. Bernard S. Bachrach, "A Reassessment of Visigothic Jewish Policy, 589–711," *American Historical Review,* February 1973, p. 13.
40. Ibid., pp. 14–33.
41. Ibid., pp. 24, 33.
42. Ibid., pp. 20–29.
43. Ibid., pp. 27, 29.
44. Solomon Grayzel, *A History of the Jews,* pp. 274, 290–291.
45. Ibid., p. 291.
46. Ibid., p. 292; Jane S. Gerber, *The Jews of Spain,* p. 99.
47. Solomon Grayzel, *A History of the Jews,* p. 294.
48. Raphael Patai, *The Jewish Mind,* pp. 122–123.

49. See, for example, Jane S. Gerber, *The Jews of Spain*, pp. xii–xiii, 31, 45, 47, 61, 62–63, 74, 86, 100.
50. Raphael Patai, *The Jewish Mind*, p. 331.
51. Stephen H. Haliczer, "The Castilian Urban Patriciate and the Jewish Expulsions of 1480–92," *American Historical Review*, February 1973, pp. 39–40.
52. Ibid., pp. 42–47.
53. Ibid., pp. 47–49.
54. Solomon Grayzel, *A History of the Jews*, p. 352.
55. Ibid., p. 365.
56. Howard M. Sachar, *Diaspora: An Inquiry into the Contemporary Jewish World* (New York: Harper & Row, 1985), pp. 229–230.
57. Nathan Glazer, *American Judaism* (Chicago: University of Chicago Press, 1957), p. 13.
58. Raphael Patai, *The Vanished Worlds of Jewry* (New York: Macmillan, 1980), p. 73.
59. Bernard Lewis, *The Jews of Islam*, pp. 112–113.
60. Jonathan I. Israel, *European Jewry in the Age of Mercantilism*, p. 33.
61. See Arthur Hertzberg, *The French Enlightenment and the Jews: The Origins of Modern Anti-Semitism* (New York: Columbia University Press, 1990), pp. 1, 137, 138–140, 314, 326, 328, 340–342.
62. Raphael Patai, *The Vanished Worlds of Jewry*, p. 73.
63. Bernard Lewis, *The Jews of Islam*, pp. 134–135; Jane S. Gerber, *The Jews of Spain*, pp. 164–165.
64. Ibid., pp. 60–61.
65. Ibid., p. 130.
66. Jane S. Gerber, *The Jews of Spain*, pp. 163–164.
67. Robert Mantran, "Foreign Merchants and the Minorities in Istanbul during the Sixteenth and Seventeenth Centuries," *Christians and Jews in the Ottoman Empire: The Functioning of a Plural Society*, edited by Benjamin Braude and Bernard Lewis (New York: Holmes & Meier, 1982), Volume I: *The Central Lands*, pp. 127–128.
68. Bernard Lewis, *The Jews of Islam*, p. 122.
69. Lord Kinross, *The Ottoman Centuries*, p. 117.
70. Bernard Lewis, *The Jews of Islam*, p. 123; Bernard Lewis, *The Muslim Discovery of Europe* (New York: Norton, 1982), p. 107.
71. Jonathan I. Israel, *European Jewry in the Age of Mercantilism*, pp. 26, 31; Bernard Lewis, *The Jews of Islam*, p. 90.
72. Aryeh Schmuelevitz, *The Jews of the Ottoman Empire in the Late Fif-*

teenth and the Sixteenth Centuries: Administrative, Economic, Legal and Social Relations as Reflected in the Responsa (Leiden, The Netherlands: E. J. Brill, 1984), pp. 135–136.

73. Ibid., pp. 128–129.
74. Ibid., p. 138.
75. Jane S. Gerber, *The Jews of Spain,* pp. 38, 94.
76. Bernard Lewis, *The Jews of Islam,* pp. 132, 133; Jane S. Gerber, *The Jews of Spain,* p. 170.
77. Bernard Lewis, *The Jews of Islam,* p. 133.
78. Ibid., p. 56.
79. Ibid., p. 129.
80. Ibid., p. 214.
81. Ibid., p. 130. The zeal with which seventeenth-century Jews responded to the claims of Sabbatai Sevi to be the long-awaited Messiah also tended to discredit Jews in the eyes of the Ottoman authorities. William H. McNeill, *The Rise of the West: A History of the Human Community* (Chicago: University of Chicago Press, 1991), p. 639.
82. Bernard Lewis, *The Jews of Islam,* pp. 143–144.
83. Ibid., p. 174.
84. Ibid., p. 131.
85. Jane S. Gerber, *The Jews of Spain,* pp. 222–223.
86. Ibid., pp. 223–224.
87. Bernard Lewis, *The Jews of Islam,* pp. 175–176.
88. Bernard Lewis, *The Muslim Discovery of Europe,* Chapter V.
89. Lord Kinross, *The Ottoman Centuries,* pp. 267–271, 335–336, 346–348.
90. Bernard Lewis, *The Jews of Islam,* p. 147.
91. Ibid., p. 170.
92. Ibid., pp. 164–168, 181–182.
93. Jane S. Gerber, *The Jews of Spain,* p. 224.
94. Ibid., p. 226.
95. Ibid., pp. 226–227.
96. Ibid., pp. 243–244; S. Ettinger, "The Modern Period," *A History of the Jewish People* (Cambridge, Mass.: Harvard University Press, 1976), pp. 953–957; Ezra Mendelsohn, *The Jews of East Central Europe between the World Wars* (Bloomington: Indiana University Press, 1983).
97. "The typical Ashkenazi Jew of the pre-Enlightenment eighteenth century differed from his Gentile countryman in all conceivable criteria of group identification: in religion and language, in education, literacy, and occupations, in clothing and manners, in morality, temperament, and

inclinations, in values, goals, and ambitions, in mentality and ethnicity." Raphael Patai, *The Jewish Mind,* p. 223.

98. Jonathan I. Israel, *European Jewry in the Age of Mercantilism,* pp. 5–6.
99. Ibid., pp. 26, 27–28.
100. Ibid., pp. 87–122.
101. Ibid., pp. 224–231.
102. Ibid., p. 254.
103. Raphael Patai, *The Jewish Mind,* pp. 222–223.
104. Arthur Hertzberg, *The French Enlightenment and the Jews,* p. 2.
105. Jonathan I. Israel, *European Jewry in the Age of Mercantilism,* p. 228.
106. H. I. Bach, *The German Jew: A Synthesis of Judaism and Western Civilization, 1730–1930* (Oxford: Oxford University Press, 1984), p. 70.
107. Ibid., pp. 73–74.
108. Raphael Patai, *The Jewish Mind,* pp. 339–340.
109. Stephen H. Haliczer, "The Castilian Urban Patriciate and the Jewish Expulsions of 1480–92," *American Historical Review,* February 1973, pp. 37–38; Bernard Lewis, *The Jews of Islam,* pp. 101–102, 208; Stephen H. Haliczer, "The Castilian Urban Patriciate and the Jewish Expulsion of 1480–92," *American Historical Review,* February 1973, pp. 39–40.
110. Arthur Hertzberg, *The French Enlightenment and the Jews,,* Chapter 8.
111. Jonathan I. Israel, *European Jewry in the Age of Mercantilism,* Chapter I.
112. Ibid., p. 27.
113. Ibid., p. 26.
114. Ibid., pp. 27–28.
115. Ibid., p. 30.
116. Ibid., p. 139.
117. Solomon Grayzel, *A History of the Jews,* pp. 394–397.
118. Ibid., pp. 397–398; Louis Wirth, *The Ghetto,* p. 89.
119. Jonathan I. Israel, *European Jewry in the Age of Mercantilism,* p. 120.
120. Ibid., pp. 120–121; Solomon Grayzel, *A History of the Jews,* pp. 440–442.
121. Jonathan I. Israel, *European Jewry in the Age of Mercantilism,* pp. 166–167.
122. Ibid., p. 170.
123. William McCagg, Jr., *A History of the Habsburg Jews* (Bloomington: Indiana University Press, 1989), p. 11.
124. Ibid., p. 15.
125. Jonathan I. Israel, *European Jewry in the Age of Mercantilism,* pp. 198–201.

126. Ibid., pp. 198–201.
127. Solomon Grayzel, *A History of the Jews,* p. 457; Jonathan I. Israel, *European Jewry in the Age of Mercantilism,* p. 215.
128. Steven J. Zipperstein, *The Jews of Odessa: A Cultural History, 1794–1881* (Stanford, Calif.: Stanford University Press, 1985), p. 12.
129. Benjamin Pinkus, *The Jews of the Soviet Union: The History of a National Minority* (Cambridge: Cambridge University Press, 1988), p. 13.
130. Solomon Grayzel, *A History of the Jews,* pp. 516–520.
131. Steven J. Zipperstein, *The Jews of Odessa,* pp. 24, 26, 27, 28.
132. Ibid., p. 30.
133. Ibid., p. 43.
134. Solomon Grayzel, *A History of the Jews,* pp. 547–548.
135. Benjamin Pinkus, *The Jews of the Soviet Union,* pp. 20–23; Solomon Grayzel, *A History of the Jews,* pp. 520–521.
136. Benjamin Pinkus, *The Jews of the Soviet Union,* pp. 27–30.
137. Simon Kuznets, "Immigration of Russian Jews to the United States: Background and Structure," *Perspectives in American History,* Vol. IX (1975), p. 39.
138. Ezra Mendelsohn, *The Jews of East Central Europe between the World Wars,* pp. 23, 26.
139. Ibid., p. 27.
140. Ibid., p. 28.
141. Ibid., p. 42.
142. Howard M. Sachar, *Diaspora,* p. 339.
143. Ezra Mendelsohn, *The Jews of East Central Europe between the World Wars,* pp. 99–101.
144. Ibid., p. 180.
145. Ibid., p. 26.
146. Ibid., p. 226.
147. Ibid., pp. 179–180.
148. Ibid., pp. 42, 70, 139, 186, 188.
149. Ibid., p. 73.
150. Ibid., p. 70.
151. Ibid., p. 237; see also pp. 106, 253.
152. Howard M. Sachar, *Diaspora,* p. 324.
153. Ezra Mendelsohn, *The Jews of East Central Europe between the World Wars,* pp. 73–74.
154. Ibid., p. 122.
155. Ibid., pp. 94, 217.
156. Ibid., pp. 113, 204.

157. Ibid., pp. 136, 137, 156, 159, 160, 176, 227.
158. Howard M. Sachar, *Diaspora,* p. 339.
159. Ibid., pp. 325–335.
160. Ibid., p. 339.
161. Ibid., pp. 339–350.
162. Ibid., p. 317.
163. Ibid., p. 377.
164. William L. Shirer, *The Rise and Fall of the Third Reich: A History of Nazi Germany* (New York: Simon & Schuster, 1960), p. 480.
165. Howard M. Sachar, *Diaspora,* pp. 377–380.
166. Ibid., pp. 381–387, 390.
167. Ibid., p. 388.
168. Ibid., pp. 392–394.
169. Ibid., pp. 388–389.
170. Ibid., pp. 431–432.
171. Ibid., pp. 448–449.
172. Ibid., pp. 407–408.
173. Jonathan I. Israel, *European Jewry in the Age of Mercantilism,* Chapter I.
174. William McCagg, Jr., *A History of the Habsburg Jews,* p. 1.
175. Solomon Grayzel, *A History of the Jews,* p. 375.
176. William McCagg, Jr., *A History of the Habsburg Jews,* p. 2.
177. Ibid., pp. 173, 177–178.
178. Ibid., p. 190.
179. ". . . the Jewish colonists . . . have made the desert bloom." Speech of May 23, 1939, *Churchill Speaks: Winston S. Churchill in Peace and War: Collected Speeches, 1897–1963,* edited by Robert Rhodes James (New York: Chelsea House, 1980), p. 689.
180. Hilary Rubinstein, *Chosen: The Jews in Australia* (Sydney: Allen & Unwin, 1987), p. 220.
181. Louis Wirth, *The Ghetto,* pp. 204–206.
182. William McCagg, Jr., *A History of the Habsburg Jews,* p. 198.
183. Peter Pulzer, *The Rise of Political Anti-Semitism in Germany and Austria,* pp. 10–13, passim.
184. Sara Gordon, *Hitler, Germans, and the "Jewish Question"* (Princeton, N.J.: Princeton University Press, 1984), p. 13.
185. H. I. Bach, *The German Jew,* p. 136.
186. Sara Gordon, *Hitler, Germans, and the "Jewish Question,"* p. 13.
187. Selma Stern-Taeubler, "Problems of American Jewish and German Jewish Historiography," *Jews from Germany in the United States,* edited by Eric E. Hirshler (New York: Farrar, Straus & Cudahy, 1955), p. 9.

188. Louis Wirth, *The Ghetto,* pp. 107–108.
189. Raphael Patai, *The Vanished Worlds of Jewry,* p. 56.
190. Ibid., p. 57.
191. Eric E. Hirshler, "Jews from Germany in the United States," *Jews from Germany in the United States,* edited by Eric E. Hirshler, pp. 42–45; Judith Laikin Elkin, *Jews of the Latin American Republics* (Chapel Hill: University of North Carolina Press, 1980), p. 37; Ezra Mendelsohn, *The Jews of East Central Europe between the World Wars,* p. 133.
192. Sara Gordon, *Hitler, Germans, and the "Jewish Question,"* pp. 13–15.
193. Donald L. Niewyk, *The Jews in Weimar Germany* (Baton Rouge: Louisiana State University Press, 1980), p. 16.
194. Raphael Patai, *The Vanished Worlds of Jewry,* p. 57.
195. Sara Gordon, *Hitler, Germans, and the "Jewish Question,"* p. 14.
196. Donald L. Niewyk, *The Jews in Weimar Germany,* p. 13.
197. Sara Gordon, *Hitler, Germans, and the "Jewish Question,"* pp. 18–23.
198. Ibid., pp. 8, 12.
199. Donald L. Niewyk, *The Jews in Weimar Germany,* p. 16.
200. Sara Gordon, *Hitler, Germans, and the "Jewish Question,"* p. 47; Raphael Patai, *The Jewish Mind,* p. 458.
201. William L. Shirer, *The Rise and Fall of the Third Reich,* p. 109.
202. Ibid., p. 118.
203. Sara Gordon, *Hitler, Germans, and the "Jewish Question,"* p. 72.
204. Ibid., pp. 120–121.
205. William L. Shirer, *The Rise and Fall of the Third Reich,* p. 431.
206. Sara Gordon, *Hitler, Germans, and the "Jewish Question,"* Chapter VI.
207. Ibid., pp. 169–170.
208. Ibid., p. 197.
209. Ibid., p. 196.
210. Nicholas de Lange, *Atlas of the Jewish World,* p. 70.
211. Sara Gordon, *Hitler, Germans, and the "Jewish Question,"* p. 119.
212. See Howard M. Sachar, *Diaspora,* pp. 13–15.
213. Ibid., pp. 15–16.
214. Ibid., pp. 10–13.
215. Sergio DellaPergola, "Jews in the European Community: Sociodemographic Trends and Challenges," *American Jewish Yearbook: 1993,* edited by David Singer and Ruth R. Seldin, p. 66.
216. Judith Laikin Elkin, *Jews of the Latin American Republics,* p. 17.
217. Ibid., p. 18.
218. Ibid., p. 7.
219. Ibid., p. 9.

220. Ibid., p. 11.
221. Ibid., p. 14.
222. Ibid., p. 15.
223. Howard M. Sachar, *Diaspora,* p. 232.
224. Judith Laikin Elkin, *Jews of the Latin American Republics,* pp. 51–52.
225. Ibid., p. 34.
226. Ibid., p. 43.
227. Ibid., p. 37.
228. Ibid., pp. 38, 41.
229. Ibid., p. 46.
230. Frances P. Karner, *The Sephardics of Curaçao* (Assen, The Netherlands: Van Gorcum & Co., 1969), p. 28.
231. Robert Weisbrot, *The Jews of Argentina: From Inquisition to Perón* (Philadelphia: The Jewish Publication Society of America, 1979), p. 177.
232. Judith Laikin Elkin, *Jews of the Latin American Republics,* p. 41.
233. Ibid., p. 46.
234. Ibid., p. 49.
235. Ibid., p. 44.
236. Ibid., p. 46.
237. Ibid., p. 50.
238. Ibid., pp. 40, 45.
239. Ibid., pp. 19, 20.
240. Frances P. Karner, *The Sephardics of Curaçao,* pp. 11–13.
241. Ibid., p. 59. See p. 3 for general designations.
242. Judith Laikin Elkin, *Jews of the Latin American Republics,* p. 18.
243. Ibid., p. 50.
244. Frances P. Karner, *The Sephardics of Curaçao,* p. 43.
245. Ibid., p. 73.
246. Judith Laikin Elkin, *Jews of the Latin American Republics,* p. 50.
247. Robert Weisbrot, *The Jews of Argentina,* p. 169.
248. Ibid., pp. 150–157.
249. Ibid., pp. 157–161.
250. Daniel J. Boorstin, *The Americans,* Volume III: *The Democratic Experience* (New York: Random House, 1973), pp. 97–99.
251. Eugene F. Sofer, *From Pale to Pampa,* pp. 100–104.
252. Judith Laikin Elkin, *Jews of the Latin American Republics,* pp. 100–102.
253. Eugene F. Sofer, *From Pale to Pampa,* p. 110.
254. Moses Rischin, *The Promised City: New York's Jews, 1870–1914* (Cambridge, Mass.: Harvard University Press, 1967), pp. 61–68; Judith

Laikin Elkin, *Jews of the Latin American Republics,* pp. 114–115; Howard M. Sachar, *Diaspora,* pp. 250, 254, 287.

255. Howard M. Sachar, *Diaspora,* p. 267.
256. Ibid., p. 233.
257. Ibid., p. 266.
258. See, for example, ibid., pp. 234–235, 237, 250, 252, 260–262.
259. Ibid., p. 262.
260. Ibid., pp. 237, 259, 276.
261. Robert A. Levine, *Tropical Diaspora: The Jewish Experience in Cuba* (Gainesville: University Press of Florida, 1993), pp. 129, 140.
262. Ibid., p. 147.
263. Robert Weisbrot, *The Jews of Argentina: From Inquisition to Perón,* p. 33.
264. Ibid., p. 25; Judith Laikin Elkin, *Jews of the Latin American Republics,* pp. 57, 127.
265. Victor A. Mirelman, *Jewish Buenos Aires, 1890–1930: In Search of an Identity* (Detroit: Wayne State University Press, 1990), p. 13.
266. Ibid., p. 14.
267. Ibid., p. 20.
268. Judith Laikin Elkin, *Jews of the Latin American Republics,* p. 54.
269. Robert Weisbrot, *The Jews of Argentina,* p. 49.
270. Victor A. Mirelman, *Jewish Buenos Aires,* p. 26.
271. Judith Laikin Elkin, *Jews of the Latin American Republics,* p. 128.
272. Ibid., pp. 133–135.
273. Ibid., p. 58.
274. Ibid., p. 128.
275. Ibid., pp. 130, 136–137.
276. Mark Jefferson, *Peopling the Argentine Pampa* (Port Washington, N.Y.: Kennikat Press, 1971), p. 156.
277. Judith Laikin Elkin, *Jews of the Latin American Republics,* p. 138.
278. Daniel J. Elazar and Peter Medding, *Jewish Communities in Frontier Societies: Argentina, Australia, and South Africa* (New York: Holmes & Meier, 1983), p. 94.
279. Ibid., p. 96.
280. Judith Laikin Elkin, *Jews of the Latin American Republics,* pp. 125, 153.
281. Robert Weisbrot, *The Jews of Argentina,* p. 71.
282. Howard M. Sachar, *Diaspora,* p. 281.
283. Robert Weisbrot, *The Jews of Argentina,* p. 70.
284. Daniel Elazar and Peter Medding, *Jewish Communities in Frontier Societies,* p. 95.
285. Howard M. Sachar, *Diaspora,* p. 281.

286. Judith Laikin Elkin, *Jews of the Latin American Republics,* p. 59.
287. Ibid.
288. Ibid., p. 72.
289. Ibid., pp. 100–108.
290. Ibid., p. 102.
291. Victor A. Mirelman, *Jewish Buenos Aires,* pp. 197–204.
292. Ibid., pp. 203–204.
293. Howard M. Sachar, *Diaspora,* p. 283. See also Victor A. Mirelman, *Jewish Buenos Aires,* pp. 206–220.
294. Judith Laikin Elkin, *Jews of the Latin American Republics,* p. 59.
295. Eugene F. Sofer, *From Pale to Pampa,* p. 94.
296. Judith Laikin Elkin, *Jews of the Latin American Republics,* pp. 110, 217; Robert Weisbrot, *The Jews of Argentina,* p. 176.
297. Robert Weisbrot, *The Jews of Argentina,* p. 177.
298. Ibid., p. 200.
299. Ibid., p. 201.
300. See Carl Solberg, *Immigration and Nationalism: Argentina and Chile, 1890–1914* (Austin: Institute of Latin American Studies, University of Texas, 1970), pp. 70, 87, 88.
301. Ibid., p. 87.
302. Ibid., p. 89.
303. Ibid., pp. 148–149.
304. Eugene F. Sofer, *From Pale to Pampa,* pp. 91–99. Whether this particular sample can be taken as representative of the fate of Jewish workers in general is open to question. Although the Chevrah Keduscha Ashnenazi at one time encompassed the great majority of Argentine Jews (ibid., p. 8), Professor Sofer himself pointed to questions as to the continuing representativeness of his sample over time, particularly as regards whether those who left the membership rolls were different from those who remained (ibid., pp. 91–92). Such a question is especially appropriate in view of the fact that five out of the six samples for this era had more "untraceable" members than those whose fate was known, including four samples where the "untraceables" outnumbered the others by from two-to-one to nearly four-to-one (ibid., pp. 95–97). Another fundamental problem is in the definitions, which treat as "downward mobility" every change from a working-class occupation—however highly skilled and well paid—to a nonworking-class occupation, even when that includes street vendors. Thus a skilled worker, temporarily unable to find work in his chosen field, might become a street vendor to make ends meet and then, when he resumed his regular occupation at a

higher income, would be counted statistically as having suffered "downward mobility." Yet the Sofer data are used to reach sweeping conclusions in Judith Laikin Elkin, *Jews of the Latin American Republics,* pp. 110–111, 215.

305. See Robert Weisbrot, *The Jews of Argentina,* pp. 176–184. Professor Weisbrot's data and conclusions seem to conflict with those of Judith Laikin Elkin, cited above, but the latter are subject to the limitations of the Sofer study and are not supported by other data for 1960 cited in Judith Laikin Elkin, *Jews of the Latin American Republics,* p. 216.
306. Robert Weisbrot, *The Jews of Argentina,* pp. 178–179.
307. Eugene F. Sofer, *From Pale to Pampa,* p. 122.
308. Robert Weisbrot, *The Jews of Argentina,* 176.
309. Moshe Syrquin, "The Economic Structure of Jews in Argentina and Other Latin American Countries," *Jewish Social Studies,* Spring 1985, p. 127.
310. Computed from statistical table in Judith Laikin Elkin, *Jews of the Latin American Republics,* p. 216.
311. Robert Weisbrot, *The Jews of Argentina,* p. 179.
312. Moshe Syrquin, "The Economic Structure of Jews in Argentina and Other Latin American Countries," *Jewish Social Studies,* Spring 1985, p. 127.
313. Howard M. Sachar, *Diaspora,* p. 287.
314. Robert Weisbrot, *The Jews of Argentina,* p. 178.
315. Moshe Syrquin, "The Economic Structure of Jews in Argentina and Other Latin American Countries," *Jewish Social Studies,* Spring 1985, p. 125.
316. Carl Solberg, *Immigration and Nationalism,* p. 182.
317. Ibid., pp. 197–199.
318. U. O. Schmelz and Sergio DellaPergola, "World Jewish Population," *American Jewish Yearbook: 1984,* edited by Milton Himmelfarb and David Singer (New York: The American Jewish Committee, 1983), p. 254.
319. Eugene F. Sofer, *From Pale to Pampa,* p. 126; Howard M. Sachar, *Diaspora,* p. 287.
320. Robert Weisbrot, *The Jews of Argentina,* pp. 206–208.
321. Judith Laikin Elkin, *Jews of the Latin American Republics,* p. 234.
322. Howard M. Sachar, *Diaspora,* p. 309.
323. Ibid., pp. 297, 299.
324. Louis Wirth, *The Ghetto,* pp. 132–133.
325. Arthur A. Goren, "Jews," *Harvard Encyclopedia of American Ethnic Groups,* edited by Stephan Thernstrom et al. (Cambridge, Mass.: Harvard University Press, 1980), p. 574.
326. Eric E. Hirshler, "The First Organized Settlement," *Jews from Germany*

in the United States, edited by Eric E. Hirshler, pp. 22, 23. See also Louis Wirth, *The Ghetto,* pp. 137–138.

327. Louis Wirth, *The Ghetto,* p. 135.
328. Eric E. Hirshler, "Jews from Germany in the United States," *Jews from Germany in the United States,* edited by Eric E. Hirshler, pp. 22–24.
329. Louis Wirth, *The Ghetto,* p. 136.
330. "Introduction," *Jews in the South,* edited by Leonard Dinnerstein and Mary Dale Palsson (Baton Rouge: Louisiana State University Press, 1973), pp. 4–5; "Jewish Life in the Antebellum and Confederate," ibid., p. 26.
331. Arthur A. Goren, "Jews," *Harvard Encyclopedia of American Ethnic Groups,* edited by Stephan Thernstrom et al., pp. 574–575; Eric E. Hirschler, "The First Organized Settlement," *Jews from Germany in the United States,* edited by Eric E. Hirshler, pp. 27, 28, 30, 31–32.
332. Abram Vossen Goodman, "South Carolina from Shaftesbury to Salvador," *Jews in the South,* edited by Leonard Dinnerstein and Mary Dale Palsson, p. 41.
333. Leon Hühner, "David L. Yulee, Florida's First Senator," ibid., pp. 52–74.
334. Eric E. Hirshler, "Jews from Germany in the United States," *Jews from Germany in the United States,* edited by Eric E. Hirshler, pp. 37, 66.
335. Arthur A. Goren, "Jews," *Harvard Encyclopedia of American Ethnic Groups,* edited by Stephan Thernstrom et al., p. 576.
336. Louis Wirth, *The Ghetto,* pp. 143–144; Solomon Grayzel, *A History of the Jews,* p. 534.
337. Eric E. Hirshler, "Jews from Germany in the United States," *Jews from Germany in the United States,* edited by Eric E. Hirshler, p. 36.
338. Ibid., pp. 41–45; Louis Wirth, *The Ghetto,* pp. 169–170.
339. Adolf Kober, "Aspects of the Influence of Jews from Germany on American Jewish Spiritual Life of the 19th Century," *Jews from Germany in the United States,* edited by Eric E. Hirshler, pp. 132–133.
340. Eric E. Hirshler, "Jews from Germany in the United States," ibid., pp. 50–52.
341. Simon Kuznets, "Immigration of Russian Jews to the United States: Background and Structure," *Perspectives in American History,* Vol. IX (1975), pp. 35n, 39.
342. Moses Rischin, *The Promised City,* p. 33.
343. Ibid., pp. 79–80.
344. Irving Howe, *World of Our Fathers* (New York: Harcourt Brace Jovanovich, 1976), p. 148.

345. Ibid., p. 148; Louis Wirth, *The Ghetto,* pp. 196–199.
346. Louis Wirth, *The Ghetto,* p. 196.
347. Ira Berkow, *Maxwell Street: Survival in a Bazaar* (Garden City, N.Y.: Doubleday, 1977), p. 223. Arthur Goldberg, Supreme Court Justice, also lived as a child in the neighborhood near Maxwell Street, in an unheated flat where everyone slept in the kitchen during the winter, near a wood stove. Out of this same neighborhood also came Admiral Hyman Rickover and William S. Paley, head of the Columbia Broadcasting System (CBS). Ibid., pp., 30, 299ff, 359ff.
348. Simon Kuznets, "Immigration of Russian Jews to the United States," *Perspectives in American History,* Vol. IX (1975), pp. 104–105, 110.
349. Moses Rischin, *The Promised City,* p. 59.
350. Eric E. Hirshler, "Jews from Germany in the United States," *Jews from Germany in the United States,* edited by Eric E. Hirshler, pp. 60–61.
351. Arthur A. Goren, "Jews," *Harvard Encyclopedia of American Ethnic Groups,* edited by Stephan Thernstrom et al., p. 576.
352. Moses Rischin, *The Promised City,* p. 63.
353. Ibid., p. 80.
354. Simon Kuznets, "Immigration of Russian Jews to the United States," *Perspectives in American History,* Vol. IX (1975), p. 113.
355. Thomas Kessner, *The Golden Door* (New York: Oxford University Press, 1977), p. 98.
356. Arthur A. Goren, "Jews," *Harvard Encyclopedia of American Ethnic Groups,* edited by Stephan Thernstrom et al., p. 589.
357. Computed from "Income, Median Age, Occupation, and Fertility, by Ethnic Group," *Essays and Data on American Ethnic Groups,* edited by Thomas Sowell and Lynn D. Collins (Washington, D.C.: The Urban Institute, 1978), p. 258.
358. Ibid., pp. 305, 365, 389.
359. Sidney Goldstein, "Profile of American Jewry: Insights from the 1990 National Jewish Population Survey," *American Jewish Yearbook: 1992,* edited by David Singer and Ruth R. Seldin, p. 159.
360. Ibid., p. 162.
361. Daniel Elazar and Peter Medding, *Jewish Communities in Frontier Societies,* p. 235.
362. Ibid., p. 241.
363. Ibid., p. 242.
364. Australian Government Commission of Inquiry into Poverty, *Welfare of Migrants* (Canberra: Australian Government Printing Office, 1975), p. 106.

365. Daniel Elazar and Peter Medding, *Jewish Communities in Frontier Societies,* p. 262.
366. Australian Government Commission of Inquiry into Poverty, *Welfare of Migrants,* p. 106.
367. Hilary Rubinstein, *Chosen: The Jews in Australia* (Sydney: Allen & Unwin, 1987), pp. 10–12.
368. Daniel Elazar and Peter Medding, *Jewish Communities in Frontier Societies,* p. 243.
369. See Hilary Rubinstein, *Chosen,* pp. 13–15, 189.
370. Ibid., p. 14.
371. Ibid., p. 30.
372. Daniel Elazar and Peter Medding, *Jewish Communities in Frontier Societies,* p. 241.
373. Hilary Rubinstein, *Chosen,* p. 9.
374. Ibid., p. 37.
375. J. Lyng, *Non-Britishers in Australia* (Melbourne: Melbourne University Press, 1935), p. 152.
376. Hilary Rubinstein, *Chosen,* p. 54.
377. Ibid., p. 89.
378. S. D. Rutland, "Early Jewish Settlement 1788–1880," *The Australian People: An Encyclopedia of the Nation, Its People and Their Origins,* edited by James Jupp (North Ryde, New South Wales, Australia: Angus & Robertson, 1988), p. 639.
379. W. D. Rubinstein, "Jewish Contribution to Australian Élites," ibid., p. 646; Hilary Rubinstein, *Chosen,* p. 42n.
380. Charles A. Price, *Jewish Settlers in Australia* (Canberra: The Australian National University, 1981), p. 9; Hilary Rubinstein, *Chosen,* p. 213.
381. Hilary Rubinstein, *Chosen,* p. 37.
382. Daniel Elazar and Peter Medding, *Jewish Communities in Frontier Societies,* p. 269; Hilary Rubinstein, *Chosen,* pp. 83–90, 101.
383. Charles A. Price, *Jewish Settlers in Australia,* p. 14.
384. Ibid., pp. 16–17, Appendix II.
385. Hilary Rubinstein, *Chosen,* pp. 130, 152.
386. Charles A. Price, *Jewish Settlers in Australia,* p. 13n; Hilary Rubinstein, *Chosen,* p. 236.
387. Hilary Rubinstein, *Chosen,* p. 133.
388. Ibid., pp. 63–64, 121–122.
389. Ibid., pp. 177, 180.
390. Ibid., pp. 189–190.

391. Charles A. Price, *Jewish Settlers in Australia,* pp. 16–18.
392. Ibid., Appendix VII (a).
393. Ibid., p. 40.
394. Ibid., pp. 38, 45, 46.
395. Ibid., pp. 43–44.
396. Ibid., Appendix V (a), V (c).
397. Australian Government Commission of Inquiry into Poverty, *Welfare of Migrants,* p. 106.
398. Charles A. Price, *Jewish Settlers in Australia,* pp. 16, 19.
399. Ibid., p. 16n.
400. Hilary Rubinstein, *Chosen,* p. 169.
401. Ibid., p. 220.
402. Charles A. Price, *Jewish Settlers in Australia,* pp. 15–16.
403. Daniel Elazar and Peter Medding, *Jewish Communities in Frontier Societies,* p. 279.
404. Australian Government Commission of Inquiry into Poverty, *Welfare of Migrants,* p. 106.
405. Hilary Rubinstein, *Chosen,* p. 213.
406. Charles A. Price, *Jewish Settlers in Australia,* p. 11.
407. Daniel Elazar and Peter Medding, *Jewish Communities in Frontier Societies,* p. 279.
408. Howard M. Sachar, *Diaspora,* p. 174.
409. Hilary Rubinstein, *Chosen,* p. 213.
410. Ibid., p. 258.
411. Ibid., p. 212.
412. Daniel Elazar and Peter Medding, *Jewish Communities in Frontier Societies,* p. 329.
413. Ibid., p. 328.
414. J. Lyng, *Non-Britishers in Australia,* p. 155.
415. Daniel Elazar and Peter Medding, *Jewish Communities in Frontier Societies,* p. 299.
416. Australian Government Commission of Inquiry into Poverty, *Welfare of Migrants,* p. 107.
417. Daniel Elazar and Peter Medding, *Jewish Communities in Frontier Societies,* p. 297.
418. Australian Government Commission of Inquiry into Poverty, *Welfare of Migrants,* p. 108.
419. W. D. Rubinstein, "Jewish Contribution to Australian Élites," *The Australian People,* edited by James Jupp, p. 646.
420. Hilary Rubinstein, "Australia," *American Jewish Yearbook: 1992,* edited

by David Singer and Ruth R. Seldin, p. 406.

421. Howard M. Sachar, *Diaspora,* p. 176.
422. Raphael Patai, *The Jewish Mind,* p. 340.
423. Ibid., pp. 441–443; Australian Government Commission of Inquiry into Poverty, *Welfare of Migrants,* p. 108.
424. Howard M. Sachar, *Diaspora,* pp. 64, 91, 97, 105, 148, 166, 191, 253, 278, 298. See also Raphael Patai, *The Jewish Mind,* pp. 532–533.

CHAPTER 7: THE OVERSEAS INDIANS

1. Hugh Tinker, *The Banyan Tree: Overseas Emigrants from India, Pakistan, and Bangladesh* (Oxford: Oxford University Press, 1977), p. 19.
2. See The Economist Intelligence Unit, *India: Country Profile 1991–92* (London: The Economist Intelligence Unit, 1991), p. 7; UNESCO, *Statistical Yearbook 1990* (Paris: United Nations Educational, Scientific, and Cultural Organization, 1990), pp. 1–5.
3. M. C. Madhavan, "Indian Emigrants: Numbers, Characteristics, and Economic Impact," *Population and Development Review,* September 1985, pp. 458, 474.
4. Ibid., p. 461.
5. Hugh Tinker, *The Banyan Tree,* p. 88.
6. Ibid., p. 461.
7. Joel Kotkin, *Tribes: How Race, Religion, and Identity Determine Success in the New Global Economy* (New York: Random House, 1993), p. 206. See also Pranay Gupte, "The Big Money in Cheap Rock," *Forbes,* August 10, 1987, pp. 64ff.
8. Joel Kotkin, *Tribes,* p. 205.
9. Ibid., p. 229.
10. Ibid., p. 209.
11. Ibid., p. 202.
12. Ibid., p. 208.
13. David West Rudner, *Caste and Capitalism in Colonial India: The Nattukottai Chettiars* (Berkeley: University of California Press, 1994), pp. 76, 80–81, 85.
14. Joel Kotkin, *Tribes,* p. 206. See also Pranay Gupte, "The Big Money in Cheap Rock," *Forbes*, August 10, 1987, pp. 64ff.
15. M. C. Madhavan, "Indian Emigrants: Numbers, Characteristics, and Economic Impact," *Population and Development Review,* September 1985, pp. 462, 466.
16. Ibid., p. 466.

17. Ibid., p. 465.
18. Kingsley Davis, *The Population of India and Pakistan* (Princeton, N.J.: Princeton University Press, 1951), p. 99.
19. Ibid., p. 98.
20. M. C. Madhavan, "Indian Emigrants: Numbers, Characteristics, and Economic Impact," *Population and Development Review,* September 1985, p. 463.
21. Ibid., pp. 468–469.
22. Chandra Jayawardena, "Migration and Social Change: A Survey of Indian Communities Overseas," *Geographical Review,* July 1968, p. 429.
23. Agehananda Bharati, *The Asians in East Africa: Jayhind and Uhuru* (Chicago: Nelson-Hall Company, 1972), p. 108.
24. J. S. Mangat, *A History of the Asians in East Africa, 1896–1965* (Oxford: Clarendon Press, 1969), p. 1.
25. Hugh Tinker, *The Banyan Tree,* p. 3.
26. J. S. Mangat, *A History of the Asians in East Africa,* p. 3.
27. Ibid., p. 7.
28. Ibid., p. 11.
29. Ibid., p. 10.
30. Ibid., p. 14.
31. Ibid., p. 9.
32. Ibid., p. 14.
33. Ibid., p. 20.
34. Ibid., p. 10.
35. Floyd Dotson and Lillian O. Dotson, *The Indian Minority of Zambia, Rhodesia, and Malawi* (New Haven, Conn.: Yale University Press, 1968), pp. 38–39.
36. Haraprasad Chattopadhyaya, *Indians in Africa: A Social Economic Study* (Calcutta: Bookland Private Limited, 1970), pp. 263–271.
37. L. H. Gann and Peter Duignan, *The Rulers of British Africa* (Stanford, Calif.: Stanford University Press, 1978), p. 281.
38. J. S. Mangat, *A History of the Asians in East Africa,* p. 37.
39. Haraprasad Chattopadhyaya, *Indians in Africa,* p. 335. Similar patterns existed among the Africans in South Africa. Ibid., pp. 21–22.
40. J. S. Mangat, *A History of the Asians in East Africa,* p. 40.
41. Floyd Dotson and Lillian O. Dotson, *The Indian Minority of Zambia, Rhodesia, and Malawi,* p. 27.
42. L. H. Gann and Peter Duignan, *The Rulers of British Africa,* p. 282.
43. J. S. Mangat, *A History of the Asians in East Africa,* p. 39.

44. Ibid., p. 37.
45. Ibid., p. 39.
46. L. H. Gann and Peter Duignan, *The Rulers of British Africa,* p. 283n.
47. J. S. Mangat, *A History of the Asians in East Africa,* p. 45.
48. Ibid., p. 46.
49. Yashpal Tandon, *Problems of a Displaced Minority* (London: Minority Rights Group, 1973), p. 10.
50. Haraprasad Chattopadhyaya, *Indians in Africa,* p. 31.
51. Ibid., pp. 21–22.
52. Agehananda Bharati, *The Asians in East Africa,* pp. 15–16, 24; Floyd Dotson and Lillian O. Dotson, *The Indian Minority of Zambia, Rhodesia, and Malawi,* pp. 125–128.
53. Mary Fainsod Katzenstein, *Ethnicity and Equality: The Shiv Sena Party and Preferential Policies in Bombay* (Ithaca, N.Y.: Cornell University Press, 1979), p. 32.
54. Yashpal Tandon, *Problems of a Displaced Minority,* p. 14.
55. J. S. Mangat, *A History of the Asians in East Africa,* p. 74.
56. Allison Butler Herrick et al., *Area Handbook for Uganda* (Washington, D.C.: U.S. Government Printing Office, 1969), p. 91.
57. Haraprasad Chattopadhyaya, *Indians in Africa,* pp. 61–62.
58. Ibid., pp. 85–86.
59. Ibid., pp. 89–90.
60. David Lamb, *The Africans* (New York: Random House, 1982), p. 153; Agehananda Bharati, *The Asians in East Africa,* p. 10; J. S. Mangat, *A History of the Asians in East Africa,* pp. 55, 58.
61. Agehananda Bharati, *The Asians in East Africa,* p. 96.
62. J. S. Mangat, *A History of the Asians in East Africa,* p. 57.
63. Ibid., p. 58.
64. Ibid., p. 61.
65. Ibid., pp. 87–88.
66. Ibid., p. 88.
67. Ibid., p. 89.
68. Ibid., p. 90.
69. Ibid., p. 86.
70. Ibid., p. 85.
71. Haraprasad Chattopadhyaya, *Indians in Africa,* p. 394.
72. J. S. Mangat, *A History of the Asians in East Africa,* pp. 87–88.
73. See, for example, ibid., pp. 8, 9, 14, 55, 61.
74. Ibid., pp. 61, 87, 95.
75. Ibid., p. 138.

76. Allison Butler Herrick et al., *Area Handbook for Uganda*, p. 266.
77. J. S. Mangat, *A History of the Asians in East Africa*, p. 139.
78. Agehananda Bharati, *The Asians in East Africa*, p. 108.
79. J. S. Mangat, *A History of the Asians in East Africa*, pp. 77–79.
80. Ibid., p. 81.
81. Hugh Tinker, *The Banyan Tree*, p. 155.
82. Allison Butler Herrick et al., *Area Handbook for Uganda*, p. 67.
83. Yash Ghai and Dharam Ghai, *The Asian Minorities of East and Central Africa (up to 1971)* (London: Minority Rights Group, 1987), p. 4.
84. J. S. Mangat, *A History of the Asians in East Africa*, p. 113.
85. Allison Butler Herrick et al., *Area Handbook for Uganda*, p. 91.
86. Dent Ocaya-Lakidi, "Black Attitudes to the Brown and White Colonizers of East Africa," *Expulsion of a Minority: Essays on Ugandan Asians*, edited by Michael Twaddle (London: The Athlone Press, 1975), pp. 88–89.
87. H. S. Morris, *The Indians in Uganda* (Chicago: University of Chicago Press, 1968), pp. 134–140.
88. Ibid., p. 141.
89. Ibid., p. 144.
90. Ibid., p. 145.
91. Yashpal Tandon, *Problems of a Displaced Minority*, p. 15.
92. Allison Butler Herrick et al., *Area Handbook for Uganda*, pp. 91–92.
93. Ibid., p. 92.
94. Yash Ghai and Dharam Ghai, *The Asian Minorities of East and Central Africa (up to 1971)*, p. 8.
95. Ibid., p. 9.
96. Allison Butler Herrick et al., *Area Handbook for Uganda*, p. 340.
97. Yash Ghai and Dharam Ghai, *The Asian Minorities of East and Central Africa (up to 1971)*, p. 7.
98. Ibid., p. 7. See also Anirodha Gupta, "India and the Asians in East Africa," *Expulsion of a Minority*, edited by Michael Twaddle, pp. 125–139; Hugh Tinker, *The Banyan Tree*, pp. 68, 125, 149.
99. David Lamb, *The Africans*, p. 88.
100. Yashpal Tandon, *Problems of a Displaced Minority*, p. 5.
101. Ibid., p. 5.
102. Ibid., p. 29.
103. Allison Butler Herrick et al., *Area Handbook for Uganda*, p. 67.
104. Yashpal Tandon, *Problems of a Displaced Minority*, p. 7.
105. David Lamb, *The Africans*, p. 155.
106. Ibid., p. 88n.

107. Ibid., pp. 264–265.
108. Scott Peterson, "Ugandan Officials Urge Asian Investors to Return," *The Christian Science Monitor,* March 17, 1992, p. 4.
109. Ibid.
110. Yash Ghai and Dharam Ghai, *The Asian Minorities of East and Central Africa (up to 1971),* pp. 4, 20.
111. Irving Kaplan et al., *Area Handbook for Kenya* (Washington, D.C.: U.S. Government Printing Office, 1976), p. 74.
112. Hugh Tinker, *The Banyan Tree,* pp. 119, 121.
113. Ibid., p. 121.
114. Agehananda Bharati, *The Asians in East Africa,* p. 150.
115. Irving Kaplan et al., *Area Handbook for Kenya,* p. 101.
116. Ibid., p. 28.
117. Ibid., p. 29.
118. J. S. Mangat, *A History of the Asians in East Africa,* p. 74.
119. Ibid., p. 75.
120. Ibid., p. 77.
121. Irving Kaplan et al., *Area Handbook for Kenya,* p. 24.
122. J. S. Mangat, *A History of the Asians in East Africa,* p. 89.
123. Ibid., p. 144.
124. Ibid., p. 90.
125. Ibid., p. 95.
126. Agehananda Bharati, *The Asians in East Africa,* p. 150.
127. Ibid., p. 103.
128. J. S. Mangat, *A History of the Asians in East Africa,* p. 98.
129. Ibid., p. 106.
130. Winston S. Churchill, *My African Journey* (London: The Holland Press, 1962), p. 34.
131. J. S. Mangat, *A History of the Asians in East Africa,* pp. 105, 111.
132. Ibid., p. 100.
133. Ibid., p. 94.
134. Ibid., p. 107.
135. Ibid., pp. 124–125.
136. Agehananda Bharati, *The Asians in East Africa,* pp. 152–153.
137. J. S. Mangat, *A History of the Asians in East Africa,* p. 136; cf. Thomas Sowell, *Ethnic America: A History* (New York: Basic Books, 1981), p. 91.
138. J. S. Mangat, *A History of the Asians in East Africa,* pp. 157, 164, 166.
139. Ibid., pp. 156–158.
140. Ibid., p. 155.
141. David Lamb, *The Africans,* p. 156.

142. See, for example, Agehananda Bharati, *The Asians in East Africa,* pp. 152–154; J. S. Mangat, *A History of the Asians in East Africa,* pp. 168–171.
143. J. S. Mangat, *A History of the Asians in East Africa,* p. 176; Haraprasad Chattopadhyaya, *Indians in Africa,* pp. 430–431; Agehananda Bharati, *The Asians in East Africa,* p. 154.
144. Agehananda Bharati, *The Asians in East Africa,* p. 105.
145. Irving Kaplan et al., *Area Handbook for Kenya,* p. 74.
146. Agehananda Bharati, *The Asians in East Africa,* p. 154.
147. Ibid., pp. 152–154.
148. Ibid., pp. 160–161.
149. Ibid., pp. 150–151, 154, 157, 160, 164.
150. Agehananda Bharati, *The Asians in East Africa,* p. 178.
151. Hugh Tinker, *The Banyan Tree,* p. 126.
152. Ibid., p. 127.
153. Irving Kaplan et al., *Area Handbook for Kenya,* p. 237.
154. Ibid., pp. 236–237.
155. David Lamb, *The Africans,* p. 155.
156. Irving Kaplan et al., *Area Handbook for Kenya,* p. 237.
157. Ibid., pp. 74, 239.
158. T. R. H. Davenport, *South Africa: A Modern History* (Toronto: University of Toronto Press, 1977), pp. 91–93.
159. W. H. Hutt, *The Economics of the Colour Bar: A Study of the Economic Origins and Consequences of Racial Segregation in South Africa* (London: The Institute of Economic Affairs, 1964), p. 121.
160. Hilda Kuper, *Indian People in Natal* (Westport, Conn.: Greenwood Press, 1974), p. xii.
161. Haraprasad Chattopadhyaya, *Indians in Africa,* p. 42.
162. Ibid., pp. 47–50.
163. Ibid., pp. 52–55.
164. Ibid., pp. 74–75.
165. Ibid., p. 69.
166. Ibid., pp. 70–71.
167. Ibid., pp. 66, 263–264.
168. T. R. H. Davenport, *South Africa,* p. 92.
169. W. H. Hutt, *The Economics of the Colour Bar,* p. 122.
170. Hilda Kuper, *Indian People in Natal,* p. 62.
171. Haraprasad Chattopadhyaya, *Indians in Africa,* p. 267.
172. Ibid., pp. 73–74, 265–266, 268.
173. Ibid., pp. 279–290.

174. T. R. H. Davenport, *South Africa,* p. 155.
175. Ibid., p. 263.
176. Ibid., p. 279.
177. Pierre van den Berghe, *South Africa: A Study in Conflict* (Berkeley: University of California Press, 1965), p. 288.
178. Ibid., p. 289.
179. Ibid., p. 304.
180. Ibid., p. 306.
181. Haraprasad Chattopadhyaya, *Indians in Africa,* p. 268.
182. *South Africa 1984: Official Yearbook of the Republic of South Africa* (Johannesburg: Chris van Rensburg Publications, 1984), p. 485.
183. Hilda Kuper, *Indian People in Natal,* pp. 18–43.
184. Ibid., p. 20.
185. Ibid., p. 60.
186. Pierre van den Berghe, *South Africa,* p. 43.
187. Ibid., pp. 44–45.
188. Ibid., p. 66.
189. Ibid., p. 4.
190. David Lowenthal, *West Indian Societies* (New York: Oxford University Press, 1972), p. 146.
191. Joan M. Jensen, "East Indians," *Harvard Encyclopedia of American Ethnic Groups,* edited by Stephan Thernstrom et al. (Cambridge, Mass.: Harvard University Press, 1981), p. 296.
192. Subhas Ramcharan, "The Social, Economic and Cultural Adaptation of East Indians from the British Caribbean and Guyana to Canada," *Overseas Indians: A Study in Adaptation,* edited by George Kurian and Ram P. Srivastava (New Delhi: Vikas Publishing House PVT Ltd., 1983), pp. 53, 59.
193. David Lowenthal, *West Indian Societies,* p. 150.
194. Ibid., p. 149.
195. Malcolm Cross, *The East Indians of Guyana and Trinidad* (London: Minority Rights Group, 1980), p. 12.
196. Dwarka Nath, *A History of Indians in British Guiana* (London: Thomas Nelson and Sons, 1950), pp. 7, 24–25.
197. Alan H. Adamson, "The Reconstruction of Plantation Labor after Emancipation: The Case of British Guiana," *Race and Slavery in the Western Hemisphere: Quantitative Studies,* edited by Stanley L. Engerman and Eugene D. Genovese (Princeton, N.J.: Princeton University Press, 1975), p. 462.
198. Ralph R. Premdas, "The Political Economy of Ethnic Strife in Fiji and

Guyana," *Ethnic Studies Report* (International Centre for Ethnic Studies, Sri Lanka), July 1991, pp. 30–31.

199. David Lowenthal, *West Indian Societies,* pp. 15–16. See also William B. Mitchell et al., *Area Handbook for Guyana* (Washington, D.C.: U.S. Government Printing Office, 1969), p. 39.
200. Dwarka Nath, *A History of Indians in British Guiana,* p. 19.
201. Malcolm Cross, *The East Indians of Guyana and Trinidad,* p. 4.
202. Dwarka Nath, *A History of Indians in British Guiana,* pp. 26, 27, 36, 37.
203. Ibid., p. 60.
204. Ibid., p. 39.
205. Walter Rodney, *A History of the Guyanese Working People, 1881–1905* (Baltimore: Johns Hopkins University Press, 1981), pp. 33–34.
206. William B. Mitchell et al., *Area Handbook for Guyana,* p. 38.
207. Dwarka Nath, *A History of Indians in British Guiana,* pp. 60–61.
208. Alan H. Adamson, "The Reconstruction of Plantation Labor after Emancipation: The Case of British Guiana," *Race and Slavery in the Western Hemisphere,* edited by Stanley L. Engerman and Eugene D. Genovese, pp. 464–465.
209. William B. Mitchell et al., *Area Handbook for Guyana,* p. 39.
210. Ralph R. Premdas, "Politics of Preference in the Caribbean: The Case of Guyana," *Ethnic Preference and Public Policy in Developing States,* edited by Neil Nevitte and Charles H. Kennedy (Boulder, Colo.: Lynne Rienner Publishers, Inc., 1986), p. 167.
211. William B. Mitchell et al., *Area Handbook for Guyana,* p. 56.
212. Ibid., p. 38.
213. Ralph R. Premdas, "Politics of Preference in the Caribbean," *Ethnic Preference and Public Policy in Developing States,* edited by Neil Nevitte and Charles H. Kennedy, p. 166.
214. Malcolm Cross, *The East Indians of Guyana and Trinidad,* p. 5.
215. William B. Mitchell et al., *Area Handbook for Guyana,* p. 57.
216. Malcolm Cross, *The East Indians of Guyana and Trinidad,* p. 5.
217. Dwarka Nath, *A History of Indians in British Guiana,* p. 206.
218. Ibid., pp. 206, 207.
219. Ralph R. Premdas, "The Political Economy of Ethnic Strife in Fiji and Guyana," *Ethnic Studies Report* (International Centre for Ethnic Studies, Sri Lanka), July 1991, p. 31.
220. Dwarka Nath, *A History of Indians in British Guiana,* pp. 203–204.
221. William B. Mitchell et al., *Area Handbook for Guyana,* p. 45.
222. Ibid., p. 205.
223. Ibid., pp. 208–209.

224. Ibid., p. 214.
225. Malcolm Cross, *The East Indians of Guyana and Trinidad,* p. 5.
226. William B. Mitchell et al., *Area Handbook for Guyana,* p. 52.
227. Ibid., p. 55.
228. David Lowenthal, *West Indian Societies,* p. 165.
229. Ralph R. Premdas, "The Political Economy of Ethnic Strife in Fiji and Guyana," *Ethnic Studies Report* (International Centre for Ethnic Studies, Sri Lanka), July 1991, pp. 31–32.
230. Ralph R. Premdas, "Politics of Preference in the Caribbean," *Ethnic Preference and Public Policy in Developing States,* edited by Neil Nevitte and Charles H. Kennedy, pp. 163–164.
231. Ralph R. Premdas, "The Political Economy of Ethnic Strife in Fiji and Guyana," *Ethnic Studies Report* (International Centre for Ethnic Studies, Sri Lanka), July 1991, p. 32.
232. Ralph R. Premdas, "Politics of Preference in the Caribbean," *Ethnic Preference and Public Policy in Developing States,* edited by Neil Nevitte and Charles H. Kennedy, p. 169.
233. Ibid., pp. 169–172.
234. Ibid., p. 177.
235. Ralph R. Premdas, "The Political Economy of Ethnic Strife in Fiji and Guyana," *Ethnic Studies Report* (International Centre for Ethnic Studies, Sri Lanka), July 1991, p. 33.
236. R. S. Milne, *Politics in Ethnically Bipolar States* (Vancouver: University of British Columbia Press, 1981), pp. 15–39, 214; The Economist Intelligence Unit, *Guyana, Barbados, Windward and Leeward Islands: Country Profile 1991–92* (London: The Economist Intelligence Unit, 1991), p. 10.
237. Ralph R. Premdas, "The Political Economy of Ethnic Strife in Fiji and Guyana," *Ethnic Studies Report* (International Centre for Ethnic Studies, Sri Lanka), July 1991, p. 33.
238. The Economist Intelligence Unit, *Guyana, Windward and Leeward Islands* (London: The Economist Intelligence Unit, 1995), pp. 10–13; Chaitram Singh, "Ethnicity and Democracy in Guyana," *Journal of Third World Studies,* Vol. 11, No. 1 (Spring 1994), pp. 417–419.
239. Jan Knippers Black et al., *Area Handbook for Trinidad and Tobago* (Washington, D.C.: U.S. Government Printing Office, 1976), p. 90.
240. Morton Klass, *East Indians in Trinidad: A Study of Cultural Persistence* (New York: Columbia University Press, 1961), p. 242.
241. Jan Knippers Black et al., *Area Handbook for Trinidad and Tobago,* p. 85.
242. Ibid., p. 53.

243. David Lowenthal, *West Indian Societies,* p. 146.
244. Morton Klass, *East Indians in Trinidad,* p. 240.
245. David Lowenthal, *West Indian Societies,* p. 170.
246. Eric Williams, *History of the People of Trinidad and Tobago* (New York: Frederick A. Praeger, 1962), pp. 115, 120.
247. Morton Klass, *East Indians in Trinidad,* p. 2.
248. Jan Knippers Black et al., *Area Handbook for Trinidad and Tobago,* p. 82; David Lowenthal, *West Indian Societies,* p. 167.
249. David Lowenthal, *West Indian Societies,* pp. 167–168.
250. Malcolm Cross, *The East Indians of Guyana and Trinidad,* p. 11.
251. Yogendra K. Malik, *East Indians in Trinidad* (London: Oxford University Press, 1971), p. 15.
252. Malcolm Cross, *The East Indians of Guyana and Trinidad,* p. 12.
253. Hugh Tinker, *The Banyan Tree,* pp. 63–65.
254. Malcolm Cross, *The East Indians of Guyana and Trinidad,* p. 11. See also Morton Klass, *East Indians in Trinidad,* p. 244.
255. Peter Xenos, Herbert Barringer, and Michael J. Levin, *Asian Indians in the United States: A 1980 Census Profile* (Honolulu: East-West Population Institute, 1989), p. 15.
256. Hugh Tinker, *The Banyan Tree,* p. 12.
257. Peter Xenos et al., *Asian Indians in the United States,* p. 15.
258. Leona B. Bagai, *The East Indians and the Pakistanis in America* (Minneapolis: Lerner Publications Co., 1972), p. 45.
259. Peter Xenos et al., *Asian Indians in the United States,* p. 4.
260. Ibid., p. 17.
261. Ibid., p. 16.
262. Ibid., p. 35.
263. Ibid., p. 22.
264. U.S. Bureau of the Census, *Asians and Pacific Islanders in the United States* (Washington, D.C.: U.S. Government Printing Office, 1993), p. 13.
265. Ibid., pp. 142, 153.
266. Peter Xenos et al., *Asian Indians in the United States,* pp. 35–36.
267. Leona B. Bagai, *The East Indians and the Pakistanis in America,* p. 37.
268. Peter Xenos et al., *Asian Indians in the United States,* p. 17.
269. Paul M. Ong, Lucie Cheng, and Leslie Evans, "Migration of Highly Educated Asians and Global Dynamics," *Asian and Pacific Migration Journal,* Vol. 1, Nos. 3–4 (1992), p. 545.
270. Robert Bellinger, "Indian EEs: Torn Between Home, Opportunity," *Electronic Engineering Times,* August 1, 1988, p. 40.
271. Joel Kotkin, *Tribes,* p. 229.

272. James P. Sterba, "Indians in the U.S. Prosper in Their New Country, and Not Just in Motels," *Wall Street Journal,* January 27, 1987, p. 1.
273. Monua Janah, "Indian Immigrants Find Room to Grow Beyond Motels," *Wall Street Journal,* August 25, 1989, p. B2.
274. Kernial Singh Sandhu, *Indians in Malaya: Some Aspects of Their Immigration and Settlement (1786–1957)* (Cambridge: Cambridge University Press, 1969), p. 61.
275. Virginia Thompson and Richard Adloff, *Minority Problems in Southeast Asia* (New York: Russell & Russell, 1970), pp. 122, 127.
276. Ibid., pp. 85, 108, 109, 129.
277. Hugh Tinker, *The Banyan Tree,* pp. 142, 143.
278. Virginia Thompson and Richard Adloff, *Minority Problems in Southeast Asia,* pp. 95, 111.
279. Ibid., p. 123.
280. Hugh Tinker, *The Banyan Tree,* p. 143.
281. Ibid., p. 141.
282. Virginia Thompson and Richard Adloff, *Minority Problems in Southeast Asia,* p. 109.
283. Ibid., p. 94.
284. Tan Loong-Woe, *The State and Economic Distribution in Peninsular Malaysia* (Singapore: Institute of Southeast Asian Studies, 1982), p. 34.
285. Virginia Thompson and Richard Adloff, *Minority Problems in Southeast Asia,* p. 111.
286. Ibid., pp. 114–117.
287. Ibid., p. 117.
288. Ibid., p. 125.
289. Ibid., pp. 96, 122.
290. Hugh Tinker, *The Banyan Tree,* p. 145.
291. Ibid., p. 142.
292. Virginia Thompson and Richard Adloff, *Minority Problems in Southeast Asia,* pp. 75, 87.
293. Hugh Tinker, *The Banyan Tree,* p. 142.
294. John William Henderson et al., *Area Handbook for Burma* (Washington, D.C.: U.S. Government Printing Office, 1971), p. 238.
295. Nena Vreeland et al., *Area Handbook for Malaysia* (Washington, D.C.: U.S. Government Printing Office, 1977), pp. 45–46.
296. Kernial Singh Sandhu, *Indians in Malaya,* p. 13.
297. Ibid., pp. 4, 13.
298. Ibid., p. 52.
299. Donald R. Snodgrass, *Inequality and Economic Development in*

Malaysia (Kuala Lumpur: Oxford University Press, 1980), pp. 39–40.
300. Nena Vreeland et al., *Area Handbook for Malaysia,* pp. 134–135.
301. Kernial Singh Sandhu, *Indians in Malaya,* p. 99.
302. Ibid., pp. 304–305.
303. Ibid., p. 185.
304. Ibid., pp. 83, 84.
305. Ibid., p. 97.
306. P. T. Bauer, *The Rubber Industry: A Study in Competition and Monopoly* (Cambridge, Mass.: Harvard University Press, 1948), p. 224.
307. Ibid., p. 234.
308. Kernial Singh Sandhu, *Indians in Malaya,* p. 152.
309. Ibid., p. 317.
310. Ibid., p. 183.
311. Ibid., p. 171.
312. Ibid., p. 184.
313. Ibid., p. 186.
314. Ibid., p. 215.
315. Ibid., p. 247.
316. Hugh Tinker, *The Banyan Tree,* p. 98.
317. Tai Yoke Lin, "Inter-Ethnic Restructuring in Malaysia, 1970–80: The Employment Perspective," *From Independence to Statehood: Managing Ethnic Conflict in Five African and Asian States,* edited by Robert B. Goldmann and A. Jeyaratnam Wilson (London: Frances Pinter, 1984), p. 46.
318. Nena Vreeland et al., *Area Handbook for Malaysia,* p. 83.
319. Donald R. Snodgrass, *Inequality and Economic Development in Malaysia,* p. 83.
320. Nena Vreeland et al., *Area Handbook for Malaysia,* p. 149.
321. Gordon P. Means, *Malaysia Politics* (New York: New York University Press, 1970), p. 20.
322. Nena Vreeland et al., *Area Handbook for Malaysia,* p. 88.
323. Ibid., pp. 134, 135.
324. Ibid., p. 144.
325. Ibid., p. 135.
326. Hugh Tinker, *The Banyan Tree,* p. 108.
327. Tai Yoke Lin, "Inter-Ethnic Restructuring in Malaysia, 1970–1980," *From Independence to Statehood,* edited by Robert B. Goldmann and A. Jeyaratnam Wilson, p. 49.
328. Mah Hui Lim, "Affirmative Action, Ethnicity and Integration: The Case of Malaysia," *Ethnic and Racial Studies,* April 1985, p. 271.

329. James Manor, "Introduction," *Sri Lanka in Change and Crisis,* edited by James Manor (London: Croom Helm, 1984), p. 3.
330. Chandra Richard de Silva, "Sinhala-Tamil Relations and Education in Sri Lanka: The University Admissions Issue—The First Phase, 1971–77," *From Independence to Statehood,* edited by Robert B. Goldmann and A. Jeyaratnam Wilson, p. 136.
331. Robert N. Kearney, *Communalism and Language in the Politics of Ceylon* (Durham, N.C.: Duke University Press, 1967), p. 8; K. M. de Silva, *Managing Ethnic Tensions in Multi-Ethnic Societies: Sri Lanka 1880–1985* (Lanham, Md.: University Press of America, 1986), pp. xv, xvi.
332. I. D. S. Weerawardana, "Minority Problems in Ceylon," *Pacific Affairs,* September 1952, p. 281n.
333. Chandra Richard de Silva, "Sinhala-Tamil Ethnic Rivalry: The Background," *From Independence to Statehood,* edited by Robert B. Goldmann and A. Jeyaratnam Wilson, p. 116.
334. H. P. Chattopadhyaya, *Indians in Sri Lanka: A Historical Study* (Calcutta: O.P.S. Publishers Private Ltd., 1979), Chapter V.
335. Ibid., p. 188.
336. R. Jayaraman, "Indian Emigration to Ceylon: Some Aspects of the Historical and Social Background of the Emigrants," *Indian Economic and Social History Review,* December 1967, p. 320.
337. Robert N. Kearney, *Communalism and Language in the Politics of Ceylon,* pp. 8, 11.
338. Kernial Singh Sandhu, *Indians in Malaya,* pp. 56–57, 159, 237. See also R. Jayaraman, "Indian Emigration to Ceylon: Some Aspects of the Historical and Social Background of the Emigrants," *Indian Economic and Social History Review,* December 1967, p. 337.
339. Robert N. Kearney, *Communalism and Language in the Politics of Ceylon,* pp. 261–262.
340. R. Jayaraman, "Indian Emigration to Ceylon: Some Aspects of the Historical and Social Background of the Emigrants," *Indian Economic and Social History Review,* December 1967, p. 349.
341. Ibid., pp. 335, 344.
342. Ibid., pp. 337, 338.
343. Ibid., pp. 350–352.
344. William McGowan, *And Only Man Is Vile: The Tragedy of Sri Lanka* (New York: Farrar, Straus, and Giroux, 1992), pp. 287–289.
345. H. P. Chattopadhyaya, *Indians in Sri Lanka,* p. 121.
346. R. Jayaraman, "Indian Emigration to Ceylon: Some Aspects of the His-

torical and Social Background of the Emigrants," *Indian Economic and Social History Review,* December 1967, pp. 322, 324.

347. Ibid., p. 322.
348. Ibid., p. 324.
349. See Hugh Tinker, *A New System of Slavery: The Export of Indian Labour Overseas, 1830–1920* (London: Oxford University Press, 1974), Chapter 6, passim.
350. C. Kondapi, *Indians Overseas, 1838–1949* (New Delhi: Oxford University Press, 1951), pp. 74–75.
351. Kernial Singh Sandhu, *Indians in Malaya,* p. 157.
352. C. Kondapi, *Indians Overseas, 1838–1949,* p. 36.
353. H. P. Chattopadhyaya, *Indians in Sri Lanka,* pp. 113, 115.
354. R. Jayaraman, "Indian Emigration to Ceylon: Some Aspects of the Historical and Social Background of the Emigrants," *Indian Economic and Social History Review,* December 1967, pp. 322, 324.
355. Walter Schwarz, *The Tamils of Sri Lanka* (London: Minority Rights Group, 1983), p. 8; Robert N. Kearney, *Communalism and Language in the Politics of Ceylon,* p. 7; Robert N. Kearney, "Language and the Rise of Tamil Separatism in Sri Lanka," *Asian Survey,* May 1978, p. 522.
356. H. P. Chattopadhyaya, *Indians in Sri Lanka,* pp. 106–108.
357. Ibid., pp. 125–127.
358. Ibid., pp. 129–130, 140–169.
359. C. Kondapi, *Indians Overseas, 1838–1949,* p. 344.
360. H. P. Chattopadhyaya, *Indians in Sri Lanka,* pp. 143, 144, 146.
361. Hugh Tinker, *The Banyan Tree,* p. 49.
362. S. J. Tambiah, "Ethnic Representation in Ceylon's Higher Administrative Service, 1870–1946," *University of Ceylon Review,* April–July 1955, pp. 125–136.
363. W. Ivor Jennings, "Race, Religion and Economic Opportunity in the University of Ceylon," *University of Ceylon Review,* November 1944, p. 2.
364. Chandra Richard de Silva, "Sinhala-Tamil Ethnic Rivalry: The Background," *From Independence to Statehood,* edited by Robert B. Goldmann and A. Jeyaratnam Wilson, p. 116. See also Chandra Richard de Silva, "Sinhala-Tamil Relations and Education in Sri Lanka: The University Admissions Issue—The First Phase," ibid., p. 136.
365. S. W. R. de A. Samarasinghe, "Ethnic Representation in Central Government Employment and Sinhala-Tamil Relations in Sri Lanka: 1948–81," ibid., p. 176.
366. Ibid., p. 177.
367. C. Kondapi, *Indians Overseas, 1838–1949,* pp. 344–347.

368. Walter Schwarz, *The Tamils of Sri Lanka,* p. 5.
369. Robert N. Kearney, *Communalism and Language in the Politics of Ceylon,* p. 27; Walter Schwarz, *The Tamils of Sri Lanka,* p. 6.
370. S. J. Tambiah, "Ethnic Representation in Ceylon's Higher Administrative Service, 1870–1946," *University of Ceylon Review,* April–July 1955, pp. 127, 128.
371. Ibid., p. 130.
372. Ibid., pp. 131, 132.
373. Robert N. Kearney, "Sinhalese Nationalism and Social Conflict in Ceylon," *Pacific Affairs,* Summer 1964, pp. 125–128.
374. Robert N. Kearney, *Communalism and Language in the Politics of Ceylon,* pp. 80–81; William McGowan, *And Only Man Is Vile,* pp. 149–158.
375. Walter Schwarz, *The Tamils of Sri Lanka,* p. 7.
376. Hugh Tinker, *The Banyan Tree,* pp. 47–48.
377. Walter Schwarz, *The Tamils of Sri Lanka,* pp. 9–10.
378. Ibid., p. 10.
379. K. M. de Silva, "University Admissions and Ethnic Tension in Sri Lanka, 1977–82," *From Independence to Statehood,* edited by Robert B. Goldmann and A. Jeyaratnam Wilson, p. 97.
380. Chandra Richard de Silva, "Sinhala-Tamil Relations and Education in Sri Lanka," ibid., p. 138.
381. K. M. de Silva, "University Admissions and Ethnic Tension in Sri Lanka, 1977–82," ibid., pp. 98–99.
382. Chandra Richard de Silva, "Sinhala-Tamil Relations and Education in Sri Lanka," ibid., p. 140.
383. S. W. R. de A. Samarasinghe, "Ethnic Representation in Central Government Employment and Sinhala-Tamil Relations in Sri Lanka," ibid., p. 178.
384. Ibid., p. 181.
385. Walter Schwarz, *The Tamils of Sri Lanka,* p. 13.
386. S. W. R. de A. Samarasinghe, "Ethnic Representation in Central Government Employment and Sinhala-Tamil Relations in Sri Lanka," *From Independence to Statehood,* edited by Robert B. Goldmann and A. Jeyaratnam Wilson, p. 178.
387. Walter Schwarz, *The Tamils of Sri Lanka,* p. 14.
388. Alvin Rabushka, "Adam Smith in Sri Lanka," *Policy Review,* Fall 1981, pp. 54–62.
389. Eric Meyer, "Seeking the Roots of the Tragedy," *Sri Lanka in Change and Crisis,* edited by James Manor, pp. 137–152.
390. James Manor, "Introduction," ibid., p. 22.
391. Eric Meyer, "Seeking the Roots of the Tragedy," ibid., pp. 139, 149.

392. "Sri Lanka Confirms Report of Army Slayings," *New York Times,* August 7, 1983, Section I, p. 5.
393. William McGowan, And *Only Man Is Vile,* p. 188.
394. Ibid., pp. 96–97.
395. Ibid., p. 191.
396. Mervyn De Silva, "Sri Lanka Rebels Defy Indian Force, Meditation," *The Christian Science Monitor,* July 21, 1988, p. 9.
397. William McGowan, *And Only Man Is Vile,* p. 381.
398. Reed Coughlan and S. W. R. de A. Samarasinghe, "Introduction," *Economic Dimensions of Ethnic Conflict,* edited by S. W. R. de A. Samarasinghe (London: Pinter Publishers, 1991), p. 12.
399. C. Kondapi, *Indians Overseas, 1838–1949,* p. 26.
400. Chandra Jayawardena, "Farm, Household and Family in Fiji Indian Rural Society," *Overseas Indians,* edited by George Kurian and Ram P. Srivastava, p. 142. See also K. L. Gillion, *Fiji's Indian Migrants: A History to the End of Indenture in 1920* (Melbourne: Oxford University Press, 1962), pp. 45–58, 202–210.
401. Adrian C. Mayer, *Indians in Fiji* (London: Oxford University Press, 1963), pp. 13–14; K. L. Gillion, *Fiji's Indian Migrants,* pp. 31–34.
402. C. Kondapi, *Indians Overseas, 1838–1949,* p. 27.
403. K. L. Gillion, *Fiji's Indian Migrants,* pp. 141–142.
404. Adrian C. Mayer, *Indians in Fiji,* pp. 19, 24–26.
405. K. L. Gillion, *Fiji's Indian Migrants,* p. 142.
406. Ibid., pp. 122–125, 144, 150.
407. Adrian C. Mayer, *Peasants in the Pacific: A Study of Fiji Indian Rural Society* (Berkeley: University of California Press, 1973), pp. 157–160.
408. Adrian C. Mayer, *Indians in Fiji,* pp. 28–29.
409. K. L. Gillion, *Fiji's Indian Migrants,* pp. 102, 142.
410. Ibid., p. 146.
411. Ibid., pp. 130–133.
412. Ibid., p. 134.
413. Ibid., p. 146.
414. Ibid., pp. 143–144.
415. Adrian C. Mayer, *Peasants in the Pacific,* p. 7.
416. Michael Ward, *The Role of Investment in the Development of Fiji* (Cambridge: Cambridge University Press, 1971), p. 21.
417. The Economist Intelligence Unit, *Fiji, Solomon Islands, Western Samoa, Vanatu, Tonga: Country Profile 1991–92* (London: The Economist Intelligence Unit, 1991), p. 18.
418. C. Kondapi, *Indians Overseas, 1838–1949,* p. 357.

419. Michael Ward, *The Role of Investment in the Development of Fiji,* p. 110.
420. Ibid., p. 109.
421. Ralph R. Premdas, "The Political Economy of Ethnic Strife in Fiji and Guyana," *Ethnic Studies Report* (International Centre for Ethnic Studies, Sri Lanka), July 1991, p. 36.
422. Wolfgang Kasper et al., *Fiji: Opportunity from Adversity* (St. Leonards, Australia: The Center for Independent Studies, 1988), p. 129.
423. Ibid., pp. 3–8.
424. "Now They'll Do It Their Way," *Time,* June 1, 1987, p. 44.
425. R. S. Milne, *Politics in Ethnically Bipolar States,* pp. 86–87.
426. Ibid., p. 236; J. S. Mangat, *A History of the Asians in East Africa, 1896–1965,* p. 40; K. L. Gillion, *Fiji's Indian Migrants,* p. 134; Hilda Kuper, *Indian People in Natal,* p. 60. Gujaratis have also been prominent and prosperous in the United States. See Monua Janah, "Indian Immigrants Find Room to Grow Beyond Motels," *Wall Street Journal,* August 25, 1989, p. B2.
427. Hugh Tinker, *The Banyan Tree,* p. 3.
428. Ibid., pp. 123–124, 154, 159.
429. Ibid., pp. x, 99.
430. M. C. Madhavan, "Indian Emigrants: Numbers, Characteristics, and Economic Impace," *Population and Development Review,* September 1985, p. 465.
431. Ibid., p. 469.
432. James Clad, "Paradise Abroad," *Far Eastern Economic Review,* April 29, 1990, p. 27; Hugh Tinker, *The Banyan Tree,* p. 9.
433. Hugh Tinker, *The Banyan Tree,* p. 10.
434. James Clad, "Paradise Abroad," *Far Eastern Economic Review,* April 29, 1990, pp. 27, 28.

CHAPTER 8: HISTORY AND CULTURES

1. Paul Johnson, *The Quotable Paul Johnson: A Topical Compilation of His Wit, Wisdom and Satire,* edited by George J. Marlin et al. (New York: Farrar, Straus & Giroux, 1994), p. 138.
2. Fernand Braudel, *A History of Civilizations,* translated by Richard Mayne (New York: Penguin, 1994), p. 17.
3. Carlo M. Cipolla, *Literacy and Development in the West* (New York: Penguin, 1969), p. 16.
4. Paul Kennedy, *The Rise and Fall of the Great Powers: Economic Change*

and Military Conflict from 1500 to 2000 (New York: Random House, 1987), p. 216.

5. Bernard Nkemdirim, "Social Change and the Genesis of Conflict in Nigeria," *Civilisations,* Vol. 25, Nos. 1–2 (197), p. 94.
6. Cynthia H. Enloe, *Police, Military and Ethnicity: Foundations of State Power* (New Brunswick, N.J.: Transaction Books, 1980).
7. Donald F. Horowitz, *Ethnic Groups in Conflict* (Berkeley: University of California Press, 1985), p. 677.
8. R. Bayly Winder, "Lebanese Emigration in General," *Comparative Studies in Society and History,* Vol. IV (1961–62), p. 309.
9. Charles Issawi, "The Transformation of the Economic Position of the *Millets* in the Nineteenth Century," *Christians and Jews in the Ottoman Empire: The Functioning of a Plural Society,* edited by Benjamin Braude and Bernard Lewis, Volume I: *The Central Lands* (New York: Holmes & Meier Publishers, 1982), pp. 262–263, 266.
10. Winthrop R. Wright, *British-Owned Railways in Argentina: Their Effect on Economic Nationalism, 1854–1948* (Austin: University of Texas Press, 1974).
11. John P. McKay, *Pioneers for Profit: Foreign Entrepreneurship and Russian Industrialization 1885–1913* (Chicago: University of Chicago Press, 1970), p. 35.
12. Carl Solberg, *Immigration and Nationalism: Argentina and Chile, 1890–1914* (Austin: University of Texas Press, 1970), p. 68.
13. Fernand Braudel, *A History of Civilizations,* p. 440.
14. Charles Issawi, "The Transformation of the Economic Position of the *Millets* in the Nineteenth Century," *Christians and Jews in the Ottoman Empire,* edited by Benjamin Braude and Bernard Lewis, Volume I: *The Central Lands,* p. 265.
15. Robert P. Bartlett, *Human Capital: The Settlement of Foreigners in Russia, 1762–1802* (Cambridge: Cambridge University Press, 1979), p. 151.
16. Seamus Grimes, "Friendship Patterns and Social Networks among Post-War Irish Migrants in Sydney," *The Irish World Wide,* Volume 1: *Patterns of Migration,* edited by Patrick O'Sullivan (Leicester: Leicester University Press, 1992), p. 171.
17. Jonathan Kaufman, "How Cambodians Came to Control California Doughnuts," *Wall Street Journal,* February 22, 1995, p. A1.
18. Pablo Macera and Shane J. Hunt, "Peru," *Latin America: A Guide to Economic History 1830–1930,* edited by Roberto Cortis Conde and Stanley J. Stein (Berkeley: University of California Press, 1977), p. 565.

19. Nena Vreeland et al., *Area Handbook for Malaysia,* third edition (Washington, D.C.: U.S. Government Printing Office, 1977), p. 303.
20. Winthrop R. Wright, *British-Owned Railways in Argentina*; Gino Germani, "Mass Immigration and Modernization in Argentina," *Studies in Comparative Development,* Vol. 2 (1966), p. 170.
21. Carlo M. Cipolla, *Clocks and Culture: 1300–1700* (New York: Norton, 1978), p. 68.
22. John P. McKay, *Pioneers for Profit: Foreign Entrepreneurship and Russian Industrialization, 1885–1913* (Chicago: University of Chicago Press, 1970), pp. 33, 34, 35.
23. Jean W. Sedlar, *East Central Europe in the Middle Ages, 1000–1500,* p. 131.
24. Charles Issawi, "The Transformation of the Economic Position of the *Millets* in the Ninetenth Century," *Christians and Jews in the Ottoman Empire,* edited by Benjamin Braude and Bernard Lewis, Volume I: *The Central Lands,* pp. 262, 263, 265, 266, 267.
25. Victor Purcell, *The Overseas Chinese in Southeast Asia,* second edition (Kuala Lumpur: Oxford University Press, 1980), pp. 7, 68, 83, 180, 245, 248, 540, 559.
26. Carlo M. Cipolla, *Guns, Sails, and Empires: Technological Innovation and the Early Phases of European Expansion, 1400–1700* (Manhattan, Kan.: Sunflower University Press, 1992), p. 31n.
27. Cynthia H. Enloe, *Police, Military and Ethnicity,* p. 75.
28. Jean W. Sedlar, *East Central Europe in the Middle Ages, 1000–1500,* pp. 97, 241–242, 267.
29. Carlo M. Cipolla, *Guns, Sails, and Empires,* pp. 59, 115, 134.
30. James M. McKeown and Joan C. McKeown, *Price Guide to Antique and Classic Cameras,* seventh edition (Hove, East Sussex, U.K.: Hove Foto Books, 1989), pp. 191, 202, 205.
31. Rudolf Kingslake, *A History of the Photographic Lens* (San Diego, Calif.: Academic Press, Inc., 1989), p. 108.
32. Ibid., p. 309.
33. See Rudolf Kingslake, *A History of the Photographic Lens,* pp. 197–313, passim.
34. Vincent Hardi, "Renaissance: The Optical Capital of the World," *Journal of European Economic History,* Vol. 22, No. 3 (Winter 1993), pp. 507–541.
35. *World Almanac and Book of Facts: 1996* (Mahwah, N.J.: Funk and Wagnalls, 1995), pp. 547, 548.
36. Roy E. H. Mellor and E. Alistair Smith, *Europe: A Geographical Survey*

of the Continent (New York: Columbia University Press, 1979), p. 3.

37. Donald Vermeer, "Here and There: Spatial Matters in Geography," *Educational Exchange and Global Competence,* edited by Richard D. Lambert (New York: Council on International Educational Exchange, 1994), p. 166.
38. Andrew Tanzer, "The Bamboo Network," *Forbes,* July 18, 1994, pp. 138–145.
39. Statements about millions of human beings' own preferences, as revealed in their own choices, are often confused with statements about an observer's personal preferences. Thus a reviewer of *Race and Culture: A World View* said: "Sowell rarely questions whether economic or industrial advancement is good." Joe Wakelee-Lynch, "Winners and Losers in the Culture Wars," *San Francisco Chronicle Book Review,* December 18, 1994, p. 8.
40. As an "illustration" of this supposed defect in my *Race and Culture,* a reviewer says: "Guns, like books, are examples of self-evident progress in tool making. But not everybody is in a position to regard the adoption of more efficient killing instruments as benign. Take the reality of inner-city life." John Stone, "Color Isn't Color: A Robust Neo-Conservative Romp through the Minefield of Race Relations," *New York Times Book Review,* November 27, 1994, p. 28.
41. Carlo M. Cipolla, *Clocks and Culture: 1300–1700,* p. 15.
42. Jean W. Sedlar, *East Central Europe in the Middle Ages, 1000–1500,* p. 139.
43. N. J. G. Pounds, *An Historical Geography of Europe: 1800–1914* (Cambridge: Cambridge University Press, 1988), p. 146.
44. Edmund Burke, *Reflections on the Revolution in France* (London: J. M. Dent & Co., 1967), p. 84.
45. T. C. Smout, *A History of the Scottish People: 1560–1830* (London: Collins, 1969), Chapter XIX; Henry Thomas Buckle, *On Scotland and the Scottish Intellect* (Chicago: University of Chicago Press, 1970), Chapter V; David Daiches et al., editors, *A Hotbed of Genius: The Scottish Enlightenment, 1730–1790* (Edinburgh: Edinburgh University Press, 1986).
46. T. C. Smout, *A History of the Scottish People: 1560–1830,* Chapter I.
47. N. J. G. Pounds, *An Historical Geography of Europe: 1800–1914.*
48. Benjamin F. Chavis, "The Farrakhan Sideshow," *New York Times,* July 12, 1994, p. A13.
49. U.S. Bureau of the Census, *Current Population Reports,* Series P-20, No. 366 (Washington, D.C.: U.S. Government Printing Office, 1981), pp. 182, 184.

50. Richard B. Freeman, *Black Elite* (New York: McGraw-Hill, 1976), Chapter 4.
51. Nicholas Eberstadt, "America's Infant Mortality Puzzle," *The Public Interest,* Fall 1991, p. 38.
52. William H. McNeill, *The Rise of the West: A History of Human Communities* (Chicago: University of Chicago Press, 1991), pp. 102–103.
53. John K. Fairbank, Edwin O. Reischauer, and Albert M. Craig, *East Asia: Tradition and Transformation,* revised edition (Boston: Houghton-Mifflin Co., 1989), pp. 38, 112.
54. Ibid., pp. 172, 243.
55. William H. McNeill, *The Rise of the West,* p. 332.
56. Ibid., pp. 260, 300–302.
57. Walter Nugent, *Crossings: The Great Transatlantic Migrations, 1870–1914* (Bloomington: Indiana University Press, 1992), p. 33.
58. N. J. G. Pounds, *An Historical Geography of Europe: 1800–1914,* p. 77.
59. Patrick Manning, "Contours of Slavery and Social Change in Africa," *American Historical Review,* October 1983, p. 854.
60. Peter Brimelow, *Alien Nation: Common Sense about America's Immigration Disaster* (New York: Random House, 1995), p. 187.
61. Carlo M. Cipolla, *Before the Industrial Revolution: European Society and Economy* (New York: Norton, 1980), pp. 100–101.
62. Alfred W. Crosby, *Ecological Imperialism: The Biological Expansion of Europe, 900–1800* (Cambridge: Cambridge University Press, 1993), pp. 280–282.
63. Peter Brimelow, *Alien Nation,* p. 287.
64. Michael Fix and Jeffrey S. Passel, *Immigration and Immigrants: Setting the Record Straight* (Washington, D.C.: The Urban Institute, 1994), p. 33.
65. Peter Brimelow, *Alien Nation,* p. 150.
66. See American Automobile Manufacturers Association, *World Motor Vehicle Data: 1994 Edition* (Detroit: American Automobile Manufacturers Association, 1994), pp. 10, 11, 329.
67. See Thomas Sowell, *Inside American Education: The Decline, the Deception, the Dogmas* (New York: The Free Press, 1993), p. 269.
68. *The Chronicle of Higher Education,* September 1, 1994, p. 18.

INDEX

Forced To Marry

Dark BWWM Mafia Romance

Amalfi Coast Brotherhood
Book 2

Jamila Jasper

www.jamilajasperromance.com

ISBN: 9798842864881

❀ Created with Vellum

Description

Grace is the only woman the young mafia prince can't break.

Enzo's new tenant isn't like any of the others.
She's a difficult African American woman...
Beautiful. Alluring. Forbidden.

And she loathes him.

She hates his grumpy attitude.
She hates his cigarettes.
She even hates Enzo's chiseled biceps.

After "taking out" Grace's degenerate Albanian boyfriend,
Enzo finally has the upper hand.

He's willing to make her problems go away,
If only Grace agrees to marry him...

If you enjoy BWWM mafia family romance stories with action and dark themes, you'll love this trilogy. Get Book #2 in this series of interconnected standalone stories. For fans of the Pagonis family from The Greek Mafia Brotherhood, strap in. The Amalfi Coast Brotherhood will blow your mind.

Series Titles

Forced To Surrogate
Forced To Marry
Forced To Submit

Content Awareness

dark bwwm mafia romance

This is a mafia romance story with dark themes including potentially triggering content, frank discussions and language surrounding bedroom scenes and race. All characters in this story are 18+. Sensitive readers, be cautioned about some of the material in this dark but extremely hot romance novel. The character in this story is ***forced by circumstance*** into her situation.

Enjoy the steamy romance story...

Dedication

Special thank you to everyone who helped me pick some characters names for this book. My instagram followers helped name the lovely dog, Ember. Thank you to my patrons Rayna, Valeria and Yolanda for your name contributions in this story!

Thank you to Christine for your patience with me, for your support on Patreon and for leaving some of my favorite reader comments. I definitely owe you a full-length shout out like this!

I hope everyone enjoys the dark & twisted tale ahead...

Been through some bad shit, I should be a sad bitch
Who woulda thought it'd turn me to a savage?
—7 Rings, ***Ariana Grande***

Chapter 1

She Will Belong To Me Forever

Lorenzo Doukas

The night I properly meet Grace West, everything changes. I stop being a man and turn into a beast, propelled forward by a powerful urge to claim something that isn't mine. From a distance, she always looked beautiful. She has nice full hips, a gorgeous butt, and she walks like a supermodel.

Grace West — my tenant. She's a woman I shouldn't touch, a woman I shouldn't want, but the moment I lay eyes on her silky smooth hazelnut skin up close, I want her so fucking bad.

Women. I've never been smitten with a woman before. I skipped the Italian penchant for romance. Most women cannot intrigue my interest past a single night, especially on the Amalfi Coast where we only have tourists and bloodsuckers hoping for a taste of Doukas money, Doukas power, and the mob life.

Italian women only want the prestige of the Doukas family name. They crave our money. They crave status. I refuse to give freely what women want. I'm too proud, too fiercely unlike my father.

Business titillates me more than women. I love money,

capisce? I own apartment complexes and many, many women need a place to live. That's how I prefer my dealings with women. Some have money, some have pussy — all find a way to pay me. I might just be the underboss in my family, but in my apartment buildings, I'm the king.

Outside of the women who come to me for help, I have no need for a woman in my life. Not a wife. Not a girlfriend. I don't need a woman. Unlike my brother, Giovanni, papa makes no financial incentives for me to have children. How would I benefit, eh? Papa wants the opposite, anyway. He pays me monthly as long as I don't father bastard children. Simple.

Keeping my distance from women has been entirely too easy. I have work to do and I'll have even more with Eddie in Long Island and the Albanians banging at our door to bring their trafficking ring into Italy.

I have no distractions, nothing to destroy my focus on our family's singular goal — until Grace.

One slight problem with beautiful, beautiful Grace. *She has a secret.*

I know I have an Albanian tenant hiding his identity under the lease by putting it in her name. She's American, this Grace woman, and harboring an Albanian man who, unbeknownst to her, has made enemies of the Doukas family. I need more information about her boyfriend. Before I meet her, I watch them for a few days, soaking in her physical appearance, allowing my obsession to grow and hating the man who freely puts his hands on her.

He's a liar, a scumbag piece of shit with the Albanian mob, and he's making her fall in love with him. I hate him for lying to her. I hate him for thinking he can hide behind a woman and make a fool of a Doukas. I hate him more with each passing day and I fall for a woman who has only met me once, who never notices me watching her from the balcony with a cigarette in one hand and a bottle of wine in another. I even go shirtless, hoping she'll look up. She never does.

That doesn't matter. She doesn't have to see me yet. When I meet her, when I finally meet Grace West for the first time, I will do everything to ensure that she never looks away from me, never leaves me. She will belong to me forever.

I don't bother telling Van about my growing fixation with my tenant when he asks me to track down the Albanian and find his reason for hunkering down on the Amalfi Coast.

I check with my Albanian contacts while I conduct surveillance. Luan doesn't recognize the name I give him or the description, but he warns me that the Dervishaj family contains several layers of cousins and bastards. He could be Luan's second cousin and an utter stranger. The message remains the same — don't fucking trust him.

I dress professionally for house calls like this one — white shirt, black trousers, Gucci belt, snakeskin loafers, a cigarette, of course, and a spare in my pocket. Okay, I'm not exactly dressed just for her. I have a wedding reception to attend. My brother Giovanni, the new boss of the Doukas family, married Jodi earlier in the day, and I have five hours before the wedding reception begins. Plenty of time for me to make a house call and do my duty with the Albanian.

This Albanian man may suspect my personal connection to the Doukas mob, but I own my properties all under my mother's maiden name for my family's security and my own.

Privacy matters.

Even if this man suspects who I am, or suspects my connection to the Amalfi Coast mob, which he must if he remains anonymous, he doesn't suspect that I'm also dangerous — if not more dangerous than the boss, my brother, Giovanni.

Liquor helps steel me for the house call, but what I really want is a cigarette. I want more than anything a fresh, hand-rolled cigarette that tastes spectacular. Ah.

I still have to be cautious, even with liquor firing me up and a time limit on my visit. I can't be late for Van's reception. I have to watch him fumble about as waitresses offer him pet chickens and old women beg him to find suitable husbands for their daughters.

Why the fuck did Eddie mess with the Albanians and get us into this? Thoughts of strangling my nephew whirl through my head as I approach the apartment door, walking through each hall of the building as I conduct a spontaneous check on the property.

Albanians are crazy motherfuckers who won't hesitate to shove a pistol up your ass and pull the trigger. The Albanian fuck can't find out what I'm up to. He might suspect I'm with the mob, but I won't give him proof unless I can get more out of him with fear. I don't know. I find you always catch more flies with honey than vinegar.

All I need from the Albanian is his name and his purpose. I don't need to bring a gun — not yet. I can't kill without a word from the boss. Van won't allow me to kill for any reason he deems frivolous.

I don't want to fuck up, but I console myself by saying that if I do screw up and kill the Albanian fuck, Van won't find out shit unless I open my big fucking mouth and tell him myself. There's no such thing as a secret kept between two people. I walk down to the apartment — 404A — a sweet little studio apartment with a king-sized bed and all the amenities you might expect in a luxury coastal apartment.

When I knock on the door, the Albanian doesn't open it. Instead, there's a vision before me with a scowl on her perfect little face. That's the moment everything changes. That's the moment I make a cruel choice, even before realizing it.

"Hello?"

My body responds the moment I hear her voice. She sounds like she's singing, even if it's just one word.

"It's me, Mr. Pazzini. Your landlord."

It's the first time she's meeting me in person and when she realizes who I am, her expression changes. A pretty smile replaces that scowl.

"Oh! I'm sorry, Mr. Pazzini. I didn't expect you to stop by. The place is a mess and I—

"Don't worry. I'm not coming in. I wanted to make sure you and... your boyfriend... enjoyed the amenities here."

Her boyfriend who isn't on the lease. Her mob boyfriend, potentially involved in some very dirty fucking business. Oh, Grace... what has she gotten herself into? Who has she wrapped herself up with?

"Shit," she mutters. Yeah, the secret resident who she conveniently forgot to add to the lease. I know about that. I wonder what I could convince her to do in exchange for ignoring this offense... *Stop it, Enzo. Focus.*

I tilt my head to the side, using the silence to coax her into saying more. The quieter you are, the more information you get. Fuck, this woman is stunning. Waiting for her to speak, I notice the subtleties of her features. Heart-shaped face. Long braids down to her waist. Large eyes with well-manicured brows and extremely full lips.

She babbles on with her explanation as I struggle to focus on anything but her tits. When did my tenants get so fucking sexy? I know this is wrong, but I can't help myself. I deeply appreciate beauty and this Grace has a mysterious allure that I can't explain. Shy, dark eyes, perfect lips. She's fucking gorgeous. My cock jumps in my pants at the sight of her breasts pushed together by her top. Fuck, I feel like a teenager. I'm too old to get this hard for a woman. Luckily, she doesn't notice and I shift my stance, enraptured again by her beautiful voice.

"I didn't add him to the lease," she says. "I admit. We just moved in together. Kinda fast... I only met him a couple months ago, but... we're in love! I'm so sorry. Let me know what I can do to rectify it."

I smile and she does that thing women do whenever I smile. Fuck, she's attracted to me. I don't know why that surprises me. It's good. Perhaps her attraction to me will come in handy later. Maybe it's just lust. Maybe I can get something out of it. There's a door I want to keep propped open...

"I'm happy for you," I tell her, incapable of stopping myself from staring at her and imbibing every inch of her body.

She bites her lower lip like she's thinking of what to say next, and all I can think is that I wish I were the one biting down on those full, sensual lips. I give Giovanni shit for his tastes, but fuck aren't women so much better when they're foreign? Different? Who wants the same old thing all the time? Italian women. I've had every variation. But I've never had a woman like her...

"Really? Happy for me? You don't seem like a romantic," she teases.

American women. They're so forward that it's impossible to tell if it's flirting or politeness. I consider her carefully, my eyes lingering on her figure as I decide. American ways take getting used to, but enough time around Jodi and Zara, and I appreciate the differences between their culture and ours. I like how the women speak their mind. Wit and beauty are a spectacular combination. It's better to have one with the other than either on their own.

My tenant, Grace, stands a few shades darker than Jodi and Zara. Her skin is a pretty, forbidden, delicate shade of brown, almost as dark as a delicious cup of espresso. I want to press my tongue against it. The forbidden thought courses through me and I do nothing to suppress my body's reaction to her.

"I'm not," I tell her. "But... I can still be happy that my tenants are enjoying the property. When your boyfriend returns, have him call me, yes? It's only a matter of paperwork. In fact... it would help if you told me his name."

"Oh," she says. "That's easy. Uksan Dervishaj. I'll have him call you."

"Thank you, Grace."

I smile at her again and enjoy the way she looks away. I want to enter the apartment with her. I want to play with her. Tease her. I want to taste every inch of her skin and then solve the mystery behind those dark brown eyes.

Fuck's sake, Enzo. She has a boyfriend. And she's clearly in love with him.

"Are you sure you don't want to come in for a glass of water or something, Mr. Pazzini?"

She doesn't know how fucking tempting she is. If I take Grace up on that offer and close the door to the apartment behind us, I won't be able to control myself. Papa's allowance has addled my brain, and it's been ages since I've allowed myself to spill a drop of my seed inside a woman.

I've never faced any temptation before her. Never. Van would say it's because I've fucked my way down the Amalfi Coast and halfway across the rest of Italy. I won't confirm or deny my youthful activities, but the fact remains—I've tasted every available treat and find the pleasures of mindless unattached sex to diminish with each incidence.

I don't want mindless sex anymore. I want a woman whose heart and body belong completely to me. Grace has a boyfriend. She can't ever fill that role. Unless I kill her boyfriend.

"I'm fine. Thank you for the offer. If you need anything, Grace... let me know."

"I will! Have a good night!"

Cheerful. American women are so fucking cheerful. She closes the door and I immediately regret not going in for a glass of water. Ah, well. I have a better idea.

I'm going to kill her fucking boyfriend.

. . .

I walk back to my apartment, finishing my cigarette before I get to the door. Van picks up and I enter my place as I greet him.

"Did you learn anything?" He growls.

He doesn't like to be bothered, and he hates it even more that he's freshly married and wants to spend the entire night cuddled up against his wife, not dealing with me and my shit. Don't worry. I don't want Van paying too much attention either.

"Uksan Dervishaj. He's one of them. I don't know if he's directly related to the boss."

"You didn't question him directly?" Van growls. He gets no fucking sleep because of the baby and insists on punishing me because of it with his attitude. He should blame his own cock for following its desires through to the end. I won't be stupid enough to have a child wantonly.

"He wasn't there. Just the girlfriend," I answer.

"I see."

"Beautiful girlfriend."

"That's enough, Lorenzo."

"I await your orders, boss."

Van makes a sound halfway between a grunt and a huff.

"Don't do anything that could get you killed."

Very open ended instructions, if you ask me.

"Yes, boss. Ciao."

I hang up on my brother and kick my feet up.

Yes. I'm going to kill her fucking boyfriend. I need information from him anyway, and I ought to wait for Giovanni's orders. But I can't. We have the reception soon and the longer this takes, the longer we'll give the Albanians a chance to make a move. What I saw on their soil haunts me. Young girls dressed like that, all available for sale. Anyone involved in such cruel business deserves to die, especially

Uksan, for daring to bring such sickness near Grace, beautiful Grace.

Papa would have let me kill the man for my own purposes, but Van wants our family to return to the old way. We can't kill for greed. We can't kill women or children. We have a truce with the Jews.

Can I kill for love? Can I kill for lust? I won't bother asking my brother for permission.

I run through a list of known hookers who frequently Jalousie in my mind. Perhaps one of them could scratch this itch and the devilish thought of murdering a man to steal his woman out of my head. No hookers appeal to me.

Unlike my brothers, I'm not a good man. I love cocaine, drinking, fucking and getting exactly what I want, including women. This woman's impossible attachment to an Albanian boils my blood. I'm the youngest brother. The loose cannon. The wild card. The sick motherfucker who would kill just for a chance at a woman.

I wonder if she knows who she is. I wonder if Grace West knows she's just that fucking beautiful that I would kill for her moments after laying eyes on her.

I wait for darkness before I move. I have cameras in all the hallways of the building and I watch the door to Grace's apartment, staring at the silent feed as I finish one cigarette after another. No one enters or leaves the apartment for at least two hours. I finish another glass of whiskey and clean my short-barreled rifle for my work. Attach a silencer on the end and I can get the job done alerting no one.

Simple.

Half an hour passes after cleaning my gun before I see Uksan approach the door. He turns the key and I see Grace's arm on the camera, dragging him into the apartment for a kiss. I hate him. My throat catches. If I leave now, I'll probably catch them in the throes of lovemaking. The mere thought of Uksan rutting between Grace's legs drives me crazy.

He doesn't deserve her.

I don't know exactly what the Albanian has done, but the mob there doesn't distinguish between clean and dirty business. They sell women, children, crack, guns, whatever the fuck they can get their hands on. Money soaked in blood still works the same. Italians at least have honor.

I keep watching the cameras until something happens. Grace. Leaving. Only a few seconds of footage of her excites me more than anything. She's only wearing sweatpants and a tight top that hugs her breasts together. She carries her purse and wears some silky thing on her head. I hear her over the hallway camera calling to Uksan.

"I'll be back in thirty minutes!"

He must respond because she replies with, "I love you."

Then she leaves, and my heart nearly leaps into my throat. Thirty minutes. I couldn't have been more blessed by opportunity. I have enough time to question Uksan and then wash Grace's floor with his blood. Technically, my floor.

Without permission, aware of the consequences, but smitten entirely, I get my gun, my balaclava and I turn off my apartment building's security system—just in case the police get off their ass for once and investigate something other than a tourist robbery.

Killing doesn't fuck with my nerves. It's the aftermath I don't like. Rigor mortis. Getting rid of the body. The gore. I don't mind the killing or the questioning. It's just work. Papa trained us well how to steel our nerves with liquor and drugs and whatever we need to serve our highest good.

Killing a woman's boyfriend isn't your highest good, Lorenzo.

I quiet that small voice in my mind and sneak my way

through the halls until I get to the apartment. I don't need to burst through the door. It's so safe here that hardly anyone locks their doors. I hear a television on the other side as I slowly crack Uksan's door open.

I check my watch for a split second. Thirty minutes. More like twenty. I have to make this quick, get answers from the Albanian and finish him before the reception and before Grace returns to watch the scene unfold. He doesn't see me coming and with the loud television, he doesn't hear me. I turn the corner of the half wall and cock my gun as the Albanian shoots straight up in bed, naked except for his boxer briefs and totally unarmed.

"Fuck," he says. "Who the fuck are you?"

"Get out of bed."

"Italian," he says. "Fuck."

He's better not make me repeat myself.

"Hands up," I snarl. "Sit at your dining table. We need to talk."

"My girlfriend's around the corner. She'll come back in five minutes. I don't care if you take the TV."

"I'm not here for a fucking television. Now sit."

Liar. I appreciate his efforts, but I know his girlfriend won't be back for long and when she comes back, she'll find her boyfriend's brains all over the floor. She'll need comfort. She'll need someone to protect her.

Uksan gives up his pretense that he has any choice but to obey my orders and he lumbers out of bed half naked, plopping down with frustration at the table.

"You're mob."

"I ask the questions."

"Which family? Pagonis? Doukas?"

"Why are you here?" I ask.

Uksan realizes he isn't dealing with an amateur.

"I don't know as much as you think," he says, cleverly attempting to bait me into revealing why I'm here. I pull out a chair and sit across from him. I don't have to get rough with him yet.

"You don't know what I think," I respond calmly, tapping my fingers on the table and allowing my heavy rings to beat out an unnerving tattoo against the hardwood. "Tell me why you're in Italy and everything you know about the Dervishaj business here. You have little time, so please... be efficient."

I flash Uksan a smile, which doesn't warm him to me.

"Please... I'm not here working. I swear. I don't involve myself in the dirty business and—

I've killed enough people to know that dead men lie around ten times more than average men, which, considering how often the average man lies, proves to be a substantial amount of fiction.

"Shut the fuck up," I interrupt him before he finishes whatever lie slithers through his fucked up Albanian mind. "I was at the last auction. I saw what your family does, Uksan Dervishaj."

Everyone knows what happened at the auction. I've never felt better about having blood on my hands.

"A fucking Doukas," he says with painful recognition that he has entirely fucked shit up. "Oh, fuck..."

He stammers in Albanian. I assume it's a prayer, but the big fuck looks like he's just cursing himself for being such an idiot as to stumble into my trap.

See, this is why I do business under my mother's name. It makes my work for papa so much easier. I have the element of surprise and a veneer of privacy, so I can lure sick fucks like this one into my trap. He knows about the auction, that means he knows his family business, which as far as I'm concerned, deserves a death sentence.

"Stop talking," I growl. "Tell me why you're here. You aren't tracking anyone, you aren't establishing a business, so I assume you're here for surveillance? Who are you watching and what do you people want here?"

"I can't tell you that. I have a family back home... If I talk..."

"You'll be dead anyway, Uksan," I point out. "Talk or not, I kill you tonight."

"But Grace... What about Grace? You can't hurt her. I won't let you."

Her name on his tongue tightens my chest with rage. I want to kill him for daring to mention her. By the end of the night, Grace will belong to me.

"Is it surveillance or something else? Answer, Uksan. Prove your value to me unless you want to end your life a little faster."

I set my gun on the table. The pungent scent of piss fills the room. They all do it eventually. It's one of the least unsavory parts of killing, but the pungent smell always forces me to suppress my nausea.

"Please... I can't tell you why I'm here, but I can give you other information you want. Please... I'm begging you for mercy."

Mercy? Does his family show mercy when they auction off little girls?

"You aren't exactly in a position to make demands."

He buries his head in his hands, a crop of blond hair falling over his severe face and square shaped forehead. Fuck the Albanians.

"I just want you to protect Grace. Please, just don't kill her. Promise to protect Grace, and I'll talk."

That's it? A promise I can make... I don't plan on letting Grace West out of my sight once I lay my hands on her.

I smile at him.

"We have a deal. Tell me what I want to know and I'll spare your beautiful girlfriend."

And can you believe it? The man fucking talks.

He's here to scout our territory and establish the likelihood that they'll have successful business here. I find out his lineage and connect Uksan to the boss of the Albanian mob. He's the underboss's son, nephew to the boss, and apparently a colossal idiot of little importance to his relatives since they sent him straight into the jaws of our family.

"What about Grace?" I ask him. "Why involve her?"

I don't want to find out she's guilty of this. Some women can be sick too and they can hurt children. My fingers tense around the trigger as I wait for his anger. Please, let this goddess be innocent.

Uksan confirms my suspicions that Grace remains ignorant of his actions.

"I needed someone here. For cover. She doesn't know who I really am, and she doesn't deserve to die. Please, spare her. She's not involved in the mob. Please..."

Grace... Trust me, she'll be spared. It's almost romantic the way Uksan cares for her. Unfortunately, that won't save him. I have more important questions.

"Which other brothers do you have here?"

"None of my brothers."

This shit again?

"Talk..."

I acquire a list of names from the Albanian — Hamza, Kazim, Verush. These three are all spread in apartments along the coast, scouting our territory and taking notes about our captains, enforcers and made men in our territory. They're gearing up for a war they don't want. To be fair, Van doesn't want a war either.

He wants a new way of life, where we exist only to protect what's ours, not to expand, not to kill for the sake of it. My brother aims for a time when we had more respect, and I can't say I disagree, despite my current actions.

"That's it?"

"Yes."

"Are you sure?'

My prisoner sounds exhausted and I'm running out of time

to kill him. Still, if I have to tell Van I killed outside his orders, I'd better come up with some fucking good information so he doesn't beat my ass to a pulp or worse, order a bullet between my eyes.

"No."

Jesus, fuck. He wants to buy time. He wants to stall so there can be a witness to this, but he can't get around my interrogations so easily.

"Speak, Uksan. Tell me."

"They're taking a girl tonight."

"What?"

"She's close with your family. She works at Jalousie. A tiny slip of a thing with dark skin..."

"Zara?"

"I don't know her name."

He's skirting around the issue, avoiding answering the question, as if pissing me off more could successfully prolong his death.

"Large eyes? Air-headed?" I describe her further, giving him a look so he'll know I'm not the man to fuck with. He won't get out of here alive, anyway.

Uksan nods. So he's met her. Shit. I have to get this information to my brother. Soon.

"Where have they taken here? What are their plans?"

Mercifully, I don't have to torture the information out of him to get it. They have a halfway house in Rome and after that, they'll take her to Albania. When I ask him why Zara, he doesn't have an answer. I'm running out of time. I need to finish the job.

"Do you have any last words?"

"No," he whispers. "I don't."

"No prayers?"

"Finish the job, Doukas."

"*Si. Padre Nostro, che sei nei cieli...*"

I pray silently for the Albanian since he has no prayers for himself and put two bullets in his chest and another in his head before I slip out the front door, leaving his door ajar, and walk back to my apartment to prepare for hell. I have anonymity, a guarantee there won't be DNA left, and no witnesses.

An easy kill. But I'm still left uneasy. I have to get to Jalousie. I call, but they tell me that everything's fine and they even allow me to talk to Zara. I have to go to the reception and then return to the apartment. Grace will have returned by then and when she stumbles upon the awful scene here… She'll need me.

Once I have Grace secure, I'll stop by Jalousie. Zara will make it, right? I warned her to be careful, that Albanians had plans. She can't screw this up.

Becoming Giovanni's underboss has been hard work and that work will only get harder when I tell him the fucked up thing I've done.

Dear brother, please understand… I only did this because I fell in love at first sight with an impossible foreign woman who belonged to someone else. I didn't mean to kill him, but my wild stallion heart got the better of me. Forgive me, brother. Don't order me to my death.

I want to live. I want Grace West.

After my brother's wedding, I'll have her. Forever.

Chapter 2

A Death On The Amalfi Coast

Grace West

Death is horrific. We can't ever escape death, but the gory reality of the dead haunts us. There's something strange about a body without a soul. I smell death before I get to my apartment door. I don't remember leaving the door open. I run for the door and thrust it open. I didn't leave Uksan with the lights off, but something tells me Uksan isn't here. I get that eerie sense that everything's out of place, but I can't put my mind on any specific thing that's fucked up.

I step into the studio and turn the light on, calling his name. With a quick couple second scan of the room, I see him — or what was Uksan, slumped over in a chair, his head on the table and blood everywhere. Death and blood smell the same — hot, metallic, intolerable. I know he's dead. There isn't a sliver of denial in my chest. I've seen too much shit in my life not to believe what's right in front of me. My boyfriend's dead and he looks like someone shot him. Adrenaline gushes through me, pumping terror into every vein.

He's not the first dead body I've found.

The scream that erupts from my chest causes every cell in my body to tremble. I scream again and race for him, wanting to save him but knowing deep down that this was just like before. He's dead. He's dead. I don't want to tell myself there's a chance, because I know there isn't one. I stopped for a few extra minutes to get a late night croissant. It was just a few extra minutes, but it was enough time for Uksan to die. He's dead.

My first thought is that he must have killed himself, but I know that can't be right. I need to get the cops. I reach for my cell phone and call the police, screaming and babbling in my extremely poor tourist's Italian.

When I tell them the address, the dispatcher replies in English.

"Sorry, we do not disturb business at Mr. Pazzini's address," the dispatcher says calmly.

Is this not the phone number you call in a damn emergency? What the hell is wrong with these people?

"What?! Excuse me!? A man died here," I screech into the phone. I want to vomit again, and the room spins around me. Stay in control, Grace, I repeat to myself in my mind as I try to figure out a way to phrase this to the dispatchers so they understand that this isn't some party animal prank gone wrong. There's actually a dead person in my apartment. My boyfriend. My boyfriend's dead... Oh God...

My phone trembles in my hand. They can't be serious. Who the hell do you call when 911 won't answer? I scream the address at them again and beg them to show up.

"He's been shot!" I screech. "How can you leave him to die if he's been shot?!"

The dispatcher replies with undue calm as I feel greater panic welling up in me. I feel myself going numb emotionally, doing what I must to survive the situation.

"We will send people for the body in the morning," the dispatcher says. "But we do not interfere in this business."

What business?

"Do something! Who else can I call? What about the hospital?"

I take Uksan's hand. It's cold. I rest his hand on the table, fighting back nausea. The hospital can't do a damn thing for him and I know it. By the time the cops or anyone else get in here, he'll be stiff and God, there's going to be so much blood.

The dispatcher finally responds, "Please, calm down. If you would like, we can send an escort to take you to the nearest embassy."

This can't really be happening.

"A man is DEAD!" I screech. "He's right here, and he's DEAD!"

"I'm sorry, miss. We cannot offer more help. Contact your landlord for assistance."

My landlord? Is Italy some kind of weird ass place where landlords can revive men from the fucking dead? I scream one more time into the phone out of frustration. I don't know who else to call, but I know I have to do something. Uksan's cold and rigor mortis already sets into parts of his body. He's over two-hundred pounds and I don't have the strength to lift him out of the chair, much less lay him on his back and cover him with a blanket.

My boyfriend's dead. He deserves respect. I can't leave him slumped over the table like this. It's disrespectful, degrading... Everything about this is utterly horrific. My thoughts are emotional and irrational at once. Who else can I call to help?

Once the dispatcher hangs up quickly, I start to feel extremely 'land of the free' about the damn police, which, trust me, ain't easy for me.

At least in America, someone shows up. Someone showed up all those years ago. Still, it didn't help. I press my fingers to Uksan's neck and he's still close to his heart, but definitely 100% dead. No pulse. No movement from his chest. I swallow and try to say his name as if that could shake a dead man from eternal sleep.

"Uksan... Uksan, wake up..."

Fifteen slow minutes pass and no help arrives. I have to do something else. I can't just stand here and watch him grow cold in front of me. I thought we would at least have the summer together. I can't stop shaking or crying and the only thing I can think to do is call our landlord — after over two hours of deliberation, which included more attempts to call the police and hospital.

No one wants to come to this building, so I have no choice but to call him up.

Lorenzo Pazzini. Maybe he can help with the police, or if I got something lost in translation. He seems like a decent guy and he speaks perfect English for an Italian. I search my phone for his number and when I find it, I call him. Mr. Pazzini answers after one ring.

"Hello?"

"Mr. Pazzini, I have an emergency! Someone broke in and shot my boyfriend! He's dead!"

"Have you tried calling the cops?"

"Yes, but they won't come," I babble hysterically. "Please, I have to do something. I've been waiting for an ambulance and there's so much blood. So much blood. I've been sitting with him, but nothing's changed."

I'm crying so damned hard, I can't keep the phone pressed to my ear. My hand shakes and I don't know what to do about Uksan. He's dead. Our love story barely had a chance, and he's dead.

Mr. Pazzini's voice soothes me instantly. He has a really pleasant voice, and it's not fair. That's the first thing I notice about him.

"I'll be there, Grace. Wait on the couch. Touch nothing. I can handle this."

"Can you get the police to help?!"

He pauses for a few seconds before responding.

"Wait for me."

He hangs up, but I keep clutching the phone to my ear. I can't listen to him. I walk over to Uksan and my stomach tightens. He's dead. I was only gone for 30 minutes and this happens. A cold-blooded murder. It doesn't hit me until he knocks on the door that Mr. Pazzini was calm on the phone. Too calm. It's like he expects this type of thing to happen with the police.

When he knocks, I don't want to tell him come in. I don't know if the person at the door could be the killer.

"It's me, Lorenzo. Signor Pazzini."

I set my phone down on the table next to Uksan's head, struggling not to look at him. It's not a long walk to the door. Italian apartments are cozy. I open the door and Mr. Pazzini stands in the doorway, exactly what I need at the moment I need it. Immediate relief washes over me. It relieves me too that he's armed. I thought only America had the second amendment, but apparently landlords here can carry weapons.

"What happened? Where is he?" He asks, with genuine concern on his face. He smells like cigarettes and booze and he looks like he's spent the night partying. Even my landlord gets into the crazy nightlife here better than I ever did. I met Uksan by complete accident after visiting a bar with a very crazy bartender named Edo who did absolutely dangerous things with gin and apple juice.

Mr. Pazzini enters my apartment with an air of leadership and goes directly to Uksan's body.

I can't look at Uksan anymore. He's changing color and I know his body must be getting stiff. He's dead.

"I don't know what happened. I stepped out. I came back... Someone shot him. The cops won't come. The hospital doesn't care. They just keep telling me to call my landlord."

"The cops won't come because the mob runs the Amalfi Coast," Lorenzo says calmly.

"The mob!?"

Uksan never mentioned we were in mob territory. Isn't this a tourist destination? People come here because of Instagram. There can't be any organized crime here. A mob? This place is for club rats and people who post all their food on the internet.

Uksan always talked about how bad things were in Albania, explaining to me in excruciating detail why we couldn't live there and why he never wanted us to go back. He told me stories about how he was in Italy to escape his horrible family, who would shoot people for a new pair of jeans.

Uksan never mentioned there was anything so dangerous in Italy. He made this seem like the safest place in the world for everything, especially falling in love. This place was supposed to be paradise. My year of healing.

Lorenzo puts his hand on my shoulder. He's so lean that I'm surprised by how heavy his hand feels against me. He's stronger than he looks, and his hand rests firmly on me, sending a soothing surge through me. I shouldn't even let him put his hand on my shoulder. Uksan was wildly jealous. Uksan's dead.

"You have nothing to fear from the mob," Mr. Pazzini says. "Nothing at all."

"What am I going to do about Uksan? I don't know his family. I don't know about a funeral... He's my boyfriend, but... we barely knew each other."

My stomach drops. We should have had more time and now this man's dead and I don't know the first thing about what I should do next. I'm only twenty-five. It's not like my boyfriends have had a habit of dying on me. Mr. Pazzini continues to reassure me. I'm a mess, but no matter what I throw at him, he's entirely calm.

"I have many contacts in Albania. I'll arrange something. You don't need to worry about this. You need to rest."

He sounds so calm that he almost makes me want to calm

down. But I can't. I can't just let this wash over me like a regular ass bad day.

"How can I rest? He's dead. My boyfriend's dead! I can't just... go to bed!"

"I'll give you the key to my apartment," Mr. Pazzini says. "I have several spare rooms with en suite bathrooms. Make yourself at home. You don't have to stay in your apartment tonight."

It's generous, but it's far too generous. Can't he put me up at one of the cockroach hostels nearby? He lives in the penthouse and rumors from the tenants say he lined the walls of his penthouse with gold. I'm sure that's an exaggeration, but Mr. Pazzini definitely looks like the type.

"I can't do that. I need to stay," I say as forcefully as possible. I can't accept generosity from this man and make him responsible for my problems. I can't imagine how much it's going to cost him to get the blood

"No," he says sternly. "You should stay out of trouble. Whoever did this could come back. I don't want you in danger."

He's right, but I can't exactly leave him in the line of fire, either.

"Mr. Pazzini—

"Please. Enzo," he interrupts.

"Enzo?"

"Short for Lorenzo. It's my name."

"Oh. Yes. Duh. But I can't—

"Please, Grace," he says firmly. "Let me handle this. Go to the penthouse. I am terribly sorry that this horrific event occurred in my building. I will sort it out for you. Now go."

He won't give me a choice. I sense he has absolutely no intention of allowing me to exercise my free will here.

"Can I... Should I say goodbye?"

I have a strange feeling that this is my last chance to say

goodbye to Uksan and once I leave here, I'll never see him again, never see a body or attend a funeral. When you've been through the shit I have, you get gut instincts about these kinds of things, you know? I bite down on my lower lip, nervously avoiding Enzo's answer. Enzo. That's a sexy name. Damn, I feel guilty as hell for thinking that, but it's from that TV show, *The Vampire Diaries*, isn't it? I suppose the name existed in Italy first.

"Si. Pack your things and say goodbye to Uksan," Lorenzo says. "This is no place for you. I'm sorry about your lease, Grace. Once I handle this, I'll assist you with other arrangements."

I hurriedly pack a bag, my hands shaking. I don't even think too hard about what to bring. Bras. Underwear. My passport. Some money. An old football t-shirt that still smells like my boyfriend. My dead boyfriend. He's dead, and he's not coming back. I put everything I can into a pink duffel and meet Lorenzo in the living room.

He's still been so calm.

"I'll take care of this and I'll make sure whoever does this faces punishment, Grace. You'll be safe. I'll put you up in my place tonight and offer you personal protection."

"Why would someone do this? Was this the mob? He wasn't involved in anything like that!"

His jaw tightens and the tattoo on his neck becomes more visible to me in the dim apartment light. I can't see the entire tattoo and feel tempted to peel his shirt open to look. It's really not the time to notice how muscular his chest looks in that shirt. Uksan's dead. I'm in shock. That's what this has to be.

"The world is cruel, Grace," Enzo says in accented English as smooth as honey. "Now go. Please. I don't want you anywhere near this business."

I take his keys and leave my studio after giving Uksan's cold body one last kiss on the forehead. I can't stop crying, even in front of Mr... Enzo. I don't know why I get the nagging feeling in my stomach that this will be my last time leaving the studio or ever seeing Uksan's body again, but I follow that feeling and say a proper goodbye. I don't get real closure, I just get this.

This isn't the worst thing I've ever been through. But fuck, it still hurts like hell. I just wish I could call someone. No one even knows I was dating a white guy. It's not like there's anyone alive who would care that he died. I close the door and walk to Lorenzo's apartment, hesitating before putting the key in.

He owns this entire building and he can't be more than a year older than me. I guess he was born rich, or he's really successful at this landlord thing. I turn the key and open the door to the apartment. There's a playful little bark as I open the door. I glance around the room, illuminated in soft, warm light. I didn't expect Lorenzo to have interior design tastes.

I glance around for a dog and finally see the source of the yelp. A black toy poodle crosses the floor to me with a wagging tail. The little dog rubs up on me and then bounds off to the couch. Okay. He has a dog, and it doesn't bite. Works for me. I walk around for a second and notice how much bigger this place looks. He must have the entire floor to himself. If Lorenzo told me which guest room he meant to be mine, I don't remember the directions. I wander past his living room, down the hallway with four bedrooms.

I touch the first door and push it open. No bedding, but a lovely king-sized bed in a really modern room. Everything looks white and pure. How the hell does a bachelor live like this without getting it all dirty? He didn't line his walls with gold, but he kept them crisp white and sterile. I'm scared to touch anything. Everything in this place is so sterile. Enzo definitely could use a woman's touch.

I could never have anything white with Uksan in the house. Maybe it was crazy moving in with a messy Albanian man I knew all of a few short weeks, but we were in love. That's what it felt like at least — like I'd taken a really hard drug and fallen so fucking fast for an attractive, blond Albanian man who never asked me questions about my past.

It's not like I've tried hard drugs, but I imagine they would feel like falling for Uksan. He was just so mysterious and so tall... and he was the first white guy who ever wanted me badly enough to go for it. Guys in Italy make it clear exactly how they feel about women who look like me. I didn't expect it to be so bad when I left all my bullshit behind in America and came here. I never came to this country to find love.

I'm here to escape some horrific shit, but that never really works, does it? Nasty shit has a way of following us across oceans and deserts. We can't escape God's plan for us, we just have to fight our way through the dark times and pray we come out okay in the end. The end. I've watched too many people fight like hell and reach that grim end, anyway. I just try to keep going, you know? There has to be something in life worth living for. A dream job. A great love. An Italian vacation.

I proceed through Enzo's apartment carefully. Tasteful art hangs on the walls and the poodle follows me around without barking or nipping at my heels, just curiously sniffing wherever I walk.

The second bedroom looks more like a guest room. It's similar to the other one and empty, with a bathroom just like Lorenzo promised. I don't want to take a shower. I don't want to move. I crawl into the bed and rest my head on the pillow, numb. The dog barks and jumps onto the bed, curling up next to me like we're old friends.

I wrap my arms around my legs and try to breathe through this. I'm in my landlord's apartment, my boyfriend's dead. In 24 hours, I'll have to start over. New apartment. Check my bank accounts. I have enough money for over a year still, I think. If I eat a little less and live in a worse neighborhood, I could keep going that long. The problem is, I didn't account for having to move and potentially having my home become a crime scene. And what about Uksan? Can I really trust Lorenzo to handle this? Maybe cops only listen to landlords or some weird cultural thing. I don't know what to make of it.

I can't believe this is happening. My boyfriend's dead. I'm all alone. Things like this aren't supposed to happen in vacation destinations. This was supposed to be about warm weather and falling in love.

I'm here to heal, not to traumatize my damned self all over again. I squeeze my eyes shut and try to stop crying. I must have fallen asleep because the next thing I know, I'm waking up. It's still dark, but I hear the heavy footfall of a man and my first instinct is to think it's Uksan. He's dead. It can't be him. I hear a soft rap on the door and then that smooth Italian accent.

"Grace, are you in there?"

I get off the bed and open the door. He smells like bleach and there's a sweet smell too, like the lavender scented disinfectant my mom mopped the floor with every Saturday when I was a child.

"Yes," I answer, choking down bile.

"It's late, but... you should have some espresso. We need to talk about your boyfriend and your situation."

"My situation?"

"Yes," he says, putting his hand on my shoulder. "How do you take your coffee?"

Only Europeans have espresso any hour of the day. Their bodies seem totally immune to caffeine. I wish I could say the same, but I'm in no position to turn down Lorenzo's generosity. He just swooped in to handle things and he didn't ask me questions or suspect me for a moment. He's a good guy deep down, I can tell. I can't imagine an American guy not questioning me or suspecting me. Where I grew up, my skin color always made me an immediate object of suspicion.

"Black," I answer.

"So do I," he says, smiling gently. I think he's trying to

make me feel better when he smiles, and it works. He's handsome, honestly. I don't want to think about how handsome he is, but it's like looking at a Van Gogh and trying not to think about quality art.

He normally looks so dour, a very European trait, so his smile softens his face considerably and draws warmth to mine. Europeans seem to think the American tendency towards smiling makes us goofy or something. Enzo gestures for me to follow him to the kitchen and he pulls up a bar stool at his fancy kitchen island. The countertops gleam.

His poodle barks and bounds over to us. Lorenzo chuckles and picks the dog up.

"Have you met Ember?"

"You named your poodle Ember?"

"Beautiful, isn't she?" Enzo answers, setting down the poodle after applying generous kisses to her forehead.

He finishes making one espresso and passes it to me, brewing his own.

"Uksan's family will come for his body. I explained the situation, but... they don't want any foreigners at the funeral."

"What? I'm his girlfriend! I have to go!"

Enzo moves on swiftly.

"I'm sorry, but... I have to tell you something important, Grace."

"What?"

"I'm afraid your boyfriend Uksan fell afoul of the wrong people. I have powerful evidence to believe this was a mob killing and the Albanian mob... they're vicious, Grace. They will want you."

"This was a mob hit? That doesn't make sense. Uksan wasn't that type of guy."

Lorenzo's jaw shifts. He pours his espresso down his throat.

"Mind if I smoke?" He asks.

"I don't really like smoking."

"I'm trying to quit. I normally smoke outside but... I've had a long night."

I give him a closer look. I don't know what time it is, but he looks tired. Something else must have happened tonight, because I don't think Uksan's death upset him that much. He must experience all this murder and violence all the time because of the mob activity here. I left America to escape violence, but apparently that doesn't work.

Enzo takes out a cigarette and puts it between his lips. It doesn't look like he's trying that hard to quit if he has an entire box of cigarettes in his pocket, but I bite my tongue. He's helping me far beyond the call of duty for a landlord, and I don't even know why. I'm just a tenant in his apartment building. Maybe he pities me for being a stupid American. I get that a lot over here, too.

Enzo lights his cigarette and I finish my espresso. I see his point now. The bitter coffee wakes me up right away, and I feel less numb and more... shocked. Terrified.

Enzo continues explaining. "Whoever wanted Uksan dead will come after you. You were his woman. You knew things."

"Clearly not if he was mixed up with the mob! How can you know that? I know nothing. If people come for me, I can't say anything and they'll figure out I don't know a damn thing and leave me alone."

Ha, that doesn't even sound believable. Enzo raises an eyebrow and then shrugs.

"I own property. I have to have connections to stay safe. I know how the mob works and what they want. Understand? I can look after you," Enzo says slowly, in English, taking a slow drag and then blowing the smoke away from me as politely as he can muster.

I don't understand at all. I thought the mob only protected their own. If Lorenzo has mob connections, that means something. My head's too foggy to challenge him. I need to process all this and get some sleep before I choose what to do next.

"Yeah."

Lorenzo interrupts my frantic thinking.

"I can protect you, Grace..."

Well, that's a relief.

He continues, puncturing that relief with his words, "But only on one condition."

His expression doesn't change. I can't read him, or tell what he wants before he says it, but holy shit — he doesn't say what I expect at all.

"What's the condition?"

"You marry me."

"What?"

He's not joking. He genuinely means it. My landlord wants me to marry him.

"I told you," he says. "I have connections, but these connections... they will only help family. They are not as generous as I am. They won't help a strange woman just because she needs it."

"W-what?"

"Grace. I want to help you. You won't be forced to marry, but if you want to survive Italy, you must marry me. Or... I can send you home. Back to America."

I can't go back to America. I have another year here. But I can't just marry this guy.

"I can't marry you," I say to him, but my mind turns around the possibility. Everything that's happened tonight makes me completely irrational.

I can't marry a man I barely know. I can't agree to marry someone hours after Uksan's death. I cared about Uksan. I don't want to disrespect him like that. There are so many other reasons this is a horrible idea, but Enzo interrupts anything that might have been about to come out of my mouth next.

"This is not a love marriage," he says, his voice growing stern. "If you wish for protection, you will agree."

"Protection against who?"

"The Albanians. Whoever. I have little time to offer you. Soon, I must leave here on business." He takes the cigarette out of his mouth for a few extra seconds. "Your boyfriend wasn't the man you thought he was, Grace. I promise not to harm you. I simply cannot think of another way."

"Marry you?" I blurt out again, as if repeating it will make this make more sense.

"Marry me. And in a year, when your lease ought to have ended, I will set you free. I promise."

"Can I get that in writing?" I blurt out. Lorenzo grins, like he already has my consent.

"If you agree," he says. "If you agree to marry me, yes."

Chapter 3

Marry The Killer

Enzo

When Van finds out what I've done, I'll pay. My only way out is convincing him I've done this for love and that I've saved Grace from a horrible fate so she can become my wife. Also, I have to prove this won't bring our family into an intense war with the Albanians. Which it might.

Fuck, he's going to kill me. Tonight was a shit show, and I had to drag him out of bed to check on the Jalousie situation.

Zara's gone. I told that ditsy child to stay out of trouble and she gets herself kidnapped while skipping the reception to pick up some extra bottles of champagne for Jalousie. Papa gave her the order, but he should have sent Lucky for protection. He knows how Zara's head is perpetually in the clouds...

It doesn't matter who made this mistake, really. Zara's gone. I never had a romantic interest in her, but it was never easy watching Eddie push her around. The girl needs to learn to stand up for herself. She won't learn that tied up in some Albanian sex pit. I've never met a woman so incapable of staying out of trouble.

I'll need to go after her soon and I have this big problem on my hands: I killed Grace's boyfriend to win her hand in marriage and she's hovering near a yes, not quite committing to me. I need her word before I give her the truth. A sensation similar to guilt nearly plagues me. Her pain isn't invisible to me.

I killed a horrible man. Since when have we cared about wicked men ending up exactly where they deserve?

If Matteo could hear my thoughts about this, he would grumble in disapproval that I sound like I'm spending too much time with my Pagonis cousins and I distinctly recall getting dodgy dating advice from the Greeks. Van has always been the last person to ask for dating advice. He had to kidnap a woman and slowly convince her to put up with him. Perhaps no one in my family gives suitable dating advice.

Dating. I don't want to date this woman. My treasure. Tesoro. She's too exquisite for dating, for me to call something as base as a girlfriend, although she's an unconventional sort of beauty. I like to think of myself as a man of taste, you know? And unlike my brother, my bloodline doesn't matter. The family will never be mine. I'm the youngest. I can do what I want... pursue women that I want. That I shouldn't want.

Van would kill me if he knew that these are the only women I like. Before Van married Jodi, I thought papa would kill me if I dared to bring a woman like Grace home. Now, he has no reason to deny me my tastes. I must be careful. I must keep my secrets. In Italy, we keep our private life private. I don't want to go public and lose her, but Grace is beautiful enough for me to take a risk.

"I can't marry you Lorenzo," she whispers again.

Her words shouldn't hurt. She has every right not to want to marry me, even without knowing that I killed her Albanian boyfriend. Even if her words pack a hard punch, I can't bring myself to look away from her. She has such full lips and a beautiful face with large features that can't help but draw my eyes in. There's no way in hell I'm letting her go.

"As you wish. I'll send you back to America," I respond calmly.

She glances up at me tentatively. Negotiation is my specialty. I wonder what Grace is good at. Given the shape of those full lips, I can only imagine. My body turns rigid just gazing at her, waiting for a response. How the fuck could anyone expect me to contain my lust for her?

If I die for a beautiful woman, then death will have been worth it. Grace crosses and then uncrosses her leg as she studies my face. I keep my jaw tight, without clenching or moving too much. I keep my gaze fixed on beautiful Grace West, staring with an intensity that matches hers.

"Wait," she says, her brows wrinkling together. She still won't meet my gaze as she continues. "This would just be... technical, right? You don't expect wife stuff from me?"

Wife stuff. She's clever, eh? She doesn't want me to use her for sex. I didn't expect that right away, but I didn't bring her into my home to wash my underwear and scrub my floors. She's far too beautiful for housework.

"What do you mean by wife stuff?" I feign ignorance.

"Never mind. I just don't want this to ruin my life. I need to be here, Enzo, but I can't get mixed up in the mob. I just want them to leave me alone."

"I can protect you. I promise."

I can feel her head spinning, thoughts whirling in her beautiful little head. Come to me, Grace. Stay with me.

"Promise?" She says. "Can you promise my protection?"

She clasps her hands over thighs, drawing my attention to her sepia thighs and her freshly manicured nails. Even with her life falling apart, she's a tastefully put together natural beauty.

"I will protect you with my life, Grace. You are my tenant. Nothing so horrible should have ever happened to you. I owe you this safety."

She pauses. She's considering it and I can see it on her face. I try not to smile too soon. *Yes, Tesoro. Consider this a gift.* Grace slowly nods. Her actions must be based on a mixture of shock and terror, but that doesn't matter. I know I'll win her over.

"Okay," she says reluctantly. "I'll marry you. I'll do it."

It's not exactly the most romantic agreement, but once I have Grace in a marriage contract, she will be mine. If I have her for a year, she won't want to leave. Look at her, wandering so beautifully into my trap. I love her already, just from the way she looks, the mystery behind her eyes and the desire that burns stronger than anything I've felt for a woman like this before. Men always know the woman they want to marry the moment they lay eyes on her. It's a tight burning in your core, a desire to pursue as deeply embedded in our genes as hunting. It's human to love and want a woman this much when fate determines that she's yours.

"I'm not doing this to disrespect Uksan. I still love him, you understand? I just... I can't get myself killed and I can't go home."

America. No rational person would choose to live in America over Italy. Then again, that's my bias. I'm a pure Italian man at heart and I never want to leave the coast. Still, there's something more going on beyond a rational displeasure with the American way of life. There's pain in her past and fuck, I want to know the exact depth of that pain.

Maybe it's because I'm lonely, but with her, I have the strongest desire to reach out, to touch her in whatever way she'll allow.

"What's going on back home?" I search Grace's soft, round face for answers. Another boyfriend? Debt? Crime? What could make Grace want to stay here after what she's been through tonight?

I ask her, "What makes you want to stay with me instead of going home?"

"It's not you," she says nervously. "It's Italy. I love it here and back home... I just can't, okay? I don't want to tell you."

"Keeping secrets from your husband?"

I hate how easy this is for me. To tease her. To play with her heart. It's for a good cause. I want to keep her and this is the only way I know how.

"You're not my husband yet," Grace replies firmly, her serious full lips pursing together as she stares at me from across the counter. "So don't play."

This is the first sign I've seen that she has a sharp side. I like it.

"Perhaps you should go to bed," I tell her. "You'll need rest."

My brother and I will have to postpone our trip to find Zara until after my wedding. I'm sure Giovanni will understand. We have men tracking her route and I know he'll want to send me across the border soon, right into fucking danger.

I need Grace to sleep, so we can marry and once we marry... I can do anything I want with her.

"I don't know if I can sleep," she whispers, reminding me that she's been through something horrific, something that I caused. Her pain tugs at my heart. I don't regret what I did, but hurting Grace isn't what I wanted.

"Then stay out here," I tell her. "I need my rest. You're welcome to enjoy the house."

I whistle for Ember, who follows me into my bedroom, bounding after me with excited little yaps.

I shut the door and try to stop myself from doing anything truly foolish, like crawling into Grace's bed and confessing the true reason I brought her here or the true reason I want her. I need to call my brother. Van's going to kill me. I call him reluctantly, and he doesn't pick up. Fuck... I'll have to tell him at his wedding.

Giovanni's going to kill me for what I've done.

I return home from a very loud early morning meeting with Giovanni to find Grace asleep. He won't kill me, but he's sending me to Albania in a week to ensure that he doesn't follow through on his desire to end my life for disobedience.

I even offer to babysit Bianca-Rose as penance, but my brother nearly throws a paper weight at my head when I suggest going near his child. I'm convinced he's inhaling fumes in that office basement of his, but when I tell him that, he insists the only fumes are my cologne. Bastard.

And why won't he allow me near his kids? Overprotective fuck. I'm great with children. Probably. I'm great with everything. Look at me—26 years old with a beautiful, foreign fiancée, soon to be my wife, luxury cars, apartments and a dog. I can handle shit just fine...

Poor Grace. Four days in my house and she barely speaks to me. She suffers deeply from Uksan's death. I never expected this grief, and frankly, her tearful sobs make me deeply uncomfortable. My attempts to console her appear to have only a moderate effect. I have her review the proposed marriage contract and all she does is nod or shake her head in response to what I say.

She's barely left her room since I took her in. I don't know what she does for money, and she barely eats, although I see signs of her having entered the kitchen when I leave to get my daily lectures from Van. Grace doesn't want to talk to me. I don't know how I'll lure her out completely. I leave her little gifts in the fridge and she enjoys those — tiramisu from a nearby cafe, pistachio gelato in the freezer, chocolate mousse, and a special iced espresso treat mama would make for me when I was a child.

Today, I want to see Grace's face, not just signs of her

around the house. Before we marry, I want her to know me and I want her to know what's coming for both of us. I'll have to visit Albania and if she expects to come with me, she'll need to know the truth about the danger we'll face. Van won't let me bring her, but I can't bear the thought of leaving her here alone, either.

Seeing Van earlier reminds me he has a family and soon, if I wanted, I could have one too. I have no brothers left. No Matteo. No Van. Perhaps it's time I settle down. I don't have any desire for children right now, but peeling layers of clothing off Grace's body and sliding into her definitely appeals to my fantasies. Babies... no babies... as long as I get to make love to a beautiful woman, I don't care.

One good fuck before Albania would soothe my nerves from the killing I'll have to do to get Zara back.

I promise myself I will wait for marriage with Grace. She's worth it, right? I have that week to earn her trust, to set her up to fall easily into my bed.

I knock on Grace's door. I don't relish telling her I will probably need to leave her here alone, despite my desires to bring her along. Work requires focus. I knock lightly, and she doesn't open her bedroom door right away. I call her name and then hear her shuffling on the other side of the door like she's hurriedly packing or unpacking something.

"Grace?"

My future wife cracks the door and a whiff of her perfume exits the room. She hasn't left the house in days, but she always smells like a garden. Wait to touch her, Enzo. Wait for her.

"Yes?" she answers nervously. "Did I eat too much of the gelato? I have a few euros I can offer for it..."

I try not to smile. I don't mind her healthy American appetite. Cigarettes killed my willingness to eat years ago, but American women are very sexy the way they eat and the way they enjoy everything with a shameless lust for sugar, fat and salt.

"No, the gelato is fine," I tell her, attempting to hide my bemusement. "I have news about our wedding. We'll have it tonight. I have arranged everything for us."

"Tonight?"

She sounds a bit panicked and I have to silence my disappointment. I can't expect her to eagerly

"Yes. I have to leave Italy soon for work. I prefer to ensure your protection before then."

She digs her nails really hard into her palm, a slight gesture that she thinks I don't notice.

"I can't come with you?"

My chest tightens. Grace doesn't want me to leave her here. I shouldn't flatter myself that she has forgotten Uksan. I hear her crying at night when I walk past her room. She cries in the shower too. Even sitting at my kitchen island, a far off look wanders across her face and not even Ember nipping at her ankles can snap her out of it. She misses him. There's a hole in her heart where Uksan lived and she won't easily allow me in.

She doesn't know how much I would do for her.

"I didn't realize this would happen so soon," she stammers uncomfortably. "I don't... I still have to..."

It's Uksan. I thought killing the bastard would quickly eliminate him from Grace's life, but now he's less of a ghost in her heart and more like an angel. She misses him. I bite my tongue from saying something more temperamental and focus on the response I wish to elicit from Grace.

"What's wrong? Is our arrangement no longer satisfactory? I won't make you stay here if you wish me to return you to America."

I'm lying, of course. But I know she has to stay. I need her to stay.

"No," she says, shaking her head. "I'll do it. But Enzo...

Who's after me? How can you leave right after you promise me protection?"

"I have armed guards. Men. My brother."

"I don't know your brother," she says through gritted teeth. I don't mind her fire, but I sense she's holding back, not wanting to taunt a man she hardly knows and doesn't completely trust.

"He's a good man. His wife, Jodi, will spend time with you. She's American."

Grace rocks her head, completely unwilling to accept my position.

"I'll have to stay here in the same building where some maniac shot my boyfriend and got away with it."

The maniac who shot her boyfriend would never hurt her. Why can't she see that? She's right that I promised her protection. I meant it.

"I don't want you traveling to Albania with me. It's too dangerous."

"Albania? Why the hell are you going to Albania? No one shot my boyfriend in Albania. Albania might just be the best place for me."

She argues with more passion than I've ever met in a woman. It's a challenge to wrestle her out of her stubbornness, but it's not a challenge I don't enjoy.

"I'm a business owner, Grace."

"Great," she says. "Then bring me along on your business. I can't stay here knowing some psycho killer could pop me in the middle of the night."

I assume 'pop' here means kill, and it's some Americanism. Fuck.

"I can't bring you along."

"Why not? You're a landlord. I can handle some real estate conventions."

Why do I feel like she's testing me?

She bites her lower lip again before I can firmly tell her

that there's no way in hell Van will let me drag her along to kill men and retrieve Zara across the sea.

Grace sighs, her body curling forward with sadness. She leans her chin on her hands and admits in that pretty American accent, "I can't enjoy Albania without Uksan. Wouldn't that be weird?"

Uksan. Just hearing his name fills me with outrage. Why do the dead never stay dead? I want to talk about my wedding, about our future, and about how I plan on keeping her, not the Albanian fuck I killed.

"You've been through hell, Grace. Perhaps you can use this opportunity to enjoy my penthouse and reflect on your relationship."

I hate the reasonable words coming from my mouth. I half expect her to argue more, but she raises an eyebrow, studying me as if she doesn't expect much wisdom from a simple landlord.

"You're right. Damn, Enzo. You be making points."

"And our wedding? Are you ready?"

"Are you?" Grace shoots back.

"I have a dress for you," I say to her. "And a ring. Give me your hand."

I reach into my pocket for the ring box. Grace eyes the box tentatively, not exactly giving me her hand, but not rejecting this first offering of my affection for her. My heart races as she considers the box. I'm a stranger to her, and she can't possibly know how deeply fucking obsessed with her I've become.

"Is this for me?"

Her breath catches despite herself. Just hearing her voice gets me so fucking hard.

"You're going to be my wife, no?"

"Yeah, but not your proper wife," she says. "It's just a contract."

I allow her to reassure herself, even if from this moment forward, nothing could force me to let go of Grace West. She'll be Grace Doukas as soon as I can tie the knot. When you meet a woman you want, why wait for her to break up? Why wait for her to be ready?

When a real man meets a woman he wants, he does whatever he must to keep her. If a man truly wants a woman, nothing on hell or earth can stop him from fighting for her.

"Yes. Perhaps it is just a contract, but you've been through hell. I want to put a little light in your life."

Tesoro. My treasure. I mean it literally when I talk about putting light into her life. I choose each stone for its luminosity, from the way I anticipate the ring glowing against her warm, brown hand. Every day I'm gone, I want Grace to think of me. When I return, Uksan will be a ghost from her past and I can have her... Forever.

I know she'll love the ring I chose. Women need luxury and real men understand this too. I open the box and allow the ring to speak for itself. She clasps her hand over her mouth and shakes her head again. No, tesoro. You're keeping this symbol on your finger. You are mine. You will always be mine.

"Enzo, this is fancy! Are these real?"

I nod. Each stone is as real as my unbridled feelings for her.

Grace keeps shaking her head even if there isn't a chance in hell I'll allow her to reject my gift.

"This is too much. I can't accept this," she insists.

She still won't take her eyes off the ring. Despite her protests, she loves it. I take her hand and slip the ring on her finger. I only guessed her size, but the ring fits perfectly with both the white and pink diamonds, making her hands look even more elegant. I don't want any opposition from Grace anymore. She deserves at least this much for what she's been through. Our hands linger against each other, and I don't want to let go of her beautiful hand.

Every man remembers when he first touches a woman.

That initial breach of physical contact sends burning through me and I can't bear the thought of letting go of her hand. I crave more of her skin beneath mine. I want to put her lips against mine and then lower her head between my legs and enter her pretty mouth.

Only touching her sends all these dirty thoughts racing through my head. I swallow as if I can push the thoughts away by sending a slow lump of spit down my throat, and then I tease the palm of Grace's hand with my thumb, enjoying the shudder my touch sends shooting through her.

"You must accept this," I insist.

Her hand drops away from mine and the lump I just swallowed returns, pressing out against my trachea and filling me with a mixture of my stubbornness and lust. She's keeping the fucking ring.

"I don't deserve your kindness," Grace says. "You've let me live in your house for days and I can't take any more from you. I don't deserve any of this. It's not your fault some criminal shot my boyfriend in cold blood. You don't have to pay."

"You deserve this ring. Trust me. I understand if you're hesitant about this wedding, Grace. I promise I will stick to my vows. I'll protect you. I'll keep you safe. I don't want this to hurt you."

Her boyfriend's dead, and she's still guilty. I should have seen that coming. She's not mafia like us. She doesn't expect her loved ones to drop dead at random. I did not expect her to kill her best friend when she was nineteen because he made the mistake of robbing her father's nightclub. She's not broken like I am. That makes what I did so much worse.

"It feels weird doing this," she says, trying to meet my gaze again. "But one year, right? Just one year?"

It's like she's too shy to look at me. My guilt tells me that a part of her knows I'm a fuckup.

"Yes. One year. That should be enough time to assure your safety."

"I should ask more questions," she says. "I'm not stupid, Lorenzo. I can see in your eyes that you know more than you say. Was Uksan involved in something that horrible? Because that's the only explanation I can have for someone killing him. He must have done something."

I know I should tell her the truth, but I can only bring myself to tell her part of the truth.

"He had involvements you didn't know about."

I don't want to taint her memory of him. I'd rather Grace forget Uksan than turn him into either a hero or a villain.

"How could he have kept that from me?" She muses. "I've turned the past couple months over in my mind and I can't imagine Uksan involved in the mob or with some criminals. I thought I knew him. I thought he was safe."

"We never really know the people we love, do we?"

"Love," she whispers, shaking her head again and tutting. "I don't understand love."

I keep staring at her, and I don't want to look away from her. She's incredibly beautiful, and she looks even more beautiful with my ring on her finger. My cock throbs. I think I have this all planned out, but the same way she hardly knows Uksan, I hardly know Grace. She could be significantly more than I bargained for. She's beautiful enough to ruin my life. I want to let her.

"I don't understand love, either. That's why I'm marrying a stranger to keep her safe."

"I don't understand, Lorenzo. Why are you doing all of this for me?"

"Because… I owe you."

Her face falls. So much sadness on that pretty brown face.

"You don't."

"This happened in my building. You were my tenant. It's my responsibility. Tonight, we will marry at the church. After supper. Nine o'clock. My family will be there."

"So late at night? And so soon?"

"Does that bother you?"

Grace shrugs. "No. I never even pictured my dream wedding. I've never been much of a romantic."

But I'm sure she never dreamed of marrying a Doukas without knowing who he really was.

"I've never been a romantic either," I tell her as honestly as I can. Before Grace, romance never occurred to me as important.

"I want to help you, Grace. So let's do this, eh?"

She nods, fidgeting with her new ring and fighting back a smile each time she moves it around her finger.

"Then we go on this business trip?"

"I go on this business trip. You stay with protection."

She's suspicious of me, I can tell, but unless Grace asks directly, I won't reveal my secrets.

"What kind of business, Enzo?"

I reach for her face and touch her gently. Her skin is warmer than I expect, like she's flushed or nervous. What about me makes her nervous? See, there's my fucking guilt again.

"I'll tell you after the wedding, Grace. Now look at your ring. Do you like it?"

She takes her hand up and gazes at the ring. Of course she loves it. The custom ring gleams, but Grace bites her lower lip, nodding, but guilty. Of course, she feels guilty.

Her boyfriend's dead, and she's about to marry his killer.

Chapter 4

What A Beautiful Wedding

Grace

My boyfriend Uksan died three days ago and I'm marrying another man tonight.

I don't know how to feel. Even if Lorenzo has been nothing but kind to me, he's devilishly handsome, and maybe if I weren't so completely fucked up, I could allow myself to feel that attraction for him, I don't have a clue what's okay for me to feel about him. Nothing, probably. I shouldn't notice anything about his eyes, his expressive eyebrows or the way his face dimples whenever he smirks.

He has a smooth voice too, like a foreign jazz singer.

I shouldn't feel this trepidation. He just wants to help me. He just wants to protect me. I don't know how well connected he is to the mob, but he must have some kind of connection, right? He must know this is the only way to keep me safe.

I don't want to tell him I've already figured him out and figured out that he might not be as perfect as he looks, but at least he's taking this investigation more seriously than the police. At least I feel safe in his apartment. Grief hit me hard, and it's still with me, and I feel too weird and guilty to celebrate this wedding. It's only one year... I can survive one year married to a man I don't love.

There's no one to tell I'm getting married aside from my cousin, Tisha. I haven't seen her in years. She ran away to Greece and rumor has it, she married a white guy several years older than her and had a bunch of babies. She's probably living her best life somewhere over there... I don't want to bother her with my unusual situation.

How the hell can I tell my sweet cousin that I might have accidentally found myself mixed up with the mob? She wouldn't want that kind of mess in her perfect Greek life.

A mobster killed Uksan, and I could be next. That's my shit to handle, isn't it? On top of all the other shit, I think I can handle that. Why is there always some fucking guy trying to kill me?

I handled everything else in my life alone. I can handle this — a spontaneous marriage for protection. If Lorenzo wanted to hurt me, he would have by now. I've been at his mercy for days, and he's been nothing but generous, bringing me all those tasty desserts. He's treating me like a real fiancée. He doesn't have to do that either. The way he looks, Lorenzo probably has women beating down his damned door.

Lorenzo brings a wedding dress to my room. He's weirdly formal about it, and quiet. I hang the dress up on the door and he reminds me about the wedding at the church.

"Isn't it bad luck for you to see me?" I ask him at the door to my guest bedroom.

Lorenzo smiles warmly. "I am the bad luck."

Before I can take him too seriously, Lorenzo continues in his fast accented English, "Don't worry. I'll have my family drive you to the church."

"Family?"

"Tonight, you meet my family," Lorenzo says. "The people pledged to protect you while I'm gone. You'll love my sister-in-law."

I hate the fact that he's leaving. I want to plead with him to let me travel with him, but I sense he won't budge and I'm just grateful he hasn't sent me back to my crime scene apartment or asked me for a dime to help with the groceries.

I work up the courage to push him for the truth.

"Before we get married, I have to ask you something."

Lorenzo leans in the doorway, that smirk still on his face. "Ask away."

My hands shake slightly, but I have to ask him. I have to know the truth from Enzo.

"Are you in the mob? Is that why you can protect me?"

"I will answer once you're my wife. Understand?"

I have my answer, don't I? He might not know that I have the answer that I need, but I do. Can I really let myself do this?

I have to be honest, I need this. It's not because of Uksan. I need this wedding to Lorenzo for reasons I can't admit to him yet. He has his secrets. I have mine. I can't go back to the United States and I can't face the Italian mob. Lorenzo might be a liar. He might play his cards close to the chest, but I'm no different.

"I understand."

He gives me that frustrating smirk, like he has me wrapped around his finger, but Lorenzo can't read me as well as he thinks.

"Will you wear the dress?"

"Yes, Lorenzo. And I'll meet your family too."

"Okay," he says, touching the cigarette box in his pocket but resisting the urge to take one out. "I'll have my sister-in-law pick you up. You'll know her."

"Okay."

He leaves and shuts the door behind him. My heart quickens. Sister-in-law. I bet she's some tall, skinny Italian chick as severe and quiet as Lorenzo. I take a shower and arrange my braids with my hair clip before slipping into a white silk dress. It's gorgeous and form-fitting with a long slit up the slide. It's nothing I would have worn into a church back home, but I guess they do things differently in Italy.

The dress fits like a dream and as for that engagement ring. I didn't want to tell Lorenzo that the whole thing was perfect, but it's flawless. I know I should expect the knock on the door, but I still jerk nervously when it comes.

"Hello? Grace? It's Jodi, Lorenzo's sister-in-law. May I come in?"

I guess she has keys to his house, and she sounds American, not Italian at all. Holy shit. I'm really going to do this. I'm marrying an Italian man tonight. I jump up and head over to the door with my high heels in hand.

"Yes, come in," I call out to her as I approach my bedroom door.

I open the door and holy shit, I'm wrong about Lorenzo's sister-in-law. She puts her hands on her hips and we both say, "You're black!?"

We bite our lips, trying to stop the words from coming out.

"I'll go first," Jodi says. "You're black. Lorenzo's future wife is black."

Jodi's really pretty, with waist-length ruby dreadlocks, curves, and what I swear is a little baby bump. Her jaw drops open, and she seems to examine me as if my skin tone is a fake tan.

"Yes. Is that... a problem?" I ask. Is there a reason she seems so surprised? Maybe she's just been in Italy a while and knows how racist most guys can be. Lorenzo isn't like that. At least, I don't think he is...

"No," Jodi says, smoothing out her facial expression. "Is it a problem for you?"

"No. I just... I didn't know there were that many black women in Italy. I haven't met many."

"Honey, same. And we just lost one of ours."

"Huh? Who? What happened?"

Jodi's eyebrows wrinkle.

"Enzo didn't tell you?"

"No."

"Then I'd better not say anything. Sorry. I don't want to be a rat."

"What's this business thing he keeps talking about? Can you at least tell me that?"

Jodi deflects masterfully. "Honey, we need to talk about how damn good you look in that dress. Did you pick that out?"

"No. Lorenzo did."

Jodi tuts. "Italian men have the best taste. I swear."

"I like the slit. Look."

I crack my first genuine smile since Uksan's death, seeing my leg peeking through the dress. The silk looks luxurious. I used to buy all my clothes at the Goodwill near my house, so real silk is a damned treat. It's fancy, like it comes from Target or something.

"This is beautiful," Jodi says. "Lorenzo has a thing for Gucci."

"Gucci!?"

"Girl, welcome to Italy."

"Gucci?! I can't wear a Gucci dress!"

I'm not a Gucci type of woman. I've never worn a designer label and there ain't ever been a time I could drop my rent money on a single belt. I can't spill a drop of water on this dress. I don't belong in luxury.

Jodi chuckles.. "Why not? You look great. If you don't mind me asking, how the hell did Lorenzo get a beautiful woman like you to fall for him?"

I bite my lip. Fall for him? Jodi must know the circumstances of our marriage, right? I wonder if I'm making a mistake, but I tell Jodi the truth, exactly what happened and exactly why I'm marrying Enzo. Her face changes, but she doesn't give me a whiff of her opinion. She reminds me of Enzo that way.

"I'm sorry for your loss," Jodi says, bringing it all to reality. I fidget with my new engagement ring. It's not like I don't feel guilty for this, but Uksan's dead and I need protection that he can't offer me anymore.

"I'm trying to cope, you know?"

"Yes. If you don't mind, I'm going to step outside for a few minutes. I need to call my husband before I take you to the church."

I nod. Jodi excuses herself, but returns only five minutes later. I'm glad she isn't leaving me alone too long. I can't let second thoughts screw me out of a marriage that I need. There's definitely a part of me that wants to back out of this. She takes my hand with a warm smile. "Let's get you to the church."

She drives a sexy as hell white Mercedes SUV with extra safety features for the babies. (Jodi informs me of this like we're in the car commercial). I walked or cycled most of my time on the coast, but it's nice being in a car that smells brand spanking new. Between the car and the Gucci, this is the closest I've ever come to feeling like a princess.

Jodi drives slowly through the streets and she doesn't talk much, which I don't mind. She mostly tells me stories about her time in Italy. She tries asking me about my life, but I give her short answers to everything.

Where are you from?

Mississippi.

You don't sound like you're from Mississippi.

I worked hard to lose that accent.

It's a nice accent!

Nobody believes that.

Why are you marrying Lorenzo?

I... Because I want to.

As long as he's not forcing you.

No. He's not.

. . .

We arrive at the church and everything blurs together as I walk inside because when Lorenzo said I would meet his family, I didn't think he meant that I would meet every family and resident of his village. Some woman even shoves a chicken in my face until a man with dark sunglasses barely concealing a pistol gently guides her out of the way.

I walk down the aisle alone in a church full of strangers. I'm scared out of my mind, but there's a man waiting for me at the end of the aisle. I know he has to be crazy, but right now, I need someone crazy enough to protect me if shit hits the fan.

I have to keep myself sane through this. I tell myself that my secret would have ended things with Uksan eventually. He shouldn't have died, but now he's gone and I can't bring him back. I have to take measures to protect myself.

I have to marry a man who's likely the furthest thing from a saint. He's not forcing me to marry him. I'm forcing myself. I need to do this. But when I look at the man waiting for me at the other end of the church, I feel this tiny tug in my stomach. He's incredibly handsome. He has gorgeous gray eyes, a clean, sharp jawline and a smile that could make anyone melt. He has a dimple in his left cheek and his tattoos make his chiseled body even more of a work of art.

He chose a light gray suit for our wedding and he shaved. I smell his aftershave as I approach the altar, and he smells delicious. All those thoughts rushing into me fill me with profound guilt. Uksan. I shouldn't feel these things or think about another man when my boyfriend just died.

But shouldn't a woman let herself go a little on her wedding day? Enzo's still going to be my husband, even if it's just a year long arrangement. I could have chosen a worse husband for looks. Lorenzo looks like a model. There's one man standing with him, his best man, and he looks terrifying, but just as handsome as his brother, even as he stands a few inches taller than him. It seems gloriously unfair that they're both so tall and handsome.

The man glowers at Lorenzo bitterly and doesn't even look at me. Is that Jodi's husband?

I don't know how someone so sweet could be married to a man who looks like he could rip me in half. I tilt my head downwards as I approach the altar and step closer towards Enzo. My mouth dries as I approach him and the smell of his aftershave started off delicious, but now brings on nausea. I know this is crazy as fuck. I'm marrying a man with secrets and he could be dangerous — more dangerous than Uksan, and Uksan tried his damndest to keep his dark side from me.

Enzo's dark side feels like it's just below the surface and I don't know what will happen tonight when, legally, I'm Enzo's wife. He's a man. I don't believe his pretty words about not expecting "wife stuff".

A priest appears and speaks in Italian. I don't understand a word, but I know my lines. Enzo's says his lines with a smile on his face, like he's won something.

"You may now kiss the bride," the priest says, in English. Enzo's hand grasps my hips and he kisses me ceremoniously. He touches his lips to my lower lip first, taking my lips between his and then slowly leading into a deep, romantic kiss. I've never had a kiss like this before. Enzo's hands grip my hips just firmly enough so I don't feel trapped and his lips taste like peppermint.

He sucks on my lower lip and pulls my body against his like he doesn't care that there's a priest hovering inches away from us. When his tongue enters my mouth, I lose it. My hands rush to his hair and I kiss him back forcefully, running my fingers through hair that's much softer than I expect. I don't want to stop touching his hair. It's light brown and feels silky. He's an incredible kisser and our kiss lasts for minutes until the scary man standing next to Enzo growls, "Can you stop?"

He kisses me a few seconds longer before pulling away.

"I simply want to enjoy my wife, Van. Allow me."

"Enjoy her in your bedroom," his older brother Van growls.

Our wedding ends quickly. No reception, just Enzo taking my arm and guiding me through blessings from what feels like hundreds of cousins, aunts, uncles and well-wishers from the coast and surrounding villages. When we get to Enzo's car, he stops me from walking with a gentle tug on my forearm.

"Wait, Grace."

"Yes?"

"I know this is just an arrangement, and you feel no love for me, but I have to be honest with you."

Honesty would be nice. I nod slightly. I like the sound of honesty.

"You look beautiful tonight," Lorenzo says. His eyes are flawless and his smile...

I have to look away from him. This feels like I'm cheating on Uksan, even if I've gone and mixed things up so much now that my emotions are a train wreck. Uksan's dead. I can't feel completely guilty about moving on. I can allow myself to get a little sentimental on my wedding night. Hell, if I want, I can even blame it on hormones. It must be the damned hormones.

"Thank you," I mutter, desperately trying to ignore all the crazy things my hormones are telling me.

He looks gorgeous. Enzo looks like he jumped out of those old Abercrombie shopping bags we used to fight over and paste on our walls as teenagers.

I bite my lip to stop those thirsty words from spilling out. I can't give myself away so easily. Lorenzo won't let me look away from him. He puts his finger under my chin and tilts my gaze towards him. I'm tall, but Lorenzo's really tall. At 6'5", he towers over me. I freeze instantly when he touches me, especially because we kissed. His touch reminds me of that kiss—that dirty, incredibly sexy kiss that betrays my dead ex-boyfriend.

Lorenzo won't let me look away from him. His gaze fixes me in place with perfect hypnosis. Women must swoon for these gray eyes. They're so pale, he looks like he's from another world.

"You already guessed about my family, but you married me anyway," he murmurs, studying my face carefully. He wants me to betray exactly what I know.

"What do you mean?"

It seems like a good time to play dumb.

"Mafia," he drawls. "My family. I'm not Lorenzo Pazzini. I'm Lorenzo Pazzini Doukas, and my family controls this coast. You guessed... at least half of that."

His face changes and there's something dark that I missed before. I suddenly feel exposed before this man and his gray eyes. He can't know everything about me. He can't know all my secrets. And surely Enzo's focus will remain on his revelation. He's mafia.

I must have known the entire time, somewhere in the back of my mind. He handled everything with Uksan too smoothly. He assured me his protection. How did I think he was going to protect me? It's not like Ember's a guard dog.

This news packs a double-punch. He isn't just in the mafia. The Doukas family controls the coast. I haven't even been in Italy that long and I've already heard rumors about an insanely wealthy family here that everyone fears and loves. I didn't assume that was Enzo's family.

The crowd at the wedding suddenly makes sense—including the chickens. And Jodi... She must know about this too. She said nothing. I feel sick to my stomach. I know Enzo isn't the only one with secrets, but holy shit. The mob. I've dealt with a lot of shit in my life, but I've never run afoul of the mob.

I steady my mind. I can't afford to freak the hell out. If Enzo wants information, so do I. I nod calmly, as if I already guessed everything he just told me and I pose a simple question that I doubt Enzo will answer. I have to try anyway. I have to piece this mess together. Maybe he knows who killed

Uksan. Maybe there's a way Enzo can help get justice. Maybe justice will make me feel less weird about marrying Enzo Doukas.

"What do you know about the Albanian mob?"

I can't shy away from him now. I plunged into this mess with both feet. I can't show any fear. I've already seen the scariest shit in my life, anyway. Even Lorenzo's secrets and revelations can't push me away. I want to know what he knows.

"They sell children, Grace. I must leave soon and I can't answer any more of your questions."

His voice tightens like I'm pestering him. Hell no, Enzo. I got into this deal for protection and I'm making damned sure that he keeps his promise, considering I've kept mine.

"What about Uksan's killer? You promised to protect me. You got your end of the deal. I want mine."

I won't let him bully me. I have rights, even by the contract I signed. Enzo has to treat this like a proper marriage, as do I. Until the end of our year, this relationship is as real as the papers we signed.

Enzo huffs like a man who isn't accustomed to explaining himself. He'll have to get used to explaining himself this year.

"Uksan's killer won't be coming for you. It's my job to protect you and even from Albania, I can do that. I swear, I won't be gone long. Only a few weeks."

My stomach knots again. A few weeks? That could mean anything, and it might even mean Enzo not returning at all. I can't let him get away with this.

"How can you be sure of that? Uksan's killer is obviously a maniac! He broke into your apartments and killed someone. You promised you would keep me safe. How the hell can you fulfill that promise from another country?."

My heart races as panic settles in. This man isn't who I thought he was. He's not a kind landlord. He's cold. Cruel. I wasn't ready for just how cruel he really was.

"I promise you'll be safe," he insists, his voice lowering until it's cold and firm.

"How the fuck can you promise that?"

He raises his eyebrows. He's never heard me swear before. I half expect him to slap me. I've certainly been slapped for the words coming out of my mouth plenty of times before.

The corner of Enzo's lips tug upward in a devious smirk that he fails so fucking hard at disguising. My stomach sinks deeper with each word out of his mouth.

"Grace, I killed Uksan."

Chapter 5

The Bathtub

Enzo

I can't lie to my wife. I should lie to my wife, but I can't. I have to watch her fall apart in front of me and know I'm the fuck who caused her all this pain. Her face contorts in disbelief at first. Grace shakes her head.

"No. You're lying. Stop."

"I killed Uksan, Grace. I walked into your apartment. I questioned your boyfriend, and I shot him in the head."

"Stop it, Enzo!" she yells. This is the most emotion I've seen from her in days. Her fire stirs me, but I don't want her to stop that burning. I want her to feel everything at once—all the pain, all the rage. She has to feel it. She has to know the truth if I ever want her to feel for me, if I ever want her to know who I really am.

I am not Lorenzo Pazzini. I am Enzo Doukas, a killer, a protector, a man who will do anything for his new wife, even if she only belongs to me for 365 ¼ days. I have her for a year, I have to win her for forever.

"I'm not lying. You know I'm not lying."

She looks fucking incredible in that dress and we're in my living room, standing inches away from each other. It's the absolute worst time, of course, but fuck, it's tempting to lose myself and pounce on her tonight. That kiss at the altar fucked with my head.

I need to be real with her, and I need to sleep with her. Tonight. That means the truth. If I don't tell her the truth, Giovanni promises he'll have me killed anyway, and I believe that.

"Let me out of here," she hisses. "You help me pack my things and you let me go."

She tries to swerve around me, but I grab her wrist and squeeze.

"No," I growl. "You aren't leaving, Grace. I killed him. I'm telling you the truth, but I'm not done."

"You murdered my boyfriend and lied to me! You're the one I need protection from."

She pushes hard against my chest with her free hand, but I catch her hands and hold them against my chest, drawing her body against mine. She trembles violently and my heart pounds in my chest. She's so fucking close to me. She looks delicious in Gucci, and I want to lick her skin from her neck all the way down to her sweet fucking pussy.

My heart pounds as sex and violence run across parallel tracks in her mind. I would kill Uksan again in a heartbeat. I would stick my tongue so deep inside her that she would have to scream my name.

Yes, I killed her boyfriend, and yes, I'm a fucked up piece of shit, but I'm not worse than Uksan. She'll see that after I've had my way with her tonight. She's too fucking gorgeous. I need her to consume me.

"Let go of me," she hisses.

"No," I snarl. "I'm not letting you out of my sight, Grace. I promised to protect you, and that's exactly what I did. Uksan helped his family sell children. Little girls. I saw their business with my own eyes, and when I discovered he was involved, I killed him."

She doesn't let the news sink in. Every word I say stings her deeply, but I refuse to allow her to deny the truth.

"That's not true!"

"It's the fucking truth!" I yell at her. "This is who I am, Grace. I lied. I understand that hurts. But I still care about you. I wouldn't have killed Uksan if it weren't for you."

She tries to kick me, but I hold her hips with my free hand, keeping her body tensed against mine. No, Grace. Stop fighting.

"Don't say that like it's supposed to be a compliment," she hisses, wriggling against my grasp and inadvertently grinding her body against my crotch. It's not fair that she's getting me hard right now. It's not fair at all.

"It's not meant to be," I snarl. "It's my job. I kill people. I killed Uksan because I had to. Because of what he's done and because a man who could hurt little girls could hurt you."

"He wouldn't..."

She shakes her head in frustration. I have to break through to her despite her resistance and show her a tiny slip of my world.

"How well do you know him? Do you know that name? Dervishaj? They're the largest mob family in Albania and unfortunately, you are not safe. I meant what I said when I said I would protect you, and I've been doing it since before I took my vows."

Grace furiously shakes her head, and her glare threatens to burn me away completely.

"How could you do this? You're a fucking sociopath."

"No, tesoro. I fell in love with you the first moment I saw you. It's not my fault your boyfriend sold children, but I don't hold it against you either."

As she wriggles violently against me, I bend my lips to hers and kiss her. She kisses back for a few moments, reminding me of the way those soft lips felt at the altar. I release her hands as I kiss her, expecting her to touch my body, feel my chest, but Grace balls her hands into a tight fist and lands a surprisingly tough punch in my stomach. I try to step back from kissing her, but she bites down hard on my lower lip, drawing blood.

"Fuck..."

I pull away and touch my lip as blood comes away on my fingers. Grace folds her arms and glowers at me with pure rage.

"You deserved that," she snarls."

"Why?"

"For kissing me."

"You enjoy kissing me," I snarl. "What? Does it make you feel guilty?"

"No," she hisses back. "But you should feel guilty. You killed an innocent man."

She sounds like she's trying to convince herself of his innocence and like it's barely working.

"That motherfucker was far from innocent," Enzo says. "He defiled you with his presence, Grace. You are the most beautiful woman I've seen in Italy and you deserve far better than a man who would use you to hide his dirty work. I take responsibility for my shit and I would never, and I mean never, put you in danger."

She freezes. I know she can't think of what to do next. She doesn't want to fuck with me.

"I don't want to be with you, Lorenzo. This isn't a romantic contract."

"Good," I growl, although it doesn't make me feel good. I don't just want this woman's body. I want every fucking inch of her. I want her heart. I want her mind. I want her delicious pussy.

"Good?"

My grasp on her tightens. Nothing could make me let her go now. She's the closest I've ever come to losing myself entirely to animal lust.

"We don't need romance for what we're about to do."

She tries to hit me again, but I grab her hands and press them against my chest.

"Feel this, Grace. It's my heart. I look you in the eye and tell you how I feel and what I want. We don't need romance, but I need you. I need your body, and you need my protection. So you will come to bed with me tonight."

I won't force her. I tell myself I won't force her, but fuck Grace gets me hard, and it's my wedding night to a dark-skinned vision in white Gucci silk. I need her naked. I need her wrapped around my cock and I need her body against mine, keeping my bed warm and keeping me sane before the dirty business in Albania.

"I will never have feelings for you," she whispers. "Never."

Right now, I don't need her heart. I need something warm, wet and delicious.

"Keep your heart, Grace. Give me your body."

"I'm only doing that on one condition," she whispers. "You keep your promise."

Van's going to kill me.

"I promise."

"Then you can have me, Enzo. Just for tonight."

No. Not just for tonight. Forever. Grace Doukas will be mine for as long as I live.

"What if I want you for more?"

"You can't," she says. "You don't kill my boyfriend and then get the girl."

"Why not?"

"Because that's not how life works, Enzo."

"I'm a Doukas, Grace, and now so are you. We always get what we want."

Before she can offer any more protest, I kiss her again. My lip still bleeds and this time, she doesn't bite me. She licks the burst part of my lip clean and then gently sucks my lower lip between her teeth. My cock stiffens instantly and I want to rip the silk from her smooth skin and have her right there on the couch.

No. It's our wedding night. This has to be perfect.

She pulls away from me with a nervous, shuddering chest. Our first time.

"Let's take a bath," I murmur, pushing her braids away from her face and kissing her forehead. "I want you in the bath, Grace West. Since it's the only time I'll have you."

Her fists unclench and she nods.

"A bath sounds nice."

"I won't hurt you tonight," I tell her. "If you don't want my body, then you stop me."

My cock protests, but the tiniest sliver of reason in my head tells me that I can't really force her. I want her... but I want her to want me back. I want her dripping and screaming for me before I enter her.

"If I do that," she whispers, as I hold her hips and keep her sweet body close. "You'll kill me."

"I've never killed a woman and I've never killed a child. I would never hurt you, Grace. Never. And I promise you, I will kill any man who hurts you. Any person. I promise."

Goosebumps break out over her arms and body. I want her close. I lean forward and kiss her again. She sucks on the part of my lip that she split again until we pull away.

"How can I believe you?" she whispers. "You lied. For days. You tricked me into marrying you."

"How could I tell you the truth about a man you love?"

"Stop," she says. "That just makes it so much worse that I'm kissing you and letting you..."

"A bath, tesoro. All I want with you is a bath."

"Is there a bath in the world that can hold your gigantic ass?"

I chuckle.

"Haven't you seen my place? Trust me, the master bathroom can hold both of us. Now come."

I find her reluctance naturally beautiful. That hesitant quiver of her lower lip gets me instantly hard. She's no fool, she's not like Zara, but she's not as brazen as Jodi about displaying her wit with various quips.

Grace is something entirely different and if I didn't know better, I would say she has a secret of her own, something that not even Uksan knew. Something she won't tell me. She moves like a woman with a secret — slow, sensual and highly arousing. I enjoy the mystery of her. Women like her only come to Italy for a reason.

Grace follows me into my bedroom, although she hesitates at the door, taking in the luxurious space. I have a cleaner and even if I didn't, I grew up obsessive and meticulous, polishing my childhood bedroom until papa swore he would spank me if I didn't stop cleaning like a slave. I live a dirty life. I like a clean fucking house.

"You will sleep here tonight," I tell her in a commanding voice, half-expecting her to argue. But what sane American tourist would argue against a California King? She doesn't argue, but she doesn't respond affirmatively either.

Grace gingerly enters my bedroom, and I slip my hand into hers and guide her to the French double doors of my bathroom. When I open the bathroom doors, Grace can't contain her response.

"Holy shit."

"Like it?"

"You didn't mention this place was huge."

"I enjoy baths."

"Is that why you needed a chandelier?"

"I enjoy chandeliers too. And wine." And women.

Grace steps forward with a gleaming, excited face. "This place is gorgeous, Mr. — Enzo. Seriously."

I place my hand gently on her lower back and guide her forward onto the black-and-white checkered tiles. She braces herself against my hand, as if reluctant to have me touch her.

That reluctance won't last long. I walk over to the giant tub, hewn out of marble with a large silver spigot arching over the basin.

"Bubbles?" I ask her.

Grace, forgetting for a moment that we'll both have to strip to nothing to enter this tub, nods excitedly.

"Would you believe I've never had a bath? Well, not since I was a little kid bathing in the sink."

"Really?"

"Really. Rent's crazy in America. I only had places with showers and some of those barely worked."

I soak up every tidbit I can about her past, and every sound of her dreamy voice and pretty little accent.

"Tonight, you have a bath."

I start the water and empty a healthy dose of sandalwood essential oils and bubbles into the bottom of the tub as it fills. Grace approaches the edge of the tub with me and peers in, closing her eyes and inhaling deeply.

"That smells incredible," she whispers.

I come up behind her and wrap my arms around her waist, allowing her to enjoy the scent while I enjoy the warmth of her body pressed against mine. If she still feels guilty about Uksan and if she still feels the horror of what happened, Grace exhibits no signs. Perhaps I'm close to having her. Just maybe. I rest my body against hers, indulging in the fresh scent of her warm brown skin and the curve of her ass resting just below my crotch. (She's not quite tall enough to press directly against it.)

My cock stiffens against her lower back, revealing my arousal to her against my will. I expect her to run away, but she just keeps making a sound of deep satisfaction and sniffing the essential oils from the tub. I lean forward, pulling the hair away from her ears and whisper into her left ear, fighting every temptation to nibble on Grace's delicious ear lobe.

"We have to get naked to enjoy the tub."

Her body shudders and her response surprises me. "You first, Enzo. You get naked first."

See? Smart. She wants me to be vulnerable. She wants to see my body before I have the pleasure of discovering hers. Grace West. She really is a treasure. I move away from her and she turns around, leaning against the edge of the marble tub to face me. The water pours into the tub behind her at a soothing pace. I have absolutely no hesitation around nudity.

Americans are the ones who are tense about it. Europeans don't give a flying fuck about getting naked and getting naked for this woman? Fuck, it's a miracle I don't already have my clothes off.

I start with my shoes, slipping off the soft black Gucci loafers and then my wool dress socks. Hardly the most exciting place to start, but Grace stares with anticipation, terror and something else. Curiosity? For all her guilt, for all her strangeness, it's clear that she feels attraction for me, something biological that defies her sense of reason and propriety. That will get worse, Tesoro, once you see my body.

Next, my shirt. White, silk, always freshly pressed and usually a custom Gucci to fit my lean, muscular frame. I work the buttons open quickly, allowing my brown hair to fall out of its knot and cascade to my shoulders as I work. Grace bites on her lower lip so hard it turns purple as I slide my shirt off and reveal my white undershirt beneath it and toned, tattooed arms.

Grace stops biting her lip and wipes away at it. Blood. She bit down so hard she drew blood. I smirk and keep stripping my shirt off, easing my tank top out of its tuck in my trousers and then sliding it over my head.

"Jesus Christ," Grace whispers. "You cannot be real."

"Like what you see?"

"Shut up."

Finally, some spunk from her. I know her boyfriend died, I

know I tricked her, I know she hates my guts, but we're married now, right? There's no reason for her shyness.

"I work hard, tesoro."

"What does that mean?"

"My treasure. If you weren't dating an Albanian, perhaps you would have learned some Italian."

"Vaffanculo," she shoots back.

"Hilarious."

Grace smirks and shrugs. "Pants off, Enzo."

I don't hesitate to work my Gucci belt off and then my trousers, dropping them to the ground so all that's left between us is my tight boxer briefs, both pure white and fastidiously clean.

"Enzo..." she whispers. "Are you serious?"

"About what?"

I step out of my trousers, enjoying the way she ogles my body. Guilt? What guilt? She's a woman, an animal just like I am, and while women are oh so coy and beautiful, they often cannot hide their animal instincts towards an attractive, healthy man more than we can hide our attraction to them.

"You have... I mean... You look... I mean... Your dick..."

"What about my cock?"

She flinches as I say the word cock.

"Nothing. I shouldn't look."

She turns around, staring back into the tub. It's nearly full. It takes everything in my power not to push her against the tub and fuck her against it before dragging her inside. Fuck, I need to control myself around her, but Grace makes it so damned hard, even with her clothes on.

"Look at me," I command her.

"No. Enzo. Look. I'm sorry, but I can't do this. I just... I can't..."

"Is it Uksan?"

She whips around, her beautiful face marked with fury.

"Yes, you asshole," she yells. "You killed my boyfriend and now you're naked and you look... you look... I just can't!"

"Why not?"

"You killed him."

"So what? He's not the first man I've killed."

"Is that supposed to impress me? Is that supposed to improve this situation at all?"

"No. It's just the truth, Grace. Now look at me."

"No," she insists. "I can't."

"Guilt?"

"Yes."

I drop to my knees slowly. My cock remains stiff, unable to respond to Grace's whirlwind of emotions with anything but pure arousal. She hasn't taken off a single article of clothing, but my attraction to her mounts just from her closeness, just from her smell. She drives me wild in a way I can't control. I killed for her before I even knew her. What other woman can say she's had that effect on me?

"Turn around, Grace."

"You're not listening," she says, leaning over the tub and turning the water off. "I can't."

"Just look. Please. Don't make me beg."

She turns around again, ready to yell at me before she notices me on my knees, pleading with her, begging with her, demonstrating my willingness to submit just enough that she knows I won't hurt her.

"Why are you on your knees?" She says.

"To show you that I won't hurt you. To show you that tonight... I just want to get to know you."

"By fucking me in your fancy ass tub?" Grace shoots back.

"No. By eating your cunt until you scream."

"Enzo!"

See? Americans are naturally very conservative about sex and beautiful Grace...

"Did Uksan eat your cunt?"

"That is none of your business," she says with such a stiff, revealing voice that I know the answer before she says it. Albanian bastard… If I had that woman in my bed, I would eat her cunt every day before breakfast passionately, obsessively and until she came buckets in my mouth.

"Okay," I tell her. "Don't tell me. Just lift your dress."

"Enzo…"

I drag my knees painfully across the tiles to trap her between my body and the tub. Grace leans back, her ass pressed over the side of the tub. She can't escape without falling in and she won't let herself fall in with those heels or with that gorgeous dress hugging her curves. I know she won't. I touch her thighs and her nostrils flare. Fuck, I wish she would hit me and take that rage out. Feel that sadness. Feel that fury. I don't want her to deny me. I gaze up at her, giving her the grey eyes that make most Italian women swoon and seem to fill Grace with unending fury.

"Let me eat your pussy," I whisper. "If you don't cum… you can drown me."

She rolls her eyes. "Cocky bastard."

"Not cocky," I whisper, running my hands over her thighs through the dress and enjoying the fact that although she's dangerously reluctant, she's allowing me to touch her through her clothes. My beautiful treasure is worth the easy pace.

"You are cocky," she insists. "I'm thirty years old, Enzo and no man has made me cum yet."

I nearly keel over and die on my bathroom floor. What the hell is this woman talking about? First, I learn that she's older than me, which isn't a problem. Next, she says the most absurd thing I've ever heard in my life.

"Are you a liar, Grace?"

"Excuse me?"

Her thighs tense between my touch and I know I've made a mistake in what I've said to her. Fuck's sake.

"You are thirty years old. Surely you've had an orgasm before."

"Have you ever heard of the dang orgasm gap?" She says uncomfortably. "And I don't need a lecture on orgasms from a man who—

"Did the world a favor by killing someone incapable of making a woman cum?"

Then she slaps me. Finally. It's a hard, brutal slap that stings and feels like it nearly snaps my neck in half. But I'm not angry. Grace's release of emotions brings a smile to my face along with the stinging on my cheek. Good fucking girl, let it all out.

"You are a bastard," she hisses.

"It was a joke."

"Life isn't a joke to me," she says. "It's not."

I kiss the top of her thighs. "Okay."

"Why do you want me?" She says. "Is it because you killed him? Do you just want something that belonged to the man you killed?"

She exposes herself here—so little faith in men. I suppose I haven't given her a reason for faith in me yet.

"No," I tell her, looking up at her again. "I want you because the moment I saw you from my apartment balcony walking home with groceries on your hip, I thought you were the loveliest fucking thing in the world and I knew I would kill for you, do anything it took, just to be close to you. And you know, tesoro, that I am not lying."

Her lower lip quivers and her eyes nearly fill to the brim with tears. "Why do you have to say such pretty words when I know you're a monster?"

"Maybe I'm a complicated monster."

"I doubt that."

I run my hands up to her hips and clasp them.

"Lift your dress," I whisper. "Let me apologize with my tongue."

"You do it," she commands. "I... I still can't..."

I don't need more permission. I slowly ease her dress over her hips, exposing her thick thighs and voluptuous curves and then the sexiest panties I've ever seen squeezed between her gorgeous pussy lips and hanging tightly to her hips. Fuck, she makes me want to cum on sight.

She holds her dress once I hike it up and I grab the underwear on her hips, my breathing quick and uncontrolled as I slide her panties down over these sexy fucking hips. When I see her pussy for the first time, I mutter a single English word. My favorite English word.

"Fuck..."

"Is there a problem?" She asks, almost hopefully. She won't get so lucky. I shake my head and run my fingers through the thick thatch of grown out hair covering her mound.

"No," I murmur. "I like your hair. It smells delicious. Your pussy smells delicious."

She swallows loudly.

"Men don't... I mean... I've never been with a guy who..."

"Do you like it?" I interrupt her nervous stammering.

"Like what?"

"Like your pussy eaten."

"I'm trying to tell you," she gasps as I spread her lower lips apart. "Men don't do that."

I seriously have no regrets about murdering her fucking Albanian boyfriend who never made her cum and doesn't eat pussy. What kind of man can live like that, eh? It's not right.

I run my tongue over her exposed nub. Her brown lower lips cover a fleshy pink center and it takes everything in my power not to tip her into the tub and have her right there. The water's still scorching hot, waiting for our bodies as we wait for it to cool. I can't wait to get her in there, but first... Grace will have her first orgasm.

She whimpers as I run my tongue over her clit.

"Real men eat pussy," I whisper.

"Real men?"

Americans. They're always so politically correct.

"Yes. Real men eat pussy. They lick it, they suck it, they put their tongue all the way inside it. Now hush..."

I kiss her thighs to relax her and then slide my tongue between her lips again, rubbing her clit as she whimpers louder. I can feel her body growing tense as she desperately tries to stop herself from losing control. I run my tongue over her clit in slow circles, easing her tension and causing her body to unravel against her will. As my tongue works her clit, I stroke her lower lips with my fingers, enjoying her furry cunt and then pushing one of my fingers against her entrance.

I know she's tight. I know she's slick. I just want to fucking lose myself in her. I wrap my lips around her clit and suck on her a little as my fingers tease around her entrance. She shows signs that she won't always keep such tight control and that despite her best efforts, she simply can't.

"Enzo..." she whimpers. "I feel... I feel..."

Grace squeezes her thighs together, trapping my face between her gorgeous brown legs. She tastes like honey and sex and everything fucking delicious about eating pussy. My finger enters her a little as I keep sucking on her clit. She edges her hips off the tub and pushes them against my face. Yes. This is what I want. I want her close. I want her lusting for it. I want her to climax all over me and I want her to let me lick her juices off those gorgeous, irresistible thighs.

I ease the rest of my finger inside her and Grace unleashes a moan that even takes her by surprise. She clasps her hand to her mouth.

"Oh my God," she gasps. "Enzo..."

"Cum," I murmur, smacking my lips between licks of her sweet pussy. "Cum for me..."

I use my finger to massage her inner walls and keep my lips firmly wrapped around her clit as I suck with gentle pressure until her moans get louder and louder. I know what will push her over the edge. I slide a second finger inside her and lick faster around her clit until Grace cries out and releases. She moans loudly and juices trickle eagerly from her pussy as her body throbs in my grasp.

She cums hard all over my face, giving me a healthy serving of her pussy juices to lick up from her thighs. She trembles and throws her head back involuntarily as I work my fingers inside her, strengthening her orgasm as I remove my lips from her clit and move my efforts to cleaning the juices off her inner thighs.

Dribbles of her creamy juices pour out of her and as I lick her thighs, she whimpers and moans. I don't want to remove my fingers from her cunt. She's tight. Insanely tight. She'll struggle to take my cock, even if I work her with my fingers. How can she have such a tight pussy between such voluptuous thighs?

I push my fingers deeper and she pleads with me. "Enzo... I can't... it feels..."

It feels like a fucking orgasm and she enjoys the hell out of it. As Grace moans, I lick her outer lips slowly, burying my nose in her pubic hair as I enjoy her scent and crave even more of her. My fingers push her to the edge of another orgasm and she releases her grip on her dress, losing herself in a deliciously sweet climax as I tease her perfect pussy.

I have this promise to stay with her for a year, to be her protector until I can ensure her safety, but I never plan on allowing Grace Doukas to leave my sight. I want her forever. She's mine... finally. I run my tongue over her lips again as the silk dress covers me and then kiss my way down her thighs, removing my head from beneath her dress and gazing up at her from my position on my knees.

"Enzo... that was..."

Fucking amazing? Beyond incredible? The best first orgasm a woman could hope for? I'm not cocky. I just know exactly what my tongue and hands can do to a woman.

Grace shudders as I release her dress and lick her juices off my lips.

"Finish your sentence, signora."

She bites down on her lower lip again. Fuck, I love that sexy as fuck nervous little habit. Everything about her drives me completely wild. This woman turns me into an animal, and I can't help but love it.

"That was... my first orgasm..."

She sighs the words in a romantic tone that I know she's desperately trying to suppress. It brings me deep satisfaction to know that Albanian fuck never pleasured her like this, that I might not be her first man, but I am the first man to show appreciation to her folds and the way her body works enough to bring her to an orgasm. Women are so fucking beautiful when they cum and this one is special. She beams with an almost visible glow and my hands can't get enough of touching her silky smooth skin.

"Please," she whispers. "Can I just... Can we take things slow?"

"You want me to lick your pussy again?"

Her teeth sink deeper into that full lower lip. She's tempted. I lick her again, and she can postpone the inevitable consummation of our relationship. If I don't... she has to do it — fuck the man who killed her boyfriend in cold blood, with no remorse, just so he could have her. The thought turns me on, but Grace West... she's far too innocent for that. That's why I want her. That's why I find myself so dangerously attracted to a woman that I should have avoided. She's foreign, too naïve to know the depth of depravity so common on the Amalfi Coast. She doesn't belong in my world and fuck, I like that.

Killing doesn't always bring me joy. I'm not like my brother. I get nightmares. Shakes. I need cigarettes to cope. I want a woman who knows nothing of my world to cradle my head in her lap. To be my peace. To save my fucked up soul from falling too far, too fast. Maybe I've already fallen too far. Maybe that's what Grace realizes.

She shakes her head. No, she doesn't want my tongue between her legs. She slips the left strap of her silk dress over her shoulder and allows it to fall away from her brown skin. Her skin color gets me hard. It's a perfect, deep brown — lighter than Zara's, darker than Jodi's, a pretty shade of brown that compares to nothing. I don't see women like her often, but when I do... desire burns through my blood.

I fix her beneath an intense gray stare as she slips the other strap off her shoulder and allows it to fall away. Easy, Tesoro. You don't know what the fuck this does to me. She has to slide the dress over her breasts. Her figure's too full for the dress to fall away. It suddenly becomes my gospel that Italian women are far too thin, far too lacking in curves in all the right places and that this gorgeous black woman does something for me that no Italian woman ever could.

She doesn't just get me hard. She makes my cock feel like it's going to break off just from watching her undress. A black strapless bra holds her voluptuous chest up underneath the dress and as the dress slides down to her hips, my lust for her naked body heightens immensely. Fuck, I want her.

"Take the rest off," I command her, struggling to conceal my impatience. She drops her gaze away from mine and moves her hips in a slight but immensely sensual manner to remove that sexy silk dress. The dress falls to her feet, revealing her bare, just-licked pussy. A mixture of my spit and her juices splatter between her thighs, which she squeezes together in a last-minute attempt to preserve some dignity from the murderer kneeling before her. I kill, but that doesn't mean I cannot love. That doesn't mean my heart is always cold, or that there's no warmth coursing through my veins.

She can only trust me on my knees, but soon I want her to trust me completely and give herself to me — not just her body, but her softly beating heart.

"You're beautiful, Grace."

"Stop," she whispers. "When you say stuff like that, you only make it worse."

"I only say what I mean."

Her gaze snaps fiercely to mine. "You're Italian. European men… Italian men…"

I kiss the top of her mound and she loses whatever fanciful words she planned to say.

"You are hot," I tell her. "Hot. Beautiful. Sexy. Cute. Every fucking English word I know for a woman. It's you."

She grabs my cheeks forcefully. Her swift movement and the aggression as she holds me surprises me, but I allow her that bit of control, the control she clearly needs to feel safe with me, to feel like I won't kill her.

"Look me in the eye and promise me you won't hurt me," she says. "Please."

We're both naked, both utterly vulnerable before each other. She knows how to get a man's honesty.

"I will die before I hurt you, Grace. Now… will you give me permission to get off my knees?"

She releases my cheeks and nods. Then she turns away from me, giving me a cock-wrenching view of her ass. Every curse word in my language floods through my mind. How the hell does this woman have an ass like that? It's thick, voluptuous, with a round shape like two watermelons pressed together. I want to bury my face in it. I want to stick my cock in it. I want to get on my knees and thrust my tongue deep inside it.

But I finally have Grace's permission to rise, so I take it before my delicious obsession changes her mind about having her killer husband take her in the bath. She leans over the marble tub and runs her hand through the water and the bubbles.

"It's warm," she whispers. "But not too hot."

"Climb in," I murmur as I rise to my feet and position

myself behind her, employing little effort to conceal my erection from her. I want this woman to know just how hard she makes me.

"I can't just climb in," she says, eyeing the edge of the tub suspiciously, like I'm asking her to launch herself in. She's so much smaller than me...

I grab the little stool and set it up for her.

"Now you can."

Grace steps up and then dips a toe into the bath, finding her footing on the step into the marble tub. I hold her hand as she slides her body into the tub, more gracefully than I imagine any other woman would. She stands in the water and then removes her bra at the last second, tossing it over the edge and quickly lowering herself into the water. That momentary glimpse of her breasts drives me absolutely wild. Her nipples. Her nipples differ from any I've ever seen and I want to touch them. Lick them. Suck on them. My patience wears thin. She sighs and visibly relaxes in the bath. Women become utterly weak in the face of essential oils and bubble baths.

She leans her head back so her head balances on the edge of the tub and I step on the stool, shedding my boxer briefs before entering the tub. She gasps once I do that. Her initial impression of my cock still didn't do the reality of the situation justice. I have to tuck into my trousers somehow, no? My dick unravels, almost like a snake, and her eyes spark open with delight and obvious desire. She may feel guilty. She may hide how she feels. But fuck, she feels something when she sees my naked body, covered in tattoos and she can't hide it despite her very human, very innocent sense of guilt.

"Your dick is way too big," she says. I grin.

"That's a first."

"No way, that's a first."

"You're right," I admit, stepping one foot into the tub I

barely use. "It's not. Most women run away screaming at this point."

"Is it... real?"

"Do men have fake cocks in America?"

"No. I mean... I don't know. But... it has to be... I mean... It's like twelve inches long."

"Yes," I tell her. "I've got a freak dick."

I sink my body into the tub and Grace quickly crosses to the other end. We play this game, then? She swims away. I chase her. Don't worry, signora. I enjoy games.

I allow her to keep her distance. For now. I imagine the warm water cleaning her thighs, soaking into her, making her warm and wet for me. I submerge my head in the water to get my hair wet and then emerge to find Grace staring with wide eyes, like prey. But I'm not her predator. I hunted her man and now I want peace with my reward — the woman I stole from him.

"We don't have to fuck right away," I tell her.

"How thoughtful."

Sarcasm. I learned that from Jodi quickly. Italians don't enjoy sarcasm with the utter delight that Americans do.

"I want to know you."

Honesty always works in any negotiation. You simply need to present honesty that you can use to your advantage.

"Most men don't kill a woman's boyfriend to get to know her."

"I'm not most men. I'm a Doukas."

She meets my wink with an eye roll.

"You're cocky."

"Yes."

There's no point in denying the truth.

"Where are you from?" I press her.

"The United States of America."

"Big fucking country."

"Yeah," Grace says. "And I'm never going back. At least... I don't want to."

She may not want to return to America, but our plan only included marriage for a single year. Grace will have to maneuver differently if she truly wishes to avoid returning to her home country.

"Why not?"

"Because I'm from Mississippi and no matter how far I run, I can't seem to escape everything that happened there."

"Is that near New York?"

She snickers and then laughs. "Are you serious?"

I shrug. I know it's a big country, but she can't expect me to know all forty states or however many there are.

"No," she says, realizing that I am indeed serious. "It's very far from New York. Trust me. My mama ran out of New York when she owed her dealer too much money to pay back. She brought me and my siblings to Mississippi and... that's just the beginning."

"It's a long story?"

"Too long."

"I have time. Wine?"

She shakes her head. "I don't drink."

I lean out of my tub. Rule #1 of being an Italian man — keep wine within arm's reach. I would keep cigarettes within arm's reach too, but there's the whole trying to quit thing making that so much more complicated. But at least there's wine. Since I don't have to share, there's no point in getting glasses. I pop the cork and drink straight from the bottle.

"Tell me the story of your life, Grace Doukas... and perhaps you'll make it out of this tub without feeling my cock in your ass."

Chapter 6

Pleasure From A Monster's Tongue

Grace

I think he's joking about the cock in my ass thing, considering the smile on his face and the way he tips that wine bottle into his mouth. He drinks almost ¼ of the bottle in one smooth gulp without pausing for the slightest breath. He smokes. He's a killer. He's a damn drunk. Could my taste in men get any worse?

Enzo doesn't want to know the story of my life, anyway. He's a rich Italian man who solves all his problems by showing his enemies the wrong end of his gun. I have to be careful with Enzo Doukas, even if he's the type of guy who makes you feel anything but careful. It doesn't matter that he's insanely handsome, he's also fucking crazy. He has to be. The look in his eye when he told me he killed Uksan scared the crap out of me, but he still has me here, completely naked in his bathtub.

He still gave me my first orgasm, and now he wants me to tell him about my life. Does he really want to know about Grace West's life? Tisha, my uncle's kid, my best friend growing up, doesn't know the first thing about my life because nobody up north does.

My mama pissed everyone off when she stole my uncle's car, sold the old BMW for a bag of crack, shoved me in the back of some guy's SUV with my brother and sister, and took us all the way down to Mississippi to live in some trailer park where the rest of the fucked up shit I want to ignore happened.

I can't tell Lorenzo what I've been through. How the hell would he look at me if he knew? He already knows too much about me and he's already been too deep inside me for me to lie to him. He can spot liars, I know that much, and it's probably because he's a damned good one. Before his confession, I never would have guessed what he did. My tongue dries in my mouth every time I remember. Enzo killed Uksan.

Enzo's gray eyes penetrate my reluctance. He won't say a word until I talk and damn, he might finish that bottle of wine before I get even one word of my story out.

"Talk," he says calmly. "I need to know my wife."

The smell of red wine fills the room along with all the other delicious sensual smells and this feels like the perfect place to get shit off my chest, even if it isn't. He sets the bottle of wine down and stares. I'd better talk before Enzo gets ideas about what he can do to me with that dick of his. Hmph. Dick. That enormous monster ain't a dick at all — that thing's a damned water snake. It's a fucking anaconda. I need to hold him off as long as possible.

I'll be honest — I don't know if I can handle a dick like that. I bite my lip, stop thinking about Enzo's dick, and try to tell him bits and pieces of my story.

"My mom did drugs. We moved around a lot. Left New York with us when we were kids, took us down to Mississippi and I never saw my family up there again."

Enzo swirls the wine bottle around and gives me a curious look. Family. If he's in the mob, family's important to him. I can't let that justify the fact that he's a killer, but I can't ignore it either.

"Us? Do you have siblings?" He questions.

"Yeah," I respond softly, hating to think about either of

them. “I do.”

“Brothers? Sisters?”

His accent drives me wild. There’s something about the way r’s sound on the Italian tongue that gets me dripping wet. I won’t lie, I love a man with an accent. That was one of the few things I loved down there — those country as hell accents that made you feel like everywhere was home. I don’t have a home. I don’t think I ever did.

I can manage telling Enzo about my siblings. Nothing to hide there.

“I’ve got one brother. One sister. My sister’s dead.”

I hate saying that out loud. I hate admitting it to myself. It’s been years — almost three years exactly — and I’m still pretending that I didn’t lose my best friend, the only person in the world who made Mississippi worth it. The great irony was that I lost her in New York — that’s where she died and where she was buried, in the home we should have had.

“What about your brother?” Enzo asks, getting closer to secrets I don’t want exposed.

“He… We don’t get along.”

Lorenzo smirks. “I don’t get along with all my brothers either.”

My relationship with my brother David is worse than normal brother sister shit. Each of us took our childhood differently. I started running away from my mama’s bullshit as soon as I could and never stopped.

My sister followed in my mother’s footsteps, trading her body for shards of meth and crack rocks from the time she was fourteen years old. And David… My skin crawls just thinking about him.

“I don’t get along with David because he pimped me out. When we got to that trailer park in Mississippi, we needed money because of my mom and… men did things to me. Lots of men.”

He was much older, and he knew better, but my brother

was caught up in shit beyond him and I don't think he ever saw me as a person. I was just little Grace — the annoying, messy, whiny baby of the family and the way he saw it, I ought to contribute to keeping logs in the fire and food on the table. I was just a kid, but that didn't matter to him. It didn't matter to any of the men he brought me to. I don't know why I bother telling Enzo this. He's a murderer. I doubt he'll give a crap considering his moral compass is all screwed up.

Lorenzo sets down his wine. His cheeks are flushed from either the warm water, the red wine or the visible rage on his face, pinching his thick Italian brows together.

"Fuck men who sell women."

"Doesn't the mob do that? Isn't that why you're having that turf war?"

"Not in Italy," Lorenzo says firmly, his voice nearly quaking with disgust. "We're Catholic. Religious men underneath the gold and the guns. We might be sick in the head, but... we don't sell women. We believe in family. You don't sell your family."

My heart wants to break, but to be honest, certain parts of who I was had to die. I think about those men and David and all that shit in the past and sometimes, it just feels like something that happened to someone else. What I'm running from now is even worse than what I ran from in the past. So far, not a word out of my dang mouth has scared him off. I don't know what to think about all that.

Another man would think I was just broken.

"So y'all don't pimp? I've never met gangsters that don't pimp."

"We aren't gangsters," Enzo says, concealing a smirk. "This is just cosa nostra. It's how we survive."

I want to believe him, but I still don't know if I can believe a word out of Enzo's mouth. He still killed Uksan, and he seems to think his good cause justifies that. He was so calm that day as he watched me wail over Uksan's stiff corpse. He betrayed no signs that he had been the one to put a bullet in my boyfriend's head. He doesn't seem to feel an ounce of guilt or remorse. If he did, he must've hid in that damn bottle of wine.

That man can keep a fucking secret, that's for sure. Maybe that's why I don't mind telling him mine. I hate that these aren't my only secrets any more. I hate that my life has become so much more fucked up than it was in that trailer park.

"When did it start?" Enzo says. "When did your brother hurt you?"

I bite my lower lip nervously.

"What matters is that it stopped."

"Not to me," Enzo says. "Is your brother still alive?"

I nod slowly, although I regret doing it as soon as I nod. I don't know what this crazy ass man could do with information about my family. I throw him off the trail of personal inquiries by telling him my story. It's so long ago that sometimes I can pretend it happened to someone else—at least when I'm not having nightmares.

"I was only twelve when it started," I continue. "I didn't know what was happening exactly. I didn't understand what he wanted from me or why men would want to hurt me. But they did. For a long, long time. I got out of it, though. I don't do that shit anymore."

"Is that why you're here? To escape your past?"

I can answer him honestly without telling the truth and something tells me it's a mistake to lie to this man, but I can't help it. I'm too scared to tell him the truth, either. I was too scared to tell Uksan.

"Partly to escape my past.."

I'm in Italy to escape a lot of shit. But I don't want Lorenzo to think I'm a fuckup. I don't want him to see me as some poor ass trailer park child prostitute. I'm more than that. I clawed my way out of hell to be more than that. I did shit I'm not proud of, but I did shit that I'm proud of, too.

"I'm not just a sad story," I tell him. "I got out of the trailer park when I was twenty. I went to college."

I dragged my sister to New York and tried to get her clean. Nothing could keep that girl away from crack. Not me, not jail, not rehab, not anybody.

"I've never been to college," Lorenzo says calmly. "So there you go. More educated than me."

He smiles warmly and for the first time since I've been with him, I feel something inside me. It's not just his feelings for me, which he's never hidden. I feel something besides guilt over Uksan. I feel something besides shame. He doesn't judge me. He doesn't loathe me for my past and he doesn't treat me like I'm delicate and incapable, either. It's nice to be appreciated, you know?

He asked me what I studied, and I have to spend five minutes explaining "Africana Studies" to an Italian man who doesn't know America has fifty states. I got a scholarship and I should have gone all the way for my PhD. I had to run before I became Dr. West. That part of my life is over now.

"What happened after college?" Lorenzo asks. "Did you ever go back to your family?"

"No," I tell him. "I don't have a home. I have people I grew up with, people I still love, but I can't ever go back there. My mom still lives with David, in and out of rehab, but life will never be the same without Amara."

"Your sister?"

"Yeah," I whisper, gazing down into the bubbles. I want to sink into them. I want to disappear beneath the water and forget every fucking thing that happened in Mississippi. The years of drug abuse in my house, the filth everywhere, the damned roaches. I worked my ass off thinking I could escape and in the end, I had to run away from everything I built and accept the truth — women like me who grow up mired deep in shit can't really ever get out. Our lives are like a black hole.

You might think you're escaping, but the gravitational pull of fucked up poverty will always pull you back in.

"But you're here now. Safe. In Italy."

"Broke in Italy," I tell him. "And married to a killer."

Lorenzo grins. "I'm not as bad as all that, am I?"

"You killed Uksan and you don't seem sorry about it."

Enzo shrugs and keeps going to town on that wine of his. How the hell can one man suck back so much damned wine?

"He's not the only man I've killed."

If I can keep him talking, I can keep him away from what he wants — sex. I know enough about men to know when they want it, and Enzo wants me badly. I don't even know why.

I want to keep away from him, but I can't keep him from moving across the tub, paddling so he's facing me in the gigantic, luxurious marble tub. Our lips are so close that I can smell his breath — mint tinged with red wine. I hate that I want to kiss him just for being a good listener, just for not treating me any differently because he knows some bullshit about my past.

"How many men have you killed?" I breathe, terrified of the answer and terrified that he'll kiss me and make the answer irrelevant.

"I lost count."

His answer is so much worse than I thought. How can he have killed so many times? If I didn't know he was a killer, I wouldn't have guessed. He looks more like a model from a slick Gucci commercial set on a yacht.

"Did you want to be a killer when you grew up?"

Lorenzo laughs as if I told a Dave Chappelle level joke. I wasn't joking at all. I want to know the truth about this man. I have to know the truth about him, even if it isn't safe for either of us for me to tell him the truth about me.

"I didn't choose who I became," He says. "My father is... I am loyal to my family. I grew up to be who they raised me to be."

And I broke away from my circumstances. We couldn't be more different, but I don't feel the desire to walk away from him the way I did before. I don't feel the desire to run.

"Your own father raised you to be a killer?"

I know I shouldn't sound so judgmental. Who the hell am I to pass judgment? My mama "raised" me to be a drug addict and a prostitute. It took me a long time to admit to myself that she knew what my brother was doing.

"He raised me to protect my country, my people, and my family. Before our families took over the coasts and cities, we were only peasants, stuck under the rule of fucked up politicians, Jews and police and anyone who wanted to fuck us out of our land and heritage."

Enzo makes it sound so noble. But it's all murder in the end, isn't it? I can't let him convince me this shit is right. I don't believe it. Men kill or whatever the hell they do for one reason only: because they want to.

"Is that why you killed Uksan? He threatened your heritage?"

"I killed Uksan because his family sells children for sex. I saw their auctions with my own eyes and I still lose sleep over what I saw."

My chest catches. I don't want to believe that I ran halfway across the world and into the arms of someone who could hurt a kid and do to someone else what someone did to me . After all that I've been through, maybe I am so damn broken that I can't tell a good guy from a bad guy.

I sense that he's telling me half of the truth, but maybe half of the truth is good enough sometimes. Everyone has secrets, right? I've peeled away plenty of Enzo's secrets and there are probably more of them. I don't need to know any more about him.

"Why would they do something like that? If you're both mafia, why does your family oppose this and their family doesn't?"

"Money, Tesoro," he says calmly. "Surely you know that some people will do anything for money."

He's right, of course. Even before I met Enzo Doukas, I knew some people would do anything for money. I scoop bubbles and warm water onto my shoulder, enjoying the warmth from the bath and wanting so badly to sink my head beneath the water and just stay there. I can't fuck up my braids completely, though. I can't imagine finding a good stylist in Italy and it's going to take me forever to get my hair together if I mess it up.

Enzo swims over to me and leans his back against the tub, sitting next to me. I squirm a little, unable to stop myself from thinking about the giant water snake he has between his legs now that it's closer to me. My hands are beneath the water and if I reached over even a smidge, I could wrap my hands easily around his big, hard cock.

Enzo leans over now that he's close and whispers into my ear.

"Have you asked me all that you wish?" He murmurs. "I'm your husband. I will answer all your questions."

One year. Didn't he tell me this arrangement was only for a year? That's plenty of time for me to get what I need and plenty of time for him to get his. I know what he wants and that there's not much I can do to stop this train from hurtling towards me. He touches my lower lip with his thumb, sending a shiver of something through me. Not fear. Despite everything, my body refuses to react with fear towards Enzo.

"Why did you marry me?" I whisper, tilting my face away from him. He touches me. I feel guilty. It doesn't matter what he does. He pulls his arm away from my face gently.

"Because you're beautiful. Because I know what I did was fucked up and I want you safe. The easiest way to keep you safe is to keep you, tesoro."

His treasure. I've never been anyone's treasure. My life just ends up one situation after another.

"Do you really think the Albanians could come all the way here to kill me? I don't know a thing about Uksan's secrets."

My stomach tightens in a disturbed knot at the thought that this man I could have given everything to could have concealed such a secret from me. We slept together. Our passionate romance exploded with sex and hours in bed cuddling, talking about our lives and sharing secrets. I felt closer to Uksan than I thought I could get to a man. Now, in this tub with Enzo, I wonder if I've ever had a fucking clue what it means to care about someone, or get close to them.

"Yes," he says. "They could. But I won't let anyone hurt you. I promise."

"I've done an okay job protecting myself so far," I tell him. "Don't worry about me."

He doesn't know half the shit I've done to protect myself.

He chuckles. "You are fierce. I can tell. What's the English phrase? Still waters run deep?"

"Yeah," I tell him. "That's me."

He doesn't know how much truth there is in that one little statement. Still waters run deep as hell. Enzo reaches under the water and puts his hand on my thigh.

"I first wanted you for your beauty, Grace... But perhaps this year, we can get to know each other. I see you're more than a pretty face and a perfect ass."

There's that handsome grin again, cutting across his harsh masculine face and softening him considerably.

"Are you that lonely?"

I don't mean to blurt out something so blunt and aggressive. I know this man kills people and it would be in my best interests to keep him happy, so he doesn't fuck me up with one of his guns. Hell, he could probably kill me with his bare hands.

"Yes," Enzo answers without missing a beat. "I am very fucking lonely and beautiful Italian women are... not like you."

He kisses my shoulder. Those lips… I have to pretend I don't feel anything when he kisses me, but it's so fucking hard when I know what he can do with those lips and with that tongue. He's the only man I've ever met who's made love to me and he hasn't even used the part of him I fear the most — the giant weapon between his legs.

He's the biggest I've ever seen — a downright freak dick. My tongue dries in my mouth and I want to sink beneath the water as his kisses move from my shoulder to my neck.

"Easy," he whispers. "I promise, I'll be easy."

I whirl away from the edge of the tub and face Enzo, just hoping for a moment away from his kisses so I can breathe and think. Steam rises from the tub, nearly suffocating me. He grips my hand beneath the water, keeping me close.

"Are you afraid?"

I was. But how can I still fear a man who uses his tongue so expertly to please me?

"No," I whisper. "But you are… really damn big."

"Yes," he says. "Most women scream."

I hate the flash of jealousy that surges through me. Most women. I can't have been so stupid as to think I was really that special in Enzo Doukas' life. He might be lonely now, but he couldn't have always been lonely. He's rich. He's well known. He owns dozens of apartments. I haven't even gotten to his looks. He's gorgeous, with these pale grey eyes unlike anything I've ever seen.

"Come," he whispers, pulling me close to him and resting my hand against his cock. He's really fucking hard.

Before I can react to my hand around his cock, he kisses me. My grasp on his cock tightens and Enzo gives a satisfied grunt, taking his lower lip between his teeth.

"That feels good," he whispers. "Very good."

"It feels like I'm trying to wrap my hand around a Thermos."

Enzo chuckles. "Not quite that thick."

"Almost," I whisper as his free hand touches my hip and Enzo draws me to him. "It's almost that big."

I allow him to pull me close to him and move my hand along his shaft. Enzo's cheeks turn brilliantly red. I don't want to pull away from him anymore. I've started something that I can't stop and I don't even know if I want to stop it anymore. He's a handsome as fuck naked man, and he smells like man musk and hot sex. He spreads his legs wide and I keep a good hold of his enormous dick as I move between them. My breasts are close to his chest and my nipples are almost uncomfortably stiff. I press my free hand against Enzo's chest and move my hand down his shaft again.

He's so thick and so long... I seriously don't know if I can fit him inside me, but I can try, can't I? If he can deliver so much pleasure with his tongue, what could he possibly do to me with that giant love stick between his legs? My fingers spread over his chest. Enzo's heart pounds furiously. If I didn't know better, I'd say a part of him was nervous. He hasn't taken his eyes off me in an instant.

"Turn around and let me take you," he murmurs. "Your hand isn't enough."

I turn around, facing away from Enzo, and he pulls me against him, letting his big cock drag against his thigh. If the water's lost any of his warmth, my body pressed against Enzo's more than makes up for it. At least we still have bubbles. He massages one of my thighs with his hands and reaches in front of me to touch my mound. Enzo slides his finger through my pubes and then spreads my pussy open to touch my clit.

I'm still ridiculously fucking sensitive from his hands and tongue, teasing and touching me. I whimper and lean back against him, pressing my ass cheeks into Enzo. He grunts again, and he kisses my shoulder.

"You're wet," he murmurs, sliding his finger inside me. "But I will still be careful."

I push the guilt out of my mind and my body succumbs to

the pleasure of Enzo's touch and the fact that he seems very talented at pleasing a woman. I gasp and allow my body to respond to the intrusion between my legs.

He slips his finger away from my pussy and moves me forward slightly so he can line the head of his dick against my entrance. Now it really feels like a damn Thermos and Enzo hasn't moved a muscle yet to thrust inside me. My pussy resists his first attempt at thrusting. He grunts and moves forward. I feel a tightening between my legs, but nothing happens as he eases forward. Water sloshes between my legs and I lean forward to allow him easier access towards me. Nothing about getting that dick in me will be easy.

"Fuck, you're tight," he grunts.

A cavern would probably feel tight to a dick that big. I bite my lower lip and as Enzo thrusts forward again in another attempt to enter me, I push back, wanting him to succeed, wanting to feel that powerfully large cock between my legs, despite all common sense guiding me against it.

I push my hips back and Enzo squeezes me tightly, finally succeeding in getting the head of his cock between my legs. I scream. It's only the head, but I feel like I've been split in two. Enzo mutters some Italian curse word underneath his breath. More water sloshes between my legs as his warm, muscular body closes in around mine.

"I can't..." I whimper as Enzo slides another inch inside me. I feel like my thighs are going to explode and my core pulses.

He presses his lips to my shoulder. "You feel very good. Incredible."

"Please..."

Tears prickle at my eyes from the pressure between my legs. Enzo pushes another inch forward. Pain hasn't yet yielded to pleasure. I whimper and despite the pain between my legs, I push my hips backward. Slowly joining with him has this emotional wave to it beyond the pain. His hands never leave my thighs or my hips as he slowly eases into me. His lips touch my neck and then my shoulders. He whispers beautiful Italian things to me and I cry as he finally enters me with a final thrust.

"Don't cry," he whispers. "Your pussy feels very nice. Very fucking nice."

"It hurts," I murmur. "You can't move..."

"Patience, signora. Let me take good care of your cunt."

As I adjust to his size, his fingers move to the front of my mound again. Enzo massages slow circles around my pussy, concentrating my attention on the pleasure at my clit instead of the intense pressure between my thighs from his big cock spearing me powerfully. I move my hips back, allowing him to settle in deeper and he swears in Italian again, but his fingers never leave my clit.

After a few minutes of his easy massage, our breathing synchronizes and the pressure between my legs yields to intense pleasure. Enzo takes my flesh between his lips and sucks on me possessively as he massages my clit. I'm close. I'm so fucking close to another orgasm. I never thought I could have so many in one night, but Enzo's fingers tease me into a bliss.

When I get close, he moves slower and uses more of his fingers until I cum hard. He still hasn't moved his cock. It's a stiff, enormous weapon spearing my pussy as he makes me cum, but he holds patiently still until I have an orgasm around it. I feel the wetness and warmth gushing between my legs. Enzo grunts and leans forward, his hips driving into me in a slow, sensual rhythm.

"Fuck," he whispers. "You are perfect."

My first orgasm with Enzo's cock inside me numbs my pain enough to enjoy the initial movements from his hips. Where I thought there would only be pain, there's euphoria and a thick movement in my pussy that feels like it's traveling up to my gut. I cry out loudly and Enzo grunts along with my moans. He's so much different from what I expected. Tender. Easy. Fantastic at sex.

His thumb massages my clit slowly as he thrusts into me from behind, his giant cock moving with greater and greater ease as I adjust to his immensity. I bite down on my lower lip to keep from cumming again too soon, but I can't hold back the wave of intense pleasure and I have no choice but to let it wash over me. As I climax again, I throw my head back so it rests on Enzo's shoulders. He calls my name and begs me to cum again, his fingers working magic between my legs as his dick takes me deep and slow.

He's a killer, but I don't think he's capable of anything other than making slow, sweet love.

I cum again and again. He shows no signs of his stamina abating. The bubbles disappear before he removes his cock from between my legs. Several orgasms later and he still isn't finished.

He turns me around so I face him and he leans his back against the side of the tub.

"I want to look in your eyes as you ride me," he whispers, his tongue darting over his surprisingly full white boy lips. "Come."

I spread my legs around his thighs and allow him to pull my body over his. My pussy aches for his dick. It's huge, but addictive. I don't think it will be possible for me to go back to a normal man after the insane orgasms Enzo's gigantic dick delivers. It's not just that dick. It's his tongue. It's his lips. It's his fingers. Every part of his body brings me unabashed pleasure, and I can't get enough of him. I don't know if I want to get enough of him.

He takes several minutes to slowly work his cock into me as I'm facing him, never removing his fingers from my clit. I cum several times before he gets inside me and then I brace my forearms on Enzo's broad, built shoulders. There's nothing like being with a man that big. He's tall, large, and with his muscles, he looks like he was carved out of a hunk of marble. I lean forward and as our lips connect, Enzo pulls me against him. My breasts tease his chest as I rock forward. My hips move as much as I can muster while impaled on his cock and finally as we kiss and as I move my hips, Enzo comes close to a climax.

I feel the big monster tensing between my legs and then his body follows, with every large muscle tensing, his face turning a brilliant shade of red and then a monstrous animalistic grunt of pleasure as his cock spills inside me. I moan loudly, unable to comprehend the force of his cock bursting between my legs. The gush of warm liquid coats my walls, and it's not a simple gush of cum. Enzo Doukas cums buckets between my legs and the thick hot pumps pummel me with surges of pleasure. I squeeze my legs around him, tightening my pussy around his cock and drawing him in deeper. He groans and leans his head back against the tub, so his long brown hair cascades away from his pale flesh.

I greedily grab his cheeks and kiss him as my fingers enjoy every inch of his flesh. I'm no longer shy about touching him. I no longer worry that I shouldn't, or feel any guilt for enjoying him. Guilt, pain, sadness and utter isolation diminish as this warm connection between my body and Enzo's builds into this feverish desire for him. I squeeze my thighs tighter. I don't want him to remove himself from me. I take his lower lips between my teeth and tug slightly. He chuckles and then I pull away, kissing his neck.

He runs his hands over my back, cupping the small of my back to keep him against him.

"Don't run away from my bed tonight," he whispers. "Come, signora. Let me make love to you again in my bed. What do you say?"

Chapter 7

Sensual Dark Skinned Woman

Enzo

She's in my bed, naked and thoroughly fucked, with my cum splattered all over her thighs. She smells clean, as do I, and she sleeps like a baby for the first night since I have her in my apartment. I love watching her body as she's asleep. Dark brown skin contrasts with crisp white sheets.

She sleeps on her stomach with her breasts pressed against her chest and her butt rises in two perfect, pillowy mounds. I could lose myself in her ass, lay my face on the cheeks and just... let myself go. I touch the small of her back and she remains asleep.

Fuck, how long has it been since I've felt like this for a woman? I roll onto my back next to her, hair spread out on my pillow, and I wonder if I could stand to let her go after a year. There's a pang in my chest. I don't want an empty bed anymore. Grace is onto me — I am that lonely. I'll always be lonely if I'm not careful with this one. I can't imagine feeling this way about another.

I don't want to go to Albania without her, but how the fuck can I subject her to the danger that awaits? Who knows what's happened to Zara, or why she's been targeted again...

Giovanni assures me that Eddie's still in Long Island and whatever has happened to her doesn't concern him, but I have different instincts from my brother. He's the leader, he's busy all the time. I'm the trickster, the man who carries out the dirty work and handles people on the ground. Giovanni understands strategy and the bigger picture, but I understand people. We didn't get everything we needed to know from the Albanian, that much I can be sure about. There are more secrets. More lies.

I roll onto my back, enjoying the soft snoring from my woman, Grace. She has a past, like anyone, but I've never met a woman with a past quite like hers. Men have brought her more pain than pleasure, and maybe I'm one of those men. I killed her boyfriend. I lied to her. There's a part of me that knows I simply don't deserve a woman like her.

I can't afford to stay in bed for long, even if a huge part of me wants to have Grace wrapped around my cock again. I can't have her yet because I have something far worse and far more pressing to attend to — 10 missed calls from Giovanni. Fuck. What's one cigarette going to hurt if I have to take calls from my brother? I plant a kiss on Grace's forehead and throw on a pair of white boxers before opening my balcony door and stepping out into the sunlight.

I don't think I can ever leave the coast forever. I'll never stop loving the warm light from the sun, the smell of the ocean breeze and the noises of Italy. Everywhere else is too different, too foreign, and not worth my time. If I don't keep my head down, Van might do what he did to Eddie — send him to be someone else's fucking problem in another country. Play it cool, Enzo. Talk your brother down.

I return Van's call and get an earful, exactly as I expect.

"You've lost your fucking mind," Van growls with outrage.

It's not exactly the wedding congratulations I would expect.

"Buon giorno, Giovanni."

I flick my lighter a few times, covering up the sound of Van growling on the other end of the line.

"I want to have a meeting, Enzo."

His voice is ice.

"Are you going to kill me?"

"Worse," he snarls. "I'm sending you to Albania this morning and you're leaving the woman behind."

Okay, at least he isn't punishing me with America, but sending me to Albania this morning has to count as some type of cruelty. I'll need men, I'll need guns and worse, I'll need to say goodbye to Grace before I can even get to know her. I'm hardly able to argue with my brother's orders. I've pushed him far enough, and he sounds like he's been drinking, so I'd better not push him any further.

"She's not 'the' woman. She's my wife."

"Jodi told me everything," Van snarls. "What the hell were you thinking?"

Great. So he already pieced things together.

"I'm not ready to leave, Van. When's the last time I got laid?"

"I can lay you to rest before the end of the day..." Van grumbles.

"Why so cranky? Has Jodi stopped sucking on your–

"Finish that sentence and I'll pluck your eyeballs out myself."

"Yes, brother."

He can probably hear my shit-eating grin over the phone.

"You will do what I say this time, Enzo. Even my mercy has limits. You leave for Albania. Two hours. Make it quick."

Van hangs up before I can give him another smart line. He's serious and I understand that. I broke rules for this woman. I can't put her in danger from my brother by further disobedience. Grace will never accept that I'm leaving her behind. It's best not to tell her. It's best to leave her with a note and a phone number — my sister-in-law's phone number specifically.

I write to her quickly...

Dear Grace,

I must leave for my business in Albania without goodbye. I will be dark on the road, but thinking of you, my treasure, every night. I have left you time to grieve, time to make peace with our arrangement. Hurting you was an unfortunate consequence of what I had to do.

I promise I will keep you safe in my absence. You can trust Jodi and Van Doukas with your life. Ember will also provide great companionship.

Do your best to think of me often. I will miss you.

— Lorenzo

... and check my phone for more details from Van. I'm taking Lucky and Dino across the border to Albania. Who could hold Zara with such little security that she only requires three men to free her?

Van texts me back a response to the question I never asked.

Van: When Zara's free, we go to Matteo. It's urgent.

Despite desperately wanting to ask why, I know I can't. My brother's the boss now and, just like with Papa, I have to obey his orders. I'm just lucky he isn't punishing me with America, but it's clear he wants to keep me away from Grace. If Jodi spoke to him, perhaps he worries I'll hurt her. I couldn't. He has to know that. They all watched me marry her. I couldn't fake my desire for her in front of a crowd.

I reconsider my theory about Van punishing me when I see the shithole he sends us to in Albania. Lucky and Dino don't deserve this. Hell, I don't fucking deserve this. It's been ages since I've had to sleep on straw. At least the cigarettes in Albania are cheap and the coffee's cheaper. Lucky and Dino have luck with the women, even if we're meant to keep a low profile. They have guns, they speak the language, the women want them… I stay out of their way.

We have to stay outside of the major cities in a small village where Luan promises us we can spend the night without detection. Lucky and Dino want to drink and play cards all night, hoping to garner more attention from the buxom Albanian women who think they're tourists and not contract killers.

I slip away from the card game after winning several hundred Euros from the idiots to make sure Jodi has Grace securely in her custody. I call my sister-in-law, disappointed to hear my brother's gruff voice on the other end of the line.

"Why are you calling Jodi?" He growls. "You have work to do."

"I promised my wife protection," I tell my brother, reminding him that Grace is not some random woman. She means something to me. "I'm ensuring that she receives that protection."

"Do you think I would hurt an innocent woman?"

"I wasn't insinuating that, which is why I called Jodi. Why are you answering her phone?"

"This is your fault," Van growls, as if he doesn't hear a fucking word I'm saying. Has the bastard finally lost his mind?

"What's my fault? Are you drunk?"

"Drunk? I'll tell you who's drunk..."

I'll be here arguing with my drunk fucking brother all night. As my voice explodes on the phone, I let my guard down. If there are any fucking rules in the mob, especially this fucking deep in enemy territory, it's never let your guard down. For all I know, Van sent Lucky and Dino out here with me to kill me. But what do I do? I scream at my crazy fucking brother on the phone and lose myself in way too much grain liquor. The Balkans love their fucking liquor.

"Van, I have to go."

"Go where? I'll tell you, Enzo... You keep fucking with me and I'll have to do shit I don't want to do. I fucking love you, idiot. But you keep fucking pushing and pushing..."

"Van... I love you too brother, ciao."

I hang up on him and polish off my drink. I miss Grace. One night with a woman that fucking beautiful isn't enough, especially since it's been so fucking long since I've been with a woman. More drinking. I need more to drink.

I don't notice the bar growing quiet, the men dressed in black surrounding the street, the tattoos on their arms marking them as dangerous. Traditional farm people don't get swastika and SS tattoos on their arms or necks. No, no, no. We're fucked. By the time I put my hand on my gun, I hear all the firearms in the room click. Everyone uninvolved in the mob—a pot-bellied drunk with a bald spot the size of the Adriatic, a pair of gaunt men muttering about football over pints of ale, and several other regular men filter out of the bar, hoping they can sneak off before bullets fly.

If any bullets fly, I'll be dead. Papa prepared us for

moments like this our entire life. You can never guarantee life in cosa nostra. You just live the way we live and pray the chips fall in your favor. A large hand thumps me on my shoulder. Guns are drawn, but no one fires. Maybe they don't plan on killing us. I fucked up and if I die because of it, that's my fault. I suppose Van and Jodi will have custody of Grace in that case. She's my one motivation to stay alive. It's bad enough I left her —I have to return for her.

"Lorenzo Pazzini Doukas."

He says my name, but his tone half questions me and half states my name as a fact. He's come for me specifically. Lucky and Dino turn to me for direction. I shake my head. No need for guns. If they draw their weapons, this Albanian fuck and his cronies will paint the walls with our brains.

"Kill us and get it over with, pussy."

The Albanian grunts. "You're coming with us."

Again, I nod in Lucky and Dino's direction. If we want a prayer's chance of dying with dignity, we obey. But if this man wanted to kill us, we would be dead. We follow him and he separates us with his men into three cars.

"Where are you taking them?"

"None of your concern," the man answers smoothly.

"Any chance in hell of me finding out my killer's name?"

"Adam."

"Well, you already know my name. Where are you taking me?"

The man's accent is thick, Albanian, indistinguishable from Luan or Uksan, or any of the others in the mob I've met. But he doesn't answer my question.

"I am half Albanian," he says. "Half Italian."

"I see."

Not the question I asked, but my life still hangs precariously in this man's hands. I know when I have the power and I know when I don't. Even now, though, there are ways to keep power in my hands.

"I thought that might answer your question," he says. He's following orders. I lean back and close my eyes. It seems insane that I would get such great sleep on the way to my death, but what can I say? I accepted dying at the wrong end of a gun as part of the inevitable a long time ago. When I wake up, Adam jerks the car to a sharp stop. He never takes my gun off me, which strikes me as foolish.

Still, I never reach for my gun. It's like my subconscious knows where I am before Adam unlocks the car and I jump out. We're in front of a castle. There's only one fucking bastard I know who would buy a house this gaudy, tacky and ancient. I glance at the castle's entrance and see him there, after five years—Matteo.

I glance behind me. That's who Adam, with his bullshit tattoos and his bullshit accent, works for. My brother. Fuck. I need to tell Van. I glance behind me and Adam has his hand on his weapon. The cars with Lucky and Dino never arrive. I know Matteo. If they caught the slightest whiff of this place, they would be dead. Hell, he may have had them killed just for showing up. We knew the consequences of coming to Albania after he explicitly told us to stay away, after we promised that we would never try to find him and bring him back.

As I follow my captor down the stone path to the castle entrance, I see a glimmer of white in the distance. My fucked up brother has a smile on his face. This isn't the version of Matteo I expect to see. No. He can't be smiling right now. Matteo cannot be happy to see me. But as I get closer, he closes the gap between us and my 6'9" brother wraps his arms around me, squeezing hard.

"Lorenzo. You've gotten so big..."

He means muscle, I hope. I'm not the shrimpy fucking kid he remembers. I can't bring myself to smile as my brother squeezes me into a tight hug.

"I didn't come to Albania to see you."

We don't have a relationship anymore. Matteo might still

be my brother, but he left our family and his son, coming here to fight his demons.

"This isn't your first time in Albania, either."

Matteo thumps me on the back. It's friendly, but it's also a warning—I'm bigger than you. I'm in control here. Fuck with me, and I'll put you in the ground.

"Adam, you're dismissed. Ensure you send Lucky and Dino on their way once they've finished."

"Papa won't be pleased if you kill them."

Matteo smirks. "Papa isn't the boss anymore, Enzo. I keep tabs on my family."

He keeps tabs on us? Matteo's fucking smirk and his fucking kidnapping trick piss me the fuck off. I could have done something stupid, thinking these fucks were there to take my life. How dare he show up like this? How dare Matteo show up in my life at all after everything?

"Then you know that your son has grown up into an embarrassment. You have your parenting to thank."

Matteo grunts, the absolute closest he comes to showing offense. He guides me through the large wooden doors. The house is cold. Empty. He doesn't have an assistant. He doesn't have anyone except that fucking dog. I hope Grace takes excellent care of Ember in my absence. Matteo's yappy bolognese barks and scuttles across the stone floors of the castle towards us.

My brother took his dog to Albania, but left his son. Vittoria, the dog in question, barks at me and then scurries toward Matteo, who scoops her up and kisses the tiny cunt of a dog on its forehead. I've always hated Vitti.

Matteo grunts when he sees the disgusted look on my face.

"She pooped in your Jeep five years ago, Lorenzo. Let it go."

"She's a bitch."

Vitti barks like she's calling Matteo to heel in her defense.

Snooty fucking dog. It isn't just the Jeep incident. She fought Ember fiercely when she was just a pup. I don't know why a giant like Matteo insists on little dogs that behave like cunts.

"Do you want to survive this encounter?" Matteo snarls, picking up Vitti protectively and planting several kisses on her furry head before releasing her to nip at my heels again. I glare at Vitti.

What does Matteo want with me?

"If you wanted us dead, we would be dead. Clearly. So tell me why you brought me here, Matteo. I'm only in Albania for Van's work."

Part of Van's work involved locating my brother. At least I've nearly killed two birds with one stone. I thought finding Zara would be easier than finding Matteo. This incident proves me very misguided in that belief.

"You're my family. Why didn't you come to me?"

Matteo can't be serious. After five years of silence, he expects us to jump to him when our family needs help? He made it clear how he felt about Italy and all of us five years ago. I take no issue with reminding my brother.

"You left after pouring an entire bottle of port down your throat and threatened to make flutes out of our windpipes if we followed you, talked to you, or attempted to find you. You abandoned your son. You left three house fires behind, bombed a yacht and caused an accident with four sports cars... Don't you remember any of that?"

My brother can be so fucking predictable. He nervously fingers the diamond earring in his ear and then shrugs. He hasn't forgotten a thing, but every emotion Matteo feels, he bottles up inside of him. Then he tries to heal those feelings with a bottle, and he ends up in deeper shit than he started off with.

"It was a long time ago."

"Yes. Eddie knows that it's been a long time."

Matteo shakes his head and sets Vitti gently on the ground.

"I left Eddie because it was the right thing to do. Between the wine and the gin... and the coke... and the pills... I couldn't think straight. I've spent the past five years getting my old self back. I miss my family."

I may be tougher than the shrimpy kid Matteo left behind, but my brother's words still provoke an instinctual response. Matteo's old self provoked fear throughout Italy. Everyone thought he would be in Van's place – everyone. He was always the most suited to cosa nostra – the most naturally ruthless.

Vitti scampers towards my legs and nips at my ankles between delighted barks, her barking growing even more delighted when she draws blood. After several fluent curse words spill from my lips, Matteo scowls and Vitti stops barking long enough to glance at Matteo with a princess-like expression on her face. Cunt of a dog. I swear, I want to drop kick her across the room, but Matteo's sharpening gaze tells me I wouldn't have a chance at survival if I dared. I dab at the blood with the end of my trousers. Fucking Vitti.

"Calm down, Vitti..." I mutter underneath Matteo's threatening stare.

"I want to help you," Matteo says. "I have my own operation here to get on my feet and I want to help the family. I'm ready."

He sounds ready, and that makes me nervous. What if Matteo wants Van's position? If there's anyone capable of starting a war, it's Matteo. Despite that, I have to keep my cool around him and I can't show a whiff of my concern for his intentions. He sniffs out weakness like a tiger shark.

"You could have helped by raising your son. He's the one who got us into this mess."

"And I'm saving him from his mess," Matteo replies. "Again. Who do you think convinced Van not to kill him?"

"You talk to Van?"

"No. I talk to Papa. Papa talks to Van."

Years. Five years, we assumed that Matteo had gone dark.

"Do you ever get tired of having secrets?"

"No," he says, but he's still smiling, so I haven't pushed any of my brother's buttons yet.

Vitti scampers off down a dark hall, barking excitedly. Matteo's allergic to light. He prefers the thicket of Albanian woods to the sunny coast, almost like he's half-Albanian himself. He's just old, I remind myself. He's seen too much shit. By the time I'm in my forties, I might want to run for the hills too. Sometimes I think the only way I'll sleep at night is if I leave my demons behind me in Italy, instead of keeping them running through my fucking head.

His thick black hair only has a few gray strands and despite his age, my brother stays in perfect shape. The creases on his face are where his brow furrows from stress or smile lines. He was always the life of the party, even if partying with Matteo normally ended with someone getting very hurt.

"What business are you involved in here?" I ask him. He's talking, so I need to take in everything I can to bring to Van. Despite my brother's belief that I'm purely selfish and disobedient, I take my work as seriously as I take my feelings for Grace. I'm allowed a personal life, no?

"Easy business," Matteo responds. "I know you're here looking for Eddie's girlfriend. That's more important business."

"Shouldn't we have wine before we discuss business?"

I'm aching for a cigarette, but I know Matteo hates them. If I can't smoke, the least he can do is get me some wine.

"I don't drink any more," He grunts. "Neither should you. I didn't bring you here for a reunion, Lorenzo."

"Pardon me for thinking you were having a change of heart."

He has our pictures on the walls. A brothers' vacation we took to Thessaloniki when I turned fourteen, trips to the Swiss

Alps, yacht vacations in St. Tropez. I think that's the yacht he blew up. Papa had to sell one of his houses in Rome to buy another one. Matteo can't help but keep reminders of us everywhere, despite himself. The sorry fuck misses us. He isn't lying, it's not one of his games. Maybe he's changed. Maybe my older brother wants a reunion as much as I do.

"I can't come back to Italy," he says. "But I must pay for what Eddie's done. I'll help you find Zara. I have only one request."

"What's that?"

"I want to keep her."

Keep her? The phrase reminds me of Grace, which everything does now. She's probably in bed without me, thinking about Uksan. Fuck that. As for keeping Zara. What business does a forty-year-old man have with a teenager?

"That's a bit fucked up, Matteo. Even for you."

My brother's brows pinch together as he reasons exactly what I mean. His cheeks darken and he stammers in frustration before blurting out, "That's not what I meant."

"Right. You simply intend to care for the vulnerable, beautiful, eighteen-year-old girl with no ulterior motive."

Matteo's fists ball up as I smirk. I miss tormenting my eldest brother. He's always been far more patient with me than Van and therefore, far more entertaining to torture.

"I want to protect her from Eddie. That's all."

"I have instructions to return her to Italy. You know Van's the boss. I've already defied him far too much."

Matteo's jaw clenches. "This is not a choice, Enzo. I sent my men after the girl with Lucky and Dino. When they get her back, she will be mine."

"You sent them into Albanian mob territory?"

Matteo grins and then chuckles. A glimmer of his old self shines in his eyes. Matteo loves drugs, and perhaps he's always loved them a little too much, but there's one drug he's never been able to resist, quit or get clean from — power.

He scoffs, "Albanian territory? It's soon going to be my territory, Lorenzo. I've taken to this godforsaken country and I have no intentions of leaving, or having the Albanian mob run my people out."

"Just what we need... you starting a war."

Matteo thumps my shoulders again, his face twisting into a wide smile. "Relax, Enzo. Let's get you that wine."

Six drinks knock me into a stupor, but I don't lose my faculties to the point where I forget that I must call Van. By the time I get to my phone, I see six missed calls from my brother. Great. I'm going to pay for that. I call back. Van's eerily calm.

"I hear you're with Matteo."

"Word travels fast."

Thank fuck those idiots Lucky and Dino got to Van while Matteo has me at his castle.

"What does he want?" Van barks.

Matteo tips the contents of a glass of water down his throat. I never thought I'd see the day when my brother quit drinking.

"Is that Van?"

"You two ought to talk," I grumble.

I always hated getting in between their vicious fights. Matteo waves off the idea as Van barks again.

"What does he want?" Van snarls.

"He wants Zara."

"What?"

Van sounds furious, but not uninterested.

"He says it's his duty to protect her and fix what Eddie's done."

"What about what Zara wants?"

I pause. Does Van mean this? What Zara wants shouldn't be a factor here. We still have to prevent a war and Zara has a nasty way of falling into trouble and into the wrong hands. The girl is like a fucking magnet for bad guys. I mean, how the fuck did she even meet Eddie?

Matteo's probably the only person in the universe that can keep her contained. We could solve all our problems. If Eddie comes back, he'll have to go straight to his father and we don't have to deal with the traitorous prick at all.

I'll never forgive Eddie for putting the target on my back. I might be a little selfish, I might like women, but I have never once faltered in loyalty to our family.

"Do you trust me?" I ask Van.

After everything last year, after everything I've done to make up for my screwups, all I can ask for is his trust.

"Yes."

For the first time in months, he doesn't hesitate. It helps that I eventually came clean about Grace, although I'm certain he's still making me pay for what I've done.

"Let me talk to Matteo. I'll decide. If I think Zara will come to any harm... I'll find a way out of here alive with her."

"You think she should stay?" Van asks. I still feel flattered that my brother considers me worthy enough to ask for advice. Not every boss feels that way. Certainly papa ruled with more fire, but that doesn't mean Van ought to be underestimated. Van groans and I know who he's thinking of. He has a special groan when he's thinking of that mischievous woman of his.

"What will Jodi say?" Van mutters.

"Blame it all on me," I tell him. "Whatever the outcome, tell her it was my fault. We both know Zara will be safe with him."

Van grunts. "Matteo in a house with a beautiful eighteen-year-old girl? Does that sounds safe to you?"

Van and I both joked over the years that half the reason Matteo stayed in Albania was to avoid all the lovers he's wronged. He's forty — he's had a fucking lot of lovers and most of them hate his guts.

"She's his son's ex-girlfriend," I say reasonably, giving Matteo a look that he ignores while drinking lemon water straight from a jug. "He won't touch her."

"You both know I wouldn't fuck a teenager," Matteo grunts. "I'm not like our father."

Van and I don't have to say a word to each other after that. We're both thinking the same fucking thing. Matteo is exactly like papa—just a younger version who hasn't settled into cirrhosis and cardiovascular disease... yet. He's gruff, tempestuous and, oh, he has a fucking thing for women.

"I trust you to make the right choice," Van says. "I have to go."

"Leaving me to deal with him?"

Matteo grunts. "If I wanted you dead, you would be dead."

His idea of a joke. Van mutters goodbye.

"Ciao, Van."

Matteo leans back, groaning and smiling before I've even said a word.

"Do we have a deal, Enzo?"

"What do you want with the girl? Be honest."

"I want to talk about my son."

"Isn't there a more efficient way to get information about your son?"

It might be the wine, but it might be my idiot brother not making any damned sense. Matteo scowls.

"He belongs in America. I heard what he did. I heard many things he did. I love him, but if he comes to Albania or to Italy... if he hurts that girl again, I'll kill him myself."

Matteo's been in the life almost twice as long as me and Van. After seeing enough shit, you can get to the point where you can kill anyone.

"If you see her, you'll want her," I warn him. "You don't have that kind of self-control. She's a beautiful girl."

I never looked at Zara like that, but the truth remains that she's petite with smooth mahogany skin and giant brown eyes that melted half the clients in my brother's night club, Jalousie. Most men find a way past their discrimination against a woman that color when they see her heart-shaped face, her white smile and, again, those eyes. She's a little problem, that one. If I have a daughter like that, I wouldn't let her out of my sight or anywhere near other men. I want Matteo to know what he's up against.

"Five years without liquor or drugs alone in the mountains," he growls. "You don't know a fucking thing about how much self-control that takes."

Surely Matteo knows that some women are harder to quit than drugs.

"She means something to our family, Matteo. Promise me you won't hurt her."

"I promise."

"Promise me you won't sleep with her."

"Christ," Matteo snarls. "She's younger than my son. She's also his ex-girlfriend. I just want to know what he was like. Judging by what I've heard, I owe her protection."

"We all owe Zara."

Mostly because Van never gave her that last paycheck before she got herself kidnapped. I think he owes her several hundred euros....

"I'll have the men who took her killed," Matteo announces.

There's nothing I can say about that. This isn't our family's territory. It's not Doukas business if he wants to start a war here. It's our business if that war gets a license to come to the Amalfi Coast.

I lean forward, studying my brother's face. I'm too drunk to tell if he's crazy, or very smart.

"How can you control so much in Albania?"

"Divided families are easy to conquer," Matteo says. "It will be their downfall and it may be our downfall too."

I don't appreciate his insinuation, because knowing my brother's history, this could be a thinly veiled threat.

"There's only one person dividing our family."

Matteo grunts. "That will soon change."

I'm too drunk to ask what he means.

"More wine?" Matteo asks. I nod. I'd better enjoy this night with my brother while it lasts.

Chapter 8

Mr. Doukas Returns To Me

Grace

Thanks to Jodi, I get to stay in Lorenzo's house at least, but I'm a prisoner with his dog and I have been for the past six weeks. Six fucking weeks! He leaves for six weeks and all I have is some damned note and for the first week at least, I had this ache between my thighs. He's big — really big — and the first few nights without him, I missed him.

It's crazy, isn't it? I'm missing my boyfriend's killer. Ex-boyfriend. Pretty sure when one guy dies and you marry another, the dead guy officially becomes your ex. Ugh. How is this happening to me? Why does shit always happen to me? I just want a happily ever after.

I won't find it with Enzo — especially not when he learns what I hid from him. I just wanted to make sure he wouldn't kill me when I told him. I have to think about my life, you know. I didn't come to this damn country to die.

But six weeks? I never expected Enzo to disappear from my life for six weeks. I thought I'd have a couple days to get myself together and tell him the truth. Now, it's going to be a damn shit show.

It's been hell hiding my secret from Jodi and Van all six

weeks. Jodi has been a peach though. One night, she got Van drunk so we could go out to Jalousie together. I only had seltzer, Jodi didn't drink either, and we got caught, but at least we got a couple hours of dancing in before Van put my ass on lockdown and banned Jodi from seeing me. I think Enzo called Jodi that night and Van had to keep our secret to keep Enzo's crazy ass from coming back over the border. Oops.

I don't know what Van did to Jodi, but I doubt he'll have her caged up for long. She acts like escaping from her mafia husband while pregnant with his baby is her part-time job. I can tell Van's crazy about her. I've never had a guy feel that way about me. I can't understand what Enzo truly feels.

Hiding my secret from the guards has been easy up in the penthouse, but I'm still hiding, still keeping a huge fucking secret I would have told Enzo if he hadn't disappeared for six weeks into Albania. If the guards find out, they'll tell Van and I don't want Van to find out first.

I also don't want Enzo to find out from anyone else.

He told me his big fucking secret and I've had six weeks to twist myself up with guilt for not telling him mine. I reread the letter he left me every night. He didn't want to leave. I can feel it. I don't blame his brother for sending him away, but it's not what they think. I'm not Enzo's victim. I might have been forced by my circumstances to marry him, but our first night together was anything but forced.

I need to tell Lorenzo the truth. I owe him that much for all he's done for me.

I beg Van to give me a chance to talk to Enzo, because once he's back, he'll know I kept this secret from him and he'll know that even if he's a murderer, I'm no angel either. Nothing works on Van Doukas. He's stern, stubborn and insists that I can't speak to my husband. At least I have his home and I have Ember, who sticks to my side most of the day, especially when she realizes how many treats I give her.

The day Enzo arrives, Van graces me with a personal

phone call. His taut voice issues commands that I 'mentally prepare' for his brother's return. My nerves are pudding and my desire to jump off Enzo's balcony heightens with each passing minute.

Enzo signed a contract too. He won't hurt me. He'll help me.

Would Enzo Doukas have signed that contract if he knew exactly who I was and exactly who he was dealing with?

I have to stop freaking the fuck out. What do we do, Grace? We fucking handle things, that's what we do.

I hear an unfamiliar engine in the complex parking lot in the early afternoon. With six weeks here and constant 'protection' from men who look like Eastern European superhero movie villains, I grew accustomed to keeping track of who was coming and going, taking notes on sheets of paper to keep myself sane during this captivity. I hear a man speaking in rapid Italian to someone downstairs and then his voice disappears. It's him. It's Lorenzo.

He climbs the stairs to his apartment, and I rush to the front door, waiting for him. I can't hide this from him. I might as well rip the bandaid off, right?

I open the front door as I hear Enzo's footsteps approaching. The armed guards on either side of the door stiffen, readying themselves to capture me (sorry 'protect me') if I bolt. Van made it clear he didn't want another runner on his hands. Enzo's gaze stops at my face and he smiles.

I can't meet his smile. Enzo's eyes drop as he notices me

properly, and he utters a string of swear words followed by, "Did I do that?"

I say the only word I can think of.

Surprise.

Enzo swears again.

"Who the hell got you pregnant?" he growls, his brows knitted in genuine fury.

Before I can answer, Enzo rushes forward, his arms wrapping tightly around me. He's hugging me, not killing me. That's a great start...

I've been all wrapped up in nerves about his arrival here and when I get too nervous, I cook. The smell of onions and sauteed mushrooms from my emergency beef stroganoff wafts into the entryway of Enzo's house. He presses his nose into my neck, pressing the baby bump against his chest. He holds me so fucking tightly that I feel genuine confusion.

I let myself lean into him, hugging him back, holding him like he's my real-life husband and like I real life love him. He moves his nose around my neck and kisses me there. I want to melt. Six weeks was far too long.

My stomach swims with guilt. I know I don't owe Enzo anything, least of all answers, but considering we slept together and considering everything that happened since I said "I do"... I owed him better. If he's upset, he doesn't show it right away. He plants a kiss on my cheek and keeping hold of my hand, he treats me to a warm smile that makes me forget how entirely fucked up this is.

"You'll answer me soon," he says. "First... What the hell are you cooking?"

Men and food... He finds out I'm carrying another man's child, but the smell of sauteed onions overrides my shocking news.

"Beef stroganoff..." I tell him, raising an eyebrow in surprise that Enzo's stomach overpowers everything else.

"Is that Albanian?" He answers, winking at me. He knows damned well there's nothing Albanian about it. I hate that he's acting all cool. I've been twisting myself up into knots for weeks about this. I'm carrying another man's child and I don't want to talk to Enzo about the damned origins of the beef stroganoff recipe I found on the internet.

"Six weeks was too long," I blurt out. "I didn't mean to hide this for so long."

Lorenzo glances down at my stomach and smirks. He's still acting way too cool. Where's the red face? The outrage? The fists flying at my head? I don't know what the hell to do with a man like Enzo, but I'd better tread carefully in case he switches it up on me.

"I can see that," he responds. "Feed me, woman. Then we'll talk about your... situation."

I hoped to talk about what he found in Albania, if he learned anything more about Uksan, or what was coming for us. He's quiet and pensive as he strips off his jacket and shoes, settling into the comfort of his home.

"Has Ember forgotten me already?" Enzo mutters as he hurries greedily over to my simmering stroganoff. I swat his hand away from the pan with a wooden spoon and lower the temperature on his electric stove. Ember's sleeping in his bedroom and she definitely misses him. She spends all day curled up on a white t-shirt belonging to him and she's nipped at me any time I've tried to grab it from her to wash it. The dang shirt's covered in black fur now.

Enzo makes another attempt to grab beef out of the pan and I give him a good swat on his hand. He winces and draws his hand away, still grinning.

"It's not ready."

"It smells ready," he says, practically drooling. I roll my eyes and give him a warning swat on his tattooed forearm.

Men are all the same with food.

"Get yourself some wine and sit down."

Wine is the fastest way to get Enzo off my case. Hell, if I wasn't pregnant, I would have needed wine to get through this shit too.

"I suppose I'll need it," he says, remarking on my obvious baby bump without remarking on it directly.

I know exactly where to find Enzo's wine after this long in his apartment, although I've been avoiding drinking on purpose since I came here. I pass him a 40-year-old bottle and hope that knocks him off his feet enough, so he doesn't take a swing at me when we talk about my pregnancy. I doubt he's the type, but you never know until you know.

Enzo cracks open the bottle as I serve up plates of delicious beef strips drenched in creamy mushroom sauce. Just what the doctor ordered. He takes a huge gulp of wine before talking, swirling around a strip of beef in the mushroom sauce afterward and indulging in the scent and texture.

"Who knocked you up?"

Considering his fixation with my Albanian ex, I want to keep things simple. This secret twisted me up for six weeks. I'm ready to let it all out and tell Enzo the truth, even if he won't like it.

"The baby isn't Uksan's."

"I'm relieved."

Enzo pokes every article on the plate with a fork first before eating. Lean men always eat like rabbits. I'm used to feeding big, beefy men who could eat twice as much as Enzo, but I suppose he has to keep his muscles tight with some type of discipline. Not my hungry, pregnant ass. My portion dwarfs Enzo's and I don't feel a lick of guilt over it. With guards delivering whatever groceries I want, I get to satisfy each one of my pregnancy cravings. Luckily Enzo didn't see what I did to a tub of gelato last week...

He gently nibbles a strip of beef before deciding it satisfying enough to chew painfully slowly. Seriously? Does he have to be that obnoxiously disciplined about everything? That's it. I can't take this restraint anymore—calmly sitting there while Enzo nibbles food and determines whether to question me. At least I can't handle this with a violently kicking baby and the smell of onions filling the room. I dig into my food myself, eating like a starving polar bear.

If he has no further questions, then maybe he won't press me for answers. He knows I'm pregnant, maybe that's all he needs to know.

"Grace?"

Shit. After two silent minutes, I'd hoped he'd given up.

"Are you enjoying the beef?" I squeak.

"It's lovely, but you haven't answered my question. Who knocked you up? I know it couldn't have been me. You look over ten weeks along."

It's my first pregnancy, so my baby bump took a long time to show. I'm twenty weeks along by my estimates, but I haven't been to the doctor, and I only took that one pregnancy test that sparked this damn journey across the Atlantic and far away from my troubles.

I bite my lip, struggling to find the words to tell him that won't make me look like the worst person in the world. I kept this from him to protect myself and I still don't know the man sitting across from me well enough to spill my heart out and risk him ending up just another monster. I've had my fill of genuine monsters. I keep trying to tell myself that not every man has that darkness in him, but life keeps trying to teach me differently.

The thing that sucks about Enzo is that I can't tell with him. I can't tell if he's a bad guy who does good things, or a good guy who does bad things. I can't tell if that even matters.

"Is this why you've left America?" He asks calmly, digging in more ferociously into the food I prepared him.

Enzo may not have a college education and he may have never left Italy, but damn he can read people. I lean back, taking a deep shuddering breath. There's no getting away from this, is there? I waited long enough.

"I didn't mean to keep this from you."

"I won't punish you," Enzo says. "I only want the truth. I've been gone for a while. I hope you haven't been busy."

"I'm way further than six weeks along."

I hate that I sound defensive. Enzo and I aren't exactly in love. One amazing sexual experience and a marriage contract don't equate to "forever love". I'm not that naïve.

"Okay."

"I have a past, Enzo. I barely know you. It's not the type of thing you want to advertise."

"There was a man in this past?"

My heart feels like it's jumping into my throat and my stomach wants to expel that tasty creamy mushroom sauce all over the counter. He keeps staring and I know this is it — the point where I have to make a choice. Can I trust Enzo Doukas?

"Not just a man," I whisper. "A husband."

Enzo reaches across the counter and grabs my hand. I expect outrage. Hurt. Pain. Instead, he tilts his head to the side and says calmly, "What did he do to you?"

His thumb massages the top of my hand, and I exhale slowly. It's okay to trust him, my gut says.

He understands. Without me saying a single word, Enzo understands.

"He did enough that I had to run and if I don't stop running, he'll find me and he'll kill me. If I go back home... I'm dead."

"How far along are you?"

"Far."

Five months. It just has to be somewhere between five and six months. I don't want to admit that to Enzo yet because I don't want to admit it to myself. He doesn't press me for details about the timing.

"Did Uksan know the truth?"

I don't know how to feel about the fact that Enzo's voice never wavers. He's a strong, calming presence and I can tell him things without worrying that he'll overreact. It's different from what I know. It's so different, that it almost feels threatening to be next to a stable man. It feels like I don't deserve this and that Enzo can't possibly be real. He gave me my first orgasm. Not even Uksan, may he rest in peace, did that for me. Enzo will always be my first.

I shake my head, struggling to stay focused beneath his gray stare. I can't meet Enzo's gaze and not for lack of trying. My body simply won't move. The shame about my past haunts me and freezes me in place. I'm expecting a fist or a slap. I'm expecting to dodge an object flying across the room.

He stands up and leans over the counter, his light brown hair falling over his face and his gray eyes focused intently on me.

"No. Uksan didn't know the truth."

He runs his fingers over my hand calmly. "Give me a name, Grace. Give me a name and I'll kill him."

"I won't ask you to kill for me."

My heart thuds. It's a secret, wicked fantasy I've had for a long time. Women in my situation know you can't help but thinking that it's the only way out. When a man turns into a monster and he exercises his complete power to terrorize you and remain above the law, your mind wanders to a dark place. If he weren't alive, he couldn't ever hurt me.

I wanted to kill my husband several times, but I never bought the gun, poisoned his supper, or got him drunk to put a pillow in his face while he slept. He got me pregnant, escalated his ass whoopings, and damn I wanted to get out. I had no money. He controlled everything. He made me drop out of school. I knew I'd fucked up letting it happen. I didn't have a choice, did I? He knew what he was doing.

He wanted to trap me with his baby and keep me saddled to his side, but the trap he tried to set gave me what I needed to get free. I knew I'd gone too far bringing another life into this. I might let him smack me around, but I'd die before he I let him wrap his fucking hands around my kid's throat or have my kid grow up watching him whoop my ass. I grew up in a broken, fucked up home, and I don't want to repeat the dang cycle.

The buck stops here. The family curse ends with me. I won't have my kid growing up in a Mississippi trailer park or a New York hood. Hell fucking no.

I knew he would try to kill me, and even if he didn't succeed, he'd hurt that precious life growing in me so damned bad. I knew he would destroy both of us, so I ran like hell.

"Why can't you let me kill him?" Enzo says calmly. Killing is his work, his business, his normal. But it isn't mine. I wanted to kill my husband, but running felt more right.

"I can't," I whisper, my voice cracking unintentionally. "You don't understand, Enzo. I fucked up. I lied to you. You can't kill for me. You shouldn't even keep up your end of our contract. You didn't know I was pregnant."

"Don't be ridiculous, tesoro."

My throat tightens as he calls me his treasure. I love the words on his lips. I love that one night we had permanently seared in my brain. I can't lie to him. I've already done enough that when he finds out the truth, he'll kill me. But I've gone too far and the words spill out of me.

"In America… I'm still married."

He doesn't miss a fucking beat. I see Enzo's nerves of steel have multiple purposes.

"Explain."

Again, he doesn't sound judgmental, just calm and centered, as usual.

"He wouldn't let me get a divorce. I filed papers. I tried. I did everything I could to free myself, Enzo. That man wanted me in the ground, so I took what I had and I came here with the last of my savings. I didn't mean to lie to Uksan, to you or to anybody, but this man will end my life. I was scared. I'm still fucking scared."

Enzo's still calm, fixing his gorgeous eyes on me. Men that beautiful make me nervous. Then again, this could also be the fact that Enzo's a killer. I know what he's capable of and that makes him more dangerous than anyone I know. He's killed too many people to keep track of.

"You sound certain of what he will do," Enzo says.

I wet my lips and struggle to get the words out. Certain? Yeah, I'm pretty damn certain of what my husband/ex-husband could do to me. He's made it pretty clear how far he's willing to go.

"He already tried."

I don't want to think about the hospital visit. The broken orbital bone. The fractured wrist. The bruises on my neck and chest. He brought me to the ER and told the nurses I fell. I was six weeks pregnant and terrified the baby wouldn't make it. I ran to save my baby.

"Give me a name, tesoro," Enzo whispers. "I left you for six weeks. Six weeks with this pain and this secret. Let me do something for you."

He kisses my hand, sending a shiver through me. How the fuck can a killer be this damned romantic? His grey eyes never leave me. They're so damn intense. I don't want to believe the man who killed Uksan in cold blood can be this romantic.

This is my fuck up, not his. I lied to him and I know I don't deserve shit. My brain feels as mixed up as mac and cheese. Monsters don't step up to care for another man's child. Where's his anger? His judgment? Could I be wrong about this man? He might be a killer, but maybe there's more to him. Maybe there's something else that I could fall in love with.

"What about the baby?" I tell him, just in case he's confused about what the hell he's signing up for. "You don't want this baby. You don't want my type of problems."

Enzo's cheeks darken, but his words betray nothing of his true feelings. His gaze carries his uninhibited intensity. The more I know him, the more those gorgeous gray eyes make me melt and tremble in equal measure. Enzo takes my hand to his lips.

"I want a year with you," he murmurs, kissing me repeatedly. "I want a year with you and your baby and your past and after that year, tesoro... I want you to stay with me. Six weeks without you and I know where I stand. If we spend only a year together... who knows how much time we'll have. I want a chance with you."

"What do you mean stay with you?"

It's not like I don't understand English or anything, but this is the last thing I expected. I might have expected Enzo to throw a slap my way for lying or take out his passions in the bedroom... but staying with him? We barely know each other. I don't know if I can risk it, but so far, Enzo's been a man of his word. He had no good reason not to kill me the night he killed Uksan. He might have lied to me at first, but the truth came quick and since then, he's been honest.

I still didn't expect this, and my face shows my blatant disbelief. Enzo won't let me move my hand away from his and he kisses me again.

"Live with me. Be mine. Don't run away. Yes, we married first... but we can still get to know each other."

"I'm pregnant with another man's child, Enzo," I reply, emphasizing his name so I can be sure that this Italian man really is listening to the words coming out of my mouth. He chuckles and then shrugs as if another man's child represents no big deal to him.

Still rubbing my palm with his thumb, he answers sweetly, "Men hurt you, Grace. Give me a name and I'll prove to you I won't be one of them. I'll prove how far I'll go to keep you safe."

He means it. There's so much temptation in his offer.

"Why?"

"Because, in my dark fucked up totally boring life, I met a woman who was very interesting. I like your mystery. I like your intensity. You, Grace Doukas, are the only woman who awakened this in me."

And I'm sure he's had many women. But can I agree to let a potentially psychopathic killer raise my unborn child? I ran away from one nut job and I don't want to flee straight into the arms of another.

Enzo swoops around the counter before I can drag my hand away and escape from his big, dramatic declaration. I've been through too much shit to think a man's going to save me, especially a man who carries guns and kills people. But this man's hands rush to my hips and he doesn't even mind the baby bump between us, although he glances down before pressing me close.

"Did you miss me?" he asks, holding me against him and putting his chin on my head. I love that feeling and I love resting my head on a man's muscular chest. Enzo has one of the warmest, firmest chests I've ever pressed my head on.

"Yes," I whisper. "But I wanted to kill you for the first two weeks for running off."

"You missed me," he murmurs. "Good. That means I treated you right."

I smile, because I'm pretty sure he's talking about his dick when he says he treated me right and yes... I still think about that orgasm and how it was the first time in my life a man put my pleasure first and genuinely gave a crap about what happened to me in the bedroom. He notices my smile and chuckles. Yup, he's definitely talking about his dick.

"I made it work," I mutter, shy because of the way his hands feel on my hips and how the gentlest touch from Enzo drives me crazy enough to want him bad.

"It's just business," he whispers. "My business. I don't want to leave you, but Grace, this is my life, you understand?"

"Yes. I don't like the thought of you killing people."

"I don't either," he says, his voice drawing deeper and slower. "I do what I'm ordered because if I don't, I die. My brother may give me one chance, but he won't give me another. Understood?"

"I understand."

"Will you stay?"

"I want to," I whisper, the truth slipping out of my mouth even if it defies all common sense. Enzo kisses the top of my head and I feel like I made the right choice. I draw back from him and stand on my tiptoes to kiss him right on the lips. That kiss melts me. I wobble on my tiptoes and nearly fall over, but Enzo clutches the small of my back and steadies me.

That's what a real man does, isn't it? He's that rock you need when everything in your life goes fucking crazy. He keeps kissing me and we stumble backwards against the kitchen counter. My fingers rush to his hair and tangle quickly in the light brown strands. His warm body presses against mine and oh God, those muscles. He is built like a damned man and I love it.

My hands drop from his cheeks to his chest and I touch every inch of him like I missed him because damn it, even if I barely know him, I want to know him better and touching him seems like a good place to start. I touch his chest and then his arms. Those thick biceps could break a metal pipe in half like a twig. He has tattoos in Italian, images, tribal patterns, ink on every inch of his arms. I plop up onto the counter and Enzo greedily spreads my legs, sliding his body between them so we can keep kissing and kissing. He pulls away from me for one moment to breathe and it's one moment too long...

. . .

"LORENZO! OPEN THE FUCKING DOOR!"

By now, I recognize Van's imperious voice. He's so much more gruff than Enzo, who has a calm and patient voice with depth and smoothness. Van sounds like he's about to rip the head off a squirrel every time he opens his mouth, even when he's not trying to be mean or rude.

Enzo tightens his grip on my hips. He doesn't want to let me go and I don't want him to move his hands away from me. I don't want to stop touching his biceps. Juices soak my thighs and I know exactly what I need – my muscular mafia man with a whole lotta dick and a whole lotta body.

Van waits patiently at the door, but Enzo ignores his yell outside.

"Fuck Van. I want you tonight," he whispers. "Right here. In this kitchen. It's been hell without you. I didn't fuck any whores. No other women..."

My thighs tingle, but I know Van won't let Enzo get away with having sex on the kitchen counter while he stands outside yelling. I already hear the key turning in the lock as Enzo presses his lips to my neck.

Van storms over and slams his hand on the table. "Enzo! Stop kissing her. Now. Grace? Good afternoon."

"Good afternoon, Van," I mutter, sliding off the counter as Enzo pulls away from me. Our reunion will have to wait, even if I feel like my body can't take the separation anymore. Pregnancy hormones and general horniness create a damned mess in my mind..

"I trust you're well?" Enzo says without a hint of humiliation that his brother walked in on us about to get it on in the kitchen. Van glowers at him, but when he turns to me, he smiles.

"Grace. I hope my brother was not molesting you..."

"He wasn't."

Van's eyes quickly dart to my now visible baby bump. Hey, I didn't have any warning, and I didn't have time to cover up. He returns his glare to Enzo.

"Irresponsible cunt," Van growls at him, and that appears to be his only comment on my pregnancy. At least he assumes Enzo's the father. Van's just as terrifying as his brother, and I don't need him up in my business. Enzo puts his arm around my shoulder and pulls me close in a protective half-embrace. His closeness does the trick and I suddenly feel more calm about the fact that Van just learned about my pregnancy.

Ember finally wakes from her nap hearing the commotion in the kitchen and she bounds over to Van first, earning a disdainful look from Enzo until she goes to him and starts licking his ankles. Ew. Enzo huffs.

"What do you want Giovanni? I was occupied."

"Just stopping by," Van grunts as Ember barks and races out of the room, zooming around the house with her black wagging tail.

"You break into my house like it's an emergency," Enzo says, although clearly he gave his brother the key for a reason.

Van turns red. "I got carried away. No emergency. Just work."

"I'm busy."

Van's cheeks turn red and Enzo grins. He loves fucking with his older brother.

Van puts his hand on his brother's shoulder in a half-friendly and half-threatening manner. They clearly have a complicated relationship.

Van orders him, "We have to work. Your woman can wait. Sorry, Grace."

Enzo kisses me and whispers that he'll return soon. I don't want him to leave.

"Where are you two going?"

Van gives me a sympathetic look. "My apologies, signora. I promise I'll bring him back in one piece."

That's as close as I get to an explanation. He's hardly been back two hours and Enzo has to leave again. I hate that part, but at least he's back in Italy and at least he took my news well.

He leaves with Van, speaking in a language I can't understand. I sit at the kitchen counter again, my stomach tightening in a weird knot. He knows my secret, and he hasn't run. Worse than that, Enzo makes me a tempting offer – he kills my enemies and I stay with him forever.

I have a damned angel on one shoulder and a devil on the other. This devil has sexy gray eyes and a body to die for. My devil has the keys to my freedom, but if I do this, what happens to my heart?Is cruelty alone what Enzo hides beneath that appearance of unshakeable calm?

He can kill my ex. I know he could get away with it too. But can I ask a man to do something so horrible for me? Has being with Enzo totally fucked with my morality?

I clean the kitchen, washing up our plates from the beef stroganoff and happy that Enzo finished his meal despite his picking at it. After tidying up, I sit at the kitchen counter with a glass of sparkling water and lemon, along with a book I've been using to learn Italian. My Italian still sucks, but at least I'm enjoying *Cinquanta sfumature di grigio*, you know, *50 Shades of Grey*? There's something sexy about mouthing the translation in Italian, even as I struggle with my pronunciation.

I'm lost in Anastasia's struggle with falling for a man she knows she should stay away from. Girl, we can all relate.

When Enzo returns, he enters so quietly, I barely hear him

and I might not have noticed him at all if Ember didn't leap up from her doggie bed and race toward the door. Ember yaps twice as Enzo picks up the tiny dog and kisses her on the head. She squirms away and runs off as Enzo approaches me, smiling with bemusement as he observes the title of my book.

"Glad to know we're on the same page," he says in slow, slurred English.

Enzo shuts my book and kisses my cheek. He smells like red wine and he slurs like he's had well over a bottle. That man can hold his liquor, but he still pushes his limits.

"Have you been drinking?"

Enzo chuckles and kisses my cheek again, this time with a wet, lusty kiss. He definitely wants to kiss more than my damn cheek. He slides the book across the counter and well away from me as he answers.

"You're pregnant," he says. "Yes, I've been drinking."

"Because of me?"

"Because I love you."

He's drunk. He's only saying this because he's drunk.

"You don't mean that."

"I love you, Grace. I married you. I killed for you. I would go to the ends of the world for you because I love you. You don't have to go back to America. Stay with me. Be mine."

He drags me out of my seat and moves me towards the kitchen counter again, to the same spot where we made out earlier when the sun was still up. Enzo's firm hands sit gently on my waist as he says this. I can't pull away from him and I don't want to. But I can't believe Enzo wants to do this out of love or the goodness of his heart.

"Why?"

It's the only question I can ask. I can't tell him that I love him. My romantic life is a mess – clearly. I'm pregnant for one man, there's another dead and then there's him – the man who doesn't care that I'm a fucking mess and I can't figure out for the life of me why. I don't bring anything to the table but another man's baby and the trouble from my past.

"Because you are everything I want."

That answers nothing, but Enzo doesn't care to answer with words half the time. He drops to his knees and gazes up at me with his lower lip between his teeth. His gray eyes tell me everything I need to know. He wants me.

"What do you want?"

"Grace," he answers, grinning. "Forgiveness. You don't look at me like I'm a monster, even if you know that's what I am."

He's more honest when he's drunk, which moves me because he's honest enough when he's sober. He tugs at the fabric around my waist, clutching me like a treasured stuffed animal. Grace. He wants my Grace. Maybe that's why he wants to help me and keep me, some way of atoning for the life he was born into.

"What happened with Van?"

"Bullshit," he whispers. "More bullshit. I don't want to think about leaving you."

He won't let everything spill from his lips, but details slip out. They must have talked about Enzo leaving again. I don't want him to leave and if he does... I want to go with him.

"You don't have to leave."

"Sit up on the counter, tesoro," he murmurs, kissing the tops of my thighs and slowly pushing me back against the counter.

I put my ass against the counter and Enzo scoops me up and pushes my ass there so I sit. His hands run over my thighs and under my linen dress. Without my iced water nearby, sweat pools almost immediately on the back of my neck. Six weeks and Italy has only become hotter. I thought we would head into a chilly, comfortable fall, but I'm sweating my ass off.

Enzo doesn't give a crap, apparently. I feel his tongue touch a bead of sweat on my thigh and he licks his way up my inner thighs, stopping just at my crotch before burying his nose between my legs and pressing it to my underwear.

I whimper as Enzo moves his lips over to my other thigh. There are no beads of sweat for him to taste away, but he savors my flesh by wrapping his lips tightly so I can't help but have a moan escape my lips. Enzo runs his finger over my mound and then cups my mound with his hand, slowly massaging me as he uses his hands to touch every inch of me. I squirm my hips forward. Pregnancy has made me extremely horny and six weeks without Enzo and without orgasms felt like complete torture.

Enzo practically rips my underwear off after kissing my thighs and working me up. By the time his tongue presses between my thighs, I'm completely soaked from my arousal. I grip the marble counters and spread my legs as Enzo presses his face deeper between them. I run my fingers through his hair and Enzo grunts as I tangle my fingers in his slightly curled brown hair.

I don't have to pull his face closer for Enzo to go deeper, his tongue slowly rolling over my clit and then sliding along my inner lips in smooth circles. I buck my hips forward and Enzo's tongue slips inside me. I cry out and my juices erupt from between my legs. Enzo pulls his head away. He kisses the tops of my thighs.

"I fucking love you," he murmurs. "I don't know why. I missed your pussy. I missed your body. Fuck, Grace... I can't live without you."

He runs his tongue over his lips, taking my juices off of them before plunging between my legs again. He slowly nibbles my outer lips before returning his attention to my clit. Every touch of Enzo's tongue against my clit drives me wild. He sucks on my outer lips as he adds a finger to massage my clit until warmth builds in my core and I can't hold myself back any longer. I cum hard and Enzo doesn't stop slurping on my pussy lips until I'm clean. He emerges from between my legs with a grin on his face.

"You taste different, pregnant."

"Enzo!"

"I mean it," he whispers.

"You know I've been pregnant the whole time, right?"

Enzo chuckles. "You taste different now. I promise. I'm an expert."

He rises to his feet and spreads my thighs forcefully, moving his hips between my legs and our bodies closer than we've been since he walked through the door. I fight my temptation to wrap my ankles around him. Enzo kisses my forehead. He runs his hands over my thighs, never moving his gaze off me.

"I wish I could have been the first to give you a baby," he whispers. "But if you stay with me, we'll have our whole life together. I can give you another baby."

My voice catches. I can't lie to him.

"I never wanted a child."

He raped me. My husband raped me before I could leave and he thought he could use this baby to trap me. But something happened during my pregnancy. I began to value the life inside me more than mine and I had to run.

"Neither did I," Enzo says. "I love you, Grace. So I love any life you create."

"I still don't know why."

"Neither do I," he murmurs. "But I would kill for you again in a heartbeat."

He kisses me, and I taste myself on his lips. When I attempt to pull away, Enzo pulls me closer. His body feels so warm and firm beneath my fingertips and I want to say yes to every single one of Enzo's offers. He wants to raise my child. He wants to keep me in Italy. I don't have to worry about the Albanian mob and I don't have to worry about my ex.

I can be safe here and protect my kid. It's going to be okay, isn't it?

My fingers find the buttons on Enzo's shirt and I follow my urge to strip him down to nothing. I want to run my hands over his tattoos, feel the spring of his firm muscles and enjoy his hard, masculine body pressing against mine.

He doesn't rush to sex. He kisses me gently, teasing my cheeks and my neck before moving to my lips. Enzo pulls on my lower lip with his and then presses his tongue into my mouth. We both move closer together after Enzo's tongue tastes mine. I push my hands up against his chest, enjoying his firm abs, his chiseled body and the sexy patterns of raised black ink covering his dusky, Italian complexion.

He certainly didn't miss the sun when he was in Albania. His skin has a perfect, unrelenting tan and up close, I spot freckles across his gorgeous face. I can't get enough of that face or those hard angles up close. He leans in to kiss my neck again and I feel his immense cock pressing into my thigh. A lump forms instantaneously in my throat.

I'll never forget how that big dick felt all balled up like a knot at the base of my stomach. Enzo entered me deeper than I ever thought possible and my body has a strange, shuddering muscle memory for the last time our bodies joined. He makes a low sound in his throat almost like a purr or a growl.

"I want you," he says. "I want you right here in my kitchen."

I'd never suggested moving our locations. There's something hot as hell about sweating with a man in the kitchen with the delicious smell of buttery sauteed onions and seasoned beef in the background of your lust. Fuck playing bedroom music — bedroom cooking gets both of you hot, horny and utterly helpless for each other.

"I want your pussy wrapped around my cock," he whispers. "I don't care if you're pregnant with another man's child, tesoro. You will always be mine. Forever."

Enzo can't help himself. He slides to his knees again and eats me out until I scream and juices drip down my thighs. Then he rises to his feet again and hurriedly unbuckles his belt. The thick bulge in his pants nearly bursts forward. I want him so damn bad it hurts. Six weeks of missing him hurt like hell. I had to push all the other feelings away — about my life in America, about Uksan, and about my baby. Now that Enzo's here, it's safe to feel again. That sense of protection returns and yes, it's confusing as hell, but right here with Enzo between my legs that confusion becomes just what the doctor ordered.

In just his boxers, Enzo leans forward to kiss me. I massage his built, muscular ass with my ankles as I kiss him and tease his chest with my fingers. Enzo grunts and leans forward, pressing his hand to my baby bump.

"The baby already feels like ours," he whispers. "Taking care of you is the most important thing in the world to me. I promise."

There he goes with those promises again. Enzo kisses my neck before I can protest his promises and I lose my will to argue with the tall Italian man who is so damned good with his lips and tongue. My juices turn cold and sticky against my bare thighs and my core yearns for more from Enzo. Six weeks and I haven't felt him entering me. My body can't ever forget that incredibly full feeling.

His hand on my baby bump distracts from the warmth building between my thighs. I haven't had a moment with Enzo that wasn't tainted by guilt and this reunion isn't any different from our delicious encounter in the bathtub. He runs his hand over my curvy stomach and then cups my mound as he makes his way over my bump and towards my soaked wetness.

Enzo's fingers part my pubic hair and he strokes my soaked clit gently as he rocks his body against mine.

"Cum on my hand," he whispers as he massages my clit

with his thumb while sliding his fingers along my slit. "We can't hurt the baby with my cock..."

A part of me feels so damn dirty that Enzo's fucking me while I'm carrying another man's child. That part of my life feels so long ago, I wanted to forget it. I escaped across the ocean, I lost one boyfriend and fell into the arms of a dangerous man. *I thought I could run away from everything that happened before Italy. That's what I love about this dreamy place.*

I wanted to pretend that the baby my ex-husband forced into me would never come. I wanted to chase away my past life by running off with Uksan and worrying about the baby later.

I never expected Enzo Doukas to drop out of the sky and promise me the fucking world. He took a life to keep me safe. It's fucked up, but in his twisted, dangerous world of guns and steel, that's love. And hell, it's more love than I ever got from any man before.

I ease my hips forward, allowing him to slide his index finger deep into me while keeping pressure on my clit. We're working so slowly to getting Enzo's cock in me I can't bear it. He acts like he's the one with all the lust. Women want sex just as much as men do and trust me, after six weeks of not getting any with all the morning sickness and back pain — dick is just what the doctor ordered.

My first climax smashes into me like a tidal wave. I can't help but push my hips forward and squirt juices all over Enzo's hand. He pushes his fingers deeper into me, massaging my inner walls as I cum and making an already intense climax unbearably powerful. My ass nearly falls off the counter, but Enzo catches me and slips me back into position. He leans forward, plucking a wooden spoon from storage and running it along my thigh.

Many black women can tell you that wooden spoons are very triggering instruments indeed. Fear and the cool ticklish pleasure from the way Enzo runs the spoon over my bare thighs intermingle in a strange sensation. He chuckles and kisses my neck as he continues rubbing my thigh with the wooden spoon.

I let my guard down for far too long because as Enzo's lips wrap tightly around my neck, he raises the spoon and strikes me on the thigh — hard. The unexpected wallop forces me to yelp and Enzo breaks our kiss. What the hell was that for?

I glare at him and rub my thigh, almost ready to kick him like a dang kangaroo if he doesn't provide a decent explanation for why he smacked me so damn hard with a wooden spoon.

"What the hell was that for?" I grumble.

"Experimenting."

"With whacking the shit out of me?"

I doubt Enzo excelled in science classes during high school if this is his idea of a scientific experiment.

"With teasing you," he whispers. "With pain."

"I'm pregnant. I have enough pain."

"Fair enough," he murmurs, taking the wooden spoon and running it along my thigh again. This time, I'm properly nervous and thanks to his first hit, there isn't a chance in hell of me letting my guard down around Enzo.

"I'm onto you," I whisper.

"It's your ass," he says, his voice straining. "I've been dreaming the past six weeks about spanking your ass and watching it... move."

I would burst into laughter if he didn't sound serious. I find it hard to believe a tough man with rock-hard muscles like Enzo's would lie up in his bed fantasizing with such intensity over my ass. I have a big ass, a curvy ass, an ass that apparently provoked men to holler at me when I was way too young. It's not exactly the type of ass you expect an Italian man to lose his mind over considering their beauty standards seem to favor being flatter than a corkboard.

Enzo turns brilliant red.

"Three gentle smacks," he whispers desperately. "Please… I promise, I'll make it up to you."

"Do I get to choose how you make it up to me?"

Visions of foot massages dance in my head. I run my toes over the back of Enzo's thighs and watch as his cock jumps excitedly in his boxers. I don't want him to spank me. I want that dick inside me.

"No," he says firmly. "Six weeks without me, Grace. I don't want you to forget that I'm the boss."

We both smile because I sense that despite his macho everything, we both are perfectly sure that I've always been the boss of Enzo Doukas. He grips my hips and lifts me off the counter, turning me around so I brace my weight against the marble and allow him complete access to my behind. He doesn't rush for my butt and he doesn't rush to smack my ass with that ferocious wooden spoon of his. Enzo presses his body against mine, allying his cock to thump gently between my ass cheeks as he holds me against him.

"Every night, I missed you," he whispers. "I hope you missed me too, tesoro."

I moved my hands to brace myself and the heavy, expensive ring Enzo gave me knocks against the counter. How the hell could I forget him with nearly a million dollars in diamonds on my ring finger?

How the hell could I forget Enzo when I had to go to sleep every night admitting that the man who killed my boyfriend gave me the best dick of my life?

Yes, I fucking missed him. It kills me to admit it, but when we're together, I can't help it. I don't care about right and wrong. I just want to be with a man who gives a crap about me and my pleasure for a change.

Chapter 9

Swear On Something Big

Enzo

Six weeks was far too long without her. It feels criminal that I kept myself away from her for so long. It seems like an impossibly foolish thing to have done now that I have Grace Doukas in my arms. I don't care that she's pregnant. Soon, I'll make myself believe that. After I kill the man who got her pregnant.

I ease her pants down and run my fingers over her gorgeous butt. Touching her feels incredible after all this time. I want to feel her baby bump. I want to touch her gorgeous ass. I crave the feeling of putting my tongue between her thighs again. She whimpers as I ease my dick out of my boxers and move her underwear away from her wetness.

My fingers slide easily between her lower lips and Grace emits a sexy, unwilling moan. Her tunnel tightens around my finger and I press deeper inside her. Grace responds by clutching the counter and moving her hips back against me. She gets slicker and wetter as my fingers move more and I lose myself in the sensation of her pretty warm pussy wrapped around me.

I take Grace's ears between my lips and whisper as I plunge my fingers into her pussy.

"You are everything," I whisper. "Everything..."

She leans against the counter as I push into her deeper and make her cum hard. Our bodies shudder together as she cums. My cock threatens to burst out of my boxers, so I release it and press my dick right against Grace's entrance. She pushes her hips back and my cock thumps against her tightness before I move my hips to ease my way in. Getting my cock into her still isn't easy.

She leans over, presenting every inch of her dripping entrance to me, driving me wild with her exposed mahogany flesh. My hands run over her thighs and I grab her hips to pull her tightly against me. My cock slides into her another inch and Grace moans from the initial violation.

"I forgot..." she whimpers.

I could have never allowed myself to forget how perfect her tight pussy felt around my dick. No, I fantasized about her gorgeous body every minute I spent apart from her in Albania. I want her. I want to take in every fucking inch of her. Animal lust takes over me and I slide my hand over the front of her hip to her mound, massaging her clit as I slide another inch inside her.

I won't last long inside her perfect cunt.

Grace cries out as I bury the rest of my cock inside her. Once I reach her depths, she moans and braces herself against the counter. Her pussy tightens around me like a vice. I feel all the blood rush to my cock and my desire to take her harder overwhelms everything else. I move inside her and Grace cries out again.

"I don't want to hurt you..." I growl as I move inside her, feeling every inch of her walls around my cock. I'm going too deep. I'm going to hurt her.

"No," she whimpers, pressing her hips back into me. "You're fine."

I press my lips to her shoulder and act on the dark urge to take her flesh between my teeth. Grace cries out again as I bite her shoulder and plunge into her slow and deep. Using my hands and my cock, I easily bring her to another orgasm. Her body responding so easily to mine threatens to push me over the edge.

"I love your ass, tesoro," I murmur, removing my finger from her clit and instead toying with her bubbly butt cheeks. She has a perfect ass and my wet finger suddenly craves something deeper. Something darker.

Grace moans as I continue pumping into her and then use my wet finger to tease her asshole. Her whimpers get weaker and juices leak furiously from between her legs as I rub slow circles around her asshole.

"Do you like how I play with your ass?" I whisper.

She nods and pushes her hips back against me, allowing my finger to penetrate her soft bottom while my cock services her. My balls tighten against my body. Fuck, she's too hot. I can't hold back. I force my own orgasm out of my mind. It's more important that Grace has whatever she wants. I slide my finger into her ass and she cries out with such pleasure that I know I have to put my cock in there.

I ease my finger out of her ass and make love to her in a slow rhythm, with a finger in her butt and my cock inside her until Grace cums so many times that she slumps over the counter, out of breath and unable to move except for shuddering as she cums. I lean my body over hers and keep teasing her ass as I make love to her pussy right until I reach the edge of my climax. I slowly remove my finger from her ass and grip her perfectly thick thighs until I cum inside her.

My cock stiffens and spills thick rivers of hot seed between Grace's legs. There's nothing like cumming inside her tightness and after so long without her, touching her drives me wild. I pull my dick out of her and a gush of my cum slides down her legs as I pull her naked body against mine and kiss her. I don't want to stop, but Grace eventually pulls away with a grin on her face.

"Sorry," she says. "I just can't walk."

"A smile?"

I can't hide my surprise. Since fucking Uksan's death, she's hardly smiled.

"I've had six weeks to mourn, Enzo. And trust me... I spent a lot of that time missing what we had."

"Hm. Does that mean you have feelings for me, tesoro?"

Because fuck, I have feelings for you.

"I don't know," she whispers. "You're my husband. It's normal, right?"

"Will you stay? Be my wife?"

Her answer rips me in two.

"Just for a year," she whispers. "Maybe that's all the happiness I can take before my life falls apart."

Ha. I'm the asshole with the life falling apart. I have apartments and work and all of that, but my brother has a family. If I don't create a family of my own, I'll be creepy Uncle Enzo with the scars and the fucked up stories. I don't want that. I'd rather have a mixed up, adopted and blended family than die all alone. Dying alone is more likely to be Matteo's fate than mine.

I clutch her body against mine, yearning for more of it.

"I promise not to leave you again," I assure her. "I won't."

"You can't promise that," she whispers. "But thanks."

And she's right. Van could send me anywhere to do anything — even back to Albania. I pull Grace against my chest, cradling her close. Her baby bump presses into me and I feel uneasy at the unfamiliar sensation. Maybe if I'd known or watched her grow, it would be different. I don't fear commitment, I fear not being good enough. I fear disappointing a woman I love more than anything.

"You are way too good at keeping secrets," I murmur, rubbing her shoulders and kissing her forehead again.

"Says the mob boss."

"Can we agree on no more secrets?" I whisper. "And we both know, Van is my boss."

Grace scoffs. "Jodi's the boss of both of y'all."

"Hm," I murmur. "We'll see about that. Now... Can I take you to bed and you tell me all about this baby and what we're going to do?"

"You won't raise this baby, Enzo. I can't let you."

She's wrong about that. I won't let her run off with that child and get herself mixed up with another thug or another loser. She deserves better than that. She was strong enough to run from her pain and what she was born into. I wasn't. I killed and I keep killing despite the drinking and the nightmares. I know I won't stop, but that doesn't mean I don't respect her or admire her for leaving behind her family curse.

"Right. But I can help you plan. I'm excellent with children."

Grace chuckles and snorts. "Really? This is the least kid-friendly penthouse I've ever been in."

"I helped raise Eddie. I have other cousins. Trust me."

Grace gives me a skeptical look that shouldn't turn me on. Then, she grabs my hands and gestures toward the bedroom. "Don't worry. I have other uses for you... in the bedroom."

Oh yes. I'd love for her to use me in the bedroom. All fucking night if that's what she wants.

"Yes, signora," I say to her. "Your wish is my command."

Three Months Later

Grace, approximately 7.5 months pregnant
Enzo, entirely smitten

Grace and Jodi stayed up late last night ordering baby supplies online with my credit card. Grace officially has a doctor, new maternity clothes and everything she needs to birth *our* baby in comfort. She's close, but not terribly close to the due date. The women act like she'll have the baby tomorrow. Ana finally meets Grace and goes nuts with preparations and demands that I pass over my credit card to support the child.

It's hard not to share in Grace's excitement, even if I constantly remind myself the child isn't mine.

There's still a man out there who could lay claim to that child. Until that man lies dead in the ground — Grace's baby won't be mine. I'll have to change that, even if she balks. She doesn't understand how it would break me to lose her and this child. I killed Uksan for less, no? This is my duty.

After our precious year passes, I have no plans to let her go. I'll kill anyone who stands in the way of us being together. I already feel like Grace saved me from loneliness. This big penthouse gets lonely, even with Ember. I don't have to worry about Grace leaving little "presents" at the foot of my bed... She's much better company than my poodle. She's a woman and an incredibly beautiful one with a gentle demeanor and eyes I could lose myself in.

Grace grunts as I wrap my arms around her. She wouldn't be so sleepy if it weren't for her late night ordering baby clothes and laughing at my pre-baby nerves with the help of my annoying sister, Ana, and my sister-in-law, Jodi.

Unfortunately, I'm about to get a taste of my own medicine. Just as I press my nose into Grace's neck and think of all the filthy ways I can enjoy her body before heading downstairs to meet with the contractor about repairing the first floor units, my phone rings.

I know it's Van before I swing my legs out of bed and pick up the phone. That doesn't make me any less annoyed.

"It's 7 a.m. Van."

My brother grunts imperiously. "You're up, what's the problem? I have work for you."

"It's not something that can wait until later?"

"Not exactly. I know you're in a complicated situation. I wanted to give you time."

I want a cigarette so fucking badly. The past three months, I've successfully quit for the baby, but Van sounds awfully close to threatening to send me back to Albania. If I have to leave Grace again, I'll definitely need a fucking cigarette.

"What do you want?" I snap.

"You should pick up smoking to relax," Van jokes. It's not like I don't deserve him fucking with me.

"Hurry. Grace is sleeping. I don't want to wake her."

Unfortunately, just saying her name is enough to rouse her slightly. She grunts and rolls over, her silk sleep shirt riding up and exposing her bare breasts to me. Fuck. How am I supposed to listen to Van when I get an instant hard-on seeing Grace's tits?

"It's about Eddie."

"Isn't Ana who you call when you want to throw a good funeral?"

"Ana's not talking to me," Van grunts. "And anyway, Eddie's not dead. But... the Vicari's want to send him back if we don't send someone right away. He needs a babysitter. They might send him back even if we go. I can't risk that."

We both know if Eddie returns to Italy, or even tries to stake out some space in the east, he'll invite trouble and possibly his own death. It's not safe for him in Europe. How could he have screwed up in America already?

"What's he done?"

"No one will talk until I send a representative from the family."

"Isn't there someone less valuable you can send?"

Van clears his throat and responds with an infuriatingly prompt, "No."

I pause before answering him, tapping my feet impatiently on the ground. If Van orders me to leave, it's my duty to obey, but I have this obligation and desire to keep my arms firmly wrapped around Grace West Doukas. I want her. I can't bear the thought of spending more time without her, especially not after the past three months.

Growing close to her makes leaving feel impossible.

"I can't leave her again," I answer my brother flatly, risking the consequences of defiance to tell him the truth. He was in love, wasn't he? He'll understand...

"This is a family matter. There's no need for you to leave her. Do you still have a safe house?"

"I promised my mother I wouldn't sell the house. I've kept that promise."

She can stay with me. My disappointment fades as I imagine taking Grace for walks along Two Mile Hollow Beach, where my mother would bring me before she left papa. I loved that beach, even if I always hated America with its loud English speakers and shitty coffee.

"I'll have a crew get the place ready and the Vicaris will send men. Announce your plans to Grace... but stay away from any frying pans. Jodi always uses those when we argue," Van says.

"You deserve it, old bastard."

"I am three years older than you, Enzo. I'm not old," he huffs sensitively. Fatherhood has definitely made Van more sensitive.

"Right. You're ancient."

He rolls his eyes and continues ignoring my comment.

"Your flights are in two days out of Rome. Paolo will send you the information."

He hangs up. Great. All I have to do is talk to Grace. She's sitting up in bed completely nude and completely tempting me. Her breasts are fucking beautiful and those nipples... dark, delicious... everything. My mouth waters.

Why talk about anything serious at all when I can climb

into bed with her and forget my irritating nephew or my imperious brother?

"What's wrong?"

"Nothing, tesoro."

"I know you way too well to believe that."

"Van's sending me to America. Long Island."

I can't mistake the expression that takes over Grace's face. It's too organic, too immediate to be mistaken for anything else.

"Does Long Island scare you?"

Grace bites her lower lip and then barrels straight past my question.

"You're going alone?"

"No. I promised I wouldn't leave you until the baby. It's a family affair. No guns necessary."

"Did you find out somehow?" she ventures, her face falling when she realizes I don't have a clue what she's talking about and she just exposed herself.

I don't understand what Grace means, and my face shows it.

"You're not going to kill my husband, are you?"

She struggles to say the word husband, but anger still courses through me. That fucking bastard has no claim to her. She's mine. You don't hurt a woman and get to keep her locked up like an insect for you to toy with. Grace deserves her freedom, and she deserves protection. Despite my intentions, killing her husband isn't the purpose of my visit.

"No. This is family business."

She rolls her eyes and gives me one of those sassy, knowing looks. "I know your family business is killing."

"Your ex-husband lives in Long Island?" Since she's giving it freely, why not probe for information?

If he's not her ex now, he soon will be. I won't leave America and leave that man alive. I've already expressed my intentions to Grace. Once I decide, I don't change my mind. Don't women like stubborn Italian men?

"Forget I said anything," she mutters as I scan her face for clues. I won't need clues to find her ex-husband if he's in New York. I have something better than clues—people on the ground who respect the mother country and those of us living the Old World mafia life.

"I won't forget," I tell her. "But since I don't even know his name, your ex-husband is, for the moment, safe."

But not for long.

"I don't want you killing people for me, Enzo," Grace announces firmly.

"What about for the baby?"

"My baby," she whispers. "My responsibility. My baby."

I smoothly breeze past the subject. She still hasn't changed my mind, and I doubt she will.

"You can come with me. You'll be safe. I have a luxurious little place in East Hampton. It was my mother's."

Grace's expression only becomes more troubling. This conversation should make her feel safer. She pulls the blanket over her nude form and sits up seriously.

"I'm not coming," Grace responds firmly.

What the hell does she mean that she's not coming? I don't want to leave without her. Yes, she'll be safe in Italy, but Grace will be safer with me. I'll be safer. If she isn't with me, I can't control how I react. I need to have a reason for being a good man.

"I promised I wouldn't leave you. Now you want to stay?"

Women have never been this confusing to me.

"I don't want to stay. If I set foot on Long Island, my first husband will find out and he'll kill me. Trust me."

I'd like to see him try. You take what's mine, I take your life.

I scoff. "I can handle him. He so much as looks as you, I end his life."

She doesn't have to worry about ex-boyfriends or ex-husbands or anyone when I'm around. I won't be alone in Long Island. Italians look after each other and even the Americans have deep ties to the mother country. We'll have respect in Long Island coming straight from the coast. Grace won't have to worry as long as she's with me, but she's giving me a very stubborn look.

"He's not just a man," Grace snaps. "He's a cop. He'll know from the second they scan my passport at LaGuardia that I'm back and he'll come for me."

"We'll fly through JFK then."

"I'm not joking, Enzo."

"Neither am I. So what, he's a cop. We have guns. We have a family. You have nothing to worry about."

My muscles tighten as I get the distinct impression it won't be so easy to change her mind. I've always liked that she was so stubborn. I still like how unattainable her heart is, trapped behind all these walls. I don't know how long I'll be in Long Island to settle family business, but I know if I leave her here, I'll be breaking a promise.

A woman never forgets a broken promise, it doesn't matter what twisted justification us men come up with. They don't forget and they don't forgive because they know just as well as we do that a man's word is his honor.

"I promised not to leave you," I say to her, moving onto the bed and sitting next to her. She's vulnerable now. What if Albanians raided the coast? It will be much easier to protect her if she's by my side, right where she belongs.

"I know. But this is my choice, Enzo. You've never stopped me from making a choice before."

She's scared. She's really fucking scared of this bastard and I hate I can't take that away from her.

"What if I want to?"

"You wouldn't," she says, denying me eye contact. "You've

done bad things, but you're not a bad person. You have a sense of honor."

"My sense of honor tells me not to abandon the woman I love."

Her eyes flit to mine. I don't care about what I've said to her out loud. It doesn't hurt to admit the truth, and it certainly doesn't hurt to admit what has been obvious the entire time.

"What are you saying, Enzo?"

"I love you," I plead with her. Can't she see that? It will break me in half to leave her here. It will break me in half if I miss any moment of our child's life. I don't want her to choose this and normally, I wouldn't give a shit what she wants. But she's Grace and I love her. I love her far too much.

"Stop it," she responds as firmly as possible with her nervous, trembling voice.

"I mean it," I tell her. "I love you so fucking much."

"What about the contract?" she says, as if that changes my feelings. The contract was part of my plan, falling in love like this wasn't. I didn't expect knowing her better to make me love Grace even more.

"You stay here, you force me to break it. I don't want to," I murmur. "Please. Don't make me break our contract. Don't make me."

"Are you asking me for a divorce?" she says, tilting her head to the side in confusion.

I don't know what the fuck I'm doing. Walking away? Running? Hoping to convince her? Doesn't Grace know that I'm a mess? I love her too much. I love her so much I killed for her before I kissed her. She doesn't understand what that obsessive love does to a man like me, how it changes me into a fucking kitten. I'll do whatever she wants, even if it breaks me into a million fucking pieces.

"No," I whisper. "I love you, so I'll grant you a divorce."

"This is very confusing."

I lean over and kiss her. She accepts my kiss, which considering everything else, counts as a good sign. Her lips are full, delicious, large lips. She has bigger lips than any I've ever kissed and I always want to take them between my teeth and tug on her. I want to consume every part of her and taste her... and please her.

"I will do anything to please you," I murmur, pushing her braids out of her face. "But if I break my word to you, I don't deserve to stay married to you."

"It's not that I don't trust you, Enzo. You don't know my first husband."

"If you trusted me, you would know there's not a chance I'd let him hurt you. I love you, Grace but... maybe this is a sign. I should let you go."

I don't know if I mean it. I never planned on letting her go, but how the fuck can I keep a woman who doesn't want me? I thought I could. I thought I could be the stubborn, imperious monster that papa raised me to become.

"What? Now this conversation is about letting me go?"

It's not what I wanted our conversation to be about, but sitting with her on the bed and thinking about the situation, I see the choice in front of me clearly. I have my suspicions that Van's doing this because he disapproves of my methods, or because he worries I'm hurting her, or he's upset I killed someone. He's right to be upset. By rights, he should have had my life for killing Uksan.

But it feels cruel that he should push me to this point — forcing me to give her up.

"I won't cast you out. You stay here, enjoy my apartment when I'm gone. When I return, I'll give you some money to help you get on your feet. I don't want you working the streets—

"I've done other jobs," she interrupts defensively. The air between us turns thick in an instant. She's angry with me. She's disappointed and worse—she doesn't understand how I can love her and do this to her. I must be gentle.

"I only meant I didn't want you desperate. That may not be my child, Grace... but I love you and that means I love every part of you, even if those parts of you are walking around in another person. I can't make you love me back. I ruined that when I shot your boyfriend."

I can't bear to look at her. It hurts too much to admit how much of a dick I've been. It hurts to realize that my first immoral action led me to this point. I killed a man, thinking I'd earn a prize, but you can't keep a free woman in a cage or a penthouse. You can't keep a free woman and expect her to bend to your will. No contract in the world can give me Grace's heart — but that's the only part of her I really want.

It's not worth it to sleep with her if I can't love her. I can't disrespect her like that.

I might have quit smoking, but there aren't any laws yet about drinking in the morning. To get through this conversation, I'll definitely need a drink. I don't bother with wine. Not strong enough. This is a job for vodka. Grace wrinkles her nose as she watches me drink.

"I'd rather talk about this when you weren't drunk."

"I'm not drunk yet."

She rolls her eyes. Stop thinking about how fucking cute she is. She's ending things.

"If we end our contract... I'll wait for you. I'll be here when you come back. I can promise that."

"I don't know when I'll come back."

"I'll wait, but I need you to promise me something."

I would give her anything.

"Don't track him down," she says. "Don't kill my first husband. Please."

"According to you, he's still your husband."

"I've been around you people too long to know that's not a promise."

"I won't kill him."

"Swear on something big, Enzo."

"I swear on my love for you, I'll do the right thing."

Let's leave the right thing up to my determination.

Grace smiles. Good. I love that fucking smile. But that won't make leaving her any easier.

Chapter 10

Missing Kidney

Grace

This time, I feel his absence. It's like someone removed one of my kidneys. Not even Ember snuggling at the foot of my bed serves as a sufficient replacement for Enzo. My ex-husband. The man I love. The man whose bed I'll keep warm until he comes back. A California King is really fucking sad when you're alone. It's not the luxury bed that draws you in, it's sharing it with somebody. I had somebody – a crazy, fucked up criminal somebody who killed for me. He would kill for me again.

I missed my chance. The thing is, Enzo doesn't understand what he's dealing with. He doesn't understand the power my first husband has. If that man finds out I'm still carrying his child, there will be a target on my back. I don't mind throwing myself into the line of danger. Lord knows I've done it enough in my life. I can't bring myself to do that to my unborn child. I can't force Enzo to risk his freedom in another country for me. I can't.

That's what I thought until the dreams started – the dreams about my past, the dreams about Uksan and the dreams about Enzo Doukas. The dreams keep me up all night, and the crazy fucked up pregnancy dreams tell me that I made a mistake. Amara was always superstitious and I know what she would say. She'd tell me that all this is a message from the baby. The baby wants Enzo Doukas back. I dream of him every night. I dream of the way he stroked my hair. I dream of his gray eyes. I dream of him whispering that one special word he calls me… tesoro. His treasure.

I wake up in the middle of the night about a week after he leaves, sweating from another nightmare involving my first husband with his hands around my neck. I can almost feel the bruises, even if it's just a dream. My body remembers what I've been through even as I do everything to forget, including shedding every bit of my identity. Some nights, sleep is just fucking impossible. I have to remind myself that I'm safe here.

There are cameras everywhere in the apartment, and guards posted at the front doors. Van arranged for my security and Jodi arranged for him to cut it down just enough so I could breathe. I miss Enzo too much tonight. I reach for Ember's furry body on the bed. She makes a low growling noise and rolls onto her back for a 1 a.m. tummy rub. I scratch her little tummy and then she gets up excitedly, barks and rushes to her food bowl. *Girl, I ain't feeding your happy ass…*

When I get out of bed wearing a black silk floor-length maternity night dress, Ember runs back over to me, jumps on the bed, rolls on her back and then rolls onto all fours and jumps off the bed, wagging her tail as she follows me to the balcony doors. I make little kissing noises to get Ember to follow me outside. I know it's especially wrong since I'm pregnant, but I especially miss the scent of tobacco on Enzo's clothes. I miss his hands. I miss his tongue.

I close my eyes and lean over the edge, surveying the apartments and the streets below. I can see my old apartment, the little place I impulsively let Uksan move into, the place I first brought my secret when I fled New York. Ember runs between my legs and barks a couple times. The streets are always noisy on the coast. Tourists and townspeople party until the morning. I can even hear the thumping music from Jalousie, the gritty accents on German tourists and then men laughing and screaming at each other in Italian.

It's not just that I don't want to be alone. I miss Enzo. I can't stand another night here without him. Hell, I'm barely sleeping through the night without him. While he works, there's no way for me to contact him. I walk back into the bedroom and search for my cell phone in the bed. I only have one of those old school flip phones to call Italian numbers and there are only two Italian phone numbers saved in the phone. It's too early in the morning, but perhaps since the nightclub's open, it won't be too late?

I call the first number saved – the one I'm only meant to use for emergencies.

Van Doukas arrives in the morning just like he promised when I called. Jodi's with the kids, he explains as he mutters commands to his security team and they allow him into Enzo's penthouse. Van glances around as if he doesn't visit the place often, which admittedly, he doesn't. Enzo's private about his personal space and too meticulous in his housekeeping for a man like Van who exudes more obvious brutishness.

After brief greetings, Van gets straight to the point. I wouldn't have guessed he were a mob boss before Enzo told me, but now that I know, I see the little signs of his leadership in his forceful attitude and the subtle ways he commands attention. He's slightly taller than his younger brother with a rougher face, but illuminated blue eyes.

"What made you change your mind?"

"I miss him."

Van raises an eyebrow. "I was under the impression that he held you here in some interminable contract."

Jodi must have told him. It shouldn't surprise me that she would have passed the information on to her husband, but I also didn't expect to have to explain my complicated situation to Van. Yes, my circumstances forced me to marry Enzo Doukas, but I had my own reasons. He didn't manipulate me entirely. I saw something in his face that made me want to say 'yes' – even before I knew he was such a lover and a monster wrapped in one deliciously hot body.

"Enzo ended our contract before he left."

"I see," Van says, raking his fingers through his hair and giving me a look of visible frustration mixed with a dash of disbelief.

"Would you like some wine?"

"Water is fine," he says. "Thank you. I don't mean to intrude."

"You aren't intruding. Believe me, it gets lonely sitting here pregnant all day."

"Jodi mentioned you might feel that way."

I hand Van a glass of water and he takes a few gentle sips, never taking his gaze off me. I've watched Enzo do the same thing. He's not ogling me, but studying me. He searches my body language for signs of deception, for clues that men in his line of work have to look for to survive. Mobsters aren't so different from cops.

"I understand if you can't help me, but I shouldn't have let Enzo go there alone. We both know he can go too far sometimes."

"Yes. If it weren't for your sake, he would have suffered further consequences over the incident."

He swirls his glass and from the look of him, I can tell exactly what he means by those vague words mobsters always use for plausible deniability. If it weren't for me, Enzo would have died for killing without orders. That's the world he lives in. Mobsters are like cops in another way too – they don't change.

"He's grateful for your mercy."

Van chuckles. "He isn't. He expects it. You... You're wary

of me and all men, including my brother. He mentions you have trouble in the States."

He's as observant as his brother, but Van doesn't put on the same arrogant displays of his intellect.

"You could say that."

"I'll help you," Van says, exhaling with an expression that appears to be relief. "But I have a few requests I want to make."

"I understand."

"You know who I am, right, Grace? My idiot brother cannot possibly be so suave as to have kept my identity from you."

I nod because I don't dare acknowledge it right now. If Enzo's a dangerous man, his brother has to be worse. He's older, more covered in scars, and I sense he would kill me in an instant if he felt it served him. Staying in his good favor would work very much to my advantage.

"Good," Van grunts. "Very good."

"Your requests?"

"I want you to tell me your honest feelings about my brother. Now."

Okay. I expected him to ask me to bring a package through JFK or something else that was at least mildly criminal. I didn't expect a visit from a mobster to be about feelings. Van senses my surprise.

"Family is very important to me," He offers as an explanation.

"I care about Enzo. I miss him. That's why I want to see him."

"That's not what I'm asking."

This feels more like an interrogation or an investigation than a 'request' as Van euphemistically put this. He's in the mob. I give the wrong answer and I'm dead. It's always best to go with the truth in situations like this, isn't it? The truth might get you killed but at least you die knowing that you did what was right. Lies are too risky with dangerous men.

"I love him."

"I see, and that baby you're carrying has nothing to do with it?"

My gaze hardens as I give Giovanni the fierce look he deserves right back. I don't appreciate his offensive insinuation in the slightest.

"I'm not using this baby to trap your brother. He knows about my past and he doesn't judge me for it. I'm not a gold digger."

My voice won't disguise my anger, even if I put my best efforts into sounding steady and unbreakable.

"I find it convenient that your boyfriend dies, my brother's smitten and you're pregnant with yet another man's child."

Enzo told him? I didn't realize they were close like that. Enzo really keeps so much to himself, especially his relationship with his older brother.

Unfortunately, I can't worry about Enzo's relationship with Van while the annoying tower of a man insults me to my face. I don't blame Enzo for telling him, but I blame Van for acting like a damned dick and insinuating shit about me. I'm not a liar. I'm not a gold digger. I didn't choose to drag Enzo into my mess.

"I have a past and I haven't hidden that past from your brother."

"My brother loves very deeply, Grace. He doesn't always see things clearly when he sets his mind on something."

Van sets his glass on the counter and then taps his fingers, not impatiently, almost as if he's keeping the conversation's rhythm and obviously, watching my responses very closely. From what I understand about the mafia, the boss doesn't come out to do busy work unless it's very important to the family.

"I'm not using Enzo. I swear. I'll admit, I agreed to marry him because I knew I had a secret and I had to stay far from a dangerous man. Enzo knows the truth about me and I know the truth about him. I love him, Van. I don't love his money or his lifestyle. I want to see him."

"It would be unfortunate if you were to betray him."

"You don't have to worry about that."

"Ensure that I don't."

As swiftly as he threatens me, all without raising his voice or laying a finger on me, Van smiles cheerily. Business is over.

"I'll get you on the next flight tomorrow morning. Given the short notice, I'll have to fly you private. I hope Enzo doesn't mind that I sent him on a commercial flight. You'll need money for the trip. My assistant will return before supper with a credit card. €25,000 ought to suffice?"

"Won't I meet Enzo there?"

"Yes," Van responds with confusion. "You'll need money for shopping at the airport. That ought to cover what you need, but I can have Paolo increase the limit if you need."

I can't tell if that man likes me or hates me. He accuses me of being a gold digger in one breath and offers me money in another. Is this a trap?

"That's generous enough. I don't even need that much..."

"I'll have an armored car take you to Enzo's place. Perhaps it will be a pleasurable surprise."

"You can't tell him?"

"I haven't heard from Enzo in a week," Van says, shrugging. "He hates New York. I'm not surprised. He probably doesn't want me gloating."

"Did you really send him there to punish him?"

Van doesn't smile. "He's lucky he isn't dead for disobedience. I'll see that you enjoy your trip."

"Thank you, Van."

"You may not be my brother's wife, but I suspect the tides will change again and you'll be family. Once a Doukas, always a Doukas."

He kisses me on both cheeks, the way I've had to get used

to over here, and then he leaves. I did it. I got the mob boss to send me to New York.

I can't resist the desire to see Enzo, but my concern for my life doesn't disappear completely. I'll be at risk the second I land in New York. I tell myself it doesn't matter, because I have Enzo, but despite all my love and all my trust, some beasts might be too big for even a pillar of a man like Enzo Doukas.

I'm tired of being his victim. I'm tired of running away. This time, I'll run headfirst into hell with the devil by my side. He won't let me down. I know it.

Chapter 11

The Long Island Mafia

Enzo

Vinnie and Mike have to be the biggest fucking idiots on the planet. Forced to use these two idiot grease-balls as hired help, I completely accept my brother sent me here to punish me. When they're not grunting like mating wild boars in my home gym, they're arguing about the fucking Islanders' game or the Giants' game or some other fucking American game that nobody gives a shit about.

I quit smoking. Can you tell? Every fucking sound annoys me and having to put up with Eddie during the day doesn't work. He's fallen to pieces, the little shit. I won't let him stay in my house, but I have eyes on him. He does more coke than Matteo did in his late twenties and the mob here hate druggies. Addicts and junkies and crackheads ruin the bonds of brotherhood. They bring trouble and the mob doesn't like that kind of trouble.

Soon, I think my nephew will have nowhere to go but back to his father. He'll be dead if he stays here and dead if he returns to Italy. Perhaps the Greeks would take him, but I don't recall Stavros Pagonis showing mercy and charity. Albania. That might be the only place he stands a chance, but I wouldn't put it past Matteo to kill his own son.

I couldn't do the same in his position. Even if I had a son like Eddie, I couldn't. I'd never admit that to my fucking brothers, but it's the truth. They already think I'm the weakest, so I'd rather not prove it to them. I would die for my child and kill for them. My child. So far away from the woman I want to be with, I can't help but yearn for her and the soft turn of her stomach. I'm ready to be a father. Blood is important, but we can sort out blood later.

I need to be ready for Grace and ready for the baby when I return to Italy with or without Eddie. I don't give a fuck what she says or what she thinks anymore.

We're divorced, officially, but I'm changing that right back around when I land in Italy. She will marry me again, I swear. I mustn't scare her but... she has to know how real my feelings are.

My soul aches without her. I thought I could be the good guy and love her so hard that I could let her go.

I'm not the fucking good guy and I never will be. Vinnie and Mike play *Dance Dance Revolution* on the ancient gaming system I pulled out of the basement. I nurse a Jagermeister on the couch, willing the fiery licorice syrup to knock me into next week. I have to meet Eddie in the morning with the Vicari boss and I don't look forward to hearing my nephew's sentence for his recent spate of unacceptable behavior.

Eddie doesn't fucking listen, that's his problem. You can be too stubborn. You can get yourself killed. Vinnie loses this round and Mike elbows him which turns into the most obnoxious slap fight of all time. Fucking bastards.

"Ay! Can you stop? Fucking idiots," I scream, pouring more Jagermeister into my mouth. It's disgusting. It's delicious. It's getting me drunk enough to handle the idiots.

Vinnie and Mike stop slapping each other like seals immediately. Mike has a heavy Long Island accent. He's a Pazzini, but his mother's a Zagarella, which means he's related to the Vicari's... The New York Italians have a far more complicated series of family connections all fucked up by intermarrying and marrying Greeks and marrying the wrong types of people. That doesn't even touch their obsession with whores and mistresses.

Who can blame them? I want to marry the wrong type of woman again. I'd make the mistake of sullying my bloodline for the sake of pleasure and love. Who wouldn't? Blood matters, but it's liquid. It shifts, it dilutes, it changes. Our mother country makes us Italian, the culture we're taught. Our thing. Our way of life. It's in just one drop of Italian blood.

"What do you want us to do, boss?" Mike asks, his white tank top gripping his sweaty, tattooed arms, each one as fat as a ham hock.

"Anything except play this fucking game. Fuck you both... Fuck drinking..."

"We're lying low, boss," Vinnie says. "Hey, you need anything – girls, cocaine, we can get it for you."

"I don't need either of those things. I need peace and quiet."

"We got two strippers at the club by the name of Peace," Mike chimes in excitedly. "But Quiet got into some trouble in Philly and we ain't seen her since."

I miss Grace.

"Don't bother with strippers."

"Boss, we'll get you some ice, okay? That'll clear your head from all the fuckin' Jager you've been drinking," Vinnie says.

"If I didn't know better, I'd say he was going through a breakup," Mike adds.

Please, Van. Give me cause to kill them both. I miss Lucky and Dino and how old world and quiet they were. I never took to America, and I never took to New York, despite owning my mother's childhood summer home here. Vinnie and Mike throw on their jackets and argue loudly about which dealer to call as they approach the front door. Mike throws it open and I anticipate a full return of my peace and quiet – which I desperately need.

"Boss! Looks like you already got a stripper outside!" Mike yells.

"Dumb fuck, when have you ever seen a pregnant stripper?"

"Some of the boys are into some weird shit, man. Weird shit," Mike says to him.

I hope I never have to see Mike again. Dumbass. Scowling, drunk and stumbling forward with my hand firmly grasped around my bottle of Jagermeister, I ooze towards the front door to chase off whatever pregnant stripper these men have ordered for me. But of course, it's not a stripper at all. I hear her before I get to the door.

"A stripper? Who the hell are you calling a stripper? I'm here to see Enzo. I thought this was his house."

Fuck. It's Grace. I don't want her to see me like this, but I'm so drunk that there isn't any other way for me to see her unless I pass out on the floor for a few minutes. My drunken mind only seems to come up with ideas for making the situation worse.

"Sorry ma'am," Mike says. "But I ain't ever seen a woman as sexy as you who didn't spend some time on the pole."

"Mike. That's enough," I snarl at him in Italian. He barely understands, but he knows I mean business.

"You know her?" Vinnie asks, gaping lewdly at Grace and slowly piecing together what's obvious.

"Yes," I growl, finally bringing myself to look Grace in the eye. "I know her. But I don't know what the fuck she's doing here."

Hurt registers on her face and there's a pang of rage and guilt right along with the bubbling pit of Jager in my stomach. Fuck. She's here. She fucking came all the way here. For me.

"Listen ma'am, he's been drinking a little," Vinnie says, putting his arm around Grace's shoulders and guiding her inside. There are guards in the car watching to make sure only our people touch her. I have nothing to fear, but just watching Vinnie put his arm around Grace sends rage coursing through me.

"Don't touch her," I snap. "Take the bottle. I'll take her upstairs."

Grace's expression twists with rage. Angry? She has no right to be angry. I'm the one who looks like shit. I'm the one who is too fucking drunk to stand. I'm the one angry with her. She stayed behind when she should have come. We got divorced when we should have stayed together. But she's back...

I won't let her go again. I lean forward and grab Grace's forearm. I'm sure she can smell the liquor on me as I kiss her cheek and she grimaces.

"You're drunk," she says with an incredibly judgmental tone.

What does she expect me to do without her? I don't care for strippers or other women. When I want something, I focus on it. I've always had that hunter's instinct. The instinct wasn't just trained into me. We were bred with killer instincts on the coast. I want to kiss her again so fucking bad.

Instead, I drunkenly slur, "Yes. You're beautiful."

"Thanks..."

That was a grumble. Definitely a grumble. I press my hand to her lower back and usher her down the hall.

"This is quite the surprise," I murmur, guiding her over the hardwood floors and watching her gawk around the family home. She can get a tour tomorrow. I want her out of sight now...

"It's nine in the morning, Enzo. You're drunk," Grace repeats. "I thought you were here working, not partying your ass off."

She thinks this is a party? It's misery. I'm mourning her like she's dead and wondering if this is the price I pay for killing her boyfriend. I'll never have her completely... I'll never get exactly what I want. She wants an answer about the drinking, I give her an answer.

"I've been watching Vinnie and Mike play old video games for weeks. It gets incredibly boring."

She stops walking and frowns at me.

"Is this really how we're going to greet each other?"

I bite my lower lip. I don't want to be cruel to her but I really didn't expect this. I really don't know why she's here. Grace made it clear that we didn't belong in each other's lives. I shrug.

"No," she snaps. "This isn't right. I'm going upstairs alone and you can knock on my door when you're sober and kind and the good man who left me in Italy."

She storms off, ignoring me when I call after her, "What if I'm not a good man?"

"Get it together, Enzo," Grace says as she supports her pregnant stomach up the stairs. She won't even turn around to look at me. I've fucked up and even if I'm drunk, I know it.

I'll have to fix things with her...

Sobering up takes longer than I hope. My stomach churns and my head spins in the opposite direction as I plaster myself on the couch and subject myself to advice about "my lady" from Vinnie and Mike.

"You gotta break down the door and show her who's boss," Vinnie says. "Dick her down."

"Fucking idiot," Mike says. "Pregnant women can't have sex."

"That didn't stop your wife fuckin' with me."

"Talk about my wife one more time and I'll crack you a shot," Mike threatens between large swigs of beer. The last thing I need to smell is beer... I hate these stupid fucks.

"Calm down, you fucking greaseball," Vinnie says chuckling at a joke that could get him killed if they weren't brothers.

"Who you calling a greaseball?" Mike's fist balls up, ready to beat the brakes off his brother over an insult they kick around like a football.

I muscle my way to sobriety through their foolish argument, which eventually turns to a brawl and a hug and a good cry. My head hurts and I must have fallen asleep for a few hours because it's dark when I get off the couch. Vinnie and Mike carried their argument to the kitchen after I fell asleep because as the sleep slowly leaves my eyes, I can hear them echoing over the stove and ribbing each other over their ma's tomato sauce recipe and who makes the best version of it.

I slip past them unnoticed and knock on Grace's door.

"No, Vinnie!" Grace yells. "I don't want to compare the damn pasta sauce for the last time."

At least we're both already annoyed by the boys. I press my head to the door attempting to soak up any detail of her I can. She's here. Grace is really here and there's something I can do about that.

"It's Lorenzo."

I might be sober, but my throat itches desperately for water. I sound raspy and still drunk enough that she might not open the door. I hold my breath, hoping she doesn't leave me to suffer desperately at her door. I want to talk to her. More than that, I want to hold her. I thought I wouldn't see her for months and the shock of seeing her angered me and first but then I remembered what I'd allowed myself to feel for her and the vow I took to myself to protect her. Always.

What changed her mind? What made her come here?

Grace opens the door, and my gaze wanders straight to her baby bump. A lump forms in my throat.

"Why did you come?" I murmur, getting straight to the point. Grace folds her arms and scans me, clearly analyzing my sobriety. I stand up as straight as possible, towering over my beautiful African American princess and the baby growing inside her.

"It doesn't matter. I clearly made a mistake."

Her warm brown eyes glow with her fire. I hate disappointing her but fuck, it's hard to think of anything but kissing her when staring into those gorgeous wide eyes. I don't want to fight, I just want to touch her.

"I'm sorry. I didn't think I would see you."

"I didn't think I would see a man I didn't recognize."

"I was only a little drunk."

"You smell like you've been drinking for days," she answers honestly. I sniff my left armpit. Fuck, she's right. Even when I'm sober, I've been living in filth, relying on Vinnie and Mike's noxious clouds of cologne to cover up my own filthy scent. If the bastards weren't arguing with each other 24/7, they would have tossed me into the shower here ages ago — or even right into the sound. Dealing with my nephew's problems stuck far away from the woman I love has had more of an effect on me than I care to admit.

I don't need to confess my emotions when I can bury them in a bottle of Jagermeister, but Grace is too irresistible and too perfect for me to lock my heart away from.

"I missed you," I murmur honestly, taking in every inch of her, including her bump. She could give birth any minute based on her appearance. It's better she's with me in that case.

"I missed you too," she says. "That's why I'm here. I'm sorry that I didn't trust you, Enzo. I was wrong."

I feel too fiercely protective of her to allow her to apologize.

"You apologize for nothing," I murmur, stepping into her bedroom and appreciating that she allows me that first little step. I run my thumb over the exquisite lips I missed since I left Italy.

"Italy wasn't the same without you," she says. "I didn't expect that. I didn't expect to feel anything for you and I didn't expect it to be so fast and so strong."

"I fell in love the second I saw you. It doesn't matter what journey you take to love, as long as you get there."

I can't resist her for another second. I grab Grace's cheeks and kiss her like it's the last fucking time I ever will. She squeals and then settles quickly, her body pressing against mine as I hold my fucking woman as tightly as I want her. When I pull away, my lips burn from the heat between us.

Her anxious squeal turns into slow, certain breathing as our bodies press together. There it is – that energy between us that changes everything. Once our lips touch the mood between us shifts and our closeness becomes something more. It's biology. It's nature. It's love. I feel like a father who needs to protect the mother of his young and care for her body and her pleasure. I run my hands over the small of Grace's back. My Grace. She's all mine.

"Bed," I murmur. "Now."

"Is that your idea of showing me you're a good man?" she says teasingly. "Taking me to bed?"

"No," I whisper, dropping to my knees. "But it's a start."

I grab Grace's thighs and pull her close before she can scamper away from me and chide me until the sun comes up. I have other plans for those lips tonight that don't involve more bickering. I was wrong for my coldness to her. We're together, and that's all I fucking want.

I slide her yoga pants over her hips and kiss the tops of her delicious dark brown thighs as I expose them slowly. The weight she's put on to carry her baby fills out her shapely body in all the right ways. My cock stiffens the instant my lips touch the top of her thighs. I slide my index finger into her underwear, peeling the fabric away from her soft flesh. I disappear beneath her baby bump to kiss gently above her furry mound once I slide her underwear over her curves and drop the silky fabric to the bedroom floor.

I slide my fingers between Grace's lower lips, plunging into her gooey center and forcing a desperate moan from her lips.

My tongue splits her lower lips as I use my fingers to massage her walls and press my pink muscle to her clit. The best apologies happen on your knees. She cries out with pleasure and hikes a thick thigh onto my shoulders as I grab her ass and pull her pussy deeper into my mouth.

I missed the sweet taste of the juices dribbling from her and the arousing, musky natural female scent between her legs. With easy effort from my tongue, Grace approaches an intense climax. Her leg digs into my shoulder, her body tenses and Grace's weight sinks into my palms, filling my hands with soft flesh from her voluptuous bottom. Her chest heaves as she cums hard and the sweet apex of her thighs fills my mouth with her juices as she finishes hard. I suck every drop of juices off of her lower lips and can't resist rubbing my tongue over her sensitive clit again.

Grace whimpers as I tease her clit to arousal and push her over the edge of one orgasm to another with no time for her to catch her breath. She loses herself in another leg-shaking orgasm. I keep sucking her juices off her lips and then slowly kiss the top of her mound as Grace trembles with pleasure.

Once she has time to recover, my tongue pries her lower lips apart and I slowly lick the length of her soaked folds, wrapping my lips around her clit until she screams. Grace's thighs wrap tightly around my head and I run my tongue over her sweet lower lips.

Oh fuck, yes.

Chapter 12

Cravings

Grace

What the fuck happened to me? I ran off to Italy to escape a monster and keep my baby out of trouble. Now I'm in the Hamptons with a sexy white man licking my pussy juices off his lips and pushing his face between my legs like a needy puppy. I rake my fingers through Enzo's hair and push him away after my fifth or sixth orgasm. My legs are soaked and as for everywhere else…

I'm dripping in sweat and totally out of breath, but Enzo doesn't give a crap. He just wants his tongue between my thighs and after that, he wants more. He wants to push that monstrous dick between my legs and move with me until we both cum. The way he enjoys sweet, slow love will remain forever imprinted on my mind. Most of the nights I don't have nightmares, I wake up having dreamed of his perfect dick.

The base of my stomach tightens in an involuntary knot at the sheer muscle memory of what my body must do to take Enzo's dick. He's beyond big. He has a fat, long and filling cock that doesn't just feel good, it's so fucking impressive that you can't look away.

Enzo tilts his head to the side, a gorgeous crop of light-brown hair falling away from his deeply tanned coastal Italian complexion.

"You want me to stop?" He whispers, his thumb noticeably pressed against my clit. The slow rubbing tempts me to tell him no and to keep his tongue or fingers pressed against my clit all night. But we can't solve all our problems with Enzo's tongue between my legs. I got here safely, but that doesn't mean I'm safe in Long Island.

I need him to stop so we can breathe and talk, and so I can remind myself this isn't a dream, and I really risked everything to be here with him. I'm trusting him with this baby and I hope I'm not fucking crazy for doing that.

"Yes," I whisper. "Stop… Just for a moment."

Enzo stops touching my pussy and regret surges through me like a thunderbolt. It's hard to explain just how fucking good he feels between my legs. Pregnancy heightens every sensation from his tongue and his fingers, turning my body into complete mush at Enzo's slightest touch. No way. He has to stop touching me if I want to keep my mind clear while talking to him.

"Get up," I whisper. "Please."

He gets off his knees and kisses the top of my forehead. "Anything for you."

I can't help touching his hair like he's a puppy. It's such a silky and weird feeling, not like my hair texture at all. I like that he's different from me, all olive-skinned and exotic.

"I'm still not safe, Enzo. Part of me thinks I shouldn't have come."

He presses his head forward sweetly, kissing me on the lips again to comfort me. He's affectionate for a killer. That's why I let him in my heart. I hope I'm not fucking up.

"Van's people got you here. That's all you need. It's a safe house. No one knows we're here."

"What exactly does Van have you doing here?"

"Mostly waiting around," Enzo says, struggling to obscure

his irritation. He never wants me thinking about his work and he thinks I don't notice the slight pout on his face whenever I try to fish for mob details he views as inappropriate for women.

"I can't have any freedom here. I risk losing everything if I do," I tell him. "I want you to know that this danger is real."

"You knew that and came, anyway."

I bite my lips, almost like I'm trying to stop myself from saying it, but I can't stop. I know why I really risked everything to come here and while I've run away from every fucked up part of my past, I don't see the sense in running away from the truth. Not with him. Not after everything he's done for me.

"I love you, Enzo."

The words come spilling out of me in a way that surprises me. I never said those words so quickly to my first husband and I definitely never said those words to Uksan. I danced around the words. With Enzo Doukas, love feels safe.

"I never filed our divorce," he blurts out. "I lied to everyone. You, Van... myself..."

"Enzo!"

I hit his chest, and he grins half-apologetically. I should have known that he'd do something like that, but it doesn't make it any more irritating. He made me sign divorce papers. He made me think that everything between us was over and once he returned to Italy, there was no chance of getting it back.

I hit him again in the stomach once I realize what he's done but Enzo catches my hand, pressing it to his lips romantically. Maybe Italian men are just this melodramatic when they're in love.

"I couldn't stand it. I love you too, Grace. I hoped you would come around."

Horror sinks into my stomach once the pleasure of his soft kisses on the back of my hand subsides.

"I'm a bigamist..."

"Not for long," Enzo grunts, moving from kissing my forehead to kissing my neck. I have to stay focused. Neck kisses make me completely weak to him and tricky ass Enzo Doukas knows that.

"What does that mean?"

"You know what I mean," he whispers, kissing my forehead again. That condescending bastard. Does he think kissing my forehead will suddenly make me okay with the insinuation that he's going to do something that I specifically asked him not to do?

"You promised you wouldn't do that," I hiss.

Enzo grabs my cheeks again and shakes his head. "I know. But what's worse? Lying to you?"

"Two things can be bad at the same time, Enzo."

He reacts to this with utter confusion, which annoys me, even if it's exactly what I expect. He rubs his thumb underneath my chin and shrugs.

"Sorry, but I've thought about it. I can't stop myself. I'm going to kill him."

"You don't even know who he is!"

"I'll find out. Van intends to punish me by keeping me here for months. I sense it."

I bite down hard on my lower lip. Enzo's right. His brother isn't happy with Enzo's disobedience and I can't blame him especially since "disobedience" from Enzo appears to amount to reckless and constant murder. Despite my stake in the matter, I certainly understand Van's perspective.

"Hmph," Enzo grunts. "I'm right. You had to ask him for help to come here, didn't you?"

"Yes. And he grilled me."

"About what?"

"Making sure I'm not a gold digger."

Enzo utters a long string of expletives half in English and half in Italian. He touches my face and then kisses my forehead apologetically. I missed that. I missed how sweet my monster could be.

"He had no right to do that," Enzo murmurs in his heavily accented English.

"I can't blame him. I've acted distant with you, Enzo. I've lied to you. I can't make you father a child that isn't yours. I can't take advantage of how you feel for me."

"Why not?"

He runs his finger over my cheek so gently that I want to sink into him and more importantly, I want to feel his body against mine. I want him completely inside me so we can finally have the closeness I yearned for every instant of our separation.

"It's not fair to you," I whisper. "This child isn't yours. I want to be safe, but I can't make a man look after another man's kid. I couldn't go through with it."

Enzo's brows wrinkle together and he shakes his head.

"Silly American girl. Once you've had this baby, don't you think I can give you another? Don't you think I plan on it?"

He grins excitedly and knowing Enzo, he has plans to give me several more children. He's insatiable and falling into bed with him can be dangerously addictive.

"So what? You're going to adopt another man's child?"

"After I kill that man... yes."

My body tenses and his hand drops away from my face. He knows how I feel about this whole killing thing and he still won't let it go.

"You don't know who he is."

"He'll make himself known," Enzo says calmly. "If everything you say about him is true."

"Of course it's true," I snap, although I can't exactly blame Enzo for doubting me since I hid my pregnancy from him for so long.

He brushes off my sharp tone with a nod. He's too thrilled with the hunt to care about my attitude.

"When he comes out of hiding, once I have proof that his existence threatens yours, I'll end his life. If he wants to live, all he has to do is leave you alone."

"He's still my husband on paper," she says. "I don't want him dead. I just want my freedom. But he won't let go, Enzo. If I try to file for divorce again, he'll kill me."

"Until then, you commit a horrible crime?" He says with a wink. Unlike Enzo, I don't find bigamy funny. I did what I had to because I thought that's what I needed to do to survive. I don't like the idea of two-timing anyone — in this case, Lorenzo. The man who would kill for me before he let any harm come to me has no claim to me while my ex and I are still married. Technically, our marriage isn't legitimate anyway until my first husband and I get divorced. But divorce is better than putting a man in the ground. I can handle divorce. It's my first husband who can't–he's the one who wants to keep me forever.

It's strange how different it is the way both men want to keep me. My first husband wanted to keep me forever in a cage. Enzo calls me his treasure, and he treats me that way. He respects me. He doesn't deserve to do something that could ruin his life for me. This isn't Italy. I don't think the Doukas family has that much power here.

I can't count on my first husband's death. I just can't.

I hate that the man who tried to take my life has so much power over me, enough to scare me and enough to keep me away from a man willing to do anything for me, even raise a baby that isn't his. I swat Enzo for his comment on bigamy and he chuckles, kissing me on the forehead again.

"Do you trust me?"

"Sometimes."

"What would make you trust me more?" he murmurs.

"The truth about Uksan. Was he really involved in child trafficking? Please, Enzo. I don't have to know why you killed him, why you really killed him, but I have to know if he could really do something so horrible."

"If he hadn't," Enzo says. "Van would have killed me for taking the life of an innocent man. I defied my brother's orders, but your ex-boyfriend helped bring girls in from Ukraine, Syria and even Ethiopia to Albanian auctions. A man like that didn't deserve you."

"Was that up to you to decide?"

"On my fucking coast? Yes," Enzo says. "Maybe that makes me a giant fucking asshole, but if that's the label I get for keeping women and children safe... I'll take it."

"You're my giant fucking asshole."

I tiptoe and kiss him on the lips. I can mourn the man I thought Uksan was, but I can't help my gut feeling about Enzo's truth. If that man hurt kids, I can't help but believing he deserved exactly what he got. Even if it's illegal. See, Enzo might be a monster, but I'm no saint. We all have a different code of morality, a different way of seeing right and wrong. At least we agree on one very important thing. Children should be protected.

"Good enough," Enzo whispers. "Now get into that fucking bed. I'm really fucking sober and I really fucking missed you."

God, I missed him too. My inner thighs ached every night I spent without Enzo Doukas. I race him to the bed and when he slides between my legs, I feel like I'm finally home. He's going to be a perfect father with an imperfect job, I know that. But at least our kids will be completely safe because of him...

I obey his orders and get into the bed with a very sober, very lusty Lorenzo.

After three weeks in Long Island, my sense of security returns. Maybe I was wrong to think my ex would still care — that he would still come after me. Enzo's even breached the subject of attempting another divorce. The Italians, naturally, are well-connected with several big shot lawyers.

"They just got Vinnie off a fraud charge and conspiracy," Enzo says proudly. "Eddie's never spent over four hours in the drunk tank. They're very good."

I still haven't met Enzo's nephew, and he claims that I don't want to. It's bad enough that I have to avoid my first husband, I'm good on meeting any shady characters so I don't press Enzo about meeting anyone in his family. Mike and Vinnie are only second or third cousins or something like that, but they're more than enough of a crazy Italian family for me.

It's been three weeks, plenty of time for my first husband to have made an attempt on my life. I start to believe that he doesn't know I landed in NYC. Maybe he doesn't have the power he used to have. A part of me muses that maybe he changed. Maybe he's forgotten all about me...

That brings a smirk to my face because I know it ain't true. Men who pleasure in hurting the weak never change. Men who hate women at their very core can't change unless they want to.

I even allow myself to muse that my first husband moved on or moved away from New York. It's nice to let my guard down and Enzo's protective approach helps. I let him take me out everywhere, and he appreciates that I don't panic every time we go to a restaurant or ice-cream shop anymore. He complains about the weak American coffee, but he doesn't miss his taking his daily espresso from the local cafe.

We go out for coffee in the nice East Hampton cafes and even if he complains incessantly about "shitty American beaches", Enzo walks with me on the beach every day, his hand clasped firmly in mine as we discuss the baby's arrival excitedly.

The baby's most likely going to be born in America unless Van calls Enzo home. Considering Van's response to Enzo during their last phone call, I doubt that's happening soon. I worried about having the baby here, but time passes and my ex stays far away. Maybe we can pull it off — staying married, Enzo finishing his work here, running back to Italy with the kid... maybe even having another.

I want a future for us and finally, I'm feeling like we can have one. I won't have to live my entire life on the run. If I weren't super pregnant, I'd feel confident enough to pick up jogging. I feel safe enough to make a request.

Enzo lounges in his pool shirtless on a giant purple float and he looks like a dream with some rum cocktail in his hand and his tanned skin glistening in the sun.

I'm glad he's been staying away from cigarettes, but his appreciation for cocktails lately has been borderline abusive. He hates being away from Italy, I can tell. Van's missions for him here involve dealing with their nephew in clandestine meetings I know little about. Again, he wants me away from the life. It's not my thing — it's theirs.

I crouch at the edge of the pool, earning Enzo's attention as I attempt to ease in. He sets his drink down in the float's cupholder and eases his lean, muscular body into the water.

"Careful!"

He acts like I'll pop without his constant vigilance. Pointing out that pregnancy doesn't make me fragile earns nothing but sharp tutting and utterances in Italian that we're both happy I don't understand. Hmph. Before I can fend him off, Enzo grabs my hips to stabilize me and slides me into the water, kissing me as my toes touch the bottom of the shallow end. I love him all wet and glistening, smelling like chlorine and sex.

Pregnancy cravings have been weird as hell but one craving I definitely understand has been my craving for a delicious, muscular Italian man. Enzo chuckles at the look of pure desire on my face. I hate being so obviously weak for him.

"Did you come here looking for your next orgasm?"

Despite the weak-at-the-knees look on my face, I have to shake my head.

"No. I have a favor to ask."

"Okay."

"I want to visit my sister's grave in Queens."

He furrows his brow. There's a little worry there, but that's become normal for him throughout this part of my pregnancy. He's like a father duck, if there's any such thing.

"Are you ready for that?"

"Maybe I exaggerated. Maybe I let my fear get the better of me. You've been patient with me and nothing has happened. I haven't heard a peep. I want to believe I'm safe."

"You are safe," he murmurs, kissing my shoulders. "I'll come with you."

I shake my head. "No way. I haven't seen her in a long time. I should go alone."

"Grace..."

"Three weeks. If he wanted to hurt me or threaten me or show his face and scare the crap out of me, he would have done it by now."

"You underestimate dangerous men."

I don't know who he's talking about now.

"If you gave me a name," Enzo whispers, kissing my shoulders again and obviously attempting to tease the name out of me with soft kisses. "I could end this for you. I could make you safe."

"I don't need you to kill. I just need a ride to the cemetery and a little space to be with my sister."

"I don't like the sound of this."

"You can drive," I relent. "But you can't follow me up there. I have to talk to her alone. Can we make a deal?"

"I'm bringing my guns."

"Perfect."

"Tomorrow?" he asks, pushing hair out of my face and kissing my cheek. I nod. We have a deal. Enzo draws me close to him and kissing quickly turns into a few more things. I guess I really did find my orgasm (or twelve) in that pool. When he finishes with me, Enzo guides me out of the pool and excitedly gushes about a new 'brain food' smoothie recipe he wants me to try for lunch — to help the baby of course.

I grimace as Enzo excitedly blends a bright green smoothie for me with way too much kale and not enough pineapple juice. My stomach wants cinnamon buns dipped in pineapple glaze. *Please, can this baby come soon...*

I don't relish getting dressed to visit Amara. I always dress respectfully to see her, but thinking about her and what happened makes me cold. I get that old deep sadness as fresh as the day it happened. I still haven't felt anything more painful than losing her.

I hate seeing that cold grey stone and pretending that standing up in front of it is anything like holding her, smelling her perfume or watching her do her hair up all fancy in the mirror. She made some bad choices — so did I. But I'm not the one cold in the ground and try as I might to come to terms with it, this just doesn't seem fair.

Enzo dresses with Italian distinction, lobbing several complaints about Americans' overly casual manner of dress, which he views as the primary reason our country is falling apart. I let him mutter bitterly about America as long as he wants until I'm ready to leave. He drives me to the cemetery without complaint, even when we nearly get into three fender benders on the way there. I forgot how crazy driving in the city can be and traffic only gets worse as Enzo speeds off the highway into Queens.

"You can stay in the parking lot," I tell him. "Her grave is up there... under the red maple."

Enzo rests a comforting hand on my thigh. The baby moves inside my belly as if he or she knows exactly how Enzo's touch feels to me. Right now, we share everything — me and this little life inside me. I can't allow anyone to hurt that little life. I can't allow fear to hold me back from being the best mother I can be.

I can't miss a chance to see Amara, even if I'm scared like hell.

"Are you sure you want me to wait?" He asks, giving me serious grey eyes. *Fuck those eyes make me weak. I want to drown in them sometimes, but I still need to do this alone.*

"I'll be fine."

He leans over and plants a soft, warm kiss on my cheek. The kiss seems to flood me with guilt-inducing euphoria. I'm at a cemetery. It's not a place where I want to feel any type of gushing. I need to hold it together and see my sister's grave while I can — while I'm still safe.

"I'll be here."

I head up the hill alone. I don't have to look back to know Enzo's behind me. He's going to protect me. I can do this.

I never thought I'd see her grave again. I thought I would always have to be on the run. Drawing nearer to her grave always hurts. Nausea builds in my stomach and the knot of grief that first implanted itself in my core when I learned about her death feels like the knife wound it was.

My throat feels itchy and tears form in every duct before I approach. We were the trashy trailer park cousins, Amara and me. We were the ones who weren't ever going anywhere, who weren't ever going to make something of ourselves. Amara never got the chance to turn her life around. I did.

"Hey sis," I whisper. "I brought your niece or nephew to say hello. I missed you."

I swear, this is the only part of Queens that's truly silent. I missed this place. I missed my home. But something about the States doesn't feel like home anymore. It's like by giving a part of my heart to Lorenzo Doukas, I gave a part of myself to Italy, and standing there in front of Amara's grave, I can't help but wonder if it's the last time I'll ever see her again — if this is my last chance to say goodbye.

Chapter 13

The Boss Approves

Enzo

Do not smoke. Enzo, do not smoke. Lorenzo Pazzini Doukas, if you think about a cigarette one more fucking time...

A matte grey Dodge Challenger eases into the cemetery parking lot. It's the type of car that would make anyone look twice. Tinted windows. Custom modifications. An engine that purrs like a snow leopard. I lean forward and stare at the car as it comes to a stop.

My killer's instincts sharpen. Hairs stand on the back of my neck and I fight competing urges. I can't pull out my gun — it's probably just some geezer reliving his glory days with a mid-life crisis induced muscle car. Then again, I can't ignore instincts bred into me my entire life. This person came here for her.

That's what cosa nostra's about — self-defense against anything in the world that threatens to crush us. I have tinted windows too and better than that, I have a gun. I glance up the hill at Grace and realize the motherfucker in the car is looking at her too. He isn't leaving the car, just watching.

It can only be one person. I calmly write the license plate down in case he drives away and then I call John Vicari for the first personal matter I've handled since coming to Long Island. John opens the casino early so the nation's elderly can get to the slot machines with their Bloody Mary's for lunch.

At least we can count on the Long Islanders for respect, which nearly makes up for those awful fucking accents.

"What's going on?"

"Does our cousin still work for the NYPD?" I ask him.

"What do you need? Coming down to gamble tonight? I've got new girls on the floor. Hot girls."

In the past, John's offer would have tempted me. Tonight, I'd rather work on keeping Grace safe. She wants me to promise to do no harm, but I'm a hunter at heart and I feel myself getting closer to sinking my teeth into my prey. I keep my eye on the Dodge Challenger as I answer John. The driver doesn't move a muscle. I crane my neck to get a better view, but there's nothing. Fuck.

"I'll pass on the girls. I need him to run a plate for me."

"Gimme the plate, I'll handle it. Give me twenty minutes."

"I need it in ten."

"You got it, boss."

Boss. I could get used to that. What I couldn't get used to is everything else about America. I love Grace, but even she must admit that everything's better in Italy, where we have blue skies instead of grey. I give John the license plate and lean back, observing my prey. Grace kneels at her sister's grave. If he gets out of the car, I'll have limited time to act to get between them.

I keep my hand on my weapon — ready to do whatever it takes to defend her. Even kill.

The man doesn't leave the car. He drives away before John calls back, but I relax once he leaves. He was watching her. He came to watch her. I just want to find out who the fuck he is.

John calls back in fifteen minutes — not quite ten, but not quite twenty.

"You know this fucking guy?" John says when I answer the

phone. The Americans appear to have lost their way with politeness and etiquette several decades ago.

"I don't know what you mean."

"He's really fucking dangerous, that's what I fucking mean."

"Give me a name."

"Head detective at a Brooklyn precinct in the NYPD. Maxwell McCarthy. You got business with this fuck?" John says.

"Yes."

"What type of fuckin' business?"

He's my cousin and I'm here due to his generosity, helping to clean up messes that my nephew Eddie helped create.

"Personal."

John pauses for a minute. "Eddie just came through the door. Listen, Enzo. Don't fuck with this guy. I don't know what he did to your people or what fucking personal business you have with him, but stay the fuck away."

"Ciao."

I don't owe John Vicari shit. At least he has Eddie tonight which makes my work simple once I drive Grace home from the cemetery. She walks down the hill towards my car wiping away tears and looking like a perfect fucking dream. I swear to fucking God, I'll never get over her.

I open her door and let Grace in. Concealing my life from others has always been simple. I don't tell her what I learned or what I plan to do. She only needs that sense of safety. She needs to know that she can walk and fall, and I'll be right behind her to catch her.

"How are you?" I murmur, kissing her cheek and letting my tongue taste the salt from her tears. I wish I could take her pain and feel it for her. I love her that much.

"Fine," she says. "It doesn't get easier, you know? You just get used to having a hole there."

"Yes. That's true."

I press my thumb beneath her eye and wipe away her tears. Grace won't have to cry for long. I don't tell her about the man in the Dodge Challenger, the husband I now know about. John doesn't ask why I needed his name because he already has his suspicions. Fuck.

I can't expect that this won't get back to Van. It doesn't matter. I might die anyway in this life and what happens to Grace then? I have to tie up all loose ends. She leans back and groans.

"The baby is officially kicking my ass. Can we go home?"

"Foot rubs and football?" I ask her.

"My kind of football," Grace insists. "Not yours. But yes, we can do that. There's a McGraw College game on tonight."

I need her nice and relaxed so she can fall asleep early and I can go out tonight to hunt the man nobody wants me to kill. If I want to get away with this, I need to do what I don't want to. I'll need to get permission from my boss.

After a night with Grace, I put her to sleep and call my brother.

"Do you know what fucking time it is?" Van growls.

"No. I need to ask a favor."

"Are you in a position to ask for favors?"

"I'm aware that I'm not."

"You disobeyed me, Enzo," Van reminds me, as if my temporary excommunication to America hasn't been punishment enough.

"I know."

"I know you'll do whatever you want without my permission."

"That's not true," I tell him. "I'm calling you. You're the boss."

"Why should I give you a favor?"

"Because I helped you get the woman you love and I need help keeping mine."

"Didn't I send her for you?" Van asks. "I've already done

you a favor."

"She's pregnant, Van. I want to care for her. I want to care for the child."

Van chuckles. I don't find this funny.

"What's your problem?"

"You? Fathering another man's child. I find that unlikely given your obsession with bloodlines."

"I've changed."

Van grunts.

"That's why I want permission to kill the father," I continue.

Van grunts, and he doesn't respond for a while.

"How can you ask me this?" Van asks. "And who do you want to kill?"

I tell Van his name and his position. I sense my brother doesn't want to answer me because he wants to reach through the phone and wrap his fingers around my neck.

"Do you seriously think you'll be able to get away with this?"

"He hurt her, Van. Imagine how you would react if someone hurt Jodi?"

"That woman..." Van growls. "You keep jumping into trouble for her."

"That woman has a name..."

Van snorts. "You're one to talk."

"I don't know if I can get away with killing him. I'll be honest."

"You're there to get Eddie out of trouble, not to get yourself into more trouble."

"I know."

I want him to give me permission. Fucking hell, I want to kill this man, but I know I'll need my brother's blessing.

"This could get us into so much fucking trouble," Van says. "Do you understand that?"

"Yes."

"You would fuck everything with the Vicari cousins for this woman?"

"That's not what I want."

"Get Eddie out of there," Van says. "Get him ready to return to Italy after this and do what you must. Then you leave, Enzo. You leave before anyone finds out."

I didn't expect Van to agree to this.

"Why are you changing your mind?"

"Because I'm going to make you pay."

Nothing in our life comes free. I must have known this was coming.

"What do you want from me?"

"Money," Van says. "And I want you to leave the Amalfi Coast when the baby comes."

"Where do you plan on sending me?"

"Albania. I need eyes on Matteo."

"What's the big dumb fuck doing now?"

"He'll be raising his son soon. It's time for our family to get back together. Especially Eddie. But that will take time and healing."

He wants updates on Eddie, but Eddie's the reason I drink. Eddie's the reason my life is in America instead of back home.

"Are you sure we shouldn't kill Eddie?"

I'm only half joking.

Van snorts. "I'm trying to fix our family for once. We need to be together. And what I'm letting you do could fuck everything up."

"They should know Italians are crazy," I murmur. "I'll try to be as clean as possible. Maybe we'll get away without them finding out. Grazie, brother."

"Don't fuck this up — and keep Grace out of trouble. I don't mind her."

From Van, that's as close to approval as I can get.

Chapter 14

Dying Without Dignity

Grace

Enzo's absence when I wake up in the morning is noticeable. My bed feels cold and I miss his lean muscles and brawny arms wrapped around me. He has the perfect, irresistible touch, not like I want to resist him anymore. The opposite. I want us to stay together forever. I can hear Vinnie and Mike arguing from the kitchen which means Enzo must not be home. I would definitely hear him yelling at them to shut the fuck up if he were awake and in the house.

I miss Ember. Van has a sitter for her, but I miss her morning kisses and the little excitable barks she would make whenever I woke up. At least the baby will get to meet her when we return to Italy. I swing my legs out of bed. I still haven't gotten used to the shift in my center of gravity. Moving around makes me feel ridiculous with that giant baby bump. I lean against the bedpost and steady myself.

The house falls conspicuously silent as I approach the bedroom door. I shriek when I open the door.

"Mike! Vinnie! What are you two doing out there..."

I have to agree with Enzo's assessment that his Long Island connections are annoying.

"The boss told us to make sure you don't move a muscle this morning or look at your cell phone."

"Where is the boss?" I grumble.

My cell phone? Why such a specific instruction? Enzo knows I don't enjoy looking at my phone in the morning, so why bother say something like that.

"He's out for the morning handling business with Eddie."

I still haven't met the man Enzo claims drove him to drink heavily ever since he's come here.

"I'm not letting Enzo keep me off my phone. I need breakfast too. I'm pregnant. What does he expect me to eat? This house is barren."

Mike elbows Vinnie hard. "Head down to the fucking corner store and get her a bacon egg and cheese, you stupid fuck."

"Ouch! How the fuck am I supposed to pay for that? Bacon egg and cheese costs five fuckin' dollars now."

Mike smacks Vinnie in the back of his head. "I don't care how you fuckin' pay for it. The boss' lady wants a bagel, you get her a fuckin' bagel."

It doesn't matter whether I truly want a bagel. I'm in New York, so I get a damn bagel. I grab my cell phone off my bedside table and begin checking it as I leave the room. Mike snatches the phone out of my hands before I can open my text messages.

"Mike!"

"Sorry, Grace. Boss' orders."

"The boss doesn't get to decide if I have a cellphone!"

"Hey, it's my head if I give this back to you. Think I want my body floating in the Hudson with fuckin' fish chewing on my dick?"

"Good one, Mike," Vinnie says, earning a glare from Mike.

"Vinnie, get the fuck outta here and get her the fuckin' bagel."

Vinnie puts his jacket on and heads out to get the bagel.

Mike has my phone in his pocket and when he catches me staring at his pocket — and thinking of ways to pickpocket him — he zips it shut and grins.

"Sorry, lady. I gotta do what the boss says."

"Is there something he doesn't want me to know about?"

"I think he wants to talk to you himself, that's all."

"Ugh. The baby is giving me hell this morning. Mind making me some tea? I'll watch some TV while I wait for Enzo to get back."

"No problem, ma'am."

Italian men can turn on the charm when they want. Even the Long Islanders have an element of old school charm that they just can't shake. They're either ghastly pale or deep tan, skin tones which both look great with dark hair and bright oceanic eyes. Mike and Vinnie would be handsome if they weren't both so young or so goofy.

I struggle to get to the couch and I seriously feel like I'm going to pop. Is it possible for my baby to come this early? I don't think I can carry this load around for another dang minute.

Luckily, Mike's quick with the tea. Vinnie will probably get distracted chatting at the bagel shop down the street, so there's no telling when I'll sink my teeth into a savory bacon egg and cheese bagel. I miss my espresso mornings, but cutting back on coffee to absolute zero for the baby has been the chest choice. I'll get my buzz back on soon enough.

Mike sits across from me and waits for my approval from that first sip of tea.

"I heard you and the boss are heading out today."

"Are we?"

"Didn't think it was a secret," Mike mutters, turning red. Hm. He probably wasn't supposed to let that slip.

"If you tell me what I need to know, I won't tell Enzo about your slip of the tongue."

"No way. This shit's too real for me to talk. I forgot how fucking crazy people from the mother country can get."

I can't help but chuckle. He has a point. Enzo thinks his cousins are crazy just because they're loud and silly. They've got nothing on the crazy I've seen or heard about in Italy. Jodi's stories while Enzo was gone served as a sufficient reminder that the Doukas family is a very dangerous group of people to be involved with.

"What do you mean by that? You don't have to spill any details."

"Our cousins start one war in Albania, but they're going to start another here. We never fucked with those people before because we know they could rain hell on our people. We count on them looking the other way, you know?"

I don't have a clue what the hell Mike's talking about. I tell him the tea tastes great and convince him to watch reality TV with me, which leads to him promptly falling asleep. I curl up on the couch, patiently waiting over forty minutes for my bagel.

When my bagel doesn't show up, I get my big girl pants on. Mike's passed out on the couch, Vinnie's gone and there's no sign of Enzo. I can run around the corner to the bagel place by myself. It's East Hampton. Nothing happens here and if we're going to leave today, I'd better appreciate my last walk through New York. I won't be spending all my time here with a newborn when Italy's much safer.

I throw on a pair of maternity pants and a hoodie before sneaking out with a twenty-dollar bill from my wallet. It's hardly sneaking out – Vinnie and Mike are both fast asleep after a grueling morning of *Dance Dance Revolution*, I'm sure.

I walk nearly half a mile to the turn at the end of the street and when the bagel place springs into view, my stomach growls knowingly. I'm so focused on walking along and shuffling there with my new extra weight that I don't notice the cream-colored

Chrysler 300 following me until it's too late. When I catch the car in my peripheral vision, I glance over my shoulder slightly and do what my instincts taught me to do. It's him. It has to be. He always drove a cream Chrysler 300. Always.

I know running is fruitless and there's no one around the quiet street this morning. The car pulls over and I hear the doors open. I'm running as fast as I can, but I know it's not fast enough. I reach into my pocket for my phone to call Enzo or the police, but my phone slips through my fingers once I get it out of my pocket and even pulling the phone out of my pocket slowed me down too much. My first husband's large hand wraps around my neck and he yanks me back. I scream and try to kick him but I end up kicking my legs out from under me. The baby. I can't do anything to hurt the baby.

Protecting my child comes first over protecting myself. He drags me off my feet and I bite his arm like hell and scream, trying to get him to let me go, but there's no one there, no one stopping him, and I'm pregnant enough to pop. My first husband drags me into the car and shoves the door closed, nearly slamming my legs shut in the door. I attempt to scramble into the front seat to escape when I try the door and find the child locks on. He gets to the front seat first and throws his elbow hard into my face.

I scream and fall back into the back seat. Blood pours out of my nose and I press my hands to my face to catch the warm gush of fluid.

"Good morning, Grace," he grunts. "We have a lot of catching up to do."

My bloody hands scratch at the door, and I leave bloody handprints all around the back seat.

"Can you stop acting crazy back there? I'm going to have to get this car cleaned."

"Take me back to where you found me," I tell him firmly, even if my voice is shaking. I can't help it. I want to be strong but this man is almost twice my size, and he put me in the hospital. I know what the hell he's capable of and my first husband's capable of putting me in the ground.

"I'm taking you where you belong," he says. "And this will be much easier for you if you calm the fuck down."

That's it. He's going to kill me.

I screwed up. I let my guard down. I knew I shouldn't have come here, but I let myself believe that love would be strong enough to fight my entire past. Who was I kidding? I was born trash, and that's how I'll die, 'cause I know this man ain't about to kill me with dignity.

I never wanted that to be my story, but fate had other plans for me. Cruel plans.

Chapter 15

The Wrong Man

Enzo

John Vicari ties a good knot, and he puts together a good basement for getting a job done. He's professional and much better to work with on a job like this than Lucky and Dino.

"I'll be in deep shit if anyone finds out I helped you," he reminds me as we head downstairs again for our second session with Maxwell McCarthy.

"I know. We won't have him for much longer."

"What's the fucking deal?" John says. "He claims he's not married to Grace?"

"He claims he's her brother."

"No offense, but the dude's the color of a caramel latte and Grace is more like... espresso with brown sugar," John says.

"John..." I interrupt, trying to get him to stay on topic.

"Sorry. I've been known to dabble with these women. Great fuckin' bodies, you know?"

"Can we focus?"

John's a decent man, but he's still a red-blooded Italian male, constantly thinking with his cock.

"Sure, boss."

"Grace's last name is West. How can this man be named McCarthy?"

"We gotta ask him. I'll do it. Let me lead."

John and I put our gloves down and walk down to the basement. Maxwell groans once we enter.

"I'm not fucking lying," he says, with a slight difference in his accent. "Don't I sound a little Mississippi? If you know my sister, you know she grew up in Mississippi."

"But you work for the NYPD. How is that possible?" I ask.

"Yo, man," Maxwell says to John. "I can't understand a fucking word of this guy's accent."

"Answer the question," John says calmly. "If you can't understand, I'll help."

John reaches for a small scalpel from his kit. Goosebumps spread across Maxwell's skin, even if he's trying to play it cool, he feels anything but cool. How can he? Vicari's a bastard and he's good at what he does.

"I swear, Grace is my sister. I changed my name to get a job and get away from my past."

His past. His past where he hurt her. One look at this guy and I know he would say anything to keep his ass out of trouble.

John presses the scalpel firmly against Maxwell's face. "Swear on your life that you're her brother."

"I swear," Maxwell says through gritted teeth, a bead of sweat dripping all over his face. I consider his appearance. Grace never mentioned it before. She never spoke about him much but what she said made me sick.

"If you're telling the truth, you can tell me about her husband, right?"

Maxwell thrusts against his binds again. Talk about Grace's husband apparently inspires him to move.

"Yo, you don't want to fuck with that guy. He's a crazy motherfucker, you hear me? You stay away from him and don't let Grace get into no mess with him. I know she don't fuck with me no more, but he's crazy, man. That motherfucker is crazy."

John pulls his scalpel away from Maxwell's face, satisfied that we're getting closer to pulling some fucking information out of this guy.

"What's his name?"

Maxwell grins. "You want something from me, you gotta give something back, man. I'm connected. Well connected."

He must be close to Matteo's age—over ten years older than his younger sister and he hurt her.

"Before you help us," I tell him. "I have questions about Grace. Questions about your past."

John toys with the scalpel, clearly making Maxwell nervous the way he balances his gloved finger over the tip.

"My past doesn't exist," Maxwell says. "I used to be somebody else, but I'm not that person anymore, man. I did some fucked up shit. Did Grace tell you about that? I don't know how she got mixed up with the fucking mob."

John tuts. "We are not the mob. We are you worst nightmare."

"Worst nightmare? You motherfuckers kill a cop and the NYPD will flush every fucking guido out of Long Island no matter how long it takes."

"Half the force is fucking guidos," John snarls. "We got nothing to fear. Now answer the man's questions if you want to live."

"I've seen your faces. I know I ain't getting out of here alive."

"If you give a shit about your sister, you'll answer my questions."

Maxwell scoffs and shakes his head. "You answer my questions first. You father that child? I see she's pregnant."

John doesn't bother glance at me. He's too smart to get involved in that side of my personal business. I'm not here to answer Maxwell's questions. I say nothing and wait for him to speak again. Silence is the most effective tool in any interrogation.

"You don't have to answer," Maxwell says. "If that kid belongs to her first husband, you've got the wrong man and y'all are wasting your time. That man ain't like me. I made myself stop hurting Grace, but he ain't man enough to leave her alone. You'd better find him or he's going to put my sister six feet under."

"We'll heed your warning," John says.

We attempt to pry as much information out of Maxwell as possible. We talk for hours, giving the dead man a last chance at conversation. He worries about Grace, but I know she's safe with Vinnie and Mike, tucked away in a Long Island house far away from danger. I followed the bastard at the cemetery and this man ended up being her brother.

Maxwell gives us little information we can use. Grace's husband is also on the force, but he won't give us anything else. John tortures him and bleeds him, but Maxwell won't give in, even if that information can ensure we save his sister. Even in his last minutes, he won't relinquish his hold on power—the one thing he has over us.

In the end, I kill him, and I try to make it painless. He's right—I have to kill him. It's not for the reason he thinks. I don't care if he sees my face. I care about what he did to Grace when she was a child. I care that he had a part in nearly breaking the woman I love. He's dead with two clean shots. We have to get rid of the body next, which is John's specialty. He's like a fucking butcher the way he cleans up his kills.

We take Maxwell out on the boat and say goodbye to him. John smokes after we finish the work and get clean as the boat sails past Montauk towards the family dock on East Hampton.

"What do you think? He never gave us a name, but do we have enough?"

"It's someone with a similar position in the NYPD or possibly someone retired."

"Retired?"

"She never mentioned her husband's age."

John chuckles. "Italians really are fucking romantic, eh?"

"What do you mean?"

"You do all this for a woman. I couldn't," John says. "Women come and they go for me. I don't need that romance shit."

Hm. I consider what my cousin says, but I'm only doing what anyone would to protect their family.

"I love her. That's all."

"Do you think she'll still love you when she finds out you killed her brother?"

I sigh, breathing in the air turned salty from the water all around us and missing home.

"I don't know," I answer him honestly. "But even if something happens to me, I want her to be safe. That's cosa nostra, protecting the ones we love."

"Amen."

We get the boat in, and John drives me back up to the house. When we get closer, I notice a big fucking problem.

"The door's open," John says. "You hear anything from Vinnie and Mike?"

No news should have been good news, right? They've been safe with Grace for weeks. Why should anything happen now? But it's late in the evening and the front door to the house is open. This can't be right. I reach for my revolver, but adrenaline bursts through me instantly.

"Not for hours."

My gut tells me something's happened. Something horrible.

"Let's get the weapons," John mutters. "Something isn't right here."

Chapter 16

Gotcha, Bitch

Grace

"Shane," I whisper. "You don't have to do this. I'm pregnant."

He pushes the button to close the garage door behind us and I'm trapped in the backseat of his car, back in that old house I promised I would never go back to. He told me he sold the house. I knew he was lying, but it's what he said and a part of me hoped that there was some new family in here, making memories and making the beautiful brick house the happy place it should have been.

"Pregnant? Did you let that man knock you up?"

Before we drove here, he drove back to Enzo's and killed Vinnie and Mike. He's still wearing his uniform, damn it. He's still sitting above the eyes of law just because he wears a uniform that makes most people trust him. That's how he gets away with everything.

"I don't know who you're talking about."

"Maybe you fucked all of them," Shane rambles. "Maybe I just killed all the motherfuckers who fucked you."

"I didn't come here to look for problems with you."

"That's right, you cheating bitch. You came here with your boyfriend."

No. I came here with my husband. That's who I have to hold on to right now. Enzo. He might not know I'm missing but when he finds out, he'll come for me. I have to stay alive until then and do my best to find a way out on my own.

"I am not cheating on you, Shane. We're broken up. We haven't been together in a long fucking time. I just want my freedom. I swear, you set me down, I'll leave and I'll never come back."

"Shut the fuck up, Grace."

He shuts the car off and gets out of the car. I'm helpless now. If I try to fight him, that will just set him off. Maybe there's another way out of this situation where I can save my baby and I can save myself. My first husband opens the back seat of the car and stares down at me.

I can't bring myself to look in his eyes. I wonder what I ever saw in him. How could I have ever believed those cold, pitch-black eyes ever contained any warmth? His anthracite stare hardens and he his lip twitches with anger.

"You look like you've been letting other men fuck you. Where the fuck have you been?"

"That's none of your business."

"I kept all those damn divorce papers," he sneers. "Irreconcilable differences? You mean the fact that you don't know your fucking place?"

"I know my place, Shane. Believe me, I know my place."

I glare at him and try to look fearless even if my tongue feels like a wad of cotton stuck in my mouth and getting air into my lungs feels like a challenge.

"You've gotten really damn uppity since I last saw you. Get out of the car."

I stand up, struggling to get there with my baby bump. Shane's lip curls with disgust as he eyes my stomach. I don't know what he's going to do to us, but I have to do everything it takes to protect my kid. I can't let anything happen — I just can't antagonize Shane to the point where he puts his fist in my stomach. I have to think clearly.

"Don't worry, I don't need help."

I walk around the car, and he shuts the door. He keeps his body between me and any potential exit, leading me towards the garage entrance of the house we used to share. I had so many of my best memories in that house. Men like Shane make sure the good times are really damned good so when they transform into monsters, we convince ourselves that it wasn't really them, that there was some demon inside them making them act wrong.

Some demons walk in human skin, right?

I finally learned that there wasn't any damned demon inside Shane — he was the demon all on his own.

I walk into the house and take my shoes off. I remember how particular he was about clean floors. That hasn't changed. You could still eat off that man's floors. He cleared away everything that reminded him of me, so the house is strangely bare. Shane shuts the door behind me.

"You're finally back where you belong. You're my wife, Grace."

"I stopped being your wife the first day you hit me. A man who hits a woman doesn't deserve to have her."

"I said sorry," he huffs. "What more do you bitches expect? You just wanna bust my balls until the end of time. Get to the bedroom. I'll see you in a minute."

"The bedroom?"

That I didn't expect. He was never one for the bedroom when we were together unless he'd been drinking or unless he had a hard day at work.

"What? You think you get to stay here without paying your way? You've caused me a lot of trouble and I've had to be very patient to get you back."

"I'm seeing someone, Shane."

I don't know why that's what the hell comes out of my

mouth. Some part of me thinks he'll respect me more if he thinks another man claimed me, if he knows that he doesn't have a chance.

"Oh? So you finally admit to cheating."

His body closes in around me and I want to throw up and shove him away at the same time. I have to be more strategic than that.

"Get your ass in the bedroom," he says. "Now."

He follows me to the bedroom, but he doesn't follow me inside. He shuts the door behind me and locks it. I hate that I'm relieved. I have time to think, plan and find a damned weapon in here. Even if he locks the door, I'm not trapped. I can find a way around this.

Shane loves control. He keeps me locked in the room without another word until nightfall. I find his gun safe, but I can't figure out the combination. I could use a lamp, but it might be awkward to hit him over the head and he might grab it from me. With hours to consider what to do, I come up with nothing. I can't physically overpower Shane. I'll have to get in his head. I'll have to look like I'm giving him what he wants, even if it makes me sick to consider it.

Shortly after sundown, Shane returns. My body still responds instinctively to the sound of his footsteps. Fear surges through me. My face still hurts from his earlier blows and my heart pounds so hard that I can't think. Enzo would tell me to stay calm. He would promise me my safety. He's not here right now, I have to handle it myself.

He bursts into the bedroom wearing a plain white t-shirt and jeans. I sit on the bed and stare at him, searching for details I can use to my advantage. Spending time with the mob, you can't help but become more observant. You notice more shit about people and places. You notice more opportunities.

"Good night, Shane."

"Take your clothes off."

"I don't want to take my clothes off. I want to talk."

"About what?"

He smirks like he's won something. I have to keep him talking and keep searching for an advantage.

"I see that I was wrong about you. About us. If you're willing to do this much to keep me... maybe we have a chance."

The words coming out of my mouth make me sick to my stomach, but maybe if I can stay on his good side I can find a way out.

"You don't deserve it," he says. "You don't deserve my forgiveness, you understand? Who the fuck knocked you up, huh? You expect me to raise your hoe ass baby?"

I want to scream at him and tell him that I don't want to be with him at all. I don't want his damn forgiveness. I want him to set me the fuck free.

"I'll take care of the baby myself," I tell him. "You don't have to do anything. I just want to be there for my man."

God, forgive me for the words coming out of my mouth.

"Come here," Shane commands. I approach him. He doesn't seem armed. I know he keeps guns in the house and he wouldn't hesitate to use them on me, but Shane's guns are all locked up which ought to be enough to buy me time.

He grabs my face and kisses me forcibly, shoving his tongue into my mouth until I physically gag and pull away. He grins and runs his thumb over my lips, forcing his thumb into my mouth and into my cheeks. I want to throw up when he pulls his finger out and sticks it in his mouth.

He's doing this to get in my head and scare the crap out of me. I have to keep my head on straight as much as possible.

"I missed those big fucking lips."

Every time he talks about me, it's just so degrading.

"You do?" I tell him, trying not to let my voice shake. "Maybe you can get more of those lips."

The door behind us is open. I'm pregnant, so escaping will

be more difficult, but if I can buy enough time to get to the neighbor's house, I can get some help and stop him from taking my life. He kidnapped me and there's still blood on my face. Even the cops would have to take me seriously.

Yes, Shane's a cop and cops don't come after cops, but it's my only chance to get away from him. I can hope that our neighbors won't let him kill me and wait for Enzo to find me. I have to try this even if it makes me sick.

"What do you mean by that?"

"I mean..." I sigh, "I can give you what you want."

I slowly drop to my knees, even if it hurts me to crouch down like that. I have to do everything in my power to keep my empty stomach from hurling up gastric juices. This is the last thing I want to do, but it's the only way out — manipulation.

"You always gave good head," Shane chuckles. "Damn, you really were the best hoe I ever had."

I made the mistake of telling Shane my past and he never let it go. He never let me forget that he thought I was worthless trailer trash. I undo the buckle of his belt and as I peel the zipper down over his bulge, the pungent scent of urine surrounds me. I gag. He greedily drops his pants and removes his underwear. The smell gets stronger. I can't let myself throw up because I have to do something way more important.

I ball my hands up in a fist and I punch Shane in the balls as hard as I fucking can. He screams in pain and drops to knees. My bones creak as I get off the floor. I'm slower than I want to be, but I got his ass good and Shane's howling and turning purple on the ground as I slip out of the bedroom, heart pounding.

I have to get out of this fucking house, but I need a weapon first. I run into the kitchen as fast as possible and grab the biggest knife out of the rack before I run to the front door. Shane's screaming gets softer, and he follows each scream with a grunt. He's on the fucking move, which means I need to haul ass out of here.

I race towards the front door and thank fucking God, it's open. I sprint down the driveway with a knife clutched in my hand and run as fast as I can...

My heart feels like it's poking out through my ribcage and each new breath of oxygen cuts through me. There's blood at the back of my throat and I still have several hundred yards to run to get to the neighbor's house. If I wasn't so damn pregnant, it would have been a piece of cake but tonight, there's this strong aching between my thighs as I run and the pain pierces me so hard, I don't know if I can make it. I cross the street and start up the grassy knoll to the property. I hope to God the neighbors are home...

As I run towards the house, I hear footsteps behind me. It's Shane... He's getting closer, I can tell. I clutch the knife even tighter, praying he doesn't catch me and that I don't have to use it. One wrong move and that knife could be in my torso, not his. I can't let anything happen to the baby and right now, I can't let anything happen to me, either.

Faster, Grace... Faster...

I can't make it up the knoll. Even with searing pain between his legs, he's not pregnant. Shane's bigger and faster than me. He knocks my legs out from under me and I clutch the knife tightly as I fall. All I can think about is not falling on my stomach. I roll so I fall on my back and make an ungodly grunt as my hard fall knocks the wind out of me. I kick my legs up wildly and slash the knife wildly.

Shane forces his body on top of mine from the side and I scream as I slash at his arms. He grunts and I see a splatter of blood erupt from the side of his arm. If I can get one good stab wound in, that's all it would take. I don't have to kill him, I just have to hurt his ass bad enough to walk away from this.

I push hard against his torso with my chest and try to move my body up. Searing pain between my thighs intensifies and I let out the wildest scream as I get to my feet and land another kick on Shane. I'm not as lucky this time and I don't hit him in the balls. He rolls away from me and before I can get to him, that pain between my legs causes me to scream and double over.

Blinding white pain cuts through me and my palms run cold. I nearly drop the knife, but the survivor in me keeps me standing.

"STAY AWAY FROM ME!" I scream at him. "You let me go, Shane! I swear to God, I'll kill your ass."

"Calm down, Grace," he says slowly. "I need you to calm down."

"NO!" I scream at him. "I'll never fucking calm down again. You took everything from me and even now, you won't leave me alone. This won't end until you're dead or I'm dead."

He runs his tongue over his lower lips. Bile rises in my throat. I don't think there's a chance in hell I'll make it out of here alive, but I'm tired of running. I have to fight and for once in my fucking life, I want to fight because I finally have something worth fighting for. My unborn child. Lorenzo Doukas. A life between America and Italy where I can stand still long enough to have a dream for myself outside of pure survival.

I don't want to be broken. I don't want to be some man's victim.

I want to be strong. I want to be the type of woman who can handle her shit and handle her mafia husband. I want to be the type of woman who lives to have a mafia husband — who lives to tell the man she's been pushing away how much she really wants this with him. The life.

"Grace," he says calmly. "I really need you to calm the fuck down and put the knife away. You cut me. See? I'm bleeding.

What the fuck did I do to you for you to abuse the shit out of me like this?"

I scream and let my anger take over me, which I know, is idiotic. But how fucking dare Shane Murray talk to me like that. How dare he accuse me of abusing him just for fighting back. I lunge at him with the knife and he sidesteps me. I have to get closer to him. I lunge again and slash at him madly, successfully nicking his torso. He yelps, but he won't give up. He's still convinced he can win — because that's what it's all about to him. He won't give up until he's sure that he's won — that he's stolen every ounce of life from me.

"If you knew what was good for you, you'd leave me alone."

"You are alone, Grace," he snarls. "Without me, you are alone. I've seen the company you keep. Thugs. Grifters. I'm the only man who could ever love some trailer park child prostitute."

"Fuck you, Shane."

I lunge at him again. This time, I get too close. I hit his arm, but Shane gets lucky. He grabs my wrist and squeezes so tightly that I drop my knife and scream. Without a weapon, he has every advantage over me. Size. Ability. Willingness to kill.

"Gotcha, bitch," he whispers. "I'm gonna make you watch as I cut that baby out of you."

I grunt and attempt to kick him again so I can get away from him and run for the knife, but Shane squeezes tighter and uses his foot to kick the knife a safe distance away. I wriggle like a rabbit in a snare, unwilling to accept that I fucked up. He might bleed for a while, but I didn't cut him badly enough for Shane to bleed out. He has plenty of energy and life in him to make good on his threats.

I do the one thing I can as he sneers in my face with vicious satisfaction. I know it's only going to piss him off, but it's the only power I have. I spit on him.

His face contorts into pure outrage.

"You deserve what's going to happen to you," he snarls, spittle flying freely from his mouth as the glob of spit rolls down his face.

"I can't wait to hear you scream as I fuck your whore ass dry."

I'm ready to spit on his ass again when I hear a loud gunshot crack across the open field. The noise is so loud that I assume I'm the one that's hit. I lose control of my body and fall into the grass.

That's it, isn't it? I'm dead. If I'm not dead yet, I'm definitely going to die here and that means my baby's dead too.

I let this happen. This is all my fault...

Chapter 17

The Vicari Family

Enzo

I know I didn't miss, but Grace falls to the ground anyway, so I run.

I run like I've never run before, faster than any race against Van on the beach and faster than I ran after Eddie the night he stole my gram of pure Colombian cocaine with his high school friends. I stumble to the ground and hold her. I have little time. I might have maimed her ex-husband, but he isn't dead and before I leave tonight, that man will be dead.

Grace is unconscious. She's warm to the touch, still breathing, but definitely in shock. It's dusk, but I can still make out all her features. There's something dark staining her legs. The baby. I think the baby's in trouble. I need to get her to a doctor, but there's something else to take care of first. I kiss her forehead and set her on the ground. She'll come to in a moment. It's better if she doesn't see this dirty work.

I walk over to Shane. This is the second person in her life I'll kill today, but I'll relish killing this one more than Maxwell McCarthy. I finally get to see the man Grace was running from. I understand her terror. How a man like that could hurt a woman, I'll never understand. He's at least my height with a face the color of caramel and black eyes. Mixed race, perhaps?

I'm not the expert. I'll risk a slap in the face and ask Jodi when I get back to Italy.

I have nothing to say to him, but I've never killed a man without talking to him first. It makes it easier to have a ritual, if killing can ever really become easy. It's always butchery, you know? Yes, you can adjust to the life of a butcher, but you never really yearn for the smell of blood.

"Fuck you for hurting her."

That's the best I can muster up for conversation. Shane groans.

"You're going to jail, you stupid fuck. You're going to jail for killing a cop."

"A disgraced cop. Of course, you never bothered telling Grace about that. You lost your power, Shane Murray."

A part of me wants to make it quick and a darker part of me wants revenge. If it weren't for Grace, I'd have my revenge, but I've already caused her so much pain. I'll give this sick fuck one more chance to say something.

He groans in pain and rolls on his side.

"Be a man and finish the job," he grunts.

"I want to know why you hurt her."

"Why the fuck do you care? Are you the one who put that baby in her? She's married. Did that whore tell you she was still married?"

I don't want him to die thinking he owned any part of her still. I want him to die knowing that he's losing everything — not just his life, but his legacy.

"Yes, I am that child's father," I murmur. "And she was married. That's no longer the case."

Before Shane can respond, I put one bullet through his skull and another through his throat. John's waiting out front with the car to clean this shit up. I just need to make a call and get Grace out of here.

I call him.

"You done?" John answers the phone.

"Yes."

"How's the lady?"

"Unconscious. I need to get her to the hospital. I need something discreet."

"Already got a few guys out front. We're only ten minutes away. I can get her there in seven."

"I'll bring her out front."

I hang up. Thank God for family, eh? I know there's not a chance in hell we can make this go away completely. Two NYPD officers missing in one night? We weren't careful enough for this to disappear. I'm the one who will have to disappear and pray that the Vicaris don't excommunicate me for the trouble I'm causing.

At least we're almost even. I'm taking Eddie back to Italy and leaving for good with Grace. That ought to sort us out.

I return to Grace's side. Her eyes flutter open and she murmurs a few nonsense words. She's bleeding. She's definitely bleeding. I can't wait for her to wake up. I need to get her out of there. I hold her as carefully as I can and hoist her against my chest. She's not the thinnest woman I've ever carried, but I never want to let her go as I press her soft, voluptuous body against mine.

She fought like hell. Before I got to her, I watched her fight and fuck, there was something so beautiful about watching her unleash that anger and rage — feeling the freedom to stand up for herself. I hope she can always feel safe standing up for herself knowing that I'll be right behind her.

I kiss her forehead as I get her to the front of the house. Sammy Zagarella and Lucky Vicari — no relation to our Lucky — help me get Grace into the backseat.

"This will be much faster than an ambulance," Lucky says. "Trust us."

Lucky and Sammy are much more serious and brooding — more genuinely Italian. They make me miss Vinnie and Mike. The poor bastards nearly bled out on the floor of the place. It'll be months before they play *Dance Dance Revolution* again or argue about the pronunciation of "bologna".

"I trust you. If she dies—

"She won't die," Lucky answers forcefully. "Trust me. Now let's go."

Lucky runs every fucking red light he can find and gets us to the hospital in one piece and in well under six minutes. I don't know how the fuck he did that, but I don't care. Sammy and I get out of the car and carry Grace into the front door of the ER. People in here recognize Sammy Zagarella. He's a big business owner and local celebrity.

"Can we get some fucking help here?" he yells. His big personality definitely plays a role in his ability to attract attention. Nurses and doctors zip around and they try to take Grace away from me, but I won't let them. I hear someone say that she's going into labor. I hear a bunch of scientific words that I don't fucking understand, but there's one thing that I definitely understand — they aren't taking Grace away from me. I don't give a single fuck what's going on, she's going nowhere without me.

I scream as much to the nurse, forgetting myself and yelling half in Italian and half in English until Lucky gets between me and the nurse and "negotiates" something in the Long Island mob language of veiled threats and subtle insinuations. I can wait in the hospital room for her, but I can't go to the operating room. It's a compromise I have to make and at least I'll get to see her.

Sammy waits with me while Lucky drives back out to Shane Murray's house to help John finish up the job over there. Two men in one night isn't exactly light work. It's nearly morning, anyway. I can't sleep and I'm not in the mood for coffee, even if Sammy can't keep his eyes open without it.

"I feel for what you're going through with Eddie," Sammy mutters. "Think he'll make it back in the old world?"

I appreciate his attempts to distract me, even if nothing could really work to keep my mind off Grace. I shake my head.

"He won't last long. We all tried to give him a chance, Sammy. Not everyone is built for the life."

"Ain't that the truth. Half the time I wonder if my son ain't going the same way."

"You could always send him to Italy to fix him up," I suggest. I've never met Sammy's son, but we're Italian, so naturally I've heard rumors. He might be an even bigger troublemaker than Eddie.

Sammy shakes his head and take a big sip of the smelly, burnt American piss water they refer to as "coffee". I wince and wish that I could hold my nose.

"No," Sammy says. "I wouldn't subject my family to my son. Whatever happens to him here... It'll be up to him. The best we can do is raise 'em and hope they do right."

"I wouldn't know," I mutter. "I'm not a father."

"Not yet, eh?"

They don't know the truth about Grace's baby and I don't bother correcting them. What's the point? From the moment that child breathes his or her first breath of air, I will be his or her father. I will be the person they come to for wisdom, advice, protection and security.

"Soon," I whisper. "I'll be a father soon."

Saying those words, I seriously underestimated how long it would take for Grace to give birth. Anxious hours inched by and I swear time slowed down just to fuck with me. It must have been about noon the next day when a sweaty nurse dressed in pink scrubs with short black hair and large gold hoop earrings emerged from the room with a smile on her face.

"Congratulations! You're a new father. Grace will be out in a few minutes."

"I can't wait a few minutes," I blurt out. Lucky puts his hand on my forearm.

"Thank you, nurse," he says. "It's been a long, anxious night for him."

"He's a very lucky man," the nurse croons. Then she really makes me wait more anxious minutes before they wheel in a hospital bed with Grace, wide awake, smiling and clutching anxiously onto two bundles. Two bundles?

"Surprise!" she says, grinning.

"Are those..."

"Twins," Grace says, her smile becoming more nervous as she says it out loud. "They're twins. This whole time, I was carrying twins, and I didn't have any idea."

"Are they..."

"Come see for yourself, daddy."

I approach and the nurses help me hold my children for the first time. The first baby is a little boy. He has skin the color of cinnamon and a shock of black hair already on his head. I kiss him and promise to protect him, praying over him in Italian before I trade babies with Grace and hold our daughter. I almost cry when I clutch her to my chest because she makes the tiniest gurgling sound, and the sound makes me feel something deep and powerful — something too strong.

I love them. They are my children and I love them... and I hope we have many more.

I kiss my daughter's forehead and say a similar prayer over her. I don't want to let her go. I want to hold them both against my chest forever and promise them a safe and happy future.

"We'll have to pick baby names," Grace says with a smile. "Maybe we can do that when we get back to Italy."

"Grace... We should talk."

I glance nervously at the nurses, and Grace's smile falls away.

"We don't have to talk," she says. "I know. I understand, Enzo. You promised to protect me."

"I did."

"So let's not talk about anything else. Let's get these babies home safe. That's all."

"Si, signora."

"Signora Doukas to you," Grace answers with a grin. Yes, tesoro. And you'll be mine forever...

I hold both babies for a while longer and wish I could spend all eternity in their first moments. They're too precious for words.

By the evening, Grace sleeps with the babies, and I plan with Giovanni for our return. Eddie meets me in the evening before the flight, coming to the house for the first time since my arrival in America. He looks worse for wear and it's clear he's been using — a lot.

He passes out on the couch. I'll have to explain him to Grace... He'll also have to explain himself to Giovanni. I don't know what trouble my nephew has gotten himself into, but he won't be able to get out easily. Drugs, pissing off the mob, the enemies he still has in Italy and Albania... All that will catch up to him. Not even Van's generosity could save him. He also has a girlfriend that he still desperately wants.

That makes me nervous. Zara might be a foolish teenager, but there's a part of me still fond of her. At least Zara will have Matteo's protection. Let us pray...

Eddie doesn't deserve a woman like Zara. When you have a good woman, you don't hurt her. You do anything to protect a woman you love, even kill for her. I hope this is the last time I have to kill for Grace because I want this to be it for us — I want this to be the end of our love story and the beginning of our happily ever after.

Chapter 18

Grace & Jodi

Grace

I can't stand living with this entitled, imperious man child for another minute. Only a few short months after the birth of our twins, he moves into the damn place with us and he's a fucking nightmare.

What's worse? Enzo leaves me alone for two weeks with this nephew of his — the man child — who makes Vinnie and Mike seem like the least annoying people ever, when they're the opposite.

I wake up to loud bachata every damn morning and Eddie doing lines of whatever it is in the guest bathroom until I knock on the door and tell him to get his ass out of there.

I'm supposed to be breastfeeding and focusing on my kids, not babysitting his annoying nephew, but what am I supposed to do? Enzo pleads with me, begging with those gray eyes that I give Eddie a chance because Van wants to kill him and Enzo thinks he can get clean. Hm. I know addicts and I know there ain't a chance in hell that brat wants to get clean. It's hard for me to say "no" to Enzo in those moments when he shows how tender he is towards his family.

It's a part of why I love him, you know?

Our boy, Renato Giovanni Doukas, gurgles as I place him

back in the crib. He's so much hungrier than Onika. I swear, Onika Amara Doukas couldn't be bothered with my boobs. Renato could drink all day and still be hungry. I kiss his forehead and make sure the baby monitor's on before I dash out to the kitchen. The nanny won't be here for another hour, and I need to get Eddie and his drug paraphernalia out of here and into the back bedroom before he starts sexually harassing her. Again.

Enzo had to pay her an extra seven hundred euros for her to come back and I think he needs to stop enabling his trashy nephew and kick that spoiled ass kid to the curb. I bang on the guest bathroom door on my way out to the kitchen. I know he's in there because he's in there every damn morning when he ought to help his uncle Van at Jalousie or at least helping Enzo keep the books for the apartment. And doesn't he have a father, anyway? Who said white men couldn't be deadbeat dads...

"Eddie!" I scream as I knock on the door. "It's time for you to go to your room."

I hate how I sound all annoying and mom-like, but guess what? That happens when you're a mom and sometimes it comes in handy. Eddie throws the door open, barely trying to disguise the fact that he was getting all drugged up in there.

"Do I smell weed in there?"

He knows Enzo hates it when he smokes in the house. It's like he's trying to set Lorenzo off and get them both entangled in an argument that lasts far too long.

"Buon giorno, beautiful Grace," Eddie slurs. "How are my cousins?"

"Get cleaned up, Eddie. Adriana's coming here soon and I don't want you trying to show her your dick. Again."

"She misunderstood my intentions."

"Do you want me to get Lorenzo to kick your ass when he gets back?"

Eddie grins. It's unfortunate that he's so handsome. What a

waste of good looks. Jodi has told me stories about his ex-girlfriend and I can totally understand how a young, innocent girl could get swept up in Eddie's ocean blue eyes or his cocky ass grin. He has that bad boy appeal women love... he's just too far gone. It's a shame because he's so young, you know? I've had shit happen to me and I can tell when a man ain't long for this world and this kid... He might be a piece of shit, but he ain't long for this world.

"Lorenzo won't be back for a while, but I don't want to upset my new aunt. Come... kisses."

"I will absolutely not be kissing your crusty ass cheeks. Take a shower, Eddie, and do something productive today."

"Can I play with the twins?"

"Absolutely not," I snap. He knows his uncle would punch him in the face just for asking. That boy is too much. He closes himself back into the bathroom, hopefully to get his ass cleaned up and not to do another bump of whatever the hell he's doing in there. I get to the kitchen and search desperately for the croissant I was saving myself for this morning. There's no croissant... Just an empty brown paper bag with a little post it note.

"Sorry — Eddie."

I swear I'm going to put my foot so far up this kid's ass...

Before Adriana gets to the house, Jodi calls and she sounds worried.

"Have you heard from Enzo today?" she blurts out.

"Um... No. Is everything okay?"

"Van promised he would check in at a particular time and he's about three hours late."

"Maybe they have bad signal. Aren't they in Albania?"

"Yes," Jodi says. "With a man who has threatened to kill them on multiple occasions. What if they're dead?!"

"They're not dead. They can't be dead."

We're always going to be like this, aren't we? Wondering if they're dead. Wondering if they're ever coming back. It's crazy, but I don't think either of us would trade what we had for the world, even with all the fear and all the uncertainty. When men like the Doukas brothers love you, there's nothing else like it. That's one thing Jodi and I have in common over everything else — we know the pain and the absolute pleasure of loving a fucking dangerous man and feeling absolutely safe and on top of the world with him.

It's a rush not even Eddie will ever understand. Especially not Eddie. I think that boy has fried his brain with drugs to the point where he can barely feel anymore. I sigh and try to offer some helpful response to Jodi.

"Why don't you come over? Bring the kids. Adriana's coming soon and Eddie's a handful. I don't want to let him out of my sight."

"He's still staying with y'all?"

"Didn't Van mention it?"

"He drinks half a bottle of whiskey every time I say Eddie's name. I try not to bring him up."

For once, I finally understand that grouchy, possibly alcoholic mafioso. Dealing with Eddie could drive anyone to the bottle. Not me. I'm breastfeeding... and I might have news for Lorenzo pertaining to future kids. I don't know yet. With everything that happened, I fear pregnancy. It's irrational, but I keep worrying that I'll only be able to have Shane's kids and that Enzo and I are doomed to never have a kid of our own. He thinks I'm ridiculous — Renato and Onika are his kids. This is why I love him.

"I'll see you in twenty?" I say to Jodi.

"I'll be there. I'm bringing Elena, by the way. She can help with the kids."

Elena's their nanny. We say our goodbyes and I have a piece of toast with orange marmalade while I wait for Jodi's arrival.

. . .

Jodi arrives right on time, but her anxiety hasn't abated in the slightest. The nannies occupy the kids while we stand on the balcony, taking in the sunlight, having one of many conversations about our husbands away on business. It's rare for Van to leave Jodi's side. He's the boss, the one giving orders instead of taking them. I feel for her and I can't hide the fact that I worry about Enzo, too.

"It's not like Van. He doesn't make a promise he can't keep. If he knew he couldn't check in, he wouldn't have said anything."

"Enzo didn't make any promises."

"They're fucking with Matteo," Jodi says. "It's a mistake. You've seen his son. What kind of man has a son like that?"

I shrug. I want to act like I'm trying not to judge but live with Eddie for a minute and you begin to wonder.

"Do you think they're making the right choice?"

"It depends," Jodi says. "Are they going to come back alive?"

Chapter 19

Matteo Returns

Enzo

"We don't know what he's done with Zara, he won't tell us a thing about what's happened the past several months. All he says is that he's coming to take his son to Albania to take responsibility for him as father. Do you trust him?"

Van glances at our brother, passed out in the backseat. For once, he's not drunk, apparently just exhausted. In his old age, Matteo has become grotesque. He snores. His beards grows out thick and dark now instead of in those curly black patches from his youth. He's still muscular, thank God. Otherwise, he would truly look like an old man. He's stayed away from the family too long and Albania has hardened him even more than he was when he left.

"We could have sent Eddie easily," Van murmurs, clearly attempting not to wake the bear. "He wants to see his son in person. That does... concern me."

"Do you think he's going to..."

Van's body stiffens like it usually does when someone has said something that brings him even the mildest displeasure.

"I don't know what he's going to do," Van interrupts before I can get my sentence out. "He hasn't exactly been a responsible parent. I hardly think that's a solution for anything."

"Yes. But you know Matteo."

Van grunts. "Yes. And he has the girl. Who knows what's happened between them."

"He says nothing will ever happen."

Van scoffs. He's thinking what I'm thinking. Zara's exactly the type of woman Matteo likes. Petite. Foreign. Needy...

Matteo grunts in the back seat. Van and I turn around nervously. He snores. Definitely not awake, thank fuck. Van grumbles to himself, "I'm in the mood to take up smoking."

"We can't let him get to us. He doesn't get to come back after all this time and raise hell in our country."

"It's his country too," Van mutters. "His family."

I understand my brother's insinuations and his fears. If there's any chance Matteo wants a leadership role in the family, that could mean war. Van worries our brother has Albanian backers and that he could turn against us in a minute. I don't want to believe that's true.

"No," I reply. "It's your family. We could arm every person in this country if he tried anything. You don't build loyalty by running away from your heritage."

"You're right," Van grunts, glancing behind him nervously again. "I want to forgive him. I really want to."

"I'm not ready either. But we don't need forgiveness. We just need to put our families first."

Van grunts again. I think he agrees. We arrive at my apartment building and Matteo awakens just as Van grinds the car to a halt in my reserved parking spot.

"Are we out of Albania yet?" Matteo responds gruffly, his voice strained and raspy from years of drug abuse and an excess of sleep.

"We're home."

"Not papa's house, I imagine," Matteo responds with a yawn, sitting upright.

"No. We're at Enzo's. Jodi doesn't know I'm bringing you."

"Excellent," I grumble bitterly. "She'll definitely react well to Matteo meeting her children by surprise."

"I'm great with children," Matteo responds, without a hint of irony.

"Father of the year," I utter sarcastically, earning a sharp glare from Van. Who cares about pissing off Matteo? Surely he deserves some criticism for forcing his brat upon us? Van hasn't had to live with Eddie for the past few weeks. He's been driving Grace crazy and frankly, it's only a matter of time before he goes after the nanny. He's my nephew and I love him, but the idiot kid is a fucking danger to himself.

Matteo grunts. "You don't know what I've been through."

"I'm sure one day, you'll tell us," Van responds. "Let's see your son."

For the first time in forever, the three of us approach the stairs to the apartment. Matteo looks nervous the closer we get. He sighs.

"It's been a long time since I've seen him."

"I wish I could say the same…" I mutter.

"I thought I was doing what was best. I wasn't fit to be a father."

"We can share our sentiments later," Van says impatiently. "Come on."

We head up the stairs together and I open the front door to my place to hear a loud argument proceeding inside. Jodi's voice rises above the din.

"Eddie, don't you dare talk to her like that."

"Don't worry Jodi, I can handle him," Grace says. "Boy, sit your white ass down."

That's my girl. Matteo clears his throat as he barges ahead and happens upon the scene. His voice echoes clearly across the penthouse.

"Eddie!" Matteo booms. "Enough."

His son, dressed in a pair of white boxers with black spades on them, drops the glass he's holding and stares at his father in utter disbelief.

"Papa?" Eddie stammers.

He turns red. Jodi and Grace fold their arms and whip around. Out of habit, I expect their ire turned in my direction or Giovanni's but instead, they glare at Matteo.

"Let me guess," Jodi says. "You're Matteo."

"Yes."

"Your son is a pain in the ass," Grace blurts out. "I'm sorry, but I've had it up to here."

Eddie and Matteo ignore them both. It's been years since they've seen each other and those years I imagine were painful for both of them in their own way. Deep down, Matteo loves his son. Maybe it's our fault for introducing him to the life too soon, for trying to teach a boy like him how to kill and how to conquer.

He's too much like his father. He's too good at turning his emotions off, even at his own expense.

Matteo's harsh face doesn't lose its intensity.

"You will come with me. Get downstairs," He snaps.

Then Matteo turns to Van, the outrage dwindling to a simmer of anger for a moment.

"I'll leave in two days. I need a new car and one of Enzo's apartments. I'll be out of your hair."

"Two days?" Van says. "Why just two days?"

"I'll be back," Matteo responds calmly. "I don't want to leave Zara alone for long."

"I see. Have you and the girl been getting along?" Van says, the implications not lost on Matteo whose face betrays nothing.

"I'm taking my son to my house and I'll return to discuss our business. I promise."

"That's nice," Grace chimes in. "I love this little family get together going on right now, but I would really appreciate somebody getting Eddie to put a shirt on and maybe leave the house."

"My apologies," Matteo says to Grace humbly, turning his warm bluish-green eyes upon her. "My son will not trouble you anymore. Eddie, pack your things."

Eddie turns around and shuffles off. He's red in the face and obedient. He knows that defying his father won't get him anywhere. His father allowed him to dally around Albania, to create havoc in Italy, to run amok in America, but Eddie's finally done enough to drag Matteo from the mountains.

I wonder if Zara had a role to play in that. I wonder if I'll ever find out. If he has slept with her, Matteo would never admit it. He'd never allow love to enter the picture, certainly. He simply isn't the romantic sort. I suppose even I have to admit to caring for that ditsy little girl. I hope wherever she is in Albania, my brother's keeping her safe. His urgency to return for her speaks well of his intentions.

Matteo strides over to my couch and plops down, gazing at the two babies in their little baby enclosure in the living room.

"Whose fucking kids are those?"

"Watch your language!" Grace calls. "Those are my kids. Your niece and nephew."

Matteo leans forward, his grumpy face cracking into a slight smile. "I see. Lorenzo is far too private."

"We don't have that type of relationship anymore, Matteo."

My brother winks. "Once I return, that will change. Trust me."

I'm not in the mood to be light-hearted and I'm glad to see that the same thing applies to Grace. She rolls her eyes at Matteo and pulls Onika into her arms. The nanny, Adriana, holds Renato for a moment until I go over and take him into my grasp. I kiss his little forehead.

"It's good to be home," I say finally. Italians. We launch into the family drama and deal with the pleasantries later. Jodi remembers she has some "pleasantries" of her own for Van and tells him off about surprising her and the kids with Matteo.

My older brother leans back and closes his eyes, but this time, he definitely isn't sleeping. He's listening. A smile breaks out on my brother's face and I understand it. I smile like that every day now.

It's family. It's the thing that makes the life worth every fucking minute of it. I'd kill a hundred or even a thousand times to protect this — my beautiful life with Grace, Onika, Renato and of course, Ember, who seems unbothered by the babies.

I glance over at Grace as she holds our daughter and she grins.

"I've got something to tell you, Enzo. I can announce it or tell you in private."

Jodi gives Grace a knowing wink. Women and their secrets...

"It appears someone else knows before I do. Tell me."

"I'm pregnant. Surprise!"

I've never been so happy before. I hand Renato over to Van, and Jodi takes Onika so that I can hug my beautiful wife. This is what I saw when I stared at the woman walking beneath my balcony. I saw a future in her eyes, a beautiful future with a beautiful woman. I saw a future with a woman who has dark skin, tightly coiled hair and the deepest brown eyes you've ever seen. I saw that future, and I chased after it as fast as I could.

I'll never regret that as long as I live.

. . .

Matteo clears his throat and raises his head. "On that note," he says. "I'd better take my son and get out of here so you can celebrate."

Jodi doesn't trust Matteo. I can tell. He ought to celebrate with us, but I know better than to ask Matteo to stay. He's the running type, isn't he? It would shock me for him to settle again, especially a grumpy old man like him.

"Where are you taking Eddie?" Grace asks. She probably hopes my brother will take his son very far away and I can't blame her. Matteo's body tenses considerably.

All my older brother does is smile — a chilling, Cheshire cat grin.

Chapter 20

My Job

Matteo

I made many mistakes with my son. I can forgive Eddie for so much of what he's done because how on earth could I expect better with the type of father I've been? This time, my son has gone too far.

There's a girl in my custody and under my protection — after months, she's finally confessed the truth to me. She's finally said something to me that changed my belief that my son could be fixed. I say goodbye to Giovanni and to Lorenzo, leaving them with their wives and their children, while I take mine into the car Van provides for me.

It's a simple, older white Jaguar, one from papa's collection with dark red leather seats and hand-rolled cigarettes in the glove compartment that are probably half a decade old. Eddie pulls his hoodie up and slips into the passenger seat, leaning back.

"I'm tired, papa," he mutters. "I'm going to sleep."

"Fine."

This will be easier if he sleeps. Easier for me, easier for him.

"Am I going to get a big room in the castle?"

"Yes. Of course."

That's what I've told my brothers, that I'm taking Eddie back to the castle and that they don't have to worry — I'll be keeping him separate from Zara. Eddie leans back and nods off as I start the long trip to Albania. Driving instead of sailing makes the entire trip a lengthy nuisance. We'll have to stop in Bari to take the ferry overnight, then head north to the countryside on the outskirts of Tirana.

Eddie sleeps the entire three hours and forty-two minute drive to Bari. I can't help but glance over at him every once in a while. I remember the day he was born and the day his mother died — six years ago, the year I left my family and left the Amalfi Coast.

I don't want to go back. I don't want to repair things with my father or my brothers. But they're my family... and in my old age, that's all I want. My family.

My heart aches when I see Eddie's pale flesh wrapped around weakened muscles and jutting bones. He's an addict, I know that, and I know that there's one thing our people do not tolerate, becoming slaves to addiction. We drink to quiet the demons but drugs that turn you into a wreck of impulses represent the utter taboo in Italian mafia families.

He's only a boy, but already I've broken him. If I don't take care of the problems I've caused, the boy's life will be nothing but misery. If I don't take care of the problem I've caused, somebody else will. This ought to be my punishment, my cross to bear.

Eddie awakens once we get to the ferry. There's no need for the car now. Mine will await me on the other side, and Enzo will come pick this car up in the morning with one of the men. His children were so beautiful and they made me feel so guilty. I am a horrible fucking father and I will never have children again.

I can't allow myself to ruin another life. Eddie yawns and gives me a nervous look. He tries to act tough, but young men wear their emotions all over their faces. It makes me wonder if

I was that obvious when I was younger about everything I felt from my lust to my fear. I shudder at the thought of being that transparent.

"Will I have to work in Albania?" Eddie asks.

I don't know what type of work he's referring to. He killed with my brothers, I know that much, but after that, in Long Island, it sounds like he didn't do much of anything except party and get the Vicari family into trouble. I've failed him and once I get him out of Italy, I'll have to set things right.

"No," I tell him. "Your first task will be getting clean."

"I'm not a junkie."

So what? He's insinuating my brothers are liars? No, my son has all the telltale signs of a user. To me, that's not his unforgivable crime. He's done something else too brutal and horrible for me to live with. I blame myself, believe me.

"You want a coffee before we get on the boat?"

"No thanks. My stomach hurts."

"Pastry?"

"Yes, papa."

I buy a pastry from a small vendor and hand it to Eddie before we board. He barely has any luggage from a whole life in America and a whole life in Italy, just a small duffel with room to spare. It hurts to see all the ways I've failed him and all the ways my own vices led to this desperate situation.

God will punish me, I know it. That's why I can't allow myself to fall harder than I have already.

Eddie eats the pastry like he's famished, but he hardly says a word until we get to our seats on the ferry. In my younger days, I'd stand at the edge and appreciate the rocking sea beneath us as we sailed across the water to Albania. I feel too old to appreciate the rocking and I'll have enough trouble fighting down seasickness just sitting in place. Eddie turns green the minute he finds his seat.

"I need a drink…" He mutters.

He won't be doing any of that in Albania. No drinking. No drugs. Nothing like that anymore.

"I won't pay for your liquor," I grunt. "Close your eyes and get some sleep."

Eddie scoffs. "You can sleep after all the shit you've done?"

I want to scold him for his words, but he has a point. When I was his age, I might have asked myself the same thing. Unfortunately, I haven't done the worst thing I'm ever going to do in my life. It's coming, and I can't avoid it, but I haven't arrived at that moment yet.

"I sleep just fine," I lie to my son. There's no more time for honesty between us. Time. We never had much of that in the first place. Cosa nostra claims to be for family, but I never had less time for my family than when I worked at papa's right hand. He thinks being the boss must grind you to a pulp. I enjoy putting in very little effort to rule.

It's exactly why I'm hesitant to leave Albania. I shut my eyes and Eddie puts his head on my shoulder. It's the first physical contact I've had with my son in years. He falls asleep instantly and I enjoy the feeling of his head on my shoulder. A single tear forms in my eye.

I lost so much with him that I'll never get back. I don't want him to know how much it kills me. Especially in our difficult situation, I have to be strong for my son.

Eventually, I fall asleep myself and wake up only a few times in the middle of the night. Eddie sneaks off to smoke against the deck twice, but I pretend I don't notice. When we land on the coast of Albania, he looks like he hasn't slept a wink, but I'm ready for the sunrise and ready for what landing in Albania means.

I want it to be a nice day. I have dirty work ahead and it's better to do your dirty work when the weather's pleasant, so at least you can take some pleasure out of the filthy deed. I let Eddie drive the car a few hours and then we switch a couple hours away from Tirani.

"I know you have Zara," he says finally, about half an hour away from the castle.

"Yes," I respond. I don't want to talk about her. She's been a problem for me — an impossible problem — and I can't talk to my son about this.

"I want to win her back," he says. "But she's not worth it, I know. She lies. She cheats. I'm just like you, eh, papa? I like sluts."

I grip the steering wheel so hard, I feel like it's going to break and on the way to the castle, I take a detour at the fork in the road, turning left instead of right and down a private road on the other end of my land.

"Fuck, this place is desolate," he says, his tongue getting far too loose and disrespectful.

"Yes," I tell him. "I enjoy the silence."

I stop the car in a clearing and tell Eddie to get out with me. He puts his hands in his pockets and steps out of the car, staring up at the trees and the sunlight filtering through them. I'm exhausted to my bones, but I still have to do what I must.

I follow my son and once I know he has his guard down, I pull out a weapon — the first pistol papa ever gave me.

"Eddie, stop right there."

My son sticks his hands up and freezes in place. He turns around slowly, his body vibrating with fear. I want to offer him comfort, but I can't.

"Papa?"

I'll never forget the hurt and betrayal in his voice.

"I love you," I whisper to him. "I always loved you. And I'm sorry. I'm very fucking sorry."

Three gunshots ring out from my pistol. It feels like somebody else pulled the trigger.

. . .

My entire world changes forever.

Zara… I hope you will forgive me, my love.

THE END

Click here to order Book #3, Matteo Doukas' story.
smarturl.it/amalfi3

Turn the page for more information on how to stay updated about my upcoming releases so you don't miss the next books in the series.

Expect more about all the characters and their families in Book #3… all your questions will have answers.

A Preview...

Sample these chapters from my Greek Mafia Brotherhood romance series while you wait for Book #3 in the Amalfi Coast Brotherhood series.

If you enjoy dark & twisted mafia romance stories, you can binge the entire completed series on your eReader.

Enjoy the free chapters.

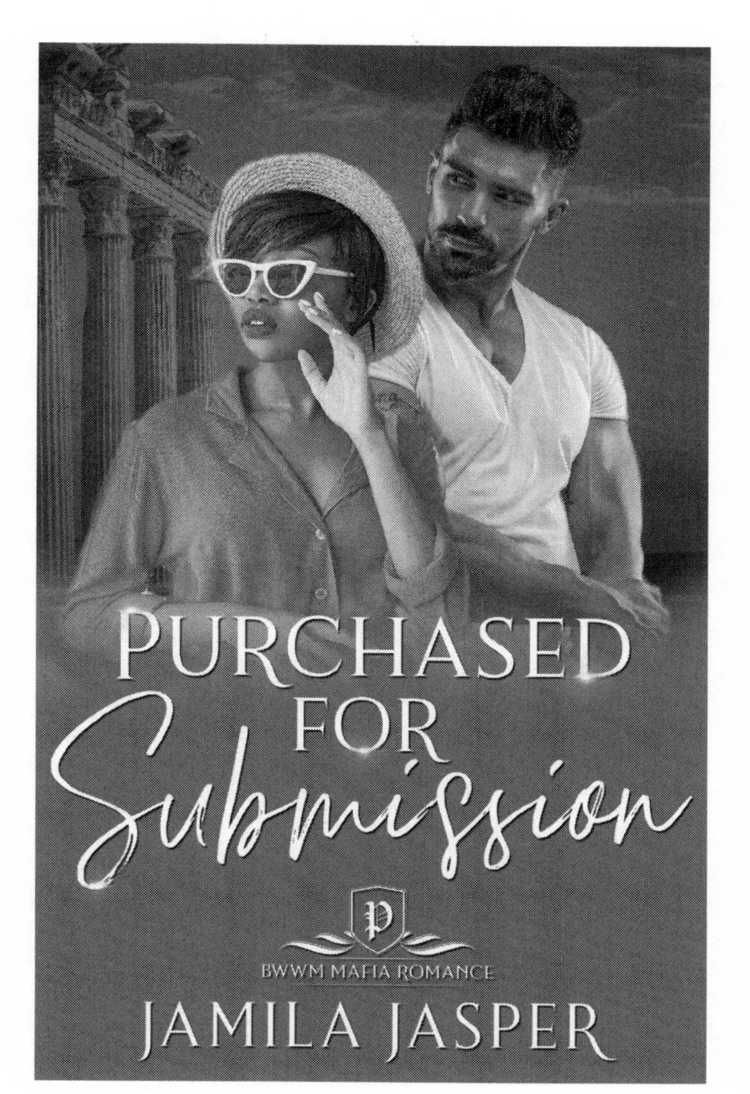
PURCHASED
FOR
Submission
BWWM MAFIA ROMANCE
JAMILA JASPER

Description

He purchases her foolishly, impulsively... guided only by his **unyielding lust.**

Stavros never wanted to hurt her.

He meant to set her free...

But Fallon's freedom comes with a steep price.

Stavros loves hard. Too hard.

As he falls for the woman he purchased for submission, he understands the darkest truth:

He can't ever let her go.

Series Titles

Purchased For Submission
Purchased For Pregnancy
Purchased For Seduction

Content Awareness

BWWM Dark Mafia Romance

This is an adults only read for fans of diverse romance, dark romance and high-heat relationships between black women and white men.

When I say dark, I mean DARK so expect mention of the following topics: rape, abuse, human trafficking, sexism, racism, sex slavery, violence, murder, and other unsavory subjects.

As this is a fictional story, Jamila Jasper does not condone any of these actions. Don't try any of this at home.

Chapter 1

Auction Block

Eight auctions a year. That's how many of these papa forces me to sit through.

"It's important you understand the men we deal with," he answers gruffly when I complain.

I loathe auctions, but when you're a part of this family, you get used to doing shit you don't want to do. At least the women are always beautiful. Too beautiful. You'd think someone would notice beautiful fucking women missing around the world.

Khalid has a knack for what he does — luring beautiful women lusting after fame or power into his clutches. Once he has them, he brings them here to the auction. You get the location the day before. The invite arrives as a mysterious text message sent to your phone with a link. You can't trace the number. Once you click the link, the web page looks like a spam website unless you expected a text message. Unless you know how Khalid operates.

Type the PIN and the location flashes on screen for 120 seconds. You can't take a screenshot without turning your phone into a brick. Khalid can pack a room wall to wall — especially when he gets back from places like Vegas or Dubai, where he finds the prettiest girls. He holds the auctions in a private club, normally owned by a friend or someone who owes him big time. Fifteen girls a night once a month.

Papa sent me here to bring back my sister. It's the only reason I'm smiling and drinking vodka with the sick motherfuckers at my table — an oil magnate and his bastard son — instead of brooding in a corner like I normally do. The auctioneer rattles off details about the first girl like he's talking about a Ming dynasty vase.

"Meet Kim, she's Korean, loves a big dominant man but willing to work for a woman. She's been pregnant once but would make a great surrogate or breed mare for individual gentlemen. We begin the bidding at €20,000."

Kim got herself on Khalid's nasty side because she has a black eye and she's whimpering, showing visible signs of distress that Khalid hates people to see. Men here like the illusion that women give a shit about them, like any chick in her right mind would get on that auction block without coercion. They tell themselves the women want it, that Khalid only finds sex freaks.

I'm here to rescue my sister from this horrible fate. But my mind ambles. Always.

If Kim's trembling and now loud whimpers affect the price Khalid and his team get for her, she might make it to her new master's house with a broken bone. My mouth is dry. There's not enough vodka in the world to desensitize you to this shit. Only time, my father tells me. I don't know if I ever want to be sick enough to enjoy these places. I hear someone call my name and look over my shoulder. But there isn't anyone there.

I've had too much vodka. Either that or I haven't had enough.

I glance over at my father and he shakes his head. We're not in the habit of buying sex slaves, although once or twice, we've purchased a girl or two — for re-sale. We mostly have Loukas to blame for that.

"We have a bidder! €20,000. Can we get €21,000?"

The bidding continues until Mr. Reichenbach buys Kim for €40,000. I wonder what happened to the girl he bought last quarter. He has a newer, younger floozy on his right arm now, desperately straining on his sleeve to tear his gaze away from the woman he's purchased. *Tick Tock, gold digger.* She may be his date to this auction and think she's not like these other chicks, but women are all disposable to him — the ones he buys and the ones he keeps as pets.

A gaunt server with a black collar around her neck approaches and offers a drink. One of Khalid's personal harem. A little "K" hangs from her neck, marking her as his personal sex slave. Her voice is raspy and strained. There are purple bruises around her neck and a placated look in her eye. Dilated pupils too.

"Vodka martini, Mr. Pagonis?"

"Dry."

"Just the way you like it," she whispers.

I grunt thanks and she seems surprised that I acknowledge her enough to say thank you.

I finish the martini in one gulp. If I have to watch female after female parading out there with horror on her face, I get sick to my stomach. Don't these women have fathers and brothers to protect them? Yiayia is the only person who enjoys these events. Not even my father enjoys them, and he's technically the boss man. Everyone knows Yiayia really calls the shots.

A Thai girl who looks nineteen sells for €14,000 because she isn't a virgin. A Duke from England buys a blonde-haired, blue eyed American from South Carolina for €65,000. He likes Southern accents and women twenty years younger than him. My father raises two fingers and I'm the only one who notices his signal. It's simple. We bid on her, we get her out of here and our year of hell ends. We all want Helen home again. Even me.

But the night doesn't go according to plan because Khalid's man on stage announces, "Sapphire. A beautiful, fertile African American with perfect proportions. She'll need a handler with a firm hand, someone willing to engage in frequent discipline. This fresh-faced adult female has never had a baby and skilled enough for domestic labor. We recommend keeping her outside the United States."

She stares ahead, unflinching and proud. Khalid hasn't broken her yet, which means he mustn't have had her long. I can't take my eyes away from her. Straight shoulders. A slender neck. Dark skin. I lick my lips.

She's not the girl I'm here for. I'm here for my sister. Helen. Khalid's a bastard and making us buy her back. One year searching for her and tonight we finally rescue her. My instincts draw me away from my purpose. Sapphire. She's beautiful, with a raw umber skin tone and perfect lips. She's fierce and sensual in a way that scares me. I can't take my eyes off her.

"Bidding starts at €13,000."

An eighty-year-old man with mottled skin raises his card. He looks older than the first Smith and Wesson.

"We have one bidder at €13,000. Anyone for €15,000?"

I raise my placard. Foolishly. Impulsively. Because I want her. Neither my father nor Yiayia can control what I do with my money, and from the second Sapphire steps onto the block, I want her. She must be an American girl.

I can tell from her proud expression, the disgust quivering in her lower lip and barely concealed. She doesn't have visible markings on her which means whoever she is and wherever she came from, she was wise enough not to piss Khalid or any of his men off. She has one bruise on her shoulder but it's healing. A week. She must have been with them a week. And Khalid's eager to rid himself of her so she must be trouble.

I stroke my stubble, poor Helen temporarily forgotten. *I"m winning this auction.*

"€15,000. Anyone for €20,000?"

That aging bastard raises his placard again. Breaking protocol, I stand and blurt out, "I'll take her for €45,000."

My hand rushes to the handle of my weapon and everyone in this room knows that you don't fuck with a Pagonis. The aging bastard might be a billionaire, but a billion dollars can't stop a bullet. I'm crazy enough to pull the trigger. Everyone in this room knows. The old man clears his throat and raises his hand.

There's one way to win a battle.

"Sold!"

Khalid sends one of his girls over with a card containing handwritten instructions on what to do next. I've been through this before. My cousin bought a sweet Syrian girl off Khalid two years ago. She stabbed him a week later. Bastard deserved it.

I glance over at my father once I sit and he's scowling. But relief floods the room because I have what I want and my hand isn't on my weapon.

I don't know why I did this, but now I owe Khalid €45,000 and he hasn't trotted my sister out yet to force my family to bid on her. It's been too long since I've seen Helen. She comes on stage after Sapphire. She's bruised and bloody. Khalid's head would end up on a platter if he was the one who did this to her. Ironically, he's the one who saved her, but the bastard refuses to give Helen back without making us pay.

"Helen Pagonis. Bidding starts at €10,000."

No one in the room is stupid enough to bid on my sister. I raise my placard. My father strokes his chin and observes the transaction silently. I've done what I came here to do. Once the auction ends, I follow Khalid's instructions to the waiting room. After a brief wait, he sends the girls in. My sister strides over to me and wraps her arms around me. I don't hug her back. I haven't seen Helen in a year and the last time I saw her, she wished me dead.

"My brother..."

Sapphire stands against the door, terrified, like she's thinking about running but smart enough to realize if she does that, she's dead meat. At a private club like this, I'm not the scariest or most powerful guy in the room. Helen pulls away from me and I think she's going to say something deeply sentimental.

I have the words balancing on the tip of my tongue. *I forgive you, Helen.*

Then, my sister slaps me across the cheek. Hard.

❖

Chapter 2

The Girl I Bought

"What the hell was that for?" I growl.

After a year sold around Southern Europe, you'd think these men would have tamed Helen by now. She's like Yiayia — unchanging.

"Bastard," she hisses, "Why did you take her?"

She gesticulates madly at the girl I bought, cowering against the door, terror in her eyes as she considers her options. Typical loud-mouthed Greek woman involving herself in my business. I remember why I don't get along with my older sister…

"I wanted her," I answer, smirking at my sister as she gazes at me in disgust.

"Fool."

"Careful, sister. I might find you another buyer. Did the ones who had you ruin you entirely?"

"You've always been a filthy chauvinist, but buying a woman..."

I push past Helen and look my new purchase in the eyes for the first time.

"Sapphire. Come."

She glances at Helen, who nods approvingly, and then she

follows me. How well do they know each other, I wonder? I don't need to drag her down the hall or look to see if she's following me. By now, she knows well that escape isn't an option. And I'm far scarier than a bastard like Khalid — without a weapon.

"Where are we going after this?" Helen inquires, nearly tripping over herself to catch up to me. She's thinner than I remember, and weaker.

"We're going to the boats."

"The boats?"

"Yiayia wants to see you."

"I don't want to see her," Helen complains.

Nobody does, I want to tell her. But I don't want to encourage Helen's dissent. Yiayia will be furious enough considering I explicitly disobeyed my father by bidding on someone else. We have business to attend to and when I'm working, they want me focused. I put Helen into her car. Papa sent a driver. I turn around and take a full look at the girl standing behind me. She's younger than me. And pretty.

The girl I *bought*.

"Sapphire. I will not hurt you. I'm taking you to my family boat. Do you speak English?"

I thump the door to Helen's car and her driver pulls away, leaving me on the curb with my new ward. Maybe my family is right to question my decision making lately. I'm in no position to drive. I'm drunk and I think this girl can tell.

"Yes. I speak English."

"Do you know where you are?"

"No."

I ask her, "How do you know Khalid?"

Most of the women he finds go with him voluntarily — at first. He buys some of them like he bought my sister. But Helen's trouble differs from my beloved's trouble. The Italians got their hands on my sister after an incident in Bosnia. Her idiot ex-boyfriend Demetrius got two in the head from all her brothers for letting her out of his sight. That was a fun night. When we find Nikola, the second ex responsible for this, he's guaranteed a bloodbath.

Sapphire doesn't answer. She glances over her shoulder once and I clear my throat.

"What are you —

She runs. Fuck. I should have known she'd try. She doesn't get far, even if she makes a solid break away from me to run. I wrap my arms around her and pull her close to me as she screams and thrashes.

"No, you don't," I growl, subduing her flailing limbs and clamping my hand over her mouth.

No one who witnesses a Pagonis putting a girl in a car would dare say a word. It's pointless to scream and most people here don't speak English.

My car isn't far, and she's easy to carry. I thrust the door open as she bites down on my hand. Hard. I'm screaming as I shove her into the back seat and lock the car doors. Then I hurry into the front seat while she screams and thrashes in the back. I start the car and she lunges forward, screeching and trying to climb into the front.

I take a sharp turn, throwing her off balance. She yells and I step on the gas.

"SETTLE DOWN! NOW!"

She screams and pulls on the door handles, but she doesn't lunge forward again. She gasps and shudders and appears to reconsider, settling into a silent sobbing in the backseat. I am in so much fucking trouble with this one. I don't have a plan for what to do with her.

I'm at the docks in ten minutes. Loukas and Gal already left on Loukas's boat. I assume my younger sister's with them. Helen and Yiayia stand on the dock in front of Papa's boat. Yiayia's blue eyes flame with rage. I park the car and look over my shoulder at Sapphire. If I was a younger man, Yiayia would never let me keep her. She'd make me throw her overboard, or worse.

"I need you to behave yourself," I tell her gruffly.

"You're a sick fuck," Sapphire hisses, "Is your dick so small that you need to kidnap women to get laid?"

I raise an eyebrow. Khalid would have broken her jaw for speaking to him like that. I wet my lips and realize I'm too drunk to come up with a clever retort. I need to get her out of the way so I can meet my grandmother.

"I'm taking you onto my boat. You'll be safe there."

She doesn't answer.

"Sapphire, I need you to answer me."

"My name isn't Sapphire," she hisses, "That's a cruel, racist joke your sicko friend played on me. My name is Fallon."

"It doesn't matter what your fucking name is," I growl.

But it matters. And now I know, I want to call her Fallon out loud and say her name until she gives a shit about me. *This is why everyone thinks I'm insane.* She quiets down.

"If you want to make it out of here alive, you'll be respectful. I show mercy, but no one in my family does. I swear, I don't want to hurt you."

She whimpers and nods.

"Come."

I lead Fallon onto the boat and lock her in my spare bedroom before I hop back off onto the dock. Yiayia sneers at me, "Is there a good reason you've purchased an African?"

I correct her calmly and tell her that Sapphire is American. The less my grandmother knows about her, the better. For now, that includes her name.

Yiayia folds her arms as a breeze blows her shoulder length grey hair off her face. She's a beautiful woman, especially for her age, but she looks as mean as she is. You would think it would make her less beautiful, but she only looks cruel.

"If you want women for sex, you can have any Greek

woman you want. There isn't a woman alive who would turn down a Pagonis."

She smiles and fixes the collar on my linen shirt, smoothing it with a perfectionist's hand. She's proud of all of us — especially her grandsons, known for their success with the ladies.

"Yes, Yiayia."

"You're looking frail, Stavros. You need to eat."

"I'll feed myself on the boat."

Yiayia. She's not like other grandmothers, but she still keeps us fed.

"Good. I need you to work tonight once we get back to Thessaloniki."

"Eh?"

She dismisses Helen and pulls me aside. When Yiayia says I have a job, she means that she wants me to kill someone and I always do what my grandmother asks. She's too old to be in charge of anything, and she's a woman. Women don't lead mafia families. Not in Greece. Helen retreats and Yiayia touches my shoulder gently, when she knows she's going to ask something I don't want to do.

"Who is it?" I ask gruffly, stroking my facial hair.

Yiayia sighs.

"Your father will not be happy with me. He doesn't understand what I do for this family."

"Tell me, Yiayia. I will always do what my grandmother asks."

Her soft expression turns harsh.

"Manipulative bastard," she hisses, "I don't need you to patronize me."

"A name."

She touches my forearm again and smiles. My grandfather would always tell us that her smile made men weak.

"Arturo Castillo. He's coming to Thessaloniki for the week and I expect him in the water before tomorrow morning."

"Yes, Yiayia."

She presents her signet ring for me to kiss. I kiss her ring.

"Good boy," she whispers.

I strut onto my boat and lean over to untie it from the dock. I don't bother saying goodbye to my grandmother.

Yiayia knows I went to university with Arturo. She could ask Loukas to do this — and it would be nice if my idiot younger brother Gal did something for this family for a change.

When there's dirty work and bodies to put in the water, they always call me. Stavros Pagonis — the Executioner.

❖

Chapter 3

Foul-Mouthed Woman

The trip to Thessaloniki would have been nice, but Fallon's screaming ruins the mood. She bangs on the door the entire time. Her gusto for escape picks up when she realizes we're moving to yet another country and I'm bringing her there with no passport, no identity, just the brand Khalid put on her nape and the chip millimeters beneath her skin on her neck. Helen will have hers deactivated once we get her home.

I hear my brother Gal calling from below deck.

"Gal!"

I remember that he isn't on the ship. I didn't hear his voice. Fuck. It's happening again. I imagined my brother's voice. I hear him calling clearly when he's nowhere around. And I believe it's real at first. Voices. Music too. But mostly voices. I ease the boat into my spot at the dock.

The girl must be hungry, but all her damn yelling pisses me off. I'll feed her later. And what was that lip back there? Doesn't she realize what a worse man would have done to her by now? I get my weapon ready on the deck, whistling as I work.

Unlike my brothers, I don't have a fetish for guns. To kill

someone, you don't need a machine gun or anything fancy. I work with a police issue hand gun. I bought it off a drunk American cop and sold him enough crystal meth that he scrubbed the serial number off the gun himself.

It's a standard weapon, not traceable, and I could kill Arturo in front of a crowd of fifty and not a single person would witness it. I don't want to do that. Unlike my brothers, I don't enjoy the way people look at us. I don't want to be a Demi-god. I do this work because it's the only thing I know how to do.

I put my family first, even if they're fucking crazy because that's who they raised me to be.

Arturo walks out of the bar with a Slavic looking slag on his arm. A tight black corset pushes her enormous breasts together, and she's hanging onto his arm like she plans to milk him for every dollar he's worth — approximately $25 million, which everyone knows since he brags about it all the time. I wait for them to turn around the corner. I cock the gun.

Arturo stops walking and the girl shrieks.

"Get out of here and shut your mouth, or I will kill your entire family."

She runs. She doesn't even attempt to get Arturo out of it. Ouch. He should be grateful I've revealed the tramp for her shallow interest in him.

"Fuck."

"Yes. Fuck. That's what you did to my sister."

"I never touched Helen," he stammers, "I swear. I never knew where she was."

"I'm not talking about Helen."

He turns pale. I take a step closer.

"I don't want to do this. But... you know the rules. You don't lay a finger on a Pagonis girl. Cassia's beautiful. I understand that. But she's my sister."

"Let me go and you'll never hear from me again. Tell them I fought back."

"Pray," I tell him, "I'll give you time to pray."

He whimpers and starts, "Dear God —

I shoot him in the head. We're close enough to the water that I drag him down the docks and get him on the boat. It's close to three in the morning. No one else is here and that girl won't say a word to anyone important — not if she wants to survive to see Christmas. I load Arturo onto the boat and put a blanket over him on the deck. I'll take him far out to sea where he can sink in peace. He was always good at cards.

"You were a human once," a gruff voice comes across the deck, like it's coming from a creature crouching on Arturo's body.

The voices will never stop, no matter how many people I kill. I walk below deck. I'm not in a hurry to leave and I want to make sure Fallon hasn't found a way out of here. I knock on the door.

"Who is it? Who are you?"

"It's me. Stavros."

"Stavros," she repeats.

I never told her my name before. And she's not from around here so she probably has never heard of me. It's possible she's heard of Gal, but not me.

"We're going for a little ride and then I'll open that door... and we can talk."

"Talk? Is that what you call it?"

"Call what?"

She doesn't answer. I rap my fingers across the door again.

"You're going to rape me," she whispers.

I stop tapping.

"I'm going to take this boat for a ride. And then we'll talk."

I walk away before she can respond. I take the boat out for an hour and drop Arturo's body in our spot. I hose the deck down with vinegar and say a prayer after I lug him overboard.

"He was a good man," I whisper, taking the ring I peeled off his finger and dropping it in the water after him, an offering to the old gods. I go downstairs. Fallon won't run away from me here. She can't. I open the door and she screeches, crawling across the bed to the corner of her room and squeezing her legs together tightly.

"I'll shit all over your dick if you try to do it," she yells, "You like that? Sick pervert? I swear, I will *shit all over your dick* if you try to rape me."

I ignore her emotional outburst. Her cursing at me doesn't bother me, although she's foul mouthed for a woman.

"Fallon. No last name?"

"I have a last name."

"Does Khalid have your documents?"

"No."

"Where are they?"

"Burned."

"You're fucked."

"Thanks," she snaps.

"Take your clothes off."

"W-what?"

I fold my arms and lean against the wall. My impulses lead the way again. I'm testing her obedience more out of instinct than any proper reason.

"Do as I say. Take your clothes off."

"No!"

"I want to see what I purchased."

"I will never let you use me like a whore," she snaps.

"If I wanted to rape you, I could have done that easily. You are mine and we are in the middle of the sea on my boat. Every inch of your body belongs to me already. I don't want to rape you. I want to see you."

"Let me go," she begs, "If you have any ounce of humanity, you'll let me go."

Her lower lip trembles and I want to kiss it and comfort her. She'd probably try to kill me if I dared. Which makes me want to kiss her more.

"Beloved, I would enjoy setting you free, but without any identification but the brand on your nape, Khalid would have you back within a week. He has people everywhere. But... I can help you."

"I don't believe you."

"I don't care. Now take your clothes off."

She takes off the clothes Khalid gave her and shivers before me entirely naked. My cock stiffens instantly. I don't know why I thought I had the strength to do this — to observe her naked body and not erupt with unimaginable lust that nearly pushes me to commit the very vile act I promised myself I wouldn't do.

"You shouldn't wear slave's clothing," I tell her, "I must keep you confined... but you are not a slave, Fallon. I won't have you dressing like one."

I reveal a surprise I brought for her. It was in my other spare room — a dress that belonged to Helen that my ex-girlfriend never returned to her. I kept the dress because I never thought Helen would come home. And it still smelled like Ana-Maria. At the time I enjoyed returning to the smell but it made me nauseous now. Fallon sniffs.

"I love this perfume."

❖

Chapter 4

I Expect Compliance

She holds the dress up, covering her body with the fresh linen. The dress smells like Helen's perfume. Clinique Happy. Cassia wears the same perfume now since she moved into Helen's room. Teenagers. The first thing Cass asked when she found out we were getting Helen was whether she'd have to move.

"You want me to wear this?"

I nod and she struggles through making conversation with me. She wants information. A sense that if she escapes, she'd find justice. But with that thing in her neck, there's no true escape from me.

"Your name is Stavros, right?"

She faces away from me, nervous goose bumps spreading down her spine as she slips the fabric over her naked body. I shouldn't ogle her. But I can't help myself. She must notice I'm hard by now. Hence the goose bumps.

"Yes."

"You kept me locked in here for hours."

"You screamed the entire boat ride over here."

"I hate boats."

"Ah."

Disappointing. Pagonis men love boats. My father's the worst out of all of us.

"And you kidnapped me."

"I bought you."

The correction is only an exercise in semantics. But it's a worthy one.

"That's better, is it?"

This is the part where I need to be romantic. I see a man standing behind her. I know a man can't possibly be there. But she's real. Fallon is real. She tilts her head cautiously to the side. I must be getting pale.

"I wanted to save you from Khalid, I know what he's like."

She scoffs.

"If you're anything like what Helen told me, you're as big a monster as he is."

I lunge forward and grab her forearm. She shrieks and starts shaking but never breaks my gaze. Even in the face of danger and death, she's unflinchingly strong.

"I am nothing like Khalid. Men protect their women. They don't sell them or hurt them. I sat there to buy back my sister and protect her chastity for her husband. I will do my best to honor yours."

Her voice drips with sarcasm, "What a hero. Now you'll take some other man's daughter. Does that make you feel powerful?"

I release my grasp on her forearm and swallow. She doesn't believe me when I tell her I will not hurt her. Why should she believe me? I'm a liar, clearly. I wet my lips and answer with what's honest on my mind.

"You look beautiful in that dress."

She steps back.

"Don't," she whispers, "Don't start flirting and think that will change things. No matter what, if you touch me, it'll be rape."

"I know that."

"Then get out of this room."

"You're in no position to make demands."

"Please..."

Her nervousness makes me hard. Everything about her makes me stiff. Fuck. I never wanted a woman this much. And I own her. Her entire purpose in life now is to submit to my will.

I want to act like I'm better than Khalid and every other mafia asshole that I know, but the truth is when I'm alone on my boat in the middle of the sea with a beautiful woman, I want to have her. I want to take her. No one would know. No one here would talk.

I can't allow myself to act on my darker impulses. I'm already a murderer. If I want God's forgiveness, I can't show up at the gates of heaven as a rapist.

"I'm taking us back to the family villa. You won't talk to anyone there. Especially none of my brothers."

She nods. I leave the room and don't shut the door. She walks into the entryway.

"You forgot to lock me in!"

I forgot nothing. She has no upper hand and I have no reason to deny her moderate freedom.

"You aren't a prisoner. Where would you go, eh? Come above deck."

She doesn't want to, I know that. But given the option of staying below deck in her prison, I'm sure she'll follow me. Fallon climbs the stairs behind me. She's quiet, but I can tell she's thinking. She's looking for an escape. The next time she tries, I'll let her succeed. But she'll regret having to deal with Khalid's men instead of me. Above deck, she wrinkles her nose.

"It smells like blood up here."

"I was working."

"What are you, a butcher?"

She teases. But I don't laugh, and her expression sobers up. She approaches gingerly, like she hasn't decided how scared she is of my bite.

"It's cold up here."

"Blankets over there," I point and answer gruffly.

She finds one and wraps it around her shoulders.

"What are you going to do with me?"

"Keep you. Sell you. I haven't decided yet."

She purses her lips. The idea of someone selling her again doesn't appeal to her. I know men who would buy her and wouldn't hurt her. Decent men, except for their relationship to Khalid.

"You'd sell me again?"

"Yes. To someone who could take good care of you."

"I can't believe this is happening to me," she mutters.

"How long has Khalid had you?"

"Two months. He hasn't raped me yet, which is more than your sister can say."

So more than a week. How did she weasel her way out of this with barely any bruising? I grip the handle of my handgun instinctively. I won't shoot Fallon, but if I ever find out who raped my sister, I'll kill them.

"Do you know who hurt my sister?"

She shakes her head and mutters an apology. She's not the one who has to apologize.

"Was it one of Khalid's men?"

She nods.

"They paid."

"Bastard..."

I utter more choice phrases in Greek and realize I look insane, muttering to myself in a strange language. I rake my fingers through my hair coolly, letting dark brown strands fall loosely in front of my face, dusting my jawline before a gust of wind pushes it all back. Fallon's hair whips around in the wind too — long black hair, well-coiffed by Khalid, no doubt to make her presentable for sale.

"You must be hungry," I grumble.

"Yes."

"I will feed you. And provide for you. I know what you think of me. And I'm worse than whatever you think. But I'm no rapist, and whoever you end up with, I'll do my best to make sure he's a good man."

"I won't thank you."

"I don't expect gratitude."

I expect compliance. And so far, she hasn't tried another escape. We approach the shoreline. The Thessaloniki shore brings a familiar jolt to my heart. Home. Greece. The most beautiful country on this earth, and the most beautiful city within it. We have the charm Athens lacks, the convenient port for our family business and old school values alongside it all.

"Have you ever been to Greece?" I ask Fallon, as her dark brown eyes widen with awe. It's like she's seen nothing this beautiful. It's so beautiful, she can forget for a moment I'm a monster and she steps even closer to me, peering over at the skyline.

"Where is this?"

"Thessaloniki. Your new home. See that giant house? With the blue roof?"

She nods.

"That's my family villa. I own two apartment buildings downtown. They do little profit, but they're very nice."

My bragging doesn't impress her. There's not a woman I know in Thessaloniki who wouldn't have swooned at the mention of my property ownership.

She wets her lips and murmurs, "It's breathtaking."

"Fallon" I enjoy saying her name more than I let on, even if she flinches when I say it, "Where did Khalid grab you from?"

A Preview...

❖

Chapter 5

Yiayia's Attack Dog

I leave her in my suite with a bodyguard and a locked door. She has two windows but there are bars on them, so she's safe and has no chance at escape. She wouldn't make it off the villa compound if she tried. It's nearly five in the morning when I amble onto the porch. Loukas sits at the table, telling a loud story about his first wife and a fat Arab gun runner who offered to buy her for his harem in Medina. I'm 200% sure he's exaggerating.

"Shut the fuck up, liar."

"Finally, Yiayia's attack dog returns," Helen taunts, tapping her cigarette in a ash tray.

Gal rests a new handgun on the table.

"Helen, look at my new baby. Stole it off Pablo in Milan last week."

"You're never going to get a girlfriend if all you care about is guns," Helen chides our younger brother.

He scoffs.

"You know nothing. I have 3 million Instagram followers. Dozens of chicks begging to fuck me in the direct messages. Look."

Helen wrinkles her nose with disgust.

"That's sick. Did she offer to eat your... I go away for one year and you people are licking each other's buttholes!?"

Helen won't look at me.

"I was telling a story," Loukas interrupts gruffly.

"No one cares," I point out, "I'm here now."

"I heard you bought a sex slave today."

"Cigarette," I command Gal.

He hands me a cigarette.

"Where's Cassia?"

"Who cares? Probably getting fucked," Gal snaps, "I want to ask about the girl you bought."

I take the cigarette and slap him across the face. Hard.

"You never talk about your sister like that. Ever. Stupid cunt."

Gal takes his gun off the table and I put my hand on the handle of mine. Gal wisely sets his gun on his duffel bag instead of making the stupid fucking moves I expect of him. None of my siblings flinch. It isn't a Pagonis get together if guns don't make an appearance. We're hot-headed Greeks with more money than we know what to do with, more guns than anyone should have, and most of the people sitting at this table have killed someone or witnessed a murder.

Cassia flits into the room, wearing red lipstick. I grab her by the forearm and growl, "Where the hell were you?"

"Helen, tell him to leave me alone!"

I snarl at her, "Where were you!?"

"Out!"

"Stavros, stop it!" Helen interjects, "I know Pagonis men never understand, but your sister isn't your possession."

Helen's scowl reminds me of Yiayia. She has Yiayia's extraordinarily beautiful face. A face that turns men's heads. I let go of my younger sister.

"When papa finds out who it is, I'm the one who will have to kill him."

Cassia's lower lip trembles.

"Is that where you were tonight? With Arturo?"

She'll find out about Arturo when rumors spread around Thessaloniki or when his body washes up from the Aegean.

"No," Gal interrupts, "He took the slave girl out to sea to rape her in peace."

Loukas snickers and puts on a mocking female voice, "Oh, don't put your cock in me, Stavros. I don't like tiny cocks."

Even Helen laughs. I light the cigarette and put my feet up with a groan.

"I need rest."

"I need a fuck. Can I borrow your girl?" Gal asks.

I ignore him.

"Seriously," my idiot younger brother goads me, "I've always wondered what it was like. To take a black girl. I had a friend who fucked a Sudanese model, and he said she was the loudest fuck he ever had with a pussy like a giraffe it was so deep — OW!"

Helen has a good hold on Gal's ear and he shrieks as she hovers a cigarette over his forearm tattoo.

"HELEN!"

Cassia snickers.

"Do it! That tattoo is stupid," she laughs as she watches Helen taunt him. Pagonis women are as fierce and unhinged as Pagonis men.

Loukas finishes his drink.

"Leave Galanos alone. I'm off to bed."

"Five in the morning. This is early for you."

Loukas grunts and storms off.

"Why the fuck is he so moody?" Helen asks once he's out of earshot, hand-rolling another cigarette mindlessly.

Cassia leans forward and whispers, "Molly died while you were gone."

"Who?"

"His third fiancée."

Loukas has a way of losing his fiancees. They all die eventually, and we're all certain he's the one killing them off. But he gets more upset with each one gone. The last time I pointed out that he could stop killing them if he wanted, he stabbed me.

"Yiayia wants you to talk to the Israeli tomorrow," Helen casually switches over to business talk, which means she's told everything about the past year to Yiayia and Papa. That explains why she's cranky enough to burn Galanos' forearm over a crude comment.

"The Israeli's a shithead. He wants to undercut us by €3,000,000. Cheap bastard."

"The Israeli is good business. He's bringing in a new client from Ethiopia. Some war lord type."

Gal's bored because the conversation hasn't been about him for over a minute.

"Will you let me fuck the girl, Stavros? I'll only take her arse if you want her intact."

Helen burns his arm. He screams and then lunges for her. Helen dodges and then artfully blows a cloud of cigarette smoke into Galanos' face. Cassia laughs. I polish off his drink. If Yiayia wants me to talk to the Israeli tomorrow, I'd better get a few minutes of sleep.

But I leave my little brother with a final warning.

"Talk about the girl again and I'll chop one of your balls off. Nobody in this house is going to rape her. Understand?"

Gal is the only one of my brothers who hasn't killed before. And he knows my body count because I wear it on my body, a tattooed fresco of dots to represent my kills. He turns ghostly pale, his eyes glittering aquamarine in the early morning light.

I walk away without another word, hearing my siblings whispering as I walk out of earshot. I turn around and they aren't saying a word to each other.

Visit this link to continue reading...
smarturl.it/4submission

About Jamila Jasper

The hotter and darker the romance, the better.

That's the Jamila Jasper promise.

If you enjoy sizzling multicultural romance stories that dare to *go there* you'll enjoy any Jamila Jasper title you pick up.

Open-minded readers who appreciate **shamelessly sexy romance novels** featuring black women of all shapes and sizes paired with smokin' hot white men are welcome.

Sign up for her e-mail list here to receive one of these **FREE hot stories**, exclusive offers and an update of Jamila's publication schedule: bit.ly/jamilajasperromance

Get text message updates on new books: https://slkt.io/gxzM

Extremely Important Links

ALL BOOKS BY JAMILA JASPER
https://linktr.ee/JamilaJasper
SIGN UP FOR EMAIL UPDATES
Bit.ly/jamilajasperromance
SOCIAL MEDIA LINKS
https://www.jamilajasperromance.com/
GET MERCH
https://www.redbubble.com/people/jamilajasper/shop
GET FREEBIE (VIA TEXT)
https://slkt.io/qMk8
READ SERIAL (NEW CHAPTERS WEEKLY)
www.patreon.com/jamilajasper

JAMILA JASPER

Diverse Romance For Black Women

More Jamila Jasper Romance

Pick your poison…

Delicious interracial romance novels for all tastes. Long novels, short stories, audiobooks and more.

Hit the link to experience my full catalog.

FULL CATALOG BY JAMILA JASPER:

https://linktr.ee/JamilaJasper

Patreon

12+ SEASONS OF BWWM ROMANCE SERIAL CHAPTERS

🔥 NEW RELEASE 🔥
Powerless: Dark Bully BWWM Romance

Read the ongoing story POWERLESS and ALL the previous releases for a small monthly cost.

📖

Instantly access all six seasons of *Unfuckable* (Ben & Libby's story) with 375 chapters.

For a small monthly fee, you get exclusive access to my all this & my recently completed serial Despicable (275 chapters) ⬇️

www.patreon.com/jamilajasper

Patreon has more than the ongoing serial and previous serial releases...

⚡ **INSTANT ACCESS** ⚡

- NEW merchandise tiers with **t-shirts, totes, mugs,** stickers and MORE!
- **FREE paperback** with all new tiers
- **FREE short story audiobooks** and audiobook samples when they're ready
- #FirstDraftLeaks of Prologues and first chapters **weeks** before I hit publish
- Behind the scenes notes
- Polls and story contribution
- Comments & LIVELY community discussion with likeminded interracial romance readers.

LEARN MORE ABOUT SUPPORTING A DIVERSE ROMANCE AUTHOR

www.patreon.com/jamilajasper

Thank You Kindly

Thank you to all my readers, new and old for your support with this new year.

I look forward to making 2022 an INCREDIBLE year for interracial romance novels. I want to thank you all for joining along on the journey.

Thank you to my most supportive readers:

Christine, Trinity, Monica, Juliette, Letetia, Margaret, Dash, Maxine, Sheron, Javonda, Pearl, Kiana, Shyan, Jacklyn, Amy, Julia, Colleen, Natasha, Yvonne, Brittany, June, Ashleigh, Nene, Nene, Deborah, Nikki, DeShaunda, Latoya, Shelite, Arlene, Judith, Mary, Shanida, Rachel,Damzel, Ahnjala, Kenya, Momo, BJ, Akeshia, Melissa, Tiffany, Sherbear, Nini, Curtresa, Regina, Ashley, Mia, Sydney, Sharon, Charlotte, Assiatu, Regina, Romanda, Catherine, Gaynor, BF, Tasha, Henri, Sara, skkent, Rosalyn, Danielle, Deborah, Kirsten, Ana, Taylor, Charlene Louanna, Michelle, Tamika, Lauren, RoHyde, Natasha, Shekynah, Cassie, Dreama, Nick, Gennifer, Rayna, Jaleda, Anton, Kimvodkna, Jatonn, Anoushka, Audrey, Valeria, Courtney, Donna, Jenetha, Ayana, Kristy, FreyaJo, Grace, Kisha, Stephanie E., Amber, Denice, Marty, LaKisha, Latoya, Natasha, Monifa, Alisa, Daveena, Desiree, Gerry, Kimberly, Stephanie M., Tarah, Yolanda, Kristy, Gary, Janet, Kathy, Phyllis, Susan